Short Story Criticism

Guide to Gale Literary Criticism Series

For criticism on	Consult these Gale series
Authors now living or who died after December 31, 1999	*CONTEMPORARY LITERARY CRITICISM (CLC)*
Authors who died between 1900 and 1999	*TWENTIETH-CENTURY LITERARY CRITICISM (TCLC)*
Authors who died between 1800 and 1899	*NINETEENTH-CENTURY LITERATURE CRITICISM (NCLC)*
Authors who died between 1400 and 1799	*LITERATURE CRITICISM FROM 1400 TO 1800 (LC)* *SHAKESPEAREAN CRITICISM (SC)*
Authors who died before 1400	*CLASSICAL AND MEDIEVAL LITERATURE CRITICISM (CMLC)*
Authors of books for children and young adults	*CHILDREN'S LITERATURE REVIEW (CLR)*
Dramatists	*DRAMA CRITICISM (DC)*
Poets	*POETRY CRITICISM (PC)*
Short story writers	*SHORT STORY CRITICISM (SSC)*
Black writers of the past two hundred years	*BLACK LITERATURE CRITICISM (BLC)* *BLACK LITERATURE CRITICISM SUPPLEMENT (BLCS)*
Hispanic writers of the late nineteenth and twentieth centuries	*HISPANIC LITERATURE CRITICISM (HLC)* *HISPANIC LITERATURE CRITICISM SUPPLEMENT (HLCS)*
Native North American writers and orators of the eighteenth, nineteenth, and twentieth centuries	*NATIVE NORTH AMERICAN LITERATURE (NNAL)*
Major authors from the Renaissance to the present	*WORLD LITERATURE CRITICISM, 1500 TO THE PRESENT (WLC)* *WORLD LITERATURE CRITICISM SUPPLEMENT (WLCS)*

ISSN 0895-9439

Volume 40

Short Story Criticism

Criticism of the
Works of Short Fiction Writers

Jenny Cromie
Editor

GALE GROUP

Detroit
New York
San Francisco
London
Boston
Woodbridge, CT

BURROUGHS LEARNING
Bethel College
325 Cherry Avenue
McKenzie, TN 38201

STAFF

Library of Congress Catalog Card Number 88-641014
ISBN 0-7876-3276-7
ISSN 0895-9439
Printed in the United States of America

10 9 8 7 6 5 4 3 2 1

Contents

Preface vii

Acknowledgments xi

Preface

Short Story Criticism (*SSC*) presents significant criticism of the world's greatest short story writers and provides supplementary biographical and bibliographical materials to guide the interested reader to a greater understanding of the authors of short fiction. This series was developed in response to suggestions from librarians serving high school, college, and public library patrons, who had noted a considerable number of requests for critical material on short story writers. Although major short story writers are covered in such Gale series as *Contemporary Literary Criticism* (*CLC*), *Twentieth-Century Literary Criticism* (*TCLC*), *Nineteenth-Century Literature Criticism* (*NCLC*), and *Literature Criticism from 1400 to 1800* (*LC*), librarians perceived the need for a series devoted solely to writers of the short story genre.

Scope of the Series

SSC is designed to serve as an introduction to major short story writers of all eras and nationalities. Since these authors have inspired a great deal of relevant critical material, *SSC* is necessarily selective, and the editors have chosen the most important published criticism to aid readers and students in their research.

Approximately eight to ten authors are included in each volume, and each entry presents a historical survey of the critical response to that author's work. The length of an entry is intended to reflect the amount of critical attention the author has received from critics writing in English and from foreign critics in translation. Every attempt has been made to identify and include the most significant essays on each author's work. In order to provide these important critical pieces, the editors sometimes reprint essays that have appeared elsewhere in Gale's Literary Criticism Series. Such duplication, however, never exceeds twenty percent of an *SSC* volume.

Organization of the Book

An *SSC* entry consists of the following elements:

- The **Author Heading** cites the name under which the author most commonly wrote, followed by birth and death dates. Also located here are any name variations under which an author wrote, including transliterated forms for authors whose native languages use nonroman alphabets. If the author wrote consistently under a pseudonym, the pseudonym will be listed in the author heading and the author's actual name given in parentheses on the first line of the biographical and critical introduction. Uncertain birth or death dates are indicated by question marks. Single-work entries are preceded by the title of the work and its date of publication.

- The **Introduction** contains background information that introduces the reader to the author and the critical debates surrounding his or her work.

- A **Portrait of the Author** is included when available.

- The list of **Principal Works** is ordered chronologically by date of first publication and lists the most important works by the author. The first section comprises short story collections, novellas, and novella collections. The second section gives information on other major works by the author. For foreign authors, the editors have provided original foreign-language publication information and have selected what are considered the best and most complete English-language editions of their works.

- Reprinted **Criticism** is arranged chronologically in each entry to provide a useful perspective on changes in critical evaluation over time. All short story, novella, and collection titles by the author featured in the entry are printed in boldface type. The critic's name and the date of composition or publication of the critical work are given at the beginning of each piece of criticism. Unsigned criticism is preceded by the title of the source in which it appeared. Footnotes are reprinted at the end of each essay or excerpt. In the case of excerpted criticism, only those footnotes that pertain to the excerpted texts are included.

- Critical essays are prefaced by brief **Annotations** explicating each piece.

- A complete **Bibliographical Citation** of the original essay or book precedes each piece of criticism.

- An annotated bibliography of **Further Reading** appears at the end of each entry and suggests resources for additional study. In some cases, significant essays for which the editors could not obtain reprint rights are included here. Boxed material following the further reading list provides references to other biographical and critical sources on the author in series published by Gale.

Cumulative Indexes

A **Cumulative Author Index** lists all of the authors that appear in a wide variety of reference sources published by the Gale Group, including *SSC*. A complete list of these sources is found facing the first page of the Author Index. The index also includes birth and death dates and cross references between pseudonyms and actual names.

A **Cumulative Nationality Index** lists all authors featured in *SSC* by nationality, followed by the number of the *SSC* volume in which their entry appears.

A **Cumulative Title Index** lists in alphabetical order all short story, novella, and collection titles contained in the *SSC* series. Titles of short story collections, separately published novellas, and novella collections are printed in italics, while titles of individual short stories are printed in roman type with quotation marks. Each title is followed by the author's last name and corresponding volume and page numbers where commentary on the work is located. English-language translations of original foreign-language titles are cross-referenced to the foreign titles so that all references to discussion of a work are combined in one listing.

Citing *Short Story Criticism*

When writing papers, students who quote directly from any volume in the Literature Criticism Series may use the following general format to footnote reprinted criticism. The first example pertains to material drawn from periodicals, the second to material reprinted from books.

Henry James, Jr., "Honoré de Balzac," *The Galaxy* 20 (December 1875), 814-36; reprinted in *Short Story Criticism,* vol. 5, ed. Thomas Votteler (Detroit: The Gale Group), 8-11.

Linda W. Wagner, "The Years of the Locust," *Ellen Glasgow: Beyond Convention* (University of Texas Press, 1982), 50-70; reprinted and excerpted in *Short Story Criticism,* vol. 34, ed. Anna Nesbitt Sheets (Farmington Hills, Mich.: The Gale Group), 80-82.

Suggestions are Welcome

Readers who wish to suggest new features, topics, or authors to appear in future volumes, or who have other suggestions or comments are cordially invited to call, write, or fax the Managing Editor:

Managing Editor, Literary Criticism Series
The Gale Group
27500 Drake Road
Farmington Hills, MI 48331-3535
1-800-347-4253 (GALE)
Fax: 248-699-8054

Acknowledgments

The editors wish to thank the copyright holders of the excerpted criticism included in this volume and the permissions managers of many book and magazine publishing companies for assisting us in securing reproduction rights. We are also grateful to the staffs of the Detroit Public Library, the Library of Congress, the University of Detroit Mercy Library, Wayne State University Purdy/Kresge Library Complex, and the University of Michigan Libraries for making their resources available to us. Following is a list of the copyright holders who have granted us permission to reproduce material in this volume of *SSC*. Every effort has been made to trace copyright, but if omissions have been made, please let us know.

Marguerite Duras
1914–1996

(Born Marguerite Donnadieu) French short fiction writer, novelist, playwright, scriptwriter, and essayist.

INTRODUCTION

Considered one of France's most original and controversial contemporary writers, Duras explores the nature and difficulties of love and the existential conflicts of the individual alone and in relationships in her work. While her output of short fiction was small, it is this genre in which Duras made the greatest popular and critical impact, particularly with her two novellas, *Moderato cantabile* and *L'amant (The Lover)*.

BIOGRAPHICAL INFORMATION

Duras was born near Saigon, Vietnam, in 1914. After her father's death in 1918, her mother unwittingly bought a parcel of worthless land in Cambodia from the corrupt colonial government. Though this purchase led to the family's financial ruin, Duras's mother managed to send her to the prestigious Lycée de Saigon, where Duras studied Vietnamese and French. At the age of seventeen Duras left Cambodia for France, eventually studying law and political science at the University of Paris, Sorbonne. She worked as a secretary for the Ministry of Colonial Affairs until 1941. Duras married her first husband, Robert Antelme, an active member of the French Communist Party, in 1939. The couple divorced in 1946, after Antelme returned from the German concentration camp where he had been held for a year during World War II. She later married Dionys Mascolo, with whom she had a son, Jean. Duras, who also joined the Communist Party and was active in the Resistance Movement during Germany's occupation of France, began writing fiction shortly after the start of the war. She published her first novel, *Les impudents,* in 1943 and published more than seventy novels, plays, stories, novellas, screenplays, and adaptations during her lifetime. In 1984, while recovering from alcoholism in a treatment center, Duras wrote *The Lover,* for which she won the Prix Goncourt, France's most prestigious literary award. In poor health as a result of her life-long addiction to alcohol, Duras died in Paris in 1996.

MAJOR WORKS OF SHORT FICTION

Duras's first work of short fiction, *Des journées entières dans les arbres (Whole Days in the Trees and Other Stories)*, was published in 1954. Consisting of four stories,

Des journées entières dans les arbres touches on several themes that Duras explored more fully in her later work—particularly the developing sexuality of young women—but in form and structure is more similar to her earlier works, which tend to be realistic and conventionally structured. Her novella *Moderato cantabile* represents the early stages of Duras's evolution into a proponent of the stylized narrative forms associated with the French *nouveau roman,* or anti-novel. Published in 1958, *Moderato cantabile* is considered among Duras's most accomplished works. The two-level structure of the story is introduced in the opening scene: while a boy's music lesson is taking place in a woman's apartment, there is a murder in the café downstairs. The story revolves around the boy's mother's growing obsession with the crime, and, as in many of Duras's works, the presence of crime sets the background for an exploration of human passion and the connection between love and death. Duras achieved international success with her novella *The Lover,* published in 1984. Considered more accessible than much of her fiction up to that point, *The Lover* draws on Duras's childhood in Indochina, focusing on her discovery of sexual passion through a love affair she experienced when she was fifteen years old as well as her turbulent relationship with her mother and two brothers. While *The Lover* is recognizably autobiographical, Duras concentrates on the recollection of events and their emotional significance rather than on the events themselves, thus creating a complex structure that conveys the illusion of simplicity.

CRITICAL RECEPTION

Critical commentary on Duras's short fiction tends to focus on *The Lover* and *Moderato cantabile*; the latter is generally considered the more remarkable work from a scholarly viewpoint. Critics have consistently commented on Duras's major themes of alienation and misunderstanding in the novella, finding her focus on her characters' compulsive fascination with the murder a dramatic and effective representation of the existential distance in human relationships. Concentrating as it does on young female sexuality, *The Lover* has received more critical coverage than most of Duras's other works. At the time of its publication, some commentators argued that it was the most effective synthesis of Duras's themes and minimalist style. Nonetheless, the novella's explicit and matter-of-fact depiction of its fifteen-year-old protagonist's affair with an older man generated much controversy.

PRINCIPAL WORKS

Short Fiction

Des journées entières dans les arbres [*Whole Days in the Trees and Other Stories*] 1954
Moderato cantabile 1958
L'amant [*The Lover*] 1984

Other Major Works

Les impudents (novel) 1943
Un barrage contre le Pacifique [*The Sea Wall*] (novel) 1950
Le marin de Gibraltar [*The Sailor from Gibraltar*] (novel) 1952
Le square [*The Square*] (novel) 1955
Dis heures et demie du soir en été [*Ten-Thirty on a Summer Night*] (novel) 1960
Hiroshima, mon amour (screenplay) 1960
La ravissement de Lol V. Stein [*The Ravishment of Lol V. Stein*] (novel) 1964
L'amante anglaise (novel) 1967
L'amante anglaise (drama) 1968

Detruire, dit-elle [*Destroy, She Said*] (novel) 1969
Les parleuses [*Woman to Woman*] (interviews) 1974
L'homme assis dans le couloir [*The Seated Man in the Passage*] (novel) 1980
Outside (essays) 1981
La maladie de la mort [*The Malady of Death*] (novel) 1982
La douleur [*The War: A Memoir*] (memoir) 1985
Le vie materielle [*Practicalities: Marguerite Duras Speaks to Jerome Beaujour*] (recorded conversations) 1986
Les yeux bleus, cheveux noirs [*Blue Eyes, Black Hair*] (novel) 1986
Emily L. (novel) 1987
L'Amant de la Chine du nord [*The North China Lover*] (novel) 1991
Le monde exterieur (essays) 1994
That's All (essays) 1996

CRITICISM

Times Literary Supplement (essay date 1966)

SOURCE: "The Boy Next Door," in *The Times Literary Supplement*, July 21, 1966, p. 640.

[*In the following review of* Moderato Cantabile, *the critic praises Duras's "controlled and hard-edged account" of her heroine's failures, but maintains that readers may feel unsatisfied with such a short book.*]

The music starts on page one [of ***Moderato cantabile***], tinkling tangentially from a sixth-floor room. It is nothing gross like a symphony, or even a concerto, but a pretty sonatina for piano, by Diabelli. The score is marked *moderato cantabile,* but it requires the intervention of a woman's scream before we are really projected into the novel of the same name, available at last in English, in an American translation which blunts a good number of sharp edges.

The pianist is a small boy having his Friday lesson, prepared to show he is quite competent only when his mother obviously cherishes him. Because he is a child he has a special openness to the world around him; he alone is properly aware of the power of the sunset and the throbbing of a passing motor boat. But he has to learn the piano, his mother says, because music is necessary, at which point one can begin to see that the lesson might be an initiation ceremony into the inexorable restraints of adult life. This all becomes much clearer after the mechanical sequence of the Diabelli has been interrupted by the scream.

It comes from a nearby café, where a young man has shot his wife through the heart. The little boy and his mother are in time to see him press himself against the corpse and be led away by policemen. The mother is now obsessed by the crime because, obviously, of the emotional deep-freeze her own social circumstances force her to live in. This is not her part of the town, down here by the docks, where men work in factories and occasionally kill; she, Anne Desbaresdes, wife of a big businessman, belongs in the cold formality of the big house right at the other end of the long Boulevard de la Mer. But now, day after day, and always at dusk, she returns ritually to the café where, her inhibitions weakened by white wine, she gets to know a workman called Chauvin, who has been sacked by her husband and who lusts after her from afar. The distance between them, social and psychological, slowly decreases as they discuss the crime that has been committed. Chauvin's pretended explanations of what had happened do little but express his own obsession with Anne, and through their shifting, oblique conversations enough pressure is created to make it conceivable that their story too must end in physical death. But it ends in emotional death only, the tension resolved by a single kiss. Anne, the condemned woman, must go back to the hell of her house and her motherhood.

Moderato cantabile is a characteristically controlled and hard-edged account of this defeat, formalized far beyond the point where anyone could easily identify themselves with the heroine. Marguerite Duras here does what she wants to do with admirable certainty, but some readers may well feel that inside a good thin novel there is an even better fat one trying to get out.

Alfred Cismaru (essay date 1969)

SOURCE: "A Short Story of Marguerite Duras," in *South Atlantic Bulletin,* Vol. XXXIV, No. 4, November, 1969, pp. 22-4.

[*In the following essay, Cismaru analyzes* Des journées entières dans les arbres, *praising Duras's realistic depiction of "the world of the dispossessed."*]

The year 1954 saw the publication of Marguerite Duras' *Des journées entières dans les arbres,* her only collection of short stories to date. The book contains four titles: **"Des Journées entières dans arbres," "Le Boa," "Madame Dodin"** and **"Les Chantiers." "Des Journées"** has attracted a considerable amount of attention, especially in its play version of 1966 under the adept direction of Jean-Louis Barrault and benefiting from the experienced play-acting of Madeleine Renaud. All four titles, however, are good examples of almost plotless compositions pursuing the vein of the New Novel through repetitions, anonymity of characters, and infrequency of incidental detail. Yet, the author does not make a clean break with the past: summaries are still possible, the totally dismal atmosphere of the masters of the New School is absent, and false, awkward hope still glitters, from time to time, in the heart of the personages.

In spite of Marguerite Duras' reputation as a novelist and film writer, in this country her short stories have given rise, so far, to practically no comment at all. The purpose of the present essay is to fill a long-standing lacuna in domestic Durasian scholarship by discussing **"Des Journées entières dans les arbres,"** the longest and perhaps the best story in the collection mentioned.

The nostalgic connotation of the words *des Journées entières dans les arbres,* pointing as it does to children climbing trees for the joy of pure ascension or the intriguing mischievousness of discovering bird nests, fills the one-hundred or so pages of the first story. There is a touching feeling of loss that grips the reader immediately, to stay with him and grow as the almost continuous dialogue of the composition unfolds, cryptically at first, but more and more plainly as the narrative advances. The loss, of course, is that of the days of old, the carefree days, the moments of sheer innocence, of play. And the void that we are left with is only poorly filled by tangible objects, by material riches that we have grown too old to enjoy or even care about.

For that is the situation of the central character, the nameless mother who returns from the Colonies to see her son, Jacques, a middle-aged man, a boy who had liked tree-climbing, frolicking, and absenting himself from school, a boy who had not quite grown up yet in spite of his chronological age. It is this son among all others whom Mother loves and whom she comes to visit, perhaps because she senses that he needs her, or perhaps, as one critic has put it, because she wants to "s'assûrer qu'il n'est pas sorti de son enfance, c'est-à-dire d'une sorte d'esclavage biologique,"[1] that she could still, secretly, enjoy. This mother, unlike Ma of the earlier *Un Barrage contre le Pacifique* (1950), has done well abroad, has become the proprietor of a factory and has acquired jewels, bracelets that she wears on each arm and rings that cover almost all her fingers. Her son, on the contrary, has not changed very much. He is lethargic, sleeps all day, and at night dances with old, single women in a night club where his concubine, Marcelle, has a somewhat similar job. Moreover, he is a drunkard, a gambler, a thief on occasion (he steals some of his mother's jewelry the one night that she sleeps in his apartment, in order to sell it and gamble with the money); but he is also a gay sort of man, capable of passion at times, sensitive and childish, a dreamer whose degradation has a measure of voluptuousness for it is willed without being calculated. His is a world of inactivity and consent, perpetuated and cultivated with care, much as that of Sara and her friends in *Les Petits chevaux de Tarquinia* (1953). In vain his mother offers him status and fortune in the Colonies: "Il est comme ça," the same critic pursues, "et c'est comme ça qu'il va vieillir, o triste et délicieuse victoire de cette femme . . . qui cache en vain sa soif de domination."[2]

In **"Des Journées,"** Marguerite Duras' pen excels indeed. Her penetrating analysis of the three main characters, mother, son, and mistress, almost exclusively by means of dialogue, is masterfully handled. The author's descriptive interventions are reduced to the barest minimum and are never more than a few lines long. In this story just about every spoken word has an intense, a pounding, dramatic value, as if the pen were that of a playwright and not of a novelist.[3] "Mais que j'ai faim," says the mother almost as soon as we meet her. "Jour et nuit . . . j'ai si faim que je rongerais un os et j'ai soif."[4] These statements, repeatedly made, act as a refrain and they constitute but one example of the writer's ability to bare immediately the psychological make-up of her personage.[5] How neatly, then, her jewelry-studded hands fall into place, and the twenty-room house she owns and boasts about but has no real use for, and the factory in which her eighty employees are busy making her a fortune that she does not quite know how to spend. Is hers a hunger for money for the power, the freedom it can provide? Not really. Rather for the *things* one can buy with it. Things to be sure, not quality: had she any real appreciation of jewelry, for example, she would purchase and wear fewer items of a more expensive and subdued character. Hers is also a hunger for much smaller, animal needs: a *choucroute,* which she eats heartily, on several occasions, during the short visit she pays to her son, a glass of Beaujolais. "Ah! les joies de la choucroute," she exclaims at one point, "on en parle aisément sans les connaître! Une bonne choucroute . . . à soixante-quinze ans passés . . . deux guerres . . . quand j'y pense. . . . En plus de tout le reste" (82).

Her apparently disconnected but closely-knit aberrations point, of course, to the infirmities of old age, to the decay humans are subjected to prior to death. She hears with difficulty, for example, does not see too well either, and is unable to think coherently or to recall except through the fluid opacity of a septuagenarian. The little that she says is replete with contradictions and reveals an unstable personality whose sensitivity only serves to enhance the pathetic quality. She is much like other aged characters of the masters of the New Novel and the New Theater, Ionesco and Beckett for example, a decrepit in dividual, physically and intellectually in an advanced stage of decomposition.[6]

The plight of growing old is even more visible in the son, for while he has aged, he still leads, essentially, the care-free existence of his tree-climbing days. And Marcelle too, the moving symbol of a cheated life (abandoned by her parents, raised in a loveless atmosphere, caught in the facile web of prostitution because of necessity, or laziness, or both), of love erased by time, of an ardent desire for something different, for a pulsating life which would not be threatened from all sides, which would be devoid of fear, of hunger, of uncertainty, Marcelle too has forgotten how to look to the future, has consented, has acknowledged and accepted that dubious state of survival in which so many of Marguerite Duras' personages sink. For her the status quo is not only possible, it is desirable because the unknown could only be worse: she might lose her job at the club, she might become ill, Jacques could leave her. She must be constantly careful, then, at work, in her conversations with Mother, in the way she dresses and exhibits her emotions. In the play version, the reviewer aptly noted her "visage nu, une marche pleine d'hesitation, des mains

tremblantes, une bouche pâle qui dénote à la fois sa tendresse et sa férocité, une voix, pure, tremblante, intense, calme, ironique, légère,"[7] for the actress's appearance and tone, changing and conflicting, denote so well the permanent inner struggle which the author wished to convey. As a matter of fact, the dramatic qualities of **"Des Journées"** descriptions and dialogue lend themselves so effectively to stage production that Christine Garnier has been moved to remark: "Saisissant auteur, admirable atrice: on ne sait, au sortir de l'Odéon . . . qui louer de plus? Mme Duras ou Mme Renaud? On a le coeur serré, on est fasciné, on sait que l'envoûtement durera *des Journées entières.* . . . Jamais mieux que dans ces *Journées entières dans les abres,* n'a-t-elle su rendre les clairsobscurs, les sable mouvants [of human relationships] et nous émouvoir avec des [mere] somnambules."[8] Yet, **"Des Journées"** pages remain the pages of a story. They never become exercises, dramatic or otherwise, and if we agree with the conclusion of Armand Hoog that "Marguerite Duras has written nothing better,"[9] it is in the story itself that we must seek the clues to its bewitching interest.

The starting point could hardly be simpler: a mother returns to visit her son after an absence of years. The visit will last approximately twenty-four hours, during which the characters will talk, eat and drink, go to the club where Jacques and Marcelle work, return home, sleep, get up. Nothing will really take place. If the son steals, gambles and loses, he simply confirms a reader's early interpretation; and the very few paragraphs that these events occupy do not give the plot any movement. What impresses, what touches, is the dialogue: the unfinished sentences, the brief, concise, incisive, staccato utterances, the alogical apostrophes, the curious interpolations, the sad and moving expressions of disenchantment and despair of the personages:

> —Parlez-moi quand même un peu de votre vie à tous les deux . . . faites un petit effort.
>
> —Toujours pareil, dit le fils.
>
> —Vraiment?
>
> —Pareil absolument, répéta le fils.
>
> (28-29)

To the familiar theme of immobility is added, repeatedly, the devastating proof of an aging person's decaying reason and loss of memory: "Pourtant, en général, ton père et moi-même . . . je ne dis pas maintenant . . . on avait plutôt de bons sentiments il me semble, chercha-t-elle dans ses souvenirs" (53).

The Existentialist's nausea is likewise an integral part of the story: "Voilà que je repense à ces hommes dans mon usine. ça me revient comme une nausée. . . . Comme une nausée . . . je ne sais pas pourquoi" (54). Much like the engulfing roots of the tree in Jean-Paul Sartre's *La Nausée* (1938) causing nausea in Roquentin's stomach, the recollection of her material possessions brings about a distasteful, physical reaction to Marguerite Duras' character. But unlike Roquentin, she is unable to reason out the origin of her response, nor does she have the intellectual or physical drive to seek even the shadow of a remedy.

The painful realization that in real life contradictions are often compatible, a theme often encountered in anti-novels,[10] and expressed frequently in **"Des Journées,"** adds to the intriguing qualities of the dialogue: "C'est la même chose en fin de compte . . . travailler . . . pas travailler . . . il suffit de commencer, de prendre l'habitude," (63) says Mother, trying half-heartedly to convince Jacques to follow her to the Colonies. As a matter of fact, all three main characters contradict themselves often, and are awkwardly unaware, at the time they speak, of what they have said a few moments before. Thus, the mother's affection for her son, the apparent reason for her visit, becomes a mere conjecture when she admits: "Si je suis là c'est pour la forme, parce que je me suis dit que mon devoir était de venir voir mon fils, tenter encore l'impossible. . . . Rien de plus, le devoir, mais mon coeur est là-bas" (71); this in spite of the fact that before, repeatedly, she had expressed scorn for riches, had commented on the too many rooms in her house and the too many workers in her factory and the excessive sums of money she had but was too old to use.

Finally, the protagonists' inability to pursue a topic for more than a few lines, their wandering minds and instability, their subjectivity and egocentricity are admirably pointed out by the author through the characters' vain efforts at real communication, at understanding. For although the story is almost exclusively made up of dialogue, **"Des Journées"** contains nothing more than subconversations and long monologues, interrupted, broken, hesitating, dangling. There are many which could be given as examples, but one of the most moving occurs in the episode in which Mother and Marcelle begin to talk on a subject of common interest, Jacques, then each reverts, from time to time, to purely personal preoccupations while apparently continuing the conversation:

—Je crois même que je l'aime, dit-elle.

La mère, à ces mots, frémit.

—Hélas, murmura-t-elle.

—Lui non, lui ne m'aimera jamais.

Mais la mère était encore une fois repartie vers le spectacle de son enfant dansant.

—Il me le dit d'ailleurs. Jamais il ne m'aimera, jamais, jamais.

La mère revint à elle, l'examina les yeux vides.

—Il ne voulait pas aller à l'école, dit-elle, jamais. . . . Tout vient de là. C'est comme ça que ça a commencé.

—Et pourquoi?

La mère ouvrit ses mains et les étendit dans l'impuissance.

—Je ne le sais pas encore, je ne le saurai jamais.

Elles se turent un petit moment puis Marcelle revint à ses propres préoccupations.

—Si au moins il me laissait rester chez lui . . . je ne demande rien d'autre que ça, qu'il me laisse rester là.

—Il y a des enfants, les autres par exemple, qui font leur chemin tout seuls, on n'a pas besoin de s'en occuper. D'autres, rien à faire. Ils sont élevés pareil, ils sont du même sang, et voilà qu'ils son si différents.

Marcelle se tut. La mère se souvint d'elle.

(65-66)

And the monologue-dialogue goes on in unaltered fashion, the two women talk mostly to themselves, only sporadically recalling the presence of the other.

"Des Journées" is also noteworthy for the brilliant stylistic sallies of the writer. Only an attentive page by page reading could do justice to the mysterious allusions, the intriguing associations, the surreptitious statements, the moving nostalgia, the paralyzing repetitions and the *choucroute* stench that emanate from Marguerite Duras' pen. Consider, for example, the sadly ironic words of Mother who, speaking of other children, of those who have made a real place for themselves in life, quips: "ils ont fait des études, eu des situations, fait des mariages, tout comme on avale des confitures" (33). Or the regret she expresses for not having been wise enough to enjoy *the good old days,* the days when she was poor financially but rich in health and in children.

Elle se toucha las bras, se les palpa comme vile marchandise.

—Plus rien, reprit-elle. Plus d'enfants. Plus de cheveux. Regarde un peu les bras que j'ai là. . . . Plus rien que cette usine. . . . Quand je pense, je vous vois encore, quand je pense que vous étiez tous là à dormir comme des anges dans tous les coins de la maison . . . à l'ombre des stores, verts, tu te souviens . . . et que moi je pleurais parce que j'avais des dettes. Que vous étiez là et que je pleurais . . . Hélas! Pleine de lait, forte comme un boeuf, et je pleurais.

(57-58)

Or the epilogue of the well-constructed scene at the night club, when Mother refuses to pay the bill on the grounds that she was overcharged for the little she has drunk, and the crowning remark she makes after she does pay: "C'est presque aussi cher qu'un matelas, c'est curieux" (79), pointing to an association between drinking and abandonment to sleep or death, a subtle, engaging association which surely originates in her intuition only. Or the profoundly poignant reasons she gives to Marcelle for leaving so soon after her arrival: "Si je pars voyez-vous, c'est parce que ça ne ressemble à rien que je sois ici . . . à rien du tout. . . . D'avoir eu des enfants, ça ne ressemble à rien, ça ne signifie rien. Rien. Vous ne pouvez pas imaginer à quel point, à vous donner le vertige. Je ne dis pas de les avoir . . . mais de les avoir eu. . . . Si je restais il ne pourrait que me tuer, le pauvre petit. Et moi, je ne pourrais que le comprendre" (86).

This is the most feared thing of all, of course, for then she would lose him entirely, he would become like the others, all of one piece, predictable, sane, safe: that is to say, he would no longer be in a state of biological slavery and she, as the mother of an infant, would cease to exist. In one of her last speeches, guarding against this possibility, she remarks: "Si tu savais . . . les autres . . . elles sont fières des leurs, et quand ils viennent les voir, qu'est-ce qu'on voit? Des bourgeois, des veaux, trop nourris, et bêtes, et qui ne savent rien. . . . Non, mon petit, je suis fière que tu sois comme ça, encore, à ton âge . . . maigre comme un chat . . . mon petit" (96). What she does not realize is that she does understand him after all, even more than her other children, for with him her intuition is her wisdom, and she can feel and display a host of emotions that she is incapable of in the case of the others. In her next to the last speech, this realization comes to the surface, porous for the reader but certainly still opaque to her own declining intellectual capacities: "C'est une autre fierté [hers] que je suis seule à comprendre. Et c'est seulement de ça que je souffre, mon petit, c'est tout, d'être seule à la comprendre et de penser que je vais mourir et que personne, après moi, ne l'aura" (96). It is obvious, then, that her haughtiness is not pleasurable because it cannot be shared: with the exception of her son, she could ill afford to show it to anyone else. It is, as she says, more a source of pain than of joy. Moreover, were she to stay close to her son for a longer period of time she would run the risk of seeing him change, hence of losing the lofty position she now appears to have. Therefore she must leave the only person she can dominate, resume the total loneliness of the Colonies and assent to distance, absence, death.

In **"Des Journées,"** then, three unfortunate people, mother, son, and mistress, spend part of a day and one night together: hardly the material for a story. A great deal of dialogue, though, a limited number of precise details: barely enough for even the briefest fictional narration. Yet, the world of the dispossessed is admirably described, the complexity of contradictory emotions is conveyed with touching simplicity, and the loneliness of immobile characters who accede to their miserable situation is perfectly identified. Certainly not a traditional story, these **"Des Journées,"** perhaps not even a story at all. But Marguerite Duras is here too close to reality to aspire to lesser goals.

Notes

1. Robert Abirached, "Marguerite Duras: *Des Journées entières dans les arbres,*" *La Nouvelle Revue française,* XXVII (1966), 345.

2. *Ibid.,* p. 345.

3. At the time of the publication of *Des Journées entières dans les arbres* the events which form the basis of her first play, *Les Viaducs de la Seine-et-Oise,* took place in France, and it is quite probable that she began thinking about the theater in 1954.

4. Marguerite Duras, *Des Journées entières dans les arbres* (Paris: Gallimard, 1954) p. 13, subsequent page numbers in parenthesis in my text refer to this edition.

5. Extreme hunger and thirst, physical and intellectual, constitute the theme of Ionesco's celebrated play *La Soif et la faim* (1966), presented in Paris at the same time as the dramatic version of *Des Journées.*

6. Yet, the paralytic characters of Beckett and the moral corpses of Ionesco differ in that their disintegration is almost always absolute.

7. Robert Abirached, *op. cit.,* p. 347.

8. Christine Garnier, "Revue dramatique," *La Revue des deux mondes* (February 1966), 455-456.

9. Armand Hoog, "The Itinerary of Marguerite Duras," *Yale French Studies,* XXIV (1959), 72.

10. Marguerite Duras had explored this theme already in *Les Petits chevaux de Tarquinia*: Sara's ultimate decision, for example, based on the principle that leaving is no different from staying.

Alfred Cismaru (essay date 1971)

SOURCE: "The Anti-Novels," in *Marguerite Duras,* Twayne Publishers, Inc., 1971, pp. 71-82, 88-95.

[*In the following essay, Cismaru discusses Duras's short stories and her novella* Moderato cantabile *as "anti-novels" in the tradition of the French New Novel.*]

"Le Boa" contains very little dialogue. It is a first-person brief memoir of a woman who looks back to the time when she was thirteen and she attended a school for girls whose directress, a virgin septuagenarian, had admitted her out of pity for her mother who was too poor to pay the full amount of the tuition.

Mademoiselle Barbet was at worst vicious, at best eccentric. While the other students were permitted to go out every Sunday, to the movies, for walks, to play tennis or otherwise amuse themselves, the narrator was subjected, each week, to two unvarying spectacles: a boa devouring a chicken at the local zoo, a free show which allowed the directress to charge her pupil's mother for "Sunday outing" expenses; and, upon returning to the seclusion of the school, the ugly nudity of the old woman who forced the girl to watch her undress so that she could boast about the quality of her underwear. These two unusual weekly events acted upon the mind of the young girl with almost catastrophic consequences, although her present ability to review them logically, clinically, points to the absence of major damage on her personality.

The intuition of the child told her that the boa's killing and assimilation of the chicken was a pure, innocent act, and that her directress' exhibitionism was the embodiment

of mature vice brought about by the frustrations of virginity. Marguerite Duras' description of the first Sunday occurrence is a blend of ferocious cold-bloodedness and poetic admiration. The spectacle of the boa's feast moves her
character to remark:

> What an impeccable crime, consumed in the warm
> snow of its feathers which added to the innocence of
> the chicken a fascinating reality. This crime was with-
> out stain, without a trace of spilled blood, without re-
> gret. The order after the catastrophe, the peace in the
> chamber of the crime [the boa's cage]. Entirely curled,
> black, shining with a purer dew than that of morning
> on berry bushes, of an admirable shape, a swelled
> roundness, tender and full of muscles, a black column
> of marble . . . replete with shiverings of contained
> power, the boa was integrating this chicken in the
> course of a sovereignly lofty digestion, as perfect as
> the absorption of water by the burning sands of the
> desert, a transubstantiation accomplished in sacred tran-
> quillity. In a formidable interior silence the chicken be-
> came boa. With a happiness to make you dizzy, the
> flesh of the biped was flowing through that of the rep-
> tile.

By opposition, the sight of Mademoiselle Barbet's nudity
fills the forced spectator with scorn and disgust:

> She would keep herself erect so that I would admire
> her, bending her eyes to look at herself lovingly. . . . It
> was too late. . . . A terrible odor emanated from the
> body of Mademoiselle Barbet. . . . I would stop my-
> self from breathing. Yet, she had her own sort of kind-
> ness. And in the whole town her reputation was se-
> cured, perfect, as virginal as her life. I would tell myself
> that, and also that she was, after all, an old woman.
> But it didn't matter. I would still stop myself from
> breathing.

In the child's mind, then, violence meant purity and virginity signified vice. To guard herself against the possibility of winding up like Mademoiselle Barbet, the narrator
would go to the window and smile to passing colonial soldiers, much like another Duras heroine, in the hope that
one would stop and kidnap her and rape her and save her
from the horrifying infirmity of a sexless existence. More
than that, she began to suspect the *good,* and to feel limitless sympathy for the dispossessed, the villain, the *evil* in
society. Confessing that she had heard only much later
about the commercial side of prostitution, she then tells of
her vision of a bordello "as a temple of defloration where,
in all purity . . . girls . . . who were not destined to get
married [because of a poor financial background], discovered their body with the aid of unknown men of the same
species as they. A sort of shrine of impudicity, the house
of prostitution had to be a silent place where no one spoke,
everything being so arranged that no word need be pronounced in its sacred anonymity." And she pursues: "I
imagined that the prostitutes put on a mask on their face
before entering. Without doubt, in order to earn the anonymity of the species, the absolute lack of personality of
the boa. . . ."

It is useless to wonder whether the narrator, who ends her
story in a beautifully poetized vision of her future, should

have been more prompted to choose the path of the boa
than that of Mademoiselle Barbet. This piece makes no
pretense at plot or credibility. It merely points, with simplicity and sobriety, to the workings of the mind of a young
girl under the imperious fatality of two events imposed
upon it from the outside and viewed now from the vantage
point of maturity. It suggests, of course, the very little
choice a child has in the difficult process of growing up
and of shaping a personality: for while not everyone contemplates a boa devouring a chicken, nor smells the decaying body of a naked septuagenarian week after week
for a number of years, other similarly uncontrollable forces
mold and petrify human life. This is a pathetic consideration, especially when made (perhaps only intuitively) by
a teen-ager. Yet, Madame Duras' approach prevents **"Le
Boa"** from becoming a soap opera type of narrative. Her
introduction of the developing feelings and ideas of the
girl remains, throughout the brief pages of the story, cautious, medical, a bit too calculated perhaps. We are left
with the impression that what we have before our eyes is
not fiction at all but rather a well-studied case history.
That the author could have accomplished this in spite of
the many poetized passages points to the writer's ability to
weave in a brilliant style even the most ludicrously violent
events to have been described by her pen. Perhaps nowhere is this more apparent than in **"Le Boa"**'s last paragraph:

> Thus the world, and therefore my life, opened up on
> two avenues which gave me two distinct alternatives.
> There existed, on the one side, the world of Mademoi-
> selle Barbet, on the other, the compelling world, the fa-
> tal world of the species considered as fatality, the world
> of the future, luminous and burning, singing and shout-
> ing, of a deft beauty, but to the cruelty of which one
> had to accede as one had to accede to the spectacle of
> devouring boas. And I would see that world pointing to
> my future, the only possible future for me, I would see
> it opening up with the music, the purity of a serpent's
> unfolding body, and it seemed to me that, when I would
> come to know it, it would be in this way that it would
> appear to me, in a development of mystic continuity
> . . . with movements of terror, of enchantment, with-
> out rest, without fatigue.

But a woman is not a boa, and for most young ladies the
fascination of the bordello decreases with maturity. It is
quite probable, then, that Marguerite Duras' narrator, who
never mentions a family, or a husband, and who confesses
having learned, eventually, of the commercial side of prostitution, never did attain the serenity and innocence of the
serpent. Did she become another Mamedoiselle Barbet, or
was she simply afraid, at the time she began to recollect
her childhood, that her emulation of the old directress was
an inevitable prospective? In either case, the reincarnation
that the young girl had dreamed of, as she smiled, naïvely,
to passing soldiers, appears to have struck the older woman
as a fanciful utopia she could only look back to with a
mixture of nostalgia and cold-blooded lucidity.

. . . . .

> The two husbands Madame Dodin had had were drunk-
> ards. She had left them both. . . . [her children,] she

did not want to see them, they bored her. She had given them a fine education . . . and for them she had worked in a factory for fifteen years. In the evening, her earnings not being sufficient, she would take in other people's washes.

"I worked so much for them," she explains, "that I've had enough. All I ask is that they leave me alone."

But the *others* hardly ever leave anyone alone, and Madame Dodin [the protagonist of **"Madame Dodin"**] caretaker of a modest apartment building, is even less in a position to aspire to the peace and quiet due a tired, old woman.

One of the duties to which she objects constantly is the daily chore of emptying the tenants' garbage cans. She has done it for years, of course, every morning of every day of every week, but she has complained about it all day, every day of every week, to tenants, to neighbors, to a streetsweeper whom she befriends, Gaston, to anyone who would listen. Specifically, she detests the odor, the weight, the contents; generally, she is bothered by the servitude that emptying other people's garbage suggests, her relegation to a position of inferiority, her intuition that, somehow, her chore reduces her to a subhuman. In her impasse, Madame Dodin, too lucid and too experienced to hope in the accepted sense of the word, cannot be aided by faith or by revolt: "God is nothing to brag about," she says, "I'm telling you. And then, the Son, just as bad as the Father . . . and the Communists, they're just like the priests, except that they say they're on the side of the workers. They repeat the same thing, that we've got to be patient, so there's no hope from them either." Dispossessed as she is, what is left for Madame Dodin to do? Not very much, not much more than other Marguerite Duras heroines have been able to devise: she unravels old pullovers, for example, and she talks a great deal. Not that she does anything with the wool or that she says anything when she speaks. Her remarks are nothing but clichés: "The sky is heavy . . . there is going to be a storm." Or else: "The sky is clear, it's going to be nice for the rich." But although she lacks both faith and the ability to revolt, she has not quite given up. Her daily complaints keep her busy, alive, and give her a measure of significance which keeps her one step above the garbage-can type of existence she leads. But there is more: she refuses to go to church, as a friend suggests, for that would mean accepting the idea of patience, of compromise with the present for the sake of an illusory future; she has visions, at times, of impossible solutions, such as "special sewer openings in which, everyone, each night, would be compelled to empty his garbage"; she has a certain passion for Gaston, with whom she laughs, quarrels, perhaps even goes to bed; she is not above stealing, on occasion, the home deliveries of the tenants, and of boasting about the thefts; finally, and more importantly since the wish is made part of the last paragraph of the story, Madame Dodin looks forward to dying with a certain sadness but also with satisfaction if, death coming during the night, there would be no one to empty the trash cans in the morning: "It's a pity," she often says, "I won't be there to see their face."

Gaston, the male counterpart of Madame Dodin, only thirty years old (she is sixty), is no different in spite of his younger age. She empties garbage, he sweeps it. As if he were already quite old, Gaston works slowly, walks painfully, his head bent, his broom dragging behind him, paying attention to no one (except, occasionally, to Madame Dodin), and is almost always indifferent, anonymous, alone. He drinks, he gets fat, he is a picture of progressive decay: "He has lived too long . . . the people in the neighborhood can die or take their First Communion, nothing moves him. He is no longer interested in human ends. They bore him. . . . And in all the human joys or mournings he perceives nothing but gradual deterioration." Because he is younger, the unchanging monotony of his work appears even more pathetic. Old or young, Marguerite Duras seems to suggest, the routine and the dirt of the subhuman functions which we must all perform to a greater or lesser degree, make life barely bearable and inconsistent with our more beautiful, more fanciful visions of it. For like his friend, Gaston too dreams: "What I need is 20,000 francs. To go to the South, take in the sun and maybe, who knows, get another job." And in this ideal location he would stop working at four in the afternoon, he would be free, he would be known, people would shake his hands, he would take part in conversations, he would meet a girl, a brunette, she would smile to him, he would smile back. There is nothing much in the meantime, however: three glasses of white wine a day, the daily exchange of banalities with Madame Dodin, the possibility, quite vague and certainly meaningless, of a physical relationship in a moment of stupor or drunkenness.

Both Madame Dodin and Gaston, then, lead the existence of previously met Duras characters: theirs is a miserable life, a human condition they are unable to change. Yet, increasingly, they become used to it, and only in moments of removal from reality are they capable of imagining something better. These moments are sufficient for survival, however. They guarantee a trace of security, they reincarnate humans into a more humane, more acceptable situation. More than that, in **"Madame Dodin"** the author inserts some of her rare humorous passages, at which readers laugh with, and sometimes more than the protagonists: the old woman's way of *kidding* Gaston by emptying, on him, from her window, her pots and pans; and Gaston's impatient wait, under the window, for Madame Dodin to appear and to splash him with the contents of her kitchen vessels. Some of the conversations between the two are particularly comic, notably the one in which Descartes and philosophers in general are taken to task for theorizing about matters that are too remote and of no immediate value to the masses:

"It urinates, therefore it drinks," Madame Dodin said.

"This reminds me of something," Gaston noted. "A philosopher said the same thing: I think, therefore I am."

"He would have done better to keep quiet," Madame Dodin said, "if he didn't discover anything better than that."

"The one who discovered it was Descartes," said the street-sweeper.

Madame Dodin burst out in laughter.

"What kind of cards? As far as cards go, I only know about ration cards . . . with all their brains . . . why didn't they find something to do away with garbage cans?"

Unlike Beckett and other anti-novelists who use humor efficiently to point to the tragic side of the human condition, Marguerite Duras takes advantage only rarely of comic devices, and the passage quoted is the lightest to be found in her publications to date.

But **"Madame Dodin,"** in spite of its aliterary aspects which place it in the larger context of Marguerite Duras' ties with the New Novel, and in spite of the fact that it points to an unsuspected, though sparingly used ability to handle jocularity, has not been, so far, the object of critical comment. Like **"Le Boa,"** it has been eclipsed by the success obtained by the first story in the collection, ***Des Journées entières dans les arbres.*** Yet, **"Madame Dodin,"** and **"Le Boa,"** are carefully written compositions suggesting unmistakably the mature pen of a novelist whose talent will result in books of increased and permanent literary value.

. . . . .

Positioned last among the four short stories under discussion, **"Les Chantiers"** does not appear to have the gripping qualities of the first three. In it Marguerite Duras plunges into the New Novel (as a matter of fact, it is barely possible to speak, in this instance, of a mere connection with it); yet, as we shall see, the ending of the brief narration constitutes a sudden and unexpected ascent from the world of the despairing and the dispossessed, and what had started as a deeply pessimistic relation of the impossibility of human communication and relationship winds up in a syrupy, semi-Hollywood type of denouement.

She and He, guests at a resort hotel, meet outside of it, in front of an enclosure where an edifice is about to be built. There is nothing remarkable about either protagonist, and their anonymity coincides with their lack of luster. As does the reader, so do She and He notice the average in the other: the plain physical appearance, the lack of excitement of their movements, the slow pace of the daily routine in which they engage. Vacation here, even more than in *Les Petits Chevaux de Tarquinia,* is synonymous with stagnation. Whereas in the previous work a number of events did take place, and dialogue was at least apparently possible, in **"Les Chantiers"** the characters are unable to exchange more than a few words, and whatever microscopic action there is, it remains locked in the mind of the personages. He, for example, takes more pleasure in observing her furtively than in talking to her or in establishing a more tangible rapport. She, on the other hand, ignores for a while that she is being watched and proceeds with the mechanical activities of her vacation: the meals,

the walks, the aimless entries into and exits out of the hotel; and when she becomes aware of his silent attention, like him, she makes a subconscious effort to avoid a meeting and to check the possibility of verbal intercourse. These subconscious attempts become more conscious later on, so that the two are able to hold on to that more subtle, more pleasurable feeling derived from indefinite waiting periods and from vague but passionate and unfulfilled desires.

In the man's case at least, the *happiness* he experiences is purely intellectual, and he soon begins to lose appetite and the ability to sleep; for it is eminently difficult to wait everywhere for a woman one hopes would never appear; and to watch everyone of her gestures without being seen and without making the interest visible to her or to others. In addition, the sight of the slightly soiled collar of a blouse she wears one day awakens in him a sexual image that leads to the discovery of more potent reasons for postponing the development of a real friendship:

> The view of this collar dirtied and wrinkled by this neck, this back of her neck half hidden under her hair, that material [of the collar], these things that he alone saw, that she did not know he saw . . . it was as if they were two to live in this body she had . . . [and] the night which followed that day the memory transformed itself into desire . . . but this desire was immediately so strong that he wanted her to be even more ignorant than she was of the life which was taking place within her [ignorant of his participation in that life]. Thus, once successful in possessing the woman he would be able to get hold of her more fully, to take advantage of her entirely, to dispose totally of this body whose sovereign negligence he had been able to uncover.

There is, then, no reason to force or to hasten an acquaintanceship; there is every reason to savor the delicious misery of waiting.

Or is there? The tone of the writer in **"Les Chantiers"** does not favor a precise conclusion. While she describes at length the protagonists' mysterious joy in the highly sophisticated game of hide-and-seek they play, she also appears to mock their *vie tranquille* (the words are repeated several times in the story and they recall, of course, her 1944 novel of the same title), the way He "plunged slowly, each day, more deeply into the red forests of illusion," the actual pleasure he feels when she passes by without recognizing him, his secret wish that she leave the hotel and his silent enumeration of all the reasons she might have for leaving, his refusal to stop her in the street and talk to her, his equally emphatic decision, "No, at the risk of losing her I would never strike a conversation in public," and, finally, "the absence of drama in his life." But over and above the derision in which she holds, perhaps, her characters, Marguerite Duras, in typical anti-novelist manner, does not fail to point with sober sensitivity to the tragedy of their condition. The few banalities which she has them exchange, not about themselves but about exterior, unimportant things (comments on the building under construction, on the men who work on it, on the changing landscape), reveal beyond doubt the emptiness of their existence. Their nervous gestures too, their forced smile and occasional laughter which "expressed neither irony, nor confusion, nor coquettishness but only a certain incertitude," their extreme care "to ignore one another as if, in this resort hotel, in the middle of the summer and in spite of their freedom love had been condemned to death," unveil brutally the personages' marginal participation in life. He and She have everything going for them, and there are no outside impediments to the birth of love. But contact beyond the mere trivial and the briefest moment is impossible since there is no inner drive, no initiative, no desire to satisfy desire. There are only certain glimpses, a number of material, solid objects (the bricks and mortars and ropes the men work with, for example), and the strangely consoling catharsis to be derived from them: "When she left again . . . the man felt like calling her back and shouting to her that this was a chance, a joy, the existence of things such as the fence around the enclosure inside of which the men were working. He did nothing of the kind. He could neither cry out to her to stay, nor could he get up in order to try and hold her back. This impotence was also mysteriously satisfying."

The very idea that satisfaction can result from a deficiency points to what extent Marguerite Duras adheres to that literature of consent mentioned in conjunction with earlier works. But unlike before, in **"Les Chantiers"** she adheres to it until the very end (or almost), and the reader has no advance notice of the possibility of even a modestly happy outcome. In a very tight structure, untainted by the slightest suggestion of sentimentality, the author appears to endow her characters with such petrified qualities of timorousness, timidity and reserve that we seem to deal more with some Beckett or Ionesco-type personages than with the more malleable, more flexible protagonists we had encountered on previous occasions. In the shorter format of the *nouvelle,* we are led to think, there is very little time for He and She to engage in any sort of liberating act which would insinuate at least the appearance of a closer rapport. Besides, He and She find, increasingly, a curious fulfillment in desire without satisfaction or in satisfaction derived from incongruous sources. That is why, when at the end of the story the two meet abruptly, at the edge of a forest, after a long walk in the course of which she had followed him with mechanical precision, we are unprepared and unwilling to accept what is obviously a contrived conclusion. The characters, it seems, had tasted such extreme pleasure in waiting, and had experienced such intense emotions in deliberately vain efforts at contact that we now view their encounter as anticlimactic if not as a non sequitur. The reader who has allowed himself to be drawn into the rhythm and tempo of the story sees himself suddenly outside it. Events which had appeared to him to lead to an essentially negative outcome in line with the characters' makeup take a turn away from the inner truth of the situation, and an artificially happy ending is constructed at the expense of the stated limitations of the personages' ability and desire to make contact. The meet-

ing in **"Les Chantiers,"** the back cover of the 1967 French edition informs us, "is the story . . . of the first beginning of love." That love can still begin after most of its emotional intensity has been experienced and consumed is as dubious a hypothesis as is the future of the now united couple, facing one another, without comment, fresh out of words (the inner dialogue has used them all) and of feelings too (He and She had waited too long, had met too often before they actually met).

The fact that Marguerite Duras ends her narrative with the unexplored union of hero and heroine points at once to the necessity of keeping within the boundaries of a short story and to the impossibility of going beyond the mass of internal reactions which had fatigued and weakened the characters. Thus, the sugar-coating of the denouement is not prolonged by sentimentality or emotional fakery. This, of course, is to the credit of the writer who will not, in the future, depart so radically from the circumscribed and limited status of the initially described reality. That she had, in a story more closely connected with the tenets of the Anti-Novel than any other, remains without explanation; unless it be that in **"Les Chantiers"** she felt suddenly that she had gone too far in a direction that she was not prepared to accept fully for fear of seeing her own, very personal fictional potentialities conform exactly to those of a semiestablished literary school. Madame Duras' integrity clashed, perhaps, with the writer's domination of plot and characters, and the writer lost. But **"Les Chantiers"** does not occupy a prominent place in the author's fiction. Except for the usual reviews concomitant with the publication of all her books, it has not given rise to critical comment. Marguerite Duras can easily afford to charge her last story to experience and emerge, as she will, in stricter control of subsequent literary endeavors. . . .

. . . . .

Three years after the publication of *Le Square* appears the very short (sixty-five pages in the Grove edition mentioned above) narrative of ***Moderato cantabile.*** It is noteworthy that only once before (the six-year period between the appearance of *La Vie tranquille* and *Un Barrage contre le Pacifique*) Marguerite Duras has taken a longer time to complete a book, and that, since 1958, no more than two years have elapsed between publications. Apparently, in spite of its brevity, this carefully written composition required an expanded period of concentration on the part of the author.

Armand Hoog, in whose opinion ***Moderato cantabile*** is not a real anti-novel but, as he cryptically states, "a novel which hesitates, which falls back upon itself, a hesitating novel, undecided and perplexed," considers it paradoxical that she should have gone with it from Gallimard to the Editions de Minuit, headquarters of the New School. It is curious, however, that the critic's article on Marguerite Duras appears in a special number of the *Yale French Review* entitled "Midnight Novelists." But more about this later.

As John W. Kneller has observed, *moderato cantabile* is to be interpreted as an antithetical term which is never used for a musical composition: the directions usually specify *moderato* by itself or in connection with *allegro* and *andante* in order to qualify the meaning of the single word; *cantabile,* which means "singable," points to a group of notes that are to be sung. *Moderato* is viewed by the same critic to signify the routine and restraint imposed by habits and by society on the novel's principal character, Anne Desbaresdes, while *cantabile,* on the contrary, is to be interpreted as the temptation, on Marguerite Duras' heroine, of ultimate freedom, of involvement, of love and violence, of metempsychosis.

The two themes unfold admirably in the brief novel, from the very first scene and through the eight chapters into which the story is divided. The author manages to create immediately a tense drama between a stubborn child, a bored mother, Anne Desbaresdes, and a stern piano teacher, Mademoiselle Giraud, whom the pupil cannot or will not obey. Largely through dialogue, Marguerite Duras succeeds in evoking a powerful inner-outer struggle. There is nothing between the three personage-enemies in the room but an indirect contact, a bond of chance. Miles separate the characters: the child goes through the motions of playing the piano, automatically and badly; the teacher insists on technicalities which are meaningless in terms of the pupil's early development of method; and the mother appears to despise her unbearable and indocile offspring. Actually, twice in the novel (once to her boy and later to a man, Chauvin, whom she will meet) she remarks that, often, she thinks she invented her son, that he does not really exist.

As the music lesson proceeds, with quiet, poetic humor Marguerite Duras points to the dramatic distance between the protagonists: the child's attention to the noises outside (of the sea, of the motorboats) and to the beauty of the sunset ("The child, motionless, his eyes lowered, was the only one to remember that dusk had just exploded. It made him shiver."); the teacher's harsh reprimands but obvious lack of interest and charity; the mother's secret pleasure in the obstinate refusal of her son to learn, to conform, which she associates with her own stifled desire to escape the conventionality and humdrum of an empty existence as wife of a rich industrialist, on vacation at a remote seaside resort. To the teacher's persistent request for an explanation of the meaning of *moderato cantabile,* the boy's ignorance, feigned or real, points, for his mother, to the possibility of eluding the routine and the monotony of her life. *Cantabile* "fights" *moderato* outside of the apartment also, for while the bickering goes on inside, a murder takes place in a café across the street. And the cry of the victim, of the gathering crowd, of the police sirens insinuates itself into the room, into the inner fibers of the three personages, like a terrible and inescapable obsession. Anne is most afflicted, for while others live and die outside, she waits and is bored and has no hope of participating in real human dramas.

Across the street the killer has been arrested, and the crowds have dispersed. No one knows exactly why the murder took place. Rumor has it that assassin and victim were too much in love. When the police arrived, the murderer stood over the body of the woman, his lips grotesquely chained to hers, her blood spotting the collar of his shirt. Anne goes into the café and meets Chauvin, one of the workers in her husband's factory. He had witnessed the murder and now attempts to satisfy Anne's curiosity about the details. As they speak, they are mysteriously attracted to each other, and they will meet, day after day, in order to drink and talk about the crime that had taken place. There is, of course, no real reason for their clandestine meetings. The simple explanation which they share at first, and which becomes more and more difficult to accept as time goes on, is that Anne must know the motives behind the murder and that Chauvin hopes to dig into these motives and relate them to her. But pressed continuously by questions, he soon runs out of details. He does not recall very much about the case, he has not been an attentive witness. "I'd like to know a little more," she keeps repeating. "Even if you're not sure of your facts." So he imagines how the *others* must have met, how their relationship must have developed, what they could have spoken about. Anne becomes intoxicated with the personality of the victim, she cannot help mimicking the gestures and movements the other woman must have made, or repeating the words she must have said, in the intonation she must have used. Her identification with the *other* is her incarnation, her participation in life, in the mystery of life, in the happiness and violence of life. Little does it matter that Chauvin, too, begins to play; that his role is that of the killer; that their perusal of the game of unbearable passion the *others* must have gone through can only come to one predictable end: Chauvin, the assassin, will have to kill Anne, the voluntary gull. But when Chauvin raises his hand and utters: "I wish you were dead," Anne responds simply: "I already am." His gesture is useless, for the woman has already discarded *moderato* and has chosen *cantabile* in its place.

Or has she? The choice is not certain, although it appears that the answer is in the negative. If we place **Moderato cantabile** in the context of Marguerite Duras' previous novels we cannot escape the fact that, for most of her characters, incarnation remained utopian. Becoming someone else, finding identification with another, are not simple operations like that of forging a passport. And the flimsiness and sketchiness of Anne and Chauvin do not point to the strong will required for the complete process of metempsychosis. Actually, what do we know about hero and heroine? We know that she is intrigued by or falls in love with Chauvin; we suspect that he is intrigued by or falls in love with Anne. But the psychological adultery in which they engage does not go past one dubious kiss in the café. And if "they lingered in a long embrace, their lips were cold and trembling . . . performing . . . a mortuary ritual." There is, of course, the much-acclaimed regurgitation scene of chapter seven, when Anne, arriving home late for a reception scheduled by her husband, goes through the hostess' motions poorly, eats the *saumon glacé,* the *canard à l'orange,* and the mocha ice on top of the many glasses of wine she had drunk before, and winds up vomiting "the strange food that had been forced upon her." This scene, interpreted by John W. Kneller as symbolizing "the end of the conventionality theme," the abandonment of *moderato,* does not make up for the fact that Anne's love for Chauvin was lived only emotionally, that there was no love affair as such, and no actual murder. In spite of the five confrontations with Chauvin, in spite of the wine and the almost accidental kiss, the heroine has remained herself, the bored, lifeless Anne who had been mimicking the *other* who was indeed assassinated because she had been alive, really alive, and because she had kindled in her husband, or lover, or whatever he was, a passion or a hatred or a madness that is only possible with the living. Likewise, in spite of Chauvin's perseverance and efforts in trying to satisfy Anne's curiousity, in spite of his emulation of the assassin's gesticulations and phraseology, he too fails in his attempt at incarnation: he does not succeed in possessing the wife of his boss, nor in killing her. And his last attempt at reaching for the woman's neck is as futile as the kiss in which their icy lips had met when he had tried, vainly, to give to their relationship the aura of passion that the other couple must have known and enjoyed.

The relationship between Anne and Chauvin proves only that an alienation from society is possible, for a short time, and that the strictures and restrictions of bourgeois respectability can be avoided without permanent danger by those rebels who repent and return within the orderly mechanism of accepted decorum. Just as the child learns eventually the meaning of *moderato cantabile,* so do hero and heroine discover the futility of stubbornness, of contradiction, of revolt, as evidenced in their final separation. However, their capitulation and consent are in no way inconsistent with the short-lived adventure and imitation of the *others.* The latter played a major role for they rekindled in the protagonists an awareness of the existence of other dimensions, other values, other rules: extralegal, violent, fiercely relentless and almost within reach. This newly acquired cognizance is sufficient to make them go on, to survive. Thus, it may be said that the unnamed town in **Moderato cantabile** is no different from Tarquinia. In both places, a number of calamitous events took palce, but even those most closely connected with them could only be touched temporarily. And characters who had attained an elusive poetic presence, a kind of purity and eternity in another, a different and forbidden world, realize that *moderato* alone is a practical sine qua non of the human condition.

The incompatability of the two musical themes of the title is beautifully interwoven in the narrative pattern. Nowhere is this more obvious than in the seventh chapter, with its description of the formal dinner scene inside the house and the relation of Chauvin circling the mansion outside the garden railings. Anne is painfully aware of the double role she must play as respectable hostess, trying desperately to behave according to the norms of the society within which she lives, and as frustrated woman prey to the stark sexual and destructive desire which she feels welling within her for the man whose nearness she guesses with every fiber of her inebriated being. An object of scandal to husband and guests inside, an object of wild passion to the man prowling outside, Anne moves and speaks with hesitation, uttering fragments of sentences and restating with every gesture and every word the dichotomy that is within her until she vomits both the wine she had drunk earlier and the socially acceptable victuals of the gala dinner of which she had been forced to partake. All this corresponds pointedly with the sonata form which is usually divided into three parts: exposition, development, and recapitulation. Two opposing themes, in this case *moderato* and *cantabile,* unfold through these stages and end in a *coda* or closing theme, in the present novel the act of vomiting. But Anne's regurgitation is neither an acquiescence in the invitation to freedom of *cantabile* nor, for the time being, a return to the security of *moderato* (it is only after the fifth meeting with Chauvin in the eighth and final chapter and following her inability to become in actuality a victim and his to become in actuality a murderer that the separation will take place); it is, in its simplest interpretation, an expected physical reaction on the part of a person that has had too much wine to drink and too much food to eat. But it is also an indication of the heroine's utopian incarnation, for while the salmon, the duck, and the mocha ice are her husband's, the wine, which is also ejected, has been bought for her by Chauvin. To see in her temporary ailment a proof of definitive metempsychosis is to be taken in by the tragic modulations of the finely controlled musical themes and to forget that no absolute emulation has taken place, for after all there has been no actual consummation of love and no actual murder.

Excellent control is evident not only in chapter seven but in the novel as a whole. For example, Marguerite Duras is extremely careful about her chronology; all episodes take place at the same time of day, the first begins on a Friday; the fifth, sixth, and seventh on the following Friday; the eighth two days later. The entire plot unfolds in clearly delineated sets, all positioned between late afternoon and evening. Control is likewise apparent in the author's use of verb tenses. While most of the composition is written in the narrative past, we are fully aware that the action takes place in the present, and the illusion of the past only serves to enhance the sense of immediacy of the situation. In the dinner scene of chapter seven there is an unexpected shift to the present tense in order to make absolutely clear the urgency of the rapidly moving events that will culminate in the vomiting incident. But the act of spewing itself and the rest of the chapter are written in the future, as if to cast additional doubt on an already complex climactic scene. Finally, there is a return to the narrative past in chapter eight, as befits Anne's and Chauvin's impending reversion to *moderato,* the inescapable solution.

The enthusiastic reception accorded this novel can be explained also by the writer's continued interest in the stylistic devices of the New School: the broken, interrupted conversations, the repetitions, the lack of specific details, the alcohol-blurred vision of the personages through which the reader must interpret the development of plot, to an extent the anonymity of characters (we learn Chauvin's name very late in the book, and those whose names we know from the beginning remain vague, sketchy, and wanting in completeness), finally, the cinematographic technique of set construction, not unlike that of Alain Robbe-Grillet's *Last Year at Marienbad* (1961), to which **Moderato cantabile** has already been linked. Much of the dialogue is also in the tradition of the New Novel:

> "I meant to ask you, you're not working today?"
>
> "No, I need some free time for the moment."
>
> "Time to do nothing?"
>
> "That's right, nothing."

Recalling a somewhat similar exchange between Sara and Jean in *Les Petits Chevaux de Tarquinia,* the passivity to which this passage points is often under the protagonists' attack during their encounters. To guard against it, to make it less visible to each other, she asks question after question and he attempts to respond, as best he can, inventing when he no longer knows what to say. But periods of silence sneak up on them just the same, and they find their awkwardness unbearable. At one point he pleads: "Hurry up and say something. Make it up." And she reacts with a long speech, without punctuation, in the film version declaimed by the actress almost in one breath: "People ought to live in a town where there are no trees trees scream when there's a wind here there's always a wind always except for two days a year in your place don't you see I'd leave this place I wouldn't stay all the birds or almost all are seagulls you find them dead after a storm and when the storm is over the trees stop screaming you hear them screaming on the beach like someone murdered it keeps the children from sleeping no I'll leave." Lack of communication and the inability to agree on even the slightest matters are likewise continuously pointed to. In this connection, Marguerite Duras appears, on one occasion, to recall another passage from *Les Petits Chevaux de Tarquinia* when she writes: "Some people declared that the day had been hot. Others—and they were the majority—did not deny it had been a beautiful day, but claimed that it had nevertheless not been hot. Still others had no opinion."

It is clear, then, that **Moderato cantabile** belongs as much to the New School as did **Des Journées entières dans les arbres** and *Le Square,* as will all of the author's subsequent fiction. "On page 77 the man who was simply The Man can no longer persist in anonymity," observes Armand Hoog. "'I am called Chauvin,' he says. How that little sentence pleases me! I have confidence in Marguerite Duras. She is a great novelist who will rise superior to the perils of the literary *school* [the Anti-Novel school]." Outside of the fact that, eventually, we learn Chauvin's name, and that Armand Hoog appears to have philosophical reservations on the merits of the anti-novel, it is difficult to see how **Moderato cantabile** can be interpreted as the beginning of a return to traditional fiction. The books which follow it deny this. And if Madame Duras rises superior to

the unspecified perils of the New School, it is because she does not follow to the extreme its abstract, disintegrated, and often cold-blooded themes; because her personages remain essentially human in their preoccupation with the problems of solitude, of communication, of desire and love tempered and frustrated by social deliberations; finally, because they rebel against the subhumanity to which they are frequently relegated, and because they fail and they consent to it, as tragic heroes and heroines do once the glossiness of revolt is erased with the passage of time.

Alfred Cismaru (essay date 1973-74)

SOURCE: "Salvation Through Drinking in Marguerite Duras' Short Stories," in *Modern Fiction Studies,* Vol. 19, No. 4, Winter, 1973-74, pp. 487-95.

[*In the following essay, Cismaru examines the meaning of alcohol consumption in* Le Marin de Gibraltar *and* Moderato cantabile, *concluding that alcohol allows Duras's otherwise hopeless characters a brief period of rebellion and salvation.*]

The following piece of dialogue from Marguerite Duras' fourth novel might well be part of the conversation of most of her personages who find in alcohol a pleasurable and solitary relief:

> "The great drinkers," she said, throwing herself back in her chair and starting to laugh, "they must be incomparably reassuring."
>
> "I should like to be the very greatest drunk of all the southern seas," I announced.
>
> "Why?" she said laughing.
>
> "Why indeed?" I said.
>
> "I don't know," she answered. "How should I know?"[1]

Marguerite Duras, widely known in this country as the author of the scenario of *Hiroshima mon amour* (1960), has, at present, one of the most distinguished reputations of any French female contemporary novelist or playwright. Her novels, almost always brief and bordering on the short story, constitute proper fare not only for the intelligentsia but serve also to introduce the American college student of French to the more intriguing aspects of Continental "aliterature": *Le Square* (1955) and **Moderato cantabile** (1958) are two cases in point. But in spite of her popularity, very few critical comments on her work exist,[2] and only one reviewer has mentioned so far, and that only in passing, the fascination that drinking entails for most of Marguerite Duras' fictional characters.[3]

Her novels have been classified, not without a certain amount of arbitrariness, as falling into two categories: American and aliterary.[4] The first includes such titles as *Les Impudents* (1943), *La Vie tranquille* (1944), *Un Barrage contre le Pacifique* (1950), and *Le Marin de Gibral-*

tar. These were, on balance, passable combinations of adventure, brutality, drunkenness, sexual aggressiveness hiding deep frustrations, and artificial gaiety obscuring poorly the most desolate sadness, loneliness, and boredom. The second incorporates *Les Petits chevaux de Tarquinia* (1953), the four short stories included in *Des Journées entières dans les arbres* (1954), the already mentioned *Le Square* and *Moderato cantabile, Dix heures et demie du soir en été* (1960), *Le Vice-Consul* (1966), and several other publications. With them Marguerite Duras moved towards a form which relinquishes the usual supports of fiction writing: the time-space pattern, the development of an action, or the presentation of characters. The author began to flirt with the anti-novel, but her present position in the aliterary or anti-literary school, whose members, incidentally, deny its formal existence, could be the subject of considerable debate. Whereas most of her works since 1953 seem to fall within the general pattern established by such writers as Nathalie Sarraute, Michel Butor, Samuel Beckett, Alain Robbe-Grillet, and others—plotless stories from which motivation, that stock prop of the traditional novel, is patently absent: nameless hero-narrators; banalities expressed by disarming clichés; disregard for psychological verisimilitude; obsessive and contradictory fragments of thoughts and souvenirs; meticulous, precise, and detailed presentation of objects—it is doubtful that she has more than an indirect association with the new school. Her stories can, after all, be summarized, and she always manages to evoke a humane atmosphere, to suggest a human situation, to seize and seal the authentic impasses of heroes and heroines dissatisfied with their condition.

But American or aliterary, drinking occupies a special place in the precarious existence of her novel's characters. To a greater or lesser degree, Chianti, Bitter Campari, manzanilla, champagne, cognac, and above all whisky constitute the vital ingredients of most Durasian personages. Because of space limitations, however, the prominence of drinking in their lives will be examined in only two novels, one belonging to the American group, *Le Marin de Gibraltar,* the other to the aliterary classification, *Moderato cantabile.*

It will be recalled that *Le Marin de Gibraltar* is the story of a civil service clerk who, for eight years, had been copying faithfully birth records, marriage licenses, and death certificates. Although he does not say so, we imagine that he had always performed his duties with the devotion of a well-lubricated machine and the efficiency of a perfectly programmed computer. Apparently periods, commas, and semicolons were his only gods. Because Jacqueline worked in the same office, and because she was handy and willing, they began living with each other. And because, after the war, people started to move again, to take vacations, to travel, the narrator and Jacqueline joined the crowd and took a trip to Italy. But changes in locale and in routine do not alter the make-up of the persons involved. In this connection, the first paragraph of the book merits our attention: "We'd already seen Milan and Genoa and been in Pisa two days when I decided we'd go on to Flo-

rence. Jacqueline made no objection. She never made any objection" (p. 3). The word *already* is used frequently by the characters of *Le Marin de Gibraltar.* It matters little whether the action has been completed, is in the process of being completed, or is simply contemplated and has not even begun yet: the personages and the reader experience a feeling of monotony, of repetition, of lassitude. There is a lack of enthusiasm, of excitement, for what the hero does appears to have been done by others, so many times before, and by himself on who knows how many previous occasions. In addition, wherever he goes he fails to see real differences, for towns are similar, and people resemble each other in spite of arbitrary frontiers. Likewise, the second glass of wine tastes the same as the first, and the tenth would also, were it not for the state of intoxication of the drinker.

To hasten the state of intoxication, and in keeping with its post-war vogue in Europe, recourse is made to whisky: "I drank whisky to restore myself," says the narrator. "I was drinking more and more of it. So was she. We both drank more and more as the voyage went on. First of all in the evening. Then in the afternoon as well. Then in the morning. Every day we started a bit earlier" (p. 72). Drinking appeals for a variety of reasons, of course, but they can all be summarized by one word: oblivion. Oblivion of the stasis of life, of its routine pleasures and dissatisfactions, of those one loves or befriends as well, and of oneself above all, that cumbersome being, that being *de trop* as Sartre used to put it. And the best of reasons for a liaison become the worst of reasons after a while; surely the couple had acquired a certain stability after the two years they had been together, and it would be unwise to disturb it; of course, there was a vague propriety about people traveling conjointly which celibates could not hope to achieve; and certainly single rooms were, proportionately, more expensive than doubles. Nevertheless, alcohol consumption, like all good things, has side effects, and these render the passably worthy arrangement impossible to continue. Intoxication, for example, allows only restless sleep and uneven eating habits. This results in extreme fatigue, and the characters complain frequently of being tired. Theirs is not a mere physical weariness; it is a lethargic condition that becomes a permanent part of their existence; it dulls sensation and emotion and thus shelters the friendly, acquiescing *victims* from actual participation in life. Finally, there is, as one might expect, very little love-making and a great deal of talk about it. But when the partners cannot even bear to sleep with each other, separation becomes mandatory, and our nameless narrator initiates it. Jacqueline goes back to Paris, not very disillusioned, we suspect, and her former lover makes the acquaintance of a yacht owner whose boat is docked nearby. She is reputed to be mysterious, beautiful, rich, and American, and although the first three adjectives apply, the last does not. She is French, but had married an American who, being old and ugly, was gracious enough to die very soon and leave her a fortune. It seems that, in her travels, she had met one day a sailor from Gibraltar with whom she had had a brief liaison. Later he had abandoned her in Shanghai, having gone to a poker game from which he failed to return. Anna is, then, the perennial searcher for a lost lover, looking for him in all the parts of the world, following the slimmest leads furnished by old cronies and ex-crew members in need of money. Little does it matter that instead of the sailor from Gibraltar she finds the owner of a filling station in Sète, a swindler in Dahomey. What counts is the endless, quixotic quest, the hope, between whiskies, that she is something else besides a drunkard. Actually, there is very little that Anna has to go by. Her memory of the sailor suggests a number of physical descriptions, and her account of the events which led to their meeting and his disappearance is not always the same. "Sometimes I get the impression that there are ten different stories of the sailor from Gibraltar" (p. 83), the narrator observes to Epaminondas, one of the boat's crew members. But no matter. Seeking gives the illusion of meaning to one's life, and Marguerite Duras seems to imply that the more remote and unattainable the object or person sought, the more significant is the persistence of those who search: for they find continuity and permanence (the continuity and permanence of absence, if nothing else) in what would otherwise be an empty and inactive existence.

"The sailor from Gibraltar appears to me to be a symbol for happiness," opined Gérard d'Houville.[5] And so there is little wonder that Anna cannot locate him, that is, that she cannot find happiness in the absolute sense. Small sources of joy to keep one going are, however, available. She is rich, possesses a luxurious yacht, a taste for liquor, and the sailors, and other lovers she picks up occasionally (such as our narrator) provide her with a modestly satisfying sexual life. Similarly, our hero is not interested in, nor can he desire, any more. His decision to "link up" with Anna was a *gradual* decision, one that he had conceived between two long drinks a while back when he had realized that "downing a pint of something or other every hour, life still seemed bearable, worth the trouble of living" (p. 74). And because on Anna's yacht there is an unlimited supply of whisky, he can now, from a narrator's vantage point, tell us nostalgically: "I drank, read, sweated, and every so often went and sat somewhere else" (p. 84). She and he, then, perceive certain glimpses, certain reflections of felicity. These are both liberating and restrictive because while they make existence bearable, they are obviously temporary: a certain disquietude about the future remains, shadowed by the act of drinking which enhances the present and hastens its passing away. For the narrator's liaison with Anna will collapse, as that with Jacqueline had. Like the critic who remarked that "We stick with them [the characters] . . . if only to drink the whiskies, hear the conversation, and see the sky and the coast as they shimmer from the yacht,"[6] the personages themselves stick with each other for the same reasons. We, as readers, will one day pick up another book; and they, as characters, undoubtedly will succumb to monotony, to the fatigue that drinking brings about, to their own burdensome existence. And if they do not become too old or die, each will find another partner, another illusion.

In *Le Marin de Gibraltar,* as in previous and subsequent works, then, Marguerite Duras points to a world which is not entirely unlivable, as it is, for example, in the corpsed universe of Ionesco or Beckett. To begin with, it is our world, and she appears to think that we should not abdicate entirely until we have made a certain number of gestures and have pronounced a certain number of words, for if we did not make those gestures and did not pronounce those words, one wonders what else we could do outside of seeking death by the most expeditious means. Thus Madame Duras' heroes and heroines walk, eat, and drink, above all drink, make love occasionally (when the partners are new to each other and before alcohol begins to interfere with their potency), go to sleep and wake up and start again, all the time painfully aware that victories are gained with the greatest efforts, remain short-lived and always end in some form of death, physical or spiritual or both.

Published six years after *Le Marin de Gibraltar,* **Moderato cantabile** is another long short story in which the role of drinking in the life of the personages emerges with extreme clarity. As John W. Kneller has observed,[7] *moderato cantabile* is to be interpreted as an antithetical term which is never used for a musical composition: the directions usually specify *moderato* by itself or in connection with *allegro* or *andante* in order to qualify the meaning of the single word; *cantabile,* which means "singable," points to a group of notes that are to be sung. *Moderato* is viewed by the same critic to signify the routine and restraint imposed by habits and by society on the story's principal character, Anne Desbaresdes, while *cantabile,* on the contrary, is to be interpreted as the temptation, on Marguerite Duras' heroine, of ultimate freedom, of involvement, of love and violence, of metempsychosis—all attainable, perhaps and partly, with the aid of liquor.

Anne Desbaresdes is the wife of a rich industrialist. Hers is a humdrum existence, replete with monotony and boredom. Occasionally she accompanies her recalcitrant son to a stern piano teacher. His refusal to learn the meaning of the term *moderato cantabile,* in spite of the efforts of the instructor, points cleverly to the mother's own inability to opt for one or the other part of the impossible combination. *Cantabile* fights *moderato* outside the apartment also, for while the bickering goes on inside, a murder takes place in a café across the street. And the cry of the victim, of the gathering crowd, of the police sirens insinuates itself through the window, into the inner fibers of the three personages, like a terrible and inescapable obsession. Anne is most afflicted, for while others live and die outside, she awaits and is bored and has no hope of participating in real human dramas.

Across the street, the killer has been arrested, the crowds have dispersed. No one knows exactly why the murder took place. Rumor has it that the assassin and the victim were too much in love. When the police arrived, the murderer stood over the body of the woman, his lips grotesquely chained to hers, her blood spotting the collar of his shirt. Anne goes into the café and meets Chauvin, one of the workers in her husband's factory. He had witnessed the murder and now attempts to satisfy Anne's curiosity about the details. As they speak, they are mysteriously attracted to each other, and they will meet, day after day, in order to drink and talk about the crime that had taken place. There is, of course, no real reason for their clandestine meetings. The simple explanation which they share at first, and which becomes more and more difficult to accept as time goes on, is that Anne must know the motives behind the murder and that Chauvin hopes to dig into these motives and relate them to her. The real reason is that they both enjoy drinking and must drink in order to go on living. Like for the seafaring couple of *Le Marin de Gibraltar,* liquor becomes a medium and a crutch overshadowing the rest of their relationship. Actually, when pressed continuously by questions on the murder, he runs out of details. He does not recall very much about the case; he has not been an attentive witness. "I'd like to know a little more," she keeps repeating. "Even if you're not sure of your facts."[8] So he imagines how the *others* must have met, how their relationship must have developed, what they could have spoken about. With the aid of liquor, Anne becomes intoxicated with the personality of the victim; she cannot help mimicking the gestures and movements the other woman must have made or repeating the words she must have said, in the intonation she must have used. Her identification with the *other* is her reincarnation, her participation in life, in the mystery of life, in the happiness and violence of life. Little does it matter that Chauvin, too, begins to play; that his role is that of the killer; that their perusal of the game of unbearable passion the *others* must have gone through can only come to one predictable end: Chauvin, the assassin, will have to kill Anne, the voluntary gull. But when Chauvin raises his hand and utters: "I wish you were dead" (p. 62), Anne responds simply: "I already am" (p. 62). His gesture is useless, for the woman has already discarded *moderato* and has chosen *cantabile* in its place.

Or has she? The choice is not certain, although it appears that the answer is in the negative. If we place **Moderato cantabile** in the context of Marguerite Duras' previous short stories, we cannot escape the fact that, for most of her characters, reincarnation remained utopian. Becoming someone else, finding identification with another, are not simple operations like that of forging a passport. Liquor may indeed give the illusion of assuming another personality, but the flimsiness and sketchiness of Anne and Chauvin do not point to the strong will required for the process of complete metempsychosis. Actually, what do we know about hero and heroine? We know that she is intrigued by or falls in love with Chauvin; we suspect that he is intrigued by or falls in love with Anne. But the psychological adultery in which they engage does not go past one dubious kiss in the café. And if "they lingered in a long embrace, their lips [were] cold and trembling . . . performing . . . a mortuary ritual" (p. 61). There is, of course, the much-acclaimed regurgitation scene of chapter seven, when Anne, arriving home late for a reception scheduled by her husband, goes through the hostess's motions poorly,

eats the *saumon glacé,* the *canard à l'orange,* and the mocha ice on top of the many glasses of wine she had drunk before, and winds up vomiting "the strange food that had been forced upon her" (p. 53). This scene, interpreted by John W. Kneller as "symbolizing the end of the conventionality theme,"[9] the abandonment of *moderato,* does not make up for the fact that Anne's love for Chauvin was lived only emotionally, that there was no love as such, and no actual murder. In spite of the five confrontations with Chauvin, in spite of the wine and the almost accidental kiss, the heroine has remained herself, the bored, lifeless Anne who had been mimicking the *other* who was indeed assassinated because she had been alive, really alive, and because she had kindled in her husband, or lover, or whatever he was, a passion, or a hatred, or a madness that is only possible with the living. Likewise, in spite of Chauvin's perseverance and efforts in trying to satisfy Anne's curiosity, in spite of his emulation of the assassin's gesticulations and phraseology, he too fails in his attempt at reincarnation: he does not succeed in possessing the wife of his boss, nor in killing her. And his last attempt in reaching for the woman's neck is as futile as the kiss in which their icy lips had met when he had tried, vainly, to give to their relationship the aura of passion the other couple must have known and enjoyed.

The liaison between Anne and Chauvin proves only that an alienation from society is possible for a short time and that the strictures and restrictions of bourgeois respectibility can be avoided without permanent danger by those alcoholics who repent and return within the orderly mechanism of accepted decorum. Just as the child learns eventually the meaning of *moderato cantabile,* so do hero and heroine discover the temporary effect of drinking and the futility of stubbornness, of contradiction, of revolt, as evidenced in their final separation. However, their capitulation and consent are in no way inconsistent with the short-lived adventure and imitation of the *others.* The latter played a major role, for they rekindled in the protagonists an awareness of the existence of other dimensions, other values, other rules: extralegal, violent, fiercely relentless, and almost within reach. This newly acquired cognizance is sufficient to make them go on, to survive. Thus it may be said that, as in the case of the characters of *Le Marin de Gibraltar,* liquor plays an important, if only partly salutary, role. In both stories it lends places an elusive, poetic atmosphere; and it bestows upon people a kind of purity and eternity in another, a different and forbidden world.

Marguerite Duras, always preoccupied by the essentially human problems of communication, of solitude, of boredom, of desire and love tempered and frustrated by social deliberations, presents us frequently with heroes and heroines who, with the aid of liquor, manage to rebel somewhat, to become partially and temporarily reincarnated, and to consent later to the mediocrity of life, later, when the glossiness of revolt has been erased by the passage of time.

In a well-known short story which bears the title of the collection of four narratives already mentioned, ***Des Journées entières dans les arbres,*** Mother, the central character, is taken by her son to a bar where he works. She drinks a bit, and when she is presented with the bill, she finds it exorbitant for the little she has consumed. "It [drinking] is almost as expensive as a mattress,"[10] she complains. But it is not really possible to do without, many of Marguerite Duras' personages seem to imply.

Notes

1. Marguerite Duras, *Le Marin de Gibraltar* (Paris: Gallimard, 1952), p. 133. All translations are mine. Subsequent references are to this edition and are given within the text.

2. An important article, "Woman's Fate: Marguerite Duras," has been published by Jacques Guicharnaud in *Yale French Studies,* 27 (1961), 106-113; the reader may also consult Germaine Brée's Introduction to *Four Novels by Marguerite Duras* (New York: Grove Press, 1965).

3. Armand Hoog, "The Itinerary of Marguerite Duras," *Yale French Studies,* 24 (1959), 68.

4. Germaine Brée, "The Contemporary French Novel (1950-1960)," *French Culture Today* (Summer 1961), 4.

5. Gérard d'Houville, "Lectures romanesques," *La Revue des deux mondes,* December 15, 1952, p. 730.

6. Anonymous, "Floating Picnic: *The Sailor from Gibraltar,*" *Time,* July 7, 1967, p. E4.

7. John W. Kneller, "Elective Empathies and Musical Affinities," *Yale French Studies,* 27 (1961), 114.

8. Marguerite Duras, *Moderato cantabile* (Paris: Editions de minuit, 1958), p. 20; subsequent references are to this edition and are given within the text.

9. Kneller, p. 118.

10. Marguerite Duras, *Des Journées entières dans les arbres* (Paris: Gallimard, 1954), p. 55.

Victoria L. Weiss (essay date 1974)

SOURCE: "Form and Meaning in Marguerite Duras' 'Moderato Cantabile,'" in *Critique,* Vol. XVI, No. 1, 1974, pp. 79-87.

[*In the following essay, Weiss discusses the cinematic techniques Duras uses to convey her meaning in* Moderato cantabile.]

As a member of the school of New Novelists in France, Marguerite Duras has attained prominence through the ability to create a sense of dramatic intensity in her fiction which few others have been able to achieve. In ***Moderato Cantabile*** (1958) Duras tells the compelling story of a thirst for passion in a modern world where the routine of everyday existence dooms one to a life of tedium and boredom.

The novella's protagonist is Anne Desbaresdes, the wife of a rich French industrialist, whose life has long ceased to embody any passion or meaning. The story begins with Anne's observing the piano lesson of her son, an event which is part of her weekly routine. Suddenly a scream from the street below rises above the sound of the child's sonatina. At the time, Anne makes light of the disturbance so as not to upset the child, but immediately after the lesson, she goes to the cafe where a large body of people have already gathered to witness the aftermath of a murder. As Anne endeavors to get closer to the scene of the crime, she sees a man kissing and fondling the woman he has just shot. From this initial vision, Anne, in her passionless existence, becomes obsessed with the idea of a passion so strong as to culminate in death. With the help of a supposed witness, Chauvin, she begins to relive what she and Chauvin imagine to have been the passionate events and feelings which perpetrated the crime.

While the characters and situation of the work are indeed conducive to the intense dramatic build-up achieved, the technique that Duras employs is perhaps most worthy of close examination. The elements of technique are rapid juxtaposition of images and phrases and the use of cinematic techniques. The effectiveness of these is demonstrated early in the book where the peaceful sounds of the child's sonatina, blending and alternating with the sound of a motorboat out at sea and the sound of the waves breaking on the shore, are violently disrupted: "In the street downstairs a woman screamed, a long, drawn-out scream so shrill it overwhelmed the sound of the sea."[1] And then: "The sound of the sea moved in again" (78). Such rapid juxtaposition provides the reader with a panoramic sense of the area—a strict sense of where everything is in space. After Anne has attempted to convince her son that the scream he heard was of no consequence, he begins to play the sonatina again, but we are kept aware of the scream and its ominous significance:

> The music rose above the murmur of a crowd that was beginning to gather on the dock beneath the window. . . . The growing clamor of voices of both sexes rose from the dock. Everyone seemed to be saying the same thing, but it was impossible to distinguish the words. The sonatina went innocently along.
>
> (79)

What Duras does with sounds here—juxtaposing and superimposing to provide the reader with all the auditory phenomena bombarding the characters—she does equally well with images in a cinematic fashion. As the novella begins, we are told that "dusk had just exploded" (75). Anne, bored by the piano lesson, sees a motorboat "framed in the open window" and notes that "the whole sky was tinted pink by the last rays of the sun" (76). Anne's attention (and the reader's) is abruptly recalled from the scene of reverie by the severe words of the piano teacher, which are suddenly interjected without speech tags or an introductory phrase: "Are you really sure, for the last time now, are you sure you don't know what it [Moderato Cantabile] means?" (76). In this way Duras sets up a contrapuntal effect which presents a multiplicity of individual scenes in the vicinity of the murder simultaneously. The tedious ritual of the piano lesson and the calm murmur of the sea provide an effective contrast to the long drawn-out scream. Such narrative style pervades the work: during Anne's daily visits to the cafe, we are always kept aware of the child outside playing in front of the cafe, the boats out on the dock, the men leaving the factory across the way at quitting time, and the progress of the patronne in her knitting and washing glasses. Duras is careful to present a complete cinematic picture which shows characters who would gladly escape the confines of space and time but are unable to do so.

Perhaps the finest examples of what Marguerite Duras can do with juxtaposition and cinematic techniques occur in the dream-like Chapter VII. Anne, drunk and late for her husband's dinner party, struggles to maintain some sort of respectability, while her impassioned lover, Chauvin, circles the house like a hungry animal and the servants in the kitchen talk about their mistress's lack of decorum. Working with three distinct scenes, Duras creates a sense of immediacy and mounting tension by providing short cinematic shots of Chauvin outside the house, the servants in the kitchen, then abruptly inserting a line of dialogue without speech tags, calling the reader back to the dinner party:

> The man [Chauvin] has left the Boulevard de la Mer and circled the garden, keeping watch from the dunes which bound it on the north, then he has retraced his steps and descended the slope to the beach . . . tosses the pebble into the sea, lies down, stretches again, and says a name out loud.
>
> Two women, alternately and cooperatively, prepare the second course. The other victim is waiting.
>
> "As you know, Anne is defenseless when it comes to her child."
>
> (129)

As Anne, afflicted by the discomfort of too much drink and aware of the inflamed man outside circling the house, agonizingly struggles through the courses of the meal, the reader is caught up in a kind of pulsating rhythm. The frequent and rapid changes of scene build in intensity and never allow the reader to forget what is happening at any of the focal points of the chapter.

At times these efforts at simultaneity have an undercutting effect reminiscent of the fair scene in *Madame Bovary*:

> A song she cannot sing comes back to her, a song heard that afternoon in a cafe at the port. The man is still alone on the beach.

> He has just spoken the name again, and his mouth is still half open.
>
> "No thank you."
>
> The man's closed eyes are caressed by the wind, and in powerful, impalpable waves, by the scent of the magnolias, as the wind ebbs and flows.
>
> (130-1)

While witnessing Chauvin in a state of passionate obsession, the reader is almost simultaneously confronted with Anne saying "No thank you." She is presumably declining an offer of some roast duckling, but her negative response at the point of Chauvin's impassioned longing ironically prefigures their inability to attain their passionate desires.

In addition to occasional undercutting and simultaneity, Duras employs the juxtaposition of scenes to create a single impression of devouring carnal appetite by blending the sense of a devouring passion in Anne and Chauvin with the avid consumption of the meal by the dinner guests:

> They murmur softly in admiration as the golden duck is passed around. The sight of it makes one of them grow faint. Her mouth is desiccated by another hunger that nothing, except perhaps wine, can satisfy. . . . They leave her alone, and begin to devour the duck. Its flesh will be digested in other bodies. A man in the street closes his eyes, his eyelids fluttering from such willful patience. His body is chilled to the bone, and nothing can warm him.
>
> (130-1)

The close relation established here between the consumption of food and the devastating passion of Anne and Chauvin points to the deleterious conclusion of their passion. To reinforce the sense of foreboding, Duras depicts the consumption of the animals in images of death, such as duck "smothering . . . in its orange-shrouded coffin" (126) and "the remains of the salmon" (128). The progressive destruction of the fish and fowl, "deep-sea salmon already disfigured by the brief moments just past, continues its ineluctable advance towards total annihilation" (126-7), combined with the grossly avaricious behavior of the dinner guests, "The women will devour it to the last mouthful. . . . They stuff themselves with mayonnaise, specially prepared for this dish" (128-9), creates a sense of devouring appetite. Such devastation highlights the passion of the strangely affiliated couple; Duras is able to create a single impression while dealing with a multiplicity of locations and events.

The dramatic intensity of the chapter is also achieved by using the present tense, changing to the future tense at the end of the chapter, while the rest of the novella is written in the narrative past. The significant departure from an established pattern creates a sense of intense immediacy, consistent with the nature of sexual passion. The present tense also heightens the sense of conflict in Anne, between the necessity to conform to society's expectations and the unrestrained nature of passion and drink.

The shift to the future tense in the concluding paragraphs, where Anne vomits, creates a dream-like atmosphere of inevitability where Anne must pay for her excessive drinking and her waywardness. As Anne's husband views her vomiting, the narrator tells us: "This time she will offer an apology. The shadow will not reply" (133). Clearly, Anne, in deviating from established social routine, has caused the dissolution of her marriage, the inevitable result of abandoning herself to drink. Duras illustrates such inevitability by placing the vomiting scene against the background of the natural process of the child's breathing: "And to the inviolable rhythm of her child's breathing she will vomit forth the strange nourishment that had been forced upon her" (133). Nature must take its course.

Everywhere in the narrative, Duras is careful to use a conventional chronology and time scheme. The events of the story take place over a period of nine days, and every scene takes place during late afternoon or early evening with the exception of the dinner-party scene. Though many experimental novelists (such as Robbe-Grillet and Beckett) distort or destroy conventional time, Duras uses it to her advantage. Anne's daily walks with her son, her trips with him to his weekly piano lesson, even her trips to the cafe at a specific time each day illustrate her enslavement to boring routine. She is trapped by time in a tedious existence from which even the promise of passion cannot release her.

In spite of her adherence to a conventional time scheme, Duras seems to be aware of the physicist's distinction between psychological time and "clock time."[2] She intermingles the two during several of the cafe scenes. During the late afternoons, Anne and Chauvin are constantly aware of the passage of time—the warnings of the patronne, the blowing of the factory whistle, and the influx of working men into the bar. The end of the work day at the factory marks the time when Anne must leave so as not to disrupt the routine of her life. As the meetings of Chauvin and Anne continue, as they begin to act like an impassioned couple, phrases about having "very little time" (96) take on additional significance. As the days get longer, "It was lighter out than it had been three days before" (99), Chauvin and Anne realize that time for acting out their passion is decreasing:

"Now, talk to me."

"Oh, let me alone," Anne Desbaresdes begged.

"I can't, we probably have so little time."

(120)

Chauvin seems to be aware of a psychological time quite different from the patronne's or society's "clock time." The subtle distinction heightens the suspense and horror of the characters' progression toward psychological death.

Chauvin seems to be instinctively aware of the time that should elapse if their passion is to reach the desired heights.

Duras' treatment of time has one more interesting aspect. Anne's visits to the cafe occupy a space in a conventional time-scheme—they are a part of the boring routine of her day. The reader sees her arrive and leave. Chauvin, an unemployed factory worker, seems to exist outside of time; aside from the scene in Chapter VII where he circles the Desbaresdes mansion, the reader sees him only in the cafe. Significantly, only here does he speak; he does not seem to have any existence apart from the cafe. In a way he seems to be a figure outside of time; Anne, whose life is utterly dictated by time, remarks upon Chauvin's temporal freedom:

"I meant to ask you, you're not working today?"

"No, I need some free time for the moment."

"Time to do nothing?"

"That's right, nothing."

(94)

Consideration of time leads to another aspect worthy of inspection—narrative point of view. As noted in discussing the narrative in Chapter VII, Duras employs metaphorical description to convey certain impressions. Frequently, in her desire to remain faithful to the cinematic technique, she restricts her narrative to what the spectator's eye can see and his ear can hear. Most obvious in the early scenes of the novella where the murder scene is depicted, Duras even seems to have some fun with the point of view as she depicts a man with a camera capturing on film the very moment which remains so indelibly imprinted on Anne's memory:

The man sat down beside the dead woman, stroked her hair and smiled at her. A young man with a camera around his neck dashed up to the cafe door and took a picture of the man sitting there smiling. By the glare of the flash bulb the crowd could see that the woman was still young, and that blood was coming from her mouth.

(81)

The reader notes that the same *voyeur* technique is employed even more distinctly when the murderer is being hauled away:

He stopped dead, again followed by inspectors to the van and got inside. Then, perhaps, he was crying, but it was already too dark to see anything but his trembling blood-stained face. If he was crying, it was too dark to see his tears.

(82)

Curiously, however, while the narration is restricted here to what those at the scene can see, the narration at other times assumes knowledge that is not readily available to the reader nor the characters: "The man lay down again beside his wife's body" (81). During the course of the narrative, the relationship between the man and the woman is never made clear. The statement that the woman is the man's wife leads the reader to question who the narrator is.

While Duras' way of telling the tale reveals a knowledge of modern media and modern concepts, the substance of her tale also betrays a world view which is particularly modern. The motives for the murder which takes place in the story are never given, and are, in fact, almost completely imagined. The notion that absolute knowledge about observable physical reality is impossible for us to possess seems to lie beneath this creative process, illustrated when Anne first begins questioning Chauvin: he answers that he wishes he could answer her question, "but I'm not really sure of anything." And Anne replies: "Perhaps no one knows?" (85). In the world Duras pictures here, everything is relative to one's frame of reference, even down to the most insignificant details: "Some people declared that the day had been hot. Others—and they were the majority—did not deny it had been a beautiful day, but claimed that it had nevertheless not been hot. Still others had no opinion" (134). As one critic has pointed out, the multiplicity of viewpoints on even insignificant matters illustrates the "lack of communication and the inability to agree"[3] which are common in the modern world.

Along with these qualities, life is basically mere existence comprised of tedium and boredom. Duras' characters confront the same kind of meaninglessness that Beckett's characters face: life is a vast void that they endeavor to fill in the best way they can. Just as Beckett's characters feel compelled to fill the void with talking, Chauvin, aware of the void, frantically urges Anne to keep talking. While Beckett's characters long for silence, Chauvin fears a disruption of the mounting intensity which talk seems to give their relationship. As Anne and Chauvin make every effort to keep the dynamo of human passion moving, Chauvin's urgings for talk and the response they incite in Anne become more frantic:

> "Hurry up and say something. Make it up."
>
> She made an effort; her voice was almost loud in the cafe, which was still empty.
>
> "People ought to live in a town where there are no trees trees scream when there's a wind here there's always a wind always except for two days a year in your place don't you see I'd leave this place I wouldn't stay all the birds or almost all are seagulls you find them dead after a storm and when the storm is over the trees stop screaming you hear them screaming on the beach like someone murdered it keeps the children from sleeping no I'll leave."

> (106)

Anne's frantic attempt to fill the void is loaded with images of death and assault to the senses. Her words bear no relationship to the sexual passion that they are supposedly simulating. The passion which is to precede the love-murder is skipped; Anne is left with only images of hideous death.

The courage to even attempt a life of passion seems to come from alcohol. Drink is required to still her trembling hands and aid her in regaining composure: "Her hands were steadier, and the expression on her face was almost normal. . . . The wine must have helped, for her voice had also become more steady. A smile of deliverance slowly appeared in her eyes" (84). Soon Anne begins to drink simply for the sensation it provides: "They drank it together avidly, but this time nothing made Anne Desbaresdes drink except her nascent desire to become intoxicated from the wine" (102). The reader realizes that, eventually, the excessive drinking leads to an end which she cannot escape: "She gulped down her glass of wine. He let her go on killing herself" (123). While drunkenness often provides a brief respite from a basically oppressive world, Anne also finds drink to be a necessary adjunct to the creation of passion. Chauvin asks: "Would it be possible if we didn't drink so much?" Anne responds: "I don't think it would be possible" (123). But the drinking eventually only leads Anne to psychological death. Ultimately, she is foiled in her attempt to find passion and meaning.

Life, as Marguerite Duras sees it, is boring and tedious, at least for women. The only avenue for escape seems to be involvement in some momentous event—in this instance, intrigue with Chauvin. Duras' ability to convey such obsessive living in the moment, to create the pulsating rhythm of suspense, and to bring together cinematically two or more scenes makes her worthy of the modern reader's consideration.

Notes

1. Marguerite Duras, *Moderato Cantabile,* in *Four Novels by Marguerite Duras,* trans. Richard Seaver (New York: Grove Press, 1965), p. 78. Subsequent references are to this edition.

2. Jeremy Bernstein in his article on Albert Einstein ("Profiles: The Secrets of the Old One—Part I," *The New Yorker,* 10 March 1973, p. 74) distinguishes between the two concepts of time: "For the purposes of physics, one must be careful to distinguish between the subjective sense of time, which by its very character must be imprecise and personal, and the objective time measured by clock. (In physics, a 'clock' is any phenomenon that repeats itself—for example, the periodic motion of a pendulum or of a balance wheel, or even a heartbeat.)"

3. Alfred Cismaru, *Marguerite Duras* (New York: Twayne, 1971), p. 94.

Evelyn H. Zepp (essay date 1976)

SOURCE: "Language as Ritual in Marguerite Duras's 'Moderato Cantabile,'" in *Symposium,* Vol. XXX, No. 3, Fall, 1976, pp. 236-59.

[*In the following essay, Zepp examines the ways in which language fails to create a sense of order for the characters in* Moderato cantabile, *arguing that the characters' response is to ritualize their meetings and dialogue to impose meaning on reality.*]

The essential quality of the world of Marguerite Duras's **Moderato Cantabile** is sound. The sea, the wind, the radio in the café, the music lesson, the sound of the factory whistle, and, of course, the scream of the dying woman are the elements which define the novel's atmosphere and structure its essential pattern of meaning.

The nexus of sensual impressions Duras creates contrasts with the language through which her characters attempt to comprehend their world. Intertwined with the few descriptions is the dialogue which composes most of the novel. A woman, Anne Desbaresdes, and a man, Chauvin, drawn to a café by the violent death of a woman which took place there, meet five times during a period of nine days, ostensibly to talk and drink. Through their conversation, they probe this crime and, in the end, their own desires. Their dialogue is fragmented, at times almost incoherent, but it makes a progression which constitutes the only real "action" in the novel.

Their queries into the unknown couple's affair become a fictional creation—Anne's and Chauvin's projection of what they imagine the couple had found and what they themselves would like to find: a relationship in which two individuals form a unity, experiencing a total and unproblematic communication. Without implying any influence on Duras, we can turn to Martin Buber, who, in his *Ich und Du,* describes this ideal: "The basic word I-You can be spoken only with one's whole being. The concentration and fusion into a whole being can never be accomplished by me, can never be accomplished without me. I require a You to become; becoming I, I say You. [. . .] The relation to the You is unmediated. Nothing conceptual intervenes between I and You, no prior knowledge and no imagination; and memory itself is changed as it plunges from particularity into wholeness."[1]

Saying the "basic word" is for Buber an act which approaches a mystical communion of spirits. Language is transparent and secondary to the relationship itself: "But how can we incorporate into the world of the basic word what lies outside language? [. . .] in every You we address the eternal You, in every sphere according to its manner" (p. 57). In language as it is conceived here, the sign and its "meaning" are equivalent.

Anne and Chauvin fail to achieve such a state because they do not realize that "Nothing conceptual [should intervene] between I and You, no prior knowledge and no imagination." In **Moderato Cantabile,** this distorting mediation is language itself, the very means by which Anne and Chauvin attempt to construct their union and whose *opacity* it is the novel's goal to establish.

Music is the key to the role of language in the novel: sound *precedes* the structuring of sound, and thus any cog-

nition or meaning. The music played by the little boy has the emotional impact of the woman's scream; Anne reacts to it in the same way, with "l'émoi dans lequel la jetait toute allusion à son existence": "Et malgré sa mauvaise volonté, de la musique fut lá, indéniablement. [Anne] écoutait la sonatine. Elle venait du tréfonds des âges, portée par son enfant à elle. Elle manquait souvent, à l'entendre, aurait-elle pu croire, s'en évanouir [. . .]. De la musique sortit, coula de ses doigts sans qu'il parût le vouloir, en décider, et sournoisement elle s'étala dans le monde une fois de plus."[2] Even though the sonatina, as a musical form, does have "structure," it is the preconscious, elemental quality of the child's playing which is stressed. As do the sounds of the sea, for example, it corresponds to some inner force which is an essential quality of the child's being.

In contrast to this is the disciplined "music" his teacher would impose upon the child. Music is reassuring for Mlle. Giraud; it is an ordering, a structuring, a discipline through which one can control the disorderly, be it sounds or little boys: "Tes gammes. Tes gammes pendant dix minutes. Pour t'apprendre. Do majeur pour commencer" (p. 68); "Vous n'avez rien à lui expliquer. Il n'a pas à choisir de faire ou non du piano, Madame Desbaresdes, c'est ce qu'on appelle l'éducation" (p. 72). The scales are almost pure form; any emotive value which the sounds might elicit is lost through their ordering process and repetition. Mlle. Giraud is the only one of the three who does not react with "émoi" to the scream. For her, it is a curiosity, just as it is for the gathering crowd, and it does not upset the stable pattern of her existence.

Order vs. disorder, the inexpressible vs. the expression which distorts, and sound vs. language—these are the novel's basic conflicts, as established in Chapter One through the imagery of music, the piano lesson and the sea, through the figures of Anne, the boy, and Mlle. Giraud, and through the event which takes place in the café.

The structure of the piano lesson is in opposition to the freedom and fluidity of the world outside the room—the world whence the scream will come. Throughout the lesson, this outside world gradually invades the room. The open window is the one outlet for the child from the rigid posture ("sa pose d'objet" [p. 11]) and the confinement of the room and the lesson. The room is so high the child cannot see outside, but he can *hear* and finds escape through the sounds which enter the room, and which the discipline of the lesson cannot keep out—sounds of the city, sounds of the sea and, finally, the scream. The sea echoes the child's resistance to the music teacher's discipline: "Le bruit de la mer s'éleva, sans bornes, dans le silence de l'enfant" (p. 12); "Le bruit de la mer dans le silence de son obstination se fit entendre de nouveau" (p. 13). The child's silence is more communicative than anything he could say; his resistance seems as limitless ("sans bornes") as the sea. The sea represents a world which is beyond restrictions, a world with which the scream is also associated. Limitless, immoderate, unordered, it contrasts with the ordered, confined, structured world represented by the music lesson, a contrast reinforced when, after witnessing the aftermath of the violent crime, Anne reminds her son of the meaning of *moderato cantabile* (p. 21). The term is an indication of control or order: the way in which sounds are to be played. In addition, the phrase carries other connotations of order. Singing (*cantabile*) might be viewed as the joint effort to control or order sound by language and music, while moderation (*moderato*) is also a control, the control over excess. The sound of the death cry, linked to the world of the sea, takes on the sea's infinite ("sans bornes") quality; death, too, is a form of the infinite. The juxtaposition of the violent crime with the musical term stresses the order-disorder contrast between the various images associated with each.

The order-disorder quality of other elements may be distinguished by their associations with the chapter's sound images (the sea and music). Coming from outside the window, the scream is automatically associated with this world, the world of the limitless sea. The extent of its force is indicated by the fact that it even drowns out the sound of the sea: "Dans la rue, en bas de l'immeuble, un cri de femme retentit. Une plainte longue, continue, s'éleva et si haut que le bruit de la mer en fut brisé. Puis elle s'arrêta, net" (p. 13).

The noise of the crowd which gathers after the scream is heard also belongs to this world. Symptomatic of the anxiety and attendant disorder created by any confrontation with the unknown and the violent, this noise completely breaks down the structure of the music lesson: "L'enfant termina sa sonatine. Aussitôt la rumeur d'en bas s'engouffra dans la pièce, impérieuse" (p. 15); "Des voix précipitées, de femmes et d'hommes, de plus en plus nombreuses, montaient du quai. Elles semblaient toutes dire la même chose qu'on ne pouvait distinguer. La sonatine alla son train" (pp. 15-16); "Le bruit sourd de la foule s'amplifiait toujours, il devenait maintenant si puissant, même à cette hauteur-là de l'immeuble, que la musique en était débordée" (p. 17). The word "débordée" metaphorically links the noise of the crowd to the sea—and thus to the world of disorder. Both the scream and this noise are pure sound, not yet subject to the discipline of music or language.

Other elements are associated with the scream because of their particular timbre, furthering the contrast between the inexpressible (or the primary experience of sound itself) and the expression which distorts (language). The resonance or reverberation of the scream ("un cri de femme retentit") is a vibration of a chord at the same pitch as the invisible waves which communicate between mother and child, and between mother, child, and the external world. We may note several examples of such a communicating "vibration" in the first chapter: "L'enfant, immobile, les yeux baissés, fut seul à se souvenir que le soir venait d'éclater. Il en frémit" (p. 10). "Une vedette passa dans le cadre de la fenêtre ouverte. L'enfant, tourné vers sa partition remua à peine—seule sa mère le sut—alors que la ve-

dette lui passait dans le sang. Le ronronnement feutré du moteur s'entendit dans toute la ville" (p. 11). "Anne Desbaresdes prit son enfant par les épaules, le serra à lui faire mal, cria presque.—Il faut apprendre le piano, il le faut. L'enfant tremblait lui aussi, pour la même raison, d'avoir eu peur" (p. 14). The significance of this vibration may account for the trembling of Anne's hands and voice and, later, the trembling of Chauvin's hands, as they attempt a similar form of communication.

In a sense, the communication between Anne and the child reaches the union between individuals Anne seeks through the unknown couple in her relationship with Chauvin. This communication takes place without the mediation of language; it is the *presence* of his mother, felt by the child, and not the *expressed* threats of the teacher which causes the child to obey: "L'enfant tourna la tête vers cette voix, vers elle, vite, le temps de s'assurer de son existence, puis il reprit sa pose d'objet" (p. 11). Nevertheless, this seemingly perfect communication with the child fails to allay her fears, for the child's dependency and immaturity prevent his understanding her needs. In fact, the child is a part of the natural environment which threatens Anne; his hair is colored by the sun (p. 12) or is "l'herbe" through which the wind blows (p. 71). The child is unaware of time; he lives "dans le désintérêt parfait du moment qui pass[e]" (p. 72). Anne and Chauvin, however, constantly comment on the passage, and pressure, of time. The night of the dinner party, which confirms Anne's adulterous desires, is for the child a "nuit innocente" (p. 101). As partner in the ritual which would control Anne's fear of death, she needs a mature adult, one who can also share this fear. Does Anne recognize this aspect of her relationship with the child when she tells Chauvin: "J'oubliais de vous dire combien je voudrais qu'il soit déjà grand" (p. 44)?

The communication between Anne and her son as evidenced in Chapter One is based on a sympathetic vibration between the two, a "note" of harmony between them. In contrast to this communication are the conversations between Anne, the teacher, and the child, which result in no communication whatsoever. Points of view are not understood, demands are met with silence, questions are not answered: "La dame ne voulut pas entendre" (p. 15). Language begins to appear as a falsification, as an obstacle to the "authentic" experience of sound—this communicating "vibration" or the scream of the woman. The crowd soon digests the facts of the crime; its own disorder of fear and anxiety gives way to the order of the police investigation and the control of the police officers who view the event with absolute boredom. "Des appels maintenant raisonnables" (p. 17) replace the first cries of fear. As soon as the scream is heard, it begins to be distorted, categorized by language, in such a way that its original intensity is lost: "D'autres cris relayèrent alors le premier, éparpillés, divers. Ils consacrèrent une actualité déjà dépassée, rassurante désormais. La leçon continuait donc" (p. 14). The word "consacrer" is pivotal. At face value, it means simply that the crowd *confirms* the fact that an event has occurred. However, it has two other possible meanings which relate the scream and the meetings between Anne and Chauvin to ritual. One meaning is "rendre durable." This moment, this "actualité," is given duration, placed into a time sequence, into "history," by Anne and Chauvin. As in a detective novel, the phenomenon becomes an *event*—part of a sequential pattern, a *fact* which is part of an order which can be determined through logical process. The final meaning of the word, to "consecrate," indicates this ritualistic nature of these meetings and this activity. Giving extension to this moment is to place it within a context; it is *ordered*.

Ritual is generally understood to be the prescribed form for a ceremony, usually a religious one. The impulses behind ritual, however, are broader than ceremony.[3] To counter the threat of disorder, man evolves patterns whose purpose is to control certain elements of his environment. Ritual may extend from the simple act of carrying a lucky charm to bring oneself "luck" (i. e., to arrange events as one would have them), or wearing the same clothes in which one was once successful as an attempt to make that success repeat itself, to the more ornate patterns of organized religions, be they an Indian rain dance or the act of communion in the Christian church (repetition of this act is intended to mold a certain result: the salvation of the penitent). In this broader sense, any action, particularly one which is repeated in the same form and which is performed in order to control the human environment in some way, may be considered ritualistic. The conversations between Anne and Chauvin are a ritual whose purpose is to control their own passions (whose violence they fear) and, through language, to place the scream of the woman (a sound without a "syntax") within a context which will "control" it by giving it meaning, by making it comprehensible.

The ritualistic nature of the meetings between Anne and Chauvin is underlined by the presence of ritual in other forms throughout the text. The piano lesson (which takes place every Friday) is ritualistic—the walk along the Boulevard de la Mer, the child's obstinacy, and Mlle. Giraud's anger are repeated over and over each week. The lesson develops into a metaphor for the ritual of the meetings between Anne and Chauvin: in both cases, the ritual begins to control the participants.

The most overt form of ritual is that of the dinner party in Chapter Seven. The chapter is satire or parody in many ways, yet it allows the extension of the pattern of ritual to the other events of the book and is the key to comprehending the necessity of the "events" which take place in the final chapter. The author herself uses the term "ritual" several times to describe the nature of the dinner party; it is a "cérémonial" (p. 92), "un rituel que rien ne trouble, sinon la peur cachée de chacun que tant de perfection tout à coup ne se brise ou ne s'entache d'une trop évidente absurdité" (pp. 91-92). The same fear of imperfection or disorder, fear that the ritual will fail to prevent the awareness of "absurdity" (in its fullest implications), is present in Anne's association with Chauvin.

The simple ceremony of the dinner hides yet another ritual element (one which Anne experiences fully): underneath the glittering gaiety and splendour of the dinner party is the pervasive presence of fear and death. The courses of the meal are presented as part of a ritual of death: "elles écorchent un canard mort dans son linceul d'oranges" (p. 92) or of sacrifice: "L'autre victime attend" (p. 97). This ritual of death is, in part, the absorption and transformation of the food—the salmon and the duck—into human form. This process reflects man's need to control by ordering his environment in human terms—the activity of ritual. Anything cast into the image of man becomes "ordered" for the mind of man, "*ritually* perfect": "Lentement, la digestion commence de ce qui fut un saumon. Son osmose à cette espèce qui le mangea fut rituellement parfaite. Rien n'en troubla la gravité" (p. 94). Duras's repetition of the term *ritual* stresses its importance and invites us to extend its application: Anne and Chauvin apply a ritual process of "osmosis" and "digestion" to the scream and the unknown couple. Through the ordering activity of their imagination and their conversation, they distort the original phenomenon and turn it into their own creation.

The presence of ritual in the chapter is extended further through the flowers which Anne wears and whose scent is carried to Chauvin as he wanders outside her house. One may note a definite progression toward an association with ritual in the references to the magnolias. At first, "De l'extrémité nord du parc, les magnolias versent leur odeur qui va de dune en dune jusqu'à rien" (p. 91). "Odeur" in French means nothing more than "scent"; at this point, before the climax of Anne's and Chauvin's muted attempts to reach each other across the barriers of the fence and the bourgeois society, the magnolias play a small role. (We may note, however, their association with the infinite, as their scent is carried "jusqu'à rien.") Next, however, it is their "parfum" (p. 92) which reaches the man and adds to his agitation; the power of the scent and the connection with Anne which it represents have increased. Finally, the scent becomes "L'encens des magnolias" (p. 96). Incense belongs to the realm of the ritualistic: it is part of the death rite which Anne and Chauvin are playing out and with which the magnolias are also connected through their "floraison *funèbre*" (p. 92). Thus, Duras insists on the presence of ritual. Through implicit and explicit means—statement and metaphor, pattern and parallel, actions and style—she establishes the ritualistic mode of the novel.

Nevertheless, the "rite mortuaire" (p. 113)—the theme is again directly expressed by Duras—of the last chapter cannot be totally comprehended until one further examines the motivations behind this ritual of death and the means by which Anne and Chauvin attempt to carry it out. Anne longs for ultimate passion and experience, yet she needs security as well. She is trapped by her respectability: "La difficulté, c'est de trouver un prétexte, pour une femme, d'aller dans un café" (Duras, p. 41) and tied to her home: "Je n'ai pas l'habitude, expliqua-t-elle, d'aller si loin de chez moi" (p. 52), yet she longs to know the intense passion she now equates with the woman's death: "Morte, dit-elle, elle en souriait encore de joie" (p. 60). Anne wants to die without actually dying. So, she hovers between a safe, enclosed world (represented by her bedroom or her home itself, "la plus calme de la ville" [p. 62]) and a world which is enticingly exciting, but violent and dangerous (represented by the window at the opposite end of the hall from her bedroom—once broken by a violent storm, through which she has, or so it is implied, adulterous thoughts about the workers who pass by—or the café, scene of the violent crime). Between these two extremes lie, in the first case, the "long" (p. 45), "grand couloir" (p. 47) and, in the second, the Boulevard de la Mer, whose "aussi longue distance" (p. 63) discourages Anne.

Anne attempts to solve her dilemma by participating in both worlds at the same time. She moves between her bedroom and the window, or to and fro along the Boulevard de la Mer, from one end of the town to the other. The ritual of her conversations with Chauvin has the same intent: the process of "osmosis" will allow her to experience the passion and ultimate relationship of the unknown couple, yet still maintain her own existence. For Anne, the couple, like the hall or the Boulevard de la Mer, is only a connection, a form empty and useless in itself. They are the kind of novelistic characters which Natalie Sarraute calls "de simples supports, des porteurs d'états parfois encore inexplorés que nous retrouvons en nous-mêmes."[4] Anne wishes to explore these states within herself through this couple. Nevertheless, one lives at either end of this connection, *not* in the connection itself. It is impossible to maintain the mixture: just as Anne is finally forced to vomit both the wine she drank with Chauvin and the food she ate at the dinner party, so she cannot maintain her fiction, the fiction which confuses her own existence with that of the dead woman.

The "facts" from which Anne and Chauvin create this fiction, as they attempt to weave a context for the scream, are few indeed. Anne sees the body of the woman and the distraught man who has apparently killed her. It is the expression in his eyes, or the lack of it (all subjectively interpreted, however, by Anne) which sets Anne's imagination in motion: "Il se tourna vers la foule, la regarda, et on vit ses yeux. Toute expression en avait disparu, exceptée celle, foudroyée, indélébile, inversée du monde, de son désir. [. . .] Apparemment, toute dignité l'avait quitté à jamais. Il scruta l'inspecteur d'un regard toujours absent du reste du monde" (pp. 18-19). Anne knows that a young woman is dead and that a man's agony at her death is intense enough to make him cling to her dead body. Beyond that, neither Anne nor the reader (who never knows any more than Anne at any time) has any further knowledge of the causes of this tragedy. The reader's vision, like Anne's, is limited—he cannot even see if the man is crying: "il suivit de nouveau les inspecteurs jusqu'au fourgon et il y monta. Peut-être alors pleura-t-il, mais le crépuscule trop avancé déjà ne permit d'apercevoir que la grimace ensanglantée et tremblante de son visage et non plus de voir si des larmes s'y coulaient" (p. 21). The man refuses to speak to the police (p. 19) and later, we learn that he has gone

insane (p. 27). The woman is dead, the man, incapable of communication—both are beyond response, beyond questioning, beyond language. There is no content which they can lend to any "expression" on the part of Anne and Chauvin. Meaning must spring from the scream (sound) alone, and from the context which Anne and Chauvin impose upon it through their own experience. A "petit fait vrai" becomes the raw material of fiction.

Anne's and Chauvin's conception of the bond between the couple and of the privileged moment of the woman's death would require of them a total commitment neither one can achieve. The closest Chauvin comes to a total sacrifice of his own being is during the garden episode the night of the dinner party. He picks up a pebble to throw at the bay window, calls out a name, but does not act (p. 97). All his anguish, desire, and need for Anne are expressed only through his convulsive gripping of the bars of the fence enclosing the garden: "L'homme s'est relevé de la grève, s'est approché des grilles, les baies sont toujours illuminées, prend les grilles dans ses mains, et serre. Comment n'est-ce pas encore arrivé? [. . .] L'homme a lâché les grilles du parc. Il regarde ses mains vides et déformées par l'effort. Il lui a poussé, au bout des bras, un destin" (pp. 100-101). Chauvin can "strangle" Anne only through the prison of the fence. He sends her a "destiny," not an action or an experience. Chauvin already lives in a fiction. Through the maze of language which they create, Anne and Chauvin gradually remove themselves from the "reality" of their own existences, and from the "authenticity" of the scream. The scream itself is actually not important to them; they need the missing "context" for it—the "destiny" of which it is a sign. And so, the scream is replaced by "quelques cris, des appels maintenant raisonnables, [qui] indiquèrent la consommation d'un événement inconnu" (p. 17). The "consommation" of the event is literal; the scream is consumed by the need for meaning. The original phenomenon is destroyed; only the context created for it remains: by the end of the novel, Anne appears to assign the full power of "reality" to language (the means by which this context was created): "Je voudrais que vous soyez morte, dit Chauvin.—C'est fait, dit Anne Desbaresdes" (p. 114). The removal of the situation from the phenomenal fact is completed; language is accepted as object or act itself (i.e., as a substitute for "reality"). This acceptance makes Anne a failure, "inauthentic," at the end of the novel, both as a creator and as a seeker after freedom.

At this point, we must distinguish between the author's manipulation of language and fiction and the way they are used by Anne and Chauvin. The author's fiction does not correspond to "reality" any more than Anne's—the novel cannot actually reproduce the sound of the scream; it can only describe it. Yet, we *can* distinguish between the fairly "neuter" description (consciously so) of the author ("plainte" is the only word in the description of the scream on page thirteen with any heavy emotional connotation) and the emotion-laden, subjective way Anne describes the situation (so subjective that she in fact finally confuses herself with the woman). These distinctions indicate the functioning of the novel on two levels. The very banality and neutrality of the surface description (and the amenities, clichés, etc. of the conversation between Anne and Chauvin) hide a second level of activity and response, "un foisonnement innombrable de sensations, d'images, de sentiments, de souvenirs, d'impulsions, de petits actes larvés qu'aucun langage intérieur n'exprime" (Sarraute, p. 115).

The overt, "conscious" level of activity of Anne and Chauvin induces in the reader a false expectation of "plot": he expects the dialogue and the meetings to define a movement, an action, which will result in some dénouement, most likely the death of Anne at Chauvin's hand. The failure of plot at the end, however, forces the reader to fall back on the dialogue itself as the only "action" in the novel. He may even be forced to reread the book, this time not in expectation of "action," but in attunement to the movement and tone of the dialogue itself. He will begin to question the situation in itself, and to be more aware of his own desires and reactions to what he has read. The dialogue appears strange and disconnected to the reader, but does not strike him as false or artificial. This is because Anne and Chauvin do not have a conversation in the usual sense: while seemingly carrying on an everyday conversation, they say things most of us leave unsaid, revealing their innermost desires. In fact, this dialogue is situated on what Natalie Sarraute terms "cette limite fluctuante qui sépare la conversation de la sous-conversation. Les mouvements intérieurs, dont le dialogue n'est que l'aboutissement et pour ainsi dire l'extrême pointe [. . .] cherchent ici à se déployer dans le dialogue même" (pp. 143-144). The dialogue thus becomes the metaphor for the communication of impulses which cannot be conveyed on the linguistic level, "une technique qui parviendrait à plonger le lecteur dans le flot de ces drames souterrains que Proust n'a eu le temps que de survoler et dont il n'a observé et reproduit que les grandes lignes immobiles: une technique qui donnerait au lecteur l'illusion de refaire lui-même ces actions avec une conscience plus lucide, avec plus d'ordre, de netteté et de force qu'il ne peut le faire dans la vie, sans qu'elles perdent cette part d'indétermination, cette opacité et ce mystère qu'ont toujours ses actions pour celui qui les vit. Le dialogue [. . .] ne serait pas autre chose que l'aboutissement ou parfois une des phases de ces drames" (Sarraute, pp. 139-140).

Thus, with the dialogue as metaphor for the evocation of "ces actions souterraines, ces drames intérieurs" (p. 117), an essential quality of *Moderato Cantabile* is the ambiguity of its signs. In this "new novel," the reader's active role is to arrange the signs or images presented to him by the author. He thus duplicates the activity of Anne and Chauvin, drawing from his own needs and desires to "invent" the details of the relationship between them just as they invent the details of the lives of the unknown couple. There is, however, no assurance from the author that any formulation of these images is "correct," "meaningful," or "better" than any other; instead, the author indirectly warns

the reader to beware of fictionalizing as she tempts the reader with plot and seemingly easy associations: "Elle regardera le boulevard par la baie du grand couloir de sa vie" (pp. 102-103). Language is not transparent; signs are not secure or fixed to a stable meaning. For example, one may associate the dark hall (and the general play of light and dark in the novel) with Anne's fear of death, or the sea with her frustrations and with her relationship to the child (who watches the constant movement of boats into and from the harbor). These associations are valid as mood-creators, but when the reader, wanting a comprehensive grasp of the novel, attempts to follow more closely the thread from one association to the next, he becomes involved in a very complex tangle. The child, the sunset, the wind, the sea, the early summer weather, and Anne, for example, are all part of a perhaps indecipherable nexus. The reader cannot "digest" the novel; its contents cannot be subsumed under one particular meaning. Even the description of a single image, the weather, is in itself problematic and does not allow one meaning or interpretation. Perception in the novel remains subjective and ambiguous: "Certains prétendirent que ce jour avait été chaud. La plupart nièrent—non sa beauté—mais que celle-ci avait été telle que ce jour avait été chaud. Certains n'eurent pas d'avis" (p. 106). What stability of meaning is left to the words "chaud" or "beauté" or to the description of the weather involved? The text engenders its own "reality," one which is problematic and which arises from the meanings attributed to signs *within the text itself* as this latter develops.

Jean Ricardou distinguishes between a "texte expressif" and a "texte producteur" in his *Pour une théorie du nouveau roman*.[5] The former is ostensibly the expression of "un *hors-texte* primordial: 'monde extérieur, univers intérieur'" (p. 40). Anne and Chauvin, as they try to give a context to the woman's scream, are engaged in the former sort of fictional activity, the production of a "texte expressif." The preceding development in our study, however, shows that *Moderato Cantabile* is itself a "texte producteur" which engenders its own "reality" from the interrelations developed between its signs. That is, the relationship between Anne and Chauvin is what it is; it does not arise as the expression of some other "reality" external to the text, although it may be comparable to or evoke some such external "reality": fact, desires, emotions, whatever. We have already stated that the dialogue appears strange, yet not artificial. The text must evoke a valid experience to the reader or he will reject it. Nevertheless, the relationship between Anne and Chauvin remains first of all a relationship of words and nothing else. The reader, confusing "texte expressif" and "texte producteur," is trapped by the fiction at the end of the book. Taking fiction for reality, he expects that Anne and Chauvin will "live" their fiction and that Chauvin will "kill" Anne at the end of the novel. That Chauvin does not do so points out the fact that, as Chauvin does with Anne, Duras has played with and entrapped the reader through language and the reader's own need to fictionalize. The end, with its *verbal* "murder," reveals the deceit of the fiction as "texte expressif." The impending murder was only a creation of language and can only take place within this mode. Language is no longer the transparent tool, the ritual which would allow the actions of the unknown man and woman to be understood and categorized; it has become an opaque obstacle, a prison imposing itself upon any attempt by Anne and Chauvin to reach originality or "authenticity." Similarly, the reader cannot categorize the ties between Anne and Chauvin; the text remains opaque to the reader's attempt to see through and digest its intricacies—he can get no further than the description (language) itself.

The music lesson is a metaphor for the ritualistic process of language undertaken by Anne. Like the fiction, the lesson was to free Anne from her environment, allow her to control it. Instead, Anne is trapped by the pattern she herself created and its new "heures fixes." Ritual control escapes its author; the lesson has begun to control Anne: "les journées sont à heure fixe. [. . .] Les repas, toujours, reviennent. Et les soirs. Un jour, j'ai eu l'idée de ces leçons de piano [. . .] à l'autre bout de la ville, pour mon amour, et maintenant je ne peux plus les éviter" (p. 82).

Though Anne loses control of her fiction, the fiction remains only that. Language cannot become "reality." When the fiction is acknowledged, the world of belief and the world of language posing as reality disintegrate: the mask of apparent truth falls away to reveal only the elements of language which compose it. This process is at work in the novel's dénouement; it is also exemplified as part of the text itself when Chauvin admits the falsity of his fiction. When he does so, Anne is left without her only support—the creative force of language—and is overcome by a paroxysm of fear in which language no longer maintains its ordering power (its role as ritual) but falls apart into its basic components—the passage is a juxtaposition of words. Anne speaks and goads Chauvin to a recognition of his "lie": "Ce que vous m'avez dit sur cette femme est faux, qu'on la trouvait ivre morte dans les bars du quartier de l'arsenal. [. . .]—Beaucoup de femmes ont déjà vécu dans cette même maison qui entendaient les troènes, la nuit, à la place de leur coeur. Toujours les troènes y étaient déjà. Elles sont toutes mortes dans leur chambre, derrière ce hêtre qui, contrairement à ce que vous croyez, ne grandit plus.—C'est aussi faux que ce que vous m'avez dit sur cette femme ivre morte tous les soirs.—C'est aussi faux. Mais cette maison est énorme. Elle s'étend sur des centaines de mètres carrés. Et elle est tellement ancienne aussi qu'on peut tout supposer. Il doit arriver qu'on y prenne peur" (pp. 58-59). Chauvin recognizes two elements of his fiction here: one, the power of imagination ("on peut tout supposer"), the other, connected to this, the ability to manipulate time ("Toujours les troènes y étaient déjà"). The first element means that "truth" is problematic. In the increasing identification of Anne and the "fictional" woman, it is *true* that "the woman" is drunk in the bars every evening, although this is at another level of complexity of the fiction. The problem illustrates the reader's freedom to "tout supposer." As Chauvin speaks, this infinite possibility of imagination is associated with fear, death, Anne's

house, and her meetings with Chauvin. Language, instead of being a means to order, becomes part of the disorder which Anne fears. This infinite imagination, precluding the security of knowledge, leads to Anne's paroxysm: "Le même émoi la brisa, lui ferma les yeux. [. . .]—Dépêchez-vous de parler. Inventez./ Elle fit un effort, parla presque haut dans le café encore désert.—Ce qu'il faudrait c'est habiter une ville sans arbres les arbres crient lorsqu'il y a du vent ici il y en a toujours toujours à l'exception de deux jours par an à votre place voyez-vous je m'en irai d'ici je n'y resterai pas tous les oiseaux ou presque sont des oiseaux der mer qu'on trouve crevés après les orages et quand l'orage cesse que les arbres ne crient plus on les entend crier eux sur la plage comme des égorgés ça empêche les enfants de dormir non moi je m'en irai" (p. 59).

Language is not here a defense against the fear of the disorder of the universe, as Chauvin envisages it when he tells Anne to *speak,* to *invent,* but a simple association of ideas and images on a horizontal plane which forms no further structure of meaning. All the disparate images which define the novel's atmosphere are present in Anne's mind: the trees are associated in the previous conversation with the sound of trees. This sound, associated with fear, elicits the sound of the storm and the sound of the sea, which elicits the sound of the cries of dying birds, which in turn creates the association with the death cry. Without punctuation, yet made up of recognizable sentences, the passage reflects not so much a complete linguistic breakdown as the loss of control over language as a means of *ordering.* Stream of consciousness is free association—signs are important not for their relationship to a total sense, but in themselves. In other words, in this passage language does not function according to its normal mechanisms; signs are related to other signs through the associations they evoke for Anne alone in the context created by the novel, not through their place in the total structure of the syntax or through their usual function as signs with a stable meaning. The sign itself takes on primary importance, rather than the relationship between signs.

The ability of fiction to manipulate time is also important to delineating the role of language in the novel. The overt time structure of the book is clear; the events take place over a period of ten days—from a Friday to a Sunday. Anne and Chauvin are highly aware of the passage of time. The factory siren marks clearly the hour for them; they continually count the days since the murder: "Il y a maintenant trois jours" (p. 40); "Il y a maintenant sept jours, dit Chauvin.—Sept nuits, dit-elle comme au hasard" (p. 78); "Vous allez rentrer boulevard de la Mer. ça va être la huitième nuit" (p. 86). The seven days between the murder and the climax of their relationship in Chapter Seven are indicative in several ways. First, along with the manner in which the passage of the days is announced, they are reminiscent of Genesis and creation. We are in fact witnessing a creation (one whose infernal side, however, may be indicated by Anne's stress on "seven *nights*"). On the other hand, seven days are a *cycle*: they complete a week. Time is bent into a circle; Friday becomes Friday again, with nothing achieved. (The last day, the Sunday of Chapter Eight, comes after the climax in Chapter Seven and seems almost removed from time—no one watches the clock or worries about the passage of time.) However, the clarity of the temporal indications is another false trail which would entrap the reader into acceptance of the fiction's correspondence with "reality"; in actuality, time is destroyed in the course of the fiction.

The meetings between Anne and Chauvin become what Ricardou calls a "récit flottant" (p. 256), a *récit* in which a single narrator presents the reader with several contradictory or repetitive versions of one or more scenes (the technique used by Alain Robbe-Grillet, for example). The narrator, through whose eyes we watch Anne and Chauvin "narrating" their versions of the ties between the unknown couple, does indeed return to a few scenes: the reception given by Anne's husband (the invisible presence in the novel, who appears only through the impersonal "on" of Chapter Seven) at which Anne is supposed to lean on the piano and wear the low-cut black dress with a magnolia placed between her breasts, the mention of a house by the seashore, the description of Anne's home and bedroom and her nocturnal restlessness, and the meetings in the café themselves. These versions, particularly in the first two instances, become more and more confusing; we cannot separate Anne's "past" existence from the "reality" of her "present" association with Chauvin, nor this "present" relationship from the "imaginary" lives of the two strangers. For example, as concerns the scene at the reception, Chauvin reaches the point of "remembering" the future, creating the scene as he moves from the memory indicated by his use of the past tense ("étiez accoudée") to a narration in the present: "—Vous étiez accoudée à ce grand piano. Entre vos seins nus sous votre robe, il y a cette fleur de magnolia / Anne Desbaresdes, très attentivement, écouta cette histoire.—Oui.—Quand vous vous penchez, cette fleur frôle le contour extérieur de vos seins. Vous l'avez négligemment épinglée, trop haut. C'est une fleur énorme, vous l'avez choisie au hasard, trop grande pour vous. Ses pétales sont encore durs, elle a justement atteint la nuit dernière sa pleine floraison.—Je regarde dehors?—Buvez encore un peu de vin. L'enfant joue dans le jardin. Vous regardez dehors, oui. / Anne Desbaresdes but comme il le lui demandait, chercha à se souvenir, revint d'un profond étonnement.—Je ne me souviens pas d'avoir cueilli cette fleur. Ni de l'avoir portée" (pp. 79-80). In the temporal unfolding of the text, Anne has not yet worn the flower; thus, in the development of the *text itself,* this event is part of the "future" at the moment Chauvin tells his "story." Yet, as narrator creating this story, in control of his "fiction," Chauvin can "remember" the event. Whether or not he actually saw Anne wearing the dress and flower a year before at a reception given by her husband for the workers at the foundry (p. 57) becomes impossible to determine, and irrelevant. For Chauvin, this scene, as part of his creation, is a "past" activity—an "actualité déjà dépassée" (p. 14). For Anne, this past which is created for her as she listens becomes a future which she will "live" at the dinner

party in Chapter Seven, in order to make it part of her "past": "Un homme, face à une femme, regarde cette inconnue. Ses seins sont de nouveau à moitié nus. Elle ajusta hâtivement sa robe. Entre eux, se fane une fleur. [. . .] Elle entra dans cet univers étincelant, se dirigea vers le grand piano, s'y accouda, ne s'excusa nullement" (pp. 92-93).

The reader cannot determine whether this scene is a repetition of a former one, or an occasion of "life" imitating "art" (Chauvin's fiction). The same scene ostensibly happened a year before Chauvin tells Anne about that same scene which will take place later in the text. The scene is past, present and future in the text; what we are witnessing is the "activité moderne d'une description se désignant elle-même" (p. 34). The reader is watching the creative process itself—and the demonstration that time is irrelevant to the creation of fiction. The novel does not depend on a progression of cause and effect. Rather, like a musical composition based on a theme and variations, the "progress" of the fiction is in fact the constant return to a few "present" moments viewed in slightly different fashion each time: the scream of the woman, the meeting in the bar, the scene with Anne wearing the flower. The fiction is little but the "story" of these returns; Duras has created characters creating characters she herself has created—the reflecting mirror effect (the "variations") of the fiction takes on an almost infinite dimension, one which the reader cannot control through the "ritual" of his attempt to derive a pattern of meaning from these scenes.

The final encounter between Anne and Chauvin, although it remains on the level of words, is described as being for them an action which requires all of their strength and will. The passion and anguish Anne and Chauvin display is strong—the "plainte" uttered by Anne during the last chapter, their bestial moans, the animal imagery of wild disarray, especially marked in Chapters Six and Seven, all convey desperation and lostness. Anne's "plainte" and the animal moans, however, do not indicate the achievement of some primal state, some golden age of natural man which precedes language. Their pain, expressed through language, never reaches the immediacy of the scream. Chauvin tells Anne: "Jamais vous n'avez crié. Jamais" (p. 62). Anne and Chauvin substitute language for action, language which creates a pattern, a ritual of which they are not unaware: "ne pouvant sans doute échapper [. . .] au cérémonial de leurs premières rencontres" (p. 52).

The vocabulary of these meetings is directly concerned with the functioning of language itself. The verbs *dire, parler,* and *savoir,* frequent words in any dialogue as part of the narrative description, assume here an active, creative role which is fundamental and central to the dialogue, not simply descriptive of it. In opposition to the force of events which can control a human destiny, and of which the scream is representative, Anne and Chauvin would impose the control of language and knowledge (represented by their active use of the verbs indicated): "Dites-moi, je vous en prie, comment elle en est venue à découvrir que c'était justement ça qu'elle voulait de lui, comment elle a su à ce point ce qu'elle désirait de lui?" (p. 43). Through Chauvin's *saying,* Anne would reach a *knowledge* of the forces at work in such a situation, even though these forces may be incomprehensible even to those involved: "Mais sans doute sont-ils arrivés très exactement ensemble là où ils étaient il y a trois jours, à ne plus savoir du tout, ensemble, ce qu'ils faissaient" (p. 46). Even the child, whose life represents the experience in Anne's life which comes closest to the intensity of the scream ("Une fois, il me semble bien, oui, une fois j'ai dû crier un peu de cette façon, peut-être, oui, quand j'ai eu cet enfant" [p. 41]), is something Anne needs to *understand*: "Je n'arrive pas à me faire une raison de cet enfant" (p. 32).

It is Anne's need to *know* more about the death and the people involved that brings her back to the café and begins the association with Chauvin: "[Anne]—Ce cri était si fort que vraiment il est bien naturel que l'on cherche à *savoir.* J'aurais pu difficilement éviter de le faire, voyez-vous. [Chauvin]—Ce que je *sais,* c'est qu'il lui a tiré une balle dans le coeur. [. . .]—Et évidemment on ne peut pas *savoir* pourquoi? [. . .]—J'aimerais pouvoir vous le dire, *mais je ne sais rien de sûr.*—Peut-être que personne ne le *sait?*—Lui le *savait.* Il est maintenant devenu fou, enfermé depuis hier soir. Elle, est morte. [. . .]—Alors, maintenant, tu le *sais,* dit l'enfant, pourquoi on a crié?" (pp. 26-27). Chauvin capitalizes on this need and "seduces" Anne through the power of his language: "Si vous reveniez, j'essaierai de *savoir* autre chose et je vous le *dirai*" (p. 33).

Chauvin demonstrates an almost demonic control over language until the last chapter, where Anne becomes the stronger of the two. The temptation to *know* was of course the temptation which led to the Fall, and it was the serpent's "oily tongue" which led Eve to persuade Adam to take the forbidden fruit. The creator is an imitator of the Creator; he who uses language mocks the Word. The name Diabelli (composer of the child's sonatina) invokes the infernal side of art; in Chapter Five, the infernal power of music is explicitly stated: "La sonatine résonna encore, portée comme une plume par ce barbare, qu'il le voulût ou non, et elle s'abattit de nouveau sur sa mère, la condamna de nouveau à la damnation de son amour. Les portes de l'enfer se refermèrent" (p. 73). As Chauvin creates through the power of his telling, he keeps Anne later and later at each meeting, until, in Chapter Six, she has moved totally into the night—into fear, the unknown, and the threat of extinction.

As with other elements of the novel, however, a simple interpretation cannot be assigned to the role played by knowledge. It may mean submitting to the control of discipline and form: "Les gammes, dit Anne Desbaresdes, je ne les ai jamais sues" (p. 76); "Un jour, dit la mère, un jour il le saura, il le dira sans hésiter, c'est inévitable. Même s'il ne le veut pas, il le saura" (p. 67), or it may be an expression of something free of form: "Anne Desbaresdes récita presque scolairement, pour commencer, une leçon qu'elle

n'avait jamais apprise" (p. 58). In this context, the verb *étonner* is a key to the usage of *savoir.* Astonishment is a direct reaction to a stimulus: a form of communication which takes place without the mediation of language. It is a reaction which is connected to the most important elements in Anne's life—to her new relationship with Chauvin (which centers upon the scream of the dying woman): "tous les jours il se passe quelque chose, vous le savez bien.—Je le sais, mais sans doute qu'un jour ou l'autre . . . une chose vous *étonne* davantage" (p. 29), and to her child: "—Quelquefois, je crois que je t'ai inventé, que ce n'est pas vrai, tu vois. / L'enfant leva la tête et bâilla face à elle. L'intérieur de sa bouche s'emplit de la dernière lueur du couchant. L'étonnement d'Anne Desbaresdes, quand elle regardait cet enfant, était toujours égal à lui-même depuis le premier jour. Mais ce soir-là sans doute crût-elle cet étonnement comme à lui-même renouvelé" (p. 35). The child yawns at Anne's worries about "truth" and "invention" and his mouth is filled with the light of the sun. Several contrasts are implied: the contrast between Anne's verbal creations and the "natural" light in the child's mouth, between Anne's verbal creations and the astounding existence of this child (a different "creation"), and between his "natural" reaction and her spontaneous astonishment and her considerations of fact and "truth." The kind of awareness, or knowledge, she has of the child's existence is not the same as the knowledge whose purpose is to sift "truth" from "fiction."

The interplay between all these verbs further dislocates the fixed meanings normally attributed to them; each takes on something of the sense usually assigned to the others. For example, Anne and Chauvin gain less and less factual "knowledge" of the couple as they continue their conversations, yet they do not stop using the verb *savoir.* Through this usage and the attendant associations with the verb, it finally loses its "meaning" as a verb which asserts fact, which asserts human control or order (man controls what he "knows"), and the security of language (to say "I know" is to assert the power of language to explain, that is, to control) and becomes nearly equivalent to the accepted sense of the verbs *dire, croire* or *inventer.* At the same time, the verbs *dire* and *parler* become active; telling no longer means passively passing on information, but becomes the *creation* of that information, and, when Anne pleads "dites-moi," can even be interpreted as an act of adultery on Anne's part, the sign replacing affection or embraces. A short examination of the first shifts in meaning of the verb *savoir* will demonstrate this process.

When Anne and Chauvin first meet, Chauvin states: "*Ce que je sais,* c'est qu'il lui a tiré une balle dans le coeur" (p. 26). The rest of the chapter tends to negate this assertion and the sense of the verb *savoir.* Chauvin immediately begins to undermine the firm foundation of knowledge indicated when he qualifies: "je ne sais rien de sûr" (p. 27). Soon, he shifts to the verb *croire*: "N'empêche, je crois aussi" (p. 28), further undermining his statements. At last, he passes into the realm of imagination and fiction: "Je n'imaginais pas" (p. 32). When, at the end of the chapter,

Anne recalls Chauvin's original statement, the dislocation of the verb is complete and the statement is voided of meaning, of its power to assert: "Elle se reprit: ce que vous avez dit, vous le supposiez?—Je n'ai rien dit. [. . .]—A l'avoir vu, on ne peut pas s'empêcher, n'est-ce pas, c'est presque inévitable?—Je n'ai rien dit, répéta l'homme. Mais je *crois* qu'il l'a visée au coeur comme elle le lui demandait" (p. 33). Chauvin's "statement" of "fact" has been negated ("Je n'ai rien dit") or has become at best a fiction, subjectively interpreted: *savoir* has been replaced by *croire.*

This dislocation of the sense of *savoir* is carried even further in the chapter which follows. Speaking of the couple, Chauvin now passes completely into imagination: "j'imagine aussi qu'il l'aurait fait de lui-même un jour" (p. 44). Finally, knowledge is *subordinated* to imagination: "*J'imagine qu'*un jour, dit-il [. . .] *elle a su* soudainement ce qu'elle désirait de lui. [. . .] Il n'y a pas d'explication, je crois, à ce genre de découverte-là" (p. 43). After this same process is repeated throughout the novel, the reader, like Anne, is unsure of what to believe.

Chauvin acknowledges the falsity of his statements about "the woman"; at another meeting, he admits "Je mentais" (p. 87). Anne is just as capable as Chauvin of fictionalizing. When she first entered the café, "Anne Desbaresdes mentit" (Duras, p. 25). Later, she states "sur le ton d'une paisible diversion": "Je pourrais vous dire que j'ai parlé à mon enfant de toutes ces femmes qui ont vécu derrière ce hêtre et qui sont maintenant mortes, mortes, et qu'il m'a demandé de les voir, mon trésor. Je viens de vous dire ce que je pourrais vous dire, voyez" (Duras, p. 83). Obviously, she is quite aware of the fictional quality of her statement. Anne's and Chauvin's manipulation of "fact" and "fiction" further dislocates the sense of *savoir*; Anne reaches the point of no longer caring about "truth" when she requests "knowledge": "Avant que je rentre, pria Anne Desbaresdes, si vous pouviez me *dire,* j'aimerais savoir encore un peu davantage. Même si vous n'êtes pas sûr de ne pas savoir très bien" (Duras, p. 85). This linguistic tangle completes the dislocation of the meanings of *savoir* and *dire,* making the latter a verb of active creation and the former a verb indicating receptivity to the fiction. Chauvin's commands "Parlez-moi" (p. 41) and Anne's requests "Je voudrais que vous me disiez le commencement même, comment ils ont commencé à se parler" (p. 44), have led to a gradual withdrawal from the original "present" phenomenon (the scream) to a fiction controlled by language, and to a dislocation of this language itself. Both the events and the signs used to describe these events are, as Chauvin states, "comme vous désirez le[s] croire" (p. 112). When Anne states: "Elle avait beaucoup d'espoir qu'il y arriverait [à la tuer]" and Chauvin answers: "Il me semble que son espoir à lui d'y arriver devait être égal au sien. Je ne sais rien" (pp. 84-85), "il" and "elle" have become ambiguous signs, which could have either third person or first person referents (the couple or Anne and Chauvin themselves). Signs are no longer reliable; through them the reader can no longer distinguish between the

"real" and the "imaginary," between what actually involves Anne and Chauvin, the couple, or the "memories" of a past, present, or even future which may belong to any of them.

Thus we can say that in the novel the "gap between word and expression" to which Renée Riese Hubert refers in a discussion of Mary Ann Caws[6] has widened for both Anne and Chauvin and the reader and that "An affirmation of the outer world perceived as a fresh vision [the scream] gradually dissolves, and, under those circumstances, the imaginary becomes indistinguishable from any possible reality. Language makes not only communication with the absolute, but communication per se, impossible" (p. 22). Through the ambiguity of signs, the distinction between the "fictional" life of the man and woman and the "real" life of Anne or Chauvin can no longer be maintained. "The imaginary becomes indistinguishable from any possible reality": "—Une dernière fois, supplia-t-elle, dites-moi. / Chauvin hésita, les yeux toujours ailleurs, sur le mur du fond, puis il se décida à le dire comme d'un souvenir.—Jamais auparavant, avant de la rencontrer, il n'aurait pensé que l'envie aurait pu lui en venir un jour" (p. 110).

Finally, Chauvin introduces his own experience as though it were part of the story he has been telling; there is no indication in the text that he makes the distinction any longer: "Le cadenas était sur la porte du jardin, comme d'habitude. Il faisait beau, à peine de vent. Au rez-de-chaussée, les baies étaient éclairées" (p. 109). The timeless nature of the description, the sense of repetition, the impersonality of the description obviate any single interpretation of the scene. The signs refuse to be rendered static; the description stands on its own in its ambiguity, free now from even Chauvin's control. The ambiguity of the signs which Chauvin and Anne consciously manipulated throughout their meetings at last traps them in this very ambiguity. They have lost control of language; they are no longer sure of their own identities nor of the course which events will take; *savoir* expresses this loss of control: "—Il faut beaucoup, beaucoup de temps?—Je crois, beaucoup. Mais je ne sais rien. Il ajouta tout bas: 'Je ne sais rien, comme vous. Rien'" (p. 111).

Submitting to the control of language was to be Anne's means of salvation: "Quand il lui disait de s'en aller, elle obéissait toujours. [. . .] De lui obéir à ce point, c'était sa façon à elle d'espérer" (p. 87). However, the ritual of language invented by Anne and Chauvin to control the sign without a context, the disordered event, finally controls them. This ritual, which removes the initial experience from "actualité," necessitates the dénouement—Anne's and Chauvin's inability to achieve authentic action. Their "life," defined by language, is on paper alone; they cannot actually "act" in any sense. The distinction between the verbal "murder" which occurs and a description of Chauvin actually "killing" Anne is false: both are only words; each is as "real" as the other. The verbal "murder," however, underlines the linguistic nature of their "existence" and of any "actions" attributed to them. Anne and Chauvin are only shadows, as indicated by a fundamental passage early in the novel: "Le mur du fond de la salle s'illumina du soleil couchant. En son milieu, le *trou* noir de leurs *ombres* conjuguées se dessina" (p. 45). A "hole" is emptiness, nothingness, a lack of existence. Their relationship, a creation of words alone, is doubly illusion since this relationship is created as the "shadow" of another fiction: the mysterious couple.

The ritualistic control of language thus may be finally described as the rigidity and the opacity of words. Once again the text itself creates a metaphor for this functioning of language. In the realm of imagination, a kiss from Chauvin has all the force and passion which Anne desires; it has "la saveur anéantissante des lèvres inconnues d'un homme de la rue" (p. 96). However, when Anne and Chauvin try to realize this kiss on the "physical" level, when they try to "act," they are overcome by a paralysis which personifies their limitation to the verbal mode which has created them: "Leurs mains étaient si froides qu'elles se touchèrent illusoirement dans l'intention seulement, afin que ce fût fait, dans la seule intention que ce le fût, plus autrement, ce n'était plus possible. Leurs mains restèrent ainsi, figées dans leur pose mortuaire" (p. 110); "Elle fit alors ce qu'il n'avait pas pu faire. Elle s'avança vers lui d'assez près pour que leurs lèvres puissent s'atteindre. Leurs lèvres restèrent l'une sur l'autre, posées, afin que ce fût fait et suivant le même *rite mortuaire* que leurs mains, un instant avant, froides et tremblantes. Ce fut fait" (pp. 112-113). The novel is thus an allegory of the nature of language and the creative process itself, in which "infinite possibility is surrendered on the altar of the form" (Buber, p. 60). The form chosen by Anne and Chauvin, the ritual of language, limits their possibilities to "act." They are trapped by their own means of attempted control and can play out the meaning-giving end, the source of authenticity, only through this ritual, through the words which rob them of the meaning and authenticity they seek. The literary tenses seem as rigid here as the figures of Anne and Chauvin; they certainly contrast with the intimacy supposedly involved. The Biblical terms ("afin que ce fût fait") support the ritualistic necessity of the scene; the linguistic prophecy must be fulfilled linguistically.

Language thus fails to bring "meaning" or to control events for Anne and Chauvin. At the end of the novel, all that is left is the empty gesture of Chauvin (p. 114) and the empty sound, the language which is only noise without meaning, of the radio (p. 115). Anne's effort to find freedom is over: "Elle ne parlera plus jamais" (p. 112); "elle accepta la peur" (p. 113). The dream of "un enfantement sans fin" (p. 17)—a human life made up of privileged moments—is renounced when Anne symbolically arrives at the café for the last meeting without her child and having made the decision to let others take him to his piano lessons (p. 107). She is in effect recognizing the ultimate inability of man to protect himself from the onslaught of the unknown and the disorder of the universe or to achieve the complete meaning or "destiny" he desires. The effort to incorporate

"sound" into "syntax," to give the scream a context which will both define and control it and enable Anne to achieve the meaning she attributes to it as an authentic experience, fails to achieve either goal.

The reader also fails to attain such control, to decipher the ultimate "meaning" of Anne's association with Chauvin and of the failure of this relationship. The meetings are fragments which the reader can associate into a "whole" as he will, just as Anne and Chauvin have only fragments of their own lives and of the lives of the couple to try to connect into a meaningful "histoire," a destiny which will bring them together. The dissociated statements, the broken, interrupted phrases which move without transition from one topic to another, and the dislocation of familiar signs frustrate the reader as he tries to unify these scenes, words, and ideas. The reader repeats the role of Chauvin and Anne—he infuses the signs with his *own* fiction, his *own* creation, springing from his own imagination, needs and desires. In spite of such a need and attempt to control on the part of the reader, however, the text refuses to accede to the order of ritual and remains an expression of nothing else but itself. Ricardou summarizes for us: "Le roman, ce n'est plus un miroir qu'on promène le long d'une route; c'est l'effet de miroirs partout agissant en lui-même. Il n'est plus représentation; il est auto-représentation. Non qu'il soit scindé en deux domaines dont l'un, privilégié, aurait l'autre pour représentation. Il est plutôt, tendanciellement, partout représentation de lui-même. C'est dire que loin d'être une stable image du quotidien, la fiction est en perpétuelle instance de dédoublement. C'est à partir de lui-même que le texte prolifère: il écrit en imitant ce qu'il lit" (p. 262). The novel becomes a parable of creation, an exposition of the ritual force of language as well as of the ultimate failure of this ritual. The repetition of the lesson, of the meeting in the café, of the siren, of the drinking (whose role may be simply to "loosen the tongue" of the participants), and, most importantly, of the few basic scenes which become the novel's own memory of itself, make the novel itself a ritual, a ritual of self-proclamation by language and by the text.

Notes

1. *I and Thou,* trans. Walter Kaufmann (New York: Charles Scribner's Sons, 1970), p. 62.

2. Marguerite Duras, *Moderato Cantabile* (Paris: Éditions de Minuit, 1958), pp. 60, 73.

3. See David I. Grossvogel, *Limits of the Novel* (Ithaca: Cornell University Press, 1968).

4. *L'Ère du Soupçon* (Paris: Editions Gallimard, 1956), p. 51.

5. (Paris: Éditions du Seuil, 1971), p. 65.

6. "The Invasions of Poetry," *Diacritics,* 4 (Spring 1974), 21-25. Reference is to p. 21.

Lloyd Bishop (essay date 1978)

SOURCE: "The Banquet Scene in 'Moderato Cantabile': A Stylistic Analysis," in *Romanic Review,* Vol. LXIX, No. 3, May, 1978, pp. 222-35.

[*In the following essay, Bishop contrasts Duras's style in the banquet scene in* Moderato cantabile *with her style in the rest of the novella, contending that all of the book's themes are contained in the banquet passage.*]

In an earlier study of **Moderato Cantabile** we analysed the banquet scene rather briefly from the point of view of neo-classical principles of composition that inform the entire novel.[1] But the scene deserves to be studied in detail for the brilliant stylistic effects that are attempted and achieved. In this single chapter Duras has distilled all of the novel's significance, summarizing all that has preceded and foreshadowing what will follow as well as presenting a memorable—although muted—moment of crisis and anagnorisis.

Until this chapter, which is the next-to-last, the novel's style has been consistently simple, intentionally (and ironically) banal, with few deviations from contemporary linguistic norms: brief, straightforward sentences encased in short paragraphs with figurative language sparse and discreet. The following passage is typical of the novel's basic stylistic context.

> Il ne resta plus qu'un seul client au comptoir. Dans la salle, les quatre autres parlaient par intermittence. Un couple arriva. La patronne le servit et reprit son tricot rouge délaissé jusque-là à cause de l'affluence. Elle baissa la radio. La mer, assez forte ce soir-là, se fit entendre contre les quais, à travers des chansons.
>
> —Du moment, qu'il avait compris qu'elle désirait tant qu'il le fasse, je voudrais que vous me disiez pourquoi il ne l'a pas fait, par exemple, un peu plus tard ou . . . un peu plus tôt.
>
> —Vous savez, je sais très peu de choses. Mais je crois qu'il ne pouvait pas arriver à avoir une préférence, il ne devait pas en sortir, de la vouloir autant vivante que morte. Il a dû réussir très tard seulement à se la préférer morte. Je ne sais rien.
>
> Anne Desbaresdes se replia sur elle-même, le visage hypocritement baissé mais pâli.
>
> —Elle avait beaucoup d'espoir qu'il y arriverait.
>
> —Il me semble que son espoir à lui d'y arriver devait être égal au sien. Je ne sais rien.
>
> —Le même, vraiment?
>
> —Le même. Taisez-vous.
>
> Les quatre hommes s'en allèrent. Le couple resta là, silencieux. La femme bâilla. Chauvin commanda une nouvelle carafe de vin.
>
> —Si on ne buvait pas tant, ce ne serait pas possible?
>
> —Je crois que ce ne serait pas possible, murmura Anne Desbaresdes.
>
> Elle but son verre de vin d'un trait. Il la laissa s'empoisonner à son gré. La nuit avait envahi définitivement la ville. Les quais s'éclairèrent de leurs hauts lampadaires. L'enfant jouait toujours. Il n'y eut plus trace dans le ciel de la moindre lueur du couchant.[2]

A brief statistical analysis will confirm the reader's impression of simplicity:

> average length of sentences—less than ten words (9.45)
>
> average length of narrative paragraphs—less than five sentences (4.25)
>
> average length of *répliques*—less than two sentences (1.37)
>
> deviations from normal word-order—none (0)
>
> stylistic devices, tropes, etc.—none (0)

The passage is typical not only of the novel's intentional banality but also of the light and swift tempo that keeps it from dragging. There is never any sustained dialogue or sustained narrative but a constant switch from one to the other as well as a constant switch from the characters within the café to nature outside. Despite the swift tempo and the airy pages, it is obvious that the entire novel could not be written in this neutral style and with this evasive dialogue and narrative. Something must happen, or something must be said, or something must be narrated to give significance to Anne's morbid curiosity about the murder, about her nervousness and incipient alcoholism. And these fleeting words and gestures must move forward to some climax and resolution. It is the banquet scene—the seventh and next-to-last chapter—that performs all these functions.

As the reader begins the chapter he is given a stylistic shock: the language suddenly becomes precious, the syntax periodic.

> Sur un plat d'argent à l'achat duquel trois générations ont contribué, le saumon arrive, glacé dans sa forme native. Habillé de noir, ganté de blanc, un homme le porte, tel un enfant de roi, et le présente à chacun dans le silence du dîner commençant. Il est bien-séant de ne pas en parler.
>
> (p. 92)

The contrast with the context established in the first ninety pages of the novel is heightened by the change of tense: the present now takes over as narrative mode. Duras has already achieved one of her goals: an abrupt change of atmosphere from that of the cheap proletarian café to the *collet monté* ambiance of upper-bourgeois *bienséance*.

The second paragraph switches the scene from the ceremonious banquet to Chauvin prowling outside. The style becomes simple and straightforward once again. The volume of the sentences gradually shrinks.

> De l'extrémité nord du parc, les magnolias versent leur odeur qui va de dune en dune jusqu'à rien. Le vent, ce soir, est du sud. Un homme rôde, boulevard de la Mer. Une femme le sait.
>
> (Ibid.)

The understatement created by the verbs of the last two sentences is reinforced by the *nouveau roman* anonymity of their subjects as well as by a convergence of contrasts:

first, the visual contrast effected by the cinematographic technique of the simultaneous scene—a device that will be continued throughout the chapter; then, the stylistic contrast between the alternating paragraphs—this device too will be sustained; and finally the inside-outside antithesis that runs throughout the novel with nature symbolizing the instinctual life as opposed to the stultifying atmosphere of upper-bourgeois respectability.

Although there is never an authorial comment nor an analysis by the non-omniscient narrator, nor even a single lyrical outburst by the protagonist, the locus, if not the precise stimulus, of her anguish is indicated by the constant juxtaposition of the natural and the artificial. With an irony bordering on the sarcastic, the anonymous characters yield stage-center to the elegant salmon. Then the camera swings abruptly away to focus once again on nature outside.

> Le saumon passe de l'un à l'autre suivant un rituel que rien ne trouble, sinon la peur cachée de chacun que tant de perfection tout à coup ne se brise ou ne s'entache d'une trop évidente absurdité. Dehors, dans le parc, les magnolias élaborent leur floraison funèbre dans la nuit noire du printemps naissant.
>
> (pp. 91-92)

The magnolia blossom has special significance for Chauvin: he once saw Anne, who likes to wear low-cut gowns, wearing such a blossom in her bosom; she is also wearing one now. However, Chauvin's feelings are not analysed; they must be devined by the contraction of his features and by the nervous gestures that the reader imagines as the camera moves in closer: "Avec le ressac du vent qui va, vient, se cogne aux obstacles de la ville, et repart, le parfum atteint l'homme et le lâche, alternativement" (p. 92). The intentional ambiguity and understatement of the verbs "atteint" and "lâche" force the reader to collaborate with the narrator in rendering Chauvin's emotional state visually. The sentence has the flavor of a discretionary stage direction or, better, a movie scenario.

Rhythmically, the scene switches once again to the superficial "ritual" going on inside. The language becomes stilted once again with ornamental epithets, precious metaphors and pedantic periphrases.

> Des femmes, à la cuisine, achèvent de parfaire la suite, la sueur au front, l'honneur à vif, elles écorchent un canard mort dans son linceul d'oranges. Cependant que rose, mielleux, mais déjà déformé par le temps très court qui vient de se passer, le saumon des eaux libres de l'océan continue sa marche inéluctable vers sa totale disparition et que la crainte d'un manquement quelconque au cérémonial qui accompagne celle-ci se dissipe peu à peu.
>
> (Ibid.)

The cumbersome "marche inéluctable vers sa totale disparition" is reminiscent of the "totale dissipation-derision-purgation" of Henri Michaux's "Clown." Duras's irony, although more muted, is as sarcastic as Michaux's.

There is one flaw in the near-perfection of the ritual: an anonymous host notices that his wife is letting her instincts show.

> Un homme, face à une femme, regarde cette inconnue. Ses seins sont de nouveau à moitié nus. Elle ajusta hâtivement sa robe. Entre eux, se fane une fleur. Dans ses yeux élargis, immodérés, des lueurs de lucidité passent encore, suffisantes, pour qu'elle arrive à servir à son tour du saumon des autres gens.
>
> (Ibid.)

This jarring note is underscored by a split-second flashback or instant replay: the abrupt *passé simple* of *ajusta* clashes with the present which by now has been established as the basic temporal context of the scene. The adverb *hâtivement* also suggests an antecedent action explaining why the dress is now so low. But since the "adjustment" of the dress follows the husband's angry gaze, the *passé simple* curiously suggests an action *future* to that gaze. The total effect is an atemporal one like that of a jarring camera shot in, say, *L'Année dernière à Marienbad,* which leaves the spectator perplexed as to the chronology of the sequence. The "saumon des autres gens" refers to Anne's alienation within her own social class and anticipates her body's rejection, through vomiting, of "cette nourriture étrangère que ce soir elle fut forcée de prendre."

The jarring note is noticed. The scandal is public.

> A la cuisine, on ose enfin le dire, le canard étant prêt, et au chaud, dans le répit qui s'ensuit, qu'elle exagère. Elle arriva ce soir plus tard encore qu'hier, bien après ses invités.
>
> (pp. 92-93)

The *passé simple* of the last verb does dual duty: it provides another sudden flashback while continuing the comments (presented in *style indirect libre*) of the kitchen-help. The flickering scene changes contribute to the general tenseness of the atmosphere.

A third and slightly longer flashback is effected by having the present collide once again with the preterite and briefly yield to it.

> Ils sont quinze, ceux qui l'attendirent tout à l'heure dans le grand salon du rez-de-chaussée. Elle entra dans cet univers étincelant, se dirigea vers le grand piano, s'y accouda, ne s'excusa nullement. On le fit à sa place.
>
> —Anne est en retard, excusez Anne.
>
> (p. 93)

The clash of tenses makes the last sentence tantalizingly ambiguous. It can of course be interpreted as the husband's apology alluded to in the preceding sentence. But it can also be interpreted as Anne's drunken speech, especially since this is a transitional sentence bringing us back to the present tense and to the table talk that takes place about an hour later. The second interpretation is plausible also because Anne is becoming increasingly drunk. She tries desperately to follow the conversation but with little success. People have to repeat their polite questions about her son, but the questions draw from her answers of only one ("déjà"), two ("ah, oui"), three ("il est vrai") and four ("Il ne savait pas"; "Il ne pouvait pas") words. Cornered, she tries the protective coloration of the fixed smile: "Elle, elle retourne à la fixité de son sourire, une bête à la forêt" (Ibid.).

Then comes a paragraph that combines three different tenses and all four themes: the stiff, strained atmosphere of the just-barely successful "ritual," the insistent appeal of nature, Chauvin's psychosexual anguish and, finally, Anne's.

> Lentement la digestion commence de ce qui fut un saumon. Son osmose à cette espece qui le mangea fut rituellement parfaite. Rien n'en troubla la gravité. L'autre attend, dans une chaleur humaine, sur son linceul d'oranges. Voici la lune qui se lève sur la mer et sur l'homme allongé. Avec difficulté on pourrait, à la rigueur, maintenant, apercevoir les masses et les formes de la nuit à travers les rideaux blancs. Madame Desbaresdes n'a pas de conversation.
>
> (p. 94)

As interesting technically as the continued collision of the present and the preterite is the conditional of the penultimate sentence. The tense—or rather the mood—of the verb, combined with its indefinite subject, suggests a concerned look by an unnamed character. The sentence would not be out of place in Robbe-Grillet's *La Jalousie*. The "voici" of the preceding sentence, suddenly short-circuiting the preciosity, is likewise reminiscent of the perennial present in the same novel; it also shifts the scene with cinematographic abruptness. The reduction of the guests to their biological process ("digestion"; "osmose") and species ("cette espèce") not only continues the sarcastic preciosity but reflects the fact that Anne is only vaguely aware of their presence and of the elegant food set before her. She is thinking of someone else and is tormented by "d'autre faim." What is impressive here is the density of the language. Duras has condensed the substance of the entire chapter, which is already a condensation of the entire novel, into one brief paragraph and has brought a plotless novel to its climax: the heroine now sits in near-catatonic silence.

Although only indirectly informed as to Anne's problem, the reader is by now in a position to interpret it for himself. A consensus would probably run along these general lines: ten years of a very proper and perhaps brilliant marriage (of convenience?), fidelity, maternity, affluence, culture, knowing the "right" people, none of this has fully satisfied Anne's subconscious longing for completeness and self-realization. The "cantabile" side of her nature is asserting itself and challenging the "moderato" side, and her ambivalence is now leaning in favor of the instincts.

But Duras has presented the "problem" with appealing subtlety, discretion, even a sense of mystery. During this very moment of crisis, she maintains the novel's low-keyed tonality. Although the heroine becomes increasingly distraught, the novel's emotional temperature does not rise significantly. There is no lyricism, no melodrama, no pathos. This muted presentation of a moment of intense psychological crisis is reminiscent of what Leo Spitzer has called Racine's *effet de sourdine* and *klassische Dämpfung*. Like Racine, Duras uses a whole arsenal of devices to achieve this cooling or muting effect. We will examine them now.

The first of Racine's *effets de sourdine* listed by Spitzer is a "désindividualisation par l'article indéfini."[3] Among his numerous examples the following—from *Andromaque*—are typical:

> J'abuse, cher ami, de ton trop d'amitié;
> Mais pardonne à DES maux dont toi seul as pitié;
> Excuse UN malheureux qui perd tout ce qu'il aime.
> Que tout le monde hait, et qui se hait lui-même.
>
> (III, 1)

> Le croirai-je, seigneur, qu'un reste de tendresse
> Vous fasse ici chercher UNE triste princesse?
>
> (II, 2)

> Voilà de mon amour l'innocent stratagème:
> Voilà ce qu'UN époux m'a commandé lui-même.
>
> (IV, 1)

The alternation of personal lyricism and de-personalized "formulas" is the very essence of Racinian style according to Spitzer (p. 208) and is accomplished here by the alternation of first-person pronouns and possessive adjectives with the indefinite article. The analogy with Duras's style in the banquet scene is both fascinating and revealing. In this climactic scene the heroine is suddenly and *totally* depersonalized, referred to simply as "une femme." This sustained anonymity is particularly appropriate since it underscores the lack of communication and real intimacy between husband and wife. The "un époux" of Racine becomes "un homme" in **Moderato Cantabile,** a husband who is *never* named: "Un homme, face à une femme, regarde cette inconnue" (p. 92). Even the would-be lover, Chauvin, is depersonalized throughout the chapter: "Un homme rôde, boulevard de la Mer. Une femme le sait." The indefinite article is also used as a pronoun to achieve the same effect.

> Les femmes sont au plus sûr de leur éclat. Les hommes les couvrirent de bijoux au prorata de leurs bilans. *L'un d'eux,* doute qu'il eut (sic) raison.
>
> Elles se pourlèchent de mayonnaise, verte, comme il se doit, s'y retrouvent, y trouvent leur compte. Des hommes les regardent et se rappellent qu'elles font leur bonheur.
>
> *L'une d'elles* contrevient ce soir à l'appétit général.
>
> (p. 95)

A poignant effect of understatement is achieved by having both Anne and Chauvin quietly hum "*a* song" that brought them together and quietly pronounce "*a* name."

The second *effet de sourdine* analysed by Spitzer is the frequent use of the indefinite and impersonal pronoun *on*.

> Eh quoi! votre courroux n'a-t-il pas eu son cours?
> Peut ON haïr sans cesse? et punit-ON toujours?
> Quel est l'étrange acceuil qu'ON fait à votre pere,
> Mon fils?
>
> *(Phèdre*, III, 5)

> . . . Mais déjà tu reviens sur tes pas,
> OEnone! ON me déteste, ON ne t'écoute pas!
>
> (Ibid., III, 2)

In ***Moderato Cantabile*** the husband's fury is attenuated by reducing him to the indefinite pronoun.

> Elle . . . ne s'excusa nullement. ON le fit à sa place.
> (p. 93)

> Cette fois, elle prononcera une excuse. ON ne lui répondra pas.
>
> (p. 103)

Thus, the vague, intentionally ambiguous pronoun turns a potentially melodramatic *scène à faire* into a gentle melody played in minor key and in *moderato* tempo, deliberately muted by the soft pedal.

The third *effet de sourdine* analysed in the *Etudes de style* is what Spitzer calls the "démonstratif de distance" (p. 214).

> Je sais de ses froideurs tout ce que l'on récite;
> Mais j'ai vu près de vous CE superbe Hippolyte.
>
> *(Phèdre*, II, 1)Nous regardions tous deux CETTE reine
> cruelle.
>
> *(Athalie*, I, 1)

Duras, too, will exploit the effect of objectification, distance and coolness of the demonstrative adjective: "*Cet* homme a quitté le boulevard de la Mer" (p. 92). The demonstrative can reinforce effectively the estrangement expressed by the substantive it accompanies: "*cette espèce*"; and "Un homme, face à une femme, regarde *cette inconnue.*"

A similar effect of distance is achieved by the use of periphrasis rather than a specific indication of the setting. Racine will write "ces lieux," "des lieux," "sur ces bords" etc. instead of "ici"; "ce jour" instead of "aujourd'hui." Spitzer very accurately suggests that the Racinian *unité de lieu* is really *l'inexistence de lieu.* Again, the analogy with Duras not only holds but is extremely relevant. The action of ***Moderate Cantabile*** takes place in an anonymous port city, and although the banquet obviously takes place in Anne's mansion, the latter is not explicitly named.

Related to this blurring of the precise setting are Racine's "PLURIELS QUI ESTOMPENT LES CONTOURS, empêchant une détermination trop nette de l'attitude des personnages." (Spitzer, pp. 230-231); the familiar *amours,*

fureurs, flammes, alarmes, vengeances that punctuate and attenuate so many lyrical passages. Duras uses the same device in describing the table talk as the banquet progresses. The wine helping, the strained cordiality at the beginning becomes innocuous good humor. But instead of reporting some of the actual conversation, the author-narrator prefers to give a vague and ironical summary, pushing the blur of the plural to a sarcastic *reductio ad absurdum.*

> Le chur *des conversations* augmente peu à peu de volume, et, dans une surenchère d'*efforts* et d'*inventivités* progressive émerge une société quelconque. *Des repères* sont trouvés, *des failles* s'ouvrent où s'essayent *des familiarités.* Et on débouche peu à peu sur une conversation généralement partisane et particulièrement neutre. La soirée réussira.
>
> (p. 95)

The superficial "success" of the banquet is deflated not only by the ironical antithesis, "généralement partisane et particulièrement neutre," and by the equally anti-climatic epithet "quelconque," but especially by the pluralization of the abstract noun "inventivités," suggesting, in subdued, *pince-sans-rire* humor, empty badinage. Thus once again Duras not only renders brilliantly the contrast between the artificiality of the banquet and Anne's instinctual urges but also indicates, subtly and *en sourdine,* the very basis of her problem. Another remark by Spitzer regarding these plurals seems particularly apposite here: "Le petit nombre de personnages du théâtre racinien est compensé par les personnages que l'on DEVINE dans la pénombre" (p. 232). ***Moderato Cantabile*** has only three named characters.

Another cooling effect employed by Racine is the use of the *épithète d'appréciation*: the "*juste* crainte," "*juste* colere," "*juste* fureur," and "*justement* irrité" that introduce a moral or intellectual judgment into the emotional situation, thus delyricizing it. Similarly, the heroine of ***Moderato Cantabile,*** although not once uttering a complaint about the artificiality of the banquet and of her life style in general, vomits the "nourriture *étrangère* que ce soir elle fut forcée de prendre." The pejorative epithet, as does the symbolic vomiting, implies a negative moral judgment not only on the guests but also on Anne herself, who has not been true to her real nature. Again, the impressive economy and compression, the "mileage" that Duras can get out of an ordinary word, is worthy of Racine.

Proust, too, has contrasted the intuition of one's "vraie vie" and "vrai moi" with the "irréalité" of one's social self, and he uses the very same image. The narrator in *Le Temps retrouvé* has just had his three illuminating "avertissements" at the Guermantes mansion:

> C'était peut-être bien des fragments d'existence soustraits au temps, mais cette contemplation, quoique d'éternité, était fugitive. Et pourtant je sentais que le plaisir qu'elle m'avait, à de rares intervalles, donné dans ma vie, était le seul qui fût fécond et véritable. Le

signe de l'irréalité des autres ne se montre-t-il pas assez, soit dans leur impossibilité à nous satisfaire,
comme par exemple les plaisirs mondains qui causent
tout au plus le malaise provoqué par l'ingestion d'une
nourriture abjecte . . . soit dans la tristesse qui suit
leur satisfaction. . . ."[4]

Duras makes the same point as Proust—just as effectively
and more economically. The latter articulates his theme
with great clarity, the former moves by equally pleasing
indirection.

The symbolism of the vomiting, replacing explicit theme
and lyrical tirade, is another *effet de sourdine* and is rich in
implications. Given the entire context of what has preceded and what will follow, the vomiting is symbolic of
several things at once. First of all, the epithet "étrangère"
makes the vomiting an explicit symbol of Anne's rejection
of the concomitant life style as mentioned above. But the
vomiting is caused chiefly by the excess of wine taken in
the cafe with Chauvin, suggesting that to live entirely on a
bohemian or "cantabile" level would not be true to her
real self either. In the final analysis, the vomiting represents a new awareness, a recognition of the irreducible duality of her nature and of the need to establish a new equilibrium: an escape from the stultifying rigidity and
conformity of her life up to now but within the context of
her present marital situation and responsibilities. Fully as
much as a rejection of upper-bourgeois values, the vomiting (as does the faded magnolia crushed in her bosom as
she vomits) foreshadows the rejection of Chauvin in the
next and final chapter. And her little boy, who constantly
bursts into the cafe to interrupt her conversations with
Chauvin, serves as a constant symbolic reminder of Anne's
responsibilities as well a the "moderato" side of her nature. She cannot imagine, she says, *not* accompanying her
child. Spitzer speaks of Phèdre as a walking or living oxymoron. Likewise, the title of Duras's novel is a discrete
oxymoron alluding to the dualism of Anne's nature and
her ambivalence toward a life of total freedom.

Racine will often de-individualize his heroines through the
personification of abstractions (Spitzer, pp. 227-228).

> UN DÉSORDRE ÉTERNEL règne dans son esprit,
> SON CHAGRIN INQUIET l'arrache de son lit:
> Elle veut voir le jour, et SA DOULEUR PROFONDE
> M'ordonne toutefois d'écarter tout le monde.
>
>   (*Phèdre*, I, 2)

Likewise, Duras, by transposing an epithet, will deperson-
alize Anne and personify the disorder "reigning" in her
mind: ". . . le désordre blond de ses cheveux." The phrase
is repeated a second and third time during the banquet
scene, the last time intensified by syllepsis: "le désordre
blond et réel de ses cheveux." Of course, it is really the
substantive that is transposed since the disorderly hair is a
symbol of an inner disorder.

Duras shares with Racine a talent for understating emotional intensity through the selection of key words, ges-

tures, even silences that are pregnant with overtones and
undertones. For example, the other women at the banquet
have been repressing *their* instincts too, as is subtly indicated by the way they eat the savory salmon. The conflict
between sensuality and "convenance" is expressed by the
careful choice of a verb, an adverb or an adjective.

> Les femmes le *dévorent jusqu'au bout.* Leurs épaules
> *nues* ont la luisance et la fermeté d'une société fondée
> dans ses assises sur la certitude de son droit, elles furent
> choisies à la convenance de celle-ci . . . Elles *se pour-
> lèchent* de mayonaise. . . .
>
>   (p. 95)

The metonymic "épaules nues" is of course a sexual syn-
echdoque, suggesting a more complete nudity just like
Emma Bovary's "main nue" seen emerging from the closed
carriage when with Léon in Rouen. Another metonymic
transfer occurs a few pages later: "Le corps de l'homme
sur la plage est toujours solitaire" (p. 99). Duras is not
simply referring to the fact that Chauvin is by himself; the
epithet creates a *double-entendre*: his body is yearning for
that of another, and on a deeper level, it is his soul, more
than his body, that is metonymically "solitaire."

Two other devices used by both authors to suggest rather
than state emotion are asyndeton and aposiopesis. Anne's
late entrance at her own party, for example, is troubled
both by her intoxication and by her fear of betraying it
through a careless word or gesture: "Elle entra dans cet
univers étincelant, se dirigea vers le grand piano, s'y accouda, ne s'excusa nullement" (p. 93). The asyndeton suggests the abrupt, nervous, mechanical gestures of a woman
trying to dominate her drunkenness. The device is repeated
nine lines later: "Elle pose sa fourchette, regarde alentour,
cherche, essaye de remonter le cours de la conversation,
n'y arrive pas" (Ibid.).

Before the banquet scene, Anne's conversations with Chauvin are filled with silences, pauses and hesitations—especially when she tries to reconstruct the crime along the
lines suggested to her by her romantic imagination.

> —A le voir faire avec elle, dit-elle doucement comme
> si, vivante ou morte, ça ne lui importait plus désormais,
> vous croyez qu'il est possible d'en arriver . . . là . . .
> autrement que . . . par désespoir?
>
>   (p. 28)

> —Elle dormait au pied des arbres, dans les champs,
> comme . . .
>
>   (p. 87)

> —C'est là, dans cette maison, qu'elle a appris ce que
> vous disiez qu'elle était, peut-être . . .
>
>   (Ibid.)

Aposiopesis is carried to an effective extreme in the banquet scene by having Anne remain silent *throughout,* except when monosyllabic responses are forced from her.

Since Duras and Racine are working in a different medium and in a different period, each has devices not at the disposal of the other. We have already mentioned the cinematographic technique of the simultaneous scene which is used throughout the chapter. It is also used in chapter five: while Anne's child plays the sonatina on the sixth floor of Mademoiselle Giraud's flat, Chauvin listens below and hums the tune. Then the direction of the camera is reversed: the voices of workers are mingled with that other symbol of instinctual freedom—the sound of the sea: "Le bruit de la mer mêlé aux voix des hommes qui arrivaient sur le quai monta jusqu'à la chambre" (p. 75). The simultaneous scene is a new device for achieving an old goal—understatement—and provides an example of the happy marriage in this novel of contemporary and classical strategies.

A *nouveau roman* contribution to *klassiche Dämpfung* is the nonomniscient point of view. Emotions are never explicitly revealed but only conjectured by a modest, tentative "peut-être," a "sans doute" or an "apparement." The characters are not lighted from within by a privileged observer; rather, the initiative is yielded to things and gestures which are seen with the innocent eye of the camera lens. Here for example is the description of the murderer being taken away by the police: "Peut-être alors pleura-t-il, mais le crépuscule trop avancé déjà ne permit d'apercevoir que la grimace ensanglantée et tremblante de son visage et non plus de voir si des larmes s'y coulaient" (p. 21). Related to these "peut-être" is the conditional mood used in the banquet scene to suggest the mere possibility of an anxious look by a depersonalized heroine: "Avec difficulté, on pourrait, à la rigueur, maintenant, apercevoir les masses et les formes de la nuit à travers les rideaux blancs."

A device used throughout the novel in the service of understatement and indirection is symbolism. Anne's unconscious desire for freedom is symbolized by open windows, the sea and ships. The narrow conventionality of her life is represented by the obsessive discussion of the "couloir" that leads off her bedroom. In the banquet scene this symbolism that has been worked out so carefully in the preceding chapters is summarized in a single sentence: "Elle regardera le boulevard par la baie du grand couloir de sa vie" (pp. 102-03). The "couloir-vie" metaphor not only suggests the basis of Anne's problem but her sudden awareness of it. It also suggests the impossibility of escape and foreshadows the end of an incipient love affair.

A neoclassical sense of decorum as well as of economy inspires Duras to have the murder take place "in the wings," i.e., through narrative exposition rather than scenic presentation. And in the banquet scene Anne's vomiting is distanced by an innovative device: the future tense suddenly takes over as narrative mode.

> Alors que les invités se disperseront en ordre irrégulier dans le grand salon attenant à la salle à manger, Anne Desbaresdes s'éclipsera, montera au premier étage . . .
> Elle ira dans la chambre de son enfant s'allongera par

terre, au pied de son lit, sans égard pour ce magnolia qu'elle écrasera entre ses seins, il n'en restera rien. Et entre les temps sacrés de la respiration de son enfant, elle vomira là, longuement, la nourriture étrangère que ce soir elle fut forcée de prendre.

(pp. 102-3)

The confrontation scene with Anne's scandalized husband is also presented *en sourdine* by having it narrated in the future tense and by having the husband represented by an indefinite article and pronoun. He is literally reduced to a shadow.

> Une ombre apparaîtra dans l'encadrement de la porte restée ouverte sur le couloir, obscurcira plus avant la pénombre de la chambre. Anne Desbaresdes passera légèrement la main dans le désordre blond et réel de ses cheveux. Cette fois, elle prononcera une excuse.
>
> On ne lui répondra pas.

(p. 103)

One cannot help being impressed by the inevitability of the banquet scene and the form that it is given. We said at the beginning that at least some hint as to the source of Anne's problem must be given the reader to prevent the novel from falling flat. But the opposite technique of explicit analysis would also have seriously damaged the novel. If Duras had explained Anne's crisis in so many words, labeling it as "frustration," "repression," "bovarysme" or what have you, **Moderato Cantabile** would read like a *roman-feuilleton* in a women's magazine. Anne cannot articulate her problem because until the vomiting scene she is not fully conscious of it. And the author refuses to articulate it because she is dealing with something mysterious and, to a large degree, ineffable. Like Jean-Jacques Bernard and his famous Theater of Silence, Duras is interested in *le mystère quotidien* that lies below the verbal level.

Duras's originality as a novelist can best be shown by comparing her work with that of the writer she most resembles, Nathalie Sarraute. We briefly sketched the main similarities and differences between Duras and Sarraute in an earlier essay:

> Both authors reject the analysis of static psychological types of essences; we do not know what these people are nor where they are going. . . . Both authors deal with *sous-conversation*, those subterranean tremors that go on below the surface of the "inauthentic" dialogue. But Sarraute locates the source of the tremors and measures the gravitational pull of surrounding bodies and of alien planetary systems; the tremors evoked by Duras remain of mysterious origin. In Sarraute's novels those swiftly-shifting molecular movements of the psyche that continually recombine to form new kaleidoscopic patterns, although unnamed and unavowed, remain precise. Sarraute's goal is clarity: she shows us—more vividly than the phenomenologists—the intentional structure of consciousness; Duras presents us with half-conscious and pre-conscious impulses, dim-

ply realized urges toward self-actualization arising from what Jung calls the Shadow side of the self.[5]

The fact that Duras is exploring territory different from that of Sarraute can be clearly shown by comparing ***Moderato Cantabile*** with one of Sarraute's *Tropismes* which deals with the same subject. The anonymous "elle" of "Tropisme XXI" is first shown as an *enfant sage* in parochial school with a religious medal pinned to her smock for her good work and behavior. Whenever she buys an adult-looking magazine or book she is careful to ask the stationer: "Il est pour les enfants, Madame, celui-là?"

> Elle n'aurait jamais pu, oh! non, pour rien au monde elle n'aurait pu, déjà à cet âge-là, sortir de la boutique avec ce regard appuyé sur son dos, avec tout le long de son dos quand elle allait ouvrir la porte pour sortir, le regard de la papetière.[6]

Then "she" is shown as an adult still repressing her instincts in favor of the approval that comes from respectability, from uttering social clichés ("ah! c'est une fois passé vingt ans que les années se mettent à courir toujours plus vite, n'est-ce pas?"), by wearing basic black ("et puis le noir, c'est bien vrai, fait toujours habillé . . ."), by keeping her hands demurely crossed upon her carefully matching handbag, by assuming—like Anne Desbaresdes—the fixed smile, and by giving—like Anne—polite answers to the polite questions ("Yes, she had heard how long their grandmother had suffered before she passed away"). But beneath the veneer of conventionality lie the seething instincts.

> Se taire; les regarder; et juste au beau milieu de la maladie de la grand'mère se dresser et, faisant un trou énorme, s'échapper en heurtant les parois déchirées et courir en criant au milieu des maisons qui guettaient accroupies tout au long des rues grises, s'enfuir en enjambant les pieds des concierges qui prenaient le frais assises sur le seuil de leurs portes, courir la bouche tordue, hurlant des mots sans suite, tandis que les concierges lèveraient la tête au-dessus de leur tricot et que leurs maris abaisseraient leur journal sur leurs genoux et appuieraient le long de son dos, jusqu'à ce qu'elle tourne le coin de la rue, leur regard.[7]

The infinitive is used of course to indicate a mere project, she will not act upon her scandalous impulse. But it is simply a lack of courage not of awareness that prevents her from doing so. On the other hand, Anne Desbaresdes, whose life and emotional situation parallel *exactly* that of "elle," cannot explain even to herself the reason her scandalous behavior: "Depuis dix ans, elle n'a pas fait parler d'elle. Si son incongruité la dévore, elle ne peut s'imaginer" (p. 93).

Bernard Pingaud has suggested that Sarraute writes not anti-novels but ante-novels since "she deals with what happens in the classical novel before either characters or plot is conceived."[8] Duras, then, has written an ante-ante-novel since she deals with subterranean tremors of the psyche before they reach even that level of consciousness

that Sarraute calls tropisms. It should be clear by now that Duras' style is not only effective but inevitable. Oblique allusions, symbolism, *Dämpfung* and understatement are the only instruments delicate enough to probe an emotional state that is pre-conscious and therefore pre-verbal. And the blurring of precise contours has enabled Duras to achieve a distinctive kind of atmosphere, at once strange and gripping. Strindberg called it an atmosphere of the soul.

Notes

1. Lloyd Bishop, "Classical Structure and Style in *Moderato Cantabile*," *The French Review,* special issue No. 6 (1974).

2. Marguerite Duras, *Moderato Cantabile* (Paris: Les Éditions de Minuit, 1958), pp. 84-85. We should like to express our thanks to the editors of Les Éditions de Minuit for its permission to reproduce this extended excerpt. This essay is based in large part upon—and at the same time offers a vivid example of—Michael Riffaterre's theory of style as contrast-with-the-context. Hence the necessity for the long excerpt. In view of the anxiety, in certain quarters, concerning the deviation-from-the-norm theory of style, Riffaterre's theory is appealing in that it analyzes the style of a literary work from the point of view of the deviations it makes from its own norms, which can be ascertained very accurately as well as objectively. Our purpose is not to defend Riffaterre's theory but to put it to work.

3. Leo Spitzer, *Études de Style* (Paris: Gallimard, 1970), p. 209. Spitzer's famous study on the *effet de sourdine* or *klassiche Dämpfung* offers support, in our opinion, to Riffaterre's theory of style. The very essence of Racinian style, according to Spitzer, is the introduction into lyrical and emotional passages of de-lyricized and de-personalized "formulas"—a good example, if ever there was one, of contrast with the context.

4. Marcel Proust, *A la recherche du temps perdu* (Paris: Gallimard, 1954), p. 875.

5. Bishop, op. cit, p. 233.

6. Nathalie Sarraute, "Tropismes" in *Monologues de Minuit* (New York: Macmillan, 1965), p. 113.

7. Ibid., p. 114.

8. Quoted in *Monologues de Minuit,* p. 93.

Bruce Bassoff (essay date 1979)

SOURCE: "Death and Desire in Marguerite Duras' 'Moderato Cantabile,'" in *Modern Language Notes,* Vol. 94, No. 4, May, 1979, pp. 720-30.

[*In the following essay, Bassoff maintains that death is the only satisfactory consummation of desire for Duras's characters in* Moderato cantabile.]

The dream reveals the reality that conception lags behind. That is the horror of life—the terror of art.

—Kafka

Marguerite Duras' fiction relies on the lyrical association of motifs rather than the progression of a story, and it defeats the separation between "real" elements and "virtual" elements (dreams, hallucinations, etc.) that is a mainstay of traditional fiction. The *mise en scène* of desire in Duras' books, moreover, is not dependent on traditional characters—known and motivated. Duras' characters are figures in a rhetorical sense; they allow her to formulate idea and mood in a dynamic way. ***Moderato Cantabile*** is about a woman, Anne Desbaresdes, who, while attending the piano lesson of her somewhat recalcitrant son, hears a terrible scream from a nearby café. On going to the café shortly afterward, she sees a young man clinging to the body of the lover he has killed. Compulsively returning to the café with her son, she imaginatively reenacts the murder and the events leading to it with a stranger she meets in the café. Becoming habitually intoxicated during these visits, she finally creates a scandal at a dinner party given by her and her husband, and throws up in her child's room with her husband as witness. After consummating in a highly ritualistic way her relation with the stranger, whose name is Chauvin, she returns home without anything, perhaps, having happened.[1] This précis, however, falsifies the lyrical function of the characters. When the murderer is introduced, he is described as follows: "Toute expression en avait disparu, exceptée celle, foudroyée, indélébile, inversée du monde, de son désir" (23). That inward look of desire creates a world for itself in which its variations can be completed. When Chauvin says, "On va donc s'en tenir là où nous sommes. . . . ça doit arriver parfois" (154), he is pointing to the form of the book, which creates something happening out of things as they are.

The theme and variations form is pointed up many times. When the child is asked to perform scales in penance for his recalcitrance, we are told: "L'enfant recommença encore d'où il était parti la première fois, à la hauteur exacte et mystérieuse du clavier d'où il fallait qu'il le fît" (93). This is also the mysterious point of departure for the text, which only appears to correspond to the beginning of a story. What appears to be the precise keeping of chronology on Duras' part is really a kind of ritual commemoration: "ça va être la huitième nuit" (119). At one point Anne says of the couple: "A le voir faire avec elle . . . comme si, vivante ou morte, ça ne lui importait plus désormais, vous croyez qu'il est possible d'en arriver . . . là . . . autrement que . . . par désespoir?" Chauvin remarks shortly afterward: "Il y a longtemps que vous le promenez . . . Je veux dire qu'il y a longtemps que vous le promenez dans les squares ou au bord de la mer" (38-39). Chauvin's insistence on one meaning forces us to consider the other: Anne's habitual walking with her son being related to the purgatorial state of the lovers. Elsewhere Chauvin conjures up an image of the man driving away the woman "très souvent" from the house. When Anne remarks that it wasn't worth the trouble, Chauvin replies: "ça va être dif-ficile d'éviter ces sortes de pensées, on doit en avoir l'habitude, comme de vivre. Mais l'habitude seulement" (118). The strangeness of this passage stems from the fact that "ces sortes de pensées," which sounds more ominous than the immediate context would justify, relates the habitual act of exclusion to the discrete act of murder. A variation of this equation occurs when Anne contrasts her walks (themselves habitual) with the fixed routine of her day. She then says of her lateness that evening: "Quand le retard devient tellement important . . . qu'il atteint le degré où il en est maintenant pour moi, je crois que ça ne doit plus changer rien à ses conséquences que de l'aggraver encore davantage ou pas" (115). The degree (more or less) of lateness in this passage is related to the degree of desire represented by the murder: "Du moment qu'il avait compris qu'elle désirait tant qu'il le fasse, je voudrais que vous me disiez pourquoi il ne l'a pas fait, par example, un peu plus tard ou . . . un peu plus tôt" (116). We learn that Anne derives from wine "une confirmation de ce que fut jusque là son désir obscur et une indigne consolation à cette découverte" (134), and we learn that her husband, watching Anne during the critical scene of the dinner party, "s'y attendait depuis toujours" (133). If at the beginning of the story, after the music teacher tells the boy to begin again, a scream causes her to say "Quelque chose est arrivé" (17), Chauvin indicates at the end that nothing has happened and remarks: "ça recommencera" (151). Duras' use of tense reinforces the accordion-like sense of time in the book—as if the sense of the habitual were compressed into a moment or as if a moment of intense desire were played out in all of its variations. The supplanting of the present tense (which has itself alternated with the preterite) by the future in chapter vii of the novel, for example, conflates the virtual with the real.

The theme of the novel is announced in its opening sentence: "—Veux-tu lire ce qu'il y a d'écrit au-dessus de ta partition? demanda la dame" (11). The word for musical score, "partition," suggests division, and the form of the score suggests the railings that surround Anne's house: "Vous allez aux grilles, puis vous les quittez, puis vous faites le tour de votre maison, puis vous revenez encore aux grilles. L'enfant, là-haut dort. Jamais vous n'avez crié. Jamais" (83). Such barriers, and the sense of their violation, occur everywhere in ***Moderato Cantabile.*** Late in the novel Anne asks Chauvin to tell the story of the lovers one last time: "Chauvin hésita, les yeux toujours ailleurs [like the inward look of the murderer], sur le mur du fond, puis il se décida à le dire comme d'un souvenir" (149). As for the scream, Anne has said, "Une fois, il me semble bien, oui, une fois j'ai dû crier un peu de cette façon, peut-être, oui, quand j'ai eu cet enfant" (54), and her smile is described as "le douloureux sourire d'un enfantement sans fin" (22), "un sourire de délivrance" (34). We will come back shortly to this motif of the smile, but for now it is important to note the overdetermined function of the child. On the one hand Anne says of him: "Il me dévore" (22), and later feels that the child's musical playing sentences her "de nouveau à la damnation de son amour. Les portes de l'enfer se refermèrent" (100). On the other hand the description of her smile as an "enfantement" immediately follows her statement "il me dévore"—as if *she* continues to contain *him*. At other times she says: "Quelquefois je crois que je t'ai inventé, que ce n'est pas vrai, tu vois" (46). Her statement "C'est un enfant qui est toujours seul" (51) is true of her also, and if we can see Chauvin too as her own invention, we can understand why the patronne of the café suddenly observes of him: "Vous êtes jeune" (101). During the colloquies between Anne and Chauvin, the child is doubled: "Les deux enfants jouaient à courir en rond" (58); and at the culmination of their ritual, Chauvin says harshly: "Je sais, pour cet enfant" (149). Anne's ambivalence toward her own existence is reflected in her ambivalence toward her son. On the one hand she says, referring to the musical catechism the child is put through: "Un jour . . . il le saura, il le dira sans hésiter, c'est inévitable. Même s'il ne le veut pas, il le saura"; and "un jour il saura ses gammes aussi . . . il les saura aussi parfaitement que sa mesure, c'est inévitable, il en sera même fatigué à force de les savoir" (92, 94). On the other hand she takes vicarious pride in his recalcitrance and does "false penitence" for her indulgence of him (98). At one point, the basic theme of closure and violation is rendered in these terms: The boy, clenching his hands (again like the inward look of the man's desire) faces the score like the object into which his teacher wants to reduce him.[2] Framed in the open window is a motorboat that passes through ("passer dans") the boy's blood—the frame of the window and the energy of the motor boat representing conflicting terms. The word "passer" joins words like "arriver" and "traverser" in the lexis of transcendence. When Chauvin evokes Anne looking from her window onto the boulevard, he says, "Endormie ou réveillée, dans une tenue décente ou non, on passait outre à votre existence" (76). When Duras sets up a counterpoint between the dinner party (and its associated "parc correctement clos") and the prowling of the unnamed man (Chauvin?) outside, we hear of the man: "Il passera," and then: "Il est passé" (139). As we reread the beginning of the book, "Quelque chose est arrivé" (17) has the same effect. Later, when Chauvin and Anne rehearse the completion of their desire, Anne wonders whether she can do it: "Peut-être que je ne vais pas y arriver, murmura-t-elle," to which Chauvin replies: "une minute . . . et nous y arriverons" (154). Just before the ritual is completed, before Chauvin wishes that she were dead and Anne replies: "C'est fait," Anne gets up from her chair and Duras writes: "Elle y arriva, se releva" (155).

Let us consider some of the variations of this theme. As the child silently repudiates his music teacher, "Le bruit de la mer s'éleva, sans bornes, dans le silence de l'enfant" (15). The sea, in turn, is "mêlé aux voix des hommes qui arrivaient sur le quai" (102), men whose memory returns to Anne at night when, as Chauvin points out, "rien ne s'y passe" (62). The two lovers, as they are conjured up by Chauvin's incantatory recitation, live, he thinks, in an isolated house by the sea (118), and Anne and her husband will vacation in such a place (139). The hallway in Anne's house is such that the inhabitants are "ensemble et séparés à la fois" (56), and one variation of the hallway, the boule-

vard, is supposed to be extended beyond the limits of the dunes and allows Anne to go beyond "ce périmètre qui lui fut il y a dix ans autorisé" (131). Part of these limits, a beech tree, overshadows Anne's room and obstructs her view of the sea (74). The black ink associated with the tree's shadow, moreover, evokes for us the blood shed by the murderer (75). When there's a wind the hedges enclosing Anne's house grate "comme l'acier" as if "on entendait son coeur," and the trees scream "comme des égorgés" (78-80). Many women, Chauvin tells us, have died in the room behind the beech tree, which has stopped growing (78-79). The wind, which has been known to smash windows, is part of the unusual period of good weather the town has been knowing during the eight days of encounters: "Le vent frais qui soufflait sur la ville tenait le ciel en haleine" (69)—like the force of Anne's desire. Windows are closed to shut out the cries of the hedges and the oppressive odor of flowers, whose unfolding is "funèbre" (125). As the dinner party progresses and the wine confirms her hidden desire, Anne experiences the following transformation: "Le feu nourrit son ventre de sorcière contrairement aux autres. Ses seins si lourds de chaque côté de cette fleur si lourde se ressentent de sa maigreur nouvelle et lui font mal. Le vin coule dans sa bouche pleine d'un nom qu'elle ne prononce pas. Cet événement silencieux lui brise les reins" (137). The passage is compacted by the repetition of "lourd" and by the consonance of "seins," "pleine," and "reins"—an intense containment broken by a "silent event" (later Anne will attempt to escape "la suffocante simplicité" of her confession—145).

The goal of Anne's desire is death. When Chauvin says that perhaps the young man wanted to kill the woman right away, Anne's fear and turmoil have to do with "toute allusion à son existence" (80). The processing of desire is carried out like a stately ritual—complete with chorus and the knitting up of fate. Throughout Anne's encounters with Chauvin the patronne knits her red sweater, and Anne keeps arranging her disheveled hair. Disapproving at first of their meetings (like the prudential community typically represented by the chorus), the patronne seems solicitous and almost "tender" in the final sequence, where "un choeur de conversations diverses" also occurs (154). The dinner party itself is "rituellement parfaite" (128-29), and at its center is a "victim"—a duck in "son linceul d'oranges" (126). Just as the duck continues "sa marche inéluctable vers sa totale disparition" (126), Anne's champagne has "la saveur anéantissante des lèvres inconnues d'un homme de la rue" (132). Anne keeps "torturing" the dying flower at her breast, and this night "le fleurissement des magnolias sera . . . achevé" (128). This consummation repeats that of the murder: "En bas, quelques cris, des appels maintenant raisonnables, indiquèrent la consommation d'un événement inconnu" (22). One is reminded of Georges Bataille's statement about the closeness between sacrifice and the act of love in antiquity: "Le partenaire féminin de l'érotisme apparaissait comme la victime, le masculin comme le sacrificateur, l'un et l'autre, au cours de la consommation, se perdant dans la continuité établie par un premier acte de destruction." What is dissolved in the erotic are the constituted forms of social life which found "l'ordre discontinu des individualités définies que nous sommes," but, as Bataille points out, this search for continuity can be effective only if it does not succeed. That is, eroticism (like reproduction) must call being into question but not condemn it.[3] Part of Bataille's thesis is that the sacred and the obscene are near allied, that both experiences trouble our sense of self-possession. In this sense, perhaps, we can appreciate Chauvin's insult. Having recapitulated with Anne her enclosure, "Chauvin proféra un mot à voix basse. Le regard de Anne Desbaresdes s'évanouit lentement sous l'insulte, s'ensommeilla" (113).[4] This sense of dissolution occurs also when Anne listens to her son play Diabelli's sonatina. Whereas earlier Anne predicts that the boy will learn his lessons by rote despite himself, now he plays movingly despite himself and Anne feels that she is on the verge of fainting ("s'en évanouir") (99). Not only Anne but also the music teacher undergoes the sense of despair associated with the two lovers—a condition in which boundaries tend to dissolve, even those between life and death: "Sa colère fléchit et elle se désespéra de si peu compter aux yeux de cet enfant que d'un geste, pourtant, elle eût pu réduire à la parole, que l'aridité de son sort, soudain, lui apparut" (14). Opposed to this word to which the boy could be reduced (in responding to his teacher) is the transgression of Chauvin's insult and the variety of screams, shouts, sirens, whistles, and vomiting that punctuate the text.

One interesting variation of the scream is laughter. The smile in **Moderato Cantabile** is associated both with a fixed mask (which, vanishing, leaves the face "brutally exposed") and with "deliverance": "Le vin aidant sans doute, le tremblement de la voix avait lui aussi cessé. Dans les yeux, peu à peu, afflua un sourire de délivrance" (34). Even dead, Anne thinks, the murdered woman "en souriait encore de joie" (80). As the "eyes" in which Anne's smile appears suggest, the smile in both of its aspects is associated with communication and recognition. Anne observes, just before she is "brutally exposed," "les yeux de cet homme qui lui parlait et qui la regardait aussi, dans le même temps" (39). At the dinner party Anne has forgotten to put on her make-up, and "un homme, face à une femme, regarde cette inconnue" (126). During the final sequence with Chauvin, we learn that she has not made herself up as carefully as usual, and when the patronne turns on the radio (the blaring of which is another variation of the scream), "Une femme chanta loin, dans une ville étrangère" (146). Laughter, however, is a kind of eruption. Like the dusk that "explodes" at the beginning of the book, laughter erupts at various times—once in explicit association with dusk: "Des cris et des rires d'enfants éclatèrent dehors, qui saluaient le soir comme une aurore" (80-81), the "comme" here suggesting the fine boundary between life and death. The connection between this eruption and the murder (which is a murder by strangling—release, ironically, by compression) is made in the following passage: "Anne Desbaresdes rit, elle aussi, cette fois à pleine gorge" (110). Like the trembling that becomes habitual with Anne when she enters the café (and that becomes transmuted by wine into the ritual of love and dying), laughter is a profound disturbance.

Wine is related both to the inky shadow of the beech tree and to the blood flowing from the murdered woman's mouth. We are reminded again of Bataille's view of eroticism (and its association with both the sacred and the infamous): "Nous n'avons de bonheur véritable qu'à dépenser vainement, comme si une plaie s'ouvrait en nous: nous voulons toujours être sûrs de l'inutilité, parfois du caractère ruineux de notre dépense."[5] When the son's mouth "s'emplit de la dernière lueur du couchant" (46), we have a kind of (paracmastic) pentecostal image, which is resumed in the following sequence: "Elle ne cessa plus de regarder sa bouche seule désormais dans la lumière restante du jour" (77). We recall that a rushing wind, also associated with Pentecost, pervades Anne's thoughts about the town and about her house. At one point, while Chauvin is drinking a glass of wine, the sun is reflected in his eyes "avec la précision du hasard" (73)—a phrase that compresses the process by which chance, in divination, is used to control chance. Chauvin is, after all, clairvoyant. At one point, having talked to Anne for a while, he announces her identity: "Vous êtes Madame Desbaresdes. La femme du directeur d'Import Export et des Fonderies de la Côte. Vous habitez boulevard de la Mer" (41). At another point, he describes the spatial disposition of the furniture in the music teacher's room, a room he presumably has never entered (109). He has returned to the café, he tells Anne, for the same reason she has (45), and he recounts at various times the daily rhythm of desire and suppression in her life. The two, as a matter of fact, seem to merge sometimes. During her second return to the café, before she and Chauvin have formally acknowledged each other, Anne says to the patronne: "Je voudrais un autre verre de vin" (51). Shortly thereafter, when Chauvin has initiated their colloquy, he says: "Je voudrais que vous preniez un autre verre de vin" (52). In fact the "osmosis" associated with the "perfect ritual" of consuming the salmon at Anne's dinner is also characteristic of her relation to Chauvin. During the dinner an unnamed man prowls the neighborhood, and his mouth utters a name (135). On the next page we read of Anne, "Le vin coule dans sa bouche pleine d'un nom qu'elle ne prononce pas" (137). The man on the beach "siffle une chanson entendue dans l'après-midi dans un café du port," and Anne recalls, "une chanson . . . entendue dans l'après-midi dans un café du port, qu'elle ne peut pas chanter" (134-35).

Duras' insistence on the mouth implies something about one of Chauvin's functions: that he is a kind of "persona of speech"[6]—like the Egyptian *ka* pointing to its own mouth in one graphic representation. Perhaps, as Julian Jaynes suggests, human nature once had two parts—an executive part called a god and a follower part called a man; and perhaps, as he suggests, poetry (or song) began as the divine speech of this "bicameral mind." Perhaps also prophecy, possession, hypnosis, and schizophrenia are vestiges of this mind in the modern world. In such a way can we understand the rushing wind and flaming tongues of

Pentecost; in such a way can we understand the inconstant wind and fading coal of poetic creation. Just as Kafka's work has the quality of a dream vision, ***Moderato Cantabile*** has the quality of a hypnotic trance or schizophrenic episode. Chauvin's role becomes more and more trance-like until, overwhelmed, "il ne la connut plus" (121). He describes the relationship between the young couple "comme d'un souvenir" (149), and at one point he uses "une voix neutre, inconnue jusque là de cette femme" (118). Anne's voice, in turn, is sometimes "raisonnable, un instant réveillée (151), but it is also "une voix de sourd" (150). Her fixation on Chauvin's eyes suggests a certain hypnotic power, as do his incantatory suggestions about her daily life. Other passages, particularly admonitory ones, suggest a schizophrenic episode. Chauvin keeps instructing her to talk to him, to make things up (79). Concerning Chauvin's clairvoyance, we know that hallucinations sometimes seem to have greater access to knowledge and memories than the patient—like the ancient gods. Unlike the gods, however, Chauvin keeps repeating: "Je n'ai rien dit" (44).

If, however, we focus less on the quality of the book's narration and more on the analogy between the two couples, we can construe Chauvin's psychic automatism in a different way—as a paradoxical function of Anne's need for transcendence. Although Bataille accounts for the transgressive aspect of desire in the book (an aspect that is eternally part of the erotic, according to him), he does not see the way in which desire is, in turn, constituted by its available models. In *Mensonge romantique et vérité romanesque* René Girard points out that desire always entails choosing a model and that one's choice is between a human and a divine model. The pride of modern man means that his need for transcendence is diverted from the *au-delà* to the *en-deçà* and that our neighbor comes to fill the role once filled by Christ.[7] Perhaps now we can understand the masochism of Anne and the murdered woman. Perhaps we can understand why Anne says of her counterpart: "De lui obéir à ce point, c'était sa façon à elle d'espérer. Et même, lorsqu'elle arrivait sur le pas de la porte, elle attendait encore qu'il lui dise d'entrer" (119-20). In the modern world, where no god (or surrogate thereof) provides a model for vertical transcendence and where democratization has undermined the qualitative differences between men, sterile rivalry (like that of conspicuous consumption) is the norm—even in erotic relationships. Recalling Flaubert's idea that in the modern world two people never love each other at the same time, we can see how the name "Chauvin" in ***Moderato Cantabile*** reinforces this sense of mutual exclusion. The lies that are so crucial in the exchanges between Anne and Chauvin relate to the deception at the heart of desire: the arbitrary differences we posit between ourselves and others so that we can overcome those differences. But since the other is discredited, made ordinary, if the difference *is* overcome, we must, like Achilles racing against the tortoise, maintain an infinite distance between ourselves and the other while constantly halving it. The ultimate meaning of our desire is masochistic since our repudiation by

the other maintains the illusion of his transcendence and the hope of our own. After Anne claims that she understands how the murdered woman became the "bitch" of Chauvin's insult, Chauvin says that he was lying, and Anne notes "la crispation inhumaine" of his face (120). The insult is a kind of repudiation, so that Chauvin is described as no longer being aware of her (121). If we think back to the main theme of the book, the variations of which we have traced throughout this essay, we can see that its sense of extension and retraction is that of "metaphysical desire." The sonatina is *moderato cantabile,* but the moan that comes out of Anne is "presque licencieuse" (44). When prompted to talk of the dead woman, Anne muses as follows: "Elle chercha, loin" (75), just as she seeks Chauvin in similar terms: "Anne Desbaresdes traversa ce temps, ce vent" (69). The rhythm of her desire is expressed as follows: "Anne Desbaresdes se retracta et, comme à son habitude parfois, s'alanguit" (76), and this rhythm pervades the novel in sequences like "resta fixe . . . fléchit vers" (96). At the threshold, then, stands the young man who represents hope for his lover—hope in her obedience and in his repudiation. She waits for him to tell her to come in, but the threshold exists only because he keeps her outside: "Il lui a poussé, au bout des bras, un destin" (138). As the reality of Anne's desire becomes confirmed, Chauvin becomes more and more a kind of psychic automaton. It is death alone, as supreme otherness and repudiation, that will satisfy Anne. As she and Chauvin accomplish their mortuary ritual, we are told that the murdered woman "n'était pas seule à avoir découvert ce qu'elle désirait de lui" (58).

Notes

1. Marguerite Duras, *Moderato Cantabile* (Paris: Les Editions de Minuit, 1958). Page references will be included in the body of the text.

2. Hands mime the essential action of the book. After the music teacher announces that something has happened, "Anne Desbaresdes prit son enfant par les épaules, le serra à lui faire mal, crier presque" (17). The murderer is first seen clutching the shoulders of the murdered woman (23). When the child clasps his mother's hand, "Elle y fut contenue tout entière. Anne Desbaresdes cria presque" (65). Hands tremble, lie side by side, and finally touch "illusoirement dans l'intention seulement" (149) as the "Pose Mortuaire" is realized.

3. George Bataille, *L'Erotisme* (Paris: Les Editions de Minuit, 1957), pp. 25-26. Anne's "sourire d'un enfantement" is pertinent here.

4. The insult is probably the word "chienne," as we see on p. 120, where that word is applied to the murdered woman.

5. Bataille, p. 190.

6. See Julian Jaynes, *The Origin of Consciousness in the Breakdown of the Bicameral Mind* (Boston: Houghton Mifflin Company, 1976), p. 192. This book provides the basis for the discussion in this paragraph.

7. René Girard, *Mensonge romantique et vérité romanesque* (Paris: Grasset, 1961). This deviated desire is "metaphysical" because it aims at the autonomy of the model rather than the concrete value of the object.

Marianne Hirsch (essay date 1982)

SOURCE: "Gender, Reading, and Desire in 'Moderato Cantabile,'" in *Twentieth Century Literature,* Vol. 28, No. 1, 1982, pp. 69-85.

[*In the following essay, Hirsch contends that the characters' oral recounting of the murder in* Moderato cantabile *constitutes a literary narration through which the characters identify with others and come to understand their own desires by reenacting the passion of others.*]

> Maybe that's what life is all about: to get into, to let yourself be carried along by this story—this story, well, the story of others.
>
> —Marguerite Duras[1]

Duras's comment might well be a description of the characters in her novels—vacant creatures who exist in a world of ruins and wait for a story that will awaken, or, as the author puts it, "ravish" them. Observation and interpretation of other lives provide Duras's protagonists with their only content: Lol Stein (*Le Ravissement de Lol V. Stein*) experiences sex vicariously by crouching in a field outside of the hotel where a friend and her lover meet; the French diplomats (*Le Vice-Consul*) can feel the suffering in Calcutta only through their observation of the vice-consul's reaction. Existence takes shape in response to others, and, therefore, it has about it much of the unreality and indirectness of fiction. "Perhaps I am an echo chamber," says Duras when speaking of her method of composition (*Les Parleuses,* p. 218).

I shall examine this structure of mediation and response in ***Moderato Cantabile,*** arguing that the characters, in their unraveling of a mysterious murder of passion, actually enact a *literary* process, namely that of interpreting an incident by recounting it in narrative form. The resulting imaginative identification with the lives of others leads the characters not to re-create, but to create, out of their own feeling and in their own lives, a version of the murder they have witnessed. Their involvement in this murder constitutes an act of reading; its mode is an empathetic *imitatio*: the only way to *know* desire is to *reenact* it. The epistemology involved is a feeling rather than a knowing, an erotics rather than a hermeneutics.[2] This reading, moreover, is not a solitary, but a communal process, one which emerges out of and becomes the basis for an evolving relationship of a woman with a man, a child, and another woman.

As the novel's protagonists become more and more involved in the activity of reading, the plot of the novel becomes a metaphor for the reading of the novel. With this metaphoric relationship as a basis, my analysis interrogates the text's implications about reading. The text suggests, for example, that the relationship between text and reader, between character and reader, differs according to the gender of that reader. Those differences, moreover, correspond to male and female developmental patterns as contemporary psychoanalysis outlines them—the male based on separation and dominance, the female on relatedness and receptivity. This essay first examines the novel's inscription of reading as a communal process of creation; by means of the inscribed readers, it then explores differences between male and female involvement in this process. Finally it looks at fiction itself as the locus for possible transformations of stereotypically binding relational patterns. The novel's own unique combination of traditional and innovative narrative strategies forces the external reader to assume both what the text designates as the "male" and the "female" reading stances. In its ultimate valorization of receptivity, fusion, and silence, however, Duras's aesthetic, centered in the reading process, is distinctly female.

My argument emerges out of two heretofore independent theoretical matrices: audience-oriented or reader-response criticism and feminist psychoanalytic analyses of gender difference. Only in very few instances have attempts been made to define gender-based variations in reader response. All of them have been speculative in nature: Annette Kolodny's "A Map for Re-reading: Or, Gender and the Interpretation of Literary Texts" demonstrates the inapplicability of Harold Bloom's patriarchal model of literary influence to women, using, as evidence for a female model of "reading," Elizabeth Stuart Phelps's short story, "A Jury of her Peers";[3] Judith Fetterley in *The Resisting Reader* analyzes the female reader's resistance to classic American literature;[4] Norman Holland and Leona Sherman in "Gothic Possibilities" document differences in response by working with an actual group of male and female readers of gothic texts;[5] and Caren Greenberg, using the myth of Echo, postulates a characteristically and distinctly female reading in her "Reading Reading: Echo's Abduction of Language."[6] My own analysis relies on psychoanalytic theories of gender difference, especially Nancy Chodorow's *The Reproduction of Mothering,*[7] Dorothy Dinnerstein's *The Mermaid and the Minotaur,*[8] and Jean Baker Miller's *Toward a New Psychology of Women.*[9]

These writers concentrate on the pre-oedipal period, especially on the infant's separation and individuation, on the formation of the self in relation to the primary parent. In our culture that immensely powerful figure tends to be the mother and, as these writers assert, the mother treats her female infant differently from her male infant. Whereas they encourage boys to become separate and autonomous, mothers see their daughters as extensions of themselves. Ego boundaries between mothers and daughters are more fluid and undefined; therefore, female personality is based on affiliations and relationships. As Nancy Chodorow says, "The basic feminine sense of self is connected to the world, the basic masculine sense of self is separate" (p. 169). The female sense of connection, fluidity, and receptivity becomes here the basis for a distinctive form of reading, "female" in character.

READERS IN THE TEXT

The beginning of **Moderato Cantabile** finds Anne Desbaresdes detached and dispossessed, a spectator at her child's piano lesson.[10] The music teacher's room shuts out the noises of the surrounding town, the brilliance of the sunset, the murmur of the sea. Outer reality remains distant and can only be sensed through the open window. Even the music is experienced indirectly, through language, the translation of the tempo indication "moderato cantabile" that the child stubbornly refuses to remember. The child, whose contact with reality is immediate and total, provides the only link to all that the room has shut out. He is "the only one to remember that dusk has just exploded . . . the motorboat passed through his blood" (**MC,** pp. 75, 76).[11]

The music lesson is interrupted by an inhuman scream which shatters all the sounds of the afternoon: the noises of the town, the women's conversation, the murmur of the sea, the child's rendition of the Diabelli sonatina. The scream jolts Anne out of her passivity; it moves her directly, viscerally. She runs to a nearby café: when she reaches the café and sees the murderer's blood-stained face as he kisses his dead lover and moans over her corpse, when she sees his expressionless state, absent and alien from his surroundings, Anne, more immediately involved than the other spectators, is almost at the point of screaming herself. The unknown woman's dying scream of passion becomes the text to be interpreted and the moment to be re-created; it is the generating pre-text of the novel.

Anne's obsessive interest in the scream and the murder can be explained primarily by the absences in her life, by the novel's ellipses. Just as the music teacher's room separates Anne from the vitality of the town and the ocean, so her entire life is subject to the constraints of routine and the bourgeois social roles she is forced to play. The scream with its echoes of madness, passion, and violence lures Anne out of her sterile and solitary existence. Only with her child has she been able to experience other modes of being—immediate, unlimited, connected—first at the moment of birth, when she also screamed, and then, day by day, by watching his openness to the brilliant sunset, by communicating with him silently and harmoniously, by understanding him without reason and without words. Anne's closeness to her child has made her particularly attuned to the scream, which communicates both the fulfillment of the dying woman and the fusion of the woman and her lover: at the moment of death the barriers of separate identity are abolished. Destruction, madness, murder provide, for Anne, the possibility of escaping from the sterile order of her life, of getting through to her "witch's loins" (**MC,** p. 132), of moving from separateness to connection. To destroy the social structures that have estranged

people from their natural inner power, to break through to the other inside herself, the other that she has had to suppress, but that, in Xavière Gauthier's words, emerges like the grass that grows between the stones of the pavement, becomes an obsessive need for Anne, a need unconscious and inexpressible, awakened by the dying scream of the murdered woman. Gauthier's comment about the discourse of women—repetitive, disconnected, disordered, unharmonious—and its source in repression and oppression gives us a clue to Anne's obsession with the scream which, similarly, emerges with "the power of that which has been long contained" (*Les Parleuses,* pp. 8, 12).

Anne's repeated visits to the lower-class café, her erotic interest in Chauvin, the factory worker she meets there, and her increasingly heavy and debilitating drinking are steps in the gradual annihilation of her individuated and civilized adult self. Anne and Chauvin meet through the common fascination with the murder of passion they almost witnessed. The relationship is nourished by their effort to understand how love between two individuals might lead to murder, and what such a culmination might mean to the two lovers. In the absence of facts, however, their dialogues are purely speculative: "Perhaps no one knows"; "I'm not really sure of anything"; "who knows?" they are forced to repeat. Anne and Chauvin's initial interpretation arises out of the passion they both sensed in the woman's scream and the man's cries, a passion they begin to re-create, or, to be more accurate, to create, within themselves. Their only authority rests on their own feelings which, as they grow, give their investigation its obsessive inevitability. As Anne says, "The scream was so loud it's really only natural for people to try and find out what happened. I would have found it difficult not to, you know" (**MC,** p. 85).

Anne's perception of the couple's union is doubly indirect: only Chauvin can help Anne comprehend the murdered woman's scream; only through the victim can Anne relate to Chauvin. Paradoxically, their only access to the couple's experience is also the greatest barrier to a reenactment of the murder and the fulfillment of their common desire—the literary activity in which they are engaged, their verbal speculations about the couple and about each other. Yet a genuine understanding of the love-murder can only take place outside of language and reason. The story must be created out of feeling; it cannot be re-created out of language because in this novel the mediating force of language is presented as antithetical to the immediacy of desire and death.[12]

The collaborative storytelling in which Anne and Chauvin are engaged thus has to go beyond the intellectual and the verbal to become erotic and sexual. They act out the couple's story *physically*: Anne drinks, becomes physically disoriented, cries, trembles, her lips turn gray, her ice-cold hands shake and an uncontrollable moan breaks from her as she approaches the moment of surrender. Anne's metamorphosis, her abandonment of her social role, is a concrete physical act—she vomits the food and wine, no longer able to control her body with an act of will. "It wasn't any longer a question of wanting or not wanting to," she says. Still, Anne and Chauvin's own adulterous union is not concentrated in the icy touch of their hands, nor does it take place at the moment of their mortuary kiss. These gestures are perfunctory; they are performed "so that it should be accomplished" (*MC,* p. 139). The real eroticism, the real sexuality of the novel is *literary* in nature; it is their common act of exploring the other couple's story. Filling the mystery of the scream with their own meaning, creating the story together, is, as Gauthier suggests in *Les Parleuses,* in itself an erotic act: "This whiteness, this emptiness is also sexual" (*MC,* p. 19). The activity of "reading" is precariously tensed between talk and action, control and abandonment.

Gender and Reading

These two plots—the other couple's unknown story and Anne and Chauvin's reconstruction/creation of that story—rest on multiple mediations both within each plot level and across plot levels. An analysis of the interaction between Anne and Chauvin, of the parallel interaction of the other couple, and of Anne and Chauvin's relationship to that other couple, reveals gender differences as profound as Chauvin's name would seem to suggest. The unusual meeting between Anne and Chauvin is as much colored by deep differences of gender and class as it is by their shared fascination: Anne is the wife of the factory owner; Chauvin has recently quit his job at that factory. Their encounters are viewed with skepticism and hostility by the other customers in the café. It could be argued that Chauvin's motive for the involvement is revenge, that he desires to reverse class categorization by making Anne into his slave. The story he tells about the other couple is about dominance and submission; the means by which he tells it—making Anne the victim—actually duplicates this master/slave relationship to the point where, when Chauvin says, "I wish you were dead," Anne responds as one does to the order of a monarch: "C'est fait" ("I am").[13]

Anne and Chauvin's ritualistic storytelling duplicates the lovers' relationship. While Anne is fascinated by the murder and begs Chauvin to tell her about the couple, even if he has to invent the details of their story, Chauvin seems initially much more interested in talking about Anne, in provoking her, through questions and comments, to reveal herself, in telling her, with great certainty, things about her own life. These two parallel processes of fiction-making, these two stories that emerge, end up nourishing each other. Only by means of Anne's own transformation and re-creation of the victim's role can the background of the murder be filled in and understood. As the dialogue moves from Anne to the murdered woman and back to Anne, we get closer and closer to the moment of death, and closer to the point where Anne and the murdered woman become one.

Chauvin describes the life Anne has led until she met him: "You go to the railings, then you go away and walk around the house, then you come back again to the railings. The child is sleeping upstairs. You have never screamed. Never" (*MC,* p. 108). Her suppressed needs gradually come to the foreground as Chauvin tells Anne about her nude breasts under the dress she wore to the reception for the workers. He gets her to admit to her erotic interest in the men who pass her house every morning. As Anne gradually surrenders to Chauvin's pressures, as she becomes the person he constructs, the story of the murder grows.

In Chauvin's version, the woman loses more and more of her individuality. First she becomes her lover's object, obeying his every command. Eventually she relinquishes all humanity, descending to an unconscious animal-like existence: "Then came the time when he looked at her and no longer saw her as he had seen her before. She ceased to be beautiful or ugly, young or old, similar to anyone else, even to herself" (*MC,* pp. 123, 124). The man prepares the scene for the inevitable murder by breaking down all of the woman's resistance, all her sense of herself. The process of working toward the murder is a common one between the two lovers; yet, even while they share the desire for destruction, emptiness, death, the only way to meet it is through aggression and dominance. The unspoken understanding between them puzzles and fascinates Anne most of all. The couple lives what most of us have been taught to suppress. Together they gradually return to a preverbal existence of silence and power, where they gain a knowledge of themselves and of each other that a novel by definition cannot express. As they turn away from society, reason, and eventually humanity, they transcend language in favor of silent understanding.

At one point, Chauvin speculates, the man simply knew that the woman wished to die, to be killed by him:

> "I'd like you to tell me now how they came not to speak to each other any more." . . . "One night they pace back and forth in their rooms, like caged animals, not knowing what's happening to them. They begin to suspect what it is and are afraid." . . . "Nothing can satisfy them any longer." . . . "They're overwhelmed by what's happening, they can't talk about it yet. Perhaps it will take months, months for them to know."
>
> (*MC,* pp. 102, 103)

Yet even beyond language, these two individuals are trapped in the structures of domination and submission that divide them.

When Anne, having projected *herself* into the story, speaks of the murdered woman in the future tense, it is clear that she is actually speaking of herself: "She will never speak again, she said." Chauvin's answer reinforces Anne's identification even while changing the story's outcome: "Of course she will. Suddenly one day, one beautiful morning, she'll meet someone she knows and won't be able to avoid saying good morning. Or she'll hear a child singing, it will be a lovely day and she'll remark how lovely it is. It will begin again" (*MC,* p. 138). While Anne has been able to accept silence and death, Chauvin pulls back. The images he uses—beautiful weather, morning, music, the child—mean life to him; for Anne they have come to represent a form of death. At this point only Anne is capable of coping with the fear of passion and destruction; Chauvin cannot even succeed in comforting her: "Anne Desbaresdes doubled over, her forehead almost touching the table, and accepted her fear" (*MC*, p. 139). Chauvin, in contrast, stops short of his identification with the murderer. He is more and more impotent before Anne's moans and laments; he is incapable of soothing her fear.

Just as the other couple are ultimately divided—the woman's knowledge is direct and immediate while the man's can never be more than vicarious—so Anne and Chauvin relate differently to the story they are interpreting—Anne identifies and merges with the victim, Chauvin remains separate and dominant. The difference in their modes of "reading" the story is a basic precondition of their access to it: for the murder to take place, for the other couple to reach that point of fusion between language and silence, between life and death, one must play the murderer and the other the victim; to understand it, Anne and Chauvin must duplicate this role division. Thus, Chauvin's entrance into the story through an understanding of the murderer's motives, of his need for dominance, differs strongly from Anne's entrance through her experience of the woman's desire to surrender and be killed. Where Chauvin needs to establish distance, Anne needs to let go of boundaries, absorb and become the other. Her identification with the murdered woman depends on her vacancy and ultimate receptivity. Where Chauvin needs to maintain control and to hold on to language (hence, his denial of Anne's "She will never speak again"), Anne must embrace silence, must learn to refuse all structure in a readiness to merge her identity with another.

The key to Anne's identification with the other woman lies in her privileged ability to hear the scream which takes her back to her child's birth. The novel equates the moments of birth and death, both situated between fusion and separation, separation and fusion. In her interaction with her child, Anne in fact lives through the process of separation and individuation as a parent; in bringing Anne back to a childhood state, her obsessive involvement in the story of the murder is meant to reverse this process. As the child moves toward individuation, civilization, language, so Anne regresses toward the fused, the preverbal, the pre-civilized. Anne can become the murder victim only at the moment when she has let go of her child, handed him over to his father and the paternal order. The intensity of the mother-child bond is both painful to sustain and devastating to break; purely nonverbal, it translates only with difficulty into the level of reason and language:

> "Perhaps it would be better if we were separate from each other once in a while. I can't seem to understand this child."
>
> (*MC*, p. 89)

> "Sometimes I think I must have invented you—that you don't really exist, you know."
>
> (*MC*, p. 90)

> "You're growing up, oh, you're getting so big, and I think it's wonderful."
>
> (*MC*, p. 100)

"My child," Anne Desbaresdes said, "I didn't have time to tell you . . ." "Sometimes," she said, "I think I must have invented him." (*MC*, p. 137)

Anne's symbiotic closeness to the child is ruptured in Chapter 6, when the crying Anne elliptically announces to him, "It's all over, darling, I think it's all over" (*MC*, p. 125), and when, in Chapter 7, she vomits food and wine on the floor of his room, ridding herself both of maternal responsibility and of maternal power. Having done so, she is free to assume the role of child herself. In the novel's last chapter, the child is absent; Anne has agreed to let someone else take him to the piano lessons.

The powerful and complicated bond between mother and child, Anne's own double identity, at once the mother who perceives the distance between them and the would-be child who denies difference, suggests the range of relational possibilities in the novel as a whole. The novel outlines two patterns: the male movement from pre-oedipal symbiosis to oedipal desire and fear of engulfment to separation which often takes the form of dominance; and the female lifelong vacillation between pre-oedipal fusion and oedipal separation. Jessica Benjamin, in "The Bonds of Love: Rational Violence and Erotic Domination,"[14] defines the long-range effects of the asymmetry all mother-raised children face in the pre-oedipal period. Male and female children separate from the mother in different ways: "Male children achieve their distinct identity by (more or less) violently repudiating the mother" (p. 147); this male experience is the basis of a fatal polarity in which the female posture is one of "merging at the expense of individuality . . . the sacrifice of independent subjectivity or selfhood" (p. 148). According to Benjamin, this splitting between male and female postures creates relationships of domination and submission between men and women.

Anne and Chauvin's relationship to the "text" of the murder is also defined by these two stances. Just as the child stands in a triangular oedipal relationship to the "parental" couple, Anne and Chauvin, or Anne and Chauvin themselves, can be said to stand in a triangular relationship to the other couple who become "parents" engaged in the consummation of their passion. "Reading," for both Anne and Chauvin, thus becomes an interrogation of an original moment of fusion and symbiosis between mother and father, between mother and child. Anne's (female) and Chauvin's (male) relation to the original "parent" couple suggest different, male and female, modes of reading: the male, based on distance and understanding, on the assertion of boundaries, responds to a fear of immersion in the text; the female, based on openness, vacancy, receptivity, has as its goal the continuity, the fusion, between reader and text. Fiction itself, as this novel's own ambivalent structure demonstrates, supports both of these forms of reading. By valorizing one over the other, however, it provides a way out of any simple binarism.

READERS OF THE TEXT

Anne and Chauvin are readers inscribed in the text. Their difficulties are reflected on the text's surface and the external reader, duplicating their experience, responds according to their model. In following Anne and Chauvin's process of interpretation, invention, and imitation, the external reader becomes implicated in the novel's structure of mediation. Not only are we twice removed from the immediacy of passion and murder, but we are also, at every step, conscious of the distorting filter of verbal narration. The novel underscores the unreality and mediation of fiction, even while using the structure of fiction and language to express something immediate which is by nature inexpressible, silent, beyond the confines of these structures. Through the novel's ambivalence, the reader comes not to understand, but to experience, to enact, that "something." Ultimately she/he may be led to relinquish the boundaries of separate selfhood and to accept a basic continuity and relatedness.

Moderato Cantabile, published in 1958 by Minuit, is a transitional work for Duras and embodies a strange mixture of traditional and modernist techniques.[15] On the one hand, it is told in the third person by an ominiscient narrator whose straightforward and detached tone suggests that expression is unproblematic. The novel's linear temporal progression and the use of the *passé simple,* the predominance of dialogue, the unquestionable reality of the crime itself, the traditional and simple syntax are all indications of a straightforward narrative. On the other hand, everything beyond the actual crime is hopelessly irretrievable; there is no truth to be uncovered and the bulk of the novel rests on conjecture and speculation. The narrator's report does reflect the strain Anne and Chauvin suffer in their interpretative process. The insecurities it produces in the reader are all the more unsettling for the apparent security of the novel's traditional forms. Just as Anne hovers between life and death, so Duras's fiction is tenuously poised between life and death, between affirming the capacities of language (fiction) and destroying them. The novel's success depends on their at least partial destruction.

The text's ambivalence emerges most forcefully in its penultimate and climactic scene, the dinner at the Desbaresdes home. This scene represents a crucial transition in the child's development from the pre-oedipal to the oedipal, the maternal to the paternal order. The opposing forces between which Anne is hopelessly caught, defined by the terms *moderato* and *cantabile,* interact most brutally during the dinner, making Anne's predicament unbearable. The mansion (inside) is opposed to the beach (outside); the formal dinner guests to Chauvin, who roams on the beach. Anne wears a magnolia between her breasts as a re-

minder of the vital and potentially destructive forces that the civilized bourgeois society suppresses and displaces. Similarly, the elegant food is opposed to the primitive wine which alone satisfies Anne's "other hunger." As these forces coexist and alternate in the chapter's counterpoint structure, without reaching any resolution (Anne vomits both food and wine; she neither joins the party inside, nor Chauvin outside), the reader vacillates hopelessly between two extremes, unable even to imagine how a resolution might be achieved.

The reader is drawn into the scene through ellipsis and absence. Names are mentioned only rarely; invariably, the characters, including those who have names, are evoked as "a man," "a woman," "this child," "the other." When Anne vomits, "a shadow" appears at the door of the room; it is the reader who invests this shadow with the identity of a husband and imagines the explanations that ensue. Equally elliptical are the transitions: Chauvin does not proceed from the beach to the garden to the town, he merely appears in each of these three places. The dinner conversation is similarly disjointed; no comment is followed up, no question answered.[16] Here the story of Anne and Chauvin is almost as cryptic as that of the other couple.

The reader's insecurity is exacerbated by the text's mixture of levels of discourse. The food is personified, the people are reified: "The salmon arrives" (literal translation), "the other waits." "Their bare shoulders have the gloss and the solidity of a society founded and built on the certainty of its rights, and they were chosen to fit this society" (**MC,** p. 128). The syntax, although it adheres to grammatical rules, is often ambiguous as we proceed from one sentence to the next: "The salmon arrives, chilled in its original form. Dressed in black, and with white gloves, a man carries it. . . ." (**MC,** p. 127; literal translation).

The narrative tone seems equally incongruous. The power of emotion in the novel derives from its displacement: the narrator as well as the characters are detached, almost uninvolved in the discussions. Except for the woman's scream and Anne's moans, the only direct expressions of emotion, the reader can extrapolate violence, passion, sadness, fear, only through indirection. It is as if emotion had abandoned individuals,[17] had left even the province of human beings, and had spread all over the surrounding scene. Throughout the novel, the modulations of the brilliant sunset, the smell of magnolia blossoms, the sounds of the beech trees in the wind, and the murmurs of the ocean contain the passion that seems to have left the characters. Instead of telling Chauvin about herself, Anne describes her house, the trees and the flowers in her garden: "Lots of women have already lived in that same house and listened to the hedges, at night, in place of their hearts" (**MC,** p. 105).

At the dinner, the salmon and duck function similarly as objective correlatives for Anne's condition. Originally free, they are now victims of a social ritual, killed and refashioned into their natural appearance, before being consumed and digested: "Meanwhile the pink, succulent, deep-sea salmon, already disfigured by the brief moments just past, continues its ineluctable advance towards total annihilation" (**MC,** pp. 126, 127). Death is in the magnolias' "funeral flowering" and in the appearance of "a duck in its orange-shrouded coffin." Disturbed by these incongruities, the novel's reader is freed to make connections between totally detached characters and an atmosphere laden with passion and death.

Not only have emotions removed themselves from the human beings who usually house them, but parts of the human body have also become autonomous and separate. The child is the only complete person in the novel; his body is integrated and contained. In contrast, Anne and Chauvin do not control their movements; their hands act independently of their volition. Each movement is a surprise: "the fingers crumple it [the magnolia], pierce the petals, then stop, paralyzed, lie on the table, wait, affecting an attitude of nonchalance, but in vain" (**MC,** p. 130). Ultimately, human fragmentation actually reaches the point of mutation: "He looks at his empty hands, distorted by the strain. There at the end of his arm, a destiny grew" (**MC,** p. 132; literal translation). The impersonal structure of this sentence suggests Chauvin's distance from his body and his fate.

The novel's most disturbing element is its confusing temporal structure. Time appears, at first, as a steady force which proceeds independently of the characters. Anne is always late; their meetings are always cut short by the factory siren. Chauvin needs to free himself from the constraints of time by passing it idly. Initially, the reader is deceived by the linear narrative: such details as the knitting of a sweater, the flowering and wilting of magnolias, the use of *passé simple,* reinforce temporal progression. Yet the *passé simple* seems as inappropriate to Anne and Chauvin's conjectural dialogues as it is ill-suited to the account of Anne's progressive degeneration. As John Kneller pointed out, the *passé simple* actually disguises the present tense which emerges in the dinner scene.[18] By obscuring the hypothetical realm in which the entire action takes place, the *passé simple* creates a disquieting incongruity at the center of the text. Even more disturbing is the sudden switch to the present and then to the future in the course of the dinner scene and in the narration of the other couple's story. How are these events related to each other? Suddenly we are forced out of the security of temporal progression into a vague duration that exists outside of known temporality.

Repetition, one of the novel's main structural principles, undermines even further the novel's apparent chronology. The scenes in the café are so similar as to appear like variations of the same scene. There are, furthermore, two piano lessons, two parties at which Anne wears a wilted flower between her breasts. The novel's regular rituals, such as the Friday piano lesson and the evening siren and the afternoon walks, are offset by the uncertainty of its tenses. When, for example, did the reception for the fac-

tory workers take place? Did Chauvin witness it, invent it, or did he anticipate the events of Chapter 7 as the conflation of the two scenes' imagery seems to suggest? Anne's moment of identification with the murdered woman is based on the anticipation of a future ("She will never speak again"), as is her regurgitation of the alien food she had been forced to eat. The ritual murder, on the other hand, is evoked as an event that had already happened at the point of the last meeting at the café ("c'est fait"). Even at the level of the fiction, the novel's main events are represented as hypothetical rather than actual, absent rather than present.

For the external reader, just as for Anne and Chauvin, the act of reading is an activity of filling gaps, responding to mystery and ambivalence, coping with contradiction and discomfort. It is both a state of reception and an act of production. The mystery-story structure is used not to involve the reader in the game of uncovering a crime, but in the game of creating it; it is not an intellectual puzzle, but an emotional gamble. This process of reading/narration—the boundaries are no longer fixed—has as its goal a transformation similar to Anne's: the destruction of the reader's own civilized self, tied to and bolstered by traditional literary structures. It is meant to create in the reader a receptivity to other modes of being, even while demonstrating the deathly dangers of that openness.

FEMALE READING/FEMALE WRITING

The responses that the novel, in its ambivalence, elicits from its readers form the basis for what could be called a female aesthetic, an aesthetic based on pre-oedipal desire, on boundless and continuous identity, and on the destruction of the unified self. Structured on a series of oppositions—moderato/cantabile, male/female, language/silence, oedipal/pre-oedipal—the novel first forces the reader to assume contrary stances and then releases her/him from duality by clearly breaking out of the first into the second terms. Both by dealing with contradiction and by choosing the female, the reader engages in the novel's female aesthetic.

In the novel, language is equated with reason and safety, with *moderato.* The first couple reach the point where words have become cumbersome, unnecessary. Their understanding is total only at the moment when, having gone through language, they have reached silence. Anne and Chauvin, afraid of the silences that begin to ensue between them, talk obsessively. "Talk to me," Chauvin commands again and again, and Anne responds by reciting parts of her life in automatic and detached fashion. Her meaningless words have become independent of feeling, independent even of truth. Both characters admit to lying; there is no truth to which they are compelled to be responsible. It is precisely this freedom of fictional language that gives it the flexibility, the creative power which allows Anne and Chauvin to *know* what the other couple have experienced. Words have become detached from their semantic content, have moved beyond denotation to self-referentiality.

Although verbal exchange provides a form of safety for the two protagonists, a distance from the immediacy of murder, it also embodies the only means by which they can project themselves into the story's affective power. From description and rational analysis they proceed to the freedom of invention which, transcending the limits of truth, makes it possible for them to relive imaginatively the couple's experience. The annihilation of self Anne experiences takes place in the *literary* process of identification with the other woman, of entering the couple's story. The freedom of fiction leads Anne and Chauvin beyond language to silence and death. Only at the moment of silence can identification take place: "She will never speak again." The woman's scream is the death of language and literature. Hence Anne's fear and hesitation. Anne's desire threatens not only her life and the very foundation of her society, but also the basis on which the novel of which she is the heroine rests. Oscillating between the conservative forces of society and language, and the destructive forces of passion, silence, and death, the novel constantly attempts to transcend its own limitations, to "consume" itself. It attempts to maintain, at all moments, the ambivalence of the murdered woman's scream which, on the threshold between chaos and civilization, expresses both plenitude (of sound) and emptiness (of speech). The process of fiction-making (interpreting reality, narrating it, then reading that narration, and so on) is precariously tensed between the two poles indicated by the terms of *moderato* and *cantabile*. This process depends on the constraints of form, yet is able, at the same time, to point beyond them, to suggest much that it does not say.

Anne's response to the Diabelli sonatina best indicates the kind of response that could lead to a fusion such as Anne experiences with the murdered woman:

> She listened to the sonatina. It came from the depths of the ages, borne to her by her son. Often, as she listened to it, she felt she was on the verge of fainting. . . . The sonatina still resounded, borne like a feather by this your barbarian, whether he liked it or not, and showered again on his mother, sentencing her anew to the damnation of her love. The gates of hell banged shut.
>
> (*MC,* p. 115)

In order to feel, as Anne does, the forces of death and damnation when experiencing a musical or literary text, we must, like Anne, come to the point of almost fainting. That is, we must relinquish the boundaries of self that tie us to our existence as civilized human beings. To enter a work we must, in one sense, stop being ourselves, only to become, as does Anne, more truly ourselves in another. This is the involvement Chauvin resists; in showing us both modes, the novel seems to uphold difference, yet in privileging Anne's response it comes to transcend any neat dualism.

I would like to argue that this process of reading/narration, dependent on openness and receptivity, is, for Duras, the basis for a female aesthetic.[19] Here, the characters and the reader enact the progressive destruction of the monolithic

traditions of our culture, in favor of endless repetition, mediation, indirection, reproduction. As one result of the process Anne undergoes, she discovers/creates within herself something totally unknown and unsuspected. As she leaves the café, she has been able to transcend the opposition of *moderato/cantabile* and to accept an existence of *moderato cantabile*: she will neither continue her bourgeois life, nor has she succumbed to the deadly lure of passion. In her identification with the other woman, she has discovered the relational base of her own identity and has been able to transcend the separation imposed by the social roles of adult, of wife and mother. Anne's gradual detachment from her child is parallel to her attachment to the dead woman whose life she interprets/invents. Structured on a number of relationships—male/female, mother/child—the novel thus ultimately relies on the relationship between Anne and the murder victim, on a female bond that precedes and supersedes the other bonds.[20]

Literature and music emerge in this novel as subversive, even destructive forces. The mediated experience of literature is, in some ways, conservative and safe; in others it can effect profound changes. Anne is transformed by her involvement with the woman's story, even though she does not die. Instead, we can imagine her going through the same process again, condemned, like Lol Stein, to endless repetition, trying to re-create in the future the moment of her symbolic murder in the café. As Chauvin says, "It will begin again."

Female aesthetic, for Duras, is here, in the endless repetition and deconstruction, in the repeated transformation of the individual subject through the fusion with others. It lies in the affirmation of death and destruction, not as an end of life, but as a means to other lives which emerge after silence and emptiness have been reached, which emerge through emptiness and silence, through fiction and beyond it.

Notes

1. Marguerite Duras, *Les Parleuses* (Paris: Minuit, 1974), p. 6.

2. I use here the terms of Susan Sontag's famous essay, "Against Interpretation," in *Against Interpretation and Other Essays* (New York: Dell, 1961).

3. Elizabeth Stuart Phelps, "A Jury of Her Peers," *New Literary History,* 11, 3 (Spring 1980), 451-67.

4. Judith Fetterley, *The Resisting Reader* (Bloomington: Indiana Univ. Press, 1978).

5. Norman Holland and Leona Sherman, "Gothic Possibilities," *New Literary History,* 8, 2 (Winter 1977), 279-94.

6. Caren Greenberg, "Reading Reading: Echo's Abduction of Language," in *Women and Language in Literature and Society,* eds. Sally McConnell-Ginet, Ruth Borker, Nelly Furman (New York: Praeger, 1980), pp. 309-30.

7. Nancy Chodorow, *The Reproduction of Mothering* (Berkeley: Univ. of California Press, 1978).

8. Dorothy Dinnerstein, *The Mermaid and the Minotaur* (New York: Harper and Row, 1976).

9. Jean Baker Miller, *Toward a New Psychology of Women* (Boston: Beacon Press, 1976). For a fuller review of this literature and its relation to French feminist theory, esp. Kristeva and Irigaray, see my review essay, "Mothers and Daughters," *Signs,* 7, 1 (Autumn 1981), 200-22.

10. In "Crime and Detection in the Novels of Marguerite Duras," *Contemporary Literature,* 15 (1974), 508, Erica Eisinger points out that Duras uses virtually no possessive adjectives in relation to Anne; her house is "this house" and even her child is referred to as "this child."

11. Parenthetical citations (*MC,* with page number) refer to *Moderato Cantabile,* trans. Richard Seaver, in *Four Novels* (New York: Grove Press, 1965).

12. See Evelyn Zepp, "Language as Ritual in Marguerite Duras' *Moderato Cantabile,*" Symposium (Fall 1976), for an excellent exposition of the distancing and mediating properties of language in this novel.

13. I am grateful to Thomas Vargish for suggesting this interpretation.

14. Jessica Benjamin, "The Bonds of Love: Rational Violence and Erotic Domination," *Feminist Studies,* 6, 1 (Spring 1980), 144-74.

15. In *Les Parleuses,* p. 59, Duras speaks of *Moderato Cantabile* as a transitional work in her career: "This woman who wants to be killed, I lived that . . . and from then on the book changes. . . . I believe that the turn toward . . . sincerity happened there."

16. See Roland Champagne, "An Incantation of the Sirens: The Structure of *Moderato Cantabile,*" *French Review,* 48, 6, pp. 981-89, for an analysis of the fragmentation in Duras's narrative.

17. See Gauthier's comment on *Hiroshima, mon amour* in *Les Parleuses,* p. 83: ". . . desire circulated from person to person, not indifferently, but still it could pass from one to another."

18. John Kneller, "Elective Empathies and Musical Affinities," *Yale French Studies,* 26 (1961), 114-20.

19. See *Les Parleuses,* pp. 146-49, for Duras's comments on passivity as the foundation of feminist politics.

20. On female friendship from a psychoanalytic perspective, see Elizabeth Abel's "(E)Merging Identities: The Dynamics of Female Friendship in Contemporary Fiction by Women," *Signs,* 6, 3 (Spring 1981), 413-35.

Jeanne K. Welcher (essay date 1983)

SOURCE: "Resolution in Marguerite Duras's 'Moderato Cantabile,'" in *Twentieth Century Literature,* Vol. 29, No. 3, 1983, pp. 370-78.

[*In the following essay, Welcher discusses Duras's use of music and mythology to express her characters' otherwise inexpressible motivations and actions in* Moderato cantabile.]

As its title announces, ***Moderato Cantabile*** by Marguerite Duras is a novel centered on contrasts.[1] These range from the paradox of murdering one's beloved; through fine discriminations—"cantabile," yes, but moderately so; to allusions and inferrable mythic parallels, especially to the myth of Dionysus.

We are struck first by the book's contrasts in style—its extraordinary limpidity, its evident complexities. In a filmmaker's approach Duras presents stark imagery, without background or depth. Her invisible narrator records appearances but virtually no interpretation or judgment. The characters are admittedly unreliable. Chauvin insists that he has no facts; Anne Desbaresdes, that she does not know even her own mind. Both she and her son lie. She confuses imagination and reality. She forces Chauvin to do the same. Everything comes to us phenomenologically: we observe, ask questions, guess answers, but what do we understand?

In a further complexity, the format of ***Moderato Cantabile*** recalls the classic drama technique of prefatory shadow play or pantomine. Because the dumb show in ***Moderato Cantabile*** displays a married woman, her lover, and their deadly passion, it seems likely that Anne will reject her husband, the shadowy, cold, faceless "directeur," for ecstatic annihilation in the embrace of the impassioned Chauvin. But she does not do so.[2] And other facets of the narrative set up quite different expectations. Preeminent are the piano lessons and Anne's son.[3] The music that the boy is studying provides title and theme. The boy himself is certainly a foregound figure, pivotal to the plot. The interplay between him and Anne frames and punctuates every scene but the last. He and Chauvin vie for Anne's attention. Tension between mother and son and its resolution are central issues.[4]

Marguerite Duras tells a simple story and simultaneously implies complexities because she is dealing with an almost inexpressible experience.[5] Music is one medium for such matter. Myth is another. The story that Duras tells here is that of mother and son. In its frequent retelling in the past, the mother-son story centers on the son, his feelings and fate. What emerges if it becomes the woman's story? The novel looks from the woman's viewpoint at the experience of bearing a son, possessing him, and losing (or loosing) him. Duras focuses on the mother, but without identifying with her. The tone of the novel is the almost impossible one of objective representation.

The first sentence of the novel, drawing attention to the musical composition, introduces the central theme: "'Would you read what's written above the score?' asked the woman, 'Moderato cantabile,' said the child. 'And what does that mean, "moderato cantabile"?' 'I don't know.'"[6] The boy is studying a sonatina of Anton Diabelli marked with this tempo.

Diabelli's sonatinas have simple themes which are set forth, interrelated, developed by means of melodic fragmentation, counterpointing, and inversion, to end in a final recapitulation. This eighteenth-century form, especially familiar as an exercise for piano students, is modest but strictly stylized, classically Apollonian in essence.

Apollo was the established model and inspiration for human artists, his art affirming existence as good in itself, setting a special value on the individual. Apollonian art is the product of study and training, involving such elements as convention, invention, symmetry, decorum, and finish. Much in the formation of Anne Desbaresdes and her son is Apollonian. They live at the exclusive end of the Boulevard de la Mer, in a large house that is classically symmetrical in design and is set in a decorously impressive ornamental garden, fenced in by hedges and iron grillwork. The ménage is one of routine, affluence, taste, and order. Among Anne's and her son's rare departures from this enclave are their Apollo-inspired trips for his piano lessons. The teacher, Mlle. Giraud, strives to evoke musical discipline and artistry from her young pupil. And Anne tries to express the necessity to the boy: "'It's necessary to learn to play the piano.'" Desperately, she repeats, "'It's necessary. It's necessary'" (p. 14). And before Chapter One concludes, "The child played. . . . Toward the end of the lesson, he gave the desired nuances, moderato cantabile" (p. 16).

The Diabelli music is a symbolic model and norm for the novel. It is its balance point: such a rigidly disciplined form as the sonatina is characteristically Apollonian: but the realm of music itself is a special province of Dionysus. Dionysus is the god of mystery and paradox, seductive, awesome, irrational, benign, terrifying. He cannot be ignored because he is the god of nature, but unlike Apollo, he lays down no laws. His art embraces disorder and destruction as well as order and creation. His devotees express themselves in violence and self-indulgence: erotic bliss, the narcotism of dreams and intoxication, insanity, the longing for death, and ultimately death itself.[7]

Anne Desbaresdes's son is a youthful Dionysus, golden-haired like the god, a would-be son of nature. His eyes are the color of the sky, he takes on the hues of the sun, breezes stir his hair like grass. His ears are tuned to the sounds of the sea "in the heart of the spring afternoon" (p. 11), the Dionysian season. As if he were the sea himself, a motorboat runs through his blood (p. 11). He is stubborn and unruly and glories in his mother's enjoyment of his unruliness.[8] When at last he cries out, "'I don't want to learn the piano,'" the sequence seems causal, not just temporal, for at that moment "in the street a woman's cry rang out, a long moan" (p. 13).[9]

The southern end of town where Anne Desbaresdes brings her son is, for her purposes, the locus of musical learning.

It is also a garish and sinister place, oppressive with the smoke and clamor of foundries and cargo boats. As mother and son climb to the studio, "A giant steam-shovel drooling wet sand passed before the last window of the landing, its famished beast's teeth closed on its prey" (p. 65).

The café is the heart of this inferno-like setting; the murder, its epitome. The presiding figure, the patronne, is a demigod, timeless and omniscient. Like Dionysus, she dispenses wine; like one of the Fates, she watches, knits, and announces the passing hours. Unlike the Fates, she is not an operative force. She foresees the crime—"three times I tried to call you" (p. 19), she tells the police—without effect, but with Dionysian imperturbability. And in this café Chauvin, who has left his job at the foundries "without giving any reasons" (p. 57), an incarnation of unreason and chaotic feelings, passes his time. He is by his own account a nightly prowler about the dunes, wildly circling Anne's house, mentally taking possession of her psyche and her flesh. He precipitately entices her to drink, to linger, to open herself to him.

Anne, while she is in the music studio, ignores the outcries from the café. But the moment she descends, she plunges into the Dionysian experience. Her compulsion to return the next day predates, we must remember, her first conversation with Chauvin. Hers is the abrupt change of a true convert to Dionysus. She abandons the ordered reason of her life, its control, sublimation, and reticence, for instant addiction and obsession. She reveals Dionysian facets of her own life: she has felt and yielded to compulsion, she too is a night prowler, the house alternately stifles her and is shaken by storms, ghosts haunt the ostensibly Apollonian domain.

At least as much as Chauvin, she invokes the hypnotic spell, confusing past and present, real and invented, herself with the dead woman. Her flaunted excesses are in sharp contrast to the behavior of the guests at her dinner party. In an orgiastic culmination, a travesty of an orgasm, she prostrates herself on the floor beside her sleeping son and "between the sacred measures of her child's breathing" (p. 103) she vomits over and over again.[10]

Marguerite Duras may not have had the Dionysian myth in mind as she wrote, though surely she knows it. Rather, the point is that our recognition of the parallels between that ancient tale and *Moderato Cantabile* clarifies the nature of Anne's ordeal, that it primarily concerns her son, only secondarily, Chauvin. Chauvin is an indispensable figure, but a catalytic agent rather than an antagonist. The adulterous temptation is an expressionistic image for Anne's passion for her boy: if renouncing a briefly known lover can imaginably cost such languorous indecision and numbing pain, how much more the severance from her flesh, her second self?

Examination of the myth, particularly as found in Euripides' play *The Bacchae*, reveals how closely the central dilemma of the novel parallels the fates of the women associated with Dionysus. In every episode, women enter the Dionysian drama not by virtue of their being female but in their relationship to men.[11] Semele, who petitions Zeus to possess her in all his splendor, is physically consumed by the white heat of the divine passion at the very moment of conceiving a son, the miraculously preserved Dionysus. Agave, Semele's sister, first denies Dionysus' divinity and denounces passion, then becomes his demented devotee, and finally, as the tool of his vengeance, tears her own son Pentheus limb from limb and eats his flesh.

Anne Desbaresdes, like Semele, has given birth to passion in the person of her Dionysus-like son. Like Agave, she has herself become impassioned toward this young god. She is symbiotically shaken by his every tremor and revels in his rebelliousness: "'What a child I have there,' said Anne Desbaresdes joyously; 'just the same, what a child I've produced there'" (pp. 12-13). She sees him as her creation, "'Lift your head,' said Anne Desbaresdes. 'Look at me.' The child obeyed, used to her ways. 'Sometimes I think I've invented you, that it isn't true, you know?' The boy raised his head and yawned in her face" (pp. 34-35).[12] He is her possession, her puppet: "she could lead him anywhere" (p. 23).

At the same time, he is sublimely self-assertive. Her promise of a red motorboat elicits a sigh. When she seeks a more effusive response, he eludes her: "She took him by the shoulders, held him back as he tried to break away to run ahead. 'You're growing up, you, oh, how you are growing up, how wonderful'" (p. 50).

The oedipal elements are all there for "Mon amour," as she repeatedly calls her son (pp. 49, 89), echoing the lament of the murderer (p. 18). The boy is "my little disgrace" (p. 67). When she is overcome by wine and inertia, "the child took her hand and firmly led her away. She followed him" (p. 63). At night she gazes on him sleeping; they are, as Chauvin says, together even when separated (p. 43). Their intimacy arouses Chauvin, when time and again their embraces interrupt his discourse: "The child appeared from outside and clung to his mother in a burst of happy abandon. She fondled his hair abstractedly. The man examined them attentively. 'They loved each other,' he said. She jumped" (p. 27). Chauvin's words ostensibly refer to the couple in the café, but the ambiguity startles Anne. The perversity of her desires is brought home by Mlle. Giraud's disapproval, scorn (pp. 13, 14, 17), denunciation: "'The education that you give him, Madame, is outrageous,' cried Mademoiselle Giraud" (p. 69).

In the Dionysus legend, every woman in her contact with the opposite sex succumbs to passion, becoming perpetuator and victim thereof. The fates of the men vary; for the women, passion always equals destruction. There is but one choice or variable for them in their association with men: to die like Semele or to kill like Agave; to be consumed or to consume.

Associated with these alternatives is the blood-red imagery that recurs throughout the novel. A roseate sunset modifies each phase of the first piano lesson (pp. 11-13). The scene in the café reveals the bleeding mouth of the dead woman, the blood-smeared face of her lover. As if in the shadow of the guillotine, the patronne knits a red sweater. "The dying daylight" fixes on Chauvin's mouth, reflects in his eyes (p. 57). As the sonatina flows from the boy's hands and Chauvin in the café below hums in tempo with him, "a colossal peninsula of clouds set aflame loomed on the horizon" (p. 75). The handling of color is equivocal. In the scene where the boy yawns in his mother's face, "The last rays of the setting sun filled his mouth" (p. 35). Who is to be victim? Who, ravager?

The images shift, but an unequivocal answer comes early in the novel. "What a martyrdom," says Anne of her own fate. And to Mlle. Giraud's ominous "'You're going to have a lot of trouble with that child,"' Anne replies, "'I already do; he devours me'" (p. 17). Duras could scarcely be more explicit. Anne says, "'He devours me'" and then "lowers her head, closing her eyes in the sorrowful smile of an eternal childbirth. Below some cries—by this time, reasonable shouts—indicated the consummation of an unknown event" (p. 17). The dying scream of the murdered woman is directly aligned with "the sad smile of an endless childbirth."[13]

From the moment Anne's child entered the world he has consumed her, a simultaneous agony and joy. She has gone through the motions of resistance—planning the lessons, paying lip service to reason, repeating and repeating "moderately and lyrically." But her struggles are perfunctory before the crime occurs. As she says to Chauvin the very next day, "'without doubt, one day or another something specially shocks you'" (p. 29). When, on top of that, she is assaulted by Chauvin's unleashed imagination and Mlle. Giraud's harsh prophecies and ultimatums, Anne sees the Dionysian vision in its totality: its seduction and its dissolution.

She relentlessly interrogates Chauvin, seeking not information but a strength that can come only from despair. She probes the tragic couple's mentality, incredulous yet already convinced, "'as if, whether alive or dead, from this point on it no longer mattered to him, do you think that you can get . . . there . . . except in despair?'" (p. 28).

Her week's sojourn in the Dionysian depths is her desperate attempt to arrive "there," at the moment of decision. The second piano lesson shatters her:

> She listened to the sonatina. It came from the depths of ages, borne to her by her child. Listening to it she kept thinking that she was about to faint. Again the sonatina resounded, lightly like a feather in the hands of this barbarian, regardless of his own desires, and once more it destroyed his mother, once more condemned her to the damnation of her love. The gates of hell swung shut.
>
> (p. 73)

She vividly sees the double truth of Apollo and Dionysus.

When she finally enters the café without her son, barely able to remark mechanically on the weather, Chauvin says, "'I'd never have thought it would happen so fast'" (p. 197)—the good weather? the failure of his dream? her disengagement from her son? She is explicit, "'After this week, some other people will take my child to his piano lesson, I've agreed that someone else will take my place'" (p. 107). Chauvin mouths commonplaces until she starts again to speak of the boy, when he brutally lashes out, "'I've heard enough of that child'" (p. 110) and then "'I wish you were dead.' 'I am,'" (p. 114) she replies. She walks away, "facing the rose-colored light that signalled the end of that day" (p. 115).

Anne's resolution is made: she will not consume; she must be consumed. The myth offers no other alternative, nor does the novel; the intransigence may not be to our liking, but it is of the essence of the work. Perhaps we are to understand that Anne is pained at not experiencing whatever rapture Chauvin could have brought her. We cannot doubt, however, that she is tortured at relinquishing her son. The smile of eternal childbirth is over; the dolor remains. In cutting the cord, she effects her own prophetic desire: "'how I wish he were already grown up'" (p. 44). As she says to him on the night of the murder, "'All the same, you could remember once for all. "Moderato," that means "moderately"; and "cantabile," that means "lyrically." It's easy'" (p. 21). The irony of the words—a mother to her son—resonates through the novella.

Notes

1. Carol Murphy quotes Marguerite Duras's self-description as "an echo chamber" (p. 850) and examines repetition and allusion in her novels. A different sort of approach is evident in Claude Roy's title of his review of *Moderato Cantabile*, "Madame Bovary réécrite par Béla Bartók," in *Liberation*, 3 Jan. 1958, excerpted in *Moderato Cantabile par Marguerite Duras suivi de l'univers romanesque de Marguerite Duras par Henri Hell et du Dossier de presse de Moderato Cantabile* (Paris: Union Générale d'Éditions, 1958), p. 149, cited hereafter as *Moderato Cantabile*, 1958. Many of the contrasts in *Moderato Cantabile* are three-sided; as Carol J. Murphy notes, "the problem of the triangular relationship" is recurrent in Marguerite Duras's work, "Marguerite Duras: le texte comme echo," *French Review*, 50.6 (1977), 852. Critical discussion, however, tends to center on the obvious "eternal triangles" and gives little attention to such spiderweb involvements as Anne/Mlle. Giraud/the boy, the murdered woman/her lover/her children, Anne/the café proprietress/Chauvin, Anne/her son/his playmate on the dock.

2. Some critics find the foreshadowing unfulfilled, the ending anticlimactic. For example Victoria L. Weiss discusses Anne's "passionless existence," in "Form and Meaning in Marguerite Duras' *Moderato Cantabile*," *Critique*, 16.1 (1974), 79. In an essay reprinted in *Moderato Cantabile* 1958, Maurice

Nadeau writes of "the art of concluding nothing" (p. 165). Gaetan Picon suggests, "perhaps nothing happens," "*Moderato Cantabile* dans l'oeuvre de Marguerite Duras," *Mercure de France*, June 1958, p. 169.

3. Roland A. Champagne provides pertinent analysis of "the sonata," but sees its function as providing "the mood for many encounters," in "An Incantation of the Sirens: The Structure of *Moderato Cantabile*," *French Review*, 48.6 (1975), 981-89. Nadeau poses questions about the boy, *Moderato Cantabile* 1958, p. 165.

4. Marianne Hirsch gives this feature astute but brief attention in "Gender, Reading, and Desire in *Moderato Cantabile*," *Twentieth Century Literature*, 28 (1982), 76-77. My reading agrees with Dominique Aury's emphasis on the indirectness of Duras's approach, but not with her denial of a denouement, as she writes: "The mystery of bodies and hearts, there it is, not explained, not resolved, but seized in its essence indirectly and by reflection," in "La Caverne de Platon," *La N.N.R.F.*, 6 Jan. 1958, as excerpted in *Moderato Cantabile* 1958, pp. 146-47.

5. Picon sees a preoccupation with the inexpressible as characteristic of Duras's later works; as he puts it, "the essential is encased in silence," *Contemporary French Literature* (New York: Ungar, [1974]), p. 70.

6. Marguerite Duras, *Moderato Cantabile*, p. 9. Quotations of this work are based on *Moderato Cantabile* 1958. Further references appear in the text: the page references are to this edition; the translations are my own.

7. Champagne (p. 981) cites Apollo and Dionysus in musical rather than mythic terms. Evelyn H. Zepp analyzes the precognitive role of the music, but without advertence to Dionysian theory, in "Language as Ritual in Marguerite Duras's *Moderato Cantabile*," *Symposium*, 30 (1976), 237-38. In *Moderato Cantabile* 1958, both Hell (p. 127) and Picon (p. 177) point out the union of love and death in the novel.

8. Anne proudly describes him as being "headstrong as a goat" (p. 13) and Charles Kerenyi notes that one of Dionysus' names is "eriphos," a young goat, alluding to the young Bacchus/Dionysus and also recalling Dionysus' own sacrificial dismemberment cited in certain legends, "Birth and Rebirth of Tragedy: from the Origin of Italian Opera to the Origin of Greek Tragedy," *Diogenes*, 28 (1959), 36. The details that I mention of the Dionysus story are found in Hesiod's *Theogony*, Euripides' *The Bacchae*, and Nietzsche's *The Birth of Tragedy*.

9. "The story . . . of almost all Duras's novels is that of a cry. The whole text is a cry," observes Carol Murphy (p. 855), stressing as befits her thesis the echoing rather than the counterpointing effect of the cry (pp. 853-55).

10. Weiss, while concentrating on the links between Anne and Chauvin, also stresses the significance of the child in this scene (p. 83). Compare Zepp, pp. 241-42.

11. Duras maintains a linguistic usage that underlies this. When Anne Desbaresdes is referred to other than by name (or, once only, by title, "sa mère"), she is "la femme." "La dame" is used exclusively for the piano teacher, never "la femme" (and not "Mlle. Giraud" until after the lesson is over). Likewise, the proprietor of the café is not "la femme," but simply and invariably "la patronne." The other "femme" of Chapter One is the nameless murdered woman. Obviously, Anne and the murder victim are meant to be seen as generically similar, however radically diverse as individuals. The primary French definition of "femme" sets these two women apart from both the unmarried Mlle. Giraud and (whether married or single) the café proprietress in that neither of the latter two is presented as, in the words of *Larousse,* "the companion of the man" (a generic sense of "woman" having no counterpart in *Larousse*).

12. As Zepp shows, "The communication between Anne and her son . . . is based on a sympathetic vibration, a 'note' of harmony between them" (p. 240). Hirsch, too, speaks specifically of symbiosis (p. 77).

13. Bruce Bassoff's "Death and Desire in Marguerite Duras' *Moderato Cantabile*" covers many aspects of the Dionysian experience, saying about this particular contrast: "the description of her smile as an 'enfantement' immediately follows her statement 'il me dévore'—as if *she* contains *him*," *Modern Language Notes,* 94 (1979), 722.

George Moskos (essay date 1984)

SOURCE: "Women and Fictions in Marguerite Duras's *Moderato Cantabile,*" in *Contemporary Literature,* Vol. 25, No. 1, Spring, 1984, pp. 28-52.

[*In the following essay, Moskos examines the relationship between language and gender in* Moderato Cantabile.]

> "Difficile d'écrire sur son propre travail. Que dire? Je parlerai d'elle, de la mère. . . . La nôtre. La vôtre. La mienne, aussi bien."[1]

A woman's cry. A woman has been killed. In the half-shadow of a café, her inert body has become a "spectacle," riveting the gaze of passersby. Her murderer, a man, lies on top of her, calling out calmly, "Mon amour. Mon amour." Another woman has heard, watches. What does she want? To know [*savoir*]. "Pourquoi?" asks Anne Desbaresdes when she returns to the café. Once again, *she* has returned to the scene of the crime: "—Ce cri était si fort que vraiment il est bien naturel que l'on cherche à savoir. J'aurais pu difficilement éviter de le faire, voyez-vous. [. . .]—Il m'aurait été impossible de ne pas revenir."[2] A man has also come back to the café: "—Je suis revenu moi aussi pour la même raison que vous,"[3] Chauvin tells Anne. In *Moderato cantabile,* over a ten-day period, Anne and Chauvin will have five conversations in which they will (re)create, verbally, the original couple and the murder.

During their first meeting, Chauvin subjects Anne to what can only be called verbal seduction. "Si vous reveniez, j'essaierais de savoir autre chose et je vous le dirais."[4] She is invited to enact the eternal return to a place where the Word is knowledge. Anne wants to know and Chauvin will tell her. In *Moderato cantabile,* language [*dire*] will become the vehicle for the imposition of a certain knowledge [*savoir*] in a relationship of power between Anne and Chauvin. In "Language as Ritual in Marguerite Duras's *Moderato cantabile,*" Evelyn Zepp precisely renders the sexual nature of this relationship by writing that *dire* is "a verb of active creation" while *savoir* indicates "receptivity" to this creation.[5] Language is Chauvin's power over Anne. Or as Michel Foucault writes: "relations of power cannot . . . be established, consolidated nor implemented without the production . . . and functioning of a discourse."[6] At the same time, if we go back to Chauvin's words of seduction, we find that the relationship between Anne and Chauvin is placed in the conditional mode from the beginning [*essaierais, dirais*]. For the most part, their conversations will be "conditional" ones. Duras prefaced *Le Camion* with Grévisse's definition of the conditional as a hypothetical future tense of the indicative mode, used to indicate "une simple imagination transportant en quelque sorte les événements dans le champ de la fiction."[7] Zepp notes that Anne's and Chauvin's relationship is "a creation of words alone." This "failure" of language will determine their "inability to achieve authentic action."[8] To the point, yet far off the mark. Their relationship *is* an eminently verbal one and should be read as such. Any questions of authenticity or action must be posed in the context of language and fiction. Indeed, the fact that Chauvin's power over Anne is created within a "field of fiction" suggests that perhaps power itself should be read as fiction.

THE NAME OF THE COUNTRY: THE NAME

The production of language in *Moderato cantabile* is dependent upon the "dialogue" established between Anne and Chauvin. The space of language, however, quickly reveals its primordial kinship with relations of power. In all but the last conversation, Chauvin is the master of Anne's displacements. Each time she returns to the café, Chauvin leads her to his table in the back room and seats her where he wants her. Having situated her, Chauvin demands only that she speak to him. His demand is an obsessively repeated one: "—Parlez-moi encore. Bientôt, je ne vous demanderai plus rien."[9] Speaking from a position chosen by the Other, however, Anne cannot but (re)produce his discourse. Indeed, Chauvin will finally speak in Anne's "place."[10]

An examination of the maneuvers that precede the first appearance of Chauvin's name in the text shows that his existence as a character, hence his very identity, depends on this appropriation of Anne's verbal space. When he asks Anne to talk to him, she begins to speak of the drunken men who occasionally walk past her house late at night. Chauvin intervenes to describe Anne in the midst of the disorder of her bedroom as she listens to the passing drunks. Anne draws back, her hands trembling from "la peur et . . . l'émoi dans lequel la jetait toute allusion à son existence."[11] It is at this moment that "Sa voix la quitta" ("Her voice left her" [p. 42]). Although Anne may continue to speak, having lost her voice she cannot constitute herself as subject of her discourse. She will try to change the "subject," but Chauvin will continue to insist: "—Vous y étiez couchée. Personne ne le savait."[12]

The conversation becomes a struggle that Anne can only lose. At the same time, this confrontation is a trial [*débat*: "phase d'un procès"][13] in which Anne is judged guilty with no real possibility of defense. Her replies are punctuated by ellipses; the only efficacious weapon on this battlefield/courtroom floor is language, and Anne has no voice. All that is left in her field—of vision, of language—is Chauvin's mouth: "Elle ne cessa plus de regarder sa bouche seule desormais dans la lumière restante du jour" ("She didn't stop looking at his mouth alone now in the waning light of day" [p. 42]). Only Chauvin's voice is left. He "narrates" Anne's presence at a reception for the foundry workers given in her home: "Au mois de juin de l'année dernière, il y aura un an dans quelques jours, vous vous teniez face à lui [le jardin], sur le perron, prête à nous accueillir, nous, le personnel des Fonderies. Au-dessus de vos seins à moitié nus, il y avait une fleur blanche de magnolia. Je m'appelle Chauvin."[14] Anne is literally objectified in/by Chauvin's language: she stands facing the garden, ready to greet the workers, but not yet moving. The use of the reflexive verb *se tenir* reinforces her immobility. Although he does not speak about himself, the true subject of this narrative is Chauvin. It is Anne's objectification, her disappearance as subject—she is literally devoured by this mouth that hypnotizes her—that allows Chauvin to name himself. The struggle is over: "Elle reprit sa pose coutumière, face à lui,"[15] there where she exists only as his reflection.

This scene of the reception for the foundry workers at which Anne *would have been wearing* a low-cut black dress with a magnolia blossom pinned between her breasts is one of the few continuing narratives in **Moderato cantabile.** Its elaboration in four parts clearly illustrates the logistics of the verbal warfare by which Chauvin attempts to reduce Anne to his language. It is during the second conversation that Chauvin first speaks of the annual event: "—Au rez-de-chausée il y a des salons où vers fin mai, chaque année, on donne des réceptions au personnel des fonderies. [. . .]—Vous aviez une robe noire très décolletée. Vous nous regardiez avec amabilité et indifférence."[16] I have shown how the second version constitutes Chauvin, not Anne, as its subject. Chauvin's accession to the status of subject permits a marked progression in the third version; it is the most detailed one and clearly demonstrates Chauvin's mastery of his material. He has become, despite his own protestations of ignorance, a quasi-omnipotent narrator:

> —Vous étiez accoudée à ce grand piano. Entre vos seins nus sous votre robe, il y a cette fleur de magnolia.
>
> Anne Desbaresdes, très attentivement, écouta cette histoire.
>
> —Oui.
>
> —Quand vous vous penchez, cette fleur frôle le contour extérieur de vos seins. Vous l'avez négligemment épinglée, trop haut. C'est une fleur énorme, vous l'avez choisie au hasard, trop grande pour vous. Ses pétales sont encore durs, elle a justement atteint la nuit dernière sa pleine floraison.
>
> —Je regarde dehors?
>
> —Buvez encore un peu de vin. L'enfant joue dans le jardin. Vous regardez dehors, oui.
>
> Anne Desbaresdes but comme il le lui demandait, chercha à se souvenir, reving d'un profond étonnement.
>
> —Je ne me souviens pas d'avoir cueilli cette fleur. Ni de l'avoir portée.
>
> —Je ne vous regardais qu'à peine, mais j'ai eu le temps de la voir aussi. . . .
>
> —Comme j'aime le vin, je ne savais pas.
>
> —Maintenant, parlez-moi.
>
> —Ah, laissez-moi, supplia Anne Desbaresdes.[17]

Although Chauvin begins in a past tense ("You were leaning"), he quickly shifts to the present. He is no longer describing a past event, but rather creating a fiction ("this story") in the present. Anne has become a character in Chauvin's fiction, to the point that she asks him whether she is (was, will be) looking outside. She tries to bring the narration back into a remembered past by observing that she has no recollection of having worn the flower. The truth or falsity of the detail and Anne's memory of the reception as a lived experience, however, are entirely secondary to the vision of the narrator, final arbiter of the "truth" of his fiction: "—I hardly looked at you, but I had the time to see it too." Anne is/was/will be as she is reflected in Chauvin's eyes, as she is spoken by his mouth. Only now will he order her to speak. That same evening Anne will "live out" Chauvin's fiction at the dinner party: she wears a black dress with a magnolia flower pinned between her breasts as she leans against the piano.

FROM PLATO'S CAVE TO THE THING

"Why?" is Anne's question. If we are to believe him, Chauvin has returned to ask the same question. Marcelle Marini writes that, up to a certain point, this scene is one of "communication . . . lieu où s'échangent deux imaginaires complices."[18] In what manner could we view Anne's involvement in it as "positive"? We do have the impression in the first conversation that Anne is speaking (of) herself for the first time since her marriage ten years before. In that other house, someone has always spoken for her. Now she herself is speaking and someone is also speaking to her about herself. A liberation? Chauvin's narrative control would hardly seem to support such an idea. Each textual element that seems to hold the promise of liberation is charged with an inverse, negative sign that finally predominates. Chauvin begins by asking Anne to speak to him and finishes with a brutal command: "Taisez-vous" ("Shut up" [p. 63]). Chauvin's desire for Anne's silence, we realize, is already contained in his request that she speak. What begins as a scene of communication between two accomplices who are there for the same reason becomes a struggle to the (second, duplicate) death.[19]

It is the cry of the murdered woman that brings Chauvin and Anne to this scene. In a movement that seems to reverse the one I described above, the "negative" cry of death evokes at the same time a "positive" one: the cry of the mother giving birth. "—Une fois," Anne tells Chauvin, "j'ai dû crier un peu de cette façon, . . . quand j'ai eu cet enfant."[20] However, at the moment the child comes into the world, the mother's cry of life will be replaced by what Duras considers the child's cry of death. The irreparable loss of the mother, of the state of perfect union, is simultaneous with birth itself; birth is a sort of death into life.[21] The cry of the murdered woman, identified in Anne's mind with the cry of birth, is described as "un cri très haut, qui s'est arrêté net alors qu'il était au plus fort de lui-même."[22] The body of the mother falls silent (or is silenced) at the most critical moment of rupture (life, death, murder?).

At least initially, Anne and Chauvin return to the same place to question this silence, their origin. Accomplices. The spatial disposition of their meeting place seems to reflect this common ground: "Le mur du fond de la salle s'illumina du soleil couchant. En son milieu, le trou noir de leurs ombres conjuguées se dessina."[23] A partially dark space, shadows projected on a wall by light coming from behind: Anne and Chauvin meet in a place that closely resembles the cave of Plato's allegory.[24] There is little need to insist on the traditional maternal symbolism of this cave: it would be the mother's womb. The often double trajectory of the text I discussed above should, however, give us pause. The disposition of the scene is perhaps not what it may appear. Indeed, Anne and Chauvin have come back to a place that, as it joins them together in desire, becomes the scene of the crime.

Even before the murder, Chauvin's fascination for Anne is a visual one; he is her spectator. The object of his "speculation" is not Anne alone, but Anne and her son together. The first time that there is an explicit textual reference to Chauvin's looking at Anne, she is literally attached to her son. Chauvin "projects" on Anne and the child what he has definitively lost and yet still seeks: union with the mother. In the "cinema" of Chauvin's imagination, the scene of childbirth is run in reverse: "L'enfant surgit de dehors et se colla contre sa mère dans un mouvement d'abandon heureux. Elle lui caressa distraitement les cheveux. L'homme regarda plus attentivement.—Ils s'aimaient, dit-il."[25] The child, rather than "appearing suddenly" from inside, comes from the outside to give himself to (to rejoin) the mother. This (re)presentation of his origin elicits Chauvin's only direct response to Anne's question: "They loved one another." The configuration of this scene is identical to the one following the murder: "L'homme s'assit près de la femme morte, lui caressa les cheveux et lui sourit."[26] Now, however, it is the mother who caresses the hair of the child and who will repeatedly call him "mon amour." In the beginning there was *not* the Word—of the Father—but the body of the mother, source of life and death. This Chauvin wishes to deny, in creating himself as narrator, as unique subject of his own fiction, as primary and autonomous. And *not* of woman born.

Chauvin is following Plato's route out of the cave; Plato exhorts the aspiring (male) philosopher to turn away "avec l'âme toute entière de ce qui naît, jusqu'à ce qu'il devienne capable de supporter la vue de l'être et de ce qu'il y a de plus lumineux dans l'être."[27] Luce Irigaray restates the philosopher's advice in the following way: "*oublier pour se souvenir du plus vrai.*"[28] In *Speculum de l'autre femme,* she examines the "phallogocentrism" of Western philosophy in an attempt to uncover what she later defined as "ce qui fait la puissance de . . . *sa position de maîtrise.*"[29] Central to this project is her rereading of Platonic metaphors that have served as models for Western philosophical discourse. She argues that the feminine is excluded from the production of this discourse—and from presence in it—by being subjected to the principle of Identity or masculine Sameness. Irigaray deconstructs the logic of binary (dichotomous) oppositions which has dominated philosophical discourse in order to show that it in fact conceals a hierarchical division into positive (male) and negative (female) poles. This strategy is "designed" to assure the repression of the negative and the mastery—and unique valorization—of the positive. Difference is thus effectively denied. To take the "prisoner" out of the shadowy (maternal) cave is to liberate him "de cette conception, de cette naissance, par trop 'naturelles,' pour le renvoyer à une origine plus éloignée, plus élevée, plus noble. A un . . . Principe, un Auteur, par rapport auquel il aurait à se re-connaître."[30] Maternal origin will be denied in/by this masculine self-identity, the logos of the Father, He who is eternal and not of woman born. Only in this way can Man become his own author: "Le Père, lui, est éternel, d'avoir à jamais refusé de naître. Son être, de ce fait, se perpétue de tout temps identique à lui-même."[31] Women serve only as a mirror to reinforce this masculine specularization, as feminine difference is negated in the endless reflection of the Same.

When Anne remembers having screamed during childbirth, Chauvin asks her if she suffered great pain. His question elicits an unexpected response: Anne smiles, remembering. Pleasure? Anne, always so immobile, rigid [*raide*] before his gaze, moves and is freed by this movement. Now it is Chauvin who stiffens, ordering her "sèchement" to speak. The adverb *sèchement* ("avec froideur, dureté") is of course derived from the adjective *sec* ("Qui n'est pas ou peu imprégné de liquide").[32] Faced with Anne's freedom—of movement, from fear—Chauvin becomes hard and dry, posing himself as the inverse of the mobility and fluidity of the sea about which Anne will speak and which her movement reflects, if only for a moment: "—J'habite la dernière maison du boulevard de la Mer, la dernière quand on quitte la ville. Juste avant les dunes. . . . Ma chambre est au premier étage à gauche, en regardant la mer."[33] Immediately prior to the passage in which Chauvin names himself, Anne speaks of a beech tree that blocks the view of the sea from her room, and that she unsuccessfully asked to have removed. Chauvin's reply will not surprise us: "A votre place, je le laisserai grandir avec son ombre chaque année plus épaisse sur les murs de cette chambre."[34] The tree's growth, like Chauvin's "dry" command, functions to block Anne's contact with the movement of the sea. Anne's physical displacement in response to Chauvin's statement makes it clear that this contact would permit her to escape his verbal hold: "Elle s'adossa de tout son buste à la chaise, d'un mouvement entier, presque vulgaire, se détourna de lui."[35] When Anne is "looking" at the sea, she is no longer face to face with Chauvin. Her turning away, her absence, would cause his verbal kingdom to fall. "—Mais, parfois," she complains, "son ombre est comme de l'encre noire."[36] It is with this "black ink" that Chauvin, author, will write his fiction on the inert and silent maternal body.

For Anne, as for Chauvin, the cry of the murdered woman elicits the memory of childbirth. Their desire to know about their origins brings them back to the café which I have compared to Plato's cave. The disposition of this scene, however, has been predetermined by Chauvin to suit the needs of his own (re)presentation: Anne sits facing Chauvin, who entirely occupies her field of vision, blocking her view of the sea. Dichotomous opposition, Chauvin-positive/Anne-negative, assures his unique valorization. Anne's immobility and her elimination as subject permit Chauvin to (re)produce himself in language. Plato's cave and its "maternal" symbolism have a curiously masculine architecture. Anne, however, is in touch with another scene that predates Chauvin's *mise en scène*—the sea. "Tu sais comment j'appelle la mer? je l'appelle: the thing," Duras tells the interviewer for *Gai Pied*.[37] Desire could also be called "The Thing": "Ce dont nous venons de parler [le désir], cette notion vacillante, divagante, je pourrais l'appeler aussi: the thing. Ton sexe. Le mien. Notre différence. Et ce troisième terme, cette triangulation incessante, par laquelle nous nous rejoignons The Thing."[38] For Duras, the perpetual movement of desire seeks always to redress "l'absence définitive de cette présence capitale et jamais remplacée par la suite, celle de ma [la] mère."[39] The divagations of love and desire all have the same origin and the same object—the mother. The movement of the sea is the image of this displacement and the circulation of desire: *la mer* rises and falls, moves without end in

the (lost) love of *la mère*. "Regarder la mer, c'est regarder le tout," Duras has written.[40] Or as Michelle Porte observed in an interview with her, "Pour vous, le paysage de la fin du monde ou du début du monde, peu importe, c'est la mer."[41] It is clear that totality and integral movement are foreign to the fixed *mise en scène* necessary for Chauvin's specularization.

THE DINNER PARTY: A SYNTAGMATIC LIFE

Movement: Anne must move. The cry of the murdered woman revives a sense of mobility associated with the birth of her child. Both childbirth and the murder take Anne outside of the ordinary, the habitual pattern of her life. I will now examine the structure of Anne's life prior to the murder. When we understand where she has been, we can better understand where she is going.

It is an understatement to refer to the habitual pattern of Anne's life. Her life is organized so meticulously as to find its faithful reflection in the "ritual" of the dinner party in chapter 7: "Le saumon passe de l'un à l'autre suivant un rituel que rien ne trouble, sinon la peur cachée de chacun que tant de perfection tout à coup ne se brise ou ne s'entache d'une trop évidente absurdité. [. . .] Lentement, la digestion commence de ce qui fut un saumon. Son osmose à cette espece qui le mangea fut rituellement parfaite."[42] Ritual is associated with prescribed ceremonial forms, normally religious ones. In a broader sense, as Zepp points out, "any action, particularly one which is *repeated* in the same form and which is performed in order to *control* the human environment . . . may be considered ritualistic. . . . Anything cast into the *image of man* becomes 'ordered' for the mind of man."[43] Repetition, control and reflection—of Man—define the limits of Anne's existence. They work together to immobilize her in a predetermined order.

Repetition: "les journées sont à heure fixe. Je ne peux pas continuer. . . .—Les repas, toujours, reviennent. Et les soirs."[44] The same adjective *fixe* will be used to describe the smile on Anne's face during the dinner party: "Un sourire fixe rend son visage acceptable. [. . .] Elle, elle retourne à la fixité de son sourire."[45] Her every action is regulated in a precise manner to ensure that she remain fixed in temporal and physical immobility. Control: Anne lives within a certain perimeter "authorized to her ten years ago," in this house surrounded by a "parc correctement clos" ("properly enclosed garden" [p. 70]). Her son's piano lessons seem to be an attempt to move outside of this control: "—J'ai eu l'idée de ces leçons de piano . . . à l'autre bout de la ville, pour mon amour, et maintenant je ne peux plus les éviter. Comme c'est difficile."[46] Repetition and order are also the principal traits of the piano lessons, which are thus assimilated into the same system of control. Anne falls unavoidably from one trap into another. There is no real movement; each activity has its set time within which it is enclosed. Like the scales that the child is forced to practice, these "measures" are repeated in an organized and inalterable pattern. Moderato cantabile. The essential function of the measures is to close out any element foreign to the predetermined activity. Like the gates of Anne's house, they set the limits beyond which she is not allowed to move. In addition to the disposition of Anne's house, we might also think of the room in which the piano lessons take place. In both cases, an opposition is established between inside and outside, immobility and movement. The high window in Mlle Giraud's apartment does not permit one to see the movement of the outside world, only to hear it. The child must remain immobile in front of his music. From the window of her room, Anne can see the ocean and from the gates she watches the couples and the workers who walk past her house. She remains immobile, never moving toward them.

Anne's "osmosis" into this pattern has been so "ritually perfect" that the bar lines between measures have been interiorized. Before the dinner party, Anne had always succeeded in conforming to the ritual: "Depuis dix ans, elle n'a pas fait parler d'elle."[47] Tonight, however, the fixed smile keeps slipping: her assimilation/reflection of this "shimmering universe" is no longer so perfect. Her husband will not recognize her: "Un homme, face à une femme, regarde cette inconnue."[48] Indeed, even Anne will not recognize herself: "Si son incongruité la dévore, elle ne peut s'imaginer."[49] Throughout the dinner, a violent interior movement is opposed to the frozen, rigid exterior that she attempts to present to her guests: "Le feu nourrit son ventre de sorcière contrairement aux autres. [. . .] Elle retourne à l'éclatement silencieux de ses reins, à leur brulante douleur, à son repaire."[50] The mordant irony with which her milieu is presented leaves no doubt in the reader's mind that Anne's interior movement and disorder are more real than the "too evident absurdity" of the ritual. (I would note, for example, the reference to the "real disorder" [désordre réel] of Anne's hair.) It is also apparent that this other Anne, the real one, is absent from the dinner party: "—Anne n'a pas entendu" ("—Anne did not hear" [p. 75]).

If Anne is absent, who is sitting in her place? Reflection, the third element of ritual, will help us to answer this question. Anne's "presence" at the dinner party is first indicated in the text by her husband's gaze: "A man, opposite a woman, watches this stranger." His position in relation to Anne is identical to Chauvin's. Tonight, he does not see what he normally sees, a perfect reflection of himself—his values, his territory. This identity is necessary for the success of the dinner party ritual, clearly a metaphor for the male social order in general: "La soirée réussira. Les femmes sont au plus sûr de leur éclat. Les hommes les couvrirent de bijoux au prorata de leurs bilans. . . . Leurs épaules nues ont la luisance et la fermeté d'une société fondée, dans ses assises, sur la certitude de son droit, et elles furent choisies à la convenance de celle-ci. . . . Des hommes les regardent et se rappellent qu'elles font leur bonheur."[51] Like so many votive statues, highly polished and covered with offerings, these women exist only as a creation of the men who gaze upon them in order to see themselves. Their immobility guarantees the solidity of the

social order. There is a smiling, silent statue occupying Anne's place at the table under the glaring chandeliers. The other Anne is barred from this ritual of identity. Where everything is brilliant light, darkness cannot be permitted to destabilize the universe. All that is foreign must be driven out of the light of day. Like a hunted animal in the forest, Anne is driven underground, into her den. The bar is lowered over this other Anne to ensure that she stay in her place. Within each measure of her life, Anne is subjected to the same ritual of identity and suffers the same elimination in favor of her husband's image. Anne's name is still not her own: Desbaresdes, *des barres raides*. These inflexible bar lines close out her difference to permit the eternal repetition of the Same.

Language is the foundation on which this linear order is built: "Le choeur des conversations augmenta peu à peu de volume et, dans une surenchère d'efforts . . . émerge une société quelconque. . . . Et on débouche peu à peu sur une conversation généralement partisane et particulièrement neutre. La soirée réussira."[52] Only Madame Desbaresdes "n'a pas de conversation" ("has nothing to say" [p. 69]). Here we should return to Irigaray's analysis of the principle of Identity as the basis of Western philosophical discourse. For Irigaray, "*La logique de tout discours*" is grounded in "*l'indifférence sexuelle.*"[53] That is to say, the feminine is reduced to a reflection of the masculine by/in language. Man uses woman as a means for reinforcing his own specularization. She permits him to (re)produce his desire, his sexuality, his representation, in sum, himself, *ad infinitum.* Irigaray uses the mirror as a metaphor for this self(male)-reflective function of discourse: "A lui seul masculin, féminin, et leurs rapports. Dérision de la génération . . . qui emprunte . . . sa *force* au même modèle, au modèle (du) même: le sujet. Au regard duquel tout *dehors* reste toujours condition de possibilité de l'image et de la reproduction de soi. Miroir fidèle, poli et vacant de réflexions altérantes."[54] If Anne is absent, it is quite simply because she does not exist on this chain of discourse. The ritual of language at the dinner party and in her marriage is rigorously identical to the *cérémonial* of the meetings between Anne and Chauvin. When Anne comes into the café for their third conversation, she remains at the counter even though Chauvin is already seated at the table, "ne pouvant sans doute échapper encore au cérémonial de leurs premières rencontres."[55] The self-reflective functioning of discourse permits Chauvin to name himself by "barring" Anne. His position of subject is dependent on her elimination. Decidedly, Anne's movement from her house to the café has not taken her far.

La donna è mobile

The murdered woman is a symbol of the violence done to women in a culture that depends for its existence (as subject) on their "elimination," their relegation to the status of object. This inert body, however, silent, passive, exactly as Man wants her to be, moves, escapes his grasp. Duras suggests that it is women's silence and passivity that make this movement possible. She speaks of a certain primal energy that *was* common to both men and women, "une énergie à venir, blanche, neutre." Men, by their "activité théorisante . . . réductrice, castratrice,"[56] have lost this energy. Women have preserved it by their silence: "ce que j'appelle leur silence, leur marginalité. C'est-à-dire qu'elles ont accumulé des masses fabuleuses de cette énergie, qui est à l'instar de celle de la mer encore enfouie mais intacte, entière."[57] Denied the status of subject, excluded from discourse, women have never been fixed in an "identity," Chauvin's hard-won name, that would block this energy. Like the sea, women's "identity" will circulate in *Moderato cantabile.*

The murdered woman's cry "breaks" [*briser*] the sound of the sea. Almost immediately after, "Le bruit de la mer ressuscita de nouveau."[58] Likewise, "la mère"—Anne, the murdered woman—will be resuscitated. The transitive definition of *ressusciter* is "faire revivre en esprit, par le souvenir."[59] Anne will resuscitate the murdered woman in precisely this sense and "assume" her identity. This identity, however, will not be the one Chauvin expects. For years Anne has "lived" with an "identity" imposed from outside. She is already "dead" when she goes to the café for the first time. As Chauvin closes Anne ever more tightly into his discourse, she *seems* to resemble more and more closely the other woman's "inert" body. She *seems* to become the product of Chauvin's fiction, to the point of living it during the dinner party. She *seems* to be headed for a repetition of the murder. Chauvin *seems* to be in complete control of his fiction. Anne, however, never learned her scales (p. 56). She may "know her place," but that does not necessarily mean that she occupies it. One is struck by the recurring references to what I would call Anne's absence from her conversations with Chauvin: "Elle le regarda, perplexe, revenue à elle"; "Elle revint de loin à ses questions"; "Anne Desbaresdes n'écoutait pas."[60] This is not to deny that at the same time she is also demanding that Chauvin tell her what happened. But as a critic complained at the moment of the book's publication, "Nous avons l'impression que l'homme n'en sait pas plus long qu'Anne et que d'ailleurs elle n'écoute guère ce qu'il lui raconte."[61]

Where is Anne? She is involved in a process of identification with the murdered woman. Although this process throws Anne into a struggle to the death with Chauvin, its continuation entirely escapes his control. What we might call the essential of Anne's identification with the other woman takes place "elsewhere," on a scene that Chauvin cannot know, of which he is ignorant. Anne will take the "place" of that other woman and move into a circulation that Chauvin can neither touch nor control.

Anne's absence during the ritual of the dinner party is an example of how this movement elsewhere precipitated by the cry could permit her to escape the grasp both of her husband and of Chauvin. While Anne's place at the table is occupied by a smiling statue, the other Anne is following the movement outside the gates: "Un homme rôde, boulevard de la Mer. Une femme le sait. [. . .] Il passera.

Elle, le sait encore."[62] The scent of the magnolia blossoms in the garden, resumed in the one that Anne is wearing, serves as the link between her "interior" and the exterior movement:

> Dehors, dans le parc, les magnolias élaborent leur floraison funèbre dans la nuit noire du printemps naissant.
>
> Avec le ressac du vent qui va, vient, se cogne aux obstacles de la ville, et repart, le parfum atteint l'homme et le lâche, alternativement. [. . .] L'encens des magnolias arrive toujours sur lui, au gré du vent, et le surprend et le harcèle autant que celui d'une seule fleur.[63]

As with all other aspects of Anne's relationship with Chauvin, the positive accompanies the negative. The flowering of the magolias is funereal—the night is black—although the season is "nascent springtime." The odor of the magnolias becomes their "incense," associating the movement between Anne and Chauvin with the ritual immobility of the dinner party. Anne's wearing of the magnolia blossom is itself "narrated" by Chauvin. On the other hand, the scent is carried by the "sea wind" [*vent de la mer*] which is not impeded by the "obstacles" of the city. The wind and the scent reach Chauvin, then leave him, continuing on their way "de dune en dune jusqu'à rien" ("from dune to dune until nothingness" [p. 67]). This nothingness is simultaneously the totality of the sea: "l'odeur franchit le parc et va jusqu'à la mer."[64] Chauvin circles around the house, ritualistically pronouncing Anne's name, in effect conjuring her presence in his territory. It is, however, impossible to seize and hold the wind: "Sur les paupières fermées de l'homme, rien ne se pose que le vent et, par vagues impalpables et puissantes, l'odeur du magnolia, suivant les fluctuations de ce vent."[65] The scent of the magnolias moves on the wind like impalpable and powerful waves, coming to rest where and when it wishes, then moving on. Neither the wind nor the sea can be fixed in his territory, by his language.

Finally, the only thing that this language can seize is language itself, that is to say, the very barriers with which it constitutes and propagates itself: "L'homme . . . s'est approché des grilles . . . prend les grilles dans ses mains, et serre. Comment n'est-ce pas encore arrivé? [. . .] L'homme a lâché les grilles du parc. Il regarde ses mains vides et déformées par l'effort."[66] As he walks back to the city, the scent of the magnolias—a product of his fiction—is replaced by that of the sea. After the dinner, Anne will vomit both the "foreign food" [*la nourriture etrangère*] she has just forced herself to eat and the wine she drank earlier with Chauvin. Both are fictions of Anne Desbaresdes that she has still been unable to refuse definitively. At the end of the dinner party she is back in her husband's shadow: "Une ombre apparaîtra dans l'encadrement de la porte . . . obscurcira plus avant la pénombre de la chambre."[67] And the beech tree's shadow surely still blocks her view of the sea.

MIMESIS: THE DEATH OF (A) FICTION

In the passages discussed above, we begin to see the suggestion of a movement that would take Anne outside of the order that has been imposed on her. At the same time, somewhat paradoxically, Chauvin appears to function as an obstacle in some sense necessary to the final realization of Anne's movement elsewhere. (In the dinner party scene, he seems to serve as a sort of relay beyond himself.) Duras has described Anne as "cette femme qui veut être tuée."[68] I would propose that in order to resurrect the murdered woman, Anne must first "voluntarily" imitate her death. Here again, memory will play an important role. I have likened her married life to death; after ten years, however, Anne has lived this fiction for so long that she has forgotten why she is so restless. She no longer remembers what happened to the other Anne, the one who never learned her scales and who screamed one day. The cry wrests her violently out of her stupor. Her meetings with Chauvin allow her to replay her own repression, to mimic her own murder, in sum, to conjure the very obstacles that deny her existence. This self-imposed submission permits her to remember what happened and puts her back in contact with the "elsewhere" she has forgotten.

Irigaray has given a "theoretical" expression to this process; she calls it *mimétisme*. Women would replay the scene of their repression "pour se souvenir de ce que celle-ci [la mise en scène masculine] aura si bien métabolisé qu'*elle* l'a oublié: son sexe."[69] For Irigaray, this *mimétisme* is a subversive activity, the first step toward a feminine displacement of language: "Jouer de la mimésis, c'est donc, pour une femme, tenter de retrouver le lieu de son exploitation par le discours, sans s'y laisser simplement réduire. C'est se resoumettre . . . à des 'idées', notamment d'elle, élaborées dans/par une logique masculine, mais pour faire 'apparaître,' par un effet de répétition ludique, ce qui devait rester occulté: le recouvrement d'une possible opération du féminin dans le langage."[70] It is by their position outside the constituted order that women survive this mimesis: "Si elle peut si bien jouer ce rôle, si elle n'en meurt pas tout à fait, c'est qu'elle . . . subsiste encore, autrement et ailleurs que là où elle mime si bien ce qu'on lui demande. . . . Hétérogène à toute cette économie de la représentation, mais qui, d'être restée ainsi 'en dehors,' peut justement l'interpréter."[71] By this distance, women are "l'éternelle ironie de la communauté—des hommes."[72]

Mimetic irony, then, cannot operate from an interior position. In their third conversation, for example, Anne tells Chauvin that what he has told her about the other women who have died in her house is false. Chauvin admits that it is false, but adds that "on peut tout supposer" ("one can imagine everything" [p. 43]). Her assertion of untruth only places Anne squarely inside a discourse that produces and mirrors truth/untruth to preserve its own position of mastery. As long as Anne unconsciously operates within this system of representation, she risks having anything she says reappropriated by it. This becomes painfully apparent immediately afterwards in the same scene. Confident that Anne can only parrot his language, Chauvin orders her to speak, to invent. Her response is a "stream of consciousness" association of most of the images that form the fab-

ric of the novel. Without interruption—or punctuation—Anne moves from the crying of the trees in the wind to the birds on the beach after a storm, whose cries, like those of someone who has been murdered, prevent the children from sleeping. As Zepp notes, the passage "forms no further structure of meaning."[73] This is precisely the problem it poses for Chauvin, who immediately begins to speak in Anne's "place" in order to incorporate what she has said into his own economy of truth/untruth. "It is true," he declares—certainly a rare statement in *Moderato cantabile*—before reducing her monologue to a banal observation on the weather. Anne, however, is no longer listening.

Only her marginality will allow irony to operate on a properly fictional level. When Chauvin tells Anne the story of the reception that she lives out at the dinner party that same evening, he for the most part abandons the tone of supposition and the use of the conditional tense that have marked his discourse since his verbal seduction of Anne. As his fiction seems increasingly to become her reality, Chauvin speaks more often in the present or the future of the indicative. On the other hand, as Anne becomes more implicated in this fiction, her language will take the inverse tack: "*Je pourrais vous dire* que je suis déjà en retard sur l'heure du dîner."[74] Chauvin responds with an assertion of truth: "—*Vous savez* que *vous ne pourrez faire autrement que d'y arriver en retard, vous le savez?*"[75] Again, Anne's response is a conditional one: "—*Je ne pourrais pas faire* autrement. Je sais."[76] Anne then changes the subject in an ironic diversion of Chauvin's conversation. She returns to his story of the other women who have died in her house. This time, however, it is not a question of the truth of the story. Anne is speaking from an entirely different position: "—Je pourrais vous dire que j'ai parlé à mon enfant de toutes ces femmes qui ont vécu derrière ce hêtre et qui sont maintenant mortes, mortes, et qu'il m'a demandé de les voir, mon trésor. Je viens de vous dire ce que je pourrais vous dire, voyez."[77] Anne's insistent reiteration of the conditional "possibility" of her statement serves to deconstruct Chauvin's narrative superiority. Her own fiction, thrown out almost as a challenge ("you see"), displaces the mirror of truth to reveal its foundation in fiction. In order to move outside of this fiction, Anne must carry her mimesis through to the end. Indeed, in their final meeting it is Anne who will complete Chauvin's text for him; then she will walk out of it, forever.

Any reading of *Moderato cantabile* that attempts to explicate a gap between language and action or, in an absolute sense, between fiction and reality, risks falling headlong into the "same" trap from which Anne finally extricates herself. Zepp convincingly demonstrates that Anne's and Chauvin's "'life,' defined by language, is on paper alone."[78] I would suggest a reading strategy that accepts Anne's and Chauvin's "literary" existence and takes *Moderato cantabile* literally [*au pied de la lettre*] as fiction or, more precisely, as the fiction of fiction. The first piano lesson is simultaneously a reading lesson, a sort of *mode d'emploi* for *Moderato cantabile*. From the first sentence, both the reader and the text itself are positioned in a "field of fiction" [*un champ de la fiction*]: "—Veux-tu lire ce qu'il y a d'écrit au-dessus de ta partition?" is the question Mlle Giraud poses to Anne's son. *Would you read what is written?* His response is immediate, "—Moderato cantabile." It is directly before his (our) eyes; he (we) cannot *not* read it. The second question is a thornier one: "—Et qu'est-ce que ça veut dire, moderato cantabile?" His response: "—Je ne sais pas."[79] This refusal is followed by silence. The invitation to read is in a sense annulled by a silence that refuses the knowledge or truth the text is "supposed" to contain. Fiction brings its own fiction into question. In an analogous movement, Anne will finally refuse to read, or to be read by, anyone else's fiction of her. When she steps out of the café for the last time, the fiction that is *Moderato cantabile* ceases.

Shoshana Felman has written that literature's basically ironic functioning permits it to deconstruct the fantasy of authority. Her argument is pertinent to our reading of *Moderato cantabile*: "Since irony precisely consists in dragging authority as such into a scene which it cannot master, of which it is *not aware* and which, for that very reason, is the scene of its own self-destruction, literature, by virtue of its ironic force, fundamentally deconstructs the fantasy of authority. . . . Literature tells us that authority is a *language effect,* the product or the creation of its own *rhetorical* power: that authority is the *power of fiction*; that authority, therefore, is likewise a fiction."[80] *Moderato cantabile* drags us back to the scene in/by which this authority constitutes itself: the murder. "My name is Chauvin." He is not of woman born, but has (re)created himself in language. He then repeats, reflects, reproduces this Name endlessly, everywhere. The coherence of his creation does not permit a place for anyone but the Same—Chauvin. His authority is indeed the power of the fiction he creates: this authority is born with the Name, is a *language effect,* and only Chauvin possesses the Word. Inscribed in this scene, however, is "another scene" which is not representable and cannot be reduced to his language: the "black hole"—of their melded shadows—where "all the other words would have been buried."[81] This "black hole" negates Chauvin's careful (re)presentation of his origin in which undifferentiated totality is *already* broken down and schematized as a face to face—binary—opposition. Constantly present at the very heart of his verbal construction, yet outside of his control due to its absence and silence, this "other scene" threatens to destroy Chauvin's fiction.

In their first conversation, when Anne speaks of the desperation that must have incited the murder, Chauvin changes the subject to Anne's own life: "Et il la ramena vers des régions qui sans doute devaient lui être plus familières."[82] More familiar, of course, because they are the only ones she has been allowed to see—someone else's territory that Chauvin knows well. Anne accompanies him, resubmitting herself to the authority of his fiction. In so doing, she rediscovers her presence/absence at his ritual of autocreation as well as her continuing existence elsewhere.

From her position in this other scene that Chauvin cannot know, she reveals that his mastery is an (auto)creation of/in language. His authority is a fiction.

MIMESIS: THE BIRTH OF FICTIONS

The last chapter of *Moderato cantabile* carries the process of mimesis/displacement to its conclusion. For the first time, Anne seems to take the initiative in their meeting. She is the one who moves closer to Chauvin. She is the one who fills his glass with wine. This has led some critics to speak of Anne as the "stronger" of the two in the last scene, a sort of reversal of roles. It would be more to the point to speak of her *active submission* to Chauvin's fiction and to her own annihilation. Like the murdered woman, she gives complete "consent." Anne is in effect pushing Chauvin to complete his fiction, inciting him to write its inevitable end.

The descriptions of their physical contact, instigated by Anne, make it clear that the goal of her activity is the re-enactment of the death that she has lived face to face with her husband and Chauvin: "Elle s'avança vers lui d'assez près pour que leurs lèvres puissent s'atteindre. Leurs lèvres restèrent l'une sur l'autre, posées, afin que ce fût fait et suivant le même rite mortuaire que leurs mains, un instant avant, froides et tremblantes. Ce fut fait."[83] The rigidity of their bodies matches that of the literary past tense. Indeed, we are in the midst of a literary illusion; pushed to its limits, Chauvin's power is reduced to so many words, cold and lifeless monuments. We read it as fiction. His ritual of language is played out to its conclusion, Anne's verbal death: "—Je voudrais que vous soyez morte, dit Chauvin.—C'est fait, dit Anne Desbaresdes."[84] Earlier in the conversation, Anne had offered to stop talking. Chauvin's reply to her voluntary silence was negative. Later, when Anne says of the dead woman and/or herself, "—Elle ne parlera plus jamais," Chauvin insists that she will: "—Mais si. . . . ça recommencera."[85] She must speak his language or he cannot control her, appropriate her space, and then silence her himself. Nothing is more threatening to him than her refusal to speak. Anne has assumed her death, accepted fear. For the first time, her movement is not dictated from the outside. She turns away from Chauvin with only her own body as a point of reference: "Anne Desbaresdes contourna sa chaise. . . . Puis elle fit un pas en arrière et se retourna sur elle-même."[86] She moves elsewhere, outside Chauvin's verbal territory. As in the dinner party sequence, Chauvin loses his grip on Anne: "La main de Chauvin battit l'air et retomba sur la table. Mais elle ne le vit pas, ayant déjà quittée le champ où il se trouvait."[87] Without Anne, on what or whom can he construct his authority? Her autodisplacement subverts his fiction and closes the text.

And opens new ones. In the last chapter, Anne comes to the café for the first time without her son. He has been replaced by a new creation, a voice. As Anne makes the first move toward her ritual death, the voice of a woman singing in a foreign city can be heard on the radio: "Une femme chanta loin, dans une ville etrangère. Ce fut Anne Desbaresdes qui se rapprocha de Chauvin."[88] We hear the voice again, even louder than before, when Anne has left the café:

> Elle se retrouva face au couchant, ayant traversée le groupe d'hommes qui étaient au comptoir, dans la lumière rouge qui marquait le terme de ce jour-là.
>
> Après son départ, la patronne augmenta le volume de la radio.[89]

Natural images of death—sunset, red light, end of the day—only prepare Anne's rebirth in another place with another voice. Just as the sound of the sea marks the resurrection of the murdered woman in the first chapter, so the new voice sings Anne's (re)entry into this same circulation. Music is a language "que nous ne pouvons pas décrypter." It is "une sorte d'annonciation . . . d'un temps à venir où on pourra l'entendre."[90] The men in the café complain that it is "trop forte à leur gré" ("too loud for their taste" [p. 84]).

After **Moderato cantabile,** Anne Desbaresdes passes into spaces that are elsewhere. The questions, Where is she going? What will become of her? are beside the point. The essential is that she continue to move. She will perhaps become Lol V. Stein, or Anne-Marie Stretter, or Aurelia Steiner, all fictions that rise up, like the child's sonatina, "in the love of the mother"—to circulate, die, and be reborn. The fiction(s) of a woman, women as fiction(s). A perpetual self-creation/destruction that refuses the immobility of any one name and the fixity of any one identity. A music that destroys all the barriers as it moves into the future: "La voici en effet, fracassant les arbres, foudroyant les murs."[91]

Notes

1. "Difficult to write about your own work. What to say? I will talk about her, about the mother. . . . Ours. Yours. Mine, as well." Marguerite Duras, "Mothers," in *Marguerite Duras* (Paris: Editions Albatros, 1979), p. 99. Translations throughout the article are my own.

2. "—That cry was so strong that it is really very natural that one should try to find out. It would have been difficult for me to avoid doing it, you see. [. . .]—It would have been impossible for me not to come back." Marguerite Duras, *Moderato cantabile* (Paris: Les Editions de Minuit, 1981), pp. 19, 25. Subsequent references in the text are to this edition. Ellipses within square brackets indicate omitted paragraphs.

3. "—I also came back for the same reason as you." *Moderato,* p. 25.

4. "If you came back, I would try to find out something else and I would tell you." *Moderato,* p. 24.

5. Evelyn H. Zepp, "Language as Ritual in Marguerite Duras's *Moderato Cantabile,*" *Symposium,* 30, No. 3 (Fall 1976), p. 255.

6. Michel Foucault, *Power/Knowledge: Selected Interviews and Other Writings, 1972-1977,* trans. and ed. Colin Gordon (New York: Pantheon Books, 1980), p. 93.

7. "a simple imagination transporting in a certain way the events into a field of fiction." Maurice Grévisse, *Le bon usage,* 9th ed. (Paris: Libr. A. Hatier, 1969), quoted by Duras, *Le Camion* (Paris: Les Editions de Minuit, 1977).

8. Zepp, "Language as Ritual," pp. 257, 256.

9. "—Speak to me some more. Soon, I won't ask you for anything more." *Moderato,* p. 43.

10. "So he spoke for her [*à sa place*]." *Moderato,* p. 44.

11. "the fear and . . . the agitation into which she was thrown by any allusion to her existence." *Moderato,* p. 44.

12. "You were lying there. No one knew it." *Moderato,* p. 42.

13. "Trial proceedings." All definitions in this article are taken from the *Micro-Robert, Dictionnaire du français primordial.*

14. "In June of last year, in a few days it will have been a year, you were standing across from it [the garden], on the steps, ready to greet us, we, the employees of the Foundry. Above your half-naked breasts, there was a white magnolia blossom. My name is Chauvin." *Moderato,* p. 42.

15. "She resumed her usual posture, across from him." *Moderato,* p. 43.

16. "—There are rooms on the ground floor where near the end of May, every year, receptions are given for the foundry workers. [. . .]—You had on a very low-cut black dress. You were looking at us in a polite and indifferent way." *Moderato,* p. 34.

17. "—You were leaning on that large piano. Between your naked breasts under your dress, there is that magnolia blossom.

    Anne Desbaresdes very attentively listened to this story.

    —Yes.

    —When you lean over, this flower brushes against the edge of your breasts. You pinned it carelessly, too high. It is an enormous flower, you chose it without thinking, too large for you. Its petals are still hard, it reached full-blossom only last night.

    —Am I looking outside?

    —Drink a little more wine. The child is playing in the garden. You are looking outside, yes.

    Anne Desbaresdes drank as he asked her to, tried to remember, came to from a deep astonishment.

    —I don't remember having picked that flower. Nor having worn it.

—I hardly looked at you, but I had the time to see it too. . . .

—I really do like wine, I didn't know.

—Now, speak to me.

—Oh, leave me alone, Anne Desbaresdes implored."

Moderato, p. 59.

18. "Communication . . . place where two concurrent imaginations come in contact with one another." Marcelle Marini, *Territoires du féminin, avec Marguerite Duras* (Paris: Les Editions de Minuit, 1977), p. 32.

19. See Marini, *Territoires,* pp. 22, 32.

20. "—Once I must have screamed somewhat in that way, . . . when I had this child." *Moderato,* p. 30.

21. See Marguerite Duras and Michelle Porte, *Les Lieux de Marguerite Duras* (Paris: Les Editions de Minuit, 1977), p. 23, and Marguerite Duras and Xavière Gauthier, *Les Parleuses* (Paris: Les Editions de Minuit, 1974), p. 66.

22. "a very long, very loud cry that stopped suddenly at its strongest point." *Moderato,* p. 30.

23. "The back wall of the room was lit up by the setting sun. In its center, the black hole of their combined shadows was outlined." *Moderato,* p. 33.

24. In "La caverne de Platon," first published in *La Nouvelle Revue Française* in 1958 and consequently included in the series of review articles that follow the text of *Moderato* ("'Moderato cantabile' et la presse française," pp. 91-93), Dominique Aury notes this similarity. The comparison is made, however, in the context of a general commentary on the "images of destiny" that would be reflected in both the cave and the text.

25. "The child came in from outside and snuggled up against his mother in a movement of happy abandon. She stroked his hair absentmindedly. The man watched attentively.—They loved one another," he said. *Moderato,* p. 20.

26. "The man sat down near the dead woman, stroked her hair and smiled at her." *Moderato,* p. 14.

27. "with all his soul from what is born, until he is capable of withstanding the sight of being and of what is most luminous in being." *La République* (Paris: Garnier-Flammarion, 1966), p. 277.

28. *"forget in order to remember what is more true."* Luce Irigaray, *Speculum de l'autre femme* (Paris: Les Editions de Minuit, 1974), p. 340.

29. "What determines the power of . . . its *position of mastery."* Luce Irigaray, *Ce sexe qui n'en est pas un* (Paris: Les Editions de Minuit, 1977), p. 72.

30. "from this conception, this birth, far too 'natural,' in order to send him to a more ancient, lofty and noble origin. To a . . . Principle, an Author, in relation to

whom he would have to recognize [know] himself [again]." Irigaray, *Speculum,* p. 366.

31. "The Father, he is eternal, having always refused to be born. Because of this, his being perpetuates itself eternally identical to itself." Irigaray, *Speculum,* p. 399.

32. "in a cold or harsh [hard] manner"; "That which contains little or no liquid."

33. "—I live in the last house on the Boulevard of the Sea, the last one as you leave the city. Just before the dunes. . . . My room is on the second floor, on the left, when one is facing the sea." *Moderato,* pp. 30-31.

34. "If I were you, I would let it grow with its shadow each year a bit thicker on the walls of that room." *Moderato,* p. 41.

35. "She spread herself back on her chair, moving her whole body in an almost vulgar way, turned away from him." *Moderato,* p. 41.

36. "—But, sometimes, its shadow is like black ink." *Moderato,* p. 74.

37. "Do you know what I call the sea? I call it: the thing." "The Thing" (interview with Rolland Thélu), *Gai Pied,* No. 20 (November 1980), p. 16.

38. "What we've just talked about [desire], this vacillating, wandering notion, I could also call it: the thing. Your sex. Mine. Our difference. And this third term, this unceasing triangulation by which we are united The Thing." Thélu interview, p. 16.

39. "the definitive absence of this fundamental presence and never since replaced, that of my [the] mother." Thélu interview, p. 16.

40. "To look at the sea is to look at totality." *Les Lieux,* p. 86.

41. "For you, the landscape of the end of the world or of the beginning of the world, it makes no difference, is the sea." *Le Camion* ("Entretien"), p. 129.

42. "The salmon passes from one to the other following a ritual that nothing disturbs, if not each one's hidden fear that so much perfection might be shattered or stained by a too evident absurdity. [. . .] Slowly, the digestion began of what had been a salmon. Its osmosis into this species that ate it was ritually perfect." *Moderato,* pp. 67, 69.

43. Zepp, "Language as Ritual," pp. 241-42. My emphasis.

44. "the days are regulated at set times. I can't go on. . . .—Meals are always repeated. And the evenings." *Moderato,* p. 60.

45. "A fixed smile makes her appearance acceptable. [. . .] She returns to the fixity of her smile." *Moderato,* pp. 68-69.

46. "—I had the idea for these piano lessons . . . on the other end of town, for my love, and now I can no longer avoid them. How difficult it is." *Moderato,* p. 61.

47. "For ten years, she has never given anyone reason to talk about her." *Moderato*, p. 68.

48. "A man, opposite a woman, watches this stranger." *Moderato*, p. 68. Accomplices in the beginning, Anne and Chauvin also become "strangers" to one another during the encounter that precedes the dinner party.

49. "If her incongruity consumes her, she cannot imagine herself." *Moderato*, p. 68.

50. "Fire nourishes her witch's womb unlike the others. [. . .] She returns to the silent explosion of her loins, to their searing pain, to her den." *Moderato*, p. 74. Duras is fascinated by Michelet's recounting of the origins of witches in the Middle Ages in *La Sorcière*.

51. "The evening will be a success. The women have never been more radiant. The men covered them with jewels in proportion to their fortunes. . . . Their uncovered shoulders reflect the brilliance and the solidity of a society whose foundations rest on the certainty of its law, and they were chosen for their suitability to it. . . . Some men watch them and remember that they make them happy." *Moderato*, p. 70.

52. "The chorus of conversations slowly grows louder and, in a concentration of effort . . . a nondescript society is born. . . . And they all gradually end up in a conversation that is generally partisan and particularly neutral. The evening will be a success." *Moderato*, pp. 69-70.

53. *"The logic of all discourse," "sexual indifference," Ce sexe*, p. 67.

54. "For him alone masculine, feminine, and their relationships. Derision of generation . . . that derives . . . its *strength* from the same model, from the model (of the) same: the subject. In whose eyes every *outside* is always the condition of possibility for the image and the reproduction of himself. Faithful mirror, polished and empty of all distorting reflections." Irigaray, *Speculum*, p. 168.

55. "undoubtedly not yet able to escape the ceremonial of their first encounters." *Moderato*, p. 38.

56. "an energy to come, white, neutral"; "theorizing activity . . . reductive, castrating." *Marguerite Duras à Montréal* (Montréal: Editions Spirale, 1981), p. 69.

57. "What I call their silence, their marginality. That is to say that they have accumulated fabulous masses of this energy, resembling that of the sea still buried but intact, whole." *Montréal*, p. 69.

58. "The sound of the sea rose again." *Moderato*, p. 10.

59. "to resurrect in the mind, by one's memory."

60. "She looked at him, confused, conscious again." *Moderato*, p. 24; "She came back from far away to her questions," p. 32; "Anne Desbaresdes was not listening," p. 44.

61. "We have the impression that the man does not know any more than Anne and that moreover she is hardly listening to what he is telling her." Jean Mistler, "Un essai non une oeuvre achevée," included in "'Moderato cantabile' et la presse," following *Moderato*, pp. 102-3.

62. "A man lurks about, Boulevard of the Sea. A woman knows it. [. . .] He will pass by. She still knows it." *Moderato*, pp. 67, 75.

63. "Outside, in the garden, the magnolias develop their funereal flowering in the obscurity of the nascent springtime.

"On the backwash of the wind that comes and goes, runs up against the obstacles of the city, then goes off again, the perfume reaches the man and abandons him, in turn. [. . .] The incense of the magnolias comes over him, drifting wherever the wind carries it and surprises and plagues him as much as would that of one single flower." *Moderato*, pp. 67, 70. The identity of the wind and the sea is established by the use of *ressac* ("backwash") to describe the wind's movement.

64. "the odor crosses the park and continues to the sea." *Moderato*, p. 73.

65. "Nothing touches the man's closed eyelids except the wind and, by impalpable and powerful waves, the odor of magnolia, following the fluctuations of the wind." *Moderato*, pp. 72-73.

66. "The man . . . comes up to the gates . . . takes the bars in his hands, and squeezes. How has it not happened yet? [. . .] The man has let go of the garden gates. He looks at his hands, empty and deformed by his efforts." *Moderato*, p. 74.

67. "A shadow will appear in the doorway . . . will darken even more the half-shadow of the room." *Moderato*, p. 76.

68. "this woman who wants to be killed." *Les Parleuses*, p. 59.

69. "in order to remember what this [masculine representation] has metabolized so well that *she* has forgotten it: her sex." *Ce sexe*, p. 148.

70. "To play at mimesis, is therefore, for a woman, the attempt to find [again] the place of her exploitation by discourse, without letting herself simply be reduced to it. It is to resubject herself . . . to certain 'ideas,' in particular about herself, developed in/by a masculine logic, but in order to render 'visible,' by an effect of ludic repetition, what is supposed to remain hidden: the covering up of a possible operation of the feminine in language." *Ce sexe*, p. 74.

71. "If she can play this role so well, if she does not die completely as a result, it is because she . . . still lives on, otherwise and elsewhere than there where she mimics so well what is asked of her. . . . Heterogeneous to this entire economy of

representation, it is she who can interpret it, precisely because she has remained in this way 'outside.'" *Ce sexe,* p. 148.

72. "the eternal irony of the community—of men." *Ce sexe,* p. 148.

73. Zepp, p. 249.

74. "*I could tell you* that I'm already late for the dinner." *Moderato,* p. 61. My emphasis.

75. "—*You know* that *you will not be able to do* otherwise than to arrive late, you know that?" *Moderato,* p. 61. My emphasis.

76. "—*I would not be able to do* otherwise. I know." *Moderato,* p. 61. My emphasis.

77. "—I could tell you that I talked to my child about all those women who lived behind this beech tree and who are now dead, dead, and that he asked to see them, my darling. I just told you what I could tell you, you see." *Moderato,* p. 61.

78. Zepp, p. 256. Unfortunately, as we have seen, she uses this observation to show their failure to achieve authenticity.

79. "And what does that mean, moderato cantabile?"; "—I don't know." *Moderato,* p. 7.

80. Shoshana Felman, "To Open the Question," *Yale French Studies,* Nos. 55/56 (1977), p. 8.

81. "tous les autres mots auraient été enterrés." Marguerite Duras, *Le ravissement de Lov V. Stein* (Paris: Gallimard, 1974), p. 48. For lack of this "mot-absence" (word-absence), a "mot-trou" (word-hole), Lol remains silent.

82. "And he brought her back toward regions that were undoubtedly more familiar to her." *Moderato,* p. 21.

83. "She drew close enough to him so that their lips could touch. Their lips rested on one another, posed, so that it be done and following the same funereal ritual as their hands, a moment before, cold and trembling. It was done." *Moderato,* p. 82.

84. "—I wish you were dead, Chauvin said.—It is done, Anne Desbaresdes said." *Moderato,* p. 84.

85. "—She will never speak again"; "—But of course [she will]. . . . This will start all over again." *Moderato,* p. 82.

86. "Anne Desbaresdes walked around her chair. . . . Then she took one step back and turned the other way." *Moderato,* p. 84.

87. "Chauvin's hand flew up in the air and fell back on the table. But she did not see it, having already left the area where he was." *Moderato,* p. 84.

88. "A woman sang far away, in a foreign city. It was Anne Desbaresdes who drew closer to Chauvin." *Moderato,* p. 78. We can almost read that the woman who sings *is* Anne Desbaresdes.

89. "She found herself facing the sunset, having crossed the group of men who were at the counter, in the red light that marked the end of that day.

"After her departure, the owner turned up the volume of the radio." *Moderato,* p. 84.

90. "that we cannot decipher." "a kind of heralding [one could almost say an Annunciation, in the religious sense] of a time to come when we will be able to hear it." *Les Lieux,* pp. 30, 29.

91. "Here it is, shattering the trees, striking down the walls." Marguerite Duras, *Détruire, dit-elle* (Paris: Les Editions de Minuit, 1969), p. 136.

Dan Gunn (essay date 1984)

SOURCE: "Life in a Moment," in *The Times Literary Supplement,* October 5, 1984, p. 1118.

[*In the following review of the English translation of* L'amant *and* Whole Days in the Trees, *Gunn finds similarities between the two books despite the thirty years between their publications.*]

Marguerite Duras is a writer whose next move only the foolhardy would predict. Yet, when viewed retrospectively, her work displays a curious singleness of purpose, an inevitability, almost, of direction. These two books are divided by thirty years yet linked by their preoccupations and prevailing currents of feeling.

Duras's recent fictions have been short, strange, and disturbing. In them, sexual acts (though not always what we presumptuously call *the* sexual act) have provided the focus, while often making themselves known only in a narrative told largely in the conditional tense, and through the mediation of a voyeuristic eye (or "I"). *L'amant,* her new novel, also has a centre which is highly charged sexually, yet the book is long, unthreatening, inviting, full of reported action and direct telling. Indeed *L'amant* is an autobiography of sorts, recounting the writer's youth in French Indochina, roughly the years which went into *Un barrage contre le Pacifique.*

Many familiar elements of Duras's early years are, then, to be found: the brothers, the despairing mother, the dead father; rivers, forest, sea, freedom; the untested commitment to writing. The reader will have few problems with these recognizable pieces of a life, which allow intriguing glimpses of the young Duras. The narrative darts now forward, now back, as memory catches fragments: the mother's moods, the younger brother's death, washday in Vietnam, the ferocious love of the mother for the older son, the ocean voyage to France, Paris in wartime. The fragments do not form a total picture, the chronology is confusing, for memory plays tricks with the writer: "L'histoire de ma vie n'existe pas." But the moments are linked by the emotions of sadness and joy, hostility and love, undiminished in intensity through the intervening years. Ambivalence is at the heart of Duras's affective world, and nowhere does it find more plain acknowledgment than here, in the context of the family life which fuelled it. The moments and fragments of *L'amant* are truly engaging, fascinating even for the reader familiar with Duras.

Yet there is a problem, one which draws us deeper into the work. It faces both writer and reader, and may be glimpsed in Duras's declared intentions:

> Avant, j'ai parlé des périodes claires, de celles qui étaient éclairées. Ici je parle des périodes cachées de cette même jeunesse, de certains enfouissements que j'aurais opérés sur certains faits, sur certains sentiments, sur certains événements.

The unsaid beckons; but Duras is one of those writers who make us aware that the path towards the unsaid is not necessarily the most obvious or direct one (her work, when difficult, is so for a reason). How, then, are we to take the central moment of this "autobiography", when the moment is one which makes quite as many demands on our imagination as any in her more obviously challenging novels? The question is not one of honesty or of belief—"Is Duras telling us the truth, when it matters most?"—since Duras never teases us with the prospect of words which would endorse (or refute) the veracity of her account (indeed the book nowhere declares itself as autobiography). The question is rather whether the writing can, through its illusion of directness and simplicity, divert the reader's interest away from the reported events in the life of a famous writer. Can the writing, when it matters most, compel an engagement so total as to correspond to the moment—not so much unsaid as unsayable—which occupies the book's heartland? The question confronts Duras the writer, as she writes, not Duras the elderly lady, as she remembers.

The moment is lived by the girl of fifteen-and-a-half, on a ferry, crossing the Mekong river. On that ferry the girl knows with an utter certainty the nature of her life, her love, her sex, her desire and desirability. And no amount of direct telling can transmit such knowledge; rather we must glean it through the love affair which the moment led to, with a fellow passenger on the ferry, a wealthy Chinese. Through him the girl initiates herself into a delirious world of passion and lust, of abandon and undying love. The telling of this love sustains the book, as it sustained the girl, with its afternoons of ecstasy, its financial exploitation, its cultural and social transgressions, its silences and declarations, its complete rightness and complete hopelessness, until she left Vietnam for France. The narrating of the love sustains the book not because it offers the most "interesting" revelation. It does so because, precisely, it takes us towards a point where, as in all Duras's finest work, certain boundaries cease to matter: between lovers; between reader and written, written and writer; between autobiography and fiction.

Each of the four stories collected in **Whole Days in the Trees** (1954; now translated for the first time) describes or alludes to an event which, though on the surface undramatic, sets the course of a life. As much as what the event contains, it is the inevitability of the course it determines, which these stories make us taste; and it is, too, the sense of the awfulness and peculiar rightness of this finality which connects them with Duras's later fictions, though it is hard not to agree with the opinion which she has expressed, that not until the late 1950s did she find a truly comfortable—and thoroughly disconcerting—narrative style.

In the title story an aging mother leaves her profitable factory to visit her son in Paris, ostensibly to persuade him to become the factory's manager. In fact she is drawn to him because, of her six offspring, he is the prodigal child: drifter, gambler, gigolo. As the mother's proposed month-long visit dwindles to a single, critical day, will she admit that his profligacy is precisely his appeal? A fatally seductive and rebarbative male figure (at best an uncaring boor, at worst an unregenerate sadist) haunts all Duras's work. Ambivalence wears thin as the son's brutishness increasingly isolates him. But the mother's obsessional old age is so deftly sketched, the dialogue so wonderfully terse, that it may be possible to overlook this and recall the cause of the son's attraction, the life-event which has singled him out: he was the one who, while his siblings studied and did what they were told, spent whole days in the trees.

In the second story, **"The Boa,"** the event which has crystallized a girl's adolescent understanding is in fact a double one: Sunday trips to the zoo to watch a boa devour a chicken, followed by being required to watch her landlady bare her ancient, virginal body to her. Cruelty and innocence, the natural and the perverse, become curiously realigned as the snake performs its fascinating ritual and the landlady vents her remorse. Two figures which haunt Duras's world rise up as heroic in the girl's imagination and sustain her reversal of conventional morality: the assassin and the prostitute. Where usually Duras only hints at the reason for the persistence and power of these figures, here an explanation is given, though perhaps not to the story's advantage.

"Madame Dodin," the third story, gives us a *concierge* who focuses her existence on her hatred of the communal rubbish-bin, which she must shift daily. As she vents her hatred on the timid tenants, Duras touchingly and humorously reveals ambivalence's less sinister aspect. But it is in the final story, **"The Building Site,"** that Duras's ability to mesh event and existence is at its strongest. A man sees a woman staring, horrified, at a building site. We will never know why her feeling is so strong, but her intensely private vision, her momentary defencelessness, draw the man inexorably towards her. At a hotel which they are visiting, he watches, waiting for her to recognize that he has seen something in her which renders their union inevitable. In the 1970s Duras moved away from fiction into filmmaking, but in this story it is almost as if the camera were already there, playing on surfaces, intimating unspeakable depths; and also the look which cuts across boundaries.

It is only to be regretted that this attractive edition is hampered by an undistinguished translation containing many elementary and unaccountable errors, and by lax typesetting, which has allowed inadmissible substitutions in which genders are changed, new sentences appear and phrases disappear.

Susan Rava (essay date 1984)

SOURCE: "Marguerite Duras: Women's Language in Men's Cities," in *Women Writers and the City: Essays in Feminist Literary Criticism,* edited by Susan Merrill Squier, The University of Tennessee Press, 1984, pp. 35-44.

[*In the following essay, Rava examines the attempts of Duras's female characters to create a linguistic voice and presence for themselves in the predominantly male urban milieu.*]

In the works of Marguerite Duras, the city inaugurates a conflict between the female search for authentic speech and the male linguistic domination. While Duras's work covers many genres, themes, and forms, her settings have frequently been cities: Duras uses those specific locations as starting points for an exploration of human relationships which concentrates on intensely charged dialogues between a limited number of characters. In Duras's earlier novels, using urban backdrops, she explores the particular difficulties a woman faces in adapting herself to the language men have created.[1] The city becomes a symbol of that language. Traversing great distances, from the mute solitude of the private home to the noisy public life of the city, women in Duras's works are typically not liberated—as they had hoped—but rather trapped by the linguistic and social constraints embodied by male language and culture. Duras's works repeatedly pose one problem: how do women participate in the activity of the city, exemplified by verbal power in the public realm, and still preserve the individual identity nurtured in the silent isolation of the home? This dilemma is the focus of my study, which will demonstrate that in cities—particularly cafés, parks, bars and hotel rooms—Duras's women struggle to seize male language, to use it, even to re-create it.

Born in Indochina in 1914 to a family of French colonials, Marguerite Duras came to France for her university studies and has remained there ever since. Her works draw on the great tradition established by nineteenth- and twentieth-century French novels which has viewed the city as embodiment of male linguistic and political power. Activists, Balzacian *arrivistes,* revolutionaries, and seducers—all have derived some of their charm from the typically urban, masculine attribute of linguistic virtuosity. For such heroes the city has served as battlefield, apprenticeship, and proving ground. Yet while men have found in the city an arena for the exercise of linguistic and cultural dominance, women have been excluded from the challenges and traits of the urban environment, because they have been excluded from the masculine language the city enshrines.

Anne Desbaresdes in *Moderato cantabile,*[2] the young maid in *The Square,*[3] and Claire Lannes in *L'Amante anglaise*[4]—focal points of my study—have all been accustomed to silent isolation from the masculine mainstream of city life. While one critic has described that typically feminine silence as a deliberate protest against the language imposed by men, the three characters reveal not a conscious refusal of language but rather a difficulty making authentic use of it.[5] Although they begin in traditionally female domestic circumstances, the characters seek a change; the core of all three novels is the moment of speech, when the women break into urban life. Claire Lannes is accused of a murder which sets public bureaucracy in motion, offering her a chance for self-expression; the maid, in contrast, finds in an afternoon outing to the public square the occasion—and audience—for storytelling; in *Moderato,* finally, an anonymous city scream breaks into Anne's private world to free her for her first verbal—and public—adventure.[6]

The city's appeal lies fundamentally in the public expression it makes possible.[7] Yet paradoxically, that very freedom is difficult for women to attain precisely because of its linguistic character. Claire's "confession," in *L'Amante,* illustrates this paradox. Puzzled detectives and citizens gather in a café to try to solve a murder; their task is impossible because the head of the dismembered body has not been found. The body, and by extension the victim, has no identity because it lacks its rational center; the crime cannot be solved. In the context of *L'Amante,* the only way to solve the crime is to find the head, whose hiding place can be revealed only by Claire.

Claire's "confession" exemplifies the tension of the female experience in the city, the tension between the masculine demand for order (in language as well as in society) and the female resistance to ordering principles. Thus, male authority says that Claire's "confession" must be clear and concise; one word would close the matter, and Claire's extraneous rumination, which seems folly to the men interrogating her, would be forgotten. Society's only concern is the coherent reconstruction of the crime so that all of its parts fit together into a decipherable, identifiable whole. Yet Claire refuses to participate in this masculine ordering activity of "confession"; she wishes, instead, for her voluminous outpouring of words to stand. Although the reporters and detectives, like the city they symbolize, have no use for Claire's incoherent ramblings, her "confession" stands as both a social statement and a personal act. Transgressing linguistic order, she flaunts masculine teleology as well. She manipulates the interrogation to her own ends, producing not the result vital to the communal interest (in the masculine system of social order), but rather creative self-expression.

Anne Desbaresdes in *Moderato* and the maid in *The Square* encounter similarly paradoxical conflicts between verbal liberty and social restrictions in the city. For Anne, the small port city of *Moderato* first seems to represent a seductive freedom from the rigid, bourgeois life she has known as the wife of a factory executive. And for the maid, the city offers the answer to a vague malaise, her desire to be free in a way as yet undefined: "'I know that women, even those who appear to be happy, often start wondering towards evening why they are leading the lives they do . . .'" (*Square,* 44). To both Anne and the maid, the unfamiliar urban world first seems to offer freedom for passion, anonymity, productive activity, even violence—all qualities outside traditional bourgeois roles for women. Ultimately, however, instead of finding social or economic freedom, purposeful physical work or emotional involvement, Anne, Claire Lannes, and the maid all discover their potential as linguistic creators. Thus, all three novels function as allegories "of the nature of language and the creative process itself."[8]

Yet while the city offers those three women the power of language use and creation, the terms of that power are dictated by men, and embodied in their world: the city. Although Anne initiates the conversation with Chauvin in *Moderato,* the bar in which they meet is an exclusively male domain, where Chauvin quickly takes control. He orders the wine, guides Anne to an isolated table, and—most important—directs their conversation. In his control of the dialogue, he even goes so far as to contradict himself, urging her at one moment to "'Keep talking to me. Soon I won't ask you anything more,'" only to intervene soon after (*Moderato,* 105). Similarly, a detective attempts to direct Claire's "confession" in *L'Amante,* while the salesman in *The Square* makes conversational overtures to the maid.

Language belongs to the masculine world, where openings and guidance are male-generated; silence and nonverbal communication are, in contrast, woman's province. Duras prizes such self-expression as a special bond between women which men often misunderstand. For instance, Anne identifies her own birthing cries with the scream of a female murder victim, leading to an implicit connection between the women; her conversation is also punctuated with nonverbal utterances, moans, and murmurs. Such primordial, nonordered expression is incomprehensible, even frightening, to men, Duras implies in *Hiroshima, Mon Amour.* There, Duras creates the tale of a Frenchwoman who is punished for crying out.[9] Punishment means banishment to the cellar until the heroine promises not to cry out anymore. The episode emphasizes woman's need to curb her sounds in order to participate in a communal life of established words.

In spite of Duras's belief in the force of nonverbal sounds, she urges women to launch themselves in the public verbal arena. She articulates this sentiment in her conversations with Xaviere Gauthier:

> If I am a professional, I take pen and paper . . . I try to translate the illegible [from within me] by using the vehicle of an egalitarian, undifferentiated language. So I deprive myself of the integrity of the inner darkness which, in me, balances my lived life. I rise from the interior mass, I project outside what I ought to do inside. . . . Woman must project out, be turned toward the outside like man.[10]

However, projecting out and talking freely do not seem to come naturally to the women in Duras's novels; for Anne, Claire, and the maid, primordial noises and maternal gestures come more easily. Furthermore, the vehicle for expression, at least within the novels, is not egalitarian. The conditions for dialogue are prescribed by men; in *Moderato* for example, Chauvin controls who speaks, when, and how. In spite of obstacles, however, the three women produce unique verbal, "works" distinct from those of their mentors. Their "works"—storytelling, dialogues, confessions, and commentaries—all reflect a rupture with customary linear or sequential constructions. Images and sensibilities welling up from the female unconscious manifest themselves in deformations of "normal" grammar and syntax.

In Claire's "confession," a sensitive intelligence (which men have construed as madness) is revealed as words pour forth unconstrained by convention:

> I had thoughts about happiness, and plants in winter, certain plants, certain things, food, politics, water, thoughts about water, cold lakes, the beds of lakes, lakes on the beds of lakes, about water, thirsty water that opens and swallows up and closes again, lots of thoughts about water.
>
> (*L'Amante,* 101)

Anthropomorphic and nonhierarchical, this sentence continues for almost a page, with fragments which—in French—are woven together by assonance or onomatopoeia. Duras also uses double-entendre, as in the passage above, and puns; for example, the title of the book, *L'Amante,* is juxtaposed to *la menthe* later in the text.

While Anne adapts externally to the routine of linear time—embodied in the city by the regular movement of the workers and by the siren—and to the masculine mode of exchange, language, she molds language to her own ends. She breaks, for example, with linear narrative chronology as she recounts the history of her house and its inhabitants simultaneously with her own past and with that of the murder victim. This she does by occasionally inserting the present verb tense into a survey of the past. Furthermore, she confounds conventional narration, where one voice concerns itself with a single narrative focus, in her multilayered recitation. Anne, thus, gives her language an individuality reflective of her inner self. In the public sphere she finds the possibility of verbal creation and of an audience as stimulus and sounding board.[11] While the city—as represented by the workers' routine—might seem to recede into the background of *Moderato,* it both goads and structures Anne's narration.

Anne's rupture with usual narrative techniques mirrors Duras's frequent transgression of novelistic conventions. Duras maximizes the evocative power of language by drawing both reader and characters into the creative moment. She does this by leaving both the sense and the structures of her texts openended; her audiences, both within and beyond the text, must help to create the work in progress. The detective in *L'Amante* clearly enunciates the shared nature of this text: "'A book is starting to come into existence about the crime at Viorne. . . . It's up to you to set the book in motion. . . . We can let the tape recite what it remembers and the reader can take your place'" (*L'Amante,* 3).

Although the verbal creations of Duras's female characters at first glance seem private undertakings stimulated by the urban environment, Duras often emphasizes the communal, even fraternal, nature of verbal enterprise. The structure and linguistic organization of several of her texts elucidate this notion of collective, city-based effort, and Duras forces her public to participate in several ways. First, she avoids the traditional propensity to delineate people or situations by names. By downplaying the individuality which a proper name bestows on a character, Duras emphasizes urban anonymity and renders dialogue in its purest form, as in *The Square.*[12] Many characters have no given name at all, are identified only once or twice, or are merely referred to by pronouns. Conversations seesaw back and forth for pages without precise demarcation of the speaker—a procedure which compels the reader to retrace his or her steps or, more important, to create a character's individuality repeatedly during the act of reading. Consequently, individuality arises not from a given name, but rather from the complicity of audience and character alike in the creative moment.

An unusual modulation of French verb tenses in *Moderato* further heightens the reader's participation. During the dramatic conclusion of the dinner scene, when Anne flees her own party, Duras suddenly switches from the past tenses of previous chapters to the present and then to the future tense to describe Anne's vomiting. The shift implies a collective public which will decide the reality of the event, and colors Anne's physical rejection of her milieu with a paradoxical tint of the inevitable, yet unrealized act of refusal: "Anne Desbaresdes [note the use of her full, married name] will go upstairs. . . . She will go into the child's room. . . . And to the inviolable rhythm of her child's breathing she will vomit forth the strange nourishment that had been forced upon her" (*Moderato,* 133).

Duras frequently blurs the antecedents of her pronouns—an equivocation rare in the rationally constructed syntax of French—giving the impression of a text-in-the-making, where meaning is not an a priori given, but must be produced by a collaboration of reader and characters. For example, in the last paragraph of the French text of *Moderato,* the *patronne* turns up the radio as Anne leaves the bar: "La patronne augmenta le volume de la radio. Quelques hommes se plaignirent qu'*elle* fût trop forte à leur gré" (*Moderato,* 115, French text, emphasis added). Even though the English translates *elle* as *it,* apparently referring to the volume of the radio, the final sentence in French is ambiguous. *Elle* may well refer to Anne, who has just passed the group of men. Understood in this way, the passage presents a final condemnation by the group of workers who have already watched, commented upon, and

judged the "adulterous" wife of one of the town's prominent industrialists. The comment reinforces the distance between Anne as an individual woman and the collective group of men—as unified, urban spokesmen. Furthermore, if taken as a collective assessment of Anne herself, the passage offers little hope that Anne can penetrate the closed and formal masculine world of the bar or—by extension—the city. *Forte* has several meanings—strong, loud, heavy in weight, for instance—as does the expression *à leur gré,* which may indicate personal taste or opinion: taken as a whole, the phrase may reflect a masculine view of Anne as object, just as the rigid finality of the formal literary past tense and imperfect subjunctive may emphasize Anne's lack of options.

In the province of prescribed language patterns no room exists for Anne's deformations; yet, paradoxically, her tools must be those of the men around her, and her audience must include that urban public. Women must, then, relate to the public when they move into the urban settings of *Moderato, The Square,* and *L'Amante;* they must measure its capacity for comprehension and extrapolation. Sometimes in Duras's texts, those urban audiences are explicit—characters like Chauvin with major catalytic roles, or like the working men in the bar in *Moderato* who function as a chorus, with a rigid moral code as basis for judgment. Sometimes, in contrast, the audience is only implicit: Duras reaches out of the text to the actual reader, urging her not only to witness but also to participate in the creative moment. So reader, intratextual listener, and character alike join in the generation of a story, spawned in the public world of the city. Not only does the city offer freedom of expression in Duras's works, then; it also holds out the possibility of communal verbal creation.

The very nature of such city-based freedom makes the city both a challenging and a problematic environment for the women in Duras's texts. Drawn initially to the city because it promises them liberation from domestic routine and the freedom to explore themselves in companionship, passion, and work, Duras's women often find self-realization difficult in a world whose routine and values are male-controlled. Urban life offers neither the private, even silent, primeval security nor the ordered confinement of the home. In contrast, in the city women must relinquish the consolations and limitations of domestic life for the urban adventures of self-discovery, creativity, and interaction with an audience. Even though the "voyage" may lead to feelings of isolation, alienation, and anonymity, its positive culmination is the use of language—or of a chosen silence. Verbal production is the end result of urban activity, producing self-discovery for the maid (and the salesman) in *The Square,* self-revelation in *L'Amante,* and self-liberation in *Moderato.* Through verbal production, Duras's woman engages in the metaphorical "search for a word which would liberate her and which might be *identity* or that feminine version of the masculine *pouvoir* (power) which is *puissance* [potential and ability]."[13] Constrained to use the given tools of collective language, Duras's women struggle courageously, even painfully, to bring their own linguistic and narrative identities into the urban, public world.

Notes

1. The theoretical base for this essay is my own, and represents an attempt to integrate theory and Duras's writings. The approach was generated in a group of women French professors which has been meeting in St. Louis since the winter of 1980. All members of the group are well grounded in French literature and in contemporary French feminist theory, be it psychoanalytic, linguistic, philosophical, or sociopolitical, according to personal bent. Each woman has brought papers, portions of readings, tapes, and thoughts on French theorists. Thus, the base for this essay developed and was tested during those meetings and was influenced by the support and thoughtful contributions of my friends Anna Amelung, Pierrette Daly, Maryann DeJulio, Mia DeWeer, Emily Guignon, Hannah Langsam, Marguerite Le Clézio, Lucy Morros, Christine Sharp, and Colette Winn. All of us have been marked by the works of Marie Cardinal, Hélène Cixous, Marguerite Duras, Luce Irigaray, Marcelle Marini, George Sand, and Monique Wittig, to name but a few.

2. Marguerite Duras, *Moderato cantabile,* trans. Richard Seaver in *Four Novels: The Square, Ten-Thirty on a Summer Night; The Afternoon of Mr. Andemas; Moderato Cantabile* (New York: Grove, 1965). Originally published as *Moderato cantabile* in French (Paris: Editions de Minuit, 1958). Future references to this work will follow the citation in this form: *Moderato,* 15.

   Moderato tells the story of a strange love affair between Anne Desbaresdes and Chauvin. Anne walks her son to piano lessons in the small port city where she lives. In the opening chapter, during a lesson, a piercing scream rises from a nearby café where Anne and her son find that a young woman has just been murdered by a lover or husband. The lure of the city, represented by the passion and violence of the crime, draws Anne back to the café where she meets Chauvin. The city as setting determines the length of Anne and Chauvin's meetings and provides commentators—workers who come and go regularly. Anne's story, therefore, is that of love and self-expression within an urban framework.

3. Marguerite Duras, *The Square,* trans. Richard Seaver in *Four Novels.* Future references to this work will follow the citation in this form: *Square,* 33.

   The Square (1955), one of Duras's earliest works, is the story of a young governess who spends the afternoon in a public square with her young charge. There, by chance, she meets a traveling salesman. The salesman is just "passing through" while the young woman feels hopelessly anchored to her servile life. The city, portrayed as the square, offers a neutral, anonymous meeting place where all is possible and restraints do not exist. It, thus, can serve as a catalyst for the exploration of human communication.

4. Marguerite Duras, *L'Amante anglaise,* trans. Barbara Bray (New York: Grove, 1968). Future references to this work will follow the citation in this form: *L'Amante,* 97.

   Originally published in French in 1967, *L'Amante anglaise* is a novel based on a news item (*un fait-divers*) about the murder and dismembering of a housekeeper—a crime probably committed by her employer. The same news item had generated an earlier play by Duras. In the three sections of the novel version, a detective interviews characters who have some apparent connection with the crime, settling finally on Claire Lannes as prime suspect. The city here is depicted as a bureaucratic, ordering force. Like other women characters cited, Claire is both stimulated and repressed by the city.

5. Marcelle Marini, *Territoires du féminin avec Marguerite Duras* (Paris: Editions de Minuit, 1977), 22.

6. Ibid., 18.

7. The notion that place confers possibility, even virtuality, upon characters marks the presentation of both men and women in French literature. In spite of romantic notions that the individual is supremely valuable and responsible, the collective potential of groups of people in towns, cities, or Paris shapes the desires, searches, and evolution of many literary figures, including some in Duras's works. See, for example, Diana Festa-McCormick, *The City as Catalyst* (Cranbury, N.J.: Associated Univ. Presses, 1979).

8. Evelyn H. Zepp, "Language as Ritual in Marguerite Duras's *Moderato cantabile,*" *Symposium* 30 (1976), 257.

9. Marguerite Duras, *Hiroshima, Mon Amour* (Paris: Gallimard, 1960), 90-91. Future references to this work will follow the citation in this form: *Hiroshima,* 21.

   Famous as a film by Alain Resnais, *Hiroshima* recounts a brief love affair between a French woman and a Japanese man. The place is Hiroshima, "le terrain commun" (11), a city where, as Duras explains, universal values are laid bare in the aftermath of disaster.

10. Marguerite Duras, *Les Parleuses* (Entretiens avec Xavière Gauthier) (Paris: Editions de Minuit, 1974), 50, 101 (my translation).

11. For further discussion of women and language, see Luce Irigaray's *Ce Sexe qui n'en est pas un* (Paris: Editions de Minuit, 1977). See discussions of women and language on 28-29, 72-82, 86-87, and 96-101.

12. Furthermore, in Duras's film, *India Song,* characters never converse directly, but instead anonymous voices emerge from the background. The viewer may or may not attach the voices to certain characters, may or may not distinguish individual traits in these disembodied sources of words.

   While the city is mere background in this film, the distinction between public life and private is a major theme. When the Vice-Consul says he must make a public act, he chooses to scream as he breaks his private silence.

13. Marguerite LeClézio, "Mother and Motherland: The Daughter's Quest for Origins," National Women's Studies Association, Bloomington, Ind., May 1980.

Gabriele Annan (essay date 1985)

SOURCE: "Saigon Mon Amour," in *The New York Review of Books,* Vol. XXXII, No. 11, June 27, 1985, pp. 11-12.

[*In the following review of* The Lover, *Annan examines Duras's motivations in the writing of the novella, as well as the book's phenomenal popular success.*]

Marguerite Duras is very much a member of the old French avant-garde. She published her first novel in 1943, wrote her first film script—*Hiroshima mon amour*—in 1959, and directed her first film in 1969. In 1968 she was a senior member of the writers' and students' revolutionary committee. So it is quite surprising that her latest novel was a runaway success in France last year, French readers being notoriously anxious to be on with the new. *L'Amant* appeared in the dead holiday month of August and is barely long enough to last through an afternoon on the beach. All the same, it quickly sold 60,000 copies and headed the best-seller list for months. In style and mood—the first cinematographic, the second a kind of dreamy melancholy streaked with anger—it is not so different from her previous work. Why did it do so sensationally well?

It is clearly an autobiographical novel. Like Duras herself, the anonymous first-person narrator is a writer who grew up in French Indochina before the war. She looks back at her adolescent self, and what happened to her then and the way she felt about it still have the power to shock, even though Duras explicitly makes her deny this right at the start:

> The story of one small part of my youth I've already written, more or less. . . . Now I'm talking about the hidden stretches of that same youth, of certain facts, feelings, events that I buried. I started to write in surroundings that drove me to reticence. Writing, for those people, was still something moral. Nowadays it often seems writing is nothing at all. Sometimes I realize that if writing isn't, all things, all contraries confounded, a quest for vanity and void, it's nothing. That if it's not, each time, all things confounded into one through some inexpressible essence, then writing is nothing but ad-

vertisement. But usually I have no opinion, I can see that all options are open now, that there seem to be no more barriers, that writing seems at a loss for somewhere to hide, to be written, to be read. That its basic unseemliness is no longer accepted.

The last statement is true, up to a point; but hardly for 60,000 readers. Whatever they may think about the existential (the word was bound to crop up in connection with a writer of Duras's generation) "unseemliness" of *The Lover,* some of them are bound to be shocked by the story and the way it is told.

The Lover is a sort of *Lolita* told by Lolita herself, and without the jokes. Humor, even just bearable lightness, has never been Duras's strong point. The original nymphet was a humorless girl too: it was Humbert Humbert who saw the ironies. Here there is no one to see them. Unlike Lolita, Duras's consciously seductive adolescent is born to like sex. She knows that, "You didn't have to attract desire. Either it was in the woman who aroused it or it didn't exist."

The girl is the youngest child in a family of poor whites. Her father is dead; her mother runs an elementary school up-country and is beset by Indian money lenders; her two brothers are ineducable. None of them has a name, and the two boys are referred to as "the killer" and "the hunter." This anthropological mythologizing adds nothing to the story or its significance. The killer is a bully and grows up to be a layabout sponging on and stealing from his mother. He torments the hunter, a backward boy with a passion for cars who gets on well with his sister. When she returns to Europe the hunter disappears from her life until she hears of his death ten years later. It comes as a cosmic trauma:

> It was a mistake, and that momentary error filled the universe. The outrage was on the scale of God. My younger brother was immortal and they hadn't noticed. Immortality had been concealed in my brother's body while he was alive, and we hadn't noticed that it dwelt there. Now my brother's body was dead, and immortality with it. . . .
>
> Since my younger brother was dead, everything had to die after him. And through him. Death, a chain reaction of death, started with him, the child.
>
> The corpse of the child was unaffected, itself, by the events of which it was the cause. Of the immortality it had harbored for the twenty-seven years of its life, it didn't know the name.
>
> No one saw clearly but I.

Well, no; and if they had, or could, the novel would lose some of its didactic point. Because, for all its dreaminess and steaminess, you feel that it is not just a recollection, still less a confession: the author is telling us something we ought to know. She is trying to pierce through our existential density, to reveal something.

Still, the narrative is very simple, though it dodges about in short takes between the present and various layers of the past. The key event—real, but also symbolic because it is a river crossing—occurs when the heroine is fifteen and a half. The brothers being what they are, her mother has pinned her ambition on her daughter: she is to get a degree in mathematics. To prepare for this, she has to attend the French *lycée* in Saigon and lodge in a state boarding school in the city. One day when she is returning there at the end of a holiday, she notices a chauffeur-driven limousine on the ferry across the Mekong River. "Inside the limousine there's a very elegant man looking at me. He's not a white man."

The shock effect of the negative "He's not a white man" is surely intentional. "Inside the limousine there's an elegant young Chinese" would be a much gentler introduction to the millionaire's feckless son who becomes infatuated with the girl. He is ten years older than she is, which is not very old since she's only fifteen. But he is always referred to as "the man" not "the young man," whereas she is "the little white girl," a description that plays up the age difference and adds to the "unseemliness" of the relationship across the color bar. The Chinese drives the girl back to the boarding school, and afterward fetches her every morning and brings her back every afternoon from the *lycée*. On the way they sleep together in his apartment in the Chinese quarter. The heat is unbearable, and only a thin blind separates them from the Chinese crowd milling about outside the ground floor window. It is the girl who encourages him to take her virginity. The first day,

> She says, I'd rather you didn't love me. But if you do, I'd like you to do as you usually do with women. He looks at her in horror, asks, Is that what you want? . . . She tells him he doesn't want him to talk, what she wants is for him to do as he usually does with the women he brings to his flat. She begs him to do that. . . .
>
> The skin is sumptuously soft. The body. The body is thin, lacking in strength, in muscle, he may have been ill, may be convalescent, he's hairless, nothing masculine about him but his sex, he's weak, probably a helpless prey to insult, vulnerable. She doesn't look him in the face. Doesn't look at him at all. She touches him. Touches the softness of his sex, his skin, caresses his goldenness, the strange novelty. He moans, weeps. In dreadful love.

The affair lasts eighteen months, until the girl's mother takes her family back to France, and the lover is forced into an arranged marriage with a sixteen-year-old Chinese heiress. The relationship is nothing but sex. The lovers never talk except to bandy banalities like tennis balls. They know nothing about each other. There is never any question of marriage. The millionaire would disinherit his son if he married a white girl; she does not want to marry at all; and the white family despises the lover so much that when he takes them to eat in expensive restaurants they won't even speak to him. The mother knows her daughter has lost all chances of marrying in the colony; she is considered a disgrace, a little whore.

The French may not be as obsessed as the British are by their colonial past, but they too feel a mixture of curiosity, shame, anger, and nostalgia about it. Duras plays up to these emotions. She writes marvelously, hauntingly, about the heat, the sweat, the vast deltas, the sunsets, the moonlit nights, the terrible tropical melancholy. As one would expect, she is particularly good on the wives:

> Some of them are very beautiful, very white, they take enormous care of their beauty here, especially upcountry. They don't do anything, just save themselves up, save themselves up for Europe. . . . They look at themselves. In the shade of their villas, they look at themselves for later on, they dream of romance, they already have huge wardrobes full of more dresses than they know what to do with, added to one by one like time, like the long days of waiting.

Duras does not incarnate the colonial presence in any subsidiary characters, but she makes it constantly felt. It is both an added interest and the *donnée* of her story, the thing that makes the girl's behavior so scandalous (the mother does not really mind). The scandal is in the eye of the beholder, the voyeur's eye of colonial society observing the child.

And she herself is a voyeur too: "I used to watch what he did with me, how he used me, and I'd never thought anyone could act like that, he acted beyond my hope and in accordance with my body's destiny." Her sexuality extends to the only other white girl at the boarding school, a dumb cluck with a beautiful body and almost the only other person in the book to have a name:

> I am worn out with desire for Hélène Lagonelle.
>
> I am worn out with desire.
>
> I want to take Hélène Lagonelle with me to where every evening, my eyes shut, I have imparted to me the pleasure that makes you cry out. I'd like to give Hélène Lagonelle to the man who does that to me, so he may do it in turn to her. I want it to happen in my presence, I want her to do it as I wish, I want her to give herself where I give myself. It's via Hélène Lagonelle's body, through it, that the ultimate pleasure would pass from him to me.
>
> A pleasure unto death.

"A pleasure unto death," or "love unto death," is repeated over and over again, one of those incantations that Duras is fond of (who can forget the tolling of the word "Nevers" in *Hiroshima?*). The phrase ends the book when, years after the war, the lover travels to Paris with his wife, telephones his former mistress, and tells her "that it was as before, that he still loved her, he could never stop loving her, that he'd love her until death."

Well, that is a comprehensible and even conventional last line. But what does Duras mean when earlier on she writes: "Both are doomed to discredit because of the kind of body they have, caressed by lovers, kissed by their lips, consigned to the infamy of a pleasure unto death, as they both call it, unto the mysterious death of lovers without love. That's what it's all about: this hankering for death."

Perhaps it doesn't mean anything so very new or strange, but is merely there to create a sexy, doom-laden atmosphere, a tropical Tristan and Isolde *Stimmung*. *The Oxford Companion to Film* entry on *Hiroshima* says that the film "contains remarkable innovations, and reveals the possibilities of a new literary cinema. . . . Sound, instead of merely explaining and supporting the visual story, is conceived as a vital and independent component; word, image, and music stand in a contrapuntal relationship, giving a new expressive resonance." Duras seems to be syphoning back into the novel what she learned on the set: how to make a *Gesamtkunstwerk* by combining sound and image, the words not necessarily having a precise meaning, but simply enhancing image, mood, and feeling.

It is with images, mood, and feeling that she is at her best, which is very good indeed (with ideas she can be affected, portentous, and irritating). In this novel she uses her incantations and other magic arts to create a powerful sexual impact. She is hypnotizing the reader into feeling what it feels like to be a highly sexed girl of fifteen. Probably she will succeed in turning him on; or anyway her. Then is *The Lover* pornography? Or an experiment to see what can be done with words? Certainly not the former. Duras herself would be the one to be shocked at that idea. But the latter probably yes. Only one must keep in mind that it is not virtuosity for its own sake she cares about, but magic, transformation, making a vent in the curtain that hides—what?

Sven Birkerts (essay date 1985)

SOURCE: "Marguerite Duras," in *An Artificial Wilderness: Essays on 20th-Century Literature,* William Morrow and Company, Inc., 1987, pp. 163-70.

[*In the following essay, originally published in the* Boston Phoenix *in 1985, Birkerts discusses the minimalistic prose of* The Lover.]

Minimalism is, for the practitioner, one of the more seductive literary modes. Like abstract painting, it looks easy, and as most of the action takes place in the realm of the unstated, the writer need not be bothered with the messy mechanics of plot or character development. Hemingway bewitched several generations of prose stylists with his primer-simple narratives and his aesthetic of exclusion: the unstated emotion, he maintained, can pack as much of a wallop as the stated one. In his hands the technique often worked—the early stories and novels, especially, quiver with repressed materials; but his legion of imitators the world over have given understatement a bad name. Few of them have bothered to learn the all-important corollary to that aesthetic—that the emotion, though not declared, must nevertheless exist. Most of us, I suspect, now balk when confronted with a page of fashionably lean prose. Dress it up how you will, I say it's spinach and I say to hell with it.

Rules make life ordinary, but exceptions make it bearable. A handful of unexpected masterpieces in the last few decades—Max Frisch's *Montauk,* James Salter's *A Sport and a Pastime,* and Lars Gustafsson's *The Death of a Beekeeper* come to mind—have shown that literary minimalism is still a viable enterprise. To this short list I would add Marguerite Duras's Goncourt Prize-winning novella, *The Lover.*

Duras's book presents, in flashback, the story of an adolescent French girl's coming of age—mostly in terms of her sexual involvement with an older Chinese man—in colonial Saigon in the 1930's. It is not, as some reviewers have suggested, a straight-faced remake of *Lolita.* The bond between these lovers is more existential than erotic. Indeed, the obsessive intensity of their coupling hints, according to minimalist precepts of exclusion, at the pervasiveness of the despair they hope to extinguish. Readers might find themselves blinking away images from Resnais's *Hiroshima Mon Amour,* for which Duras wrote the script.

The narrator—I will not make so bold as to call her Duras, though the biographical particulars seems to match up—begins her telling with an encounter from the present. An old acquaintance approaches her on the street and delivers the following compliment: "Everyone says you were beautiful when you were young, but I want to tell you I think you're more beautiful now than then. Rather than your face as a young woman, I prefer your face as it is now. Ravaged." The word echoes like a pistol shot in an empty street. We know we are in for anything but a lighthearted romp through the past.

The first third of the book hovers around a single image, a memory from the narrator's youth that is as composed and static as a photograph. "It might have existed," she writes, "a photograph might have been taken, just like any other, somewhere else, in other circumstances. But it wasn't. The subject was too slight." A girl, age fifteen and a half (the specificity tells us at once of the struggle between girlishness and precocity), stands by herself at the rail of a ferry crossing the Mekong River. She is on her way to her boarding school in Saigon; she's dressed in a hand-me-down silk dress, an exotic pair of gold lamé high heels, and a flat-brimmed pink hat with a broad black ribbon. Duras devotes several pages to her apparel, describing the acquisition of each item. But what we are really getting is a series of glimpses into a melancholy, fatherless childhood. An observation like the following tells us more about the family situation than pages of patient characterization:

> When my mother emerges, comes out of her despair, she sees the man's hat and the gold lamé shoes. She asks what it's all about. I say nothing. She looks at me, is pleased, smiles. Not bad, she says, they quite suit you, make a change. She doesn't ask if it's she who bought them, she knows she did.

There is, of course, another reason why the image is so painstakingly examined. The girl at the rail is just moments away from her fateful encounter. She has already taken note of the long black limousine and the gentleman watching her through the window; the promise of his otherness has already begun to penetrate her self-absorption.

A solitary, beguiling girl at a turning point in her life, inhaling the last air of innocence . . . The fantasy is an easy one to fall in with. But, as the puzzle books put it, something is wrong with this picture. And the more Duras keeps returning to it, the more we sense that. Carefully inserted vignettes and background details gradually force us to abandon the Pollyanna drift of our reverie. The girl on the barge is inwardly cauterized. Living in gloomy tropical houses with a half-mad mother and two tormented brothers has long since destroyed any joyous freshness in her. She is going through the paces of late adolescence with a cool detachment. Not lust, but a need even deeper—a need to be touched, to be certified as existing—makes her respond to the man's overtures.

Readers lured on by the promise of titillation will be disappointed. They will find no elaborate seduction scene, no fetishism (the gold lamé heels are a bit of naturalism, not a come-on), no variations on the themes of master/slave or colonialism-in-the-boudoir. These are just two strangers, adrift, frightened, and almost entirely opaque to themselves. He—no name is given—is a rich man's son, uncentered by wealth and idleness; he trembles when he offers her a cigarette and later can scarcely bring himself to touch her. She, in turn, tells him: "I'd rather you didn't love me. But if you do, I'd like you to do as you usually do with women." Their interchanges go largely unreported. But Duras does not need conversation to bring across the shuddering immediacy of the first bodily encounter or the emergent contours of their relationship:

> The skin is sumptuously soft. The body is thin, lacking in strength, in muscle, he may have been ill, may be convalescent, he's hairless, nothing masculine about him but his sex, he's weak, probably a prey to insult, vulnerable. She doesn't look him in the face. Doesn't look at him at all. She touches him. Touches the softness of his sex, his skin, caresses his goldness, the strange novelty. He moans, weeps. In dreadful love.

We wonder, momentarily, about that "dreadful love" but dismiss it as a young girl's ignorant perception. Neither do we find, as months pass, that anything resembling love develops between them. They have their ritual. He picks her up at school in his limousine, they go to his room in the city's Chinese quarter, he drives her back. We almost never hear them exchange words; their lovemaking is fierce, but in Duras's telling affectless: there is no apparent progress in their affections. When, from time to time, he takes the girl's mother and brothers out to dinner, no one talks. She explains to him that they are like that with everyone. The dominant impression is of claustrophobic unreality, as if this man and girl had been excerpted from the space-time continuum.

The affair continues for a year and a half. Then, one day, the girl is told that the family is returning to France, that passage has been booked. There is no shock or panic; any tremors they might feel travel inward. We get this flat report: "Once the date of my departure was fixed, distant though it still was, he could do nothing with my body any more."

The parting is simple, cinematic. The girl sees the black limousine on the pier as her boat pulls away. They will never see each other again. Years later she will learn that he has married a girl chosen for him by his parents. The unhappy business is consigned to memory, becomes a painful episode in what the French fondly call *l'éducation sentimentale*. Until, suddenly, in a time near the present ("years after the war, after marriage, children, divorces, books . . ."), he calls her. He is in Paris, traveling with his wife. He has followed her career, her literary successes. They converse nervously. "They didn't know what to say. And then he told her. Told her that it was as before, that he still loved her, he could never stop loving her, that he'd love her until death." With these words the book ends.

A sketchy chronicle like this cannot account for the power of *The Lover,* which derives as much from its silences as from its narrative. Duras's decision to present the story as a memory, to let a half century of vanished time function as a sounding chamber, is a brilliant one. Had the story been told in the present, the reticence, the terse notations, would have seemed mannered. This way, though, the spareness reveals as nothing else can the harsh abrasions of time. The woman with the ravaged face has given us a disturbing picture of the workings of destiny.

The Lover is saturated with a peculiarly Gallic ennui. As a result, the final lines break in on the gloom swiftly and unexpectedly. The telephone conversation transfigures everything. Both man and affair take on a retroactive profundity, invalidating our dismissal. This, in turn, makes the image of the limousine on the pier the very emblem of ill-starred love. The tale is rewritten in the space of a breath; its density, depth, and hopelessness become even more pervasive. Now, however, his love—its mysterious persistence—flings a beam of light into the darkness. And we can't help but steer our way toward it.

The Lover was published here in 1985 to considerable acclaim, garnering for Duras the wider recognition that had eluded her before through a long career as a novelist and script writer. Readers were as much taken with the trembling staccato of her narrative style as they were with the narrative itself. That eerie and lacerating work will doubtless be invoked in most assessments of *The War: A Memoir* (1986). For this prose, too, is voiced through a numbed, life-scarred "I," and concerns itself, at least in part, with the ambiguities of love and the immense difficulty of bridging the space that exists between even the most kindred of souls.

Similarities do abound, but it is the primary difference that is most instructive. *The Lover* was written in the near present, after the passing of decades had stripped off emotional clutter and had left only the bleached residues of event. *The War,* on the other hand, comprises a diary and several memoirs and stories written by Duras in the 1940's; the main sections, she claims in a short preface, were put down in exercise books and forgotten. The first of these, "The War," is still mysterious to the author: "I recognize my handwriting and the details of the story. . . . But I can't see myself writing the diary. When would I have done so, in what year, at what times of day, in what house?" The congruity between works—the one remembered, the other forgotten—almost suggests that there is a deeper "writing self" that stands apart from the movements of time and circumstance.

The War has five sections. The longest of these, "The War" and "Monsieur X, Here Called Pierre Rabier," are directly autobiographical, and form, along with the thinly disguised (Duras admits it) story "Albert of the Capital/Ter of the Militia," the compelling core of the book. The two slight tales grafted to the end, "The Crushed Nettle" and "Aurelia Paris," lack the peculiar quiver that Duras's manipulation of her own persona invariably provides.

"The War" is, quite simply, a diary that was begun by the author when she heard that the German camps were being liberated. Her husband, identified only as Robert L., had been shipped to Belsen during the occupation for his resistance activities. Duras would not find out for a month if he was among the survivors or not. The entries—sometimes several for a single day—forge a nearly unendurable chronicle of fear and morbid fantasy. Time is registered not on the clock but in the nerve endings:

> You don't exist anymore in comparison with this waiting. More images pass through your head than there are on all the roads in Germany. Bursts of machine gun fire every minute inside your head. And yet you're still there, the bullets aren't fatal. Shot in transit. Dead with an empty stomach. His hunger wheels around in your head like a vulture.

Duras tries to quell her agony by giving up hope. But, alas, one cannot control the mechanism with a resolve. She can only endure her dread. She works, spends long days in transit centers, helping others. Still, she cannot stop herself from prowling among the endless lines of returnees, scanning faces. The horror of it all nearly finishes her off. Then the call comes: Robert L. is alive.

Duras's pain does not end with Robert L.'s return—it just becomes more specific. For now the worst imaginings have been replaced by a reality that almost defies language. Every resource, we sense, is mustered to get the words to the page. No other choice is allowed. Only through the most precise accounting will history be served. Man must be able to look at what Man has done:

> The head was connected to the body by the neck, as heads usually are, but the neck was so withered and shrunken—you could circle it with one hand—that you wondered how life could pass through it; a spoonful of gruel almost blocked it. . . . You could see the verte-

brae through it, the carotid arteries, the nerves, the pharynx, and the blood passing through: the skin had become like cigarette paper.

This, I may add, is the mildest of her reports.

The love we find here is not romantic, but biological. We feel Duras's struggle to reverse, through the most patient ministrations, the destruction wrought by an enemy that despised the human miracle. Astonishingly enough, the body is revealed to be the vessel for an entity more precious still: ". . . it was then, by his deathbed, that I knew him, Robert L., best, that I understood forever what made him himself, himself alone and nothing and no one else in the world. . . ." The diary breaks off with Robert L.'s recovery.

The other autobiographical sections are not nearly as harrowing. Both, however, give us sustained insight into the hectic and treacherous life in resistance cadres. In "Monsieur X," the more complex of the pieces, Duras depicts her desperate cat-and-mouse involvement with a young Gestapo officer (he claims to know the whereabouts of Robert L.). Fear, anxiety, and—yes—fascination are plaited with a slender filament of pity. Her devotion to justice—she finally denounces the man to her comrades—does not blind her to the uncertainty they share. Indeed, this is the quality that distinguishes Duras as a writer. On every page we hear a woman who is unable to hide from the truth, whose strength must take root in the hardest place—the far side of vulnerability.

Anna Otten (essay date 1987)

SOURCE: "Fiction," in *The Antioch Review,* Vol. 45, No. 1, Winter, 1987, pp. 112-13.

[*In the following review, Otten deems* The Lover *a "parable of French colonialism."*]

Winner of the prestigious Prix Goncourt in 1984, *The Lover* was acclaimed as a major literary event and has been translated into all major world languages. Labeled nonfiction, the work repeats autobiographical material already present in *The Sea Wall* (*Un barrage contre le Pacifique,* 1950). The narrative presents the life of Saigon in the 1930s under the rule of French colonialism, where the life of the heroine parallels that of Duras, who was born there in 1914. Duras was brought up by her mother after her father's death, had two brothers, left Saigon in 1932, studied mathematics in Paris, and wanted to write. Yet the work cannot be classified as memoir because it is primarily fictional and a parable of French colonialism.

This love story, compared to the world's great tales of passion, is rather simple. A poor middle-class French high-school girl of fifteen becomes the mistress of a rich Chinese, twelve years older than herself, from whom she accepts money. Divided by age and racial and social barriers, they cannot marry but still cling together passionately. The story has a sad ending: he marries a rich girl and she leaves for France. Yet this potentially banal story is fascinating because of Duras's art as a storyteller. The colonial upper class is set off from the gray existence of the natives who struggle for survival amidst corruption, oppression, and human degradation. The heroine considers herself a prostitute. She sometimes loves but later hates her mother. She exchanges banalities with her lover. Yet the story fascinates us because of the revelation of hidden feelings and forgotten events that gradually assume form in the mind of the narrator and of the reader. Written unemotionally, this tale of masters and servants is much like a film scenario where a great variety of images fly by. There is passion, serenity, chatter, tenderness, servility, beauty, despair, abject poverty, rebellion, and dream. Life around the child/woman is full of contrasts and diversity, like the people along the shores of the Mekong. Like the Mekong, everything moves on, forever. Two lovers, separated by time and space, have always been a favorite subject matter for myth. In a humble way, this book is a myth of our time.

Sharon Willis (essay date 1987)

SOURCE: "Introduction," in *Marguerite Duras: Writing on the Body,* University of Illinois Press, 1987, pp. 1-11.

[*In the following introduction to her book* Marguerite Duras: Writing on the Body, *Willis focuses on* The Lover *in her examination of Duras's "transgressive" texts.*]

Long a respected figure on the French literary scene, Marguerite Duras eludes any effort to situate her work in a fixed area. In the over forty years she has been publishing, her work has always resisted easy classification, in part because she produces novels, plays, and films simultaneously. To date, she has produced over twenty novels, nearly as many plays, numerous essays in the lively exchanges of French journals, and a number of films, her filmic production having evolved from early scriptwriting and collaborative efforts on *Hiroshima mon amour* and ***Moderato cantabile*** to her more recent work as a director executing her own concepts. Occupying several fields at once, Duras' work sets up a series of exchanges among them, particularly because it often produces narrative, theatrical and filmic incarnations of the same themes and scenes.

Duras' texts resist generic convention: films without narration (*La Femme du Gange, Nathalie Granger*), novels composed of visual figures (*Le Ravissement de Lol V. Stein, India Song, L'Homme atlantique*), film scenarios that read like novels (*India Song, Hiroshima mon amour, Aurélia Steiner*), theater and films in which the actors read, rather than perform, their roles (*Le Camion, La Maladie de la mort*). Her significance in the French literary scene no doubt derives in part from that position—between novels, theater, and film—as if no medium could convey a final version of a story. Significantly, most of her titles carry a generic label as well, as if we would not be able to determine the status of the object without it.

Duras disappoints—or perhaps deceives? French has an admirable double meaning for the word *décevoir,* which can mean either disappoint or deceive. In their invariable display that something is missing, her fictions are about expectations unfulfilled. Perhaps it is this potential for deception and withholding that makes her fiction alluring. This is not a passive disappointment, for Duras' force lies in her active subversion of expectation and demand. Her novels, films, and theater effectively defy generic bounds because they are inevitably rewritings or restagings of scenes that persist throughout her work. But even as repetition, they fail to satisfy *that* expectation entirely—the repetition is never quite the same. Something similar might be said of the writer herself, as a figure on the literary scene. The elusiveness of her texts is replicated in the mobility of her own position; as film producer, playwright and novelist, she is difficult to situate. As such, she may figure the subterranean contradictions and exchanges that ground literary production as a political and historical field as well. Reading her work may be a means of reading certain shifts and contradictions that make literary production what it is today in France, a complex exchange between theoretical and artistic production that yields perpetual efforts to explore and transform the encoding of literary and cinematic practice. Along with the constant repositioning that characterizes her work, Duras' elusiveness as a literary figure is no doubt one of the sources of fascination for readers—the artist exploring a variety of practices that contest and criticize one another.

Part of the task of situating Duras as a figure is to explore the sources and effects of the fascination she exercises upon the reader. Her obsessional method yields a variety of effects, not the least of which is a curious tension between familiarity and estrangement produced by the reappearance of figures in a series of texts, since these repeated figures inscribe an obsession that has all the features of a private, personal drama, despite its near-anonymous character, its feeling of authorlessness. The sense of uncanny familiarity then extends to figurations of the author within the work, as the origin of their obsessions. It becomes difficult to separate the figure of the author from her work, the life story from the emblems it inscribes in the obscurity of its textual references. That is, part of the reader's fascination depends on the effort to locate the author's traces in the work, to follow the clues, reconstruct *her* figure.

Duras' earliest narratives, beginning with *Les Impudents* (1943), and including her better-known *Un barrage contre le Pacifique* (1950) (which has just appeared in English as *The Sea Wall* [London: Hamish Hamilton, 1985]), *Le Marin de Gibraltar* (1952), and ***Moderato cantabile*** (1958), all present a linear narrative development, even though they bear the traces of the later textual obsession with memory and desire, locked together in repetition, which will become the performance of repetition that characterizes the later texts, from the 1960s onward—*Dix heures et demie du soir en été, L'Après-midi de Monsieur Andesmas*, and the Lol V. Stein cycle. These texts perform the repetition they thematize, reducing narrative movement to a minimum. Increasingly, each text recalls previous ones, isolating fragments, scenes, details, and figures that appeared in a larger context in an earlier text. Duras' work, taken as a whole, appears based on fragmentation and dispersion. This serial focus on the fragment is consistent with a certain "postmodern" concern for the broken piece, for the shattered totality and for serial repetition of a minimal set of elements. However, in their refusal of textual boundaries—their intertextual recall and perpetual rewriting—the texts from the 1960s to the present resemble more one long narrative than a series. They constitute a sort of inverted *A la recherche du temps perdu,* substituting dispersal for recollection. It is this feature that establishes Duras' difficulty of access. Beginning with the Lol V. Stein texts—*Le Ravissement de Lol V. Stein, Le Vice-consul, L'Amour* and *India Song* and *La Femme du Gange*—it is difficult to read one Duras text without the support of the others. To read *one* is to become caught in a cycle of repetition and to know it, so that the reader follows a set of relays through other texts in a search that parallels the texts' own obsessive repetition. While it is possible to read a text in isolation, one only feels the force of the narrative mechanism, or strategy, through retroaction, a retroaction that develops after several readings, producing a sense that what one reads was "already read."

As such, Duras' texts exemplify a resistance to consumption and disposability. Instead, they demand perpetual re-readings; they do not consolidate a singular message that, once received, is finished off in the act of consumption. These are not books to consume and throw away. Rather, they offer an apprenticeship in another form of reading, based on repetition and intertextual circulation. At the same time, however, they demand an engagement, a commitment on the part of the reader, a willingness not to finish, not to advance, but to return, to repeat, to read the entire corpus, since the legibility of a given text is dependent upon the others. Such repetition then calls into question and reframes literary reception as being itself a process of inscription.

This picture of Duras' work has just taken yet another shape, and with it, the picture of Duras herself. The publication of *L'Amant* (1984) and its nearly immediate translation into English as *The Lover* (translation Barbara Bray [New York: Pantheon, 1985]) marks Duras' first really popular success. Heretofore, as a novelist, she has not had such popular success in France, although her plays have been produced with regularity in the past few years. In the United States, her work is virtually unknown, and is considered rather inaccessible, at best. With the publication of *L'Amant,* which won the Prix Goncourt and subsequently sold over 700,000 copies within six months of its publication in France, I find myself wanting to account for such an unexpected phenomenon. Once again, Duras disappoints, deceives?

It's not just a compulsion to account for literary phenomena, to situate them in fixed and irrevocable categories, that motivates my explorations here, but rather the desire to take into account the fact that Duras' work is again crossing boundaries and thereby throwing them into question. In this case, the work questions the boundaries between "high" and "low" culture, between academic and popular, or mass-reception, literature, which may be emblematic of certain conjunctions and certain shifts in literary production and reception.

While Duras' most recent text is structured according to a more familiar and legible narrative order, it also displays the ambivalences that characterize her more difficult work. The June 9, 1985, issue of the *New York Times Book Review* carried a full-page advertisement for **The Lover** which highlights, unconsciously, the text's doubleness. First, there is the contrast between the external face of the text—its cover, or, more figuratively, the publishers' and critics' discourse surrounding it, as a sort of packaging within which it is offered to the public—and the contradiction it strikes with the text's inner face—the content, the letter of the text. The ad announces "Duras' incandescent novel of first love," and includes a *Saturday Review* comment that "this exotic, erotic autobiographical confession will deservedly become one of the summer's hottest books." Catchy as that sounds, one is most struck by the doubleness and the contradiction within the ad, between "novel of first love" and "autobiographical confession," a contradiction never resolved. One might argue that this is more than an oversight; in its groping way, this superficial, perfectly ordinary copy has hit the mark: **The Lover** is profoundly ambivalent, undecided. In its narrative vacillation between "I" and "she," this mostly linear textual organization will not be pinned to the conventional confessional or fictional modes.

Indeed, one suspects that part of the appeal of this text lies in its duplicity, its pretense to confession coupled with its refusal to swear to truthfulness (thereby replicating a standard feminine icon, the woman who seduces by her duplicity). The reader's pleasure is that of hearing the private "exotic and erotic" confession, these qualifiers not to be taken at all lightly. Clearly, despite the third person narrative intervention, many will want to read this text as strict autobiography, taking pleasure in its erotic side (this is the story of a sexual initiation and a first love affair), and its exotic side (set in Indochina in the 1930s, it recounts a "forbidden," or at least socially proscribed, affair between a Chinese man and a European woman). Not only does the text contain many parallels with Duras' own life (she was born in Cochin China, a part of what was then Indochina and is now Vietnam, in 1914), but it opens with a lyrical but brutal description of the narrator's/author's face. It is that description that has prompted critics to turn to Duras' face, to images from her youth and contemporary ones, in focusing their comments. Diane Johnson concludes her review of **The Lover** (*New York Times Book Review,* June 25, 1985) with a reference to its author's beauty. And Michel Tournier, in *Vanity Fair,* July, 1985, devotes most of his article on *The Lover* to scrutiny of Duras' face, study of her image, speculation on her ethnic origins. A text that begins with the face of its author, although it contains no images, and that elaborates a prolonged description of the author as a subtext to the love story, is, in a sense, a book about shaping a figure. The disfiguration of the face (figura) may be its real subject.

At the same time, as a result of a particular coincidence with the literary market, Duras is cutting a figure in the commercial scene, cutting a figure that cuts across literary boundaries—between popular and high culture, between the novel and autobiography, between the figure and the face. And, I think, her new success is in part due to her capacity to be a figure, and the coincidence of that capacity with readers' desire for a fascinating woman author-figure. Like her book, it seems, she is an erotic and exotic figure.

But what is this figure, exactly? What is singular about Duras is her resistance to a single reading or appropriation, immobilization in a fixed frame. Similarly, the complex configurations of her texts raise hard questions about the connections between eroticism, pleasure, and power, sometimes in violent forms. Therefore, we must see the figure of prostitution in *The Lover* as having several faces, or registers. It might be read as the literalization of a persistent metaphor for the marginal economic status of literary production in Western culture: the author as prostituted to the literary market. In that case, *The Lover* is an ironic figure for the writer's ambivalence about her insertion into market relations, or for the public's discomfort with that insertion, a discomfort based, on the one hand, on a false separation between art and the profane matter of making a living, and, on the other hand, on a resistance to the appropriation of all artistic practice as an object of consumption. As readers and consumers, then, we can't escape certain reflections on our own position.

But *The Lover* is also a figure of transgression, and not just in the common way, as a woman writing her erotic memoirs, "telling all" about an affair. Rather, Duras the author can be linked to the woman of her story—the alcoholic woman, parading her devastation and her survival, and recounting her past as an "exotic" seductress. She was raised in Indochina, and grew up bilingual, although she spoke Vietnamese everywhere but at home until age eighteen, when she departed to study in France. She is thus the "Other" within, a strangely familiar, or familiarly estranged, figure—a "non-Western" Western woman. In this double-faced figure of Duras, we might then read our own anxiety about the Other, as well as our desire to incorporate the other, to reduce difference. However, given the text's strategy of veiling and unveiling, where "I" veils herself as "she," but where "she" just as frequently masquerades as "I," we cannot maintain a rigid and secure separation of same and other, interior and exterior. Nor can we as readers determine and fortify a fixed vantage point, and the reassuring distance that that would entail. We are implicated in the issues the text raises and refuses to put to rest.

It is not accidental that it is with a novel that is explicitly erotic that Duras gains popular recognition. No doubt this is one of the pleasures of the text—the woman represented here passes from virgin to prostitute, a passage motivated by transports of passion unleashed by the appeal of the forbidden. But what differentiates this text from a pornographic scenario is precisely its attentiveness to the complex of erotic impulses that motivate both the affair and the narcissistic confessional enterprise. This text explores with subtlety the subtext of a passionate affair, a subtext filled with violence and brutality, since it takes up the problems of separation and loss, power and domination, within a social and familial scene, as well as the private space of the two lovers. The text displays the complex connections of sexual pleasure and violence, and sexual pleasure and economics, as the woman more or less prostitutes herself to the man, allows herself to be kept, and uses her power over him to extort money for her brothers' entertainment.

Like some other recent Duras texts (*L'Homme assis dans le couloir*, *Agatha*, *La Maladie de la mort*), this is a text whose erotically appealing passages are linked to a devastating violence and negativity. Traces of this effect appear in most of her love stories, and the conjunction of domination and desire appears in better-known early texts like *Hiroshima mon amour* and ***Moderato cantabile,*** and even as early as the short story **"Whole Days in the Trees"** (1954). Until *The Lover,* however, these earlier narratives seemed to be the form in which these configurations could be most easily tolerated; the violent fragmentation of their more recent embodiments render them too disturbing. This version, in fact, retroactively facilitates our access to the earlier texts of the 1980s, since it repeats the scenes they offer. Consequently, to read them in view of *The Lover,* and to read *The Lover* as part of a series of narratives rooted in erotic fantasies and exploring their lability, clarifies the stakes of this form of representation.

The figure of an exhibitionist female subject should have special force for feminist readers. Duras has long been a central figure for feminist readers and critics, in both the United States and France, in part because she is one of the most prominent contemporary French woman writers. More important, her work centers on issues of concern to most feminist theoretical enterprises: desire and sexuality, gender and biology, the relation of the body to language.

The Lover reinscribes the exhibitionist scenario in a woman's active self-display, a presentation of her life as spectacle—active, that is, as opposed to the passive form of woman as object of spectacle for a mastering gaze, that of reader or spectator. As such, the text is a complex structure: an erotic tale which is not based on representation of a woman as object, but which constitutes a narcissistic parade. Its seductive effects operate not only within the narrated scenes, but also, and perhaps most powerfully, in the autobiographical register, as the "I" veils itself in "she," giving us a new version of the seductive intermittence of erotic spectacle. Duras evades us, as she attracts us, in an alternating play of veiling and unveiling.

A similar ambivalence is central to readings of the sadistic edge to eroticism, as it is depicted in *The Lover* and, even more powerfully, in texts like *La Maladie de la mort, Agatha, Détruire, dit-elle,* and *L'Homme assis dans le couloir.* And this ambivalence is crucial, since it firmly links pleasure and violence, demanding that the reader confront their imbrication in desire and sexuality. Duras' transgressive impulse extends to an area of particular concern for feminist thought at the moment: the politics of pleasure, the relation between pleasure and power. Where her texts raise the question of how pleasure and power, desire and violence, are related, they invite us to imagine other forms in which these terms might be configured. In order to do so, we must give up our impulse to maintain a rigid separation between pleasure and power, desire and violence, just as we recognize the complex construction of gender identification as part of a process, a social articulation of the body. For these reasons, Duras is not only a compelling figure for feminist critics, but a crucial site of interrogation for theoretical enterprises concerned with the articulation of pleasure and power in representation and sexuality.

Finally, the transgressive nature of this text operates on another level as well; transgressing the conventions of erotic literature, and crossing the boundary between "difficult" and popular fiction, this text allows us to explore the complexity and ambivalence entailed in representing feminine sexuality within a more popularly available form than her previous texts. It may allow us to map the effects of such representation within the framework of popular consumption. Certainly, feminist theory has long debated the historical significance of these boundaries and their effects on women's production and reception of art and literature. Does one betray a feminist project, origins, or goals by becoming popular? Or by refusing to be popularly accessible? And here, my own position is uncertain, as I try to render Duras more accessible. Do I mislead by proposing that the uninitiated reader explore her work? Do I subvert the force of her project by trying to make it more available, more legible; do I situate it within a false framework of interest? These final questions, significant for a literary critic and a feminist, indicate the range and scope of the terrain Duras' textual transgressions open for us, since they demand nothing less than the reconsideration of our operative categories of literary production and reception.

Doris T. Wight (essay date 1988)

SOURCE: "A Game Played: 'Moderato Cantabile,'" in *The USF Language Quarterly,* Vol. XXVI, Nos. 3-4, Spring-Summer, 1988, pp. 32-4.

[*In the following essay, Wight asserts that the principal characters of* Moderato cantabile *work out their issues through Freudian game-playing.*]

Game-playing can surely provide a major sport for both participants and viewers. And game-playing can supply dangerous sport—both psychologically (in actual life) and allogorically (in literature). In Marguerite Duras' story *Moderato Cantabile,* for instance, a real-life problem faced by many women is depicted on the page, here, while a little boy watched by his mother takes a lesson from his piano teacher, a certain meaningful play is being played.

Sigmund Freund described another game played by another child that might throw light on the piano lesson scene in *Moderato Cantabile.* The child Freud watched was seeking to solve a personal problem. The little boy suffered agonies whenever his mother left his sight. Now, in an instinctive effort to work this out, the child has invented a game about his mother's occasional disappearances, and he plays this game with himself. The child has an object tied to a string, a treasure representing his mother. As he plays, the child by dropping the object behind something makes it disappear from sight, upon which he anxiously cries out "Fort!" (*away*; *gone*). Next, by pulling his string, the little boy causes the treasure to reappear and himself to joyously call out "Da!" (*here*; *le voici*). After a moment, the child symbolically makes his mother go away again, ("Fort!"), brings her back to prove to himself that he is the one truly in control after all ("Da!"), and so on. Through the game, painful anxiety is mastered, at least in the symbolic realm. Jacques Lacan makes these observations on the Fort/Da game described by Freud:

> This game shows in its radical features the determinacy which the human animal receives from the symbolic system. . . . The game provides an illuminating insight into the individual's entry into an order the mass of which supports and welcomes him in the form of language, and which superimposes the determination of the signified.

(*Écrits,* pp. 46-47)

Back now to that Duras story with a game being played in the opening scene, the piano lesson. At first glance, the situation might seem to reënact Fort/Da, with the piano teacher analogous to Fort/Da's little boy with the piano student becoming the object manipulated on the string, and with mother watching as a stand-in spectator for us, readers about Fort/Da. In no time, however, we find that such an interpretation won't work. *Moderato Cantabile* is not about a piano teacher's effort to work out her frustration with a troublesome pupil. And as we read on, watching the child's relatively-happy, relatively-normal, relatively-secure and untroubled behavior, we know that the story's undercurrent does not center on some life-and-death struggle within the little boy. Instead, as we live through the events' unfolding, we feel developing an excruciating tension within, and a strange love parable developing without, the child's mother.

From the first scene on, Anne Desbaresdes is anything but the passive observer she appears to be. It is she who will not allow the little pianist's sonatina to be played, as the teacher desires, *moderato cantabile.* She does not even permit her child to answer his instructor's question about the definition of the term, although he knows it perfectly well. How is this? What game can this be, enacted before us late on a Friday afternoon with the sun—again symbolically—just about to set in a great bloody-golden blaze? What problem needing solution dictates this game being played in the lives of Mlle. Giraud, teacher of the upper-class children in this little seacoast town living off its foundries, off the only son of the town's wealthiest inhabitant, and off the wife of that unseen powerful figure?

Let us begin afresh to try to understand the game's playing board. Yes, the child sitting there captive at at the piano beneath a window through which comes the enticing sounds of the sea and at the same time of the voices of lower-class but free children, that child signifies something dominated, an object, ostensibly of his music teacher. And that music teacher, Mlle Giraud, signifies what dominates: authority, the subject, operating will.

Yet this subject is herself an object, is she not? Is she not subject to pleasing Mme Desbaresdes, who has hired her? In this case Mlle Giraud herself is an object, an economic object hired to play the role of subject over her little false-object pupil. At the moment this little pupil responding to subtle commands of his mother ten feet away across the room, is resisting the authority of his teacher. By his resistance to his teacher he, false object to the teacher, represents an antagonist for her, a counter-subject, an equal and resisting will to hers. However, although he is not his teacher's object but yet acts out the desires of someone outside of himself (left to himself, he hums the sonatina happily, plays scales well, performs *moderato cantabile* perfectly), the child functions after all, truly, as symbolic object. The boy represents, in short, an object for his own beloved mother. Obedient to her felt desires, her proxy, he is defying an authority representing the symbolic 'authority' Anne Desbaresdes senses is strangling her.

> "Will you please read what's written above the score?" the lady asked.
>
> "*Moderato cantabile,*" said the child.
>
> The lady punctuated his reply by striking the keyboard with a pencil. The child remained motionless, his head turned toward the score.
>
> "And what does *moderato cantabile* mean?"
>
> "I don't know."
>
> A woman, seated ten feet away, gave a sigh.

This passage, which opens the story, gives us a scene in which three characters function. These characters defined by their functions, not their names (so far in Duras' story the game pieces do not even have names), are: [1] the authority figure, [2] the externally-resisting figure (one secretly acting out the desires of the third figure), and [3] the internally—resisting figure, the true antagonist to authority.

One will find this triad again and again in *Moderato Cantabile.* Now the authority figure will be the piano teacher; now the *patronne* in the bar; now the unseen husband and children of the murdered drunken woman of the allegorical tale-within-the-tale; now the men in the bar who call Anne Desbaresdes "adulteress" despite her actual innocence; but now (and always) Anne's rich husband. The externally-resisting figure will be the child in the piano lesson; the lover who murders his sweetheart publicly; Anne sitting in public view drinking with Chauvin and so drawing down the accusation of cuckold on her husband, and Anne appearing drunk at her own dinner party in humiliating display. The internally-resisting figure who causes another to act out his or her challenge will be Anne at her child's music lesson; the murdered woman in the street scene; Chauvin, long-disgruntled and rebellious foundry worker, employee of the omnipotent Desbaresdes, at the bar with Anne and later prowling about outside while she faces her husband and guests within the mansion, and so on.

But let us return to the opening scene where all this which will happen again and again first happens.

> "Are you quite sure you don't know what *moderato cantabile* means?" the lady repeated.
>
> The child did not reply.

Of course, the child's not replying is his reply. It is the beginning of the resistance he is going to act out now for his mother.

> The lady stifled an exasperated groan, and again struck the keyboard with her pencil. The child remained unblinking.
>
> The lady turned.
>
> "Mme Desbaresdes, you have a very stubborn little boy."
>
> Anne Desbaresdes sighed again.
>
> "You don't have to tell me," she said.

Of course, Anne does not have to be told about her child's stubbornness, because she herself is its author.

> The child, motionless, his eyes lowered, was the only one to remember that dusk had just exploded. It made him shiver.

Duras' metaphor for sunset, the dusk's exploding, represents also the violence soon to break out, bursting through repression in this narrative of tension and contradiction. The title itself, **Moderato Cantabile,** oxymoronically announcing singing ("*cantabile*") which is innately unbound, free, and yet calls for that song of the lyrical self to be girdled, enslaved ("*moderato*"). This is the tension of Anne Desbaresdes' life, and everyone's life. The dusk's exploding into magnificent-bloody red-ink prefigures the murder, requested by the victim herself, in the play-within-the-play to be enacted a few minutes from now across the street by the café as well as the more immediate violence threatened by the music teacher's pencil-weapon. Mlle Giraud now openly threatens while the child shivers in anticipation of violence.

> "I told you the last time, I told you the time before that, I have told you a hundred times, are you sure you don't know what it means?"
>
> The child decided not to answer. The lady looked again at the object before her, her rage mounting. . . .
>
> "You are going to say it this minute," the lady shouted. The child showed no surprise. He still did not reply.
>
> Then the lady struck the keyboard a third time, so hard that the pencil broke. Right next to the child's hands. His hands were round and milky, still scarcely formed. They were clenched and unmoving.

Those round, milky hands, scarcely formed little child hands cannot help but win the reader's sympathy for the threatened child. And they link up in our minds with the round, milky breasts of the boy's mother, those vulnerable breasts that Anne's future lover Chauvin, once having seen, will remember vividly for an entire year. Mother and child are linked, interchangeably, as victims, but resisting victims.

> "He's a difficult child," Anne Desbaresdes offered timidly.
>
> The child turned his head towards the voice, quickly towards his mother, to make sure of her existence, then resumed his pose as an object facing the score. His hands remained clenched.

The breaking pencil, splintering bludgeon of authority, signifies victory for the child in the immediate moves of the game because he himself does not lose face, does not 'break' like the pencil, but sits there whole, unbowed, showing no surprise, defiantly clenching his fists. Yet the child's victory is double-edged. The martyr's victory. Still openly victorious is the phallic pencil. This power symbol, wielded so far by the music teacher, represents ultimately the child's father, almighty owner of the great mansion on the Boulevard de la Mer(e), chief capitalist governing everyone's lives in this poor little town of three factories, its bourgeois rulers, and nothing else. In resisting his murderous father, the child responds unconsciously to his mother's unconscious, doomed demand.

> "I don't care whether he's difficult or not, Mme Desbaresdes," said the lady. "difficult or not, he has to do as he's told, or suffer the consequences."

We are no farther along in this story than two-thirds down the second page, yet in a sense Marguerite Duras' tale—the important part of it—is already told. Louis Althusser discussed the problem of Anne Desbaresdes (indirectly, of course) when in *Lenin and Philosophy* he theorized about State Ideological Apparatuses. As Althusser points out, successful patterns of production are successful only if, in addition to producing their products, they also reproduce themselves for the next generation.

Now we can understand how essential it is for the Desbaresdes' heir to learn how to play the piano and for the wife of the capitalist leader to sit in appropriate beauty and grace and submission to her wealthy husband at their dinner parties. These acts maintain the distance between workers and their master. This conspicuous consumption (to borrow the term and idea similar to Althusser's, from Thorstein Veblen's *Theory of the Leisure Class*), this intimidating display helps to preserve the stratifications within society and the reproducing of these same social pattern and stratifications.

Take those piano lessons. They are given to the children of the upper classes only. One of the other mothers at the Desbaresdes party mentions to Anne comments made to her child by their mutual employee Mlle Giraud. At the other end of the social scale, the *patronne* of the café and the foundry workers listen to the these piano lessons of the wealthy. Chauvin, on the day Anne stays too late with him and arrives late and drunk at her own dinner party, has heard, from the bar where he awaited Anne, every note her child has played across the street.

Unfortunately for Anne Desbaresdes, she is ignorant on a conscious level of the necessity that State Ideological Apparatuses reproduce themselves and so maintain the economic base. It was inevitable that the Desbaresdes heir should learn to play the piano and so maintain his superior position of "higher learning"—to use another of Veblen's terms. Yet Anne believes that the idea of having her child study music was her own. Exposing her ignorance of the system which is causing her misery, she tells Chauvin this about her son:

> "I somehow got the idea that he had to learn music, you know. He's been studying for two years."

To this, Chauvin, who had a year ago been with the other foundry workers a gaping guest at the impressive Desbaresdes mansion, replies:

> "Sure, I understand. So this grand piano, to the left as you go into the room?"

Grand pianos, and the room to house them in, do not belong to the world of the town's factory workers. Dimly, Anne grasps how the music lessons function but she cannot clearly formulate her ideas. Yes, she has picked up the proper social signals counseling her to have her son taught piano, and she is obeying them, but something within her doubts and resists.

> "Yes." Anne Desbaresdes clenched her fists and struggled to maintain her composure. "But he's still so little, such a little child, you have no idea. When I think about it, I wonder whether I'm wrong."

Two hours earlier, on the way to the lesson with her child, Anne had again struggled with the question of the piano lessons. "Music is necessary, and you have to learn it. Do you understand?" she tells the child, and she grooms him to be able to define *moderato cantabile* this time. Yet she sends the child signals to the contrary as well, and again the child's behavior at the lesson is unsatisfactory to the teacher, is frankly appalling. Now not only her child, but Anne herself is openly admonished by the representative of authority, the teacher.

> "Perhaps he didn't hear."
>
> "He heard perfectly well. One thing you'll never understand, Mme Desbaresdes, is that he does it deliberately."
>
> The child turned his head slightly towards the window. . . . His mother was the only one who could see his eyes.
>
> "Shame on you, darling," she whispered.
>
> "In four-four time," the child said listlessly, without moving. . . .
>
> "Some day," his mother said, "some day he'll know it, and he'll say it without hesitating, it's inevitable. Even if he doesn't want to, he'll know it."
>
> She laughed gaily, silently.
>
> "You ought to be ashamed, Mme Desbaresdes," said Mlle Giraud.
>
> "So they say."

The rebellion against their rôles is there in both mother and child, and varying degrees of punishment will be meted child and mother if they rebel too far. At the moment, the child must do a penance of ten minutes of scale playing, which he hates.

> "Its good for the fingers as well as the character," she [the piano teacher] said.

Let us return to the child's first rebellion, there in the opening scene when the little boy at last bursts out, "I don't want to learn how to play the piano." At that moment the open window shows pink sky exploding in a final burst of bloody brillance. And at that crucial moment the story's mythic center, the anecdote of the love-killing, occurs:

> In the street downstairs a woman screamed, a long drawn-out scream so shrill it overwhelmed the sound of the sea. Then it stopped abruptly.

A woman had screamed, a woman of commoners downstairs, outside. But another woman had screamed too, Anne Desbaresdes was screaming. She, too, was rebelling, protesting her unknown enemy, those sleepless nights without love. With the beautiful weather and the scent of magnolias, love-longings (socially-conditioned metaphor for the desire to escape captivity, as every woman's heart has experienced), love-restlessness has been aroused in her confused, bored, tormented soul.

Anne Desbaresdes has two signifiers for her love cravings. One is her child, whom at the story's end she will have so far lost that she is not even allowed any longer to accompany him to those infamous piano lessons. The other signifier is a lover, existent initially only in her fantasies. This lover comes to life for another woman, embodied there in the man who kills his mistress to put her out of her misery. Then this fantasy lover comes to life for Anne herself in Chauvin, who pointedly resembles the lover-murderer, and with whom Anne shares nine days of meeting and drinking wine.

Seldom, however, has a romantic love affair been described so unromantically as this courtship of Anne Desbaresdes, wife of the town's rich capitalist, and Chauvin, discontented worker who had once seen, and coveted, his wealthy neighbor's wife wearing a magnolia between naked breasts. Come together against all odds, these lovers drink and talk together in meetings dark and dismally unfulfilling, climaxing in a final triste so morbidly chilling the page ices over.

> Anne Desbaresdes moaned again, louder than before. Again she put her hand on the table. His eyes followed her movement and finally, painfully, he understood and lifted his own leaden hand and placed it on hers. Their hands were so cold they were touching only in intention, an illusion, in order for this to be fulfilled, none other, it was no longer possible. And yet, with their hands frozen in this funeral pose, Anne Desbaresdes stopped moaning.

A moment later, rhythmically identical in structure, the narrative shows the lovers' lips meeting, again in death-ambience:

> She moved close enough to him for their lips to meet. They lingered in a long embrace, their lips cold and trembling, so that it should be accomplished, performing the same mortuary ritual as their hands had performed a moment before. It was accomplished.

It was accomplished, yes. We readers feel and acknowledge this. But what is accomplished? What is accomplished, as after a moment one recognizes, is the replaying of the scene of the other two lovers, that pair whose hopeless, mythic passion of the love/death vignette has brought Anne and Chauvin together. These two other failed lovers, the woman empirically dead in his mental derangement, these two joined in blood as the red stain stains the lover's face from his kisses on his sweetheart stilled lips—these two predecessors had shown Anne and Chauvin the way, had revealed to them their desire for each other and what it might signify. Revealed beyond even love in this vision, perhaps, is hate: two people's unvoiced, bodily enacted conspiratorial rebellion against the repressions of the established order.

Of course, the brave mute effort at revolution proves to be a failure. Chauvin has prowled the mansion grounds of his envied, detested late employer, mouthing with silent passion the name of the wife of the town's uncrowned god in vain, to no avail. To no avail, except that he has, standing behind Anne, willed her to openly defy authority and, like the vignette's lover, had obeyed his sweetheart's desire to be destroyed.

>"I wish you were dead," Chauvin said.

>"I am," Anne Desbaresdes said.

Love is no longer possible, and even hate is of no use now.

>She passed the cluster of men at the bar and found herself again moving forward into the fiery red rays of the dying day.

The game tortuously played *moderato cantabile* for so long has finally ended, has been lost.

Trista Selous (essay date 1988)

SOURCE: "The Blanks," in *The Other Woman: Feminism and Femininity in the Work of Marguerite Duras,* Yale University Press, 1988, pp. 97-111, 127-32.

[*In the following essay, Selous examines the significance of what she describes as the "blanks" in Duras's writing, suggesting that those periods of silence or emptiness represent, particularly in* Moderato cantabile, *the "unsayable."*]

[As] opposed to *Un barrage contre le Pacifique,* which recounts events and gives insights, usually through free indirect style, into the psychology of the characters, 'in ***Moderato cantabile,*** not only does it not say what happened, but it may be that nothing happens at all'[1] and, even supposing something is happening, 'who can give a name to what happens between strangers, to what is happening now between Anne Desbaresdes and Chauvin?'[2] In this text, according to one critic, Duras refuses 'to name, to recount, to entertain, to fill the blanks.'[3] It is possible, however, to give a brief reconstruction of the events described, as Jean Mistler does:

>Anne Desbaresdes was a chance witness to a crime of passion in a quayside café, whilst her little boy was having his piano lesson. She goes back to this café several times and questions a man whom she meets there each time. We have the impression that the man knows no more about it than Anne and moreover that she scarcely listens to what he tells her. After five or six meetings, there has been no action, but we have a vague feeling that the psychological positions have been transformed.[4]

Mistler, as his article clearly shows, is not impressed. But those who are praise Duras's ability to produce silence and 'blanks' in her writing. So what is happening in this text, and how does Duras do it?

Perhaps the first point to make is that a large part of ***Moderato cantabile*** is taken up with a reconstruction of events which culminate in the shooting at the end of the first chapter. This reconstruction is undertaken by two figures, Anne Desbaresdes and Chauvin, neither of whom 'know what really happened' and will never be able to know, since one of the protagonists is dead and the other mad. Because of the way in which the text is narrated, this story is always out of reach of the authoritative narration and is equally out of reach of Anne and Chauvin. It has already happened before the chronological point where the text begins and is thus produced as an unattainable object of knowledge a 'blank.'

However, even in the events actually narrated by the text, there are gaps and silences. I have taken two passages for analysis in order to see how Duras produces effects of silence; the first is representative of the dialogue which makes up much of the text and the second is taken from the section recounting the dinner party, which contains little dialogue, but where a similar process is at work as in the first passage. The first passage is taken from the end of Anne Desbaresdes's first conversation with Chauvin:

>Les premiers hommes entrèrent. L'enfant se fraya un passage à travers eux, curieux, et arriva jusqu'à sa mère, qui le prit contre elle dans un mouvement d'enlacement machinal.
>
>—Vous êtes madame Desbaresdes. La femme du directeur d'Import Export et des Fonderies de la Côte. Vous habitez boulevard de la Mer.
>
>Une autre sirène retentit, plus faible que la première, à l'autre bout du, quai. Un remorqueur arriva. L'enfant se dégagea, d'une façon assez brutale, s'en alla en courant.
>
>—Il apprend le piano, dit-elle. Il a des dispositions, mais beaucoup de mauvaise volonté, il faut que j'en convienne.
>
>Toujours pour faire place aux hommes qui entraient regulièrement très nombreux dans le café, il se rapprocha un peu plus d'elle. Les premiers clients s'en allèrent. D'autres arrivèrent encore. Entre eux, dans le jeu de leurs allées et venues, on voyait le soleil se coucher dans la mer, le ciel qui flambait et l'enfant qui, de l'autre côté du quai, jouait tout seul à des jeux dont le secret était indiscernable à cette distance. Il sautait des obstacles imaginaires, devait chanter.
>
>—Je voudrais pour cet enfant tant de choses à la fois que je ne sais pas comment m'y prendre, par òu commencer. Et je m'y prends très mal. Il faut que je rentre parce qu'il est tard.
>
>—Je vous ai vue souvent. Je n'imaginais pas qu'un jour vous arriverez jusqu'ici avec votre enfant.
>
>La patronne augmenta un peu le volume de la radio pour ceux des derniers clients qui venaient d'entrer. Anne Desbaresdes se tourna vers le comptoir, fit une grimace, accepta le bruit, l'oublia.
>
>—Si vous savez tout le bonheur qu'on leur veut, comme si c'était possible. Peut-être vaudrait-il mieux parfois que l'on nous en sépare. Je n'arrive pas à me faire une raison de cet enfant.

—Vous avez une belle maison au bout du boulevard de la mer. Un grand jardin fermé.

Elle le regarda, perplexe, revenu à elle.

—Mais ces leçons de piano, j'en ai beaucoup de plaisir, affirma-t-elle.

L'enfant, traqué par le crépuscule, revint une nouvelle fois vers eux. Il resta là à contempler le monde, les clients. L'homme fit signe à Anne Desbaresdes de regarder au dehors. Il lui sourit.

—Regardez, dit-il, les jours allongent, allongent. . . .

Anne Desbaresdes regarda, ajusta son manteau avec soin, lentement.

—Vous travaillez dans cette ville, Monsieur?

—Dans cette ville, oui. Si vous reveniez, j'essayerai de savoir autre chose et je vous le dirai.

Elle baissa les yeux, se souvint et pâlit.

—Du sang sur sa bouche, dit-elle, et il l'embrassait, l'embrassait.

Elle se reprit: ce que vous avez dit, vous le supposiez?

—Je n'ai rien dit.

Le couchant était si bas maintenant qu'il atteignait le visage de cet homme. Son corps, debout, legèrement appuyé au comptoir, le recevait déjà depuis un moment.

—A l'avoir vu, on ne peut pas s'empêcher, n'est-ce pas, c'est presque inevitable?

—Je n'ai rien dit, répéta l'homme. Mais je crois qu'il l'a visée au coeur comme elle le lui demandait.

Anne Desbaresdes gémit. Une plainte presque licencieuse, douce, sortit de cette femme.

—C'est curieux, je n'ai pas envie de rentrer, dit-elle.

Il prit brusquement son verre, le termina d'un trait, ne répondit pas, la quitta des yeux.

—J'ai dû trop boire, continua-t-elle, voyez-vous, c'est ça.

—C'est ça, oui, dit l'homme.

Le café s'était presque vidé. Les entrées se firent plus rares. Tout en lavant ses verres, la patronne les lorgnait, intriguée de les voir tant s'attarder, sans doute. L'enfant, revenu vers la porte, contemplait les quais maintenant silencieux. Debout devant l'homme, tournant le dos au port, Anne Desbaresdes se tut encore longtemps. Lui ne paraissait pas s'apercevoir de sa présence.

—Il m'aurait été impossible de ne pas revenir, dit-elle enfin.

—Je suis revenu moi aussi pour la même raison que vous.[5]

[The first men came in. The child pushed his way through them, curious, and reached his mother, who pulled him against her in an automatic clasping movement.

'You are Madame Desbaresdes. The wife of the head of Import Export and of Coastal Foundries. You live on Sea Boulevard.'

Another siren sounded, quieter than the first, from the other end of the quay. A tugboat came in. The child freed himself, quite roughly, ran off.

'He's learning the piano', she said. 'He's got ability, but I must admit, he's very unwilling.'

Again to make space for the men entering the café at regular intervals and in very large numbers, he drew a little closer to her. The first clients left. Still more came in. Between them, in the play of their comings and goings, one could see the sun setting in the sea, the sky which was aflame and the child who, on the other side of the quay, was playing all alone at games whose secret was indiscernible at that distance. He was jumping over imaginary obstacles, must have been singing.

'I want so many things at once for that child that I don't know how to go about it, where to begin. And I go about it very badly. I must go home because it is late.'

'I have often seen you. I never imagined that one day you would come up here with your child.'

The café owner turned up the volume of the radio a little for those of the later clients who had just come in. Anne Desbaresdes turned towards the counter, made a face, accepted the noise, forgot it.

'If you knew all the happiness that one wants for them, as if it were possible. Perhaps it might be better sometimes if they took them away from us. I can't seem to be reasonable about this child.'

'You have a beautiful house at the end of Sea Boulevard. A large walled garden.'

She looked at him, perplexed, brought back to the present.

'But these piano lessons give me great pleasure,' she stated.

The child, harried by the dusk, came back towards them once more. He stayed there contemplating all the people, the clients. The man gestured to Anne Desbaresdes to look outside. He smiled at her.

'Look,' he said, 'the days are getting longer, longer . . .'

Anne Desbaresdes looked, rearranged her coat carefully, slowly.

'Do you work in this town, Monsieur?

'In this town, yes. If you come back, I'll try to find out something more and I'll tell it to you.'

She lowered her eyes, remembered and grew pale.

'Blood on her mouth,' she said, 'and he was kissing her, kissing her.'

She pulled herself together: 'what you said, you were just supposing it?'

'I said nothing.'

The sun had sunk so low now that it touched the man's face. His body, standing, leaning slightly on the counter, had already been catching it for some time.

'Having seen it, one can't stop oneself, don't you think, it's almost inevitable?'

'I said nothing,' the man repeated. 'But I think he aimed for her heart, as she asked him to do.'

Anne Desbaresdes groaned. A soft, almost licentious moan came from the woman.

'It's odd, I don't want to go home,' she said.

He took up his glass abruptly, finished it at one go, did not answer, turned his eyes away from her.

'I must have drunk too much,' she went on, 'you see, that's it.'

'That's it, yes,' said the man.

The café had almost emptied. People came in more rarely. As she washed her glasses, the owner watched them out of the corner of her eye, intrigued, no doubt, at seeing them stay on so long. The child, who had gone back to the door, was contemplating the now silent quayside. Standing in front of the man, turning her back on the harbour, Anne Desbaresdes stayed silent for a long time more. He did not seem to notice her presence.

'It would have been impossible for me not to come back,' she said at last.

'I also came back for the same reason as you.']

This passage, like the rest of **Moderato cantabile,** is written in the past historic, constructor of universes and of the observer who records them. However, unlike the passage from *Un barrage contre le Pacifique* which I have discussed above, it does not produce a narrator with a point of view in the sense of an attitude, such as irony, with regard to what is narrated. The discourse is not disturbed in the way that it was in the previous passage by conflicting meanings. This makes the style appear almost hyper-realist, like the transcription of a photograph. It appears to be a simple description of the events, a recording, as if by a kind of verbal camera, with no comment on the part of the narrator. This allows the language to appear 'transparent', with none of the colouring or 'distortion' which can be read into a text where the reader infers a narrator with a 'personality' who is directing the former's perception of events.

So the 'impersonal narrator' is reduced almost to transparency, disappearing into the language, only seeming to encroach on the recording of events at points of uncertainty ('whose secret was indiscernible at that distance,' 'must have been singing'). This encroachment does set up a point of view, but in a spatial sense. The passage is written in such a way as to make it possible for the reader to construct a fantasised image of the café by the quay, with workers coming and going, and where two people, Anne Desbaresdes and Chauvin, are talking by the bar. This is all put forward with little or no apparent mediation or in-

terpretation on the part of the narrator. An unthreatened illusion of reference is maintained throughout.

Anne and Chauvin are produced as 'real people,' seen as if by a camera. But 'real people' are more than surfaces; Anne and Chauvin have names, a vaguely defined social status, and by realist implication, psychology and desires. The main thread running through the passage is the dialogue between them. Nevertheless, their conversation does not proceed unproblematically. In the first half of the passage they do not appear to be talking about the same thing. Anne is talking about her child, whilst Chauvin is talking about Anne. Furthermore, the dialogue is punctuated by descriptions of the child's actions, the café owner turning up the radio, or Anne's own actions. These actions are, for the most part, written in the past historic, the tense used to mark the speech of Anne and Chauvin, the tense of definite, completed action. The effect of this is that the utterances of Anne and Chauvin and the actions or descriptions which punctuate them are given equal importance and appear to follow each other chronologically. The difference this makes to the flow of the narration can be seen when the above passage is compared to the following exchange between Suzanne and M. Jo in *Un barrage contre le Pacifique,* when M. Jo is trying to get Suzanne to open the door and let him see her washing.

—Dire que vous êtes toute nue, dire que vous êtes toute nue, répétait-il d'une voix sans timbre.

—Vous parlez d'une affaire, dit Suzanne. Si vous étiez à ma place j'aurais pas envie de vous voir.

Quand elle évoquait M. Jo, sans son diamant, son chapeau, sa limousine, en train par exemple de se balader en maillot sur la plage à Ram, la colère de Suzanne grandissait d'autant.

—Pourquoi vous ne vous baignez pas à Ram?

M. Jo reprit un peu de sang-froid et appuya moins fort.

—Les bains de mer me sont interdits, dit-il avec toute la fermeté qu'il pouvait.

Heureuse, Suzanne se savonnait. Il lui avait acheté du savon parfumé à la lavande et depuis, elle se baignait deux et trois fois par jour pour avoir l'occasion de se parfumer. L'odeur de la lavande arrivait jusqu'à M. Jo et en lui permettant de mieux suivre les étapes du bain de Suzanne rendait son supplice encore plus subtil.

—Pourquoi les bains vous sont-ils interdits?

—Parce que je suis de faible constitution et que les bains de mer me fatiguent. Ouvrez, ma petite Suzanne . . . une seconde. . . .

—C'est pas vrai, c'est parce que vous êtes mal foutu.

Elle le devinait, collé contre la porte, encaissant tout ce qu'elle lui disait parce qu'il était sûr de gagner.

—Une seconde, rien qu'une seconde. . . .[6]

[—'To think that you're completely naked, to think that you're completely naked,' he repeated in a toneless voice.

'Some bargain,' said Suzanne. 'If we swapped places, I wouldn't want to see you.'

When she pictured M. Jo, without his diamond, his hat, or his limousine, walking along in a swimming costume, for example, on the beach at Ram, Suzanne's anger grew all the greater.

'Why don't you go bathing at Ram?'

M. Jo recovered his cool a little and pushed (against the door) less hard.

'I am not allowed to bathe in the sea,' he said, as firmly as he could.

Suzanne was soaping herself, happily. He had bought her some lavender scented soap and ever since she had been bathing two or three times a day so that she could cover herself in perfume. The scent of the lavender floated out to M. Jo and, by allowing him to follow the stages of Suzanne's bathing more easily, rendered his torture all the more subtle.

'Why aren't you allowed to bathe?'

'Because I have a weak constitution and bathing in the sea tires me. Open up, my sweet little Suzanne . . . just one second. . . .'

'That's not true, it's because you're ugly.'

She could imagine him, pressed up against the door, swallowing everything she said to him because he knew he would win.

'One second, just one second. . . .']

In this exchange the dialogue is interrupted by two fairly long passages, the one beginning *Quand elle évoquait . . .* ('When she pictured . . .') and the other beginning *Heureuse, Suzanne se savonnait* ('Suzanne was soaping herself, happily'). However, both these passages have their main verbs in the imperfect tense, the tense of indefinite time. This means that the actions described in the imperfect do not interrupt the actions described in the past historic, but can be read as happening at the same time, providing a background for the words. In the ***Moderato cantabile*** passage this is not the case. The result is that the reader/narratee assumes a gap between two parts of the dialogue in which, for example, the café-owner turns up the radio, Anne turns towards the bar, makes a face, resigns herself to the noise and forgets it, before speaking. This produces a gap in the dialogue, when neither speaks while these actions are performed. Thus a dialogue full of silences can be produced without the narration having to make this explicit; the silences arise in the spaces between the utterances of the figures, made by the intercalation of narration in the past historic between instances of direct speech.

The passage also produces effects of silence in what the speakers actually do say, by creating the impression that there is something they are not saying, or are avoiding saying. In the first part of the passage it would appear that what Anne and Chauvin each say bears no relation to the words of the other. Alone, this section of the dialogue would appear absurd(ist). The speeches of Anne and Chauvin would appear to be lacking in 'pertinence'; the reason for their existence would at best be obscure in terms of accepted conventions of dialogue, which uphold the view that when two people talk together their utterances have some relevance to each other. For here, whilst each independently appears to be capable of coherent thought, they seem unable to follow each other's drift. However, after Anne asks Chauvin if he works in the town, the conversation picks up and each speech appears to be connected in some way to the previous one. Although the connexions may not be immediately obvious, the reader can assume that when Chauvin says, 'I'll try to find out something more', he is referring to the shooting, that the memory of the latter event makes Anne turn pale and that it is the man's kissing of the dead woman to which she refers when she says 'Having seen it.' 'One can't stop oneself' can be referred back to a previous speech of Anne's: 'I've thought about it more and more since yesterday evening . . . since my child's piano lesson. I couldn't have stopped myself from coming today, you see.'[7] 'It' here refers to the shooting. After Chauvin has said he will try to find out more, both figures appear to be talking about the incident, after the disconnected conversation they had been having before. The reader can then reasonably infer that that shooting is of interest to both of them, following the idea that these are 'real people,' whose utterances are not completely random. Continuing in this vein, the reader can also assume that Chauvin's words about the shooting have the effect of making Anne groan in a way which was 'almost licentious,' since the groan immediately follows them. The proximity of the two suggest cause and effect. The reader might then assume that Anne's loss of desire to go home is also something to do with what has just been said and the 'almost licentious' sound that she has just made. Because, with a little effort, the reader can find or invent a 'pertinence' in this part of the dialogue, s/he can continue to read Anne and Chauvin as 'real people,' and assume that there is something which Anne is trying to justify when she says, 'I must have drunk too much . . . That's it,' even if it is totally unstated what 'it' might be. Such an assumption is also possible in relation to Chauvin's words: 'I also came back for the same reason as you.' No reason has been given but 'real people' have reasons for doing things, or say they do, or even say they have not when they really have. So runs the convention. From the vantage point of the all-seeing, but not necessarily all-comprehending eye of the narrator, the reader may not know exactly what the reason that Chauvin refers to is; but since the latter apparently does, s/he assumes it exists.

It is then by compelling the reader to make the associations necessary to find the 'pertinence' of the utterances attributed to Anne and Chauvin that the text produces an effect of things left unsaid. The reader supplies the associative links, but notices they are missing. With the hindsight of Anne and Chauvin's exchange on the subject of the shooting, the reader can also infer a suppression of this topic during the disconnected part of the conversation, since their willingness to talk about it has apparently carried over from an earlier exchange. Perhaps, the reader might think, it was that suppression which made their conversation so fragmented and disconnected. Perhaps not. We cannot know for sure.

The second passage from **Moderato cantabile** that I want to discuss also relies on the reader's desire to find the 'pertinence' of the words s/he reads. However, here it is not the utterances of the figures in the text which require interpretation, it is the narration.

> Le pétale de magnolia est lisse, d'un grain nu. Les doigst le froissent jusqu'à le trouer puis, interdits, s'arrêtent, se reposent sur la table, attendent, prennent une contenance, illusoire. Car on s'en est aperçu. Anne Desbaresdes s'essaye à un sourire d'excuse de n'avoir pu faire autrement, mais elle est ivre et son visage prend le faciès impudique de l'aveu. Le regard s'appesantit, impassible, mais revenu dèjà douloureusement de tout étonnement. On s'y attendait depuis toujours.
>
> Anne Desbaresdes boit de nouveau un verre de vin tout entier les yeux mi-clos. Elle en est déjà à ne plus pouvoir faire autrement. Elle découvre, à boire, une confirmation de ce qui fut jusque-là son désir obscur et une indigne consolation à cette découverte.
>
> D'autres femmes boivent à leur tour, elles lèvent de même leurs bras nus, délectables, irréprochables, mais d'épouses. Sur la grève, l'homme siffle une chanson entendue dans l'après-midi dans un café du port.
>
> La lune est levée et avec elle voici le commencement de la nuit tardive et froide. Il n'est pas impossible que cet homme ait froid.[8]

> [The magnolia petal is smooth, with a naked grain. The fingers crush it, tearing it, then, forbidden, stop, lie on the table once more, wait, adopt an attitude of composure, which is illusory. For one has noticed. Anne Desbaresdes tries a smile of appology for having been unable to do otherwise, but she is drunk and her face takes on the shameless appearance of confession. The look grows heavier, impassive, but it has already painfully recovered from all astonishment. One has always expected this.
>
> Anne Desbaresdes drinks another glass of wine all at once her eyes half closed. She has already reached the point of being unable to do otherwise. She discovers, in drinking, the confirmation of what had been until then an obscure desire and a shameful consolation in this discovery.
>
> Other women drink in their turn, they likewise raise arms which are naked, delectable, irreproachable, but are those of wives. On the beach, the man whistles a song heard in the afternoon in a quayside café.
>
> The moon has risen and with it here is the beginning of the cold, late-coming night. It is not impossible that the man is cold.]

Here the first link to be made is between the magnolia flower worn by Anne as a corsage at the dinner-party and the one Chauvin has described her as wearing when he saw her before:

> —Vous étiez accoudée à ce grand piano. Entre vos seins nus sous votre robe, il y a cette fleur de magnolia.
>
> Anne Desbaresdes, très attentivement, écouta cette histoire.
>
> —Oui.
>
> —Quand vous vous penchez, cette fleur frôle le contour extérieur de vos seins. Vous l'avez négligemment épinglée, trop haut. C'est une fleur énorme, vous l'avez choisie au hasard, trop grande pour vous. Ses pétales sont encore durs, elle a justement atteint la nuit dernière sa pleine floraison.[9]

> ['You are resting your elbows on the grand piano. Between your breasts, which are naked beneath your dress, is that magnolia flower.'
>
> Anne Desbaresdes, very attentively, listened to this story.
>
> 'Yes.'
>
> 'When you lean over, the flower brushes against the outline of your breasts. You have pinned it carelessly, too high. It is an enormous flower, you chose it at random, too large for you. Its petals are still hard, in fact it reached its full flowering just the night before.']

In Chauvin's description, the magnolia is associated with Anne's breasts. The reader is encouraged to infer Chauvin's sexual interest in Anne from his clear memory of how the flower touched her breasts. The magnolia flower worn by Anne during the dinner-party scene carries the weight of this earlier magnolia with it. The very use of the word 'magnolia,' followed by *grain nu* ('naked grain'), echoing the earlier *seins nus* ('naked breasts'), is almost bound to recall for the reader the sexual connotations of the earlier conversation, whether or not it reminds her/him of the actual words previously used. The magnolia has become the symbol for something sexual, for Chauvin's desire, which has never been explicitly articulated. Chauvin's sexual desire is a fantasy of the reader's, an inference, unstated. The magnolia refers to it as something which has been kept silent, whose articulation is absent, left 'blank.' The same process is at work with the wine, which can be read as a symbol for Anne's (sexual) desire, having potentially acquired this meaning (to add to the ancient bacchanalian symbolism that it carries amongst others) in the preceding chapters. And in this case, the symbolic value of the wine is confirmed. Reinforcing the impression of the presence of Anne's desire, the reader is then told that other women besides Anne 'likewise raise arms which are naked, delectable, irreproachable, but are those of wives.' The 'but' marks them out as different from, even inferior to, Anne. Anne is also a wife, the reader might remember but straight after these words comes a reference to the man on the beach and the 'quayside café.' Although this sentence brings a complete break with the last in terms of the place and person it refers to, because it is in the same paragraph it appears to be linked to what precedes it and the reader assumes the connexion.

At this point the reader, if s/he is going to be able to 'make sense' out of what is being recounted, must almost inevitably infer that the man is Chauvin, that Anne's desire has something to do with him and their meetings in the café, that that desire is sexual in some way and that it makes her different from the other women, because it is for a man who is not her husband. None of this is stated instead it is left 'blank,' to be more or less unconsciously assumed by the reader.

The other notable 'blank' to be found in this passage is around the use of *on* ('one'). In the preceding part of the chapter, *on* recurs, excusing Anne for lateness.[10] In the passage cited above, *on* has noticed Anne fingering the magnolia and becomes the source of a look and an opinion. *On* has become someone specific. This is, of course, inference on the part of myself as reader, but it is an inference which nothing contradicts and which everything suggests. Later, at the end of the chapter, *on* will look into the child's room and see Anne lying on the floor. *On* here takes the form of *une ombre* ('a shadow').[11] It would be almost perverse not to assume that *on* is Anne's husband but he is never mentioned by name. He is without any explicit existence in the text other than as *on* (and when Chauvin refers to him) but because the reader can infer him as the referent of *on,* he is constructed as a man to whom reference has been avoided, evaded, or perhaps suppressed. He has become a 'blank.'

In *Moderato cantabile,* 'blanks' may be produced by means of the juxtaposition of sentences which then seem to be connected, as above and, as I have indicated earlier, in dialogue. Alternatively, they may be produced by the use of symbolism, as in the case of the magnolia or the wine, where the signifiers *magnolia* and *vin* both become loaded with resonances, so that their significance seems to the reader to exceed the possibility of its articulation and so becomes constructed as inarticulable. The 'blanks' are thus those elements of the reader's fantasy which the text produces by means other than explicit articulation. They are created through the operations of the reader's desire to 'make sense' of the text. The reader can only embark upon such an enterprise if s/he assumes that there is a sense to make, that is, if s/he assumes the presence of an effort of coherent representation, a desire on the part of the author to mean something by the text,[12] in terms of which the elements s/he is given do 'go together.'

Of course, most, if not all works of fiction require some work of inference on the part of the reader. For example, in the passage from *Un barrage contre le Pacifique,* the reader's inference is required to produce the irony of the narrator; and other authors besides Duras have used similar techniques to create an effect of 'blanks.' A notable example of such an effect can be seen in Alain Robbe-Grillet's *Le Voyeur,* in which the reader is invited to understand that the central character, Mathias, has committed a murder which is not actually recounted. Like *Moderato cantabile,* this is a third person narration. However, it is entirely in free indirect style, which gives the reader/narratee insight into Mathias's thought processes throughout. This allows the reader to explain the 'blank' in terms of Mathias's psychology: he has suppressed the murder and the text can be read as an attempt to render his confused, disavowing thought processes.

In *Moderato cantabile,* the reader might be able to understand the 'blanks' in dialogue in psychological terms but the narration itself is too impersonal and detached to make its 'blanks' appear effects of a personalised narrator's suppression of things s/he does not want to describe, or think about. However, the reader's confidence that the elements of the narrative do 'make sense' is aided by apparently transparent reference to the 'real world.' And the story is clearly not out of control; on the contrary, it is fixed and finished in the past historic, seen through the eyes of this impartial narrator, told in the most apparently impersonal of language. Because of the apparent impartiality of the narration, and thus its authority as source of objective knowledge, the reader is not led to infer that the 'blanks' are the result of any deliberate omission of information. The narration appears simply to record what there is to tell, rather than having been 'edited down' from some fuller original version. The result is that where things are left unsaid, it seems that they are in some sense unsayable.

Notes

1. Gaëton Picon, 'Moderato cantabile dans l'oeuvre de Marguerite Duras,' in *Moderato cantabile,* Paris, Minuit, 10/18 series, 1958, p. 169.

2. Ibid, p. 171.

3. Madeleine Alleins, 'Un langage qui recuse la quiétude du savoir,' in Ibid p. 159.

4. Jean Mistler, 'Un essai non une oeuvre achevée,' in Ibid, p. 162.

5. Ibid, pp 30-4.

6. *Un barrage contre le Pacifique,* pp. 104-5.

7. *Moderato cantabile,* p. 30.

8. Ibid, pp. 97-8.

9. Ibid, pp. 79-80.

10. Ibid, p. 93.

11. Ibid, p. 103.

12. Something which Jean Mistler seems unsure about. 'Critics are with their rights to ask why this second attempt; for it cannot be anything other than an attempt, with the aim of creating a finished work later on.' (*Moderato cantabile,* p. 162)

Leslie Hill (essay date 1989)

SOURCE: "Marguerite Duras: Sexual Difference and Tales of Apocalypse," in *The Modern Language Review,* Vol. 84, No. 3, July, 1989, pp. 601-14.

[*In the following essay, Hill explores the function of repetition in* Moderato cantabile.]

> Elle se promène encore. Elle voit de plus en plus précisément, clairement ce qu'elle veut voir. Ce qu'elle rebâtit, c'est la fin du monde.

> *(Le Ravissement de Lol V. Stein)*

A number of Duras's books are written indifferently as plays, film-scripts, or novels. In at least two of these texts, *India Song* and *Détruire, dit-elle,* there is an enigmatic passage: if these texts were to be staged in a theatre, declares a peremptory editorial voice, 'il n'y aurait pas de répétition générale'.[1] This apparent distaste for dress rehearsals is strange, but revealing. Behind it lies a paradox. If no dress rehearsals may be allowed for these texts, it is most likely so that the continuity between rehearsal and performance may be preserved. Performance itself becomes a rehearsal, or, since the French word, 'répétition', cannot distinguish between a rehearsal and a repetition, it becomes a rehearsal as well as a repetition. The act of repeating in Duras's texts turns towards the future as well as facing into the past. From the very beginning, performance repeats a loss of origin, it is a circular event having no originating moment.

But even before the question of dress rehearsals arises, self-reflexive repetition and circular self-rehearsal are already the preferred terms of reference of Duras's fictions. In the context of her work, the borderline between what is and what is not fundamentally a repetition becomes difficult to draw, and the idea of repetition or rehearsal can take in phenomena as diverse as self-adaptation (the reworking, for instance, at a distance of some twenty-five years, of the novel *Un Barrage contre le Pacifique* into the play *L'Eden Cinéma*), self-quotation (as in the figure of Anne-Marie Stretter, who, 'différemment toujours', travels across texts, as a name, at any rate, from one fiction to another),[2] structural circularity within narrative and the ritualistic re-enactment of plot events (as, for example, in **Moderato cantabile,** or *Le Ravissement de Lol V. Stein*), and the use of various echoing leitmotifs both within and between texts. Here, the phenomenon of textual repetition is more than a simple consequence of the entropy of the signifier. The questions which arise from repetition can be extended to apply in principle to all Duras's films, plays, and novels, and it becomes clear that the use of repetition as a structuring device is central to her whole strategy as a writer and film-maker.

But if in all her texts, repetition, both thematically and structurally, is an undeniable source of enigma and fascination, what remains unclear (and this is the fundamental disturbance created by all repetition) is what it is that is being repeated, or what lies behind the apparent compulsion to repeat. Repetition is never easy to interpret, and readers (and readings) of Duras have in the past diverged in deciding on the function of repetition in her work: that is, whether it reflects a desire to recapture the past and thus retrieve it from oblivion, or somehow the reverse. In the latter case the point of the compulsion to repeat would be to transform the past into a radical absence of foundation, into a catastrophic loss of beginnings that would throw into question all the guarantees which derive from identifiable origins.[3]

Part of the fascination caused by repetition no doubt derives from this double status. In itself (if it were possible to assign an identity to it), repetition is Janus-like. It is always possible to postulate a dual function for it. On one level, repetition operates in Duras's work as a memory of origins, and a rehearsal of the past, but at the same time, it also appears in the guise of a diabolical process dedicated to destroying the original status of what it is repeating. It disrupts the idea of the hierarchical primacy of the original time or event. (Not for nothing is it traditionally associated with death, sexuality, loss of identity, the uncanny, or the music of the devil.)

The effect of repetition is melancholy, to the extent that it records loss. However, in Duras's work, it should not be taken to imply monotony, or dreary sameness. It is also a movement that refuses to be controlled by the past. If repetition tells of a loss of origins, it also recounts the failure of canonic and binding models of truth to control meaning. It possesses its own diabolic autonomy, which allows it to steal, purloin, and usurp effects from elsewhere. Repetition has a multiple identity. It becomes difficult to set any bounds to what is potentially a repetition. As Gilles Deleuze has argued, this excess of repetition over itself, which gives it its protean lack of identity and its capacity for renewal and endless proliferation, is itself another name for the process of fundamental variation which makes repetition possible (and of which repetition in the familiar sense is a localized instance) and gives it its creative and shifting energy (*Différence et répétition* (Paris, 1968)). Repetition in Duras's work is not a changeless reproduction of sameness; rather, as in music, it is an effect of an underlying movement of perpetual variation. Duras indicates as much herself by her insistent and repetitive use of Beethoven's Diabelli variations in films such as *India Song* and *Le Camion*. In Duras, as in Beethoven, what is repeated is not identity but variation and difference. The effect of textual repetition is to bring about, by adaptation, textual transposition, or internal replication, a constant circulation of meaning which cannot be arrested by the appeal to an origin or stable model.

If repetition suggests despair and finality, Duras argues, it is a despair which no longer mourns what it has lost. Rather it affirms the absence of faith, and the insubordination of despair, a state that she sometimes refers to as a 'gai désespoir'.[4] She explains what is at issue most clearly in the text of *Le Camion*. This is a film which takes the form of a speculative conversation between Duras and Gérard Depardieu, seemingly playing themselves. Their dialogue is conducted in the hypothetical mode, and the two actors perform, by word alone, the story of a male lorry-driver and a woman hitch-hiker, which in turn is illustrated or sketched in by various inserted sequences depicting a blue Saviem articulated lorry on its journeys up and down the Channel coast. Two locales, the outside world of the lorry and the darkened inside room occupied by the actors, mime and repeat each other, like two images which reflect each other but refuse to coincide, except as variations on common possibilities. As a result, *Le Camion* is a film which, in its own way, can be seen as entirely unrehearsed, almost improvised by Duras and Depardieu, or, just as much, to consist of nothing more than a series of rehearsals for a film which will not have been made, but which will have been enacted in the very process of its being rehearsed and repeated.

Within the world of circular paradoxes explored by *Le Camion,* where events take place without their taking place, where the actors both remain themselves and become the provisional understudies of characters who are spoken about only as conjectures, the world survives its own finality with a desperate intensity. Duras explains: 'On croit plus rien. On croit. Joie: on croit: plus rien.'⁵ Here, as the audience is invited, in the words of 'la dame du camion', as embodied, quoted, or rehearsed by the author-narrator herself, to 'regarde[r]: la fin du monde' (p. 21), Durassian repetition takes on what is properly its apocalyptic dimension. The idea of apocalypse signifies not only irreversible catastrophe but also revelation: no doubt, too, here, the one as the other, calamity as illumination, revelation as disaster. In the context of Duras's work, the apocalypse, as in Biblical tradition, denotes both an end and a beginning, destruction and resurrection. It implies, for instance, an end to story-telling, an admission that the world will no longer fit the bounds of narrative representation, and yet affirms the survival of writing as an act of discovery and invention. While it challenges all inherited notions of value, it still asserts the capacity of writing, in the aftermath of the catastrophic collapse of meaning which *Le Camion* recounts, to be a vehicle for revelation, and the ability of the cinema to cast its own peculiar, apocalyptic, half-light onto the scattered images and reflections of the world.

Under cover of a radically pessimistic account of politics and meaning in general, what is being repeated, then, in Duras's work (as in the musical analogy) is an awareness of fundamental variation, a knowledge of discord, separation, and incommensurability at the heart of the world. This division and duplicity at the centre of things, however, is not a secondary or derived phenomenon but a primary one, and therefore pre-exists the notion of an established universal model, and it seems clear, in Duras's work, that the originating difference within the human order itself, the division between the sexes, is the prime focus of this awareness of difference. That difference, which lies beyond the purview of each human, who is irremediably differentiated as male or female from the outset of life, both figures (as a metaphor) and embodies (literally) the absolute, the unspeakable or unsayable, on which Duras's writing, like the apocalyptic revelations of the Bible, is suspended.

Writing, Duras argues, is an exploration of this infinity which founds the human order: 'L'homme', she says to Dominique Noguez, '. . . est fondé justement sur l'inconnaissable, l'insondable, l'inconcevable de l'inconcevable de quoi participe sa vie. Et interminablement, infiniment, l'homme écrit de cet infini. C'est de cette difficulté qu'il vit. Dans un monde fini, explorable, l'homme n'écrirait pas.'⁶ Downstream of their singular conception and their gender identity, humans, male and female, can only repeat and vary, in a state of perpetual non-resolution, their relation to the uncontainable absolute of sexual difference. This relationship to the infinite, to what escapes boundaries, limitations, or confinement, is fundamental. This is why, in turn, Duras's stories are so often structured and staged as repetitions and rehearsals of absolute passion, as stories of sexual difference, and of the enigmatic and unstable tracing and retracing of that difference. Like her own texts themselves, her love stories are tales of repetition and variation, accounts of the space between the sexes, and the compulsions, enigmas, and divisions which structure that space.

Of Duras's many stories of love, the novel **Moderato cantabile** is probably one of the best known.⁷ Its plot is characteristically dual in structure as well as melodramatic, even lurid. The narrative opens with the murder (by her male lover) of an unnamed woman, and traces the effects of that crime on two of its chance (and partial) witnesses: Anne Desbaresdes, the mother of a small boy taking music lessons, and Chauvin, the man she subsequently meets in the local café and with whom she questions, explores, reinvents, and, finally, re-enacts the murder in metaphoric manner. The novel itself is mainly taken up with exploring the parallels, repetitive echoes, and divergences between these two series of events as Anne's and Chauvin's amorous encounter is set against the backdrop of the murder which initiates it.

In the first instance, reading **Moderato cantabile** becomes essentially a matter of unravelling the complex network of recurrent motifs running through the text, and following up its self-mirroring and repetitive plot patterns. Within the book itself (if one reads it self-referentially), the task of interpretation is presented primarily as a question of framing: of matching, for instance, the words of the title with the music (and narrative) they surround. (Subsequently, the challenge will be to relate the major plot events, those dealing with Anne and Chauvin, to the frame story of the murder.) It is clearly not by chance that the text begins with an invitation to read and with the music teacher's question to the boy: '—Et qu'est-ce que ça veut dire, moderato cantabile?' (p. 7). The boy, rather like the reader at this stage, can only reply that he (or she) does not know.

Significantly, however, as though to forestall the search for a regular and recognizable frame, the novel is, from the very beginning, staged in a world of margins, edges, and border-zones. Locations are rendered indeterminate, and a sense of otherness becomes everywhere present. Lines of separation are established in the text only to be suspended and blurred. Within the opening chapter, the theme of the sea-board works as a powerful source of such effects of 'in-betweenness'. The music-room, in which the first chapter is set, is itself, characteristically, poised between the town and the sea, and the sounds of both echo within the room, which is given over to the small boy's struggle to master the Diabelli sonatina of the title. In much the same way, the young child's attention is wayward: he cannot (or will not) settle on the matter at hand and is half distracted by the spectacle of the sea and the sky. Anne, his mother, too, is half reluctant in her commitment to the music lesson and hesitates between indulgence and strictness. The time of day is mid-afternoon, and the colour of the sky is poised midway between light and dark, clear and obscure. (This reference to the half-light of evening as an intensification and engulfment of light is a constant apocalyptic motif in this novel and elsewhere in Duras's work, where the reader, or spectator, is continually exposed to the idea that half-light, like the final rays before nightfall, is a source of peculiarly vivid illumination. *Aurélia Steiner* speaks, for example, of the existence of a 'forte clarté, juste avant l'obscurcissement général que répand le rougeoiement de la nuit' (*Le Navire Night* (Vancouver), *Césarée, Les Mains négatives, Aurélia Steiner, Aurélia Steiner, Aurélia Steiner* (Paris, 1979), p. 148).

In this world of indecision and unresolved contrasts, where space, character, and time echo each other according to an underlying rhythm of repetitive variation, something happens. Or rather, more appropriately, something takes place which is also perhaps nothing. For this is how the murder event is first described:

> Dans la rue, en bas de l'immeuble, un cri de femme retentit. Une plainte longue, continue, s'éleva et si haut que le bruit de la mer en fut brisé. Puis elle s'arrêta, net.
>
> —Qu'est-ce que c'est? cria l'enfant.
>
> —Quelque chose est arrivé, dit la dame.
>
> Le bruit de la mer ressuscita de nouveau. Le rose du ciel, cependant commença à pâlir.
>
> —Non, dit Anne Desbaresdes, ce n'est rien.
>
> (p. 10)

One of the central paradoxes of the novel is caught in this exchange. What has happened is an event which hesitates between being something and nothing, between a rehearsal and a performance, a quotation and a reality, an event and a figment of the imagination, and this indeterminacy is reflected in the quality of the cry itself, which is sustained yet abrupt, as well as in the surrounding sky, as it fades into pale pinkness and darkness, and in the sound of the sea, which is silenced only to re-emerge a moment later.

However, even if it seems, when it happens, that the event is almost without consequence for the protagonists, the scene which Anne now witnesses comes entirely to dominate the rest of the novel. For the major part of the plot is

structured like a repetitive reworking of the murder incident, its metaphoric re-enactment and ritualistic rehearsal, whereby Anne and Chauvin project onto one another the roles of murderer and victim, and become caught up in a lengthy fictional transference in the course of which it is no longer entirely clear what is real and what is fantasized or imagined. (And I use the term transference in the Freudian sense of a reactualization of unconscious material in the relation between Anne and Chauvin. All transference is repetition, and, at the limit, all repetition is transference. This is at any rate the case with Duras's two protagonists, and potentially, also with Duras's readers, who, if the act of reading is repetition and transference, cannot avoid being drawn into the scene of the text as its witnesses, its martyrs.)

From this point on, the murder scene, in repetitive, diabolical fashion, takes possession of ***Moderato cantabile.*** It does so in two ways. The first is the result of its inherent impact as a scene viewed by Anne, and, by extension, visualized by the reader. This comes about partly because of the violence and potent melodrama of the scene, which Duras underlines with the use of some readily apparent colour symbolism (the darkness of the woman's blood, for instance, echoing the dying glow of the sunset) or by recourse to blood as a sexual motif (blood is dripping from the mouths of both murderer and victim, and links them in some kind of ritualistic or sacrificial embrace, suggesting perhaps that the presence of the diabolical, even in the form of sexual vampirism, is not restricted to the structure of the plot). More important, however, is the point of view adopted by the text, which, after an introductory section, stages the scene of the crime from the viewpoint of Anne herself:

> Anne Desbaresdes se renseigna.
>
> —Quelqu'un qui a été tué. Une femme.
>
> Elle laissa son enfant devant le porche de Mademoiselle Giraud, rejoignit le gros de la foule devant le café, s'y faufila et atteignit le dernier rang des gens qui, le long des vitres ouvertes, immobilisés par le spectacle, voyaient.
>
> (p. 14)

Intriguingly, the act of seeing, or looking ('voir'), takes an absolute status, and the word is used here as an intransitive verb. Seeing the crime, imagining, or reimagining it on the basis of its aftermath, becomes, in its own right, a compelling, even compulsive, act. The scene is described by Duras as a spectacle, as a spectacle, moreover, which roots its spectators to the spot. This is important, for it puts Anne in the position of someone viewing a fantasy or dream image of her own, or, alternatively, in the position of someone looking on at an imaginary scene like that performed on a cinema screen. (What makes being in the cinema most like dreaming, it is sometimes said, is that everything except the screen is in darkness and that it is impossible, or undesirable, for people to move.) To reinforce the parallel, Duras incorporates within the fictional scene a press photographer, by the light of whose flash-bulb Anne is able to distinguish the age of the murdered woman as well as the blood disfiguring her mouth and that of her lover. The scene is framed in a single ray of light (a 'lueur' (p. 15), like that of the setting sun), and begins to stand out in the novel not only as a kind of screen image to be visualized by the reader and the hero but also as a screen memory, which condenses into one vivid scene, un-located in both time and space, a whole complex of poten-tial other meanings and associations.

The position occupied by Anne is crucial. She is a witness at the scene of the crime and thus involved as a spectator, but she is also kept at a distance as though she were the viewer of a more private scene taking place on a different stage. As she looks on, with the other bystanders, the things she sees are 'au fond du café, dans la pénombre de l'arrière-salle' (p. 14), as though they were at the back of a stage set. Her own special implication in the vision before her is underlined, as she stands looking, by her hearing the man repeat (as though it were a dream) her own earlier words to her son, 'Mon amour. Mon amour' (p. 14), and there are a number of other common elements detailed in the murder scene and in the seemingly unconnected music lesson: these range from disgust (an anonymous bystander seeing the blood on the murderer's mouth finds it all 'dégoûtant' (p. 15), as does Anne when describing her son's obedient attitude to his teacher), to the theme of vio-lent suffering and martyrdom, evoked both in the murder and by Anne's remark (already prefiguring her parting words to Chauvin) that her son causes her pain, that 'c'est déjà fait, il me dévore' (p. 13). Etymologically, to be a martyr is to be, like Anne, a witness.

Childbirth is another repetitive motif. Later, in talking with Chauvin, Anne compares the woman's dying moan to the sounds Anne made during the birth of her son. Earlier, too, as the sounds of the murder had begun to merge with the boy's piano-playing, Anne had closed her eyes (and this privileging of inward seeing again makes the point) to display 'le douloureux sourire d'un enfantement sans fin' (p. 13) (and just afterwards the murderer himself is photo-graphed 'assis et souriant' (p. 15)). A complex patchwork of verbal echoes is set up across the text, and the result is not only to create suspense by the forging of oblique and enigmatic verbal connexions but also to modify the status of the scene Anne witnesses by transferring it from the outside world into a more hallucinatory inner one. At the same time, the effect is also, arguably, to invite the reader to inquire into his or her own position as a voyeur looking on at this scene of violent murder.

As a result, as Madeleine Borgomano suggests, the murder scene functions in the novel rather like a primal scene (or *Urszene*) in the Freudian sense of the term (pp. 113-39). These are vivid, hallucinatory scenes, based on real memory, but substantially reinvented and overlaid with other meanings by the unconscious. They work as densely-woven miniature scenarios dramatizing in fantasy form what, according to Freud, can be interpreted as the view-er's or dreamer's first (traumatic or dramatic) encounter with sexuality, and the moment of his or her initiation into the secrets of sexual difference. As Borgomano argues, in Duras's novels the density and energy of scenes like the murder in *Moderato cantabile* (and many other scenes of this type could be cited here) derive from their capacity to condense into one luminous scene or narrative tableau a complex but necessarily latent drama of sexual insight and awareness.

In the Freudian context, such memories are usually thought of as childhood memories, and it is worth stressing in this respect the role played at the scene by Anne's child. Clearly, Anne's son is used in the first chapter in part as a realistic device, to emphasize Anne's role as wife and mother (and there are few enough major novels which ex-plicitly deal with this dimension of parenthood). But there is a further important aspect to the child's presence, for it is implied later that the child is almost an imaginary cre-ation of Anne's, and she declares to him, accordingly, that 'quelquefois je crois que je t'ai inventé, que ce n'est pas vrai' (p. 25). The child becomes almost an integral part of Anne herself, not just her child but a part of herself, and thus, to some degree, herself as a child. But also, what the child encapsulates for Anne is Anne herself as sexually differentiated, not only in the sense that childbirth pre-sumes a knowledge of the sexual difference between male and female but also in the sense that she, a woman, has borne this male child.

This sexual knowledge, then, is what, from Anne's per-spective, seems to be at issue in this scene she has wit-nessed. The insight it gives is clearly visible, in so far as the scene can (and perhaps can only) be viewed, but the scene also seems to speak silently of the unseen. The child is instructed not to look ('ne regarde pas', Anne says to him, without elaborating (p. 15)), and the discussion is im-mediately covered up by the question of the meaning of the words 'moderato cantabile'. Admittedly, this serves to underline how the vision of the scene touches on a social and sexual taboo, but it also achieves the second and equally important purpose of linking music with the theme of sexuality. Music, as a structure of repetition and varia-tion, and as a process of (non-verbal) differentiation, be-comes a means of dramatizing the very instability of sexual difference, the separation but also the apparent fusing of identities, the violence but also the erotic union displayed in the murder scene. It is not coincidental in this respect that by the end of the first chapter the two major enigmas posed by the text are the significance of the words 'mod-erato cantabile' and the meaning of the murder incident.

Yet much of the ambivalence of the murder appears to de-rive from the mixture of generic registers at work in the text and the expectations of reading which accompany them. The scene Duras unfolds seems to hesitate between low crime and high romance, between brutal realism and passionate melodrama, and, ultimately, between sensation-alism and seriousness. It is far from self-evident how read-ers are to react to this spectacle of the *crime passionnel*.

The generic clues seem to be working at cross-purposes, and readers are invited by the text to respond in a number of possible ways: with disgust, shock, sympathy, annoyance, indifference, curiosity, fascination, or even rapture, depending on which position in the text readers decide to share.

One of the characteristic traits of the apocalyptic genre as such, Derrida argues, is precisely this mixing of genres, the combining of the pious with the lurid, the extravagant with the reverential. This can be pushed to such a degree that the notion of a message to be revealed becomes gravely compromised by the text's own inability to exhaust the absolute, unspeakable, or infinite which is its object.[8] The same paradox seems to affect Duras's text. The more the murder scene takes on the semblance of a scene of revelation or recognition, the more Anne Desbaresdes's vision or insight recedes into enigma, and the more unclear it becomes what it is that is being revealed. Indeed, the uncertainties readers may have about the generic conventions the novel may be following (romance, crime fiction, 'women's' fiction, psychological thriller, or high art?) reflect disturbances at work on the level of gender as well as of genre. It is far from clear not only what Duras's novel actually implies in terms, say, of its sexual politics, but also what the novel's own position (if it has one) is towards the sexual violence it depicts. National tradition also plays a part and it is no doubt the case that French readers are more attuned to the mythic dimensions of the theme of the *crime passionnel* than English-speaking ones. The connexion claimed between eroticism and violence has become, in France, a rather dreary contemporary commonplace, one which, some readers might well argue, Duras's own novel reveals in its apparent refusal to frame the murder in any other way than as an act of violent and excessive desire.

What Duras does in ***Moderato cantabile,*** by way of answering her own question about the meaning of the title, is to produce a set of contradictory frames of reference, the effect of which is to challenge the existence of any unified interpretation or intent behind the text. What happens instead is that readers are exposed, uncomfortably, to the puzzles and enigmatic implications of sexual difference and sexual relations in a way which bypasses convenient rationalizations. On one level, Duras's text revamps in overtly melodramatic fashion a number of canonic and mythical images on the subject of the interpenetration of love and death. The notion of orgasm as 'la petite mort' lies tremulously in wait in the margins of Duras's text for any over-enthusiastic commentator. The scene rehearses, albeit in fantasy form, a myth of romantic passion, set in a seaside town in modern France, and at the heart of that myth is a theme of passion, of love and desire as a fusing of identity between sexual partners. It is the same loss of difference, of the boundaries which exist between individuals, between me and you, which is implied in the actions of the murderer as he lies across his dead lover, mingling his blood with hers in a moment of sadistic oral communion (and we must be wary here of assuming that

Duras's novel unproblematically endorses the myth of love as erotic fusion):

> Dans la lueur du magnésium, on put voir que la femme était jeune encore et qu'il y avait du sang qui coulait de sa bouche en minces filets épars et qu'il y en avait aussi sur le visage de l'homme qui l'avait embrassée.
> . . .
>
> L'homme se recoucha de nouveau le long du corps de sa femme, mais un temps très court. Puis, comme si cela l'eût lassé, il se releva encore. . . . .
>
> Mais l'homme ne s'était relevé que pour mieux s'allonger, de plus près, le long du corps. Il resta là, dans une résolution apparemment tranquille, agrippé de nouveau à elle de ses deux bras, le visage collé au sien, dans le sang de sa bouche.

(p. 15)

While Duras evokes this theme of merging identities, she simultaneously highlights the irreducible gap which is inherent in the relation between male and female. For unmistakably (and the story of Anne and Chauvin perhaps stresses this more than the opening murder scene) the murder is also an act of aggression which has as its outcome the suppression of the difference existing between the couple (which had made it possible for this 'relationship' to exist, however furtively, between them). A fundamental question mark is raised here as to the nature of that relationship between the sexes. The novel itself provides no answer to the question, because the novel itself is the dramatic enactment of that question, its rehearsal and repetition, and, by refusing to answer, is proof of the fact that there can be no universalizing answer to the question, only singularly different ones, since sexual difference is precisely what ruins the claim to existence of universal truths. There can be no single frame of reading which would resolve these issues. What Duras's readers are given instead is the puzzling terms of a scene of literature which has to be deciphered and read, not only by the book's readers, male and female, but also by the novel's protagonists, Anne and Chauvin. And this, as Marianne Hirsch suggests, is largely what happens in the remainder of the novel ('Gender, Reading and Desire in *Moderato cantabile,*' *Twentieth-Century Literature,* 28, no. 1 (Spring 1982), 69-85 (p. 78).

Here, the murder scene comes to dominate ***Moderato cantabile*** in a second important way. The incident reverberates throughout the novel as more than just a powerful beginning. Though it occupies less than three pages in the first chapter, the scene comes to programme, rather like some fascinating but impenetrable subtext, almost all the subsequent actions of Anne, especially in her relationship with Chauvin, as soon as she encounters him in the café at the beginning of Chapter 2. The story of the murder provides them with their major topic of conversation, and thus, in the theatrical sense of the term, with their text. As Anne is attracted to Chauvin as a witness who might cast some light on the perplexities of the primal scene, she begins to repeat the scene in her talks with him (and Chauvin's behaviour suggests his willingness to repeat the scene, too). Numerous elements recur: the café locale serves as a common theatre or stage for the murder and the meeting with Chauvin, the colour symbolism of the wine Anne drinks (and does so to excess) in the course of her flirtatious relations with the man echoes that of the blood in the earlier scene, while the timing of the meetings, at dusk, is the same, and allows the glow of the sunset, like a theatrical spotlight, to pour in through the windows in the same way as in the last paragraphs of the first chapter ('le mur du fond de la salle', we read in the middle of the third chapter (p. 33), 's'illumina du soleil couchant. En son milieu, le trou noir de leurs ombres conjuguées se dessina').

The compelling presence of the murder as an object of Anne's and Chauvin's fascination and as an enigma they seek to resolve but end up repeating means that the boundary between the central plot and the frame story of the murder is effectively blurred, and it is no longer clear which of the two takes logical precedence over the other. In *Moderato cantabile,* as elsewhere in Duras's novels, notably in *Le Vice-consul,* meaning is organized by use of a rhetoric of contagion (in *Le Vice-consul* and *India Song* this is thematized with the aid of the motif of leprosy or untouchability). Rather than subordinating themes hierarchically, though, Duras's text sets up its own logic of association, creating connexions by metonymic juxtaposition or repetition. The relation between the murder and its re-enactment, for instance, remains indeterminate. No chain of causality is established in the text and a circular structure results, by which the murder is a preliminary section of a larger story, which itself is a subsection of the story of the murder, itself the culmination of an earlier story which is withheld from the reader and suspended in oblivion. The inquiry into the crime becomes part of the crime just as much as the crime is itself part of the inquiry, and it is no longer evident which story events are repeating or rehearsing which, or which set of events is the metaphoric transposition or transference of which other. Narrative hierarchy is perturbed and it is no longer possible to distinguish with confidence between what is literal and what is figurative, or what terms are available to formulate the enigmas of love, desire, and sexual difference.

Typical of this process is the way the words exchanged by Anne and Chauvin take on a slippery ambivalence. Few of Duras's pronouns (in this novel or in any other texts) are made explicit, and it is at times questionable whom they refer to. On one occasion, for example, the pair remain silent for some moments, and Anne asks:

> —Je voudrais que vous me disiez maintenant comment ils en sont arrivés à ne plus même se parler. . . .

> —Je ne sais rien. Peut-être par de longs silences qui s'installaient entre eux, la nuit, un peu n'importe quand ensuite et qu'ils étaient de moins en moins capables de surmonter par rien, rien.

> (p. 40)

Unmistakably, the referents of the third-person 'ils' have changed. They are no longer the earlier couple but Anne

and Chauvin themselves, who have forfeited their own personal pronouns and become the participants in some romantic 'cérémonial' (p. 38), a ritualistic sexual encounter which dissolves their sense of identity and, like the sunset, turns them into silhouettes of themselves who remain who and what they are, but also exist as the shadows and reflections of someone or something else.

As the novel proceeds, then, Anne and Chauvin become actors in a scenario which, though it seems not to be of their making, they reinvent, repeat, re-enact, and make their own. The dividing line between real and imaginary, between knowledge and simulation, between self and other, is erased. The plot of *Moderato cantabile* as a whole takes the form of a series of self-mirroring events to which it is impossible to assign an origin or a root cause. This style of reflexivity works counter to the idea of the mirror as a controlling device (and continues to inform much of Duras's work, notably the film of *India Song,* in which almost all the interior shots, either totally or in part, are done through a mirror). Both the relation between Anne and Chauvin and the murder earlier become versions, rehearsals, or repetitions of something else, which is not named and is lost as an absent and forgotten memory. This most of all is what lends Duras's novel its air of compelling mystery. None of the enigmas announced in the first chapter (the reasons for the murder, or the significance of the words 'moderato cantabile') is resolved; they are simply repeated and reworked, rehearsed, and varied (like a musical excerpt) in a spiralling movement which takes the reader forward, but also leads back in time towards an unlocated and effaced memory to which access is denied.

Structured as a series of repetitive mirrors, what the novel does is to describe and to put into crisis a whole array of frames, divisions, and borderlines, which no longer serve to stabilize meaning but become blurred and uncertain. It is difficult, if not impossible, to resolve the enigma of desire or sexual difference dramatized in the murder scene by recourse to a readily-available frame of reference. On the contrary, frames slip and slide, and borderlines become areas of confusion, not demarcation zones affording clarity. This is the lesson behind the famous and no doubt programmatic set-piece dinner scene (Chapter 7), where Anne faces the implications of her experiences on the borderline (between sea and shore, promiscuity and maternity, seeing and not seeing). The dinner party is another inquiry into borderlines and the turbulence they conceal, an exploration, for instance, of the gulf now apparent between Anne and her social world, of the scandalous nature of her relation to Chauvin, and of the limit between the inside and outside of the house and park, as well as that between the inside and outside of Anne's own body.

On this frontier, limits are paradoxically undone, and Anne is able to stage her revolt against the masculine order of her social world, against the well-policed divisions of a 'société', as Duras puts it, 'fondée, dans ses assises, sur la certitude de son droit' (p. 70). But while Anne does rebel against the profligacy and rituals (indeed, the 'cérémonial'

(p. 68)) of the world of her husband and family, she does so in the name of a different excess and a different ritual, and in response to a different man, one who comes prowling, and invades the 'parc correctement clos' (p. 70) of her matrimonial home, like the agent of some primeval sexual disturbance, revealing the deep complicity of desire now present between Anne and Chauvin. 'Un homme rôde, boulevard de la Mer', writes Duras. 'Une femme le sait' (p. 61).

It would seem that in the Bible, Derrida suggests, the idea of apocalyptic disclosure has to do with the improper unveiling of sexuality, that of the father, for example, within the family circle, with the public exposure of private parts (*D'un ton apocalyptique,* pp. 13-14). As in the Bible, so it is in Duras's novel, where, moreover, the enactment of desire, the dramatization of the space between Anne and Chauvin is performed by way of the motif of overpowering, sweet-smelling, cup-shaped magnolia flowers. (Later, in *India Song,* leprosy is described as having 'comme une odeur de fleur' (p. 19).) 'Dehors, dans le parc', ***Moderato cantabile*** has it, 'les magnolias élaborent leur floraison funèbre dans la nuit noire du printemps naissant' (p. 67), and there follows a whole string of allusions to the magnolia blossom Anne wears in her cleavage (marking her sexual identity) and finally crushes as the culminating gesture of this love scene carried out at a distance.

Sexual desire, like the magnolias, overpowering, excessive, funereal, and deadly, irrupts into Anne's domesticated world with catastrophic force. 'Il lui faut fracasser les arbres, foudroyer les murs', mutters Stein in *Détruire, dit-elle* (p. 136), speaking of the music of Bach as it floods in across the park from the forest, and the effect of desire in Duras's work is much the same, objecting turbulence, disorder, excess to the carefully circumscribed borderlines of established society. Anne herself, responding to the call of Chauvin (who, like her, throughout this chapter, pronounces a name, which Duras leaves unspoken), vomits the sumptuous food at the dinner-table, thus rejects her family, and forfeits her child as a result. Her social identity is effaced, and the structured lines of that life give way to a catastrophic blurring of borders. The margins of her life, those areas where her sense of self had mysteriously been held in abeyance (as she discovers by witnessing her own primal scene in the border-zone of the docks), move to the centre.

It is possible, as some critics have argued, that Anne achieves here some form of self-emancipation (see David Coward, *Duras: **Moderato Cantabile*** (London, 1981), pp. 51-53). But that would imply a view of subjective freedom which the self-mirroring circularities of ***Moderato cantabile*** seem not to accommodate. In the closing scene, as it rehearses once again the frame story of the murder, it still remains enigmatic between Anne and Chauvin whether their relationship has been merely a game, or a faithful re-enactment of the past (but whose past?), or a real sexual encounter, whether it culminates in freedom from a compulsive model or in the ritualistic endorsement of a mur-

derous confrontation, and what it is that distinguishes the ritual of their daily meetings from the rituals of middle-class domesticity. Duras provides a dual, or even triple, story, a modern love-story, which tells a tale of merged identities, but also of irreconcilable differences, indeed a story of the enigmatic and unspeakable character of sexual desire. She manages to subscribe to and to confront at one and the same time two of the major modern (fictional and literary) myths of human sexual relations: the myth of sexuality as the fusing of selves, and the myth of inescapable and remorseless difference, both *Tristan and Isolde* and *Sodome et Gomorrhe,* while subjecting both to the catastrophic sense of their inadequacy and fragility. In this regard it is unsurprising that the novel has an ending which is both a completion of a ritualized enactment and its deliberate effacement, both a repetition and a refusal to repeat:

> Anne Desbaresdes se releva et tenta encore, par-dessus la table, de se rapprocher de Chauvin.
>
> —Peut-être que je ne vais pas y arriver, murmura-t-elle.
>
> Peut-être n'entendit-il plus. Elle ramena sa veste sur elle-même, la ferma, l'étriqua sur elle, fut reprise du même gémissement sauvage.
>
> —C'est impossible, dit-elle.
>
> Chauvin entendit.
>
> —Une minute, dit-il, et nous y arriverons.
>
> Anne Desbaresdes attendit cette minute, puis elle essaya de se relever de sa chaise. Elle y arriva, se releva. Chauvin regardait ailleurs. Les hommes évitèrent encore de porter leurs yeux sur cette femme adultère. Elle fut levée.
>
> —Je voudrais que vous soyez morte, dit Chauvin.
>
> —C'est fait, dit Anne Desbaresdes.
>
> (pp. 83-84)

As Anne gets up and, with the courtesy of a passing reference to the Bible, emerges once more into the apocalyptic sunset, the reader of these closing lines is put in the position of not really being able to say what it is that he or she has witnessed, or what has just been carried out: the final acting-out of an obsessive fantasy, a symbolic enactment of death, murder, and ritualized desire, or the ironic relegation of that fantasy to the past (with Anne offering a final gesture of mock compliance to Chauvin). But, if that is true, the reader is treated no differently from the protagonists of the novel. In some ways the reader's only option seems to be to behave like Anne and Chauvin, who, as I have said, become caught up in a scenario over which they have no apparent control, but which dictates to them, as though from some pre-established script, the enigmas of sexual difference as though these signified revelation and as though that revelation itself were to imply, in fact, like some blood-red visionary sunset, nothing less than the end of the world.

But what does the end of the world mean? The use of the formula 'c'est fait', with its overtones of biblical martyrdom, is not isolated in Duras's writing. It occurs notably in the first version of the story *L'Homme assis dans le couloir* which, on its publication in 1980, was criticized by some readers as little short of pornographic in its explicit coupling of sexual enjoyment and violence.⁹ (In it, for example, as an aftermath to orgasm, during 'la lente remontée du désir' (p. 32), the woman asks the man to strike her and to continue beating her to the point of insensibility.) Marcelle Marini suggests that the text, together with *La Maladie de la mort* (and presumably, too, the more recent *Les Yeux bleus cheveux noirs*), needs to be read as to some extent detached from the rest of Duras's work, almost as its infernal doublet, though it is she who points out that in the early version of *L'Homme assis dans le couloir* published in *L'Arc*, the woman character is named as Anne-Marie Stretter. Moreover, as Madeleine Borgomano shows (pp. 172-73), various fragments from this version survive in *Le Vice-consul*, where they are presented as a fantasy of Charles Rossett's concerning Anne-Marie Stretter.

Given this close connexion between *L'Homme assis dans le couloir* and some of Duras's major novels, it is difficult to see how the text can be relegated to some purgatorial antechamber. For in each of the various texts concerned, the two versions of *L'Homme assis dans le couloir* as well as *Le Vice-consul* and **Moderato cantabile,** there seems clearly to exist an underlying but none the less recurrent scene, which takes on different guises, but which insists on the coupling of erotic fusion with beating, violence, death, even murder. That the scene also has its voyeuristic component is made clear not only in **Moderato cantabile** and *Le Ravissement de Lol V. Stein* but also by the changes made in the published version of *L'Homme assis dans le couloir,* which, Duras notes in *Les Yeux verts,* hinged in part on the introduction of a spectator, a voyeur, as witness to the actions of the couple, and on the realization that 'cette vue était, devait être mentionnée, intégrée aux faits'.¹⁰ Why, in turn, this voyeur should make her appearance in a text initially intended for the *Cahiers du cinéma,* is something which must be reserved for another occasion.

In the *L'Arc* version of *L'Homme assis dans le couloir,* the phrase 'c'est fait' marks the conclusion of a scene which, unmistakably, is a transposed description of sexual intercourse, executed by a phallic male hand labouring the lips, teeth, and mouth of a compliant Anne-Marie Stretter. The rhythm of his beating hand is clearly crucial, since it recurs in both versions of *L'Homme assis dans le couloir* as well as in *Le Vice-consul* (p. 203). 'La main bat', says each of these texts, and it is no surprise to realize the importance given to hands and lips in the closing pages of **Moderato cantabile,** as Anne and Chauvin join in some deathly sexual partnership (and on the last page of the novel we read: 'La main de Chauvin battit l'air et retomba sur la table' (p. 84)).

Though the level of explicitness is quite different, the distance is not vast between **Moderato cantabile** and texts such as *L'Homme assis dans le couloir.* In both there is within sexual relations the same depersonalization, the same extremity of violence, of participants being engulfed by an absence of memory, a primeval blankness, an apocalyptic emptiness such that, as in the concluding words to the first version of *L'Homme assis dans le couloir,* 'le non-sens s'installa'. In the later version, like the red sunset that greets Anne Desbaresdes as she gets up to go, what happens is the colour violet, as though to bear witness to some catastrophic, apocalyptic disclosure. The colour violet, offering as its homophonic doublet the spectre of destruction, rapture, and rape, is another reference, this time to the film *India Song* and the death of Anne-Marie Stretter, to Venice, and the blinding white light which, in the film, floods the screen as though to reveal the decaying mortality of white supremacy and the political crises changing the landscape of colonialist Europe. The vision is that of a world collapsing, it is the aftermath of a vision, the vision of an apocalyptic aftermath which, as a man lies weeping across his lover's body, rehearses yet again the murder scene of **Moderato cantabile.** This is how the 1980 version of *L'Homme assis dans le couloir* ends:

> Je vois que la couleur violette arrive, qu'elle atteint l'embouchure du fleuve, que le ciel s'est couvert, qu'il est arrêté dans sa lente course vers l'immensité. Je vois que d'autres gens regardent, d'autres femmes, que d'autres femmes maintenant mortes ont regardé de même se faire et se défaire les moussons d'été devant des fleuves bordés de rizières sombres, face à des embouchures vastes et profondes. Je vois que de la couleur violette arrive un orage d'été.
>
> Je vois que l'homme pleure couché sur la femme. Je ne vois rien d'elle que l'immobilité. Je l'ignore, je ne sais rien, je ne sais pas si elle dort.
>
> (pp. 35-36)

Irredeemably, then, this scene of apocalypse stands at the various turnings of Duras's text or texts: as a figure of disaster and violence, separateness and flow, origin and finality, insight and puzzlement. It signals the coupling of male and female in death and melancholy; it traces, too, the unbridgeable difference between female and male against the background of the summer monsoon. Its contours remain blurred, filling the frame of reading but refusing to settle as a simple object of voyeuristic inquiry. What it does, in tune with the whole of Duras's cinema and much of her fiction, is to raise the very question of the frame through which Duras's readers, as sexed bodies, gaze on, with fascination, at the mysterious spectacle of these bodies, one male, one female. Apocalypse as revelation gives way to apocalypse as violent conundrum. Love as transcendence becomes love as abolition and the only meaning of sexual difference that of an obsessive but none the less empty and inhospitable space of division.

Notes

1. Marguerite Duras, *Détruire, dit-elle* (Paris, 1969), p. 139. A similar formula appears in *India Song* (Paris, 1973), p. 10, where the restriction is lifted for countries other than France.

2. Anne-Marie Stretter appears in *Le Ravissement de Lol. V. Stein, Le Vice-consul, India Song, Son nom de Venise dans Calcutta désert,* as well as in the early published version of *L'Homme assis dans le couloir.* It is from the 1980 version of *L'Homme assis dans le couloir* (Paris, 1980), p. 9, that the phrase 'différemment toujours' comes. (I shall return to this text later.) Anne-Marie Stretter's initials are also those of Aurélia Steiner. Madeleine Borgomano makes the odd but suggestive point that all Duras's female characters (including the woman of *Moderato cantabile*) seem to be called Anne (*Duras: Une lecture des fantasmes* (Brussels, 1985), p. 178).

3. The diversity of arguments on this and other issues is reflected in the following collections of essays devoted to Duras's work: *Marguerite Duras,* edited by Joël Farges and François Barat (Paris, 1975); *Marguerite Duras à Montréal,* edited by Suzanne Lamy and André Roy (Montreal, 1981); *Ecrire dit-elle: Imaginaires de Marguerite Duras,* edited by Danielle Bajomée and Ralph Heyndels (Brussels, 1985); *L'Arc,* 98 (1985), a special number devoted to Duras's work, as is the *Revue des sciences humaines,* 202 (1986).

4. See, for example, the interview entitled 'La Voie du gai désespoir', published in *Le Monde* in 1977 to coincide with the release of *Le Camion,* and reprinted in Marguerite Duras, *Outside* (Paris, 1981), pp. 171-79. The term is clearly calculated to echo that of 'le gai savoir', but it also perhaps owes something to the use of 'gai' in the same sense as the contemporary English 'gay'.

5. Marguerite Duras, *Le Camion* (Paris, 1977), p. 73. Further references in the text are to this edition. This article was already completed when Julia Kristeva's essay on apocalyptic themes in Duras became available, published in her *Soleil noir: Dépression et mélancolie* (Paris, 1987).

6. From the interviews included on the video collection of eight of Duras's films, issued by the Ministère des relations extérieures in 1984. They are reproduced in the accompanying booklet, *Marguerite Duras: uvres cinématographiques* (Paris, 1984), p. 58.

7. Marguerite Duras, *Moderato cantabile,* collection 'double' (Paris, 1958, 1985). All references to the novel are to this edition.

8. See Jacques Derrida, *D'un ton apocalyptique adopté naguère en philosophie* (Paris, 1983), pp. 76-78. It cannot be coincidental in this context that the story of *Moderato cantabile* is spread out over seven days (the book has been translated as *Seven Days and Seven Nights*), and that seven should be the apocalyptic number *par excellence.*

9. See Marcelle Marini, 'La Mort d'une érotique', *Cahiers Renaud-Barrault,* 106 (September 1983),

37-57. As Marini points out, there exist (at least) two published versions, in French, of *L'Homme assis dans le couloir.* The first, which appears to be fragmentary (and has suspension points in various places), but none the less gives the woman's name as Anne-Marie Stretter, appeared in *L'Arc,* 20 (October 1962), 70-76. Totally rewritten, except for a few portions of the text, the story (initially intended for Duras's special *Cahiers du cinéma* issue) reappeared as a separate volume in 1980, published by Éditions de Minuit. This later version differs considerably in detail, though much of the structure of the earlier version is retained. Similar material is found also towards the end of *Le Vice-consul* (Paris, 1966), pp. 203-04.

10. Marguerite Duras, *Les Yeux verts,* Special number of *Les Cahiers du cinéma,* 312-13 (June 1980), 33. It might be argued (this is to some degree the position put forward by Marcelle Marini) that, by coupling sexuality with violence in this way, Duras is dramatizing sexual violence as an inherent component of heterosexual relations. It is important to note, however, that the voyeur viewing, witnessing, and inventing the scene (like Anne in *Moderato cantabile*) is not a male fetishist or pornographer, but Duras herself, as she admits: 'J'ai trouvé', she says, 'que les amants n'étaient pas isolés mais vus, sans doute par moi' (*Les Yeux verts,* p. 33). The whole question of gendered looking and sexual knowledge is an important and recurrent theme in her work, particularly in her films, but limitations of space prevent me from going into it here.

Nina S. Hellerstein (essay date 1989)

SOURCE: "Family Reflections and the Absence of the Father in Duras's 'L'Amant,'" in *Essays in French Literature,* No. 26, November, 1989, pp. 98-109.

[*In the following essay, Hellerstein suggests that the father's death in* The Lover *"deprives all the members of the family of a source of emotional, economic, and sexual definition."*]

The theme of absence plays a major role in Marguerite Duras's works, as has been shown by the studies of Carol Murphy and others.[1] *L'Amant* is no exception to this rule, and indeed Duras indicates the importance of the theme from the very beginning of the novel: her own identity appears as an unnameable void, and the family relations which form one of the major subjects of the book are described as "le lieu au seuil de quoi le silence commence", a "mystère", a "porte fermée".[2] However, these family relations are not only a form of ontological, emotional absence, a mysterious, unknowable void; they are themselves based on one primordial absence which is a literal and physical fact: the absence of the father. The death of the narrator's father deprives all the members of the family of a source of emotional, economic and sexual definition. The consequences of his absence, although they are rarely explicitly mentioned, affect all the characters, and are a central factor in the narrator's search for self-definition and fulfilment with her lover.[3]

On a social and economic level, the father's death deprives the family of security, and this feeling of instability extends to all its members' relations with others:

> Je lui dis qu'on était dehors, que la misère avait fait s'écrouler les murs de la famille et qu'on s'était tous retrouvés en dehors de la maison, à faire chacun ce qu'on voulait faire. Dévergondés on était.
>
> (58)

The father's traditional role is to represent external society within the family, to mediate between the personal interactions of the family and the economic, institutional, impersonal world outside. With the father's absence, the female members of the family are forced to assume the heavy burden of its economic survival. Thus the narrator, by her success in school and its promise of future professional success, takes on the economic and professional aspects of the father's role.

There is, however, one major form of the Father figure in the novel: the Chinese lover's father. This character represents the traditional values of patriarchal society in their most archaic form: he is the jealous possessor of untold millions which he has extracted from the poor by somewhat dubious methods; he supervises his son's activities with a suspicious eye; and, most of all, he forbids his son's marriage with the narrator in the name of his family's ancestral lineage, the purity of his race and regional origin. All of these qualities contrast with the narrator and her family, with their poverty and social marginality. The Chinese father is a builder; whereas the walls around the heroine's family have collapsed. The contrast is even more direct in the domain of sexuality: the paternal obligation is to create "l'héritier du nom" (141), and this preoccupation with reproduction is opposed to the narrator's free, hedonistic, uncontrollable sexuality.

The contrast between the two situations reveals that, in spite of the hardship and suffering it has imposed on the heroine and her family, the absence of her father has also had a liberating effect. It has freed her from the constraints of convention, family stability and society, as represented in their most extreme form by the lover's father, and forced her to create another kind of strength and identity, which are destined to be realized in her writing. But this existential freedom and self-creation are irreconcilable with the conventionality and permanence of marriage; for this reason, the narrator and the lover's father both agree that marriage between her and the lover is impossible. Their love affair, "leur histoire", will never become a part of History as it is inscribed in permanent form in marriage or children; this permanent form of History is the history of

the Father, of institutions, inheritances and lineage. But the love affair will live on in another kind of history, a more fluid and impalpable one, that which has taken form in this book. History on the institutional, public level has overwhelmed the two lovers, but like the strain of music, the lover's voice, which comes back to the heroine at the end of the book, is a personal form of history which has continued to defy the Father's interdiction.

Thus, the absence of the father is a form of negation, a blank space which affects the life of the narrator and her family in many adverse ways, but which also forces them to search for new roles and qualities, in order to replace what has been lost. Her mother, with the courage the narrator describes as "cette vaillance de l'espèce, absurde" takes on the greatest part of the burden, and the narrator finds in this courage "la grâce profonde" (117) which inspires her own hard work and strength of will. Yet in spite of this solid, reasonable, practical kind of courage, there is another, much more troubling side to her mother's role. The little we learn about their relationship suggests that her mother is a symbolic accomplice in her father's death: she seems to question the value of her marriage and her husband, and she refuses to follow him back to France before his death. Moreover, she possesses the occult power to foresee his death and to communicate with the ghost of her own father as well; the association of these two apparitions, in the paternal sanctuary which is the father's office, in the King of Cambodia's palace, suggests that the mother exercises a kind of mysterious domination over these paternal figures.

This sinister side of the mother's role is most fully embodied in her relationship with her sons. The disappearance of the father leaves a gap which is destined to be filled by the sons. From a psychoanalytic point of view, it is a continuation of the infantile, Oedipal relationship, in which the mutual sexual complementarity of mother and son creates a self-contained, complete unit.[4] The infantile nature of the sons' relationship to their mother is shown by the fact that neither of them is able to succeed in his studies, to become independent intellectually and professionally. But the Oedipal bond of mother and son is the most overt and important in the case of the elder son: "Jusqu'à sa mort le frère aîné l'a eue pour lui seul" (72). The mother is capable of giving life, but this symbiotic, Oedipal bond prevents her from teaching her son to grow beyond her into an adult who is capable of nourishing himself. The episode of the chicken-raising shows this inability in a symbolic, concrete form:

> Ce qu'elle avait fait, elle, de son château est proprement inimaginable, cela toujours pour le fils aîné qui ne sait pas, lui, l'enfant de cinquante ans, gagner de l'argent. Elle achète des couveuses électriques, elle les installe dans le grand salon du bas. Elle a six cents poussins dun coup, quarante mètres carrés de poussins. Elle s'était trompée dans le maniement des infra-rouges, aucun poussin ne réussit à s'alimenter. Les six cents

poussins ont le bec qui ne coïncide pas, qui ne ferme pas, ils crèvent tous de faim, elle ne recommencera plus.

(39)

The symbiotic, infantile relationship of mother and son thus leads ultimately to death, where it finds its most complete expression. Death reunites the son and the mother in a circular, timeless space which is both tomb and maternal uterus.

Elle a demandé que celui-là soit enterré avec elle. Je ne sais plus à quel endroit, dans quel cimetière, je sais que c'est dans la Loire. Ils sont tous les deux dans la tombe. Eux deux seulement. C'est juste. L'image est d'une intolérable splendeur.

(99)

This connection with death confers upon the mother the aura of a mother-goddess, with the power to create and to destroy life. She exercises these powers in both positive and destructive ways. Yet in spite of these occult connections with the principle of life and death, or perhaps because of them, the mother conceives her relationship to the world as that of a victim. She is the prophet crying in the wilderness, in the desert of her wastrel sons' incompetence, in the solitude of her poverty. "Autour d'elle c'est les déserts, les fils c'est les déserts, ils feront rien, les terres salées aussi, l'argent restera perdu, c'est bien fini" (33). She exercises her terrible power over her children even as a victim, since their most basic conception of themselves, each other and the world is determined by this view: "A cause de ce qu'on a fait à notre mère si aimable, si confiante, nous haïssons la vie, nous nous haïssons" (69). The hate that each child feels for himself or herself, and for each of the others, is hate for the image of accomplice which he sees within himself and in the mirror of the others' faces. Their crime is to be separate human beings who will have to make their own way in the world, and who have independent faculties of judgment which they can turn on their own mother, condemning her as society does.

Elle nous fait honte, elle me fait honte dans la rue devant le lycée, quand elle arrive dans sa B.12 devant le lycée tout le monde regarde, elle, elle s'aperçoit de rien, jamais, elle est à enfermer, à battre, à tuer.

(32)

The children know things about the mother that she does not know about herself: they know that she has remained a child, symbolically, because she has never known sexual pleasure. Yet the mother's innocence, which has the effect of inducing a terrible, destructive guilt in the children who do not share it, also represents her most admirable quality. Washing the family's house becomes a celebration of this innocence, as the house becomes full of the perfume of "la pureté, [. . .] l'honnêteté, celle du linge, celle de la blancheur, celle de notre mère, de l'immensité de la candeur de notre mère" (76-7).

Here the beneficial qualities of water are associated with the mother's innocence, in contrast with the arid deserts of corruption and complicity which she sees around her. This mythical, elemental purity is also associated with her refusal to compromise. Not only does she reject the intervention of external, institutional powers, but this rejection and refusal are in fact based on a kind of existential refusal, a profound despair which extends to every part of her life. "J'ai eu cette chance d'avoir une mère désespérée d'un désespoir si pur que même le bonheur de la vie, si vif soit-il, quelquefois, n'arrivait pas à l'en distraire tout à fait" (22). This basic rejection of life's pleasures is an example, a way to put into perspective whatever good things may momentarily come one's way, a reminder that no joys can really answer human beings' overwhelming, total needs. In her toughness, her unrelenting battle against the senseless forces of a corrupt and crushing world, the mother represents the purity of an absolute.

Thus the positive and the negative, the creative and the destructive sides of the mother are intricately related. As children, the narrator and her brothers admire their mother's seemingly supernatural knowledge and powers, but this knowledge concerns death as well as life. Her courage against the patriarchal institutions of society and the state is exemplary, but within the tangled web of family relationships caused by the disappearance of the father, she is as weak as she is strong outside it. By allowing her eldest son to usurp the position of the other two and to occupy alone the role of her "child", she becomes the accomplice in her younger son's death, and it is therefore her association with death which finally dominates the heroine's evaluation of her mother's role in her life.

The narrator herself is the only child with the emotional and professional ability to escape this jungle. It is, paradoxically, the child of the same sex, and moreover the child who is closest to her mother in her assumption of responsibilities for the family, who is destined to make the cleanest break. Students of the mother-daughter relationship, such as Nancy Chodorow and Luce Irigaray, have emphasized the continuity between mother and daughter, a kind of confusion of self-images which makes it harder for the daughter to grow up and become a separate person.[5] Our heroine, however, is unable to overcome this danger. Because her brothers are of a different, complementary sex from their mother, they are already from birth in an "ideal" relationship with her and do not develop the resources to free themselves from it, since their father is not present to force this Oedipal crisis. In contrast, the narrator is from the very beginning excluded from her mother's love. Her sexual definition will have to come from her difference with her mother, and this is the function of the affair with the lover. By discovering the "jouissance" which her mother never knew, the narrator matures beyond the mother's own childish state, and this enables her to conquer independence in other areas as well.

To some extent, the absence of the father from his daughter's life is simply a more extensive and permanent form of the traditional and "normal" father's absence, caused by his customary lack of involvement in child-raising. Olivier has shown how this paternal absence deprives the daughter of a source of sexual complementarity similar to that provided to the son by the mother, and creates a lifelong feeling of dissatisfaction and need for male approval.[6] The heroine of *L'Amant* shows many of these reactions, but the irremediable and permanent character of her father's absence inspires her to assume them consciously and voluntarily, to utilize her need and her search for satisfaction to conquer independence. When her mother's older men friends are attracted to her, she plays the charming role they expect, but instead of experiencing the alienation of the passive female object, the narrator voluntarily takes control of the process of image creation, in order to utilize the regard of others in her search for self-definition.

> Ce que je veux paraître je le parais [. . .] tout ce que l'on veut de moi je peux le devenir. Et le croire. [. . .] Dès que je le crois, que cela devienne vrai pour celui qui me voit et qui désire que je sois selon son goût, je le sais aussi.
>
> (26)

The Chinese lover is the narrator's most important partner in this formative exchange of regards and desires; and in this role, he takes on the symbolic attributes of the father, understanding the narrator's needs and responding to them in a way that suggests the father's creative, constructive function.[7]

> Je regardais ce qu'il faisait de moi, comme il se servait de moi et je n'avais jamais pensé qu'on pouvait le faire de la sorte, il allait audelà de mon espérance et conformément à la destinée de mon corps. Ainsi j'étais devenue son enfant. [. . .] C'était avec son enfant qu'il faisait l'amour chaque soir.
>
> (122)

The sexual character of this paternal influence shows that the lover is stepping in to replace the narrator's missing father in the formation of his female "child"'s sexuality. However, the lover is not the original Father, the genitor, the origin of the name and being. He is taking on the father's functions, but this is only playing a role, and in fact, it is not the only role that the lover plays in the book. Upon closer examination, the relationships among the main characters appear as a complex and changing system in which one character can play several different roles, at different times and with different partners. For example, the lover also takes over the mother's function of protecting the narrator as she crosses the river to Saigon, thus replacing the mother as the heroine crosses symbolically from childhood to adulthood. Moreover, it is due to her affair with the lover that the heroine is able to develop a new kind of detachment, which enables her to judge her mother for the first time, and this also suggests that the lover is replacing her mother as the dominating force in her life.[8]

In addition to these parental roles, the lover seems to have other functions as well. The physical resemblance between himself and the heroine suggests that they are like brother and sister:

> Lui, l'amant de Cholen, il croit que la croissance de la petite blanche a pâti de la chaleur trop forte. Lui aussi il est né et il a grandi dans cette chaleur. Il se découvre avoir avec elle cette parenté-là.
>
> (120)

The physical resemblance accentuates their mutual slenderness and fragility, emphasizing their youth, weakness and helplessness in the confrontation with the disapproving Father and Mother figures who refuse to accept their affair. In addition, the lover shares some important traits with the narrator's brothers. Like them, he is unable to complete his studies, to grow up professionally and economically. He most resembles the younger brother, in his uncontrollable fear of the world and of his father, and the narrator finds a physical resemblance between the two as well.[9] The lover is the narrator's most important partner and spectator; as such, he plays many different roles, alternately parental and fraternal, in the course of the heroine's exploration of herself through her relationship with him.

But this multiplicity of roles is present in the case of other characters as well. In particular, the relationship between the narrator herself and her brothers is a complex network of reflections, centred around the ambiguous figure of the Double. The foundation of their relationship is their love for their mother, which is both a bond and a cause for rivalry. On one level, the two brothers are themselves doubles of each other, rivals for their mother's love and for the power that comes with it. Here, once again, the older brother is the usurper:

> Reste cette image de notre parenté: c'est un repas à Sadec. Nous mangeons tous les trois à la table de la salle à manger. [. . .] Il nous regarde manger, le petit frère et moi, et puis il pose sa fourchette, il ne regarde plus que mon petit frère. Très longuement il le regarde et puis il lui dit tout à coup, très calmement, quelque chose de terrible. La phrase est sur la nourriture. Il lui dit qu'il doit faire attention, qu'il ne doit pas manger autant. Le petit frère ne répond rien. Il continue. Il rappelle que les gros morceaux de viande c'est pour lui, qu'il ne doit pas l'oublier.
>
> (98)

The heroine clearly identifies with her younger brother, here and throughout the book. "Le corps de l'enfant" refers by turn to herself and to her younger brother (see 123, 128); and the younger brother's death leads his sister to feel that she herself has died. The two are doubles in their youth and in their position of victim in relation to the older brother.

However, the heroine and her older brother are also doubles of each other, since the older brother is the narrator's principal rival for their mother's love. He has many of the attributes that scholars of the Double, such as Rank and Keppler, have defined in this figure. Most notably, he is a dark, sinister figure who has the diabolical qualities often associated with the double.[10] Significantly, the narrator feels his influence on her as disturbing but almost irresistible.

> Je ne danse jamais avec mon frère aîné, je n'ai jamais dansé avec lui. Toujours empêchée par l'appréhension troublante d'un danger, celui de cet attrait maléfique qu'il exerce sur tous, celui du rapprochement de nos corps.
>
> Nous nous ressemblons à un point très frappant, surtout le visage.
>
> (68)

The double figure, as defined by scholars of the subject such as Rank and Keppler, is essentially a projection of the fears and guilt feelings which the primary personality is unable or unwilling to accept. This function is present in the relationship between the heroine of *L'Amant* and her elder brother: her brother appears as the incarnation of her own murderous, jealous impulses. But this relationship is much more complex than the standard double situation, since the narrator's murderous desires are described as the response to the elder brother's own essentially evil, usurping nature. She wishes to kill him because he wishes to kill the younger brother and to possess the mother and her resources all for himself.

> Je voulais tuer, mon frère aîné, je voulais le tuer, arriver à avoir raison de lui une fois, une seule fois et le voir mourir. C'était pour enlever de devant ma mère l'objet de son amour, ce fils, la punir de l'aimer si fort, si mal, et surtout pour sauver mon petit frère, je le croyais aussi, mon petit frère, mon enfant, de la vie vivante de ce frère aîné posée au-dessus de la sienne.
> . . .
>
> (13)

The older brother plays the role that Keppler has called the Tempter: the older brother's monstrous impulses create their own mirror image in the heroine, his evil desires tempt the heroine to respond in kind in order to prevent him from realizing them.[11] Within this tangled web of reciprocal images of destruction, there intervenes a third form of double: the narrator's external image, which, like the Picture of Dorian Gray, becomes the concrete embodiment of the hate which the narrator has discovered in herself.

> Non, il est arrivé quelque chose lorsque j'ai eu dix-huit ans qui a fait que ce visage a eu lieu. ça devait se passer la nuit. J'avais peur de moi, j'avais peur de Dieu.
>
> (13)

Like the text we are reading, this face, lined with the wrinkles of suffering and fear, is a "readable" double of the inner person. But we have seen that all the characters of the novel have this function; the same elemental drama of love, jealousy, hate and death plays itself out through a multiplicity of roles, all centred around the heroine herself.

Thus, we return to the problem which is the underlying cause of all the role-playing and the questions of perception throughout the book: the absence of the father. The narrator's driving search for herself, and the complex interplay of roles and attributes which this evokes in those who surround her, are all responses to the one primordial and original lack of definition which the father has not been there to supply. Moreover, the father's absence is reflected in the absence of the Father figure *par excellence*: God. The death of the Father is the disappearance of a fixed, eternal, cosmic system of definition which would be the guarantee of permanent meaning and truth.

The narrator, and various characters, refer frequently to God. He is the guarantee that the narrator's murderous feelings toward her elder brother will be punished; the only witness to the narrator's crossing of the river who had the power to foresee its importance; the invisible reader of the truth about the relationship between the mother and the eldest son; the ironic name by which the narrator designates her exploration of sexual ecstasy; and the cosmic principle which tolerates the scandal of her younger brother's death. But we know, from the beginning of the book, that there is a place in the narrator's heart which God was unwilling or unable to occupy, and that his absence has opened up a void which the narrator has filled by drinking. "L'alcool a rempli la fonction que Dieu n'a pas eue, il a eu aussi celle de me tuer, de tuer" (15). The absence of God has permitted this murder, and his absence, thus, extends itself to all the other circumstances in which his name is invoked. In none of them is God able to manifest his presence and his aid in a positive way. He is reduced to a name, the reminder of an empty promise, the recollection of an absent omnipotence and omniscience, the nostalgia for a totality and an absolute which have to be replaced by something else.

Thus the absence of God and of the Father is the absence of a fixed centre, of an immutable essence of the truth and of human character.

> L'histoire de ma vie n'existe pas. ça n'existe pas. Il n'y a jamais de centre. Pas de chemin, pas de ligne. Il y a de vastes endroits où l'on fait croire qu'il y avait quelqu'un, ce n'est pas vrai il n'y avait personne.
>
> (14)

But the narrator has sought to fill this void: in place of the paternal Name and fixed definition, she has substituted a fluid, mobile, open circulation of meanings which depends on relationships and not on essences, on the collectivity instead of the individual. This system is opened up by her discovery of sexuality, which represents a form of communication, a passage from the individual to the collective.

> Soudain je me vois comme une autre, comme une autre serait vue, au-dehors, mise à la disposition de tous, mise dans la circulation des villes, des routes, du désir.
>
> (20)

This idea of "circulation" is continued in the symbolism of the sea, which is identified with the narrator's sexual pleasure. "La mer, sans forme, simplement incomparable. [. . .] La mer, l'immensité qui se regroupe, s'éloigne, revient" (50, 55). The language of the body is impersonal, but for that reason it is authentic.

> Il me traite de putain, de dégueulasse, il me dit que je suis son seul amour, et c'est ça qu'il doit dire et c'est ça qu'on dit quand on laisse le dire se faire, quand on laisse le corps faire et chercher et trouver et prendre ce qu'il veut, et là tout est bon, il n'y a pas de déchet, les déchets sont recouverts, tout va dans le torrent, dans la force du désir.
>
> (54-5)

Thus, the system of "circulation", desire and open communication has replaced the old, paternal system of essences and Source. And this new system is reflected in the various textual problems we have studied. In the absence of a paternal Origin, it is the narrator, her emotions and her search which are the origin of meaning. The meaning roles, the system of doubles and mirror reflections show that all meaning comes from her. There is no more transcendent Authority as a source of definitions; the narrator's identity is the product of a continuing process, an open system of relationships which enable her to see herself as others do, to explore the diverse echoes which she has awakened in others.

In the same way, the narrator imagines writing which would be "open", more an unfinished, continuous process or project than a perfected technique: ". . . je vois que tous les champs sont ouverts, qu'il n'y aurait plus de murs, que l'écrit ne saurait plus où se mettre pour se cacher, se faire, se lire . . ." (15). This open, fluid, anti-patriarchal conception of writing has recently become the object of study by many critics and feminist theoreticians, who have shown its increasing importance in Duras's literary practice, especially during the last few years.[12] *L'Amant* shows that its origin is the blank space left by the absence of the Father.

Notes

1. See Carol J. Murphy, *Alienation and Absence in the Novels of Marguerite Duras,* Lexington: French Forum, 1982. See also Sarah J. Capitanio's study of "négation," in "Perspectives sur l'Ecriture Durassienne," *Symposium,* Vol. XLI, No. 1 (Spring 1987), pp. 19-20; Madeleine Borgomano, "Romans: La Fascination du Vide," in *L'Arc,* No. 98, "Marguerite Duras," (1985), pp. 40-8, and Gisèle Bremondy, "La Destruction de la Réalité," in *L'Arc,* No. 98, pp. 51-5. The present study is the development of a paper presented to the section on Romance Literary Relations at the December 1988 Modern Language Association, and entitled "The Mother-Daughter Conflict in Marguerite Duras's *L'Amant.*" I would like to thank Ms. Catherine Slawy-Sutton for the helpful bibliographic

suggestions in her paper, presented before the same group, "Beyond the Female Bond in *La Maison de Claudine* and *Sido.*"

2. Marguerite Duras, *L'Amant* (Paris: Minuit, 1984), pp. 34-5. All subsequent references will be to this edition.

3. See the treatment of this general theme in Duras's works by Marc Saporta, "Les Yeux Fermés," in *L'Arc,* No. 98, pp. 68-9.

4. See Christiane Olivier, *Les Enfants de Jocaste: l'empreinte de la mère* (Paris: Denoël-Gonthier, 1980), p. 58.

5. See Nancy Chodorow, *The Reproduction of Mothering* (University of California Press, 1978), pp. 95-104, and Luce Irigaray, *Et l'Une ne bouge pas sans l'autre* (Paris: Minuit, 1979), p. 14. The problem of the mother's insanity in *L'Amant,* and its reflection in the heroine's fear, shows that she is not immune to the problem of confusion between herself and her mother.

6. Olivier, pp. 55-65.

7. The lover treats the narrator as "son enfant," whereas the mother refuses to use this term either for her daughter or her younger son. See Marcelle Marini, "Une Femme sans Aveu," in *L'Arc,* No. 98, p. 15.

8. See Germaine Brée, review of *L'Amant, International Fiction Review* (Vol. 12, No. 2, summer 1985), p. 119, for other indications that the lover is a replacement for the mother.

9. Capitanio points out this resemblance, p. 18.

10. See for this diabolical aspect the numerous examples examined by Otto Rank, *The Double* (University of North Carolina Press, 1971), and his conclusion, 76; and C.F. Keppler, *The Literature of the Second Self* (University of Arizona Press, 1972), for example pp. 27-8.

11. See Keppler, pp. 56-77.

12. See notably Trista Selous, *The Other Woman* (Yale University Press, 1988), and Sharon Willis, *Marguerite Duras, Writing on the Body* (University of Illinois Press, 1987).

Marianne Hirsch (essay date 1989)

SOURCE: "Feminist Family Romances," in *The Mother/ Daughter Plot: Narrative, Psychoanalysis, Feminism,* Indiana University Press, 1989, pp. 125-61.

[*In the following essay, Hirsch provides a psychoanalytic reading of the relationship between the narrator and her mother in* The Lover.]

"The story of my life doesn't exist," asserts the (again) nameless narrator of ***The Lover.*** "Does not exist. There's never any center to it. No path, no line" (p. 8). The text begins with a long self-portrait, a reflection of the narrator's aged face, first as it is described to her by a young man she encounters in a public space, then as she herself sees it evolve from the age of eighteen to the present moment of utter devastation. The entire text revolves around an earlier recollection, the moment just preceding that laying to waste: the crossing of the Mekong River on a ferry at the age of fifteen and the visual image (a photograph never taken) of the young girl dressed in a low-cut silk dress, evening shoes, and a man's fedora. This tension between narrative and image, movement and stasis, controls the text, as does the tension between the external objective perception of the narrator by others and her self-perception, between the third and the first person, and between speech and silence.

The Lover is already a revision of a *fabula* which has appeared, in different guises, in several of Duras's works. Both the 1958 novel, *Un Barrage contre le Pacifique* (*The Sea Wall*) and the 1977 play *L'Eden Cinéma* deal with aspects of the same plot: the young girl's adolescence in colonial Indochina, the broken dreams of her disturbed and impoverished mother, the hated and adored brother(s), and the rich older lover who promises the entire family an escape from hopelessness. But, as Duras explains in *The Lover,* "Before, I spoke of the clear periods, those on which the light fell. Now I'm talking about the hidden stretches of that same youth, of certain facts, feelings, events that I buried" (p. 8). The darkness and silence, the difficulty of telling and the need to retell, again and again, the narrator explains, is connected to the figure of her mother, the figure around whom these texts revolve. "In the books I've written about my childhood I can't remember, suddenly, what I left out, what I said. I think I wrote about our love for our mother, but I don't know if I wrote about how we hated her too. . . . It's the area on whose brink silence begins. What happens there is silence, the slow travail of my whole life. I'm still there, watching those possessed children, as far away from the mystery now as I was then. I've never written, though I thought I wrote, never loved, though I thought I loved, never done anything but wait outside the closed door" (p. 25). In this remarkable passage, the narrator is both mother and child, mother as she stands watching "those possessed children," and child as she enacts the unspeakable primal scene "outside the closed door."

The Lover, then, is but one of several repeated attempts to open that door, to illuminate the area of supreme darkness "hidden in the very depths of my flesh, blind as a newborn child" (p. 25). To tell the story of passionate mother-child attachment and identification, Duras uses images similar to Colette's—mystery, darkness, something hidden beyond view, unavailable to narrative. And, like Colette, Duras identifies this search for the "darkest plots" with the process of what she elsewhere calls "feminine literature," defined as "an organic, translated writing . . . translated from blackness, from darkness." But Duras identifies her "feminine writing" in specific contrast to Colette who, she

says, wrote "'feminine literature' as men wanted it." Whereas, in Duras's view, Colette writes for the enjoyment of men, the feminine literature she herself envisions and practices, is "a violent, direct literature" which aims to "make women the point of departure in judging, make darkness the point of departure in judging what men call light, make obscurity the point of departure in judging what men call clarity" (p. 426).

Interestingly, Duras's judgment of Colette resembles Rich's reading of Woolf—too much attention paid to men, too much compromise and not enough anger and violence. Whereas, unlike Colette's texts, Duras's do indeed present a past full of anger and violence, pain and suffering, her search through "the darkest plots" of mother-daughter attachment is, like Colette's, mediated by a heterosexual love narrative which is also ultimately and radically rejected. If the figure of the mother appears as both the point of departure and the destination of the narrative, the narrative places her in a multiple network of mediations with the male brothers and the lover whom she ultimately displaces in her daughter's passionate and disturbed attachment. Although these male figures function as pre-texts leading to the mother, their presence complicates and confuses the narrative of daughterly desire.

In a post-script to *L'Eden Cinéma,* Duras's adaptation of *The Sea Wall* for the stage, the author apologizes for one particularly disturbing passage of her play, giving license to directors to remove it. The passage is a letter written by the mother to the cadastral agents who had leased her a plot of land which, since it turned out to be totally infertile, robbed her of all her savings and of any possible future livelihood. Providing (like Sido's letters included in *Break of Day*) a glimpse into the mother's own discourse and imagination, this letter is a long and uncontrolled outpouring of rage and complaints, culminating in detailed threats on the agents' lives, with concrete plans for their violent murder. It is this violence, written in the mother's voice, that Duras feared might be unacceptable to the audiences of her play: "I hesitated to keep—in 1977—the murderous threats that the mother's last letter to the cadastral agents contained. . . . Then I decided to leave it in. As inadmissible as this violence may appear, it seemed to me more serious to silence it then to disfigure with it the figure of the mother. This violence existed for us, it cradled our childhood." Continuing in detail to describe the pain, sadness, and despair contained in the letter, Duras concludes: "If the violence of this woman, the mother, is, however, apt to shock or not to be heard at the very point of its greatest legitimacy, then that passage of the letter can be deleted" (p. 150, my translation). The letter in *L'Eden Cinéma* is reprinted from *The Sea Wall,* where Joseph and Suzanne discuss it at length. Joseph also silences the mother's rage—he decides not to mail the letter since he feels it would be more useful to him and his sister than to the insensitive agents. It would teach him to keep alive his own anger, and, for his sister, it would function as a negative example: "You must remember these stories about the Eden cinema [the theater where the mother played piano to accompany silent movies] and you must always do just the opposite of what she did" (p. 224). Maternal identification threatens and unsettles disturbingly the daughter's process of subject-formation; yet the reasons for this threat transcend the patterns of psychology.

In *The Lover,* where no such letter appears, the act of silencing the mother is more comprehensive. Yet the mother does express similar rage in her dialogue and is reported to have done so throughout the narrator's childhood and adolescence. In this last text Duras's narrator focuses on her own relation to the mother's rage and violence, especially on how maternal anger and maternal madness affect and inform her own imagination and her own writing. It is as though the mother's own discourse could be better rewritten, revised, by the daughter if it were excised from the text: "I tell him that when I was a child my mother's unhappiness took the place of dreams. My dreams were of my mother, never of Christmas trees, always just her, a mother either flayed by poverty or distraught and muttering in the wilderness, either searching for food or endlessly telling what's happened to her, Marie Legrand from Roubaix, telling of her innocence, her savings, her hopes" (p. 46). When the mother is present, she only causes fear and anger in the daughter: "There was no longer anything there to inhabit her image. I went mad in full possession of my senses." Faced with the mother's mad alterity, the terrified daughter comes to inhabit the mother's body, herself taking the place the mother has left empty during the attack.

This account and experience of the mother's pain and her madness, her hysterical outbursts, her absences, her radical otherness, terrifying for her children, dominates the pages of *The Lover,* although the mother's own words are absent. Not only does the mother not write, she also discourages, even forbids, the narrator to write. The daughter's text, emerging from that prohibition, can no longer contain the voice of the enraged mother, even though it takes shape around that missing voice in the effort to give it life, to keep it alive, to open the door that might allow her to understand it. This pattern of maternal presence/absence very much resembles that of *Break of Day,* even though the quality of the mother's elided and sought-after subjectivity is radically different. Whereas the memory of "Sido" represents the idealized garden of the narrator's childhood, a paradisiacal realm of which "Colette" is no longer worthy, which she needs to recapture and may never be able to, the memory of Marie Roubaix reflects the hardships of widowhood and single motherhood, the colonial existence of a teacher and her family in Indochina, war, hunger, poverty, and the resulting madness. Nevertheless, the outlook of both protagonists is shaped by their mothers', and Duras's narrator needs the access to and the distance from the mother's madness as much as "Colette" needs access to her mother's plenitude. "Because of what's been done to our mother, so amiable, so trusting, we hate life, we hate ourselves" (p. 55). Here, however, the pre-oedipal world of mother-child union is no Eden to recapture. Not only does it fail to offer an alternative to the violence of civilization, it is very much a product of that violence.

The relationship between the narrator of *The Lover* and her mother is filtered through a complex structure of mediating relationships which include the two brothers, the older Chinese lover, and even a female friend, Hélène Lagonelle. Through each of these figures, the narrator gains access to the others and ultimately seeks to gain access to the mother, the figure behind the closed door. Some significant changes have taken place since *The Sea Wall,* however. The single adored brother Joseph, clearly a "man-who-would-understand," has been replaced by two brothers—a revered younger brother who has all of Joseph's positive and none of his negative qualities, and a despised older brother, the image of an authoritative patriarch who, although powerless in the world, destructively dominates the lives of his family members. The lover has also shifted both in character and plot. No longer French, he is Chinese; although he is rich, he occupies a lower social status than the narrator and her family. It is this shift in power and status, perhaps, that makes it possible for the narrator to desire him sexually, whereas in the earlier text she could barely tolerate his presence. The older brother, revered and preferred by the mother, serves as a repressive object of jealousy and rage, later contempt, throughout the narrative. The younger brother is the narrator's adored twin whose early death nearly causes her own destruction. Vastly different from each other, the three siblings are united only through the passionate love they share for their mother, and through their sorrow for her ruined life. In this family, the primal psychic triangle defining the narrator's individuation does not consist of mother/father/daughter but of mother/son/daughter, with the brother split into two, one good, one bad. Whereas the father is totally absent from the narrative, an object of memory and longing only for the mother, the brothers remain important psychic forces throughout the space of the text. Yet in the course of the plot they also come to be displaced—the younger brother dies and the older brother eventually loses his authority, becoming a traitor, even a thief, before his demise.

It is not the lover, however, who displaces the brothers from the narrator's affection or from the center of the narrative. During her affair with the lover, all three male figures coexist in her forever shifting affections—between her love for the younger brother, the physical passion for the lover, and the murderous hatred for the older brother. The affair does not represent a rupture in her affections, then, but merely another element in the structure of mediation that defines them. From the beginning of their affair, the lover's presence is entangled with the very material being of the mother, the brothers, and Hélène Lagonelle. When they meet and go out to dinner together, the lover and the brothers do not speak. But during the narrator's moments of extreme bodily intimacy and togetherness with the Chinese lover, the brothers are there, approving or disapproving, similar to him or different: "The shadow of another man must have passed through the room, the shadow of a young murderer, but I didn't know that then. . . . The shadow of a young hunter must have passed through the room too, but that one, yes, I knew about, sometimes he was present in the pleasure and I'd tell the lover from Cholon, talk to him of the other's body and member, of his indescribable sweetness" (p. 100). Rather than a simple break from childhood and familial attachments, the lover offers, through mediation, a way to remain embedded in those attachments, even while finding enough distance from them to be capable of describing their intensity. In fact, I would argue that he offers a privileged form of access to her mother: during their passionate scenes of lovemaking, the lover becomes her mother, as she becomes his child. The passion she feels gives her access to the mother's body: "So I became his child. And he became something else for me too. I began to recognize the inexpressible softness of his skin, of his member, apart from himself" (p. 100). As the narration moves from first to third person during the moments of passion, the protagonist gains distance from herself and access to the mother's mad self-abandonment by way of the sexual passion she shares with the lover.

The Lover is the story of the narrator's coming to writing. Even at the moments of greatest childhood and adolescent despair, she knows that she will write and that to do so she must leave behind her family and the lover. It is only when she has left Saigon and is traveling on the boat to France that the narrator understands the depth of her love for the Chinese man from Cholon; it is only after the younger brother dies that she accepts the "unfathomable mystery" of her love for him which also makes her want to die. Even as she separates from the figures of her adolescence, they establish themselves as permanent fixtures in her imagination, to be examined again and again in their complex relations to each other, providing the obsessive themes and images of Duras's oeuvre. The novel ends as, years later, the lover calls her in Paris to tell her that he will always love her, that nothing has changed. It is *his* declaration. For her, for the older woman novelist, love and the lover need to recede into the background of the fiction. Like the brothers, the lover is not the object of nostalgia or longed-for recovery, but an important marker in the shifting structure of mediation which creates not only the space for writing in Duras's work, but also its obsessive preoccupation.

The mother, however, functions as more than such a pretext; one could argue that she is the ground on which all the other relationships rest and to which they lead. But she is, in many respects, an absent ground. Although she is featured in many of Duras's texts, she often remains silent. The most dramatic staging of her silent presence is in *L'Eden Cinéma,* where the stage directions read as follows:

> The mother sits on a low seat and the others gather around her. . . . Then they speak about the mother. About her past. About her life. About the love she elicited. The mother will remain immobile on her seat, expressionless, like a statue, distant, separated—like the stage—from her own story. The others touch her, caress her arms, kiss her hands. She allows it: what she represents in this play surpasses what she is and she is

not responsible for it . . . the mother—object of the narrative—will never speak for herself.

> (p. 12; my translation)

The Lover, as do the other texts which tell the same story, presents a version of the feminist family romance that differs from the ones we encountered earlier. If mother-daughter entanglement serves as a narrative focus here, it does so as the privileged relationship in a nexus of shifting attachments, each mediating a series of others. If Duras's text seeks to open a closed door, she can do so only to find that it leads to other doors, each connected to all the others, but none providing an ultimate point of origin. Does the desire for the lover allow her to seek the mother, or is it the reverse? Does the love for her younger brother enable her to recognize her love for the lover or vice versa? How is power distributed in these relationships: does the lover hold the power because he is older, richer, and male, or does the narrator because she is white? Duras overturns and complicates such dichotomies and divisions. No relationship and no point in the process of subject-formation is immune from the struggles of power and from the degradations of a civilization engaged in war and imperial expansion. No alternative can be offered, none can even be envisioned. The process of repeated revisions and shifting mediations allows Duras and her narrators to go over the same ground again and again, making discoveries but reaching no ultimate illumination. As the narrator says: "Sometimes I realize that if writing isn't, all things, all contraries confounded, a quest for vanity and void, it's nothing. That if it's not, each time, all things confounded into one through some inexpressible essence, then writing is nothing but advertisement" (p. 8).

Yet *The Lover* suggests that the figure of the mother is this "inexpressible essence" which confounds all other things into one, thereby making writing possible. She does so not by offering a destination to which to return, but by functioning precisely as "vanity and void"; she may be a privileged point in the nexus of relationships defining the structures of desire, but she is not the "center" which would make the story of the narrator's life "exist" or cohere. She does so not by providing an alternative realm to cultural complicity, but through her very entanglement in the culture and the relationships which define it.

Such a reading lies outside of the confines of a feminist family romance based in psychoanalysis alone. Julia Kristeva's recent article on Duras illustrates the limitations of a psychoanalytic perspective. Interestingly, her reading of Duras's writing is preceded by a reflection on the literature that might best approximate the politics of our age, the psychic pain inflicted by the gas chambers, the bomb, and the gulag. Duras, she feels, possesses the discourse of "blunted pain," the art of "non-catharsis" which brings the reader to the edge of silence and not beyond. After this haunting and suggestive beginning, two related aspects of her reading are particularly striking: her insistence that "political events . . . are internalized and measured only by the human pain they induce," that "public life becomes profoundly unreal, whereas private life is intensified to the point that it invades the real and invalidates all other pre-occupation," and in contrast, her identification of maternal abandonment as *the* traumatic structure which lies at the basis of all of Duras's writing, of all the internal pain. In her narrative of this pervasive structure of maternal abandonment, Kristeva represents the mother as other, as the "archaic, uncontrollable" object, the icon of madness whose function it is to disrupt all efforts at identity and sameness. Kristeva's internalization of the political, and her location of its force in the figure of the abandoning, mad, and unfaithful mother, is symptomatic of the moves of psychoanalytic feminism (especially insofar as it is allied with French deconstructive theory, but also in its American object-relations incarnation). In eclipsing the mother's own voice, her own story, and allowing her only the status of object, or of "Other," Kristeva, and to an extent Duras also, eclipse the political dimensions of women's lives, conflating them with the psychological. Here, I believe, lies a major limit of psychoanalytic feminism.

What Kristeva sees as the structure of maternal violence and abandonment, leading to "reduplication" and ultimately stasis and "nothingness," can be read through a lens different from the lens of subjectivity and identity. Another obsessive figure in Duras's work illustrates the need for such a shift in perspective—the beggar woman from Vinlongh or Savannakhet who returns in many of the novels and films from *The Sea-Wall* to *The Vice Consul to India Song, Love,* and ***The Lover.*** Poor, at times pregnant, at other times trying to sell her child to another mother (the somewhat less poor white woman), this figure of lament, whose delirious song and cry punctuate Duras's novels, serves, in Madeleine Borgomano's terms, as the "generative cell" for Duras's entire narrative project and, in Kristeva's terms, as the double of her other characters. In a taped interview, cited by Borgomano, Duras relates the autobiographical incident which constituted the generative cell of this generative cell: "My mother once came back from the market having bought a child . . . a six-month old little girl . . . that she only kept for several days and who died. . . . I still see my mother crossing the garden with this woman who followed her. . . . My mother cried . . . she was always enraged by such misery. . . . I remember this stubbornness, this fantastic will to give away her child. . . . I have tried to transform this monstrous and adorable act into literature but I have not succeeded." The obsessive and unnarratable nature of this memory emerges quite clearly in this oral account, as it does in the many scenes of her work Duras has devoted to it; what emerges with equal force, however, is Duras's interest in sustaining the irrevocable *strangeness* and *opacity* (these are her terms) of the beggar woman's shocking maternal act. In so doing, Duras can perhaps minimize its monumental threat, a threat so great that in ***The Lover*** she describes it as the fear of a state worse than death, of entering the beggar woman's madness, or perhaps of becoming the child who is killed by it. The dangers of maternal identification are here.

Yet, the scene Duras describes in that taped interview has obvious significances beyond the psychological, significances which, interestingly, emerge more clearly in the early texts in which the mother screams and speaks than in the later ones in which she remains silent so as to be spoken about. The Indian beggar mother, ostracized by her own mother and reduced to dire poverty, sells her child to the white woman while the white daughter looks on; the white second mother, although she dresses the child in a lace gown, is incapable of keeping her alive; in *The Sea Wall* the white brother buries the child, and the white mother swears she will never care for children again. The white mother herself is too poor to care for her own children. She watches her own children's failure to thrive and all around her she watches many other children die of hunger and disease. She is the colonizer, yet, as a woman, she is also the colonized. Certainly she is the victim of colonialism. She is more and more angry, more and more depressed. A doctor (the text's image of a "psychiatrist") warns that her fits of angry screaming may be fatal. But the third person narrator's voice argues with the doctor's diagnosis: "The doctor traced these attacks of hers to the crumbling of the sea wall. Maybe he was mistaken. So much resentment could only have accumulated very slowly, year by year, day by day. There was more than one single cause: there were thousands, counting the collapse of the sea walls, the world's injustice, the sight of her children splashing in the river . . ." (p. 17). While the doctor sees only one cause, the narrative voice understands the complexity and vastness of the problems faced by the mother. Whereas in a psychoanalytic reading the crumbling of the sea wall represents a psychic disintegration pervasive in Duras's texts, the text itself, I would argue, demands a more multifaceted reading which goes beyond the psychological to the economic and the political and which places the mother's madness in that context. Similarly, the white eight-year-old, terrified of the beggar woman's touch in ***The Lover,*** is afraid of the touch of poverty as well as of the touch of the madness of mother-child fusion. The fear and the power of "all things confounded into one" need to be traced back not only to their roots in the psyche and their connection to writing, but also to the connections between that psyche and the biological and social body it inhabits. Such contextualization might perhaps make it possible to take the maternal out of the realm of silence and unrepresentability and to include, in the feminist family romance and on the stage of feminist self-presentation, the perspective and the voice of mothers as well as of daughters.

Susan D. Cohen (essay date 1990)

SOURCE: "Fiction and the Photographic Image in Duras' 'The Lover,'" in *L'Esprit Createur,* Vol. XXX, No. 1, Spring, 1990, pp. 56-68.

[*In the following essay, Cohen explores Duras's "intergenre" use of visual imagery in* The Lover.]

> Le seul sujet du livre [*L'Amant*] c'est l'écriture,
> L'écriture, c'est moi. Donc moi, c'est le livre.
>
> —Marguerite Duras

Most of Marguerite Duras' work focuses on the referent's essential absence. Duras writes this absence with visual metaphors, but in ways that deconstruct the dominant, centralizing primacy of seeing as documentation. Although much critical comment has been made about her cinematic innovations, on the one hand, and about vision as a theme in her books, on the other, critics have rarely situated seeing with regard to absence and to language in her work. Further, this has not been linked to a form of intertextuality that crosses from one genre to another, which might be called "inter-genre."

In her films, Duras disconnects the sound track from the screen images, which causes the viewer to reconsider a coincidence hitherto largely unquestioned. With Duras, this dislocation deemphasizes the visual in favor of the verbal. Directed towards the invisible and the unknown, unstuck from concrete objectal representations, the gaze becomes a *verbal* instrument productive of open-ended imagination and textuality. Often the narrative structures play on several levels of visual absence. In the films *India Song* and *La Femme du Ganges,* for example, speakers who never appear on screen narrate a mixture of the story and their personal reactions to it and to each other. We "hear" them "see," since we know they are looking only because they say so, and we know what they are "seeing"—the story—only because they tell it. The envisaged tale is not enacted on the screen, which simply shows people dancing or lying down (*India Song*) or people walking (*La Femme du Ganges*). Thus no direct visual representation is provided, either to the public or to the speakers. For the latter recount events that occurred in the past, events they not only did not themselves witness, but the "original" narrative of which they have largely forgotten. The fact that what they are reconstituting is, most probably, a text, places the visual at an even further remove. These films consist, then, mainly of verbal embroidering on an absent textual referent. Visual evidence is replaced, both for the speakers and the spectators, by imagination understood primarily as linguistic. This basic valorisation of the verbal over the visual occurs in many of Duras' films, with various interesting structural variations.

The protagonists of the film *Le Camion* never appear. We do see the speakers, one of whom is the author. They do nothing but read aloud, on and off screen, the text of a possible film, from manuscripts they hold in their hands. A "stage direction" in the published text specifies that the room in which Duras and Depardieu read the text is called a "reading room" (*chambre de lecture*)—a term evoking verbal rather than visual images.[1] *Son Nom de Venise dans Calcutta désert* and *Aurélia Steiner* show no human figures at all. Spoken words evoke the absent characters while unpeopled images fill the screen. Finally, during a lengthy segment of *L'Homme atlantique* the screen remains completely blank. The narrating voice, identified as that of a woman writer and film-maker abandoned by a man, articulates the absence of her lover and films it as such, filling the void with her *words.* She defines her cinematic undertaking as primarily verbal, actually predicated on visual absence. The narrator relates how, after her lover left, she cleaned her house, ridding it of all "signs."[2] This cleared a space, metaphorically a blank page on which, first of all, she could write: "Everything was cleaned of life, exempt, emptied of signs, and then I told myself: I am going to begin writing, to cure myself of the lie of an ending love. . . . And then I began to write" (17-18). Filming, the visual medium, came second, after the written text: "You remained in the state of having left. And I made a film of your absence" (ibid., 22).[3]

Considered eminently cinematic, these techniques hark back nevertheless to schemas already present in Duras' novels more than 30 years ago. In *Le Marin de Gibraltar* (Gallimard, 1952), the male narrator accompanies a woman on her quest for a vanished lover, whom they never see, but about whom they speak incessantly. Emanating from his absence, the woman's stories about him provide the impetus for the relation between her and the narrator, for the text we read, and for a novel the narrator plans to write. Again, textuality emerges from a visual void. The cinematic analogy, of a verbal cinema based on visual referential absence, applies more strikingly to **Moderato Cantabile** (Minuit, 1958), in which the protagonists meet at a café and attempt to "perceive" the relationship leading to the crime of passion they did not see, but which fascinates them. They meet as though in order to train their "vision" on a blank screen which they fill with words, their own projected images conjointly "narrated." Their voices have fundamentally the same function as those in the later films. In *Le Ravissement de Lol V. Stein* (Gallimard, 1964), after Lol's fiancé abandons her for another woman, her desire to see her own absence in the couple that excludes her leads her to project it phantasmically, on a "screen" she carefully leaves blank. This "cinema of Lol V. Stein" (55) consists of another couple making love in a hotel room while Lol lies in a rye field beneath their window (the figure of the screen), which remains doubly "blank": she has positioned herself too far from it to see inside, and she lies with her eyes closed. But she is not the speaker of her story, for the words that replace vision and constitute the text belong to the male narrator, who endeavors to "see" Lol's memory of her own absence, and who tells the story in her place.[4] Thus, these texts full of "cinematic" structures already disconnect the verbal and the visual within the written form itself. Narrators or protagonists project words onto a space cleared to make room for them, and textuality exists as a function of a visual blank.

If Duras' texts pass so easily from one genre to another, it is largely because of the inherent transportability of these blank "screens," which enables the author to favor the verbal even in essentially visual media. Writing predominates in her theater and cinema, then, as it does in her novels. Duras confirmed this in an interview: Q: "How do you combine literature, theater, and movies?" Duras: "The secret is discovering that they are similar media. When I direct a play I also write."[5]

The Lover offers a good illustration of the relation of the verbal to the visual in Duras' work. While it does not announce its inter-genre nature in the manner initiated with *India Song,* whose subtitle is "text, theater, film," it pointedly claims a correlation with the medium of photography. The first-person narrator informs us that her text was articulated around two photographs, which she "shows," or, to use the appropriate metaphor, "develops" before the reader, directly addressed as "you." Repeatedly referred to simply as "the image," the first "picture" figures Duras, the ostensible speaking "I," at fifteen, as she imagines she appeared to a young Chinese man who saw her on a ferry boat in Indochina. The author presents it piecemeal, as though in several narrative takes, and invokes it with photographic terminology. However, she quickly asserts that the picture was never taken. As such, a nonexistent photograph becomes an agent of literature, the "absolute" of a memory not confined to a single, adequate representation. Memory of a "real" event—the river crossing—merges with imagination in a literary projection of what the writer *says* the snapshot would have reflected had it been made. Because the image was never "removed" (*enlevée*) from time, made concrete and invariable, its very "blankness" acts as a literary catalyst, the text's non-visual, verbalized support, its "author":

> It could have existed, a photograph could have been taken like any other, elsewhere, in other circumstances. But it wasn't. That is why this image—and things could not have been otherwise—does not exist. It was omitted. It was forgotten. It was not detached, removed from the total (*la somme*). It is to this lack of having been made that it owes its power, that of representing an absolute, precisely of being its author.

> (*L'Amant,* Minuit, 1984, 16-17)

Indeed, as Duras confides to an interviewer, she had originally intended to entitle her text *The Absolute Image.*[6] One notes the connection in the quoted passage between an absolute and its "representation" by something that does not exist. Otherwise stated, there can be no adequate representation; the open field of literature emanates from "absolute," irreducible referential absence. If the absolute image existed, it would preclude others, and inhibit imagination. Its absence, like that of God for Duras, constitutes *the* principle of creativity, and forms an explicit theme in this text. Although *The Lover*'s opening has notes of devastation (her "destroyed face," p. 10, and her alcoholism, which "filled the position God never had," including that of "killing her," p. 15), the story is essentially one of creativity, in particular the self-making of a woman and of a writer whom we watch in the process of creating out of that very initial non-presence.

Duras situates the unsnapped but verbally pictured photograph on the same level as other things the book "figures," such as the boat, the countryside, and the country itself. Since everything has receded equally into the past, the same literary status applies: everything resuscitates via written images:

> That image, that unphotographed absolute photograph, entered into the book. . . . That central image, as well as that ferry boat which doubtless no longer exists, that countryside, that country also, destroyed . . . but it [the image] will have been and will remain indicated (*signalé*); its existence, its "retinian" permanence will have been placed there, in that book.

> (*Nouvel Observateur* 52)

But it will have been "placed there" with words. Whatever the genre, Duras treats vision as a verbal phenomenon: to see means to imagine with words. And to write or utter those words constitutes a favored mode of intersubjectivity. Duras recognizes verbally communicated imagination as the agent of shared experience, from its beginnings in childhood play. It generates and fosters community. In *The Lover,* the contrast between words and visual images (here photographs), in its relation to literary intersubjectivity, forms a thematic as well as structural component of the text. The narrating author explains that as long as she simply "sees" the "absolute image" she remains alone: "I often think of that image which I am still alone in seeing, and of which I have never spoken." Appearing on the first page, this first reference to a central but unsnapped photograph announces that the author is about to end her solitude by writing. Writing the image makes it verbally visible to the "you" Duras continually addresses, that is, to readers, who will now "envision" it with the author as they read.

Further, the non-being of the "absolute image" allows Duras to write memory in terms of desire, when she steps back to "look" at her young self. What she remembers of her appearance combines with her preferred imaginary vision of herself to compose the image. From among all "real" photographs or images of herself, the unreal, "absolute image" is not only the one that "pleases and enchants" her, it is the one in which she "recognizes herself" (9). This work of memory and imagination and of imaginary memory emanating from a necessarily absent source throws into relief processes at work in autobiography in general. In literature, of which autobiography is a part, the selected, imagined past *is* the past. While describing the clothing she recalls wearing on the boat, for example, Duras expresses uncertainty as to which shoes she had on. Then she imagines a possibility, which immediately becomes fictional fact: "That day I must be wearing the famous pair of gold lamé high heels. I see nothing else that I could wear that day so I am wearing them" (19). When, after recounting the cutting of long hair in Paris at age 23, Duras returns to "the image," she invites the reader to join her in "seeing" her long hair, which she "still" has: "On the ferry, look at me, I still have it" (24).

As in many others of her books, the use of the present tense resituates the temporal relation to the text. For Duras, imagination itself and the imagination of memory take place in the present, and the reader's experience takes place now, as one reads. Duras emphasizes this when she completes the description of the gold shoes with a sentence whose conjoined clauses recount both "then" and "now" in a simultaneous present of imagination, desire, and memory: "I go to the lycée in evening shoes decorated with little sparkling patterns. That is my will. I can only stand myself with that pair of shoes, and still now I want myself like that" [*Je me veux comme ça*] (19). Thus the text functions in the deictic register. Pointing to her various literary "pictures," the author urges the reader to "look" at them with her, here and now.

Like the first image, with which it interacts contrapuntally, the second photograph has a name: "the photo of despair" (41). According to the narrating author, however, this second main picture actually did exist. Taken in Hanoi, it showed Duras with her brothers and mother, who indeed felt perpetual despair at their poverty: "The book does not start from that real picture, but it returns to it each time it speaks of the mother and her despair" (*Nouvel Observateur* 52). Yet this photograph's material reality does not account for its textual productivity. Beyond the fact that it, too, remains perforce absent in a purely written text, and that the only proof of its existence resides in the author's written word, the memory it represents had to fade from her "eyes" in order for her to write. In other words, its visual referential power had to be neutralized for it not to inhibit the flow of textuality by imposing a finite, documentary image. The author can only *write* the picture because of the gulf between photographs and memory. Despite the picture's ostensible presence, she has "forgotten" her mother's looks, and this visual mnemonic absence affords the precondition of Duras' ability to write about her so copiously:

> For memories also it is too late. . . . I've left them [her mother and brothers]. I no longer have the perfume of her skin in my head, nor in my eyes the color of her eyes. . . . It's over. I don't remember any longer. That is why I write so easily about her now, so long, so stretched out; she has become fluent writing.
>
> (38)

"Ecriture courante," translated here as fluent writing, is a pun on "eaucourante," running water, as well as on "parler couramment," to speak fluently. The liquid connotation of flowing writing applies most aptly to Duras' symbolic universe, in which water has so great a part. Additionally, "courant" means common. Faded visual memory enables the author to transform the singularity of experience by communicating it through language. Common to all readers and directly related to imagination, of which it is a vehicle, language communalizes.

Sensate experience, then, does not provoke involuntary memory as it did for Proust. Voluntary verbal efforts produce an imaginary "memory," on the one hand, and involuntary forgetting of a real photograph-memory spurs imagination, on the other. After that, what incites memory and textuality in *The Lover* is writing itself. By dint of an

inherently metonymical power, the word on the page catalyzes simultaneously memory and the literary process. On several occasions, Duras explicitly attributes her recollection of certain details to the fact that she has just *written* a passage about other things connected to them. For example, while describing the tension between her older brother and her lover during the dinners that bring them together in the Chinese restaurant, Duras suddenly "remembers" the former's facial expression, which appears, metonymically summoned forth by the words immediately preceding: "Speaking about it [her brother's hostility] now makes me rediscover the hypocrisy of his face, the distracted air of someone looking in another direction" (67).

Later, metonymy functions so to speak in absentia, in the cleaning episode, which presents a rare happy scene, with the family and several neighbors participating in hosing down the house. Only upon writing does the author "see" that "everyone" did not include her older brother. The "sight" of her written memory conjures up the memory of his absence: "I remember, at the very moment I write, that our older brother was not at Vinhlong when we washed the house" (77). This recovered memory, fictional or not, blends with the text's other levels. In a final example, a statement of shaky memory attracts its own corrective. At the beginning of the brief story of a young man who committed suicide by jumping off a ship, Duras notes that she does not really know any longer whether the event happened during the voyage she has just described or at some other time (137). A few lines later, as if invoked suggestively by writing itself, "memory" awakens: "No, writing it now, she doesn't see the boat but another place, where she heard the story" (137).[7] Significantly, the "correct" version turns out to be remembrance, not of a witnessed event, but of a text, as is so often the case for Duras' narrators. Again, verbal expression of memory's visual uncertainty produces remembrance and textuality.

Contrary to the assumptions of many reviewers, who have tended to dichotomize the text of *The Lover,* it would be misleading to posit an antagonism between the two central images. Although a river crossing is involved, which entails a passage to sexual initiation at once symbolic and concrete, it signals no definitive departure from one place to another. One must not neglect the fact that the rite of passage takes place on a ferry, which, rather than transporting one to a permanent destination, shuttles back and forth. The ferry has neither port of origin nor end port. Moreover, the alternation between the two "ports," here the two photographic scenes, brings them closer and produces metonymical links. Rather than institute a dichotomy between her lover and her family, Duras associates them. The two interpenetrate. One "port" interprets the other, which it resembles:

> I am still in that family, that is where I live to the exclusion of any other place. . . . The hours that I spend in the bachelor flat in Cholen [with the lover] make that place appear in a fresh, new light. It is an irrespirable place, close to death, a place of violence, of pain,

of despair, of dishonor. And such is Cholen. On the other side of the river.

(93)

The sexual affair coordinates with Duras' erotic feelings towards her two brothers, whose "shadows pass through the bedroom" where she and the Chinese man make love (122). Orchestrated so that they bring the two "ports" together, the dinner scenes show a polarity maintained not by her but by the others involved. To be sure, she perceives an essential difference between herself and her mother,[8] when her own sexual experience leads her to realize that her mother has probably never known sexual pleasure, and she "leaves" her in that sense:

> The sons knew it already. The daughter, not yet. They will never speak about the mother together, about this knowledge they have and which separates them from her, about this decisive, final knowledge, of the childhood state [*enfance*] of the mother. The mother has never known sexual pleasure.

(50)

But if there is separation, it distances Duras equally from her family and from her lover. For she also knows that she has not left her mother for the lover. Nor will she leave her lover for her family. She learns that she will never consign herself, either symbolically or concretely, to one or the other of the river banks: "I told him to regret nothing. I reminded him of what he had said, that I would leave everywhere, that I could not control my behavior" (102-03). It is not for other lovers, or to return to her family, that she will "betray" him; it is for writing.[9] The mother understands this desire of her daughter:

> I answered that what I wanted above anything else was to write, nothing else, nothing. Jealous, she is. No answer, a brief glance quickly turned away, the small, unforgettable shrug of her shoulders. I will be the first to leave. . . . She knew it.

(31)

Yet she "leaves" only to return to them, to shuttle back and forth on the ferry boat of her writing, which these two "images," of family and sexual love, have always informed. She takes up permanent quarters on a figure of impermanence: a vehicle riding on water, that central Durassian symbol of the constant flow of feminine creativity and sexuality. The Mekong carries everything in it. Generous, full, "the river flows dully [*sourdement*]; it makes no noise, blood in the body" (30). In the hazy sunlight "the river banks have disappeared" and everything remains suspended for the moment, as does this magnificent metaphorical description placed between two declarations of the young girl's intention to write, each of which corresponds to one of the central "photographs." With its promise to overflow, the river figures the writer herself, a young girl on the brink of reaffirming her own vocation to overflow, ink on the page, fluids from the body, the metaphor of feminine creativity. Just prior to this passage, Duras takes up the "picture" of herself at 15, adding brush strokes

to her physical portrait, describing her body, her breasts, her make-up and provocative attire. Lest the reader miss the profoundly literary message, Duras concludes the description with a summary of its meaning:

> At fifteen and a half the body is slender, almost puny, breasts still those of a child, make-up pale pink and red. And then that outfit. That could make people laugh but no one does. I see very well that everything is there. Everything is there and nothing is played out yet. I see it in the eyes, everything is already in the eyes. I want to write.

(29)

Thus *The Lover* is also, and perhaps primarily, the story of an artistic vocation.

Several other pictures are written into *The Lover*, such as that of the author's son (21) and a second one of her mother (118), as well as flash descriptions of Marie-Claude Carpenter (79) and Betty Fernandez (82), two wartime acquaintances whose "portraits" suddenly interrupt the text, as though Duras had just happened upon them in a drawer where they had inadvertently been mixed in with the batch of "pictures" from Indochina. Or as though she had turned a page in an album and found them. The entire text is composed of brief scenes, or verbal snapshots set off by blank spaces, a photo album consisting solely of captions. Indeed, Duras had originally planned to publish a collection of photographs accompanied by a text depicting the unphotographed boat scene: "The text of *The Lover* was at first called *The Absolute Image*. It was to thread through an album of photographs of my films and of me" (*Nouvel Observateur* 52). Once again, one notes an interesting artistic progression. Duras abandons the structure of a picture book, whose main status would have been one of that documentary truth Roland Barthes declared to be the essence of photography, proof that "that really was."[10] Instead, she opts for a non-visual poetic "that is, in my imagination and now in the reader's." The flowing, musical temporality of poetic prose replaces photography's visual and temporal stasis. Duras describes the writing of *The Lover* in musical terms: Like music, a sort of literary "Pictures at an Exhibition," the text unfolds in the temporal mode of the present in contrast to photography's inherent past tense of recorded fact. Just as in musical composition, juxtaposition constitutes a unifying principle, and Duras recognized this sort of metonymy as central to *The Lover*:

> I wrote it measure by measure, beat by beat, without ever trying to find a more or less profound correspondence between the beats. I let this correspondence work unconsciously. . . . When I reread it, I notice it. There is constant, incessant metonymy in The Lover.

(*Nouvel Observateur* 52-53)

As she does in every instance where several artistic media are involved, Duras uses the musical analogy to elucidate literary techniques. She equates music, or the sounds and rhythms of words, with writing: "All composition is musical. In every instance, it is this adjustment to the book that is musical. If one does not do that, one can always make other books, those whose subject is not writing" (ibid.). Verbal music, then, composes the "captions" that make up this non-visual photo album.

In French the word for caption and for legend is the same: *légende,* as if, by adapting an older word to the modern context of photographic images in texts of all kinds, the French language intuitively recognized the mythical nature of commentary embodied in captions. Contemporary thought distanced all language from objective fact or truth when it accepted the implications of Saussure's contention, later elaborated by Benveniste, that the relation between the linguistic sign and its referent is arbitrary. This implicitly attributes an inherently fictional nature to language itself. Roland Barthes, who considers language essentially fictional, contrasts it to photography, whose relation to its referent he declares factual, albeit in the past tense: ". . . in Photography, I can never deny that *the thing was there*" (*Chambre Claire* 120), and "language is by nature fictional [. . .] but photography [. . .] is authentification itself" (*Chambre* 134). Couching the viewer's attitude in phenomenological terms, Barthes maintains that "one must link photography to a pure spectator consciousness, not to a fictional consciousness."[11] At other times, he uses linguistic concepts to make the same distinction, calling the factual essence of photographs denotative and the fictional essence of language connotative.

Discussing the relation of the photographic image, Barthes notes that despite their connotative nature, captions usually try to pass themselves off as denotative, as the factual definition or explanation of what photographs represent. Therefore, the presence of the two together tends to undermine the captions' fictional status. Whenever a photograph is present, the denotative element predominates (*Obvie* 20). One can conclude that in literature this remains true, so that a mixed structure is produced, in which the balance tips towards the factual register.

By excluding photographs from her text, Duras avoids this sort of ambivalent relation between captions and their visual, referential support. Indeed, she uses the absence of pictures to reverse the habitual relation between them, situating both commentary and "fact" in the fictional realm of language. Instead of the image eliciting the caption, the "caption" produces a non-material, verbally evoked image: "Betty Fernandez. Another foreigner. As soon as the name is pronounced, here she is, she's walking down a street of Paris, she's nearsighted . . ." (82). In the wake of verbal invocation and visual absence, once again associative metonymy triggers textuality.

Thus disconnected, Duras' "captions" are free to present the relativized idiolect of her personal (but public, because literary) mythology, which she opens to readers. Unambiguously removed from the sphere of the documentary, they move into that of the legendary. Duras martials a number of techniques that combine with this one to lend her text the legendary qualities suggested by the French "légende." She creates a quasi-sacred atmosphere common to so much of her fiction, through use of rhythmically repeated invocations, the anaphorical charge of intertextual references to numerous others of her works that spin the same setting (nine or ten films and novels, from the 1950 *Sea Wall* to *India Song* to *The Lover*), recurring characters and passages, and through the manipulation of the definite article when speaking, for example, of "the" image, "the" lover, "the" mother. This enables the author to leave the personal possessive for the general, to make public property of her private mythology. "When I speak of my lover I do not say that I see *his* face again, I say I see *the* face again, and that I remember the name. That takes it outside. To you. I give it to you" (*Libération* 29). Photographs would have restored the possessive adjective pictorially, since they would have been received as pictures of "her" lover, "her" mother, etc.

Moreover, the very musicality of Duras' prose harks back to ancient oral traditions of the transmission of legends situated, like *The Lover,* in a semi-mythicized past made present with each telling. But in Duras, for whom the binary opposition oral/written has little pertinence, telling is close to (if not the same as) writing, as well as to reading. Her narrators are mostly either "real" or "potential" writers of the text we read (Hold in *Le Ravissement,* Peter Morgan for the beggar section in *The Vice-Consul,* Aurélia in the *Aurélia Steiners,* the interrogator in *L'Amante anglaise,* the male protagonist in *Le Marin*) or readers of a text materially present (*The Truck, Agatha, Le Navire Night, La Maladie de la Mort*) or absent (*India Song, Savannah Bay*).[12] These structures add another dimension to reading, activating the etymological meaning of "légende": to be read. In addition, frequently the text is explicitly designated as legendary. In *India Song* the narrating voices evoke a story expressly designated by the author in the text as a legend (12). Duras does the same in a "stage direction" in *Savannah Bay* (32). Combined with the effects of this sort of performative discourse, the awed attitude of the narrators in *India Song,* in *The Lover,* and in many of these texts, contributes further to the legendary air of Duras' work.

The Littré dictionary defines "légende" as "a popular (folk) narrative with a more or less altered historical foundation, or at least a self-styled (*prétendu*) historical foundation." "Popular": of the people; the deprivatizing of Duras' texts generalizes the particular into a sacralized commonality. And, as with legends, since the telling and reading of the "historical" event occurs in the present, it presupposes the material absence of the referent. In *The Lover,* beyond temporal distance, the marked absence of visual reproductions of the referent—photographs—most specifically conditions the text's legendary character.

To conclude, two quotations seem particularly apt. Barthes quotes Kafka in the epigraph to *Roland Barthes par Roland Barthes* (Seuil, 1975): "One photographs things to chase them from one's mind. My stories are a manner of closing one's eyes." And Verena Conley cites the following remark by Hélène Cixous in *Boundary 2* (Winter 1985): ". . . despite the temptation, I will not tell the most tragically tragic of stories, which are those of people who never had the good fortune to be able to transform their fatality into legend."

Notes

1. Marguerite Duras, *Le Camion* (Paris: Editions de Minuit, 1977) 11.

2. Marguerite Duras, *L'Homme atlantique* (Paris: Editions de Minuit, 1982) 17. All translations from the French are mine.

3. Marguerite Duras has frequently affirmed that her films partake, first and foremost, of the act of writing: "Talking in the theater after a rehearsal of *La Musica,* she says she makes films between books in order to keep writing" (interview with Mary Blume in *The International Herald Tribune,* March 22, 1985). In *Les Yeux verts,* she makes the following comment about film scenarios, or "manuscripts": "A manuscript is not neutral. It is that which can not be seen" (*Les Yeux verts, Cahiers du cinéma* [Paris: Editions de l'Etoile, 1980] 87). If it was "perhaps not worth the effort" to film *Agatha,* it is because "The text would have said it just as well. Because the text says everything. The totality of the cinematic potential contains the text, is said by it, the text. The film is an accident, a sort of consequence of not great importance. . . . [*Agatha*] is a listening proposition, a reading proposition. They are there, for one and a half hours, they read 70 pages. That's all. . . . [I made the film] for the reading of the voice, not for the voice, for the reading of the text" (*Marguerite Duras à Montréal,* eds. Lamy and Roy [Montreal: Editions Spirale, 1981] 18).

4. Cf. Susan D. Cohen, "Phantasm and Narration in *The Ravishing of Lol V. Stein,*"*The Psychoanalytic Study of Literature,* eds. Reppen and Charney (New Jersey: The Analytic Press, October, 1985): 255-77.

5. Marguerite Duras and Paulo Leite, "Veja, excerpts from an interview with Marguerite Duras," *World Press Review* (September, 1985): 57.

6. Marguerite Duras and Hervé Masson, "L'Inconnue de la rue Catinat," *Le Nouvel Observateur* (Paris: September 28, 1984): 52.

7. A characteristic technique of Duras, the switch from the first person to the third, effects a distancing from the writer and the character, which attenuates the immediacy of (self)-identification. This undermining of potential autobiographical readings of *The Lover* contributes to a dispossession peculiar to Duras, which generalizes the textual experience, as I shall discuss later.

8. The words "mother" and "brother" each signify "the family," an indissoluble unit for Duras. The younger brother's death, for example, signals the death of the family as such: "The little brother died in three days, of bronchial pneumonia; the heart could not hold on. That is when I left my mother. . . . Everything ended that day. . . . She died, for me, of the death of my little brother. So did my older brother" (37).

9. Duras has equated writing with a certain betrayal: "What is writing? What is that parallel road, that fundamental betrayal of everyone and of oneself?" (Marguerite Duras, "Sublime, forcément sublime," *Libération* [Paris: September 4, 1984]: 29).

10. Roland Barthes, *La Chambre claire* (Paris: Gallimard, 1980) 120.

11. Roland Barthes, *L'Obvie et l'obtus* (Paris: Seuil, 1982) 36.

12. In the case of *Savannah Bay,* I use the term "reading" in the widest sense, to include imagining and remembering a "text." Cf. Susan D. Cohen, "La Présence de rien," *Les cahiers Renaud-Barrault, 106,* ed. Simone Benmussa (Paris: Gallimard, September, 1983): 17-37.

Janice Morgan (essay date 1991)

SOURCE: "Fiction and Autobiography/Language and Silence: 'The Lover' by Marguerite Duras," in *Redefining Autobiography in Twentieth-Century Women's Fiction: An Essay Collection,* edited by Janice Morgan and Colette T. Hall, Garland Publishing, Inc., 1991, pp. 73-84.

[*In the following essay, Morgan discusses the autobiographical significance of the silences in* The Lover.]

> To write is not to comment on what one already knows but to look for what one doesn't know yet.
>
> —Viviane Forrestier[1]

In 1984, Marguerite Duras surprised the French literary world by producing **L'Amant (***The Lover***)**, a lyrical, darkly-candid autobiographical book about her adolescence in Indochina during the late 1920s. The book, which opens with the young Duras crossing the Mekong river on a ferry and closes one and a half years later with her departure on an ocean liner for France, traces the young woman's passage from childhood to adulthood. In many ways, ***The Lover***—written toward the end of what has been a long, distinguished career as an author—is the retelling of events described earlier in a novel called *The Sea Wall* (1950). More than thirty years separate the two works, more than thirty years of relative silence on this evidently formative part of Duras's life. It is as if until just recently, Duras wished to forget—both publicly and privately—about this very different childhood she experienced in what remains for Westerners an alien land. Gradually, however, the past has re-surfaced in Duras's writing—first in fiction, as in the Indian cycle beginning with *The*

Vice-Consul (1966), then later in the growing number of photographs, interviews, and frankly autobiographical texts the author has published during the last few years.

In re-reading *The Sea Wall,* it is clear what Duras would have wished to forget—the poverty, isolation, and the lack of opportunity endemic to the remote, tropical outpost where the family, a widowed mother and her two children, lives. Informing the whole is the legend of how the mother, in a heroic but doomed attempt to become a wealthy land-owner for her children's benefit, suffers one legal defeat after another at the hands of a corrupt, colonial administration. With their mother living afterwards in despair and close to madness, the son and the daughter have no one to turn to for consolation but each other and their romantic fantasies of a better life. An erotic liaison with a wealthy lover becomes for both of them the preferred avenue of escape.

Though *The Sea Wall* is based on personal situations and events that actually occurred, the novel is nonetheless a very public narrative: the story is told in the third person (yet closely tied to the daughter Suzanne's point of view) and develops in a conventionally linear, chronological fashion. Throughout, its realistic settings and terse dialogue recall the American novel style à la Hemingway so fashionable in France during the 1950s.

The Lover, while covering the same brief period in the author's life, differs dramatically from the earlier version. Narrated largely in the first person, the text is composed of fragments taken from shifting time frames, fragments that are related not in an external, linear way, but in circular, associative patterns that convey the more intimate, psychological rhythms of that experience. At times etched with a sharp sense of realism (the strident sounds and exotic mixture of smells in the night streets of Cholon, for example), yet at other times, passing with a dream-like fluidity beyond any set boundaries of place and time, *The Lover* creates a distinctive style all its own.

It is clear that Duras assumes the two different texts to be complementary, for each provides a certain content that the other leaves out. In this way, the first text becomes a kind of narrative *repoussoir* for the second, a foil against which the new text, this new interpretation of events, will be played. "Before, I spoke of clear periods, those on which the light fell. Now I'm talking about the hidden stretches of that same youth, of certain facts, feelings, events that I buried" (8). In thus characterizing the interdependency of the two texts, Duras asserts her need to clarify what had been written before, to re-discover a remembered vision of her past life and self that had previously been disguised. The author tells her readers that she now feels free to tell the true story of how things happened, now that her mother and her brothers are dead, now that the moral strictures governing literary culture (and women's writing in particular) have been unbound.

Yet though Duras pursues the past with a relentless candor, it would be naive to conclude that she is writing the book merely to settle accounts or that she is uncovering the past in an effort to reveal all. Estelle Jelinek, in her introduction to *Women's Autobiography,* speaks of a dual or conflicting intention in the writing of autobiography. While on the one hand authors "wish to clarify, to affirm, and to authenticate their self-images" (15), a writer will also tend to camouflage or in some way distance herself from intimacy in the projection of that self-image. Certainly, the psychological tension between intimacy and distance, self-revelation and self-effacement accounts for much of the fascination and allure *The Lover* exerts upon its readers. Central to this issue is the enigma of Duras's feelings for the man who first became her lover and with that, the sense we have of how much the author reveals or conceals, first from the lover and secondly, from the reader. For perhaps the real subject of this autobiography, unlike the earlier version in *The Sea Wall,* is writing—that is, the origins of Duras's desire to write and with that, her means of access to that writing.

To begin, many readers are struck by her tendency to slip from a predominantly first-person narration to a more distant third-person narration and to do so precisely in those scenes with the man from Cholon, scenes which are among the most intimate in the book. The more obvious explanations for this are not at all satisfying. For example, the split between the first person (1) and the third person (she) does not seem to convey, as one might anticipate in an autobiographical work, the distinction between the young girl of then as she lived her experiences and the mature woman of today looking back on those experiences. For the narrative, rather than shifting back and forth from the present tense to the past, is written very dominantly in the present tense (regardless of the particular time period being evoked) and with a high degree of vividness and immediacy that effectively erases the very distinction between past and present. Rather, the appearance of the third person seems to mark the deliberate intrusion in autobiography of a fictional artifice; that is, Duras, the public figure and author *narrating,* becomes Duras, a literary character, *narrated,* in her own story.

For some critics, this fictional intrusion compromises the transparency of Duras's early statement that this book is one of self revelation. Sharon Willis, for example, views the narrative split consciousness in *The Lover* as a kind of literary smokescreen, one highly characteristic of Duras's tendency to *décevoir* (in the dual sense of the French word *to deceive; to disappoint*) her public (4). The author would seem to stand accused, then, of intentional duplicity, "given the text's strategy of veiling and unveiling, where 'I' veils herself as 'she', but where 'she' just as frequently masquerades as 'I'" (6). In other words, one may well gain the suspicion that Duras, the writer, is playing the same game of seduction and evasion with her readers that the young girl played, then, with her lover.

As compelling as this interpretation might seem, I would like to propose another—namely, that is precisely through a certain artifice and duality that Duras's narrative is able

o achieve its authenticity. Moreover, the tension that ex-
sts in the written text between intimacy and distance, deception and sincerity, language and silence is, in fact, in-
rinsic to the experiences as she lived them.

From the outset, Duras describes her erotic adventure as
"the experiment," revealing already not only a taste for
pleasure but a taste for speculative distance on that pleasure. From her opening statement about what constitutes a
woman's beauty, her seductiveness, Duras shows a keen
awareness of women's iconic value, their particular qual-
ty of (in Laura Mulvey's words) "to-be-looked-at-ness"
Mulvey 11). Having identified that quality in herself
through a somewhat elaborately detailed description of
her clothing and makeup), she goes on to describe the
Chinese man's approach, his interest—but also his apprehension because of the racial difference, her youth. It is at
the moment when he approaches her that Duras slips into
third-person narration, and thereafter, a dual awareness in-
uses the narrative. From the moment she describes her
gaze going out to the man on the ferry, there is another
gaze, beyond the couple, looking back—Duras consciously
watching herself being watched, being enchanted by the
phenomenon, writing about it. When Duras slips into the
third person, she effectively transposes the transparency of
the first-person account of an individual experience into a
more complex kind of theater, one which transcends the
limits of the personal.

The rhythmic force of the prose carries events forward as
relentlessly as the Mekong River current, the girl being
embarked with the man in what she calls "everyone's
story,"[2] the knowledge which she says she already possessed, "in advance of time and experience" (9). Clearly,
the balance of passion is weighted on his side, while the
balance of power (the passive power of a desired woman)
is on hers. Far from stressing the uniqueness of her experience—as we might expect—the young girl insists instead
on maintaining almost an enforced impersonality with her
lover. Alone with him for the first time, she asks the man
to do with her what he "usually does with the women he
brings to his flat" (37, 38) and later confides to him that
she enjoys the idea of being curiously "one of them, indistinguishable [from them]" (42). No names are mentioned
in the narrative; Duras refers to the man and to herself
through third-person epithets: "the child" (35), "the man
from Cholon" (74), "the little white girl" (83), "the Chinese millionaire" (91)—terms which not only convey the
way each is viewed by a certain segment of society, but
also the way the lovers inevitably view each other; they
are attracted to and defined for each other by their separateness, their difference.

The young girl never equates the undeniable pleasure she
receives from him with love for the man she meets each
night; part of her is always outside the room where they
are, beyond the space their two bodies occupy. Their affair
s characterized, from the first night they are together, by
an unbridgeable solitude: "He says he's lonely, horribly
lonely because of this love he feels for her. She says she's

lonely too. She doesn't say why" (37). Because of this
solitude, her intense physical pleasure with him seems abstract, austere—almost brutal. The first person narration
resumes suddenly in the memory of her mother, then in
the vivid evocation of the particular atmosphere of the
room where they are—so open to the Chinese streets outside its windows. In the midst of their lovemaking, the
young girl hears the sounds of wooden clogs on the
crowded streets, the strident sounds of merchants mingled
with the rich aroma of roasted peanuts, soups, the sudden
mountain fragrance of wood-smoke, and it is as if all the
individuality, the unforgettable particularity of the event
lay there, strangely outside herself.

Between the ebb and flow of physical desire, the girl tells
the Chinese about her family in Sadec; soon surrounding
the lovers' bodies alone in the room grows the shadowy
presence of the mother, the two brothers, and their familiar
"inspired silence" (34). After their first evening together,
the narrative flickers back and forth from the nights in
Cholon to the remembered days in Sadec. Thus, at the
same time that Cholon inaugurates her separation from the
family in Sadec, it also curiously confirms that original experience; both Sadec and Cholon share the identity of "a
place that's intolerable, bordering on death, a place of violence, pain, despair, dishonor" (75). Gradually, the nights
in Cholon, with their distinctive mixture of pleasure-in-
pain, in their essential ambivalence, seem to parallel with
the lover the same silent relationships of desire and difference, pride and shame, power and fear that existed within
her family. It is undoubtedly to the intensity of this ambivalence—in recognition of these silences—that Duras
owes the uniqueness of her vision as a writer. About Sadec
she writes, "It's in its aridity, its terrible harshness, its ma-
lignancy, that I'm the most deeply sure of myself, at the
heart of my essential certainty, the certainty that I'll be a
writer" (75). Here, in the powerful comfort Duras takes in
the knowledge of her destiny as a writer, one can only
conclude, as does the critic Yvonne Guers-Villate, that
writing performs a very important and specific function for
this author: it is through the writing of books that she will
be able to transpose—in an aesthetic form—the wealth of
contradictions, the polarities and distances, the emotional
intensities and ambiguities of life as she experienced them.[3]
Her desire here is not to *resolve* these conflicting tensions,
but rather—as in death—to free herself from them, to transcend them.

All these elements participate in the distances established
by the oscillations in the narrative, of which the shift between she and I is but one indication. Yet there is another
facet to this layered consciousness in the story. For also
intertwined with the nights in Cholon are the remembered
images of certain women: Marie-Claude Carpenter, Betty
Fernandez, Helen Lagonelle. *The Lover* is a hymn to these
women—to the desire they evoked in those around them,
their mystery, their beauty, and also their peculiar absence,
their silence. Among these women, one reigns supreme in
memory, referred to here as "the Lady" (89), the wife of
the French ambassador in Vinh Long, the one whose young

lover committed suicide in Savanna Khet when she left there to join her husband in Vinh Long. This particular woman, first encountered by Duras at the age of eight, seems to have incarnated for her an unforgettable model of femininity—one strongly implicated in a precocious obsession with death.[4] The model also for a literary character, Anne-Marie Stretter, who dominates several of Duras's most well-known works—notably *The Vice-Consul* and *India Song,* embodies for the young Duras a dual power and possesses a dual identity: first, as a wealthy woman of society, wife and mother, an elegant sustainer of the status quo and then, underneath that identity, a woman who contained within the sensuality of her body "this power of death, to create death, to bring it on" (*Lieux* 65).[5]

Duras's use of the third person (she) to introduce and frame her own erotic initiation, that curious fusion of she/I, works to connect her own individual story to this other myth of passion. In fact, the author draws a clear parallel between that other woman, then almost forty, and the fifteen-year-old girl; both alike "doomed to discredit because of the kind of body they have, caressed by lovers, kissed by their lips, consigned to the infamy of a pleasure unto death, as they both call it, unto the mysterious death of lovers without love" (90). The nights spent with the lover in Cholon repeat, too, the litany of "a pleasure unto death" (43, 90), and one senses strongly that Duras's account of this experience represents, for her, a personal access to a legend; one senses that the narrative enacts her own entry into the necessarily impersonal myth of passion and desire.[6] It is this quality of the relationship that accounts, no doubt, for the externality of its narration: in the text, for example, Duras refers to the man as "the" not as "my" lover; and further on, she writes about him using once more the definite article where the possessive would be more customary, "I can still see the face, and I do remember the name" (44).[7] This same externality, this implicit allusion to a legend of erotic passion that exists curiously *beyond* the two lovers also provides the essential dimension to the young girl's previously expressed wish with her lover to be among all the other women "he'd had," to be "'mixed in' with them, indistinguishable" (42). In this wish, the lover becomes her accomplice (and, to a certain extent, her victim): "He understands what I've just said. Our expressions are suddenly changed, false, caught in evil and death" (42). "It was as if he loved the pain, loved it as he'd loved me, intensely, unto death perhaps, and as if he preferred it now to me" (110).

Nowhere does the force of this myth seem more striking than in the closing pages of the book when, again, the fictional register resumes in the telling of her departure on the ocean liner and, with that departure, the young girl's sudden realization one night—after their separation—that perhaps she had loved him after all, "with a love she hadn't seen because it had lost itself in the affair (*l'histoire,* the story) like water in sand" (114; *L'Amant* 138). The distanced, fictional mode here, the story, becomes a way of revealing the depth of illusion behind the experience as she lived it—a way of unveiling the self-deception that in-

formed (or perhaps better, de-formed, concealed) the emotion contained within that experience. Thus, as in Duras's novels, even as the narrative weaves its spell of fantasy or illusion, it also reveals a lucid awareness of the central delusion it depicts. The text's duality, its "duplicity"—far from compromising the validity of the fundamental experience—becomes, in fact, the hallmark of its genuineness. Ultimately, for the writer, it is the "story" that triumphs years afterward, through the man's phone call, we hear once more in the book's final pages the echoing testimony of a mythic love undiminished by time, of a passion that would endure until death. Here, personal event has been fully transposed into literature: autobiography has passed into legend.

We began by observing that *The Lover* is a work of revelation. In Duras's avowed intentions in writing the book to tell those parts of her experience that were not expressed before, the text assumes the role of a testimonial or a confession. Yet in comparing this later book to the earlier *Sea Wall,* we note a peculiar irony: it is the earlier novel that is filled with movement, character, event, and dialogue—speech that passes even into invective and diatribe—whereas the later autobiographical book remains largely a record of silences. In effect, the text is saturated with silence, silences that exist at the level of the experience itself: in speaking of the family in Sadec, for example, "Never a hello, a good evening, a happy New Year. Never a thank you. Never any talk. Never any need to talk. Everything always silent, distant. It's a family of stone, petrified so deeply it's impenetrable" (54); about the subject of marriage between herself and the Chinese "They never speak of it any more" (97); about their night together in Cholon, "He scarcely speaks to her any more. Perhaps he thinks she won't understand any longer what he'd say about her, about the love he never knew before and of which he can't speak" (99); or at the moment when the young girl nearly confides her story to her mother: "I almost told her about Cholon. But I didn't. I never did" (93).

But silences occur also in the gaps and fissures of the narration, in the fragmentation and dislocation of memory as the text slips from one time-place to another. One cannot avoid the impression—confirmed even on the printed page punctuated as it is by blank spaces—that a mysterious content must have been left out. Curiously, however, in comparing *The Lover* to *The Sea Wall,* one discovers that this later book is, at once, more fragmented yet more thematically coherent than its fictional predecessor, more elusive, yet more complete. Clearly, there is something here that goes beyond the contingencies of youthful reticence, the accidents inherent in either willful or unwillful failure to communicate; for the silence at the heart of Duras's childhood experience lies also at the heart of her aesthetic practice. One need only compare the style and structure of the text to those of her mature, fictional works: *Moderato Cantabile, Hiroshima mon amour, The Ravishing of Lol V. Stein, The Vice-Consul*—to recognize that the writing of silence represents for this author a deliberate, aesthetic choice. Both the fiction and the autobiography are based on a central conviction deeply held by the author, that language (the spoken) exists precisely to suggest, to evoke that which remains unspoken in life; that writing serves, therefore, primarily to render the substance of things imagined, the evidence of things not said.

Duras's own comments on the complex, hidden filiations between desire, silence, and writing in this autobiographical work make this conviction evident (25, 75, 103). Furthermore, in an interview, the author states that the intense, youthful affair in Cholon about which she has written "has eclipsed the other loves of my life, those that were declared, married"[8] and has done so precisely because it was "unspoken, undeclared" (Apos). In its silence, then, Cholon and all that it represents rejoins the imaginary photograph that opens the book, the one of the seductive young girl on the ferry crossing the river, the one that was never taken. Because it was never taken, she says, never "detached or removed from all the rest" (10), the tenuous, remembered image holds a great power, that of representing an absolute: it is precisely because their content was never expressed, never acknowledged or fixed in either image or words that both the absent photograph and the silent nights in Cholon have come to hold—much later in the author's life—an inexhaustible richness.

Here, a certain suspicion of language prevails, one shared by other contemporary writers (notably Maurice Blanchot, whom Duras admires)—a belief that language, even as it calls into being and names our past experience, can also betray that experience, can contain and kill its sensuous strangeness, its unrepeatable magic. The goal of the writer, then, is to create a style that does not attempt to directly express its ever-elusive content but only to suggest the contours, the dimension, or the shadow of that content. It is this quality that gives a literary text (like a memory) the power to resonate beyond itself, to engender other texts, other forms.

And this can be true, it seems, of autobiography as well as of fiction. In this way, Duras would not have us view this particular book as an endpoint or a conclusion to the past but rather as another possible point of departure and rediscovery of that past.[9] In its elusiveness, its fluidity, its ritual imperative of looking again, of saying again, *The Lover* asserts the re-performing of a self in writing that ultimately cannot be fixed, seized, rendered captive or named in words and images. Paradoxically, then, it is through a certain artifice, through the use of fictional registers, and through the shaping of silence that the writer is able to evoke a composite portrait of herself, one that in its complex facets of event and illusion begins to attain the fullness of authenticity.

Notes

1. This epigraph by Forrestier is borrowed from a book about writing by Suzanne Lamy entitled *Quand je lis je m'invente* (*When I Read, I Invent Myself*). Translation my own.

2. This citation is from a special interview with Marguerite Duras conducted by Bernard Pivot on the French television program *Apostrophes*. This particular program, broadcast by Antenne 2 on September 28, 1984, is available on video upon request from the French Cultural Services in New York (FACSEA), 972 Fifth Avenue, NY 10021. Further references to this particular interview will be indicated in the text by the abbreviated (Apos) in parentheses. Translations are my own.

3. For a sensitive and highly perceptive discussion of this subject, see the chapter "Ambivalence and sentiment de contradiction" in *Continuité/Discontinuité* by Guers-Villate: "Without a single doubt, literary creation was the means chosen very early by the novelist to permit her to exorcise her own conflicts through transposing them" (58). Translation my own.

4. Duras speaks at length about the influence of this mysterious red-haired woman in *Les Lieux de Marguerite Duras,* an interview with Michelle Porte (61-69).

5. Far from being merely an idiosyncratic obsession, the eight-year-old's fascination with this particular woman's story seems to connect with a primal reverence and fear of the power of women's bodies that reaches back into the mists of recorded time. The dual feminine identity that the young Duras found so compelling touches upon ancient myths and rituals where "woman became recognized as both benign goddess and mysterious power, both a life giver and life destroyer, to be feared and desired, loved and scorned" (Arms 11-12). Even today, a deep ambivalence regarding the myth of "Woman" is very much in evidence, taking many curious forms in popular culture: the role of women in advertising, in *film noir,* in the presence of cult personalities such as Madonna, for example.

6. Though Duras's affair (as well as her fiction) is steeped in the mystique of "Woman," she nonetheless reveals a sardonic awareness of how women are often betrayed by this mystique. She describes the not-to-be-envied plight of the upper-class colonial women she knew of, cloistered in their mansions, saving their fragile white beauty through the tropical seasons while waiting for some vague future romance to change their empty lives (26-28). Duras's own story in *The Lover,* though it participates fully in this romantic mystique, also asserts a much bolder, more controlling approach to the satisfaction of feminine desire within that mystique.

7. These observations are made by Duras herself in an interview with Marianne Alphant in *Libération.*

8. Citation from the interview with Marianne Alphant, op. cit.

9. In the above-cited interview with Alphant, Duras suggests that this same brief period of her youth

may well give rise to two or three other autobiographical books, each of them different. Further on, she quotes Stendhal, saying that no other part of her life holds as much meaning for her as a writer: "interminably, childhood."

Works Cited

Arms, Suzanne. *Immaculate Deception: A New Look at Women and Childbirth.* New York: Bantam/Houghton-Mifflin, 1975.

Alphant, Marianne. "Duras à l'état sauvage" and interview with Marguerite Duras. *Libération* (4 September, 1984).

Duras, Marguerite. *L'Amant.* Paris: Minuit, 1984.

―――. *Un Barrage contre le Pacifique.* Paris: Gallimard, 1950.

―――. *Hiroshima mon amour.* Paris: Gallimard, 1960.

―――. *India Song.* Paris: Gallimard, 1973.

―――. et Michelle Porte. *Les Lieux de Marguerite Duras.* Paris: Minuit, 1977.

―――. *The Lover.* Trans. Barbara Bray. New York: Perennial, 1986.

―――. *La Maladie de la mort.* Paris: Minuit, 1982.

―――. *Moderato Cantabile.* Paris: Minuit, 1958.

―――. *Le Ravissement de Lol V. Stein.* Paris: Gallimard, 1964.

―――. *The Sea Wall.* Trans. Herma Briffault. New York: Perennial, 1986. c. 1952.

―――. *Le Vice-Consul.* Paris: Gallimard, 1966.

Guers-Villate, Yvonne. *Continuité/Discontinuité de l'oeuvre durassienne.* Brussels: Editions de l'Université de Bruxelles, 1985.

Jelinek, Estelle C. "Introduction: Women's Autobiography and the Male Tradition." *Women's Autobiography: Essays in Criticism.* Ed. Estelle Jelinek. Bloomington: Indiana UP, 1980.

Lamy, Suzanne. *Quand je lis je m'invente.* Montréal: L'Hexagone, 1984.

Mulvey, Laura. "Visual Pleasure and Narrative Cinema." *Screen* 16: (1975): 6-18.

Willis, Sharon. *Marguerite Duras: Writing on the Body.* Urbana: U of Illinois P, 1987.

Suzanne Chester (essay date 1992)

SOURCE: "Writing the Subject: Exoticism/Eroticism in Marguerite Duras's 'The Lover' and 'The Sea Wall,'" in *De/Colonizing the Subject: The Politics of Gender in Women's Autobiography,* edited by Sidonie Smith and Julie Watson, University of Minnesota Press, 1992, pp. 436-58.

[*In the following essay, Chester examines colonialism and autobiographical representation in* The Lover *and* The Sea Wall.]

Until now, the main body of critical work on Duras has explored the relationship between her writing and the category of the feminine—defined variously in cultural, linguistic, and psychoanalytic terms.[1] However, the colonial aspect of Duras's work has been largely ignored and is, I argue, crucial to a reading of sexual difference and the construction of a gendered writing subject. Therefore, my essay will focus on Duras's representation of the particular power relations emerging from the confrontation of the female Other with the "exotic" Other in a French colonial situation. In my reading of *Un barrage contre le pacifique* (*The Sea Wall*) and *L'Amant* (*The Lover*), I will examine the relationship between structures of dominance and strategies of representation, especially as the latter pertain to questions of autobiography.[2]

Since my analysis of Duras lays special emphasis on the notion of a gendered writing subject, my reading of colonial discourse is to be distinguished from Abdul R. JanMohamed's theory of "colonialist literature."[3] Basing his analysis on Frantz Fanon's account of the Manichean structure of the colonizer/colonized relationship, JanMohamed identifies "colonialist literature"—writing produced by the European colonizer—as a monolithic discourse constructed around the central trope he calls "Manichean allegory."[4] He defines this trope as "a field of diverse yet interchangeable oppositions between white and black, good and evil, superiority and inferiority, civilization and savagery, intelligence and emotion, rationality and sensuality, self and Other, subject and object."[5]

While JanMohamed's approach is important in that it emphasizes the historical, social, and political context of colonial discourse, his argument is ultimately reductive insofar as it suggests that colonial power is possessed entirely by the colonizer. As a result, it cannot account for the conflicting textual strategies occasioned by a split in the colonial writing subject, a split that may occur when this subject is a woman and, as such, already defined as the Other of patriarchal society. Because JanMohamed's analysis relies on an absolute opposition between colonizer and colonized, it cannot engage with what I consider the specificity of writing produced by certain women in a colonial society. I maintain that the factors of gender and class produce a split in the colonial writing subject that challenges the fixed opposition between subject and object and the stable process of othering central to JanMohamed's conception of Manichean allegory.

Another pitfall in JanMohamed's approach to colonialist literature lies in its tendency, as Tzvetan Todorov has observed, "to elicit a similarly Manichean interpretation with good and evil simply having switched places; o[r] your right the disgusting white colonialists; on your left the innocent black victims."[6] My analysis of two texts written by, and dealing with, the female Other in the patriarchal society of French colonial Indochina examines how the intersection of gender and colonialism in Duras's writing avoids the trope of Manichean allegory, thereby generating readings that escape the moralistic tendencies of Manichean interpretation. In *The Sea Wall* and **The Lover,** the factors of gender and class problematize the relationship of the colonizer to the colonized, and consequently disrupt the economy of colonial discourse as defined by JanMohamed.

Published in 1950, *The Sea Wall* is Duras's third novel. As she has made clear in interviews with Michèle Porte and Xavière Gauthier, this novel contains many autobiographical elements dealing with her childhood and adolescence in colonial Indochina.[7] In 1914, Duras was born into the family of two French schoolteachers attracted to French Indochina by colonial propaganda, tales of exotica, and the promise of making their fortune. When Duras was four years old, her father died, leaving her mother with three young children. After teaching in a French colonial school by day and playing the piano in a cinema by night for twenty years, the mother put all her savings into the purchase of a concession from the colonial administration. Realizing that the administration had deliberately allotted her an unworkable piece of land that was periodically flooded by the salt water of the Pacific, she employed a group of local peasants to help build a series of dams to prevent the sea from invading. After the collapse of the dams, the mother's anger and bitterness at her exploitation by the colonial administration plunged her into depression and near insanity. Duras spent her first seventeen years in French Indochina, now southern Vietnam, and received her education in the *Lycée de Saigon*. In 1931, the family moved to Paris, where Duras obtained degrees in law and in political science before embarking on her career as a writer.

As a *roman à thèse, The Sea Wall* is an ironic indictment of the French colonial administration, from its corrupt policy of allocating infertile concessions and its collusion with the colonial banks, speculators, and property holders to its callous refusal to alleviate the abject poverty of the indigenous population. The novel also contains an implicit critique of the status of women in patriarchal, colonial society, structured as it is around the endeavors of Suzanne's mother and brother to secure her marriage to a series of white colonial suitors: Mr. Jo, son of a wealthy planter; John Barner, sales representative for a cotton factory in Calcutta; and Jean Agosti, local pineapple farmer and opium smuggler.

The Lover, published in 1984 and an international best-seller, explores the issues raised in *The Sea Wall* through an autobiographical account of Duras's childhood in Indochina and her relationship with her family. Centered on the affair Duras had with a Chinese man, **The Lover** rewrites the cultural and sexual politics of *The Sea Wall*.

This rewriting is exemplified by a shift from the representation of the protagonist as a object of prostitution and of male desire in *The Sea Wall* to the construction of a female subject with an active relationship to desire in **The Lover,** Related to this transformation of the status of the female protagonist is the move from the overt anticolonialism of *The Sea Wall* to the feminization and subordination of the exotic Other in **The Lover.** An analysis of the representation of the female protagonist in *The Sea Wall* as an object of prostitution and of male desire provides the backdrop for an understanding of the subversive strategies at work in **The Lover.** *The Sea Wall* is a narrative in which the protagonist has no active relationship to desire. As a commodity in a colonial, patriarchal society, Suzanne shares the characteristics of both virgin and prostitute, neither of whom has the right to her own pleasure.[8] Suzanne's status as a young girl with neither money nor looks emerges from the following exchange concerning plans for a visit to Ram, the capital city of the colony.

> "So it's not tonight that we're going to Ram," said Suzanne.
>
> "We'll go tomorrow," said Joseph, "and it's not in Ram you'll find what you're looking for. They're all married, except Agosti."
>
> "I'd never give her to Agosti," said the mother, "not even if he came and begged for her."
>
> "He'll not ask you for anything," said Suzanne, "and it's not here I'll find what I'm looking for."
>
> "He wouldn't ask better," said the mother. "I know what I'm saying. But he can go on chasing her."
>
> "He never even thinks about her," said Joseph. "It's going to be hard. Some girls manage to marry without money, but they have to be awful pretty and even then it's a rare thing."[9]

(27)

Occurring early in the novel, this exchange among Suzanne, her brother Joseph, and their mother establishes class as one of the determining factors in the quest to find a husband for Suzanne. It also points to important hierarchies within the dominant group of white colonialists. Since the family's poverty severely limits their choice, the chances of finding Suzanne a suitable husband are slim. What emerges from this conversation is that the mother and Joseph will ultimately decide whom Suzanne will marry. Therefore, although the father is absent from the novel, his traditional function within patriarchal society, as the one who controls the daughter's sexuality, is assumed by the mother and the older brother.

Once Mr. Jo falls in love with Suzanne, her status is radically transformed from that of a liability to that of a highly lucrative asset. As the only son of rich colonial speculator, Mr. Jo represents a potential source of enormous wealth for the family. Consequently, the mother does everything in her power to expedite his marriage to her daughter. Referring to Mr. Jo's daily visits to the house to see Suzanne, the narrator observes: "These visits delighted the mother. The longer they lasted the higher her hopes rose. And if she insisted they leave the bungalow door open, it was in order to give Mr. Jo no alternative but marriage to satisfy his strong desire to sleep with her daughter" (p. 53; translation modified).[10]

The mother recognizes the role Mr. Jo's desire plays in the family's quest for a suitable husband. Such desire is the basis upon which a daughter's value is established, as Luce Irigaray argues in her elaboration of the commodified status of women in patriarchal society. Since a woman's value in society lies in her capacity to be exchanged, her value is not intrinsic to her but is a reflection of a man's desire/need for her: "The exchange value of two signs, two commodities, two women, is a representation of the needs/desires of consumer-exchanger subjects: in no way is it the 'property' of the signs/articles/women themselves."[11] This dynamic is clearly at work in the bathroom scene in *The Sea Wall*. As Suzanne prepares to take a shower in the bathroom, the frustrated and pathetic Mr. Jo begs her to open the door and show him her naked body. While her first reaction to Mr. Jo's entreaty is a decisive refusal, Suzanne gradually begins to wonder if her body is not, after all, intended to gratify the male gaze.

> He had a great desire to see her. After all, it was the natural desire of a man. And there she was, worth seeing. There was only that door to open. And no man in the world had yet seen this body of hers that was hidden by that door. It was not made to be hidden but, on the contrary, to be seen and to make its way in the world, that world to which belonged, after all, this Mr. Jo.[12]
>
>   (57)

Suzanne is on the point of opening the door when Mr. Jo promises to give her a new record player. Realizing that he is trying to prostitute her, she opens the door only to spit in his face.

Although the young girl rebels against this overt prostitution of her body, she does not recognize that the marriage being arranged for her is an institutionalized form of prostitution orchestrated by her mother and Joseph. Thus, despite her initial rebellion, Suzanne comes to appreciate the value of her body when Mr. Jo, his humiliation notwithstanding, presents her with the promised record player. While a glimpse of her body was enough to secure the record player, the sexual favors demanded and the rewards offered begin to increase in direct proportion. Next, Mr. Jo promises her a diamond in exchange for a three-day visit to the city with him. Suzanne's perception of her body as a valuable entity temporarily blinds her to the alienation inherent in her newly commodified status: "And it was thanks to her, Suzanne, that it was now there on the table. She had opened the bathroom door just long enough for Mr. Jo's loathsome and unwholesome gaze to penetrate her body and now the record player lay there, on the table" (p. 59; translation modified).[13]

Similarly, in *The Lover,* the narrator repeatedly acknowledges the ways in which the white colonial woman becomes the object of the gaze and desire of both the indigenous and the colonial male: "I'm used to people looking at me," the narrator remarks, and then explains: "People do look at white women in the colonies; at twelve-year-old girls too. For the past three years white men, too, have been looking at me in the streets, and my mother's men friends have been kindly asking me to have tea with them while their wives are out playing tennis at the Sporting Club" (p. 17).[14] Her awareness of the objectification of the white woman by the male gaze of both colonizer and colonized indicates that sexual difference functions in a particular way in a colonial situation.

While the narrator of *The Lover* alludes to the male gaze that constructs the young girl as an object of desire, *The Sea Wall* vividly stages the negativity of her self-alienation and indicates that, far from being in the dominant position of the subject, as JanMohamed's argument implies, the lower-class white colonial woman is objectified and prostituted by the male gaze. This self-alienation emerges clearly when Suzanne goes to the colonial capital to sell Mr. Jo's diamond. Carmen, the resident prostitute in the Hotel Central, suggests that, since her marriage prospects are limited by the family's poverty, Suzanne earn her living through prostitution, thereby forcing on the young girl a certain image of her precarious status. Unaware of the class divisions within the colonial capital, Suzanne wanders alone through the fashionable district, attracting the attention of the wealthy white residents and unwittingly making a spectacle of herself: "People looked at her. They turned to look, they smiled. No young white girl of her age ever walked alone in the streets of the fashionable district" (p. 149).[15] Furthermore, as Suzanne walks through the white, upper-class district, her consciousness of herself as an object of another's gaze causes her to see herself as she believes others see her: "The more they looked at her the more she was convinced that she was something scandalous, an object of complete ugliness and stupidity" (p. 150).[16]

Finally, the price of being the object of the male gaze results in the fracturing of any residual sense of identity as Suzanne's perception of her body now centers on its fragmentation, each part an object of shame, revulsion, and ridicule:[17] "She herself, from head to foot, was contemptible. Her eyes—where to look? These leaden, obscene arms, this heart, fluttering like an indecent caged beast, these legs that were too weak to bear her along" (p. 151; translation modified).[18]

Subjectivity is further denied to the protagonist of *The Sea Wall* as a result of the omniscient narrator, who, like the proverbial fly on the wall, effaces its own subject position within the text while aligning the reader with its disembodied point of view. Although there is an implicit critique of the objectification of the young girl, the ominiscient narrator also contributes to her objectified status by remaining a hidden observer of this process. Duras's use of a realistic, novelistic convention that depends on an un-problematized narratorial gaze makes both narrator and reader of *The Sea Wall* complicitous in the voyeurism that objectifies the female protagonist.

JanMohamed's Manichean allegory is further problematized by the class divisions within white colonial society—divisions that reveal the structures of dominance existing within that society. In *The Sea Wall,* Suzanne's body becomes the site of the class conflict between her family and the colonial powers. When Suzanne's brother Joseph refuses to allow Mr. Jo to have sex with her before marriage, he is not interested in the morality of the issue but in the measure of power such an interdiction affords the family. Helpless in the face of the colonial powers that have thwarted them, namely, the administration and the banks, their only remaining power lies in the control of Suzanne's body. By forbidding her to sleep with this wealthy planter's son, Suzanne's mother, situated at the bottom of the colonial hierarchy, finds a way to avenge herself psychologically on the whole colonial system. Joseph brazenly tells Mr. Jo where they stand on the issue of his sister's sexuality: "She can sleep with whoever she likes. We don't stop her. But in your case, if you want to sleep with her, you've got to marry her. That's our way of saying to hell with you" (p. 75).[19]

This censorship of Suzanne's relationship to her body reaches a climax when her mother physically beats her, refusing to believe she has not slept with Mr. Jo in exchange for the diamond he has given her. In fact, it is this diamond that really arouses the mother's wrath, since for her it symbolizes an object that has no use value, only exchange value: "There's nothing more disgusting than a diamond. It has no use, no use at all" (p. 108; translation modified).[20] The mother's revulsion at the diamond is related to her ambivalent feelings about her own part in the prostitution of her daughter, feelings that alternate between shame at handing her daughter over to Mr. Jo, who epitomizes the worst aspects of the dominant white colonials, and pride in the economic rewards that result from the relationship. The mother's ambivalence is symptomatic of her own alienated position within this colonial society, since it is the family's impoverishment—a direct result of colonial corruption—that predisposes her to use Suzanne's body as bait to lure Mr. Jo into a marriage with her daughter.[21]

As an object of pure exchange value, the diamond symbolizes the commodification of the daughter by a society in which a woman's value is realized in exchange. The final sale of the diamond at the end of the novel coincides with Suzanne's first experience of sexual pleasure with Agosti, the local pineapple farmer, an experience that is above all a "useful" one in bringing to an end the circuit of exchange, violence, and prostitution in which the young girl has been involved.

> The mother knew about it. No doubt she thought it was *useful* for Suzanne. She was not mistaken, for it was

during that week, from the time of the first excursion to the pineapple field to the time of her mother's death, that Suzanne at last unlearned her senseless waiting for the hunters' cars and abandoned her empty dreams.[22]

(p. 281; translation modified; emphasis mine)

However, Suzanne's sexual pleasure with Agosti is itself a direct result of the mother's authority in relation to her daughter's sexuality: "Still, they had made love together every afternoon for a week until yesterday and the mother knew, she had left them together, she had given him to her so that she might make love with him" (p. 284; translation modified.)[23] While *The Sea Wall* ends with the sexual awakening of the protagonist, her life remains circumscribed by the desires and authority of her mother, lover, and brother. After the death of her mother, Suzanne must choose between remaining with Agosti or leaving with Joseph.

> "It's not important whether she stays with me or someone else, for the time being," said Agosti suddenly.
>
> "No, it's not very important," said Joseph. "It's up to her to decide."
>
> Agosti had begun to smoke and had turned a little pale.
>
> "I'm leaving," Suzanne said to him. "I can't do anything else."[24]

(p. 288)

Although the protagonist of *The Sea Wall* achieves some small degree of autonomy, and a real, if circumscribed, relationship to sexual pleasure, the overriding emphasis of the novel, both formally and thematically, is on the young girl's body as the site of domination by both colonizer and colonized, and on the marginalized position of the lower-class, white colonial woman.

More than thirty years later, Duras rewrote the autobiographical material of *The Sea Wall*, this time availing herself of the possibilities offered by the autobiographical "I" in order to establish her own subjectivity and an active relationship to desire. In 1984, **The Lover** appeared—an "exotic, erotic autobiographical confession" that, I maintain, radically transforms the subordinate status of the female protagonist of *The Sea Wall*.[25] Given that some critics regard the genre of **The Lover** as ambiguous, vacillating as it does between a confessional mode in the first person and novelistic narration in the third person, I will first suggest a reading of the text that resolves what Sharon Willis calls "the text's doubleness" and its refusal "to be pinned to the conventional confessional or fictional modes."[26]

The narrator of this text both adheres to and transgresses the conventions of confessional autobiography. On the one hand, in typical modernist fashion, she points to the impossibility of transposing her life into a story with a consistent identity at its center, saying: "The story of my life doesn't exist. Does not exist. There's never any center to it. No path, no line. There are great spaces where you pretend there used to be someone, but it's not true, there was no-one" (p. 8).[27] The use of the novelistic third person is also evidence of Duras's departure from a traditional autobiographical mode, a point I shall return to later.

On the other hand, the text is presented as a traditional autobiography in that its goal is the seemingly unproblematic reconstruction of personal identity. Alluding to *The Sea Wall* in her reference to the autobiographical content of her previous work, Duras indicates her intention to fill in the blanks and restore the omissions necessitated by the conditions of her life as a writer at that time.

> The story of one small part of my youth I've already written, more or less—I mean, enough to give a glimpse of it. Of this part, I mean, the part about the crossing of the river. What I'm doing now is both different and the same. Before, I spoke of clear periods, those on which the light fell. Now I'm talking about the hidden stretches of that same youth, of certain facts, feelings, events that I buried. I started to write in a milieu that drove me to modesty.[28]

> (p. 8; translation modified)

Despite the narrator's claims of merely elucidating what had previously been concealed, Duras's rewriting of this "one small part" of her youth radically transforms her own subject position within the economy of sexual desire.

By designating herself as the subject of *The Lover,* Duras avails herself of the autobiographical "I" in order to realize her own subjectivity. As Emile Benveniste has observed, language provides the possibility of subjectivity because it is language that enables the speaker to posit herself as "I," the subject of discourse.[29] Instead of being subjected to the voyeuristic gaze of the ominiscient narrator/reader, Duras claims control over the representation of her body, transforming it into an active display of her life as spectacle. Referring to the image of herself as a young girl, Duras writes: "It could have existed, a photograph could have been taken, just like any other, somewhere else, in other circumstances. But it wasn't. . . . And it's to this, this failure to have been created, that the image owes its virtue: the virtue of representing, of being the author of, an absolute" (p. 10; translation modified).[30]

Duras's image of herself is thus likened to a nonexistent photograph. It is this nonexistent photograph that allows Duras to create her own image of herself, an image in which "I" and "me" coincide and subjectivity is realized:[31] "It's the only image of myself I like, the only one in which I recognize myself, in which I delight" (pp. 3-4).[32] Whereas the reader of *The Sea Wall* is aligned with the disembodied point of view of the omniscient narrator, the reader of *The Lover,* by contrast, is a spectator whose presence and gaze are actively solicited. "Look at me" (p. 16), commands the narrator, as she constructs a new image that replaces the negative self-alienation of the young girl in *The Sea Wall.*[33]

The narrative vacillation between "I" and "she" that occurs at different points in the text has provided some crit-

ics with evidence of the failure of the narrator's search for identity. Sarah Capitanio, for example, argues as follows:

> Quant à la focalisée toutefois, sa designation comme 'elle' à ce moment marque une séparation définitive entre elle et la narratrice et, par la, la non-résolution de cette recherche si fondamentale.[34]

I read the question of narrative identity differently: the autobiographical "I" allows Duras to posit an identity between the narrator of *The Lover,* the young girl in the nonexistent photo, and the protagonist of *The Sea Wall,* thereby enabling her to reconstitute an identity fragmented by her experience as a white woman in the colonies. By designating herself alternately by the pronouns "I" and "she," Duras in fact undermines the objectification to which she was subjected. She appropriates the masculine position of the observer and, as we shall see, she rewrites the traditionally femininized position of the observed. In the following description, for instance, the actions of the Chinese man, later to become her lover, take place as though before the eye of a moving camera. Through this discursive strategy, the narrator ultimately appropriates the position of the mastering gaze as she watches the man from Cholon watching the young girl: "The elegant man has got out of the limousine and is smoking an English cigarette. He looks at the girl in the man's fedora and the gold shoes. He slowly approaches her" (p. 32).[35]

In the narrative shift to the third person, the young girl is also designated by the way white colonial society perceives her—that is, as "the little white slut" (passim). However, through the device of reported speech, Duras subverts the tone and meaning of the original utterance by permeating the reported speech with her own ironic intonation.[36]

> Fifteen and a half. The news spreads fast in Sadec. The clothes are enough to show. The mother has no idea, and none about how to bring up a daughter. Poor child. Don't tell me that hat's innocent, it means something, it's to attract attention, money. The brothers are layabouts. They say it's a Chinese, the son of the millionaire, the villa in Mekong with the blue tiles. And even he, instead of thinking himself honored, doesn't want her for his son. A family of white layabouts. . . . It goes on in the disreputable quarter of Cholon, every evening. Every morning the little slut goes to have her body caressed by a filthy Chinese millionaire.[37]

> (pp. 88-89)

By drawing attention to the clichéd speech, dogmatic worldview, and racist doxa of colonial society, Duras undercuts its tone of scandalized self-righteousness.

The representation of her lover as the exotic Other constitutes the second discursive strategy that enables Duras to appropriate the position of the subject. This construction of subjectivity is inextricably linked to her position of domination and power as she constructs it in relation to the Chinese man. In *The Lover,* the narrative strategies that effect the subordination of the cultural Other belong to what Edward Said terms the discourse of "Oriental-ism."[38] The most significant of these strategies are the eroticization of the exotic, the feminization of the figure of the Other, and the representation of the Orient as an onto-logical and unchanging essence. The Orient of *The Lover* figures as a set of topoi that Duras deploys for aesthetic and personal/political reasons. Thus, her exploitation of Orientalist discourse is instrumental in the textual transfor-mation of the subordinate status of the poor white woman in French colonial patriarchal society and the construction of a female subjectivity. Although *The Lover* exemplifies many aspects of "Orientalism," the text is not structured by the Manichean allegory that JanMohamed sees at the heart of colonialist literature. Rather, Duras's inscription of many of the themes of Orientalist discourse is in ser-vice to the constitution of a subject position for the female protagonist of *The Sea Wall,* who, although she belongs to the group of French colonizers, is already defined as object/Other.

The eroticization of the exotic—figured by Indochina and the lover's Chinese heritage—is a key element of Duras's text. Said has identified the association of sex with the Orient as a persistent motif in Orientalist discourse.[39] The formal structure of the text reflects the binary opposition of intellect and sensuality that informs the representation of Europe and the Orient. While the erotic theme domi-nates in Indochina, intellectual and political affairs take place in France.

While Mr. Jo in *The Sea Wall* and the man from Cholon in *The Lover* represent two different versions of "the rich man in the black limousine," the transformation of the Eu-ropean Mr. Jo into an Asian is particularly important. By making the lover a Chinese man, Duras takes advantage of the erotic topoi associated with the Orient. Indeed, the ex-otic and the erotic are so inextricably merged in the text that even Duras's French school friend, Hélène Lagonelle, is imbued with Eastern eroticism. As object of the young girl's homoerotic desire, Hélène is "orientalized" through association with the Chinese lover: "I see her as being of one flesh with the man from Cholon. . . . Hélène Lag-onelle is the mate of the bondsmen who gives me such ab-stract, such harsh pleasure, the obscure man from Cholon, from China. Hélène Lagonelle is from China" (p. 74).[40] Here, the geographical referent, China, disappears and is appropriated as a trope for the private sexual fantasy of the narrator. Nor is it insignificant that this orientalized body provokes fantasies of sadistic power: "[Hélène Lag-onelle] makes you want to kill her, she conjures up a mar-vellous dream of putting her to death with your own hands" (p. 73).[41] Similarly, the conflation of the erotic with the exotic and the related dynamic of sexual domination are implicit in the narrator's incestuous desire for her younger brother, whose body she compares to that of an Indian servant: "Even the body of my younger brother, like that of a little coolie, is as nothing beside this splen-dour" (p. 72).[42]

A similar configuration of power and desire is suggested by the feminization of the Chinese lover. This feminiza-tion results from the description of his body and his role during sex. In the former, the emphasis is on traditional markers of femininity: smooth skin, fragile physique, and hairless body. The only sign of virility, the penis, is under-mined by the lover's inability to carry through the initial seduction: "The skin is sumptuously soft. The body. The body is thin, lacking in strength, in muscle, he may have been ill, may be convalescent, he's hairless, nothing mas-culine about him but his sex, he's weak, probably helpless prey to insult, vulnerable" (p. 38).[43] Far from being a pas-sive object of this man's desire, the young girl orchestrates and controls her initiation into sex and pleasure: "She was attracted to him. It depended on her alone. . . . She tells him she doesn't want him to talk, what she wants is for him to do as he usually does with the women he brings to his flat" (pp. 37-38). And then again, "She tells him to keep still. Let me do it. And she does. Undresses him" (p. 38). The act of penetration, traditionally associated with activity and virility, is reduced to an elliptic "And weep-ing, he does it" (p. 38), with the emphasis more on his feminine tears than on the act of penetration itself.[44]

The lover's feminization also results from his position in relation to the discourse of love. As Roland Barthes has noted, this discourse has historically been elaborated by woman in the absence of her beloved.[45] As a result, some-thing feminine is revealed in the man who speaks in the voice of love. In Duras's text, these roles are exchanged: the female protagonist speaks from the place of desire, and the Chinese lover elaborates that of love and passion (passion as suffering): "He's started to suffer here in this room, for the first time, he's no longer lying about it. He says he knows already she'll never love him. . . . He says he's lonely, horribly lonely because of this love he feels for her" (p. 37).[46]

Similarly, the fickleness of the traditional male lover is transposed onto the narrator as a young girl as the Chinese man anticipates her future unfaithfulness: "Talks to me, says he knew right away, when we were crossing the river, that I'd be like this after my first lover, that I'd love love, he says he knows now that I'll deceive him and deceive all the men I'm ever with" (p. 42).[47]

Sailing away on the boat to France and leaving behind her lover, the narrator also usurps the position of the man whose seduced and abandoned women grieve in his ab-sence. Years after their affair, the lover telephones the nar-rator to tell her he is still in love. This reversal of the gen-dered economy of the discourse of love is echoed in the shift in roles related to the traditional departure.

> Departures. They were always the same. Always the first departures over the sea. Men always left the land in the same sorrow and despair, but that never stopped them from going, Jews, philosophers, and pure travel-lers for the journey's own sake. Nor did it ever stop women from letting them go, the women who never went themselves, who stayed behind to look after the birthplace, the race, the property, the reason for the re-turn.[48]

(p. 109)

The father's authority over his son and his refusal to allow him to marry "the little white slut" place the Chinese man in the feminine position of the woman, entrusted with the care of the domestic hearth and the perpetuation of the race. Reinforcing the young girl's position of dominance as she constructs it in relation to her lover is her explicit identification with the authority of his father: "Then I said I agreed with his father. That I refused to stay with him" (p. 83).[49] Later, the narrator confirms the finality of the young girl's decision: "The man from Cholon knows his father's decision and the girl's are the same, and both are irrevocable" (p. 97).[50] In this manner, Duras's text constructs a subordinate position for the Chinese lover through a variety of textual strategies that contribute to his feminization. By making him occupy the traditionally subordinate feminine position, Duras appropriates a position of dominance for herself.

This configuration of power is also related to the racial politics of the text. The transformation of the European Mr. Jo of *The Sea Wall* into "the man from Cholon" in *The Lover* is significant in that race is integral to the balance of power in the relationship. Although the young girl prostitutes herself to the Chinese man, and thereby places herself in what is typically a subordinate position, the fact that he does not belong to white colonial society relegates him to the subordinate position in the eyes of her family, who maintain their sense of superiority by believing the girl is sleeping with the "Chinese scum" only for his money. The young girl's failure to disabuse her family of this assumption allows her to continue to enjoy the intense sexual pleasure she experiences in her relations with him.[51]

> My brothers never will say a word to him, it's as if he were invisible to them, as if for them he weren't solid enough to be perceived, seen or heard. This is because he adores me, but it's taken for granted I don't love him, that I'm with him for the money, that I can't love him, it's impossible that he could take any sort of treatment from me and still go on loving me. This because he's a Chinese, because he's not a white man.[52]
>
> (p. 51)

Although the narrator exposes and denounces her complicity as a young girl in her brothers' exploitation of the Chinese man, Duras reinscribes this exploitation through the discursive strategies she deploys in her own representation of her Asian lover. Belonging to the discourse of "Orientalism," these strategies reinforce the subordinate racial status of the "man from Cholon."

Moreover, the lover's superior economic status—which enables him to "colonize" the young white girl through prostitution—is specifically connected to his Chinese origins. The wealth of "the man from Cholon" is tarnished through his association with the colonial history of the Chinese in Indochina and their continuing financial exploitation of the French colony. By drawing attention to the colonialist activities of the father and his son's complicitous attitude, the narrator transforms the superior economic power of her lover into a position of moral inferiority.

I ask him to tell me about his father's money, how he got rich. He says it bores him to talk about money, but if I insist he'll tell me what he knows about his father's wealth. It all began in Cholon, with the housing estates for natives. He built three hundred of these "compartments," cheap, semi-detached dwellings let out for rent. Owns several streets. . . . The people here like living close together, especially the poor, who come from the country and like living out-of-doors too, on the street. And you must try not to destroy the habits of the poor.[53]

> (pp. 47-48)

In *The Lover*, the significance of the gaze further reinforces the Chinese man's subordinate position, as constructed by the narrator. Duras rewrites the semiotics of the gaze by transforming the negative associations of the gaze, which subordinates and reifies its object in *The Sea Wall*, into an action that signifies the recognition of the value of the other in *The Lover*. Referring to the hostile relations within her family, the narrator observes:

> It's a family of stone, petrified so deeply it's impenetrable. Every day we try to kill one another, to kill. Not only do we not talk to one another, we don't even look at one another. When you're being looked at, you can't look. To look is to feel curious, to be interested, to lower yourself. No one you look at is worth it. Looking is always demeaning.[54]
>
> (p. 54)

To be looked at, then, is to enjoy the privilege of exciting interest and curiosity. The Chinese lover, however, is denied the recognition of this gaze because his liaison with "la petite blanche" transgresses the racial arrangements of French colonial society. "My brothers never will say a word to him, it's as if he were invisible to them, as if for them he weren't solid enough to be perceived, seen or heard" (p. 51). By contrast, the narrator flaunts the heroine's transgressive behavior in the face of the reader/spectator by actively soliciting the latter's attention with her imperious "regardez-moi," thereby demanding the recognition implicit in this gaze.

Duras's naturalization of the young girl's French identity further contributes to her position of authority over her lover. The narrator both relates the young girl's mockery of the Chinese man's French pretensions—"I tell him his visit to France was fatal. He agrees. Says he bought everything in Paris, his women, his acquaintances, his ideas" (p. 49)—and undercuts these pretensions through the use of irony—"He talked. Said he missed Paris, the marvellous girls there, the riotous living, the binges, ooh là là, the Coupole, the Rotonde, personally I prefer the Rotonde, the nightclubs, the 'wonderful' life he'd led for two years" (p. 34).[55] This ironizing of the lover's predilection for things French stems from the split between the narrated "I" and the narrating "I." While the former—the subject of the narration—refers to the white fifteen-year-old born and raised in colonial Indochina, who has never been to France, the latter—the narrating subject—is the narrator whom the text explicitly associates with the authorial identity of

Marguerite Duras—the embodiment of a certain Frenchness. It is this split that both authorizes the mockery of the young girl and enables the narrator to undercut the Chinese man's pretensions by infiltrating his reported speech with ironic authorial intonation.

Another textual strategy that effects the subordination of the cultural Other is the representation of the Orient as an unchanging essence of which the lover clearly partakes. That he remains nameless is the first sign of his lack of individuality, a characteristic that is reinforced by the generic nature of the epithets used to designate him—"the lover," "the man from Cholon," and "the Chinese man" (passim). Although an individual, the lover functions as a representative type who embodies the atmosphere of the Orient. Years later, when he calls the narrator in France, his fear and his trembling voice are represented as belonging to the very essence of the Orient: "He was nervous, afraid, as before. His voice suddenly trembled. And with the trembling, suddenly, she heard again the voice of China" (p. 116).[56]

The idea of the Orient as timeless and unchanging is conveyed by the absence of a history to which the lover can lay claim since his affair with the young girl. In contrast to the narrator's development as a writer, his life is defined by his love for her, which dissolves the future into an inescapable, eternal present: "He knew she'd begun writing books, he'd heard about it through her mother whom he'd met again in Saigon. . . . Then he didn't know what to say. And then he told her. Told her that it was as before, that he still loved her, he could never stop loving her, that he'd love her until death" (p. 117).[57]

In this display of her life as spectacle, Duras is also the ultimate spectator. By exploiting the possibilities of autobiographical discourse, Duras appropriates the privileged masculine position of observer and rewrites the feminine position of the observed. By constructing a position of dominance in relation to the "man from Cholon," the author of *The Lover* radically transforms her relationship to both desire and prostitution in order to establish a female writing subject.

Because JanMohamed's trope of Manichean allegory posits a stable process of othering in which the colonizer occupies the position of subject and the colonized that of object/Other, it fails to account for the ways in which gender and class affect the economy of colonial discourse. As a lower-class woman in the patriarchal society of French colonial Indochina, Duras was *already* in the position of Other. Her subordinate status as object of both prostitution and the male gaze is clearly represented in *The Sea Wall*. In *The Lover,* Duras establishes a female subjectivity through the appropriation of the masculine position of the observer, through the construction of an active relationship to desire, and by recourse to a variety of Orientalist topoi—the eroticization of the exotic, the feminization of the Asian lover, and the representation of an unchanging Oriental essence. Despite Duras's overt anticolonialism in *The Sea Wall* and her occasional contestation of the discourse of colonialism in *The Lover,* in which the narrator both satirizes and explicitly denounces the racist doxa espoused by her family and by French colonial society, she nonetheless also *reinscribes* a variety of Orientalist/colonialist themes in order to transform her own marginalized position as Other and to achieve a position of power and dominance in relation to her Chinese lover. Through her participation in colonialist politics in service to a "white" female subjectivity, Duras engages in textual strategies that have disturbing implications for the politics of women's autobiography.[58] This gendered subject position is also constructed through Duras's use of the rhetorical strategies made possible by autobiographical discourse. Just as the nonexistent photograph provides Duras with the means to authorize her favorite image of herself as a young girl, so autobiography affords the possibility to *create* a self/subject liberated from the oppressive realities of poverty, prostitution, and the patriarchal order of French colonial society.

Notes

1. For a psychoanalytic reading of the feminine in Duras's *oeuvre,* see Sharon Willis, *Marguerite Duras: Writing on the Body* (Urbana: Illinois University Press, 1987). Willis uses hysteria as a metaphor for Duras's narrative discourse and analyzes how her texts explore "the limits of narrative representation"—a discursive space coded as feminine within a particular historical moment. See also Michèle Montrelay, "Sur le Ravissement de Lol V. Stein," *L'Ombre et le nom* (Paris: Minuit, 1977). Situated within a psychoanalytic framework, Montrelay's article offers a reading of Duras's *Le Ravissement de Lol V. Stein* as an example of a text that gives a place to femininity defined as nonsense, silence, and nonspeech. In *Territories du féminin avec Marguerite Duras* (Paris: Minuit, 1977), Marcelle Marini reads Duras's disruptive writing style and her creation of silences and gaps as a feminine space that attempts to circumvent women's oppression within patriarchy. Trista Selous, in *The Other Woman: Feminism and Femininity in the Work of Marguerite Duras* (New Haven, Conn.: Yale University Press, 1988), offers a cultural critique of the representations of women in Duras, challenging the claims that Duras's work is truly feminist.

2. All citations will include page numbers in parentheses in the text from the following editions, except where otherwise noted. Marguerite Duras, *The Sea Wall,* trans. Herma Briffault (New York: Harper & Row, 1986); *The Lover,* trans. Barbara Bray (New York: Pantheon, 1985). I have altered the English translations in places in order to stress nuances of the French text that are important to my analyses. I shall indicate "translation modified" wherever such changes occur. French quotations are provided in the notes and are from the following editions: Marguerite Duras, *L'Amant* (Paris: Minuit,

1984); *Un Barrage contre le pacifique* (Paris: Gallimard, 1950).

3. Abdul R. JanMohamed, "The Economy of Manichean Allegory: The Function of Racial Difference in Colonialist Literature," *Critical Inquiry* 12 (Autumn 1985): 59-87.

4. Frantz Fanon notes that "the colonial world is a Manichean world." *The Wretched of the Earth,* trans. Constance Farrington (New York: Grove, 1968), 41. He demonstrates the mechanism of this Manichean world in *Black Skin, White Masks,* trans. Charles Lam Markmann (New York: Grove, 1967).

5. JanMohamed, "Economy of Manichean Allegory," 63.

6. Tzvetan Todorov, "Critical Response III: 'Race', Writing Culture," trans. Loulou Mack, *Critical Inquiry* 12 (Autumn 1985): 178.

7. Marguerite Duras and Michèle Porte, *Les Lieux de Marguerite Duras* (Paris: Minuit, 1977); Marguerite Duras and Xavière Gauthier, *Les Parleuses* (Paris: Minuit, 1974).

8. For a more extensive discussion of this issue, see Luce Irigaray, *This Sex Which Is Not One,* trans. Catherine Porter (Ithaca, N.Y.: Cornell University Press, 1977). Irigaray describes women's censored relationship to desire as follows: "Mother, virgin, prostitute: these are the social roles imposed on women. The characteristic of (so-called) feminine sexuality derive from them: the valorization of reproduction and nursing; faithfulness; modesty; ignorance of and even lack of interest in sexual pleasure; a passive acceptance of men's activity; seductiveness, in order to arouse the consumers' desire while offering herself as its material support without getting pleasure herself. . . . Neither as mother nor as virgin nor as prostitute has woman any right to her own pleasure" (pp. 186-87).

9. "'Ce n'est pas ce soir qu'on ira à Ram,' dit Suzanne.

'On ira demain,' dit Joseph, 'et c'est pas à Ram que tu trouveras, ils sont tous mariés, il y a qu'Agosti.'

'Jamais je ne la donnerai à Agosti,' dit la mère, 'quand même il me supplierait.'

'Il ne demande pas mieux,' dit la mère, 'je sais ce que je dis, mais il peut toujours courir.'

'Il ne pense même pas à elle,' dit Joseph. 'Ce sera difficile. Il y en a qui se marient sans argent, mais il faut qu'elles soient très jolies, et encore c'est rare.'"

(p. 35)

10. "Ces tête-à-tête enchantaient la mère. Plus ils duraient et plus elle espérait. Et si elle exigeait qu'ils laissent la porte du bungalow ouverte, c'était pour ne laisser à M. Jo aucune issue que le mariage à l'envie très forte qu'il avait de coucher avec sa fille."

(p. 68)

11. Irigaray, *This Sex,* 180.

12. "Il avait très envie de la voir. Quand même c'était la l'envie d'un homme. Elle, elle était là aussi, bonne à être vue, il n'y avait que la porte à ouvrir. Et aucun homme au monde n'avait encore vu celle qui se tenait là derrière cette porte. Ce n'était pas fait pour être caché mais au contraire pour être vu et faire son chemin de par le monde, le monde auquel appartenait quand même celui-là, ce M. Jo."

(p. 73)

13. "C'était grâce à elle qu'il était maintenant là, sur la table. Elle avait ouvert la porte de la cabine de bains, le temps de laisser le regard malsain et laid de M. Jo pénétrer jusqu'à elle et maintenant le phonograph reposait là, sur la table"

(p. 76)

14. "J'ai déjà l'habitude qu'on me regarde. On regarde les blanches aux colonies, et les petites filles de douze ans aussi. Depuis trois ans, les blancs aussi me regardent dans le rues et les amis de ma mère me demandent gentiment de venir goûter chez eux à l'heure ou leurs femmes jouent au tennis au Club Sportif."

(p. 26)

15. "On la regardait. On se retournait, on souriait. Aucune jeune fille de son âge ne marchait seule dans les rues de haut quartier."

(p. 185)

16. "Plus on la remarquait, plus elle se persuadait qu'elle était scandaleuse, un objet de laideur et de bêtise intégrale."

(p. 185)

17. For a more extensive discussion of women's relation to their bodies in patriarchal society, see John Berger, *Ways of Seeing* (London: Penguin, 1972). According to his analysis, a woman is constantly accompanied by her own image of herself because she is the object of the male gaze. Consequently, a woman's sense of self is split into two and "she comes to consider the surveyor and the surveyed within her as two constituent yet always distinct elements of her identity as a woman" (p. 46).

18. "C'était elle, elle qui était méprisable des pieds à la tete. A cause de ses yeux, ou les jeter? A cause de ses bras de plomb, ces ordures, à cause de ce coeur, une bête indécente, de ces jambes incapables."

(p. 187)

19. "C'est pas qu'on l'empêche de coucher avec qui elle veut, mais vous, si vous voulez coucher avec elle, faut que vous l'épousiez. C'est notre façon à nous de vous dire merde."

(p. 96)

20. "Il n'y a rien de plus dégoutant qu'un bijou. Ca sert à rien, à rien. Et ceux qui les portent n'en ont pas besoin, moins besoin que n'importe qui."

(p. 135)

21. See Marianne Hirsch, "Feminist Family Romances," in *The Mother/Daughter Plot: Narrative, Psychoanalysis, Feminism* (Bloomington: Indiana University Press, 1989), for an illuminating reading of the mother-daughter relationship in *The Lover*. Hirsch argues that Julia Kristeva's psychoanalytic reading of Duras in "The Pain of Sorrow in the Modern World: The Work of Marguerite Duras," *PMLA* 102 (March 1987): 138-52, ends up "eclipsing the mother's own voice, her own story, allowing her only the status of object, or of 'Other'" (p. 152). I concur with Hirsch that the figure of the mother in *The Sea Wall* and *The Lover* needs to be read in the political and economic context of colonialism in order to avoid "conflating [the political dimensions of women's lives] with the psychological" (p. 152).

22. "La mère le savait. Sans doute pensait-elle que c'était utile à Suzanne. Elle n'avait pas tort. Ce fut pendant ces huit jours-là, entre la promenade au champs d'ananas et la mort de la mère que Suzanne désapprit enfin l'attente imbécile des autos des chasseurs, les rêves vides."

(p. 357)

23. "Pourtant ils avaient fait l'amour ensemble tous les après-midi depuis huit jours jusqu'à hier encore. Et la mère le savait, elle les avait laissés, le lui avait donné pour qu'elle fasse l'amour avec lui."

(p. 360)

24. "'Ca n'a pas d'importance qu'elle soit avec moi ou un autre, pour le moment,' dit brusquement Agosti.

'Je crois que ça n'a pas tellement d'importance,' dit Joseph, 'elle n'a qu'à décider.'

Agosti s'était mis à fumer, il avait un peu pâli.

'Je pars,' lui dit Suzanne, 'je ne peux pas faire autrement.'"

(p. 365)

25. The 9 June 1985 issue of the *New York Times Book Review* carried an advertisement for *The Lover* that included a *Saturday Review* comment that "this exotic, erotic autobiographical confession will deservedly become one of the summer's hottest books."

26. Willis, *Marguerite Duras*, 5.

27. "L'histoire de ma vie n'existe pas. Ca n'existe pas. Il n'y a jamais de centre. Pas de chemin, pas de ligne. Il y a de vastes endroits où l'on fait croire qu'il y avait quelqu'un, ce n'est pas vrai, il n'y avait personne."

(p. 14)

28. "L'histoire d'une toute petite partie de ma jeunesse, je l'ai plus ou moins écrite déjà, enfin je veux dire, de quoi l'apercevoir, je parle de celle-ci justement, de celle de la traversée du fleuve. Ce que je fais ici est différent, et pareil. Avant j'ai parlé des périodes claires, de celles qui étaient éclairées. Ici je parle des périodes cachées de cette même jeunesse, de certains enfouissements que j'aurais opérés sur certains faits, sur certains sentiments, sur certains événements. J'ai commencé à ecrire dans un milieu qui me portait très fort à la pudeur."

(p. 14)

29. See Emile Benveniste, *Problèmes de linguistique générale* (Paris: Gallimard, 1966), 258-65.

30. "Elle aurait pu exister, une photographie aurait pu être prise, comme une autre, ailleurs, dans d'autres circonstances. Mais elle ne l'a pas été. . . . C'est à ce manque d'avoir été faite qu'elle doit sa vertu, celle de représenter un absolu, d'en être justement l'auteur."

(p. 17)

31. Susan Cohen notes that "the story [of *The Lover*] is essentially one of creativity, in particular the self-making of a woman and of a writer whom we watch in the process of creating out of that very initial non-presence." "Fiction and the Photographic Image in Duras' *The Lover*," *L'Esprit Créateur* 30 (Spring 1990): 59. Cohen's article explores the relationship of absence to seeing and creativity.

32. "C'est entre toutes celle qui me plaît de moi-même, celle où je me reconnais, où je m'enchante" (p. 9).

33. Although I consider *The Lover* a feminist autobiography, it needs to be distinguished from the definition of "feminist confession" offered by Rita Felski in *Beyond Feminist Aesthetics* (Cambridge, Mass.: Harvard University Press, 1989). Whereas Felski's examples of feminist confession belong to the realist convention and continually refer to the question of truth as their ultimate legitimation, Duras is clearly less concerned with producing an image of herself faithful to a preexisting reality and more interested in the rhetorical and creative possibilities offered by the autobiographical genre. Felski makes the interesting observation that feminist confession is a rare phenomenon within the Catholic and rhetorically conscious French tradition on account of the strong Protestant element in the feminist preoccupation with subjectivity as the discovery of an authentic self (p. 114).

Clearly, Duras's writing of the "subject" differs from the pervasive quest for truth and self-understanding that Felski finds in the Protestant tradition of feminist confession. As Sharon Willis remarks, "Part of the appeal of *The Lover* lies in its duplicity, its pretense to confession coupled with its refusal to swear to truthfulness," *Marguerite Duras*, 5. In *The Lover*, the autobiographical "I" uses a variety of formal and rhetorical strategies in order to create a subject position for the female Other within a specific sexual and cultural economy. Rather than seeking validation through an appeal to authenticity, Duras's construction of a female subject relies on the colonialist politics of *The Lover* and a specific use of the autobiographical mode, both of which rework the sexual and cultural economy of *The Sea Wall.*

34. Sarah J. Capitanio, "Perspectives sur l'écriture durassienne: *L'Amant,*" *Symposium* 41 (Spring 1987): 18. The English translation of the cited passage is as follows: "The designation of the focalized as 'she' at this point, however, indicates a permanent split between her and the female narrator and, consequently, the nonresolution of this fundamental search [for personal identity]."

35. "L'homme élégant est descendu de la limousine, il fume une cigarette anglaise. Il regarde la jeune fille au feutre d'homme et aux chaussures d'or. Il vient vers elle lentement."

(p. 42)

36. See V. N. Volosinov, *Marxism and the Philosophy of Language* (Cambridge, Mass.: Harvard University Press, 1973), 115-23, for an analysis of the infiltration of reported speech with authorial intonation.

37. "Quinze ans et demi. La chose se sait très vite dans le poste de Sadec. Rien que cette tenue dirait le déshonneur. La mère n'a aucun sens de rien, ni celui de la façon d'élever une petite fille. La pauvre enfant. Ne croyez pas, ce chapeau n'est pas innocent, ça veut dire, c'est pour attirer les regards, l'argent. Les frères, des voyous. On dit que c'est un Chinois, le fils du milliardaire, la villa du Mékong, en céramiques bleues. Même lui, au lieu d'en être honoré, il n'en veut pas pour son fils. Famille de voyous blancs. . . . Cela se passe dans le quartier mal famé de Cholen. Chaque soir cette petite vicieuse va se faire caresser le corps par un sale Chinois millionaire."

(pp. 108-10)

38. As Edward Said demonstrates, the Orient represents "one of Europe's deepest and most recurring images of the Other." *Orientalism* (New York: Random House, 1979), 1. For political and economic reasons, the relationship between the West and the Orient has been one of power and domination. Said defines "Orientalism" as the discourse produced by the West about the Orient, a discourse in which the Orient is less a place than "an idea that has a history and a tradition of thought, imagery and vocabulary, that have given it presence and reality for the West" (p. 5).

39. Ibid., 188.

40. "Je la vois comme étant de la même chair que cet homme de Cholen. . . . Hélène Lagonelle, elle est la femme de cet homme de peine qui me fait la jouissance si abstraite, si dure, cet homme obscur de Cholen, de la Chine. Hélène Lagonelle est de la Chine."

(p. 92)

41. "Hélène Lagonelle donne envie de la tuer, elle fait se lever le songe merveilleux de la mettre à mort de ses propres mains."

(p. 91)

42. "Même le petit corps de petit coolie de mon petit frère disparaît face à cette splendur."

(p. 89)

43. "La peau est d'une somptueuse douceur. Le corps. Le corps est maigre, sans force, sans muscles. Il pourrait avoir été malade, être en convalescence, il est imberbe, sans virilité autre que celle du sexe, il est très faible, il paraît être à la merci d'une insulte, souffrant."

(p. 49)

44. "Il lui plaît, la chose ne dépendait que d'elle seule" (p. 48); "Elle lui dit qu'elle ne veut pas qu'il lui parle, que ce qu'elle veut c'est qu'il fasse comme d'habitude il fait avec les femmes qu'il emmène dans sa garçonnière" (p. 49); "Elle lui demande de ne pas bouger. Laisse-moi. Elle dit qu'elle veut le faire elle. Elle le fait. Elle le déshabille" (p. 49); "Et pleurant il le fait" (p. 50).

45. Roland Barthes, *A Lover's Discourse,* trans. Richard Howard (New York: Hill & Wang, 1978).

46. "Il a commencé à souffrir là, dans la chambre, pour la première fois, il ne ment plus sur ce point. Il lui dit que déjà il sait qu'elle ne l'aimera jamais. . . . Il dit qu'il est seul, atrocement seul avec cet amour qu'il a pour elle."

(p. 48)

47. "Il dit qu'il a su tout de suite, dès la traversée du fleuve, que je serai ainsi, après mon premier amant, que j'aimerais l'amour, il dit qu'il sait déjà que lui je le tromperai et aussi que je tromperai tous les hommes avec qui je serai."

(p. 54)

48. "Les départs. C'était toujours les mêmes départs. C'était toujours les premiers départs sur les mers. La séparation d'avec la terre s'était toujours faite dans la douleur et le même désespoir, mais ça n'avait jamais empêché les hommes de partir, les juifs, les hommes de la pensée et les purs voyageurs du seul voyage sur la mer, et ça n'avait jamais empêché non plus les femmes de les laisser aller, elles qui ne partaient jamais, qui restaient garder le lieu natal, la race, les biens, la raison d'être du retour."

(p. 132)

49. "Alors je lui ai dit que j'étais de l'avis de son père. Que je refusais de rester avec lui."

(p. 103)

50. "L'homme de Cholen sait que la décision de son père et celle de l'enfant sont les mêmes et qu'elles sont sans appel."

(p. 119)

51. Although the relationship between the young girl and her lover is a form of prostitution in that it involves monetary exchange, it needs to be distinguished from Suzanne's prostitution in *The Sea Wall* and the notion of prostitution elaborated by Irigaray in *This Sex*, 187-88. In *The Lover*, it is the exchange of money that makes the young girl's relationship with the Chinese man tolerable in the eyes of her family. Consequently, it serves as a screen for the sexual pleasure the young girl derives from the affair, and thereby enables her to continue the relationship.

52. "Mes frères ne lui adresseront jamais la parole. C'est comme s'il n'était pas visible pour eux, comme s'il n'était pas assez dense pour être perçu, vu, entendu par eux. Cela parce qu'il est à mes pieds, qu'il est posé en principe que je ne l'aime pas, que je suis avec lui pour l'argent, que je ne peux pas l'aimer, que c'est impossible, qu'il pourrait tout supporter de moi sans être jamais au bout de cet amour. Cela, parce que c'est un Chinois, que ce n'est pas un blanc."

(p. 65)

53. "Je lui demande de me dire comment son père est riche, de quelle façon. Il dit que parler d'argent l'ennuie, mais que si j'y tiens il veut bien me dire ce qu'il sait de la fortune de son père. Tout a commencé à Cholen, avec les compartiments pour indigènes. Il en a fait construire trois cents. Plusieurs rues lui appartiennent. . . . La population ici aime bien être ensemble, surtout cette population pauvre, elle vient de la campagne et elle aime bien vivre aussi dehors, dans la rue. Et il ne faut pas détruire les habitudes des pauvres."

(pp. 60-61)

54. "C'est une famille en pierre, pétrifiée dans une épaisseur sans accès aucun. Chaque jour nous essayons de nous tuer, de tuer. Non seulement on ne se parle pas mais on ne se regarde pas. Du moment qu'on est vu, on ne peut pas regarder. Regarder c'est avoir un mouvement de curiosité vers, envers, c'est déchoir. Aucune personne regardée ne vaut le regard sur elle. Il est toujours déshonorant."

(p. 69)

55. "Je lui dis que son séjour en France lui a été fatal. Il en convient. Il dit qu'il a tout acheté à Paris, ses femmes, ses connaissances, ses idées" (p. 62). "Il parlait. Il disait qu'il s'ennuyait de Paris, des adorables Parisiennes, des noces, des bombes, ah là là, de la Coupole, de la Rotonde je préfère, des boîtes de nuit, de cette existence 'épatante' qu'il avait menée pendant deux ans."

(p. 45)

56. "Il etait intimidé, il avait peur comme avant. Sa voix tremblait tout à coup. Et avec le tremblement, tout à coup, elle avait retrouvé l'accent de la Chine."

(p. 142)

57. "Il savait qu'elle avait commencé à écrire des livres, il l'avait su par la mère qu'il avait revue à Saigon. . . . Et puis il n'avait plus su quoi lui dire. Et puis il le lui avait dit. Il lui avait dit que c'était comme avant, qu'il l'aimait encore, qu'il ne pourrait jamais cesser de l'aimer, qu'il l'aimerait jusqu'à sa mort."

(p. 142)

58. Gayatri Spivak argues that a certain body of liberal feminist criticism "reproduces the axioms of imperialism" through "a basically isolationist admiration for the literature of the female subject." "Three Women's Texts and a Critique of Imperialism," *Critical Inquiry* 12 (Autumn 1985): 243. I concur with this argument and have emphasized the colonialist politics involved in Duras's constitution of a female subject position.

Peter Brooks (essay date 1993)

SOURCE: "Transgressive Bodies," in *Body Work: Objects of Desire in Modern Narrative,* Harvard University Press, 1993, pp. 257-86.

[*In the following essay, Brooks analyzes what he considers Duras's subversive techniques of dealing with the problem of the visual in* The Lover.]

The body quickened through sexuality remains the object of most intense interest for our culture. It is worth dwelling on one example that will serve to draw attention, once again, to the problematics of the gaze directed at a body which is conceived as the object of a writing project, this time by a woman. The author, Marguerite Duras, is particularly sensitive to issues of looking, and has indeed worked successfully in the cinema, as well as in the theater and narrative fiction. Duras accepts the tradition of the body in the visual field but works subtle and subversive displacements within it. Although any and all of her work would be pertinent to this discussion, I shall focus on the novel that transformed her from an avant-garde novelist into a best-seller: *L'amant* (*The Lover*), which is a narrative of somewhat deceptive limpidity.

L'amant tells the story of a fifteen-year-old girl in French Indochina in the 1930s who has her first sexual relationship with a Chinese financier. The affair is thoroughly scandalous from all points of view: the transgression of racial lines, the youth of the girl, and the girl's refusal to delude herself with romance. She knows from the outset that she is not in love with her lover (who is very much in love with her) but only with love itself, with the erotic transaction, and with the pleasure experienced by her body. In the social isolation that her transgression brings—other girls in the lycée are forbidden to associate with her—she makes an imaginary identification with the "woman of Vinh Long," whose young lover killed himself in despair when she announced the end of their liaison. The identification of the girl with the isolated and stigmatized woman of

Vinh Long comes from the experience of their bodies: "Alone, queens. Their disgrace is a matter of course. Both of them destined to disgrace because of the kind of body they have, caressed by lovers, kissed by their mouths, given over to the infamy of a pleasure to die from, as they call it, to die from in this mysterious death of lovers without love."[1]

What particularizes the girl, from the moment she is observed by her future lover while crossing the Mekong River on the ferry, is the capacity of her body for erotic pleasure—*jouissance,* or orgasmic bliss.[2] It separates her from her mother: as soon as she has been to bed with her lover, she knows that her mother has never known this pleasure. It separates her from her family, and the tyrannical law of her elder brother. It gives a special destiny to her body, as removed from the contingencies, indignities, and displeasure of her everyday existence. She becomes the body of the beloved, and this confers on her a special status.

This status is created by the desiring gaze of the other, the lover. A key moment of the novel comes when the lover, in bed, looks at her: "Il la regarde" (121), and the text continues to describe her observation of his observation of her:

> I used to watch what he was doing with me, how he made use of me, and I had never thought that one could do anything like that, he went beyond my hope and in accordance with my body's destiny. Thus I had become his child. He had also become something else for me. I began to recognize the inexpressible softness of his skin, of his sex, beyond himself . . . Everything worked to his desire and made him take me. . . .
>
> He takes her as he would take his child. He would take his child in the same way. He plays with his child's body, he turns it over, he covers his face, his mouth, his eyes with it. And she, she continues to abandon herself in the very direction that he took when he began to play. And suddenly it's she who begs him, she doesn't say what for, and he who yells at her to be quiet, who cries that he doesn't want her anymore, that he doesn't want to take pleasure in her anymore, and there they are again caught between themselves, locked between themselves in terror, and then this terror undoes itself again, and they give in again, in tears, in despair, in happiness.
>
> (122-23)

If she is her lover's child, it is because she is to a degree his creation, something created in the act of lovemaking, a body fashioned for his pleasure which is also a body fashioned for its own pleasure and destiny: her body become what it was supposed to become. In response, she is able to espouse the direction of his desire, and her body follows the inflections given to it by his caresses toward its own pleasure. The body is here both hyper-conscious—"I used to watch what he was doing with me"—and the place of a knowledge of inexpressible pleasure.

The passage quoted bears witness to a narrative peculiarity of *L'amant* that is closely related to the status of the body

as I have been attempting to describe it. The first of the two paragraphs is in the first person, a retrospective narrative in which the girl, now a woman of some years, and explicitly a writer (and indeed, explicitly Marguerite Duras), recalls her youth. The second paragraph is in the third person: the "I" has become "she." The shift between first and third person in *L'amant* doesn't necessarily take place between paragraphs; it can happen from one sentence to another. And the play of the subjective and objective perspectives is not limited to presentation in these two pronominal modes. Consider, for instance, her reflections on the desirable body of her friend Hélène Lagonelle: "These flour-white forms, she bears them without any knowledge, she shows these things for hands to knead them, for the mouth to eat them, without holding them back, without knowledge of them, without knowledge also of their fabulous power. I would like to eat the breasts of Hélène Lagonelle as he eats the breasts of me in the room in Chinatown where I go each evening to deepen the knowledge of God. To be devoured by these flour-white breasts that are hers" (91). Translating Duras is extremely difficult: her style is deceptively limpid and simple, achieving astonishing effects by slight distortions of normal diction. In this passage, for instance, "elle montre ces choses pour les mains les pétrir, pour la bouche les manger" resorts to an almost childish syntax to express the value of Hélène Lagonelle's breasts in terms of their pleasurable use by a putative lover. "Je voudrais manger les seins d'Hélène Lagonelle comme lui mange les seins de moi" skews normal usage ("mes seins") in order to suggest her own bodily parts as experienced by her own lover. What is at issue in such moments is precisely the body known as the site of pleasure by way of the pleasure that a lover takes in it. By experiencing her own desire for Hélène Lagonelle's body, she can experience her own body as the object of the lover's desire. Point of view, the use of pronouns and perspectives, the place of the subject and the object, have to do with positions in respect to desire.

One of the prime effects of desire, in this novel, seems to be to make subject into object, to allow or to force the subject to grasp itself as it is for the desire and in the perspective of the other. Marguerite Duras' fiction has been praised by Jacques Lacan as a confirmation of his doctrine, and the view of desire presented in *L'amant* is in fact quite Lacanian. For Lacan, the unconscious is "the discourse of the Other," which means, *inter alia,* that the individual's desire is always structured for him or her by that impersonal Other that defines the individual's ego, at the mirror stage, as alienated, that is, as the product of others' gazes and perspectives. In Lacan's conception, the demand for love is always absolute, a demand for recognition that never can be fulfilled, based on infantile scenarios of original lack. Desire, born in the discrepancy or lack between need and demand, is thus not desire for this or that, but desire *tout court,* driven by radical unsatisfaction, for which any given object is a stand-in, an "imaginary" and hence deceptive simulacrum. What a lover desires is "the desirer in the other," that the lover be "called to as desirable" by the person chosen as the object of desire.[3]

The Chinese lover resembles Lacan's *"objet petit a"*—the other, not the Other—in that he is simply in the place where desire seeks an object. He is an imaginary object, as he himself understands after he has first made love to the girl, when he tells her that he has known from their first meeting on the ferry that she would "love love," and that she will deceive him and all the men who will be her lovers in the future (54). And she understands "that he does not know her, that he will never know her, that he has no way of understanding such perversity" (48)—the "perversity" being her desire for desire, without regard for the person that is its pretext. "There is no such thing as a sexual relationship," Lacan says in one of his famous dicta. The knowledge that she obtains—that she "deepens"—in her erotic encounters is expressed, in the passage quoted above, as the "knowledge of God": that is, of something transindividual, impersonal, desire in itself.

The discourse of desire in *L'amant* is especially about the place of the body in the economy and discourse of desire. The girl's place in the economy of desire is originally and insistently a product of the gaze. The first encounter with the lover, on the ferry, is initially presented by way of a photograph that might have been taken and wasn't. The girl's mother regularly arranges for photographs to be made of the family, as testimonials to its existence, somewhat in the manner that the Indochinese have themselves photographed in old age in order to be remembered after their deaths and, through the effects of age and the photographer's retouching, all end up looking the same. That the decisive encounter with the girl's lover was not photographed gives the image of their meeting its "virtue, that of representing an absolute" (17). The lacking photograph subtends the presentation of the scene as insistently visual. In the visual field thus established, our attention is insistently called to a single detail: the men's felt hat worn by the girl which, by its "determining ambiguity," transforms her looks and her very identity. Her "awkward thinness of form" becomes something else: "It ceased to be a brutal, fatal, given of nature. It became quite the opposite, a choice against the grain of nature, a choice of the mind. Suddenly, here's what one wanted. Suddenly, I see myself as an other, as an other would be seen, from the outside, made available to all, made available to all gazes, put into the economy of towns, roads, desire [mise dans la circulation des villes, des routes, du désir]" (20).

In the following pages, the narrator develops this awareness of the gaze of others (essentially, of other men) as an experience of the girl's adolescence; the gaze by definition conveys an understanding of the potential for erotic encounter with its object: "It wasn't a matter of attracting desire. It was in her, the woman who provoked it, or it didn't exist. It was already there from the first glance or else it had never existed. It was the immediate understanding of sexual relation or else it was nothing" (28). Thus

the girl, marked by the hat that transforms her into the object of the erotic gaze, has already entered the circulatory economy of desire when she is approached by the Chinese financier—who immediately comments on the hat. She conceives of her body as that which will henceforth be defined by that economy, and no longer by the domestic economy of the family. When she enters the Chinese financier's black limousine, she knows that her "obligations toward herself" mean that she will now have to deal with an exogamous system, that she has passed—in the direction that the hat has made her appearance pass—as it were from nature to culture, where culture is defined as the positions assigned by desire. The Chinese financier's approach to her is the first time in the text where the first person is replaced by the third, where she does not directly assume her subjectivity but rather sees herself as seen by the other: "He looks at the girl with the man's hat and the gold shoes. Slowly he comes toward her. It's evident that he is intimidated" (42).

The play of gazes in *L'amant* subtly displaces the traditional field of vision of novels in the realist tradition. Woman is the object of the male gaze. She is defined by her position in relation to desire, which is expressed by way of the male gaze. She assumes that defining property of the male gaze, adopts her identity in relation to it. And yet, the capacity of the girl in *L'amant* to assume her identity in relation to male desire consciously and deliberately, and to manipulate desire in order to realize the "destiny" of her own body, subverts the traditional model. The play of subjective and objective narrative perspectives suggests that she controls positions in regard to desire: she is no longer the passive object of the gaze (as postulated in much film theory) but actively exhibitionist. Lacan claims that woman's sexuality is inseparable from the representations through which she comes to know it: "images and symbols *for* the woman cannot be isolated from images and symbols *of* the woman . . . It is . . . the representation of feminine sexuality, whether repressed or not, which conditions how it comes into play."[4] By assuming control of representation of her sexuality—by becoming the scenarist of her own body as it comes into play—the girl of *L'amant* makes woman's relation to the displayed body active and conscious, and indeed complicates accepted notions about activity and passivity in spectatorship.[5]

One might say that Duras seems both to espouse and to subvert Freud's declaration that there is only one libido, and that it is male. Freud's somewhat cryptic statement appears to mean that there is no separate libido for women since libido is signified by the phallus as the marker of desire, and perhaps also that libido has been defined throughout history as male. Woman's freedom, on this model, is her capacity to understand and to use libido so defined, to make its masculine definition serve her own pleasure and thus to make the lover only the excuse for love, an impersonal goal. The girl in *L'amant* bears affinities with such earlier (male-created) heroines as the Marquise de Merteuil, in *Les liaisons dangereuses,* and the adolescent protagonist of Stendhal's *Lamiel.* All three work a reversal of perspectives within the male-generated and male-dominated system. Men, in the words of the Marquise de Merteuil, are "dethroned tyrants become my slaves."⁶

The liaison of the girl in **L'amant** with the lover develops, then, as a realization of the desire of the other, experienced as the true "destiny" of her own body as part of an erotic economy in which she has found her place, precisely by being displaced from the subjectivity, and the familial economy, in which she began. Upon her first assignation with the lover in his apartment, we have the comment: "She is there where she must be, displaced there" (47). Displacement, like the "perversity" she finds characteristic of her emotions a few pages later, marks a new position in regard to desire. And after her first experience of sex with the lover, as they lie together in bed: "I realize that I desire him" (Je m'aperçois que je le désire) (51). Desire comes as a realization, a perception, as it were as the result of a mental operation on the body which now has entered into the system of desire. The erotic, one might say, is the intelligence of the body. It is the body become sentient and self-aware by way of the other.

It is illuminating to return, in this context, to the passage that evokes her desire for the body of her friend Hélène Lagonelle. "I am prostrated by the beauty of Hélène Lagonelle's body stretched out against mine . . . Nothing is more extraordinary than this surface roundness of the breasts she carries, this exteriority held out toward the hands. Even my younger brother's little coolie body disappears next to this splendor. Men's bodies have stingy, internalized forms" (89). Then follows the passage cited earlier ("These flower-white forms, she carries them without any knowledge . . ."), which leads to a phantasy scenario in which she would take Hélène with her to the place where every evening "I have myself given the pleasure that makes one cry aloud." The passage continues:

> I would like to give Hélène Lagonelle to the man who does that to me so that he might to do it in turn to her. This in my presence, so that she do it according to my desire, that she give herself there where I give myself. It would be by way of Hélène Lagonelle's body, by the passage across her body, that pleasure would come from him to me, in its definitive form.
>
> Pleasure to die from.
>
> (92)

As I understand this difficult passage, it is about the intellection of desire, about desire becoming knowledge. Hélène Lagonelle's body as intermediary between the lover and the narrator—as the medium through which his desire is transmitted—serves, in phantasy, as a vehicle for the expression of desire in a form that she can see, realized before her eyes, and thus understand. Her lover's desire and her own would meet and become visible when acted out on Hélène Lagonelle's body. One is reminded of Balzac's *La fille aux yeux d'or,* where the body of Paquita Valdès becomes the place where the desires of Henri de Marsay

and the Marquise de Saint-Réal are inscribed, in a way that represents the "infinitude" of their (ultimately incestuous) desire, and murders Paquita. It is as if another body had to be in place in order to realize fully the eroticism of the visual that is so much the definition of desire in the novel. To be "definitive," pleasure, orgasm, must be seen.

Pleasure and knowledge are products of positioning the body in relation to desire. So are suffering, sadism, and the imposition of the law. The girl's affair with her Chinese lover violates the social taboos of the European colony in Indochina, and in particular disqualifies her for the colony's marriage market. She has lost status; she risks never being able to "place" herself in society. This realization periodically drives her mother into a rage in which she locks the girl in her room and strips her, seeking the smells and signs of the lover's body on her underwear and her body, and then strikes and beats her. As she is beaten, her elder brother is listening through the walls, with pleasure. He encourages the mother to strike, in the name of the need to discover the truth, and in the name of the law according to whose standards the girl stands condemned. Meanwhile, the younger brother begs the mother to stop; he is afraid his sister will be killed, and afraid also of his older brother. His fear finally calms the mother, rage dissolves in tears. The girl cries with her, and denies that she is having sex with the Chinese financier. The account of this repeated incident ends: "I know that my older brother is riveted to the door, listening, he knows what my mother is doing, he knows that his younger sister is naked, and being beaten, he would like that to go on and on, till it became dangerous. My mother is not unaware of this obscure and terrifying intention on the part of my brother" (74).

The scene bears a close resemblance to a typical scenario analyzed by Freud in his essay "A Child Is Being Beaten" ("Ein Kind wird geschlagen," 1919). Here, Freud also emphasizes positions in relation to desire and its repression. A girl will typically move through three positions, the first and third sadistic—another child is being beaten—the second masochistic, erotic, and deeply repressed: she is the child being beaten, by her father. For a boy, in a yet more complicated process of transformation, a first phantasy, "I am loved by my father," is transformed into the conscious phantasy "I am being beaten by my mother."⁷ Without attempting to find direct correspondences between Freud's scenarios and Duras' beating scene, one can note a general resemblance of the positions of the three children in relation to the beating and the various positions that can be assumed by one child according to Freud. In particular, the older brother's excitement at his naked sister's beating suggests both sadistic and masochistic urges, and the desire to be in the places both of beater and beaten. As in Freud's essay, positions in relation to desire in **L'amant** are virtually a matter of grammatical transformations. The subject finds and takes up positions in relation to desire, active and passive, sadistic and masochistic, in processes capable of reversal and contradiction. Freud's essay, read in conjunction with the beating episode of *L'amant,* suggests again the crucial importance of where one stands in relation to desire, including its negative transformations. Desire is always desire of the other, and of the other's desire; there is no such thing as a simple, unmediated, unproblematic desire on the part of the subject. The girl creates desire on the part of her future lover from the moment he looks at her, while his desire creates her, as part of that circulatory system which, in the description given by Freud in this essay, allows the subject to take up multiple positions within it.

To return once again to the girl's lovemaking, and particularly to the moments that describe her lover's gaze at her, one further passage needs quotation:

> He looks at her. His eyes closed he looks at her still. He inhales her face. He breathes in the child, his eyes closed he breathes in her breathing, the warm air that comes from her. He discerns less and less clearly the limits of this body, this one is not like the others, it is not finite, in the room it keeps growing, it is still without fixed forms, being made at every moment, it's not only there where he sees it, it is also elsewhere, it extends beyond his view, toward risk, death, it's supple, it embarks whole into pleasure as if it were grown up, adult, it is without guile, it has a frightening intelligence.
>
> (121)

Besides offering a remarkable view of herself in terms of the desiring gaze directed at her, and an understanding of her own capacity to serve as the object of desire, this passage suggests the importance of desire and the erotic as potential transgressions of human finitude.

For Georges Bataille, in *L'érotisme,* the erotic is fundamentally transgressive of taboos and limitations. Human beings are "discontinuous"—finite, closed, incapable of deep communication with others because the bodies of others are closed to them. In the erotic encounter discontinuity and finitude are breached, if only momentarily. One body accedes to another, breaches its walls, enters its bodily orifices. Bataille writes:

> All the work of eroticism has as its principle a destruction of the structure of the closed being that each partner in the game is in the normal state.
>
> The decisive action is making naked. Nudity is opposed to the closed state, in other words, to the state of discontinuous existence. Nudity is a condition of communication, which reveals the quest for a possible continuity of being, beyond the closing in on oneself. Bodies open to continuity by these secret passages that give us the feeling of obscenity. Obscenity signifies the trouble that disorders a condition of bodies in possession of themselves, a possession of a durable and affirmed identity. . . .
>
> What is at stake in eroticism is always a dissolution of constituted forms . . . But in eroticism, even less than in reproduction, discontinuous life is not doomed, de-

spite Sade's claim, to disappear: it is simply put into question. It must be troubled, maximally disordered.[8]

Putting one's body at risk in this manner creates a disequilibrium in which one consciously puts oneself into question. The erotic thus offers a momentary transcendence of limits, of discontinuity. It is comparable to sacrifice, as the revelation—and creation—of the sacred. "The sacred is precisely the continuity of being, revealed to those who fix their attention, in a solemn rite, on the death of a discontinuous being" (92). Death offers the final transgression or transcendence of the closed body. Eroticism as an act of transgression indicates that "the sacred and prohibition are bound up together, and that access to the sacred takes place in the violence of an infraction" (139). Bataille thus redefines the age-old intimacy of love and death: eroticism is "the affirmation of life all the way unto death" ("l'approbation de la vie jusque dans la mort").

I cite Bataille because he so well captures the transpersonal state achieved in erotic realization by the protagonist of *L'amant,* and how this state opens onto a sacred state ("the knowledge of God," she calls it) that is also akin to death. For both Bataille and Duras, the erotic is a state of expenditure and excess. These are key terms for Bataille, since they underlie his attempt—given its fullest statement in *La part maudite*—to found a social economy based not on saving and capitalization but on expenditure (*la dépense*), waste, and unproductiveness, which are necessary to regain a sense of the sacred beyond the utilitarian. Art is in this sense also expenditure, waste, excess. Poetry, says Bataille, is "creation by means of loss . . . the pursuit of inconsistent shadows that provide nothing but vertigo and rage. The poet frequently can use words only for his own loss."[9] The view of writing advanced in *L'amant* is quite similar.

L'amant closes with a phone call from the Chinese lover to the girl, now married and divorced, and a mother, many years after her return to France, during his visit to Paris. The call ends with his avowal that he loves her still, that he could never stop loving her, that he will love her unto death. The desire created in *L'amant* is absolute, beyond the specific circumstances in which it is enacted. The episode of the phone call is immediately preceded by the narrative of the lover's arranged marriage with the Chinese wife chosen by his father—events which the girl did not witness and could not know. According to her account, the lover must for a long time have been impotent with his new wife, unable to consummate the marriage because of his memory of the white girl, as if her body stretched sideways across the marriage bed:

> She must have remained for a long time the ruler of his desire, the personal reference of his emotion, of the immensity of his tenderness, of somber and terrible carnal depth. Then the day came when it must have been possible. Precisely when desire for the white girl must have been so strong, so unbearable that he could recall her image in its totality as in a raging fever and could penetrate the other woman with this desire for her, the

white girl. It must have been by way of a lie that he found himself inside this woman, and by a lie that he engendered what the two families, Heaven, his ancestors in the North, all expected from him, that is, an heir to his name.

(140-41)

In the manner of the phantasmatic scenes played out on the body of Hélène Lagonelle, the body of the girl serves as intermediary in the realization of desire, indeed takes on the role of the phallus: it is with this desire that the lover finally succeeds in entering his bride. But whereas the phantasmatic body of Hélène Lagonelle serves the intellectual comprehension of desire, here the hallucinated body of the girl—invoked as in a fever—serves rather the lie, the substitution of sexual objects. One may then ask which kind of phantasy or hallucination presides at the writing of this passage, which narrates not what the girl has witnessed and knows to be the case, but rather the way things "must have been." Is this a lie? Or is it the kind of phantasy that creates truth, the truth dictated by desire? Is it, in this sense, an emblem of the very fiction-making process, of the capacity to narrate not only events but also the history of desire underlying events, the history in which events are merely symptoms of a determinative, hidden narrative? It is not to cast doubt on the truth of the events recounted in **L'amant** to suggest that the guiding thread of the narrative, and the dynamic of the plot, have less to do with the relatively sparse and simple events of the novel than with the force of desire, as the source of hallucinated and phantasized bodies, of bodies that have a corporeal reality but become significant in their placement in relation to desire. The writing of the book also has to do with positions in relation to desire. The writing body retraces the eros of the story in a state of deprivation and hallucination.

There is a moment in the novel, following the girl's fantasy of Hélène Lagonelle in the arms of her lover, when the place of erotic encounter with the lover, the Cholon apartment, is analogized to the place of writing. Within the aridity and hardness of her family the girl gains her essential conviction that she will be a writer. She has come to understand her family in a new light because of the hours she spends in the Cholon apartment. "It is an unbearable place, it borders on death, a place of violence, of pain, of despair, of dishonor. And such is the place in Cholon" (93). That is, the place of writing, its spiritual space, is one of agony and despair, also of eroticism and death. We are reminded of a passage early in the novel where the narrator refers to her vocation of writing, which she discovers along with eroticism at age fifteen, as characterized by an "inconvenance fondamentale," a fundamental impropriety. Writing is a violation of accepted norms, a transgression of limits, an experience of pain and of orgasmic pleasure. Writing indeed (as I have suggested) may originate in the erotic. And the erotic espouses the mission of writing when it is the source and the object of an act of intelligence, when it is seized intellectually as a testing of limits.

Writing for Bataille is linked in much the same manner to the lucid, willed transgression of proprieties and prohibitions, the creation of value through the experience of infraction and loss. Bataille's essays in literary criticism, in *La littérature et le mal,* turn around the issue posed in Baudelaire's phrase, from the poem "L'irrémédiable," "la conscience dans le mal," consciousness of evil and consciousness within evil, the transgressor's awareness at the moment of transgression. It is not so much that wrongdoing is pleasurable, as that taking pleasure is seen as evil. "Evil is not transgression, it is transgression condemned. It is precisely sin."[10] The importance of sin lies in its conceptualization, as that kind of transgressive act that changes one's spiritual condition and entails sanctions. In sinning, one may choose the state of damnation, and therefore know it in full lucidity. Eroticism, for both Bataille and Duras—as also for Baudelaire—offers the most direct experience of *mal*: transgression condemned, turned into sin. The act of erotic transgression is a moment of heightened consciousness beyond the normal limits and conventions. The transgression of writing—another form of "communication"—is fundamentally similar; it assumes the impossible, as place and as state of being, a condition akin to mortal sin where pleasure is derived from the knowledge of *mal,* of one's wrongdoing, and knowledge itself is that pleasure.

Notes

1. Marguerite Duras, *L'amant* (Paris: Editions de Minuit, 1985), p. 111; English trans. Barbara Bray, *The Lover* (New York: Pantheon, 1985). The translation of this stylistically challenging text by Barbara Bray is excellent. I have preferred to give my own translations, however, in an attempt to remain closer to the peculiar syntax of the original, although this often results in an English version less fluent and graceful than Bray's. Duras in 1991 published another, very different version of her story, *L'amant de la Chine du Nord* (Paris: Gallimard, 1991), which apparently was begun as a screenplay for the film of *L'amant* and, not used in this capacity, developed into a novel, though one with indications to the maker of a possible film of the original novel. It is a strange performance, much less subtle and compelling than *L'amant.*

2. In the wake of of Roland Barthes' use of *jouissance* in distinction to *plaisir,* it has been usual to translate the former term as "bliss." But the connotations of "bliss" strike me as hopelessly wrong for designating intense, orgasmic bodily pleasure. I note that Barbara Bray also uses "pleasure" to translate *jouissance.*

3. See Jacques Lacan, "Hommage fait à Marguerite Duras du ravissement de Lol V. Stein," in François Barat and Joël Farges, eds., *Marguerite Duras,* rev. ed. (Paris: Editions Albatros, 1979), pp. 131-37. Lacan writes, "Marguerite Duras s'avère savoir sans moi ce que j'enseigne" (p. 133). Lacan's piece was originally published in the *Cahiers Renaud-Barrault*

(December 1965). I adapt here especially material from Lacan, *Le séminaire,* book 8, *Le transfert* (Paris: Editions du Seuil, 1991), p. 415.

4. Lacan, "Propos directifs pour un Congrès sur la sexualité féminine," in *Ecrits* (Paris: Editions du Seuil, 1966), pp. 725-36; I quote from the translation by Jacqueline Rose, "Guiding Remarks for a Congress on Feminine Sexuality," in *Feminine Sexuality: Jacques Lacan and the Ecole Freudienne,* ed. Juliet Mitchell and Jacqueline Rose (London: Macmillan, 1982), p. 70. For Rose's comments on this passage, see p. 43.

5. Sharon Willis makes a similar point in the context of feminist theory: "The figure of an exhibitionist female subject should have special force for feminist readers. . . . [Duras'] work centers on issues of concern to most feminist theoretical enterprises: desire and sexuality, gender and biology, the relation of the body to language. *The Lover* reinscribes the exhibitionist scenario in a woman's active self-display, a presentation of her life as spectacle—active, that is, as opposed to the passive form of woman as object of/spectacle for a mastering gaze, that of reader or spectator." *Marguerite Duras: Writing on the Body* (Urbana and Chicago: University of Illinois Press, 1987), p. 7.

6. Choderlos de Laclos, *Les liaisons dangereuses,* in *Oeuvres complètes* (Paris: Bibliothèque de la Pléiade, 1979), Letter 81, p. 169.

7. Sigmund Freud, "A Child Is Being Beaten," *Standard Edition* 17:179-204.

8. Georges Bataille, *L'érotisme* (1957; Paris: Union Générale d'Editions/10/18, 1965), pp. 22-23. The evident affinities of Bataille's thinking about eroticism with Lacan's are not accidental: Lacan was much influenced by Bataille.

9. "The Notion of Expenditure," in Georges Bataille, *Visions of Excess: Selected Writings, 1927-1939,* ed. Allan Stoekl, trans. Allan Stoekl with Carl R. Lovitt and Donald M Leslie, Jr. (Minneapolis: University of Minnesota Press, 1985), p. 120.

10. Bataille, *L'érotisme,* p. 140.

Marilyn R. Schuster (essay date 1993)

SOURCE: "Coming of Age Stories: Defining the Woman and the Writer," in *Marguerite Duras Revisited,* Twayne Publishers, 1993, pp. 13-62, 105-45.

[*In the following essay, Schuster discusses female sexuality and subjugation in "The Boa."*]

In 1954, Duras published four short stories under the title *Des Journées entières dans les arbres* (*Whole Days in the Trees*).[1] Just as *The Tranquil Life* tells a story of female subjectivity, one of the stories in this volume, **"The**

Boa," presents a story of female sexuality. Although the story is told in the first person, both temporal and geographic distance between the adult narrator and her younger self is carefully established at the beginning: "This happened in a large city in a French colony, around 1928" (*WD,* 71; *J,* 99). The use of an impersonal, reflexive construction ("cela se passait") reinforces the distancing of the narrator and is the first mark of split female subjectivity in this text, in which the woman tries to read her own adolescence. In the story, the adult narrator situates her thirteen-year-old self between two spectacles that provided the only terms available to her to understand her awakening sexuality.

The narrator describes her younger self as a poor student at Mademoiselle Barbet's boarding school for girls. The other girls have friends in town, and every Sunday their developing minds and bodies are nourished by endless adventures: cinema, teas, drives in the country, afternoons at the pool or tennis courts. The narrator, however, has no such social life and spends all her time with the seventy-five-year-old spinster, Mlle Barbet. Mlle Barbet provides the girl with the two spectacles that mark her coming of age. Every Sunday she takes her to the zoo, where, with other fascinated onlookers, they watch a boa constrictor consume a live chicken. If they arrive too late, they contemplate the boa napping on "a bed of chicken feathers" (*WD,* 72; *J,* 100). They remain transfixed because "there was nothing more to see, but we knew what had happened a moment before, and each of us stood before the boa, deep in thought" (*WD,* 72; *J,* 100-101).

The other spectacle is provided by Mlle Barbet herself, with the girl as an unwilling witness. In a routine as certain as the boa's, Mlle Barbet calls the girl into her room. Under the pretext of showing the girl her fine lingerie, Mlle Barbet exhibits her seminude body. The old woman had never shown her body to anyone before and would never show it to anyone else because of her advanced age. She instructs the girl that beautiful lingerie is important in life, a lesson she learned too late.

The narrator adds that Mlle Barbet's body exudes a terrible odor that permeates the entire boarding school; she had noticed the odor before, but could not locate it before seeing the woman's exposed body. The old woman sighs during their secret sessions, saying "I have wasted my life. . . . He never came" (*WD,* 74; *J,* 105). The girl is induced by her own impoverished circumstances to tell the woman that she has a full life, that she is rich and has beautiful lingerie: The rest is unimportant.

This Sunday double feature, repeated weekly for two years, is developed in great detail by the narrator, who spends most of the story linking, contrasting, and interpreting the two spectacles because they illuminate the only two avenues through which the young girl could imagine her future. The narrator insists that one weekly event without the other would have led to other effects. If, for example, she had witnessed only the boa's devouring of the chicken, she might have seen in the boa the force of evil and in his victim, goodness and innocence; she might have understood the world as an eternal struggle between these two forces revealing the presence of God. Or, she could have been led to rebel (*WD,* 73; *J,* 102). She could have internalized the weekly lesson at the zoo, that is, as a morality tale, a story of good and evil leading to conformity or rebellion.

The spectacle of Mlle Barbet alone might have led the girl to understand social inequities and the "multiple forms of oppression" that result. Coupled with the zoo experience, the second spectacle shifts the meanings of both because of the terrifying glimpse of aging female flesh, undiscovered by the male gaze and imprisoned in its own virginity. Together, the two events become not a morality tale of good and evil, of inequity and injustice, but a cautionary tale of female sexuality. The terms the narrator uses to reconstruct each event and the conclusions she draws articulate a specific construction of the female body and heterosexuality. Within the terms of the story—shown especially in the contrast between the young narrator and her school friends—she seems to suggest that this is an anomalous construction. At the same time, fatalistic language and implications of social determinism suggest that this is a distilled experience of female sexuality rather than an anomalous one. In any case, the highly individualized definition of female sexuality elaborated in this text will be generalized in other texts by Duras, passing imperceptibly from one woman's story to the story of "woman." For that reason, as well as the fact that this is one of the few texts with explicit autobiographical references situated in Indochina and written before *The Lover,* **"The Boa"** merits close consideration.

From the start, the narrator insists that she is an involuntary, yet complicit, solitary voyeur of Mlle Barbet. The girl undergoes this weekly drama and keeps Mlle Barbet's secret in exchange for Mlle Barbet's silence about her mother's poverty. The girl is in the school because her mother thinks that it is the only way she will meet a husband and thus find a way out of poverty and marginalization in the strictly ordered society of the colony.

The girl shares her mother's belief that Mlle Barbet is better suited to help her find a husband, even though the old woman's "secular virginity" exudes the odor of death that permeates the school (*WD,* 74; *J,* 105). The narrator specifies that Mlle Barbet is consumed by lack, by "the lack of the man who never came" (*WD,* 74; *J,* 105). Each week, after leaving the old woman, the girl returns to her room, looks at her own body in the mirror, and admires her white breasts. In a gesture that superimposes the boa and female sexuality, she says that her breasts provide the only source of pleasure for her in the entire house: "Outside the house there was the boa, here there were my breasts" (*WD,* 76; *J,* 107).[2] Feeling trapped in the school, the girl goes out on the balcony to attract the attention of passing soldiers.

The spectacles of the old woman and of the snake involve consumption and violence valued in opposite ways. Mlle Barbet is consumed by lack, and the private viewing of her enclosed, undiscovered sexuality inspires disgust and dread. The boa consumes his prey, and his public act is characterized as a sacred crime inspiring horror and respect. The boa itself is described in hyperbolic, highly sexualized terms: "Curled into himself, black . . . in admirable form—a plump roundness, tender, muscular, a column of black marble . . . with shudders of contained power, the boa devoured this chicken in the course of a single process of digestion . . . transubstantiation accomplished with the sacred calm of ritual. In this formidable, inner silence, chicken became serpent" (*WD,* 72; *J,* 101). This spectacle in the open daylight attracts spectators who are fascinated, entranced by the vital beauty and violence of the beast. In sharp contrast, the narrator calls Mlle Barbet's secret "hidden" and "nocturnal."

The narrator does not read the formative stories of her youth as a simple contrast between powerful male and sterile female sexuality, two stories of devouring desire—one the passionate devouring of an innocent, the other the passionless devouring of the self by a hypocritical innocence. In her work on reader theory, Jean Kennard talks about the shaping role of both gender and sexuality in the recognition and interpretation of literary conventions.[3] She shows how new meanings can be assigned to conventions to subvert their apparent or traditional sense. The narrator of **"The Boa"** can be read as a woman thinking back on the cultural texts available to her to understand and revalue her sexuality through a complex negotiation between her needs and the stories available. Duras accomplishes this negotiation by mapping a story of female sexuality onto the spectacle of the boa constrictor so that *both* stories recount possibilities for female sexuality. Female sexuality is redeemed by the power of the phallus in the first story, condemned by its own inadequacy in the second.

To map a story of female sexuality onto the story of the boa, the narrator must negotiate a complex series of substitutions and displacements. Her narrative sleights of hand recall the convoluted associations and displacements of a Freudian map of female sexuality—one that privileges the penis and defines woman by lack. The slippage that results from this imperfect, if ingenious, mapping compounds the division within the woman/girl's experience of the female body marked thematically by the two spectacles.

In an increasingly intense meditation on the links between the spectacle of the boa and of Mlle Barbet, the narrator expresses the despair she felt as a girl: unable to flee the closed world of Mlle Barbet, "nocturnal monster," unable to join the fertile world revealed by the boa, "monster of the day." In a passage presented as a waking fantasy, she imagines the world represented by the boa. She fantasizes a green paradise, a scene where "innumerable carnal exchanges were achieved by one organism devouring, assimilating, coupling with another in processes that were at once orgiastic and calm" (*WD,* 78; *J,* 110). The contrast of this paradise with the prison of Mlle Barbet leads her to define two types of horror. One horror—hidden vices, shameful secrets, hypocrisy, concealed disease—inspires a deep aversion. The other—the horror of assassins, crime, the outlaw—inspires admiration. The boa is the "perfect image" of this second kind of horror that elicits respect. In a series of substitutions she expresses contempt for those who would condemn certain species such as "cold, silent snakes . . . cruel, hypocritical cats." She establishes one category of human being that could be considered among these privileged outlaws: the prostitute. She parenthetically links assassins and prostitutes, imagining both in "the jungle of great capital cities, hunting their prey which they then consumed with the impudence and imperiousness of fatalistic temperaments" (*WD,* 79; *J,* 112). She thus establishes a train of associations that shifts the story from the masculine figure of the snake to the male assassin/outlaw to the feminine figure of the prostitute, from the jungle to the city.

The transfer of value from the snake to the prostitute also takes place at a deeper, linguistic level. The boa consumes a chicken, put in the masculine in the French: "un poulet." A common word for prostitute in French, which is implied though not invoked in the story, is the feminine form of chicken: "une poule." The prostitute figure in the story, like the chicken that is ingested by the boa and becomes one with his flesh, is absorbed into the values of the phallic figure of the snake. Another substitution and transfer of values is hinted at more explicitly in the story. The same soldiers who walk under her balcony are also spectators at the zoo. She would attract their gaze, fascinate them, in the same way as the boa, substituting herself for the great serpent in her fantasy.

At the moment that she transfers values from the male figures to the female, the image of Mlle Barbet erupts into her fantasy as a reminder of the body she is fleeing. She tells herself that if she does not marry, at least the brothel would provide an escape for her. This leads her to a fantasy of the brothel: "a sort of temple of defloration where, in all purity . . . young girls in my state, to whom marriage was not accorded, would go to have their bodies discovered by unknown men, men who belonged to the self-same species" (*WD,* 79; *J,* 112). The brothel, painted green, recalls the zoo garden as well as the tamarind trees that shade her balcony, where she tries to attract the gaze of passing soldiers. She imagines this as a silent place, marked by a sacred anonymity; girls would wear masks in order to enter. Anonymity pays homage to "the absolute lack of 'personality' of the boa, ideal bearer that he was of the naked, virginal mask" (*WD,* 79; *J,* 113).[4] The ritual initiation and anonymity shift this from the story of one girl to the story of woman, from a specific sexual awakening to a model of female sexuality. She imagines cabins in which one could "cleanse oneself of one's virginity, to have the solitude removed from one's body" (*WD,* 80; *J,* 113).

The oscillation between the brothel fantasy and the memory of her despair on the balcony, between the snake and the prostitute, situates her as both spectator and par-

ticipant in an initiation where phallic sexuality is worshiped and woman is freed of the isolation and lack of her body. She invokes another, earlier childhood memory as "corroboration" of this way of seeing the world. One day her brother asked her to show him her sex. When she refused, he said "girls could die from not using it, and that hiding it suffocated you and made you seriously ill" (*WD,* 80; *J,* 113). The spectacle of Mlle Barbet's body seems to confirm her brother's dire prediction. Her brother's voice, like the "fraternal image" that Francine sees in the mirror in *The Tranquil Life* and the voice of "virility and truth" that Suzanne hears in Joseph's stories, is the voice of male authority. In an image that recalls Suzanne's pleasure in Monsieur Jo's gaze, the narrator generalizes the power of male authority by saying, as she remembers Mlle Barbet's decaying body: "From the moment a breast had served a man, even by merely allowing him to see it, to take note of its shape, its roundness, its firmness—from the moment a breast was able to nourish the seed of a man's desire, it was saved from withering from disuse" (*WD,* 80; *J,* 114).

While admitting the terror of being consumed that the boa inspired, the narrator appropriates that story to imagine the female body and female sexuality redeemed by the male gaze and desire. In **"The Boa,"** female heterosexuality defined by the phallus is intrinsically linked to a loathing of the female body. The key transition in her fantasy chain of images that allows the narrator to transform the story of the boa into the story of the prostitute and, hence, into a model for female sexuality, is the glorification of crime and the figure of the outlaw. And yet, I would argue, Duras has not written a story of outlaw female sexuality. Her representation of female sexuality is outlaw only in its flamboyant display and excess, without the pretense of monogamy. Far from being deviant, the construction of desire and the deployment of erotic power in this representation remains conventional. Rather than disrupt sexual and social order in this narrative, she imagines a way for woman to fit into the dominant construction of heterosexuality that privileges the phallus and demeans the woman's body.

Notes

1. Marguerite Duras, *Des Journées entières dans les arbres* (Paris: Gallimard, 1954); hereafter cited in the text as *J*; and Anita Barrows, translator, *Whole Days in the Trees* (New York: Riverrun Press, 1984); hereafter cited in the text as *WD*.

2. Potentially, the maternal body could provide an alternative to the horror of Mlle Barbet's body. She thinks of her mother's body having nourished four children and the freshness of its smell. But this is a quick, undeveloped aside.

3. Jean E. Kennard, "Convention Coverage or How to Read Your Own Life," *New Literary History* 13, no. 1 (1981): 69-88, and "Ourself behind Ourself: A Theory for Lesbian Readers," in *Gender and Reading: Essays on Readers, Texts, and Contexts,* ed. Elizabeth A. Flynn and Patrocinio P. Schweickart

(Baltimore: The Johns Hopkins University Press, 1986), 63-82.

4. The published translation has "individuality" instead of "personality" in this passage. However, in the French, "personnalité" is set off by quotation marks, adding emphasis both to the word and the choice of that word. Given the anthropomorphism of the image, I prefer to keep the word *personality* in the English.

James H. Reid (essay date 1994)

SOURCE: "The Cafe Duras: Mourning Descriptive Space," in *French Forum,* Vol. 19, No. 1, January, 1994, pp. 45-64.

[*In the following essay, Reid discusses the ways in which the café setting represents an "ideal inner space" in Duras's fiction.*]

> . . . écrire, c'est ça aussi, sans doute, c'est effacer. Remplacer.
>
> (*Emily* 32)[1]

The café, like so many places in Marguerite Duras's novels, is less a material than a mental space that her characters construct and deconstruct in their minds. Within this inner, and some would say feminine, space, or rather, within the descriptive space that makes the fiction of space possible, desire and narrative are born and die in a seemingly unending repetition outside time, history, and narrative.[2] However, unlike the other interiorized spaces discussed by recent Duras criticism (Willis 168), Duras's café is a space in which characters exchange words and desires, not only as lovers, but also as traders buying and selling commodities. It is a place of business as well as love. This not-so-privileged *locus amoenus* plays a privileged role within the body of Duras's texts. The café highlights a process of commodification that puts into question the reality of Duras's inner descriptive space. It also foregrounds a process of mourning the death of this space, a process that structures her text. By repeatedly mourning the death of the descriptive discourse with which they construct the inner space of an "amour absolu" (*Ravissement* 7),[3] Duras's characters reopen the question, but only the question, of time, history, and narrative.

Duras dramatizes the mourning of her characters for the death of an ideal inner space of desire in *Moderato cantabile* (1958) and *Emily L.* (1987). On the surface, her allegory of this mourning has changed very little over the course of 30 years: in both works, a man and a woman enter a café and reinvent the story of two real lovers who have frequented the same café. In their story, the male lover helps the female lover create an atemporal inner space in which her desire for death is satisfied, literally or figuratively. The storytellers then realize that they have told their story out of a need to mourn the death of their

belief in such an inner space of desire. Finally, in an attempt to renounce desire and resolve the process of mourning, they leave the café.

The manner in which Duras's two novels repeat this allegory foregrounds not only the continuity, but the evolution, of her meditation on space, desire, and the descriptive. Between *Moderato* and *Emily L.*, Duras's writing ceases to thematize a mental space of consciousness, as did French existentialism, and comes to speak of a descriptive space of writing, as did French poststructuralism. The reappearance of time that marks the attempt to end the process of mourning begins to be accompanied by references to history. A deceptive reconciliation of writing and desire, art and life, becomes an explicit rejection of the possibility of such a reconciliation.

Moderato and *Emily L.* construct and mourn the fiction of an ahistorical space of desire by redefining traditional descriptions of the café. Conventional representations of the café began to appear along with cafés in the late seventeenth century, soon after the introduction of coffee into France.[4] In contrast to the cabaret, which was often associated with drunkenness and lewdness, the café came to be seen, especially during the eighteenth century, as a respectable place in which serious opinions, particularly on theater, literature, and politics, could be exchanged by men (Lemaire 17-20).[5] Given that some authors, as early as Diderot, also began to write in cafés, the café was to represent a place where art and (social or intellectual) life were reconciled (Fosca 161). For bourgeoisie and workers and in the nineteenth century, however, the café was a place where the men could share a bottle of beer, often in the company of their families. It represented social respectability and cohesiveness (Fosca 36).[6]

In *Moderato* and *Emily L.*, Duras redefines the traditional café in a manner that constitutes it as a place of subversive, rather than respectable, desire (life) and storytelling (art). She describes her version of the traditional café in an early novel, *Le Square* (1955). In *Le Square,* a young female servant constructs in her mind what she believes to be an ideal, working-class café. Her fantasy café is a commercial place where the exchange and consumption of money, drinks, gestures, and words enable clients to satisfy their desire to constitute and reaffirm their conventional social selves. Having never visited such a place, she does not, she believes, have an identity: "vous ne pouvez pas savoir ce que c'est que de n'être rien," she tells the traveling salesman sitting beside her on the park bench (*Square* 32).[7] One day, however, she will enter a café and satisfy her wish to be someone rather than nothing. She will become part of society: "Je serai là, au comptoir, au bras de mon mari et nous écouterons la radio . . . nous y serons à la fois ensemble et avec les autres" (*Square* 47). She will *be* ("je serai") when she is *there* ("là") *with* others (Membrado 89). Duras's description of a traditional café that makes being possible differs little from Roquentin's description, in Sartre's earlier *La Nausée* (1938), of clients in the café Mably. There "tout est toujours nor-mal": "Eux aussi, pour exister, il faut qu'ils se mettent à plusieurs."[8]

The social space of Duras's café, like that of Roquentin's, constitutes identity synecdochically and metaphorically. *Being with* someone ("nous") produces a sense of indi-vidual identity through the mediation of a shared notion of community. The price of drinks buys the right to sit and exchange words, gestures, and glances. The resulting ex-changes are speech acts and these speech acts are indiffer-ent to the content of the words and sentences they ex-change, to their use value:[9] "On nous parlera de choses et d'autres et nous répondrons. . . ." (*Square* 47). Rather than be dictated by content, speech acts in the café are dictated by rules distinguishing felicitous from infelicitous performances:[10] "Tout le monde avait eu peur d'une autre question qu'elle aurait pu poser" (*Emily* 37). The commu-nal, ritualized repetition and exchange of acceptable speech acts constitutes the café as an identifiable social space: a community of felicitous and similar speech actors who are—politically, artistically, or socially—someone rather than nothing (Membrado 94-96).

The concept of a fixed social space is the product of a ritualized observance of the conventional rules that distin-guish a legitimate or sacred discursive inside from an ille-gitimate or profane outside (Membrado 73). Only ex-changes that are felicitous, that satisfy the desire for identity, are allowed in the café. Exchanges that are infe-licitous, like those between servant and anonymous sales-man, are kept outside.[11] To be unable to perform the speech acts appropriate to the café is to be condemned, as is Ro-quentin (Sartre 17-20), to desire (for identity), solitude, and dissatisfaction: "Parfois l'envie me prend d[e] . . . faire un tour [au café], mais, seule, voyez-vous, une jeune fille de mon état ne peut pas se le permettre" (*Square* 47).

Felicitous speech acts that respect the rules of the café make discourse on the café appear to be a realist descrip-tion: a fixed, paradigmatic discursive space. Descriptive space produces the fiction of fixed spatial relationships and this fiction makes possible the concept of a social and ma-terial space in which proprietor and clients have their proper places and identities.[12] Duras's traditional café pre-supposes, therefore, the repetition of an irreversible story that gives it a circular, mythic temporality (Membrado 79): entry into the café after work, social confirmation of indi-vidual identity through ritual observance of society's rules, departure for home (Hamon, *Personnel* 315, 323).

Moderato puts into question the servant's distinction be-tween a rule-governed social inside, the café, and a rule-less social outside by constructing the fiction of an atem-poral, mental space of desire. The novel juxtaposes passages on a working-class café with a passage on the formal dining room of an upper-class home, the descrip-tion of each place being outside in relation to the other, but both being governed by rules similar to those regulat-ing the servant's café. In the dining room of the home, so-

ciety's wealthy producers and powerful leaders, like the servant in *Le Square,* reconstruct their description of com-munity and self: "Le chur des conversations augmente peu à peu de volume et, dans une surenchère d'efforts et d'inventivités progressive, émerge une société quelconque" (*Moderato* 69).[13] The periodic coming together of mem-bers of the same social class, the ritualized exchange of acceptable words and gestures, "la crainte d'un manque-ment quelconque au cérémonial" (*Moderato* 68), consti-tute this upper-class dining room, like the servant's café, as a seemingly unchanging set of relationships between a social whole and its parts: "'Nous sommes toutes pareilles, allez'" (*Moderato* 71). Host and guests construct a social space in which society's dominant upper-class inside, al-though socially superior to the working-class inside of the café, nonetheless repeats the ridgity of the implicit dis-course of the latter on a fixed social space.

Moderato questions the discourses of home and café on a fixed, rule-governed social inside by reducing them to commercial and exchangeable commodities and by subor-dinating both social "insides" to a seemingly privileged, mental, inner space. Anne Desbaresdes, an upper-class ma-tron, enters a working-class café and begins drinking and conversing, over a period of days, with an unemployed worker from her husband's factory. Her ritualized crossing of society's descriptive boundaries transgresses the rules with which social discourse constructs an unchanging so-cial space:[14] "Deux clients entrèrent. Ils reconnurent cette femme au comptoir, s'étonnèrent" (*Moderato* 19); "La pa-tronne s'exécuta sans un mot, déjà lassée sans doute du dérèglement de leurs manières" (*Moderato* 29). As in An-dré Breton's *Nadja,* a transgressive couple reveals the tra-ditional rules that govern the café clientele's social space to be ritualized deceits which hide and reveal a desire for what they exclude: anonymity and death (Membrado 16).[15] And like Sartre's solitary, self-conscious individual, Ro-quentin (Sartre 19), Duras's couple reinterprets the café as a place in which social identity is emptied of, rather than filled with, meaning, where both characters come to re-semble, in each other's eyes, things rather than people.

The café in *Moderato,* like Breton's surrealist café, is thus a space in which a couple's desire demystifies the logic with which society constructs (its members' consciousness of having) a fixed identity. It is not at all clear, however, that Duras demystifies the logic of the café in order to open up the romantic or surrealist possibility of an authen-tic or unconscious self, here a feminine self, or in order to raise the existentialist possibility of an inner consciousness of nothingness.

Anne begins constructing the subversive space of her café after she hears, coming from a café, the cry of a woman being murdered by her lover. When she enters on the next day, she meets the unemployed worker, Chauvin. Together they invent the story of how the two lovers came to desire and carry out their murder/suicide. The immediate goal of this story is allegorical and performative. It figuratively represents and performatively enacts a murder of the hierarchical, social paradigm that constitutes Anne's and Chauvin's social identities, as if storytelling expressed the teller's desire that his or her identity die (Willis 155).[16] The prospect of this death makes Anne feel, not Roquentin's nausea, but a sado-masochistic combination of desire and fear.[17]

Anne's and Chauvin's performative allegory reverses the servant's fantasy in which entry into the café transformed nothing into someone. Their account of how a man murders his female lover is a speech act by which the worker reduces his boss's wife from someone to nothing: "'C'est là, dans cette maison, qu'elle a appris ce que vous disiez qu'elle était, peut-être par exemple. . . .'—'. . . Oui, une chienne. . . .'" (*Moderato* 64); "Chauvin proféra un mot à voix basse. Le regard d'Anne Desbaresdes s'évanouit lentement sous l'insulte, s'ensommeilla" (*Moderato* 60). Verbal degradation is a "rite mortuaire" that replaces society's rites of community and identity (*Moderato* 82): "Leurs mains étaient si froides qu'elles se touchèrent illusoirement" (*Moderato* 80). Identity, community, presence, and life become masks hiding anonymity, solitude, absence, and death: "'Je voudrais que vous soyez morte. . . .' 'C'est fait'" (*Moderato* 84).

Anne and Chauvin erase exterior signs of identity and community by replacing realist signs of an economic, historical, and social exterior—cranes, tugboats, factories, and workers outside the café—with the lovers' perceptions of each other, then with an erasure of all consciousness of difference between self and other, subject and object. The couple tries to go beyond Roquentin's philosophical consciousness of nothingness, which remains within the definition of the café as a place to exchange ideas, and to return to the less socially-acceptable model of the cabaret as a place of drunkenness and forgetting. As Anne and Chauvin drink more and more wine, they imagine that the two lovers performed a methodical, Rimbaldian "dérèglement de tous les sens" (*Moderato* 270). The lovers' sensory signs of presence, the couple fantasizes, became progressively indistinguishable from signs of absence. First auditory signs: "'Je voudrais que vous me disiez le commencement même, comment ils ont commencé à se parler. C'est dans un café, disiez-vous . . .'" (*Moderato* 32); "'Alors ils ont parlé . . . et parlé, beaucoup de temps, beaucoup, avant d'y arriver'" (*Moderato* 33); "'Je voudrais que vous me disiez maintenant comment ils en sont arrivés à ne plus même se parler'" (*Moderato* 40). Then visual and tactile signs: "'Puis le temps est venu où quand il la regardait, parfois, il ne la voyait plus comme il l'avait jusque-là vue. Elle cessait d'être belle, laide, jeune, vieille, comparable à quiconque, même à elle-même'" (*Moderato* 64); "'Puis le temps est venu où il crut qu'il ne pourrait plus la toucher autrement que pour . . .'" (*Moderato* 65). The desire to kill the sensory signs with which they identify each other can only be satisfied by death ("'Le cri a dû s'arrêter au moment où elle a cessé de le voir'" [*Moderato* 30]) or by a death of consciousness: "il se débattit en silence, échappa aux inspecteurs et courut en sens inverse, de toutes ses forces, vers le café. Mais, comme il allait

l'atteindre, le café s'éteignit. Alors il s'arrêta, en pleine course, il suivit de nouveau les inspecteurs jusqu'au au fourgon et il y monta" (*Moderato* 16); "'Il est maintenant devenu fou . . .'" (*Moderato* 20).

Anne's and Chauvin's story of the lovers' search to die, physically or mentally, indirectly recounts their own search, through wine and conversation, for a non-existentialist, mental space that will satisfy a similar desire: "'Je voudrais que vous partiez'" (*Moderato* 65). They do not care whether their story is literally true: "'C'est comme vous désirez le croire, ça n'a pas d'importance'" (*Moderato* 82). Their story is only an allegory of their fantasized transformation of their consciousness of being someone into a consciousness of being nothing in each other's eyes, then into an absence of consciousness: "Anne Desbaresdes fixa cet homme inconnu sans le reconnaître" (*Moderato* 64); "Anne Desbaresdes releva ses mains vers son cou nu . . ."; "Chauvin resta assis, accablé, il ne la connut plus" (*Moderato* 65).

Anne and Chauvin murder their consciousness of being (someone) by negating their means of recognizing (the objects of) their sensations: society's conventional descriptive discourse on social space. After Anne returns home drunk and late to her own dinner party and as Chauvin roams outside on the beach, her upper-class sensations of the inside of her home and his lower-class sensations of the outside become oxymoronic figures of each other. Tastes and smells of her elite social world become indistinguishable from signs of his working-class world, and vice versa: "le Pommard continue d'avoir ce soir la saveur anéantissante des lèvres inconnues d'un homme de la rue" (*Moderato* 71); "Elle soulève une nouvelle fois sa main à hauteur de la fleur qui se fane entre ses seins et dont l'odeur franchit le parc et va jusqu' à la mer" (*Moderato* 73); "L'encens des magnolias arrive toujours sur lui, au gré du vent, et le surprend et le harcèle autant que celui d'une seule fleur" (*Moderato* 70).

In the lovers' minds, upper-class dining room and public beach lose their symbolic class meaning. Ceasing to signify fixed class relationships, inside and outside take on differential exchange values as consumable and disposable commodities (Baudrillard 53-59, 66-68), not unlike the prostitute (Irigaray 171, 181) to which Chauvin has compared Anne and to which the narrator has implicitly compared the wives at the dinner party: "Les hommes . . . couvrirent [leurs femmes] de bijoux au prorata de leurs bilans. L'un d'eux, ce soir, doute qu'il eût raison" (*Moderato* 70). Anne prefers to see herself for what she and the other wives are, commodities. She thus identifies with the gradually disappearing food they consume: "le saumon . . . continue sa marche inéluctable vers sa totale disparition" (*Moderato* 67-68; see Willis 158 on the implications of orality in this scene); "Anne Desbaresdes implorera qu'on l'oublie"; "Anne s'éclipsera, montera au premier étage." Effacement of signs of class identity culminates in Anne's forgetting of and being forgotten by, not only her class, but her worker: "Elle regardera le boulevard par la baie du grand couloir de sa vie. L'homme l'aura déjà déserté. Elle ira dans la chambre de son enfant, s'allongera par terre, au pied de son lit, sans égard pour ce magnolia qu'elle écrasera entre ses seins" (*Moderato* 75).[18]

By trying to forget their socially-imposed identities, Anne and Chauvin deny any consciousness of gender, as well as class, difference.[19] When they first met in the café, he offered her a drink and seduced her, or so it appears, into satisfying their desire to kill her identity. But when they last meet, "Ce fut Anne Desbaresdes qui se rapproacha de Chauvin" (*Moderato* 78). She kisses, seduces, and leaves him.[20] In her mind, as in his, he is as much the object of seduction and the producer of desire as she. She is as much its agent and consumer as he. The speech act of seduction has become reversible. But if that is true, it can no longer be said that an act of seduction, a crime, has taken place at all.[21] Indeed, when Anne leaves the café, she disposes of Chauvin the way a man might dispose of a prostitute after he has finished with her. She simply becomes indifferent to him, the way he will become indifferent to her: "elle ne le vit pas, ayant déjà quitté le champ où il se trouvait" (*Moderato* 84). Forgetting the social parameters of class and gender identity, Anne forgets identity itself. Her seemingly stable class relationship with a worker becomes what Fredric Jameson characterizes as a "coexistence of . . . sealed subjective worlds and their peculiar interaction, which is in reality a passage of ships in the night."[22]

The last chapter of *Moderato* seems to transform the café into a mental space (Anne's and Chauvin's) in which all class and gender differences are reversed. Like the murdered woman's dying cry or Anne's (false) memory of having screamed when her son was born, signs of the emergence of life (the pleasure, presence, memory, and difference of a touch and kiss) become indistinguishable from signs of its disappearance (pain, absence, forgetting, and indifference) (Moskos 33, 40). The café, or rather its description, takes on the appearance of a juxtaposition of contrary, logically reversible, signs in which identity and difference die, but where art (the story of this death) and life (the desire to die or the consciousness of dying) coincide (Hamon, *Introduction* 253-55).

However Anne's departure from the café puts this inner fusion of art and life—whether or not it be called feminine—into question. After the dinner party, Anne vomits not only the food she has eaten at home, but the wine she has drunk in the café. The café like the home, the lover like the husband, the male like the female, all become equally disposable, exchangeable, and forgettable commodities. Entry into the café demystified the husband's discourse on the production of a fixed differential world because the wife bought into the worker's counter-discourse on a mental world in which binary distinctions are reversed and consumed. Departure from the café disposes of the worker's counter-discourse, as one might throw away a used-up commodity. Whereas the café enabled Anne to create a mental space that negated the hier-

archical differences structuring her husband's world, it now leads her to question the negative space of desire with which she replaces this world, and, by extension, any romantic, surrealist, or feminine attributes of self that one might associate with it.

If neither the husband's description of an exterior space of social life nor the worker's description of an inner space of death and anonymity are referential, then are both fundamentally homogeneous and meaningless? Does Anne work through her mourning by recognizing that Chauvin's discourse on an inner space is simply one more commodity to be consumed and rejected in a contemporary market of signs?[23] Is the inner world of Duras's "amour absolu" simply one more metaphor of desire in a world market, where the social fiction of the group and the psychological fiction of the desiring or conscious individual are equally disposable, and fundamentally homogeneous, commodities (Jameson 412-13)?

Neither this reading of Duras's café as a commodified, empty space nor its reading as a privileged space of desire can account for the return of narrative signs of difference and of linear historical time at the end of the novel.[24] Anne goes back, it would appear, to her husband. Because she has encouraged her son to rebel against his piano teacher's discipline and left him to play untended while conversing and drinking with an unemployed worker, her husband has decided that someone else, someone who obeys and enforces society's differential codes, must accompany the child to his piano lessons. This reappearance of discipline subordinates the space of the child's and mother's present consuming pleasure to the production of a future social skill, playing the piano. It posits a temporal difference between present ignorance and future knowledge. Descriptive space gives way to the appearance of a narrative transformation.

When Anne leaves the café, Duras's description of an inner space, in which all exterior differences are erased, thus does not give way to the description of the commodified space of a world market. Rather, the very categories of space and of the descriptive seem to be transformed into narrative functions, into means by which Anne completes the process of mourning, of rejecting the ahistorical, inner space of her desire for the temporal and historical reality of the world in which she lives with her husband.[25] This return to narrative, an apparent resolution of the mourning process, is highly ambiguous. Is it a mere repetition of Anne's initial repression of desire, one imposed on her by her husband? Or is it a real choice to subordinate desire to action and historical change, as Sartre's Roquentin leaves his café to act, by writing a book?

Much of Duras's writing after *Moderato* might be read as a repetition of and meditation on Anne's ambiguous departure from a negative space of desire like the café. *Emily L.* interprets this departure, and with it Duras's tendency to transform the descriptive into the narrative, as marks of an irreducible gap between desire and writing. This gap prevents life and art from coinciding as they seem to do in the traditional literary café. *Emily L.* interprets departure from the café as a mourning both of the death of writing in Duras's negative space of desire and of the death of desire in the time of writing.

From the beginning of *Emily L.,* writing and desire seem to inhabit discrete spaces. Inside a café are two non-working consumers, here perpetual consumers: a wealthy woman and the husband who captains her yacht. They spend their leisurely life traveling from Asian port to Asian port, café to café, drink to drink, purchasing desire and dream. Outside the café is a working port, here a real-world market port, Quillebuf, with its river Seine, oil tankers, Asian sailors and tourists. Mediating between the fiction-producing inside of the café (Membrado 48) and its historical, working outside are the first-person narrator, a working writer, and her writer/companion, whose names, like those of wife and captain, are not given. The writing couple's entry marks their temporary abandonment of the space of writing—the home—for a space of desire and fiction, the café. In their minds, the café is not a place to drink and forget, as it is for Anne or the wealthy couple; rather it is a place to remember, think, and converse as in the original cafés. But it is not a place to write. When the writing couple goes home to write, therefore, they repeat their implicit renunciation of desire, fiction, and life within the café. Because they resemble Duras and her male companion, Yann Andréa, entry and desire coincide with an effacement of the autobiographical and historical context of the novel. Withdrawal and writing coincide with its reinscription.[26]

The aging narrator enters the Quillebuf café out of a fear of death: "ça avait commencé par la peur" (*Emily* 9). Asian tourists or sailors make her fear that civilization itself will die: "'La mort sera japonaise. La mort du monde. Elle viendra de Corée'" (*Emily* 14). The death of civilization means the destruction of difference and the advent of commodification and cruel indifference: "'Ces gens paraissent n'avoir qu'un seul et même visage, c'est pourquoi ils sont effrayants'" (*Emily* 11); "'Voyez comme ils sont indifférents'" (*Emily* 46). But flight from death outside only brings the narrator face to face, inside, with her desire for death and, eventually, with her mourning.

Whereas entry into the café in *Moderato* seems to abandon historical signs outside for an ahistorical poetics of death and desire inside the café, entry into *Emily*'s café unveils a life-or-death struggle between history and fiction, writing and desire (Ladimer 63). Desire, the narrator tells her companion, blocks writing: "'Ce qui m'empêche d'écrire, c'est vous'" (*Emily* 56). But writing, like the world market outside, kills desire: "'Quand j'écris, je ne vous aime plus'" (*Emily* 26). There results a double fear: that desire will kill writing—"'C'est la peur, vous croyez?'" (*Emily* 57)—and that writing will kill desire—"'Ce sont des mots qui font peur'" (*Emily* 27; Ladimer 65). The battle between the historical outside of the café and its ahistorical inside, market and desire, thus figures a

struggle inside between writing narrator and desired companion. This struggle in turn represents a sado-masochistic conflict within the narrator herself, between the writer and the lover (Ramsay 94): "'c'est une cruauté nue, muette, de moi à moi'" (*Emily* 51). And this mental conflict can be traced back to a real sado-masochistic struggle between Duras's desiring mother, who beat her, and the writing career with which she, like Anne's child, devours her mother: "la scène où une mère battait son enfant, se transforme en désir d'une scène où un enfant battrait sa mère."[27]

The inside of *Emily L.*'s café is a place where the writing narrator mourns the death of desire and mother. Within the autobiographical story she later writes at home—the one we are theoretically reading ("j'avais décidé notre histoire" [*Emily* 21])—she embeds the fictional story of the wealthy woman, dubbed Emily L., and her lover, the Captain, whom she and her companion see drinking at the bar and whose story they invent. Unlike the narrator, Emily has chosen desire over writing, or so the writers imagine. As a result, she spends her life mourning the writing self she has killed.

The narrator's story of Emily's life is a performative allegory. Like Anne, the narrator constructs, and recounts the construction of, a negative descriptive space, one in which her writing self, rather than just social and gender selves, dies. This space is a narcissistic, as well as sensual, space. Not only does the narrator identify with Emily's choice of desire over writing, she desires Emily physically ("j'éprouve pour elle une sorte de désir" [*Emily* 131]) as the male murderer desired the murdered woman in *Moderato* (Ramsay 98): "Je la regarde, elle, la femme du bar. Je pense que j'aurais pu prendre son bourbon et le boire. . . . Je sais mal pourquoi j'aurais fait ça, qui aurait été dangereux pour moi. Peut-être le désir de cette peau de sel, de l'odeur marine et gercée de sa bouche sur le verre" (*Emily* 96-97). In the narrator's visual image of the anonymous woman at the bar, she combines identification and sensual desire to construct the portrait of a self-destructive woman, a portrait that recalls the author's gaze at her mother and at herself during her bouts with alcoholism.[28]

For Emily and the Captain, the café is a place where entry has become a departure, life a death, writing an erasure: "On aurait dit des plantes, des choses comme ça, intermédiaires, des sortes de végétaux, des plantes humaines, à peine nées que déjà mourantes, à peine vivantes que déjà mortes" (*Emily* 17). Their entry into each successive café simply prepares their departure and prefigures the departure of those Emily has known: "'Vous voyez, Madame,'" the Captain tells the narrator, "'c'est le malheur de cette vie que nous avons sur la mer, ces personnes des cafés et des restaurants que nous connaissons si bien, qui sont nos amis, et qui nous laissent, qui quittent l'endroit ou qui meurent. . . .'" (*Emily* 34). By going from café to café, Emily, like the departing Anne (who seems to have forgotten Chauvin), tries to erase even the story of her life of erasure: "ce sont les histoires les plus terribles, celles qui ne s'avouent jamais, qui se vivent sans certitude aucune, jamais" (*Emily* 56).

Flight enables Emily to forget, repeatedly, the murder of her writing self. She yielded to the Captain's jealous hate of her writing after he began to fear that it was destroying her desire for him: "Rien n'apparaissait de leur vie, de leur amour, de leur bonheur" (*Emily* 83). She quits writing altogether after he burns, unbeknownst to her, her last and incomplete poem about the winter light: "le criminel qui avait assassiné Emily L., c'était le Captain" (*Emily* 124-25). But Emily is not only a victim; she is also an accomplice in her own murder. She thus prefers to deny the very existence of the published volume of her poems: "'Pour moi, ce livre n'existe pas'" (*Emily* 117). It is she who pays for the endless voyage on which her husband captains her boat (*Emily* 130), a voyage through Asia where her growing, European reputation as a poet poses no threat to her forgetting. The husband simply captains the poet's search to erase any trace of her writing self. Together, they perform a murder and suicide whose story the narrator now invents.

In the narrator's fable, Emily forgets her writing self in order to carve out an imaginary space that preserves her desire to write (Hofmann 31).[29] Emily only appears to devote her life to her love for the Captain: "'Contrairement à toutes les apparences, je ne suis pas une femme qui se livre corps et âme à l'amour d'un seul être, fût-il celui qui lui est le plus cher au monde'" (*Emily* 135). Her love is a more abstract desire: "'il fallait toujours garder par-devers soi . . . une sorte d'endroit personnel . . . pour aimer . . .'" (*Emily* 135). In Emily's imaginary, private space, she preserves a desire for an ideal nurturing reader who, unlike the Captain, encourages rather than discourages her writing. She once found such a reader in the young caretaker of her family home. It was he who first showed her the volume of her poems that her father had published on her behalf and it was he who later dubbed her Emily L. "'Vous voulez dire,'" she told him, "'que, même sans rien savoir de l'histoire, si vous, vous l'aviez trouvé [the poem burnt by the Captain], que ce soit avant ou après la mort de mon père, il serait dans le recueil?'" (*Emily* 119). She kissed her ideal reader once, then, like Anne, left him forever: "'Ne gardez aucun espoir de me voir'" (*Emily* 136).

In the inner "endroit personnel" that Emily carries from café to café, she mourns her desire to write. She flees the caretaker in order to preserve his memory, a metaphor for her desire to write that she no longer reads: "'Vous êtes devenu à vous seul la face extérieure de ma vie, celle que je ne vois jamais'" (*Emily* 135-36). By effacing yet preserving her desire, forgetting transforms her personal place into "'la place . . . de l'attente d'un amour, . . . de l'amour'" (*Emily* 135). The desire for "un amour," the desire to write, becomes a desire for "l'amour," a desire for desire, where desire is subject as well as object: "'Je voulais vous dire que vous étiez cette attente'" (*Emily* 135). Emily thus erases her desire to write (which she associates with father and caretaker) and identifies with a desire for desire itself, just as the narrator, in her visual space, identifies with and desires Emily's desire.

The desire for desire in Emily's "endroit personnel" recalls the self-sufficient space that Duras criticism has associated with the feminine ("'L.'*elle*" [Ladimer 71]) and the body (Willis 168). This theoretically feminine space is constituted by a "permeability of self boundaries" between mother and daughter (Ramsay 97). Like Anne's final indifference to distinctions between home and café, Emily's "endroit personnel" presupposes the logical reversibility that grounds some contemporary definitions of the descriptive. Desire for desire performs yet defers, effaces yet preserves, satisfaction. Continually reversing polarities, it encloses yet preserves time within a dynamic, rather than a static, space. In the manner of a perpetual motion machine, desire for desire theoretically produces the same quantity of energy it consumes. If it exists, desire for desire overcomes narrative, entropy, temporal change, and death.

Emily can enclose her mind within Duras's ahistorical and reversible space only by endlessly fleeing one consumer space, like the café, after another. She must repurchase and reconsume her feeling of desiring only desire by repeatedly repressing, and preserving, her grief over the writing self she has killed. Sometimes she expresses her grief indirectly, by mourning the loss of her dog: "Elle . . . est toujours à chercher Bownie, elle l'appelle tout bas. *Here, boy.* Elle pleure. Puis elle oublie . . ." (*Emily* 131); "elle dit au Captain qu'il devrait la laisser parler de Bownie de temps en temps, qu'elle finirait comme ça par moins en souffrir" (*Emily* 140). Saturating herself with alcohol, she awaits departure and blinds herself to her flight, to the signs of death that time writes on her aging body, to the "jour qui se consume," and to the "train de pétroliers descend[ant] vers la mer" (*Emily* 54, 32, 131) outside the café.

The oil tankers, dying day, and "la mort . . . à nu sous . . . la peau" (*Emily* 32) that Emily refuses to see are unwelcome reminders that, according to the law of entropy, consumption inevitably outstrips individual and social production. Whether it be conceived as a private mental space or a homogeneous world market space that consumes its own consumption, desire for desire necessarily produces its own historical demise. Behind Emily's "humilité devant la mort," therefore, hides her repeated murder of her writing self (*Emily* 19). Like the cruel Asiatics who, according to the narrator, "s'amusaient à écraser les chiens" (*Emily* 47), she consumes her producing self in order to chase the illusion that this self, the desire to write, will never die.

While the narrator's imaginary Emily pursues the fleeting illusion of a self-consuming, self-producing space, the narrator repeatedly tries to renounce the visual space that links her to, yet separates her from, Emily. She wants neither "'d' . . . appeler [un amour au secours], ni d'en espérer. Seulement d'en écrire'" (*Emily* 138). Her writing is not the expression of a prior or present desire for desire. It is the production of a text about desire that defers desire.

The narrator explores what it means to write "about" desire when she discusses Emily's lost poem describing the pale winter light. If we interpret the rays of light as metaphors for a writing that "illuminates" desire, then writing, like Anne's allegory, destroys the very differences it illuminates, the differences that create desire: "les blessures que nous faisaient ces mêmes épées de soleil . . . ne nous blessaient ni ne nous soulageaient" (*Emily* 85). The poetic illumination of desire neither wounds nor consoles writer or reader. It is a reversible speech act which, like desire in Emily's "endroit personnel," produces indifference to what words do. But whereas Emily's desire for desire blinds itself to the indifference it produces, writing's illumination of desire accepts this indifference and renounces desire. Renunciation of difference is itself a "blessure" that produces "la perception de la dernière différence: celle, interne, au centre des significations" (*Emily* 85). By illuminating desire's reversibility and indifference, descriptive writing paradoxically awakens a last difference, a desire for a future end: "c'est seulement l'idée de la mort qui réveille" (*Emily* 61).

The identity of this final difference may be inferred, I believe, from the despair it discloses: "cette différence interne était atteinte par le désespoir souverain dont elle était en quelque sorte le sceau" (*Emily* 85). Despair, an insurmountable obstacle to the resolution of mourning, arises in *Emily L.* out of the unbridgeable gap between the lover's desire for desire (which kills writing) and the writer's description of desire (which kills yet reproduces desire). The desire to write and the writing of desire cannot be united in a spatial metaphor, such as Anne's visual memory of the dead lover, Emily's "endroit personnel," the narrator's vision of Emily, or Duras's memories of her mother or her self. Desire and writing can coincide only metonymically, like companions rather than lovers: "Le jeune gardien était sûr aussi que c'était elle, Emily L., qui avait été là, dans la pièce, à écrire, quand le poème s'était fait" (*Emily* 123-24).

In order to write, the narrator must renounce her desire for a metaphorical relationship between writing and desire, daughter and mother: her desire for a metaphor that eliminates her writing self.[30] Feminine writing, if it exists in Duras, is a repeated matricide, the murder and mourning of a fantasized maternal space outside writing and narrative.[31] Rather than try to preserve desire by clinging to the fantasy of an inner space, a body, or a fetishized past text, the writer mourns the death of this fantasy by accepting her complicity in bringing about its demise.[32]

After stating her decision to write "notre histoire," therefore, the narrator, upon returning home to write, recounts her renunciation of "un amour" ("'Je ne vous aime plus'"), then her replacement of love for Yann with love for Emily's desire for desire ("l'amour"), finally her renunciation of desire itself when she left the café (*Emily* 21, 27). But renunciation reproduces desire, if as a temporally discontinuous future rather than the temporal duration of a present and preserved space: "'Je crois sincèrement que j'aurais pu ne pas vous aimer. Puis ça revient'" (*Emily* 137). Effacement and repetition demystify and temporalize the fiction of a space of desire.

The narrator's relationship to her companion plays out the metonymical difference between writing and desire, art and life. They can leave the café and go home together precisely because he is neither a nurturing reader like the caretaker nor a jealous lover like the Captain. Or he is both. His alternation between supporting and obstructing her writing helps maintain her despairing awareness of the gap between writing and desire. It prevents her from staying and drinking in the café (she orders tea) but also from remaining home to write: "je suis toujours près de vous dans le désespoir que je vous procure" (*Emily* 25). *Emily L.* ends with the two writers' return to the place where they, like writing and desire, co-exist metonymically in separate bedrooms. This metonymical space is temporalized by the falling asleep and the reawakening of desire: "Votre corps et le mien ont été dans le même endroit, enfermés. . . . Et puis je me suis réveillée. . . . J'ai été à votre porte . . ." (*Emily* 152-53). The writer's home is constantly ceasing to be a descriptive production of space and becoming, but never quite being, a narrative of temporal change, of its own writing of desire: "'Notre histoire . . . ne sera jamais tout à fait écrite'" (*Emily* 55).

If writing in Duras mourns the death of the fantasy of a feminine descriptive space in which writing and desire are metaphors, if it repeatedly takes on the appearance of a seemingly male, irreversible, historical, autobiographical act of narrative transformation ("'Cette histoire, encore . . .'"), this repetition is no more a representation of the real than is the novel's repetition of descriptive appearance (Ramsay 98): "'Ce n'est pas possible'" (*Emily* 22). Duras cannot say that her allegory of desire is motivated by an irreversible masculine desire to enter into and appropriate a feminine, descriptive space of desire any more than by a feminine desire for narrative to die and be reborn (Selous 83, 235): "Comment on arrive à le faire, je ne sais pas non plus, ni pourquoi" (*Emily* 57). To write about desire is to write about a Beckettian impossibility and necessity of expressing desire in writing:[33] "ce n'était pas assez . . . de faire accroire que c'était sans pensée aucune, guidé seulement par la main, de même que c'était trop d'écrire avec seulement la pensée en tête qui surveille l'activité de la folie" (*Emily* 153).

Duras's most recent novels signify her renunciation of desire, I believe, not only by an apparent return to narrative, but also by marks of the autobiographical and social historical context of the text (Vircondelet 418). *Emily L.* ends with signs of linear time ("le fleuve coulait dans les eaux de la mer"), linear writing ("il fallait écrire sans correction"), and the destruction of monopoly capitalism and imperialism ("l'usine allemande, immense, évidée, aux vitres détruites"): "ce que j'écris en ce moment, c'est autre chose dans quoi [notre histoire] serait incluse, perdue, quelque chose de beaucoup plus large peut-être . . ." (*Emily* 151, 153, 145, 22-23).

The evolution of Duras's writing on the café from *Moderato*'s deceptive formalism—in which form and content, writing and desire, seem to be substitutable metaphors—to

Emily L.'s apparent fragmentation and referential illu-
~~s~~ion—in which desire and historical writing are clearly
~~m~~etonymical—repeats the same renunciation of the nega-
~~ti~~ve descriptive space of life that both novels on the café
~~li~~nk to, yet separate from, art. Whether descriptive space
~~b~~e interpreted in realist terms as a fixed differential struc-
~~tu~~re or in more contemporary terms as a reversible indif-
~~fe~~rent one, as satisfaction of or as desire for desire, it is an
~~ar~~tificial construct that can only repeat the temporal signs
~~it~~ erases. It would appear that Duras's novels are always
~~to~~o late to be descriptions of an inner, feminine space of
~~de~~sire or an exterior, market space of commodification.
~~B~~ut they are always too early to be a narrative of temporal
~~or~~ historical change. They are too late to be a literary café
~~an~~d too early to be an historical event in which writing
~~an~~d life coincide.

Notes

1. Marguerite Duras, *Emily L.* (Paris: Minuit, 1987).
   All quotations from Duras's novels will be followed
   by a shortened title and the page number in
   parentheses.

2. Luce Irigaray, *Ce sexe qui n'en est pas un* (Paris:
   Minuit, 1977) 26. See Sharon Willis, *Marguerite
   Duras: Writing on the Body* (Urbana: U of Illinois P,
   1987) 27-31, for a discussion of the feminine as
   maternal and the maternal as "the mouth as locus of
   speech, incorporation and expulsion, acceptance or
   refusal of food" in Duras's texts. Also see 167-69
   for a discussion of the spatial. Many Duras scholars
   seem to take for granted that this space exists and
   that it is feminine in essence. I will question its
   existence. See Philippe Hamon, *Introduction à
   l'analyse du descriptif* (Paris: Hachette, 1981) for a
   discussion of the relation between fictional space
   and descriptive space.

3. Marguerite Duras, *Le Ravissement de Lol V. Stein*
   (Paris: Gallimard, 1964).

4. Gérard-Georges Lemaire, *Les Cafés littéraires*
   (Paris: Henri Veyrier, 1987) 31.

5. François Fosca, *Histoire des cafés de Paris* (Paris:
   Firmin-Didot, 1934) 66-69; Peter Stallybrass and
   Allon White, *The Politics and Poetics of
   Transgression* (Ithaca: Cornell UP, 1986) 94.

6. Monique Membrado, *Poétique des cafés* (Paris:
   Publisud, 1989) 16. To the best of my knowledge
   Membrado's work is the only extant study that
   interprets the ways in which the space of the café
   functions in French literature. Although Membrado
   does not treat the question of an inner descriptive
   space, her Bachelardian analysis does provide
   evidence that many twentieth-century novels have
   questioned the traditional notion of the café.

7. Marguerite Duras, *Le Square* (Paris: Gallimard,
   1955).

8. Jean-Paul Sartre, *La Nausée* (Paris: Gallimard,
   1938) 16.

9. Jean Baudrillard, *For a Critique of the Political
   Economy of the Sign,* trans. Charles Levin (St.
   Louis: Telos, 1981) 29.

10. J. L. Austin, *How to Do Things with Words*
    (Cambridge: Harvard UP, 1962) 6, 14; Stanley J.
    Tambiah, "A Performative Approach to Ritual,"
    Proceedings of the British Academy 65 (1979)
    113-69.

11. The café "was an important instrument in the
    regulation of the body, manners and morals of its
    clientele in the public sphere" (Stallybrass 96).

12. Philippe Hamon, *Le Personnel du roman* (Geneva:
    Droz, 1983) 32.

13. Marguerite Duras, *Moderato cantabile* (Paris:
    Minuit, 1958).

14. Evelyn H. Zepp, "Language as Ritual in Marguerite
    Duras's *Moderato cantabile,*" *Symposium* 30 (1976)
    236-59 (242).

15. André Breton, *Nadja* (Paris: Gallimard, 1964). See
    in particular the following statements made in cafés.
    On anonymity: "Elle me dit son nom, celui qu'elle
    s'est choisi . . ." (74); "'Qui êtes-vous?' Et elle,
    sans hésiter: 'Je suis l'âme errante'" (81). On death:
    "Nadja commence à regarder autour d'elle. Elle est
    certaine que sous nos pieds passe un souterrain. . . .
    'Et les morts, les morts!' . . . 'Il y avait aussi une
    voix qui disait: Tu mourras, tu mourras'" (94).

16. Irène Pagès, "*Moderato cantabile, L'Amant,* et le
    non-dit, ou dans les trous du discours," *French
    Literature Series* 16 (1989) 141-48.

17. Raylene Ramsay, "Through a Textual Glass, Darkly:
    The Masochistic in the Feminine Self and
    Marguerite Duras' *Emily L.,*" *Atlantis* 17 (1991)
    91-104 (93).

18. Marianne Hirsch, "Gender, Reading, and Desire in
    Moderato cantabile," *Twentieth Century Literature*
    28 (1982) 69-85 (82).

19. See Leslie Hill, "Marguerite Duras: Sexual
    Difference and Tales of Apocalypse," *Modern
    Language Review* 84 (1989) 601-14.

20. George Moskos, "Women and Fiction in Marguerite
    Duras's *Moderato cantabile,*" *Contemporary
    Literature* 25 (1984) 28-52 (29-30, 50).

21. Anne Tomiche, "Writing and Crime: A Reading of
    an Article Published by Marguerite Duras in
    Libération," *Romance Languages Annual* 1 (1989)
    337-42 (340).

22. Fredric Jameson, *Postmodernism: Or the Cultural
    Logic of Late Capitalism* (Durham: Duke UP, 1991)
    412.

23. "We must therefore also posit another type of
    consumption: consumption of the very process of
    consumption itself, above and beyond its content
    and the immediate commercial products" (Jameson
    276).

24. Roger McLure, "Duras *contra* Bergson: Time in *Moderato cantabile*," *Forum for Modern Language Studies* 25 (1989) 62-76 (75).

25. For an interpretation of the descriptive as a narrative function, see A.-J. Greimas, *Du sens II,* 2 vols. (Paris: Seuil, 1970-83) 2: 144 ff.

26. Bethany Ladimer, "The Space of a Woman's Autobiography in *Emily L.,*" *Dalhousie French Studies* 18 (1990) 61-80 (62).

27. Madeleine Borgomano, *Duras: une lecture des fantasmes* (Petit-Rulx: Cistre, 1985) 172; see also Carol Murphy, "Duras's 'Beast in the Jungle': Writing Fear (Or Fear of Writing) in *Emily L.,*" *Neophilologus* 75 (1991) 539-47 (544), and Moscos 43.

28. Carol Hofmann, *Forgetting and Marguerite Duras* (Niwot: U of Colorado P, 1991) 26; Alain Vircondelet, *Duras* (Paris: François Bourin, 1991) 61. For the café as narcissistic mirror, see Membrado 90.

29. "Le café est à la fois ce lieu du transitoire—on ne l'habite pas—et de l'immuable—on veut le croire et s'y croire éternel . . ." (Membrado 18).

30. Melanie Klein, "Mourning and Its Relation to Manic-Depressive States," *Love, Guilt and Reparation* (New York: Dell, 1977) 344-69 (352).

31. Barbara Johnson, "My Monster/My Self," *Diacritics* 12.2 (1982) 2-10 (8). See also Ramsay 97; Hofmann 150.

32. Trista Selous, *The Other Woman: Feminism and Femininity in the Work of Marguerite Duras* (New Haven: Yale UP, 1988) 147.

33. ". . . [t]here is nothing to express, nothing with which to express, nothing from which to express, no power to express, no desire to express, together with the obligation to express." Samuel Beckett, "Three Dialogues," *Samuel Beckett* (Englewood Cliffs, NJ: Prentice-Hall, 1965) 16-22 (17).

Graham Dunstan Martin (essay date 1994)

SOURCE: "The Drive for Power in Marguerite Duras' 'L'Amant,'" in *Forum for Modern Language Studies,* Vol. XXX, No. 3, July, 1994, pp. 204-18.

[*In the following essay, Martin examines power in* The Lover *as it is used by and against the narrator.*]

The nature of power has not been discussed in relation to *L'Amant.*[1] Power evokes desire, obedience, the forbidden, terror and fear, especially the fear of suffering and death; it is rendered still more powerful when those who provoke desire do not entirely reciprocate it; when there is conflict with the pleasure principle; when the forbidden is no longer kept secret but deliberately rendered public. It is on the basis of these thoughts that I propose to examin *L'Amant* and the power relationships in this autobiographi cal novel.[2] I shall focus first on the origins of the heroine drive for power, seen in the complex nature of her rela tionships with her mother, her brothers and her Chines lover. I shall then explore the heroine's power itself: ho it is exercised over others and over society; finally I sha examine her violence against herself.

Let us begin with the appalling *silence* in the heroine family. It expresses hatred and is the result of fear.

> Jamais bonjour, bonsoir, bonne année. Jamais parler. Jamais besoin de parler. Tout reste, muet, loin. C'est une famille en pierre, pétrifiée dans une épaisseur sans accès aucun. Chaque jour nous essayons de nous tuer, de tuer. Non seulement on ne se parle pas mais on ne se regarde pas. Du moment qu'on est vu, on ne peut pas regarder. Regarder c'est avoir un mouvement de curiosité, c'est déchoir. Aucune personne regardée ne vaut le regard sur elle. Il est toujours déshonorant.
>
> (*A* 69)

Silence is seen as expressing hostility to the other mem bers of the family. She notes the absence of what Mal nowski called "phatic communion". This he defined a "meaningless" verbal gestures, such as words like "bo jour"—which in fact rather express ordinary human goo will. Communication, even at the visual level, has reache absolute zero. The absence of reciprocal gaze implies th (1) to allow someone close is to become perilously vulne able, (2) one must be self-sufficient to prevent shame, ar (3) one must feel indifference for others. But it must als be added: if being looked at dishonours you, then there an implicit challenge here which might lead to a reactior

The family, and particularly the mother, are depicted a having victim status. But why should the evil done to th family from outside it *necessarily* tear the family apar rather than binding it closer together? The explanation insufficient. On investigation of the family relationshij one sees that they are imbued with cruelty, violence ar contempt. The children thieve from their mother, which usually a sign of unmet need, of lack of love. It is lov which is being, symbolically, stolen (*A* 32).

> The two sons continually fight each other with alarm ing savagery. The elder brother
>
> dit au petit: sors de là, tu gênes. Aussitôt dit, il frappe. [. . .] Quand ils se battaient on avait une peur égale de la mort pour l'un et pour l'autre.
>
> (*A* 74-5)
>
> [La mère] a toujours parlé de la force de ses fils de façon insultante. [. . .] Elle était fière de la force de ses fils [. . .] Comme son fils aîné elle dédaignait les faibles.
>
> (*A* 71-2)

The mother's failure to intervene when they fight, h melodramatic shrieking while they do so, points to her b sic incapacity to cope. The noise she makes *encourages* their behaviour, since it effectively makes them the centre of attention. Her weakness is therefore in part responsible for the violence of her sons. So is her overt favouritism. It is only of the elder brother (Pierre) that the mother says "mon enfant" (*A* 75). This of the most violent member of the family, who terrorises his younger brother (Paulo). She says of him

> Que s'il avait voulu c'était le plus intelligent des trois. Le plus "artiste". [. . .] Et aussi celui qui a le plus aimé sa mère. [. . .] Je ne savais pas, disait-elle, qu'on pouvait attendre ça d'un garçon, une telle intuition, une tendresse si profonde.
>
> (*A* 98)

On her request, he ends up buried with her. "L'image est d'une intolérable splendeur," writes Duras (*A* 99). One almost suspects incest, one of the locuses of silence and secrecy in this family. But, incest or no incest, the complicity between mother and elder son is an enormity. To single Pierre out as "her only child" constitutes a cruelty practised by the mother against her younger children. The indictment is clear, the implications tragic.

Not only are relations with the living impossible, so also are relations with the dead. It is explicitly said that no death is celebrated in the family (*A* 72). This refers most obviously to the dead father, and the fact that he is not mentioned in so many words is an act of concealment which demonstrates that the failure to celebrate his death has particular significance. Perhaps this is the resentment of his wife against him for his death, more probably for something else (for she failed to return with him to France [*A* 41]). Here is yet another unforgiving silence, likely to have had an important effect upon the 15½-year-old narrator.

No situation could be more full of dramatic suspense than this theatre of silence interrupted occasionally and unpredictably by an angry and hysterical screaming. The very fact that the family *does not* look, *does not* speak, *does not* listen, paradoxically shows that attention, watching, speaking, reveal hidden sources of power—which will in due course be used by the heroine.

Because both younger son and daughter know themselves to be unloved, this is a likely source of inferiority feelings, which may lead to a desire for compensatory power. In Alfred Alder's psychology, the Inferiority Complex arises from continuous humiliation (whether real or merely perceived). "The neglected, the hated, the undesired and the ugly" may, as children, contract the Inferiority Complex very easily (Orgler 69-71).[3] Adler writes:

> When the feeling of inferiority is intensified to the degree that the child fears she will never be able to overcome her weakness, the danger arises that [. . .] she will not be satisfied with a simple restoration of the balance of power. She will seek to tip the scales in the opposite direction. In such cases the striving for power

and dominance may become so exaggerated [. . .] that it must be called pathological, and the ordinary relationships of life will never be satisfactory.

> (*UHN* 71)[4]

The members of the family are deprived of love, care, concern and approval. They will therefore try (as Adler suggests) to compensate for this lack by seeking weapons of power. There is a power-vacuum in this family, and the children seek to fill it. The weapons of the elder brother (Pierre) are crude: sudden explosive anger, physical brutality. The heroine's tussle with her mother, however, takes subtle, unexpected paths, which ultimately bring a terrifying potency.

The mother takes care to demean the heroine. She takes pleasure in her daughter's dressing, not merely badly, but absurdly: the man's hat, the gold lamé shoes, the cheap prostitute's get-up: "Elle me regarde, ça lui plaît, elle sourit. [. . .] Elle doit trouver que c'est un signe réconfortant cette imagination de la petite, d'inventer de s'habiller de cette façon. [. . .] Cette inconvenance lui plaît" (*A* 32-3). In other words she finds the clothes make her daughter a laughing-stock; and she herself is amused and delighted by this. The heroine, however, uses this absurd dress to take vengeance on her mother. Wearing it with panache, she openly flaunts the whore-status her mother has imposed on her. She goes further, she acts out this accusation, using her outlandish clothes to land the Chinese millionaire's son. At only 15½ it shows some power to turn the insult round and transform it into a victory! Moreover this adds doubly to her self-esteem, because it is she and she alone who turns the clothes to her advantage, she who achieves it through her own personal magnetism. Besides, the narrator uses this episode as revenge in her novel to underline the mother's lack of taste, lack of social know-how, lack of concern for her children's (and daughter's) welfare, thereby asserting her superiority over her mother after the latter's death.

When the mother interrogates her daughter about her relationship with the Chinese, she repeatedly beats her (*A* 72-4). Physical violence is here (as so often) a sign of weakness, and of fear: it stems from the terror of being unable to control the world. She elicits no confession, and her daughter is still denying at the end of the book that she actually sleeps with the Chinese (*A* 114). Duras writes:

> Derrière les murs de la chambre fermée, le frère.
>
> Le frère répond à la mère, il lui dit qu'elle a raison de battre l'enfant [. . .]
>
> (*A* 73)

The mother's complicity with Pierre's violence is again confirmed. As with the scene where she accompanies her sons' fighting with "un opéra de cris" (*A* 75), so in this case the mother is incapable of anything but a hysterical, noisy fuss, which simply underlines the power of her daughter, and her freedom to do what she likes. When she strips her, this emphasises how exciting and important her body is! The daughter's sense of power is reinforced. Here are (1) parental authority, (2) anger, (3) physical violence, helpless before "l'enfant/la petite". The elder brother's threatening presence outside the closed door also constitutes *attention,* and provides the heroine with an exciting feeling of power. The mother's behaviour, both in respect of this interrogation of her daughter and of her sons' violence, is in fact contradictory: it is calculated to have an effect opposite to its ostensible purpose, and harmonises with the later claim (*A* 114) that the mother has "une connaissance si profonde de ses enfants". I deduce that the mother's true desire is (1) for her sons to continue to fight, and (2) for her daughter to continue her affair. For the mother knows very well, and may even enjoy, the damage she is inflicting on her younger children. If Duras is sincere in thinking she had a "connaissance si profonde", it could be only this (perhaps unconscious) knowledge.

The mother's interview with the directress of the boarding school confirms this reading (cf. *ACN* 119). Such complicity on the mother's part with her daughter's behaviour points to other powerful, concealed emotions:

> La mère parle, parle. Elle parle de la prostitution éclatante et elle rit [. . .] je parle, dit-elle, [. . .] de cette jeune enfant qui [. . .] tout à coup arrive au grand jour et se commet dans la ville au su et à la vue de tous, avec la grande racaille milliardaire chinoise, diamant au doigt comme une jeune banquière, et elle pleure.
>
> (*A* 113-4)

The mother's tears at the end of this sentence are the cloak and the clue to her motivation, whether conscious or unconscious. She is envious of her daughter's daring, delighted by the money she can pass on from her Chinese lover (33-4), awed by her blatant sexuality and brazen flaunting of her affair. It is the daughter who has the upper hand.

In regard to the mother's attitude, Adler's remarks about criminal negligence are alarmingly apposite:

> In law, the fact that the criminally negligent act is not consciously intended is considered an extenuating circumstance. There is no doubt, however, that an unconsciously hostile act is based upon the same degree of hostility as a consciously hostile one.
>
> (*UHN* 186)

If one applies this sort of thinking to the problem, one may conclude that the mother's lack of concern for her daughter is equally a reality.

Later in this scene the mother-daughter relationship might be interpreted more positively: "Elle a attendu longtemps avant de me parler encore, puis elle l'a fait, avec beaucoup d'amour: tu sais que c'est fini? que tu ne pourras jamais plus te marier ici à la colonie?" (*A* 114). Perhaps for once Duras wishes to assert her mother's status as an authority, because at this point the mother is explicitly acknowledging her daughter's magnetism, charisma and sexual allure.

This is why her words are described as "inoubliables": "Elle me regarde et elle dit les choses inoubliables: tu leur plais? Je réponds: c'est ça, je leur plais quand même. C'est là qu'elle dit: tu leur plais aussi à cause de ce que tu es toi" (ibid.). These unusually tender statements could be interpreted, that is, as a cry of triumph: "At last she acknowledges my power!" However, this episode provides clear evidence that the mother's approval is normally *never* given, for it is presented as a unique occurrence. It is from the mother's self-hatred and self-doubt that everything stems. Having no self-confidence herself, she is neither able nor willing to provide any for her children. This is totally disabling to them.

The mother's hostility to her daughter is also directed at her intellectual ability:

> Le proviseur lui dit: votre fille, madame, est première en français. Ma mère ne dit rien, rien, pas contente parce que c'est pas ses fils qui sont les premiers en français, la saleté, ma mère, mon amour, elle demande: et en mathématiques? On dit: ce n'est pas encore ça, mais ça viendra. Ma mère demande: ça viendra quand? On répond: quand elle voudra, madame.
>
> (*A* 31)

The mother's resentment of her daughter's brilliance in French is, however, not because she would rather it were her sons, but rather because she cannot bear her daughter to succeed. This little episode is a *double* mark of the daughter's power. For (1) she proves her intellectual ability—a quality her mother desires her to have. She cannot therefore despise her daughter. But (2) she demonstrates this ability in precisely the way her mother doesn't want it shown, thereby becoming her superior. This observation leads naturally to a further point: the ultimate expression of her power over her mother is her writing of this novel. Furthermore, in writing it she has the novelist's liberty to demonstrate her contempt for her mother, even going so far as to allege that the latter had always been mad: "Elle l'était. De naissance. Dans le sang. Elle n'était pas malade de sa folie, elle la vivait comme la santé" (*A* 40).

In addition, the narrator claims (*A* 50) that her mother "n'a pas connu la jouissance". Since she cannot know this, why does she wish to believe it? (1) In what is for her possibly the most important of all areas, namely the female sexual experience, it asserts her superiority over her mother. Equally importantly, (2) she wishes to deny that her mother was a complete adult.

The narrator's achievement (both social and literary) is, however, at the terrible cost of never establishing a proper relationship with her mother.

We turn now to the other members of her family, to her Chinese lover, and to society. Are the power relations here any different?

The key to the elder brother (Pierre) is anger: verbal and physical brutality. Anger among children is often a response to feelings of loss, abandonment, or to needs not being fulfilled.[5] He terrorises the younger brother (Paulo). Indeed the narrator calls him a "murderer" (he is not literally one) and asserts that, when Paulo dies young (*A* 37-8), this is because Pierre had stolen his life-will during childhood (*A* 13-14).

We have already seen Pierre's violence, and his overt sexual sadism when he encourages the mother to beat the narrator. But maybe Duras understands him all too well in this respect. We shall return to the subject of sadomasochism in a moment, but, as she says, she is most like her elder brother, even physically (*A* 68). She takes care never to dance with Pierre, on account of the implicit, incestuous sexual threat (*A* 68). We may connect this detail perhaps with his attempt to rape the Vietnamese servant Dô (*A* 28). On p. 13 she refuses to disclose the facts about a later episode ("lorsque j'ai eu dix-huit ans") about which a possible guess is that her elder brother attempted to rape her:

> Non, il est arrivé quelque chose lorsque j'ai eu dix-huit ans qui a fait que ce visage a eu lieu. ça devait se passer la nuit. J'avais peur de moi, j'avais peur de Dieu. Quand c'était le jour, j'avais moins peur et moins grave apparaissait la mort. Mais elle ne me quittait pas. Je voulais tuer, mon frère aîné, je voulais le tuer, arriver à avoir raison de lui une fois, une seule fois et le voir mourir. C'était pour enlever de devant ma mère l'objet de son amour, ce fils, la punir de l'aimer si fort, si mal, et surtout pour sauver mon petit frère, je le croyais aussi [. . .].
>
> (*A* 13)

The use of ellipsis here, the suppression of any explanation, leaves room, however, for any number of hypotheses. In *L'Amant de la Chine du nord* we learn nothing more about this episode. We are however told something that is not hinted at in *L'Amant,* namely that Paulo used to come into the heroine's bed, and that when Pierre saw this, he tried to beat up Paulo (*ACN* 54-5). It would seem that this incest does not involve the defloration of the heroine (since in both books she is still a virgin when the Chinese makes love to her for the first time [*ACN* 77, *A* 50]), but expresses her domination of her brother:

> L'enfant l'appelle tout bas: Paulo. Paulo était venu dans la salle de bains par la petite porte du côté du fleuve. Ils s'étaient embrassés beaucoup. Et puis elle s'était mise nue et puis elle s'était étendue à côté de lui et elle lui avait montré qu'il fallait qu'il vienne sur son corps à elle. Il avait fait ce qu'elle avait dit. Elle l'avait embrassé encore et elle l'avait aidé. Quand il avait crié elle s'était retournée vers son visage, elle avait pris sa bouche avec la sienne pour que la mère n'entende pas le cri de délivrance de son fils.
>
> (*ACN* 200)

In this scene of incest, once again the powerful heroine ("the child") is the instigator. Her fear of the elder brother is less a fear for herself than for her younger brother: "Il 'a battu (Paulo). C'est là que ça a commencé, la peur

qu'il le tue" (*ACN* 55). In fact, "La seule personne que craint le frère aîné [. . .] c'est moi" (*A* 68). It seems that "the child" exercises a universal ascendancy over the other members of her family, and particularly its most violent member.

From an Adlerian perspective one must point above all to Pierre's anger. Anger is a reaction to feelings of helplessness and deprivation (*UHN* 213-14). That this anger is most violently directed against Paulo is suggestive. The novel provides no evidence on which to found a theory, but Pierre's jealousy of his younger brother must be due to his feeling rejected, and to his seeing Paulo as the competitor for his mother's love.

The elder brother's ineffectuality as a criminal can also be elucidated by Adler: "Criminals are in fact cowards. They do not dare to follow the straight path, but choose instead crooked ways, dark, secret paths to their goal" (Orgler 112). Criminals are often spoilt children, says Adler. This explains Pierre's weakness, dependent as he is to her life's end on his mother.[6]

In *L'Amant* the heroine's lover too is afraid of Pierre. When he is ignored by her brothers at the "Source" nightclub, he is on the verge of tears (*A* 68).

> En présence de mon frère aîné il cesse d'être mon amant. Il ne cesse pas d'exister mais il ne m'est plus rien. Il devient un endroit brûlé. Mon désir obéit à mon frère aîné, il rejette mon amant. Chaque fois qu'ils sont ensemble vus par moi je crois ne plus jamais en supporter la vue. Mon amant est nié dans justement son corps faible, dans cette faiblesse qui me transporte de jouissance. Il devient devant mon frère un scandale inavouable, une raison d'avoir honte qu'il faut cacher.
>
> (*A* 66-7)

This evidently has incestuous overtones. Mainly, however, the heroine must always measure herself against strength. Her lover is a "weakling", and this is a source of sexual triumph to her when she is with him, but when she sees him with her brother she immediately transfers her competitive power-instinct from her lover to the latter. It is now *he* who must be overcome, *he* against whom she must measure herself.[7] Her competitive power-impulse appears to be of the classic male variety.

In the affair with the Chinese, she does not have to fight for dominance as with the elder brother, but emphasises her ascendancy from the outset:

> au moment où il est descendu de la limousine noire, quand il a commencé à s'approcher d'elle, et qu'elle, elle le savait, savait qu'il avait peur.

> Dès le premier instant elle sait quelque chose comme ça, à savoir qu'il est à sa merci. Donc que d'autres que lui pourraient être aussi à sa merci si l'occasion se présentait. Elle sait aussi quelque chose d'autre, que dorénavant le temps est sans doute arrivé où elle ne peut plus échapper à certaines obligations qu'elle a en-

vers elle-même. [. . .] L'enfant maintenant aura à faire
avec cet homme-là, le premier, celui qui s'est présenté
sur le bac.[8]

(*A* 45-6)

Though he is an experienced lover and knows how to give
her pleasure, it is she who exercises the supreme power in
the bedroom: "Il dit qu'il est seul, atrocement seul avec
cet amour qu'il a pour elle. Elle lui dit qu'elle aussi elle
est seule. Elle ne dit pas avec quoi" (*A* 48). Indeed, because he is "un homme qui a peur, il doit faire beaucoup
l'amour pour lutter contre la peur" (*A* 53). His fear of losing her is much greater than hers of losing him: "Il vit
dans l'épouvante que je rencontre un autre homme. Moi je
n'ai peur de rien de pareil jamais" (*A* 79). His fear of her
at the outset of the affair is still there when he speaks to
her on the phone years later: "Il était intimidé, il avait
peur comme avant. Sa voix tremblait tout à coup" (*A* 141).

As for that other principal, but impersonal, "character" of
the novel, the Grand Passion—it may overpower him, but
not the dominating 15½-year-old heroine. Her tone, as she
speaks of her destiny and duty as a *femme fatale,* is full of
pride and power (*A* 45-6, quoted above). As far as passion
is concerned, *she knows* and possesses the power of that
knowledge. We have seen her asserting that, if it were not
the Chinese, it would be another. We have seen her prudent refusal to protest undying love in response to her lover's protestations. She is just as determined as the Chinese
father that she will leave her lover: "Alors je lui ai dit que
j'étais de l'avis de son père. Que je refusais de rester avec
lui. Je n'ai pas donné de raisons" (*A* 103). She feels pity
rather than contempt. But pity too is the emotion of a "superior", as he recognises; for, despite the fact she gives no
reasons, he submits without argument to her decision:

> L'homme de Cholen sait que la décision de son père et
> celle de l'enfant sont les mêmes et qu'elles sont sans
> appel. [. . .] [Leur histoire] n'est pas de la sorte qu'il
> faut pour être mariée, qu'elle se sauverait de tout mar-
> iage [. . .].

(*A* 119)

The decisions of both father and mistress are thus spoken
of in the same breath, as if both have equal authority. He
hears and obeys. Now for a young man from this kind of
society to put his mistress' authority on the same level as
his father's is indeed a striking instance of her power!

The one respect in which—superficially—the heroine
might not seem to be so powerful is that (in public) she is
regarded as a prostitute—and in private (or in fantasy) accepts at times the prostitute's role:

> Elle devient objet à lui, à lui seul secrètement prosti-
> tuée. Sans plus de nom. Livrée comme chose, chose
> par lui seul, volée. [. . .] diluée dans une généralité pa-
> reillement naissante, celle depuis le commencement des
> temps nommée à tort par un autre mot, celui d'indignité.

(*ACN* 96)

Il devient brutal, son sentiment est désespéré, il se jette
sur moi [. . .]. Il me traite de putain, de dégueulasse, il
me dit que je suis son seul amour [. . .].

(*A* 54)

From the man's point of view, it seems to me that he is
seeking power: the power to influence the woman's view
of herself by calling her names. At the end of the name-
calling he thinks he will lift her into gratefulness by calling her "mon seul amour".

From the woman's point of view the situation is more interesting. Her images of rape, of prostitution, of becoming
an anonymous sexual object, are nonetheless an unmistake-
able expression of sexual pride and joy. The fact is that
sexual pride and sexual self-abasement are not so easy to
separate from each other. In view of Adler's claim that
prostitutes have a deep sense of inferiority (Orgler 135),
do they therefore crave the contempt of others? Lack of
self-esteem, as we have seen, is the source of the heroine's
power-struggle. As we shall see later, her sex-drive is
deeply infected with self-hatred. It is also, however, well
known that prostitutes despise the men who seek their services. Could this explain a part of the heroine's motivation
in *L'Amant*? She seeks self-abasement so as to abase the
supposedly superior male sex and be able to despise them.
One might ironically hypothesise, therefore, that fantasies
of raping are an expression of sexual inadequacy, while
fantasies of being raped are an expression of sexual dominance. A power which dares to fantasise its own loss is
perhaps power indeed.

I would link all this with the lack of names. Why, for instance, is the Chinese lover anonymous? Why, for that
matter, is the heroine's own name never once pronounced
throughout the novel? The explanation is that anonymity is
erotic. French lovers may sometimes address each other as
"vous", playing at not knowing each other, adopting the
roles of a couple who have picked each other up in the
street, mimicking the immediacy of an overpowering lust.
The absence of names indicates the immediate compulsive
power of the sexual impulse, and its ability to override social conventions.

Furthermore the traditional power-trick by which the male,
by sleeping with a woman, turns her into a "slut"[9] is here
reversed. The young Chinese sleeps with a white woman.
She according to the racist mores of the time would consider herself racially superior, though he naturally, being
Chinese, considers her racially inferior. But she turns the
tables on him, for this is at least equally her conquest of
him; she will love him and leave him, as male Don Juans
are supposed to do.

At times indeed she appears more than superior: she is su-
perhuman or supernatural. She claims he sees her as a
many-dimensional Super-Being:

> Il respire l'enfant [. . .] cet air chaud qui ressort d'elle.
> Il discerne de moins en moins clairement les limites de
> ce corps, celui-ci n'est pas comme les autres, il n'est

pas fini, dans la chambre il grandit encore, il est encore sans formes arrêtées, à tout instant en train de se faire, il n'est pas seulement là où il le voit, il est ailleurs aussi, il s'étend au-delà de la vue, vers le jeu, la mort, il est souple, il part tout entier dans la jouissance comme s'il était grand, en âge, il est sans malice, d'une intelligence effrayante.

(*A* 121)

Here, like a Hindu divinity, her body is expanding into the universe. She is air, warmth, life. She is "à tout instant en train de se faire", like the continuous creation of the world out of Brahma. Her body has no limits, it is infinite, and infinitely expandable, it is not only here but everywhere else as well, it is linked with the secrets of death (and therefore of life), it is all-power, and all-wisdom!

Is there a countervailing touch in the fact that she feels she is his child? Perhaps it is the lost father she finds in him, also the lost (because inadequate and threatening) mother. In him she finds the tenderness which her mother never gave her. But let me emphasise this: for her he is not an incarnation of the godhead; he is merely one of the concrete manifestations behind which the shadows of her desires lurk. There is nothing metaphysical about him.

The young Chinese may remain anonymous, but his race is frequently mentioned. This again is a constant reminder that social conventions of power are being flouted. This transgression reaches a further peak when the affair becomes public—when everyone, French, Chinese and Vietnamese, knows that "la petite prostituée blanche" is sleeping with her Chinese lover. *A disgraceful passion, seen in public as disgraceful, and gloried in, is all the more powerful.* It might be thought that society can operate at least one powerful sanction on transgressors of this sort: ostracism. But to the heroine, this is but another ordeal to be victoriously overcome. She will have the power to be alone in triumph (though others think she is alone in suffering). Thus: "La même différence sépare la dame et la jeune fille au chapeau plat des autres gens du poste. [. . .]. Isolées toutes les deux. Seules, des reines" (*A* 110-11). The dangers of solitude are clear; this passage terminates with a mention of them: "de la peur, de la folie, des fièvres, de l'oubli". But this is no contradiction: without such dangers, the courage and strength of her who surmounts them would be less remarkable! The heroine, then, is not seeking that conventional but elusive state called "happiness". On the contrary, it is power that she is seeking, and at no point does she describe her affair with the Chinese in terms of "happiness":

Mes cheveux sont lourds, souples, douloureux [. . .].

(*A* 24)

C'est un lieu de détresse [. . .] Je lui demande si c'est habituel d'être tristes comme nous le sommes.

(*A* 56)

[. . .] c'est toujours terrible. [. . .] cette tristesse [. . .] je pourrais presque lui donner mon nom, tellement elle me ressemble.

(*A* 57)

Rather, her desire is a tyrant. It operates in and through pain. The pleasure of the heroine and her lover seems almost to vanish and be engulfed by pure suffering. The strength of passion is seen as all the greater because it overcomes even the obstacle of suffering. And to the extent that the heroine has this passion at her command and under her control, then it is *her* power which is vaunted as supreme.

We have seen that not only does she assert her power against these principles of (1) crude force, (2) desire, (3) prohibition, (4) suffering. She has become herself the object of desire; herself that which is forbidden; herself that for which one must suffer. In raising herself to this status, she avenges herself against mother and elder brother. "The child" has satisfyingly turned the tables upon those different forms of violence which she had suffered—the violence of brute force, of love rejected, of actions disapproved, of aspirations despised, of tears unnoticed.

Her transgression of social taboos, however, is not without its cost, and we have already spoken of the suffering in the bedroom. Her childhood experience had been one in which violence was done to her by others, in the interests of making her appear weak. Now she continues the process "under a different sign", doing violence to herself and her emotions in the interests of her own strength. We see that the quest for power may have its self-destructive side, and may entail violence against herself.

The heroine's childhood created in her a need for attention, a hunger for importance. Now, the more elements of a person's psychic needs are embodied in an emotion, and the more fundamental they are, the more powerful it will be. *When many needs converge, giving this emotion explosive power, there emerges that most exciting of states, "passion".* In her case her needs can be most excitingly achieved when she manages to provoke sexual desire, anger, violence, incomprehension, social disapproval, even danger (when her lover fantasises about sex-murder). These are precisely the reactions which constitute for her the most satisfying triumph over her past experience, because (1) they reflect and repeat that experience, but (2) in doing so they turn her former weakness in those similar situations into present active power. "Therefore" (as Adler would say) her emotions throw her into a relationship which will provoke these various reactions.[10]

Pleasure is aroused by the overcoming of fear (as when she overcomes her fear of the elder brother). Fear is aroused by danger, and above all by the danger of death. The pleasure of orgasm is heightened by the thought of, or the closeness of, death. Thus, when the heroine mentions other women who have disgraced themselves by taking lovers, she links sex and death, talking of "une jouissance à en mourir [. . .] de cette mort mystérieuse des amants sans amour. C'est de cela qu'il est question, de cette humeur à mourir" (*A* 111). A passion which incurs the danger of death is more powerful than lesser passions; most powerful of all is a passion which leads to actual death.

Hence the fascination of the heroine with the unfaithful "Dame de Sadec" and with her lover who commits suicide in public in the great square at Savannakhet (*A* 109, 112). The scandal thereby created is another example of passion transgressing (transcending) the social proprieties. In *L'Amant* the heroine has a fantasy about watching her lover make love to her friend Hélène Lagonelle (*A* 91-2, cf. *ACN* 92-3). Can this be understood as a wish to have power over Hélène? A vicarious rape of her friend by her lover? We must not, however, overlook the remark: "Hélène Lagonelle donne envie de la tuer, elle fait se lever le songe merveilleux de la mettre à mort de ses propres mains" (*A* 91). The extremities of desire, for Duras, push towards sex-murder.[11] Anything, to be really powerful, must be really dangerous, so that overcoming it, controlling it, or even merely playing with it, becomes a mark of one's own power. A monstrous love is more powerful than a normal love because it projects fear—which is in turn a challenge which has to be overcome, because, once overcome, it confers a sense of enormous power. Passion reaches the zenith of its power, and of its ability to confer power on those who feel it, when it becomes an overwhelming threat to the self, to consciousness, to life. The dark undertow of this threat accompanies all Duras' work. Thus, to briefly illustrate this point, we read in *La Maladie de la mort*:

> Le corps est sans défense aucune, il est lisse depuis le visage jusqu'aux pieds. Il appelle l'étranglement, le viol, les mauvais traitements, les insultes, les cris de haine, le déchaînement des passions entières, mortelles.
>
> (*MM* 21)

In *Les Yeux bleus, cheveux noirs* the anonymous woman puts a black silk scarf over her face and when the man questions her, she replies:

> La soie noire, comme le sac noir, où mettre la tête des condamnés à mort.
>
> (*YBCN* 34, 37)

> Elle lui demande si cette nuit-là l'idée lui est venue de la tuer. Il dit:—L'idée m'est encore venue, mais comme celle d'aimer.
>
> (*YBCN* 135)

In *L'Homme assis dans le couloir*, we find: "Il lui dit qu'il voudrait ne plus l'aimer [. . .] Il lui dit qu'un jour il va la tuer" (*HAC* 31-2).

On the basis of this kind of evidence, Danielle Bajomée in her excellent *Duras ou la douleur* argues that "Il n'est, pour Duras, de désir que sadique [. . .]."[12]

I suggest therefore that Duras sees sado-masochism and the urge towards sex-murder as marks of passion's all-conquering power. In view of her belief that women are stronger than men, how can one understand this obsession with the female as victim? It should be noted that, in the quotations given above, the woman often incites the man to contemplate sex-murder. Duras' heroines are delighted

when their men have thoughts of this kind, and give every encouragement to them.[13] It shows that they have inspired a genuine grand passion; it proves the power of their female sexuality, creating in men a desire so great that it cannot be satisfied, and whose agonised insatiability therefore tempts them towards murder. It is not that the man is violent; it is that he is driven to violence by his love for the woman. She therefore is the source and origin of his violence, which is doubly an evidence of her power, for (1) she has inspired this murderous emotion; and (2) she is able to face it, face it down, or welcome death. Sex-murder is thus in Duras not so much a mark of metaphysical frustration, but rather of woman's invincible power and thus of a kind of metaphysical triumph.

It is here that the logic of power can be admired in its full perversity. How can the desire for power (whose source is originally the need for self-protection) lead to a desire for one's own destruction? But, let us ask, "What is the greatest conquest of fear? Is it (1) to conquer your fear of X by defeating X? No, for then you eliminate fear by defeating the cause of it. Is it (2) to conquer your fear of X by defeating fear? No, for if you no longer feel fear, then its power has been reduced to a nullity. Is it (3) to know your fear justified, yet to willingly continue to experience it, feeling it ever more acutely (like the heroine of *L'Homme assis dans le couloir*, wilfully submitting to obscene brutality [*HAC* 32-3, 34-5])?"

Logically, the last is the greatest conquest of the demon Fear—for it neither reduces nor dismisses him, it stares into his face and, as he expands like a night darker than the night, till he covers the last glow of horizon, the last glimmer of starlight, her grim determination still refuses to flinch. The brutalities to which the woman submits in *L'Homme assis dans le couloir* cannot be understood except in these terms. Namely that what she seeks is—by an extraordinary paradox—power: that supreme power which is constituted by welcoming the ultimate threat to her own survival *in all its extremity*. Here it can be seen how the drive for power may lead to someone's committing the ultimate violence against herself.

Leslie Hill writes:

> It is misleading to argue that Duras [. . .] is somehow endorsing violence against women or automatically linking heterosexuality with oppression. [. . .] Rather, the disturbing intensity of Duras's text lies in its refusal to moralise sexuality or normalise the excessive nature of desire. Sexuality [. . .] falls beyond meaning and cannot be rationalised or contained within recognisable limits. [. . .] Desire, it seems, is like some kind of radical disaster that cannot be held within bounds; and it comes into its own when it pushes humans to the very limit of what they are.
>
> (Hill 63)

I agree with Hill that this is indeed very close to what Duras *believes* she is doing. But is this not to present sado-masochistic transgression as something particularly revelatory and profound? It would seem that to understand sex as fundamentally sado-masochistic is being held up as privileged knowledge.[14]

Moreover, I would question whether it is really sexuality which is the source of the "radical disaster" of which Hill speaks, which "pushes humans to the very limit of what they are". No, sexuality and the sexual act are merely its *occasion* in Duras. The true motive of the drive to death is the loss of self-esteem and tenderness in infancy. Furthermore, since the woman who feels desire is killed, her desire is killed, and *this shows an unconscious hatred of desire*. Duras' sado-masochistic sexuality does not fall beyond meaning or morality. It is entirely meaningful, once it is seen as the tragic result of (1) a childhood loss of love and (2) the consequent drive to power. It does not fall beyond morality because we must, as we should, feel pity for its perpetrators and horror for what they perpetrate. Duras obsessively shows us women who fall helplessly at the feet of murderous violence, worshipping it. The impulsions described in these novels are singularly dark: they are akin to the psychology of suicide. For her this suicide is exciting only if it involves, as wielder of the death-blow, a male executioner-accomplice. The crucial moral question therefore is: is she presenting this to us as the ultimate meaning of sexuality? If she is, then Duras is endorsing violence, and we must condemn her doing so. Duras' transgressive sex is "revelatory", "apocalyptic" only in the sense that it reveals the hidden roots of such transgression—the fact that her understanding of sex was crippled during childhood, and overlaid with the power impulse. For Duras, I believe, it is normal tender sex that would take her outside her own psychological limits, and therefore be "revelatory" and "apocalyptic".

Adler is again valuable here: for him, sexual perversion is a sign of frustration, of distance between the sexes, but it is important to point out that he does not accept that such distance is inevitable: healthy sexual relationships *are* possible:

> 1. Every perversion is the expression of an increased distance between man and woman.

> 2. A perversion indicates a more or less deep revolt against the acceptance of the normal sexual role *and expresses itself as a planned though unconscious trick to raise the lowered self-esteem.*

> (Orgler 146, my italics)

Thus, for Adler, sado-masochistic "triumphs" of this kind are the tragic outcome of damaged self-esteem. There is no surer sign of damaged self-esteem than wilful self-destruction, the desire for which is the projection of a tragically misunderstood self-interest.

In *L'Amant,* the heroine does not use her power to satisfy her sexuality. She uses her sexuality to express and exalt her own transcendent power, to make it public and manifest to all. In some of Duras' novels, this drive to power becomes so wanton that it threatens the survival of the

woman herself. And this psychological process is probably masculine in kind, deriving from that childhood period when, in a family that was not merely fatherless but contained a power-vacuum, she and her elder brother competed for the dominant role.

There is little love in Duras' novels—there is only that lesser, though fiercer thing, passion, and the drive for power.

Notes

1. As far as I can see, the question of power has not been discussed in relation to *L'Amant*. It appears as a momentary tangent in Yvonne Givers-Villate's perceptive "M. Duras's *La Maladie de la mort*: feminist indictment or allegory?", in: Sanford S. Ames, *Remains to be Seen* (New York: Peter Lang, 1988), pp. 127-35.

2. But of course, to what extent is it fiction, to what extent autobiography? These questions perhaps are not entirely soluble. Its consistency, however, both with itself and with other works by Duras, show its closeness to the roots of the author's psychology.

   Works by Marguerite Duras are referred to by the following initials (the place of publication is Paris in each case):

   A=L'Amant, Minuit, 1984;

   ACN=L'Amant de la Chine du Nord, Gallimard, 1991.

   BCP=Un Barrage contre le Pacifique, Gallimard, 1950.

   DDE=Détruire, dit-elle, Minuit, 1969.

   HAC=L'Homme assis dans le couloir, Minuit, 1980.

   MC=Moderato cantabile (1958), 10/18, 1962.

   MM=La Maladie de la mort, Minuit, 1982.

   YBCN=Les Yeux bleus, cheveux noirs, Minuit, 1986.

3. Hertha Orgler, *Alfred Adler, the Man and his Work* (London: Sidgwick & Jackson, 4th ed., 1973).

4. *UHN=*Alfred Adler, *Understanding Human Nature* (Oxford: Oneworld, 1992). The first version of this essay mentioned Adler, but I had not returned to him as a source, and I am grateful to Mary Orr for encouraging me to consult him properly: he turns out to be a potent ally. While this will not be an Adlerian reading, such an approach unlocks interesting connexions which I will in part be following up.

5. E.g. Claudia Jewett, *Helping Children Cope with Separation and Loss* (London: Batsford, 1984), pp. 65-6.

6. Confronted with strength, he is helpless. During the episode where the Chinese offers the mother money, he does his best to create a scene, to prevent it happening, using the ineffective weapons of rudeness, anger, insult (*ACN* 125-32). The Chinese

lover simply treats him as if he were not there. In this scene in *L'Amant de la Chine du Nord* he appears particularly ineffectual, even pathetic.

7. The passage ends, "Autour du souvenir la clarté livide de la nuit du chasseur. ça fait un son strident d'alerte, de cri d'enfant." Again these enigmatic references to "the hunter's night". Is this the night of the attempted rape? (Frankly, despite *A* 13, I suspect that this took place well before the age of 18.) Leslie Hill claims in his *Marguerite Duras, Apocalyptic Desires* (London & New York: Routledge, 1993; hereafter referred to as *MD*) that this refers to Charles Laughton's film *The Night of the Hunter,* in which a murderous preacher pursues two children. However, as both Mary Orr and I have independently noticed, there are references to the brother as hunter in *BCP,* which antedates the film by several years.

8. In *L'Amant de la Chine du Nord* she is perhaps the more active instigator of the affair. For, once "L'enfant" is in his limousine, the young man does most of the talking . . . but during a long initial silence, she picks up his hand and turns it over and over, as if fascinated (*ACN* 42).

9. If an academic reference is needed, let me suggest David G. Winter, *The Power Motive* (London: Macmillan, 1973), p. 170.

10. As Duras carefully explains, the scene with the Chinese has recurred in most of her books in one way or another; around it her imagination has obsessively revolved. It is clear why: this was the moment when her emotional needs came together for the first time, in the most satisfying combination. Passion resulted.

11. Cf. *L'Amant de la Chine du Nord* where the lover proposes to take the heroine to Long-Hai:

Elle se retourne, se blottit contre lui. Il l'enlace. Il dit qu'elle est son enfant, sa sur, son amour. Ils ne sourient pas. Il a éteint la lumière.

—Comment tu m'aurais tuée à Long-Hai? Dis-le-moi encore.

—Comme un Chinois. Avec la cruauté en plus de la mort.

Elle récite la fin de la phrase comme elle ferait d'un poème.

(*ACN* 110)

12. D. Bajomée, *Duras ou la douleur* (Bruxelles: Éditions Universitaires, Université de Boeck, 1989), p. 180.

13. Of the woman murdered by her lover at the opening of *Moderato cantabile*:

—Son consentement à elle a été entier?

—Emerveillé. (*MC* 110)

14. E.g. Hélène Lagonelle in *L'Amant* "ne saura jamais ce que je sais" (*A* 91). There is in *DDE* a privileged group of the sexual elite—Alissa, Max Thor and Stein—who truly grasp the transgressive and tragic nature of sex.

FURTHER READING

Criticism

Cousineau, Diane. "The Image and the Word, History and Memory in the Photographic Age: Marguerite Duras's *The Lover.*" *Letters and Labyrinths: Women Writing/Cultural Codes,* pp. 128-68. Newark: University of Delaware Press, 1997.

A postmodern feminist examination of Duras's use of the photographic image in *The Lover.*

Le Sage, Laurent. "Marguerite Duras." *The French New Novel: An Introduction and a Sampler,* pp. 85-91. University Park, Penn.: Pennsylvania State University Press, 1962.

Briefly examines Duras's works that fall into the *nouveau roman* category.

Thormann, Janet. "Feminine Masquerade in *L'Amant*: Duras with Lacan." *Literature and Psychology* XXXX, No. 4 (1994): 28-39.

Provides a Lacanian analysis of *The Lover,* noting that "to read . . . *L'amant* through Lacanian theory is to foreground the movement of desire through language."

"A Clean, Well-Lighted Place"

Ernest Hemingway

American short story writer, novelist, essayist, nonfiction writer, memoirist, journalist, poet, and dramatist. For further information on Hemingway's short fiction, see *SSC*, Vols. 1, 25, and 36.

INTRODUCTION

"A Clean, Well-Lighted Place" is considered a prime example of Hemingway's craftsmanship and insight into the human condition. In this brief story, which was initially published in *Scribner's Magazine* in 1933, he evokes an atmosphere of despair and loneliness almost entirely with dialogue and interior monologue. Through these stylistic techniques Hemingway renders a complex series of interactions between an old waiter and his young colleague as the two men reflect on the ephemeral nature of happiness and the inevitability of death. Much of the critical commentary on the short story focuses on a series of unattributed lines of dialogue. For decades, commentators have speculated on Hemingway's stylistic technique in "A Clean, Well-Lighted Place," turning to the author's original manuscript and correspondence to determine the proper configuration and attribution of the dialogue of the story.

PLOT AND MAJOR CHARACTERS

Rendered almost completely in dialogue, the main action of "A Clean, Well-Lighted Place" is set in a small café in Spain, as two waiters prepare to close the establishment for the night. The place is empty except for a regular customer, a deaf old man drinking alone at one of the tables. Realizing that the old man is drunk, one of the waiters informs the other that the customer attempted suicide the week before. After the waiters watch a young man and woman pass on the street, the young waiter serves the old customer another brandy and voices his impatience to the old waiter, complaining that the old man is keeping him from his warm bed and the comfort of his wife. They discuss the old man's suicide attempt and his possible reasons for such a desperate act. When the old man gestures for another brandy, the young waiter tells him that it is closing time. After the old man pays his bill and leaves, the old waiter chides the young waiter for his lack of patience and empathy for the old man. He compares himself to the man, saying he understands the need for a clean, well-lighted place to be at night. After the café closes, the old waiter stops at a bar for a drink before he goes home, dreading his return to an empty room.

MAJOR THEMES

In his short fiction Hemingway depicted a disillusioning environment in which his protagonists address the precariousness of existence, the evanescence of happiness, and the universality of suffering. This is certainly true in "A Clean, Well-Lighted Place," as the old waiter shows a sensitivity to and understanding of both the young waiter's impatience to get home and the old man's utter hopelessness. Critics have noted a series of contrasts in the story: light and dark, clean and dirty, noisy and quiet, youth and age, and nihilism and religious idealism. In fact, many believe that the major thematic concern of the story is the conflict between generations. This is illustrated by the contrast between the two major characters: for many critics, the young waiter represents materialism and the callousness of youth and the old waiter symbolizes the perspective and wisdom of age, which is illustrated by his empathy for the old man's profound despair and alleged suicide attempt. Some critics have suggested that the old waiter's repetitive use of the term "nada" (translated as "nothing" or "nothingness") suggests his nihilistic tendencies because he faces loneliness and advancing death like the old man. A few commentators have viewed the three main characters in the story as an implied progression from youth through middle age to old age.

CRITICAL RECEPTION

In 1959 controversy about the dialogue in "A Clean, Well-Lighted Place" began when two critics noted a few confusing and illogical passages of conversation between the two waiters. Hemingway rarely identified the speaker of each line of dialogue, and confusion ensued about which character was speaking each line. In fact, some of the dialogue seemed to be uttered by the wrong character. At first, commentators speculated that there was a mistake in the text: Hemingway or his publisher, Scribner's, had forgotten or omitted a line of dialogue, throwing off the entire exchange between the two characters. In 1959, Otto Reinert challenged the prevailing theory that Hemingway employed metronomic dialogue and that each indented line implied a new speaker. Instead, he theorized that Hemingway utilized anti-metronomic dialogue—allowing a character to speak consecutive lines of dialogue in a few places. This could explain the discrepancy and allow the dialogue to be logical and idiosyncratic.

A few years later, commentators began to challenge Reinert's theory. Joseph Gabriel contended that the dialogue was metronomic and that the resulting confusion was viewed as an integral aspect of the story. John Hagopian rejected these theories, maintaining that the confusion stemmed from a typographical error and urged a revision of the story. In 1965 the story was amended as recommended and reprinted in *The Short Stories of Ernest Hemingway*. This revised version of "A Clean, Well-Lighted Place" unleashed a torrent of protest from critics who repudiated Hagopian's view and agreed with Reinert's theory of Hemingway's use of anti-metronomic dialogue. Many scholars furnished additional examples of anti-metronomic dialogue in Hemingway's short fiction and novels, discovering further evidence for Reinert's theory in the author's correspondence with friends and publishers, as well as the original manuscript of the story. In recent times, Reinert's view has become the prevailing theory, as many scholars have urged a republication of Hemingway's original version of "A Clean, Well-Lighted Place."

PRINCIPAL WORKS

Short Fiction

Three Stories and Ten Poems 1923
In Our Time 1924

Men without Women 1927
Winner Take Nothing 1933
The Fifth Column and the First Forty-Nine Stories 1938
The Portable Hemingway 1944
The Old Man and the Sea 1952
The Hemingway Reader 1953
The Fifth Column and Four Stories of the Spanish Civil War 1969
The Nick Adams Stories 1972
The Complete Short Stories of Ernest Hemingway 1987

Other Major Works

The Sun Also Rises [*Fiesta*] (novel) 1926
The Torrents of Spring: A Romantic Novel in Honor of the Passing of a Great Race (novel) 1926
A Farewell to Arms (novel) 1929
Death in the Afternoon (nonfiction) 1932
Green Hills of Africa (nonfiction) 1935
To Have and Have Not (novel) 1937
For Whom the Bell Tolls (novel) 1940
Across the River and into the Trees (novel) 1950
A Moveable Feast (autobiography) 1964
Islands in the Stream (novel) 1970
The Garden of Eden (novel) 1986

CRITICISM

Charles A. Allen (essay date 1955)

SOURCE: "Ernest Hemingway's Clean, Well-Lighted Heros," in *The Pacific Spectator: A Journal of Interpretation*, Vol. IX, No. 4, Autumn, 1955, pp. 383-89.

[*In the following survey of the major characters of Hemingway's fiction, Allen asserts that anxiety is the defining feature of the characters in "A Clean, Well-Lighted Place."*]

The Hemingway stories and novels are dominated by heroes who conduct a retreating battle with nature and the world's hostility. But they fight against their loss with pleasure, skill, and courage. The world of nature and humanity robs health, hope, and love, leaving in the end only *nada*, nothingness. Nothingness is opposed skillfully and zestfully with stoical integrity and courage, Hemingway's two chief themes.

This limited philosophy is not altogether satisfying, but even less satisfying is a tendency for Hemingway to mistake emotional immaturity for maturity. The "code" behavior of his stoical heroes and the motivation of the behavior are often a trifle suspect: to some degree anxiety would seem the motivation and "defense mechanism" the behavior. Both anxiety and defense are expressions of unconscious hostility.

Of course for Hemingway and his admirers the code is not defensive and the motivations are rationally and maturely rather than anxiously inspired.

Hemingway's stories usually emphasize conflict within the individual. Thus **"Big Two-Hearted River"** (1925) is, on the surface, a quiet, slow-paced narrative of a young man out trout fishing. Nick Adams leaves the train up in Michigan, unhurriedly tramps over a fire-burnt area, takes a nap under the pines, and arrives on time at his camp site beside the river. Methodically, he pitches camp and prepares food; he sleeps in the precise knowledge that he has earned his rest. The next day he expertly fishes the river until it enters a swamp. The swamp he will save until another time. This is the action. The conflict is, as in **"A Way You'll Never Be"** and **"Now I Lay Me,"** Nick's struggle to hold an unnamed fear in check, to calm his nerves, to maintain his equilibrium before the threat of collapse. He does this through a series of rituals—preparing his food carefully, pitching his tent efficiently, catching his grasshoppers in the right way at the right time, handling his undersized trout with wet hands so as not to damage them. He believes that such ritualistic gestures can prevent the recurrence of threatening memories and can heighten his awareness and enjoyment of the world about him. He is apparently fighting successfully, and one knows that he will win his fight when he decides not to enter the swamp. This climactic decision forcefully illuminates the humanistic theme of the story—the necessity for discipline, for skillful and pleasurable fighting against the enemy.

Structurally the story is impeccable. All of the elements of language, method, and meaning work in dramatic harmony. The cause of Nick's anxiety is never directly named. The author may well be, as both Carlos Baker and Philip Young suggest, hinting that Nick's trouble is rooted in the memory of the violence and destruction of war, such a memory, for example, as swerves the protagonist of **"A Way You'll Never Be"** to the brink of insanity, or the memory of such wounds as Frederic Henry of *A Farewell to Arms* and Colonel Cantwell of *Across the River and into the Trees* have experienced. Certainly the burnt town and surrounding country support the theory. But the genesis of the anxiety state is indefinite. The clear-running stream, the fragrant pine forest, the warm tent—all images that contrast sharply with the charred town and countryside—represent peace and serenity.

The anxiety and defense pattern is apparent in almost all of Hemingway's work, but perhaps anxiety as the invisible enemy is most clearly defined in **"A Clean, Well-Lighted Place,"** and defense most obvious in **"Soldier's Home."** An intense anxiety feeling afflicts the old waiter and the old customer in **"A Clean, Well-Lighted Place"** (1933). Of the two characters the focus is on the aging waiter. His sympathy and understanding for the customer are based on a recognition that he too is "someone who needs the café," who, having lost youth and confidence, needs cleanness and order and good light as a defense against the black night. "What did he fear? It was not fear or dread. It was a nothing that he knew too well. It was all a nothing and a man was nothing too."

Krebbs, a young American just returned from the trenches of Europe to the routine of his middle-class parents' home, is the protagonist of **"Soldier's Home"** (1925). He eats and sleeps with satisfaction, enjoys shooting pool, finds it pleasant to read about the war, and likes to watch the pretty girls. But he does not want to become involved with them or with his family. He simply wants to keep his life uncomplicated, to remain a spectator. He is, in brief, attempting to defend himself against his depressed insecurity by erecting an intellectual barrier of serene detachment. The story is superior to **"A Clean, Well-Lighted Place,"** largely because the author vividly dramatizes the genesis of Krebbs's neurotic detachment. It is not the war experience but the hostile overprotectiveness of his mother and the hostile rejection of his father which have driven him into his shell of apathy. This is the one story in which Hemingway most clearly and accurately estimates the meaning of frustration, anxiety, and defense, but even here one has the uncomfortable intimation that the author is placing too much weight on the rationality and reality of Krebbs's defense rather than on his anxious and unrealistic motivations.

The conviction of *nada* suffered by the protagonists of these three stories is what the psychiatrist, I suspect, would define as depression anxiety. Such anxiety is at bottom a suspicion of one's own inadequacy, failure, worthlessness. It is an irrational, self-destructive feeling which has as its foundation the childhood fear that one is unwanted and unloved, a recognition that one's parents really consider one a little nuisance. It is a feeling that may lead to a yearning for escape from ordinary worldly concerns, to a seeking of an isolation such as Nick, Krebbs, and the two old men attempt to build for themselves: a camouflaged desire to escape guilt feelings about one's parents. It may lead one in a long search for soothing rituals and the peace and serenity of clean, well-lighted places: a disguised need for respectable, loving parents, and a respectable and loving conscience.

Sanitation and ritual as hostile defenses against the anxious conviction of *nada* are evident in most of Hemingway's protagonists and in all his heroes. But before outlining in more detail this evidence, I should like to note certain other emotional defenses which the Hemingway hero reveals, frequently to his dismay and chagrin.

Stoical integrity and courage verge on arrogant pride for Robert Wilson of **"The Short Happy Life of Francis Macomber"** and Colonel Cantwell of *Across the River.* Both men are resplendent in their array of code virtues: efficient, quick-witted, well-mannered, compassionate, brave, they are a bit boastful of their virtue. Both are proud of their self-reliant professionalism; one is a big game hunter and the other a military man. Both are loyal to their hard-won standards and are contemptuously willing to break society's rules to preserve their own code. They are both willing to preach with an edgy abruptness their airtight philosophy, to condescendingly gather disciples—and to show signs of intolerant impatience and sarcastic "roughness" toward those who are incapable or undesirous of becoming converts. This tendency toward arrogance is not altogether lacking in a good many other heroes in Hemingway's stories and novels. Arrogance is one form of hostile insecurity.

Stoical integrity and courage collapse into brutality for the two Harrys of **"The Snows of Kilimanjaro"** and *To Have and Have Not.* In his effort to save his soul, the dying author in **"The Snows"** engages in a masochistic tongue-lashing of himself and a sadistic attack on his loving but unloved wife. A recognition and acceptance of frailties does not demand brutality. In the novel, Harry Morgan's cold-blooded murders are inexcusable, code or no code. Both men might have been made endurable if they had been satirically interpreted as hostile.

Stoical integrity and courage threaten to break under the strain of emotional rebellion for heroes Jake Barnes of *The Sun Also Rises* and Frederic Henry of *A Farewell to Arms.* Emotional rebellion against one's biological fate and against society is a symptom of anxious immaturity. Like arrogance or sadism, rebellion against the world of nature and society is at bottom primarily an expression of ambivalent love and hatred for one's parents: an attempt to capture their attention and love and a need to offend and reject them. Society—the military, the nation, the "they"—"threw you in and told you the rules and the first time they caught you off base they killed you," complains Frederic Henry in the last chapter of *A Farewell to Arms.* "Or they killed you gratuitously like Aymo. Or gave you the syphilis like Rinaldo. But they kill you in the end. You could count on that." This rhetorical "they" kills Catherine Barkley in childbirth, a "dirty trick," as Catherine says and Frederic agrees. Jake Barnes also shows a degree of unrealistic sentimentalism about his emasculation; Nick Adams of **In Our Time** has a wretched time accepting the world's inevitabilities; even Robert Jordan has not yet fully learned acceptance of man's fate. The reader—*this* reader, at least—does not relish such self-pity in the heroes.

Although Frederic Henry and Catherine Barkley speak well of marriage, they are not handicapped without it—and without parents, church, and state. Everywhere they are suspicious of society's authority. "If they shot floorwalkers after a fire in the department store because they spoke with an accent they had always had, then certainly the floor-walkers would not be expected to return when the store opened again for business." This metaphor pretty accurately sums up Frederic Henry's reservations not only about the Italian army but about all organized society. And so the heroes concoct their own standards.

But rituals and sanitation are the primary defenses against anxiety.

Rituals are potent weapons against a hostile world; and they give physical delight. Ritualized eating and drinking and love-making are as effective and pleasurable as Nick's trout fishing. As Frederic Henry passionately avows: "I was not made to think. I was made to eat. My God, yes. Eat and drink and sleep with Catherine." Henry might also have added a list of sporting rituals: fishing, hunting, skiing, swimming, and the great art and death pageants of bullfighting and military campaigning. These are the physical rituals of the code, the outward show. They are often, too, the emblem of the inward struggle against *nada.*

But the pleasurable ritual act, and the consequent spiritual pleasure, are defenses not only against *nada* but also against the socially unacceptable defenses of arrogance, brutality, and rebellion which sometimes victimize the heroes. The rituals have helped subdue these uglier defenses, and finally come near to dominating them. Obviously the struggle to build the code, to make it appear impregnable, has meant hard and often bitter toil.

An obsessive urge toward cleanness, order, and light is common to most of the protagonists of Hemingway's short stories and to the admirable characters of all his longer works, fiction and nonfiction. Consider for a moment the places in which the heroes dwell.

The bright, clear Gulf Stream is the home of Harry Morgan of *To Have and Have Not* and of Santiago of **The Old Man and the Sea.** Sunny days, piney woods, and long vistas of uncontaminated landscape are the setting of *The Sun Also Rises* and *For Whom the Bell Tolls.* The spaces in *A Farewell to Arms* and *Across the River* are not so wide and sparsely inhabited, but Milan, a center of action in the earlier novel, is an open friendly place; and Venice is the most beautiful city in the world. Both have their neat and cheerful eating, drinking, and love-making nooks. Both have their spacious, well-scrubbed plazas, tidily designed for fresh air strolls.

It is interesting, too, that all these works bubble with cleansing water imagery. Water is usually exhilarating, though the rains of *A Farewell to Arms* and the snows of *For Whom the Bell Tolls* are depressing and bad. There are a variety of sparkling streams, rivers, lakes, and oceans (not to mention purifying sweats and tasty drinks). Jake Barnes finds refreshment in the Spanish trout streams, on the motherly heave and fall of the Atlantic breast. Frederic Henry finds a river and a lake as allies in his fight against a hostile world. The Gulf Stream is almost a mother (and garbage disposal) for both Harry Morgan and Santiago. And there is certainly well-arranged good cheer around the rivers and lakes of Colonel Cantwell's Venice and Pop's green hills of Africa. The mountain streams relieve Robert Jordan's arduous pilgrimage.

In brief the locales of Hemingway's works are quite tidy and clean. These locales which the protagonists and heroes either find or make become a clear symbol. They become the primary indicators of the defensive insecurity which is the bottom nature of all the Hemingway protagonists and heroes. They also become the primary emblems of the hero's obsessively motivated sanitary code.

The most recent statement of the finicky code is in *The Old Man and the Sea.*

The novella's tragic hero, Santiago, has been out of luck for eighty-four days, has not caught a fish, and so decides to probe the deep waters farther out than fishermen should venture. On the eighty-fifth day, with the aid of his young apprentice, Manolin, Santiago puts to sea in his rowing and sailing skiff. By daylight he is far from Havana, trolling steadily and with skillful calculation in the current of the Gulf Stream. He hooks a great marlin that is designed if ever fish was to test the limits of man's endurance and courage. Implacably and without panic fish and man engage each other for all of two nights and the better part of two days. Santiago finally circles his mighty antagonist in for the kill. Having efficiently lashed the marlin to the side of his boat, he hoists sail before a fine breeze and points for home. But long before he arrives his prize is attacked and largely destroyed by sharks. In the realm of tangible gain he is still in bad luck; but in the universe of spiritual values he has proved once again, despite his sin of pride in venturing too far out, that he is worthy of Manolin's respect and love, and of his own.

The plot stated so barrenly reads like a detective story. There are the excitement of the chase, and the wily and experienced protagonist and antagonist, both of whom act rather nobly within the limits of their self-defined codes. But again the conflict is only superficially with the exterior enemy, with the fish and with the boy's parents; the real enemy is one's potential frailty. Santiago is declining physically, and there is his fear that he will fail spiritually: and so he must constantly test himself against his icy code. He must not only endure his poverty, ill luck, and pain, but triumph over them. The moment of climax, when Santiago shows that he will not collapse in his struggle to bring the fish within harpooning distance, is approached superbly as tension and as demonstration of the old man's muscular and moral strength. He proves to be full of self-reliance, alertness, efficiency, and courage, full of all the usual code virtues. In addition he shows a deeper understanding of humility and compassion, of acceptance and of love, than any of the previous heroes.

If Santiago is the rigid code hero in his most highly developed and admirable state, he is not a complex or variously motivated character. He is a didactic type, a memorable idea—as well-lighted and as pure as the ocean on which he dwells.

Santiago's code has considerable moral dignity. But he is emotionally a trifle too spotless, too humorless, too didactic; perhaps also too aggressively loving and humble and compassionate. One is a bit disturbed by the strenuous, self-righteous quality of his code, which often seems no more than a façade for an obsessive and irrational need.

Santiago's code is the statement toward which the Hemingway heroes (and romantic heroines) have been aspiring for a quarter of a century. The struggle can be traced through the even more complex and camouflaged defenses of Nick Adams, Jake Barnes, Frederic Henry, and Robert Jordan. All along they have been haltingly approaching Santiago's idealized virtue.

Hemingway's code hero has accomplished a difficult and astonishing feat—he has reared a monolithic defense which is not easily attacked. Yet psychological defense is always vulnerable under pressure, is likely to crumble periodically, like the defenses of the two Harrys and Colonel Cantwell. One can only wish the heroes luck with their further visions of clean, well-lighted life.

William B. Bache (essay date 1956)

SOURCE: "Craftsmanship in 'A Clean, Well-Lighted Place,'" in *The Personalist,* Vol. XXXVII, No. 1, January, 1956, pp. 60-4.

[In the following essay, Bache contends that "A Clean, Well-Lighted Place" is "valuable both as a comment on and as a representation of Hemingway's craftsmanship and insight."]

At first glance the short story **"A Clean, Well-Lighted Place"**[1] by Ernest Hemingway may seem slight; yet if it is slight, it is so only in length and not by any other standard. The intrinsic value of the story has been well recognized by Mark Schorer, who has said of it: "'**A Clean, Well-Lighted Place**' is not only a short story, it is a model of the short story, with all the virtues that attend it as a *genre* singularly lighted."[2] The importance of the story, moreover, not so much for itself as for its place within the corpus of Hemingway's fiction, has been noted by Robert Penn Warren. He has said that **"A Clean, Well-Lighted Place"** is the best description of the world that underlies Hemingway's world of violent action.[3] The pertinent and obvious implications of this last statement are that Hemingway's subject matter is limited in scope and that his fictional world is essentially violent in nature. The purpose of this discussion is not only to substantiate what the above critics have said but also to suggest that **"A Clean, Well-Lighted Place"** is valuable both as a comment on and as a representation of Hemingway's craftsmanship and insight. A study of this short story therefore should enable us to understand more fully Hemingway as a creative artist.

The main action of the story takes place in Spain in a café, clean and well lighted. The important characters are three: an old man who has tried to kill himself and who is now drinking alone at one of the tables in the café, a young waiter, and an older waiter who are waiting for their customer to finish drinking and to leave. Until the time that the café is closed, the bulk of the story is a dialogue between the two waiters, first about the old man and later about each other. There are two muted conflicts in the story: one between the young waiter and the old man; the other between the young waiter and the older waiter. The old man's presence in the café is the immediate cause of both conflicts: the young waiter feels antagonism for the old man, whereas the older waiter feels sympathy for him.

Hemingway's fiction being what it is, one would expect to find points of similarity between **"A Clean, Well-Lighted Place,"** published in 1933, and *Death in the Afternoon,* published the preceding year, and it is not even surprising to find in the book a passage that, if not an expositive germ for the short story, at least tells us how Hemingway feels toward the old man of the story, a man who has out-lived his wife and who has tried to commit suicide:

> There is no lonelier man in death except the suicide, than that man who has lived many years with a good wife and then outlived her. If two people love each other there can be no happy end to it.[4]

It might be maintained that this passage does more than give us Hemingway's feelings, that it helps to interpret and to explain the old man's actions. Thus we should be led to ask ourselves if it is only by chance that the older waiter does not have a wife and that the young waiter does. We should notice, too, Robert Heilman's suggestion that the old man and the older waiter are in reality the same character, since they both feel the need of going to a clean, well-lighted place and since they both cannot sleep.[5]

In Hemingway's fiction "the interest in conduct and the attitude toward conduct is central."[6] To express this focus on conduct in **"A Clean, Well-Lighted Place"** Hemingway seems to have represented—his fiction, rather than being a report, is always a suggestive, dramatic representation—two ways of life: the young waiter standing for a materialistic way of life; the older waiter and the old man standing for a nihilistic (notice the parody of the Lord's Prayer) way of life. These two ways of life, since both are devoid of spiritual values, lead us to an awareness of the theme of the story: the dilemma of contemporary man living in a world of spiritual emptiness. The clean, well-lighted place is a symbolic substitute for the spiritual life. It is clean and orderly and well lighted, but it is only a substitute, and as such it is sterile. It signifies a nothingness, but a known and tangible and dignified nothingness; it is opposed to the intangible blackness and the unknown.[7] The clean, well-lighted place is, like materialism, an opiate of the spirit.

Since the older waiter and the old man have much in common, it can be said that there is really only one conflict in the story: the conflict between the young man and the two older men. In a sense, then, this is the conflict of youth with age. The young waiter represents materialism because youth is not rarely materialistic, though with the passage of time materialism often loses its meaning. But reading the story with care, one discovers that the young waiter is even now clutching at the straws of materialism. There are numerous suggestions that the young waiter is aware, perhaps not intellectually but certainly emotionally, of the pit-

falls and insecurities of a life based solely on materialism: the young waiter admits that there is a difference between drinking at home and drinking at the café; the young waiter takes offense at his fellow waiter's mild joke about his wife, although a few lines later he is to assert that he is all confidence; in brief, throughout the story the young waiter seems to be protesting too much. From all this we can assume that the two waiters are not of two different kinds as the older waiter says; rather, the young waiter's attitude toward life is more akin to the older waiter's than he would care to admit.

John Peale Bishop has said of the many Spaniards found in Hemingway's fiction:

> Plenty of things can happen to his drunken expatriates, but nothing they do, nothing that is done to them, can have any significance. For they are all of them, amusing as they are, aimless and will-less; they are so completely devoid of spiritual life that neither stupefying drink nor the aware intelligence can save them.[8]

That this is a true description of many of Hemingway's characters and that these characters are true pictures of many Spaniards cannot be disputed, but this is not to say that only the Spanish people have this *malaise* of the spirit. The spiritual deficiency as Hemingway sees it is more inclusive than that; Hemingway simply knows the Spanish people well, and he has known them under conditions that have particularly adapted them to serve as a vehicle for his expression of the lack of spiritual values in contemporary life. If this is not so, **"A Clean, Well-Lighted Place"** is not so great as critics have maintained.

If the assumption is granted that the true purpose of this short story is the expression of the dilemma and insecurity of contemporary life, the three main characters are more than they seem: they are symbols of modern man. And as symbols of modern man they tend to function as parts of a more pervasive symbol of man: the young waiter is youth; the older waiter, middle age; the old man, old age. The contention that this was Hemingway's purpose is supported by the manner in which he designates the important characters. No name as such is used: rather, it is largely the force of the adjective—"young," "older," "old"—applied to each character that differentiates one from the other. These adjectives—and perhaps the same thing can be said of the word "waiter"—perform a function similar to that performed by the names in the morality plays. The absence of names, too, implied that these characters should be regarded not so much as identifiable persons but as symbols.

The two older men are now, as Heilman suggests, the same character. The older waiter is different from the old man in that he has a job and in that he has not tried to kill himself. From the older waiter to the old man lies a progression in despair, for the three characters are actually parts of an implied progression from youth through middle age to old age. The focus of character is on the older waiter because he is in the process of going from youth to old age and because he can best appreciate the positions of youth and old age. The older waiter is the truest symbol of modern man. The young waiter and the old man, while they are parts of the pervasive symbol, are, in effect, poles to the older waiter; they help to explain the dilemma of modern man, who is living in a world that has lost its spiritual values and who is caught on the horns of the selfish and cruel materialism of youth and the insomnious nihilism of old age.

Notes

1. Ernest Hemingway, "A Clean, Well-Lighted Place," *Scribner's Magazine,* XCII (March, 1933), 149-150.

2. Mark Schorer, *The Story: a Critical Anthology* (New York, 1950), p. 425.

3. Robert Penn Warren, introduction to *A Farewell to Arms* (New York, 1949), p. xv.

4. Ernest Hemingway, *Death in the Afternoon* (New York, 1932), p. 122.

5. Robert B. Heilman, *Modern Short Stories: a Critical Anthology* (New York, 1950), p. 391.

6. Delmore Schwartz, "Ernest Hemingway's Literary Situation," *Ernest Hemingway: the Man and His Work,* ed. John K. M. McCaffery (Cleveland, 1950), p. 116.

7. At the end of the story we are told: "The older waiter would go home to his room. He would lie in the bed and finally *with daylight,* he would go to sleep." (Italics added.)

8. John Peale Bishop, "The Missing All," *Ernest Hemingway: The Man and His Work,* p. 303.

Frederick P. Kroeger (essay date 1959)

SOURCE: "The Dialogue in 'A Clean, Well-Lighted Place,'" in *College English,* Vol. 20, No. 5, February, 1959, pp. 240-41.

[In the following essay, Kroeger considers the confusing dialogue in Hemingway's story.]

Ever since the first printing of **"A Clean, Well-Lighted Place"** in *Scribner's Magazine* (March, 1933), there has been what appears to be an insoluble problem in the dialogue. Hemingway, or someone, has been careless enough about this story so that at one time one main speaker seems to have information about the old man's suicide attempt which the other one does not have, and at another time the situation is reversed. If the young waiter has the information about the suicide attempt, all the lines which describe details of the attempt should be ascribed to him. Unfortunately, this cannot be done in the second dialogue between the two waiters, which begins right after the young waiter has served the old man and has said, "You should have killed yourself last week." Assuming that the "He" carries through as the young waiter we have:

. . . The [young] waiter took the bottle back inside the café. He [young waiter] sat down at the table with his colleague again.

"He's drunk now," he [young waiter] said.

"He's drunk every night."

Old waiter or young waiter? If this is the young waiter it should not be indented, so it must be the old waiter. The next line is the young waiter's: "What did he want to kill himself for?" The old waiter says he doesn't know, and the young waiter says, "How did he do it?" The rest of the dialogue seems to indicate that the young waiter doesn't know anything about the suicide attempt. The old waiter knows that the old man tried to hang himself with a rope and that his niece cut him down for the "good of his soul." Unfortunately for our line identification, right after the old waiter has told the young waiter all about the suicide we find the young waiter saying, "He's lonely. I'm not lonely. I have a wife waiting in bed for me." Continuing in alternate lines we find the young waiter saying that the old man couldn't use a wife because he is too old, and besides his niece looks after him. Then the old waiter says, "*I know. You said she cut him down*" (italics mine). This certainly indicates that it is the young waiter who knows about the details of the suicide, and not the old waiter as the earlier dialogue indicates. (There is other evidence of carelessness: the old waiter says his niece cut him down, and the young waiter asks why *they* did it.) Well, which one knows all about the suicide attempt? Hemingway's intent was certainly not to have them both know about it or he would have added, "I know." to the "Why?" of the second line of the beginning dialogue.

The first ten lines of dialogue in the story are different enough once one knows the character of the two waiters. If the first line of the beginning dialogue is given to the old waiter, then he is the one who knows about the suicide. Since the second long dialogue begins with a line that must be given to the young waiter or there would seem to be an error in pronoun reference, it can be seen that the old waiter is still the man with the information. Since the story is about the word *nada,* chaos, it does not seem reasonable that in the first dialogue the young waiter would say that the old man tried to commit suicide because he was in despair. The old waiter would naturally say that he tried to commit suicide about nothing because the old waiter understands that even with money, the old man can be in despair with his knowledge that all is *nada,* even the blessed Mary who intercedes for our souls. The kindred feeling that these two men have with each other is thus established, as it should be, at the beginning of the story. Later on the old waiter says that the niece cut the old man down out of "fear for his soul." Since the old waiter by reciting his Hail Mary with the word *nada* in it shows his fear that there is no organization that will save his soul, this line should be assigned to him. The young waiter would naturally be concerned with money, so the line "How much money has he got?" is his. These two lines can be assigned to speakers without the benefit of counting, but the line count also shows that they have been assigned to the proper characters.

Otto Reinert (essay date 1959)

SOURCE: "Hemingway's Waiters Once More," in *College English,* Vol. 20, No. 8, May, 1959, pp. 417-18.

[*In the following essay, Reinert perceives the inconsistent and confusing dialogue in "A Clean, Well-Lighted Place" as a result of Hemingway's utilization of anti-metronomic dialogue.*]

In the February *College English* Mr. Kroeger and Professor Colburn find "confusion" and "inconsistency" in the distribution of speeches between the old and the young waiter in Hemingway's **"A Clean, Well-Lighted Place."** I don't presume to know what "this generation of close readers has been doing" about the problem "all this time," but I suspect they have been assuming, as I have, that the difficulty arises from Hemingway's violation of one of the unwritten rules of the art of presenting dialogue visually. The rule is that a new, indented line implies a new speaker. It is a useful rule, but it is not sacrosanct. I believe Hemingway has broken it here, possibly from carelessness, possibly deliberately. It seems to me preferable to preserve the unity and plausibility of the two waiters' characters and the consistency of their function in the moral drama, than to find "an insoluble problem in the dialogue" (Kroeger) or an irreconcilable conflict between artistic intent and execution (Colburn). We can do so if we assume that Hemingway did not observe the typographical convention.

My premise (and, according to Professor Colburn, Warren's, Schorer's, Heilman's, and Oldsey's premise also) is that the speech "He has plenty of money" in the first dialogue is the young waiter's, and that this speech first establishes him in our mind as a callous materialist. To him, suicide when one has money would be suicide about "nothing"—an ironic anticipation of the *nada* motif later in the story. If we assume, as surely we must, that in a question and answer sequence the speaker *does* change with each new line, the young waiter is the one who knows all about the suicide and the old waiter the one who asks questions about it. This means that the questions in the second dialogue ("What did he want to kill himself for?" "How did he do it?" "Who cut him down?" "Why did they do it?" and "How much money has he got?") are the old waiter's. But if we assume that the speaker *always* changes when the line changes and take "He's drunk now" to be the old waiter's also (since only one line intervenes between it and "What did he want to kill himself for?"), then we run into difficulty with the pronoun reference, for the second "he" in "'He's drunk now,' he said" ought to refer to the young waiter and, I think, does. On this last point Mr. Kroeger, Professor Colburn and I are in agreement.

The inflexible use of the alternating line count fails again later in the second dialogue. "He's got plenty" is spoken by the young waiter. Its identity in content and attitude and near identity in wording with "He has plenty of money" in the first dialogue leaves the identification beyond any doubt, even without the assumption that it is the old waiter who asks the question the speech answers. And "I wish he would go home. I never get to bed before three o'clock. What kind of hour is that to go to bed?" is certainly the young waiter's also. That leaves two speeches in between: "He must be eighty years old" and "Anyway I should say he was eighty." Whose are they?

I submit that it is the young waiter who speaks *both* "He's drunk now" (because the pronoun reference demands it) *and* the next speech, "He's drunk every night." And that it is the old waiter who speaks *both* "He must be eighty years old" *and* "Anyway I should say he was eighty." Except in question and answer sequences, there is no need to assume regular alternation of speakers with each new, indented line—if, as here, such assumption presents difficulties.

It is possible that Hemingway, "or some one," as Mr. Kroeger prudently adds, was careless in distributing speeches between the two waiters. But the difficulty need not be so explained. Hemingway may have violated the convention in order to suggest a reflective pause between two sentences in a single speaker's uninterrupted utterance. "He's drunk every night" *may* be the old waiter's speech, but it seems to me to have more meaning as the young waiter's afterthought to his "He's drunk now." Similarly, either "He must be eighty years old" or "Anyway I should say he was eighty" *may* be the young waiter's, but I much prefer to assign both to the old waiter. The second sentence strikes me as a difficult disclaimer, an admission of subjectivity, that qualifies, after a pause, the objective certainty of "He must be eighty years old." Such qualification is in character, I think, only if it is the old waiter's.

The above, obviously, does not amount to proof. But it is common sense, and it has the added advantage of assuming Hemingway's ability to develop a major theme in his story by means or consistent characterization and without slipshod craftsmanship. It does not bother me at all that Hemingway may have violated the convention that new line means new speaker, but it would bother me to to think that he was confused as to the thematic function of his two waiters.

Joseph F. Gabriel (essay date 1961)

SOURCE: "The Logic of Confusion in Hemingway's 'A Clean, Well-Lighted Place,'" in *College English,* Vol. 22, No. 8, May, 1961, pp. 539-46.

[*In the following essay, Gabriel revisits the confusion regarding the dialogue in "A Clean, Well-Lighted Place," and contends that "there is no error made in the dialogue . . . in short, the inconsistency in the dialogue is deliberate, an integral part of the pattern of meaning actualized in the story."*]

Recent criticism of Hemingway's much admired and frequently anthologized **"A Clean, Well-Lighted Place"** has attempted to demonstrate that this story contains a damaging flaw. Indeed, two critics, F. P. Kroeger ("The Dialogue in 'A Clean, Well-Lighted Place,'" *College English,* Feb. 1959) and William E. Colburn ("Confusion in 'A Clean, Well-Lighted Place,'" *College English,* Feb. 1959), working independently of each other, appear to have arrived simultaneously at the same conclusion—that, to quote Professor Colburn, "The dialogue does not fit a logical pattern." Inasmuch as the story consists almost entirely of dialogue (principally a brief conversation between an older waiter and a younger waiter about an old man who recently attempted suicide and who is on this occasion the only customer in their care) this charge is a serious one—serious enough to warrant careful examination.

The difficulty presented by the story derives from the fact that in only a few instances does Hemingway identify the speaker. Throughout most of the dialogue the reader is faced with the task of inferring the speaker from the context. This initial difficulty is compounded, however,—turns into what Mr. Kroeger calls "an insoluble problem"—when the reader, proceeding on the natural assumption that he can assign each alternate line to one of the two waiters, attempts to trace out a consistent pattern in the dialogue. For when he works back and forth from lines which can be assigned with certainty, he finds himself involved in an apparently hopeless contradiction. The procedure and the contradiction which it makes manifest are succinctly outlined by Professor Colburn:

> One line . . . we can assign to the younger waiter, because of information which is brought out later. "'He's lonely. I'm not lonely. I have a wife waiting in bed for me.'" Using this line as a reference point, we can trace backwards in the story the alternate lines and discover that it is the younger waiter who is asking about the old man's attempt at suicide and it is the older waiter who knows the details as to method and who prevented him. Counting forward in the story from our reference line, however, we find the older waiter saying, "'I know. You said she cut him down.'" Obviously there is an inconsistency here.

In short, as Mr. Kroeger asserts, it would appear that "Hemingway, or someone, has been careless enough about the story so that at one time one main speaker seems to have information about the old man's suicide attempt which the other does not have, and at another time the situation is reversed."

This inconsistency would of itself be only a minor flaw were it not for the fact that it throws some doubt upon the first exchange, a part of the dialogue which has been seen by all previous commentators as an important key to the story because it helps establish the characterological and philosophic differences between the two waiters:

> "Last week he tried to commit suicide," one waiter said.

"Why?"

"He was in despair."

"What about?"

"Nothing."

"How do you know it was nothing?"

"He has plenty of money."

Though, as Professor Colburn observes, Robert Penn Warren ("Introduction," *A Farewell to Arms,* Scribner's, 1949, p. xv), Mark Schorer (*The Story,* p. 427), Robert Heilman (*Modern Short Stories,* p. 391), and Bernard Oldsey ("Hemingway's Old Men," *Modern Fiction Studies,* Aug., 1955, p. 32) all carefully avoid explicitly assigning the lines in this initial passage, their comments make inescapable the inference that it is the younger waiter who, because he is a materialist, because he does not understand what Mr. Warren so aptly calls "the despair beyond plenty of money," must be given the word "'Nothing'" here and that, therefore, it is he to whom one must attribute the knowledge of the old man and his suicide attempt. Inasmuch as Carlos Baker (*Hemingway: The Writer as Artist,* p. 124) and Otto Reinert ("Hemingway's Waiters Once More," *College English,* May, 1959), the two Hemingway critics who are specific in assigning the lines in the above passage, arrive at a similar reading, it is clear that these conclusions represent the prevailing interpretation of the initial dialogue.

It so happens that Professor Colburn is inclined to agree with the prevailing interpretation, Professor Kroeger is not. But the point upon which they concur—the burden of the argument presented in their papers—is that whatever the inclination of one's literary instincts in this matter, whatever the weight of critical opinion, the text does not literally support any consistent interpretation. Indeed, it is Professor Colburn's contention that this logical inconsistency in the dialogue calls into question the thematic unity of the story. For if, as part of the contradictory evidence would suggest, it is the older waiter who knows about the old man and his suicide attempt, then he would be the one to utter the word "'Nothing'" in the first exchange, and thus he too would presumably believe that there is no reason for despair except the lack of money. But if this is the case, then both waiters are materialistic, the story no longer presents two clearly differentiated and contrasting characters, and we are faced, not only with an inconsistency in the dialogue, but an inconsistency in the whole fabric of meaning.

The case for confusion in **"A Clean, Well-Lighted Place"** appears to be a solid one, and I cannot agree with Professor Reinert, who attempts to refute the charge by arguing that Hemingway simply ignored the convention whereby each new indented line implies a new speaker. Nevertheless, my purpose in this paper is to take issue with the thesis elaborated by Messrs. Kroeger and Colburn. Not that I deny the logical inconsistency of the dialogue. I am quite willing to accept this as fact. I dissent, however, from the use to which Professors Kroeger and Colburn appear to put their discovery. Thus, my intention is to redeem the story; that is, to establish, through an alternative reading, the validity of the dialogue just as we have it. What specifically I contend is that there was no error made in the dialogue, either by Scribner's or Hemingway himself; that we have here one of the most artfully contrived pieces in the Hemingway canon; and that, in short, the inconsistency in the dialogue is deliberate, an integral part of the pattern of meaning actualized in the story.

Despite the uncertainties and inconsistencies of the dialogue, the critic is not totally adrift. We have reasonably good grounds for assuming that the younger waiter and the older waiter are substantially different types: "'We are of two different kinds,' the older waiter said"; and indeed, if one ignores temporarily those parts of the dialogue which are in dispute, he does find sufficient evidence among those lines which can be assigned with certainty to arrive at a clear differentiation of the two waiters. But wherein do these differences lie? Since the story is about the word *nada* (a point on which all the critics agree), the reasonable inference is that the two waiters differ most importantly with respect to this word; that is, that all concomitant characterological and philosophic differences are reflected in their divergent interpretations of this word and its English equivalent, *nothing*.

It is apparent, as Carlos Baker has indicated (*Hemingway*, p. 124), that the older waiter uses the word *nada* in a special sense. For him the term represents, not a mere negativity, the absence of something, but a real constituent of the universe—the essence of life and of each life: "It was all a nothing and a man was nothing too." The most dramatic representation of this nihilism is to be found in the older waiter's ironic parody of the Lord's Prayer: "Our nada who art in nada, nada be thy name." He prays; but though, on one level, his prayer is a nostalgic glance at a pattern of belief, obviously Catholicism, which once gave meaning to the whole of life, on another level, it is a denial that any system is capable of conferring order upon the chaos. And in the place of the absent God and the missing Mary, he enthrones the Nothingness which he sees all around him: "Hail nothing full of nothing, nothing is with thee."

Yet it is evident that despite the older waiter's perception of chaos, of the impossibility of adhering any longer to a value system which made belief possible, he continues to betray a religious consciousness. The prayer which he utters, though involving an inversion of religious values, is nevertheless a prayer. We recognize it as a spiritual act. And though, paradoxically, what he apotheosizes is nothingness, it is obvious that his philosophy continues thereby to include the idea of God. Indeed, though the older waiter is acutely conscious of the impossibility of belief, he cannot free himself from the tendency to think religiously. Thus, his dilemma is the most acute. A religious man who finds no system acceptable, he must bear at the same time his intense spiritual hunger and the realization of the im-

possibility of its fulfillment. For no reconciliation is possible. The crack in his universe is beyond repair; the gap between chaos and order, nothingness and meaning, is infinite. And it is this infinite distance which is the measure of his despair.

It is a tribute to the heroic quality of the older waiter's aspiration that he does not settle for the philosophy of nothingness to which he is driven. A religious man and therefore, by implication, one who seeks for patterns, he constructs out of the infinite *nada* something which is not *nada*. This accomplishment is symbolized in the dominant visual image in the story: the radical contrast between the minute spot of light represented by the café and the infinite surrounding darkness outside. The intensity of the older waiter's commitment to the café—"'I am one of those who like to stay late at the café. . . . With all those who need a light for the night.'"—is to be traced to the fact that for him it is the single patch of meaning in the void of *nada*. Its qualities of cleanliness, order, and light stand in direct contrast to the attributes which so overwhelmingly prevail in the universe outside. But that the only order and meaning he can find is offered by a clean, well-lighted café is an indication of the extremity to which he is driven, as well as of the crisis of our age. Nor can we miss the irony and the pathos inherent in so extremely limited a faith. This is brought home to us the moment we compare it with the conventional religious belief in an omniscient and omnipotent God. To the question everywhere implied in the text: In what do you believe? the older waiter can reply only with the virtually absurd, "I believe in a clean, well-lighted place."

The younger waiter has none of the heroic qualities of the older waiter and nothing of his spiritual aspiration. A thoroughgoing materialist, he offers us the image of man reduced, man stripped of every spiritual dimension. Only the physical satisfactions interest him. His vision extends only as far as his wife waiting at home in bed for him. And he knows nothing of that despair with which the older waiter is consumed. He is, as he admits, "'all confidence,'" because he sees the universe, not as an objective lack, but as a plenitude. It is equal to his desire. Indeed, it is only money which is lacking, money with which to purchase those purely naturalistic satisfactions, which are all that he can conceive. Only money stands between him and complete fulfillment.

It will be seen that the value system embraced by the younger waiter entails an alternate concept of *nada*. To him *nada* can only signify a personal physical privation. *Nothing* refers simply to the absence of those objects capable of providing material satisfactions. And by extension he applies the term to all behavior which does not grant the sufficiency of things. Any behavior of this sort strikes him as motiveless, lacking in sufficient reason, and, therefore, grounded in nothing. But, thus, to him, the despair of a man who has plenty of money would appear absurd, and he would use the word "'Nothing'" to signify that absurdity—that is, to mean "for no reason." Hence the prevailing interpretation of the first exchange:

Y.W. "Last week he tried to commit suicide," one waiter said.

O.W. "Why?"

Y.W. "He was in despair."

O.W. "What about?"

Y.W. "Nothing." (For no reason)

O.W. "How do you know it was nothing?"

Y.W. "He has plenty of money." (With plenty of money, there is no reason for despair.)

This is an eminently reasonable inference. Yet, if we are to understand the story, it is vital that we see that it is not only the only hypothesis which is consistent with the facts. There are, as our analysis has attempted to make clear, at least two concepts of *nada* in the story, the *nada* which each waiter sees. And the truth is that as soon as we are able to make a precise differentiation between the two, we realize that it is equally reasonable to assign the word in question to the older waiter, except that he would use the word "'Nothing'" to refer, not, as the younger waiter does, to any senselessness or absurdity in the old man's behavior, but to that which is his own obsessional concern, the chaos, the lack of objective meaning in the universe. And thus we arrive at an alternate reading of the initial dialogue:

O.W. "Last week he tried to commit suicide," one waiter said.

Y.W. "Why?"

O.W. "He was in despair."

Y.W. "What about?"

O.W. "Nothing." (Chaos, meaninglessness)

Y.W. "How do you know it was nothing?" (Misunderstanding the older waiter's use of "'Nothing.'")

O.W. "He has plenty of money." (Inasmuch as he has plenty of money, his despair does not derive from any merely material want.)

It might appear that the foregoing analysis only serves to substantiate the charge of confusion in **"A Clean, Well-Lighted Place."** On the contrary, however, as I shall try to demonstrate, it helps to establish the rationale of the story. The position taken here is that the several concepts of nothing inhere simultaneously in the word "nothing" as it is spoken in the first exchange and that therefore it is attributable to either waiter and to both waiters. Hence my operating assumption is not that this initial dialogue is in any way defective, but that it is part of an experiment in multiple meaning and that Hemingway, in making use of the range of semantic possibilities inherent in the words *nada* and *nothing,* has, in the manner of Henry James, constructed a perfect ambiguity. This is the reason I can agree neither with the proponents of the prevailing inter-

pretation (Baker, Reinert, Colburn, etc.) nor with Professor Kroeger when he says:

> Since the story is about the word *nada,* chaos, it does not seem reasonable that in the first dialogue the young waiter would say that the old man tried to commit suicide because he was in despair. The old waiter would naturally say that he tried to commit suicide about nothing because the old waiter understands that even with money, the old man can be in despair with his knowledge that all is *nada.*

For the point is that it is not a matter of either/or; the dialogue should be read on both levels. All merely one-valued interpretations of its meaning are simplistic and therefore inadequate.

These contentions are confirmed in the analysis of other elements in the story. It is generally assumed that, in the dialogue following the one just discussed, it is the older waiter who expresses fear that the soldier and the girl will be caught ("'He had better get off the street. The guard will get him. They went by five minutes ago.'") and it is the younger waiter who says, "'What does it matter if he gets what he's after.'" Thus Professor Colburn says, "No doubt most readers will agree that the older waiter should be the one . . . to be concerned that the soldier with the streetwalker will get into trouble. And most readers probably will agree that the younger waiter should be the one with the completely materialistic attitude toward life." Certainly this accords with what we already know about the two waiters. We have witnessed the importance which the younger waiter attaches to sex. Furthermore, knowing as we do the older waiter's solicitude for the old man, it seems likely that this sympathetic quality manifests itself here, too, in his concern for the welfare of the soldier.

But though this hypothesis is quite reasonable, it is equally logical to read the dialogue in the opposite fashion, attributing the "'What does it matter if he gets what he's after'" speech to the older waiter. The older waiter is the one who, conscious of the infinite gap between chaos and order, is in the grip of despair. And from the perspective of despair, what can it matter that the soldier might be picked up by the guard. In a virtually meaningless world, one takes one's desperate chances, because, in fact, all chances are desperate, and one makes one's little meaningful moments as one can. It is only from the perspective of the younger waiter that such prudent considerations as are expressed in the above quotation can have any weight. Indeed, it is the materialist who is always finally the practical man, the one who is constantly absorbed in the calculus of probability, balancing possible success against possible failure. Prudence, practicality, calculation: these are the pragmatic virtues, the virtues that bring material success; and these are precisely the qualities we attribute to the younger waiter. In short, again there are two equally good ways of reading the dialogue; again we have a dialogue constructed on the pattern of ambiguity.

At this point two observations are in order: that the story contains something less than fifteen hundred words and that, within this brief compass, it is possible to cite, in addition to the inconsistency of the third dialogue and the ambivalence of the first and second dialogues, still other instances of "confusion." Thus, to produce one final example, when near the conclusion of the story the older waiter speculates upon the strange fear that has gripped him ("What did he fear? It was not fear or dread. It was a nothing that he knew too well"), the language is such that no simple logical reduction is possible. The passage is really a dialectic of contradictory implications: that what is feared is not feared; that what is not known, because known only negatively (in terms of what it is not), is known only too well; and that what is a nothing is a something, and a something of such importance that it consumes his every thought and gives decisive shape to his existence. The answer is plain enough. The actualization of multiple meaning is so pervasive an element here that obviously no attempt to explain it as the result of a single lapse in artistic control or of an error in the process of publication can possibly be successful. Clearly it can only be accounted for as part of a deliberate plan, a function of the author's mode of execution. And, indeed, careful attention to the structure of the story demonstrates the truth of a general observation about Hemingway's method made by Professor Carlos Baker—that below his purely naturalistic surfaces, Hemingway undertakes a conscious exploitation of the possibilities inherent in the symbolistic technique and makes major use of the specific devices of this style: ambiguity, irony, symbol, and paradox (*Hemingway,* pp. 289-292).

But it might be said that ambiguity is one thing, inconsistency quite another. Why should Hemingway deliberately create an inconsistency? We know that the story is an exploration of the word *nada,* that it develops by playing upon the several meanings inherent in this word and its English equivalent. But if the word "'Nothing'" when spoken in the first exchange is to be a complex term, conveying the full range of meanings and especially those contradictory ones we have already discussed, then it becomes necessary that its speaker not be identified. But this in turn demands that the waiter who knows about the old man and his suicide attempt not be identified, or at least that the reader not be able to make any consistent identification; conclusive identification would be inimical to the creation of multiple meaning. Thus such inconsistency as we find in the long dialogue is the necessary means toward a higher consistency. Indeed, it is only through this inconsistency that the ambiguity of the first exchange can be maintained.

But if it is clear enough that the inconsistency in the long dialogue guarantees the ambiguity of the initial exchange, wherein lies the ultimate necessity or justification for either ambiguity or inconsistency? This question might be answered in part by attempting to show that ambiguity is one of the fundamental norms of the symbolist, that is to say, the modern aesthetic. But this procedure would appear to be less expedient and less relevant than another. We can assign a more immediate reason for those plurisignificant structures which we find here. Though, as even a casual

reading of the story demonstrates, Hemingway employs the words *nada* and *nothing* as if he were weaving a musical motif, and though he is interested in all the variations on his theme; nevertheless, it is the meaning which the older waiter attaches to these words which is the more important. Clearly it is his problem which is central, and the story is fundamentally about the kind of world which he sees. But though it has more than once been observed that the older waiter's world is ruled by chaos and that, therefore, its major constituents are uncertainty, inconsistency, confusion, and ambiguity, it has not been observed that the constituents of his world are precisely the constituents of the dialogue—that, in short, there is a structural similarity between this world and the dialogue.

Indeed, it is the principal thesis of this [essay] that the dialogue in the story operates on two levels: it operates in the conventional manner, discursively conveying the essential features of the older waiter's vision; and it operates symbolically, actually representing through its construction the kind of world he experiences. Not only does the dialogue tell of the *nada* of existence, but it re-creates it by raising for the reader the very problems which confront the older waiter and the old man as they apprehend their world. The experience of the reader duplicates their experience, for the reader, too, is called upon to bear uncertainty, inconsistency, confusion, and ambiguity, as he attempts to fashion some pattern of meaning out of the chaos of the dialogue. Thus, the confusion in **"A Clean, Well-Lighted Place"** is neither a mistake nor an accident. It is deliberate. Hemingway has brilliantly actualized in the dialogue the very conditions which obtain in the world as it is perceived by modern man—a world where meaning is no longer guaranteed by omniscience.

It might be noted in passing that just as the structure of the dialogue symbolically represents the theme of chaos, so the structure of Hemingway's language symbolically portrays the older waiter's limited faith. Thus, the denial of rhetoric implies the impossibility of the elaborate system-making of traditional metaphysics. And the restricted diction, the uncomplicated grammatical patterns actualize on the purely linguistic level the values of cleanliness, order, and light to which the older waiter clings amid the massive chaos.

But we need to carry our analysis one step further if we are to understand fully the necessity behind Hemingway's method of construction here. We have already observed that the story is about the word *nada,* that it emerges out of the contrast of two wholly different concepts of nothing. What we need to recognize, however, is that this preoccupation with the *nada* of existence establishes a crucial connection between the story and the most important philosophic movement of our time—existentialism. Indeed, it can be said that this story is about the word *nada* in the same way that the phenomenological ontologies of Heidegger and Sartre are about the concept of nothingness. It is no accident, for example, that Sartre's major work bears the title *Being and Nothingness.* But it is only with the realization that **"A Clean, Well-Lighted Place"** is itself an existentialist document that we are likely to understand the way in which it actualizes still another concept of nothing, one which has been the special concern of existentialist literature. And, in turn, it is only when we possess this knowledge that we can understand the total relationship between theme and structure in the story.

The humanistic wing of the existentialist movement has really been conducting an examination of the consequences of living in a world where, as Nietzsche put it, "God is dead" (See Walter Kaufmann, "The Death of God and the Revaluation," *Nietzsche,* pp. 80-100). This is the subject to which Sartre addresses himself (See Hazel E. Barnes, "Translator's Introduction," *Being and Nothingness,* p. xxix), and this, as we have seen, is the condition in which the older waiter and the old man find themselves. But if Nietzsche's assertion truly defines the modern predicament, then it follows that man alone now has the responsibility for actualizing being and creating values. As the existentialists have realized, however, this total freedom which thus devolves upon man is ambivalent. It is felt as a burden, a dreadful freedom. Man, in the words of Sartre, is "condemned to be free" (*Being and Nothingness,* p. 439). For inasmuch as man's existence is no longer grounded in the noncontingent, that is, in God, man is stripped entirely of his dependence upon the objective, and neither an objective guarantee of meaning nor an objective justification for behavior is possible. Man is thus faced with the necessity for assuming the contingency of all of his projects and even of his own existence. But to perceive every being essentially as pure contingency is to assert, not only that every being is suspended in nothingness—in the chaos which the older waiter discerns—but that nothingness is itself contained in every being. In short, the metaphysics which the older waiter embraces, his metaphysics of chaos, entails an ontology, that is, says something about the very nature of being. And what is said has been succinctly summed up by Sartre himself: "Nothingness lies coiled in the heart of being—like a worm." (*Being and Nothingness,* p. 21).

Here we have a clue to that mysterious fear or dread which the older waiter feels is not fear or dread in the usual sense: "What did he fear? It was not fear or dread. It was a nothing that he knew too well." This dread comes not from the fear of any particular object, but is rather the consequence of the older waiter's perception, however dim, of pure contingency, of that nothingness which in part defines human nature. It is thus an existential anguish which the older waiter feels, a psychological concomitant of the existential ontology. To quote Hazel Barnes, the translator of *Being and Nothingness,* this anguish is "The reflective apprehension of the Self as freedom, the realization that nothingness slips in between my Self and my Past and Future so that nothing guarantees the validity of the values I choose. Fear is of something in the world, anguish is anguish before myself (as in Kierkegaard)" (*Being and Nothingness,* p. 628). Thus, in addition to the two major meanings already assigned to the word *nada* in the

story, there is a third: nothingness is synonymous with man's radical subjectivity, with his total freedom. Indeed, man may be defined as that being who is forced to renounce the idea of finding a guarantee for his existence outside of himself. (See Simone de Beauvoir, *The Ethics of Ambiguity,* trans. by Bernard Frechtman, p. 14).

It is this third meaning of nothingness which partially escapes the older waiter. He is, after all, no philosopher. And he does not fully understand what he feels. In the end he wonders whether it isn't only insomnia from which he suffers. Nevertheless, despite the limitations in the older waiter's understanding of his predicament, Hemingway manages with consummate skill to incorporate this third meaning of nothing into the texture of the story. As its creator, the God behind its world, he refuses to guarantee the meanings which it actualizes. The dialogue is so constructed that the reader, in his attempt to impose order upon the chaos of inconsistency and ambiguity, is stripped of his dependence upon the objective. In so far as the dialogue fails to conform to the norms of logic, the reader himself is, like the older waiter, plunged into the existentialist predicament and made to confront the absurd. In his attempt to make sense out of the story, the reader too is forced to assume contingency, is forced to deal with values and meanings which cannot be given objective justification, and is even brought finally to a recognition of his own radical subjectivity.

John V. Hagopian (essay date 1964)

SOURCE: "Tidying Up Hemingway's Clean, Well-Lighted Place," in *Studies in Short Fiction,* Vol. I, No. 2, Winter, 1964, pp. 140-46.

[*In the following essay, Hagopian rejects earlier attempts to attribute Hemingway's dialogue in the story—particularly Joseph Gabriel's above—and considers the flaw in the dialogue as an obvious typographical error.*]

Interpretation of Hemingway's **"A Clean, Well-Lighted Place"** has always been dogged by the problem of the confused dialogue between the two waiters, and it seems to me unfortunate that the discussion of it remains where Joseph F. Gabriel left it in *College English* (May, 1961). Gabriel was responding to three earlier articles in the same journal (February and May, 1959), in the first of which F. P. Kroeger had accurately interpreted most of the dialogue up to the line "I know. You said she cut him down," which he assumed to be incorrectly attributed by Hemingway to the young waiter because it suggests that it is he who "knows about the details of the suicide, and not the old waiter as the earlier dialogue indicates." William E. Colburn concurred with this view, but went further in asserting that such an error raises doubts about the first conversation in which the old waiter replies "He has plenty of money" in answer to the younger waiter's question "How do you know it [the reason for the old customer's suicide attempt] was nothing?" Colburn felt certain that "probably most readers will agree that the *younger* waiter should be the one with a completely materialistic attitude toward life"; and he took to task such critics as Robert Penn Warren, Mark Schorer, Robert Heilman, and Bernard Oldsey for "carefully" or "cleverly" failing to identify the speaker of the line "He has plenty of money."

Then Otto Reinert announced that he and all of the aforementioned critics, except Kroeger, proceed on the premise that the first reference to money in the story is made by the younger waiter and that it "establishes him in our mind as a callous materialist." By what authority Reinert spoke for the others remains unclear, but he developed from that premise a complex set of confusions and misinterpretations: "If we assume, as we surely must, that in a question and answer sequence the speaker *does* change with each new line, the young waiter is the one who knows all about the suicide and the old waiter the one who asks questions about it." But since this would create impossible difficulties about the identity of the speaker of "He's drunk now," Reinert was forced into ingenuity by assuming that Hemingway violated convention in having the same speaker for alternating lines of a dialogue which is not a question-and-answer sequence "in order to suggest a reflective pause between two sentences in a single speaker's uninterrupted utterance." And he presumed that this occurs twice, without any sign from the author, with two different speakers in the same dialogue sequence! "I submit that it is the young waiter who speaks *both* 'He's drunk now' (because the pronoun reference demands it) *and* the next speech, 'He's drunk every night.' And that it is the old waiter who speaks *both* 'He must be eighty years old' *and* 'Anyway I should say that he was eighty.'" This was presumably such good "common sense" that it required no "proof."

It seems to me, however, that this solution to the problem would be valid only if (1) by the law of parsimony, it is the simplest solution; (2) an examination of the rest of Hemingway's fiction shows that the author often, or even occasionally, employed such a technique; and (3) the context supported, as it does in Joyce's *Ulysses,* the notion that the author violates standard conventions without explicit hints or clues to the reader. On none of these grounds can one support Reinert's interpretation. It is neither the simplest solution nor is it at all supported by the context, which makes it quite clear that it is the old waiter who is obsessed with the awareness of *nada* and who recognizes and sympathizes with a fellow sufferer in the old man at the café. Furthermore—though this is by no means an absolute test—nowhere else in *The Short Stories of Ernest Hemingway* (Modern Library) is there an instance of a reflective pause between two lines of dialogue by the same speaker without some indication of the fact:

in **"The Battler"**:

> Bugs: ". . . She sends him money."
>
> He poked up the fire.
>
> "She's a mighty fine woman," he said.
>
> (p. 235)

in **"The Killers"**:

> "Maybe it was just a bluff."
>
> "No. It ain't just a bluff."
>
> Ole Andresen rolled over toward the wall.
>
> "The only thing is," he said, talking toward the wall, "I just can't make up my mind to go out. . . ."
>
> (p. 385)

in **"A Pursuit Race"**:

> "Good," said William Campbell. "Because really I don't know anything at all. I was just talking." He pulled the sheet up over his face. "I love it under a sheet," he said.
>
> (p. 449)

in **"Now I Lay Me"**:

> "I think it's all bull, myself," he said. "I just heard it somewhere. You know how you hear things."
>
> We were both quiet and I listened to the silk-worms.
>
> "You hear those damn silk-worms?" he asked.
>
> (p. 466)

in **"The Sea Change"**:

> "Yes," she said. "I have to and you know it."
>
> He did not say anything and she looked at him. . . .
>
> "Couldn't you just be good to me and let me go?" the girl asked.
>
> (p. 497)

Joseph F. Gabriel does not refute Reinert; he merely dismisses him in order to take issue with Messrs. Kroeger and Colburn: "What specifically I contend is that there was no error made in the dialogue, either by Scribner's or Hemingway himself; that we have here one of the most artfully contrived pieces in the Hemingway canon; and that, in short, the inconsistency in the dialogue is deliberate, an integral part of the pattern of meaning actualized in the story." But if there is anything that is "artfully contrived," it is Gabriel's interpretation, which is one of the most ingenious *tours de force* of explication that I have ever seen. Although I have no quarrel with his existentialist reading of the story and, in fact, consider it the most profound and thoroughgoing to date, I cannot accept his contention that such a reading is dependent upon logical inconsistency in the dialogue. For the most part he is quite right about the meaning, but far too cleverly wrong about the technique. Gabriel would have us believe that the confusion in the third dialogue is a clue to the necessity of an either-or alternation of speakers in the first two dialogues: "The experience of the reader duplicates [the old man's and the old waiter's] experience [of nada], for the reader, too, is called upon to bear uncertainty, inconsistency, confusion, and ambiguity, as he attempts to fashion some pattern of meaning out of the chaos of the dialogue."

However, once again, submitted to the tests of validity that I have suggested above, this reading collapses. It is by no means the simplest solution to the problem, it is a technique employed nowhere else in the Hemingway canon, and it is not supported by the context—especially the ending, which clearly attributes to the two waiters different and incompatible sets of values, each of which can, except for the line isolated by Kroeger, be clearly traced without any difficulty in the opening dialogues. Furthermore, this solution endows Hemingway with the absurd aesthetics of a Tristan Tzara by suggesting that an artist can validly embody the idea of chaos by being chaotic. Gabriel confuses the *perception of ambiguity* with the *feeling of confusion,* and he seems to believe that a "pattern of meaning" can be "actualized in a story" even when its creator "refuses to guarantee the meanings which it actualizes." Each of the multiple meanings of any artistically successful ambiguity must be clear, complete, and meaningful. The Gestaltists long ago showed how this is possible in the famous figure of the Rubin vase, which—depending on whether the center is taken as figure or as ground—can be seen either as an ornate Grecian vase or as the profiles of two people looking at each other, but not as both at the same time! Hence, there is no confusion, no chaos—merely "plurisignificance." William Empson demonstrated in *Seven Types of Ambiguity* that there are many ambiguous (i.e., multiply meaningful, but not confused) substructures *within* literary works. But I know of no work which is the successful *total* ambiguity that Gabriel proposes **"A Clean, Well-Lighted Place"** is (unless John Donne's "The Relique" fills the bill).

In any case, the very nature of art requires order, meaning, and form, even if what is being rendered into art is the absurd. And if, like Gabriel, we are to discuss the art of fiction in terms of existentialism, it would be well to remember the dicta of Albert Camus, who though he recognized the world to be absurd did not therefore conclude that art forms and techniques must be absurd. He says in *The Rebel* (trans. by Anthony Bower, London, 1953):

> Artistic creation is a demand for unity and a rejection of the world (p. 222). . . . The artist reconstructs the world to his plan (p. 224). . . . What, in fact, is a novel but a universe in which action is endowed with form, where final words are pronounced, where people possess one another completely and where life assumes the aspect of destiny (p. 231). . . . Whatever may be the chosen point of view of the artist, one principle remains common to all creators: stylization, which supposes the simultaneous existence of reality and of the mind which gives reality its form.
>
> (p. 239)

Hence the artist shapes the absurdity of the world in such a way that we are enabled to perceive it; he does not fling the absurd into our faces. But Gabriel would have us believe that in Hemingway's story "the dialogue is so con-

structed that the reader, in his attempt to impose order [as if that were the reader's and not the writer's task] upon the chaos of inconsistency and ambiguity, is stripped of his dependence upon the objective. In so far as the dialogue fails to conform to the norms of logic, the reader himself is, like the older waiter, plunged into the existentialist predicament and made to confront the absurd." This, I submit, is a misinterpretation. It is far kinder to Hemingway to label a single line of dialogue as the obvious typographical error than it is to torture his prose into ambiguous chaos.

My German colleague Martin Dolch has offered an interpretation of **"A Clean, Well-Lighted Place"** which is consistent with that of Gabriel, but without his radical twisting of the form (cf. Hagopian and Dolch, *Insight I: Analyses of American Literature,* Frankfurt, 1962, pp. 105-11). On the basis of Dolch's discussion, the three opening dialogues might be interpreted as follows:

I.

O.W. "Last week he tried to commit suicide." [According to the final dialogues of the story, it is the older waiter who knows and understands the despair of the old man at the café.]

Y.W. "Why?" [All the questions demanding answers are uttered by the young waiter. The older waiter never seeks information from the younger, all his questions being purely rhetorical: "What does it matter if he gets what he's after?" "How should I know?" "Why didn't you let him stay and drink?" "What is an hour?" "And you? You have no fear?"]

O.W. "He was in despair." [The younger waiter knows nothing about despair; it is the older waiter who in his prayer to *nada* proves himself the authority on this subject.]

Y.W. "What about?"

O.W. "Nothing." [A controlled, ambiguous substructure; its double-meaning would be: "For no reason that you would understand" and "Because of the nada of the universe."]

Y.W. "How do you know it was nothing?"

O.W. "He has plenty of money." [Again ambiguous: "Since you insist on a reason, I'll give the only one a man like you could possibly understand—there couldn't be a good reason because he has plenty of money" and "It wasn't the lack of money; it was his awareness of nada."]

II.

(After a girl and a soldier walk by in the street) Y.W. "The guard will pick him up." [A bit of Schadenfreude, quite consistent with his remark to the deaf old man, "You should have killed yourself last week."]

O.W. "What does it matter if he gets what he's after?" [Consistent with his indifference to the usual social norms, with his nihilism, and with his awareness of the value of youth and confidence: "those things are very beautiful."]

Y.W. "He had better get off the street now. The guard will get him." [The young waiter wants everybody to get off the streets, including the old man, so that he can go home to his wife. It is he who is keenly aware of the time, who complains that he never gets into bed before three o'clock, and who is impatient. He is later identified as "the waiter who was in a hurry," while the older one is dubbed "the unhurried waiter."]

III.

Y.W. "He's drunk now," he said. [All critics recognize, with varying degrees of distress, that the speaker must be the young waiter who has returned from serving the old man.]

O.W. "He's drunk every night." [The intonation of the young waiter's remark should indicate indignation, while the old waiter's reply indicates recognition and acceptance of the fact with tolerance and sympathy, as if to say "Of course the old man is drunk tonight and every night—he has good reason to be!"]

Y.W. "What did he want to kill himself for?" [Resuming the earlier dialogue in which he was the questioner.]

O.W. "How should I know." [reluctant to discuss the subject with a man of whom he says later, "We are of two different kinds" and "You do not understand."]

Y.W. "How did he do it?" [If you won't tell me why, at least tell me how."]

O.W. "He hung himself with a rope."

Y.W. "Who cut him down?"

O.W. "His niece."

Y.W. "Why did they do it?" [Perhaps suggesting that they should have let him hang, in which case he would not now have to wait about while his wife lies in bed waiting for him.]

O.W. "Fear for his soul." ["You know how some people are—they have no awareness of nada and think that a man has a soul, the credulous fools."]

Y.W. "How much money has he got?" ["You said earlier that he has plenty."]

O.W. "He's got plenty." ["What difference does the exact amount make? How much money a man has isn't important anyway."]

Y.W. "He must be eighty years old." [Old enough to die."]

O.W. "Anyway, I should say he was eighty." ["Perhaps he is, but that, too, doesn't matter much."]

Y.W. "I wish he would go home. . . . " [Impatient.]

O.W. "He stays up because he likes it." [Again, it would be futile to try to explain the importance of a clean, well-lighted place *to* a man who is unaware of the nada of the universe.]

Y.W. "He's lonely. I'm not lonely. I have a wife waiting in bed for me." [Supplying the only motive that he can understand, again perhaps with a bit of Schadenfreude, especially considering his boast.]

O.W. "He had a wife once, too." ["Having a wife isn't sufficient guarantee that nada will not catch up with you. You are by no means superior to that old man, merely less aware."]

Y.W. "A wife would be no good to him now." [Again a boast with Schadenfreude.]

O.W. "You can't tell. He might be better with a wife." [Recognizing, as in Camus, that love might not eliminate nada, but might make it bearable. He is irritated into disputing with the cocksure young waiter.]

Y.W. "His niece looks after him. You said she cut him down." ["The only services that a wife could render him, those of nurse and caretaker, are being supplied by his niece."]

O.W. "I know." ["I am perfectly aware of what happened and why—much more than you, you young puppy!"]

And the line "you said she cut him down" clearly belongs to the speech of the young waiter; it has all the overtones of his sadistic irony. All the texts to date have merely perpetuated a typographical error. The answer to Colburn's enquiry, "How do we evaluate a story which has 'mistakes'?" is that we make a distinction between artistic and mechanical errors. The latter, like the reversal of the chapters in Henry James's *The Ambassadors,* are not very serious and are easily corrected. They certainly do not warrant a torturing of the text or critical pyrotechnics to convert them into dubious virtues. I would suggest that in the future editions of this story Scribner's simply move the line to its proper place and avoid any further fuss.]

Y.W. "I wouldn't want to be that old. An old man is a nasty thing." [Consistent with his sadism, his boasting, etc.]

O.W. "Not always. This old man is clean. He drinks without spilling. Even now, drunk. Look at him." [He is a defender of the Hemingway code: with the awareness of the absurdity that death makes of human life, one must be congratulated if he maintains a certain poise and grace in his external behavior while within he is in despair. Nick Adams in **"The Big Two-Hearted River"** is one of many variations on the theme.]

Though I am certain that my glosses can be improved upon, I do not believe it is possible to supply a similar set of glosses derived from the total context of the story to justify a reversed alternation of speakers. All that Hemingway's story needed was a little tidying up by its first proofreader, a mere sweep of the broom; there was no need to call out the reconstruction crews to convert **"A Clean, Well-Lighted Place"** into the absurd house of Samuel Beckett.

Warren Bennett (essay date 1970)

SOURCE: "Character, Irony, and Resolution in 'A Clean, Well-Lighted Place,'" in *The Short Stories of Ernest Hem-*

ingway: Critical Essays, edited by Jackson J. Benson, Duke University Press, 1975, pp. 261-69.

[In the following essay, which was originally published in American Literature *in 1970, Bennett proposes that Hemingway's use of verbal irony provides insight into the main characters as well as evidence as to the attribution of dialogue in "A Clean, Well-Lighted Place."]*

Interpretation of Hemingway's short story **"A Clean, Well-Lighted Place"** has always been confronted with the illogical dialogue sequence between the two waiters. Since analysis probably became stalled on the question of which waiter knew about the old man's attempted suicide, interpretation has tended to center on either the older waiter's *nada* prayer or the problem of the illogical sequence itself.[1] The result seems to be a partial misinterpretation of the character of the younger waiter, a failure to see the wide play of irony in the story, and the absence of any interpretation of the story's ironic resolution.

However, before these latter matters can be successfully dealt with, the story's troubled dialogue must still be preliminarily considered. Scribner's claims that the dialogue inconsistency occurred when a slug of type was evidently misplaced in the first printing of the story in *Scribner's Magazine* in 1933, and since reprint plates were made from that printing and not from the original manuscript, which is no longer extant to anyone's knowledge, the error was perpetuated until 1965.[2] At that time Scribner's issued a new edition of **The Short Stories of Ernest Hemingway** and made an "editorial" correction in the illogical sequence because the dialogue dictated it.

All texts from 1933 to 1965:

"His niece looks after him."

"I know. You said she cut him down."

The 1965 text and all subsequent printings:

"His niece looks after him. You said she cut him down."

"I know."[3]

This solved the problem of the illogical sequence, but because it gives the knowledge of the old man's attempted suicide to the older waiter instead of the younger waiter, it is contrary to some critical opinion and compatible with others. The correction, therefore, traded one kind of question for another kind: since Hemingway did not correct his own story during his lifetime, does that make the old text Hemingway's story and the new text his publisher's story? Should the critic use the old text or the new text?

In order to put my own interpretation on a firm footing, I hope to demonstrate, first of all, that even though no corrections were made in the story, it is still possible to determine that the older waiter is the one who knows about the old man's attempted suicide.

The structure of the story is based on a consistent polarity: "despair," characterized by depth of feeling and insight into the human condition, in opposition to "confidence," characterized by a lack of feeling and, therefore, a lack of insight. Each pole is seen as an attitude, or stance, in relation to Hemingway's *donnée,* which is a nihilistic concept of life: nothingness or *nada.* The spark which ignites the conflict of stances is the deaf old man who has tried to commit suicide and needs a clean, well-lighted café in which to stay late. The denouement is an irony of fate, presented by image and understatement, which will shatter "confidence" against the hard truth that "it [is] all a nothing and a man [is] nothing too."

The tension of the conflict is rendered almost exclusively through the dialogue of the two waiters, who are said to be of "two different kinds," and we can identify one waiter by tracing the use of the word "kill." When the younger waiter returns from taking the old man's brandy order, he says to the older waiter, "'I'm sleepy. I never get into bed before three o'clock. He should have *killed himself* last week'" (italics mine). Then when the younger waiter takes the brandy out to the old man, he says to him, "'You should have *killed yourself* last week'" (italics mine). Since there is no textual basis for transferring the younger waiter's mode of expression to the older waiter, the text clearly establishes that it is the younger waiter who asks for further information: "'What did he want to *kill himself* for?'" (italics mine). Consequently, it is the older waiter who knows the history of the old man and speaks the first line of dialogue in the story: "'Last week he tried to commit suicide.'"

This is supported by a structural pattern, utilizing verbal irony, which is repeated in three separate scenes—two formerly in question and one not in question. For the pattern to emerge clearly, it is necessary to look at the scenes in reverse order, beginning with the scene where the lines are not in question. The scene is the bodega where the older waiter stops for a drink.

"What's yours?" asked the barman. [Serious question.]

"Nada." [Verbal irony: the older waiter.]

"Otro loco mas," said the barman and turned away. [Dropping the subject.]

"A little cup," said the waiter. [Serious reply.]

The bodega barman, of course, must be equated with the younger waiter because he has an "unpolished" bar, equivalent to the younger waiter pouring into the old man's brandy glass until it "slopped over and ran down the stem." Also, the barman calls the older waiter "another crazy one," as the younger waiter has accused the older waiter of "talking nonsense." But for our purposes, the important aspect is the pattern: serious question, verbal irony by the older waiter, a dropping of the subject, and then a serious reply. The significant factor in the pattern is the older waiter's use of verbal irony in response to a serious question.

The complete pattern appears earlier in the story, in that exchange concerned with why they cut the old man down.

"Why did they do it?" [Serious question.]

"Fear for his soul." [Verbal irony: the older waiter.]

"How much money has he got?" [Dropping the subject; serious question.]

"He's got plenty." [Serious reply.]

The third scene is the first exchange between the two waiters, near the beginning of the story. The pattern here is abbreviated, repeating only the older waiter's use of verbal irony in response to a serious question. One waiter says the old man was in despair, and the other waiter asks,

"What about?" [Serious question.]

"Nothing." [Verbal irony: the older waiter.]

"How do you know it was nothing?" [Serious question.]

"He has plenty of money." [Verbal irony: the older waiter.]

In this last scene, the reply, "nothing," and the reply, "he has plenty of money," both carry an undertone of irony, regardless of which waiter speaks the lines.[4] The irony is inherent in them as answers to the serious questions asked. For example, if the younger waiter answered that the old man was in despair about "nothing," the reply still carries the charge of double meaning, meaning: i.e., a serious meaning: there was, in fact, no apparent reason; *and* a malicious meaning: the reason seems ridiculous and unimportant to me: he was only feeling sorry for himself.

Since verbal irony is employed, we must look to the text for hard evidence of which waiter employs it as a mode of speaking, and that evidence is in the scene with the bodega barman. It is the *older* waiter who uses verbal irony; he even thinks ironically: "After all, he said to himself, it is probably only insomnia. Many must have it." There is no definite evidence, anywhere in the story, that the younger waiter has mastered such a manner of speaking, or thinking. On the contrary, the younger waiter is consistently serious and changes his form of address only once, "speaking with that omission of syntax stupid people employ when talking to drunken people or foreigners."

Once it has been established that the older waiter is the one who knows about the old man, it is then possible to see the characters of the two waiters in correct perspective.

Essentially, the younger waiter is not a "materialist," as critics, explicitly or implicitly, have tried to make him. Expressing interest in money and sex does not automatically relegate one to the pigeonhole labeled "materialist," which critics like to use in a pejorative sense, although it should not be so used. Materialism denotes a complex set of ideas,

and to the extent that the story is held to have philosophical import, the philosophical senses of "materialism" must be recognized.

Briefly, a materialist is one who affirms matter as the only reality, or one who gives it an effective priority. Looking at the two waiters in this light, it is the older waiter who holds the view which is most compatible with philosophic materialism, not the younger waiter.

It is better, undoubtedly, to avoid classifying the younger waiter at all, than to misclassify him. The most we can do with the younger waiter is describe him, an effort which results in showing him to be something of a "type," the average individual, "in a hurry." He is self-interested and indulges himself with believing an hour is "'more to me than to him [the old man].'" He does not especially like work, and accuses the old man of having "'no regard for those who must work'"; nevertheless, he seems to accept it as economically necessary and is quite an efficient waiter, making sure the shutters are closed before he leaves. He is satisfied with his marriage and is eager to get home to his wife "waiting in bed" for him. He is a legalist in his attitude toward the soldier, although even when refusing to serve the old man, he does not "wish to be unjust. He was only in a hurry." He is no Christian zealot but accepts the church with its transcendent values, illustrated by his changing the subject to money when told the niece cut the old man down because of "fear for his soul." In short, he is one of those who have "confidence," or faith in the established system in which they live. He has "'youth, confidence, and a job . . . everything.'" His job gives him a sense of economic success within the community. The institution of marriage has provided him with a "waiting" wife who satisfies the biological drive and gives him a sense of male effectiveness. His youth gives him a sense of life as infinite continuum, and the institution of the church confirms such immortality for him. "'I have confidence,'" he says, "'I'm all confidence,'" and as long as he has this confident faith in the value and permanence of these cultural structures, he has "everything."

The older waiter, on the other hand, is unable to muster such faith or confidence. He *is* a materialist and beyond the material there is "nothing." "Some lived in it and never felt it but he knew it all was nada y pues nada y nada y pues nada." The individual "cannot find anything to depend upon either within or outside himself."[5] There is no *a priori* order or value system, either providential, natural or social, on which man may intelligently depend and predict a future. "'No. I have never had confidence and I am not young.'" The material world, which includes the mental processes, is the only reality and has priority, but it is found lacking: life is a net of illusions. "'And what do you lack?'" asks the younger waiter. "'Everything but work,'" replies the older waiter. And even the ability to "work" has been taken from the old man, as it evidently was from Hemingway by July 2, 1961.

This profound, but masked "difference" between the two waiters is imbedded in the casual-appearing conversation about the old man. When the younger waiter asks, "'How do you know [the old man's despair was about] nothing,'" the reply, "'He has plenty of money,'" is more philosophically precise than an entire chapter of discursive contortions. *Nada* can be described only in terms of an opposite because to make some-thing out of nothing is not only incomprehensible but impossible.[6] And "plenty of money" provides the most nearly perfect polar opposite to "nothing." The holes in a fish net are perceptible because of the net. When a man has the power of money and the plenty which it makes possible, it also makes the "lack," *nada,* that much more apparent and unbearable. "Plenty" intensifies what is lacking to the psychological breaking point. The old man's severe despair, and the serious despair of the older waiter, are not caused by some-thing, and are not *about* anything. Despair is a negation, a lack. The lack of life after death, the lack of a moral order governing the universe, the lack of trustworthy interpersonal relations, the lack of an ordering principle in the individual consciousness, the lack of the ability to work, and the lack, therefore, of even self-respect and dignity. The old man lacks any-thing to live *for.* "'It was a nothing he [the older waiter] knew too well.'"

However, to quit the story on the philosophical level is to leave the primary question of "confidence" or "despair" artistically unanswered. The younger waiter would go confidently home to his "waiting wife" and live happily ever after: a winner who takes everything.[7] The older waiter's *nada* is "probably only insomnia" and will pass with daylight, which, if not a happy ending, is at least a very tolerable ending. This is essentially an uncommitted balance, which is where interpretation to date has left it.

But this is to understand only the "literal" ending of the story; that is, what happens to the older waiter after *he* leaves the café. It does not reveal what happens when the younger waiter arrives home. For this insight, which Hemingway refers to as the "real end," which may be "omitted" on the basis of his "new theory," it is necessary to go back into the story.[8]

In the silence that takes place immediately following the older waiter's ironic "'He has plenty of money,'"

> A girl and a soldier went by in the street. The street light shone on the brass number on his collar. The girl wore no head covering and hurried beside him.
>
> Y.W. "The guard will pick him up," one waiter said.
>
> O.W. "What does it matter if he gets what he's after?"
>
> Y.W. "He had better get off the street now. The guard will get him. They went by five minutes ago."

The younger waiter emphasizes the military guards because to him they represent guardians of a culture in which one may be confident of success. He is not concerned about the soldier. Individual needs, whether they are the need of a girl or the need of a drink for a lonely old man, must be sacrificed to the punctualities of the job, the igno-

rant securities of rule and routine. The younger waiter wants everyone off the street, as he wants the old man out of the café. He wants to be off the streets himself, and is, in fact, also a kind of guard. "'No more tonight. Close now,'" he says to the old man and begins "pulling down the metal shutters."

But the older waiter does understand that agonizing lack in an individual: "'What does it matter if he gets what he's after?'" Company punishment will be minor compared to the anguish of being alone. Everything is a temporary stay against despair: a light for the night, another drink, relations with a girl. "'You can't tell,'" even the old man "'might be better with a wife.'"

The soldier's kinship with the older waiter and the old man is illustrated by the metaphor of light and something clean or polished. "The street light shone on the brass number of his collar." They are all of a "kind," the soldier as disillusioned with the military machine as the older waiter and the old man are disillusioned with the machine of the world. The soldier is not concerned about curfew as the older waiter is not concerned about closing the café on time, and the old man is not concerned about letting the café close. The soldier needs the sexual intoxication of this girl as the older waiter and the old man need a drink. The soldier is no more concerned about military regulations than the old man is concerned about financial regulations, and "would leave without paying" if he became too drunk. "As Hemingway once put it, 'There is honor among pickpockets and honor among whores. It is simply that the standards differ.'"[9]

The scene—a prostitute and a soldier—is the epitome of a meaningless and chaotic world full of loopholes: an interwoven fabric of ironies punctured by nothingness. Everything is possible through love or aggression, but paradoxically nothing is permanent. There is a constant, desperate struggle against the coefficients of adversity. Living becomes a deadly affair, or conflict, essentially devoid of humor because everything is ultimately a "dirty trick."[10]

This is the basis for the older waiter's not so funny "joke" later in the story. The younger waiter has just suggested that the old man could buy a bottle and drink at home, to which the older waiter replies, "'It's not the same.'"

> "No, it is not," agreed the waiter with a wife. He did not wish to be unjust. He was only in a hurry.
>
> "And you? You have no fear of going home before your usual hour?"
>
> "Are you trying to insult me?"
>
> "No, hombre, only to make a joke."
>
> "No," the waiter who was in a hurry said . . . "I have confidence. I am all confidence."

The joke is crucial and hinges directly on the scene with the girl and the soldier. Structurally and texturally they establish the love wound motif which is so dominant in

Hemingway that it becomes the other side of the same psychic coin as the war wound. Through either the death of one of the partners or the inability of one partner to fulfill the promise of love—satisfy the other's needs—an individual is isolated and pushed to despair by the failure of the love alliance.

The complete working out of this motif is the "real end" which Hemingway omitted, and the phrase "waiter with a wife" preceding the joke, functions as a lens to bring into focus the catastrophe which the younger waiter will face. When the younger waiter goes home before his "usual time," his wife will be gone, or perhaps, though at home in bed, engaged in another desperate relationship. The girl and the soldier appear again like ghosts, only this time the girl without a "head covering," ironically "hurrying," is suggestive of the younger waiter's wife.

The story now becomes superbly charged with dramatic as well as verbal irony. The younger waiter's confidence dissolves into tragic hubris, and his statements, such as "'I'm not lonely,'" are imbued with an impending doom that is near classic. Situations become ironically transferred. The old man's despair and loneliness without a wife, the older waiter's insomnia and need of light, the soldier's risk for temporary sexual meaning—all are now the younger waiter's future. At the very moment that he is playing the heartless and uncompromising judge, he is also reality's dupe and victim. Whatever he has said about the others may soon be said about him. And with equal irony, he has "hurried" to his own undoing. His all-confident intentions will be reversed. His recognition of another truth is imminent. The radical contingencies of life will have taught him the absurdity of the human condition, and the twist of events will topple him from his pinnacle of confidence into the phantasmagoria where the older waiter and the old man cling despairingly to their clean, well-lighted place. The younger waiter will become a new member of Hemingway's collection: ***Winner Take Nothing.***

Notes

1. See Robert Penn Warren, Introduction, *A Farewell to Arms* (New York, 1949), pp. xv-xvi; Mark Schorer, ed., *The Story: A Critical Anthology* (New Jersey, 1950), p. 427; Carlos Baker, *Hemingway: The Writer as Artist* (New Jersey, 1952), p. 124; F. P. Kroeger, "The Dialogue in 'A Clean, Well-Lighted Place,'" *College English*, XX (Feb., 1959), 240-241; William E. Colburn, "Confusion in 'A Clean, Well-Lighted Place,'" *College English*, XX (Feb., 1959), 241-242; Otto Reinert, "Hemingway's Waiters Once More," *College English*, XX (May, 1959), 417-418; Edward Stone, "Hemingway's Waiters Yet Once More," *American Speech*, XXXVII (Oct., 1962), 239-240; Joseph F. Gabriel, "The Logic of Confusion in Hemingway's 'Clean, Well-Lighted Place,'" *College English*, XXII (May, 1961), 539-546; John V. Hagopian, "Tidying Up Hemingway's 'Clean, Well-Lighted Place,'" *Studies in Short Fiction*, I (Winter, 1964), 140-146.

2. Information concerning the correction is in letters to the author from Mr. L. H. Brague, Jr., editor, Charles Scribner's Sons, and from Professor Philip Young of Pennsylvania State University. I would like to express my appreciation to Mr. Brague and Professor Young for their help.

3. *The Short Stories of Ernest Hemingway* (New York, 1965), pp. 379-383. All subsequent references will be to this text.

4. It is interesting to note that the line, "He has plenty of money," is reminiscent of the famous exchange between Hemingway and F. Scott Fitzgerald which Hemingway recorded in "The Snows of Kilimanjaro": "He remembered poor Julian and his romantic awe of them and how he had started a story once that began, 'The very rich are different from you and me.' And how some one had said to Julian, Yes, they have more money" (p. 72). The story was "The Rich Boy," which appeared in *Red Book Magazine* in January and February, 1926.

5. Jean Paul Sartre, "Existentialism Is a Humanism," *Existentialism from Dostoevsky to Sartre*, ed. Walter Kaufmann (Cleveland, 1956), p. 295.

6. Jean Paul Sartre seems to fall into this linguistic trap when he describes nothingness in *L'Etre et le néant*: "c'est au sein même de l'être, en son coeur comme un ver" (Paris, 1943, p. 57).

7. "A Clean, Well-Lighted Place" was included by Hemingway in a collection of rather bitter stories *Winner Take Nothing* (New York, 1933), pp. 17-24.

8. Ernest Hemingway, *A Moveable Feast* (New York, 1964), p. 75. The complete statement is as follows:

It was a very simple story called "Out of Season" and I had omitted the real end of it which was that the old man hanged himself. This was omitted on my new theory that you could omit anything if you knew that you omitted and the omitted part would strengthen the story and make people feel something more than they understood.

Well, I thought, now I have them so they do not understand them. There cannot be much doubt about that. There is most certainly no demand for them. But they will understand the same way that they always do in painting. It only takes time and it only needs confidence.

Professor Philip Young refers to the passage in his book *Ernest Hemingway: A Reconsideration* (New York, 1966), p. 285, and cites three stories for which we already have an answer: "Out of Season," "Fathers and Sons," and "Big Two-Hearted River." Suicides are omitted from the first two stories, and the fact that Nick Adams has just returned from the war is omitted in the third.

9. Young, p. 64.

10. Ernest Hemingway, *A Farewell to Arms* (New York, 1957), p. 331. Shortly after Frederic Henry ha-

prayed "Please, please, dear God, don't let her die," Catherine says "I'm not a bit afraid. It's just a dirty trick."

David Lodge (essay date 1971)

SOURCE: "Hemingway's Clean, Well-Lighted, Puzzling Place," in *Essays in Criticism*, Vol. XXI, No. 1, January, 1971, pp. 33-57.

[*In the following essay, Lodge contrasts the older and younger waiters in the story and concludes that Hemingway "deliberately encourages the reader to make an initially incorrect discrimination between the two waiters which, when discovered and corrected, amounts to a kind of peripetia."*]

'A Clean Well-Lighted Place' is one of Ernest Hemingway's best-known and most often reprinted short stories; yet until very recently its text contained a curious anomaly: curious, especially, in that it for so long apparently escaped the attention both of Hemingway himself and of his readers. For this crux is not a minor, incidental matter, but one that vitally affects one's reading of the whole story. In fact, the text which appeared in *Scribner's Magazine* in March 1933, and was reprinted in all editions until 1966 (and which is still appearing in textbooks and anthologies[1]) simply doesn't make sense.

I first discovered this for myself a few years ago in the 1963 Scribner's paperback edition of *The Snows of Kilimanjaro and Other Stories.* Enquiries revealed that a number of articles had appeared on the problem, beginning in 1959, and that Scribner's had emended the text in their 1967 edition of *The Short Stories of Ernest Hemingway,* adopting a solution proposed by John V. Hagopian.[2] This solution seems to me the right one; and I discuss the problem here, not in order to suggest an alternative solution, but as a starting-point for an analysis of the story as a whole.

The original unemended text (here reprinted by permission of Jonathan Cape and the Executors of the Ernest Hemingway Estate), which obtained up until 1966, is as follows:

"A Clean Well-Lighted Place"

It was late and every one had left the café except an old man who sat in the shadow the leaves of the tree made against the electric light. In the day time the street was dusty, but at night the dew settled the dust and the old man liked to sit late because he was deaf and now at night it was quiet and he felt the difference. The two waiters inside the café knew that the old man was a little drunk, and while he was a good client they knew that if he became too drunk he would leave without paying, so they kept watch on him.

'Last week he tried to commit suicide,' one waiter said.

'Why?'

'He was in despair.'

'What about?'

'Nothing.'

'How do you know it was nothing?'

'He has plenty of money.'

They sat together at a table that was close against the wall near the door of the café and looked at the terrace where the tables were all empty except where the old man sat in the shadow of the leaves of the tree that moved slightly in the wind. A girl and a soldier went by in the street. The street light shone on the brass number on his collar. The girl wore no head covering and hurried beside him.

'The guard will pick him up', one waiter said.

'What does it matter if he gets what he's after?'

'He had better get off the street now. The guard will get him. They went by five minutes ago.'

The old man sitting in the shadow rapped on his saucer with his glass. The younger waiter went over to him.

'What do you want?'

The old man looked at him. 'Another brandy', he said.

'You'll be drunk', the waiter said. The old man looked at him. The waiter went away.

'He'll stay all night', he said to his colleague. 'I'm sleepy now. I never get into bed before three o'clock. He should have killed himself last week.'

The waiter took the brandy bottle and another saucer from the counter inside the café and marched out to the old man's table. He put down the saucer and poured the glass full of brandy.

'You should have killed yourself last week', he said to the deaf man. The old man motioned with his finger. 'A little more', he said. The waiter poured on into the glass so that the brandy slopped over and ran down the stem into the top saucer of the pile. 'Thank you', the old man said. The waiter took the bottle back inside the café. He sat down at the table with his colleague again.

'He's drunk now', he said.

'He's drunk every night.'

'What did he want to kill himself for?'

'How should I know.'

'How did he do it?'

'He hung himself with a rope.'

'Who cut him down?'

'His niece.'

'Why did they do it?'

'Fear for his soul.'

'How much money has he got?'

'He's got plenty.'

'He must be eighty years old.'

'Anyway I should say he was eighty.'

'I wish he would go home. I never get to bed before three o'clock. What kind of hour is that to go to bed?'

'He stays up because he likes it.'

'He's lonely. I'm not lonely. I have a wife waiting in bed for me.'

'He had a wife once too.'

'A wife would be no good to him now.'

'You can't tell. He might be better with a wife.'

'His niece looks after him.'

'I know. You said she cut him down.'

'I wouldn't want to be that old. An old man is a nasty thing.'

'Not always. This old man is clean. He drinks without spilling. Even now, drunk. Look at him.'

'I don't want to look at him. I wish he would go home. He has no regard for those who must work.'

The old man looked from his glass across the square, then over at the waiters.

'Another brandy', he said, pointing to his glass. The waiter who was in a hurry came over.

'Finished', he said, speaking with that omission of syntax stupid people employ when talking to drunken people or foreigners. 'No more tonight. Close now.'

'Another', said the old man.

'No. Finished.' The waiter wiped the edge of the table with a towel and shook his head.

The old man stood up, slowly counted the saucers, took a leather coin purse from his pocket and paid for the drinks, leaving half a peseta tip.

The waiter watched him go down the street, a very old man walking unsteadily but with dignity.

'Why didn't you let him stay and drink?' the unhurried waiter asked. They were putting up the shutters. 'It is not half-past two.'

'I want to go home to bed.'

'What is an hour?'

'More to me than to him.'

'An hour is the same.'

'You talk like an old man yourself. He can buy a bottle and drink it at home.'

'It's not the same.'

'No, it is not', agreed the waiter with a wife. He did not wish to be unjust. He was only in a hurry.

'And you? You have no fear of going home before your usual hour?'

'Are you trying to insult me?'

'No, hombre, only to make a joke.'

'No', the waiter who was in a hurry said, rising from pulling down the metal shutters. 'I have confidence. I am all confidence.'

'You have youth, confidence, and a job', the older waiter said. 'You have everything.'

'And what do you lack?'

'Everything but work.'

'You have everything I have.'

'No. I have never had confidence and I am not young.'

'Come on. Stop talking nonsense and lock up.'

'I am of those who like to stay late at the café', the older waiter said, 'With all those who do not want to go to bed. With all those who need a light for the night.'

'I want to go home and into bed.'

'We are of two different kinds', the older waiter said. He was now dressed to go home. 'It is not only a question of youth and confidence although those things are very beautiful. Each night I am reluctant to close up because there may be some one who needs the café'.

'Hombre, there are bodegas open all night long.'

'You do not understand. This is a clean and pleasant café. It is well lighted. The light is very good and also, now, there are shadows of the leaves.'

'Good night', said the younger waiter.

'Good night', the other said. Turning off the electric light he continued the conversation with himself. It is the light of course but it is necessary that the place be clean and pleasant. You do not want music. Certainly you do not want music. Nor can you stand before a bar with dignity although that is all that is provided for these hours. What did he fear? It was not fear or dread. It was a nothing that he knew too well. It was all a nothing and a man was nothing too. It was only that and light was all it needed and a certain cleanness and order. Some lived in it and never felt it but he knew it all was nada y pues nada y nada y pues nada. Our nada who art in nada, nada be thy name thy kingdom nada thy will be nada in nada as it is in nada. Give us this nada our daily nada and nada us our nada as we nada our nadas and nada us not into nada but deliver us from nada; pues nada. Hail nothing full of nothing, nothing is with thee. He smiled and stood before a bar with a shining steam pressure coffee machine.

'What's yours?' asked the barman.

'Nada.'

'Otro loco mas', said the barman and turned away.

'A little cup', said the waiter.

The barman poured it for him.

'The light is very bright and pleasant but the bar is unpolished', the waiter said.

The barman looked at him but did not answer. It was too late at night for conversation.

'You want another copita?' the barman asked.

'No, thank you', said the waiter and went out. He disliked bars and bodegas. A clean, well-lighted café was a very different thing. Now, without thinking further, he would go home to his room. He would lie in the bed and finally, with daylight, he would go to sleep. After all, he said to himself, it is probably only insomnia. Many must have it.

The attentive reader will have observed a logical inconsistency at line 78, in the long dialogue between the two waiters beginning at line 55. It is clear that it is the younger waiter' who is serving the old man (see line 33). It is therefore the younger waiter who (lines 52-5) rejoins the older waiter at the table and reopens the conversation:

The waiter took the bottle back inside the café. He sat down at the table with his colleague again.

'He's drunk now', he [the younger waiter] said.

The same identification can be made by working backwards from line 72, 'I have a wife waiting in bed for me', which must be spoken by the younger waiter.) Taking this as a key to the attribution of dialogue, it is clear that it is the younger waiter who is asking the questions about the old man's suicide attempt, and the older waiter who is answering them. The young waiter asks, 'Who cut him down?'. The older waiter replies 'His niece' (61-2). But when the younger waiter seeks to dismiss the old man's lack of a wife by saying, 'His niece looks after him', the older waiter says: 'I know. *You* said she cut him down' (77-8, my italics).

Two short articles by F. P. Kroeger and William E. Colburn, printed side by side in *College English* (1959),[3] first drew attention to this contradiction. Mr. Kroeger implied that the story had been carelessly written and/or edited. Mr. Colburn castigated Hemingway's critics for overlooking or evading the problem. Both writers recognised that the crux affected the attribution of the first dialogue between the two waiters (12-19). For the long third dialogue, beginning at line 55, is the only *logical* guide to the correct attribution of the first dialogue. If in the long dialogue it is the younger waiter who is asking all the questions about the suicide attempt, and the older waiter who is answering them, then it is logical to attribute the opening exchange as follows:

Older Waiter: Last week he tried to commit suicide.

Younger Waiter: Why?

O.W.: He was in despair.

Y.W.: What about?

O.W.: Nothing.

Y.W.: How do you know it was nothing?

O.W.: He has plenty of money

In this case the older waiter is being consciously ironic at the younger waiter's expense. By '"Nothing"' the older

waiter refers privately to the sense of 'nada' which, as we later discover, he himself shares, and which is quite enough to drive a man to suicide. His younger colleague, however, as we also discover later, has no perception of 'nada', and no sympathy for those who are afflicted by it, so 'Nothing' will also serve to mean that, in common-sense terms, the old man had no reason to despair. '"How do you know it was nothing?"' indicates that the younger waiter does indeed interpret the word in this sense; and the older waiter underlines the impossibility of explaining the suicide attempt in the rational, materialistic terms the younger waiter would understand by saying, '"He has plenty of money."'

If, however, we ignore the logical key provided by the opening of the long, third dialogue (which is itself, in our original text, logically confused) it is possible to attribute the lines of the opening dialogue in reverse order, as, for instance, Carlos Baker does:[4]

Younger Waiter: Last week he tried to commit suicide.

Older Waiter: Why?

Y.W.: He was in despair.

O.W.: What about?

Y.W.: Nothing.

O.W.: How do you know it was nothing?

Y.W.: He has plenty of money.

In this case the younger waiter reveals his unimaginative materialism by '"Nothing"' (in its ordinary colloquial sense) and '"He has plenty of money"'; while the older waiter anticipates his later development of the meaning of 'nothing' by his question, '"How do you know it was nothing?"' As regards the overall meaning of the story there is little to choose between these two, opposite attributions, since both can be interpreted as making the same distinction between the two waiters—one through the older waiter's concealed, conscious irony, and the other through an ironical, but unconscious self-betrayal by the younger waiter. Superficially, the lines '"Nothing"' and '"He has plenty of money"' seem entirely appropriate to the coarser sensibility of the younger waiter as it is later displayed in the story.

Otto Reinert placed so much weight on this last point that, in the next published contribution to the discussion[5] he made it the keystone of his argument. His premise was that it is the younger waiter who says '"He's got plenty of money"', and therefore it is he who knows all about the suicide attempt of the old man. To reconcile this reading with the third dialogue beginning at line 55, he suggested that here Hemingway violated the usual convention that in a printed dialogue a new, indented line implies a new speaker, 'in order to suggest a reflective pause between two sentences'. He suggested that the younger waiter says *both* '"He's drunk now"' and '"He's drunk every night"' (55-6) and that the older waiter says *both* '"He must be eighty years old"' *and* '"Anyway I should say he was eighty"' (67-8). This, of course, has the effect of making the older waiter ask all the questions, and the younger waiter answer them, so that there is then no inconsistency about line 78.

It is true that "'He's drunk every night'" and "'Anyway I should say he was eighty'" *could* be afterthoughts by the speakers of the previous lines, and would be accepted as such without question if they had been printed continuously. Reinert also argues, with some plausibility, that "'Anyway I should say he was eighty'" seems more natural as an amplification of the preceding remark than as a response by the other speaker. However, on this last point, Edward Stone has observed that 'Anyway' here is an attempt to render a phrase in colloquial Spanish indicating agreement or confirmation.[6] The main objection to Reinert's theory, as John Hagopian later pointed out,[7] is the implausibility of Hemingway's having deliberately violated a well-established typographical convention in a way for which there is no precedent elsewhere in his work (nor, one might add, anywhere else), for a purpose that could have been easily accomplished by other means. Had Reinert suggested that the placing of the 'afterthoughts' on a new, indented line was a printer's error, his case would have been more plausible. For, contrary to Hagopian's assertion, the idea that it is the younger waiter who knows about the suicide attempt is quite compatible with the idea that 'it is the old waiter who is obsessed with the awareness of nada and who recognises and sympathises with a fellow sufferer in the old man at the café', because, as we have seen in the opening dialogue, so many lines are capable of being read in two opposite ways. One can only say that it is slightly more fitting, in emotional and aesthetic terms, that the older waiter should be acquainted with the old man's history and background; and that if he is being ironical in the opening dialogue (as we *must* suppose if he is the first speaker) then this is consonant with his more overt irony at the younger waiter's expense later in the story. The superior merit of Hagopian's solution is that it is simpler, inherently more plausible, and deals directly with line 78, the justification of which is the only logical support for Reinert's hypothesis.

Between Reinert and Hagopian, however, came Joseph F. Gabriel, ingeniously but perversely arguing that the text of the story was sound, and that the 'inconsistency in the dialogue is deliberate, an integral part of the pattern of meaning actualised in the story. . . . In so far as the dialogue fails to conform to the norms of logic, the reader himself is, like the older waiter, plunged into the existential predicament and made to confront the absurd.'[8] Gabriel's article was the longest, and in many ways the most critically perceptive of those that had so far appeared. He was the first commentator to point out that the dialogue in the first two exchanges could be attributed in different ways without affecting the qualitative contrast between the two waiters, and that this ambiguity was probably deliberate. It is not, however, legitimate to assimilate the inconsistency of line 78 into the concept of literary ambiguity. The *ambiguities* which Gabriel rightly observes in the text are all, in the end, capable of resolution or, if left open, do not affect

the authority of the story. This cannot be said of the *inconsistency* in line 78, and it is its uniqueness in this respect which makes it a problem. A logical inconsistency of this kind, if deliberate, can only have the effect in narrative of radically undermining the authority of either the narrator or the characters or both; but this will always entail the sense of some authorial mind behind both narrator and characters who *is* reliable, to the extent that we can infer that he has some literary purpose in exploiting inconsistency. This purpose could be to expose the deceptiveness of fictions; or, in this case, it could be to reveal that neither of the two waiters really knows anything for certain about the old man—that they are making up a story about him for their own psychological purposes, and forget their respective roles in the process, as sometimes happens in the theatre of the absurd. The situation from which **'A Clean, Well-Lighted Place'** starts *might* have been explored in this way. Unfortunately for Mr. Gabriel's argument, it wasn't. There are no other equivalent inconsistencies which would confirm the radical unreliability of the narrator. And so far from the two waiters being ironically distanced and presented as equally confused (as would happen if we believed neither of them knew what they were talking about), the story turns on a discrimination between them and a resolution of the story's ambiguities by a change of presentation—the shift into the older waiter's consciousness. That the facts about the old man are 'true' and that the older waiter is a reliable character, are essential preconditions if the latter's interior monologue is to be at all moving or persuasive. The story works by packing meanings under its realistic surface, not by undermining that surface so that it collapses.

Hagopian's solution is simply to emend the text by moving the words, "'You said she cut him down'" to the preceding line, thus:

> Younger Waiter: A wife would be no good to him now.
>
> Older Waiter: You can't tell. He might be better with a wife.
>
> Younger Waiter: His niece looks after him. You said she cut him down.
>
> Older Waiter: I know.
>
> Younger Waiter: I wouldn't want to be that old. . . .

Gloss: the younger waiter discounts the older waiter's suggestion that the old man might be better if he had a wife by saying that the only use he would have, at his age, for a woman, i.e. someone to look after him, is already supplied by his niece—a fact he has deduced from the information given earlier that the niece cut him down. The older waiter's 'I know' is a conventional phrase of agreement, but, like some of his previous remarks carries an ironical implication: what you say is true but it doesn't take my point, which I'm not going to try and explain to you because you wouldn't understand it. With this emendation, the whole dialogue, beginning at line 55, becomes quite coherent and consistent, and provides a reliable basis for deciding that it is the older waiter who knows the facts about the old man and who opens the first dialogue at line 12.

Hagopian does not speculate how, when or by whom the words "'You said she cut him down'" were misplaced, and unless and until the original MS. is available for scrutiny, it is impossible to answer these questions—or even to know for certain that he is right. But his solution is clearly the best of those that have been proposed. Everything we know about Hemingway's working habits—the immense concentration and care that he brought to the act of composition—suggests that it is highly unlikely that he himself was careless or confused about which of the two waiters had the information about the old man. It is odd that he did not pick up the error in proof or print. But it is even odder that none of his readers and critics commented publicly on the inconsistency in line 78 until twenty-five years after the story first appeared.

Presumably the inconsistency remained unnoticed for so long because so much of the dialogue in the first half of the story is presented dramatically, with no specific indication of who is speaking. Is this just an irritating mannerism, creating unnecessary confusion? It seems to me more reasonable to regard it as a deliberate rhetorical device. As we begin reading the story for the first time, we probably form the expectation that the story is going to be 'about' the old man; but as we read on we discover that it is about the difference between the two waiters. The ambiguity concerning which of the two waiters is speaking at any one time, therefore, keeps the reader's attention partly preoccupied with distinguishing between them, even though the main focus of the narrative is initially upon the old man; it thus prepares the reader for the subsequent development. Moreover, as I will try to show in the third part of this essay, Hemingway deliberately encourages the reader to make an initially incorrect discrimination between the two waiters which, when discovered and corrected, amounts to a kind of peripetia. Hemingway, in short, is making things deliberately difficult for his readers in this story. Ironically, he succeeded so well that a quite gratuitous and non-functional difficulty has passed unnoticed by most of them (including himself).

II

There are four well-established categories in the critical discussion of Hemingway's fiction—particularly his earlier fiction, and particularly the short stories: the Hemingway universe, the Hemingway code, the Hemingway hero and, embracing and articulating these three, the Hemingway style. The Hemingway universe is the metaphysically vacant waste land of much modern literature, but with a special emphasis on meaningless suffering.

"'What have we done to have that happen to us?'" complains the woman in **'The Snows of Kilimanjaro,'** referring to Harry's fatal infection. Harry replies with deliberate literalism, "'I suppose what I did was to forget to put

iodine on it when I first scratched it. Then I didn't pay any attention to it because I never infect. Then later, when it got bad, it was probably using that weak carbolic solution when the other antiseptics ran out that paralyzed the minute blood vessels and started the gangrene." He looked at her. "What else?"' Harry's reply is determinedly positivist, ruling out any attempt to explain suffering by reference to a moral or metaphysical scheme. Suffering and death are essentially arbitrary, part of the order—or rather the disorder—of things. Hence the emphasis in Hemingway's work is not upon seeking explanations or solutions for the problems of existence, but upon the question of how to live with them.

The answer, in part, is the Hemingway code: the cultivation of the masculine virtues of courage, dignity and stoic endurance. These qualities are represented by such characters as the gambler in **'The Gambler, the Nun and the Radio,'** and the Major in **'In Another Country.'** There is no suggestion that the code can reduce suffering—the gambler tells Mr. Frazer that only consideration for his fellow patients prevented him from screaming aloud in his pain. Still less can the code *avert* suffering: the Major has schooled himself to accept his mutilation without illusions of being cured, but he is then struck from behind by the cruel and totally unpredictable death of his wife, whom he had carefully abstained from marrying until he was out of the war. His words to the narrator—"'A man must not marry. . . . He should not place himself in a position to lose. He should find things he cannot lose'" is not intended as practical advice, but implies that it is a necessary condition of our being human that we lay ourselves open to the pain of loss.

As Philip Young, from whom I take these concepts of the code and the hero, has perceptively shown,[9] the Hemingway *hero* is not defined by the simple terms of the Hemingway code. The hero is a man who admires the code and aspires to it, often by seeking to harden himself in the direct experience of violence and suffering. But whether such experience has been willed (as in the case of war) or involuntary (as in childhood) the hero is never entirely able to reconcile himself to it. It leaves him with wounds both physical and psychological, which never entirely heal, and whose pain he tries to assuage in a number of ways: by attaching himself to those who live by the code, by private rituals such as hunting, fishing, drinking or playing the radio, by writing, or by the process, akin to writing, of recovering and ordering the past by concentrated efforts of memory.

This brings us to the Hemingway style. Out of the commentaries of various critics[10] we can draw its profile fairly sharply. It is characterised by extreme grammatical and lexical simplicity: short, simple sentences, often linked together by conjunctions, especially *and,* to form compound sentences; precise, plain, colloquial diction, in which only the occasional foreign or technical word causes any difficulty of understanding; a heavy reliance on basic verbs, particularly the verb *to be,* and on the most ordinary adjectives, *big, fine, nice, etc.,* thus putting maximum emphasis on nouns. Such a description, however, might apply equally well to the style of Defoe, from whom Hemingway is far removed, not only temporally and culturally, but in terms of literary effect. How are these linguistic features combined and exploited to create the special quality of Hemingway's style? We might begin by saying that it is a style almost easier to define by what it avoids than by what it does—avoiding complex or periodic syntactical structures, elegant variation, consciously 'literary' language of any kind. *Avoids* is the operative word, for Hemingway's style, unlike Defoe's, communicates a sense of the austere poetics on which it is based; we are always aware of the easy, decorative or evasive formulations which have been scrupulously rejected. This is partly a historical matter, for without the foil of English (and American) narrative prose as it developed through the eighteenth and nineteenth centuries Hemingway's stark simplicity would lose much of its effectiveness. Superficially naive, his style is highly sophisticated and demands a sophisticated reader for the full appreciation of its effects.

By its scrupulous avoidance of what is usually thought of as rhetoric, Hemingway's style itself functions as a powerful rhetoric of sincerity, bearing horrified, or traumatized, witness to the ugliness of life and death. At the same time, this style, particularly in its avoidance of syntactical subordination—the linguistic tool with which we arrange the items of our knowledge to show priorities or relationships of cause and effect—carries a large philosophical implication: the denial of metaphysics and the suggestion that life is ultimately meaningless.

III

Nowhere in Hemingway's work is this view of life more bleakly presented than in **'A Clean, Well-Lighted Place.'** The key word of the story is certainly 'nothing' or 'nada', and the way it invades the prayers, the 'Hail Mary' and the 'Our Father' at the end, makes explicit the rejection of any metaphysical explanation or consolation. God is very dead in this story. The only positive values it endorses are the very limited ones of light and cleanliness. The richer dimensions of the physical life, for example sexuality, mentioned in connection with the soldier and the younger waiter, are implicitly devalued as vain or transient or vulnerable.

The Hemingway code, as defined above, is not fully embodied in his story. The code is something to which both the old man and the older waiter aspire, but incompletely, unconfidently. The old man's unsuccessful suicide attempt is an index of his failure, but though he is a broken man he still preserves certain features of the code, which are remarked approvingly by the waiter or the narrator:

> 'This old man is clean. He drinks without spilling. Even now, drunk.'

(81-2)

(In contrast, the younger waiter pours the brandy so that it slopped over and ran down the stem into the top saucer of the pile (50-1).)

> . . . a very old man walking unsteadily but with dignity.

(98-9)

'Nor can you stand before a bar with dignity' the older waiter reflects later, 'though that is all that is provided for these hours' (147-9). The clean, well-lighted café is, therefore, valued because it permits a very limited practice of the code.

The hero of the story, again in the sense defined above, is clearly the older waiter. This only gradually becomes evident, as the difference between the two waiters becomes more perceptible, and as the point of view from which the story is told shifts from an impersonal authorial mode to that of the older waiter's consciousness. These two processes—the shift in point-of-view, and the gradual discrimination between the two waiters—are the basic rhetorical strategies of the story.

We begin with the spectacle of the old man, described by the impersonal narrator, sitting alone at the café in the small hours. The second sentence is interesting for the way in which its appearance of logical explanation dissolves under scrutiny. It seems to be saying that the old man likes to sit in the café late at night because by then the dust has settled, but then a different physical reason is produced—the quietness of the street at night, which is also a little unexpected because he is deaf and so, one might have supposed, less sensitive to noise. The statement appears to be a privileged authorial comment on the old man's behaviour, but the haziness of the logic suggests that it is, if not an unreliable, at least an inadequate explanation; and this is confirmed by the later development of the story. The old man's behaviour is a puzzle, an enigma, a provocation, and this is reflected in the conversation about him between the two waiters. He is, for the purpose of the story, an image of the Human Condition. To use such a portentous abstraction is to fall into the dishonest habits of language Hemingway's art implicitly criticises, but he has taken steps to stress the representative nature of his three characters. None of them is named, nor are they distinguished by any descriptive particularity of dress, personal appearance, etc., such as we normally expect from realistic fiction. We don't even know where the story is set until line 115, where the word *hombre* indicates that the setting in Spain. This singular anonymity, as well as stressing the representative or symbolic significance of the characters, means that the very limited terms of reference in which they *are* distinguished carry enormous weight. The old man is just that—the old man. He is referred to once as 'the deaf man' (48) to explain the waiter's callous remark, '"You should have killed yourself last week"', but otherwise he is referred to as 'the old man' or 'a very old man' (95, 99). It is highly significant, therefore, that the first time one waiter is explicitly distinguished from the other is by the word 'younger' in line 33: 'The younger waiter went over to him.' In other words the primary distinction made between the two waiters belongs to the same category as that used to describe their customer: age. Thematically, this is obviously important. It is strongly suggested in the story that hope (or 'confidence') can only be entertained by the young (see lines 119-20), and that since youth is transient hope is a vain illusion.[11] Going back to line 33, we now know that one waiter is younger than the other, and it follows that the other waiter is older; but this formula, 'the older waiter' is not in fact introduced for another eighty lines. In fact no *explicit* distinction is made between the two waiters between line 33 and lines 87-8 ('The waiter who was in a hurry', followed by 'the unhurried waiter' 100-1). As we have seen, the reader must attend very carefully to attribute the dialogue correctly in this part of the story, and before line 33 he has no means at all of keeping the two waiters distinct in his mind.

The last sentence of the first paragraph presents the two waiters as a single unit of consciousness:

> The two waiters inside the café knew that the old man was a little drunk, and while he was a good client they knew that if he became too drunk he would leave without paying, so they kept watch on him.

This authorial comment, like the preceding sentence, is somewhat misleading—deliberately so. It presents the two waiters as being in complete accord and agreement, professionally allied against the old man. The story goes on to reveal an ever-increasing gap between the sensibilities of the two waiters, and to suggest a spiritual alliance between the older waiter and the old man against the younger waiter. It is some time before this becomes clear, however, because the reader has difficulty in distinguishing between the two waiters.

The first exchange of remarks between them (12-19) reveals a difference in the information each possesses about the old man, but not, at this stage, a definable difference of attitude towards him. The next piece of dialogue (28-31) reveals a difference of attitude—but not towards the old man (this should perhaps alert us to the possibility that the story is not going to be 'about' the old man, but about the difference between the two waiters—otherwise the introduction of the soldier and his girl will seem an irrelevant distraction). It is therefore impossible to match, with any confidence, the lines of the second dialogue with those of the first. When we come to the first explicit distinction between the two waiters with 'the younger waiter' in line 33, we may refer back to the two passages of dialogue to see if we can now identify which lines were spoken by the younger waiter, but we still cannot do so. As the story proceeds, however, the character of the younger waiter is sharply defined by his callous attitude towards the old man, especially his remark to the older waiter, "'He should have killed himself last week'" (42), repeated to the old man himself at line 47. If, with this clearer picture of the younger waiter, we refer back once more to the opening dialogue, we shall probably decide that the line, "'He has

plenty of money'" has a callous cynicism that fits the character of the younger waiter, and that it is therefore he who opens the dialogue at line 12. We may then find the same callous cynicism in the line "'What does it matter if he gets what he's after?'" in the second dialogue, and so assign this line also to the younger waiter. The remarks of the other waiter in this dialogue, about the guard, will then, by contrast, appear to express a humane solicitude, and we may find a similar quality in the question 'How do you know it was nothing?' which we have assigned to the older waiter in the first dialogue. It all seems to be fitting together.

But when we come to the long dialogue beginning at line 55 this hypothesis crumbles. For reasons given above, it is clearly the younger waiter who opens this dialogue, and who goes on to ask questions about the old man's suicide attempt. It must therefore have been the older waiter who opened the first dialogue at line 12 by saying 'Last week he tried to commit suicide'. As the long third dialogue continues it becomes more and more evident that the older waiter is compassionate towards the old man, so that we have to revise our interpretation of the lines "'Nothing'" and "'He has plenty of money'" in the first dialogue. To do this we have to read further into the story. That "'He has plenty of money'" was ironic is supported by the older waiter's obviously ironic references to 'job' and 'work' in lines 122 and 119. The real import of the first "'Nothing'" (17) does not become evident until we reach the older waiter's long meditation on nothing, beginning: 'It was a nothing that he knew too well.' (150). Then a kind of electric spark travels back to the earlier occurrence of 'Nothing', and we realise that when the older waiter said the old man was in despair about nothing, he didn't mean that the old man had no reason to despair, but that it was an awareness of nothingness, nada, the meaninglessness of existence, that caused his despair; and that in this respect he, the older waiter, feels an affinity with the old man. With this enhanced understanding of the characters of the two waiters, we can agree fairly confidently with Hagopian's attribution of the second dialogue, as follows:

> Younger Waiter: The guard will pick him up.
>
> Older Waiter: What does it matter if he gets what he's after?
>
> Younger Waiter: He had better get off the street now. The guard will get him. They went by five minutes ago.

Hagopian takes the younger waiter's remarks as an expression of malicious pleasure in another's impending misfortune and of his preoccupation with the lateness of the hour. The older waiter's remark is 'consistent with his indifference to the usual social norms, with his nihilism, and with his awareness of the value of youth and confidence.'

This affinity has already been established by increasing emphasis on the difference between the two waiters. In the middle of the story we are helped to discriminate between the two waiters by more distinguishing phrases than before:

the waiter who was in a hurry

(88; 116)

the unhurried waiter

(100)

the waiter with a wife

(110)

the older waiter

(119; 128; 132)

At line 107, the younger waiter says to the older waiter, 'You talk like an old man yourself.' The older waiter says to him: 'We are of two different kinds.' (132).

The 'two kinds' are, on the one hand, those who, like the younger waiter 'lived in it and never felt it' (153-4) and, on the other, those like the old man and the older waiter who live in it and *do* feel it. What is 'it'? The story asserts the impossibility of defining 'it' any more precisely than 'nothing' or 'nada'. It is worth nothing how often, and how ambiguously, the word 'it' is used in lines 149-54. When the older waiter actually names 'it' as 'insomnia' in the last line of the story—'After all, he said to himself, it is probably only insomnia. Many must have it.'—the naming is plainly meant to be ironically inadequate to the experience presented. The symptoms are those of insomnia, but the clinical diagnosis is irrelevant. The darkness of night (a recurrent archetypal motif in Hemingway's work) heightens the sense of *nada* and makes sleep impossible—hence the importance of erecting some defence against it for 'these hours'. Here it is the refuge of the café, the clean, well-lighted place, its light and order opposed to the darkness and disorder of existence. "'I am of those who like to stay late at the café'" the older waiter says (127), "'With all those who do not want to go to bed. With all those who need a light for the night.'"

With this speech the theme of the story—the idea of some community or brotherhood of those who are oppressed by nada—becomes explicit. The effect of resonant emphasis is imparted mainly by the parallelism of rhythm and structure in the three sentences. For there is nothing particularly striking about the *diction* of this speech—there is no word in it which has not already occurred several times in the story. *Stay, late, café, bed, light, night*: these are staple words in the remarkably limited vocabulary of the story, especially *night* and *light*, which occur twelve times and nine times respectively in this very short text, but never in such close juxtaposition as here: 'a light for the night'.

This is a characteristic example of Hemingway's very artful use of repetition. I call it artful because it manages to generate a kind of verbal intensity of the kind that we associate with lyric poetry, while maintaining a surface of realistic illusion, an impression of straight, objective reporting. The high degree of repetition which we cannot be unaware of seems, on one level, to be merely a function of the austerely exact, simple, unpretentious narrative tone, that reports every action and speech without selection,

compression or elegant variation. But the words that are repeated define experience in a very basic way: we have a sense of life pared down to its bare essentials. *Clean, light, late, café, old man, shadow, leaves, tree, street, night, waiter, drunk, brandy, money, table, saucer, bottle, glass, bed, wife, kill, home, lonely, hurry, fear, confidence, bar, nothing*—these are the basic terms in which experience is presented in the story—these are the words which occur and recur in the flat, neutral descriptions of the impersonal narrator, or in the rambling, realistically redundant conversation of the two waiters. It only needs a slight adjustment—a shift into a slightly artificial rhythm or syntactical structure—to transfigure the apparently banal particulars of the story and to invest them with moving significance. The effect is closely comparable with Joyce's stories in *Dubliners*, where the 'epiphany' is usually marked by the lifting of the language from its normative 'scrupulous meanness' (as Joyce described it) to a more poetically heightened mode—for example, at the end of 'Araby':

> Gazing up into the darkness I saw myself as a creature driven and derided by vanity; and my eyes burned with anguish and anger.

Hemingway's most extravagant use of repetition and incantatory rhythm is in the long 'nada' passage, where it is licensed by two factors; firstly, that it is parodying prayers which are themselves rhythmically and rhetorically patterned, and secondly that the story has now shifted its centre from the impersonal narrator to the point of view of the older waiter. One might also note here that considerable literary advantages accrue from the fact that the story is set in Spain. To some readers the prayer-parodies will always seem contrived, but clearly they would arise most naturally in a mind conditioned by a Catholic religious culture. All the speech, both in dialogue and in interior monologue, is by implication a rendering of Spanish, so that the sceptical reader cannot test its authenticity with any confidence. The sprinkling of Spanish words in the text follows a familiar narrative convention for giving 'local colour', but it has other more subtle effects. The word *nada*, for instance, is obviously far more resonant, mysterious and sinister as a foreign word appearing in an English language context than it would be in a wholly Spanish context.

The shift in point of view is managed so discreetly that we are scarcely aware of it. The impersonal narrator withdraws with the forgiving remark à propos the younger waiter, 'He did not wish to be unjust. He was only in hurry' (110-11). But this withdrawal is covered by the ongoing dialogue, and the movement into the 'older waiters' consciousness is presented as a continuation of the dialogue: 'Turning off the electric light he continued the conversation with himself.' (143-4). This device doesn't seem unnatural because it has already been established that communication between the two waiters has broken down. It was always tenuous—as we have seen, many of the older waiter's remarks have a private meaning unperceived by the younger waiter, and when he tries obliquely to communicate what oppresses him, the younger waiter says 'Stop talking nonsense'. (126). (This moment is re-enacted later, in a more extreme form, when the older waiter orders 'nada' in the bodega, and the barman dismisses him as a madman (lines 163-5).) Thus, when the older waiter says, "'I am of those who like to stay late at the café,'" he is already in a sense talking to himself rather than to the younger waiter, he is embarked on an effort of self-definition, a declaration of faith, or rather of scepticism, the slightly incantatory rhythm of that declaration "'of those . . . with all those . . . with all those'" preparing for the prayer-pardoy that is to come.

The parody of the Lord's Prayer rises to a kind of climax as the word *nada* replaces more and more of the meaningful words of the prayer, so that at the beginning the words, *who art, name, kingdom,* etc., are retained, but towards the end of the parody all the nouns and verbs are replaced by *nada*—'and nada us our nada as we nada our nadas and nada us not into nada,'—and then comes a significant reversion to the actual prayer: 'but *deliver* us from nada' (159, my italics). **'A Clean, Well-Lighted Place'** implies very strongly that there is no deliverance from nada.

Notes

1. E.g., *The Essential Ernest Hemingway,* Penguin Books, 1969.

2. John V. Hagopian, 'Tidying Up Hemingway's "A Clean, Well-lighted Place,"' *Studies in Short Fiction,* 1 (1964), 140-6.

3. F. P. Kroeger, 'The Dialogue in a "A Clean, Well-lighted Place"'; William E. Colburn, 'Confusion in "A Clean, Well-lighted Place,"' *College English,* 20 (1959), 240-2.

4. Carlos Baker, *Hemingway: the Writer as Artist* (1963), p. 124.

5. Otto Reinert, 'Hemingway's Waiters Once More,' *College English,* 20 (1959), 417-18.

6. Edward Stone, 'Hemingway's Waiters Yet Once More,' *American Speech,* 37 (1962), 239-40.

7. Hagopian, op. cit.

8. Joseph F. Gabriel, 'The Logic of Confusion in Hemingway's "A Clean, Well-lighted Place,"' *College English,* 22 (1961), 539-46.

9. Philip Young, *Ernest Hemingway; A Reconsideration* (1952, revised 1966).

10. See, for example, Robert Penn Warren, 'Hemingway,' *Kenyon Review,* 9 (1947), 1-28; Harry Levin, 'Observations on the Style of Ernest Hemingway' in *Contexts of Criticism* (1957); Baker, op. cit., and Young, op. cit.; Charles A. Fenton, *The Apprenticeship of Ernest Hemingway; the Early Years* (1954).

11. In an otherwise rather simple-minded essay (which makes no reference to the problem of line 78) William B. Bache comments perceptively, 'From the

older waiter to the old man lies a progression in despair, for the three characters are actually part of an implied progression from youth through middle age to old age'. See 'Craftsmanship in "A Clean Well-lighted Place,"' *The Personalist,* 37 (1956), 60-64.

Charles E. May (essay date 1971)

SOURCE: "Is Hemingway's 'Well-Lighted Place' Really Clean Now?," in *Studies in Short Fiction,* Vol. VIII, No. 2, Spring, 1971, pp. 326-30.

[*In the following essay, May rejects John V. Hagopian's reading of "A Clean, Well-Lighted Place" and offers his own interpretation of the dialogue of the story.*]

> "Every professional artist has met the questioner who asks of some detail: 'Why did you do it so clumsily like that, when you could have done it so neatly like this?'"
>
> —Joyce Cary, New York *Times Book Review*, April 30, 1950.

Everyone seems satisfied and perhaps a bit relieved now that John Hagopian has tidied up Hemingway's **"A Clean, Well-Lighted Place"** (*Studies in Short Fiction,* Winter 1964). The dialogue discrepancy that had scholars counting lines in *College English* in 1959 and 1961 was only a typographical error after all—a thirty-year-old typographical error. And thus, following Mr. Hagopian's suggestion, Charles Scribner's Sons have cleaned up the messy **"Place"** in their most recent edition of *The Short Stories of Ernest Hemingway* by changing the two bothersome lines:

> "His niece looks after him."
>
> "I know. You said she cut him down."

to Mr. Hagopian's tidier arrangement:

> "His niece looks after him. You said she cut him down."
>
> "I know."

We should congratulate Mr. Hagopian for his influence. Not only has the text of a story, read by thousands since it first appeared in *Scribner's Magazine* in 1933, been changed for the sake of "tidiness," but Mr. Hagopian has fulfilled the secret desire of all critics at one time or another—to rewrite the work of an author to fit his own interpretation of that work. As a result of his "tidying," Mr. Hagopian can now assert that it is undeniably the old waiter who knows about the old deaf man's suicide attempt. And based on this, he further can create an elaborate and sophisticated gloss of the double meanings of many of the old waiter's lines. For example, in the first dialogue section it is the young waiter who asks what the old man was in despair about and the old waiter who replies "Nothing," which, according to Mr. Hagopian, is "a controlled ambiguous substructure," meaning *both* "For no reason that you would understand" *and* "Because of the nada in the universe." It is also the young waiter who asks "How do you know it was nothing?" and the old waiter who replies "He has plenty of money," which again, according to Mr. Hagopian, is ambiguous, meaning *both* "Since you insist on a reason, I'll give the only one a man like you could possibly understand—there couldn't be a good reason because he has plenty of money," *and* "It wasn't the lack of money; it was his awareness of nada." With his one typographical change Mr. Hagopian is able to gloss the following dialogue lines revealing that all the old waiter's replies to the young waiter's questions are ambiguous, impatient, or sarcastic.

Although Mr. Hagopian's main quarrel seems to be with Joseph Gabriel's elaborate justification of the confusion in the dialogue as functional ambiguity (*College English,* May 1961), he first takes issue with Otto Reinert's suggestion (*College English,* May 1959) that Hemingway violates the typographical convention that each new indented line in a dialogue implies a new speaker. Reinert says "it is the young waiter who speaks *both* 'He's drunk now' (because the pronoun reference demands it) *and* the next speech, 'He's drunk every night.' And that it is the old waiter who speaks *both* 'He must be eighty years old' *and* 'Anyway I should say he was eighty.'" Reinert, however, does not support his assertion very well, and Mr. Hagopian says his solution would only be valid if "(*1*) by the law of parsimony, it is the simplest solution; (*2*) an examination of the rest of Hemingway's fiction shows that the author often, or even occasionally, employed such a technique; and (*3*) the context supported, as it does in Joyce's *Ulysses,* the notion that the author violates standard conventions without explicit hints or clues to the reader." Of course, Mr. Hagopian tries to show that Reinert's suggestion fails on all three counts, but I'm not so sure that he isn't a little too hasty to get on with his "mere sweep of the broom."

As to the first objection, it seems to me that *assuming* Hemingway has violated a typographical convention (a functional violation) is "simpler" than *presuming* the rather drastic measure of rewriting the text of a work—especially a story by Hemingway. Is it really such a simple solution to believe that Hemingway, with his consummate care for the individual word, would have allowed the supposed typographical error to be perpetuated for so long?

As to the second objection, I can offer at least one other instance in which Hemingway does violate the dialogue indentation convention. At the end of chapter ten of *A Farewell to Arms* when Rinaldi is chiding Frederick Henry about Catherine Barkley, this dialogue occurs:

> "I will send her. Your lovely cool goddess. English goddess. My God what would a man do with a woman like that except worship her? What is an Englishwoman good for?"
>
> "You are an ignorant, foul-mouthed dago."

> "A what?"

> "An ignorant wop."

> "Wop. You are a frozen-faced . . . wop."

"You are ignorant. Stupid." I saw that word pricked him and kept on. Hemingway has violated the indentation convention here and for a good reason. Frederick is trying to rouse Rinaldi, sees a slight response when he calls him an "ignorant wop," then tries to find out which word has the effect—first trying *wop,* then *ignorant,* which is the word that "pricked him." Thus, Hemingway does violate the convention when it serves the purpose of conveying pause and reflection.

As to Mr. Hagopian's third objection about context justifying such a violation, I might only point out that the entire story violates expected dialogue conventions from the very beginning. The reader goes through three dialogue scenes (almost half the story) before he is able to distinguish between the two waiters. Not until one waiter says, "I wouldn't want to be that old. An old man is a nasty thing," do we know that this is the young, impatient waiter. I can only agree with Joseph Gabriel, at least on this point, that the mystery here is a deliberate effect of the story—a functional violation of the convention of identifying speakers to convey a certain significant impression of the story. If we can accept this major violation, why can we not accept the relatively minor one of breaking the indentation convention?

But the real objection I have to Mr. Hagopian's facile "sweep of the broom" is that it changes the meaning of the story in a major way. The difference between whether the young waiter or the old waiter knows about the old man's suicide attempt is the difference between seeing the story as a static or a dynamic action. If the old waiter knows, then the old waiter (and I assume that everyone agrees he is the character we are concerned with) remains essentially the same at the end of the story as he was at the beginning. However, if it is indeed the young waiter who tells the old waiter about the suicide attempt, then the story is about the old waiter, who, forced to confront his affinity with the old man's despair, arrives at his nada prayer at the end as a *result* of the story. This makes for a simpler, yet more pertinent reading of the story than if we assume the old waiter has already realized and articulated the significance of nada to himself before the story begins. It is the difference between seeing the story as an excuse for a preconceived philosophic concept or as a dramatic realization of such a concept.

Before proceeding with this reading of the story, I first wish to suggest why Hemingway violated the dialogue indentation convention in the four lines Reinert has already pointed out. First it is the young waiter who says in disgust, "He's drunk now," and, getting no response from the old waiter, who doesn't mind, says "He's drunk every night." Hemingway breaks the convention to show the young waiter's impatience with the old man for being drunk again as he has for several nights and for once more causing him to have to stay late at the café. The old waiter makes no response to the second statement either, for he is still considering the old man's suicide attempt and asks, "What did he want to kill himself for?" Mr. Hagopian glosses this as the young waiter's line, "resuming the earlier dialogue in which he was the questioner." But this is not a resumption of the dialogue. It is a repetition of the question asked earlier—a question the young waiter would not care enough about to repeat. However, it is a question the old waiter is concerned with—a question the young waiter gave no satisfactory answer to earlier. It is the old waiter who says, "He must be eighty years old," and then after a reflective pause says, "Anyway I should say he was eighty." This is an even more significant pause because it is the old man's age that made him try to kill himself, and it is this suicide attempt that makes the old waiter reflect on his own advancing age. This again seems more convincing than Mr. Hagopian's gloss of the line "Anyway I should say he was eighty" as being a response to the young waiter meaning, "Perhaps he is, but that too doesn't matter much." I should think it would matter a great deal—both to the old man and to the old waiter. Moreover, in this connection, it is not accidental that the first dialogue line in the story positively identified is the young waiter saying "I wouldn't want to be that old. An old man is a nasty thing." For it is just the young waiter's youth that makes him disgusted and impatient with the old man and the old waiter's age that makes him understanding and sympathetic. This is not only the source of the difference between the two, but also the source of the old waiter's increasing realization of his own age and resultant despair.

Understanding the story this way, we do not need Mr. Hagopian's elaborate gloss. The rest of the question and answer exchange about the old man is quite clear. The first dialogue scene opens with the young waiter watching the old man and idly noting that he tried to commit suicide last week. (If the old waiter is really as cynical about the young waiter's understanding of this as Mr. Hagopian says he is, I don't see why the old waiter would have mentioned it in the first place.) When the young waiter says this, the old waiter is immediately interested because the similarity in their ages and resultant despair make the act relevant to him. We can then see (without worrying about "ambiguous substructures") that when the old waiter asks what the old man was in despair about, the young waiter answers "Nothing" and "He has plenty of money" because the young waiter cannot understand a man with plenty of money trying to kill himself. Later, the old waiter again asks "What did he want to kill himself for?" and then continues by asking "How did he do it?" "Who cut him down?", and "Why?" because such questions vitally concern his own situation. Not only would the young waiter not bother to ask such questions, but he answers the old waiter in short replies without comment because he doesn't care. To the old waiter's question about why he did it, the young waiter says "How should I know?"

This reading allows us to see the story as following basically a cause and effect structure. The presence of the old man in the café so late causes the ensuing dialogue between the two waiters; the knowledge the old waiter gains about the old man's suicide attempt in the dialogue causes the old waiter's reflections about nada at the end of the story. At the end of the dialogue section when the old man leaves, the old waiter, having recognized his affinity in despair with the old man, now explicitly affirms it by admitting that he too is one of those, like the old man, "who like to stay late at the café. . . . With all those who need a light for the night." Then after the young waiter leaves, the old waiter, reflecting on his recognition, recalls the word the young waiter used when asked earlier what the old man was in despair about—*nothing*. He transforms this non-answer, meaning "No reason" as the young waiter understands it, to the most real answer of all—a concrete and terribly felt "nothingness" as the old waiter himself now understands it.

Finally, in the understated conclusion of the story when the old waiter decides to go home knowing he will lie awake all night, he tries to dismiss the "nothing that he knew too well" with "It is probably only insomnia." But it is a "nothing" he has been forced to confront in the story by confronting his affinity with the old man—an affinity that makes him realize "Many must have it."

Thus, I would like to suggest that Mr. Hagopian might have been a little too hasty with his broom, and Scribner's a little too precipitous in tampering with the text of Hemingway's story. The story may be "tidier" as a result of Mr. Hagopian's efforts, but is it really "clean" now?

Scott MacDonald (essay date 1973)

SOURCE: "The Confusion Dialogue in Hemingway's 'Clean, Well-Lighted Place': A Final Word?," in *Studies in American Fiction*, Vol. 1, No. 1, Spring, 1973, pp. 93-101.

[*In the following essay, MacDonald concurs with Charles Mays's interpretation of the dialogue in "A Clean, Well-Lighted Place," contending that Hemingway ignored normal dialogue conventions in several other fictional works.*]

In his generally sensible, but somewhat precipitant article, "Is Hemingway's 'Well-Lighted Place' Really Clean Now?" Charles E. May shows how the long critical debate about the confusing dialogue in Hemingway's **"A Clean, Well-Lighted Place"** resulted in Charles Scribner's Sons changing the text of the story.[1] Until recently **"A Clean, Well-Lighted Place"** was printed so that near the end of the long exchange which has caused so much confusion, the younger waiter says, "His niece looks after him," and the older waiter responds, "I know. You said she cut him down." In the last few years, however, the passage has been printed so that the younger waiter says, "His niece looks after him. You said she cut him down," and the older waiter responds, "I know." Clearly this is a crucial difference. By changing the identity of the waiter who knows about the attempted suicide Scribner's has altered much of the story. One would expect that a change of this magnitude in one of the most highly respected and widely read of Twentieth Century short stories would be based either on a request by Hemingway himself or on evidence from a manuscript of the story. Unfortunately, neither was the case. As May points out, the change was apparently a result of the critical article "Tidying Up Hemingway's Clean Well-Lighted Place" in which John V. Hagopian concluded that modifying the text was the only way of satisfactorily solving the difficulties caused by the dialogue.[2]

Hagopian recognized that to assume the passage was correct as originally published, it is necessary to suppose that in two instances during the exchange between the two waiters, Hemingway ignores conventional dialogue expectations and has a single speaker say two consecutive indented lines of dialogue. Hagopian refused to accept this possibility, he said, because it was not the simplest solution to the problem, because he felt there was no supporting evidence in the text, and because of his contention that nowhere else in Hemingway's fiction is such a device used even occasionally. As May suggests, however, Hagopian's arguments simply don't hold water. The contention that a change in the text is the simplest way to solve the problem of the confusing passage is clearly ridiculous. Obviously, to alter a text and develop a wholly new interpretation of a story is more complicated than to suppose that Hemingway failed to follow normal conventions in a passage of dialogue. May also points up the weakness of Hagopian's contention that there is nothing in the text itself to support the suggestion that in two instances a single speaker says two consecutive indented lines. A careful look at the text shows that it is quite possible that the younger waiter says, "He's drunk now" and then after a pause, continues with the next indented line, "He's drunk every night"; and that later in the same passage the older waiter says, "He must be eighty years old" and then after a pause continues, "Anyway I should say he was eighty."[3] The one important weakness in May's article is his failure to prove that, despite what Hagopian says, Hemingway does ignore normal dialogue conventions in other works.

May cites a passage from *A Farewell to Arms* in which he believes that Hemingway has a character speak several consecutive indented lines. In the passage Rinaldi and Henry are discussing Catherine Barkley:

> "I will send her. Your lovely cool goddess. English goddess. My God what would a man do with a woman like that except worship her? What else is an Englishwoman good for?"

> "You are an ignorant foul-mouthed dago."

> "A what?"

> "An ignorant wop."

> "Wop. You are a frozen-faced . . . wop."

> "You are ignorant. Stupid." I saw that word pricked him and kept on.

"Uninformed, Inexperienced, stupid from inexperience."[4]

May apparently feels that Henry says "An ignorant wop" and both the following statements. While it may not be impossible to read the passage in this way, May's interpretation is strained and unnecessary. There is nothing in the text which indicates that Rinaldi does not say, "Wop. You are a frozen-faced . . . wop." In fact, the repetition of the single word "Wop" and the pause indicated by the ellipsis suggests the Italian's difficulty in coming to grips with Henry's American slang. Further, the use of "frozen-faced" seems to be Rinaldi's mocking prediction of what will happen to Frederic Henry as a result of being in contact with a "cool" Englishwoman. The passage, in other words, is best read in the conventional manner. Though May fails to support his belief that Hemingway ignores normal dialogue conventions, this contention can and should be substantiated. If enough critics can be made aware of the weakness of Hagopian's arguments, it may be possible to convince Scribner's that the revision of **"A Clean, Well-Lighted Place"** was a mistake.

As has been mentioned, Hagopian's arguments are based to a significant extent on his contention that "nowhere else in *The Short Stories of Ernest Hemingway* . . . is there an instance of a reflective pause between two lines of dialogue by the same speaker without some indication of the fact. . . ."[5] While Hagopian indicates that the lack of such instances is not an absolute test, it is crucial to his reasoning. His article even lists a series of passages from the stories in which a single speaker speaks twice in succession, but in which intervening lines of description and the repetition of nouns or pronouns act as clear signals of what Hemingway is doing, passages such as this one from **"The Killers"**:

> "Maybe it was just a bluff."

> "No. It ain't just a bluff."

> Ole Andreson rolled over toward the wall.

> "The only thing is," he said, talking toward the wall, "I just can't make up my mind to go out. I been in here all day."

and this one from **"Now I Lay Me"**:

> "I think it's all bull, myself," he said. "I just heard it somewhere. You know how you hear things."

> We were both quiet and I listened to the silk-worms.

> "You hear those damn silk-worms?" he asked.[6]

Hagopian's implication is that in all cases Hemingway either abides by standard procedure or supplies these indications that he is not doing so. The fact is, however, that Hemingway *does* deviate from standard procedure without supplying explicit clues to the reader and that he does so with some regularity. Passages in which Hemingway ignores normal dialogue conventions by indenting two consecutive speeches by a single speaker occur frequently enough and obviously enough in both the stories and the novels that one wonders how Hagopian was ever able to make his original assertion. In **"The Three-Day Blow,"** for example, Nick Adams is talking about G. K. Chesterton with Bill:

> "That's right," said Nick. "I guess he's a better guy than Walpole."
>
> "Oh, he's a better guy, all right," Bill said.
>
> "But Walpole's a better writer."
>
> "I don't know," Nick said. "Chesterton's a classic."[7]

It is obvious from the context that Bill says Chesterton is a better guy and then emphasizes in the succeeding, indented line that Walpole is the better writer. And it is clear that Hemingway supplies no explicit clue in the story that he is disregarding normal conventions for writing dialogue. A similar instance occurs in **"The Gambler, the Nun, and the Radio."** As Mr. Frazer sits talking with the Mexican "friends" of Cayetano, the Mexican who does not drink asks him,

> "How many tubes has the radio. . . ."
>
> "Seven."
>
> "Very beautiful," he said. "What does it cost?"
>
> "I don't know," Mr. Frazer said. "It is rented."
>
> "You gentlemen are friends of Cayetano?"
>
> "No," said the big one. "We are friends of he who wounded him."[8]

It is obvious that Mr. Frazer says, "I don't know . . . It is rented," and then asks if the men are Cayetano's friends. As is true in **"The Three-Day Blow,"** it is clear in **"The Gambler, the Nun, and the Radio"** who is saying what, but the reader's knowledge results from his understanding of the characters and their situations, not from specific indications in the text. In each of the above instances Hemingway's disregard of normal dialogue conventions functions to create a reflective pause. Bill's second, indented statement indicates his brief hesitation before qualifying his agreement with Nick. The indenting of Mr. Frazer's second comment emphasizes the difficulty the American is having making conversation with the Mexicans.

Passages of dialogue in which Hemingway indents lines of dialogue without changing speakers are also found in various novels. Near the end of *For Whom the Bell Tolls,* for example, as Robert Jordan lies wounded, he talks with Pablo about what he and his band should do:

> "Does it hurt much?" Pablo asked. He was bending close over Robert Jordan.
>
> "No. I think the nerve is crushed. Listen. Get along. I am mucked, see? I will talk to the girl for a moment. When I say to take her, take her. She will want to stay. I will only speak to her for a moment."
>
> "Clearly, there is not much time," Pablo said.

> "Clearly."
>
> "I think you would do better in the Republic," Robert Jordan said.
>
> "Nay. I am for Gredos."
>
> "Use thy head."
>
> "Talk to her now," Pablo said. "There is little time. I am sorry thou hast this, *Inglés.*"[9]

It is obvious from the context that Jordan responds, "Clearly" and then in the next line advises Pablo against going to Gredos. The indenting of the second statement indicates a short pause during which Jordan presumably decides to try to convince Pablo to escape to the Republic. Another instance, one in a passage of dialogue as long as the confusing passage in **"A Clean, Well-Lighted Place"** and with as few identifications of speaker, occurs earlier in *For Whom the Bell Tolls.* As Robert Jordan talks with El Sordo, the Spaniard asks Jordan if he likes the whiskey he has been served:

> "Very much," said Robert Jordan. "It's very good whiskey."
>
> "Am contented," Sordo grinned. "Was bringing tonight with information."
>
> "What information?"
>
> "Much troop movement."
>
> "Where?"
>
> "Segovia. Planes you saw."
>
> "Yes."
>
> "Bad, eh?"
>
> "Bad."
>
> "Troop movement?"
>
> "Much between Villacastin and Segovia. On Valladolid road. Much between Villacastin and San Rafael. Much. Much."
>
> "What do you think?"
>
> "We prepare something?"
>
> "Possibly."
>
> "They know. Prepare too."
>
> "It is possible."
>
> "Why not blow bridge tonight?"
>
> "Orders."
>
> "Whose orders?"
>
> "General Staff."
>
> "So."[10]

It is clear that Jordan says, "Bad" and then in the next line asks, "Troop movement?" Again, the use of two consecutive indented lines seems to indicate a pause, in this case a pause in which Jordan and El Sordo contemplate the danger indicated by the increased troop movement and the presence of the planes.

Similar instances in which normal dialogue conventions are ignored occur in *The Sun Also Rises*. Near the end of Book II, for example, Jake Barnes returns from a walk with Brett, and, having promised her to look after Mike, goes by the Scotchman's room:

> Mike lay on the bed looking like a death mask of himself. He opened his eyes and looked at me.
>
> "Hello, Jake," he said very slowly. "I'm getting a little sleep. I've wanted a little sleep for a long time."
>
> "Let me cover you over."
>
> "No. I'm quite warm."
>
> "Don't go. I haven't got ten to sleep yet."
>
> "You'll sleep, Mike. Don't worry, boy."[11]

It is clear from the context that Mike tells Jake, "No. I'm quite warm" and then in the following line asks Jake not to leave. The indenting of Mike's second statement seems to indicate a pause during which Jake begins moving toward the door in the hope that Mike has fallen asleep. It is even possible that normal dialogue conventions are ignored again on the same page of *The Sun Also Rises* within a few lines of the last example. When Jake leaves Mike, he goes to his room:

> Bill was in my room reading the paper.
>
> "See Mike?"
>
> "Yes."
>
> "Let's go and eat."
>
> "I won't eat down-stairs with that German head waiter. He was damned snotty when I was getting Mike upstairs."
>
> "He was snotty to us, too."

It seems clear that Bill begins this exchange by asking Jake if he has seen Mike. When Jake and Brett arrive at the hotel, the German head waiter tells them that Mike and Bill have gone up to their rooms, and it is likely that Jake would assume that Bill has seen Mike. The opening question thus makes most sense if Bill asks it. Since the reader knows that Jake was with Brett when Bill and Mike went to their rooms, it is clear that Bill must say the fourth line of the exchange. It follows then that either Jake responds, "Yes" and then says, "Let's go and eat," or that Bill says, "Let's go and eat" and then says that he won't eat downstairs. Of course, if Bill asks the opening question, the exchange can be read in conventional fashion, but it does seem possible that for the second time in less than a page Hemingway ignores conventional rules without supplying the reader with any signals that he is doing so. Other passages in Hemingway's work during which a single character speaks two indented lines in succession can be found. There are two instances in **"The Battler,"**

for example.[12] It should be clear from the examples which have been discussed, however, that Hemingway ignores normal dialogue conventions with enough regularity to show that Hagopian's arguments are based to a significant degree on incomplete investigation.

The existence of passages in Hemingway's fiction in which Hemingway clearly ignores dialogue conventions, of course, does not prove that he ignores the conventions in **"A Clean, Well-Lighted Place."** At the same time, these instances do indicate that Hagopian should have given a good deal more consideration to this possibility than he was willing to give. Literary conventions, after all, are not laws. They are assessments of what authors have done, not of what they must do. It is true that most authors have consistently indented during passages of dialogue in order to indicate that a new speaker is speaking, but this is far from saying either that all writers always adhere to this way of doing things, or that all writers should always adhere to this way of doing things. The fact that at one point the original text of **"A Clean, Well-Lighted Place"** clearly indicates that the younger waiter is the one who knows about the attempted suicide must override any interpretation based on the assumption that Hemingway's dialogue must be conventional.[13] Even if one were to agree that the interpretation Hagopian derives from the altered text is a fully consistent one, the conclusion would not be changed, for Hagopian's interpretation is surely no more consistent with the text as a whole than is the traditional interpretation. Surely, a consistent interpretation based on a significant change in an author's text cannot, and must not, override a consistent interpretation based on the assumption that an author disregards certain conventional rules, especially when they are rules which the same author has clearly broken in other places.

There is no doubt that Hemingway's disregard of convention in **"A Clean, Well-Lighted Place"** is misleading, far too misleading to be effective. The fact remains, however, that the problems which the story creates can and should be solved without recourse to alterations in Hemingway's text. It is highly unfortunate that the long critical discussion about the confusing dialogue resulted in a change in the way Scribner's prints the story, a change which Charles Scribner, Jr. admits was made, not on the basis of manuscript evidence or at the suggestion of Hemingway himself, but solely on the basis of the advice of critics and "common sense."[14] It might be common sense to alter the way a passage of dialogue was printed if the change eliminated confusion and caused no significant modification in the meaning of the text. But that is not the case here. The alteration in the dialogue of **"A Clean, Well-Lighted Place"** changes the meaning of the text significantly and, as a result, cannot help but create more confusion than it was meant to solve. Those readers who are introduced to the story through the "corrected" version will be forced to develop an interpretation of the two waiters—and of much of the rest of the story—which is very different from what is called for by Hemingway's original text. One can only hope that concerned scholars will be able to prevail upon

Scribner's to reverse the recent policy and once again print the story Hemingway wrote and saw through numerous printings.

Notes

1. Charles E. May, "Is Hemingway's 'Well-Lighted Place' Really Clean Now?" *SSF*, 8 (1971), 326-30.

2. John V. Hagopian, "Tidying Up Hemingway's Clean Well-Lighted Place," *SSF*, 2 (1964), 140-46. Only two alternatives had been suggested. One was Joseph F. Gabriel's contention that the confusing dialogue is an attempt by Hemingway to purposely confuse the reader and thus place him in the same existential position as the characters. See "The Logic of Confusion in Hemingway's 'A Clean, Well-Lighted Place,'" *CE*, 22 (May, 1961), 539-46. The other was Otto Reinert's suggestion that Hemingway ignores conventional dialogue expectations and twice during the long exchange between the two waiters has a single waiter say two consecutive indented lines of dialogue. See "Hemingway's Waiters Once More," *CE*, 20 (May, 1959), 417-18. Hagopian correctly demonstrated why Gabriel's interpretation was over-ingenious. As is shown in the present discussion, however, Hagopian's reasons for dismissing Reinert's sensible suggestions were poorly thought out.

3. This is made all the more clear by the fact that the second of these instances is actually easier to understand if one does not attempt to alternate speakers. Were the reader to suppose that "He must be eighty years old" and "Anyway I should say he was eighty" are spoken by two different waiters, it would be difficult to understand the purpose of "Anyway" in the second sentence. As Reinert explains, the second sentence seems to indicate an admission of subjectivity on the part of the speaker of the previous line; it seems to be an attempt to disqualify after a pause, "the objective certainty of 'He must be eighty years old'" (Reinert, p. 418). While it is not impossible to read the two lines as though they were spoken by two different speakers, the feeling of continuity which is created by the use of "Anyway" makes it at least as acceptable to read the lines as spoken by the older waiter.

4. Ernest Hemingway, *A Farewell to Arms* (New York: Scribner's, 1957), p. 69.

5. Hagopian, p. 141.

6. Ernest Hemingway, *The Short Stories of Ernest Hemingway* (New York: Scribners, 1953), p. 287.

7. *The Short Stories of Ernest Hemingway,* p. 119.

8. *The Short Stories of Ernest Hemingway,* p. 476.

9. Ernest Hemingway, *For Whom the Bell Tolls* (New York: Scribner's, 1940), p. 462.

10. *For Whom the Bell Tolls,* p. 143.

11. Ernest Hemingway, *The Sun Also Rises* (New York: Scribner's, 1954), p. 210.

12. One of these instances occurs as Ad is speaking angrily to Nick: "'How the hell do you get that way?' came out from under the cap sharply at Nick." Ad then says the following indented statement: "Who the hell do you think you are? You're a snotty bastard. You come in here where nobody asks you and eat a man's food and when he asks to borrow a knife you get snotty" (*The Short Stories of Ernest Hemingway,* p. 135). The other example occurs at the end of the story when Bugs says the long paragraph which ends, "'Would you like to take some of that ham and some bread with you? No? You better take a sandwich,' all this in a low, smooth, polite nigger voice," and then says the next indented line, "Good. Well, good-bye, Mister Adams. Good-bye and good luck!" (*The Short Stories of Ernest Hemingway,* p. 138). There are additional examples in other works, too. It is likely, for example, that near the beginning of Book II of *The Sun Also Rises,* Brett says both, "Might" and the next indented statement, "I needed that" (*The Sun Also Rises,* p. 83).

13. As all critics have agreed, it is clear that at one point in the original text the younger waiter says, "His niece looks after him," and the older waiter replies, "I know. You said she cut him down." The question about these lines has never been how they should be read, but only if they are correct as they are printed, for if they are correct then it is clear that Hemingway does ignore dialogue conventions in "A Clean, Well-Lighted Place."

14. Information in a letter to the author from Charles Scribner, Jr., April 5, 1971.

Annette Benert (essay date 1974)

SOURCE: "Survival through Irony: Hemingway's 'A Clean, Well-Lighted Place,'" in *Studies in Short Fiction,* Vol. XI, No. 2, Spring, 1974, pp. 181-87.

[In the following essay, Benert explores Hemingway's use of imagery and characterization in "A Clean, Well-Lighted Place."]

"A Clean, Well-Lighted Place" has with justice been considered an archetypal Hemingway story, morally and aesthetically central to the Hemingway canon. But its crystalline structure and sparse diction have led many critics to judge the story itself a simple one, either about nothingness, "a little *nada* story," or about the author's positive values, a story "lyric rather than dramatic."[1] I would like to suggest that it is in neither sense simple, but that the feelings and ideas which lie behind it are complex and are expressed dramatically, chiefly through the characterization of the older waiter. The latter is a man of enormous awareness continually torn between what might be called religious idealism and intellectual nihilism, a combination that surfaces in irony in several places in the story. This tension between two modes of viewing the world is developed through imagery that functions as a setting, through characterization, and, more abstractly, through a theme which I take to be the barriers against *nada*.

The most obvious source of imagery is the words of the title, the qualities of light and cleanness, to which one may add quietness. These terms admirably illustrate what Richard K. Peterson calls the "use of apparently objective words to express values";[2] they may be followed with profit throughout Hemingway's stories, novels, and nonfiction. But in this story each of these qualities exists also in its negative aspect, its shadow side.

Light provides the most striking image pattern. The café has an "electric light"[3] that the older waiter eventually turns off (p. 382). A street light is picked up by the brass number on a passing soldier's collar (p. 379). The older waiter is "with all those who need a light for the night" (p. 382).[4] The café where he works is "well lighted"; its "light is very good" (ibid.). In the bodega where he buys coffee "the light is very bright and pleasant" (p. 383). After going home he would be able to sleep "with daylight" (ibid.). Obviously, light is not only the antithesis of darkness but an effective barrier against it, or, rather, as Randall Stewart puts it, the light "at any rate, must be made to do."[5]

But it is stated twice that the patron, the old man, "sat in the shadow of the leaves" (p. 379), and the older waiter likes the café not only because its light is good but because "now there are shadows of the leaves" (p. 382). Further, the old man particularly liked sitting in the café at night because "the dew settled the dust" of the day and "it was quiet and he felt the difference," though he was deaf (p. 379). Here shadow clearly has a positive connotation, in the sense of shade, of protection from the glare of the light, perhaps because the light is artificial but more likely because any direct light hurts the eyes and exposes the person.[6] In addition, the night is clean and quiet, positive values contrasted to the day's dirt and noise.

The older waiter is equally concerned that his "place" be clean. He contradicts the younger waiter's remark that "an old man is a nasty thing" with "this old man is clean. He drinks without spilling. Even now, drunk" (p. 381). In contrast to the younger waiter, who wipes "the edge of the table with a towel" (ibid.) to emphasize that the old man should leave, but earlier had poured brandy so that it "slopped over and ran down the stem into the top saucer of the pile" (p. 380), the older waiter emphasizes several times the necessity of cleanness (pp. 382, 383). Bars and bodegas are open all night, and they have light, but one cannot "stand before a bar with dignity, with correctness."[7]

Its natural occurrence, however, is at night, when "the dew settled the dust" (p. 379). Its negative aspect is even more evident in that statement of the younger waiter that "an old man is a nasty thing" (p. 381), which, as a generalization, the older waiter does not contradict. Since age, as opposed to youth, is specifically associated in this story with

greater awareness and sensitivity, in Hemingway terms "imagination," cleanness may be linked with ignorance and insensitivity.

The third positive quality of the café is its quietness; the old man, in addition, is deaf. There is the suggestion that another thing wrong with bars is that they may have music, but, in any case, "you do not want music. Certainly you do not want music" (p. 382). Any form of noise, then, like darkness and dirt, is to be avoided.[8]

In this quality is the negative side of all three most evident. The old patron not only cannot tolerate direct light and can be classified with "nasty things," but also he is actually deaf so that no sound even has relevance for him. That the shadow side of quietness is its extreme, in the form of a negation of one whole sense faculty and a major art form, reminds the reader that all three qualities are in some sense negations. Light functions as an absence of darkness, cleanness as an absence of dirt, quietness as an absence of sound. Yet all three are posited as barriers against the ultimate negation, against Nothingness itself—perhaps, for once in literature, a genuine paradox, but certainly a major source of irony in this story.

Other images are less important but function in the same way. Liquor, the "giant killer" of other stories, is a weapon against the darkness, but it also impairs physical functioning, making the old man walk "unsteadily," so that the older waiter notices with pride that he can drink "without spilling. Even now, drunk," walk "with dignity" (p. 381). The younger waiter is "not lonely" because he has "a wife waiting in bed" (p. 380), but for the old man who "had a wife once" now "a wife would be no good' (p. 381), making women, a relationship to a woman, a material, but very temporary and thus illusory, protection against nothingness. All Hemingway's sleepless heroes desire sleep, but the old waiter, acutely conscious of the darkness lurking behind the light, cannot allow himself to lose that consciousness until he has light to protect him. There is a synonymity between being aware and being awake that overrides the psychologically negative connotations of insomnia. Thus, the man who can sleep is unaware and insensitive.

But in **"A Clean, Well-Lighted Place"** characterization is even more important than imagery. Though the old patron is the main topic of conversation between the two waiters, he is less important as a character than either of them. He functions more as part of the setting, a demonstration of the way things are, and as an indirect means for the characterization of the other two men. The younger waiter, also called "the waiter who was in a hurry" (p. 381) and "the waiter with a wife" (p. 382), is not the villain he is often cast to be; he after all "did not wish to be unjust" (ibid.), He is merely *l'homme moyen sensuel,* lacking that moral and aesthetic sensibility Hemingway calls "imagination." He alone should serve as a refutation of the "locker-room" Hemingway, if such is still needed, but he is much less important than his co-worker, indeed serving as a kind of foil for him.[9]

That the older waiter is also called "the unhurried waiter" (p. 381) makes evident the pun in the appellation. The younger man is "waiting" impatiently to go home and the older is "waiting" patiently or has transcended "waiting" altogether, has gone one step beyond Beckett's tramps, having learned that there is nothing to wait for. As Joseph Gabriel has it, he "must bear at the same time his intense spiritual hunger and the realization of the impossibility of its fulfillment."[10] His alienation is dramatized, as Robert Weeks has noted, by his being "in the presence of others who either do not even notice him, or if they do are unaware of his ordeal and of the gallantry with which he endures it."[11] But he is also something more, and something more complex, than these tragic, heroic qualities would suggest.

He first appears in that initial dialogue, which, by its lack of speech tags and the ensuing possible mis-assignment of them, has plagued so many readers. The second long dialogue makes clear that the older waiter provides the younger with information concerning the old patron's attempted suicide, and that the older man possesses the greater degree of sensitivity and awareness. This characterization is then read back into the first dialogue, making the younger waiter tell about the old man's act, so that he may be given the line "Nothing" to describe the old man's despair.[12] That Hemingway, nothing if not a craftsman of the first rank, could have made such a major error is simply beyond belief. The passage surely must be read as follows:

> Older waiter: "Last week he tried to commit suicide."
>
> Younger waiter: "Why?"
>
> Older waiter: "He was in despair." [as he of all men would understand]
>
> Younger waiter: "What about?"
>
> Older waiter: "Nothing." [that is, *nada*, Nothingness]
>
> Younger waiter: "How do you know it was nothing?" [that is, nothing tangible or material]
>
> Older waiter: "He has plenty of money." [that is, his despair must have had metaphysical, rather than physical, grounds].
>
> (p. 379)

Ambiguity exists, not as Joseph Gabriel would have it, in that the speeches may be assigned either way,[13] but, in addition to the above, in the possibility of the older waiter's sarcastic response to a man after all incapable of understanding either old man anyway. Perhaps he means also something like "of course, what could any man possibly despair over—he has plenty of money?" This possibility is underscored by his response later to the query, "What did he want to kill himself for?" with the abrupt "How should I know."

The older waiter manifests this kind of double vision repeatedly. He remarks that the old patron "might be better with a wife" (p. 381); yet he clearly knows the transitory nature of such a comfort. He has just informed his colleague that, like the latter, the old man "had a wife once too," implying that she is dead, and later (p. 382) hints in jest that wives may be unfaithful. As they close up the café, the older waiter states that the younger has "everything," meaning "youth, confidence, and a job" (ibid.); yet such attributes are temporary and at best can counteract only the young man's "nothing," not the old man's "nothingness." With some justice does the former accuse the latter of "talking nonsense" after the remark, but without sensing its latent sardonic quality.

The strongest evidence of the older waiter's double awareness is of course the long paragraph of the two parodic prayers (pp. 382-383). *It* is used eleven times with references varying from the café, to the merely grammatical subject of the verb *is*, to the anguish he tries to define, to the world, to nothingness itself. The fragments of the two prayers follow naturally from the catechetical dialogues at the beginning of the story and from the repetitions of *it* and *nothing*. Like the world and man himself, religious form is hollow at the core, filled with "nothing," or, rather, "nothingness," in existential terms, the abyss. Though there is "nothing" to be gained, the older waiter does profit by thus saying his prayers. Such a vision—of lost "everything" and of realized "nothing"—does not send him into Byronic heroics. We read instead that "he smiled and stood before a bar with a shining steam pressure coffee machine" (p. 383). He could smile and remain upright because he knew that the world and himself, even his prayer, were "nothing," and by that act of awareness could survive with dignity, could transcend "it."

This hyper-consciousness, of course, keeps him awake at night. Thus perhaps his definitive act of self-perspective is the observation, "After all, it is probably only insomnia. Many must have it" (ibid.). Calling his condition "insomnia" is an act of humility eliminating the last possibility of error, of assuming himself, by his consciousness, to be more than "nothing." Even as an act of reassurance, a whistling in the dark, it forestalls the dangers of pride by an admission of uncertainty even about the existence of "*nada*." It is an act of merciless self-consistence, thus liberating him from messianic responsibilities, and enabling him to continue to smile at himself and to keep that café open at night. The older waiter, then, can look at the world both ways—as a man of deep religious sensibility he can see the Nothingness of existence, and as a man who "knew it all was nada" he can make jokes and, above all, smile.

Perhaps belatedly, but at least on the evidence of imagery and characterization, we may now discuss the theme of the story. Most readers take the latter to be *nada*, making **"A Clean, Well-Lighted Place,"** despite the title, a story about Nothingness and the pessimism and despair of the human response to it.[14] This view ignores both the definition of *nada* inferable from the story and the nature of the old waiter's response to it.

Despite Hemingway's manipulation of the pronoun *it*, the reader must not confuse Nothingness with the responses it produces, nor the response of the older waiter with that of the old man. *Nada* is depicted primarily spatially, as an objective reality, out there beyond the light; it is a final hard fact of human existence, though "some lived in it and never felt it" (p. 383), e.g., the younger waiter. In addition, it becomes temporal with the older waiter's repetition of "*y pues nada*" before the prayer. Though Carlos Baker, with great sensitivity, calls it "a Something called Nothing which is so huge, terrible, overbearing, inevitable, and omnipresent that, once experienced it can never be forgotten,"[15] which "bulks like a Jungian Shadow,"[16] its mythic qualities are perhaps not even that well defined.

More important, the response of the old patron—the search for oblivion through drunkenness or suicide—is not the only one, and certainly not the one of the older waiter. John Killinger observes that "the only entity truly capable of defying the encroachments of Nothingness is the individual,"[17] and Cleanth Brooks that "the order and the light are supplied by *him*,"[18] the old waiter, the individual. Carrying this affirmation one step further, Wayne Booth notes "a mood of bitterness against darkness combined with a determination to fight the darkness with light—if only the clean, well-lighted place of art itself."[19] But, as we have seen, all the positive imagery, including light, is ironically undercut by the presence of a shadow side, and the "darkness" is counteracted on more levels than that simply of "light."

The older waiter in fact acts in various ways against Nothingness. He expresses solidarity with the old patron, and would willingly keep the café open as long as anyone wants it; he is instrumental in keeping the lights on. But his acquaintance with *nada* is intimate enough to keep him awake all night, every night; yet this hyper-awareness leads him neither toward self-destruction nor toward egocentricity. He can fuse religious sensibility with existential anxiety into a parodic prayer, after which he can smile. Truning off the light in the café and going home to bed is a daily act of courage done silently, without complaint. His sensitivity to places which make dignity possible gives us the verbal clue that his life is one of survival with dignity.

Thematically, then, the older waiter actively demonstrates that life against *nada* is achieved by awareness, sensitivity, human solidarity, ritual (verbal and physical), humor, and courage. Together these qualities make dignity, or, to use Jamesian terms, style or form; we encounter them also in the good bullfighters in *Death in the Afternoon*, [. . .]. Such attributes also lead to a double vision and a mode of expression which may be called irony, a potent antidote to both despair and pride. The older waiter, against the heaviest odds, is a man in control.

"A Clean, Well-Lighted Place" is, without cheating, a totally affirmative story, one of the very few in our literature. It assumes a world without meaning, life on the edge of the abyss, but that is not what it is about.[20] It assumes a protagonist of acute awareness and minor characters of

lesser consciousness, but it is not about that difference. It is, rather, a dramatization of the possibility, given the above conditions, of man continuing to act, to feel even for others, to think even about metaphysics, to create (with a smile), to control and thereby to humanize both himself and his environment. The older waiter is neither a hero nor a saint, but, to borrow from Camus, that more ambitious being, a man.

Notes

1. Cleanth Brooks, *The Hidden God* (New Haven: Yale University Press, 1963), p. 10.

2. *Hemingway: Direct and Oblique* (The Hague: Mouton, 1969), p. 26.

3. Ernest Hemingway, *Short Stories* (New York: Scribner's, 1938), p. 379. All further references to this story will be made parenthetically in the text.

4. That company includes, of course, Jake Barnes, Frederic Henry, Nick Adams; and, by implication, Mr. Frazer of "The Gambler, the Nun and the Radio."

5. *American Literature and Christian Doctrine* (Baton Rouge: Louisiana State University Press, 1958), p. 135.

6. Earl Rovit, *Ernest Hemingway* (New York: Twayne Publishers, 1963), p. 115, makes the surely unwarranted parallel between "the leaves of the trees" which "throw shadows into the café" with "the nothingness" which "can invade and disrupt the imposed order at any time." They seem to me to serve rather to qualify light as an anti-*nada* symbol.

7. I find a link here with *Green Hills of Africa* (New York: Scribner's, 1935), p. 272, "I did not mind killing anything, any animal, if I killed it cleanly," clearly a statement about moral/aesthetic style, in other terms, about dignity.

8. This would seem to parallel Mr. Frazer's hushed radio.

9. William Bache, "Craftsmanship in 'A Clean, Well-Lighted Place,'" *Personalist,* 37 (1956), 64, calls the older waiter "the truest symbol of modern man, . . . caught on the horns of the selfish and cruel materialism of youth and the insomnious nihilism of old age." The story seems to me to dramatize instead three responses to the modern world, none as simple as Bache's description would imply.

10. "The Logic of Confusion in Hemingway's 'A Clean, Well-Lighted Place,'" *College English,* 22 (1961), 541.

11. "Introduction" to Robert F. Weeks, ed., *Hemingway: A Collection of Critical Essays* (Englewood Cliffs: Prentice-Hall, 1962), p. 12.

12. See the debate in *College English*: Frederick P. Kroeger, "The Dialogue in 'A Clean, Well-Lighted Place,'" 20 (1959), 240-241; William E. Colburn,

"Confusion in 'A Clean, Well-Lighted Place,'" 20 (1959), 241-242; Otto Reinert, "Hemingway's Waiter Once More," 20 (1959), 417-418; also Edward Stone, "Hemingway's Waiters Once More," *American Speech,* 37 (1962), 239-240.

13. "The Logic of Confusion," pp. 542-543. I disagree, however, that "the structure of the dialogue symbolically represents the theme of chaos," p. 545; neither dialogue nor theme seems to me to be chaotic.

14. See Ray B. West, *The Short Story in America, 1900-1950* (Chicago: Gateway Editions, 1952), p. 93; Joseph DeFalco, *The Hero in Hemingway's Short Stories* (Pittsburgh: University of Pittsburgh Press, 1963), p. 216; Sheridan Baker, *Ernest Hemingway: An Introduction and Interpretation* (New York: Holt, Rinehart and Winston, 1967), p. 86.

15. *Hemingway: The Writer as Artist* (Princeton: Princeton, University Press, 1963; rpt. 1970), p. 124.

16. Ibid., p. 132.

17. *Hemingway and the Dead Gods: A Study in Existentialism* (Lexington: University of Kentucky Press, 1960), p. 14.

18. *The Hidden God,* p. 10.

19. *The Rhetoric of Fiction* (Chicago: University of Chicago Press, 1961), p. 299. Sean O'Faolain, "A Clean, Well-Lighted Place," in Weeks, ed., *Hemingway,* p. 113, comments likewise that Hemingway's "art is, in fact, a very clean, well-lighted place."

20. In the comment of Robert Penn Warren, "Ernest Hemingway," *Kenyon Review,* 9 (1949), 5, that this story is "the best description of the world in which underlies Hemingway's world of violent action," I would therefore substitute "man" or "response" for "world."

John Leonard (essay date 1974)

SOURCE: "'A Man of the World' and 'A Clean, Well-Lighted Place': Hemingway's Unified View of Old Age," in *The Hemingway Review,* Vol. 13, No. 2, Spring, 1974, pp. 62-73.

[*In the following essay, Leonard considers the common thematic concerns of Hemingway's "A Clean, Well-Lighted Place" and "A Man of the World."*]

Scholars and critics lately have put to good use the companion pieces among Ernest Hemingway's short fiction. Susan Beegel has achieved insights into **"The Undefeated"** and **"A Lack of Passion"** from side-by-side analysis of these two antithetical companion stories. Robert Fleming, in "Dismantling the Code: Hemingway's 'A Man

of the World,'" opens up the riches of that short story when he aligns it with **"The Undefeated"** and **"Fifty Grand"** by interpreting all three narratives as "structured around 'code heroes'"(6). By comparing **"A Man of the World"** with **"The Battler," "The Killers,"** and **"The Short Happy Life of Francis Macomber,"** Fleming sees an initiation story, although he concludes that the protagonist of **"A Man of the World,"** Blindy, is a parody of the "code hero" and, underneath "his stoic insistence on the sacredness of that [heroic] identity," a "hollow man" (9).[1] For Fleming, **"A Man of the World"** is an ironic code story.

Applying the same critical method, I offer a comparison between **"A Man of the World"** and its more famous counterpart, **"A Clean, Well-Lighted Place."** The close reader quickly discovers a large number of elements common to both stories. This is not to say that **"A Man of the World"** replicates the conscious and hidden symbols and actions of its renowned predecessor. There are differences, most notably the memorably foregrounded nihilism in **"A Clean, Well-Lighted Place,"** which as Fleming points out is not found in **"A Man of the World,"** and the use of a first-person narrator (Tom) in the later story.

The reader should bear in mind that the stories were published nearly a quarter century apart: **"A Clean, Well-Lighted Place"** in 1933 and **"A Man of the World"** in 1957, the latter about four years before the author's suicide. But given the two stories' common themes, one must acknowledge the author's uniform and sustained attitude toward age. Hemingway's wisdom concerning age came early, and he seems to have kept that counsel all his life. In *The Garden of Eden,* David Bourne has the same recognition: "He [David Bourne] must remember that. He had only a sorrow that had come from his own tiredness that had brought an understanding of age. Through being too young he had learned how it must be to be too old" (1-2).

Age is a central theme in both short stories, and it is the older characters, the old man and older waiter versus the younger waiter in **"A Clean, Well-Lighted Place,"** and Frank the bartender and Blindy versus the young fellow/ stranger in **"A Man of the World,"** who carry the ideological burden. Tom the narrator stresses the generation gap throughout **"A Man of the World"**: Blindy has been "on lots of roads" (*CSS* 493); Frank the bartender was a witness to Blindy's brawl with Willie Sawyer during the former's "fighting days," making him coeval with Blindy; the outsider who learns about Blindy's history is "the young fellow" during the first half of the story. In **"A Clean Well-Lighted Place,"** opposing viewpoints due to differences in age and experience create dramatic conflict. Julian Smith calls **"A Man of the World"** a "technically perfect story" (10), and also notes that it takes its meaning from "the reactions inspired in others" (Willie Sawyer, Frank, Al Chaney, Tom, and the young fellow) by Blindy (10). Actually all of the older characters seek the young fellow's response in one way or another: Tom by denying that he knows anything about how Blindy lost his sight

(494), Frank by setting the record straight, Blindy by justi-fying his name ("I earned that name" 495). Each older subject has a specific restless need to initiate youth.

Readers of Hemingway know well the brief plot of **"A Clean, Well-Lighted Place."** They may however need re-minding of the abbreviated action in **"A Man of the World,"** narrated by Tom and set in Wyoming. Blindy nightly cadges money from the patrons of saloon slot ma-chines in The Flats, and then travels on foot or hitchhikes to Jessup, where he works that town's two saloons, The Pilot and The Index. On the night the story takes place, Tom asks Blindy why he looks frozen and Blindy explains that he had to walk part of the way to Jessup. Blindy re-fuses a drink from Al Chaney, and when a young fellow hits twice on the machines, Blindy begs a quarter from him each time. After serving the young fellow and Tom a drink, Frank the bartender tells the young stranger how years earlier Blindy lost both eyes in a brawl with Willie Sawyer, whose face Blindy mutilated in the same fight. Blindy overhears the narration and with pride adds a detail or two. He also notes that it was Willie Sawyer who put him out of the car on the way to Jessup, because Blindy placed his hands on Willie's face. After insisting that his name is now Blindy and not Blackie, he accepts from Frank a drink and an offer to sleep overnight in the back of The Pilot. The story is brief, but a detailed reading re-veals that a lot happens in the span of four pages.

The consolation of light is crucial in both stories, most ob-viously in **"A Clean, Well-Lighted Place"** (*CSS* 290). "Well" is an important qualifier: the café is shadowed by leaves so as not to be "very bright" (291). In addition it is "clean and pleasant" (290). The bodega has a "shining steam pressure coffee machine" (291), but unlike the café is "very bright" (291). Its excessive brightness and "unpol-ished" bar repel the older waiter (291). In **"A Man of the World,"** approaching cars pick up Blindy in "their lights" (492) as he stops along the road between The Flats and Jessup, and his fight with Willie Sawyer took place in the lights from the doors of The Pilot and The Index (494). Blindy regrets not being able to "see sometimes" (495), but darkness does not undermine his ebullient persona. He puts a heroic face on his tragic life.

Annette Benert interprets the "Light" of **"A Clean, Well-Lighted Place"** as one of the "barriers . . . against Noth-ingness itself" (183). Steven K. Hoffman sees the light of the same story as a metaphor for "a special kind of vision, the clear-sightedness and absolute lack of illusion to look into the darkness and thereby come to grips with the *nada* which is everywhere" (176). One can argue that Blindy also has this "special kind of vision." He is well aware of the odds against him, of his lowly and disadvantaged posi-tion in a difficult society, of the incessant demands life puts on his wits and will-power, yet he never despairs. To-ward the end of the story Tom describes a brief, passing gesture of Blindy's: "His hand reached out and found the glass and he raised it accurately to the three of us" (495). Blind though he is, Blindy performs his toast "accurately,"

as if he could see and did not live in darkness. The accu-rate toast becomes an implicit metaphor for the daily rou-tines of Blindy's life. He is careful on the roads, drinks moderately, works the slot machines nightly, and is ever alert to the sounds from the machines. He lives as if he actually experiences light with little or no psychic or physi-cal disorientation. His is a very limited life but one that is admirably functional. At times he rejoices with manic glee over his bits and pieces of good fortune.

As a frequently discussed symbol or as a special kind of vision (Hoffman 176), light opens to wide view "the dig-nity of movement" that is the surface of Blindy's daily life and, to a lesser degree, the hidden "seven-eights" below. I should note that many still question the "dignity of move-ment" in the one-eighth above the surface of **"A Man of the World"**—according to Paul Smith, "Carlos Baker dis-missed both these stories [**"A Man of the World"** and **"Get a Seeing-Eyed Dog"**] as trivial and there is always the off chance that he was right" (392).[2] Much of what is subtextual is arguable, conjectural, and enigmatic; as well as ultimately indistinguishable from the voice of Heming-way. But what is there must be formidable enough to sus-tain the resilience of Blindy's surface life.

Another signifier common to both short stories is concern over money, specifically in the context of age. The old man in **"A Clean, Well-Lighted Place"** has "plenty of money" (298), but Blindy must "work" the slot machines of the two towns (492). Both characters evince a middle-class fiscal conservatism, of the same sort George Cheatham, following Scott Donaldson, finds in Jake Bar-nes. Cheatham defines it this way: "Just exchanges [Jake's term in *The Sun Also Rises*] are also equitable exchanges, legal, correct, proper, exact, accurate, uniform exchanges" (29). Note how the old man accounts and pays for his drinks in **"A Clean, Well-Lighted Place"**: "[He] slowly counted the saucers, took a leather coin purse from his pocket and paid for the drinks, leaving half a peseta tip" (290). The exchange is "proper, exact, accurate," even given the old man's inebriated condition.

Blindy may lack the wealth of the old man but he imbues his financial and social affairs with the same spirit of "just exchanges." Blindy has to scramble for quarters, but his transactions are always enacted with the assiduous sense of the honest business deal. Blindy gets his first quarter from the young fellow despite the latter's reluctance to give it to him. On the "pretty good" second jackpot Blindy politely accepts a single quarter; he raises no quarrel about a bigger jackpot entitling him to a bigger cut, and when the young fellow's luck turns, Blindy does not badger him with any undue pleas for money. Nor does Blindy follow the young fellow after he leaves the machines and returns to the bar; Blindy continues to stand by the machines "waiting for someone else to come in and make a play" (493). Blindy will "earn" his quarters. His diligence, his obsessive concern about *justly* earning his quarters, his name, and even his social worthiness, overshadows his physical ugliness, his lack of personal hygiene, and his formerly violent nature. The narrator again and again attests to the assiduity of Blindy's vocation: "it must have taken him quite a time" "to learn the sounds of all the different machines" (492). For a blind man to walk the often frozen road between The Flats and Jessup every night is a considerable feat—"He'd stop by the side of the road when he heard a car coming and their lights would pick him up and either they would stop and give him a ride or they wouldn't and would go on by on the icy road" (492). The narrator uses the word "worked" twice in the first paragraph of the story and in the second "threw his trade" to emphasize the economic propriety of Blindy's cadging in these difficult circumstances. Blindy also uses financial terms to describe the acquisition of his nickname: "[I] earned that name. You seen me earn it" (495).

The old man and Blindy live out their lives with the diminishment or loss of the male sexual drive. In **"A Clean, Well-Lighted Place"** the younger waiter boasts that he has "a wife waiting in bed" (289) and then scornfully avers that "A wife would be no good to him [the old man] now" (289). The compassionate older waiter counters: "You can't tell. He might be better with a wife" (289), a response abundant with meanings: a wife might be an antidote to the loneliness and depression the old man experiences, someone to care for him or someone for whom he could care, someone with whom perhaps to have conjugal relations. The older waiter's sympathy for the old man's conjugal deprivations finds a responsive chord in Hemingway's correspondence. In a letter written in 1954 to Bernard Berenson, Hemingway observed: "But B.B. there is nothing like Africa as there is nothing like youth and nothing like loving who you love or waking each day not knowing what the day will bring, but knowing it will bring something" (*SL* 838).

A reader might lose sight of the lost sexuality theme amid the sensational violence and repellent physical ugliness described in **"A Man of the World."** But despite all that has befallen Blindy since his memorable brawl with Willie Sawyer, and despite his current squalor, only once in the story does he evince sadness or discouragement and that by understatement. In "his high-pitched voice" (494) Blindy tells the young fellow that after blinding him Willie Sawyer "stomped me when I couldn't see" (494). He then discursively adds the judgment: "That was the bad part" (494). Blindy could reconcile himself to being blinded by Willie Sawyer; being castrated by him, however, is horrible and morally reprehensible, a wanton act of humiliation. The "youth . . . and loving" Hemingway described to Berenson is lost forever.

In the aftermath of these irreversible traumas Blindy has shown what Julian Smith calls "lifelong endurance under pressure" (9). His stoical acceptance of his dire fate inspires Smith to add: the "dignified, stigmata-bearing Blindy [is] . . . like Christ, a man of the world, a man of all the world" (12). Between Smith's effusive judgment and Howard L. Hannum's estimate of Blindy as "Hemingway's final, sardonic comment on the boxer-brawler" (342)

lie the upbeat elements, amid preponderant squalor and ugliness, of Blindy's life: his speaking "without any rancor," his narrating "happily" how he touched Willie Sawyer's face earlier that night, and his raising his glass "accurately to the three of us" (495). His élan is the manic antipode to the sad though dignified life of the old man in **"A Clean, Well-Lighted Place"**. Both characters, however, play out their biases as a response to losing the consolatory joys of human sexuality.

Another theme common to both stories is social isolation. The old man is a widower; the younger waiter calls him "lonely" (289), and the older waiter agrees. The older waiter, arguably the story's protagonist but certainly the "mentor," lives much like the old man, apparently also with no wife and with no niece. At the end he is to "go home to his room"; his profoundest "thinking" is shared with no one: he keeps his thoughts "to himself" (291). In **"A Man of the World"** the cars that pass Blindy on the road, Blindy's positioning himself "down at the far end of the machines" (494), his sleeping by himself in the back of The Pilot, and Tom's assertion that it "was always hard for me to look at him" (493) demonstrate the reality of Blindy's loneliness. Considering Blindy's social isolation, **"A Man of the World"** is an ironic title; that Blindy tries to sustain this view of himself is a tribute to his lonely heroism. Isolation envelops other characters as well. Even though Blindy's life is tied to Willie Sawyer's in a perverse and unrelenting way, Blindy states the truth simply: Willie Sawyer is "Probably alone home by himself" (495). The "young fellow" becomes "the stranger" in the second half of the story, following the narrator's denial of having witnessed the brawl between Blindy and Willie Sawyer. That the older characters in the Hemingway canon must suffer in isolation seems to be a constant. David Bourne in *The Garden of Eden* sounds the knell: "That was all he took from the elephant except the beginning of the knowledge of loneliness" (16).

Three other themes cluster about loneliness, adding their dismaying significance to the view of age presented in both stories. Consider physical debility. That the body withers and loses its prowess and beauty is a commonplace but worrisome fact. The drama lies in the eventual allotment of debilities to each person and how he or she responds spiritually. In **"A Clean, Well-Lighted Place"** the old man counts "slowly" and walks "unsteadily" (290). He is deaf, "in despair" (288), and according to the younger waiter, "a nasty thing" (289). The older waiter argues against that judgment, observing, "He [the old man] drinks without spilling" (289), a thrust at the younger waiter having "poured on into the glass so that the brandy slopped over and ran down the stem into the top saucer of the pile" (289). The older waiter too has lost "youth" (290), "confidence" (291), sleep ("only insomnia" 290), and by implication joy. But his sadness yields compassion ("Each night I am reluctant to close up because there may be someone who needs the café" 290).

In **"A Man of the World"** physical debility is shockingly fore-grounded in Willie Sawyer and Blindy. Sawyer's face has a hole big enough so that "the whole inside of his face . . . [could] catch cold" (495). And then there are Blindy's eyeless sockets covered with "small pus icicles" (493), his body which smells "plenty strong" (492), and his "high-pitched" voice (494). He is so physically repellent that it is "hard for [Tom] to look at him" (493). He looks "so awful" (493) that the young stranger "quit playing [the slots] and came over to the bar" (493). In both stories, the younger characters are unsympathetic to the infirmities inherent in age. A "nasty thing" says the younger waiter of the old man, and "Him fight?" asks the young stranger of Blindy (494). Empathy for the aging subjects proceeds from their cohorts, the older waiter in **"A Clean, Well-Lighted Place"** and Frank the bartender in **"A Man of the World."**

Depression bordering on despair dogs the older characters in these stories. The old man is "drunk every night" (289), is quite capable of becoming "too drunk," and has "tried to commit suicide" (288). Depression pervades the story linguistically and dramatically. The old man's drunkeness, despair, loneliness, and attempted suicide dominate the conversation between the waiters and gloom even infects their observations on the "girl and a soldier [who go] by in the street": "The guard will pick him up" (288). The younger waiter becomes a pitiless agent of despair, telling the unhearing old man to his face "You should have killed yourself last week" (289). The older waiter too bears a melancholic burden; lacking "Everything but work" (290), he fully comprehends that "a man was nothing too" (291). Only in the final paragraph does the pall of despair begin to lighten, with "sleep" and "daylight" finally becoming achievable ends.

In **"A Man of the World,"** depression, both from trauma and shame, drives the self-imposed and unchanging social isolation of Willie Sawyer. Depression nags at Blindy's spirit also, though paradoxically acted out. He exhibits a hale and happy resilience even to strangers ("Your night is my night" 493); a laudable prudence governs his bibulousness (he has "to be careful on the roads" 493). It is true that by cadging drinks, in addition to husbanding his meager store of coins, he guarantees that he never has to drink alone. Yet Tom, the narrator, clearly alludes to the dark underside of Blindy's nature. (Blindy placed himself "at the far end of the machines," figuring "no one would come in if they saw him at the door" 494). Even though he tries to get tauntingly "funny" with Willie Sawyer, Blindy states emphatically that they "have never made friends" (495). On two occasions he angrily tells Tom and Frank that "Blindy's the name," "just don't call me Blackie" (495). A sense of unworthiness, bitterness over the castrating injury, sadistic humor, and suppressed anger exact their depressive levy on Blindy's spirit. Only Frank's quick action defuses Blindy's anger and melancholic mood: "Have a drink, Blindy" (495), Frank says, offering alcohol-induced tranquility and safe sleep at the story's end.

In the Hemingway oeuvre, from ***In Our Time*** to *The Garden of Eden,* the essential characteristic of all experience

is threatened or actual violence. The old man in **"A Clean, Well-Lighted Place"** is an unsettling reminder that age is no protection against violence. Violence is the primary raw material of the critical industry surrounding the Hemingway canon. From Malcolm Cowley's, "In no other writer of our time can you find such a profusion of . . . morally wounded people who also devour themselves" (40-41) to Amberys R. Whittle's observation that many "of Hemingway's stories . . . are parables of . . . violent death" (287), the question is one of how the subject deals with violent, often lethal experience. **"A Clean, Well-Lighted Place"** and **"A Man of the World"** are no exceptions.

Consider **"A Clean, Well-Lighted Place."** The old man tries to commit suicide by hanging. The soldier for a night of passion risks arrest by the guard. The young waiter urges the deaf old man to commit suicide. Only accidental good fortune forestalls violence in the first half of the story: the niece prevents the old man from dying, the guard does not arrest the soldier, and the old man cannot hear the younger waiter's brutal taunt. In the second half of the story, only the ameliorating actions of the older waiter and the old man defuse two potentially violent incidents. The old man responds cooperatively to the younger waiter's "Finished"; and the older waiter/mentor backs off his "insult" to the younger waiter by saying he was only trying "to make a joke" (290).

The violence in **"A Man of the World,"** both past and present, is actual. Violence at its most sensational occurs in Frank's narrative and Blindy's coda about the fight between Blindy and Willie Sawyer. Based on those two paragraphs, Howard L. Hannum logically concludes that Blindy's story is "Hemingway's final, sardonic comment on the boxer-brawler," representing "the final stage of such violence" (342). The reader must stretch to find "dignity of movement" in the fight passages, and may incline either to share "Carlos Baker's estimate" (340) or to follow Paul Smith's lead and link up the story with "Mark Twain and the tradition of the tall tale" (393).

Putting aside the sensational "fight" passage, the reader will discover violence in other guises. Willie Sawyer puts Blindy out of his car to "be frozen up so bad" (493). Later Blindy confesses he started the altercation in the car by once again putting his hands on Willie Sawyer's face (495). Although their "fighting days" are long past, the urge to assault or humiliate each other is still present (495). Even if Blindy is just using his hands to "see" and remind himself of his past accomplishments, his action is abusive and malevolent, an assault on Willie's forlorn dignity.

Reprising the subtle, psychological, and diminishing violence in **"A Man of the World"** requires an extended dramatic example involving Blindy, Tom, and Frank. First, one should note that Paul Smith, following Julian Smith, is correct in ascertaining that the "drama [in **'A Man of the World'**] rests in the reaction of the three others [Frank, Tom, the young fellow/stranger] at the bar" (393). Secondly, Julian Smith in his critical study has noted certain parallels with the New Testament:

> Blindy, I am suggesting, is, like Christ, a man of the world. . . . But whereas Blindy has accepted his fate, Tom the narrator would turn away could he. Thrice he denies Blindy, once by claiming not to know his story, once by claiming he has not heard of the fight though he was there, once by calling him by his old name. Tom is a doubting Thomas unwilling to put his hands, metaphorically, into Blindy's wounds—unlike Blindy who can touch Willie's wounds.
>
> (12)

This religious interpretation does not lack cogency, although it is arguable. However, the dramatic import of Tom's denial is evident. When the outsider asks Tom how Blindy lost "his sight," Tom belligerently replies, "I wouldn't know" (494). Immediately Tom, who up until then had identified the outsider seven times as "the young fellow," calls him "the stranger" and will do so twice more in the remainder of the narrative:

> "I wouldn't know," I told him.
>
> ["In a fight," Frank told him.][3]
>
> "Him fight," the stranger said. He shook his head.
>
> "Yeah," Frank said.
>
> (494)

Tom, obviously unnerved, estranges himself from the young outsider. And he also grows testier with Frank's and Blindy's recapitulation of the brawl, a testiness exacerbated by Frank's deliberately curt retorts, "In a fight" and "Yeah," aimed at jogging Tom's memory and conscience. His testiness is also demonstrated when he angers Blindy by using his old name: "Give Blackie a drink," I [Tom] said to Frank. "Blindy's the name, Tom. I earned that name. You seen me earn it." (495).

Blindy goes on to explain to the stranger what he did to Willie Sawyer's face earlier that night, arousing the disapproval of Frank, who reproves the blind man by calling him Blackie: "'Blackie, you have one on the house,' Frank said." Blindy, of course, takes vehement exception once again to being called by his old name: "That's mighty good of you Frank [to offer me sleeping quarters]. Only just don't call me Blackie. I'm not Blackie any more. Blindy's my name." Frank, unlike Tom, wisely and compassionately corrects himself and adds a fillip: "Have a drink, Blindy" (495). Just as the older waiter in **"A Clean, Well-Lighted Place"** defuses a potentially violent altercation by making "a joke," Frank also becomes the peacemaker who facilitates the swing of the narrative from abhorrent violence to social amity and eventually to the tranquility of isolated but secure and consolatory sleep.

The stories share positive as well as negative themes. There is a merging of voices into a kind of spiritual bond. In **"A Clean, Well-Lighted Place,"** the voices of the older waiter and the old man, who, as Carlos Baker notes, never speak a single word to each other, join to express a common ethos, by implication Hemingway's as well. In **"A Man of the World"** there is a similar bonding between Frank and Blindy. Tom is uneasy about Blindy's loquacious presence, but it's Frank the bartender who should want Blindy gone from The Pilot. Blindy is bad for business: he "had run . . . [the young fellow] out" from the slot machines (493), the patrons threaten to "go next door to The Index," "no one would come in if they saw him at the door" (494). And yet Frank tells the story of the fight, pacifies Blindy by using his correct name, and offers him a drink and a room for the night "in the back of the place" (495). Like the older waiter in **"A Clean, Well-Lighted Place,"** one "of those who like to stay late at the café" (290), Frank signals his spiritual closeness to Blindy with various offers of comfort and security.

Blindy "reached out and found the glass and he raised it accurately" (495) and gratefully for the bartender's respect and compassion for him. As the "accurate" toast shows, Blindy never forgets his manners. Good manners, indeed dignity and self-esteem, found in such an unlikely subject, only reinforce the argument that the need to act with grace is universal and lifelong. In **"A Clean, Well-Lighted Place"** the old man and the older waiter certainly embody this virtue. The old man walks "unsteadily but with dignity" (290), he says "thank you" (289) to the insulting younger waiter who pours him a brandy, and he pays for all his drinks, "leaving half a peseta tip" (290). The older waiter too exercises good manners. Although the younger waiter does "not understand" (290), the older waiter never sinks to rude or provocative behavior, but responds with a well-mannered "Good night" (291). And even though the older waiter "disliked bars and bodegas," his final words in the story, addressed to the barman, naturally are: "No, thank you" (291)—laconic but polite.

Strange to tell, a politeness born of earned self-esteem is also Blindy's strong suit in public. He too says "thank you" each time to the young man who gives him a quarter from his jackpots. He stays "at the far end of the machines" (494) so as not to drive away any new patrons, and he is politely grateful to Frank for allowing him to stay the night ("That's might good of you" 495) and for offering him a drink, accepting with a "Yes, sir" (495) and a formal toast. As for the mentor/code hero of the story and his patience, wisdom, generosity, business savvy, and deference toward Blindy, especially in the matter of Blindy's correct name—all these I have already alluded to as elements of Frank's persona.

And so both short stories converge dramatically on these common themes: age, the consolation of light, a conservative viewpoint toward money, the loss or diminishment of sexuality, aloneness, the deprivation of physical powers and beauty, lurking depression and despair, violence (here eventually attenuated), the lifelong need for dignity and self-esteem, spiritual bonding among men, and the wisdom of age duly earned. In **"A Clean, Well-Lighted Place"** the abundance of naturalistic detail, some of it unpleasant, does not undercut the dignity of movement in the text and most readers come away "unusually stirred," as Sean O'Faolain once put it (112). A "dignity of movement" occurs, perhaps arguably, in **"A Man of the World,"** especially if the reader perceives the overall movement toward amity and tranquility in the narrative and if he or she acknowledges that the tall-tale part of the story, the two paragraphs in which Frank and Blindy respectively recount the brawl, represents action that is prior, off-stage and verbally reprised to suit the occasion.

There is much in age that is a "nasty thing." But the older subjects in both these stories face it with exceptional dignity, some with more (the older waiter and Frank) and some with less (the old man and Blindy). The adversities that confront the latter, perhaps even the greater flaws in their characters (Blindy's sadistically violent nature and the old man's brooding aloofness) diminish their heroism. In the case of **"A Man of the World,"** Blindy's durably happy and fun-loving disposition is a partial counterweight to the increased dross of violence that weighs down his heroism. It's a dicey trade-off that Hemingway made late in his career, making **"A Man of the World"** appear to be a "final, sardonic comment on the boxer-brawler" and clouding over the unexpected similarities between this story and **"A Clean, Well-Lighted Place."** Ironically, the less despairing of these two short stories comes just four years before that fateful 2 July 1961 date. The singular event of that day in American letters prevented Ernest Hemingway from experiencing the aspects of age he had creatively prefigured in these two short stories.

Notes

1. "Hollow man" that Blindy is, Fleming does not take his heroism away from him: "Not all heroes have the good fortune to die at the most heroic moment of their lives as Francis Macomber does. Some are left long years to meditate on the meanings of their actions as Blindy does in 'A Man of the World'" (9).

2. Carlos Baker's memorable putdown reads: "In its place he wrote a short story called 'A Man of the World' about a malodorous old bum named Blackie who had been blinded in a tavern brawl in Jessup, Wyoming. 'I think it is a good story' said Ernest. If he really thought so, his judgment was slipping" (*Life* 538).

3. This line, "'In a fight,' Frank told him," is missing in the Finca Vigía Edition of Hemingway's stories, but present in the November 1957 issue of *The Atlantic Monthly,* where "A Man of the World" first appeared. A missing line of dialogue, albeit tagged, invites comparison with the famous missing line of dialogue in "A Clean, Well-Lighted Place." It also shows an incipient curtness and anger in Frank that he quickly brings under control two lines later when with verbal irony and a parenthetical remark he lets Tom off the hook: "'No. You wouldn't of,' Frank said. 'Of course not. You wasn't here, I suppose.'"

Works Cited

Baker, Carlos. *Ernest Hemingway: A Life Story.* New York: Scribner's, 1969.

Beegel, Susan F. "Ernest Hemingway's 'A Lack of Passion.'" In *Hemingway: Essays of Reassessment.* Ed. Frank Scafella. New York: Oxford U P, 1991. 62-78.

Benert, Annette. "Survival Through Irony: Hemingway's 'A Clean, Well-Lighted Place.'" *Studies in Short Fiction* 11 (1974): 181-89.

Cheatham, George. "'Sign the Wire with Love': The Morality of Surplus in *The Sun Also Rises.*" *The Hemingway Review* 11.2 (Spring 1992): 25-30.

Cowley, Malcolm. "Nightmare and Ritual in Hemingway." *Hemingway: A Collection of Critical Essays.* Ed. Robert P. Weeks. Englewood Cliffs: Prentice-Hall, 1965.

Fleming, Robert. "Dismantling the Code: Hemingway's 'A Man of the World.'" *The Hemingway Review* 11.2 (Spring 1992): 6-9.

Hannum, Howard L. "Hemingway's Tales of 'The Real Dark.'" *Hemingway's Neglected Fiction: New Perspectives.* Ed. Susan F. Beegel. Ann Arbor: UMI Research, 1989.

Hoffman, Steven K. "Nada and the Clean, Well-Lighted Place: The Unity of Hemingway's Short Fiction." In *New Critical Approaches to the Short Stories of Ernest Hemingway.* Ed. Jackson Benson. Durham: Duke U P, 1990. 172-191.

Hemingway, Ernest. *The Complete Short Stories of Ernest Hemingway.* Finca Vigía Edition. New York: Scribner's, 1987.

———. *The Garden of Eden.* 422.1—Folder 29, Hemingway Collection, J.F.K. Library, Boston.

———. *Ernest Hemingway: Selected Letters, 1917-1961.* Ed. Carlos Baker. New York: Scribner's, 1981.

O'Faolain, Sean. "A Clean, Well-Lighted Place." In *Hemingway: A Collection of Critical Essays.* Ed. Robert P. Weeks. Englewood Cliffs: Prentice-Hall, 1965. 76-79.

Scholes, Robert. "Decoding Papa: 'A Very Short Story' As Work and Text." In *New Critical Approaches to the Short Stories of Ernest Hemingway.* Ed. Jackson Benson. Durham: Duke U P, 1990. 33-47.

Smith, Julian. "Eyeless in Wyoming, Blind in Venice: Hemingway's Last Stories." *Connecticut Review* 4 (April 1971): 9-15.

Smith, Paul. *A Reader's Guide to the Short Stories of Ernest Hemingway.* Boston: G. K. Hall, 1989.

Lawrence Broer (essay date 1976)

SOURCE: "The Iceberg in 'A Clean Well-Lighted Place,'" in *Lost Generation Journal,* Vol. IV, No. 2, Spring-Summer, 1976, pp. 14-15, 21.

[*In the following essay, Broer explores the bond between the old waiter and old customer in "A Clean, Well-Lighted Place."*]

"I always try to write on the principle of the iceberg," Ernest Hemingway said about his craft. "There is seven-eights of it under the water for every part that shows." In drawing attention to the often unsuspected depths in his work, Hemingway provides the ground for instruction in one of the major aesthetic principles of modern fiction: the art of indirection. What most modern writers have realized, and what Hemingway achieves so well in **"A Clean, Well-Lighted Place,"** is that it is possible to convey a great many things on paper without stating them at all. The art of implication, of making one sentence say two or more different things with a minimum of description, and the possibilities of conveying depths of emotion and the most intimate and subtle of moods through the interplay of image and symbol are grasped by Hemingway as well as by any writer of our time.

Especially in the case of a story like **"A Clean, Well-Lighted Place"** must the reader be warned against a too easy acceptance of what happens literally in the tale. The tale begins as an infirm old man drinks alone one night in a café that is about to close, proceeds through a rather laconic dispute between two waiters over the propriety of closing the café early, and concludes as the older of the two waiters muses over the difference between a bar and a clean, well lighted café, has a nightcap at a nearby bar, and finally retires to his room for the night.

Obviously, a description of the mere tip of the iceberg scarcely begins to account for the compelling power and poignancy of Hemingway's story. Its art resides rather in the author's ability to create the dramatic illusion of nothingness through resonant images of isolation and aloneness, through ironic juxtapositions, through symbolic characterizations, and through a momentary glimpse into the despairing consciousness of the old waiter.

From the very first line of the story Hemingway causes the reader to dwell on the hopeless void within and around the old man who comes nightly to drink at the café. Not only is it late in his life, but he is now reduced to drinking alone and in the *late night shadows* of an *empty café*. Even the dust on the street outside seems a grim reminder that the old man's life has come to a close, a symbolic hint of the fate nature has in store for him. We furthermore learn that he is deaf—that, literally, his life has become a hermetically sealed compartment, and that the old man's imprisonment of isolation and inevitable suffering has produced in him a despair so terribly frustrating that he contemplates suicide as an answer. The very bleakness of the conversation of the two waiters—unadorned and terse—conspires to emphasize the deadly stale monotony of the final days of his life.

As with the paucity of dialogue, just as with the lack of emotional commentary on the part of the author, the very absence of background information in the story about the past life of the old man augments the readers's sense of the vacuum that has formed around him. We are given the present form of his despair—he has attempted suicide in a hideous fashion and manages to bear life now only by drugging himself on liquor—but we are given little direct information about the source of that despair. When, in fact, the young waiter asks his colleague why the old man attempted suicide, he answers flatly that it was over "nothing." It is an answer, of course, which assumes dramatic symbolic importance later in the story. But for the moment, taken literally, it hardly suffices to explain the forces which have created his predicament—forces which the reader is made to feel unconsciously due to the movement of the submerged portion of the iceberg.

It is through the careful placing together of highly ironic scenes and images that the author comments on those things in the old man's past which, having now been denied him, explain and greatly intensify his sense of void, or "nada," which old age has created. The old man's sense of emptiness and futility is stressed in the obvious contrast between the vitality of youth and the passivity of old age. "You have youth, confidence and a job," the old waiter tells his impatient, youthful co-worker. "You have everything." Hemingway suggests that it is not the passing of youth in and of itself that frustrates and embitters the old waiter, but the passing of the fuller, more active and productive life that youth makes possible. The "everything" includes the ability to make love, the capacity for excessive drinking, and the confidence and energy to work at a worthwhile job.

In dismal contrast to the young waiter who rudely reminds his colleague that he has a wife waiting home in bed for him, the old waiter must return alone each night to an empty room, and the burned out old man who drinks alone in the café has only a niece who pityingly "looks after him." Thus, the isolation and loneliness of both old men becomes considerably more tragic, especially in view of an explicit statement Hemingway makes on this subject in *Death in the Afternoon*.

> All stories, if continued far enough, end in death, and he is not a true story teller who would keep that from you. Especially do all stories of monogamy end in death, and your man who is monogamous while he often lives most happily, dies in the most lonely fashion. There is no lonelier man in death, except the suicide, than that man who has lived many years with a good wife and then outlived her.

That the solace of companionship and sexuality with a good woman has been denied the two old men is further emphasized in the juxtaposition of the solitary figure of the old man drinking alone in the shadows of the café, and the eager young couple hurrying by him in the night to fulfill a romantic adventure. Against the expectancy and intensity of the soldier and the young waiter, the two old men have nothing to look forward to in the night but thoughts of death and nothingness.

The contrast between the insensitivity and unconcern of the young waiter and the understanding and compassion of the older waiter amplifies still further the pathos of isolation in old age. But it also serves to set up the crucial identification—the essential oneness—of both old men in the story, and hence the symbolic statement of theme in the old waiter's embittered recitation of the Lord's Prayer. From the very beginning of the story we see that the old waiter has more than a passing interest in the old man's plight. It is he, for instance, who has knowledge of the suicide attempt, and who identifies the source of the old man's despair as "nada." And it is he who recognizes and appreciates the old man's attempt to preserve some semblance of dignity amidst the despair and personal dissolution of old age. In contrast to the young waiter, he feels he understands the needs of a proud man grown old, and the obtuseness and insolence of the younger waiter provokes a defense of the old man's virtues. "This old man is clean," he instructs his colleague. "He drinks without spilling. Even now, drunk. Look at him." Then, as if to vindicate the older waiter's faith, the old man is particularly careful about counting his saucers, paying the bill and leaving a tip. And when he leaves, we sense that it is with considerable pride that the old waiter observes him "go down the street, a very old man walking unsteadily *but* with dignity." The old waiter knows that an old man, despite the disintegration of his body, may still affirm his worth as a man by keeping himself under control, by facing his ordeal without asking any favors or making any concessions to his age, and thus showing himself superior to circumstances until the final moment of death—until nada's will is done.

For the two old men in the story, the capacity for stoic endurance—the faculty for control and manly bearing—provides at least one positive standard by which an old man might gain honor and dignity in the face of inevitable defeat. In the manner of Hemingway's other embattled and aging heroes, Santiago and Colonel Cantwell, these two old men act in keeping with the author's belief that there is very definitely a correct way to live and a correct way to die, and that the manner of dying may demonstrate man's indomitability beyond his physical destruction. Certainly we do not find the old men in this story asserting their manhood in the conspicuous fashion of Santiago or Cantwell, yet the image of the old man enduring his physical hardship quietly and alone, attempting to make the best of a bad situation, signals a positive connection with these other proud and disdainful figures. Even the old man's decision to meet death head-on—to initiate his own destruction violently and quickly—rather than live on in the perpetual horror of nothingness, dying a slow and humiliating death by degrees—is consistent with the defiant attitudes of the author's most prominent heroes.

Despite the resemblance of the old men in this story to the familiar figure of the Hemingway hero, they differ in one very crucial respect; and in this difference lies the particular pathos of their condition. Whereas Hemingway's other aging heroes are able to combat the forces of nada through immersion in the life of the senses, by seizing the intensity of the moment and an indifference to the consequences of intense and dangerous action, circumstances have rendered these old men passive. It is their frustration and vulnerability that we feel—not their ability to dominate. Their senses hardly serve anymore, and capacity for defiance has become limited to pose and gesture. And whereas Hemingway's other aging heroes achieve a partial triumph over despair—a ray of light in a darkened world—through love and human compassion, these old men are completely cut off from contact with their fellow human beings. Despite their attempt to endure their last days with dignity and courage, we see through the introspective reverie of the old waiter that they have been forced into an impotent despair so obsessive that only death offers any hope for relief.

The final bond of sympathy between the two old men, ironic, since it affords them no solace in their mutual isolation, is established when the older waiter informs his colleague, "We are of two different kinds . . . I am of those who like to stay late at the café. . . . With all those who do not want to go to bed. With all those who need a light for the night." Because of the insight given him through the power of suffering, the old waiter comprehends the horror of "nada" to which the old man has been condemned for the night, i.e., thoughts of dissolution and death and perpetual void that loneliness in the night shall surely produce. Hence, he is able to appreciate the fact that the order and cleanliness and light of the café provides a temporary stay against such despair, and explains, consequently, that "each night I am reluctant to close up because there may be some one who needs the café." The contrast between the bodega and the café climaxes the series of juxtapositions of light and dark, early and late, youth and old age—with the attendant association of life and death—that have accumulated from the opening line of the story.

But it is the old waiter's answer to the barman's question, "What's yours?" that indicates the symbolic merging of identities of the two old men, as well as the full measure of their common fate. "Nada," the old waiter replies, thus establishing that his is the same condition and the same state of mind underlying the old man's suicide attempt mentioned earlier in the story. His is a life without relation to any other human being, without hope for the future, and worse, as we see through the embittered reading of the Lord's Prayer, without the light and order that religion can sometimes bring to life. Beneath the stiff control of the facade, we see that the old waiter has taken to brooding over the futility of life—its essential meaninglessness, injustice, and cruelty. His recognition that he lives in a world totally indifferent to human aspirations, that God as well as man is nothing, and hence, that no relief is due his suffering, causes him to reduce the values and promises embodied in the Lord's Prayer to nothingness. The substitution of "nada" for every important word in the prayer is a symbolic way of saying that each of these phrases means "nothing," that they have failed to make men better, or to order the world, or to bring justice, and, most important, that they are as powerless as the other illusions of youth against the ultimate reality of death and void, from which there is no deliverance. It is noteworthy that we find the old waiter offering up his prayer to nothingness before "a bar with a shining steam pressure coffee machine," no altar, no religious shrine, but a gleaming machine, banal and totally devoid of spirituality, a fitting symbolic mockery of spiritual aspiration. It is no doubt a sardonic smile of acknowledgment with which the old waiter ponders the machine.

It is the old waiter's sense of cosmic alienation that culminates and makes unbearable the feeling of void in old age. And yet it is just this tragic awareness of life's essential meaninglessness which marks his moral superiority to the young waiter in the story. When the older waiter says that "we are of two different kinds," a basic value judgment is implied which makes the unrelieved arrogance of the young waiter even more ironic and unpardonable. The older waiter recognizes that nothing in the young waiter's life has allowed him to glimpse the tragic side of life and the inevitability of death that old age has brought to him and the old man. "Some lived in it and never felt it." the old waiter concludes. He realizes that the enjoyment of the daily material things, family, security, position, and money has dulled the edge of the younger waiter's perceptivity, and thus provided him with the ability temporarily to ignore the ultimate, ever-present realities of nada. In contrast, experience and observation have taught the older waiter that, in Hemingway's words, "our bodies all wear out in some way and we die. . . . that no man can avoid death by honest effort. . . ." The older waiter has acquired the tragic perception which is at the center of the author's nihilistic vision: "That death is the unescapable reality, the one thing man may be sure of; the only security; that it transcends all modern comforts."

Once again, it is the lack of emotional commentary on the part of the author, and the use of ironic contrast, which makes so terrible the prospect of the old waiter going home alone to him room. "He would lie in the bed and finally with daylight, he would go to sleep," the old waiter muses. "It is probably only insomnia." The irony of understatement here calls to mind the famous line at the end of chapter one in *A Farewell to Arms*. "At the start of the winter came the permanent rain and with the rain came the cholera. But it was checked and in the end only seven thousand died of it in the army." In both cases it is the jarring incongruity between the casualness of the utterance and the actual grimness of the situation which creates the tension—the emotional impact—in the reader. In dreary fact, it is not the relatively innocent state of "insomnia" that awaits the old waiter in the dark of his room, but the certain torment of thoughts of death and nothingness, intensified, probably, by the haunting memory of an old man hanging grotesquely from a roof beam.

In explaining his reliance upon the art of indirection to convey meaning in his stories, Hemingway has written that

I have tried to eliminate everything unnecessary to conveying experience to the reader so that after he or she has read something it will become a part of his or her experience and seem actually to have happened.

In **"A Clean, Well-Lighted Place,"** what the author has eliminated are certain devices and patterns which have been the skeletal bones of traditional narrative literature—expository structure, turning points, climax and symmetrical plot. In order to obtain a maximum emotional response from his reader, he has employed instead the connotative devices of image, symbol, and irony of statement and circumstance. This is no doubt disheartening news for those readers whose tastes run more to the literal truths of "Sheena, Queen of the Jungle." Upon encountering the stylistic subtleties of **"A Clean, Well-Lighted Place,"** such a reader is likely to close his book after a few moments because "nothing is happening," or to throw up his hands in despair, or cry out in exasperation, "Why can't these authors say what they mean?" It is hoped that for such a reader the preceding sounding of depths in Hemingway's classic tale of spiritual and social isolation will enable him to perceive that complexity, indirection—in particular, the elements of imagery, symbolism, and irony—may be a necessary integral part of the "saying," and the "meaning," and that these differences in quality often distinguish the story of genuine value from a piece of competent trash, the kind of fiction produced by the pulp magazines to provide mindless entertainment and which leaves no residue, no aftermath of deeply stirred emotion, no moral implications to think over, no particular insights into life, behavior, or human character.

C. Harold Hurley (essay date 1976)

SOURCE: "The Attribution of the Waiters' Second Speech in Hemingway's 'A Clean, Well-Lighted Place,'" in *Studies in Short Fiction,* Vol. XIII, No. 1, Winter, 1976, pp. 81-5.

[*In the following essay, Hurley takes issue with Hagopian's attribution of the some of the dialogue in the story, maintaining that the dialogue should be "consistent with the characters as revealed elsewhere in the story."*]

John V. Hagopian's emendation of the much-disputed dialogue of Hemingway's **"A Clean, Well-Lighted Place"** establishes that it is the older waiter, not the younger waiter, who knows of the old man's suicide attempt.[1] Each of the waiters' statements can now be identified unequivocally, except the controversial second exchange concerning the soldier and the girl. This passage, made more difficult by the omission of all explicit identifying tags, must be attributed correctly if the waiters are to be viewed as separate character types. But despite the lack of identifiers, the text contains several patterns that differentiate the speakers of this crucial exchange and maintain the waiter's distinctiveness, which, according to the older waiter's remark to his colleague, "'We are of two different kinds,'" is what Hemingway intended.

Professor Hagopian's solution to the problem of the dialogue, since adopted by Scribner's,[2] is to move the words, "'You said she cut him down,'" to the preceding line, thus:

> Younger Waiter: "A wife would be no good to him now."
>
> Older Waiter: "You can't tell. He might be better with a wife."
>
> Younger Waiter: "His niece looks after him. You said she cut him down."
>
> Older Waiter: "I know."

This exchange, the only logical guide to the correct attribution of the opening dialogue, indicates that it is the older waiter who knows about the deaf old man's suicide attempt. The first exchange, then, can be attributed as follows:

> Older Waiter: "Last week he tried to commit suicide," one waiter said.
>
> Younger Waiter: "Why?"
>
> Older Waiter: "He was in despair."
>
> Younger Waiter: "What about?"
>
> Older Waiter: "Nothing."
>
> Younger Waiter: "How do you know it was nothing?"
>
> Older Waiter: "He has plenty of money."

Critics, unable to match with confidence the lines of the first and third exchanges with those of the second, are divided over the attribution and interpretation of the second exchange. William Colburn, who early called attention to the confused dialogue, stated what was then the prevailing view: "No doubt most readers will agree that the older waiter should be the one to feel that money and a wife in bed are not enough and that he should be concerned that the soldier with the streetwalker will get into trouble" (p. 242). Several years later, Joseph F. Gabriel reiterated the view: "It is generally assumed that it is the older waiter who expresses fear that the soldier and the girl will be caught . . ." (p. 543). This reading, though correct, is difficult to confirm because of the omission of identifying tags.

Professor Hagopian, ignoring earlier opinion, altered the general view by attributing the opening line of the second exchange, "'The guard will pick him [the soldier] up,'" to the younger waiter, with the gloss, "a bit of Schadenfreude, quite consistent with his remark to the deaf old man 'You should have killed yourself last week'" (p. 144). "The younger waiter," Hagopian adds, "wants everybody to get off the streets, including the old man, so that he can go home to his wife. It is he who is keenly aware of the time, who complains that he never gets into bed before three o'clock, and who is impatient . . ." (ibid.). To the

older waiter Hagopian assigns the line, "'What does it matter if he gets what he's after?'" with the gloss, "consistent with his indifference to the usual social norms, with his nihilism, and with his awareness of the value of youth and confidence . . ." (p. 144). David Lodge and Warren Bennett, the latest contributors to the controversy, accept Hagopian's attribution of the waiters' second exchange; but the text supports only one interpretation—the former.

Joseph Gabriel's contention that "there are two equally good ways of reading the dialogue" (p. 543), though a compromise between the opposing opinions, is contrary to Hemingway's intention of delineating two distinct characters. As the story unfolds, Hemingway distinguishes between the main characters with the following tags: "the younger waiter," "the older waiter," "the waiter who was in a hurry," "the unhurried waiter," and "the waiter with a wife." Unfortunately, these tags do not apply to the passage in question; but Hemingway does provide a consistent set of patterns in differentiating between the waiters, which, when taken with the context, enable us to resolve the controversy over the second exchange.[3]

The attributions of the first and third exchanges, now generally unquestioned, reveal a simple pattern: the younger waiter asks the questions and the older waiter provides terse answers that, as we shall see momentarily, have meanings known only to himself.[4] This pattern is maintained in the disputed speech, attributable as follows:

> Older Waiter: "The guard will pick him up," one waiter said.
>
> Younger Waiter: "What does it matter if he gets what he's after?"
>
> Older Waiter: "He had better get off the street now. The guard will get him. They went by five minutes ago."

In addition to maintaining the question-answer pattern in the first three exchanges, Hemingway employs a second pattern of distinguishing between the waiters that further supports this attribution. The opening line of the first exchange, ascribed to the older waiter, reads:

> "Last week he tried to commit suicide," one waiter said.

The opening line of the disputed exchange reads:

> "The guard will pick him up," one waiter said.

These lines, in close proximity in the text, have much in common. Both are similar structurally; both initiate the exchange and express compassion, first for the old patron, and then for the young soldier; and both have the "one waiter said" tag, used nowhere else in the story. These parallels are purposeful and enable us to match the speakers of the second exchange with those of the first and third. The older waiter, who unquestionably speaks the opening line of the first exchange, should be attributed with the opening line of the disputed exchange.

Hemingway, employing the "one waiter said" tag to refer to the older waiter, utilizes a similar device to designate the younger waiter. Except when explicitly identified, the younger waiter is referred to simply as "the waiter." In the scenes where the men appear together, the designation "the waiter" is used seven times to refer exclusively to the younger waiter, and is used to refer to the older waiter only after he is alone and cannot be mistaken for his colleague.

The context of the controversial scene, together with these distinguishing patterns, indicates that the initial line of the second exchange, "'The guard will pick him up,'" should be attributed to the older waiter, and the line, "'What does it matter if he gets what he's after?'" to the younger waiter; and not the other way around. As Carlos Baker observed (p. 124), the waiters' first exchange dramatizes the unspoken bond between the older waiter and the old man. The older waiter, recognizing the old man as a fellow-sufferer, is reluctant to close, because he, too, needs the light, cleanness, and order that the café provides against the dark. In the next scene, the older waiter extends his compassion for the old patron to embrace the young soldier, since he perceives in them, and himself, a progression in despair that moves from youth through middle age to old age.[5] The despondent old man is what the others may become. The younger waiter, unconcerned with the old man and the soldier, is simply concerned with going home to his wife.

That the older waiter, the old man, and the soldier are all of a kind is further exemplified by the metaphor of light and something clean or polished in the line, "The street light shone on the brass number of his collar." The soldier, on the street past the curfew hour, is disillusioned with the military just as the older waiter and the old patron are disillusioned with the world; and just as they find a momentary stay against nothingness in a clean, well-lighted café and a drink, the soldier finds a momentary respite in relations with a girl.[6]

In this scene, the younger waiter does not recognize the implications of the older waiter's remark, "'The guard will pick him up.'" With a wife waiting in bed for him, the younger waiter queries, "'What does it matter if he gets what he's after?'" Actually, the older waiter, knowing that the soldier might be better off with a girl just as the old man might be better off with a wife is not concerned that the soldier "gets what he's after" but that "the guard will pick him up." The older waiter realizes that sex, even with a streetwalker, is an interpersonal relationship, more desirable by far than nothingness.

Finally, critics who would reverse the attribution of the second exchange misinterpret the younger waiter as well as the older waiter. The younger waiter's interest in money and sex is normal and does not make him a "callous materialist." Nor does he derive pleasure in thinking the soldier may be picked up or in hastening the old patron from the café. He even agrees with the older waiter that buying a bottle and drinking at home is not the same. With "youth,

confidence, and a job," the younger waiter has "everything," and, as yet, is unaware of the despair surrounding his colleague and the old man. Hemingway himself indicates that the younger waiter "did not wish to be unjust. He was only in a hurry."

In summation, the older waiter's remark to his colleague that "'We are of two different kinds'" and the explicit identifying tags express Hemingway's intention of delineating the waiters as distinct character types. As such, the dialogue of the disputed second speech should be read in a way consistent with the characters as revealed elsewhere in the story. The several patterns employed to distinguish between the waiters, taken with the context of the dialogue, suggest that the lines which express concern for the soldier being picked up should be attributed to the older waiter, and the line that deals with the soldier having relations with the girl should be attributed to the younger waiter. And not the other way around.

Notes

1. John V. Hagopian, "Tidying Up Hemingway's Clean Well-Lighted Place," *Studies in Short Fiction,* 1 (1964), 140-146. In addition, see: Robert Penn Warren, "Ernest Hemingway," *Kenyon Review,* 9 (Winter 1947), 1-28; F. P. Kroeger, "The Dialogue in 'A Clean, Well-Lighted Place,'" *College English,* 20 (Feb. 1959), 240-241; William E. Colburn, "Confusion in 'A Clean, Well-Lighted Place,'" *College English,* 20 (Feb. 1959), 241-242; Otto Reinert, "Hemingway's Waiters Once More," *College English,* 20 (May 1959), 417-418; Joseph F. Gabriel, "The Logic of Confusion in Hemingway's 'A Clean, Well-Lighted Place,'" *College English,* 22 (May 1961), 539-546; Edward Stone, "Hemingway's Waiters Yet Once More," *American Speech,* 37 (1962), 239-240; Carlos Baker, *Hemingway: The Writer as Artist,* 3rd ed. (Princeton, New Jersey: Princeton University Press, 1969), p. 124; Sheridan Baker, *Ernest Hemingway: An Introduction and Interpretation* (New York: Holt, Rinehart and Winston, Inc., 1967), p. 87; Warren Bennett, "Character, Irony, and Resolution in 'A Clean, Well-Lighted Place,'" *American Literature,* 42 (1970), 70-79; David Lodge, "Hemingway's Clean, Well-Lighted Puzzling Place," *Essays in Criticism,* 21 (1971), 33-56; and Charles E. May, "Is Hemingway's 'Well-Lighted Place' Really Clean Now?" *Studies in Short Fiction,* 8 (1971), 326-330.

2. Hagopian does not speculate how the words came to be misplaced, only that "all the texts to date have merely perpetuated a typographical error" (p. 146). Charles Scribner, Jr. indicated to me in a letter that the confused dialogue in the original version of the story "was unquestionably the result of an error," but "whether this error was made by the author or a typist, or a typesetter we cannot tell because we do not have the original manuscript." Mr. Scribner adds that "in editing other works of Hemingway's (e.g. *Islands in the Stream*) I have noted more than one

place where he 'skipped a beat' in a long passage of dialogue in which the speakers are not identified. Accordingly, I feel all the more confident in having changed the text [of 'A Clean, Well-Lighted Place'] as we have." I wish to express my appreciation to Mr. Scribner for his assistance.

3. Warren Bennett established that the older waiter knew of the old man's suicide attempt through Hemingway's use of several other patterns: the "serious question, verbal irony by the older waiter, a dropping of the subject, and then a serious reply" pattern (p. 72), and the younger waiter's use of the word *kill* (p. 71).

4. Professor Hagopian's contentions that "all the questions demanding answers are uttered by the young waiter" and that "the older waiter never seeks information from the younger, all his questions being purely rhetorical" (p. 144) need to be refined. The older waiter's response to the younger waiter's "'What did he want to kill himself for?'" is "'How should I know,'" "which is not a question at all (the text has no question mark), but a statement; and the older waiter's "'Why didn't you let him stay and drink?'" "is not a rhetorical question, nor is it so construed by the younger waiter who answers, "'I want to go home to bed.'" Hagopian, however, was aware that the pattern of the waiters' dialogue provides a clue to the attribution of their speeches.

5. William B. Bache, "Craftsmanship in 'A Clean, Well-Lighted Place,'" *The Personalist,* 37 (Winter 1956), p. 64.

6. For this interpretation of the second scene, I am indebted to Warren Bennett, p. 77.

Hans-Joachim Kann (essay date 1977)

SOURCE: "Perpetual Confusion in 'A Clean, Well-Lighted Place': The Manuscript Evidence," in *Fitzgerald/ Hemingway Annual,* 1977, pp. 115-18.

[*In the following essay, Kann examines Hemingway's original manuscript and concludes that it was the author who inserted an uncharacteristic line of dialogue for the older waiter.*]

Ever since the appearance of the first articles by F. P. Kroeger and William E. Colburn in 1959,[1] it has been clear that, apart from the apparent ambiguity in the first dialogue, the third dialogue section of **"A Clean, Well-Lighted Place"** is obscure (or even messy) at the end. Numerous attempts have been made[2] to explain the contradiction and to restore order in the two waiters' dialogue. Otto Reinert wanted to have two indented and quotation-marked lines read as one line of dialogue; Joseph F. Gabriel saw the confusion as an intended literary device; John V. Hagopian pleaded for splitting the line, "I know. You said she cut him down," and redistributing the two sentences (the

1965 Scribners edition of the stories followed this advice). in 1973, Scott MacDonald[3] argued in favor of reverting to the original text; in between, Warren Bennet[4] suggested as a solution the assumption that a slug of type was misplaced[5] and Nathaniel M. Ewell[6] saw two slugs of type lost.

The tearsheets from the first publication in *Scribner's Magazine*[7] do not offer any assistance—the proofreading marks do not affect the lines in question.

More can be learned from the manuscript[8] (an interpretative investigation of what, how, and why Hemingway altered or deleted—for instance, the last twenty-nine words of the original draft—is a rewarding undertaking, but it would go beyond the limited scope of this note).

Hemingway began with an undifferentiated "boys," changed his mind on page 2, between line 2 and line 15, crossed out "boys"/"boys," and put in "waiter"/"waiters" instead.

He must have felt the need of a differentiation beyond "one waiter"/"the other waiter"; thus, on page 2, "One of the waiters" is changed to "The younger waiter," although this must have happened when Hemingway had already been writing for some time because the correction is written with a thicker, worked-down pencil. Hemingway obviously saw the danger of ambiguity in other parts, too, as is demonstrated by the alterations "the waiters came over"/ "the waiter who was in a hurry came over" (p. 4), "the waiter"/"the unhurried waiter" (p. 5), "the waiter"/"the waiter who was in a hurry" (p. 6).

The separation of "with his colleague again" and "He's drunk now,' he said" (p. 3) through paragraphing and indentation made the identification of the "he" somewhat difficult—Hemingway connected the two lines with a run-in indication. Unfortunately the printed version disregarded his proof-reading mark.

Another printing mistake was the deletion[9] of the period after "Anyway" in "Anyway I should say he was eighty." Here, the manuscript supports Edward Stone's[10] theory that "Anyway" is supposed to be a literal translation from the Spanish dialogue and that it functions as an affirmative.

In two places, Hemingway was confused himself. In the first instance when he had already written the younger waiter's utterance ". . . three o'clock." / "He should have killed himself . . ." as two separate lines, he corrected himself by a simple run-in mark (p. 3). In the second instance he saw that the alternating line count attributed "His niece looks after him." to the younger waiter positionally, just as the next line, "I wouldn't want to be that old. An old man is a nasty thing." (p. 4) was the younger waiter's line. To restore the alternating count Hemingway inserted a line,[11] however with the wrong semantics: the older waiter might say "I know." but not "I know. You said she cut him down." Hemingway must not have recognized the mistake either at the time of writing or later—otherwise he would not have written in 1956 that the dialog "made perfect sense to him."[12]

Thus, although the passage does not make sense, it is still Hemingway's original—the teacher, however, may, for his students' sake, point out that, since the whole line is "filling material," the second sentence might be quietly disregarded.

Notes

1. Both in *College English,* XX (February 1959), 240-2.

2. For a discussion of Kroeger, Colburn, Reinert, Stone, Gabriel, Hagopian, and Hagopian/Dolch see Hans-Joachim Kann, *Ubersetzungsprobleme in den deutschen Übersetzungen von drei anglo-amerikanischen Kurzgeschichten: Aldous Huxley's "Green Tunnels", Ernest Hemingway's "The Killers" und "A Clean, Well-Lighted Place"* (München, 1968), Mainzer Amerikanistische Beitrage, X, pp. 59-61. Most of these articles are reprinted in Morris Friedman and David B. Davis, eds. *Controversy in Literature: Fiction, Drama and Poetry with Related Criticism* (New York: Scribners, 1968), pp. 121-141. More recent items are listed in Nathaniel M. Ewell, "Dialogue in Hemingway's 'A Clean, Well-Lighted Place,'" *Fitzgerald/Hemingway Annual 1971,* 306, n. 1, and in Audre Hanneman, *Supplement to Ernest Hemingway: A Comprehensive Bibliography* (Princeton: Princeton University Press, 1975), pp. 9-10.

3. "The Confusing Dialogue in Hemingway's 'A Clean, Well-Lighted Place': A Final Word?" *Studies in Short Fiction,* 1 (Spring 1973), 93-101.

4. "Character, Irony, and Resolution in 'A Clean, Well-Lighted Place,'" *American Literature,* 42 (March 1970), 70-79.

5. *Ibid.,* 70.

6. *Ibid.,* 305.

7. # 222, Hemingway Collection, John F. Kennedy Library, Waltham, Massachusetts.

8. #337, Hemingway Collection. The author is indebted to Mrs. Ernest Hemingway for her permission to quote from the MS.

9. Except for one instance of a stylistic change, the printed version differs from the manuscript only in unimportant details of spelling, punctuation and grammar (definite article deleted twice), besides the two important changes mentioned above.

10. "Hemingway's Waiters Yet Once More," *American Speech,* 37 (October 1962), 240. For Hemingway's repeated attempts to have the speech in this story sound like a literal translation from Spanish, see Kann, pp. 62-64.

11. The line is squeezed in and even slightly indented to fit.

12. George Monteiro, "Hemingway on Dialogue in 'A Clean, Well-Lighted Place,'" *Fitzgerald/Hemingway Annual 1974,* p. 243.

Warren Bennett (essay date 1979)

SOURCE: "The Manuscript and the Dialogue of 'A Clean, Well-Lighted Place,'" in *American Literature: A Journal of Literary History, Criticism, and Bibliography,* Vol. 50, No. 4, January, 1979, pp. 613-24.

[*In the following essay, Bennett reiterates the importance of Hemingway's original manuscript of "A Clean, Well-Lighted Place" and asserts that it shows "evidence of two mistakes, one by a typist or typesetter, and one by Hemingway himself; and it clarifies Hemingway's intention as to which waiter knows about the old man's suicide attempt."*]

The known manuscripts of Ernest Hemingway are in the possession of Mrs. Mary Hemingway, who on several occasions since 1972 has deposited short story material at the John F. Kennedy Library. This has been inventoried and arranged for examination, and was opened to research in 1975. In this material is a previously undiscovered pencil manuscript of Hemingway's much debated short story, **"A Clean, Well-Lighted Place."**[1] This discovery seems to resolve many of the questions about the original dialogue sequence and how the confusion in the story came about.

"A Clean, Well-Lighted Place" was first published in *Scribner's Magazine* in 1933. It has been the subject of a critical debate concerning the inconsistent dialogue between the two waiters since F. P. Kroeger and William E. Colburn first drew attention to the confusion in their articles published in 1959. Colburn argued that

> The major difficulty in analyzing the dialogue arises because there are in the story several separate conversations between the waiters, and in only a few places is the speaker identified by the author. One line, however, we can assign to the younger waiter, because of information which is brought out later: "'He's lonely. I'm not lonely. I have a wife waiting in bed for me.'" Using this line as a reference point, we can trace backwards in the story the alternate lines and discover that it is the younger waiter who is asking about the old man's attempt at suicide and it is the older waiter who knows the details as to the method and who prevented him. Counting forward in the story from our reference line, however, we find the older waiter saying, "'I know. You said she cut him down.'" Obviously there is an inconsistency here. It is the older waiter who knows about the suicide attempt and is enlightening the younger.[2]

Otto Reinert, in an article the same year, disagreed with Colburn's assigning of the dialogue and took the position that it was the "young waiter," a "callous materialist," who knew about the attempted suicide of the old man.[3] He preferred to

> preserve the unity and plausibility of the two waiter's characters and the consistency of their function in the moral drama, than to find 'an insoluble problem in the dialogue' (Kroeger) or an irreconcilable conflict between artistic intent and execution (Colburn). We can do so if we assume that Hemingway did not observe the typographical convention [that a new, indented line implies a new speaker.]

He suggested that in two different places in the story "Hemingway may have violated the convention in order to suggest a reflective pause between two sentences in a single speaker's uninterrupted utterance."

> I submit that it is the young waiter who speaks *both* "he's drunk now" (because the pronoun reference demands it) *and* the next speech, "He's drunk every night." And that it is the old waiter who speaks *both* "He must be eighty years old" *and* "Anyway I should say he was eighty."

Joseph F. Gabriel then entered the debate with what he called an intention to "redeem the story . . . ,"

> What specifically I contend is that there was no error made in the dialogue, either by Scribner's or Hemingway himself; that we have here one of the most artfully contrived pieces in the Hemingway canon; and that, in short, the inconsistency in the dialogue is deliberate, an integral part of the pattern of meaning actualized in the story.
>
> The experience of the reader duplicates their [the older waiter's and the old man's] experience, for the reader, too, is called upon to bear uncertainty, inconsistency, confusion, and ambiguity, as he attempts to fashion some pattern of meaning out of the chaos of the dialogue. Thus, the confusion in **"A Clean, Well-Lighted Place"** is neither a mistake nor an accident. It is deliberate.[4]

John V. Hagopian, however, found it "unfortunate that the discussion . . . remains where Joseph F. Gabriel left it," because "if there is anything that is 'artfully contrived,' it is Gabriel's interpretation." Hagopian suggested that, "it is far kinder to Hemingway to label a single line of dialogue as the obvious typographical error than it is to torture his prose into ambiguous chaos." Arguing on the basis of a series of glosses, Hagopian determined that the "obvious typographical error" was in the line of dialogue previously pointed out by Colburn, "I know. You said she cut him down." He assigned the place of this dialogue to the older waiter but also concluded that "the line 'you said she cut him down' clearly belongs to the speech of the younger waiter; it has all the overtones of his sadistic irony. All the texts to date have merely perpetuated a typographical error." Hagopian suggested that "in future editions of this story, Scribner's simply move the line to its proper place and avoid any further fuss."[5]

In 1965, a year after the appearance of Hagopian's article, Scribner's issued a new edition of *The Short Stories of Ernest Hemingway,* and in **"A Clean, Well-Lighted Place"** made an editorial correction in the dialogue.

> All texts from 1933 to 1965:
>
> "His niece looks after him."
>
> "I know. You said she cut him down."[6]
>
> The 1965 text and all subsequent printings:
>
> "His niece looks after him. You said she cut him down."
>
> "I know."[7]

This correction, however, only compounded the existing debate.[8] Because it changed the story in a major way, critics began to argue not only the assigning of the dialogue and the consequent interpretation but also the ethics and efficacy of the Scribner's editorial change.[9]

The recent discovery of the pencil manuscript is therefore of significant importance. It reveals how the illogical dialogue sequence may have occurred; it shows evidence of two mistakes, one by a typist or typesetter, and one by Hemingway himself; and it clarifies Hemingway's intention as to which waiter knows about the old man's suicide attempt.

The story was, by all appearances, written at one sitting, with surprisingly little revision after an initial "false start." The insertions and revisions, judging from the thickness and texture of the pencil lead, were evidently made at three different stages: almost immediately after the first phrasing; relatively late or as the story neared completion; and much later, perhaps another day, with a sharp pencil.

The first line of the false start reads, "In Zaragossa the," but this incomplete sentence is crossed out (p. 1). The second and third sentences are about "an old man," and although X'ed out they are essentially the same description of the street, tree, light, and dust as in the true draft. A title was written below the false start and erased; the only legible word remaining is the last word: "Nothing." "A Clean, well lighted place," is written over the erasure (p. 1).

Initially there were no "waiters" as such. There were "two boys," reminiscent of the two-boy situations in the Nick Adams stories, although the term "boy" may also be an attempt to render Spanish idiom. The manuscript, without revisions, reads,

> The two boys inside the café knew that the old man was a little drunk and that if he . . . became too drunk he would leave without paying so they kept watch on him.
>
> "Last week he tried to commit suicide," one boy said.[10]

It is not until after the scene with the soldier and the prostitute that the word "waiter" appears: "'The guard will pick him up,' one waiter said" (p. 2). There is no descriptive distinction between the two waiters, such as age, until page six where the manuscript reads, "'You have youth, confidence and a job,' the older waiter said. 'You have everything.'" Then Hemingway evidently went back to page two of the manuscript and inserted a reinforcing reference to the "younger" waiter, because the thickness and texture of the pencil point at the time of this revision is about the same as in the writing on page 6. (Insertions by Hemingway are indicated here by pointed brackets.)

> The old man sitting in the shadow rapped on his saucer with his glass. ~~One of the~~ <The younger> waiters went over to him.[11]

The descriptions of the waiters as the waiter "in a hurry" (pp. 4 and 6) and the "unhurried" waiter (p. 5) are also insertions but may have been made almost immediately after the first phrasing. The line which describes the younger waiter as "speaking with that omission of syntax stupid people employ when talking to drunken people or foreigners," is also an insertion, written over the length of the righthand margin of page five. It was probably made much later, after the story was completed, because the pencil used is again a sharp pencil, and the writing is smaller and tighter. The same sharp pencil (again with small, tight writing) was used to add three lines to the story—all three of which were then lined out:

> . . . not know. It would be easier if one knew.
>
> One feels certain things but one
>
> knows nothing. Certainly there is no one who
>
> knows another.
>
> (p. 12)

What all of these particular insertions and revisions suggest is that at the beginning of the story Hemingway had not preconceived any significant distinction between the two main characters—with the exception, perhaps, that he intended one of them to have a "wife," for the reference to the younger waiter's wife is not an insertion but appears in the first phrasing on page four. Perhaps Hemingway discovered their significant difference as they began to speak in the dramatic context of the situation with the drunk old man who had attempted suicide. He then enhanced the difference by developing the difference in ages, the difference between being "hurried" or "unhurried," and finally the statement, "'We are of two different kinds,' the older waiter said" (p. 7).

If the characters did develop as they spoke and as the story itself developed, that might explain the origins of the obscurities which have produced so much debate. These involve three problematic sections in the story. One relates to the question of which waiter says of the old man, "'He's drunk now,'" and whether or not the same waiter speaks the following line, "'He's drunk every night.'" The second problem arises in that crucial sentence which was editorially reassigned by Scribner's. The third appears in the conversation between the two waiters concerning the soldier and the prostitute.

In the first problematic section, the manuscript reads,

> "You should have killed yourself last week," he said to the deaf man. ~~who~~ The old man motioned with his finger, "A little more," he said. The waiter poured <on into> the glass so that the brandy slopped over and ran down the stem into the top saucer of the pile. "Thank you," the old man said. The waiter took the bottle back into the café. He sat down at the table with ~~the other waiter~~ <his colleague> again <"He's drunk now," he said.>
>
> "He's ~~stewed~~ <drunk> every night."
>
> "What did he want to kill himself for?"
>
> ~~Christ~~ "How should I know?"
>
> (p. 3)

It has been argued in the debate over which waiter should know about the old man's suicide attempt that the younger waiter speaks both the line "'He's drunk now,' he said," and the line "'He's drunk every night.'" But a run-on line drawn in the pencil manuscript indicates that the dialogue, "'He's drunk now,' he said," should be the last line of the preceding paragraph, which negates the "reflective pause" argument. That the published story did not properly place the line suggests a mistake by either a typist or a typesetter. In any case, however, the pencil manuscript registers Hemingway's original intention about the speakers of the two lines of dialogue. The younger waiter says, "He's drunk now," and the older waiter says, "He's [stewed] drunk every night" (p. 3).

This is supported by Hemingway's diction, his changing the word "stewed" to "drunk." The younger waiter would hardly say, "He's drunk," in one line, and then "He's stewed," in the next. The obvious intent was for the older waiter to say, "He's [stewed] drunk every night," and the younger waiter to ask the following question, "'What did he want to kill himself for?'" (p. 3). This establishes the fact that it was the older waiter who knew about the old man's attempted suicide.

The second problematic section concerns those two lines changed by Scribner's. In attempting to sort out Hemingway's intention with this dialogue, the spacing of the manuscript becomes important. The story was written on unlined paper, and the spacing of the writing is relatively consistent throughout the manuscript, increasing from about ten millimeters on the early pages to about twenty millimeters on the later pages. The only time there is less than ten millimeters between the lines is when Hemingway has made an insertion or a revision. Regarding the lines in question there are only five millimeters between the line "His niece looks after him" and the following line "I know." This indicates that an insertion was made. And the text suggests that the insertion was made because Hemingway evidently noticed that he had "missed a beat"—

there was an inconsistency in the dialogue. If the first writing were reconstructed the manuscript would read,

> YW: "He's lonely. I'm not lonely. I have a wife waiting in bed for me."
>
> OW: "He had a wife once too."
>
> YW: "A wife would be no good to him now."
>
> OW: "You cant tell. He might be better with a wife."
>
> YW: "His niece looks after him." ~~They treat~~
>
> YW: "I wouldnt want to be that old. An old man is a nasty thing."

Hemingway must have noticed the inconsistency of the above dialogue and so inserted another line of dialogue.

> YW: "His niece looks after him." ~~They treat~~
>
> OW: "I know."
>
> YW: "I wouldnt want to be that old. An old man is a nasty thing."[12]

The other published sentence, "You said she cut him down" (the line moved by Scribner's in their correction) seems to have been added in the pencil manuscript *after* the first revision. It is written in a noticeably thicker and darker pencil and it begins at a level slightly higher than the "I know":

> "His niece looks after him." ~~They treat~~
>
> "I know. <You said she cut him down.">
>
> "I wouldnt want to be that old. An old man is a nasty thing."

(p. 4)

The manuscript indicates that during the first writing Hemingway followed the statement "His niece looks after him" with what might have been, "They treat [him well enough]." The intention of the line may have been to reflect ironically the younger waiter's "stupidity" in not knowing what a wife could give the old man that the niece could not. The reason Hemingway did not finish the statement was probably that the subject of the old man's treatment was information beyond the characterization of the younger waiter. But sometime later, after he had inserted "I know" to correct the dialogue sequence, Hemingway evidently still felt dissatisfied with this exchange. So he added a second revision, "You said she cut him down." Perhaps he intended the statement to replace "They treat [him well enough]," but more probably he forgot the context and simply felt that the weak line "I know" needed support. In this case, one may conjecture that the first confusion in the dialogue sequence must have still lingered in Hemingway's mind. When he read "His niece looks after him," he probably thought it was the older waiter speaking, since earlier in the story it was the older waiter—not the younger waiter—who knew about the niece: "His niece [cut him down]." It was an unfortunate *lapsus memoriae* on the part of Hemingway, and "bad luck" for the story,

because Hemingway now introduced a new inconsistency into the sequence he had previously corrected.[13] But however the mistake occurred, the manuscript evidence still clearly establishes that it is the older waiter who knows about the old man's suicide attempt. And on the basis of the manuscript, the Scribner's emendation makes sense of a nonsensical passage while properly giving information about the old man to the older waiter.

Hemingway, however, as a matter of artistic form, had been omitting dialogue identification to a dangerous extreme anyway. An example of that appears in the problematic section of the story concerned with the soldier and the prostitute. The story as published reads,

> A girl and a soldier went by in the street.
>
> The street light shone on the brass number on his collar.
>
> The girl wore no head covering and hurried beside him.
>
> "The guard will pick him up," one waiter said.
>
> "What does it matter if he gets what he's after?"
>
> "He had better get off the street now. The guard will get him. They went by five minutes ago."[14]

The question has always been, which waiter is emphasizing the guards and which waiter is interested primarily in the soldier getting "What he's after?" Assigning this dialogue to speakers seems to be made easier by the pencil manuscript, which reads,

> . . . A girl and a soldier went by in the street. The ~~light~~ <street light> shone on the brass number on his collar. The girl wore no head covering [following three words are part of the preceding line] and hurried beside him.
>
> "The guard will pick him up," one waiter said.
>
> "What does it matter if he gets ~~his tail~~?" <what he's after?">
>
> "He <had> better get off the street. <now.> The guard will get him. They went by five minutes ago."

(p. 2)

The line, "The girl wore no head covering and hurried beside him" is an insertion, but of greater importance is the change of diction from "his tail," to "what he's after." There are two similar changes in the story, and in each case the changed dialogue belongs to the older waiter. Both changes occur in that scene where the younger waiter returns from serving the old man brandy.

> "He's drunk now," he said.
>
> "He's ~~stewed~~ <drunk> every night."
>
> "What did he want to kill himself for?"
>
> "Christ "How should I know?"

(p. 3)

There, as in the scene with the soldier and the prostitute, the original language suggested a tough "realism" associated with the older waiter. Its ultimate extension will be the older waiter's parody of the Lord's Prayer, "our nada who are in nada" (p. 10) and his "Hail Mary" parody, "Hail nothing full of nothing, nothing is with thee."[15] Thus from the evidence of changed diction in the manuscript, it seems certain that it is the older waiter who says, "What does it matter if he gets what he's after?"

But regardless of the correct assigning of the dialogue, my feeling is that in Hemingway's mind both waiters knew more about the deaf old man than just that he was a "good client" (p. 1). When one waiter says the old man's niece cut him down, referring to a single person, the other waiter replies in the plural, "Why did *they* do it?" (p. 3, italics mine). And in the manuscript the next line reads, "~~They~~ Fear for his soul" (p. 3). *Both* seem to know that the niece was not alone in saving the old man's life. And, although it is the older waiter who says that the old man's "niece" "cut him down," it is the younger waiter who remarks that the niece also "looks after him" (p. 4). Again, both know something about the old man. If such mutual knowledge was envisioned in Hemingway's imagination, it may have caused Hemingway himself to become confused, first, as to the early characterization of the waiters; second, as to just how much each waiter knew about the old man; and third, as to which waiter was speaking at certain times.

This argument, of course, presents not the stereotyped image of Hemingway the ideal craftsman, weighing each word and revising each sentence to perfection. It sees Hemingway the writer as a fallible human being—and perhaps also as a writer in a hurry, eager to record his vision and lock it up. The manuscript certainly bears out the impression that the story was written and brought to completion in one rapid session. The first two and one-half pages were written with a sharp pencil, the handwriting relatively small, the lines sloping only slightly downward across the page. Gradually the handwriting enlarges, the words and lines become more spaced out. By pages ten and eleven, which involve the nada prayer and the bodega barman, the pencil has become blunted and the lettering heavy; the handwriting is significantly larger, the words well spaced out, the lines slanting dramatically downward across the page; and there are only about half as many lines per page as on the beginning pages. This pictures not Hemingway the slow perfectionist, hovering over each word and detail, but an artist "fired up," and writing at considerable speed in producing what must be regarded, in spite of the flaw in the dialogue, as classic Hemingway: expressing much by showing little.

Notes

1. Ernest Hemingway. "A Clean Well-Lighted Place" 337. Manuscript. Titled pencil manuscript w/one false start. pp. 1-12. See also #222. Hemingway Collection. John F. Kennedy Library, Waltham, Massachusetts. Unless footnoted for explanatory purposes, all subsequent references will be by page number in parentheses after the quotation.

I want to thank Mrs. Mary Hemingway for the permissions she has granted me to work with this manuscript, and to publish page four of it. Also, I want to thank Jo August, Curator of the Hemingway Collection, and E. William Johnson, Senior Archivist, for their helpfulness in my research.

2. William E. Colburn, "Confusion in 'A Clean, Well-Lighted Place,'" *College English,* XX (Feb., 1959), 241-242; see also, F. P. Kroeger, "The Dialogue in 'A Clean, Well-Lighted Place,'" *College English,* XX (Feb. 1959), 240-241.

3. Otto Reinert, "Hemingway's Waiters Once More," *College English,* XX (May, 1959), 417-418.

4. Joseph F. Gabriel, "The Logic of Confusion in Hemingway's 'A Clean, Well-Lighted Place,'" *College English,* XXII (May, 1961), 540, 545.

5. John V. Hagopian, "Tidying Up Hemingway's 'A Clean, Well-Lighted Place,'" *Studies in Short Fiction,* I (Winter, 1964), 140, 142, 143-144, 146.

6. Ernest Hemingway, "A Clean, Well-Lighted Place," *Scribner's Magazine,* XCIII (March, 1933), 149.

7. Ernest Hemingway, "A Clean, Well-Lighted Place," in *The Short Stories of Ernest Hemingway* (New York, 1965), p. 381. Hereafter cited as *Short Stories.*

8. See, for example, Warren Bennett, "Character, Irony, and Resolution in 'A Clean, Well-Lighted Place,'" *American Literature,* XLII (March, 1970), 70-79. Reprinted in *The Short Stories of Ernest Hemingway: Critical Essays,* ed. Jackson J. Benson (Durham, N.C., 1975), 261-269. In this interpretive article, I establish first that it is the older waiter who knows about the old man's attempted suicide by analysing Hemingway's pattern of verbal irony on the part of the older waiter; also, it is the younger waiter who uses the phrase "kill himself."

9. In addition to the critics to which I have already referred, the following is a checklist of other pertinent criticism related to the problem of the dialogue. Robert Penn Warren, "Ernest Hemingway," *Kenyon Review,* IX (Winter, 1947), 1-28; Edward Stone, "Hemingway's Waiters Yet Once More," *American Speech,* XXXVII (Oct., 1962), 239-240; Carlos Baker, *Hemingway: The Writer as Artist,* 3rd ed. (Princeton, N.J., 1969), p. 124; Sheridan Baker, *Ernest Hemingway: An Introduction and Interpretation* (New York, 1967), p. 87; Nathaniel M. Ewell, III, "Dialogue in Hemingway's 'A Clean, Well-Lighted Place,'" *Fitzgerald/Hemingway Annual 1971,* 305-306; David Lodge, "Hemingway's Clean, Well-Lighted Puzzling Place," *Essays in Criticism,* XXI (Jan., 1971), 33-56; Charles E. May, "Is Hemingway's 'Well-Lighted Place' Really Clean Now?" *Studies in Short Fiction,* VIII (Spring, 1971), 326-330; Scott MacDonald, "The Confusing Dialogue in Hemingway's 'A Clean, Well-Lighted

Place': A Final Word?" *Studies in American Fiction,* I (Spring, 1973), 93-101; George Monteiro, "Hemingway on Dialogue in 'A Clean, Well-Lighted Place,'" *Fitzgerald/Hemingway Annual 1974,* p. 243; and C. Harold Hurley, "The Attribution of the Waiters' Second Speech in Hemingway's 'A Clean, Well-Lighted Place,'" *Studies in Short Fiction,* XIII (Winter, 1976), 81-85.

10. In all the quotations from the manuscript I have tried to be as faithful to the original as it is possible to be with print. In this particular quote, the "g" in the second line ("he g became") is probably the beginning of the word "got" which Hemingway changed to "became."

11. In this quote I have again tried to accurately render the manuscript. The word "waiter" in the second line was originally plural, "waiters." When Hemingway crossed out "One of the" and inserted "The younger," he X'ed out the "s."

12. In this mock up, I have placed a quotation mark after the word "know." In the manuscript, it appears to me that Hemingway had so closed the quotation. But when he inserted the sentence, "You said she cut him down," he wrote the "Y" of "You" over the first apostrophe of the closing quote; the second apostrophe of the quote appears to be over the "o" of "You."

13. The question which arises is why Hemingway felt under the compulsion—in working on this section a second, or even a third, time—to insert a sentence which repeats information which the reader already knows. It is even a bit incongruous within the context of the discussion. And why does Hemingway use "she" instead of "they," as he evidently originally intended? But then, why is it a "niece" instead of a daughter—or sister, brother, son or nephew?

14. *Short Stories,* p. 379.

15. "Hail Nothing full of nothing, nothing is with thee," is an insertion of the third category, i.e., after completion of the story, or on another day, with a sharp pencil.

Steven K. Hoffman (essay date 1979)

SOURCE: "Nada and the Clean, Well-Lighted Place: The Unity of Hemingway's Short Fiction," in *Essays in Literature,* Vol. VI, No. 1, Spring, 1979, pp. 91-110.

[In the following essay, Hoffman explores Hemingway's thematic concern with "nada," or nothingness, in his short fiction.]

One of his most frequently discussed tales, **"A Clean, Well-Lighted Place"** is justly regarded as one of the stylistic masterpieces of Ernest Hemingway's distinguished career in short fiction. Not only does it represent Hemingway at his understated, laconic best, but, according to Carlos Baker, "It shows once again that remarkable union of the naturalistic and the symbolic which is possibly his central triumph in the realm of practical aesthetics."[1] In mere five pages, almost entirely in dialogue and interior monologue, the tale renders a complex series of interactions between three characters in a Spanish café just prior to and immediately after closing: a stoic old waiter, a brash young waiter, and a wealthy but suicidal old man given to excessive drink.

Aside from its well-documented stylistic achievement, what has drawn the most critical attention is Hemingway's detailed consideration of the concept of *nada.* Although the old waiter is the only one to articulate the fact, all three figures actually confront nothingness in the course of the tale. This is no minor absence in their lives. Especially "for the old waiter," Carlos Baker notes, "the word *nothing* (or *nada*) contains huge actuality. The great skill in the story is the development, through the most carefully controlled understatement, of the young waiter's mere *nothing* into the old waiter's Something—a Something called Nothing which is so huge, terrible, overbearing, inevitable and omnipresent that once experienced, it can never be forgotten."[2] Because the terrifying "Something called Nothing" looms so very large, and since **"A Clean, Well-Lighted Place"** appeared in a 1933 collection in which even "winners" take "nothing," critics have generally come to see the piece as a nihilistic low point in Hemingway's career, a moment of profound despair both for the characters and the author.[3]

If this standard position does have a certain validity, it also tends to overlook two crucial points about the story. First is its relation to the rest of Hemingway's highly unified short story canon. In the same way that two of the three characters in **"A Clean, Well-Lighted Place"** meet *nada* without voicing the fact, all of the major short story characters also experience it in one of its multiple guises. Thus **"A Clean, Well-Lighted Place,"** a rather late story written in 1933, is something of a summary statement of this recurrent theme; the tale brings to direct expression the central crisis of those that precede it—including the most celebrated of the Nick Adams stories—and looks forward to its resolution in the masterpieces that come later: **"The Short Happy Life of Francis Macomber"** (1936) and **"The Snows of Kilimanjaro"** (1936).

Second, because *nada* appears to dominate **"A Clean, Well-Lighted Place,"** it has been easy to miss the fact that the story is not about *nada per se* but the various available human responses to it.[4] As a literary artist, Hemingway was generally less concerned with speculative metaphysics than with modes of practical conduct within certain *a priori* conditions. The ways in which the character triad in **"A Clean, Well-Lighted Place"** respond to *nada* summarize character responses throughout the canon. The fact that only one, the old waiter, directly voices his experience and manages to deal successfully with nothing ness is also indicative of a general trend. Those few Hemingway characters who continue to function even at the razor's edge do so in the manner of this heroic figure—by establishing for themselves a clean, well-lighted place from which to withstand the enveloping darkness. For these reasons, **"A Clean, Well-Lighted Place"** must be termed the thematic as well as the stylistic climax of Hemingway's career in short fiction.

Although the difficulty of attributing certain individual statements in the tale creates some ambiguity on the subject, it is clear that the young waiter's use of the term *nada* to convey a personal lack of a definable commodity (*no thing*) is much too narrowly conceived. In his crucial meditation at the end, the old waiter makes it quite clear that *nada* is not an individual state but one with grave universal implications: "It was a nothing that he knew too well. It was *all* a nothing and a man was nothing too" [my italics].[5] According to William Barrett, the *nada*-shadowed realm of **"A Clean, Well-Lighted Place"** is no less than a microcosm of the existential universe as defined by Martin Heidegger and the existentialist philosophers who came before and after him, principally Kierkegaard and Sartre.[6] Barrett's position finds internal support in the old waiter's celebrated parody prayer: "Our nada who art in nada, nada be thy name thy kingdom nada thy will be nada in nada as it is in nada. Give us this nada our daily nada and nada us our nada as we nada our nadas and nada us not into nada but deliver us from nada; pues nada" (p. 383). The character's deft substitution of the word *nada* for all the key nouns (entities) and verbs (actions) in the Paternoster suggests the concept's truly metaphysical stature. Obviously, *nada* is to connote a series of significant absences: the lack of a viable transcendent source of power and authority; a correlative lack of external physical or spiritual sustenance; the total lack of moral justification for action (in the broadest perspective, the essential meaninglessness of *any* action); and finally, the impossibility of deliverance from this situation.[7]

The impact of *nada*, however, extends beyond its theological implications. Rather, in the Heideggerian sense ("das Nicht"), it is an umbrella term that subsumes all of the irrational, unforeseeable, existential forces that tend to infringe upon the human self, to make a "nothing." It is the absolute power of chance and circumstance to negate individual free will and the entropic tendency toward ontological disorder that perpetually looms over man's tenuous personal sense of order. But the most fearsome face of *nada*, and clear proof of man's radical contingency, is death—present here in the old man's wife's death and his own attempted suicide. Understandably, the old waiter's emotional response to this composite threat is mixed. It "was not fear or dread" (p. 383), which would imply a specific object to be feared, but a pervasive uneasiness, an existential anxiety that, according to Heidegger, arises when one becomes fully aware of the precarious status of his very being.[8]

That the shadow of *nada* looms behind much of Hemingway's fiction has not gone entirely unnoticed. Nathan

Scott's conclusions on this issue serve as a useful summary of critical opinion: "Now it is blackness beyond a clean, well-lighted place—this 'nothing full of nothing' that betrays 'confidence'; that murders sleep, that makes the having of plenty of money a fact of no consequence at all—it is this blackness, ten times black, that constitutes the basic metaphysical situation in Hemingway's fiction and that makes the human enterprise something very much like a huddling about a campfire beyond which looms the unchartable wilderness, the great Nada."[9] The problem with this position is that it tends to locate *nada* somewhere outside of the action, never directly operative within it. It is, to William Barrett, "the presence that had circulated, *unnamed* and *unconfronted*, throughout much of [Hemingway's] earlier writing" [my italics].[10]

The clearest indication of *nada*'s direct presence in the short stories is to be found in the characters' frequent brushes with death, notably the characteristic modern forms of unexpected, unmerited, and very often mechanical death that both Frederick J. Hoffman and R. P. Warren consider so crucial in Hemingway.[11] Naturally, these instances are the climactic moments in some of the best known tales: the interchapters from *In Our Time,* **"Indian Camp," "The Killers," "The Capital of the World,"** and **"The Snows of Kilimanjaro."** But death or the imminent threat of death need not be literally present to signal an encounter with *nada*. What Philip Young and others have called Nick Adams's "initiation" to life's trials is actually his initiation to *nada*.[12] In **"The End of Something"** and **"The Three Day Blow,"** Nick must cope with the precariousness of love in a precarious universe; in **"The Battler,"** with the world's underlying irrationality and potential for violence; in **"Cross-Country Snow,"** with the power of external circumstance to circumscribe individual initiative. In several important stories involving the period in Nick's chronology after the critical "wound," *nada*, as the ultimate unmanageability of life, appears as a concrete image. In **"Big Two-Hearted River,"** it is both the burntout countryside and the forbidding swamp; in **"Now I Lay Me,"** the night; in **"A Way You'll Never Be,"** a "long yellow house" (evidently the site of the wound).

Other imagistic references to *nada* appear in the non-Nick Adams tales. In **"The Undefeated,"** it is the bull, a particularly apt concrete manifestation of active malevolence in the universe, also suggested by the lion and buffalo in **"The Short Happy Life of Francis Macomber."** These particular images, however, are potentially misleading because *nada* does not usually appear so actively and personally combative. An example to the contrary may be found in **"The Gambler, the Nun, and the Radio"** where *nada* is the distinctly impersonal and paralyzing banality of life in an isolated hospital, as well as the constant "risk" of a gambler's uncertain profession. Regardless of its specific incarnation, *nada* is always a dark presence which upsets individual equilibrium and threatens to overwhelm the self. And, as Jackson Benson has pointed out, "A threat to selfhood is the ultimate horror that the irrational forces of the world can accomplish."[13] In that each story in the canon turns on the way in which particular characters respond to the inevitable confrontation with *nada,* the nature of that response is particularly important. The only effective way to approach the Void is to develop a very special mode of being, the concrete manifestation of which is the clean, well-lighted place.

Again, it is the old waiter who speaks most directly of the need for a physical bastion against the all-encompassing night: "It is the light of course but it is necessary that the place be clean and pleasant. You do not want music. Certainly you do not want music. Nor can you stand before a bar with dignity" (p. 382). In direct contrast to the dirty, noisy *bodega* to which he repairs after closing and all the "bad" places that appear in Hemingway's fiction, the pleasant café at which the old waiter works possesses all of these essential attributes: light, cleanness, and the opportunity for some form of dignity. Perhaps the most direct antithesis of this legitimate clean, well-lighted place is not even in this particular story but in one of its companion pieces in *Winner Take Nothing,* the infernal bar in **"The Light of the World"** (1933). Here, light does little more than illuminate the absence of the other qualities, the lack of which moves one of the characters to ask pointedly, "'What the hell kind of place is this?'" (p. 385). Thus, in an inversion of the typical procedure in Hemingway, Nick and his companion are impelled outside where it is "good and dark" (p. 385).

Evidently, well-lighted places in Hemingway do not always meet the other requirements of the clean, well-lighted place. Moreover, since the café in **"A Clean, Well-Lighted Place"** must eventually close, even the legitimate haven has distinct limitations. These facts should be enough to alert us to the possibility that tangible physical location is not sufficient to combat the darkness. The clean, well-lighted place that is, is not actually a "place" at all; rather, it is a metaphor for an attitude toward the self and its existential context, a psychological perspective which, like the café itself with its fabricated conveniences and electric light, is man-made, artificial. The "cleanliness" of the metaphor connotes a personal sense of order, however artifical and temporary, carved out within the larger chaos of the universe, a firm hold on the self with which one can meet any contingency. By "light" Hemingway refers to a special kind of vision, the clear-sightedness and absolute lack of illusion necessary to look into the darkness and thereby come to grips with the *nada* which is everywhere. At the same time, vision must also be directed at the self so as to assure *its* cleanness. With cleanness and light, then, physical locale is irrelevant. Whoever manages to internalize these qualities carries the clean, well-lighted place with him, even into the very teeth of the darkness. The degree to which the Hemingway character can develop and maintain this perspective determines his success (or lack thereof) in dealing with the Void.

The man who does achieve the clean, well-lighted place is truly an existential hero, both in the Kierkegaardian and Heideggerian senses of the term. In the former, he is con-

tent to live with his *angst,* and, because there is no other choice, content to be in doubt about ultimate causes. Nevertheless, he is able to meet the varied and often threatening circumstances of day-to-day living, secure in the knowledge that he will always "become" and never "be." In the latter, he can face the unpleasant realities of his own being and the situation into which he has been "thrown," and can accept with composure the inevitability of his death. In both instances, he is an "authentic" man.[14]

Two of the main characters in **"A Clean, Well-Lighted Place,"** as well as a host of analogous figures in other tales, fail to develop this attitude either for lack of "light" (the young waiter) or for lack of "cleanness" (the old man). As is evidenced by his inability to grasp the full impact of his partner's use of the word *nothing,* the egotistic young waiter has not even grasped the fact of *nada*—has not *seen* clearly—and therefore can hardly deal with it. "To him," comments Joseph Gabriel, "*nada* can only signify a personal physical privation. *Nothing* refers simply to the absence of those objects capable of providing material satisfaction. And by extension he applies the term to all behavior which does not grant the sufficiency of things."[15] Unable to see that the old man's wealth is a woefully inadequate bulwark against the Void, he is, in his ignorance, contemptuous both of the man and his predicament. Perhaps as a direct outgrowth of this lack of light, the young waiter also violates the principle of cleanness by sloppily pouring his customer's desperately needed brandy over the sides of the glass. Thus, he easily loses himself in a fool's paradise of blindness and illusion. Still young, secure in his job, and, as he boasts, "'I'm not lonely. I have a wife waiting in bed for me,'" (p. 380), he is "all confidence": as such, a particularly patent example to the old waiter of those who "lived in it [*nada*] and never felt it" (p. 383).

Yet, in the course of the story, even this naif has an unsettling glimpse of the fundamental uncertainty of existence and its direct impact on his own situation. What else can account for his sharply defensive reaction to the old waiter's joke? [Old Waiter]: "'And you? You have no fear of going home before your usual hour?'" [Young Waiter] "'Are you trying to insult me?'" [Old Waiter]: "'No, hombre, only to make a joke'" (p. 382). The youth's subsequent grandiose claims to security notwithstanding, the force with which he objects to the merest possibility of marital infidelity clearly underscores the shaky foundations of his "confidence." This bogus self-assurance does not emanate from a mature awareness of himself and his world, but is based on the most transitory of conditions: youth, present employment, sexual prowess, and the assumed loyalty of his wife. The young waiter depends for his very being on factors over which he has no control, leaving him particularly vulnerable, in the case of marital uncertainty, to what Warren Bennett calls the "love wound," a common form of deprivation in Hemingway.[1] But because he is essentially devoid of light or insight, he is not cognizant of the significance of his testy reply; his vision is so clouded by putative "confidence" that he fails to see through the ephemeral to the underlying darkness in his own life. Consequently, he cannot even begin to reconstruct his existence upon a more substantial basis.

Hemingway must have reveled in such naifs, aflame with so obviously compromised bravado, for he created many of them. Perhaps the most notable is Paco, the would-be bullfighter of **"The Capital of the World"** (1936), who even in the face of his own death, is "full of illusions." For many of these characters, moreover, blindness is not a natural state but a willed escape from *nada.* Conscious flight from reality is particularly prevalent in the early stages of the "education" of Nick Adams. In **"Indian Camp"** (1924), for instance, one of the first segments in the Adams chronology, Nick has a youthful encounter with *nada* both as the incontrovertible fact of death (the Indian husband's suicide) and as human frailty, the intrinsic vulnerability of mankind to various species of physical and psychic suffering (the Indian woman's protracted and painful labor). The pattern of avoidance set when he refuses to witness the Caesarean section climaxes in his more significant refusal to recognize the inevitability of death itself at the end. Lulled by the deceptive calm of his present circumstances—a purely fortuitous and temporary clean, well-lighted place—he maintains an internal darkness by retreating into willed ignorance:

> They were seated in the boat, Nick in the stern, his father rowing. The sun was coming up over the hills. A bass jumped, making a circle in the water. Nick trailed hand in the water. It felt warm in the sharp chill of the morning.
>
> In the early morning on the lake sitting in the stern of the boat with his father rowing, he felt quite sure that he would never die.
>
> (p. 95)

In another early story, **"The Killers"** (1927), the somewhat older Nick is again faced with harsh reality, but his reaction to it has not appreciably altered. Again, death (the Swede's) is the primary manifestation of the Void. But here the manner of its coming is also particularly important as a signature of *nada.* As represented by the black-clad henchmen who invade the café—another inadequate place of refuge—*nada* is totally impersonal; in the words of one of the killers, "'He [the Swede] never had a chance to do anything to us. He never even seen us'" (p. 283). Moreover, *nada* displays its tendency to disrupt without warning any established external order, and, ironically, is visited upon its victims not without a certain macabre humor. Naturally, as Nick learns from the intended victim, its effects are totally irremediable. Thus, in spite of their suggestive black clothing, the killers do not represent forces of evil unleashed in an otherwise good world, as so many critics have claimed: rather, they stand for the wholly amoral, wholly irrational, wholly random operation of the universe, which, because it so clearly works to the detriment of the individual, is *perceived* to be malevolent and evil.

In spite of the clearly educational nature of his experience, Nick once again refuses initiation. Only now his unrea-

soned compulsion to escape is more pronounced than that of his younger counterpart. Deluded into thinking that this is the kind of localized danger that can be avoided by a mere change in venue, Nick vows not only physical flight ("'I'm going to get out of this town'") but psychological flight as well: "'I can't stand to think about him waiting in the room and knowing he's going to get it. It's too damned awful'" (p. 289). Both versions of Nick Adams, then, are "young waiter" figures because they neither will allow themselves to look directly at the fearsome face of *nada* nor recognize its direct applicability to their own insecure lives.

That such an attitude is ultimately insupportable is exemplified by a third early tale, **"Cross-Country Snow"** (1925). Here, yet another Nick employs a physically demanding activity, skiing, as an escape from yet another incarnation of *nada,* entrapping circumstance. This appearance of the Void is also ironic in that the specific circumstance involved is the life-enhancing pregnancy of Nick's wife. Nevertheless, its impact on the character is much the same as before in that it serves to severely circumscribe independent initiative, even to the point of substituting an externally imposed identity—in this case, fatherhood—on the true self.[17] Once again misled by the temporary security of the "good place," this Nick also attempts to escape the inescapable, and, at the height of his self-delusion, is moved to raise his pursuit of physical release to the level of absolute value: "'We've got to [ski again] . . . It [life] isn't worth while if you can't'" (p. 188).

The ski slope, however, offers only apparent protection from *nada,* for even in his joyous adventure, Nick encounters its own form or hidden danger: "Then a patch of soft snow, left in a hollow by the wind, spilled him and he went over and over in a clashing of skis, feeling like a shot rabbit" (p. 183). Unlike the others, this story ends with clarified vision, and Nick does come to terms with the inevitable external demands upon him. Finally, he is no longer able to pretend that the pleasures of the ski slopes—themselves, not always unmixed—are anything more than temporary, in no way definitive of human existence or even a long-lived accommodation to it. Thus, in response to his companion's suggested pact to repeat their present idyll, Nick must realistically counter, "'There isn't any good in promising'" (p. 188).

In this relationship to *nada,* the old man of **"A Clean, Well-Lighted Place"** is cast as the polar opposite of the young waiter. Said to be eighty years old, virtually deaf, and recently widowed, he is "in despair" in spite of his reputed wealth, and has attempted suicide shortly before the story begins. Unlike the young waiter, he has the light of unclouded vision because he has clearly seen the destructive effects of time and circumstance on love and the self and directly witnessed *nada* in its death mask. But unlike the old waiter, he has not been able to sustain a satisfactory mode of being in the face of these discoveries. He therefore seeks escape from his knowledge either through the bottle or the total denial of life in suicide. Undoubtedly, the old man senses the importance of the clean, well-lighted place, but to him it is very literally a "place" and thereby no more helpful in combatting *nada* than Nick's ski slope. That it is inadequate is suggested imagistically at the outset; darkness has indeed invaded this character's "place," for he sits "in the shadows the leaves of the trees made against the electric light" (p. 379).

What seems to offer the old man the little balance he possesses, and thus helps keep him alive, is a modicum of internal cleanness and self-possession, his dignity or style. Of course, this is an issue of great import in Hemingway in that an ordered personal style is one of the few sources of value in an otherwise meaningless universe. The old waiter draws attention to this pitiful figure's style when he rebukes the young waiter for callously characterizing the old man as "'a nasty old thing'": "'This old man is clean. He drinks without spilling. Even now, drunk'" (p. 381). But even this vestige of grace has been compromised over time. While the old man leaves the café "with dignity," he is "walking unsteadily" (p. 381).

The product of a series of encounters with *nada,* the old man's despair is mirrored in two Nick Adams stories on the period immediately following the critical war wound. In **"Now I Lay Me"** (1927), the emotional dislocation stemming from his brush with death is continued in an almost psychotic dread of the night and sleep. *Nada* is imaged both as the night itself and, as Carlos Baker has suggested, by the disturbing and seemingly ceaseless munching of silkworms, just out of sight but most assuredly not out of Nick's disturbed mind. Paradoxically, the protagonist's abject terror in the face of potential selflessness—permanent in death; temporary in sleep—has resulted in a severe dissociation of the self. Using Paul Tillich's descriptive terminology from *The Courage To Be,* one can say that he is burdened by "pathological" anxiety: a condition of drastically reduced self-affirmation, a flight from nonbeing that entails a corresponding flight from being itself:[18] "I myself did not want to sleep because I had been living for a long time with the knowledge that if I ever shut my eyes in the dark and let myself go, my soul would go out of my body. I had been that way for a long time, ever since I had been blown up at night and felt it go out of me and go off and then come back" (p. 363).

Awakened to the fact of his own death, Nick experiences *angst* so strongly that he is virtually paralyzed. Unwilling to sleep in the dark and not yet able to develop an internal light and cleanness to cope with his trauma, he depends entirely on external sources of illumination: "If I could have a light I was not afraid to sleep" (p. 363). In the absence of this light, however, he attempts to pull back from the awareness of *nada* by reliving the happier times of his youth, a period of cleanness and assured order. But the search for a good "place" in the past is ultimately fruitless; his memories of favorite trout streams tend to blur in his mind and inevitably lead him to unpleasant reminiscences of his father's ruined collection of arrowheads and zoo-

logical specimens, a chaotic heap of fragments that merely mirrors his present internal maelstrom.

In **"A Way You'll Never Be"** (1933), Nick's dissociation has not been remedied and is suggested initially by the post-battle debris with which the story opens. Plagued by a recurring dream of "a low house painted yellow with willows all around it and a low stable and there was a canal, and he had been there a thousand times and never seen it, but there it was every night as plain as the hill only it frightened him" (p. 408), he is close to an old man's despair. He now intuits something of the significance of the vision: "That house meant more than anything and every night he had it [the dream]. That was what he needed" (p. 408). But he is still too traumatized by the experience there to examine it more closely, and can only ramble on in self-defense about the "American locust," another familiar item from his childhood. In his present condition, Nick is an oddly appropriate choice for the absurd mission on which he has been sent, to display his American uniform in order to build morale among the Italian troops. At the moment, his "self," like the entire American presence in the region, is solely the uniform; the clothes are as dimly suggestive of a more substantial identity as they are of the substantial military support they are designed to promise. For the present, though, this barely adequate package for his violently disturbed inner terrain is Nick's only semblance of the clean, well-lighted place. Still insufficiently initiated into the dangerous world in which he is doomed to live, he desperately clutches at any buffer that will hold *nada* in abeyance.

The other side of Hemingway's "old man" figure is epitomized by Manuel Garcia, the aging bullfighter of **"The Undefeated"** (1925). After numerous brushes with death in the bullring, he too depends for his very being on style. Garcia's style has also eroded, leaving him defenseless against the bull, Harold Kaplan's "beast of *nada.*"[19] Banished from the brightly lit afternoon bouts, he now performs in the shadowy nocturnals for a "second string" critic and with bulls that "'the veterinaries won't pass in the daytime'" (p. 237). The performance itself is merely "acceptable" if not "vulgar." Largely as a result of his diminished capabilities, he is seriously (and perhaps mortally) wounded, and, at the conclusion, is left with only his *coletta,* as is the old man his shred of dignity. With these all-important manifestations of internal cleanness sullied, the fates of both are equally uncertain: Manuel's on the operating table, and the old man's in the enveloping night.

Of all Hemingway's short story characters, however, the one who most fully recapitulates the "old man" typology is Mr. Frazer of **"The Gambler, the Nun, and the Radio"** (1933). Confined to a backcountry hospital as a result of a riding accident, Frazer too experiences *nada,* "the Nothingness that underlies pain, failure, and disillusionment alike,"[20] in the form of his own incapacity and that of the broken men who share his predicament. He also experiences banality, one of the less overtly disturbing but nonetheless ominous visages of *nada,* in the form of the numbing routine of this claustrophobic, but clean and well-lighted place. If Frazer has an old man's clear perspective on nothingness, he is no better able to achieve the cleanness of character necessary to cope with it. As is suggested by Hemingway's first title for the story, "Give Us a Prescription, Doctor," Frazer too seeks external anodynes for his *nada*—induced pain. His compulsion to monitor random radio broadcasts and so imaginatively transport himself from his present circumstances is analogous to the old man's drinking because each involves a flight from, rather than a confrontation with reality. His very choice of songs—"Little White Lies" and "Sing Something Simple"—serves to underscore the escapism of this pastime.

In the end, however, neither escape succeeds. The old man remains in despair, and Frazer is given to periodic fits of uncontrollable weeping. In the same way that the former cannot entirely banish the specter of loneliness and death from his consciousness, neither can Frazer, nor any man, completely cloud his view of *nada* with the various "opiums" at his disposal. The very consideration of the question of release leads Frazer through the opium haze to the terrible truth that lies beneath:

> Religion is the opium of the people. . . . Yes, and music is the opium of the people. . . . And now economics is the opium of the people; along with patriotism the opium of the people in Italy and Germany. . . . But drink was a sovereign opium of the people, oh, an excellent opium. Although some prefer the radio, another opium of the people, a cheap one he had just been using. . . . What was the real, the actual opium of the people? . . . What was it? Of course; bread was the opium of the people. . . . [Only] Revolution, Mr. Frazer thought, is no opium. Revolution is a catharsis; an ecstasy which can only be prolonged by tyranny. The opiums are for before and for after. He was thinking well, a little too well.

(pp. 485-87)

The old waiter definitely stands apart from the other two characters in **"A Clean, Well-Lighted Place."** If the running controversy over dialogue attribution has thrown some doubt on whether he or his young partner first learns of the old man's attempted suicide, it has done nothing to contradict earlier assumptions on which of the two is more sensitive to the reasons for it. It is evident throughout that the old waiter's insight into the word *nothing* he so frequently uses is much broader. He recognizes from the first that the old man's despair is not a reaction to a material lack but to a basic metaphysical principle. Thus, he is unable to delude himself into a bogus "confidence." When he responds to the youth's boasting with "'You have everything'" (p. 382), he is clearly being ironic; the latter indeed has "everything," *except* a firm hold on the "nothing" which underlies "everything." They are "of two different kinds" (p. 382) because the old waiter knows the ability to withstand the dark "is not only a question of youth and confidence although those things are very beau-

tiful" (p. 382). In spite of their superficial beauty, both the transitory condition of youth and the illusory confidence that so often goes with it are clearly inadequate tools with which to combat the darkness.

There is a closer connection with the old man, however, initially because the news of his attempted suicide begins the old waiter's formal consideration of the reasons for it. In this sense, at the beginning of the tale, the old waiter is a representation of Earl Rovit's "tyro" and Philip Young's "Hemingway hero" (as opposed to the "tutor" and "code hero") in that he is in the process of learning about the dark underside of life. But while the old man's plight is a necessary goad for the old waiter's musings on his own situation, the latter certainly outstrips his "mentor" in the lengths to which he pushes his speculations on *nada*: "What did [the old waiter] fear? It was not fear or dread. It was a nothing that he knew too well. It was all a nothing and a man was nothing too. It was only that and light was all it needed and a certain cleanness and order. Some lived in it and never felt it but he knew it all was nada y pues nada y nada y pues nada" (p. 382-83).

Like the old man, then, the old waiter sees clearly, in fact more clearly, the fearsome nothing, but he reacts far differently to his discovery. Instead of lapsing into despair or escaping into drunkenness, this character displays true metaphysical courage in raising the concept of *nada* to a central article in his overtly existentialist creed, climaxing with his mock prayer of adoration, "Hail nothing full of nothing, nothing is with thee" (p. 383). Perhaps even more importantly, he refuses to limit himself to abstract speculation but willingly embraces the impact of universal nothingness on his own person. Thus, in response to the barman's question, "'What's yours?'" he demonstrates the ironic sense of humor that typifies him throughout by unflinching answering, "'Nada'" (p. 383). No other statement in the tale so clearly designates the old waiter as the central figure of Hemingway's 1933 collection: he is the "winner" who truly takes "nothing" as his only possible reward.

If his stoic courage in the shadow of the Void differentiates the old waiter from the old man, so does his method for dealing with it. Again, the old waiter provides some grounds for confusing the two modes of existence when he insists upon the importance of a purely physical haven: "'I am one of those who like to stay late at the café. . . . With all those who do not want to go to bed. With all those who need a light for the night'" (p. 382). Yet, he does more than merely accept the dubious protection of an already established "place"; he is, in fact, the keeper of the "clean, well-lighted place," the one who maintains both its cleanness and its light. To cite Cleanth Brooks on this subject, "The order and light are supplied by *him*. They do *not* reflect an inherent, though concealed, order in the universe. What little meaning there is in the world is imposed upon that world by man."[21] Given the stark contrast between his café and the distinctly unclean and ill-lighted bar he frequents after work, his almost ritualistic efforts to furnish and consistently maintain these essential qualities are definitely not representative of those around him. Finally, the old waiter's clean, well-lighted place is distinctly portable—transcending "place" altogether—because it is so thoroughly internalized. He carries it in the form of equanimity and dignity to the shabby *bodega,* and he carries it home as well.

Thus, it is the old waiter, a man who can see clearly the darkness surrounding him yet so order his life that he can endure this awareness, who most fully attains the attitude symbolized by the clean, well-lighted place. In the society presented by this tale, and in the Hemingway canon as a whole, he is indeed *"otro loco mas"* when set against a standard of sanity epitomized by an egotistical partner, unfeeling barmen, lustful soldiers, and suicidal old men. Both realist and survivor, epitome of "grace under pressure," he is by the end of the tale an exceptional man and very much a representation of the highest level of heroism in Hemingway's fictional world, whether it be denoted by Young's "code hero" or Rovit's "tutor." Even his insomnia, which he regard as a common trait ("Many must have it"), is a mark of his extraordinary character: his vision is too clear, his sense of self too firm, to allow him the ease of insensate slumber. One need only compare this insomnia with Nick Adams' pathological fear of sleep in **"Now I Lay Me"** to appreciate the qualitative difference between the old waiter and other men.

Some of Hemingway's most important tales also contain characters who either presage an achievement of or actually attain the old waiter's clean, well-lighted place. A notable early example is the Nick Adams of **"Big Two-Hearted River"** (1925). Again, the confrontation with *nada* is critical here, but the appearance of *nada* is more artfully veiled than in other tales. There are hints of the Void in the description of the burned-over countryside at the beginning, in Nick's vision of the trout "tightened facing up into the current" (p. 210) shortly thereafter, and in the methodical series of tasks that comprise the central action of the story. As Malcolm Cowley first suggested and Sheridan Baker has since amplified, the ritualistic series connotes a desperate attempt to hold off something "he had left behind" (p. 210); in Philip Young's reading, the "something" is the memory of the traumatic war wound that so discomfits other versions of Nick in **"Now I Lay Me"** and **"A Way You'll Never Be."**[22] But *nada* is most overtly suggested by the forbidding swamp: "Nick did not want to go in there now. . . . In the swamp the banks were bare, the big cedars came together overhead, the sun did not come through, except in patches; in the fast deep water, in the half light, the fishing would be tragic" (p. 231). Aside from the old waiter's prayer, this is Hemingway's most detailed characterization of *nada:* it too is dark; its depth is ungauged but considerable; and, with its swiftly moving current and bare banks, it is most assuredly inhospitable to man.

As the "patches" of sunlight suggest, though, the *nada/* swamp can be discerned and therefore analyzed by human

vision. And, by the end of the story, Nick seems to have gained the light necessary to see into the Void—at the very least, to realize that he can never truly leave it behind him. Yet Nick still lacks the inner cleanness to delve further into *nada;* he is still too dependent on a distinct physical locale as a buffer zone. As he says early on, "He was there, in the good place" (p. 215). But the very ritualistic behavior that alerted Cowley to the possibility of a mind not right also suggests progress toward an internalized order. Like the trout's in the potentially destructive current, this discipline could hold Nick steady in the dangerous eddies of life and so enable him eventually to enter the swamp. Thus, while the tale ends with a temporary withdrawal from direct confrontation, Nick strikes a positive note when he says, "There were plenty of days coming when he could fish the swamp" (p. 232).

Two characters in the late short stories actually do "fish" the swamp of *nada,* the sportsman Macomber in **"The Short Happy Life of Francis Macomber"** (1936) and the writer Harry of **"The Snows of Kilimanjaro"** (1936). The two men approach the clean, well-lighted place from different directions, however: Macomber, from an old man's despair; and Harry, from a young waiter's naive faith in transitory material security. For Macomber, the master of "court games" and darling of drawing rooms, it is necessary to leave the protective enclosures of the rich to meet his *nada* in the African tall grass in the figure of the wounded lion, an epitome of pure destructive force: "All of him [the lion], pain, sickness, hatred and all of his remaining strength, was tightening into an absolute concentration for a rush" (p. 19). The brush with externally conceived *nada* triggers Macomber's cowardly flight, but more importantly leads him to an appreciation of his own inner emptiness, a Sartrian version of nothingness, as well as a Sartrian *nausea* at his inauthenticity. Granted, Macomber responds to the threat with fear, but it is also more than fear, "a cold slimy hollow in all the emptiness where once his confidence had been and it made him feel sick" (p. 11). Thus Macomber comes face to face with the fact that *nada* need not destroy the physical being to make man a "nothing"; man *is* a nothing unless and until he makes himself "something."

The black despair that follows his initiation to *nada* without and within is not Macomber's final stage. Through the ministrations of the hunter Wilson and the familiar, secure place (the jeep), he undergoes a significant and almost miraculous change at the buffalo hunt. As Wilson describes it, "Beggar had probably been afraid all his life. Don't know what started it. But over now. Hadn't had time to be afraid with the buff. That and being angry too. Motor car too. Motor cars made it familiar. Be a damn fire eater now" (p. 33). The jeep is indeed useful as a means for facing *nada* analogous to the old waiter's café and Nick Adams' peaceful campsite, but Macomber's real "place" is distinctly internal. Again, Wilson furnishes the analysis: "Fear gone like an operation. *Something else grew in its place.* Main thing a man had. Made him into a man [italics mine]" (p. 33). Macomber's real achievement, then, is the creation of an ordered "something" to fill the inner void. It not only prepares him for the buffalo hunt but enables him to see clearly, as if for the first time, his inauthentic condition, not the least important facet of which has been his sacrifice of personal identity to an unfulfilling marriage and social expectation. With his "place" securely inside him, he can face with dignity and courage another brush with *nada* in the "island of bushy trees" (p. 35), a hostile testing ground certainly reminiscent of Nick's swamp.

In **"Snows of Kilimanjaro,"** Harry too has multiple confrontations with *nada,* the first of which is with the ultimate manifestation of the Void, death: "It came with a rush; not as a rush of water nor of wind; but of a sudden evil-smelling emptiness" (p. 64). As we learn later, this appearance certainly fits Carlos Baker's oxymoronic designation for *nada* as the "nothing that is something," for "It had no shape, any more. It simply occupied space" (p. 74). The immediate effect of the experience is to lead Harry to an appreciation of the underlying absurdity of an existence that could be doomed by such a trivial injury—a small scratch which becomes gangrenous for lack of proper medication. With this awareness of his radical contingency, the protagonist can defuse death of its terror: "Since the gangrene started in his right leg he had no pain and with the pain the horror had gone and all he felt now was a great tiredness and anger that this was the end of it. . . . For years it had obsessed him; but now it meant nothing in itself" (p. 54).

Like Macomber's, Harry's brush with imminent death also awakens him to a second face of *nada,* the inner nothing caused by his failure to preserve artistic integrity, his very self, against the lures of the inconsequential: material comfort, financial security, hedonistic pleasure. Every bit as much as Macomber, this most autobiographical of Hemingway's short story characters suffers a hollowness at the very core. Therefore, the basic thrust of the tale is Harry's effort to cleanse and reorder his life through a pointed self criticism. Gradually he manages to "work the fat off his soul" (p. 60) by jettisoning the excess baggage of a young waiter's facile confidence in the material and replaces it with something more substantial, a pledge to take up his writing once more. Again, the process is facilitated by his being situated in a tangible clean, well-lighted place: "This was a pleasant camp under big trees against a hill, with good water, and close by, a nearly dry water hole where sand grouse flighted in the mornings" (p. 53). But again, the important "place" is actually within. According to Gloria Dussinger, Harry's difficult rite of purification leads, as it should, to a reclamation of his own identity: "Harry is left with his naked self, the irreducible *I am* that defies chaos."[23] Though the climactic dream flight from the plain is decidedly ambiguous, it does seem to vouchsafe Harry's success at this endeavor, for the author allows him imaginative entry into the cleanest and best lighted of all the places in the short story canon: "great, high, and unbelievably white in the sun, was the square top of Kilimanjaro. And then he knew that there was where he was going" (p. 76).

Although Harry and Macomber both achieve the clean, well-lighted place, their premature deaths deprive them of the opportunity to bring additional value to their lives, as the old waiter most assuredly does. Having controlled his own life through the implementation of a clean, well-lighted place, he fulfills the remaining provisions of Eliot's *Waste Land* credo by sympathizing with the plight of others and aiding them in their own pursuits of this all important attitude. In so doing, he becomes an existential hero in Martin Buber's particular sense of the term, a champion of the "I-Thou" relationship. His "style" is essentially compassion, the willingness to treat others as valid, subjective "Thous" rather than depersonalized "Its."[24] This facet of his personality is implicit as early as his expression of sympathy for the pleasure-seeking soldier who risks curfew violation. As he himself comments on the risks involved, "'What does it matter if he gets what he's after?'" (p. 379). But his capacity for true compassion is made most explicit near the end, particularly in his admission, "'Each night I am reluctant to close up because there may be some one who needs the café'" (p. 382).

The ability to extend outward to others from a firmly established self is once again in direct contrast to the narrow, selfish pride of the young waiter, who is unmoved by the needs of the old man and sees love as a matter of blind loyalty (verging on bondage) and physical gratification. This inclination is made all too clear by his insensitive comment on the old widower's plight: "'A wife would be no good to him now'" (p. 381). The old waiter's attitude is also contrasted to that of the old man, who is so absorbed by his own misery that he is barely cognizant of others. This admirable figure passes beyond Rovit's "tyro" stage to that of "tutor" when he humorously, but pointedly, attempts to instruct the youth on the evanescence of "confidence" and the latter's serious misuse of love (*e.g.,* by the joke). Moreover, he tries to provide the morose old man with some basis upon which to reconstruct his shattered life by rendering to this wretched figure the respect and sympathy he so desperately needs. Thus, in Buber's sense as in Heidegger's, Kierkegaard's, and Sartre's, the old waiter "authenticates" his life by fulfilling his responsibilities both to himself and to others.

The picador Zurito in **"The Undefeated,"** the dignified major in **"Another Country"** (1927), and the guide Wilson of **"The Short Happy Life of Francis Macomber"** all transcend the limits of self-sufficiency by sympathizing with and proferring aid to those who most need it. But the character who most closely approximates the old waiter's multi-faceted heroism is Cayetano Ruiz, the luckless gambler of **"The Gambler, the Nun, and the Radio,"** a story whose three main characters (Ruiz, Frazer, Sister Cecilia) form a triadic grouping analogous to the hero, victim, and naif of **"A Clean, Well-Lighted Place."**[25]

That the gambler does attain the exemplary attitude is implicit in William Barrett's summary characterization of him: "Cayetano is the absurd hero who carries on his code, even if it is only the code of a cheap gambler, defiantly and gracefully against the Void."[26] Cayetano, of course, earns his heroism in that he too encounters the death mask of *nada.* Like Harry's, his wound comes totally without warning, and, given the rather unreliable aim of his assailant, almost totally by accident. Yet even before this crisis, the perspicacious gambler with eyes "alive as a hawk's" (p. 468) has undoubtedly sensed its presence in the form of chance and the ever-present risk of his chosen profession. In spite of the fact that his work takes him into places that are anything but clean and well-lighted, he has so internalized the "place" that he can calmly face external hostility and internal suffering, and face them with honor and exemplary courage. Consequently, he refuses to inform on his assailant and also refuses opiates to dull the physical pain that serves as metaphor for the metaphysical pain *nada* induces.

But Ruiz is far more than Barrett's "cheap," albeit heroic, gambler because he strives to communicate his insights on life to others. Indirect proof of his compassion is to be found both in his embarrassment over the offensive odor of his peritonitis and in his considerate silence even in periods of terrible pain. Direct evidence is available in the conversations with Frazer. Here Ruiz incisively analyses the untreatable ills of the human condition—the absurd irony, the prevalence of accident and risk, and, most of all, the difficulty of maintaining a self amidst the vagaries of fortune that have driven his auditor to tears. Like the old waiter, he is quite capable of humbling himself, denigrating his own considerable courage, in order to provide comfort to one less able to withstand *nada.* Surely he consciously misstates fact when, in an attempt to assuage Frazer's shame at lapsing into tears, he declares, "'If I had a private room and a radio I would be crying and yelling all night long'" (p. 482). Evidently this self-described "victim of illusions" (p. 483) also possesses the old waiter's ironic consciousness, for it is at the very heart of his dispassionate self-analysis, also delivered principally for Frazer's benefit: "'If I live long enough the luck will change. I have bad luck now for fifteen years. If I ever get any good luck I will be rich'" (p. 483). Although he fully realizes that "bad luck" will continue to predominate, like the other residents of the *metaphoric* clean, well-lighted place, the gambler is content to "continue, slowly, and wait for luck to change" (p. 484). In the interim, he will continue to try to instill in others some of the light and cleanness essential to the authentication of the self.

In their dealings with the various faces of *nada,* then, the old waiter figures represent the highest form of heroism in the Hemingway short story canon, a heroism matched in the novels perhaps only by the fisherman Santiago. Those who manage to adjust to life on the edge of the abyss do so because they see clearly the darkness that surrounds them yet create a personal sense of order, an identity, with which to maintain balance on this precarious perch. The failure either to see the significance of the encounter with *nada* or, if seen, to constitute an inner cleanness vitiates the lives not only of the young waiter and old man of **"A Clean, Well-Lighted Place"** but also of a host of similarly flawed figures throughout the canon.

Because of the frequency with which *nada* appears in the short fiction, we can only assume that the Void also played a major role in Hemingway's own life, whether as the shattering war wound or the countless subsequent experiences, both real and imagined, that threatened to make him a "nothing." Carlos Baker concluded as much in his biography: "**'A Clean, Well-Lighted Place'** was autobiographical . . . in the sense that it offered a brief look into the underside of Ernest's spiritual world, the nightmare of nothingness by which he was still occasionally haunted."[27] But if we are justified in seeing Hemingway's life in terms of his encounters with *nada,* are we not equally justified in following Earl Rovit's lead and thereby treating his fiction as one of the by-products of these encounters—in fact, as a primary strategy for dealing with *nada?*[28]

Both the fiction itself and the author's comments on it seem to support us in this regard, for Hemingway's basic aesthetic suggests precisely the sort of perspective symbolized by the clean, well-lighted place. The need for clearsightedness, for instance, is the essence of the writer's celebrated remark on art in *Death in the Afternoon* (1932), a personal testament published just a year before **"A Clean, Well-Lighted Place"**: "Let those who want to save the world if you can get to see it clear and as a whole. Then any part you make will represent the whole if it is made truly."[29] But unclouded vision alone, not uncommon among his fictional progeny, could guarantee neither a psychological nor an aesthetic clean, well-lighted place. A careful and conscious ordering of disparate material was also required in order to fill the Void of nothing (the blank page) with an enduring something. Thus, the characteristic Hemingway style: the clean, precise, scrupulously ordered prose that so often serves to illuminate shimmering individual objects against a dark background of chaos.[30] As for his old waiter figures, the actual places that inspired the author's descriptions pale against the deftly constructed "places" that *are* the descriptions; because the latter are no longer subject to the random, transitory world of fact but rather interiorized and subsequently transmuted into art itself, they are much more secure, and certainly more permanent, strongholds against nothingness.

In spite of the apparent disdain for utilitarian art in the passage from *Death in the Afternoon,* Hemingway also performed some of that function, albeit indirectly, by probing the sources of our well-documented modern malaise and offering at least tentative solutions to it in the form of resolute personal conduct. In this way he too displayed some of the Buberesque qualities of his short story heroes. It should come as no surprise, then, that Granville Hicks' summary of the author's artistic mission has a rather direct applicability to that of the old waiter as well. For in their potential impact on an attentive audience. Hemingway and his extraordinary character are virtually one and the same. Like the latter, "The artist makes his contribution to the salvation of the world by seeing it clearly himself and helping others to do the same."[31]

Perhaps nothing so effectively demonstrates the difficulty of maintaining the clean, well-lighted place than Hemingway's own failure to do so in the years immediately preceding his death. Like so many of his "old man" figures, he never lost sight of *nada* but did lose the essential inner cleanness, without which the light must eventually be overpowered by darkness. With his internal defenses in disarray, Hemingway turned to an old man's despairing act. In effect, in his suicide, he opted for the release from turmoil offered by the metaphorical "opiums" of Mr. Frazer: "He would have a little spot of the giant killer and play the radio, you could play the radio so that you could hardly hear it" (p. 487).

Notes

1. Carlos Baker, *Hemingway: The Writer as Artist,* 4th ed. (Princeton, N.J.: Princeton Univ. Press, 1972), p. 128.

2. Baker, p. 124.

3. Of course, "A Clean, Well-Lighted Place" is not the only story in *Winner Take Nothing* (New York: Scribner's, 1933) that conveys the sense of desolation. "After the Storm," "The Light of the World," "A Natural History of the Dead," and "A Way You'll Never Be" are apt companion-pieces and Hemingway's epigraph firmly sets the tone for the entire collection:

   Unlike all other forms of lutte or combat the conditions are that the winner shall take nothing; neither his ease, nor his pleasure, nor any notions of glory; nor, if he win far enough, shall there be any reward within himself.

   In addition to the commentary of the *nada* theme, at least a dozen articles have been written on the difficulty of attributing certain portions of dialogue in "A Clean, Well-Lighted Place." In perhaps the most provocative of them, Joseph Gabriel argues that the speeches of the old and young waiter were intentionally confused so that the reader might not only witness but actually experience the uncertainty of nothingness in the very act of reading the tale. See "The Logic of Confusion in Hemingway's 'A Clean, Well-Lighted Place,'" *College English,* 22 (May 1961), 539-47. For an overview of the dialogue controversy, see Charles May, "Is Hemingway's 'Well-Lighted Place' Really Clean Now?" *Studies in Short Fiction,* 8 (1971), 326-30.

4. Annette Benert also stresses the response to *nada* in this particular tale, but only the old waiter's, in "Survival Through Irony: Hemingway's 'A Clean, Well-Lighted Place,'" *Studies in Short Fiction,* 11 (1974), 181-89.

5. *The Short Stories of Ernest Hemingway* (New York: Scribner's, 1966), p. 383. All subsequent references to Hemingway's stories and all page references are to this volume. Dates provided for individual stories refer to their initial publication.

6. *Time of Need: Forms of Imagination in the Twentieth Century* (New York: Harper, 1972), pp.

83-92. For a useful, if overly systematic, study of Hemingway and existentialist thought, see John Killinger's *Hemingway and the Dead Gods: A Study in Existentialism* (Lexington: Univ. of Kentucky Press, 1960). See also Richard Lehan's section of Hemingway, Sartre, and Camus in *A Dangerous Crossing: French Literary Existentialism and the Modern American Novel* (Carbondale: Southern Illinois Univ. Press, 1973), pp. 46-56.

7. For more detailed theological and linguistic analyses of the old waiter's prayer, see John B. Hamilton, "Hemingway and the Christian Paradox," *Renascence,* 24 (1972), 152-54; David Lodge, "Hemingway's Clean, Well-Lighted, Puzzling Place," *Essays in Criticism,* 21 (1971), 33-34; and Earl Rovit, *Ernest Hemingway* (New York: Twayne, 1963), pp. 111-14.

8. Evidently leaning heavily on the old waiter's statement "and man was a nothing too," Joseph Gabriel sees *nada* from a Sartrian perspective. In *Being and Nothingness,* Sartre posits that the human self ("pour soi") is by its very nature a "nothing" with only the possibility of becoming "something." Although I claim no direct influence, in most of his stories Hemingway seems to be operating under the Kierkegaardian and Heideggerian senses of *nada* as an external "force." He does appear to be more Sartrian, however, in "The Short Happy Life of Francis Macomber" and "The Snows of Kilimanjaro"; I will treat the consequences when discussing those tales.

9. "Ernest Hemingway: A Critical Essay," in *Ernest Hemingway: Five Decades of Criticism,* ed. Linda Wagner (East Lansing: Michigan State Univ. Press, 1974), p. 214.

10. *Irrational Man* (Garden City, N.Y.: Doubleday, 1958), p. 284. Carlos Baker seems to come closest to my viewpoint in *Hemingway: The Writer as Artist.* He sees a rather explicit appearance of *nada* in "Now I Lay Me" and connects it generally with the idea of "not home," a significant image in the short stories and novels alike. See especially pp. 133 ff.

11. See Frederick J. Hoffman, "No Beginning and No End: Hemingway and Death," *Essays in Criticism,* 3 (Jan. 1953), 73-84, and Robert Penn Warren, "Ernest Hemingway," in *Ernest Hemingway: Five Decades of Criticism,* pp. 75-103.

12. Without dealing directly with *nada,* Young traces Nick's initiation and the frequent refusals of initiation in *Ernest Hemingway: A Reconsideration* (New York: Harcourt, 1966), pp. 29-55.

13. *Hemingway: The Writer's Art of Self-Defense* (Minneapolis: Univ. of Minnesota Press, 1969), p. 130.

14. For more information on their versions of nothingness and the existential "authentication" of

the self, see Kierkegaard's *Either/Or,* trans. D. Swenson and W. Lowrie (1843; rpt. Princeton, N.J.: Princeton Univ. Press, 1944), and Heidegger's *Being and Time,* trans. J. Macquarrie and E. Robinson (1927; rpt. London: SCM Press, 1962).

15. "The Logic of Confusion," p. 542. See also John Hagopian's discussion of the young waiter's limited sensitivity to the word *nothing* in "Tidying Up Hemingway's 'A Clean, Well-Lighted Place,'" *Studies in Short Fiction,* 1(1964), 141-47.

16. "Character, Irony, and Resolution in 'A Clean, Well-Lighted Place,'" *American Literature,* 42 (1970), 78. Reacting to Hemingway's own claim that he often omitted the real ending of his stories, Bennett proceeds to speculate that the omitted ending here is the fact that the young waiter's wife has indeed left him, presumably for the soldier who passes by the window of the café.

17. Delmore Schwartz expanded on this idea in his discussion of "Cross-Country Snow" in "The Fiction of Ernest Hemingway":

    Skiing and activities like it give the self a sense of intense individuality, mastery and freedom. In contrast, those activities which link the self with other beings and are necessary to modern civilization not only fail to provide any such self-realization but very often hinder it. The individual feels trapped in the identity assigned him by birth, social convention, economic necessity; he feels that this identity conceals his real self; and the sense that he is often only an anonymous part of the social mass makes him feel unreal.

    See *Selected Essays of Delmore Schwartz,* ed. Donald Dike and David Zucker (Chicago: Univ. of Chicago Press, 1970), p. 257.

18. Tillich distinguishes between the three forms of "existential" anxiety (of death, meaninglessness, and condemnation), which "belong to existence as such and not to an abnormal state of mind," and "pathological" anxiety, which represents an escape into neurosis, in *The Courage To Be* (New Haven, Conn.: Yale Univ. Press, 1952), pp. 64-70.

19. In using this term, Kaplan underscores the unintelligent natural violence, the concentrated destructiveness of the bull. See *The Passive Voice* (Athens: Ohio Univ. Press, 1966), p. 106.

    There are many who see Garcia, and the old man as well, as representations of the Hemingway "code hero" precisely because of their dignity in the face of potentially catastrophic external circumstances. These critics, and Kaplan is one, point to Garcia in particular because as a bullfighter, he is in constant touch with danger yet maintains a certain grace by virtue of his role in the bullfight, a ritualistic form of order imposed upon the chaos of life.

    Granted, both the old man and Garcia display admirable courage, but they lack the firm internal order I see necessary for the true Hemingway hero. As his desperate attempt at suicide and very unsteady balance suggest, the old man's place of refuge is now totally external. Garcia's form has also eroded to the point that he can hardly be considered an exemplar of dignity. There is a certain desperate foolhardiness in his stubborn insistence on making a comeback and his unrealistic hope for "an even break" after his recent disasters in the ring; as his friend Zurito admits, these are signs of empty pride. On the other hand, the picador himself, though aged, is still a thoroughly professional craftsman. Thus, I agree with Arthur Waldheim's view in *A Reader's Guide to Ernest Hemingway* (New York: Farrar, 1972) that Zurito, along with the old waiter, is much more fully representative of the "code hero."

20. Edward Stone, "Hemingway's Mr. Frazer: From Revolution to Radio," *Journal of Modern Literature,* 1 (1971), 380.

21. *The Hidden God* (New Haven, Conn.: Yale Univ. Press, 1963), p. 6.

22. See Malcolm Cowley, "Nightmare and Ritual in Hemingway," in *Ernest Hemingway: A Collection of Critical Essays,* ed. Robert Weeks (Englewood Cliffs, N.J.: Prentice-Hall, 1962), pp. 40-52; and Sheridan Baker, "Hemingway's 'Big Two-Hearted River,'" in *The Short Stories of Ernest Hemingway,* ed. Jackson Benson (Durham, N.C.: Duke Univ. Press, 1975), pp. 150-59. In addition to the ritual series in the tale, Baker finds a suggestion of desperate defensiveness against a shadowy threat in the image of Nick's tent, "stretched as tightly as his own state of mind, equally protective in its static tension" (pp. 151-52).

23. "'The Snows of Kilimanjaro': Harry's Second Chance," *Studies in Short Fiction,* 5 (1967), 58.

24. Buber's most detailed consideration of this ethic is in *I and Thou,* 2nd ed. 1923, rpt. trans. R. Smith (New York: Scribner's, 1958).

    Randall Stewart has also noted the old waiter's proclivity for compassion and sees it as crucial both to the clean, well-lighted place and to the tale's quasi-Christian ritual:

    The café is a place where congenial souls may meet. The older waiter, particularly, has a sympathetic understanding of the elderly gentleman's problem. Living in a clean, well-lighted place does not mean solitary withdrawal so long as there are others who also prefer such a place. One can belong to a communion of saints, however small.

    See *American Literature and Christian Doctrine* (Baton Rouge: Louisiana State Univ. Press, 1958), p. 135. See also Richard Hoving's discussion of the need for communion in *Hemingway: The Inward Terrain* (Seattle: Univ. of Washington Press, 1968), p. 25.

25. Because of her faith in the transcendent forces "A Clean, Well-Lighted Place" negates and her naive ambition for sainthood, Sister Cecilia seems an apt equivalent for the unrealistic young waiter. Indeed, as Paul Rodgers has pointed out in "Levels of Irony in Hemingway's 'The Gambler, the Nun, and the Radio,'" *Studies in Short Fiction,* 7 (1970), 446, her blindness—also the young waiter's defect—is suggested by the very etymology of her name (from the Latin *caecus,* or "blind").

Upon closer examination, two other stories reveal a similar triad, "The Undefeated" has its own version of the old waiter (Zurito) and the old man (Garcia), but it also has a young waiter in the person of the young bullfight critic. He too neither empathizes nor sympathizes with the victim's plight and thus engages in facile criticism of him. Moreover, like the young waiter, he is far more interested in a midnight tryst; consequently, he too hurries away, leaving the old man figure to his fate. In "The Battler" (1925), the naive Nick Adams meets only confusion in his encounter with the despairing, jumbled Ad Francis (old man), and fails to fully appreciate the compassionate efforts on both his and Francis's behalf of the eternally watchful Bugs (old waiter).

26. *Time of Need,* p. 94.

27. *Ernest Hemingway: A Life Story* (New York: Scribner's, 1969), p. 305.

28. Rovit convincingly argues that *nada* was both a challenge to and a stimulus for Hemingway's art in *Ernest Hemingway,* pp. 168 ff. See also Jackson Benson, *Hemingway: The Writer's Art of Self-Defense* on this point.

29. *Death in the Afternoon* (New York: Scribner's, 1932), p. 278.

30. See Ihab Hassan's illuminating discussion of Hemingway's literary pointillism in "Valor Against the Void," in *The Dismemberment of Orpheus: Toward a Postmodern Literature* (New York: Oxford, 1971), pp. 80-110.

Tony Tanner makes a similar point about the Hemingway style in *The Reign of Wonder* (New York: Cambridge Univ. Press, 1956), pp. 241-50. In Tanner's terms, Hemingway characteristically resisted disorder by erecting a verbal "cordon sanitaire" around each individual image, thus creating any number of miniature, aesthetic clean, well-lighted places.

31. *The Great Tradition: An Interpretation of American Literature Since the Civil War,* 3rd ed. (Chicago: Quadrangle, 1969), p. 277.

David Kerner (essay date 1979)

SOURCE: "The Foundation of the True Text of 'A Clean, Well-Lighted Place,'" in *Fitzgerald/Hemingway Annual,* 1979, pp. 279-300.

[*In the following essay, Kerner determines the possible sources for Hemingway's confusing and unconventional use of dialogue and urges a restoration of the author's original text.*]

It is almost sixty years since Hemingway silently patented a small change in the way we arrange dialogue; but many readers still refuse to acknowledge the innovation, so that we have had, over the past twenty years, not only twenty conflicting articles on the dialogue of **"A Clean, Well-Lighted Place"** but even the publisher's unwarranted emendation of the text. Like the justice of the peace at the end of Faulkner's "Spotted Horses," we want to cry, "I can't stand no more! This court's adjourned! Adjourned!" The latest misleading testimony, from both sides of the North Atlantic, is that the "error" has been traced to the pencil manuscript: inserting a one-line speech, Hemingway gave it to the wrong waiter. Hans-Joachim Kann suggests we advise students to ignore the insertion as obvious filler, intended merely to restore the conventional alternating pattern for two speakers.[1] But that convention is what Hemingway's innovation modifies: at least twenty-five times—in five novels and seven stories, not counting **"A Clean, Well-Lighted Place"**—Hemingway deliberately (and sometimes confusingly) assigned consecutive, separate speeches to a single speaker. The manuscript of **"A Clean, Well-Lighted Place"** cannot be interpreted without an awareness of this unconventional practice, which removes the alleged inconsistency. (This solution was proposed by Otto Reinert the year the controversy began and was later amplified by Scott MacDonald.)[2]

Since the innovation antedates the manuscript, the genetic approach must go back to the moment Hemingway wrote the following lines in **"The Three-Day Blow"**:[3]

"That's right," said Nick. "I guess he's a better guy than Walpole."

"Oh, he's a better guy, all right," Bill said.

"But Walpole's a better writer."

"I don't know," Nick said. "Chesterton's a classic."

There are only two speakers here, so at first we suspect that the third speech was mistakenly indented (since the smooth continuity does not suggest that a line was dropped); but the probability that exactly this sort of mistaken indention occurs twenty-seven times in so careful a writer as Hemingway is very slight, especially when from the start he took pains to be obvious in his insistence that a character be permitted to pause, then speak again, without the author's having to label the pause—as in **"The Undefeated,"** which Hemingway wrote in 1924.

"I was going great till I got hurt," Manuel offered.

"You ought to have seen me, Manos," Manuel said, reproachfully.

And in **"Fifty Grand,"** written in 1925:

"That was a fine bunch out here this afternoon," he said. "They don't take any chances, those two."

Then a little later, "Well," he says, "they're right. What the hell's the good in taking chances?"

"Don't you want another, Jerry?" he said. "Come on, drink along with me."[4]

By first using "Then a little later" and then omitting it for the third paragraph, Hemingway was educating his readers.

But even with these early examples, the genetic approach has not quite reached its goal. One reason that readers have been unwilling to accept Otto Reinert's solution is their belief that Hemingway's innovation is not to be found in any other writer—as though, if it can't be shown where Hemingway learned the trick, he never did it.[5] The fact is that the "innovation"—in its original, modest form—is at least a hundred years old.[6] On 28 December 1921, a week or two before the first draft of **"The Three-Day Blow,"** Hemingway had joined Sylvia Beach's rental library, where he "started with Turgenev and took the two volumes of *A Sportsman's Sketches*" (*A Moveable Feast*, p. 36).[7] These volumes were the Constance Garnett translation, where, in "The Hamlet of Shtchigri District," Hemingway found this:

'Honoured sir!' he cried, 'I am of the opinion that life on earth's only worth living, as a rule, for original people; . . . but I am not to be reckoned among them!'

'And yet,' he went on, after a brief silence, 'in my youth what expectations I aroused! . . .'

And this:

'And now,' he went on warmly, '. . . The beam is still there in my barn, to which I repeatedly made up my mind to hang myself!'

'Some pears,' he began again, after a brief pause, 'need to lie in an underground cellar for a time. . . .'[8]

Garnett's back-to-back juxtaposition of end and opening quotation marks, with indention, for a single speaker appears twice also in "A Living Relic" (II, 239, 246) and once more in "The Peasant Proprietor Ovsyanikov" (I, 96). Did Hemingway immediately borrow—and extend—Garnett's unconventional indention? All we know is that the new arrangement was in the version of **"The Three-Day Blow"** that he wrote between the spring of 1923 and September 1924; and after reading Turgenev, Hemingway tells us, he went on to read "the Constance Garnett translations of Tolstoi" (p. 130). In *Anna Karenina* (one of his favorite books) Hemingway would have found the following passage, in which there are only two speakers:

"If only Countess Marya Borissova were Minister of War . . . ," said a gray-headed, little old man in a gold-embroidered uniform, addressing a tall, handsome maid of honor. . . .

"And me among the adjutants," said the maid of honor, smiling.

"You have an appointment already. . . ."

"Good-day, prince!" said the little old man to a man who came up to him.

And near the end of the novel:

"I can never see these collecting-boxes unmoved while I've money in my pocket," he said. "And how about today's telegrams? Fine chaps those Montenegrins!"

"You don't say so!" he cried, when the princess told him that Vronsky was going by this train.[9]

It is unlikely that Hemingway read these translations without noticing a single instance of Garnett's unconventional practice of pointing with indention. *In Our Time*, which Hemingway finished in 1923, shows him experimenting with every style of pointing dialogue: he uses inverted commas, and he omits them; he uses the European dash, and he omits it. Could he, then, have missed in Garnett a new style of pointing that he found attractive? Even as a beginner, Hemingway was so concerned with the ways typography can affect meaning that he would go "to a printer's shop in the late evening to learn how to set up type so as to know exactly how his manuscripts, to the last comma, would look on the printed page."[10] And can one believe that Hemingway arrived at his innovation while reading Garnett's translations, which he admired, and yet never noticed it in her own practice?

In fact, the difference between her practice and the first instance of Hemingway's, in **"The Three-Day Blow,"** permits us to reconstruct, with some reasonableness, the process of Hemingway's inspiration. He evidently wondered why Tolstoy and Turgenev should have felt obliged to explain that the same speaker was continuing after a pause or interruption. The convention was at fault in fostering the notion that two speakers always alternate in actual conversation. That Hemingway acknowledged the effectiveness of the conventional English multi-paragraph pointing for a continuing speech, we see in Frances Clyne's diatribe at the end of chapter 6 of *The Sun Also Rises*; but if a speaker pauses between consecutive speeches, why must the novelist throw in a dead expository phrase, breaking the rhythm of the dialogue, merely because a typographical metronome has conditioned the reader not to expect a certain perfectly natural irregularity? Hemingway decided to recondition his readers: by only implying the pause he would jolt them into an appreciation of the need to modify the convention.

But can we be sure it was Garnett's practice alone that inspired Hemingway's? Might he have found it in other translators whom he had read before 1922?[11] In the United States, too, he could have read Gertrude Stein's *Three Lives* (1909), where, at the very beginning, he would have found this:

"You bad dog," Anna said to Peter that night, "you bad dog."

"Peter was the father of those pups," the good Anna explained to Miss Mathilda. . . .

But nothing before **"Up in Michigan,"** which Hemingway wrote in 1922, suggests the influence of Gertrude Stein; and perhaps he delayed meeting her—he waited until March 1922—because he had not read *Three Lives*. Similarly—despite reasonable conjectures—Hemingway seems not to have read the excerpts from *Ulysses* that had run in *The Little Review.*[12] In "Episode XI," in the August 1919 number, which the post office did not seize, we find this:

> —Sweet tea Miss Kennedy having poured with milk plugged with two ears with little fingers.
>
> —No, don't, she cried.
>
> —I won't listen, she cried.
>
> (p. 44)

And this:

> —Here's fortune, Blazes [Boylan] said.
>
> He pitched a broad coin down. Coin rang.
>
> —Hold on, said Lenehan, till I . . .
>
> —Fortune, he wished, lifting his bubbled ale.
>
> —Sceptre will win in a canter, he said.
>
> —I plunged a bit, said Boylan winking and drinking.[13]
>
> (p. 50)

But Hemingway's fondness for his innovation may have been due in part to his belated discovery of these passages in *Ulysses.*[14] He probably realized that here he was seeing the unconventional Russian punctuation whose effect Garnett had captured in English pointing.[15] He would, I suspect, have known by this time that in Russian, as in French, there is only an indention, without a dash, when the same speaker is continuing; an indention with a dash indicates a change of speaker.[16] Joyce, like Tolstoy and Turgenev, was using an indention with a dash for the consecutive speeches of a single speaker; and like the Russians, Joyce identified that speaker every time. Did Hemingway smile to see the bold Joyce so timid a follower?[17] And did Joyce's timidity encourage Hemingway to display his own virtuosity? In **"The Three-Day Blow"** we have the only instance of Hemingway's innovation in 1922-1924; then, in 1925-1926, he gave us seven new ones. In **"The Three-Day Blow"** he had merely indented; in 1925 he risked Garnett's juxtaposition of end and opening quotation marks, and he did it without identifying the speaker. Was this flowering due only to the self-confidence brought by the publication in 1925 of **In Our Time**? Or—a third possibility—was the new pattern of the innovation in *The Sun Also Rises* influenced by E. M. Forster? In *A Passage to India* Mrs. Moore speaks first, to her son and his fiancee, in this exchange:

> "One knows people's characters, as you call them. . . . I have heard both English and Indians speak well of him, and I felt it isn't the sort of thing he would do."
>
> "Feeble, mother, feeble."

> "Most feeble."
>
> "And most inconsiderate to Adela."
>
> Adela said: "It would be so appalling if I was wrong. I should take my own life."[18]

This novel came out at the beginning of June 1924, while the manuscript of **In Our Time** was still in Hemingway's hands, but no evidence has turned up that Hemingway read Forster's book that summer.[19] In any case, one cannot expect to be able to trace every step in the genesis of Hemingway's disputed practice; what matters here is that the precedents supply an international foundation for the "violation" that establishes the true text of **"A Clean, Well-Lighted Place."**

Given this historical background, Hemingway's disputed practice no longer seems anomalous. But the other reason Scribner's 1965 emendation has had support is that no one had shown yet that Hemingway's innovation is to be found elsewhere in his work.[20] In 1973 Scott MacDonald identified nine instances. Some of these, and some of the fifteen others I have found, are especially useful for an understanding of the "inconsistency" in **"A Clean, Well-Lighted Place."**[21] In *The Sun Also Rises* Jake Barnes advises Brett to write Cohn that she and Mike are joining Jake and Bill in Pamplona; Cohn would then realize he should stay away.

> I did not see Brett again until the night of the 24th of June.
>
> "Did you hear from Cohn?"
>
> "Rather. He's keen about it."
>
> "My God!"
>
> "I thought it was rather odd myself."
>
> "Says he can't wait to see me."
>
> (p. 86)

This exchange occurs on the page after one of the passages MacDonald cites, and the two other instances he finds in this novel appear on a single page. There are also two on one page in *Across the River and into the Trees,* two in **"The Battler"** (cited by MacDonald), and two in **"Homage to Switzerland,"** as well as two in **"A Clean, Well-Lighted Place."** Surely it is no coincidence that so many of the twenty-seven instances of the violation come in pairs: discovery of the same breach of convention assures us—as Hemingway learned from Turgenev—that the first one is not a typo. And one of MacDonald's other examples in *The Sun Also Rises*—again illustrating the pattern in which the speaker is not identified either time (the reverse of the most obvious pattern)—provides a precedent for the elusiveness of the violations in **"A Clean, Well-Lighted Place"**:

> Bill was in my room reading the paper.
>
> "See Mike?"

"Yes."

"Let's go and eat."

"I won't eat down-stairs with that German head waiter. He was damned snotty when I was getting Mike up-stairs."

"He was snotty to us too."

(p. 218)

Since Jake knows that Bill brought Mike back to the hotel, Bill must be the first speaker; but we will never know whether it's Jake or Bill who says, "Let's go and eat." Even more inscrutable, perhaps, is a passage in *Across the River and into the Trees,* where the waiter begins:

"We don't have fiascos. This is a good hotel, you know. It comes in bottles."

"I forgot," the Colonel said. "Do you remember when it cost thirty centesimi the liter?"

"And we would throw the empty fiascos at the station guards from the troop trains?"

"And we would throw all the left over grenades away and bounce them down the hillside coming back from the Grappa?"

"And they would think there was a break-through when they would see the bursts and you never shaved, and we wore the *fiamme nere* on the grey, open jackets with the grey sweaters?"

"And I drank grappa and could not even feel the taste?"

"We must have been tough then," the Colonel said.

(pp. 120-121)

But the most persuasive example is the one in *To Have and Have Not* whose pattern parallels that of the crucial exchange in **"A Clean, Well-Lighted Place."** The speakers are Harry Morgan and the lawyer he calls Bee-lips.

"I'm going to get out," Bee-lips said.

"When are you going to get the boat out?"

"Tonight."

"Who's going to help you?"

"You."

"Where are you going to put her?"

"Where I always put her."

(pp. 109-110)

On first reading, we think Bee-lips speaks the third, fifth, and seventh lines. But the boat is Harry's, so the last line must be his; this inference is confirmed when Harry says, within the page, "I'm going to put her up in the creek right where it crosses the road"; and Harry, being the owner, is the one who would know when "to get the boat out." So the second speech, as well as the first, belongs to Bee-lips, despite the indention; and the third, fifth, and seventh speeches are Harry's, reversing our first reading.

Hemingway forces us to reread this passage and reassign the speeches. The passage illuminates what Hemingway had done four years earlier in **"A Clean, Well-Lighted Place,"** where the dialogue containing the alleged inconsistency begins with the younger waiter.

"He's drunk now," he said.

"He's drunk every night."

"What did he want to kill himself for?"

"How should I know."

Unaware of Hemingway's innovation, we naturally think the second speech is the older waiter's, and the following question the younger waiter's; so the fourth line establishes the older waiter as the one telling of the suicide attempt. But a few lines later the older waiter says, "You said she cut him down." We are stopped short—exactly as in the passage above from *To Have and Have Not.* Forced to retrace our steps, we surmise (after much confusion) that at the beginning of this dialogue—

"He's drunk now," he said.

"He's drunk every night."

—the younger waiter speaks both lines: the pattern of these lines duplicates exactly the initially confusing lines:

"I'm going to get out," Bee-lips said.

"When are you going to get the boat out?"

and, from **"The Three-Day Blow,"** Hemingway's first use of his invention:

"Oh, he's a better guy, all right," Bill said.

"But Walpole's a better writer."[22]

What distinguishes the innovation in **"A Clean, Well-Lighted Place"** is that the second instance of it that turns up does more than assure us that we have read the first instance correctly—it asserts itself in its own right as indispensable to the dialogue's coherence.[23]

Readers who have accepted Scribners's emendation will still want to know how Warren Bennett's argument for it, based on the manuscript evidence, can be refuted. Here are the lines containing the alleged error, from page 4 of the manuscript:

"He's lonely. I'm not lonely. I have a wife waiting in the bed for me."

"He had a wife once too."

"A wife would be no good to him now."

"You can't tell. He might be better with a wife."

"His niece looks after him."

"I know. You said she cut him down."

Bennett argues that Hemingway—when he added "You said she cut him down" to the earlier insertion, "I know"— "probably thought" that the immediately preceding speech was the older waiter's since the older waiter is the one who has been telling of the suicide attempt (in Bennett's opinion), and that Hemingway, "one may conjecture," was still suffering from the "confusion" that had caused him to omit a speaker in the alternating sequence (pp. 620, 622). Mistakenly thinking, therefore, that it was the younger waiter who was saying "I know," Hemingway added "You said she cut him down" to "I know." So Hagopian and Scribners are right in assigning "You said she cut him down" to the younger waiter—by adding it to "His niece looks after him"—because Hemingway meant to give the line to the younger waiter.

But Hemingway could not have thought that "His niece looks after him" was the older waiter's line, since it contradicts the immediately preceding speech, "You can't tell. He might be better with a wife," which indisputably belongs to the older waiter. So Hemingway, perfectly aware that he had inserted "I know" as the "missing" speech of the older waiter, added the explanation "You said she cut him down." This new line—far from being either the filler Hans-Joachim Kann finds it or the redundancy Bennett calls it (p. 622n.)—is, of course, the one line in the story proving that the younger waiter has been telling of the suicide attempt. (The line became redundant only when Scribners assigned it to *him*.) Furthermore, the two insertions support Hemingway's characterization. To the younger waiter's argument "His niece looks after him," the older waiter is made to reply dryly, "I know [how well she 'looks after him': the old man wants to die, and she won't let him]. You said she cut him down. [I said, just now, 'He might be better with a wife,' because you had already made clear to me how 'his niece looks after him']"[24] The unsupported "I know," which the gratuitous emendation leaves the older waiter, is uncharacteristically fatuous.

If Hemingway had made the alleged error, we can be sure he would have caught it. On the same page, he at first wrote:

> "This old man is clean. He drinks without spilling. Even now, drunk."
>
> "I wish he would go home. . . ."

Revising, Hemingway added two lines:

> "Even now, drunk. Look at him."
>
> "I don't want to look at him. I wish he would go home. . . ."

How could Hemingway have been attentive to this small break in continuity and have been suffering a few lines earlier from the inattention Bennett imagines?

Moreover, that Hemingway was not confused but at first meant to follow "His niece looks after him" with "I wouldn't want to be that old [and have to be looked after by a nursemaid]. An old man is a nasty thing"—without an intervening reply—can be surmised not only from our antecedent awareness of this unconventional practice of Hemingway's but also from an earlier instance of it in this manuscript: Hemingway originally juxtaposed the lines

> "I never get into bed before three o'clock."
>
> "He should have killed himself last week."
>
> (pp. 2-3)

—both speeches belonging to the younger waiter; later, Hemingway ran the two lines together. In the disputed passage, he inserted "I know. You said she cut him down" when he decided that here he had to end his riddling refusal to tell us which waiter was saying what—the second insertion went hand-in-hand with other late clarifications of identity: "the other unhurried waiter" on page 5 and "waiter who was in a hurry" on page 6.

The final flaw in the notion of Hemingway's "confusion" here is the implicit charge that Hemingway was again confused when he read the typescript and the *Scribner's Magazine* proofs and whenever he reread the published story.

Bennett does not open his case with Hemingway's crucial insertion; proceeding chronologically, Bennett argues that "You said she cut him down" must be made consistent with the beginning of the passage. But since the later line is the one that tells us which waiter knows of the suicide attempt, any earlier line that at first seemed to indicate otherwise must be reconstrued. The logic of this order— the technique of retroactive correction imposed by Hemingway's innovation—is demonstrated conclusively by the passage quoted above from *To Have and Have Not*. All the same, we have to meet the rest of Bennett's argument on his own ground. He quotes from the manuscript, showing two deletions and one insertion:

> "He's stewed drunk every night."
>
> "What did he want to kill himself for?"
>
> "Christ "How should I know?"

Because Hemingway—after originally indenting "'He's drunk now,' he said"—drew a line attaching this speech to the end of the preceding paragraph, and because he had indented and had at first written "stewed" in the second speech of the exchange (in contrast to "drunk" in the first speech), Bennett argues that Hemingway's original intention was to assign "He's stewed every night" to the older waiter; the question following would then establish that the older waiter is the one telling of the suicide attempt (p. 619). To this argument three objections may be made.

First, Bennett only assumes that the indention of "'He's drunk now,' he said" in the published story is an error. Since *Scribner's Magazine* did not set the story from the pencil manuscript, one may assume, instead, that Hemingway changed his mind about the run-on line. After all, there are other legitimate differences between the manuscript and the published version: "waiting in the bed" becomes "waiting in bed"; "It was no fear" (on page 9) is changed to "It was not fear"; and where the manuscript, on page 3, says clearly that the waiter "walked out to the old man's table," the published story has "marched." So, knowing that the older waiter's line "You said she cut him down" would be surprising, Hemingway must have been paying careful attention to his management of the ambiguity responsible for the surprise; and he could not have failed to correct an unwanted indention in "'He's drunk now,' he said," the first of the two lines creating the ambiguity. Originally, Hemingway meant the younger waiter to say this first line and then sit down; the "he said" was clear then, following immediately "The waiter took the bottle back inside the café"; and the implied sitting down would explain the pause calling for the second indention.[25] Then Hemingway decided to insert "He sat down at the table with his colleague again" before the first speech, and he drew the run-on line to make clear that the "he said" does not refer to "his colleague." The second indention now implied only a pause, without action—a pause that Hemingway's innovation sufficiently explains. But in typing, or going over the typescript, Hemingway evidently decided that a single indention here would indicate, even to him, a new speaker; *two* indentions for a single speaker was what Hemingway had educated his best readers to be on the lookout for. A pleased confession of the trap laid for unwary readers of this most delicate instance of his still unrecognized innovation may be detected in the tone of Hemingway's dismissal of the query Judson Jerome sent him in 1956 about the "'messy' dialogue" in the story: "oh so sorry to disappoint."[26] In any case, why should Bennett find the run-on line sacred when he goes so far as to take "You said she cut him down" away from the speaker Hemingway never stopped assigning it to, from 1933 to 1956?

Similarly, if, by Bennett's own argument, Hemingway would hardly have used "stewed" if the younger waiter were still speaking, then as soon as Hemingway changed "stewed" to "drunk," he may well have been suggesting that the younger waiter *is* still speaking. The younger waiter likes to say things twice: "He should have killed himself last week" is followed by "you should have killed yourself last week"; "I never get into bed before three o'clock" is said twice; "I wish he would go home" is said twice; pressed to amplify "plenty of money," the younger waiter bullishly repeats, "He's got plenty"; and "You'll be drunk" turns into "He's drunk now" and "He's drunk every night."

Third: the deleted "stewed," "Christ," and "tail" (in "What does it matter if he gets his tail? what he's after?") do force us to assign all three speeches to one waiter—but why not the younger waiter? First of all, can we, with Bennett, hear—in the wit and longing of the older waiter's parody of the Lord's Prayer and the Hail Mary—an "ultimate extension" of the "tough 'realism'" of the banal "stewed," "Christ," and "tail" (p. 623)? Could Hemingway

have given "stewed" to the older waiter, when the word is pejorative, intensifying the preceding "He's drunk now"? Is the rebuff "Christ how should I know?"—a crude, impatient denial of empathy with the old man—characteristic of the older waiter, who sensitively and patiently wishes to explain things to his young colleague? And last, may not "tail" show that the soldier's urgency confirms the machismo of the younger waiter, who boasts of having a wife "waiting" in bed? The soldier is in a hurry, like the younger waiter, who "marches." Krebs, in **"Soldier's Home,"** thinks, "a fellow boasted that he could not get along without girls, that he had to have them all the time, that he could not go to sleep without them. That was all a lie"; similarly, the older waiter may wonder whether the soldier still on the street may not end up paying too much for his whistle—"tail" is not a wife. In **"The Gambler, the Nun, and the Radio,"** Mr. Frazer includes "sexual intercourse" among the opiums of "some of the best of the people," but he does not include love: one may distinguish between an opium and a clean, well-lighted place. Would it be more reasonable to find the older waiter condoning the young soldier's desperation as much as the old man's?[27] Hemingway, to make his readers think, deleted the three banal words, which would have mechanically identified the younger waiter.

We are left, then, with the unprecedented spectacle of a gratuitous emendation that defies the author's endorsement of his text, the confirmation of the text by the manuscript, and the text's consistency with a fairly common practice of Hemingway's (the genesis of which we have been able to trace, more or less), not to mention the corresponding consistency in characterization and dramatic development. Furthermore, since Charles Scribner, Jr., claims that in the posthumously published manuscripts Hemingway more than once "skipped a beat" in dialogue between unidentified speakers (Hurley, p. 82n.), scholars will have to compare these passages with the edited versions, to make sure the publisher has not presented us with other silent "corrections" of Hemingway's innovation.

Besides restoring Hemingway's text, retraction of the unwarranted emendation would grant his innovation official recognition at last. Not everyone has dismissed the device. We can see its usefulness in Bernard Malamud's "The Magic Barrel"[28] and in two post-Hemingway translations in passages where the practice was not used in the original Russian;[29] and Faulkner borrowed it almost at once—we find it three times in *The Sound and the Fury,* most notably as follows:

> "You know how come your name Benjamin now." Versh said. "Your mamma too proud for you. What mammy say."

> "You be still there and let me dry my legs off." Versh said. "Or you know what I'll do. I'll skin your rinktum."[30]

No one, probably, has or will come closer than Forster did to the extreme form Hemingway confused us with, but the transparent unidentified reversal of the conventional alternation of speakers is worth borrowing, as the examples prove; and Hemingway's dramatic underground resistance to the convention—and the torture that at least one of his texts has suffered as a result—dictate that we not only recognize the innovation but name it after him.

Notes

1. "Perpetual Confusion in 'A Clean, Well-Lighted Place': The Manuscript Evidence," *Fitzgerald/Hemingway Annual 1977,* pp. 115-118. The other new witness, who will be examined below, is Warren Bennett, in "The Manuscript and the Dialogue of 'A Clean, Well-Lighted Place,'" *American Literature,* 50 (January 1979), 613-624. In his "The New Text of 'A Clean, Well-Lighted Place,'" *Literary Half-Yearly,* 14, i (1973), Bennett wrote, "The new text is by Hagopian and Scribner's" (p. 124)—that is, not by Hemingway; but the manuscript seems to have persuaded Bennett that the emended text *is* Hemingway's. The emendation was suggested by John V. Hagopian, in "Tidying up Hemingway's 'A Clean, Well-Lighted Place,'" *Studies in Short Fiction,* 1 (Winter 1964), 140-146.

2. Otto Reinert, "Hemingway's Waiters Once More," *College English,* 20 (May 1959), 417-418; Scott MacDonald, "The Confusing Dialogue in Hemingway's 'A Clean, Well-Lighted Place': A Final Word?" *Studies in American Fiction,* 1 (Spring 1973), 93-101.

3. Hemingway first wrote "The Three-Day Blow" in January 1922, but this version was in the suitcase stolen from Hadley in December, and we have no date for the version in the manuscript of *In Our Time,* which Hemingway sent to New York "towards the end of September" 1924. See *A Moveable Feast* (New York: Scribners, 1964), pp. 5, 73-75; and Carlos Baker, *Ernest Hemingway: A Life Story* (New York: Scribners, 1969), pp. 103, 539, 580, and *Hemingway: The Writer as Artist,* 4th ed. (Princeton: Princeton University Press, 1972), p. 352.

4. *The Fifth Column and the First Forty-Nine Stories* (New York: Scribners, 1938), pp. 217, 342, 409; later page references to this volume will accompany the quotations. Ten years after "Fifty Grand," in *To Have and Have Not* (New York: Scribners, 1937), we find Hemingway taking the same pains to make obvious the first (p. 57) of the innovation's three appearances in the book; and in *Across the River and into the Trees* (New York: Scribners, 1950), again we find this pedagogical technique—three obvious instances come first (pp. 70, 80, 97), the third of which is conventional, like the one in "The Undefeated" (so that I exclude both of these from the total count of twenty-seven), and the seventh instance too is obvious (p. 142).

5. The British critic David Lodge has pointed to "the implausibility of Hemingway's having deliberately violated a well-established typographical convention in a way for which there is no precedent elsewhere in his work (nor, one might add, anywhere else)," in "Hemingway's Clean, Well-Lighted, Puzzling Place," *Essays in Criticism,* 21 (January 1971), 44, rpt. in *The Novelist at the Crossroads* (Ithaca, N.Y.: Cornell University Press, 1971), pp. 184-202.

6. The intention behind Hemingway's innovation is perfectly clear in a nineteenth-century instance he never saw—a passage in the manuscript of *The Way of All Flesh,* which Samuel Butler set aside in 1884 with the instruction "Revised, finally corrected and ready for the press without being further looked at":

   "I can afford the luxury of a quiet unobtrusive life of self-indulgence," said he laughing, "and I mean to have it."

   "You know I like writing," he added, after a pause of some minutes. . . .

   This passage, in the only text published before 1964, concludes "'and I mean to have it. You know I like writing,' he added after a pause of some minutes. . . ." See *Ernest Pontifex; or The Way of All Flesh,* ed. Daniel F. Howard (Boston: Houghton Mifflin, 1964), pp. xxiii, 336; and the Streatfeild edition as published by the Modern Library, p. 531.

7. Noel Fitch, "Ernest Hemingway—c/o Shakespeare and Company," *Fitzgerald/Hemingway Annual 1977,* pp. 158, 162.

8. London: William Heinemann, 1906; II, 122-123, 134-135. The title Hemingway uses is Garnett's, and the two-volume translation Hemingway borrowed in later years was Garnett's (Fitch, pp. 165, 175, 181 n.3). Sherwood Anderson, who may have introduced Hemingway to *A Sportsman's Sketches,* always refers to the book as *Annals of a Sportsman* (F. A. Abbott's translation [New York: Holt, 1885]); Isabel F. Hapgood's title is *Memoirs of a Sportsman* (New York: Scribners, 1907).

9. New York: The Modern Library, 1950, pp. 604, 901. This is the original Garnett translation (London: Heinemann, 1901); the last speech in the first passage begins a three-line omission from the revised Modern Library translation (1965). Garnett's end quotation marks and indention are to be found also in Isabel Hapgood's translation (New York: Scribners, 1899) and the first Louise and Aylmer Maude translation (London: Oxford University Press, 1918).

10. Bryher, *The Heart to Artemis* (New York: Harcourt, Brace & World, 1962), p. 213. In *In Our Time,* see chapters 6-8, 11, 13, 15, and "L'Envoi." "On the Quai at Smyrna" was added in 1930.

11. In *A Moveable Feast* Hemingway says to Evan Shipman, "I remember how many times I tried to read *War and Peace* until I got the Constance

Garnett translation" (p. 137); so, since he says he took out *War and Peace* the day he joined Sylvia Beach's library, evidently when he was writing *A Moveable Feast,* he believed he had been reading the Russians before coming to Paris. Garnett's unconventional practice appears in the Hapgood translation of Turgenev's *Fathers and Children* (New York: Scribners, 1907), p. 317, and as early as Eugene Schuyler's translation (New York: Leypoldt & Holt, 1867)—as well as in virtually all the recent translations. In Schuyler the passage goes:

"There is youth!" said Bazarov tranquilly; "but I count on Katerina Sergheivna! She will console you in less than no time."

"Goodbye brother!" he said to Arcadi when he had already climbed into the *telega.* . . .

(p. 223)

12. The Post Office's confiscation of four of the *Little Review* Joyce numbers and the obscenity trial in February 1921 admittedly stimulated Hemingway's appreciation of Joyce; but Hemingway claims that at that time *Ulysses* did not influence him directly—see *Writers at Work: The Paris Review Interviews,* Second Series (New York: Viking, 1963), p. 226.

13. The dashes at the margin follow Joyce's manuscript: see James Joyce, *Ulysses—A Facsimile of the Manuscript* (New York: Octagon, 1975). The passages are pointed the same way in the first Shakespeare and Company edition (pp. 248, 254-255) and the first Random House edition (New York, 1934; pp. 255, 261).

14. We don't know how soon Hemingway read all of *Ulysses.* In the fall of 1923, in Toronto, while he was telling Morley Callaghan, "James Joyce is the greatest writer in the world" (*That Summer in Paris* [New York: Coward-McCann, 1963], p. 28), Hemingway was writing Edmund Wilson that *The Enormous Room* was "the best book published last year that I read" (*The Shores of Light* [New York, 1952; rpt. Vintage, 1961], p. 118).

15. Having learned from Turgenev and Tolstoy that French was the language of the Russian gentry, Hemingway had probably deduced that the Russian practice followed the French. Also, Paris in the early 1920s was full of literate Russian emigres: for example, a White Russian prince preceded Hemingway as a subeditor on *Transatlantic Review,* the first number of which was printed on a Russian press (see Bernard J. Poli, *Ford Madox Ford and the "Transatlantic Review"* [Syracuse, N.Y.: Syracuse University Press, 1967], p. 26); and one friend whom proofreader and typesetter Hemingway could easily have questioned, early in 1924, about the Russian pointing of dialogue is Nathan Asch, who was born in Warsaw in 1902 and attended the Russian Lycee in Paris in 1910-1915.

16. Anyone who has never noticed this can see it in *Red and Black,* trans. Richard M. Adams, who preserves Stendhal's punctuation (New York: Norton, 1969): Book I, chapter 23, and Book II, chapter 1, pp. 122-123, 184. In Chekhov's story "Gooseberries," the translator's omission of end quotation marks while Ivan Ivanich's speech continues through several paragraphs is an accurate rendering of Chekhov's omission of opening dashes.

17. In "The Dead" and *A Portrait of the Artist* Joyce merely substitutes the dash for the opening quotation marks of an obviously continuing speech: he had borrowed the form of the Russians' juxtaposition but robbed it of its point. See the Viking Critical Editions of *Dubliners,* ed. Robert Scholes and A. Walton Litz (New York, 1969), pp. 202-204, 225, and *A Portrait of the Artist as a Young Man,* ed. Chester G. Anderson (1968), pp. 109-111, 117-124, 127-134, 205. In *Ulysses* Joyce changed his system: indention alone, without a dash, introduces the second paragraph of a continuing speech (New York, 1934; pp. 143-144, 186). Judging by Joyce's practice, the six unidentified speeches in six lines on page 21 of *A Portrait* do not anticipate Hemingway's innovation, but one cannot be sure. In January 1907 Joyce had been reading *A Sportsman's Sketches* in French, and he wrote "The Dead" late that summer (*Letters,* ed. Richard Ellmann [New York: Viking, 1966], II, 207, 212, 64); in 1905 he had written his brother that Turgenev is "useful technically" (p. 90).

18. London: Edward Arnold, 1924; pp. 206-207. For month of publication, see P. N. Furbank, *E. M. Forster: A Life* (New York: Harcourt Brace Jovanovich, 1978), II, 122. Forster in 1914-1915 was working at a book on Samuel Butler (Furbank, II, 3-4).

19. See Michael S. Reynolds, *Hemingway's Reading: 1910-1940* (Princeton: Princeton University Press, 1980).

20. For example, in "The New Text" (see above, n. 1), Warren Bennett writes that "Hemingway never uses reflective pauses anywhere else in his short fiction" (p. 119). By "short fiction," Bennett shows awareness of Charles E. May's "Is Hemingway's 'Well-Lighted Place' Really Clean Now?" *Studies in Short Fiction,* 8 (Spring 1971), 326-330, which claims the discovery of an instance of the "violation" in *A Farewell to Arms*; but Edward Stone had already identified an actual instance, in "The Gambler, the Nun, and the Radio"—see "Hemingway's Mr. Frazer: From Revolution to Radio," *Journal of Modern Literature,* 1 (March 1971), 376.

21. In *Across the River and into the Trees,* the eighth instance, not mentioned below, is on p. 210. The twenty-fifth example is in Stone, "Hemingway's Mr. Frazer," p. 376n.

22. The pattern does not confuse when it concludes a dialogue, as on p. 70 of *Across the River and into the Trees*. Not specifically useful for our purposes—though every instance strengthens the general precedent that establishes the text of "A Clean, Well-Lighted Place"—is the fourth pattern, identifying the speaker's second speech only. At the end of "Homage to Switzerland," Harris reveals that "last year" his father had "shot himself."

"I am very truly sorry. I am sure his loss was a blow to science as well as to his family."

"Science took it awfully well."

"This is my card," Harris said.

(pp. 532-533)

In "Fathers and Sons":

"Come out after supper?" [Trudy]

"No." [Nick]

"How you feel?" [Trudy]

"Good." [Nick]

"All right." [Trudy]

"Give me kiss on the face," Trudy said.

(p. 593)

And *To Have and Have Not*:

"Well, I never killed anybody," Bee-lips told him.

"Nor you never will. Come on, let's get out of here. Just being with you makes me feel crummy."

"Maybe you are crummy."

"Can you get them from talking?"

"If you don't paper your mouth."

"Paper yours then."

"I'm going to get a drink," Harry said.

(p. 134)

This would seem to be the pattern, too, of the last two of the inscrutable set of speeches at pp. 120-121 of *Across the River and into the Trees*, but how can we be sure the speakers alternate in the earlier speeches?

23. Otto Reinert assigns the older waiter both "He must be eighty years old" and "Anyway I should say he was eighty," so that the preceding speech—"He's got plenty"—confirms that the younger waiter is the one who has been telling of the suicide attempt. Edward Stone suggests that "Anyway" is an attempt to translate a Spanish idiom of agreement ("Hemingway's Waiters Yet Once More," *American Speech*, 37 [October 1962], 239-240); and, as Kann points out, a period follows "Anyway" in the manuscript. But even if the younger waiter does say "Anyway. I should say he was eighty," he still has the next line, "I wish he would go home," so the principle of Reinert's solution still holds.

The closest approximation to the double use of the innovation in "A Clean, Well-Lighted Place" is in *Across the River and into the Trees* (p. 131), where, within one short exchange, a waiter speaks twice consecutively two times without typographical clue or expository identification, and the passage is clear. This waiter's appreciation of the value of a pause helps us understand the point of Hemingway's innovation—on p. 144 we have

"But if you would like some Perrier-Jouet—"

"Bring it," the Colonel said and added, "Please."

And on p. 147:

"Take it to the room, please."

"You said please without a pause before it."

24. Martin Dolch, who accepts Hagopian's emendation, also offers this interpretation of "I know"; but the meaning no longer applies if "I know" follows "You said she cut him down." See John V. Hagopian and Martin Dolch, eds., *Insight I: Analyses of American Literature* (Frankfurt am Main: Hirschgraben, 1962), p. 108.

25. We see this in "Homage to Switzerland" when Harris is drinking alone, and the old man comes over.

"I beg your pardon if I intrude," he said in English.
. . .
"Please sit down," Harris said. The gentleman sat down.

"Won't you have another coffee or a liqueur?"

"Thank you," said the gentleman.

(p. 530)

The action in "The gentleman sat down" explains the original indention of "He's drunk every night." The unidentified pause for an omitted action between two speeches is nowhere more obvious than in "Hills Like White Elephants," between "Yes, with water" and "It tastes like licorice" (p. 372).

26. George Monteiro, "Hemingway on Dialogue in 'A Clean, Well-Lighted Place,'" *Fitzgerald/Hemingway Annual 1974*, p. 243. And Hemingway of course said: "When it is all finished, naturally you go over it. You get another chance to correct and rewrite when someone else types it, and you see it clean in type. The last chance is in the proofs. You're grateful for these different chances" (*Writers at Work*, p. 222). In the final text of "A Clean, Well-Lighted Place," we may see Hemingway's hand not only in the removal of the period after "Anyway" but also in the removal of the question mark from "How should I know"—since the period here was the original choice in the manuscript, before Hemingway changed it to the question mark we find in *Scribner's Magazine* (March 1933): the manuscript question mark is a thick-leaded curve above the thin *x* Hemingway used for periods,

whereas his typical question mark, as seen immediately above and below in the manuscript, consists of a thin curve above a point. Further, in the preface to *The First Forty-Nine,* Hemingway names "A Clean, Well-Lighted Place" as one of the stories that continue to be his favorites after a new reading.

27. C. Harold Hurley, in "The Attribution of the Waiters' Second Speech in Hemingway's 'A Clean, Well-Lighted Place,'" *Studies in Short Fiction,* 13 (Winter 1976), argues that the repeated pattern in the opening line of the first and second dialogues—"'Last week he tried to commit suicide,' one waiter said" and "'The guard will pick him up,' one waiter said"—identifies the older waiter as the speaker both times (pp. 83-84). But this reasoning, besides requiring Hagopian's emendation, overlooks the fact that "one waiter said" is the formula of a riddle—it underscores rather than resolves the problem of identification: the point of the second "one waiter said" is that it does *not* mean "the first waiter said."

28. *The Magic Barrel* (New York: Farrar, Straus & Cudahy, 1958), p. 196:

[Salzman] placed the card down on the wooden table and began to read another:

"Lily H. High school teacher. . . . Wonderful opportunity."

"I know her personally," said Salzman.

Malamud writes me (4 October 1979): "I remember punctuating paragraphs in that way, at that time, in order to work up a pause before a subsequent remark in a faster rhythm. The device basically related to bringing out the true quality of the characters' speech."

29.* Leo Tolstoy, *Ivan Ilych* and *Hadji Murad,* trans. Louise and Aylmer Maude (London: Oxford University Press, 1934), p. 64:

"I was going up in public opinion, but to the same extent life was ebbing away from me. And now it is all done and there is only death."

"Then what does it mean? Why? It can't be that life is so senseless and horrible. But if it really has been so horrible and senseless, why must I die and die in agony? There is something wrong!"

"Maybe I did not live as I ought to have done," it suddenly occurred to him.

In the original, Tolstoy uses neither dashes nor quotation marks for the first two of these paragraphs. More interesting for us is Richard Hare's change in *Fathers and Children* (London, 1948; rpt. San Francisco: Rinehart, n.d.), p. 84:

"Who is that you were standing with," [Madame Odintsov] asked him, "when Mr. Sitnikov brought you over to me?"

"So you noticed him?" asked Arkady in his turn. ". . . That's my friend Bazarov."

Arkady went on to discuss "his friend.. . ." Meanwhile the mazurka was drawing to a close. . . .

The music stopped.

"*Merci,*" murmured Madame Odintsov, rising.

"You promised to pay me a visit; bring your friend with you. . . ."

Doesn't one think, at first, that it is Arkady who is saying "You promised to pay me a visit"? No other translator indents after "rising"; nor did Turgenev (see the first published text, in the *Russian Herald* [Russkiy Vestnik], 37 [March 1862], 540, or the corrected manuscript at the Bibliotheque Nationale, Paris). Hare's indention, suggesting a pause, parallels Hemingway's

"He's drunk now," he said.

"He's drunk every night."

30. New York, 1929; offset reprint (Vintage, 1954), pp. 85-86; and 36, 78. Since these instances do not go beyond the usage in Joyce, the assumption that Faulkner borrowed it from Hemingway needs the support of a passage in *Sanctuary* (New York: Jonathan Cape & Harrison Smith, 1931) that has confused two Faulkner scholars (and many other readers probably):

"Oh, I know your sort," the woman said. ". . . Take all you can get, and give nothing. 'I'm a pure girl; I don't do that.' . . . just let a man so much as look at you and you faint away because your father the judge and your four brothers might not like it. . . ." Across the child Temple gazed at the woman's back, her face like a small pale mask beneath the precarious hat.

"My brother said he would kill Frank. . . . I climbed down the gutter and headed Frank off and told him. I begged him to go away. . . . He said he'd drive me home to get my suitcase. . . . We came up the path and father reached around inside the door and got the shotgun. . . . Frank shoved me behind him and held me and father shot him and said 'Get down there and sup your dirt, you whore.'"

"I have been called that," Temple whispered. . . .

(pp. 66-67)

Olga Vickery, in *The Novels of William Faulkner* (Baton Rouge: Louisiana State University Press, 1959), p. 108, and Edmund Volpe, in *A Reader's Guide to William Faulkner* (New York: Noonday, 1964), p. 145, have taken the second indention—in conjunction with the preceding sentence describing Temple—to indicate that the new speech is hers, even though this speech ends with quotation marks and is followed by an indented speech of Temple's.

Faulkner would then be doing what Hemingway does. But doesn't the middle speech belong to "the woman," Ruby, despite the indention? Is Temple's father, the respected judge, another hillbilly Eupheus Hines with a shotgun inside the door, who would assassinate her lover and say, "Get down there and sup your dirt, you whore"? And would Temple's lover be driving a buggy? Yet Ruby has just told us of Temple's protective brothers, so "My brother" can seem to be one of these. Faulkner, evidently, did not indent the sentence describing Temple because the indention might imply that Temple *is* the next speaker. But did he have to indent the second speech? He is indicating a gap. This, together with his decision to let the reader identify the middle speaker, comes close to Hemingway's confusing practice. (In the second edition of her book [1964], Mrs. Vickery dropped her reference to the passage.)

David Kerner (essay date 1982)

SOURCE: "The Manuscripts Establishing Hemingway's Anti-Metronomic Dialogue," in *American Literature: A Journal of Literary History, Criticism, and Bibliography,* Vol. 54, No. 3, October, 1982, pp. 385-96.

[*In the following essay, Kerner finds several examples of Hemingway's use of anti-metronomic lines of dialogue in his fiction and concurs with other critics who want to restore the original text of "A Clean, Well-Lighted Place."*]

The one remaining step in the demonstration that two instances of anti-metronomic dialogue resolve the notorious crux in **"A Clean, Well-Lighted Place"** is an examination of the manuscripts containing the forty other instances in the books Hemingway saw through the press.[1] This examination confirms beyond question thirty-eight of those passages, including—in manuscripts Hemingway wrote in pencil or typed himself—all seven instances of the pattern in **"A Clean, Well-Lighted Place"** when the older waiter is understood to be speaking both of these consecutive, unattributed lines:

> "He must be eighty years old."
>
> "Anyway I should say he was eighty."[2]
>
> (p. 478)

Insofar as the charge of error (elsewhere in the story) depends on the conventional alternation of speakers in these two lines, the unquestionable precedents for finding the lines anti-metronomic expose the gratuitousness of the need to postulate an unprecedented (and incredible) error. Judging by two instances in *The Sun Also Rises*,[3] Hemingway planted this second, easily acceptable juxtaposition in the story in order to teach us how to read the earlier, more elusive passage (for then the crux is resolved):

> "He's drunk now," he said.
>
> "He's drunk every night."[4]

This pattern too appears seven times in the other work Hemingway saw into book form—but the holographs and typescripts confirm only five beyond question: two raise the possibility of the sort of error (a second error) that Warren Bennett alleges at this point in the pencil manuscript of **"A Clean, Well-Lighted Place."**[5]

Bennett argues that the run-on line connecting "'He's drunk now,' he said." with the end of the preceding paragraph proves that the following speech is the other, the older, waiter's; the third speech in the exchange, therefore ("What did he want to kill himself for?"), belongs to the younger waiter, establishing that he is the one asking the questions about the suicide attempt, so that later the older waiter cannot be the one saying, "You said she cut him down." Thus, for Bennett, the indentation of "'He's drunk now,' he said." in the published story is an oversight that happily confirms the Scribners emendation (suggested by Martin Dolch and John V. Hagopian), which attaches "You said she cut him down." to the preceding speech, spoken by the younger waiter. But the confirmation is illusory: one cannot logically claim that the preserved indentation is an error unless one has already assumed that the attribution to the older waiter of "You said she cut him down." is an error—and the only support for that assumption is the prior assumption that Hemingway overlooked his run-on line. This circular reasoning proves nothing. It does help us see, however, that the abandoned run-on line is crucial: all the arguments in the twenty articles on the crux in this story can be reduced to the single question, is there any substantial evidence that Hemingway did overlook the run-on line canceling the indentation of "'He's drunk now,' he said."? And the possibility that Hemingway made that mistake seems plausible suddenly when one discovers in two typescripts the possibility of precisely such an oversight in anti-metronomic passages of the same pattern.

The simpler of the two passages is in **"The Three-Day Blow"**:

> "That's right," said Nick. "I guess he's a better guy than Walpole."
>
> "Oh, he's a better guy, all right," Bill said.
>
> "But Walpole's a better writer."
>
> "I don't know," Nick said. "Chesterton's a classic."
>
> (p. 217)

In Hemingway's typescript (the only surviving manuscript), Bill's first speech in the quoted exchange is the last line on page 6 and ends at the right margin; and his second speech, at the top of page 7, can seem an unindented continuation of the first:

> "But Walpole's a better writer."
>
> "I don't know," Nick said. "Chesterton's a classic."
>
> "Walpole's a classic too." Bill insisted.[6]
>
> (Item 96, p. 41)

The placement of the first "classic" shows that that second speech of Bill's begins at the left margin. One can argue, therefore, that Hemingway forgot to indent Nick's speech here—a mistake that Hemingway noticed as soon as he typed the first "classic" (since he then began, and continued, to indent one space for each new speech). But if Hemingway had intended no indentation for Bill's second speech, wouldn't he have naturally indented Nick's, knowing he was at the left margin? Hemingway's absorption as he began this page may be surmised from the fact that, after he typed the first "classic," he indented only one space for the nine little speeches that follow—he did not want his attention diverted by even the slightest unnecessary mechanical movement. (The six variations in the number of spaces for the indentations throughout page 7 indicate that Hemingway was using the space bar to indent.) It would be arbitrary to suppose that the urgency of his imagination led Hemingway to neglect to indent only when he reached the second speech on the page, rather than when he began the page, for his absorption led him to type a "6" at the upper left margin—a mistake that he did not correct until later, as is shown by the slightly higher horizontal alignment of the "7" he then typed next to the x'd out "6." That Hemingway was not aware he had not indented Bill's speech would then explain why Nick's first speech on the page begins directly below the beginning of Bill's. And that Hemingway could forget to indent as he began a new page of this typescript, we see on page 4: the first line, unindented, is "Bill stood up." (following a line of dialogue at the bottom of page 3)—and in the left margin is an inserted "¶" symbol. Furthermore, since Hemingway was thus quite capable of inserting this symbol, why didn't he do so in front of "'I don't know,' Nick said." if he thought Bill's opening line unindented? Or why didn't Hemingway insert a "no ¶" in front of Bill's line, to distinguish it from Nick's and the speeches that follow? In the absence of either insertion, Bill's line must be considered to have as much of an indentation as Nick's. Evidently Hemingway thought the column of opening quotation marks running halfway down the page a clear indication that all the speeches are indented. He may, however, have decided he should make those first two indentations clearer: the margin for the second and third lines of the narrative paragraph below the middle of the page is one space closer to the left edge of the sheet. Why would Hemingway go to the trouble of resetting the margin? (It would have to be reset, since he could not get the first "classic" any nearer the left edge of the paper.) Did he intend the new margin to establish a one-space indentation for those first two lines of dialogue? Nine times in a row, in the top half of the page, he shows himself to have been satisfied with one-space indentations. Finally, why should one strain to claim an error here when two anti-metronomic passages—without any possibility of error—turn up in the first draft of *The Sun Also Rises* the same year Hemingway was very carefully correcting proof for *In Our Time*?[7] One concludes that Bill's anti-metronomic line in the typescript of **"The Three-Day Blow"** cannot be used as a pre-

cedent supporting the charge that Hemingway overlooked an unintended indentation in **"A Clean, Well-Lighted Place."**

The other problematic passage is in *To Have and Have Not*:

> "I got *cojones*. Don't you worry about my *cojones*. But I'm figuring on keeping on living here."
>
> "I'm not," Bee-lips said.
>
> Jesus, thought Harry. He's said it himself.
>
> "I'm going to get out," Bee-lips said.
>
> "When are you going to get the boat out?"

(p. 109)

That the last speech too is spoken by Bee-lips (as the reader learns by paying attention to the rest of the scene) is confirmed by the surviving first handwritten draft of the passage:

> "I got *cojones*. Don't you worry about my *cojones*."
>
> "When you going to get the boat out?" Bee-lips asked.

When, in this draft, Hemingway squeezed three new line between these two speeches, the second of the lines went "'I'm not,' Bee-lips said. 'I'm going to get out.'"; but ther Hemingway deleted "'I'm going to get out.'" and wrote i in at the end of the third of the added lines, curving "Bee-lips said" up the right edge of the sheet and drawing a line from there to the opening of the next speech, from whicr he now deleted "Bee-lips asked." That run-on line would seem to indicate that "'When are you going to get the boa out?'" in the setting copy should not have been indented (and then there would have been no confusion). Yet we know that Hemingway typed that page himself, since a space is skipped consistently after each opening quotatior mark, a few of the indentations are irregularly spaced, the error "Whose" for "Who's" perpetuates itself even though it was corrected in the holograph, and there is a revision in syntax.[8] Then did Hemingway overlook his own run-on line (as Bennett suggests Hemingway did in **"A Clean, Well-Lighted Place"**)?

In that page of typescript, between the two speeches the line in the holograph connects, one notices that the vertical distance (for the first time on the page) is more than a double space and less than a triple and that the letters in the two lines are not aligned vertically; in addition, the space between the two lines is narrower on the carbon than on the original, and the two sheets have lost their earlier alignment. That is, before Bee-lips's second speech here was typed, the page, with its carbon, was removed from the typewriter. Why? Neither an interruption nor an abrupt decision of his own to quit work for the day is the likely explanation: years later, writing a letter longhand, he explains that he hates his new typewriter and "I must not write letters on any [sic; "my"?] old one because it has page 594 of the [African] book in it, covered over with the dust cover, and it is unlucky to take the pages out" (*Selected Letters*, p. 847). Since the *To Have and Have Not* typescript was to be the setting copy, Hemingway evidently wanted to use the machine to see how the crowded handwritten insertion would look. Two other circumstances support this inference. First, one notices an earlier and different disalignment of original and carbon at the line "'Jesus,' thought Harry. 'He's said it himself.'"—which has no quotes in the holograph: Hemingway apparently tried the quotes out on the machine, liked how they looked, and then rejected them when he saw them in print.[9] Second, when *Scribner's Magazine* was serializing *A Farewell to Arms*, Hemingway would copy a passage he wanted to work on—he did not experiment on the typescript Scribners would be using for the book (*Selected Letters*, p. 299). Such written and typed testing of a revision would have led Hemingway to the "are" added to Bee-lips's last speech, since the pause implied by the preserved indentation is inconsistent with the casual syntax of the holograph's "'When you going to get the boat out?'" The added "are" makes the question grave and more calculated. Furthermore, Hemingway later corrected at least the original of that typed page, for only he could have changed "'cutting you in on'" to "'letting you in on.'" All this evidence of Hemingway's attention to the passage in typescript and galleys is especially significant since Hemingway of course always knew that Bee-lips has the two consecutive speeches (it is Harry Morgan who will "get the boat out"): there was never a question here of that "confusion" Warren Bennett attributes to Hemingway in the manuscript of **"A Clean, Well-Lighted Place."** Consequently—and, again, in the light of Hemingway's practice elsewhere—the typescript does not support a claim that Hemingway's indentation was an oversight. The abandoned run-on line in *To Have and Have Not* cannot, then, be used to buttress the otherwise untenable claim that the abandoned run-on line in **"A Clean, Well-Lighted Place"** was an oversight; and the charge that Hemingway made a mistake in assigning "You said she cut him down." to the older waiter loses its one possible support.

In fact, instead of confirming that alleged error in the story, the three pages from the manuscripts of *To Have and Have Not* uphold the authority of the text of **"A Clean, Well-Lighted Place"** as originally published. If Hemingway had followed the holograph run-on line in *To Have and Have Not,* he would have eliminated the momentary confusion the indentation causes the reader. But if Hemingway had followed the run-on line in **"A Clean, Well-Lighted Place,"** he would have multiplied the confusion endlessly: the older waiter *would* then be saying "He's drunk every night." and he would then be answering the questions about the suicide attempt; so he could never say "You said she cut him down."—and the reader would be permanently lost. Therefore, since the evidence of Hemingway's close attention to the minimal difficulty caused by Bee-lips's consecutive, indented speeches indicates that the run-on line joining them was canceled only after some hesitant deliberation, how much more likely that the cru-

cial cancellation of the disputed run-on line in **"A Clean, Well-Lighted Place"** was the result of careful consideration.

All the same, in neither manuscript do we catch Hemingway in the act of canceling the run-on line. But in the setting copy of **"Homage to Switzerland"** we do catch him in the act. The pencil manuscript (Item 476-2, p. 4) confirms the indentation of Harris's second speech in this published passage:

> "Please sit down," Harris said. The gentleman sat down.
>
> "Won't you have another coffee or a liqueur?"
>
> "Thank you," said the gentleman.
>
> (p. 530)

But in Hemingway's typescript the smudged remains of an erased run-on line connect Harris's second speech here with the end of the first paragraph (Item 477, p. 11). That is, Hemingway indented in the pencil manuscript and typed the indentation, then canceled the indentation by drawing the run-on line, and ended up erasing the run-on line. Can we be sure it was Hemingway who drew the line? On sending this story to *Cosmopolitan,* he warned, "It is submitted to be published as it is with no changes and no deletions" (*Selected Letters*, p. 367); and at Scribners, where the story went next, no one needed to be warned—Maxwell Perkins told a correspondent, "Nobody ever edited Hemingway, beyond excising a line or two for fear of libel or other legal dangers."[10] This external evidence (and there is more of it)[11] is confirmed by internal evidence: another anti-metronomic passage appears in **"Homage to Switzerland"**—

> "Science took it awfully well."
>
> "This is my card," Harris said.
>
> (pp. 532-33)

—and in the pencil draft a squiggle runs through the quotation marks after *well.* and before *This* (Item 476-2, pp. 11-12); but no run-on line links the two paragraphs, and Hemingway's typescript restores these canceled quotation marks (Item 477, p. 14). That is, the squiggles catch Hemingway in the act of musing over his use of unattributed anti-metronomic dialogue here—and this musing parallels his drawing and then erasing the run-on line canceling the anti-metronomic indentation earlier in the story. These hesitations are strong support for the inference that such deliberations, rather than oversights, explain the published indentations canceling the holograph run-on lines in **"A Clean, Well-Lighted Place"** and *To Have and Have Not.*

There are other, less dramatic examples of Hemingway's attention to his anti-metronomic indentations. In the setting copy of *To Have and Have Not,* on a page which Hemingway did not type, an indentation between two speeches made by Harry Morgan's mate, Eddy, creates an anti-metronomic passage exactly like the younger waiter's in **"A Clean, Well-Lighted Place"** (Item 213, p. 45; 212,

chose not to elaborate, but at that time he had no stomach for the objections that he knew would be made to unattributed anti-metronomic dialogue—a practice so elusive that, despite some thirty appearances in thirty years, it had never been subjected to public scrutiny: his recent encounters with the scrutiny of Charles Fenton and Philip Young had left him vowing, "I'm never going to answer one [a critic] again. Not answer a letter, no explanations, no permissions to quote, no nothing. Whatever is written is written and they can cut it up among them."[15]

And "cut it up"—beyond anything Hemingway could have foreseen—is what Dolch and Hagopian did to **"A Clean, Well-Lighted Place,"** for their emendation violates Hemingway's characterization: how can the insensitive, indifferent younger waiter, who can't wait to throw the old man out, be at the same time concerned enough to persist in asking about the suicide attempt? If any emendation were to be made—not to "correct" the text but to spare the uninitiated reader—what that change should be is suggested by the manuscripts of **"The Three-Day Blow"** and *To Have and Have Not*: the indentation of "'He's drunk every night.'" would be canceled. That is the only acceptable way out of the difficulty created by the older waiter's having the line "You said she cut him down.": the change would call for no untenable assumptions and would recognize Hemingway's anti-metronomic practice, and his characterization would be preserved. The manuscript does not, however, authorize even that change; and the authority of that manuscript is left intact after close examination of the forty other passages of anti-metronomic dialogue in the manuscripts Hemingway saw through the press.

Notes

1. Twenty-five of these are cited in "The Foundation of the True Text of 'A Clean, Well-Lighted Place,'" *Fitzgerald/Hemingway Annual 1979,* pp. 279-300; the others (and fourteen more, from the posthumously published books) will be identified in a third article. I do not here include the posthumous volumes, to forestall the charge that the passages do not reflect Hemingway's final intentions.

2. For the stories, page references are to *The Fifth Column and the First Forty-Nine Stories,* since the passages cited are the same there as on first publication; for each novel, the reference is to the first U.S. edition.

3. The famous first draft, in the *Fiesta* notebooks (Item 194), shows—at both 194-3, p. 14, and 194-6, p. 6—only one instance of anti-metronomic dialogue; to each, Hemingway added an educational preliminary instance in the typescript (within a page), for the two close doublings would prove to the careful reader that the juxtaposition of unattributed indented speeches for one speaker was intentional.

4. The two anti-metronomic passages were Otto Reinert's solution of the crux, in "Hemingway's Waiters Once More," *College English,* 20 (May 1959), 417-18.

5. "The Manuscript and the Dialogue of 'A Clean, Well-Lighted Place,'" *American Literature,* 50 (Jan. 1979), 613-24.

6. Item 96 is the setting copy for *In Our Time.* The original page numbers of Hemingway's typescript of this story appear at the upper left; the new ones, for the book, at the upper right.

7. To estimate this care, see Hemingway's 1924-25 comments on typographical errors and on Liveright's editing of the punctuation, in *Selected Letters 1917-1961,* ed. Carlos Baker (New York: Scribners, 1981), pp. 126, 145, 161. When Scribners reissued *In Our Time* in 1930, Hemingway rejected more of the Liveright changes—see James B. Meriwether, "The Text of Ernest Hemingway," in O. M. Brack, Jr., and Warner Barnes, eds., *Bibliography and Textual Criticism* (Chicago: Univ. of Chicago Press, 1969), pp. 323-24.

8. For the holograph passage, see Item 204-8, p. 16; the original typescript, Item 213-4, p. 86; and the carbon, Item 212-3, p. 13.

9. Galley 27-16522, opening chapter 11, at the Monroe County Public Library, Key West, Florida.

10. *Editor to Author: The Letters of Maxwell E. Perkins,* ed. John Hall Wheelock (New York: Scribners, 1950), p. 228.

11. In Perkins's letters (at Princeton) there is no reference to the indentation. Considering his policy (he kept his staff's hands off even the many gross misspellings in Fitzgerald's *Tender Is the Night* in 1934) and the note by Hemingway in the upper left-hand corner of page one calling for return of the typescript with the proof, no copy-editor would have drawn so bold a line or erased the line so crudely, leaving a heavy smudge. Nor would Alfred Dashiell, then managing editor of *Scribner's Magazine,* have risked such exposure—in 1926 he had outraged Hemingway by venturing to cut 2500 words from "Fifty Grand," and Hemingway was still furious six years later: offering the *Magazine* "Homage to Switzerland" and other new stories, Hemingway warns Perkins "for christ sake" not to turn him over to "that little . . . Dashiell" and says he "would rather use them for bungroad" than argue about them with "that twirp" (9 August 1932). Dashiell's own retreat from further encounters is suggested by the introduction he wrote in 1932-33 for his anthology of stories, *Editor's Choice* (New York: Putnam's, 1934): "There are, on the other hand, authors who are so sure they are great artists that they consider the editor only an irritating commercial necessity whose opinion they value not at all. The editor's prayer is 'From this sin and these people, Good Lord deliver us'" (pp. 7-8). Moreover, Hemingway had established his pre-eminence in 1929 when *Scribner's Magazine* paid more for *A Farewell to Arms* than it had ever paid for a serial.

12. See n. 3 for additional confirmation of the deliberateness of Hemingway's anti-metronomic practice in *The Sun Also Rises*.

13. *Scribner's Magazine* has Frederick Henry say to Captain Rinaldi, "You were sweet to tell me"—but what Rinaldi told him is not there; compare the bottom of p. 651, col. 2, with the book, p. 71, where the missing lines are restored.

14. Jerome's letter, with Hemingway's handwritten reply at the bottom, was discovered by George Monteiro in 1974 at the Mugar Memorial Library of Boston University. Quoted with Mr. Jerome's and the Library's permission.

15. Letter to Charles Poore (23-28 February 1953), excerpted in Matthew J. Bruccoli and C. E. Frazer Clark, Jr., comps., *Hemingway at Auction 1930-1973* (Detroit: Gale Research, 1973), p. 170.

C. Harold Hurley (essay date 1982)

SOURCE: "The Manuscript and the Dialogue of 'A Clean, Well-Lighted Place': A Response to Warren Bennett," in *The Hemingway Review*, Vol. II, No. 1, Fall, 1982, pp. 17-20.

[*In the following essay, Hurley maintains that Warren Bennett's "misinterpretation of the waiters' speech in the problematic exchange concerning the soldier and the girl compound rather than resolve the existing debate."*]

Working from a recently discovered manuscript of Hemingway's **"A Clean, Well-Lighted Place,"** Warren Bennett resolves many of the questions concerning the story's much debated dialogue.[1] As Bennett contends, the manuscript indeed "reveals how the illogical dialogue sequence may have occurred" (p. 616); "clarifies Hemingway's intention as to which waiter knows about the old man's suicide attempt" (p. 616); and demonstrates that Hemingway was himself to blame for "the problem that arises in that crucial sentence which was editorially reassigned by Scribner's" (p. 618). But in addressing "the problematic section of the story concerned with the soldier and the prostitute" (p. 622), Bennett misinterprets the evidence of the manuscript and consequently misattributes the waiters' dialogue—a misattribution that alters our conception of the waiters. As I have indicated elsewhere, however, the story's text provides a set of patterns authorizing the reversal of Bennett's attribution and the proper assignation of the line dealing with the soldier having relations with the girl to the younger waiter and the lines expressing concern for the soldier being picked up by the guard to the older waiter.[2] The manuscript, properly interpreted, supports this reading and presents the waiters, as Hemingway intended, as "two different kinds."[3]

Bennett, on the basis of the manuscript, establishes that the waiters' illogical dialogue concerning the old man's suicide attempt was neither "deliberate,"[4] nor "a typographical error,"[5] nor "Hemingway's violation of one of the unwritten rules of the art of presenting dialogue visually" (the "reflective pause" theory).[6] Writing the story at a single sitting with few revisions, initially making little descriptive distinction between the waiters, and omitting dialogue identifiers to an extreme, Hemingway, although clearly intending the older waiter to know of the deaf old man's attempted suicide, himself erred in attributing the dialogue.

These issues resolved, Bennett seeks in the manuscript the solution to a second longstanding question of dialogue—the correct attribution of the waiters' controversial exchange concerning the soldier and the girl. The text as published reads:

> A girl and a soldier went by in the street. The street light shone on the brass number on his collar. The girl wore no head covering and hurried beside him.
>
> "The guard will pick him up," one waiter said.
>
> "What does it matter if he gets what he's after?"
>
> "He had better get off the street now. The guard will get him. They went by five minutes ago."

This exchange, made difficult by the omission of explicit identifying tags, must be attributed correctly if the waiters are to emerge as distinct characters. The critics, however, have long been divided on the attribution and interpretation of the passage. William Colburn, who early drew attention to the confused dialogue, stated: "No doubt most readers will agree that the older waiter should be the one to feel that money and a wife in bed are not enough and that he should be concerned that the soldier with the streetwalker will get into trouble."[7] Several years later Joseph F. Gabriel reiterated the view: "It is generally assumed that . . . it is the older waiter who expresses fear that the soldier and the girl will be caught . . . and it is the younger waiter who says 'What does it matter if he gets what he's after?'" (p. 543). Shortly thereafter, John V. Hagopian altered the earlier view by attributing the first line of the exchange, "'The guard will pick him [the soldier] up,'" to the younger waiter with the gloss, "a bit of Schadenfreude, quite consistent with his remark to the deaf old man, 'You should have killed yourself last week'" (p. 144). "The younger waiter," Hagopian adds, "wants everybody to get off the streets, including the old man, so that he can go home to his wife. It is he who is keenly aware of the time, who complains that he never gets into bed before three o'clock, and who is impatient. . . ." (p. 144). To the older waiter Hagopian assigns the line, "'What does it matter if he gets what he's after?'" with the gloss, "consistent with his indifference to the usual social norms, with his nihilism, and with his awareness of the value of youth and confidence. . . ." (p. 144). David Lodge and Warren Bennett, the latest commentators on the issue, agree with Hagopian's attribution;[8] but as I have indicated in an article entitled "The Attribution of the Waiters' Second Speech in Hemingway's 'A Clean, Well-Lighted Place,'" the text supports only one interpretation—the former. The recently discovered manuscript, properly interpreted, confirms this reading.

In the aforementioned article, I have demonstrated that Hemingway, despite omitting conventional dialogue identifiers, provides the following set of patterns to distinguish between the two waiters: (1) in the first three scenes the younger waiter asks the questions and the older waiter provides short answers; (2) in the first two scenes the "one waiter said" tag, used nowhere else in the story, refers to lines spoken by the older waiter; and (3) "the waiter" tag is used seven times to refer exclusively to the younger waiter and refers to the older waiter only after he is alone and cannot be mistaken for his colleague. When applied to the scene in question, the first two patterns enable us to attribute to the younger waiter the line dealing with the soldier having relations with the girl and to the older waiter the lines expressing concern for the soldier being picked up by the guard.

Bennett, disregarding these patterns,[9] finds in the manuscript version of the scene where the younger waiter returns from serving the old man brandy a key to the correct attribution of these lines. The scene as published reads:

> "He's drunk now," he said.
>
> "He's drunk every night."
>
> "What did he want to kill himself for?"
>
> "How should I know."

The second and fourth lines of the manuscript version of this scene, indisputably attributable to the older waiter, read "'He's stewed [drunk] every night'" and "'Christ How should I know?'" Bennett contends that in the disputed scene the published line "'What does it matter if he gets what he's after?'" in the manuscript "'What does it matter if he gets his tail? [what he's after?]'"[10] should also be attributed to the older waiter—the original language in both scenes suggesting a tough "realism" associated with the older waiter that finds its ultimate expression in his parody of "Hail Mary" and "The Lord's Prayer" (p. 623). But Bennett's argument, offering no explanation for the deletion of the older waiter's tough realism in the published version of the above scenes and its retention in the prayer scene, is unconvincing. Rather, Hemingway altered the original language of both scenes simply to differentiate more clearly the two waiters.

As Bennett demonstrates, there were initially no "waiters" as such, only "two boys." Apparently discovering their individuality as they spoke about the old man's attempted suicide, Hemingway went back through the manuscript and enhanced the waiters' differences in age, in being hurried or unhurried, and in their degree of compassion for the old man. (From the outset, Hemingway seems to have intended one of them to have a wife.) In the scene with the undisputed dialogue, Hemingway deleted from the manuscript the manuscript the word "Christ" and changed

"stewed" to "drunk" to refine the older waiter's original coarseness and to heighten his compassion for the old patron. Recognizing the old man as a fellow sufferer, the older waiter is "reluctant to close up." He, too, likes "to stay late at the café . . . With all those who do not want to go to bed. With all those who need a light for the night." In the scene with the soldier and the girl, the older waiter's lines are further expressions of compassion, this time directed toward the young soldier. The older waiter, knowing that the soldier might be better with a girl even as the old man "might be better with a wife," is not concerned that the soldier "gets what he's after," but that "the guard will pick him up." Sex, the older waiter realizes, even with a streetwalker, provides a momentary stay against nothingness.

Just as the line "'The guard will pick him up'" is consistent with the older waiter's compassionate nature, so the line "'What does it matter if he gets what he's after?'" is consistent with the younger waiter's more prurient but not altogether incompassionate nature. At this point, Hemingway's alteration of "his tail" to "what he's after" has nothing to do with the older waiter, as Bennett argued. Hemingway is simply being kinder to the younger waiter whose interest in sex, as his interest in money, is normal. Unlike his older colleague, the younger waiter cannot envision an eighty-year old man being "better with a wife"; but being young himself and having "a wife waiting in bed," the younger waiter can identify with the soldier. Despite his impatience and unkind words, however, the younger waiter does not really wish the old man dead nor does he take pleasure in hastening him from the café before the usual closing hour. He even agrees with his colleague that buying a bottle and drinking at home is not the same. With "youth, confidence, and a job," the younger waiter has "everything." As one who "lived in it and never felt it," he is as yet oblivious to the nothingness that for the older waiter and old patron lurks in the darkness beyond the clean, well-lighted café. "Sleepy now" and "anxious to get into bed before three o'clock," the younger waiter, Hemingway reminds us, "did not wish to be unjust. He was only in a hurry."

In summation, Bennett's reading of the manuscript of **"A Clean, Well-Lighted Place"** answers questions that have plagued critics for a generation, but his misinterpretation of the evidence of the manuscript and subsequent misattribution of the waiters' speech in the problematic exchange concerning the soldier and the girl compound rather than resolve the existing debate. A reinterpretation of Hemingway's revisions, when taken with his intention of portraying the waiters as "two different kinds" and with the patterns employed to distinguish between them, suggests that the line dealing with the soldier having relations with the girl should properly be attributed to the younger waiter and that the lines expressing concern for the soldier being picked up by the guard should properly be attributed to the older waiter, and not, as Bennett would have it, the other way around.

Notes

1. "The Manuscript and the Dialogue of 'A Clean, Well-Lighted Place,'" *American Literature*, 50 (Jan., 1979), 613-624.

2. C. Harold Hurley, "The Attribution of the Waiters' Second Speech in Hemingway's 'A Clean, Well-Lighted Place,'" *Studies in Short Fiction*, 13 (Winter, 1976), 81-85.

3. *The Short Stories of Ernest Hemingway* (New York: Scribner's, 1965), pp. 379-383. Citations to the published version of the story are to this text.

4. Joseph F. Gabriel, "The Logic of Confusion in Hemingway's 'A Clean, Well-Lighted Place,'" *College English*, 22 (May, 1961), 545.

5. John V. Hagopian, "Tidying Up Hemingway's Clean, Well-Lighted Place," *Studies in Short Fiction*, 1 (Winter, 1964), 146.

6. Otto Reinert, "Hemingway's Waiters Once More," *College English*, 20 (May, 1959), 417-418.

7. William Colburn, "Confusion in 'A Clean, Well-Lighted Place,'" *College English*, 20 (Feb., 1959), 242.

8. David Lodge, "Hemingway's Clean, Well-Lighted, Puzzling Place," *Essays in Criticism*, 21 (Jan., 1971), 51; Warren Bennett, "Character, Irony, and Resolution in 'A Clean, Well-Lighted Place,'" *American Literature*, 42 (March, 1970), 77. Bennett's interpretation of the manuscript may have been influenced by his conclusions on the story published earlier. In addition to those already cited, the following items are related to the problem of dialogue: Robert Penn Warren, "Ernest Hemingway," *Kenyon Review*, 9 (Winter, 1947), 1-28; F. P. Kroeger, "The Dialogue in 'A Clean, Well-Lighted Place,'" *College English*, 20 (Feb., 1959), 240-241; Edward Stone, "Hemingway's Waiters Yet Once More," *American Speech*, 37 (Oct., 1962), 239-240; Sheridan Baker, *Ernest Hemingway; An Introduction and Interpretation* (New York: Holt, Rinehart and Winston, Inc., 1967), p. 87; Carlos Baker, *Hemingway: The Writer as Artist*, 3rd ed. (Princeton, New Jersey: Princeton University Press, 1969), p. 124; Charles E. May, "Is Hemingway's 'Well-Lighted Place' Really Clean Now?" *Studies in Short Fiction*, 8 (Spring, 1971), 326-330; Scott MacDonald, "The Confusing Dialogue in Hemingway's 'A Clean, Well-Lighted Place': A Final Word?" *Studies in American Fiction*, 1 (Spring, 1973), 93-101; George Monteiro, "Hemingway on Dialogue in 'A Clean, Well-Lighted Place," *Fitzgerald/Hemingway Annual 1974*, 243; Annette Benert, "Survival Through Irony: Hemingway's 'A Clean, Well-Lighted Place,'" *Studies in Short Fiction*, 11 (Spring, 1974), 181-187; Hans-Joachim Kann, "Perpetual Confusion in 'A Clean, Well-Lighted Place': The Manuscript Evidence," *Fitzgerald/Hemingway Annual 1977*, 115-118.

9. In his earlier article (see not 8) Bennett established that the older waiter knew of the old man's suicide attempt through Hemingway's use of several other patterns: the "serious question, verbal irony by the older waiter, a dropping of the subject, and then a serious reply" pattern (p. 72), and the younger waiter's use of the word "kill" (p. 71).

10. Hemingway's insertion in the manuscript of "drunk" and "what he's after" are here indicated by pointed brackets. "Stewed," "Christ," and "his tail" are crossed out in the manuscript. Note, incidentally, that the published line "'How should I know'" appears in the manuscript as "'How should I know?'" A typist or typesetter inadvertently deleted the question mark.

George H. Thomson (essay date 1983)

SOURCE: "'A Clean, Well-Lighted Place': Interpreting the Original Text," in *The Hemingway Review*, Vol. II, No 2, Spring, 1983, pp. 32-43.

[*In the following essay, Thomson examines the controversy surrounding the waiters' dialogue regarding the soldier and the girl.*]

I. The Nature of the Textual Problem

Hemingway's story begins late at night in a café. An old man is drinking, watched by two waiters who are not differentiated. In Dialogue 1, comprising seven speeches, there is no way of knowing who begins the exchange, hence no way of knowing which waiter refers to the old man's attempted suicide and which asks questions about it. In Dialogue 2, comprising three speeches, there is similar indefiniteness. Only when the old man asks for another drink does the reader learn that one of the waiters is "younger," is sleepy, and never gets to bed before three o'clock. Even at the beginning of Dialogue 3—I have for convenience divided it into two parts, 3a and 3b—it is still not possible to identify with assurance the opening speaker. Finally, with the third speech in Dialogue 3b it can confidently be asserted that the "younger" waiter says "I never get to bed before three o'clock." Assuming normal conventions of paragraphing, it can be deduced that in Dialogue 3a the younger waiter asks the following question about the old man's suicide: "Who cut him down?" And the older waiter replies "His niece." Similarly it can be deduced that in Dialogue 3b the younger waiter says, "His niece looks after him." And the older waiter says to the younger, "I know. You said she cut him down." This statement seems at odds with the deduction that it was the older waiter who first mentioned the niece.

How to explain this apparent anomaly? The following propositions will be considered:

(1) The text is confused and needs emending

(2) The text violates normal conventions for presenting dialogue

(3) The text is correct but has not been correctly interpreted

Hemingway wrote **"A Clean, Well-Lighted Place"** in 1933. The story was published that same year both in *Scribner's Magazine* and in the collection *Winner Take Nothing.* The three dialogues are as follows in the 1933 text:

1.

"Last week he tried to commit suicide," one waiter said.

"Why?"

"He was in despair."

"What about?"

"Nothing."

"How do you know it was nothing?"

"He has plenty of money."

(p. 17)

2.

"The guard will pick him up," one waiter said.

"What does it matter if he gets what he's after?"

"He had better get off the street now. The guard will get him. They went by five minutes ago."

(p. 18)

3ᴀ.

The waiter took the bottle back inside the café. He sat down at the table with his colleague again.

"He's drunk now," he said.

"He's drunk every night."

"What did he want to kill himself for?"

"How should I know."

"How did he do it?"

"He hung himself with a rope."

"Who cut him down?"

"His niece."

"Why did they do it?"

"Fear for his soul."

"How much money has he got?"

"He's got plenty."

(p. 19)

3ʙ.

"He must be eighty years old."

"Anyway I should say he was eighty."

"I wish he would go home. I never get to bed before three o'clock. What kind of hour is that to go to bed?"

"He stays up because he likes it."

"He's lonely. I'm not lonely. I have a wife waiting in bed for me."

"He had a wife once too."

"A wife would be no good to him now."

"You can't tell. He might be better with a wife."

"His niece looks after him."

"I know. You said she cut him down."

"I wouldn't want to be that old. An old man is a nasty thing."[1]

(pp. 19-20)

It was not until 1959 that two critics, William Colburn and F. P. Kroeger, drew public attention to the problem with the dialogue.[2] Their articles began an ingenious critical debate which has continued to this day.

II. Explanations of the Textual Problem

In 1964 John Hagopian said that the simplest solution was to suppose that initially "a typographical error" had been made which should now be corrected.

Original Version:

> "His niece looks after him." [Younger waiter]
>
> "I know. You said she cut him down." [Older waiter]

Revised Version:

> "His niece looks after him. You said she cut him down." [Younger waiter]
>
> "I know." [Older waiter][3]

Frank L. Hoskins, Jr., the editor of *Studies in Short Fiction,* published the following comment in summer 1964:

> Mr. L. H. Brague, Editor at Charles Scribner's Sons . . . has written Dr. John V. Hagopian that when Scribner reprints Hemingway's short story **"A Clean, Well-Lighted Place,"** it will emend the text as suggested by Dr. Hagopian in an article in *Studies in Short Fiction.* . . . The transposition in speech attribution must have occurred, reported Mr. Brague, during setting of the story for its first appearance, which was in *Scribner's Magazine,* XCIII (March 1933). Scribner decided to change the text after conferring with Professor Carlos Baker and with Mrs. Mary Hemingway.[4]

In the process of elaborating on Hagopian's argument, Warren Bennett in 1970 records that he has been in correspondence not only with L. H. Brague, Jr., but with Philip

Young. The result: "Scribner's claims" he tells us, "that the dialogue inconsistency occurred when a slug of type was evidently misplaced in the first printing of the story. . . ."[5] Thus it can be seen that an impressive array of Hemingway luminaries has lent itself to this speculative enterprise culminating in a slug of type.

Shortly thereafter, in 1971, Scott MacDonald succeeded in wringing from Charles Scribner, Jr., the admission that the textual change to the story had been made—to quote Mac-Donald's summary—"not on the basis of manuscript evidence or at the suggestion of Hemingway himself, but solely on the basis of the advice of critics and 'common sense.'"[6] Of course this had been obvious from the beginning, but outright speculation had been lent a specious probability by the casual simplicity of a "typographical error" and the apparent solidity of a "slug of type." How a typed phrase or a "slug" comprising six words got so inconveniently shuffled about poses logistical problems nowhere confronted by Hagopian, Brague, Bennett, or anyone else.

Against this background three explanations of the state of Hemingway's 1933 text will be evaluated.

1. The text is confused and needs emending.

Since 1964, when the proposal to emend the text was first made, three pieces of evidence have come to light. The first and second provide new information; the third, discussed under (2) below, impugns Hagopian's scholarship. As a result the "slug of type" theory is rendered untenable but the essential difficulty remains.

The first piece of evidence is as follows: On 31 November 1956, Judson Jerome, an Assistant Professor of English at Antioch College, wrote Hemingway a breezy letter saying in effect: why should I sweat over this problem in **"A Clean, Well-Lighted Place"** when you can tell me the answer. Jerome clearly sets out the difficulty. Hemingway, in his thirteen word autograph reply, neatly inserted at the bottom of the letter, says that he has read the story again and that it continues to make perfect sense to him.[7] Unless one assumes that Hemingway is here being mischievous, one has no choice but to conclude that the original text is authoritative.

The second piece of evidence is a MS [manuscript], long thought lost, but in fact in the possession of Mrs. Mary Hemingway. This MS, described in detail by Bennett in 1979, is now housed in the Hemingway Collection of the John F. Kennedy Library.[8] It is not easy to discuss Bennett's analysis of the MS, for to do so thoroughly would require almost as much space as he himself takes to present the evidence and then almost as much space again to show to what degree his presentation is a tissue of speculation and assumption. I must be content to highlight only the most important issues.

Of course, the crux must be the speech "I know. You said she cut him down." And indeed the MS has a good deal to tell us here. The MS originally read:

"His niece looks after him."

"I wouldn't want to be that old. An old man is a nasty thing."

The comment about the niece—because of the clear statement-and-response pattern of the four preceding speeches—must be made by the younger waiter. The next speech is also made by him, for it is specifically replied to by the older waiter. Hemingway presumably noticed this inconsistency and—as the spacing of MS page 4 makes obvious (it is reproduced by Bennett)—inserted the additional speech "I know." Later in the writing of the story, Hemingway came back and, slightly higher on the same inserted line, added with a blunter pencil: "You said she cut him down." Thus after two stages of revision the MS read:

"His niece looks after him." [Younger Waiter]

"I know. You said she cut him down." [Older Waiter]

"I wouldn't want to be that old. . . ." [Younger Waiter]

(pp. 620-21)

Only one thing is certain from this evidence. It was not a misplaced slug of type but an afterthought—whether misplaced or not—by Hemingway himself that caused this now-famous sentence to be inserted after "I know."

Bennett conjectures that Hemingway first became confused in writing "His niece looks after him." He was then going to add how the niece, etc. ("they") looked after the old man, but, realizing the younger waiter would not possess this knowledge, struck "They treat." When he came back to add "You said she cut him down," he knew that it was the older waiter who spoke of the niece and assumed mistakenly that the first speech was by the older waiter. Hence the inserted statement was intended as the younger waiter's but got attached to "I know" and so became the older waiter's (p. 620). It is notable that Bennett entertains only casually the possibility, which one imagines would be the first to cross Hagopian's mind, that Hemingway might have carelessly misplaced the second insertion, intending the dialogue to read "His niece looks after him. You said she cut him down," thereby providing the younger waiter with a justification for what might otherwise be regarded as a rather curious statement on his part. But it is equally notable that neither interpretation acknowledges Hemingway's reply to Judson Jerome. When that evidence is taken into account, Hemingway appears not only confused at the time of writing but irresponsible after the event.

To be fair to Bennett's position, it is necessary to set out the assumptions on which it is based and the evidence for those assumptions.

The story was, by all appearances, written at one sitting, with surprisingly little revision after an initial "false start." The insertions and revisions, judging from the thickness and texture of the pencil lead, were evidently made at three different stages: almost immediately after the first phrasing; relatively late or as the story neared completion; and much later, perhaps another day, with a sharp pencil.

(p. 616)

What all of these particular insertions and revisions suggest is that at the beginning of the story Hemingway had not preconceived any significant distinction between the two main characters—with the exception, perhaps, that he intended one of them to have a "wife," for the reference to the younger waiter's wife is not an insertion but appears in the first phrasing on page four.

(p. 618)

If the characters did develop as they spoke and as the story itself developed, that might explain the origins of the obscurities which have produced so much debate.

(p. 618)

All the pieces of evidence for these assumptions cannot be rehearsed. Among the most important: the story begins with a false start, followed by an erased title; the handwriting is consistent, vigorous, flowing; there are relatively few revisions; in paragraph one the characters are originally "The two boys," they become waiters only on page 2 in the episode with the soldier and the girl; no age difference is specified until two-thirds of the way through the story when the "older waiter" says to his younger colleague, "You have youth, confidence, and a job"; at this point—to judge from the bluntness of the pencil and Bennett's elaborate assumptions—Hemingway went back to page 2 and, in the scene in which "One of the waiters" went over to the old man, he revised the text to read "The younger waiter went over to him."[9]

f this evidence is adequate, then it proves that we possess *he* MS of **"A Clean, Well-Lighted Place."** But what if he evidence is not adequate? What if a different set of circumstances prevailed? Consider the following. Hemingway had already a MS draft of this story. He sat down to make some final revisions and a fair copy. He began to opy: "In Zaragossa the," instantly grew dissatisfied with uch specificness, and struck the phrase. Next he copied ut the opening sentences, grew dissatisfied and struck hem. (Alternatively, his opening paragraph was not yet ully formed.) He now wrote the title. Then or later he rased it and inserted the title we now know. The original s illegible except for the word "Nothing" (p. 616). Clearly lemingway knew what the theme of his story was to be. le now began with his opening sentences, practically the ame as those he had just struck. He planned to call his haracters boys, then waiters, and only after that would he listinguish between them. Though one of the two waiters vas from the beginning intended to carry the theme of *ada,* Hemingway had in the first draft made no distinction of age between them. He had, however, made other escriptive distinctions (contrary to Bennett's statement, p. 17). The "sleepy" waiter, who turns out to have a wife, is omplaining and impatient in serving the old man. The lder waiter, as we see a little later, is patient and considrate. As Hemingway worked his way through Dialogue b something went wrong. Adding "They treat" to a speech y the younger waiter was clearly a mistake. He corrected

that. Maybe this distraction caused him to overlook the next line of dialogue in his draft and instead he copied out the younger waiter's next speech. He then had to go back and insert the overlooked line. Here one could invent a dozen different possibilities. For instance, Kerner argues that "His niece looks after him" and "I wouldn't want to be that old" were at first intended to be consecutive indented speeches by the younger waiter; "You said she cut him down" was added later as a concession to help the reader identify the speakers in Dialogues 1 and 3a (pp. 288-89). As Hemingway copied the final dialogue between the two waiters in which the distinction between them is made more decisive, it struck him that a difference in age would reinforce his theme and further separate the two waiters. He went back and inserted "younger" on page 2. (Alternatively, he had always had the age difference in mind but had worked at first on the principle of letting the reader know as little as possible—compare the boy-waiter case above; on reflection, however, he decided it wise to give the reader a few more props.) As Hemingway approached the last part of the story he wrote with increasing speed and vigor because this part of the narrative was most fully and completely developed in his preliminary draft.

I do not for a moment propose that this reconstruction is true, only that it has something like the same degree of probability as Bennett's reconstruction. All that can be said with certainty is that the extant MS is fair, that it is closely related to the printed text, and that Hemingway is responsible for Dialogue 3b in its original published form. Since Bennett is driven to support Hagopian's revision on the ground that Hemingway was confused (p. 622), the MS cannot be said to have improved our ability to interpret this part of the text. Whether it can help to resolve other problems will become apparent in what follows.

2. The text violates normal conventions for presenting dialogue.

This proposal was first offered by Otto Reinert (1959), and later supported by Charles May (1971).[10] At the beginning of Dialogue 3—so the argument runs—the younger waiter returns from serving the old man and says "He's drunk now." Then he adds in a newly indented speech "He's drunk every night." The typographical set-up is intended to indicate a reflective pause between the two speeches and, of course, silence on the part of the older waiter. Similarly at the beginning of Dialogue 3b the older waiter says, "He must be eighty years old." After a pause he adds, "Anyway I would say he was eighty."[11] As a result of this arrangement, the older waiter asks the questions and the younger waiter knows all about the old man's attempted suicide. It then becomes entirely appropriate in Dialogue 3b for the older waiter to say to the younger concerning the old man's niece, "You said she cut him down." From this theory it follows also that Dialogue 1 is opened by the younger waiter. The question to be asked at this point is a technical one. Is such an arrangement of dialogue at all probable?

239

Hagopian objected that Hemingway nowhere violated the convention that indented speeches are always alternating, unless of course the contrary is explicitly indicated (p. 141). There the matter rested until 1973 when MacDonald pointed to four instances from the short stories and three or possibly five from the novels in which Hemingway had assigned two consecutive indented speeches to one character without any other indication than the logic of the context. In 1980 Kerner went further, finding at least twenty-five examples of this innovative technique in five novels and seven stories.[12] In face of such evidence, Hagopian's position is demolished. It is not at all improbable that Hemingway, in writing **"A Clean, Well-Lighted Place,"** might have violated normal conventions of dialogue.

At this juncture the MS appears to come to our aid. It reads, in Bennett's transcription, as follows [square brackets indicate insertions]:

> The waiter took the bottle back into the café. He sat down at the table with the other waiter [his colleague] again ["He's drunk now," he said.]
>
> "He's stewed [drunk] every night."
>
> "What did he want to kill himself for?"
>
> "Christ "How should I know?"
>
> (MS p. 3) (p. 618)

The inserted sentence at line three was originally introduced as a new paragraph, which is the way it has always appeared in print. But, as Bennett explains,

> a run-on line drawn in the pencil manuscript indicates that the dialogue, "'He's drunk now,' he said," should be the last line of the preceding paragraph, which negates the "reflective pause" argument.
>
> (p. 619)

Kerner has subjected Bennett's interpretation and the MS evidence to minute analysis which I will not elaborate upon here. His conclusion is this: it is reasonable to suppose that at some point between MS and final typeset Hemingway realized he had miscalculated; as a result he restored "'He's drunk now,' he said" to its original position as a separate paragraph. The "reflective pause" argument is not negated by the MS. Kerner adds—devastatingly, one may feel: "In any case, why should Bennett find the run-on line sacred when he goes so far as to take 'You said she cut him down' away from the speaker Hemingway never stopped assigning it to, from 1933 to 1956?" (p. 290)

A further conclusion could also be drawn from the MS. With the single exception of Kann, every specific comment I have seen on the printed version of this scene either assumes or asserts that because the younger waiter is the subject (He) of the last sentence of the long paragraph, he must also be the author of the following speech, "'He's drunk now,' he said."[13] If that argument is so widely acceptable, it must follow that before Hemingway inserted

that very sentence, the next one "He's stewed every night" was spoken by the younger waiter. Unless the insertion was then made immediately, a further consequence is that the older waiter asks the question "What did he want to kill himself for?" The MS, then, far from demolishing the "reflective pause" theory of Reinert and May, can effectively be used to support it, and in supporting it confirm the view that it is the younger waiter who knows about the old man's wish to die.

3. The text is correct but has not been correctly interpreted.

By correct, I mean that no violation of conventions is needed to make sense of the text as it was originally published. What is needed, rather, is an interpretive strategy that can sweep the difficulty away. Such a strategy begins with the assumption that the older waiter is thoughtful, disillusioned, and has an ironic attitude toward the confidence and callow worldliness of the younger waiter. The older waiter tells his colleague that the old man hanged himself with a rope, after which the dialogue continues.

> "Who cut him down?" [Younger Waiter]
>
> "His niece." [Older Waiter]
>
> "Why did they do it?" [Younger Waiter]

Though told it was the niece, the younger waiter goes on to use "they," typical of the impersonal and thoughtless speech so common in social discourse. Alternatively, the younger waiter assumes without any evidence that "his niece" is short for "his niece and her family." The casual use of "they" is not the only way in which the younger man's mind is shown to be cliche-ridden. He has no knowledge of the suicide attempt except what the older waiter tells him, yet he unthinkingly assumes that the old man was rescued by being cut down, by popular presumption the commonest mode of deposition in cases of hanging by rope. But in certain circumstances it might be easier to untie a knot around a beam or to stand on a chair or table and lift up a frail old man so that the noose could be loosened and pulled over his head. These, of course, are idle speculations. But so are the assumptions of the younger waiter. As we look back on this exchange, we may conclude that the older waiter in his cynicism lets the "cut him down" cliche pass. Later, however, when the younger man jumps to a further conclusion, "His niece looks after him"—something he cannot know; the niece could accidentally have come by at the moment of the suicide—the older waiter quietly chastises his colleague's propensity to jump to conclusions: "I know [which is more than you do]. *You said* she cut him down [but you don't know at all what happened]." (The italics here are my suggested rhetorical emphasis.) The younger waiter, entirely missing the point of this barb, goes on to expound his conventional attitude to age.[14]

On this interpretation it is the mature waiter who from the beginning knows about the old man and answers the younger waiter's questions. The contrast between the two speakers is sharpened, no paragraphing convention is violated, and no confusion on Hemingway's part need be invoked.

III. INTERPRETATIONS OF THE TEXT

Of the three explanations of the textual problem, the first—that the text is corrupt—may be judged untenable; the second—that normal conventions for presenting dialogue are violated—may be judged distinctly possible and sufficient to justify the interpretation that it is the younger waiter who is aware of the old man's history; and the third—that the text is correct but has not been correctly interpreted—may also be judged distinctly possible and sufficient to justify the interpretation that it is the older waiter who is aware of the old man's history.[15]

Before attempting to choose between these interpretations, it is appropriate to introduce the one piece of textual evidence so far neglected, namely Dialogue 2. The soldier with a girl, her head uncovered, hurries by. One waiter says the guard will catch the soldier; the other says, "What does it matter if he gets what he's after." Unlike Dialogues 1 and 3 which are logically connected, Dialogue 2 is independent; the only way to determine the speakers is through the character revealed in their words. As one might expect, disagreement has resulted. Colburn (1959), Hurley (1976), and Kerner (1980) insist that the older waiter is the opening speaker; Dolch (1962), Hagopian (1964), Bennett (1970), and Lodge (1971) argue that the younger waiter begins the exchange.[16]

Gabriel presents a convincing case for both views. He quotes Colburn: "No doubt most readers will agree that the older waiter should be the one . . . to be concerned that the soldier with the streetwalker will get into trouble. And most readers probably will agree that the younger waiter should be the one with the completely materialistic attitude towards life." Gabriel adds that the younger waiter has already shown his interest in sex and the older waiter solicitude about the old man (p. 543). An equally good argument can be made for precisely the opposite attribution. Now it is the younger waiter who begins the exchange and the older waiter who says, "What does it matter if he gets what he's after." Gabriel writes: "In a virtually meaningless world, one takes one's desperate chances . . . and one makes one's little meaningful moments as one can." The younger waiter, untouched by such insights, is concerned rather with prudential and practical considerations (p. 543).

My own view is distressingly simple: the evidence is not sufficient to make a conclusive determination. It is possible, however, to entertain a preference based on one's general interpretation of the story. If the younger waiter is the one who recounts the history of the old man, his greater authority in the early part of the story increase the likelihood that it is he who makes the rather conclusive statement: "What does it matter if he gets what he's after."

Even so, that likelihood scarcely balances the factors to be mentioned below. Conclusion: on this interpretation, the assigning of speeches in Dialogue 2 is a toss up. If, on the other hand, the older waiter is the one who recounts the history of the old man, his greater authority prevails throughout the story. For him to wish that the soldier get what he's after is consonant with his philosophy that there is little to be got in a world of *nada*. Likewise, for the younger waiter in the following speech to be concerned about guards and regulations is consonant with his conventional attitude towards things worldly. The style of the concluding speech is also conventional and may therefore point to the younger waiter: "He had better get off the street now. The guard will get him. They went by five minutes ago." Such choppy rhetoric lacks the dignity and eloquence typical of the older waiter. Conclusion: on this interpretation, the assigning of speeches in Dialogue 2 is tentatively possible. The younger waiter opens the exchange and the older replies: "What does it matter. . . ."

The text, however, does not stand alone; we have the evidence of the MS. Though Bennett considers it to be decisive, in fact it is not so. The key MS variant in the dialogue about the soldier is in the second speech, which reads: "What does it matter if he gets his tail." The change to "what he's after" can be related to the emendations at the beginning of Dialogue 3a where the second speech is changed from "stewed" to "drunk" and the fourth speech drops "Christ." Bennett considers that in all three cases tough "realism" is being toned down to better accord with the more philosophical character of the older waiter to whom he assigns all three statements (pp. 622-23). But since the line "He's stewed every night" must originally have been assigned to the younger waiter, there is no way of knowing whether Hemingway carried out the revision of this line with the younger or the older waiter in mind. Certainly "tail" is not right for the tone of the older waiter. But then, neither "tail" nor "stewed" seems right for the tone of the story as a whole. In sum, the MS does not resolve the difficulty of assigning the speeches in Dialogue 2, even if one adopts Bennett's view that it is the older waiter who tells about the attempted suicide.

If one adopts Kerner's view, however, the MS takes on new significance. Kerner's argument, granted his primary assumption, is relentlessly logical. We can be certain it is the older waiter who says "I know. You said she cut him down." Therefore it is the younger waiter who tells about the suicide attempt (primary assumption). Therefore it is our obligation to adjust our reading of the rest of the dialogue to this primary assumption (p. 289). Since we know Hemingway with some frequency consigned consecutive indented speeches to the same character, we must assume that "He's drunk now" and "He's drunk every night" are both spoken by the younger waiter and that the two statements about the old man being eighty years old are both spoken by the older waiter. (Alternatively, the last statement about age and the next "I wish he would go home" could both be spoken by the younger waiter.) (pp. 286-87, 297). Given such an arrangement, the dialogue is consistent.

Further, the MS offers supporting evidence. On Kerner's primary assumption, the speeches "He's stewed every night" and "Christ How should I know" belong to the younger waiter and accord with the MS speech in the soldier dialogue: "What does it matter if he gets his tail" (pp. 290-91). Since on almost any assumption, as I have already argued above, the MS speech "He's stewed every night" must originally have been assigned to the younger waiter, it follows that the MS evidence can be used to support the view that all three of the above speeches belong to the younger waiter and that it is he who tells his colleague about the old man.

Were Kerner's primary assumption indisputable, the matter would be settled. Since it is not indisputable, we have still the possibility of an alternative interpretation for the statement "You said she cut him down." Both interpretations require ingenuity on the reader's part. In the one case he must assign two consecutive speeches to the same speaker and must do this not once but twice. In the other, he must notice the assumptions the younger waiter makes about hanging, assumptions not easily perceived for the very reason of their conventionality; for only then is it possible to appreciate the ironic value of the older waiter's "*You said* she cut him down."

Of these two interpretations of **"A Clean, Well-Lighted Place,"** which is most compatible with the evidence of the text? One further resource is available to help us make that decision, a careful look at the characters of the two waiters. Such an inspection, to be successful, must begin by concentrating on those portions of the text where no doubt exists as to who is speaking.

The younger waiter. After serving the old man, he complains that he never gets to bed before three o'clock. His serious annoyance is indicated by his adding that the old man should have killed himself last week. His tendency to complain is confirmed in Dialogue 3b and in his further conversation. Of his twenty speeches before saying goodnight, five return directly to the theme of wanting to go to bed, two are refusals to serve the old man any more brandy, and one—in reply to the older waiter's question "What is an hour?"—is the complaint "More to me than to him."

The young waiter is also rather argumentative. "An old man is a nasty thing." he says. "I don't want to look at him." When the older waiter says of himself that he lacks everything but work, the younger denies it, saying "You have everything I have." Then he returns for the last time to his persistent theme of wanting to go home. The younger waiter appears complaining, argumentative, and superficial. The latter quality shows in his attitude to old age, and in such things as his inability to appreciate what a wife might mean to an old man. "A wife would be no good to him now," he says. The failure of understanding is accentuated by the contrast with the older waiter who, though he seems to be alone in the world, knows that the old man might be better with a wife.

The older waiter. His character begins to shape itself in our minds near the beginning of Dialogue 3b when, for the first time, a statement can unquestionably be attributed to him. He replies to the younger waiter's complaints about the old man by asserting: "He stays up because he likes it." Here the older waiter's tone is one of quiet authority and judgment. Later, in the final dialogue between the two, he politely but firmly lectures his colleague about closing early, about confidence, and about the difference between them. He is the authority figure: ironic, thoughtful, laconic, and compassionate. He insists to his complaining colleague: "This old man is clean. He drinks without spilling. Even now, drunk. Look at him." Such simple appreciation suggests that the older waiter identifies with the old man, who is also described as "walking unsteadily but with dignity." The waiter shares this dignity. It is reflected in the finality both of his thought and rhetoric.

> "I am of those who like to stay late at the café," the older waiter said. "With all those who do not want to go to bed. With all those who need a light for the night."

("I want to go home and into bed" replies the younger waiter, like a complaining child in face of this eloquent utterance.) This distinction of the older waiter's character is sustained when the narrator enters his consciousness. For the remainder of the story he becomes the focus of insight and authority in the narrative.

The analysis of character offers, in my judgment, the most conclusive evidence for interpreting **"A Clean, Well-Lighted Place."** It seems more appropriate that the older waiter, rather than the younger, know the history of the old man. But to so interpret the story, it is essential that the older waiter's crucial statement—"I know. You said she cut him down"—be read as an ironic jibe at his presumptuous colleague. Otherwise, assuming it to be a straightforward reply, there seems no alternative but to conclude that the younger waiter is the one who knows of the old man's attempted suicide. Either interpretation is possible. Either requires some ingenuity of reading. But that is not unfair, for either interpretation can lead us to confront the desolation of Hemingway's narrative with its bare bright place and its fragment of light, in a night of enclosing nothingness.

Notes

1. Ernest Hemingway, *Winner Take Nothing* (New York: Scribner's, 1933). This text was revised in the June 1965 printing of the uniform edition of *The Collected Short Stories* and in the subsequent paperback edition of the same. See Andre Hanneman, Supplement to *Ernest Hemingway: A Comprehensive Bibliography* (Princeton: Princeton University Press, 1975), p. 10. However, the original text was retained in the paperback edition of *Winner Take Nothing* in the Scribner Library of Contemporary Classics (SL 155), first issued in 1968. This edition is identical in pagination with the first edition of 1933.

2. William E. Colburn, "Confusion in 'A Clean, Well-Lighted Place,'" *College English* 20 (Feb. 1959), 241-42; F. P. Kroeger, "The Dialogue in 'A Clean, Well-Lighted Place,'" *College English* 20 (Feb. 1959), 240-41.

3. John V. Hagopian, "Tidying Up Hemingway's Clean, Well-Lighted Place," *Studies in Short Fiction* 1 (Winter 1964), 146.

4. "Editor's Comment," *Studies in Short Fiction* 1, No. 4 (Summer 1964), ii.

5. Warren Bennett, "Character, Irony, and Resolution in 'A Clean, Well-Lighted Place,'" *American Literature* 50 (March 1970), 70.

6. Scott MacDonald, "The Confusing Dialogue in Hemingway's 'A Clean, Well-Lighted Place': A Final Word?" *Studies in American Fiction* 1 (Spring 1973), 99.

7. Jerome's letter is housed in Special Collections, Mugar Library, Boston University, and is paraphrased with the generous consent of Dr. Howard Gottlieb. It was first brought to public attention by George Monteiro, "Hemingway on Dialogue in 'A Clean, Well-Lighted Place,'" *Fitzgerald/Hemingway Annual* 1974, p. 243.

8. Warren Bennett, "The Manuscript and the Dialogue of 'A Clean, Well-Lighted Place,'" *American Literature* 50 (Jan. 1979), 613-24. For other discussions of the manuscript see Hans-Joachim Kann, "Perpetual Confusion in 'A Clean, Well-Lighted Place': The Manuscript Evidence," *Fitzgerald/Hemingway Annual* 1977, pp. 115-18; and David Kerner, "The Foundation of the True Text of 'A Clean, Well-Lighted Place,'" *Fitzgerald/Hemingway Annual* 1979, pp. 279-80, 286-92.

9. Bennett (1979), p. 617. Speculations on the degrees of bluntness of Hemingway's pencil(s) are of dubious value. How can one know *when* Hemingway picked up a sharp or blunt pencil?

10. Otto Reinert, "Hemingway's Waiters Once More," *College English* 20 (May 1959), 417-18; Charles E. May, "Is Hemingway's 'Well-Lighted Place' Really Clean Now?" *Studies in Short Fiction* 8 (Spring 1971), 326-30.

11. For another possibility see Edward Stone, "Hemingway's Waiters Yet Once More," *American Speech* 37 (Oct. 1962), 239-40, who argues that "Anyway" translates a colloquial Spanish affirmative. Kann supports this proposal by noting that in the MS "Anyway" is followed by a period (p. 116).

12. MacDonald, 93-101; Colburn, p. 242; Kerner, pp. 279-300.

13. See Kann, p. 116; and Bennett (1979), p. 619; Hagopian, p. 145; Kerner, pp. 286-87; Kroeger, p. 240; David Lodge, "Hemingway's Clean, Well-Lighted, Puzzling Place," *The Novelist at the Crossroads. . . .* (Ithaca, New York: Cornell University Press [1971]), pp. 190, 199; MacDonald, p. 94; May, p. 328; Reinert, p. 418.

14. Bennett (1979) used the same evidence concerning "they" and the niece to argue that both waiters seem to know a good deal about the old man. "If such mutual knowledge was envisioned in Hemingway's imagination, it may have caused Hemingway himself to become confused. . . ." (p. 623). Such may be the case, but since it is an unnecessary assumption, I prefer not to make it.

For a different view, see Joseph F. Gabriel, "A Logic of Confusion in Hemingway's 'A Clean, Well-Lighted Place,'" *College English* 22 (May 1961), 539-46. He proposed that the story is itself an existentialist document (p. 545) and that the "inconsistency in the dialogue is deliberate, an integral part of the pattern of meaning actualized in the story" (p. 540). "In so far as the dialogue fails to conform to the norms of logic, the reader himself is, like the older waiter, plunged into the existentialist predicament and made to confront the absurd" (p. 546). This argument is more ingenious than convincing. Moreover, as Lodge has persuasively argued, it has implications respecting the reliability of the narrator which are unacceptable (pp. 191-92).

15. The position that the younger waiter is the knowledgeable one has been implied or asserted on a variety of grounds by Robert Penn Warren, "Introduction," *A Farewell to Arms* (New York: Scribner's, 1949) p. xv; Robert B. Heilman, *Modern Short Stories* (New York: Harcourt, Brace [1950]), p. 391; Mark Schorer, *The Story: A Critical Anthology* (New York: Prentice, Hall, 1950), p. 427; Carlos Baker, *Hemingway: The Writer as Artist* (Princeton: Princeton University Press, 1952), p. 124; Bernard Oldsey, "Hemingway's Old Men," *Modern Fiction Studies* 1 (Aug. 1955), 32; Reinert (1959), p. 418; Thomas E. Saunders, *The Discovery of Fiction* (Chicago: Scott, Foresman, 1967), p. 359; May (1971), pp. 327-28; MacDonald (1973), pp. 93-94; and Kerner (1979), pp. 286-87. The contrary position that the older waiter is the knowledgeable one has been entertained by Kroeger (1959), p. 241; Martin Dolch, "A Clean, Well-Lighted Place," in *Insight I: Analyses of American Literature,* eds. John V. Hagopian and Martin Dolch (Frankfurt: Hirschgraben, 1962), pp. 107-08; Hagopian (1964), pp. 144-46; Hoskins (1964), p. ii; Bennett (1970), pp. 71-74; Bennett (1979), pp. 619-23; Ewell (1971), p. 306; Lodge (1971), pp. 191-93, 198-200; Sheldon N. Grebstein, *Hemingway's Craft* (Carbondale: Southern Illinois University Press, 1973), p. 228; Annette Benert, "Survival through Irony: Hemingway's 'A Clean, Well-Lighted Place,'" *Studies in Short Fiction* 11 (Spring 1974), 184-85; C. Harold Hurley, "The Attribution of the

Waiters' Second Speech in Hemingway's 'A Clean, Well-Lighted Place.'" *Studies in Short Fiction* 13 (Winter 1976), 81-82; and Kann (1977), pp. 115-16.

16. Colburn, p. 242; Hurley, pp. 83-84; Kerner, p. 291; and Dolch, pp. 106, 110; Hagopian, p. 144; Bennett (1970), p. 77; Lodge, p. 199. Dolch thinks that the speech "They went by five minutes ago," is one that "would best fit into the younger waiter's mouth: he is impatient and therefore keeps looking at his watch and counting the minutes" (110). But is not the older waiter the kind of man who could gauge five minutes without even looking at a clock? One might as convincingly make an argument based on continuity of action. The younger waiter speaks, concluding: "They went by five minutes ago"; the old man raps for service; the younger waiter goes over to him.

Robert E. Fleming (essay date 1989)

SOURCE: "Wallace Stevens' 'The Snow Man' and Hemingway's 'A Clean, Well-Lighted Place,'" in *ANQ: A Quarterly Journal of Short Articles, Notes, and Reviews*, Vol. 2, No. 2, April, 1989, pp. 61-3.

[*In the following essay, Fleming speculates on the possible influence of the poet Wallace Stevens and his concept of nothingness on Hemingway's short story.*]

The relationship between Wallace Stevens and Ernest Hemingway is best remembered for the one-sided fist fight between the two in February of 1936. According to a letter Hemingway wrote on 27 February 1936, Hemingway knocked Stevens down several times because he had insulted Hemingway's sister Ursula at a party. According to Hemingway, Stevens spent several days in the hospital, but an impartial witness said that the poet was seen in public the day after the fight, wearing sunglasses to conceal bruises.[1]

It is possible, however, that there is a more meaningful connection between the two. In "The Snow Man," first published in *Poetry* in 1921, Stevens uses the same existential image that Hemingway was to use in **"A Clean, Well-Lighted Place,"** first published in *Scribner's Magazine* in 1933.[2] The image is that of nothing; not *nothing* as one normally uses the word, but what Carlos Baker describes as "Something—a Something called Nothing which is so huge, terrible, overbearing, inevitable, and omnipresent that, once experienced, it can never be forgotten."[3]

No external evidence that Hemingway had read "The Snow Man" exists. Both Michael Reynolds in *Hemingway's Reading, 1910-1940* and Brasch and Sigman in *Hemingway's Library: A Composite Record* indicate that the only Stevens work owned by Hemingway was *The Man with the Blue Guitar* (1937), and that the only copy of *Poetry* in his personal library was the January 1923 issue which

contained six of his own poems.[4] Nevertheless, Hemingway borrowed books regularly during his Paris years and could easily have seen "The Snow Man" either in *Poetry* or in *Harmonium* (1923).

After detailing a barren, snowy landscape observed by a "mind of winter," suggestive of modern life as perceived by modern existential man, Stevens concludes his fifteen line poem by stating that his protagonist, "nothing himself," sees "Nothing that is not there *and the nothing that is*" (my emphasis).[5] The distinction is exactly the same as that paraphrased by Baker, writing of Hemingway's depiction of *nada* or nothing: the second *nothing* in Stevens' last line is not the mere absence of something, but an entity in itself, a force so powerful that only the strongest mind can perceive it and survive.

In his five-page story, Hemingway explores the theme more fully and goes a step beyond Stevens. After closing the café where an elderly customer has been lingering, trying to forget his loneliness and his suicidal thoughts, one of Hemingway's two waiters discloses that he shares the old man's sense of horror at the nothingness that pervades the universe: "It was a nothing that he knew too well. It was all a nothing and a man was nothing too. It was only that and light was all it needed and a certain cleanness and order. Some lived in it and never felt it but he knew it all was nada y pues nada y nada y pues nada. Our nada who art in nada, nada be thy name thy kingdom nada thy will be nada in nada as it is in nada."[6]

To modern man, nothingness is such a powerful force that only the strongest can bear to perceive it; furthermore, since it is the only force in the universe, the wise man will worship it, however ironically.

Whatever their personal differences, Stevens and Hemingway shared a bleak view of the universe. It seems quite possible that Hemingway, reading the last line of "The Snow Man," felt moved to write his own artistic response to the plight of modern humanity.

Notes

1. *Ernest Hemingway: Selected Letters, 1917-1961*, ed. Carlos Baker (New York: Scribner's, 1981), pp. 438-39. See also Baker, *Ernest Hemingway: A Life Story* (New York: Scribner's, 1969), p. 285, and Jeffrey Meyers, *Hemingway: A Biography* (New York: Harper & Row, 1985), pp. 273-75.

2. *Poetry*, 19 (Oct. 1921), 4-5. *Scribner's Magazine*, 9 (March 1933), 149-50.

3. Carlos Baker, *Hemingway: The Writer as Artist* (Princeton: Princeton Univ. Press, 1963), p. 124.

4. Michael S. Reynolds, *Hemingway's Reading 1910-1940* (Princeton: Princeton Univ. Press, 1981), pp. 85, 188; James Brasch and Joseph Sigman, *Hemingway's Library: A Composite Record* (New York: Garland, 1981), p. 356.

5. Wallace Stevens, *Poems* (New York: Vintage Books, 1959), p. 23.

6. Ernest Hemingway, "A Clean, Well-Lighted Place," *The Short Stories of Ernest Hemingway* (New York: Scribner's, 1961), p. 383.

Paul Smith (essay date 1989)

SOURCE: "A Note on a New Manuscript of 'A Clean, Well-Lighted Place,'" in *The Hemingway Review,* Vol. VIII, No. 2, Spring, 1989, pp. 36-9.

[In the following essay, Smith heralds a typescript version of Hemingway's story, known as the "Delaware typescript."]

Some three years have passed since the last article on the controversy over the two waiters' dialogue in **"A Clean, Well-Lighted Place."** In March 1985 David Kerner returned to the argument he had entered in 1979, bringing further evidence—almost an anthology—of instances of "anti-metronomic dialogue," including several from Hemingway himself, to argue that the text of the story should be restored to its original form. From its first publication in *Scribner's Magazine* (March 1933) to 1965, the crucial lines of dialogue read:

> [Younger Waiter] "His niece looks after him."
>
> [Older Waiter] "I know. You said she cut him down."

The inconsistency in that dialogue—earlier the *Older* Waiter has said "His niece [had cut him down]"—was resolved when Scribner's printed the lines in the 1965 edition of **The Short Stories** with this revision:

> [Younger Waiter] "His niece looks after him. You said she cut him down."
>
> [Older Waiter] "I know."

The dialogue's inconsistency may have been resolved with that revision, but not so the controversy among the competing "authorities" on the true text: the publisher of the 1933 version (*Scribner's Magazine* in March and **Winner Take Nothing** in October); Hemingway scholars who, after a quarter century of stony sleep, noticed in 1959 that seeming inconsistency; or Hemingway with the evidence of the story's one surviving manuscript and the tear-sheets from *Scribner's Magazine* used as setting copy for the **Winner Take Nothing** version (Items 337 and 222 in the Hemingway Collection, Kennedy Library. For three differing summaries of the controversy, see Kerner, Lodge, and Thomson.)

When the manuscript was made available in the mid-1970s, Warren Bennett followed the lead of Hans-Joachin Kann to argue that the crucial sentence, "You said she cut him down," was a late insert and should be added to the Younger Waiter's line above it, not the Older Waiter's be-

low it. That argument might have been conclusive but for the supposition that Hemingway read carefully whatever proofs he received of the publications in 1933 and the fact that, when the inconsistency was called to his attention in 1956, he noted that the story still made "perfect sense to him" (paraphrase of Hemingway's note on a letter sent to him by Judson Jerome, 30 November 1956 [Monteiro 243]). Although, by now we should suspect the presumption of Hemingway's or his editors' concern or skill reading proofs of his fiction as well as his latter-day recollections of that work.

But the argument over the attribution of that crucial line to either of the two waiters was weakened on both sides by the fact that there was no version between the earliest extant pencil manuscript and the magazine tear-sheets. For most of Hemingway's stories there is at least an original manuscript, one of his typescripts, and another typed by someone else and submitted for publication. So, for those on either side of the question of whether Hemingway took pains or nodded over his manuscripts, the appearance of an intermediate version of **"A Clean, Well-Lighted Place"** would be of some critical moment. A typescript, for example, by him or someone else, might reveal his intention or confirm a copy editor's mistake that Hemingway had overlooked.

Now one has come to light, but whether it enlightens the crucial issue of the two waiters' dialogue is still arguable.

In the summer of 1987 it was announced that the University of Delaware Library had acquired, among several other Hemingway manuscripts, "the only recorded copies of a draft of '**A Clean, Well-Light Place**'" (*College and Research Libraries News* 411). It is a five-page typescript and carbon, titled, on 8 1/2 x 14" pages, with a few minor typed corrections and one marginal typed insertion (enclosed here in slashes): "he said / speaking with that omission of syntax stupid people employ when talking to drunken people or foreigners / 'No more tonight'" (see *SS* 381). And it bears one editorial transposition mark over the incorrectly typed line: "'No,' the waiter said who was in a hurry" (*SS* 382). It is neither a Hemingway typescript, bearing none of his typing idiosyncracies, nor, with its typed corrections and insertion, does it seem the work of a professional typist.

It is likely that this "Delaware typescript" was one of those Hemingway referred to in a letter to Maxwell Perkins of 7 December 1932: "Pauline had 3 of the last stories copied when she had to go to St. Louis. Will send 3 and you can pick what you want." Carlos Baker suggests that Hemingway was referring to the last three stories submitted for publication in *Scribner's Magazine*: **"Homage to Switzerland," "Give Us a Prescription, Doctor"** (later titled **"The Gambler, The Nun, and The Radio,"**) and **"A Clean, Well-Lighted Place"** (*Selected Letters* 380). Pauline left for St. Louis in late October 1932, the probable date for this typescript.

Hemingway's note to Perkins, however, leaves in doubt whether Pauline typed this version or had it typed by someone else. That question is of interest for it bears on another: Is there a lost *Hemingway* typescript of **"A Clean, Well-Lighted Place"**? In the fall of 1932, Hemingway was working apace on the stories that would complete his 1933 collection—"have so damned much vitality now that I cannot sleep and only knock off writing when my damned eyes get too bad" (*Selected Letters* 377). If Pauline typed the Delaware version, then Hemingway might have trusted her familiarity with his handwriting enough to let her copy his original manuscript. If someone else typed it, Hemingway probably would have typed a copy of his manuscript himself.

That second question bears, of course, on a third: Who was initially responsible for assigning the line, "You said she cut him down," to the Older rather than to the Younger Waiter? That question might be answered with the discovery of a Hemingway typescript, if one exists. For now, however, the Delaware typescript may well relieve Scribner's typesetters from some of the onus of the typographical crime some critics have placed on them. If this typescript was submitted to *Scribner's Magazine* as setting copy for the March 1933 publication, they set the type properly. The typescript assigns the crucial sentence— "You said she cut him down"—to the Older Waiter. So, if that line was misplaced, it occurred at some time between the writing of the original manuscript and the Delaware typescript.

Finally, there is some equally inconclusive evidence on the matter of Hemingway's use of anti-metronomic dialogue. Those who have been following this controversy will recall that Mr. Kerner's argument depends in part on evidence that Hemingway departed from the convention of "metronomic" dialogue, successive indented lines indicating a change of speakers (let us say, the "tick-tock" convention), to adopt the "anti-metronomic" liberty, assigning successive lines to one speaker (perhaps the "tick-tick" variant). In the Delaware typescript, immediately following that crucial passage, there are two indented lines obviously spoken by the Younger Waiter:

"I don't want to look at him."

"I wish he would go home. He has no regard for those who must work."

In the original manuscript Hemingway wrote the first line of dialogue here at the same time he wrote the crucial line confusing the waiters' dialogue five lines above. With this one, however, he added a mark of insertion to indicate that the two lines (printed above) should be joined. If whoever typed the Delaware typescript was working from the manuscript, that editorial mark was ignored, leaving another instance of anti-metronomic dialogue. But by the time copy was set for the *Scribner's Magazine* version, the two lines were combined in one indented speech (*SS* 381).

This began as a "note" and would have ended sooner had the Delaware typescript not presented some seemingly simple questions that resurrected important issues of inter-

pretation of **"A Clean, Well-Lighted Place."** That typescript seems to narrow the time when Hemingway, deliberately or not, confused the dialogue of the two waiters to sometime in October of 1932. By December a clean typescript was ready to send to Perkins, who at most would have scanned it for a lurking obscenity and sent it to the *Scribner's Magazine* editor and on to the typesetter, both of whom did their jobs, no questions asked.

But from the moment Hemingway received this typescript in the fall of 1932 until a quizzical college teacher raised the question in 1956, the confusion of the waiters' dialogue never crossed his mind. And the question, in spite of all the answers, still abides—Why not?

Works Cited

Bennett, Warren. "The Manuscript and the Dialogue of 'A Clean, Well-Lighted Place,'" *American Literature,* 50 (1979): 613-24.

College and Research Libraries News (July/August 1987): 411.

Hemingway, Ernest. *Ernest Hemingway: Selected Letters, 1919-1961.* Ed. Carlos Baker. New York: Scribner's, 1981.

———. *The Short Stories of Ernest Hemingway.* New York: Scribner's, 1966.

Kann, Hans-Joachim. "Perpetual Confusion in 'A Clean, Well-Lighted Place': The Manuscript Evidence," *Fitzgerald/Hemingway Annual* (1977): 115-118.

Kerner, David. "Counterfeit Hemingway: A Small Scandal in Quotation Marks," *Journal of Modern Literature* 12 (November 1985): 91-108.

———. "The Foundation of the True Text of 'A Clean, Well-Lighted Place,'" *Fitzgerald/Hemingway Annual* (1979): 279-300.

Lodge, David. *The Novelist at the Crossroads and Other Essays on Fiction and Criticism.* Ithaca: Cornell UP, 1981.

Monteiro, George. "Hemingway on Dialogue in 'A Clean, Well-Lighted Place." *Fitzgerald/Hemingway Annual* (1974): 243.

Thomson, George H. "'A Clean, Well-Lighted Place': Interpreting the Original Text," *The Hemingway Review* 2.2 (Spring 1983): 32-43.

Warren Bennett (essay date 1990)

SOURCE: "The Characterization and the Dialogue Problem in Hemingway's 'A Clean, Well-Lighted Place,'" in *The Hemingway Review,* Vol. IX, No. 2, Spring, 1990, pp. 122-23.

[*In the following essay, Bennett compares Hemingway's "A Clean, Well-Lighted Place" and "The Gambler, the Nun, and the Radio."*]

I

"A Clean, Well-Lighted Place," although long recognized as one of Hemingway's best short stories, has nevertheless been plagued by controversy because of Hemingway's proclivity for writing dialogue without identifying the speakers. The story was first published in *Scribner's Magazine* in 1933 and then republished the same year in Hemingway's collection of stories **Winner Take Nothing.** In this 1933 text, Hemingway's failure to identify the speakers created a contradictory dialogue sequence which resulted in a confusion as to which waiter knew about the deaf old man's attempted suicide. No one, however, seemed to have noticed the contradictory sequence and its resulting confusion until 1956—twenty-three years later—at which time Judson Jerome wrote Hemingway about the "'messy' dialogue" (Monteiro 243) in the story. Hemingway replied, "oh so sorry to disappoint" (Monteiro 243); the dialogue, he said, "made perfect sense to him" (Monteiro 243). Jerome evidently did not pursue the matter, but the contradictory sequence eventually sparked a serious scholarly debate and in 1959 three articles were published on the subject: F. P. Kroeger's "The Dialogue in 'A Clean, Well-Lighted Place,'" William E. Colburn's "Confusion in 'A Clean, Well-Lighted Place,'" and Otto Reinert's "Hemingway's Waiters Once More." Then, in 1964, three years after Hemingway's death, John V. Hagopian, "Tidying Up Hemingway's 'Clean, Well-Lighted Place',," suggested that the confusing text was flawed by a typographical error and should be emended. He suggested that the line, "I know. You said she cut him down," should be split and the second sentence reassigned to the previous speaker who says, "His niece looks after him." Finally, when Scribner's was preparing to published **The Short Stories of Ernest Hemingway** in 1965, they decided to follow Hagopian's suggestion. The old 1933 text which read,

> Older waiter: "You can't tell. He might be better with a wife."
>
> "His niece looks after him."
>
> "I know. You said she cut him down."
>
> "I wouldn't want to be that old. An old man is a nasty thing."
>
> (*WTN* [*Winner Take Nothing*] 20)

was changed to read,

> Older waiter: "You can't tell. He might be better with a wife."
>
> Younger waiter: "His niece looks after him. You said she cut him down."
>
> Older waiter: "I know."
>
> Younger waiter: "I wouldn't want to be that old. An old man is a nasty thing."
>
> (*SS* [*The Short Stories of Ernest Hemingway*] 381)

The 1965 emendation solved the dialogue contradiction and resolved the confusion as to which waiter knows about the deaf old man's attempted suicide, but the becomes even more exasperated and more irritated: the more the brandy the longer the old man will stay. Caught between his training as a waiter and his urge to go home, he pours angrily into the glass so that the brandy does not just spill over the rim but slops over the rim (the younger waiter later "wipes the edge of the table" (21). The old man, of course, has no idea that the waiter is so angry—and that he wishes he had killed himself last week. The old man thinks the waiter has shown him a real generosity and he politely says, "Thank you" for the gratuity. A superb little irony of the mean-spirited and the innocent.

It is of some importance to a complete understanding of the significance of the younger waiter and the younger waiter's wife to point out that Cayetano Ruiz, in **"The Gambler, the Nun, and the Radio,"** tells Mr. Frazer,

> "No gambler has luck with women. . . . He works nights. When he should be with the woman. No man who works nights can hold a woman if the woman is worth anything.
>
> (*SS* 484)

Since **"Give Us a Prescription, Doctor"** (later titled **"The Gambler, the Nun, and the Radio"**) and **"A Clean, Well-Lighted Place"** were written during approximately the same period—and were both accepted by Scribner's at the same time—it is not unlikely that Cayetano's philosophy that "No man who works nights can hold a woman if the woman is worth anything," was in Hemingway's mind (and by authorial extension in the older waiter's mind) when he had the older waiter ask the younger waiter, "You have no fear of going home before your usual hour?" Cayetano's philosophy, however, does not change the character of the younger waiter nor does it justify the younger waiter's attitude toward his wife.

David Kerner (essay date 1992)

SOURCE: "The Ambiguity of 'A Clean, Well-Lighted Place,'" in *Studies in Short Fiction*, Vol. 29, No. 4, Fall, 1992, pp. 561-74.

[*In the following essay, Kerner offers a "comprehensive demonstration of the accuracy of Hemingway's text."*]

Since Warren Bennett's 13,000-word defense—concluding, "All printings of [**"A Clean, Well-Lighted Place"**] should, therefore—in fairness . . . most of all, to Hemingway—follow the 1965 emended text" (120)—has passed muster with Paul Smith,[1] the earlier cries of "Enough!" were premature:[2] a comprehensive demonstration of the accuracy of Hemingway's text is needed, lest we wake up one day to find the emendation enshrined in the Library of America. The need is evident too when Gerry Brenner can write: "*must* we know which waiter answers the question

'How do you know it was nothing?' with 'He has plenty of money.'? I think not" (252-53). One cannot take this answer away from the younger waiter without redistributing 19 other speeches; and to think that this can be done without damaging the intention in a story that so sharply differentiates the two waiters is to reveal once again that the story being read is not yet the one Hemingway wrote.[3]

Anyone drawn to the notion that in Hemingway's text, whether by accident or design, there is an inconsistency that cannot be resolved has failed either to consider or to study the context of the crucial disputed line. No one, when first reading the story, can know which waiter is saying, as the dialogue opens, "Last week he tried to commit suicide." The deliberateness of the uninformative "one waiter said" is undeniable, for in the second short dialogue (about the soldier), critics will never agree that it is possible to *know* which waiter is saying what. The third dialogue continues the challenge, as the younger waiter begins:

"He's drunk now," he said.

"He's drunk every night."

"What did he want to kill himself for?"

By habit we assign this question and the succeeding ones to the younger waiter, so we are surprised, some lines later, to find the *older* waiter saying, "You said she cut him down," for *he,* it would seem, has been answering the questions. But since this apparent inconsistency complements the riddling "one waiter said"s, the context of controlled ambiguity assures us that when Hemingway decided to insert "You said she cut him down," he knew that his assignment of this indispensable line was decisive, and consequently he knew which waiter he was giving it to.[4] The function of this dual ambiguity is clear even before we know it is dual: once we have heard about "nada," the withholding of identification throws a spotlight on the opening "Nothing":

"What [was he in despair] about?"

"Nothing."

Then, after we have detected the apparent inconsistency, we realize that without the disputed insertion, we might decide that this "Nothing" (whose overtones Hemingway must have been aware of before he began) is the older waiter's "nada," and the insertion is there to tell us we would be mistaken. But it tells us ambiguously, not immediately ending the puzzle of the "one waiter said"s, prodding us to see *why* "Nothing" cannot be the older waiter's "nada" and must be the younger waiter's line. If the opening "Nothing" *were* the older waiter's line, there would be no reason for the web Hemingway took pains to weave. In pulling that web apart without studying it, the emenders, like surgeons cutting blindly, destroyed its function and lopped off an organic part of the story's meaning, for the younger waiter's "Nothing" opens up a kind of flanking attack that turns out to be the central location of the battle.[5]

Bennett argues that the reply to "Why [did the old man try to commit suicide]?"—"He was in despair"—indicates the speaker's familiarity with "nada," and therefore the older waiter must be the one answering the questions. True, in the whole story this "despair" is the one word that can make us hesitate, but what follows it only supports our seeing the younger waiter throw up his hands mockingly as he replies, "He was in despair"; for, coming from him, these words are a vacuous formula, forcing the questioner to repeat his question, and the mockery is confirmed when we see that the proffered answer "Nothing" is a set-up for a joke:

"How do you know it was nothing?"

"He has plenty of money."

Because the older waiter could not think that anyone with "plenty of money" can have no reason to kill himself, Bennett is forced to construe "Nothing" as the later "nada." But a premature, ambiguous "Nada" here, followed by an equally unenlightening, mocking deflection of the appeal for an explanation, would make the whole passage a pointless, as well as a misleading, anticipation, and it would also make the older waiter uncharacteristically glib and smug:[6] it would be inconsistent with his patience as a teacher ("You do not understand. This is a clean and pleasant café"), with his feeling for the old man, and with the fact that, as he begins his interior monologue, he is not out to explain the old man's suicide attempt—he is asking, rather, why he himself has "never had confidence," why does *he* "need a light for the night," "What did he fear?," as though he is only now, for the first time, naming his trouble (see May 328-29).[7] If "Nothing" were the older waiter's reply and meant what Bennett claims, this waiter's next reply would make sense—for example:

"How do you know it was [nada]?"

"He has a loving wife."

That is, what but "nada" can explain the suicide attempt when even such affection fails?[8] The hypothetical answer helps us see the actual answer as a coarse joke; but that it *is* such a joke and stays a joke, Hemingway makes clear when the persistent questioner asks, "What did he want to kill himself for?" The new answer is not an explanation of "nada" but a callous dismissal—"How should I know"—which shows us again that behind the answer "Nothing" there was no idea the speaker might expand on; he now openly shrugs the question off, as though saying, "What are you asking foolish questions for? What difference does it make? Who cares?" Three times the older waiter has asked "Why?" and three times there has been no genuine answer. This persistent rebuff of a serious question is not the way of the older waiter. Bennett is insensitive to the tone of "How should I know" when he hears in it the older waiter's "existential uncertainty" (119), not the crude impatience that Hemingway helpfully suggested by removing the question mark and restoring the period with which he had originally ended the line (MS 3). And since the opening "Nothing" was meant as a set-up for a wise-guy answer, the older waiter cannot be said, in his monologue, to be expounding already, with stunning eloquence, on the "'despair'" he had just "'learned' about from" his insensitive colleague (116).

The principal argument, however, against attributing "Nothing" to the older waiter is in what Hemingway meant by contriving this line for the younger waiter. Bennett asserts that since the older waiter "knows and understands the 'nothingness' behind suicidal thoughts," *he* "could not 'stupidly' ask 'Why [did the old man try to commit suicide]?'" (115; see also 117). This distortion makes us think immediately of Hemingway's suicide. We are still asking "Why?"—as Hemingway himself asked, more than once, about his father (*Winner* 228; *Bell* 339). In *Darkness Visible* William Styron concludes that clinical depression, even when it does not end in suicide, is an "all but impenetrable mystery" (77).[9] The older waiter's persistent return to the question "Why?"—an effort to learn what may be known—reflects the compassionate, intelligent involvement behind his pursuit of the subject—"*How* did he do it?," "*Why* did they do it [cut him down]?" (emphasis added). But the more important mistake in Bennett's distortion here is his failure to realize that the older waiter neither says nor implies that "nada," as he defines it, causes suicide. His monologue laments the loss of the traditional image of a fatherly God; what it says is what Freud says in *The Future of an Illusion* (had Hemingway read it?), though Freud, arguing, like the waiter, "light was all it needed," exhibits rather more confidence in the café he had opened. In this context, "a man was nothing too" has two meanings, which Hemingway, with grim humor, had recently explained in "A Natural History of the Dead," puncturing the rhetoric of Mungo Park: our individual survival means nothing to the universe, and what happens to an untended corpse ridicules our exalting ourselves above natural law. No more than Hemingway there does the waiter here connect this atheism with suicide. Rather, he is raising the question, What *are* we (the human race), now that the God who marks the sparrow's fall is gone and we are no longer immortal? The answer, "a man was nothing too," means we are only another kind of animal, so that our "place" now is merely a refuge, a sort of wildlife sanctuary, like the café for the old man. The symbolic meaning of this refuge is not the older waiter's—he is too modest ("it is probably only insomnia"); behind him, it is Hemingway who is suggesting that religion—and every other kind of home we carve for ourselves out of this harsh cosmos that doesn't know we are here—is no more than such a refuge.

But the story does not stop with the monologue: having shown us how different the waiters are, Hemingway has maneuvered us into going back to see what he is up to with those "one waiter said"s—a challenge that is reinforced when, as we puzzle over it, we detect the apparent inconsistency; and now we discover that the younger waiter's role is to dramatize *how* "a man was nothing too," in the way his behavior answers "What *are* we?" with the complementary question "Who am I?" His bristling when his colleague teases, "You have no fear of going home before your usual hour?," implies that under the boast "I am all confidence" is a man who does not know himself, and who is fated, like Oedipus, to find out who he is, disastrously. This ominous ignorance is equally noticeable when he tells the deaf old man, "You should have killed yourself last week": such self-satisfied callousness is excessive, a gratuitous display of this waiter's assurance that he has nothing in common with the despairing old man; and the excess, like a neurotic symptom, is a measure of the strength of the anxiety the waiter is hiding from himself. Our understanding of this defensiveness is enlarged by Mr. Frazer's interior monologue at the end of **"The Gambler, the Nun, and the Radio,"** which Hemingway was finishing around the time he wrote **"A Clean, Well-Lighted Place"**: life, Frazer thinks, is surgery without anesthesia—what Dr. Adams does in **"Indian Camp"** is how the universe operates—and we block the pain openly, with alcohol or other drugs, or covertly, with the protective coloration or identity we assume. Frazer's catalogue of such identities includes the macho facade—the anxiety-pacifying use of "sexual intercourse"—that is the younger waiter's "opium." Hemingway leaves it to us to figure out that the incident of the soldier hurrying with the girl is meant to give this waiter the rope to hang himself, when he says, in a display of his own sexual powers, "What does it matter if he gets what he's after?"[10] We hear the choral commentary on this line when Frazer, learning that the nun wants to be a saint, tells her, "You'll be one. Everybody gets what they want. That's what they always tell me." Behind the restrained, good-humored irony of this speech is Frazer's knowledge of how we disappoint ourselves (the rodeo rider "now, with a broken back, was going to learn to work in leather and to cane chairs"). The younger waiter needs to delude himself that he is "of those" who get "what they want," *he* "gets what he's after."

So when the old man's "despair" is said to be about "Nothing"—and we listen carefully, rereading, because the ambiguity has forced us to wonder what this means (Is it a contemptuous dismissal? Is it the older waiter's "nada"?)—the conjunction of these alternatives, now that we have seen what thin ice the younger waiter is on, suddenly makes *him* the concealed subject of the inquiry when his unwitting "Nothing" explodes into a revelation of a second kind of "nada": since he is "of those" who "lived in it and never felt it," we realize that the cause of *his* eventual despair, when his macho conception of himself collapses, will not be the older waiter's metaphysical, outer "nada," but a psychological, inner "nada"—the younger waiter's own nothingness that, unconsciously, he is anesthetizing with his sexual persona—which we are being asked to hear in the resonance of that spotlighted "Nothing," as though Hemingway, whose symbolism looms behind the older waiter's monologue, could here be heard murmuring in the wings, like Bugs in **"The Battler,"** "'Nothing,' eh? Ah, Buster! You've 'got a lot coming to' you." With this, we have discovered the initial purpose of the ambiguity: we have been driven to see that the story is a tale of *two* "nadas." The conclusion "a man was nothing too," which is contestable when the older waiter infers it from the silence of the cosmos, is reached unarguably from below, in the human condition the younger waiter's insubstantial identity reveals; for it is this inner "nada" that turns out to be fundamental, since it still takes its toll when the outer "nada" is vigorously denied (as in Hemingway's view of his father's suicide, for Dr. Hemingway was a lifelong devout Christian).

The initial purpose of the ambiguity is joined by a corollary purpose when we realize the relation between the two "nada"s. The young waiter's "bogus self-assurance," as Steven Hoffman has observed (177), is matched in **"Indian Camp"** when little Nick Adams, with "willed ignorance" (178), feels "quite sure he would never die." Hoffman does not explore where this leads. In **"Three Shots,"** the discarded original opening of **"Indian Camp,"** three times we are told that "Nickie" (like Mr. Frazer) tries to avoid thinking, about either his shame or his fear. A few weeks before, the hymn "Some day the silver cord must break" had made him realize for the first time "that he himself would have to die sometime," and he had sat up all night in the hall, reading. That is no small feat for a little boy—it expresses intolerable anxiety, which returns now when he is alone in the tent, where no "silver cord" ties him to his source. "Nickie" here—can he be more than 10?—knows nothing of "the death of God"; the absence frightening him is that of his earthly father, for his fear goes away, and he falls asleep, as soon as he fires the signaling shots, since he has complete faith his father will return at once, and the firing itself identifies him with his father—which shows that the threat facing the boy was not death but separation, the inescapable demand that he be himself, with an identity of his own to protect him. So his concluding denial of how he must end expresses his unwillingness to relinquish the Nirvana of his "silver cord" beginnings.

In little Nick this childish denial is healthy; in the younger waiter it has become a sick denial that exposes his whole character structure as a defense against the reactivation of an intolerable indelible infantile threat. Hemingway's appreciation of this threat is clear in Frazer's belief that we are being operated on without anesthesia when we are stripped of the illusory identity that is all we have. And since, from the older waiter's mock prayer and "A Natural History of the Dead," we see that for Hemingway, as for Freud, the God who marks the sparrow's fall can be nothing but a projection of the infant's experience of omnipotent parental protection, then the older waiter's sense of cosmic desolation is a recapitulation of the primal psychological loss the younger waiter has unsuccessfully buried. Astonishingly, we now gather that the ambiguity, by leading us to entertain the possibility that either waiter might be saying certain significant lines, has as a corollary purpose a dreamlike blurring of the explicit difference between the waiters: though the older one says, "We are of two different kinds," we are meant to see that the younger one's overpowering need to deny the residue of his smol-

dering infantile helplessness makes his blustering "confidence"—his assurance that the old man's despair is "a way [he'll] never be" (see **Winner** 76)—an illusion, which may well be identified before long as the mask of the first stage of the depression that, when catastrophe strikes, may overwhelm *him* with the older waiter's insomnia, and may in the end bring him too to suicide (just as little Nick's confidence "he would never die" presages that he too will one day suffer the Indian husband's unanesthetized anguish). (This psychological relation between the waiters does not, of course, make their speeches interchangeable.) The older waiter himself—with his protesting "What did he want to kill himself for?"—does not yet realize where he is heading. The three characters in the story are an allegory for the stages of our encounter with our inner "nada"—a post-theological pilgrim's progress that Hemingway's life has mapped for us.

The "clean, well-lighted place," then, insofar as it symbolizes a refuge one can achieve for oneself, is only a resting place, a holding action, as Hemingway intimates by the sly echo when Frazer attributes his climactic discovery ("Bread is the opium of the people") to "that well-lighted part of his mind that was there after two or more drinks in the evening; . . . (it was not really there of course)." In **"Big Two-Hearted River"** Nick Adams builds "the good place" of his own tent and camp, his "home where he had made it"—he has learned how fishing can control his anxiety, whatever its roots;[11] but when Frazer concludes, "He was thinking well, a little too well," it is not fellow-traveling book reviewers he is afraid of, if he lets them read, in 1933, his judgment on the Russian revolution[12]—he is afraid that in another minute he will be asking himself why he has omitted fishing and hunting from his catalogue of opiums (for the story is autobiographical), and his next question would be, Why did he omit art—his stories? Does the "clean, well-lighted place" his talent makes available certify his salvation? Hemingway does not have to identify for us the personal failings implied in "Usually [Frazer] avoided thinking all he could, except when he was writing"—such failings are universal, and Hemingway could be a merciless judge of his own, as in **"Hills Like White Elephants."**[13] In **"The Snows of Kilimanjaro,"** which too is autobiographical, Hurry's dream of heavenward flight as he dies—a remorse-inspired illusion rising from his betrayal of his talent—is only one of the story's echoes of Tolstoy's *The Death of Ivan Ilych*, perhaps the most devastating story ever written about inauthentic identity as a defense against the anxiety radiating from the buried soul. For though the loss of the parental God has again brought our professed identity into question, the unique willingness of the human animal to submit to judgment survives. "Fear for his soul" on the lips of the younger waiter is part of the Sophoclean irony.[14] He does not know what danger his own soul is in, since he has not permitted himself to learn that the soul is no imaginary religious atavism—it is still, as it always was, inescapably, the self we create by our choices (insofar as we have them). That Hemingway, after his affair with Jane Mason (following his choice of Pauline Pfeiffer), could make the younger waiter a withering caricature of his own macho bristling,[15] and then imagine for himself an inauthenticity that evoked for him *The Death of Ivan Ilych*, reinforces the allegory revealing the "clean, well-lighted place" as hardly more secure than the heaven that has dissolved like a mirage.[16]

But we have yet to see the range of Hemingway's insight into the younger waiter's insubstantial identity as representative of the human condition. The younger waiter unwittingly betrays himself by overeagerly proclaiming that *he* is something (he is not "nothing too"), while Hemingway, behind the older waiter, is telling us that our need to establish a "clean, well-lighted place" of our own is due to the failure of our social institutions to live up to *their* claims that we are something (they have provided us such well-lighted mansions of meaning as the one that sustained Mungo Park in the desert); and this parallel between the younger waiter and civilization—a bristling "confidence" in the solidity of a shaky identity—is what gives the story its fundamental unity, climaxing the significance our attention to the ambiguity has found in the younger waiter. The range of the parallel is immense—it takes us immeasurably back and forward. For the older waiter's "What are we *now*?" is not new—it goes back to the emergence of the human race, when there was no question of "the death of God" or the "meaninglessness" of life: we alone among animals had to ask ourselves what we were, now that we'd been ejected from the closed programming of our animal Eden; we were already bristling, like the younger waiter, the first time a tribesman shrouded his head and trunk in an animal hide to reassure himself (and all others concerned) who his ancestors were; and the problem is permanent, as Hemingway learned from the collision of Oak Park with the twentieth century, which we see in **"Soldier's Home."** In *Winner Take Nothing* Frazer's monologue is followed immediately by the first paragraph of **"Fathers and Sons,"** where "the traffic lights" "would be gone next year when the payments on the system were not met." As an allusion to Prohibition (the story before **"The Gambler, the Nun, and the Radio"** is **"Wine of Wyoming"**), this introduces a bristling theocratic eagerness to overregulate; for Dr. Adams's contribution to the sexual education of his son advises us that a system of rules telling us when to stop and when to go, permitting us to go about our business without slaughtering each other, must be inspired by a mistaken image of ourselves when it comes at a price we cannot afford (Dr. Adams will pay with his life).

In **"A Clean, Well-Lighted Place"** Hemingway faces us with such a system in the injunction against suicide, the dereliction the girl's uncovered head represents, the hurry of this couple, the curfew, and the patrolling police. As **"Fathers and Sons"** opens, a detour sign has not been removed, though "cars had obviously gone through," so Nick Adams does not detour; but the soldier's graceless infraction classes him with the drunks the Fontans turn away in **"Wine of Wyoming."** What his hurry exposes (emphasized by the contrast with the "very old man walk-ing unsteadily but with dignity") is less a self than a sexual urgency that we are invited to see as an inner uniform—a biological herding that pacifies us with an illusion of identity; and this implicit metaphor explains why "walked out to the old man's table" in the holograph (3) was changed to "marched" in the typescript (2).[17] We are not told precisely how the younger waiter's macho uniform will one day explode, but the strength his behavior leads us to attribute to the unresolved threat he has buried urges us to realize that when a man murders his estranged wife and her lover and then kills himself (a news item we've seen often), he has found that losing her robs him of his identity—without her he is *nothing*—and this is a danger that makes death preferable. In **"The Battler"** Bugs says of Ad Francis's wife, "one day she just went off and never come back." ". . . He just went crazy." But whether or not the crazy violence with which the punch-drunk ex-fighter hallucinates his old identity in the ring may be expected, in one form or another, from the similarly dependent younger waiter, his double, the soldier, is there so that we may ponder the possible imminent collision with the police, which adumbrates the younger waiter's problem in its broadest, tragic significance; for the state or culture, when *its* uniform—its bristling profession of a deep-rooted illusory identity (like the primitive animal hide)—is seriously threatened, knows no restraint, and lesser groups often claim such juggernaut authority. In this way, the younger waiter's desperate flailing when he feels his identity escaping him becomes a microcosmic suggestion of the suicidal extremes that erupt in all racial, religious, ethnic, and political hostilities where persecution of a scapegoat is needed to shore up a precarious identity.

This is what Frazer is thinking in 1933 when he sees patriotism as "the opium of the people in Italy and Germany": the "doctor," it would turn out (in *Scribner's Magazine* the story was called **"Give Us a Prescription, Doctor"**), was prescribing, for those people's tranquility, 50 million deaths. Every culture struggles, with its back to the wall, against the realities threatening the identity it claims. For Socrates, wisdom begins when we admit we do not know; but society, denying to the end what its professed identity will not permit it to admit, must bristle like the younger waiter, and self-destruct. From the older waiter's rejection of the bodega, with its "shining steam-pressure coffee machine," we gather that Hemingway foresees no salvation in the identity technological civilization offers. Our effort to discover what the human race is turns out to be back-breaking Sisyphean labor—a cruel joke—if our vaunted openness to cultural development is an endless, savage turmoil of one self-deception after another. But Hemingway does not believe it endless. Whether justifiably, or only reflecting his own depression, he gives us, in his next book, *Green Hills of Africa,* his opinion of our ability to solve our problem. He compares what the human race will leave behind—after "the systems of governments, the richness, the poverty, the martyrdom, the sacrifice and the venality and the cruelty are all gone"—to the five loads of garbage dumped on a good day outside Havana, turning the Gulf Stream to "a pale green to a depth of four or five fathoms": "in ten miles along the coast it is as clear and blue and unimpressed as it was ever before the tug hauled out the scow" (149-50). There, for Hemingway—after the floating debris is gone ("the worn light bulbs of our discoveries and the empty condoms of our great loves") and as long as the sun rises—is the lasting "clean, well-lighted place."

Notes

1. Smith finds Bennett's defense a "persuasive counterstatement, that—is it too much to hope?—may settle the issue" (385).

2. Reviewing Joseph Flora's *Ernest Hemingway: A Study of the Short Fiction,* James R. Frakes expostulates at once: "Would you believe that . . . [he] offers us here, without grimacing, still another effort to straighten out the two waiters' dialogue . . .?" (275-76). And Hershel Parker says: "Everyone wants to know the right assignment of speakers in" the story, "but the attention paid to this problem has been excessive" (19-20). But if we haven't determined how to read what James Joyce, who knew only the unemended text, reportedly called "one of the best short stories ever written" (Power 107), can the "attention paid" have been sufficient?

3. Are we to suppose that Hemingway, when he wished Hotchner would adapt "A Clean, Well-Lighted Place" for television (Hotchner 164), expected him to provide the audience with *two* versions, distributing the lines both ways? The reasonable inference is that Hemingway believed that a careful reading resolves the ambiguity. After a work was published, "no explanations or dissertations [from the author] should be necessary" (*Writers at Work* 230; see Kerner, "Manuscripts" 394-95).

4. In addition, the holograph shows that Hemingway, from the beginning, meant to obscure identification of the two waiters. After the second short patch of dialogue, about the soldier, Hemingway originally wrote, "One of the waiters went over to [the old man]" (2); and even after the third dialogue, when the old man asks for "Another brandy," Hemingway originally wrote, "One of the waiters came over" (4). In the first instance, the waiter says, "What do you want?," "You'll be drunk," and "You should have killed yourself last week" (2-3); in the second, "Finished. Close now" and "No. Finished" (5). Clearly, in both instances it's the same waiter who goes over to the old man, and Hemingway knew this—it wasn't something he still had to decide; yet he chose, originally, not to say it's the same waiter, and not to tell us it's the younger waiter. This was no casual omission of attribution; it was a challenge. Later Hemingway realized that since these speeches were transparent, the withholding of identification here was superfluous and could be damaging—it might arouse an impatient mistrust of the serious ambiguity he had in mind.

5. Strangely ignoring the context of deliberate (and therefore presumably purposeful) ambiguity, Dolch and Hagopian conjectured that there had been a printing error—"You said she cut him down" belonged at the end of the preceding speech, spoken by the younger waiter; and Scribner's put it there. In 1965 no one seemed to know that Hemingway was fond of juxtaposing two separate speeches for a single speaker, even without attribution, and that he had learned this from writers he had read and admired in his youth, like O. Henry and Marryat (Kerner, "Origins" and "Hemingway's Trail"). (Few of us, apparently, realized that in English the typographical convention for dialogue includes the possibility of an anti-metronomic disruption. Since we omit end quotes when a speech continues in a new paragraph, the inclusion of those end quotes when the speaker does not change can imply [among other things] a pause or gap—the speaker does not *continue* to speak, but speaks again [Kerner, "Counterfeit" 91-100]; and identation alone, after unspoken words [like "he said"], can serve the same purpose ["Hemingway's Trail" 189-92].) Yet Otto Reinert, suspecting this, had proposed in 1959 that it is the younger waiter who, after a "reflective pause," adds, "He's drunk every night" (in a reiteration that we soon learn is characteristic of this waiter). The thoughtful older waiter sees no need to respond to "He's drunk now" (our own silent response might be, "So what else is new?"); nor would he think that "He's drunk every night" needed saying after he has just heard that the old man tried to kill himself last week. We see what this waiter is thinking about when he asks, "What did he want to kill himself for?" So the younger waiter is the one answering the questions; there is no discrepancy. When the holograph turned up and confirmed Hemingway's placement of the troubling line, Hagopian and Dolch were silent. But Mr. Scribner, undeterred, continued to print the line where "common sense" told him it belonged (MacDonald 99). Echoing Hagopian's exclamation of incredulity (141), Bennett, in objecting to "the conclusion that Hemingway . . . used anti-metronomic dialogue in" the story "not only once but *twice*" (98), fails to see that the doubling simplifies the problem: the second instance—the older waiter's

"He must be eighty years old."

"Anyway I should say he was eighty."

—is meant to confirm the deliberateness of the first instance (as in *The Sun Also Rises* and elsewhere: see Kerner, "Foundation" 284-85; "Manuscripts" 385n; "Counterfeit" 104-05). Bennett argues that Hemingway wrote anti-metronomic dialogue only "inadvertently," when he "lost track" of the speakers in unattributed dialogue (100-04), and that comparison of the holograph and the typescript shows there is no anti-metronomic dialogue in "A

Clean, Well-Lighted Place" (107-12). For my detailed refutation, see "Hemingway's Attention."

6. Launching his artillery at the first opportunity, the older waiter would be something of a soapbox orator, which he is not—he is not the Mexican whom Mr. Frazer mocks in "The Gambler, the Nun, and the Radio":

"I was acolyte," the thin one said proudly. "Now I believe in nothing. Neither do I go to mass."

"Why? Does it mount to your head?"

(*Winner* 206)

7. What can Bennett mean when he writes that "'plenty of money' symbolizes all that it is possible for a person to have and it is the polar opposite of nothingness" (117; also "Character, Irony" 75)? "In Another Country" teaches us that there is nothing we cannot lose, and money of course is one of the easiest things to lose, as Hemingway's father learned; nor does "having" it keep it out of the "black hole" of nothingness (117). Hemingway's title identifies the possible "opposite" of "nada" available.

8. The change in plot would not affect the theme. Like the older waiter, who suggests that the old man "might be better with a wife," William Styron tells us, "I would hazard the opinion that many disastrous sequels to depression might be averted if the victims received support such as [my wife] gave me" (57); but her devotion did not keep Styron's depression from taking him to the brink of suicide.

9. The obscurity of the causes of suicidal depression is darkened further by Carol Iannone's review of Styron's book and the letters her review provoked.

10. Hemingway's manuscript revision of "He better get off the street now" to "He had better . . ." is a refinement of grammar expectable from the older waiter, while "What does it matter if he gets <what he's after>?" is a young cock's crow (2). Correspondingly, for the younger waiter, Hemingway crossed out the grammatical "hanged" and substituted "hung" (3).

11. Writing in the third person, Hemingway says: "Since he was a young boy he has cared greatly for fishing and shooting. If he had not spent so much time at them, at ski-ing, at the bull ring, and in a boat, he might have written much more. On the other hand, he might have shot himself" (Schreiber 57).

12. John Dos Passos reportedly said that when he told Hemingway in 1937 "he was going back to the United States to tell the truth about what was going on" in Spain, "Hemingway responded, 'You do that and the New York reviewers will kill you. They will demolish you forever'" (Ludington 496).

13. As with the suppressed causes of Thomas Hudson's suicidal depression in *Islands in the Stream* (Hovey), the omission of what Frazer tries not to think about signals the presence of autobiography.

14. Bennett believes that when the younger waiter asks, "How much money has he got?," he is merely changing the subject, the preceding answer, "Fear for his soul," having made him nervous ("Character, Irony" 74). Besides turning "How much money . . .?" in itself into a meaningless question, this interpretation gives the younger waiter a religious sensitivity inconsistent with his telling the old man, "You should have killed yourself last week," and saddles the older waiter with the uncharacteristically crude dismissal "He's got plenty." In Hemingway's version, when the older waiter moves directly from "Why did they [cut him down]?" to "How much money has he got?," skepticism (as in the "joke" about the risk the younger waiter may run by coming home early) has made this waiter wonder how much of a temptation the old man's heirs faced.

15. For the inveterate insistence on his prowesses that associates Hemingway with the younger waiter, see Tavernier-Courbin and Brenner.

16. Hemingway in 1949: "Only suckers worry about saving their souls. Who the hell should care about saving his soul when it is a man's duty to lose it intelligently, the way you would sell a position you were defending, if you could not hold it, as expensively as possible. . . ." (Ross 48). *If you could not hold it* is not a reference to death. In 1926 he'd written Fitzgerald, ". . . I'm now all through with the general bumping off phase. . . . Am continuing my life in original role of son of a bitch sans peur et sans reproche" (*Letters* 232); and in 1945 he wrote Mary Welsh, "Half the time, too, if they had real justice we'd all be shot" (599). In 1954, reportedly: "I would be tempted to say . . . fattening of the soul, but I don't know anything about the soul" (Manning 176).

17. Had Hemingway in November or December 1932 already read *Light in August* and seen what Faulkner finds lurking under the uniform that means so much to Percy Grimm?

Works Cited

Bennett, Warren. "Character, Irony, and Resolution in 'A Clean, Well-Lighted Place.'" *American Literature* 42 (1970): 70-79.

———. "The Characterization and the Dialogue Problem in Hemingway's 'A Clean, Well-Lighted Place.'" *Hemingway Review* 9 (Spring 1990): 94-123.

Benson, Jackson J., ed. *New Critical Approaches to the Short Stories of Ernest Hemingway.* Durham, NC: Duke UP, 1990.

Brenner, Gerry. "A Lamp on the Anxiety in Hemingway's 'Vital Light.'" Scafella 246-55.

Dolch, Martin. "'A Clean, Well-Lighted Place.'" *Insight I: Analyses of American Literature.* Ed. John V. Hagopian and Martin Dolch. Frankfurt am Main: Hirschgraben, 1962. 105-11.

Frakes, James R. Rev. of *Ernest Hemingway: A Study of the Short Fiction,* by Joseph M. Flora. *Studies in Short Fiction* 27 (1990): 275-77.

Hagopian, John V. "Tidying Up Hemingway's 'Clean, Well-Lighted Place.'" *Studies in Short Fiction* 1 (1964): 140-46.

Hemingway, Ernest. "A Clean, Well-Lighted Place," pencil ms. Item 337. John F. Kennedy Library, Boston. © The Ernest Hemingway Foundation.

———. "A Clean, Well-Lighted Place." ts, ribbon copy and carbon. Items SS381, 382. U of Delaware Library, Newark. © The Ernest Hemingway Foundation.

———. "Ernest Hemingway." *Writers at Work: The Paris Review Interviews*, Second Series. Ed. George Plimpton. New York: Viking, 1963. 215-39.

———. *For Whom the Bell Tolls.* New York: Scribner's, 1939.

———. *Green Hills of Africa.* New York: Scribner's, 1935.

———. *Winner Take Nothing.* New York: Scribner's, 1933.

Hoffman, Steven K. "*Nada* and the Clean, Well-Lighted Place: The Unity of Hemingway's Short Fiction." Benson 172-91.

Hotchner, A. E. *Papa Hemingway.* New York: Random, 1966.

Hovey, Richard. "*Islands in the Stream*: Death and the Artist." *Hemingway: A Revaluation.* Ed. Donald R. Noble. Troy, NY: Whitston, 1983. 241-62.

Iannone, Carol. "Depression-as-Disease." *Commentary* 90 (November 1990): 54, 56-57.

———.et al. Letters. *Commentary* 91 (March 1991): 10-13.

Kerner, David. "Counterfeit Hemingway: A Small Scandal in Quotation Marks." *Journal of Modern Literature* 12 (1985): 91-108.

———. "The Foundation of the True Text of 'A Clean, Well-Lighted Place.'" *Fitzgerald/Hemingway Annual 1979*: 279-300.

———. "Hemingway's Attention to 'A Clean, Well-Lighted Place.'" *Hemingway Review* 12 (1993), forthcoming.

———. "Hemingway's Trail to British Anti-Metronomic Dialogue." *Literary Research* 12 (1987 [1990]): 187-214.

———. "The Manuscripts Establishing Hemingway's Anti-Metronomic Dialogue." *American Literature* 54 (1982): 385-96.

———. "The Origins of Hemingway's Anti-Metronomic Dialogue." *Analytical & Enumerative Bibliography* ns 2.1 (1988): 12-28.

Ludington, Townsend, ed. *The Fourteenth Chronicle: Letters and Diaries of John Dos Passos.* Boston: Gambit, 1973.

MacDonald, Scott. "The Confusing Dialogue in Hemingway's 'A Clean, Well-Lighted Place': A Final Word?" *Studies in American Fiction* 1 (Spring 1973): 93-101.

Manning, Robert. "Hemingway in Cuba." *Conversations with Ernest Hemingway.* Ed. Matthew J. Bruccoli. Jackson: University Press of Mississippi, 1986. 172-89.

May, Charles E. "Is Hemingway's 'Well-Lighted Place' Really Clean Now?" *Studies in Short Fiction* 8 (1971): 326-30.

Parker, Hershel. "Textual Criticism and Hemingway." Scafella 17-31.

Power, Arthur. *Conversations with James Joyce.* Ed. Clive Hart. New York: Barnes, 1974.

Reinert, Otto. "Hemingway's Waiters Once More." *College English* 20 (1959): 417-18.

Ross, Lillian. *Portrait of Hemingway.* New York: Simon, 1961.

Scafella, Frank, ed. *Hemingway: Essays of Reassessment.* New York: Oxford UP, 1991.

Schreiber, Georges. *Portraits and Self-Portraits.* New York: Houghton, 1936. Rpt. Freeport, NY: Books for Libraries, 1968.

Smith, Paul. "A Partial Review: Critical Essays on the Short Stories, 1976-1989." Benson 375-91.

Styron, William. *Darkness Visible: A Memoir of Madness.* New York: Random, 1990.

Tavernier-Courbin, Jacqueline. "'Striving for Power': Hemingway's Classical Neurosis and Creative Force." *MidAmerica V.* Ed. David D. Anderson. East Lansing: Michigan State University Press, 1978. 76-95.

David Kerner (essay date 1993)

SOURCE: "Hemingway's Attention to 'A Clean, Well-Lighted Place,'" in *The Hemingway Review*, Vol. 13, No. 1, Fall, 1993, pp. 48-62.

[*In the following essay, Kerner rejects Warren Bennett's position regarding the dialogue controversy and interprets the questionable passages in the story as Hemingway's deliberate use of anti-metronomic dialogue.*]

If our professed boredom with the controversy over the emendation in **"A Clean, Well-Lighted Place"** is how we deny our evasion of Hemingway's challenge—for no one has explained the purpose of the clearly deliberate ambiguity in the dialogue—two new pieces of evidence may soften our reluctance to trust the unemended text. We haven't forgotten that in 1956 the poet Judson Jerome wrote Hemingway that since the third patch of dialogue opens as follows—

"He's drunk now," he said.

"He's drunk every night."

"What did he want to kill himself for?"

—and the first speech here is the younger waiter's, it "does not make sense" for the *older* waiter, in speech 22, to be found saying, "'You said she cut him down,'" since this waiter has been *answering* the questions that begin with speech 3. Hemingway replied, "Dear Asst Professor Jerome: I just read the story over and it makes sense to me. Sorry."[1] *We* are sorry he did not explain. In 1965, knowing nothing of this exchange, Scribner's accepted the Dolch/Hagopian conjecture that a printer had misplaced the apparently inconsistent line, and the line was tacked onto speech 21, spoken by the younger waiter. We seem to have been able to live with this wholesale alteration, which, without further tampering, redistributes 19 other unattributed speeches. The most intelligent discussion of the story (still Steven K. Hoffman's) deftly sidesteps the problem, as though we understand well enough what Hemingway was up to, whether the speeches are distributed his way or Hagopian's. In thirty-four years, only Joseph F. Gabriel has ventured to decipher what the ambiguity does for the story. He, unfortunately, like Hagopian, failed to weigh his hypothesis, for either credibility or usefulness, against an interpretation based on the suggestion Otto Reinert had made. In the second line of dialogue above, the younger waiter (Reinert suggested) unexpectedly speaks again after a "reflective pause"—an attribution that makes dramatic sense (the younger waiter needs to hear himself talk—he says things twice); and Reinert inferred a second such juxtaposition, this time for the older waiter, in speeches 13-14.[2] Since then, in the other work Hemingway proofread, we have found 40 such deviations from the typographical convention for dialogue, 10 of them without attribution in either line. We know too where he learned the practise.[3]

Before examining the new evidence, one must realize that the case for the emendation rests on the supposition that Hemingway, after writing the story at white heat, never reread it attentively, either in typescript or proof or when Jerome questioned the confusing line. What makes this supposition necessary can be demonstrated by a simple experiment: visualizing Hemingway rereading the third patch of dialogue. Warren Bennett, in his latest defense of the emendation, argues that "Hemingway was *not* writing antimetronomic dialogue" in this story (110). Let us follow where this leads. The question in speech 3 above is the first in a series of five questions—all, according to Bennett, asked by the younger waiter; and each time, the answer is given by the older waiter. Hemingway, rereading, swings back and forth, and does so again in lines 13-14. Line 15 begins a six-speech set of protests and defenses—the younger waiter complains about the old man, and the

older waiter counters the complaint: here, no reader, let alone Hemingway, could have any question who is speaking. And when the older waiter, in speech 18, says, "'He had a wife once too,'" this line, according to Bennett (115), reaffirms in Hemingway's mind that this waiter is the one who knows about the old man's life and therefore is the one who has been telling about the suicide attempt.[4] Then come speeches 19-22:

"A wife would be no good to him now."

"You can't tell. He might be better with a wife."

"His niece looks after him."

"I know. You said she cut him down."

In lines 19-20, which complete the six-speech set of complaint and defense, Hemingway knows, obviously, that 19 is the younger waiter's complaint, and 20 the older waiter's defense. Line 21, therefore, by its resistance to line 20, is just as obviously the younger waiter's. Well, after swinging metronomically, without deviation, from younger waiter to older, younger waiter to older, for 20 very short speeches—during which Hemingway, from the start, has the great advantage over us of *knowing* (according to Bennett) that it is the younger waiter who is asking the questions—nevertheless, when Hemingway comes to the eleventh consecutive metronomic swing from younger waiter to older, he does not notice that "'I know'" *precedes* "'You said she cut him down.'" This reversal of his alleged intention does not jar him (though it would mean that in his own mind he had misassigned 19 other speeches), he does not say to himself, "Wait a minute. That's not where I put the line." Try it. The conjectured oversight is not possible when you "know" that the older waiter is the one telling of the suicide attempt, and that all the speeches are metronomic. Overlooking the alleged inconsistency is possible only for someone without prior knowledge of which waiter is saying what, someone with no notion that it matters which waiter is telling of the suicide attempt—someone who can read the third dialogue without noticing the problem. And as Scott MacDonald pointed out in 1973, if speeches 21-22 "are correct as they are printed" in the original version, "then it is clear that Hemingway does ignore dialogue conventions" in this story (101n). There is no alternative.

To prove, then, that "'You said she cut him down'" belongs where Hemingway put it, we need do no more than establish that he reread the story attentively at least once.[5] And this is what the typescript that surfaced in 1987 establishes, in conjunction with the following unpublished handwritten note, which Hemingway, in Key West, sent Alfred Dashiell, managing editor of *Scribner's Magazine,* on 26 January 1933:

Thursday

Jan

Dear Dashiell,

Here is the proof—Am sending it air-mail—Hope you get it in time. The corrections wont be difficut [sic] to make! Two semi-colons to go in and one word—(the word) (not) to come out.

Just got here last night—send this off—air mail—Special Delivery today.

Yours always—

Ernest Hemingway[6]

The corrections identify **"A Clean, Well-Lighted Place"** now that we have the typescript: there are only two semi-colons in the story as it appeared in *Scribner's Magazine* in March, and neither of them is in the typescript, so the deletion must have been of the duplicate "not" in "nada us not not into nada" (4).[7] The identification is confirmed by Dashiell's reply on the 30th:

> Thanks for your promptness in returning the proofs. They got under the wire and the changes are made.
>
> We expect to use **"Homage to Switzerland"** in the April number, and hope very much that we may have the third story for the May Scribner's. If it can be longer than the first two, so much the better.

Since Hemingway had mailed the corrected proof of **"Homage to Switzerland"** on 28 September 1932, and "the third story" had not been submitted, the "proofs" Dashiell had been in a hurry to have were the two pages **"A Clean, Well-Lighted Place"** filled in the March issue.[8]

Now, if Hemingway could twice be stopped by what struck him as a defective rhythm—for neither of the semi-colons he inserted is conventional, and at least one of them would never have been suggested by a copy editor or proofreader (it was removed in ***Winner Take Nothing***)[9]—then Hemingway, reading the page proof, was hearing what he read. Nothing, then, authorizes a conjecture that when he came to the line "'You said she cut him down,'" he did not hear the older waiter say it; and since its meaning was inescapable and crucial, we must infer that Hemingway wanted the line where it was.

In a less obvious way, his deletion of the "not" leads to the same conclusion. Though the possibility that a proofreader or copy editor had queried the two "not"s cannot be dismissed, nothing in Hemingway's letter warrants that conjecture. The exclamation point gives his announcement the air of a news bulletin meant to reassure an apprehensive audience: Dashiell, with the March issue locked up, was concerned what troublesome changes Hemingway might want to make, and Hemingway was happily reporting how simply the corrections could be made. Moreover, if the extra "not" had come with a query, Dashiell, with his concern, would have noticed it, and Hemingway then should have felt no need for the caution that impelled him, despite his hurry, to take a moment, in his letter, to identify what word he had deleted—a caution doubly evident in his finding the identification incomplete until, in the grip of an afterthought, he had squeezed "the word" above the "*not.*"

Whatever doubt these inferences may fail to dispel loses its significance when we realize that the letter proves Hemingway had been attentive to the typescript, where he had missed the duplicate "not" because the first "not" ends the line—the eye cannot take in the two "not"s in a single glance. Since the "not not" was in the page proof—whether with or without the query the typescript's placement of these two "not"s should have prompted—we cannot reasonably doubt that the "y y" in "It all was nada y pues nada y y pues nada" (4) would also have been in the page proof if this error had been uncorrected in the typescript Hemingway had sent Maxwell Perkins. That the "y y" was not in the page proof, we know from Hemingway's letter: the duplicate "not" was the only substantive error transmitted from typescript to proof. Therefore Hemingway himself must have restored the "nada" omitted between the two "y"s: *we* know a "nada" is missing from the surviving typescript, because we know the published story; the typesetter, copy editor, and proofreader who kept the "not not" (probably without querying it) allow us no grounds for conjecturing that they, without the holograph, could have seen through the "y y" and inserted the missing "nada." One concludes that Hemingway had restored this "nada" on the lost carbon that became the setting copy,[10] since neither of the surviving copies of the typescript carries a single printer's mark, and there is no date. On receiving a typescript, the Scribner Press would stamp the date in an upper corner of the first page.[11]

Of the other serious mistakes in the surviving typescript, the one we might expect a copy editor or proofreader to have noticed (if Hemingway had not already corrected it) is the missing comma in "The old man stood up slowly counted the saucers" (3; see JFK 337:5). But if Hemingway was queried here—as he would have had to be—where was the query made? It was not in the proof he corrected in Key West, and the evidence indicates he had not seen earlier proof when he was in New York. In any case, nothing permits us to assume that anyone but Hemingway initiated the three remaining significant changes. Where the holograph has a period followed by a capital "W" beginning "'With all those who do not want to go to bed'" (7), the typescript has a comma and lower-case "w" (4). Since the comma was mechanically correct, and the possibility of a faulty rhythm was not the sort of thing the Press was invited to look for in Hemingway's work, one must doubt that the people who let the "not not" through would have paused here. At best—a remote best—there would have been a query. The letter of 26 January shows there was no such query. Even more clearly, where the typescript reads "It was no fear or dread" (4), *Scribner's Magazine* substitutes "not" for the "no," because Hemingway (one must assume) had repaired the typescript's omission of the immediately preceding sentence in the holograph ("He did not fear."[9]). This was a revision, not a correction. With Hemingway, the mission of the Press was to correct routine errors, not volunteer "improvements." The last mistake was here:

> "I don't want to look at him."

"I wish he would go home. He has no regard for those who must work."

(3)

In the holograph the first of these speeches is only an insertion (4) inside the opening quotation mark of what the typist set off as a second speech. The reasonable inference here is that Hemingway, in the setting copy, restored the single speech he had written. No one at the Press knew what Hemingway had written, so it is unlikely that anyone there would have made this correction, since the Press left unchanged the two anti-metronomic juxtapositions in **"Homage to Switzerland"** in April and the one in **"Give Us a Prescription, Doctor"** in May.[12]

The other new piece of evidence may not, at first, seem particularly relevant. The emendation, we must remember, asks us to believe that Hemingway, reading page proof for *Winner Take Nothing,* again was inattentive. Yet there was a single obvious substantive mistake in the book, and no one at the Press noticed it—Hemingway is the one who caught it. The untold story of this incident must be reported in enough detail to leave the reader no doubt of its bearing here.

On 2 August 1933, writing Hemingway that the *Winner Take Nothing* galleys would be going out to Havana that afternoon, Perkins advised him not to keep **"The Light of the World"** first, and added, "I have underlined the words and phrases I think you ought to get around." The galleys did not reach Hemingway before he sailed for Spain. In an undated handwritten letter, probably sent when a second set of galleys went out, now to Madrid, on 14 August, Perkins said again: "I'm enclosing the places marked that seem to me to be especially questionable." This gave Hemingway an extra copy of the first galley of **"The Light of the World"**; and here, in pencil, he crossed out what Perkins had underlined in ink—"'Up your ass'" and two "'bugger'"s—and substituted "'You know where'" and two "'interfere with'"s that *he* found questionable, for in the left margin he posted two question marks (JFK 222a). But on the galley he returned he crossed out one word too many:

"Ever interfere with a cook?" he said to me.

"No."

"You interfere with this one," he looked at the cook. "He likes it."[13]

The mistake is Hemingway's: the handwriting in the substituted words is the same as that on the galley he kept.[14]

On 22 September, the day after Scribner's mailed Hemingway the page proof, Perkins wrote him, "If you strike anything wrong, and can wire it, do that." On 25 September Perkins assured Hemingway that "a few . . . obvious little typographical errors have been corrected. Don't bother about them. The proof has been very carefully read, minutely." On 5 October: "We are going right ahead with the book. . . . And if there are any small things you want to change that won't upset the re-paging, we can do it even in the first edition in unbound copies. . . . But I do not think anything will be wrong." Perkins never mentions the mistake. On 20 October Hemingway cabled: "PROOF OK PAGE THIRTY SHOULD READ YOU CAN INTERFERE WITH THIS ONE." But I have yet to find the "can" in a copy of the first edition, and later printings too leave the mistake uncorrected, indicating that neither Perkins nor the Press found it anything to get excited about, so we have no reason to imagine that Hemingway's correction may have been a response to a lost query.[15] Consequently—since the page proof, according to Perkins, had been read at the Press "very carefully . . . minutely," and the correction was not made even when Hemingway's cable came in—the incident lends no support to a conjecture that anyone at the Press would have stopped or even queried the "not not," "y y," and at least three of the four other serious errors in the Delaware typescript. The reasonable inference, once more, is that it was Hemingway who caught those errors, just as he caught the missing "can."

The indications that Hemingway went over **"A Clean, Well-Lighted Place"** attentively at least four times—in the setting copy, the *Scribner's Magazine* proof, and the *Winner Take Nothing* galleys[16] and page proof—permit a thorough reappraisal of Warren Bennett's conjecture in 1979 that Hemingway was confused when he inserted "'You said she cut him down.'"

First: In the holograph, precisely at the point of the alleged inconsistency (see Bennett's reproduction, 621), Hemingway, at first, again juxtaposed two speeches for the younger waiter:

"His niece looks after him."

"I wouldnt want to be that old. An old man is a nasty thing."

(4)

Between these speeches, there is silence—the older waiter keeps his comment to himself, as at the opening of the third dialogue. The silence invites the younger waiter to speak again: he has been thinking of the unpleasantness the niece must endure—she must have to clean up, for example, where the old man, shaky, misses the toilet. The coherence linking these two speeches makes it impossible for Hemingway to have been unaware that the speech he later inserted between them—"'I know'"—was the older waiter's response to the younger waiter's "'His niece looks after him,'" which had expressed this waiter's resistance to the older waiter's immediately preceding "'He might be better with a wife.'" For Bennett, however, the coherent juxtaposition of those two speeches by the younger waiter was a "confusion in the dialogue sequence" that "must have still lingered in Hemingway's mind" when Hemingway returned again to the passage (620), since now, Bennett conjectured, Hemingway added "'You said she cut him down'" to "'I know'" because "he probably thought" "'His niece looks after him'" was the *older* waiter's line, and "'I know'" the younger waiter's.

Second: The mechanics of the insertion indicate Hemingway's care in placing "'You said she cut him down.'" He added it on the same line-level as "'I know'"; writing the "'Y'" over the quotation mark closing "'I know,'" he obliterated the first of the inverted commas and left the second a meaningless speck (see the reproduction), and he did nothing to the quotation mark closing "'His niece looks after him.'"[17] Clearly, Hemingway *wanted* the second insertion to follow and join the first—and there are no grounds for imagining he could not remember he had given "'I know'" to the older waiter. Yet Bennett asks us to believe that at the very moment Hemingway was adding the indispensable line informing us that the younger waiter is the one who has been telling of the suicide attempt, Hemingway could have thought "'His niece looks after him'" was the older waiter's line because *this* waiter (according to Bennett) has been telling about the suicide attempt.

Third: Since "'I know'" was inserted *first* (meaning "'[Yes,] I know [his niece looks after him (though I hadn't heard he tried to kill himself)—but a niece is not a wife].'"), how can this insertion have been meant as a response to the second insertion, which had not yet been written? The second insertion makes sense only as a continuation of the first: "'I know [*how* the niece 'looks after him':] You said she cut him down [—she was not doing him a favor].'" Moreover, when we switch the second insertion, making it precede the first, the direct response of "'I know'" to "'His niece looks after him'" is clumsily deflected—the older waiter can seem to be saying, incongruously and fatuously, "'I know [I said she cut him down].'" And the switch presumes that the dialogue has been metronomic throughout, which means we already know who said the niece "'cut him down,'" so the second insertion, which was crucial where Hemingway put it, becomes pointless when it is given to the younger waiter, since "'His niece looks after him.'" in itself needs no explanation.[18]

Fourth: The assurance with which Bennett attributes to Hemingway a manifestly impossible misreading and reverses the intention of the two insertions, dismantling their coherence, was based on the assumption that the typographical convention of alternating speakers is inviolate. Yet by 1973 Scott MacDonald had identified, in Hemingway's other work, 9 abrogations of this convention. One must ask why Bennett—instead of investigating what this resolution of the problem might do for our understanding of the story—preferred to see, in the two originally juxtaposed speeches of the younger waiter here, a "confusion" inviting a cluster of untenable conjectures.

Fifth: The insertion of "'I know'" was not a mechanical restoration of metronomic rhythm. Though the anti-metronomic juxtaposition Hemingway had written here (a third one) was obvious, he saw that this clarity would not stop us from reading speeches 1-2 and 13-14 metronomically; we would still think the older waiter is telling of the suicide attempt, and the far-reaching purpose of the ambiguity in the first and second dialogues would be lost. (The

emendation blithely disregards this context of the alleged inconsistency.) The third anti-metronomic passage, serving no purpose, offered Hemingway an opening for the information we needed. But after inserting "'I know,'" he decided we could easily miss the implied "'[though I hadn't heard he tried to kill himself].'" The disputed insertion itself, then, establishes Hemingway's awareness of the two anti-metronomic passages he was keeping: we infer their presence because he would not otherwise have found it necessary to surprise us with "'You said she cut him down,'" which, by forcing us to wrestle with the apparent inconsistency, underscores the opening ambiguity, warning us that its purpose is not to be shrugged off.

So the argument that the passage shows confusion is as gratuitous as it is groundless. The notion that Hemingway was confused here is a projection of the uninitiated reader's own initial confusion, when there seems to be no way out of the apparent inconsistency.

In 1990, in lieu of the conjectured confusion, Bennett "documents" the "particularly serious trouble [Hemingway was having with his eyes] in 1932, from April through November"; for "difficulty with blurred vision . . . can cause lines on a page to appear to be where they are not" (104). That is, what Hemingway actually saw on page 4 of the holograph (and saw again in the typescript, galleys, and page proof) was what he (according to Bennett) had *meant* to write:

> "His niece looks after him. You said she cut him down."
>
> "I know."

By limiting this fantasy to 1932, does Bennett spare himself the need to search for 40 other such recurring hallucinations in the work Hemingway proofread?

The two holograph details Bennett relied on in 1979, he again depends on in 1990, without considering the objections that undermine his use of them. (See Appendix A.) He can now admit "it is possible to find instances of anti-metronomic dialogue in Hemingway's published work" (98); but when he runs across such a passage (as in **"Fathers and Sons,"** *WTN* 238.9-10), he calls it "inadvertent" and a "lapse" (100) and asks, "Why did Hemingway [do this]? Did he himself become confused?" (103), for Hemingway "preferred, if he caught it, that the dialogue be metronomic" (100), but "on numerous occasions he lost track of who was speaking" (104). Bennett fails to establish either part of this linkage. Only three of the "numerous occasions" are offered, and not one of them supports the charge. (See Appendix B.) When we include some of the posthumously published books, there are at least 55 instances of anti-metronomic dialogue in Hemingway's work; but, except for the passage in **"Fathers and Sons,"** which Bennett tries, unsuccessfully, to dispute, he doesn't mention them, not even the fourteen-line exchange in *Across the River and Into the Trees* that matches the dual instance in **"A Clean, Well-Lighted Place"** (Kerner, "Counterfeit" 104-105). Moreover, when Hemingway was questioned point-blank about the troubling line, he stood firm and made no change. This alone should prove that the emendation has no authority; for Bennett, however, the rebuff to Jerome means, somehow, that Hemingway was tacitly admitting his "mistake" (107).[19] Yet the emendation distorts the characterization and hamstrings Hemingway's achievement, cutting off what the ambiguity does to enlarge our understanding of the story.

APPENDIX A. SPEECHES 1-2 AND 13-14

1. Bennett argues (108-09) that since a run-on line on page 3 of the holograph attaches speech 1, "'He's drunk now,' he said," to the end of the preceding paragraph, this canceled indentation (left uncanceled by the typist) shows that Hemingway meant speech 2, "'He's drunk every night,'" to be the older waiter's—an inference Bennett thinks is confirmed by the original shift from "'tanked'" in speech 1 to "'stewed'" in speech 2. The canceled pejorative slang, however, indicates that the younger waiter had both speeches—an inference confirmed by the repeated substitution "'drunk'"; and since the run-on line was drawn before the two "'drunk'"'s were substituted (the line was partly erased when Hemingway erased the word superseded by the first "'drunk'"), the line could not have been meant to indicate that the younger waiter does not have speech 2.[20] (To buttress his argument here, Bennett calls Hemingway's pencil line inserting "'I don't want to look at him'" another "run-on line" "the typist did not understand" [109]. But that insertion-line is no different from seven other such lines, of varying length, all of which the typist followed, beginning with one on page 2.) Bennett again relies on the surface of diction, rather than its substance, when he argues that the waiter who says, "'You should have killed yourself last week'" must be the one who says "'What did he want to kill himself for?,'" and could not be the one saying, "'Last week he tried to commit suicide.'" Both these expressions are in the public domain, without power to characterize the speaker. And the plaintiveness of the protest "'What did he want to kill himself for?'"—a plaintiveness echoing "'How do you know it was nothing?'"—is inconsistent with "'You should have killed yourself last week.'"

2. In the holograph an "x" (Hemingway's period) follows "Anyway" when the older waiter modifies his assurance in speech 13:

> "He must be eighty years old."
>
> "Anyway I should say he was eighty."

Bennett argues that the typist's omission of the period destroys Hemingway's use of "'Anyway'" as a rendition of a Spanish expression that shows the older waiter agreeing with the younger waiter. But if speech 13 is the younger waiter's, then speech 2 ("'He's drunk every night.'") has to be the older waiter's—the entire passage would be metronomic. This puts us back where we started: if Hemingway could misassign "'You said she cut him down'" when he knew the entire passage was metronomic and the

younger waiter was asking the questions, then Hemingway never reread the passage attentively—and the evidence makes this supposition untenable. Just as with the run-on line, Bennett assigns the "x" a significance it did not have for Hemingway. Also, how is it logical for Bennett to find the holograph sacrosanct in the case of the "x" but without authority in the placement of "'You said she cut him down'"? For one thing, we should not dismiss the possibility that the "x" may be a comma: in the holograph of "Homage to Switzerland" we find "'Hmx' said the gentlemanx" (JFK 476-3:8). And while the alleged period disappears, the disputed line stays in one place, from holograph through typescript to magazine and book. Since Hemingway, in the magazine proof, took the trouble to insert two insignificant semi-colons, it is reasonable to infer that he did not want a period after "'Anyway.'" (Similarly, he preserved the typescript "marched," which he could not have failed to know was not the "walked" he had written [in "walked out to the old man's table" (3)]. Who the typist was is a mystery of some importance. One is at a loss to explain how a careless typist could have turned the clear "walked" into the highly significant "marched" [2], and on page 3 dropped "opened it, chose coins from among the silver," which had been made redundant by the holograph revision "leaving <half a peseta> tip" [5], and also, on page 4, deleted the redundant "He did not fear" [9], *and* restored the meaningful "too" [4] that Hemingway had buried under a scribble, inserting a new period before it [9]. Moreover, from the bottom of page 3 to the end, skipped spaces appear before closing quotation marks, as well as after opening quotation marks—a characteristic of Hemingway's typing.) Finally, Bennett argues that since speech 13 is the last line on page 3, and "'Anyway'" begins page 4, this separation is "visual evidence . . . that the two lines are not anti-metronomic" (110). This is a non sequitur. The second anti-metronomic juxtaposition in "Homage to Switzerland" (*WTN* [*Winner Take Nothing*] 126.9-10) is similarly divided between two pages of the holograph (3:11-12), and so is the first such passage Hemingway published (Kerner, "Manuscripts" 387).

APPENDIX B. HEMINGWAY'S OTHER
ANTI-METRONOMIC DIALOGUE

1. First, Bennett quotes Hemingway on an early draft of "My Old Man": "When I finished it it was stinko. Had gotten all mixed up with the people" (99). "My Old Man," however, has almost no dialogue—where can Hemingway have "lost track" of who was saying what? The phrase "mixed up with the people" criticizes a maudlin identification with the characters (see Hemingway on Sherwood Anderson, in connection with "My Old Man" ["Art" 12]). Then:

(a) Bennett does not deny the juxtaposition of Trudy's "'All right'" and "'Give me kiss on the face'" (*WTN* 238.9-10)—he is merely puzzled. The preceding lines of dialogue are no less deliberate—only less clear. The gun and shells, however, are Nick's, so Billy can't assume the squirrel he has shot belongs to him; the right to make the offer "'You can have the squirrel'" is Nick's—and the line's syntax, as well as the authority, matches Nick's "'You can take the gun'" in the preceding scene. Nick is not asking Trudy if *she* "'want[s] to hunt tomorrow'"— she doesn't need the euphemism, nor does he need to question her availability. Billy too—not only Trudy—says "'All right.'"

(b) In the rejected passage from **"Fathers and Sons"** (unfinished and therefore inadmissible) Bennett again attributes to Trudy two clearly juxtaposed speeches, so there is no basis for a claim that Hemingway had "lost track"; nor may Bennett claim that "Hemingway cut the entire scene" because "he was not interested in anti-metronomic dialogue" (102), since there is no escaping Trudy's two speeches at 238.9-10.

(c) Bennett quotes as follows a passage from *Fiesta*:

> "Let us rejoice in our blessings. Let us utilize the product of the vine. Will you utilize a little Brother <?">
>
> "After you."
>
> Jake Bill took a long drink.

Bennett comments: "Here, Hemingway momentarily confuses, first himself with Jake, and then Jake with Bill . . . once he crossed out 'Ernest,' he evidently lost track of who says "'After you,'" and who it is who takes 'a long drink'" (103). But the quotation mark before the deleted "Jake" indicates that Hemingway was thinking of giving Bill a speech here, possibly a toast. And what Hemingway wrote, in ink, and then lined out, was not "Ernest" but "Barnes" (JFK 194, notebook 4, page 10, right leaf).

2. The insertion of Cayetano's "'Truly'" (*WTN* 215) is offered as proof that Hemingway "consciously tried to write 'metronomic' dialogue . . . even if he had to insert a dead line to do so" (100). Why, then, does Bennett withhold the following passage in the story?

> "I don't know," Mr. Frazer said. "It is rented."
>
> "You gentlemen are friends of Cayetano?"
>
> (203)

Only Frazer could speak the second line—Hemingway did not "lose track." This is equally true of the revised passage:

> "Truly?"
>
> "And what is there to do?"
>
> (JFK 417:16)

Hemingway could not have carried these lines from holograph to typescript without being aware that both lines were Frazer's. The later insertion would then be not a correction but a revision, with a dramatic purpose, and this conclusion holds if there was no holograph. *Is* the "'Truly'" "a dead line"? Frazer wants to know whether Cayetano's bad luck "'with everything and with women'"

was comic hyperbole, and silence could be misinterpreted. Such an inference is indisputable in the "'bugger'" passage from **"Fathers and Sons"** (*WTN* 229.19-23): Bennett concedes that the answer Hemingway interpolated for Nick is dramatically appropriate, not a mechanical metronomic swing (99-100).

Notes

1. Mugar Memorial Library, Boston University.

2. The doubling simplifies the difficulty: each passage confirms the other, assuring us that both are deliberate. See Kerner, "Foundation" 284-85; "Manuscripts" 385n; "Counterfeit" 104-05. Warren Bennett argues that Hemingway had no interest in "trying to educate his readers" to recognize anti-metronomic dialogue ("Characterization" 100). Only such an interest, however, can explain why, in the 259 pages of SAR, with perhaps 3000 lines of dialogue, the four anti-metronomic passages appear in two close pairs (on the same page [218] or within a page of each other [85-86]) when only one passage from each pair is found in the holograph.

3. Kerner, "Counterfeit" 99-104; "Origins" 13-15; "Trail" 189-96.

4. Nothing prevents our taking "'He had a wife once too'" as common knowledge. That the account of the suicide attempt is given by the younger waiter is indicated by his having waited until he is eager to close the café—the delay makes the account merely an offshoot of his impatience to go home.

5. This could have been taken for granted. The revisions in the holograph show close attention; and why should Hemingway have been less careful with this story for the March 1933 *Scribner's Magazine* than he was with his stories in the April and May issues? In "Homage to Switzerland," in April, there is a single substantive change—"'drink'" (206.1.4)—which one naturally attributes to Hemingway, since "'drinken'" (JFK 477:6) was obviously part of Mr. Johnson's initial "clowning with the language." In "Give Us a Prescription, Doctor" (later retitled "The Gambler, the Nun, and the Radio"), there are forty-six substantive deviations from the latest surviving typescript (JFK 420), all of them authorial—they are revisions and additions.

6. This letter and those quoted later are at Princeton, in the Firestone Library, Manuscript Collection, The Charles Scribner's Sons Archive I, Ernest Hemingway, AM 21984, Boxes 2 and 3. The computer's embrace of "the word not" is the closest the machine could come to Hemingway's single set of plain but roomy parentheses.

7. University of Delaware Library (SS 381, 382).

8. Lest anyone be misled by Carlos Baker's note reporting that Hemingway's letter of 26 January included the proofs of "Homage to Switzerland"

(606), one must add that there are six semi-colons in the magazine version, and all six are in the setting copy (JFK 477).

9. The one in "'No,' the waiter who was in a hurry said; rising from pulling down the metal shutters." The other is in ". . . deliver us from nada; pues nada."

10. If Hemingway saw galleys when he was in New York in January, the "not not" could not have been queried there, since it got through to the page proof. One must therefore assume that the printer would have printed the "y y" too if it had been in the typescript; this error would then have reached the copy editor or proofreader, who did their work on foul galleys (see Hinkle 53-54); and their approval of the "not not" without a query gives us no reasonable grounds for conjecturing that they would have queried the "y y." So since the "y y" was not in the page proof, either Hemingway had caught it himself in the galleys, or it was not in the setting copy. The first of these alternatives requires us to conjecture, arbitrarily, that Hemingway, in New York, while catching the "y y," not only missed the "not not" in the same passage but also neglected the need for punctuation before the "pues nada" in the same line as the "not not" (though it was he who made both of these corrections in the page proof). Moreover, Perkins visited the Hemingways in Piggott, Arkansas, in mid-December, but Hemingway did not give him the story—it was mailed at the last minute, on 4 January, the day Hemingway drove off. This delay indicates he had not finished going over the typescript. Yet the surviving copies show no authorial attention: the single handwritten correction, a transposition symbol added in ink on the carbon as well as on the ribbon copy (see Smith, "A Note" 37), must have been made by the typist—Hemingway would not have limited himself to this one minor correction, nor would he have entered it on both copies, since he did not bother to record on either copy the corrections that only he could have made on the lost carbon.

11. Such a date (SEP 10) can be seen on the setting copy of "Homage to Switzerland." For the Scribner Press—the "separate establishment" at 311 W. 43rd Street that handled Scribner's copy editing, proofreading, and printing (Hinkle 54)—see also Scribner 43-44 and Burlingame 91-93, 111-12. These accounts raise a question about the quality of editorial attention at the Press—Hinkle identifies sixty oversights in the copyediting of *The Sun Also Rises* (50-51). In addition, the more than one hundred errors in *Tender is the Night* show that Perkins, as late as 1934, was still protecting Fitzgerald from editors at Scribner's—the typescript went directly from Perkins to the Press; and this was his practice with Hemingway too, who, in offering Perkins three stories for *Scribner's Magazine* in

1932, warned that he wanted no editorial interference from Dashiell (9 August). See Kerner, "Manuscripts" 392n and "Counterfeit" 106n40.

12. *WTN* 121.8-11 up; 126.9-10; 203.1-3 up.

13. Monroe County Public Library, Key West.

14. Haste alone, probably, does not account for the mistake: the haste facilitated a Freudian slip, for Hemingway was aware that "interfere with" in this sense applies only when it is used defensively, in protest (as in *AMF* 18.5 up), but he was too annoyed to care—the mistaken deletion exposes his chagrin that here *he* was yielding to "interference."

15. For the continuing omission of the "can," see the British first edition (London: Jonathan Cape, 1934) and the Scribner's editions coded D-10.61[MH] and H—9.69 (MC), as well as others. Yet a copy of Perkins's 20 October memo directing the printer to insert the "can" survives. What did the Press do with it?

16. Here Hemingway seems to have made one last revision: he substituted a period for the *Magazine* question mark in "'How should I know?'" We have no reason to attribute this change to anyone at the Press, or to suspect a typo, since the period was Hemingway's original choice in the holograph (3). Reading the galleys, then, Hemingway again heard the waiters' speeches: the period suggests the younger waiter's impatience and indifference.

17. Paul Smith (*Guide* 278) follows Bennett ("Manuscript" 620) in describing the second insertion as "slightly above 'I know'"—a meaningless distinction that is made to seem meaningful by the printer's placement of the new insertion (in Smith's attempt at typographical facsimile) on the line-space between "'I know'" and the preceding line, "'His niece looks after him.'" Smith then compounds this misrepresentation by omitting Hemingway's quotation mark closing "'His niece looks after him'" and keeping the quotation mark Hemingway canceled, that had closed "'I know.'" These mistakes make Hemingway seem to have meant "'You said she cut him down'" to go with "'His niece looks after him'"—an impression reinforced by Smith's asking, "Who was initially responsible for assigning the line, 'You said she cut him down,' to the Older rather than to the Younger Waiter?" ("A Note" 37), as though the holograph doesn't show clearly which waiter Hemingway assigned it to.

18. Bennett himself wonders "why Hemingway felt under the compulsion . . . to insert a sentence which repeats information which the reader already knows" ("Manuscript" 622n).

19. George Monteiro, who discovered Jerome's letter, describes Hemingway's reply, at the bottom, as "scrawled" (which Bennett twice embellishes with a "hastily" [106, 107]), though the writing is clear and

neat, as George Thomson reports (34). Why didn't Hemingway explain? For two reasons. First: ". . . it is very bad for a writer to talk about how he writes . . . it is not the writer's province to . . . run guided tours through the more difficult country of his work" (Interview 230). He didn't explain the "Kilimanjaro" leopard: "I know, but I am under no obligation to tell you. Put it down to *omertà*" ("Art" 8). Second: Since Hemingway had no intention of going into the complex purpose of the ambiguity, mere information about anti-metronomic dialogue would only have made matters worse, as the continuing resistance to recognition of this practice shows (see Kerner, "Foundation" 293n5, "Manuscripts" 394-95, Donaldson 87, and Bier).

20. For what the run-on line seems to have meant, see Kerner, "Foundation" 290.

Works Cited

Baker, Carlos. *Ernest Hemingway, A Life Story.* New York: Scribner's, 1969.

Bennett, Warren. "The Manuscript and the Dialogue of 'A Clean, Well-Lighted Place.'" *American Literature* 50 (1979): 613-24.

———. "The Characterization and the Dialogue Problem in Hemingway's 'A Clean, Well-Lighted Place.'" *Hemingway Review* 9 (Spring 1990): 94-123.

Benson, Jackson J., ed. *New Critical Approaches to the Short Stories of Ernest Hemingway.* Durham: Duke UP, 1990.

Bier, Jesse. "Tornado in a Thimble." *Analytical & Enumerative Bibliography* n.s. 2 (1988): 58-60.

Burlingame, Roger. *Of Making Many Books.* New York: Scribner's, 1946.

Dolch, Martin. "'A Clean, Well-Lighted Place.'" In *Insight I: Analyses of American Literature.* Ed. John V. Hagopian and Martin Dolch. Frankfurt am Main: Hirschgraben, 1962: 105-11.

Donaldson, Scott. "Censorship in *A Farewell to Arms*." *Studies in American Fiction* 19 (Spring 1991): 85-93.

Gabriel, Joseph F. "The Logic of Confusion in Hemingway's 'A Clean, Well-Lighted Place.'" *College English* 22 (May 1961): 539-46.

Hagopian, John V. "Tidying Up Hemingway's 'Clean, Well-Lighted Place.'" *Studies in Short Fiction* 1 (1964): 140-46.

Hemingway, Ernest. *The Sun Also Rises.* New York: Scribner's, 1926.

———. Interview. In *Writers at Work: The Paris Review Interviews.* Second Series. Ed. George Plimpton. New York: Viking, 1963: 215-39.

———. "The Art of the Short Story" (1959). In Benson: 1-13.

———. *A Moveable Feast.* New York: Scribner's, 1964.

Hinkle, James. "'Dear Mr. Scribner'—About the Published Text of *The Sun Also Rises*." *Hemingway Review* 6 (Fall 1986): 43-64.

Hoffman, Steven K. "*Nada* and the Clean, Well-Lighted Place: The Unity of Hemingway's Short Fiction" (1979) Rpt. in Benson: 172-91.

Kerner, David. "The Foundation of the True Text of 'A Clean, Well-Lighted Place.'" *Fitzgerald/Hemingway Annual 1979*: 279-300.

———. "The Manuscripts Establishing Hemingway's Anti-Metronomic Dialogue." *American Literature* 54 (1982): 385-96.

———. "Counterfeit Hemingway: A Small Scandal in Quotation Marks." *Journal of Modern Literature* 12 (March 1985): 91-108.

———. "The Origins of Hemingway's Anti-Metronomic Dialogue." *Analytical & Enumerative Bibliography* n.s. 2 (1988): 12-28.

———. "Hemingway's Trail to British Anti-Metronomic Dialogue." *Literary Research* 12 (1987 [1990]): 187-214.

MacDonald, Scott. "The Confusing Dialogue in Hemingway's 'A Clean, Well-Lighted Place': A Final Word?" *Studies in American Fiction* 1 (Spring 1973): 93-101.

Monteiro, George. "Hemingway on Dialogue in 'A Clean, Well-Lighted Place.'" *Fitzgerald/Hemingway Annual 1974*: 243.

Reinert, Otto. "Hemingway's Waiters Once More." *College English* 20 (1959): 417-18.

Scribner, Charles, Jr. *In the Company of Writers: A Life in Publishing.* New York: Scribner's, 1990.

Smith, Paul. *A Reader's Guide to the Short Stories of Ernest Hemingway.* Boston: G. K. Hall, 1989: 277-88.

———. "A Note on a New Manuscript of 'A Clean, Well-Lighted Place.'" *Hemingway Review* 8 (Spring 1989): 36-39.

Thomson, George H. "'A Clean, Well-Lighted Place': Interpreting the Original Text." *Hemingway Review* 2 (Spring 1983): 32-43.

Ken Ryan (essay date 1998)

SOURCE: "The Contentious Emendation of Hemingway's 'A Clean, Well-Lighted Place,'" in *The Hemingway Review*, Vol. 18, Fall, 1998, p. 78.

[*In the following essay, Ryan maintains that Scribner's 1965 emendation of "A Clean, Well-Lighted Place" is invalid and should be retracted.*]

For nearly forty years, a war of words has been waged, the battlefield being a short passage of dialogue in Hemingway's **"A Clean, Well-Lighted Place"** originally published in *Scribner's Magazine* in March 1933 and reprinted in the short story collection **Winner Take Nothing** in October of the same year. The battle has revolved around an apparent inconsistency in dialogue with relation to the identifies of the story's two now-famous waiters. The discrepancy seemed to go unnoticed for nearly twenty-six years, until February 1959, when articles by F. P. Kroeger and William Colburn sparked the conflict. In 1965, Charles Scribner Jr. emended the original text, thus "correcting" the inconsistency, but with the unfortunate side-effect of interchanging the identities of the two waiters. The current situation, as noted by Warren Bennett, is "that there are two different stories by Ernest Hemingway, both titled **'A Clean, Well-Lighted Place'**" ("Characterization" 95).

With the 1965 emendation, the skirmish quickly escalated, pitting those who supported the emendation against those who favored the original text. The battle has been long, and both sides seem to have exhausted their ammunition. Perhaps, then, this temporary lull marks an appropriate opportunity for a review of the history of this conflict, with an eye towards its resolution. In the years since the emendation, a wealth of information and analysis has come to light, and literary responsibility demands that the entire body of evidence be tested against what I consider to be the central question of the controversy: Is the emendation valid?

It is important to recognize from the outset that two conditions must exist before any author's work can rightfully be considered for emendation: 1) substantial evidence that an error has in fact been made, and 2) a substantial lack of evidence that what is perceived as an error is actually a deliberate device of the artist.

Thus, the existence of a "perceived error" is not in and of itself justification for emendation; there is yet another consideration. If the suspected error occurred as an integral part of the act of creation (as opposed to an error of reproduction), one must examine the possibility that it might actually contribute to the art, at least in the eye of the artist. After all, what is creativity if not experimentation? Experimentation implies trial and error, and the line between error and creative genius is not always clearly defined. In other words, a mistake is not always a bad thing; it is possible to have "happy accidents" which actually contribute to the overall effect that the artist is seeking. The artist, while recognizing that his work may be perceived as flawed, sometimes prefers the "imperfection."

With these guidelines, and in this period of relative calm, let us turn now to the story and its rich history of interpretation. The story takes place in a Spanish café. It is late at night, and two waiters are talking. The subject of their conversation is the only other person in the café, an old man who comes in frequently and stays late, drinking. The reader does not know which waiter speaks first.

"Last week he tried to commit suicide" one waiter said. "Why?" "He was in despair." "What about?" "Nothing." "How do you know it was nothing?" "He has plenty of money."[1]

A soldier and a girl walk by, evoking a second conversation between the two waiters, again with no indication as to who begins.

> "The guard will pick him [the soldier] up," one waiter said.
>
> "What does it matter if he gets what he's after?"
>
> "He had better get off the street now. The guard will get him. They went by five minutes ago."

The old man, who is deaf, signals for another brandy. The younger waiter, clearly perturbed that the old man won't leave, marches out to the old man's table, and hastily serves him his brandy. "You should have killed yourself last week" he says to the deaf man. The younger waiter returns to his colleague. Even here, critics have disagreed over the question of who begins the conversation:

> "He's drunk now," he said. "He's drunk every night." "What did he want to kill himself for?" "How should I know." "How did he do it?" "He hung himself with a rope." "Who cut him down?" "His niece." "Why did they do it?" "Fear for his soul." "How much money has he got?" "He's got plenty." "He must be eighty years old." "Anyway I should say he was eighty." "I wish he would go home. I never get to bed before three o'clock. What kind of hour is that to go to bed?" "He stays up because he likes it." "He's lonely. I'm not lonely. I have a wife waiting in bed for me." "He had a wife once too." "A wife would be no good to him now." "You can't tell. He might be better with a wife." "His niece looks after him." "I know. You said she cut him down."

At this point in the dialogue, the reader may have noticed a problem in assigning the speeches to the different waiters. With regard to this problem, Colburn notes:

> One line . . . we can assign to the younger waiter, because of information which is brought out later: "'He's lonely. I'm not lonely. I have a wife waiting in bed for me.'" Using this line as a reference point, we can trace backwards in the story the alternate lines and discover that it is . . . the older waiter who knows the details [about the suicide attempt]. . . . Counting forward in the story from our reference line, however, we find [that it is the younger waiter who knows]. . . . Obviously there is an inconsistency here.

(241)

Colburn's analysis does seem to indicate the possible existence of an error, one which Kroeger went so far as to label "an insoluble problem" (240). Before making such a judgment, we are obliged to examine the possibility that the "perceived error" is actually a deliberate device of the artist. When the author is unable to speak for himself, it seems the assumption must be that the text reads correctly, with the onus of proof resting on those who would rewrite his story.

Working from this assumption, Otto Reinert finds:

> [The inconsistency] arises from Hemingway's violation of one of the unwritten rules of the art of presenting dialogue visually. The rule is that a new, indented line implies a new speaker. It is a useful rule, but it is not sacrosanct.
>
> (417-8)

Reinert suggests that Hemingway breaks this rule:

> [I]t is the young waiter who speaks both "He's drunk now" (because the pronoun reference demands it) and the next speech, "He's drunk every night." And . . . it is the old waiter who speaks both "He must be eighty years old" and "Anyway I should say he was eighty."
>
> (418)

Reinert justifies the original text, saying "Hemingway may have violated the convention in order to suggest a reflective pause" (418) between consecutive speeches by the same speaker. In defense of Reinert's position, David Kerner notes that genuine dialogue is not "uniformly metronomic . . . [like] a tennis match" ("Origins" 12), and that Hemingway breaks convention not once, but twice, as if to "confirm the deliberateness of the first instance" ("Ambiguity" 563). He also offers a possible explanation for why Hemingway might have turned to such an innovation:

> [I]f a speaker pauses between consecutive speeches, why must the novelist throw in a dead expository phrase, breaking the rhythm of the dialogue, merely because [the reader has been conditioned] not to expect a certain perfectly natural irregularity?
>
> ("Foundation" 282)

Kerner's reasoning is particularly applicable to a writer such as Hemingway, who once told his son Gregory, "Never use more words than you have to" (G. Hemingway 105). Scott MacDonald justifies Hemingway's possible departure from the conventional with the following observation:

> Literary conventions, after all, are not laws. They are assessments of what authors have done, not of what they must do. It is true that most authors have consistently indented during passages of dialogue in order to indicate that a new speaker is speaking, but this is far from saying either that all writers always adhere to this way of doing things, or that all writers should always adhere to this way of doing things.
>
> (98)

Reinert's reading, combined with Kerner's and Mac-Donald's defenses, casts grave doubt upon the validity of the emendation, because it supports the hypothesis that the apparent inconsistency results from Hemingway's intentional violation of standard dialogue conventions.

Edward Stone notes that it is possible to view the dialogue as a translation from Spanish to English. Regarding the possibility that "He must be eighty years old" and "Anyway I should say he was eighty" are both spoken by the same speaker, he maintains "this would be truer of conversational idiom in English than in Spanish" (240). But, as Kerner points out, "even if the younger waiter does say 'Anyway. I should say he was eighty,' he still has the next line, 'I wish he would go home,' so the principle of Reinert's solution still holds" ("Foundation" 297).

Returning to the English language, notice the similarity of the lines in question: "He's drunk now" and "He's drunk every night"; "He must be eighty years old" and "Anyway I should say he was eighty." In each instance, the second utterance is little more than a reconfirmation of the first. It is also true that all four lines in question can be completely removed from the story without the loss of any important information; we already know that the man is old, and that he is frequently drunk. The similarity of the four lines in question, the fact that they provide the reader with no important new information, and the fact that they occur in a story that is consummately distilled and concise all reinforce the idea that Hemingway chose these lines carefully.

Joseph F. Gabriel, in 1961, offered a different opinion regarding the inconsistency in the long dialogue. His explanation is founded in his observations concerning the ambiguities in the first two dialogues. On first reading the first dialogue, it is impossible to know the respective identities of the two waiters. As Kerner observes, "the deliberateness of the uninformative 'one waiter said' is undeniable" ("Ambiguity" 561). The second dialogue is equally unrevealing, using the same uninformative tag line.

A closer study of these first two dialogues reveals far deeper ambiguities. Gabriel reminds us that we have good reason to believe that the waiters may be different types: "We are of two different kinds, the older waiter said." From here, Gabriel postulates:

> Since the story is about . . . nada . . . the reasonable inference is that the two waiters differ most . . . in their divergent interpretations of this word and its English equivalent, nothing
>
> (541)

Gabriel then demonstrates how, in the first dialogue, the reference to "nothing" can be logically attributed to either or both of the waiters. He utilizes the following glosses:

> Y.W. "Last week he tried to commit suicide," one waiter said.
>
> O.W. "Why?"
>
> Y.W. "He was in despair."

O.W. "What about?"

Y.W. "Nothing." (For no reason)

O.W. "How do you know it was nothing?"

Y.W. "He has plenty of money." (With plenty of money, there is no reason for despair) and:

O.W. "Last week he tried to commit suicide," one waiter said.

Y.W. "Why?"

O.W. "He was in despair."

Y.W. "What about?"

O.W. "Nothing." (Chaos, meaninglessness)

Y.W. "How do you know it was nothing?" (Misunderstanding the older waiter's use of "'Nothing.'")

O.W. "He has plenty of money." (Inasmuch as he has plenty of money, his despair, does not derive from any merely material want.)

(Gabriel 542)

Next, Gabriel shows how the second dialogue can also be attributed to either or both of the waiters. The line "What does it matter if he gets what he's after," Gabriel points out, can be attributed to the younger waiter because he is preoccupied with sex; with equal validity, it can be attributed to the older waiter because "from the perspective of despair, what can it matter that the soldier might be picked up by the guard. In a virtually meaningless world . . . one makes one's little meaningful moments as one can" (543).

Further evidence points toward a purposeful blending of the identities of the two waiters. As David Lodge observes, "the last sentence of the first paragraph presents the two waiters as a single unit of consciousness" (49). Nothing that Hemingway does not give any of the characters a name, William B. Bache finds that this absence implies "that these characters should be regarded not so much as identifiable persons but as symbols . . . the three characters are actually parts of an implied progression from youth through middle age to old age" (64). Furthermore, the line "An hour is the same" can be seen as uniting all three characters into one, if it is viewed as an assertion of man's mortal nature. An hour is the same insofar as it brings each of them one hour closer to death.

With regard to the actualization of multiple meaning, Gabriel concludes: "Clearly it can only be accounted for as part of a deliberate plan, a function of the author's mode of execution" (544). Gabriel's analysis presents strong evidence pointing toward the apparent likelihood that Hemingway's ambiguity in the first two dialogues is indeed carefully crafted, and therefore purposeful. This observation gives rise to Gabriel's comments with regard to the inconsistency in the long dialogue:

[I]f the word "'Nothing'" when spoken in the first exchange is to be a complex term . . . it becomes neces-

sary that the speaker not be identified . . . [which] in turn demands that the waiter who knows [about the suicide] not be identified. . . . Indeed, it is only through this inconsistency that the ambiguity of the first exchange can be maintained.

(544)

The inconsistency in the third dialogue does create an undeniable sense of unreliable narration. This troubling quality is heightened by Hemingway's use of the plural pronoun "they" to refer to the singular nouns "the guard" and "his niece" as well as by his use of the period to punctuate the question "How should I know." Gabriel explains such unreliability, nothing how the dialogue in the story operates on two levels. . . .

in the conventional manner, discursively . . . and . . . symbolically, actually representing through its construction the kind of world . . . [the older waiter] experiences. . . . [creating for the reader] a world where meaning is no longer guaranteed by omniscience.

(545)

The third dialogue is not vexed by the same uninformative "one waiter said" that plagues the first two dialogues; rather, this dialogue is introduced with the marginally more revealing "he said." Regarding this pronoun, John V. Hagopian notes, "All of the critics recognize, with varying degrees of distress, that the speaker must be the young waiter who has returned from serving the old man"(145). At least one critic disagrees: Bennett observes that "he" can justifiably be attributed to either the younger waiter or "his colleague" ("New Text" 119).

Hagopian attacks Reinert's analysis, rejecting the notion of anti-metronomic dialogue:

[T]his solution to the problem would be valid only if (1) by the law of parsimony, it is the simplest solution; (2) an examination of the rest of Hemingway's fiction shows that the author often, or even occasionally, employed such a technique; and (3) the context supported . . . the notion that the author violates standard conventions without explicit hints or clues to the reader. On none of these grounds can one support Reinert's interpretation.

(141)

Hagopian extends his quarrel to Gabriel, proclaiming that the reading collapses when "submitted to the [same] tests of validity" (142). On the basis of an interpretation by Martin Dolch, Hagopian suggests the dialogue be "tidied up" with the following emendation:

Original dialogue:

Y.W. "His niece looks after him."

O.W. "I know. You said she cut him down."

Hagopian's suggested dialogue:

Y.W. "His niece looks after him. You said she cut him down."

O.W. "I know."

Hagopian then glosses the three dialogues, seeming to proceed from the assumption that the burden is on the text to match his interpretation. When it doesn't, he makes the above change, claiming that the text suffers from an "obvious typographical error" (144). Just how Hagopian knows that any typographic error was made, let alone the specific one he proposes to correct, is a mystery. He gives no holograph evidence, no typescript evidence, indeed no evidence at all. Referring to Hagopian's method of inquiry, Bennett calls it "not critical analysis . . . [but rather] theological persuasion" ("New Text" 16). Astoundingly, Scribner agreed with Hagopian and implemented his suggestion. In reaching his decision, Scribner later admitted that he relied not on manuscript evidence but rather on the advice of critics and "common sense" (MacDonald 99).

Regarding his criticism of Reinert and Gabriel, even by his own criteria, Hagopian's argument fails. Let us first consider Reinert's proposition of anti-metronomic dialogue and Hagopian's assertion that "it is a technique employed nowhere else in the Hemingway canon" (142). With at least thirty recorded examples of Hemingway's use of anti-metronomic dialogue (see MacDonald, Kerner 1979, 1982, 1987, 1988), George H. Thomson notes, "In the face of such evidence, Hagopian's position is demolished" (37). With regard to Hagopian's mandate that the solution be as simple as possible, Charles May writes, ". . . it seems to me that assuming Hemingway has violated a typographical convention . . . is 'simpler' than presuming the rather drastic measure of rewriting the text of a work" (327), while Paul Smith simply notes that "Hagopian's principle does confuse a simpler editorial solution with a simpler interpretation" (*Reader's Guide* 282).

As to Hagopian's claim that the context of the story doesn't support Reinert's or Gabriel's interpretations, consider the essential effect of Hagopian's emendation: It positively gives the information of the attempted suicide to the older waiter. Some agree with this interpretation, while many others do not. May, for example, writes:

> [I]f it is indeed the young waiter who tells the old waiter about the suicide attempt, then the story is about the old waiter . . . [who] arrives at his nada prayer at the end as a result of the story. This makes for a simpler, yet more pertinent reading . . . than if we assume the old waiter has already realized and articulated the significance of nada. . . . It is the difference between seeing the story as an excuse for a pre-conceived philosophic concept or as a dramatic realization of such a concept.
>
> (328)

Carlos Baker explicitly acknowledges that it is the young waiter who knows of the attempted suicide (124). In addition, in what is an implicit reference to the young waiter's use of the word "nothing" in the first dialogue, Baker maintains that the story is about

> the development . . . of the young waiter's mere nothing into the old waiter's Something—a Something

called Nothing which is so huge, terrible, overbearing, inevitable and omnipresent that once experienced it can never be forgotten.

(124)

In 1971, Lodge agreed with Hagopian and Scribner, declaring the implausibility of Hemingway's having deliberately violated a well established typographical convention in a way for which there is no precedent elsewhere in his work . . . for a purpose that could have been easily accomplished by other means. (41)

As to Lodge's contention that Hemingway never uses anti-metronomic dialogue in his other works, we have already seen this to be patently incorrect. As to his assertion that the same purpose could have been easily accomplished by other means, because he fails to elaborate what "other means" he has in mind, I am at a loss to comment on whether or not they would achieve the "same purpose."

Lodge does bring to the battlefield a perceptive distinction between the ambiguities in the first two dialogues and the logical inconsistency in the third. He notes how such an inconsistency "can only have the effect in narrative of radically undermining the authority of either the narrator or the characters or both" (42).

Lodge says, "There are no other equivalent inconsistencies which would confirm the radical unreliability of the narrator" (42). He ignores or does not notice the use of the plural pronoun "they" for the singular nouns "the guard" and "his niece," or the unusual punctuation of the question "How should I know." While it is true that this last line functions in the story as an answer to a question, it is merely an example of a question being answered with a question. The more conventional punctuation in such a situation would be a question mark. Later, in the same article, Lodge seems to contradict his own argument when he notices that the narrator's description in the second sentence "is interesting for the way in which its appearance of logical explanation dissolves under scrutiny" (48).

Lodge is correct in his observation that the ambiguity of the first two dialogues and the inconsistency of the third are two different beasts. He goes one step too far, however, by suggesting that they cannot possibly be related. He states that it is not "legitimate to assimilate the inconsistency . . . into the concept of literary ambiguity" (42), but he offers no convincing argument to counter Gabriel's suggestion that Hemingway desires that "the reader, in his attempt to impose order upon the chaos of inconsistency and ambiguity, [be] stripped of his dependence on the objective" (546).

The next major event in the conflict came when Thomson offered an alternative reading, one that made logical sense of the third dialogue without violating any conventions. Thomson's reading proceeds from the prevalent assumption that the younger waiter opens the third dialogue. He further assumes that the dialogue proceeds metronomically with the younger waiter then speaking the line "Who cut him down?"

Thomson notes that the younger waiter "has no knowledge of the suicide attempt . . . yet he unthinkingly assumes [emphasis added] that the old man was rescued by being cut down [emphasis added]" (38). The older waiter lets this cliche pass, but when the younger waiter jumps to another conclusion, "'His niece looks after him'—something he cannot know . . . the older waiter quietly chastises [him]. . . . 'I know [which is more than you do]. You said she cut him down'" (38).

With regard to the validity of the emendation, Thomson's reading presents an interesting wrinkle, casting doubt upon the very existence of an inconsistency, much less an error. This doubt, combined with the doubt raised by Reinert's and Gabriel's alternative explanations (and the failure of Hagopian and Lodge to counter them), constitutes a very strong case against the emendation. Before we reach a conclusion, however, we must return to the issue that Hagopian raised but failed to substantiate: that a typographical error resulted in the seemingly illogical inconsistency in the waiters' dialogue.

When Hagopian proclaimed the existence of a typographical error, he was voicing pure speculation, since there was no manuscript or typescript evidence available for inspection. Now there are both. Hemingway's original pencil manuscript was discovered in 1975, and, in 1987, *College and Research Libraries News* announced that the University of Delaware had acquired "the only recorded copies" of a draft of **"A Clean, Well-Lighted Place"** (411).

Much has been written about these two documents. Hans-Joachim Kann, Warren Bennett, Paul Smith, and David Kerner have studied the texts and each other's arguments in excruciating detail. In the light of their work, one thing becomes evident: Because the suspected error appears in the original holograph, the Delaware typescript, the magazine story, and the short story collections, and because Hemingway did not see fit to change it in his lifetime, the inconsistency in the long dialogue must be considered Hemingway's responsibility, not the responsibility of some errant typist or typesetter.

Much of the debate concerning the manuscript has focused on speculation concerning at what point and for what reason Hemingway wrote the sentence, "You said she cut him down" I submit that no matter when he wrote it, and regardless of his reason, the more important point is that the inconsistency appears on the original holograph. This does not prove that no error was made; it merely classifies the "possible error" by type: an error of production, not an error of reproduction. There is no reason to believe that a typographical error is responsible for the inconsistency. Because the inconsistency in the long dialogue occurred as an integral part of the creative process, we are obliged to consider whether or not Hemingway may have perceived

the "error" as actually strengthening the story. Hemingway himself once gave the inconsistency his direct and open endorsement. In 1956, Judson Jerome wrote to Hemingway specifically inquiring about the inconsistency. Hemingway responded that he had just reread the story, and it "continued to make perfect sense to him" (Monteiro 243). It can also be argued that Hemingway gave his tacit approval of the original text when he said, "I guess the story that tops them all for leave-out was **'A Clean, Well-Lighted Place.'** I left everything out of that one. . . . May be my favorite story" (Hotchner 164).

The debate since the 1965 emendation has revolved around which of the two waiters knows about the old man's attempted suicide. The assumption has been that a "truthful" answer to this question would determine the validity of the emendation. Ironically, one result of this scholarly debate has been to suggest that the question of which waiter knows about the suicide attempt may be irrelevant to the emendation's validity; for if Hemingway perceived the inconsistency in the third dialogue as improving the story, then there can be no justification for "correcting" it.

Those still intent on seeing **"A Clean, Well-Lighted Place"** published in its emended from have a responsibility to consider whether what they perceive as an error—and others perceive as creative genius—may have been seen by Hemingway as contributing to the story's effect. Given the weight of the evidence, it seems entirely plausible that even if Hemingway did lose track "of which waiter is saying what" (87), as Sheridan Baker suggests, he may well have considered the confusing dialogue to be a "happy accident." Hemingway may have liked the way the confusion clouds the identities of the two waiters, despite the difficulty it presents to the reader.

After twenty-six years of silence, six years of skirmishing, an emendation, and more than thirty years of sometimes vicious critical warfare, we find ourselves in an ironic position not unlike that of the older waiter—a man, as suggested by Robert Penn Warren, "who hungers for the certainties and meaningfulness of a religious faith but who cannot find in his world a ground for that faith" (6). We find ourselves hungering for a certainty in Hemingway's text, but no such certainties are forthcoming. The inconsistencies and ambiguities of the story create within the reader a discomfort not unlike that which plagues the older waiter.

Whether by accident or design, whether skillfully or instinctively, Hemingway places the reader not only in the position occupied by the older waiter, but indeed by every thoughtful person. Clarence Darrow once said, "I do not pretend to know where many ignorant men are sure—that is all that agnosticism means." Just as no one can have certain knowledge of the existence or nonexistence of God, neither can the reader of the original text of **"A Clean Well-Lighted Place"** know with certainty whether or not a new line of dialogue indicates a change in speakers; belief in either option represents an act of faith. The corruption of Hemingway's original text does more than simply impose a clarification of the identities of the two waiters; it serves to deprive all readers of the opportunity to decide for themselves what, if anything, they believe.

Notes

1. Except where otherwise noted, all quotations from "A Clean, Well-Lighted Place" are from the 1933 *Scribner's Magazine* edition.

Works Cited

Bache, William B. "Craftsmanship in 'A Clean, Well-Lighted Place.'" *Personalist* 37 (Winter 1956): 60-64.

Baker, Carlos. *Hemingway: The Writer as Artist.* Princeton: Princeton UP, 1956.

Baker, Sheridan. *Ernest Hemingway: An Introduction and Interpretation.* New York: Holt, 1967.

Bennett, Warren. "The New Text of 'A Clean, Well-Lighted Place.'" *Literary Half-Yearly* 14 (1973): 115-125.

———. "The Characterization and Dialogue Problem in Hemingway's 'A Clean, Well-Lighted Place.'" *The Hemingway Review* 9.2 (Spring 1990): 94-123.

Colburn, William E. "Confusion in 'A Clean, Well-Lighted Place.'" *College English* 20 (Feb. 1959): 241-242.

College and Research Libraries News (July/August 1987): 411.

Dolch, Martin. *Insight I: Analyses of American Literature.* Frankfurt: Hirschgraben-Verlag, 1962.

Gabriel, Joseph F. "The Logic of Confusion in Hemingway's 'A Clean, Well-Lighted Place.'" *College English* 22 (May 1961): 539-546.

Hagopian, John V. "Tidying up Hemingway's Clean, Well-Lighted Place." *Studies in Short Fiction* 1 (1964): 140-146.

Hemingway, Ernest. "A Clean, Well-Lighted Place." *Scribner's Magazine* (March 1933): 149-150.

Hemingway, Gregory H. *Papa: A Personal Memoir.* Boston: Houghton Mifflin, 1976.

Hotchner A. E. *Papa Hemingway: A Personal Memoir.* New York: Random House, 1966.

Kann, Hans-Joachim. "Perpetual Confusion in 'A Clean, Well-Lighted Place': The Manuscript Evidence." *Fitzgerald/Hemingway Annual* (1977): 115-118.

Kerner, David. "Hemingway's Trail to British Anti-Metronomic Dialogue." *Literary Research* 12 (1987): 287-214.

———. "The Ambiguity of 'A Clean, Well-Lighted Place.'" *Studies in Short Fiction* 29 (1992): 561-74.

———. "The Foundation of the True Text of 'A Clean, Well-Lighted Place.'" *Fitzgerald/Hemingway Annual* (1979): 279-300.

———. "The Manuscripts Establishing Hemingway's Anti-Metronomic Dialogue." *American Literature* 54 0982): 385-396.

———. "The Origins of Hemingway's Anti-Metronomic Dialogue." *Analytical and Enumerative Bibliography* (1988): 12-28.

Kroeger, F. P. "The Dialogue in 'A Clean, Well-Lighted Place.'" *College English* 20 (Feb. 1959): 240-242.

Lodge, David. "Hemingway's Clean, Well-Lighted Puzzling Place." *Essays in Criticism* 21 (1971): 33-56.

MacDonald, Scott. "The Confusing Dialogue in Hemingway's 'A Clean, Well-Lighted Place': A Final Word?" *Studies in American Fiction* 1 (1973): 93-101.

May, Charles E. "Is Hemingway's 'Well-Lighted Place' Really Clean Now?" *Studies in Short Fiction* 8 (Spring 1971): 326-330.

Monteiro, George. "Hemingway on Dialogue in 'A Clean, Well-Lighted Place.'" *Fitzgerald/Hemingway Annual* (1974): 243.

Reinert, Otto. "Hemingway's Waiters Once More." *College English* 20 (1959): 417-418.

Smith, Paul. "A Note on a New Manuscript of 'A Clean, Well-Lighted Place.'" *The Hemingway Review* 8.2 (Spring 1989): 36-39.

———. *A Reader's Guide to the Short Stories of Ernest Hemingway.* Boston: G.K. Hall, 1989.

Stone, Edward. "Hemingway's Waiters Yet Once More." *American Speech* 37 (1962): 239-240.

Thomson, George H. "'A Clean, Well-Lighted Place': Interpreting the Original Text." *The Hemingway Review* 2.2 (Spring 1983): 32-43.

Warren, Robert Penn. "Hemingway." *The Kenyon Review* 9 (Winter 1947): 1-28.

FURTHER READING

Criticism

Campbell, Harry M. "Comments on Mr. Stock's *Nada* in Hemingway's 'A Clean, Well-Lighted Place.'" *Midcontinent American Studies* III, No. 1 (Spring 1962): 57-9.

Finds fault with Ely Stock's translation of the term "nada" in Hemingway's story.

Kerner, David. "Counterfeit Hemingway: A Small Scandal in Quotation Marks." *JML* XII, No. 1 (March 1985): 91-108.

Deems the amended version of Hemingway's "A Clean, Well-Lighted Place" counterfeit.

Monteiro, George. "The Education of Ernest Hemingway." *Journal of American Studies* VIII, No. 1 (April 1974): 91-9.

Determines the influence of Henry Adams's *The Education of Henry Adams* on Hemingway's short fiction, especially "A Clean, Well-Lighted Place."

———. "Ernest Hemingway: Psalmist." *JML* XIV, No. 1 (Summer 1987): 83-95.

Explores the role of Psalm 23 in "A Clean, Well-Lighted Place."

Stone, Edward. "Hemingway's Waiters Yet Once More." *American Speech* XXXVII, No. 3 (October 1962): 239-40.

Asserts that there is "evidence in the story that Hemingway was trying to reproduce not only the conversation of the two waiters but the flavor of their speech."

Additional coverage of Hemingway's life and career is contained in the following sources published by the Gale Group: *Authors and Artists for Young Adults*, Vol. 19; *Contemporary Authors*, Vol. 77-80; *Contemporary Authors New Revision Series*, Vol. 34; *Concise Dictionary of Literary Biography*, 1917-1929; *Contemporary Literary Criticism*, Vols. 1, 3, 6, 8, 10, 13, 19, 30, 34, 39, 41, 44, 50, 61, 80; *DISCovering Authors*; *DISCovering Authors: British*; *DISCovering Authors: Canadian*; *DISCovering Authors Modules: Most-studied Authors, Novelists*; *DISCovering Authors 3.0*; *Dictionary of Literary Biography*, Vols. 4, 9, 102, 210; *Dictionary of Literary Biography Documentary Series*, Vols. 1, 15, 16; *Dictionary of Literary Biography Yearbook*, Vols. 81, 87, 96, 98; *Major 20th-Century Writers*, Vols. 1, 2; and *World Literature Criticism*.

Alun Lewis
1915–1944

Welsh short story writer and poet.

INTRODUCTION

Lewis is considered one of the most significant short story writers of World War II. While critics are divided over whether or not his stories take critical precedence over his poetry, most agree that Lewis's short fiction is an important contribution to the canon of war literature written during the twentieth century.

BIOGRAPHICAL INFORMATION

Lewis was born in Cwmaman, Wales, in 1915. The family briefly moved to Yorkshire, England, during World War I so that Lewis's father could enlist in the army. When he was wounded in 1918, they returned to Cwmaman and then moved to Glynhafod, where Lewis began school in 1920. Lewis entered Cowbridge Grammar School in 1926, where he contributed short stories to the school journal, *The Bovian.* In 1932 Lewis enrolled at the University College of Wales in Aberystwyth, majoring in history, and began contributing stories to the university's literary journal, the *Dragon,* in 1934. Lewis graduated in 1935 and in September of the same year, began attending Manchester University. In 1937 he earned a master's degree in medieval history, but soon grew disillusioned with scholarly research. Lewis did, however, continue to write short fiction, most of it published once more in a student journal. In May 1937 Lewis attended a retreat in France, but his dissatisfaction and unhappiness continued. He returned to Aberystwyth to work for a teacher's diploma and spent the next months as a student teacher in Dolgellau before he obtained his diploma the following year. In 1939 he began working as a teacher at Lewis School in Pengam, Wales. Throughout the autumn of that year Lewis was torn between his desire to serve in World War II and his ambivalent feelings about killing. In March 1940 he registered in the reserves, as a way of serving in the war without having to kill. A few months later he changed his mind and went into active service on the railroad at Longmoor, Hampshire, England. In 1941 Lewis married Gweno Ellis. Lewis was sent to serve in India in 1942, where he was made an intelligence officer. Stationed on Lake Kharakvasla, Lewis was offered a captaincy, but refused the promotion. Having suffered most of his life from frequent bouts of depression, Lewis again succumbed while in India and also was hospitalized for malaria. In 1944 his battalion was transferred to Burma, where he volunteered to join a patrol in the Goppe Pass. Lewis was killed by a shot from his own pistol. While the official inquiry ruled that the shooting was accidental, many fellow soldiers who were aware of his struggle with depression were convinced that Lewis committed suicide.

MAJOR WORKS OF SHORT FICTION

Lewis published only one volume of short stories, *The Last Inspection,* during his lifetime. The rest of his short fiction was published in magazines and journals and collected in several volumes after his death: *In the Green Tree* (1948), *Alun Lewis: Selected Poetry and Prose* (1966), *Alun Lewis: A Miscellany of His Writings* (1982) and *Alun Lewis: Collected Stories* (1990). While his stories generally are categorized as either war stories or non-war stories, many contain common themes, such as the isolation of the individual in a world hostile to human aspirations. Many of Lewis's early stories, such as "The Tale of a Dwarf," "The End of the Hunt," and "They Say There's a Boat on the River," contain elements of neo-Gothic fables and explorations of nature and ideal beauty. In others—notably "If Such Be Nature's Holy Plan" and "The Whirligig of Fate"—Lewis probed the dark side of nature's powers. Lewis's early stories also frequently reflect his training as a medievalist and his Welsh heritage and have been compared favorably with the fiction of D. H. Lawrence. Around the time Lewis enlisted in the service, his subject matter shifted to issues surrounding World War II. Most of the stories in *The Last Inspection* evidence Lewis's ambivalent feelings about war. Some, such as the title story "The Last Inspection" and "It's a Long Way to Go," are satirical depictions of what Lewis saw as the military's cold and uncaring attitude toward civilian suffering during wartime. Others are often tragic and ironic examinations of the confusing and alienating effects of war on both soldiers and civilians, including one of Lewis's best-known stories, "Almost a Gentleman."

CRITICAL RECEPTION

While Lewis is well known as a war writer, many critics feel that his other stories, which range widely in tone and theme, have been unjustly neglected. Others find his war stories pedestrian and overly intellectualized, evidence of the emotional distance of the upper-middle classes from the harsh realities of life during wartime. But Lewis's proponents point out that by concentrating many of his war stories on civilian suffering rather than on soldiers fighting on the front, Lewis democratized the experience of war for all social classes. These and other critics contend that

Lewis made a significant contribution not only to war literature of the twentieth century but also to Anglo-Welsh literature.

PRINCIPAL WORKS

Short Fiction

The Last Inspection 1942
In the Green Tree 1948
Alun Lewis: Selected Poetry and Prose [edited by Ian Hamilton] 1966
Alun Lewis: A Miscellany of His Writings [edited by John Pikoulis] 1982
Alun Lewis: Collected Stories [edited by Cary Archard] 1990

Other Major Works

Raiders' Dawn and Other Poems (poetry) 1942
Ha! Ha! Among the Trumpets: Poems in Transit (poetry) 1945
Letter from India (letters) 1946
Alun Lewis: Letters to My Wife [edited by Gweno Lewis] (letters) 1989

CRITICISM

John Hampson (essay date 1943)

SOURCE: "Fiction," in *The Spectator*, Vol. 170, No. 5983, February 26, 1943, pp. 204, 206.

[*In the following essay, Hampson reviews* The Last Inspection, *praising the volume and calling the stories "both touching and beautiful."*]

Readers who enjoy out-of-the-ordinary books should . . . make a point of reading Alun Lewis's first collection of short stories, **The Last Inspection.** Lewis is a poet, and his themes are lit by tenderness and sensibility. In a brief foreword he explains that eighteen of his twenty-three stories "are concerned with the Army in England during the two years' attente since the disaster of June, 1940." He, too, presents the problems and conflicts of individuals caught up in the struggle of nations. He is a serious writer, using courage, sympathy and humour for his critical interpretation of life in the Army, with its sudden isolation of the individual from his familiar community. The full implications of this commonplace, yet most difficult problem, are

sensitively illumined and realised. His characters, ranging from the small child and the simple recruit to the conscious and intellectual adult, are recognisable human beings. Lewis, like Leslie Halward, can explore the province of the inarticulate, and bring back riches, but his range is not confined to the proletariat. **"Private Jones," "Lance-Jack," "Interruption," "Acting Captain,"** and **"They Came,"** contain a wealth of experience transformed by imagination into exciting prose. The last-named story reveals the mind of a soldier whose wife was killed in an air-raid on the first night of his leave, as he returns to his unit. In its economy of effect it is both touching and beautiful. This collection carries a recommendation from the Book Society.

Philip Toynbee (essay date 1943)

SOURCE: "New Novels and Stories," in *The New Statesman and Nation*, Vol. 25, No. 630, March 20, 1943, pp. 191-92.

[*In the following essay, Toynbee praises Lewis's stories in* The Last Inspection *but offers reservations about the authenticity of Lewis's depiction of war.*]

Had Mr. Alun Lewis spent as many years in the army as Mr. Phelan spent in prison, his stories might have achieved the same assurance and unity. But where Phelan moves almost too slickly among his "mugs" and "grasses," Lewis is less at ease with "Jerry Planes," "Civvy Street" and the "Boss Class." His reactions to army life are intensely interesting, for he is the 1943 equivalent of Siegfried Sassoon and Robert Graves. As a prose-writer he is inferior to both, but his reactions may be contrasted. Graves and Sassoon were civilised human beings, outraged by the stupidity and horror of trench warfare. Their reactions were more or less clear-cut and clearly expressed. Lewis, who has seen only the home-duty incidentals of war, is far more confused and uncertain. His attitude to the army oscillates between disgust and fascination. Very consciously left-wing he is anxious to establish the democracy and comradeship of an army in which he recognises the obstacles to both. The attitude is sympathetic, but leads to indifferent writing. He is at his best in the story called **"Almost a Gentleman,"** the portrait of an O.C.T.U. candidate who fails to get his commission. The study of Burton is free from any preconceptions. He is plausible, ingratiating and pathetic—condemned to the ranks not through any direct snobbery of situation, but because his social background has rendered him truly unsuited to command. This concise and brilliant tragedy is a far grimmer indictment of a class-ridden society than are any of the more obvious tilts at Blimps and gentleman-majors. So far as the actual writing is concerned, Mr. Lewis is again caught between two stools. As an intellectual observer he must write intellectually, but as a democrat and a good chap he is obsessed by the guilt of intellectual isolation.

Unfortunately, good writing is doomed to be as undemocratic as the current level of appreciation. "Jerry Planes" are too thin a sugar for Mr. Lewis's pill, and I doubt whether his book will be widely read in the Forces.

Times Literary Supplement (essay date 1943)

SOURCE: "Soldier Tales," in *The Times Literary Supplement*, No. 2147, March 27, 1943, p. 149.

[*In the following essay, the anonymous reviewer provides a mixed assessment of* The Last Inspection, *finding only some of the stories to be successful.*]

The best stories in this collection of short stories [*The Last Inspection*], by which is meant those that probably struck the author, too, as presenting fresh facets of truth, include the title-piece. This account of the Brigadier's last rounds before retirement comes from the ranks, from the crew of the service train, from below the windows of the saloon that holds all the food and all the speeches. It is comic, critical, and above all in relief: the reader shares the author's view of the world as he might a painter's. Another indisputable success is **"They Came,"** the sketch of a soldier returning from the leave on which his wife was killed in an air-raid.

In a slightly different class are such tales as **"The Wanderers"** and **"The Prisoners,"** tales which now and again sound the right note but not, to some ears, all the time; tales in which, one suspects, the author, confident of giving great pleasure to a great many people anyhow, has let his attention wander and his energies flag. When a writer has promise he is exposed to dangers from which the dullards are safe. The danger in this case is that Mr. Lewis may find it easier, especially while on active service, to turn out the work of a slick but second-rate literary "school." That he is not quite alive to this danger is suggested by one or two of these pieces, pieces that *may* be heartfelt but read rather more like exercises on the sanctioned themes of poverty and hardship and grime. They express feelings on these subjects that it is proper and even fashionable to have, but they do not seem yet to express the particular and unique feelings Mr. Lewis may be expected to have.

John Lehmann (essay date 1952)

SOURCE: "A Human Standpoint," in *The Open Night*, Longmans, Green and Co., 1952, pp. 109-16.

[*In the following essay, Lehmann provides an overview of Lewis's life and work.*]

The first thing I knew of Alun Lewis's death was when I was rung up from the editorial offices of a daily newspaper, and asked if I could write a short obituary note. The news was a great shock to me, and I found it quite impossible to say anything then and there. Up to that moment the war had seemed miraculously to spare the young English writers and artists whose work I most believed in, but in that moment I knew there were going to be no miracles, and my mind was trapped in a miserable foreboding. But I was also embarrassed by the newspaper's request, because I had never met Alun Lewis, though we had corresponded for several years, and I was critical of him as a poet, though I had published several of his poems.

I still feel something of the same embarrassment, because Alun Lewis had many friends who knew him intimately and loved him, and many who had never met him loved his poetry with an unqualified enthusiasm I could never muster. To all those I offer my apologies for writing as I shall in these pages, but it would be wrong of me to pretend that I thought he was comparable in his poetic achievement with Edward Thomas or Wilfred Owen, the victims of an earlier war, and his own admired masters, or even with some of his own contemporaries who survived the war. It would be unfair to those survivors as well as insincere, because death in battle does not by some mysterious magic immediately make a young man a better poet. But I do think the war, not the bullet that killed him, made Alun Lewis a writer: a writer who was capable of very big things indeed. I had read his volume of stories *The Last Inspection* with the feeling that prose, not verse, might turn out in the end to be his proper medium; and when he sent me from India his story **"Ward O 3 (b),"** which is still to me one of the most brilliant stories written by anyone during the war, this feeling became a conviction. Alun Lewis knew I felt that way about his work, but it didn't offend him, and I think he was as sorry as I was that his posting to India prevented our meeting. In a letter he wrote to me just before embarkation, he said 'My job looks like being fast, violent and very technical. I contemplate it vaguely just at the present through a haze of farewells one of which, although I've never met you, I hereby send to you.'

That letter and the tragedy that followed, sent me on a quest to discover glimpses of him from his friends and those who had been nearest to him at various times in his life. From what they have written to me, as I shall show, I have been able to form some pictures for myself of the features of the poet I shall always regret not having talked with or known personally; and nothing in them has contradicted the impression his writing had already given me.

Alun Lewis left us two books of poems, *Raider's Dawn* and *Ha! Ha! Among the Trumpets*, the volume of stories I have just referred to, and a posthumous collection (*In the Green Tree*) consisting of letters—originally published as *Letter from India*, selected by his widow—together with his last stories, including **"Ward O 3 (b)"** and the almost equally remarkable **"The Orange Grove."** I have just read all these again, and I am more than ever impressed by a quality that runs right through them, a natural human warmth but also something more than that. There is a passage in the long poem, the last he ever wrote and perhaps the best, called "The Jungle," which expresses it very beautifully:

Some things we cleaned like knives in earth,
Kept from the dew and rust of Time,
Instinctive truths and elemental love,
Knowing the force that brings the teal and quail
From Turkestan across the Himalayan snows
To Kashmir and the South alone can guide
That winging wildness home again. . . .

t is this sureness about the things that matter, above all
ove, this rootedness in life and faith in the sensual world
hat seem to me so important about Alun Lewis. One of
he reasons for this sureness may well have been the unusually happy childhood and home life that he had experi-
nced. He was the eldest of a family of four, with two
brothers and a sister, who all adored one another and re-
iprocated equally their parents' love for them. In a letter
o me his mother has written:

> As a family we seem to have laughed our way through
> the years between the wars. Money was never suffi-
> cient to supply all our family's needs, and they knew
> that scholarships had to be the order of the day. But if
> they worked hard, they played hard too, and tennis,
> hockey, swimming, hiking, rugger were their enthusias-
> tic pastimes. Then there were those Bohemian holidays
> in secluded Penbryn, to pay for which my husband did
> extra evening work; and when we played and laughed,
> swam, read and lazed to our heart's content, and when,
> in looking back, the sun seems always to have been
> shining, the sky and sea blue and the sand shimmering
> gold.

n the same letter his mother also reveals another point of
o little significance: that she had always wanted to be a
vriter, and that his becoming a writer had been felt to be
n affair in which the two of them were specially and inti-
nately associated. 'One day when he was about fifteen,'
he recalls, 'he came hurriedly into the house from one of
is solitary strolls on the mountains, calling excitedly to
ne: "Look, Mother, I can do it." And he showed me five
hort poems that had come to him on the mountain top.
One was 'Five Silver Birches' to be seen in *Raiders' Dawn*,
nother was "Vanité" published by *The Sunday Times* soon
fterwards. . . .'

his belief in life and the touchstone of the heart, quali-
es, it is worth remembering, that made Wordsworth a
reat poet, are all too rare today, when literature in so
nany countries is in danger of being dominated by pseudo-
hilosophies and the ingenious constructions of the intel-
ct that really deny the heart; and this makes Alun Lewis's
eath particularly tragic for us. He was always striving to
xpress his faith and vision more clearly and completely
n his art, and in one of his letters he says:

> I find my memory, in my 29th year, is taking a new
> and definite shape to itself. It's discarding everything it
> doesn't need to write and dream upon. It retains the
> bare necessities of soldiering: otherwise it forgets. All
> the stuff I learnt at College and Pengam has gone by
> the board, and it tunes itself more and more to the
> simple human material of life and of itself. It won't
> even acquire the economic statistics of the Beveridge

> Report, newspaper articles or Oxford pamphlets. It's
> going native, quite definitely and all its reasoning is
> done from a human standpoint. My longing is more
> and more for one thing only, integrity, and I discount
> the other qualities in people far too ruthlessly if they
> lack that fundamental sincerity and wholeness. So I
> only hope that I will be able to write, for I'm sure I
> won't be able to do anything else half as well.

Alun Lewis may have felt that the best part of him went
into his writing, that secret soul he kept inviolable from
the life of a soldier; but soldiering is not merely marching
and shooting, it is relationships with other soldiers, and
about that Lewis really cared. I have had testimony from
many of his fellow writers who were in close contact with
him at one point or other during his army career, and all
tell the same story. 'He was a quiet, undemonstrative man,'
says Jack Aistrop who was with him in the early days of
the war at a big R.E. camp in the south, 'and once he had
accepted one as a friend, quieter still. But with some
strangers he would be awkward and extremely shy. He
was practical and always knew what he wanted and the
best way to get it. . . . And despite his quietness he had
great store of energy. This energy was largely used in
fighting against the stupid things of army life, and he was
a thorn in the side of visiting lecturers and brass-hats. If
they made stupid remarks a lone figure would invariably
get to his feet and launch polite but scathing questions.
. . .' Another fellow-writer, who met him a little later,
Julian Maclaren-Ross, has also described this shyness and
his contempt for 'the stupid things of army life', especially
when it prevented sympathy between man and man even if
one man was an officer and the other a soldier in the ranks.
Maclaren-Ross also noted as a dominant trait his 'deep
tenderness towards life itself', and his nostalgia for the elemental simplicities of his Welsh home. This nostalgia
saturates many of his early poems and stories: it was so
strong an emotion that it was a long time before he got it
under control in his art—but he did get it under control, as
"Ward O 3 (b)" is there to witness, with its beautiful balance of satiric observation and warm human insight, and
what I can only call a kind of poetic wisdom transmuting
the violent feelings that his theme must have had for him.
At the time when he wrote this story, the last few months
of his life, he seems indeed to have travelled far towards
the attainment of that 'wholeness' he speaks about in the
letter. Since his death, many people have told me they
agree that **"Ward O 3 (b)"** is his masterpiece, and that
they are as certain as I am that prose would have been his
master-medium; and I have been particularly interested to
find his mother—though she believed that, given the
chance, he might have excelled in drama, poetic or non-
poetic—among them. In the letter from which I have already quoted, she says:

> Prose was to be his major work. I know it by the same
> intuitive process as I knew he was going to be a writer.
> Generally speaking, his poems came to him too easily,
> out of the blue; though I knew there were exceptions,
> with which he wrestled in the black silences as Jacob
> struggled with the Angel. But in his prose, he had the
> joy and pride of the true craftsman. Often he refers to

it in his letters, always as his future life's task. Of the story of a British battalion on foreign service, which he had in his mind on entering the Arakan, he wrote: 'I will give you bigger fruit than ever came out of the Orange Grove.'

It is impossible justly to compare the young British writers who were lost in the Second World War—and Alun Lewis in my opinion is one of them most bitterly to be regretted, together with Sidney Keyes and Dan Billany—with those who were mourned in 1918. Promise can always be interpreted in so many ways, is always so obscure in relation to events that had not been foreseen; and the writers of the First World War had different spiritual fronts to wage their war on. Nevertheless, even though I feel almost certain that *as a poet*—that is in the medium of verse—Alun Lewis was not and would not have been the peer of Wilfred Owen, there are many points of similarity in the total personalities of the two soldier writers. And one of them is their sense of comradeship and identity with their men. Bernard Gutteridge describes Lewis as follows:

> He was Intelligence Officer in the regiment and quite obviously efficient and extremely popular. He was one of those rare, quiet, sympathetic people whom one met as officers in the army who were both good officers and well-loved. . . . He was called 'our poet' throughout his brigade in a thoroughly affectionate way—and that says a lot, I think . . . Incidentally, he could have got promotion and a safer job months before, but was absolutely insistent that he should go into action with the boys.

Alun Lewis refers in more than one letter to this feeling about not being separated from his men. It was something more complex than liking and the sense of human trust. He says in one place: 'I'm frightened of leaving them. They seem to have some secret knowledge that I want and I will never find out until I go into action with them and war really happens to them. I dread missing such a thing, it seems desertion to something more than either me or them.' In his story **"The Orange Grove,"** he says of one of his characters: 'He was experiencing one of those enlargements of the imagination that come once or perhaps twice to a man, and recreate him subtly and profoundly. . . . Such an enlargement of the imagination came to Alun Lewis, I feel sure, in India. It was a disturbing experience, too, rather like that sudden sense of 'unknown modes of being' that came to the boy Wordsworth when he was rowing across Ullswater. Only it was complicated for Alun Lewis by the *sky* of India, the sense, as E. M. Forster has described it, that outside the arch there seemed always another arch, beyond the remotest echo a silence'. And in this experience the categories of thought and value which he had accepted in his youth, in England, seemed gradually to be losing their meaning, to be swallowed up in something vaster. Here again his last poem "The Jungle" gives us clues:

> But we who dream beside this jungle pool
> Prefer the instinctive rightness of the poised
> Pied kingfisher deep darting for a fish

> To all the banal rectitude of states,
> The dew-bright diamonds on a viper's back
> To the slow poison of a meaning lost
> And the vituperation of the just. . . .

Alun Lewis was lost, like Staff-Captain Beale in **"The Orange Grove,"** driving on and on through the unknown landscape with his dead driver in the back of his truck—an image that has always reminded me of Yeats's lines about the soul 'sick with desire and fastened to a dying animal.' The whole story indeed is like a parable of the spiritual experience that Alun Lewis was going through. It is the gipsies who rescue Captain Beale when his truck finally sticks in the river bed, people he cannot understand, going in a direction he cannot guess, but elemental, smiling, and guided by some secret certainty. 'He wished, though, that he knew where they were going. They only smiled and nodded when he asked. Maybe they weren't going anywhere much, except perhaps to some pasture, to some well.' Those are the last sentences of **"The Orange Grove."** And if Alun Lewis was lost in one sense to 'the banal rectitude of states', he still had with him the 'instinctive truths and elemental love' that he had kept 'cleaned like knives in earth', and the presentiment that he was on the verge of discovering something far greater than he had lost. All his hints about the search for integrity, and reasoning only from a human standpoint, and the bonds with the men under his command which he found so difficult to analyse, are pointers to that, and pointers too to the role he might have played in literature if he had lived. But there was a sense of darkness also, and it invades the last lines of 'The Jungle':

> A trackless wilderness divides
> Joy from its cause, the motive from the act;
> The killing arm uncurls, strokes the soft moss;
> The distant world is an obituary,
> We do not hear the tappings of its dread.
> The act sustains, there is no consequence,
> Only aloneness, swinging slowly
> Down the cold orbit of an older world
> Than any they predicted in the schools,
> Stirs the cold forest with a starry wind,
> And sudden as the flashing of a sword
> The dream exalts the bowed and golden head
> And time is swept with a great turbulence
> The old temptation to remould the world.
> The bamboos creak like an uneasy house;
> The night is shrill with crickets, cold with space.
> And if the mute pads on the sand should lift
> Annihilating paws and strike us down
> Then would some unimportant death resound
> With the imprisoned music of the soul
> And we become the world we could not change?
> Or does the will's long struggle end
> With the last kindness of a foe or friend?

That poem reached England after he was dead. For the annihilating paws struck only too soon. He was out on patrol in the Maya Hills, following a difficult and dangerous path. Then the fatal accident occurred: we are told that he slipped on a stone, and the loaded revolver he was carrying went off, mortally wounding him. A stupid accident one might say on hearing such a piece of news and knowing nothing of the persons involved, just the kind of thing that happens in a war. . . . But, whatever happened in that still mysterious episode, the person happened to be a young writer whose fame, even on the slender remains of his work we have, has already spread to many countries, and will continue to spread and grow as his 'cryptic message' expands and sinks itself in our hearts.

John Stuart Williams (essay date 1964-65)

SOURCE: "The Short Stories of Alun Lewis," in *The Anglo-Welsh Review*, Vol. 14, No. 34, Winter, 1964-65, pp. 6-25.

In the following essay, Williams examines major themes in Lewis's stories, contrasting them with the themes of Lewis's poems.]

The short stories of Alun Lewis were first published in periodicals as different as *Lilliput* and *The Welsh Review*. Twenty-three of them were collected in *The Last Inspection,* published by George Allen and Unwin in 1942, and six appeared, with selections from his letters, in *In the Green Tree,* also published by Allen and Unwin, in 1948. Another story, **"Manuel,"** was re-printed in *First View,* a collection of short stories chosen by G. F. Green published by Faber and Faber in 1950. His achievement in this genre is perhaps easier to assess than his achievement as a poet. Certainly some critics who, like Glyn Jones, found it difficult to 'get the wavelength' of the poet, found no such difficulty with the writer of short stories. Yet both came out of the same sensibility, the same experience and the same pre-occupations, and Lewis's virtues and faults as a poet and as a short-story writer are not surprisingly often related. Perhaps we are less critical when we read prose; perhaps in poetry, especially lyric poetry, a single line out of place can unbalance the poem, whereas in the short story the virtues are more able to carry the faults.

I would suggest that both points are relevant. In England (and I use the word to distinguish the Saxon from the Celt) many of us have tended in the past to look on the short story as of secondary importance, a yarn, an anecdote or a characterization, something which is either a sort of short novel or an extract from a novel. Yet the two forms are different in essence. In a novel, development of character, the inter-relation of character and plot as a means of exploring a theme over a period of time, may be accepted, but in a short story the focus needs to be sharper and the significant point in time or development which a novel may lead up to and away from, must now be presented in itself. What has gone before and what may follow must be implicit in the moment: to explain them is to weaken it. In other words the short story may have the same sort of genesis as the lyric poem; its writing demands the same kind of sensibility and its virtues are similar. They are both crystallizations of experience, they both

demand a ruthless exegesis of the inessential and both are the better for that economy of statement in which each word is strictly relevant to the needs of the form and the aims of the writer. Sean O'Faolain in his book, *The Short Story,* suggests that a short story is as much a personal statement as is a lyric poem. The short story then should be judged with much the same critical standards in mind as the lyric. This has not often been the case in this country. The Irish, the Scots and the Welsh, together with the Americans, have been more aware of the distinctive qualities of the form both in writing and in criticism than have the English.

Perhaps this is an accident. Perhaps the opportunities for publication have something to do with it. Perhaps these writers are more aware of a European tradition, or perhaps, as O'Faolain suggests of America, Ireland and France, they see things in a more "assertively personal way," which English diffidence finds lacking in decorum. But this is speculation which needs to be qualified. The relevant fact here is that the short story is a significant part of the Anglo-Welsh contribution to literature. Three collections have been published, one by Faber edited by George Ewart Evans, one by Oxford University Press in the World's Classics edition edited by Professor Gwyn Jones, and another from the same editor by Penguin Books. All three are somewhat uneven in quality, although what is good is very good. They form a useful guide, nevertheless, to the pre-occupation of writers in the Anglo-Welsh heyday which was heralded by the rude trumpet of Caradoc Evans in 1915.

They are concerned with the working out of now familiar themes, the evocation of time past, the preservation of individual 'Welshmen' under the pressure of economic circumstances and Anglicisation, the attack on a Nonconformity already routed by Caradoc Evans, the creation of a 'cap and muffler' archetype, pathetic, sometimes humorous, sometimes, in short, a self-contemplation which often became self-conscious. They were often too concerned with themselves and what they were, to take time off to be themselves and write from that viewpoint. This need for a self-definition was valid enough at first, but by the late thirties it had become a habit, a way of doing things into which a man might fall without thought, and which made difficult any attempt at a wider view which might relate the parochial to the universal. The 'Anglo-Welsh' short story had become a manner, its first impetus lost in a formula. Alun Lewis in his short stories moved in another direction, a direction we have already traced in his poetry, towards a deeper exploration of the self and a deeper understanding of its relationship to others, not only in his own Welsh back-yard, which he never forgot was his starting point, but in the wider context of humanity and the world. He was born in Aberdare in 1915 and grew up at a time and in a place in which political solutions seemed not only relevant but comparatively straightforward. His life in the army in England seemed only to confirm this. In an unpublished letter to Robert Graves dated 2/5/42 he wrote that he was "a bit dubious" about the stories in *The Last Inspection.*

They're all very objective, the stories; and I imagine you'll lay them aside for pointing too regularly to the social moral. I'm becoming very left: and my prose is tinged.

It is thus reasonable to accept that in the story, **"Flick,"** the left-wing young officer, is Lewis's mouthpiece, and although its ending is uncomfortably close to cliché, and although the laconic style seems a little self-conscious, it illustrates clearly, perhaps too obviously for the sake of art, the politcal direction of his thought. Left-wing idealism of the sort which takes the brotherhood of man seriously is, I suggest, a source of his future development. His concern with the problems of common humanity is not unrelated to his concern for the problems of the individual caught up in self, time, and place. That he often appears more concerned with love and compassion need not imply a rejection of politics but a shift of emphasis and a realization that politics, while necessary, sometimes seemed in Europe an over-simplification and, perhaps to a British officer in war-time India, a complication which increased the complexity of his emotional and intellectual response. **"The Raid,"** in which a young terrorist is captured in an Indian village, is a well-written example. Here the question of 'whose side is one on' seems an irrelevant simplification in the face of human tragedy. Lewis is more like Keats than Shelley. In Keats the politics is there, a background to his concern with the problems of the individual; in Shelley it provides the answer to the problem of humanity.

Lewis's Welsh egalitarianism and his concern for individual values were heightened by the war until they became a kind of self-defence. He wrote in a letter that

> . . . although war is so monstrously arbitrary and violent that personal values seem as futile and ineffectual as art for art's sake, I still hold them, like thousands of others, because there is nothing else to save one or make one worth saving.

His Welshness is a starting point for his understanding of himself and of others, both as individuals and as part of the pattern of humanity. Those of us who write today at the fag-end of the 'Anglo-Welsh hiatus' could find worse guidance than this.

The themes of his poetry are often paralleled in his stories and their treatment is characterized by a seriousness of purpose even when humour breaks in. He sees man, shaped by his past, attempting to come to terms with himself and his fellow men and with his environment, in spite of the sense of alienation imposed by consciousness of himself as an individual. This alienation becomes in the army stories that of the 'landless soldier lost in war.' Technical ease came earlier than in poetry. **"The Wanderers,"** which was first published in 1939, has a satisfying unity in which the poetic and the realistic are balanced. It is passionate and sensuous, tender and clear-sighted, and its prose is concrete and evocative, suggesting a sureness of touch which he attained with any consistency only in a handful

of his war stories in **The Last Inspection.** The late stories in **In the Green Tree** in general show this certainty and command of his material. The same difficulty, that of relating form and language to subject matter under the pressure of war, which we noticed in his poetry is present but perhaps to a lesser degree in the stories written in between. Eighteen of the twenty-three stories in **The Last Inspection** are concerned with the army in England during the two years following "the disaster of June 1940." Alun Lewis in an 'author's note' describes them as "studies of 'hangover.'"

> Death in battle, death on a large scale, and all the attendant finalities and terrors—these are outside. They are the bread and water of our comrades overseas; we have the cakes and ale. The only deaths in these stories are from air raids and accidents; the main motif is the rootless life of soldiers having no enemy, and always, somehow, under a shadow.

Their subject then is the 'landless soldier' of the poetry. He also describes them as

> written out of immediate experience, typed upon leave, impelled by a perpetual sense of urgency; they are rather personal observations than detached compositions . . .

This suggests that he is aware of a fault in these stories that we have noticed in some of his poems, the too immediate involvement of the author, for it is one of the paradoxes of writing that the author must be both detached and involved in much the same way as an actor playing a part must be at the same time the character he is playing and an actor aware of the need to shape and control his performance. Some of these stories are not far from reportage, some are character studies; but others are perceptive examinations of crises in relationships arising out of the running together of the lines of circumstance. **"Lance Jack,"** for example, reads more like a journal than a short-story. **"Flick"** and **"Almost a Gentleman"** are studies of a central character, cooler in tone, more objective, perhaps because of the social criticism behind them, and therefore, to me, more acceptable. **"Acting Captain"** is concerned with the relationships of clearly-defined characters, but even here, in a story which is largely successful, Lewis himself intrudes and tells us what he has failed to imply. Curly Norris in this story sometimes appears to be the author's mouthpiece for making plain what should have been plain in the story itself. Curly, however, is a not unacceptable mouthpiece because he figures as a kind of chorus rather like those characters in the earlier novels of William Faulkner who live on the fringe of the action, at once involved and detached. He is not, like most chorus-figures, impersonally complete, but an imperfect man who understands out of his own imperfections.

The question of reportage in these stories is not easy to resolve. While the word implies the reporting of events, the photographing of circumstance, to dismiss it, like journalism, as of little value except in the context of its time, to forget that behind the eye which sees there is a mind which selects what is significant, whether this selection is done consciously or not. Someone must point the camera and develop the film. In the writer's mind and sensibility lies the grammar which relates a single experience to the pattern of the whole. It is often a matter of degree, of concentration, and, while much in these stories may seem at first glance to be merely factual recording, I would suggest that in as many cases such facts are the concrete equivalents of thought and emotion. What seem to be merely descriptive passages often have a deeper significance which might not at first be apparent. The last paragraph of **"They Came,"** for example, leads up to and supports the conclusion in a way which foreshadows the very fine later story **"Ward 0.3 (b)"** in which the description of the garden pond is significant to the whole meaning of the story.

The main criticism I have to make of the stories in *The Last Inspection* is, indeed, not that they verge on reportage, not that they are too factual, but that, to quote O'Faolain writing about his own early stories, they are "full of . . . personalizations and sensations which belong to the author rather than to the character." In other words the charge is not of reportage, not of too much objectivity, but of woolliness, of telling too much himself and allowing his characters in their words and by their action or inaction to tell us too little. One of the 'civilian' stories illustrates this well. In **"The Housekeeper"** he tells us a great deal where a little would do much better, and writes around and about his subject creating, it is true, an atmosphere, but doing it clumsily. Indeed parts of this story read like *Cold Comfort Farm*:

> Myfanwy watched her husband stir the boiler. He sat hunched over the fire, his eyes following the circling swirl of the brown liquid. As he stirred a warm dirty smell came from the boiler. Myfanwy shuddered.

But we cannot dismiss the story; its opening is skilful, and in its last pages what has become flabby suddenly becomes taut and significant again and the narrative moves with economy and force. In general, however, it is fair to say that if he wrote out of urgency, that urgency is not always as apparent as he would have wished. His prose is sometimes too full of qualifying phrases which only confuse the sense and diffuse the focus. His language is often heavy with adjectives, which sometimes result in a rich and satisfying texture, sometimes in a slowing of the pace and slackening of tension. Sometimes, too, it seems self-conscious, as in the opening conversations of **"Private Jones,"** when his attempt at conveying the idioms of Welsh speech seems almost, but not quite, condescending in a story which is anything but that. That this is the last fault anyone could attribute to Lewis himself suggests an uncertainty of control over language that occasionally disconcerts the reader in an otherwise successful story. It is worth noting in passing that as this story develops Lewis appears to find that balance of involvement and detachment which is part of his mature strength. The language becomes simpler and as a result his compassion and understanding are communicated without the intrusion of unnecessary explanation or qualification.

The criticisms already made are of faults that perhaps seem more important than they are in comparison with the undeniable quality of his best work. It is possible that the sureness of touch of **"The Wanderers"** would have developed slowly into a different kind of maturity. But war, the army and India gave him no time and it is scarcely surprising that his writing should not always be free from unevenness. Whatever faults in technique are apparent the honesty of his purpose is never obscured. He writes to know himself and to know others as aspects of humanity and in approaching his subject he is aware of the need for humility. In another unpublished letter to Robert Graves he wrote:

> If you read any of my work, please know beforehand the source from which my writing comes *Humility*. A dangerous thing to have in one but without it one is useless to do good. It is the source of all my long struggles, for it brings me into conflict with self-pity and pity for the world with authority and presumption on the part of those who are not humble, with intolerance and cruelty, and with submission.

The self-awareness and the awareness, too, of the necessity for understanding is evident in such stories as **"They Came," "Private Jones," "Picnic"** and others in *The Last Inspection.* They were already present in **"The Wanderers,"** but they increase in importance in the work written in war-time. Lewis's trouble is one of form and method not of conception or of purpose. In Tchehov's play *The Seagull* the unsuccessful writer Tryeplyev has this to say:

> The poster on the fence announced. . . . The pale face framed by dark hair . . . Announced . . . Framed. . . . It's banal (striking the words out). I'll begin with the hero awakened by the noise of the rain, and away with all the rest. The description of the moonlit evening is long and laboured. Treegorin has worked out certain methods for himself, it's easy for him. . . . He says, the neck of a broken bottle glistens on the dam, and the shadow of the mill-wheel is growing blacker—There's a moonlight night all complete; while I describe the tremulous night, the gentle gleaming of the stars, and the distant sounds of the piano dying away in the still, scented air. . . . It is tormenting. . . .

Alun Lewis in *The Last Inspection* was sometimes like Tryeplyev, but there are already signs that he is developing into a Treegorin. In his last stories, those re-printed in *In the Green Tree,* his virtues are those of Treegorin. Here we find true objectivity, the realism which is imaginative because it is selective. Thus he gains in power without losing any of his skill in the evocation of atmosphere or his sensitivity to the link between natural objects and man.

These last stories are for the most part admirable in structure, in the felicitousness of the relation of language to content and in the way in which action, character and imagery are related in the expression of the theme. The sureness of touch of **"The Wanderers"** is now at the service of a deeper understanding of the human predicament. He wrote to his wife about his later poems in *Ha! Ha! Among the Trumpets!*:

> Each version I've worked to simplify and abbreviate.

The discipline implied in this process is evident in these stories, at least one of which seems to me worthy of inclusion in any anthology of short stories written in English in the last forty years. The simplification of style, this sureness of touch in selecting what is significant, is perhaps related to his mature awareness of the paradox of beauty and ugliness, of life and death. The Indian scene provided many examples:

> . . . Indian dirt always has its beautiful surprises and there was the most vivid kingfisher you've ever dreamed of, a brilliant little flying rainbow sedately watching us and the native boys who splashed themselves in the black water like sparrows in a puddle.
>
> (Letter to Mrs. Lewis.)

The 'ripeness' that 'is all' is the dominant theme in most of these stories, but it is more than a passive acceptance of the inevitable. Death and life are seen as together encompassing the circle of being and the tone, with one notable exception, is one of grave compassion and understanding. He has found a secure footing on the point of balance between involvement and detachment. In any comprehensive study of Alun Lewis the influence of Edward Thomas and Rilke must be considered. There is no space in a brief introduction such as this, but it is necessary to notice that the movement towards and away from death in Lewis's writing is reminiscent of Keats in *The Ode to a Nightingale*. In **"The Earth is a Syllable"** death is almost a mother figure. The wounded man in the stranded truck

> wanted to get up and enter the darkness and enter the silent village under the hill and enter it with his wife alone. . . .
>
> So he went across the plain in the night. . . .
>
> The driver found him five yards away from the truck.

In **"The Reunion,"** however, there is no acceptance, but savage protest. This is a violent little story with traces of the imbalance that disturbs some of his earlier stories. The opening is somewhat literary in style but establishes situation and atmosphere effectively; it is followed by some revealing conversation which is admirably laconic. Then we have a passage of a kind we have read before in Lewis, which tells us a little too obviously what we should have been able to deduce, before the story erupts into a wholly convincing violence. Lewis's use of a central symbol to concentrate the theme of his story is exemplified here in the sea-shell which one brother gives to another only for it to be destroyed. It stands for something rare and delicate, love and its sensitive relationships, home, the integrity of the individual, all of which are brutally beaten by the lunatic world of reality in the war-time Army in India. **"The Raid,"** one of the few stories in which the narrator is not

a 'Lewis' figure, is also concerned with violence and with protest, but the point is made more obliquely and economically and therefore, with more force.

In the other stories, from **"Night Journey"** to **"The Orange Grove,"** we meet the familiar lost figure of the 'landless soldier' who serves not only as a symbol of the paradoxical alienation of the individual in the mass but also as a chorus figure who is at one and the same time detached and involved. In the two stories mentioned values belonging to other times and other places are suggested. Another world is contrasted with the predicament of the present. This other world, a world of individual values, may exist only in the mind or memory. It may be idealized, but it is this which preserves a man in alien circumstances:

> "I was born just over them fields, sir" the prisoner said, heavily, slowly, peaceably. "See that level crossing there? Used to go over that to school every day."
>
> "Never mind," said the Officer. "We'd better go back now. Both of us."
>
> **("Night Journey")**

In **"The Orange Grove,"** a story rich in association, an officer and his driver are travelling in a truck in an India full of "unrest and rioting." They talk over their attitudes and their personalities grow into contrast. The officer, Beale,

> couldn't understand hate. War hadn't taught it to him, war was to him only fitness, discomfort, feats of endurance, proud muscles, a career, irresponsible dissipation. . . .

The ranker had started in a reformatory, moved into the regular army, and served in Palestine. "Seen them collective farms the Jews got there, sir? Oranges. . . ." His life had been bitter, but he was without self-pity. The orange groves casually mentioned are later remembered by Beale.

> They were good places, those farms?

And the ranker, who significantly remains anonymous, replies:—

> Aye, they were . . . They didn't have money, they didn't buy and sell. They shared what they had . . . and I would like to go back there.

In thinking of this Beale experienced an "enlargement of the imagination" which was to "recreate him subtly and profoundly." The driver is killed and Beale's last journey with the body is a spiritual pilgrimage during which he first becomes passionately involved with the life of the dead man, and then moves through sympathy to understanding not only of himself and the driver but of all lost people on the face of the earth. The orange grove is the symbol of perfect belonging, which may or may not be available to any one man in reality, but is profoundly significant even as a symbol alone. In **"The Orange Grove"** form and content are fused. The language is felicitous, the pattern of character, event, and background is treated with assurance. Narrative and theme are inter-related. It is a short story of unusual quality.

"Ward 0.3 (b)" tells of a group of wounded officers in a convalescent ward in India awaiting a medical board's decision on their futures. Some hope to be sent home, others to return to active service. The hospital itself "is, by 1943 standards, a good place to be in." The backgrounds and foibles of the characters are revealed in their re-action to each other, to the beautiful Sister Normanby (no cardboard heroine this), and to the tension occasioned by the imminence of a decision which will radically alter their lives, with an insight and understanding free from sentimentality. Weston, the savagely wounded young man who wants to "have a look at Burma" and doesn't "want to see England" is somehow the most balanced character in the story, even if his balance is a delicate one based on unresolved tension, and his poise is related to that understanding in which "ripeness is all." The description of the garden pool at the end of the story is significant. It is a point of rest, of a suspension of tension for the moment in the contemplation of, and in the identification with, things outside the press of human circumstance.

> And he felt glad tonight, feeling some small salient gained when for many reasons the men whom he was with were losing ground along the whole front to the darkness that there is.

As in **"Night Journey"** the return to the reality of the trivial yet inescapable is recognised:

> "The mosquitoes are starting to bite," he said. "We'd better go now."

The story is finely balanced and written with unobtrusive control of technique. I consider it one of his finest achievements.

Of all Anglo-Welsh writers he is the one who most clearly relates what he is to the world outside. His concern with alienation reflects the situation of the English-speaking Welshman who carries the tension of two worlds within himself. Technical assurance comes easily to some writers; their problem is to find something worth saying. For others, the importance of what they have to say distorts both subject and form in the difficulty of expression. They have to work hard to learn their craft, to turn a facility into a talent. But when they succeed their work is always considerable. Alun Lewis started with more than facility, he became a poet and a craftsman with something more than talent. He felt confident in his ability at the end:

> can draw comfort and power from knowing that I can write short stories.

"Ward 0.3 (b)" and **"The Orange Grove"** show that confidence to be fully justified.

Jacqueline Banerjee (essay date 1972)

SOURCE: "Alun Lewis: The Early Stories," in *The Anglo-Welsh Review,* Vol. 20, No. 46, Spring, 1972, pp. 77-82.

[*In the following essay, Banerjee examines Lewis's early stories, finding in them evidence of the success of the later, better-known stories and poems.*]

The relative merits of Alun Lewis's poetry and short stories have long been in dispute. Was he basically a prose-writer, who only turned to poetry under the stress of service conditions, or was he, as one reviewer suggested, "a natural poet fascinated by the problems of the short story, which he once or twice brilliantly solved?"[1] One clue is to be found in a letter to Freda Aykroyd in India, where Lewis tries to define the impulses which lie behind the poetry and the prose, and himself suggests that the two represent different but complementary aspects of his art: "I think the poems are an act of daring, always daring, to plunge and tear and enter; the stories are an act of recognition and steadiness . . . the stories . . . stick to things the poetry sweeps above or below."[2] But it may be significant that his earliest interest was, in fact, in prose; and that his development in this form was more even. It was soon apparent that his achievement here was to rank with that of other writers who have used the medium, not simply to tell a lively tale, but to explore and extend their vision of the universe.

With the exception of one or two slight poems, Lewis's frequent contributions to school and college magazines (*The Bovian* at Cowbridge Grammar School, *The Dragon* at Aberystwyth, and *The Serpent* at Manchester University) were in prose, almost all of them being short stories. To the critical eye his earliest attempts, quite understandably, betray the same bad tendencies as the earlier poems— unnecessary and over-sensuous description, romantic flourishes, cliche endings, and a general unevenness of tone. Yet from the very beginning the stories are remarkable for showing Lewis's preoccupation with suffering, his capacity to understand and sympathize with it wherever he encountered it. And just as the right word or the memorable phrase redeems many of the slighter poems of *Raiders' Dawn,* so an unusual dramatic power in the portrayal of suffering redeems many of these stories. In one story written at school he describes vividly the terror of the hunt; in another, **"The Tale of a Dwarf,"** he depicts the misery of a circus dwarf, whose fate is shown in all its irony:

> On the little wooden stool inside sat a human figure, like a small child, hugging the darkness, indistinct and fantastic in the fitful light of the little stove. Hunched up as he sat, in the gloom, distorted by a hundred quips of light and shade; a creature of angles and mystery as he rocked to and fro in silent misery, beating a ceaseless echoing tattoo on the unseen floorboards. Felix the dwarf he was, price 2d. for the fairgoer. 'Felix means happy,' he thought, eyes brimming with tears of irony.
>
> (*The Bovian,* March 1931, p. 4.)

The common theme of suffering, and the desire to find a positive solution to it, link nearly all the stories written at school. In the last of these, **"They say there's a Boat on the River,"** Lewis demonstrates the need to reject the alluring, relaxing charms of an idyllic land, presumably in favour of the harsher but more vital world of reality. His progress here, as later in the poems, may be seen to stem from his determination to get to grips with the essentials of life.

The stories published in the college magazines show a marked improvement in style and technique. They still have some romantic touches, but these are not expanded into full-length descriptions—except for dramatic purposes in one story, **"Dwellers in the Valley,"** where a long opening paragraph raises and then shatters the illusion of pastoral calm. Here, and throughout these stories, it is clear that Lewis is learning to subject his lyrical impulses to the particular demand of the short story—that every element of the writing should tend towards the central action. In **"Tudor Witch,"** for instance, the first of the stories to be published in *The Dragon,* an ominous atmosphere is evoked in a few sentences by a quick sketch of the scene, and of the background events of the story: a small party of villagers is making its way timidly through a silent, shadowy glade after a visit to a local miracle play. Thereafter, the plot is developed neatly, and the onward pressure of the narrative never falters. The central character, one of the villagers who takes it into his head to destroy a reputed witch, is drawn with insight, and his victim is sketched with compassion. Although the story does not escape touches of melodrama, especially at the end, the various ironies of the witch-hunt are well brought out, and the story is far in advance of any of the school stories.

Two of the other pieces written at college are re-creations of historical events—**"The Diary of a Knight of King Arthur"** (a skit on the legend of Sir Gawayne and the Green Knight) and **"Old Unhappy Faroff Things . . ."** (an impassioned account of an incident in the War of the Sabines). So Lewis's mother may well be right in linking the improvement in his prose with his academic pursuits: she feels that the disciplines involved in the study of history (his subject at Aberystwyth) helped him to approach his writing with greater detachment and precision. But equally important in the development of his prose at this time is his steadily growing interest in people, rather than the wild creatures and fictional characters of the earlier stories, or the historical figures which sometimes inspire him now. He becomes aware that the sufferings which he saw in the hunted fox or the captive circus dwarf are experienced by ordinary human beings, in their ordinary, everyday lives. He begins to deal with the Welsh folk—the sour old farmer who realizes his cruelty in holding on to his only daughter, but dies too late to decide on any generous action; the old man whose market trap has been made redundant by the motor car, and whose comical efforts to get some business end in tragedy. This interest in simple country people leads Lewis to describe familiar ways of life, and in itself prompts him to seek a stricter realism.

"The Wanderers" was written at about this time, although it appears with later stories in *The Last Inspection* (1942). It became, as his mother notes, a favourite with the publishers, and it was this story which established his reputation as a short story writer. Firmer control, particularly in the use of descriptive passages and poetic diction, and the selection of strictly relevant and realistic detail, are linked here with the dramatic power which Lewis has shown from the beginning, and the understanding of human nature which he is beginning to win, early in his life, through his ready sympathy with suffering. The plot, like that of **"Tudor Witch"** is well-turned and moves quickly: typically enough, it concerns people who seem to be swept along by forces beyond their control. A gipsy is unfaithful to his wife, who guesses, and turns passionately to a roaming Breton onion-seller; she sets out to follow the Breton to Cardigan, but decides to return for the sake of her son; husband and wife confront each other at the door of their caravan and the tensions which have long been growing between them explode in a physical struggle—and then subside in passionate love-making. Gradually we have become aware of the deeper causes of resentment between the two—the gipsy's wife is the daughter of a Cardiganshire farmer, not wholly suited to the way of life which once attracted her; but we have also been prepared for the ending, by the violence of the woman's reactions to her husband's unfaithfulness. The story is a translation into human terms of that paradoxical mingling of beauty and brutality in nature which fascinated Lewis, and which he was now finding in the simple people who live close to the instinctive life of nature.

Although one is tempted to find the influence of D. H. Lawrence in the story, it clearly expresses Lewis's own interests: the prototype of this gipsy is perhaps the gipsy who appears, with his son, as the cruel captor of a small bird, in **"The Death of Monga,"** one of Lewis's earliest contributions to *The Bovian.* Significantly, it is through the reactions of the young boy in **"The Wanderers"** that our response is evoked; he becomes the register of the emotional ebb and flow of the story. Here, for instance, is the ending:

> After an hour lying in the deepest part of the wood, Micah came back slowly and fearfully to the clearing. Slowly he tiptoed up the steps of the caravan, apprehensive of the silence, and found them lying together under the red blanket, face to face and fast asleep.
>
> The child did not wake them. Instead he sat quietly on the steps and carved a whistle out of a sycamore branch, knowing that when they woke everything would be the way he liked it.
>
> (p. 106.)

Throughout, the restraint and yet richness of the writing is remarkable. In another passage we see the family just before the split occurs:

> They decided to spend the night in a little pasture by the river, and after unharnessing the mare and tethering her to a hazel, the gipsy stripped and swam in the stream. The cold green water seemed to flow through him, dissolving his tired sweaty body into energy and delight. He climbed onto the bank and lay in the long grass, biting off the leaves of sorrel with his teeth and

tasting the bittersweet juice on his tongue. Micah was playing near him, yellow as a bee with rolling in the buttercups. His wife was sitting hunched up on the steps of the caravan.

(p. 92.)

The contrast between the gypsy's vitality and his wife's sullen withdrawal from the family helps to explain the gipsy's sudden desertion—but at this moment the young boy's carefree world is still intact. The quality of this writing is such that Lewis is able now to suggest undercurrents of frustration, and now to realize full-blooded passion. Apart from some awkwardness in the dialogue, it is a very successful story, and is certainly, as his mother says, unusually mature and sophisticated for a young man of eighteen years old.

As in the other stories of farming folk, Lewis presents the central conflict of emotions in **"The Wanderers"** objectively: here he makes his comments on it through the small boy, rather than in his own person; and two incidents in the plot, the gipsy's pawning of his wife's ear-rings, and the redemption of them at the end, also serve as indirect indications of the course of the relationship. This growing ability to write with the necessary detachment was put to the test in two stories about boarding school, which appeared, one in Lewis's last undergraduate year at Aberystwyth, the other in his first year at Manchester. These show him beginning to explore himself, rather than nature or the lives of other people. He had already contributed an autobiographical essay to the school magazine, and perhaps projected himself into the young schoolmaster of an earlier contribution to *The Dragon*, **"If Such be Nature's Holy Plan. . . ."** But here, in the sensitive young boy of **"Whit Monday"** and **"Chestnuts,"** Lewis seems to be presenting an imaginative reconstruction of his own adolescence. Bristow, in **"Chestnuts,"** is an earnest, studious schoolboy who must put up with taunts from another boy in his dormitory:

"I say, Bristow," he called, "saying your prayers?"

"Don't try and be funny," came a voice from the next bed.

"Well, you're soft enough to do that," said Mottram, lying on his back while his legs explored the cold sheets. A chap that reads Keats and bloody Shelley's soft enough for anything."

(*The Serpent*, December 1936, p. 39.)

Lewis keeps some measure of detachment here by the gentle humour with which he portrays the boy's first romance: "'Of course, I know *your* name—you're Anne Ellis—it rhymes with rose trellis.'" (p. 39.) This vein of humour, which appears in Lewis's prose from the beginning, and which in the best of his stories is mingled with pathos or edged with irony, does perhaps suggest that it is a more balanced statement of his personality than his poetry.

A slightly later story, **"Attitude,"** is much less successful, and represents the kind of failure which could occur when

Lewis got *too* close to his own experiences: here his activities as a student in London, writing poetry, working on his research projects, and forming relationships, are thinly disguised as the thoughts of a girl recalling the events which led to her marriage. But of course it was only to be expected that, at a time when he was beginning to realize the potential of the short story, Lewis should occasionally lose the objective standpoint which he already saw the need for.

And indeed, his last contribution to *The Dragon*, **"Squibs for the Guy,"** prepares us for some of the best stories in *The Last Inspection*. This brief glimpse of a poverty-striken Welsh family is given with a compassion which never overflows into personal emotion. A father collects his small boys from school and takes them gathering ferns to stuff a guy. The grandmother greets them at home with the news that the rent-collector is there, armed with an ultimatum, and the boys are sent out to the shed together with the rent-collector's son, to stuff their guy. The other boys' excited prattling, revealing their poverty and bringing out the death of their mother, keeps the rent-collector's son in awkward silence. When the father eventually comes out to the shed, he seems to be hiding some unpleasant news, and the rent-collector calls his son back sharply. Before he hurries out, the son yields to an impulse of pity (something his father had evidently been unable to do) and timidly hands the boys a threepenny bit. Lewis's attitude may well appear in this act of embarrassed generosity, but it is never directly expressed, and the blend of humour, irony and pathos in the story is never disturbed by unnecessary comment.

It does appear from a study of this early work that Lewis had a special interest in the short story: his progress in this medium quickly yielded something more than occasional success. It is no surprise, then, to find him writing to Lynette Rhys in later years:

I'm growing more and more into a mere short story writer, Lynette. I *love* it, just *love* it. I get all the feeling of poetry, with something less miraculous and more credible in the act of writing. I can never believe I write *poetry*. I can draw comfort and power from knowing that I can write short stories.

("A Sheaf of Letters from Alun Lewis, 1941-1943—First Selection," *Wales*, February-March 1948, p. 426.)

Alun Lewis could, of course, write poetry. But it soon became clear that his achievement as a prose-writer was to be perhaps even more considerable.

Notes

1. *The Times Literary Supplement*, June 24, 1949, p. 408

2. "Some Letters of Alun Lewis," *Modern Reading*, Summer 1952, p. 24.

Walter Allen (essay date 1981)

SOURCE: "Thomas, Alun Lewis," in *The Short Story in English,* Oxford at the Clarendon Press, 1981, pp. 299-305.

[*In the following essay, Allen discusses Lewis's story "The Wanderers," which Allen considers his best story.*]

A South Wales man, Alun Lewis was killed in an accident while on active service in India in 1943. He was then a lieutenant in the South Wales Borderers. Lewis's primary reputation was and remains that of a poet, but he left behind a handful of stories of great promise which suggest also that he might have become a novelist of stature. It would be easy to believe that it was the experience of war that wrenched Lewis out of a narrow, parochial tradition of English writing in Welsh. That this was not so is shown conspicuously by **"The Wanderers,"** one of the five stories in his volume *The Last Inspection* that do not deal with the war. It is perhaps the finest story he ever wrote; in its suggestion of a kinship with the young Lawrence it indicates the nature of his talent and his affinities.

The opening sets its scene and ambience:

> The heat inside the caravan was too much for her. The wooden wall-boards were warped and the paint bubbled and flaked by the burning hot noon. She fell asleep in the middle of stitching a corner of the red quilt in the boy's trousers. Running up the steps in nothing but his rough green jersey, the boy found her lolling open-mouthed in the chair, beads of sweat on her pale face. He twined his grubby fingers in the fall of her black hair and pulled gently.
>
> 'Wake up, mam,' he said, 'Dad's coming across the fields.'
>
> She woke with a start, surprised to find herself sleeping.
>
> 'Jewks!' she muttered, rubbing her eyes. 'I'm that sleepy. Where is he, Micah?'
>
> 'Just crossing the river,' Micah replied. 'He's got two rabbits.'
>
> 'We'll have a change from bread and dripping, then,' she said, yawning.

She—we never know her name—is a farmer's daughter who has run away with and married a gipsy. From the beginning of the story we are conscious of tension and lack of trust between them. She discovers that he has been unfaithful to her and she has her own back by being unfaithful with Johnny Onions, an itinerant Breton onion-seller. She begs him to stay with her but he refuses, and next day she runs away intending to join him. At sunset there are still fifteen miles to go.

> She took her shoes off and bathed her swollen feet in a little brook. The water prattled like ice over her toes. She moved them up and down and her body sighed with relief. She took a handful of cress, broke off the

roots, washed it and put it in her mouth. It was cool on her tongue, and yet it burnt her like a remorse. Ever since she had seen the gipsy come out of the cowshed, dusting his knees, she had been helpless in the whirlpool of her mind and body. She saw it clearly, looking down upon herself. She must go back to the caravan. If he had stayed in town overnight, he would never know. And Micah there alone—God! She pulled her sandals on, fingers trembling with haste, and started back along the lane.

She reaches the caravan at first light. Her husband is waiting for her, drunk; they trade insults and recriminations and then they fight. They fight each other into reconciliation. And the story ends:

> After an hour lying in the deepest part of the wood, Micah came back slowly and fearfully to the clearing. Slowly he tiptoed up the steps of the caravan, apprehensive of the silence, and found them lying together under the red blanket, face to face and fast asleep.
>
> The child did not wake them. Instead he sat quietly on the steps and carved a whistle out of a sycamore branch, knowing that when they woke everything would be the way he liked it.

What is impressive in this story of sexual passion is the sense of being in the presence of a young writer who is ready to confront unflinchingly the great subjects of literature. He sees his action from a great height, and this allows us more than one point of view. We find ourselves, for instance, identifying with the small boy as well as with his mother; and this without strain.

The qualities conspicuous in **"The Wanderers"** similarly distinguish the stories of Army life. Among the best, and characteristic of them all, is **"Cold Spell,"** which narrates the course of the love of a Naafi counterhand, Gracie, for a flight sergeant in the Royal Air Force. The first paragraph sets the tone of the story:

> Gracie worked in the Naffy on the aerodrome and it had begun with him buying coffee from her during the morning break, or before taking off of a winter morning on practice, or after dark on a raid. She always saw to it that his coffee was piping hot; the very first time she served him a cup she had heated it up for him.

We are told next to nothing about their antecedents and backgrounds and we never learn the flight sergeant's name, but both spring to life under Lewis's pen. The course of their love flows smoothly enough, though always checked by the constraints of their situation, by the knowledge, particularly for Gracie, that it may have no future.

> And gradually, by herself, she made terms with life, figuring out just how it was. He had never said a word about the future. Marriage wasn't in his mind. And how could it be when he didn't expect to live? She wasn't blaming him for that. Their whole life was limited in a way, limited to the aerodrome, its routine and conventions and personnel and operations . . . They were just part of the aerodrome, that was all, a little

corner of the war. And he was more a part of it than she. He belonged to his kite, and was part of its crew. He talked of her engines and controls and guns with the intimate quietness of a lover. . . . She meant more to him than Gracie did. And she wasn't blaming him for that, either.

With its strong yet unemphatic rhythms, its colloquial ease, this is surely a beautiful piece of unstudied prose, which again may recall early Lawrence. Then in mid-December the ground freezes up, and one afternoon he takes Gracie to the neighbouring town. They walk by the lake in the public park.

> 'Look, Gracie,' he said, stopping and turning to her and kicking a stump of gorse with his toe, 'I've been thinking it out this week. Shall I tell you what I think?'
>
> 'Yes,' she said, her whole life suddenly pausing. If after all it was just this Saturday afternoon beside the lake for which she had been waiting with such fixed frightened endurance?
>
> 'Well, I've been thinking about the kite and the boys,' he said.
>
> Something flared up in her, blind anger, like a heath fire half-stamped-out that breaks again into flame with a gust of wind.
>
> 'Yes?' she said. 'That's not unusual, is it?'

And he tells her that Micky, the rear-gunner, who had been wounded on the flight back from the last trip, had died that day.

> After kicking the stump of gorse for a long time he said, 'I can't forget the stink of blood, and the clots of black flesh congealed in his clothes and the mess on the floor his face was sprawled on—I can't get it out of my mouth, Gracie, the filthy mess it was, and the stink.'

Then he proposes marriage to her; and the story ends with a beautiful image that seems the perfect resolution of everything that has gone before:

> 'Oh, look!' he said. 'Look at those two swans.'
>
> A brace of swans, swift and white, cut like arrows slantwise through the lemon clouds of misty sunlight over the pines, wings firm-spread and glittering white in their downrushing and furling, scarcely disturbing the surface of the lake.
>
> 'Perfect landing!' he said. 'Wasn't it? Couldn't have done it better myself.'

Lewis left behind him half a dozen further stories, which are published together with letters from India to his wife and parents. They show the direction he might have gone, had he survived the war. The best of them is probably the best-known, **"Ward O 3 (b),"** which focuses on the fortunes of the four officers in the officers' convalescent ward of a British military hospital in southern India in the autumn of 1942. There is no plot in any usual sense; rather, it is as though the occupants of the ward and the ward-sister exist in the spotlight of Lewis's totally objective and unsentimental compassion. The ease with which Lewis passes from one to another of them and builds up relationships between them suggests that he would have gone on to writing novels; we know that he was planning a work on much the same theme as *A Passage to India.* He did not live to begin it, but enough of his writing survives, the two volumes of verse and the score and a half of short stories, to indicate how great a loss to English literature his death was.

FURTHER READING

Biography

Pikoulis, John. *Alun Lewis: A Life.* Mid Glamorgan, Wales: Seren Books, 1991, 322 p.
>   Provides a critical biography of Lewis.

Criticism

John, Alun. *Alun Lewis.* Cardiff: University of Wales Press, 1970, 98 p.
>   Examines Lewis as a distinctly Welsh writer.

Jones, Gwyn. "Postscript." In *In the Green Tree,* by Alun Lewis, pp. 137-41. London: George Allen and Unwin, Ltd., 1948.
>   Offers a personal reminiscence of Lewis as a writer and correspondent.

Stegner, Wallace. "Waiting." *New York Times Book Review* (20 June 1943): 4-5.
>   Admits some flaws in *The Last Inspection* but finds that the stories provide a valuable artistic service in their examination of the ordinary, non-heroic, aspects of army life.

Additional coverage of Lewis's life and career is contained in the following sources published by the Gale Group: *Contemporary Authors,* **Vol. 104;** *Dictionary of Literary Biography,* **Vols. 20, 162; and** *Twentieth-Century Literary Criticism,* **Vol. 3.**

Frank Moorhouse
1938–

Australian short story writer, novelist, screenwriter, and essayist.

INTRODUCTION

Moorhouse is considered one of the most important and influential contemporary short story writers in Australia. Critics praise his deft portrayal of the urban landscape in modern Australia, particularly the changing sexual and social mores of post-World War II society. His experiments with the genre of the short story have spurred critical commentary, and many critics have compared his work to that of Sherwood Anderson and William Faulkner.

BIOGRAPHICAL INFORMATION

Moorhouse was born in Nowra, New South Wales, on December 21, 1938. In 1956 he moved to Sydney and began working as a journalist for the *Daily Telegraph*. For the next several years he worked as a journalist and editor in Sydney, an experience that contributed to his literary style and the thematic concerns of his short fiction. In 1969 he published his first volume of short stories, *Futility and Other Animals*. With fellow Australian writer Michael Wilding he co-founded the influential literary magazine *Tabloid Story* in 1972. Moorhouse has been a writer-in-residence for several Australian universities. In 1985 he adapted stories from *The Americans, Baby* and *The Electrical Experience* for the film "The Coca-Cola Kid." Throughout the 1980s Moorhouse traveled extensively and settled in France in 1991.

MAJOR WORKS OF SHORT FICTION

Moorhouse refers to his short fiction as "discontinuous narratives," which indicate his attempt to link his stories through characters, locations, and themes. Two of Moorhouse's recurring themes are the effects of American culture on Australians and the changing sexual mores of Australian society. Several of his stories examine the impact of an American visitor on his Australian hosts. In his collection *The Americans, Baby,* "The American, Paul Jonson" introduces an American businessman who gets involved in a sexual relationship with Carl, a young Australian college student. At first, Carl believes he has the moral responsibility to exploit Jonson to counter the deleterious effect of American culture, but the story ends on Carl's discovery of his homosexuality. Yet Moorhouse's main focus in his fiction is on the complexity and vicissi-

tudes of contemporary Australian life. *The Electrical Experience* features stories from the life of T. George McDowell, a self-made manufacturer of soft drinks in Australia. In *Conference-Ville* the stories revolve around an academic seminar, with its concomitant rituals and affectations. In *Forty-Seventeen,* the stories involve an affair between a forty-year-old man and a seventeen-year-old schoolgirl in Australia. As the affair continues over several years, Moorhouse examines the nature of sexual attraction, love, and commitment and how it changes with age and responsibility.

CRITICAL RECEPTION

Moorhouse's tendency to link his stories across different short fiction collections by character, location, and thematic concerns has prompted critics to view his work in short story cycles. In this way, he has been compared to such short story writers as Sherwood Anderson, William Faulkner, J. D. Salinger, and James Joyce. With his focus on topical contemporary themes such as the change in sexual attitudes and Australia's relationship to American culture, commentators often discuss his work as anthropology, sociology, or social history. In his realistic portrayal of contemporary urban, academic, and suburban life, reviewers praise his ability to draw material from everyday existence to illustrate the moral issues of his generation.

PRINCIPAL WORKS

Short Fiction

Futility and Other Animals 1969
The Americans, Baby 1972
The Electrical Experience 1974
Conference-Ville 1976
Tales of Mystery and Romance 1977
The Everlasting Secret Family and Other Secrets 1980
Room Service 1985
Forty-Seventeen 1988
Loose Living 1995

Other Major Works

Grand Days: A Novel (novel) 1993

CRITICISM

Brian Kiernan (essay date 1973)

SOURCE: "Notes on Frank Moorhouse," in *Overland*, Spring, 1973, pp. 9-11.

[*In the following essay, Kiernan provides a brief overview of Moorhouse's short fiction.*]

With his *The Americans, Baby* (Angus & Robertson), Frank Moorhouse seems to have won some long deserved general recognition. The book has been received enthusiastically, though more interest has been shown in the trendy nature of his material—the Sydney push, the drug scene, student radicalism, sexual permissiveness, women's liberation *et al.*—than with his handling of it. Partly, one suspects, this enthusiasm is a matter of general consciousness catching up with the individual talent. Although Moorhouse, at thirty-four, is still regarded as a "young writer," he has been writing about his urban tribe and their now suddenly 'relevant' preoccupations for most of the past decade, slowly winning an audience who could appreciate his sort of story and the sometimes uncomfortable in-

tegrity that was behind it. Perhaps also that old chestnut about Australian writers being obsessed with the outback and the mythic past helps explain the excited discovery that Moorhouse, like young dramatists and poets, is writing about contemporary urban Australian society. Whereas the new men are cool as spreading fern over the cultural dilemmas of Ern Malley's generation, accepting the society they know as the natural, familiar and substantial background to what they want to write about, their audiences still tend to be fascinated with the background itself.

Not that Moorhouse himself objects to this fascination with the sub-culture he has drawn upon for his fiction. "I find it complimentary that people are totally taken in by the performance and talk to me about the characters and the situations as though they were real. But they're realistic or naturalistic stories in their observed details only. There was a party for Rexroth which attended, but that story (**"The American Poet's Visit"**) was written long after and isn't a record of what actually happened. It's all been adjusted from a distance." Another example of adjustment to reality is **"The Jack Kerouac Wake,"** a story not yet published that turns up at Sydney readings in different versions. One version is by Michael Wilding (whose own collection, which includes stories of Sydney push life, has just been published by Queensland University Press), others are by Moorhouse. Each claims to present the "true" account of a chaotic night. Each is close to the truth—but what is truth? What mainly come out of his adjustments to reality in *The Americans, Baby,* Moorhouse feels, are allegorical or politically representative characters. "If I were a literary critic, I'd suggest that Becker (his Coca-Cola sales executive and the anti-hero of a sequence of stories) is a human trying to be a technological giant—in fact playing one of America's major roles."

Moorhouse's interest in Americans goes back to his boyhood memories of U.S. servicemen during the war and business associates of his father. They always seemed visitors from a remote and powerful land. When last year he went overseas for the first time his destination was New Orleans, the place that, particularly from his reading, had most excited his imagination, With Becker, the American who appears most frequently in his stories, Moorhouse twists a number of conventional expectations. In a time-honored American tradition, Becker is an innocent abroad; but it is the New World of Australia that corrupts him, a world that seems to him as remote from his home town of Atlanta, Georgia, as the moon. Becker's view of Australia is fresh and comic:

> Becker was thinking this: how rarely in this foul country did the milk carton open up as the printed directions promised, "to open push up here"—push up where, for goddam. It had to do with the spread of talent across the land. For a country with a population so small they should, in terms of technology, still be peasants. That was his feeling, harsh as it may be. The way he figured it, the high-performance five-percenters were spread over too diversified an economy. By accident of history. The accident of history, as Becker saw it, was

that they were English speakers. They attempted the higher technology of the main English nations. That was it. Result: milk cartons which wouldn't spout.

Becker is an outsider to Australian society as a whole, as well as to the worlds of the drag queens, speed freaks and liberated females he stumbles into. As an outsider, he is like a number of other characters who are affected by sub-cultural in-groups. Another example of the outsider, and of what Moorhouse sees as 'allegorical' or socially representative characterization, would be in **"Dell Goes Into Politics."** Dell returns to her country town after an unsatisfactory affair with a Trotskyist schoolteacher in Sydney. Wanting to appear sophisticated, she speaks out boldly on Vietnam, to the amazement and embarrassment of all in the local pub. Yet, as she admits to herself at the end of the story, this has only been to evade what is really troubling her. The gulf between her political 'awareness,' which is no more than the holding of fashionable attitudes, and her personal experience seems to offer a more general comment about the impact of the Vietnam war on public consciousness.

For someone who sees himself partly motivated as a writer by his interest in politics and social theory, Moorhouse is cooly detached from his characters and their beliefs. As the author, he seems interested in ideology only as it affects people, and his political autobiography is relevant here:

> When I was an adolescent I became a socialist and atheist, in the usual adolescent way. After school I went into journalism, first of all as a cadet on the *Telegraph,* and met a lot of communists. By twenty, I was a co-operative socialist believing in worker's control. Then I went to Wagga and for a year edited a paper in Lockhart (population 12,000). I came back from that with a broken marriage, badly demoralized after a period of social isolation and intellectual discomfort. My reformist zeal to change society by peaceful means took me out of journalism and into the W.E.A. I had this 1920s evangelical fervor about adult education, and felt that once workers were informed and critical they would adopt the socialist alternative.

> I had three or four years as an organizer and publicist in the W.E.A. These were influential in developing my political awareness of the difference between the authoritarian and the non-authoritarian Left. This was something I had been slow to recognize. At this time I was sexually recruited into the Libertarian Society and in their atmosphere of totally free communication and interaction I felt comfortable, and able to develop as a writer.

> Previously, when I was a socialist, I often found that my fiction wouldn't fit the "class struggle" as expected by doctrinaire socialists. I still find that at a certain stage the story itself takes over, and that I can later find myself agreeing with interpretations of the story which weren't consciously in my mind at the time of writing. Anyhow, when I started to see myself as a writer rather than a socialist it was a great relief. The Libertarians don't appeal to feelings of brotherhood and compassion

that aren't genuinely felt, or pretend to share the interests of groups that they don't know, like blue-collar workers. Instead their sense of community is found within their sub-culture, and many hold the enclave view that it is possible in Western society to carry on interaction and critical enquiry with only marginal harassment. This corresponds to the classical position of the writer in terms of his detachment from society and his relationship to authority.

> A lot of my writing is a natural associate of my libertarian politics but it is not intended to be their servant. The difference between the consciously political writer and someone like myself is that the former would see the holding of positions as central, whereas I would see them as superstructure for deeper personal dynamics. People adopt ideologies to suit their personalities, and writers who take up traditional or contemporary stances are playing personality roles, posturing, dramatizing themselves.

Moorhouse's stories can be seen as a series of role performances by his characters. They dramatize themselves, and sometimes, like Dell, discover the false roles they have been playing in subscribing to stereotyped life styles. But Moorhouse's belief that any stance adopted by the writer is the playing of a role opens up in turn the question of his own stance. In his *Bulletin* review, Ian Turner provided an interesting sociological analysis of the themes of *The Americans, Baby,* and unhesitatingly delivered the right literary judgement—these are "the best short stories we've had in Australia for a long time." Yet his assumption that the stories are "deeply disturbing because the writer himself is so clearly disturbed and deeply involved" seems wide of the mark. These are the best short stories for a long time because, first of all, they *are* stories, not raw, still-quivering slices of life. They are sharply dramatized with the characters presenting themselves and their anxieties and ambivalences. If some of the dramatized attitudes and conflicts should correspond to the author's, then this doesn't show in the telling. Moorhouse's own position comes through as an ironic, often amused, scepticism towards any schematization of life. His stance is one of detachment combined with what he calls 'empathy through curiosity'—curiosity about what it would be like to be Becker, Dell, the narrator of **"The Girl from the Family of Man,"** or any of the characters who don't belong to the sub-culture and who react to the attempted manipulations of revolutionaries and reformists with bewilderment.

His Rotarians, he points out, are not baddies. They're just playing their adopted roles, as are the apparatchiki or the revolutionary. The question Moorhouse asks himself is whether, having shed black and white moralism, he is accommodating evil too readily. One answer to this would be that although his empathy is ironic, it is empathy all the same, and can convey more sympathy for Dell, say, then for her Trotskyist lover. The stories in his earlier collection (*Futility and Other Animals*, 1969) presenting Nish, the seedy, randy chief clerk, lacked this empathy, or human insight. They are attempts to flesh out stereotypes of 'suburban man,' and the 'irony' is indistinguishable from disgust or contempt. Many of the stories in the later collection however reveal the classic morality of the writer—a concern with individuals rather than with the rigidities of any ideology. They can often be classical too in their structuring. The seemingly casual ways in which characters, settings and situations are established conceal a skilful dramatic economy. Because of this tight selectivity, the stories frequently re-read better than they read at first, not because they are 'difficult' in any stylistic or formal way, but because they seem so straight-forward and yet disappoint expectations that they will finish on a high note, as well-made stories—instead they usually leave the reader to grasp the implications himself.

Apart from his fiction, Moorhouse has written two Current Affairs Bulletins on the mass media, which draw on his own newspaper experience and the two years he spent with the A.B.C., and he gives W.E.A. lectures in this field. As one of the group producing *Thor* (previously *Thorunka*) he is associated with 'porno-politics' and a university guest lecturer on the subject. He has recently completed a chapter on censorship for Henry Mayer's book on Australian politics. His anti-censorship activities stem from both theoretical convictions and freely admitted self-interest. As a writer who accepts Freudian assumptions of the primacy of the sexual instinct, he wants to be free to explore previously taboo areas in his writing, and feels that at a time when the roles of the sexes are changing it would be dishonest for a writer not to explore them. His own books have not been interfered with, contrary to perhaps hopeful expectations in the case of *Futility and Other Animals.* His explanation is that books are privileged in comparison with magazines.

Moorhouse's interests in the mass media are also partly in liberating the short story from the straitjacket of the book, an interest shared by other young short story writers in Sydney. The secret, rapid mass-printing of *Thorunka* in defiance of the law demonstrated the revolution that has occurred in printing techniques. Recently the Commonwealth Literary Fund made a grant to launch *Tabloid Story,* which takes advantage of these techniques and will, it is hoped, make the short story as popular as poetry. Other Sydney writers associated with the project are Michael Wilding and Carmel Kelly and they hope to attract new writers from all over Australia to *Tabloid Story.*

Although he does not see them as influence on his own work—pointing instead to Bartleme, Borges and the New Zealander Janet Frame—Moorhouse admires many local short story writers: Lawson ("naturally"), Gavin Casey, Barbara Baynton . . . But why short stories?

> Well, it wasn't any conscious choice. I grew up reading short stories and wanting to write short stories. I was just fascinated by them from about the age of eleven. I read novels and plays and verse as well, but when people asked me what I wanted to be, I always said a short story writer. I suspect that the short story is a natural form whereas the novel isn't. The short story is related to dream and fantasy and the episodic breaking

up of life into incidents. However, the creative span is limited by the form and I like the idea of a larger unity and clusters of stories.

> In the fifties and sixties something went wrong with the short story. TV stultified the form by taking away the light fiction role. However, the mainstream tradition continued in a purified way. It's now a minority form rather than a popular form. In 1930, the A.B.C. ran a competition and got three thousand entries. This year, as editor of *Coast to Coast,* I got 280. However, It's one of the few creative fictional forms which can be communicated outside the covers of a book, and when there aren't taboo areas I think that it will be revitalized as a form by the application of new talent.

Don Anderson (essay date 1976)

SOURCE: "Frank Moorhouse's Discontinuities," in *Southerly,* Vol. 36, No. 1, March, 1976, pp. 26-38.

[*In the following essay, Anderson explores stylistic aspects of Moorhouse's fiction, in particular his use of the "discontinuous narrative."*]

Frank Moorhouse "writes short stories and does not intend to write a conventional novel. At present completing another discontinuous narrative called *The Americans, Baby*. Is opposed to all censorship." Thus, in the biographical note to the first edition of *Futility and Other Animals* (Gareth Powell & Associates, Sydney, 1969), Moorhouse threw down his gages. Both have been taken up. Publishers, distributors, and governments have continued to censor him; reviewers have insisted on referring to his books as "novels." One can only wonder which he finds the more offensive.

In a prefatory note to *Futility and Other Animals,* which is subtitled "a discontinuous narrative," Moorhouse adumbrates his themes and insists upon his method.

> These are interlinked stories and although the narrative is discontinuous—there is no single plot—the environment and the characters are continuous. In some ways, the people in the stories are a tribe—a modern, urban tribe—which does not fully recognise itself as a tribe. Some of the people are central members of the tribe while others are hermits who live on the fringe. The shared environment is both internal—anxieties, pleasures and confusions—and external—the houses, streets, hotels, and experiences.

Jos Davies, interviewing Moorhouse on the University of Sydney's "Television Tutorial" at the time of the book's publication, criticized the anthropological, "tribal," analogy on the grounds that there were no children in the book. Nancy Keesing, on the other hand, reviewing the book in *The Bulletin* (12 July 1969) asserted that "Since I put away my invaluable Dr Spock I doubt I've read quite so much about babies between one set of covers." It may have been these observations that led to the addition of a sentence to the prefatory note when a second edition was produced (Angus & Robertson, 1973): "The central dilemma is that of giving birth, of creating new life."

Reviewers of Moorhouse's books have been quick to respond to his themes, often seeing his fiction as anthropology, or sociology, or social history (currently fashionable academic studies, as literature seems not to be). Stephen Knight, an early admirer of the "Nish" stories, claimed that they showed "the violent and anarchical lunacy that is just below the surface of human behaviour". (*Australian Highway,* Winter 1965). For Peter Cowan, Moorhouse's "external environment is the modern city, contemporary urban life, and it is featureless, anonymous. The stories are set nowhere, yet everywhere." (*Westerly,* October 1969) Michael Wilding responded to *Futility* as Cowan had: Moorhouse's characters make connections "not with the hinterland of their own continent, but with other centres in the global village." (*Southerly,* XXIX (1969) 232) Ian Turner read *The Americans, Baby,* as social history:

> There are three central themes in Moorhouse's stories: the contradiction between preservation of self and involvement with others; the irreconcilability of libertarian (personal) and radical (social) values: and the conflict between the demands made of the individual by the institutions of capitalist (or any other?) society and the desire for self-realisation.
>
> (*The Bulletin,* 19 August 1972)

Ian Bedford saw the second volume in the following terms:

> In its small compass, this book of stories affords a more exact and relevant observation of peculiarly Australian social tensions than any recent work of politics or sociology that I can think of.
>
> (*Nation,* 22 July 1972)

Other readers have seen *The Americans, Baby* as an antipodean psychopathology of sexual aberration. The Victorian Board of Publications in mid-1975 awarded the book an R certificate on the grounds that the dialogue and descriptions were rich in gross obscenities. "An obscenity is often juxtaposed with blasphemy," the report said. "Some of the episodes deal with sodomy, homosexuality, transvestism, bestiality, fellatio, cunnilingus and free love, with co-habitation and adultery." (See Brian Kiernan, "Under the Counter Culture," *The Australian,* 18 August 1975.)

The responses of critics and censors give some indication of Moorhouse's content and themes. He is the chronicler of urban, and in his most recent volume *The Electrical Experience,* small-town tribes; he is an analyst of contemporary Western urban life and of its peculiar New South Welsh manifestations; his work is a rich mine for historians and sociologists (*The Americans, Baby* has been prescribed reading for Australian Literature students at the University of Sydney, and for students of Political Science at the University of New South Wales); and he is unquestionably a chronicler of sexual anxieties and of changing sexual mores. But he is, above all, an imaginative writer;

and it is the business of this essay to examine how appropriate the "discontinuous narrative" is to the world as Moorhouse sees it, and his critics have described it.

Robert Burns reacted to *Futility* rather like the reviewers of Hemingway's 1924 volume, *In Our Time*—he would not allow that the book was composed of short stories, but preferred to call them "episodic reminiscences" (*Nation,* July 1969), pointing at once to their structure but apparently questioning their imaginative status. Michael Wilding, however, was more perceptive about the structure of the volume—"Plotting for a bohemian milieu is a severe problem . . . Moorhouse has to search for his plots in sexual behaviour." Wilding asserted further that *Futility* succeeded by "hint, association, by a careful cumulative process". Hemingway (his theory of "omission") is again conjured up in Brian Kiernan's assertion with respect to *The Americans, Baby* that Moorhouse "conceals his art so well that the reader unfamiliar with his manner needs to be alerted to look for what has been left out, and left unsaid". (*The Australian,* 29 July 1972)

Moorhouse himself has stressed the essential nature of his fiction. *Futility,* as has already been noted, was subtitled "a discontinuous narrative"—in fact, in the often bizarrely printed first edition, it was insistently if perhaps accidentally *super*-titled "a discontinuous narrative." *The Americans, Baby* (Angus & Robertson, 1972) was subtitled "a discontinuous narrative of stories and fragments," while in *The Electrical Experience* (Angus & Robertson, 1974) Moorhouse returned to his original form, "a discontinuous narrative"—though his table of contents subdivides into "narratives" and "fragments." In an interview in *The National Times* (1-6 July 1974) Moorhouse asserted what many may have suspected; that his insistent structure was an objectification of how he saw the world: "It's got a lot to do with seeing life as a series of fragments. I don't see any underlying harmony or unity in life." Again, in *The Australian*'s annual "pick-the-best-books" opinion poll at the end of 1974, advocating Donald Barthelme, he asserted: "The short story is probably a natural form akin to the dream, the fantasy, the moment of self-awareness, the snatched glimpse of reality. It has going for it all the technological advantages plus some others."

Before proceeding to a detailed examination of Frank Moorhouse's discontinuities, it may be worth considering whether the short story form is in itself essentially discontinuous. Such an account of the form is implied in George Lukács's definition of the short story (*The Theory of the Novel,* 1920; London, 1962, pp. 51-52):

> In the short story, the narrative form which pin-points the strangeness and ambiguity of life, such lyricism must entirely conceal itself behind the hard outlines of the event: here, lyricism is still pure selection: the utter arbitrariness of chance, which may bring happiness or destruction but whose workings are always without reason, can only be balanced by clear, uncommented, purely objective depiction. The short story is the most purely artistic form; it expresses the ultimate meaning

of all artistic creation as *mood,* as the very sense and content of the creative process, but it is rendered abstract for that very reason. It sees absurdity in all its undisguised and unadorned nakedness, and the exorcising power of this view, without fear or hope, gives it the consecration of form: *meaninglessness as meaninglessness* becomes form: it becomes eternal because it is affirmed, transcended and redeemed by form.

"Clear, uncommented, purely objective depiction"; "meaninglessness become form"—Lukács might have been describing Moorhouse's fiction, where absurdity and meaninglessness are represented in discrete yet interlinked, essentially discontinuous structures, objective correlatives of a meaningless, godless, disconnected, universe. E. M. Forster's plea, "Only connect," cannot find fulfilment in Moorhouse's world.

For Moorhouse's characters are alone, isolated in an indifferent universe. Nish, an early Moorhouse creation and—in terms of age, occupation, interests—an atypical one, in fact may serve as a paradigm of Moorhouse's characters, He sits, isolated in the toilet, spitting on the wall, gloating over having destroyed files, "seeing the day when all his life would be secret and hidden and he would be alone, serene, in a toilet world." Donnie, the middle-aged homosexual narrator of **"Bread, Sugar, and Milk"** does not relish but bewails the isolation: "why must I live alone in this loneliness without mother, without anyone?" In the final story in *Futility,* Cindy, pregnant ("The central dilemma is that of giving birth, of creating new life") is isolated from her mother's middle-class cleanliness and her father's industrial world and political conservatism. Like many Moorhouse characters, she is uncertain of the moral value of isolation: "Were you in the vanguard or simply impatiently running on ahead—to find yourself without society—isolated and scared with other isolated and scared people." The ambiguity of "without" is an objectification of the ambivalence with which Cindy greets her isolation. Later in the story, Cindy ruminates:

> Her baby would be born into a time when granddaughters would not understand their grandmothers. Already mothers and daughters were having difficulty. Perhaps, we are creating an orphan generation—no parents and no god—where had she heard that—someone in the common room? She corrected herself—it was not the whole world that was alienated from its parents—only the teenagers and they for only a short time. It was the intellectually rebellious and the neurotics who went on feeding and nursing their alienation—proceeding further in the direction away from their parents. But her daughter would be freer.

It might be noted in passing that Moorhouse's sentence structure, those staccato utterances linked and cut off from each other by those insistent hyphens, echo Cindy's alienation, her discontinuity with the worlds around her. At the story's, and the book's, end, having ordered her mother out, she is alone, except for the unborn child inside her.

Turning to *The Americans, Baby* ("a discontinuous narrative of stories and fragments") we find further evidence

for the conviction that isolation is Moorhouse's theme. Dell's commitment to the anti-Vietnam-involvement cause isolates her from her family and the people in her home town; further, she is in some way isolated from herself, for she realizes that the words which she speaks are not really hers, but Kim's. There is no conviction in her claim to be a Trotskyite—she is truly inauthentic. And Kim himself has known isolation and inauthenticity:

> He became aware of his own body, his feet, legs, torso, hands, arms neck and head, standing there in an upright position on a floor, in a club, in a town, on an orbiting planet,—standing in stark isolation as the world orbited the sun.

(**"The Coca-Cola Kid"**)

We might take the metaphor in which the "he" of **"The Girl Who Met Simone de Beauvoir in Paris"** objectifies his condition as definitive of Moorhouse's world.

> The world was a panorama. A panorama of which he was, he sometimes felt, the only isolated spectator. Perhaps the only passenger in the dim observation car travelling without destination.

But it is Becker, the American Coca-Cola agent stranded in "this godforsaken country," who is not only perhaps Moorhouse's finest fictional creation, but also his most extreme and most complex isolate. Becker both bewails his isolation and courts it, delighting in the ultimate expression of contemporary discontinuity and estrangement—the motel room.

> Motels. Now a motel was five-star living. Bourbon, a jar of hot mix, of which he was inordinately fond, a pre-war movie or perhaps a Dashiell Hammett, cleanliness, air-conditioning, and refrigeration. Motels kept him a today man because there was no yesterday around to hold him back.

(**"The St. Louis Rotary Convention 1923, Recalled"**)

Neither the comfort of motel anonymity nor human contact with people so unlike himself that he gets along with them—Terri the kook, her father T. George McDowell. Becker's playing Pat Hobby to Sam's Jack Berners at Coca-Cola headquarters—can redeem Becker from loneliness:

> He knew he was dying. He knew that being an ocean away from Atlanta and the sparkle, in an alien distribution zone, was killing him. He'd read of cases. People died from being isolated from their intimates and people lost control that way.

> Environmental isolation and stress put him in the lavatory with Terri that frosty Friday.

(**"Jesus Said to Watch for 28 Signs"**)

"Environmental isolation" is a common condition in Moorhouse's world. There is no shortage of frosty Fridays. The "environmental isolation" of the *writer* finds its formal celebration in the final narrative in *The Americans, Baby,*

"The Letters to Twiggy." It is not only the isolation of the character, that masturbator of ill conscience, who copes with his isolation by writing letters to the androgynous English model, but the isolation of the *form* (*meaninglessness as meaninglessness* becomes form" in Lukács's Germanic phrase) that must be stressed. The unanswered (save by a mass-produced photograph and note) letters are a formal objectification of isolation (cf. Bellow's use of the epistolary form to demonstrate his hero's schizophrenia in *Herzog*). As the urgent, unanswered, or unread letter is a closed world, so the writer is imprisoned in his loneliness. Which only makes the last sentence of the book more painfully ironic: "We have so few rare chances to reach out and pursue boldly the perfect mate. . . ." Those three dots belie that lunatic optimism. In a discontinuous universe there are no conclusions, no final affirmations, no full stops. (For an informative contrast, consider the final sentence of John Barth's novel. *The End of the Road*. It reads "Terminal".)

Though there are no affirmations, or none that are not undermined, in Moorhouse's work, there is much irony. Irony is hardly exclusively a Sydney phenomenon, though Ward is described in one of Moorhouse's "Around the Laundromats" columns as possessing an "affected, Sydney anti-life irony." More significantly, irony is a defining characteristic of Modernism, a tradition that Moorhouse continues—not for him the new Romanticism. Anyone familiar with Moorhouse's writing will recognize that, no matter how different a given situation, age group, or locale—inner urban, South Coast: radical young, conservative old—there is a consistency found everywhere in narrative tone, and that tone is best described as ironic, self-conscious, self-deprecating. It is an ironic tone that derives from the awareness of one's ridiculousness, and that ridiculousness in turn derives from an ineffectuality born of isolation. Here is Becker, *eiron*-extraordinary:

> They're not going to remember me as a great lover but I'm considerate to a limited degree which is all we can ask of one of God's less radiant servants.

> **("Becker on the Moon")**

That irony is also present in the narrator's voice in **"The American Poet's Visit,"** a fictional version of a party organized for Kenneth Rexroth in Sydney.

> The evening begins in a relaxed way with Cooper introducing him as "Rex Kenroth." The evening also begins good naturedly with me asking him if he is here on a Congress for Cultural Freedom grant. J-o-k-e. Like some of the people in our group he is unable to detect the delicate irony of the remark and takes it seriously and defensively. I have to hint that I am j-o-k-i-n-g without insulting his sense of humour. I do this by digging him in the ribs.

Moorhouse, unlike his character, does not have to s-p-e-l-l out his jokes, his ironies. His control of tone is perfect. Irony is, of course, a form of self-defence, a way of building walls around the self to protect it from the ravages of other selves—but there is always the risk of walling the self in, of imprisoning the self in a defensive irony. Thus the narrator of **"The American Poet's Visit"** soon finds himself moving "to sit on the edge of the table—edge of the world—nonchalantly ill at ease."

Similarly T. George McDowell, the "hero" of *The Electrical Experience,* finds himself perpetually at the edge of the world (Martin Johnston acutely dubbed him "a South-Coast Martian"), forever "ill at ease." The ironies of *The Electrical Experience* are extremely complex and subtle. There are the more apparent ironies of plot, such as our finding out in the final narrative (**"Filming the Hatted Australian"**) that the worker whom T. George self-righteously rewarded and the one he bawled out were in fact the wrong ones—he should have bawled out the one and rewarded the other. But the very inclusion of **"Filming the Hatted Australian"** is the book's supreme structural irony. It brings Moorhouse's two worlds (urban, young: rural, old) into mutually uncomprehending connexion. There are *no* bridges between the wandering islands. But Moorhouse does not labour his ironies, as his character had to labour his "j-o-k-e" (Moorhouse didn't labour *that* irony, either). He lets the juxtaposition of his narratives and the utter incompatibility of his sets of characters do that. His ironies generate a sense of cosmic isolation. He is truly a Modernist writer in his structures. He is the descendant of Flaubert, who spoke of the author's being "everywhere present, but always invisible," or of Stephen Dedalus and his creator, who maintained that the artist "like the God of creation, remains within or behind or beyond or above his handiwork, invisible, refined out of existence, indifferent, paring his fingernails."

Moorhouse achieves a most complex yet delicate tonal irony through shifting narration. The opening pages of **"The End of Ice"** are a particularly clear and fine example of this. The narrative opens in quoted speech, which will become dialogue, followed by authorial directions:

> "We are but the engine-drivers of progress," T. George McDowell said, moving a paperweight as if by calculation, as if it were a driving-lever, a switch, a throttle.

We, the readers, instantly recognize that homely, machine-age, pragmatic, metaphor as typical of McDowell. We also recognize the ironies implicit in McDowell's assumption that human relations can be controlled like machines. It is, you might say, his fatal flaw. When we consider the authorial description of McDowell's utterance, however, we recognize that the tone and sphere of reference of the character's image has been carried on in the authorial comment. There is, in fact, a delicate shift of narration into McDowell's mind, though the method is not stream-of-consciousness. It is as though the author is speaking for McDowell, but still detached from him. It is this intimacy between author and character, with its accompanying critical distance, that generates an irony of disparity. To maintain a critical detachment (which Moorhouse does) given the degree of affection (which is very high) is a narrative feat of a very considerable order. It generates in the reader a critical detachment from, and an immense affection towards. T. George McDowell—which is an ethical feat of a very considerable order. One of which the young men and women of **"Filming the Hatted Australian"** are not (yet?) capable, as their author is.

Let us turn from Moorhouse's larger discontinuities, thematic and structural, to more local manifestations of them—to his smaller structures, his paragraphs, sentences, sub-divisions, and punctuation, all of which, it will be argued, demonstrate in small his larger discontinuities, the isolation and inauthenticity of his characters. Moorhouse's writing is strikingly stylistically consistent (as, for example, Truman Capote's is not) and we are not surprised, therefore, to find a typical Moorhouse paragraph on the first page of *Futility.*

> "All things pass," he said, "that's folk fatalism. Perhaps the time of the knife is over." How affected, Fey. The time of the knife. She did that to him. Twenty-year-olds were always saying things like that. The knife was stolen. There was nothing portentous about that. In fact the duffle coat was stolen—the knife just happened to be in it.

That paragraph announces what attuned readers will recognize as the distinctive Moorhouse paragraph rhythm. It does not move smoothly and confidently (as Jane Austen's paragraphs do), it does not flow and eddy (as Faulkner's do), it does not progress with a relentless rhetorical logic (as Mailer's do), rather it is tense, staccato (the sentences much briefer than even Hemingway's), moving through isolated sentence itemizations of experience to create, in the paragraph unit, a rhythm of discontinuity, underscoring Roger's growing estrangement from the twenty-year-old Anne. In the story **"Watch Town,"** published in *The Illegal Relatives* (a pirated, unauthorized collection), we find the paragraph structure employed to underline the discontinuities of life and social groups in a country town:

> The town divides.
>
> The blow-in, "transients," and the settlers.
>
> Those who work for wages and those who work for self.
>
> Those whose families were there from the beginning and those who came later.
>
> Between those who work in a tie and those who work in overalls.
>
> Between those who drink publicly and those who don't drink or don't drink publicly.
>
> Those who farm and those who live in town. . . .

The itemization of "division" continues for another twelve paragraphs. While this page of *The Illegal Relatives* may look, at first glance, like a page of Whitman's *Song of Myself,* the resemblance is misleading. Whitman parallels his lines to assert social equality between various individu-

als—his is a democratic form. Moorhouse's paragraphs, on the other hand, create a sense of social isolation.

In the story **"Jesus Said to Watch for 28 Signs"** (*The Americans, Baby*) we find Beckar (mis-spelled "Becker" in a newspaper; a further cruel reminder of his inauthenticity) in Surfers' Paradise, playing jazz piano. Again, the paragraphs underscore the discontinuity of his world, its fragmentariness. The irony with which Becker copes with this fragmentation ("If we are the last of the bourbon generation, let's be good at it") in no way diminishes his tragedy. But the paragraphing is crucial. In the final three pages of the story we find sixty-one paragraphs, none longer than four lines of type, none containing more than three "sentences." Consider how the end of the story encapsulates the sense of cosmic loneliness and lack of continuity which is its subject:

> Terri says he is free now.
>
> That is a joke. But Terri speaks like that. He has an inkling that stress and pollution are what the world is all about.
>
> He sometimes misses stress and pollution. He sometimes misses Sam. Coca-Cola.
>
> He has a scheme for manufacturing cassette programmes of unusual material which would be delivered with the milk on Sundays.
>
> He is fond of saying, "If we are the last of the bourbon generation, let's be good at it."
>
> He also likes to say that he is the best jazz pianist from Atlanta who has ever worked for Coca-Cola.
>
> Becker wears maroon bow tie, fancy arm bands, floral braces and drinks Old Crow while he plays at the Silver Spade.

Turning to *The Electrical Experience*, we find that the paragraphs similarly reinforce T. George McDowell's isolation. Consider the opening page of **"The Annual Conference of 1930 and South Coast Dada,"** and the whole of **"Tell Churchill that T. George McDowell is on His Feet,"** of which the final two pages are particularly striking. Indeed, the entire media-presentation of *The Electrical Experience* must be considered in this regard. The "Narratives" are interlinked by "Fragments" (printed white on black like negatives), photographs, an advertisement. Gwenth McDowell's "Statement" about her sister Terri appears as if typed. In this pre-eminently discontinuous work, the medium is indeed the message. As Rosemary Creswell observed in her review of the book on the ABC programme "Books and Ideas":

> What T. George really fears is a loss of selfhood, and that selfhood is so vulnerable precisely because it consists in *things*: in a persona he has erected out of the mores of objectified systems of behaviour and belief. Moorhouse's technique of dispersing what he calls 'fragments' through the series of connected narratives is a concrete correlative of McDowell's mind. Consisting of various wise-saws, recipes for soft-drinks and

for living, local sayings and an occasional wry comment from the narrator, these fragments act as structural links but also seem to present us with the inside of McDowell's head. And that the inside of his head happens to be *printed* seems exactly right.

Having considered Moorhouse's paragraphs, let us turn to the sentences of which they are constructed, and the words of which those sentences are composed. We will not be surprised to find the overwhelming impression of discontinuity reinforced. Consider the following two paragraphs from **"Bread, Sugar, and Milk"** in which the forty-eight-year-old homosexual narrator, Donnie, is at home alone, sick in mind and body ("why must I live alone in this loneliness, without mother, without anyone?"):

> Now I've spewed on the bed. That's all I bloody needed. What a bloody mess—all over the cover—vile—how putrid. What's happening to me? I'm going mad. Why? Cry, go on cry. It used to taste so beautiful. And it's good for sick people. Good things turn bad. The world is a miserable cheat. It cheats me even when I'm sick. Pieces of bread like turds in white piss. Why was everything so good when I was little and now so foul? It's a foul life. Life is foul.
>
> Who wants to be forty-eight?—no one gives a bugger about you when you are forty-eight—miserable old fool. Feel sorry for yourself. Pull the cover off and put it on the floor. Mess, Cry, cry, cry. Take three nembutals and sleep it off. Take the lot why don't you? You never have the guts and it's what you want to do.

Through the words—principally monosyllabic or bisyllabic, unlearned, unadorned, often unattractive to certain moral sensibilities—by way of the sentences—often simple or compound, less often complex and when so, not involvedly so; often themselves broken up by dashes or the three dot convention—the rhythm of the paragraph is established. It does not seem fanciful to call that rhythm discontinuous, as it does not seem fanciful to assert that those terse, staccato sentences establish at the level of functional detail Moorhouse's drama of isolation. Even the simile contributes to our sense of Donnie's aloneness and self-disgust: "Pieces of bread like turds in white piss" is an effective emblem of *s'emmerdement.*

Another typical sentence is the paratactic itemization of objects, Consider this example from **"I Am a Very Clean Person."**

> It was her flat and she had made it the way it was before him. It was her tv and her chiming clock and her carpets and her standard lamp and her bedspread and her maple china cabinet and her maple radiogram. It was all hers. And the flat was clean and spick and span because of her. He was the one who made the mess in it. Not her. And he made a mess in her and on the sheets.

"Her" selfhood is so vulnerable precisely because it consists in *things.* "Her" sexual neurosis is reified, and that process is objectified in Moorhouse's prose through the paratactic structure. The co-ordinate conjunctions stress the separateness of the objects, and their separateness from her, while her "because" clause and her possessive pronouns express her delusion that she dominates them. An emphasis on things *via* nouns is symptomatic of Moorhouse's description, and his critique, of life. Things are, for his principal characters—e.g. T. George McDowell, Becker—an attempt to find value and support outside the self, for the Australian bourgeois self is inauthentic. Moorhouse recognizes the tragic, isolating discontinuities of life in Australia. Things are substitute gratifications for the inauthentic self—but they are inadequate substitutes. Throughout Moorhouse's work, there is a sense of inadequacy, isolation, and loss.

Frank Moorhouse (essay date 1977)

SOURCE: "What Happened to the Short Story?" in *Australian Literary Studies,* Vol. 8, No. 2, October, 1977, pp. 179-91.

[*In the following essay, Moorhouse traces the development of his career, the structure of his short fiction collections, and the continuing influence of American literature and culture on his work.*]

What now seems to characterise my work, five books published, is a persisting with related short stories or episodic structure—what I've called the discontinuous narrative. It now seems that my work grows in clusters of stories which make fragmented perceptions of characters and situations.

The discontinuous narrative appears to relate to my preoccupations with the accidental, the unintended consequence, the non-rational factors of human conduct and behaviour.

The clusters form larger unities of book length (a hugely flexible term) and the books themselves have interconnections not only in theme but in character and situations. Some of the clusters I am working on at present are of more awkward lengths and shapes, perhaps novella length.

I have written a film script, *Between Wars,* and I am working on another which draws on *The Americans, Baby.* The films, too, interconnect with the books. The main character of *Between Wars* is a minor character in *The Electrical Experience,* Dr. Trenbow, and appears in the work in progress. *The Americans, Baby* script develops and continues with Becker, the Coca-Cola executive, Terri, and T. George McDowell. Terri, for example, appears in *Futility and Other Animals, The Americans, Baby* and *Electrical Experience*.

In *The Americans, Baby,, The Electrical Experience* and *Tales of Mystery and Romance* I have played around with the physical layout of the books. In *AB* [*The Americans, Baby*] I used three interludes and notes, in *EE* [*Electrical Experience*] I used non-fictional materials and fictionally modified non-fictional material (slight alterations to fit the narrative), pictures and notes. In ***Tales of Mystery and Romance*** a designer illustrated the titles of the stories in magazine style and I included also non-fictional material—a diagram, a footnote, an appendix.

I suppose my motive for working with the physical layout of the books is to enhance the fragmentation so that the books do not look like conventional novels, but also to give something of a carnival or playful impression.

My story writing began at school and when I left school I submitted to the literary magazines *Meanjin, Southerly, Westerly, Australian Letters* (now defunct) and *Overland. Meanjin* and *Southerly* were brought to my attention by school teachers. I guess I found my way to the others. *Southerly* published my first short story **"The Young Girl and the American Sailor"** (I was interested in the American presence even then) in 1957. It was edited by Kenneth Slessor. *Westerly* published **"One Night in Bed"** in 1960, *Meanjin* published **"The Uniformed Stray"** in 1962 and *Overland* published **"Spider Town"** in 1964. *Westerly* gave me most support, publishing four stories in the early years. As I developed away from the humanist tradition of the Australian story—sympathetic to the working class and kind to kangaroos—my stories were rejected from the literary magazines. From 1965 to 1970 I was consistently rejected and published only one story—in *Southerly* (**"The American Poet's Visit"**) which was censored. At least I was continuing with the American theme. For these five years I published wherever I could, forcing myself into unlikely magazines including *The Pluralist* and *The Red and the Black*. A commercial men's magazine *Squire* began to accept stories without restriction and was a crucial encouragement. We also organised readings of prose and verse at Balmain.

From 1970 I began to find wide acceptance including *The Bulletin, Nation Review, Chance, Overland* again, *Hemisphere,* the ABC, *Cosmopolitan* and finally again *Meanjin* under the editorship of Jim Davidson after 13 years of rejection.

I don't put down the years of rejection solely to the magazines' adherence to older formulas of the story and to moralism. In fairness, I was also in a highly developmental stage, plunging about, impatient for publication which meant that I often submitted premature work. I had not yet understood the process of creative revision.

It is difficult to know the size and nature of the audience for my work. I realise now that it takes years to find one's readership, even in a population as small as Australia. I still get letters from first time readers who have stumbled on say ***Futility and Other Animals***, my first book. Right from the start I thought that it was worthwhile presenting my work as widely as possible although I know now that I do not have mass appeal. This was behind the setting up of *Tabloid Story* as a show-case supplement of story writing which could appear in widely different host magazines.

In my report to the Literature Board I noted that in the three years of my Fellowship (1973-76) my stories have appeared in twelve different publications including UNESCO book *Man and the Biosphere* (following upon a reading of a story at a conference), *Cosmopolitan, Ear in a Wheatfield,* a book on political theory *Liberty and Politics, Meanjin, Gayzette* (a defunct homosexual magazine), *Forum, Nation Review, Sydney Morning Herald, Quadrant, National Times,* and the *New Literature Review.*

My readership, as far as I can see my work, is likely to remain Australian. I think my perception of my material, and the limitations of the material, would make it surprising if it was widely read outside of Australia. I no longer have any serious expectations of this happening. Some of my stories have been published overseas but these tend to fall outside the body of my work. But standards and stimulus still come from the American and English traditions and contemporary writing—especially in the US. I couldn't say that any Australian writer has consciously had a stimulus affect on me (which is not to say that I do not enjoy reading other Australia writers).

Looking at the records I've kept I see that I have written 103 stories since leaving school and have published 94 of these—82 in book form.

In 1973 a pirated edition of three stories was published without my permission titled *The Illegal Relatives.* These stories in revised form appear in ***Tales of Mystery and Romance***. The pirated edition was first put together as an anti-censorship publication which was abandoned by the organisers and then stolen by the printer.

Bruce Bennett (essay date 1978)

SOURCE: "Frank Moorhouse and The New Journalism," in *Overland,* 1978, pp. 6-14.

[*In the following essay, Bennett considers the relationship between journalism and literature in Moorhouse's short fiction.*]

Various attempts have been made by critics and commentators to define "literature" and "journalism". But there is a broad measure of agreement that a distinction between the two needs to be made. Writers as different in outlook and historical circumstances as T. S. Eliot and Walter Benjamin agree on this issue, though for different reasons. Eliot defines his journalist as a 'type of mind' whose best writing is done 'under the pressure of an immediate occasion'.[1]

Benjamin distinguishes between 'news' or 'information' and 'literature', using the story as his epitome of literature:

> The value of information does not survive the moment in which it was new. It lives only at that moment; it has to surrender itself to it completely and explain it-

self to it without losing any time. A story is different. It does not expend itself. It preserves and concentrates its strength and is capable of releasing it even after a long time.[2]

In spite of qualifications to their main assertion, these two writers share a common view of the inferiority of journalism to literature on the grounds that the one product is durable while the other is not.

Every assumption of this kind is subject to reexamination in the light of changes in writing techniques and intentions, reading habits and tastes, new technologies and varying concepts of literary culture in different societies. Developments in American writing since the mid-1960s have led to a questioning of the assumption that journalism is a kind of ancillary to the novel.

In Australia, grounds for further questioning of the relationship between literature and journalism, and fiction and nonfiction, are evident in the work of Frank Moorhouse, especially in his latest book, *Conference-Ville.*[3] Tom Wolfe's championing in America of 'new journalists' such as Gay Talese, Truman Capote, Joe Eszterhas, Terry Southern, Hunter S. Thompson, Norman Mailer and himself, is in part a reaction against what he sees as a retreat from realism by recent fiction writers: "Fiction writers, currently, are busy running backward, skipping and screaming, into a begonia patch that I call Neo-Fabulism".[4] This begonia patch is becoming increasingly attractive to Australian writers of short fiction. Peter Carey and Murray Bail, for instance, enjoy its exotic colors and their experiments in it are to be applauded. But the fabulists must not have it all their own way. Frank Moorhouse's work gives hope of developments in another garden closer to the streets: his attempts to forge an alliance between reportage and the techniques of prose fiction give grounds for hope of a renovated realism.

In an age of advertising, "new" is one of the most overworked words in a limited stock of vocabulary. It is therefore perhaps necessary to remind ourselves of some forebears of Tom Wolfe's "new" journalism. They include Boswell's Johnson, Defoe's *Journal of the Plague Year,* Cobbett's *Rural Rides,* Dicken's *Sketches by Boz,* Mayhew's *London Labour and the London Poor,* Mark Twain's *Innocents Abroad.* With the exception of Cobbett and Mayhew, these writers are remembered chiefly for other, more 'literary' achievements and even Cobbett's and Mayhew's works are chiefly known as accessories to literature courses on the Romantics and the Victorians.

Tom Wolfe argues that this "literary" attitude persisted into the 1960s in America: journalists typically regarded the newspaper as "a motel you checked into overnight on the road to the final triumph" (i.e. the novel). But in the last decade or so the "new journalists", according to Wolfe, have added a dimension to American writing: artistic excitement has entered the field and the *lumpenprole* journalists now threaten the security of their literary masters, the novelists and literary critics. Some novelists have turned

directly to nonfiction. Some, such as Gore Vidal, Herber Gold, William Styron and Ronald Sukenick, have tried forms that are part fiction, part nonfiction. Others place real people with their real names into fictional situations The boundaries are blurring. At the same time, according to Wolfe, a more cunning journalism that grows from the best traditions of social realism in the novel is becoming worthwhile end in itself. Magazines such as the New Yorker, the Herald Tribune's Sunday magazine, New York Atlantic, Harper's and Esquire have been leading publishers of this "new" journalism.

The value of Wolfe's essay is not so much in his enthusiastic championing of a dubiously "new" form as in the attention that he gives to the aesthetic dimension of reporting; and further, its implications, in our time and place, for an understanding and assessment of a writer such as Frank Moorhouse. Moorhouse, now in his late 30s, worked as a journalist for city and country newspapers in New South Wales before becoming a full-time writer.

The experience of day-to-day journalism is apparent in Moorhouse's first book, *Futility and Other Animals* (1969), in which close observation of manners and social setting and an ear for dialogue are allied with a clipped carefully sub-edited style: these qualities are adapted to the more impressionistic demands of his 'discontinuous narrative'. He adapts also Australian newspapers' habitual bracketed reference to the age of persons named in news items: the precise ages of members of his urban tribe are significant in their different responses to the pressures and strains of a search for alternative life styles to those of their parents. Already apparent, too, is Moorhouse's knack of finding the catchy phrase, the right headline, that encapsulates a person's 'story'. The author seems also aware, in his first book, of the impact of changing technologies on modes of thinking and feeling. He seems aware of the need for his prose to move to different the question, what is it to live naturally?

The Americans, Baby (1972) shows a sharpen-rhythms in it is to capture the often unspoken needs and desires of a generation moving towards social awareness in Australia [. . .] Also noticeable is a growing interest in American influences on Australian life. As a whole, though, the second book does not signify a great aesthetic advance on the first. It is in the third book, *The Electrical Experience* (1974), that an artistic breakthrough occurs. In this book Moorhouse's dextrous use of material from a variety of sources coincides with an ability to recreate not only the gestures and attitudes of his central character, but also his thought processes. T. George McDowell, an apparently forgettable soft drink manufacturer from a New South Wales country town, becomes memorable to us both as a father figure and as a living exponent of free enterprise capitalism as it has grown up in Australian country towns fostered by Rotary and the Reader's Digest. A clash of values and attitudes between generations, and between country and city, is suggested. A new maturity is evident in the author's ability to portray sympathetically the per-

sonality and outlook of a character whose values he rejects, creating an atmosphere in which both irony and
compassion can co-exist.

T. George McDowell seems to emerge from the author's
autobiographical experience as well as from research in
contemporary newspapers, magazines, recipe books and
other receptacles of folk wisdom. Consequently, he comes
across as more than "good news"; indeed, as a human being. In spite of some technical experiments that do not
wholly succeed, *The Electrical Experience* does, in Benjamin's words, 'preserve and concentrate its strength and
is capable of releasing it even after a long time'.

The durability of *Conference-Ville* (1976), first published
in serial form in Nation Review, is less assured. However,
as Wolfe has pointed out, we should not be overwhelmed
by traditional academic criteria when faced with contemporary writing that uses and extends the techniques of
journalism. And anyhow, on the question of durability,
who can predict the tastes and reading interests (if any) of
the next generation?

Conference-Ville, as its title suggests, is about the various
behaviors that come into play when a conference comes to
town—or rather, when a conference creates its own community of interests, aspirations and antagonisms and becomes a microcosm of the larger society outside. It is a
phenomenon of our times: the conference, otherwise
known as seminar or symposium (seldom simply a "meeting" or "discussion") is now big business, and as such is
in process of creating its own rules of procedure, patterns
of behavior and a mystique that is designed to impress the
uninitiated. Moorhouse lifts the lid on these pretensions
but, as in his earlier fiction, he is not content merely to
ridicule: he is also concerned to analyse motives and the
assumptions that lie behind present actions. We can best
understand how he does this in relation to Tom Wolfe's
account of the new journalism.

A cornerstone of Wolfe's argument is that the best American journalists in the 1960s were relearning the techniques
of realism of the sort found in Fielding, Smollett, Balzac,
Dickens and Gogol. They "re-discovered" four main techniques: scene-by-scene construction, the use of realistic
dialogue, third-person point of view and the recording of
details symbolic of people's "status life". It is clear that
Moorhouse has also worked at these aspects of his writing.
Conference-Ville, for example, consists of twelve carefully orchestrated scenes, beginning with the narrator's in-
flight encounter *en route* to the conference with the academic who is to introduce his paper and concluding with
an encounter after the conference that brings the narrator's
identity and loyalties into question. These sections frame a
series of scenes that highlight significant behavioral or
ideological aspects of the conference. For example, there
is a demonstration against one of the speakers, an American who is alleged to have CIA connections, and there are
moves at a breakaway meeting to set up an 'alternative'
conference:

The counter-conference boy, urged by his friends, went
out to the front of the auditorium and turned his back
on Eric, setting up a new boundary to the meeting. He
said, "A planning group should be set up . . . we
should all be bound by its decisions. . . ."

"Speak up," someone shouted. The noise level was
high. The meeting was disintegrating.

"Sorry," the boy said, and haltingly repeated his proposal. But then he stopped as if he had seen something.
I felt that what he'd seen was the hopelessness of his
proposal, of arranging, executing and achieving agreement—first of all among those listening, let alone
among the 900 others who had not stayed for the meeting. Cumbersome, lumbering reality was rolling over
him.

(p. 38)

Moorhouse is concerned to show not only the farcial element in this scene, but also, through the brooding reflections of his narrator, its wider ramifications. The politics
of society are writ small in the micro-society of the conference hall.

The scenic approach is heavily dependent on dialogue. Realistic dialogue involves the reader more than any other
single device and, effectively controlled and co-ordinated,
it can define character. In *Conference-Ville,* the voice and
social matrix of Eric Bottral, the ubiquitous trades union
speaker and former English shop steward, are quickly and
effectively revealed in conversation with the narrator:

"You know, boyoh, we're the radicals at this wank—
you and me," he said, poking me playfully with his
rolled up newspaper, which was, I noted, the *Financial
Review.*

I laughed and said, "I seem to have only small opinions on the big issues these days." But I didn't mind
being Eric's sidekick. One of the outlaws.

He took out the program. "Professor this and that," he
said, "a bloody wank they are."

"It's the Parliament of Intellectuals, Eric—and you're a
senator. And you like it." Parliament of Fowls.

(p. 12)

Along with the recording of characteristic phrases, rhythms
and gestures, we see here an aspect of the author/narrator's
shifting relationship with the political left, which becomes
one of the book's sustaining interests. Later, with a clutch
of academics at dinner, he subverts his alliance with the
trade unionist by falling in with their condescending gossip about him:

"Oh, he's probably socially intimidated," said Mrs
Henderson. "All we heavies—professors and so on—
and a writer." She glanced at me, weighing me up to
see if I made it.

Mr Henderson added a note and comment to his wife's
thesis, "I know this is the thing we don't say—but I
make it as a value-free observation—it may be simply

that he can't handle table customs—the wrong fork anxiety—probably as simple as that."

I glanced to my own forks.

"Yes, yes," said Newell Smith grumpily, while showing appreciation for the table's supportive remarks, "but you can still be a revolutionary and have good form— Bevan, for instance, was great value at a dinner table."

Bevan.

"I hear Eric's got a drink problem," Julia contributed.

(p. 17)

The dialogue here, as elsewhere, almost does away with the need for historical narrative or explanation.

Moorhouse has experimented with third person, first person and shifting points of view, but in **Conference-Ville** he achieves a degree of cohesiveness by using his first person narrator as barometer and interpreter of the conference's changing moods. He is clearly aware of different narrative methods that could be employed, as references to Dos Passos (p. 13) and Mailer (p. 39) show. But he takes his own path between the cinematic 'objectivity' of the former and the rampant egotism of the latter. There is a danger that his laconic, ironic narrator will be too colorless (his understatement certainly contrasts with the fervid verbal acrobatics of most American 'new' journalists) but his interior monologues or brief spoken comments are often pertinent and penetrating. Occasionally there is a triumph, as when a video playback gives the narrator a wounding insight into himself:

But the picture then steadied. When it was steady up came Charles and me on the screen.

It concentrated on Charles' university tie. Panned up to his expansive gestures. We were talking in the lobby of the auditorium. I don't remember being conscious of it being shot. It held on Charles' laugh.

It came in on me. I seemed nondescript, in that I had no social comment embodied in my appearance. There was no word commentary to accompany the video. The camera caught the identity tag from the conference. It roved over both of us.

But something had been caught by the video shot of me. Something about the way I was smiling with Charles. It hadn't been the intention of the video shot. It was just something that hit me about the smile. About the smile and the nodding of my head. It wasn't nice. My mind was slow to present a word to describe the smile, to describe what was worrying me about the smile. The word came to me, the word was *fawning.*

Fawning, that was what it was.

A weak ego suggested, "Maybe passive, not fawning."

No. It was *fawning.*

(pp. 86-7)

The word "fawning" implants itself in his mind, recurring in different contexts as the film proceeds, and the mind broods upon it like a toothache. Simultaneity of external stimuli and the mind's internal filtering devices is successfully suggested.

But first person narration brings its problems. especially with the ostensible reporting of a contemporary event. An autobiographical approach can encourage a trivialising curiosity about the author's actual involvement in the event described instead of focusing on the events themselves. Moorhouse seems uncertain about how much latitude to give his narrator. Typically, he allows him a laconic, self-deprecating irony (one is inclined to think this typically Australian) whereas Mailer would almost certainly have turned it into an outrageously entertaining display of ego. Where there is an excess of ego in the one, there is sometimes a thinness and uncertainty in the other.

The curiosity that can be aroused about the author/narrator in this kind of writing also spills over into a curiosity about the named persons who take part in the action. In this respect, the American "new" journalist has greater scope than his Australian counterpart, thanks to more liberal libel laws in his country. In Australia, Moorhouse can only barely characterise the named members of the literary and political intelligentsia who attend his conference. He does little more than sketch in their roles as part of the interacting "positions" taken up at his conference; as such they are not allowed to assume the autonomous existence that the narrative elsewhere seems to move towards.

Frank Moorhouse's work is notable for its deft recording of everyday idioms, gestures, manners, habits, customs, styles of furniture and clothing, of travelling and eating. At his best, Moorhouse achieves both verisimilitude and symbolic extension. But in **Conference-Ville** he is less interested in the physical and material contexts of his characters than he was in **The Electrical Experience**: the conference is an occasion that uproots people from their normal surroundings. In this book he concentrates instead on landscapes of opinion, gossip and belief—landscapes from which the natural man seems to have fled, to be found, if at all, behind the potted plants of a motel's Hawaiian bar or, considerably diminished, in the hands of a woman from a massage parlor. Ironically, a conference which sets out to investigate "communications", "media access", and the like, becomes an ideological battleground and although the battle imagery is at times overdone, it does serve to point up the tensions and conflict that underly the games that conference-goers play.

Crossing the borders between literature and journalism, each with its traditionally conceived conventions and expectations, is necessarily a hazardous exercise. At best, an uneasy alliance can be expected. But Moorhouse is a writer who exercises his considerable talents and his interest in contemporary political and social realities from just such a border outpost. His narrator's inner drama (how close to Moorhouse's own?) is cleverly interwoven in his latest book with the events of his conference: it depicts the writer's uneasy and shifting reactions to the human and ideological dilemmas around him. He is duped neither by the 'Genial Right' nor by the 'Urbane Left' as he jousts with the representatives of both sides and with his own conscience. In the process, he addresses himself to some central human concerns as well as to topical issues and paves a way for further Australian experiments in the disputed territory between journalism and literature.

Notes

1. T. S. Eliot, 'Charles Whibley' (1931) in *Selected Essays* (Faber, London, 1963).

2. Walter Benjamin, *Illuminations* (Collins/Fontana, 1973).

3. Frank Moorhouse, *Conference-Ville* (Angus and Robertson, Sydney, 1976). Page references are given for the longer quotations.

4. Tom Wolfe, *The New Journalism* (Pan Books/Picador, London, 1975).

Brian Kiernan (essay date 1981)

SOURCE: "Frank Moorhouse: A Retrospective," in *Modern Fiction Studies,* Vol. 27, No. 1, Spring, 1981, pp. 73-94.

[*In the following essay, Kiernan discusses the defining characteristics of Moorhouse's short fiction, in particular the recurring theme of the impact of American culture on Australia.*]

Publication in the United States today represents for probably most Australian writers, and readers, the same kind of recognition that publication in England did for so long in the past. Until toward the end of the nineteenth century, when the establishment of local presses coincided with conscious efforts to develop a native literature, London or Edinburgh offered the Australian writer virtually his only chance of publication. A consequence of this cultural colonialism for this century has been a tendency to distinguish between "characteristically" Australian writing published locally and the more "international" writing by Australians published elsewhere—even though this has often had similar characters, settings, and themes. The reception of works has often been confused by consideration of a writer's country of birth or residence, his concerns, and the continuance from last century of the debate over the appropriateness of absolute "universal" or relative "local" critical criteria. There is nothing unusual about this in the history of a comparatively new literary culture, nor that "metropolitan" recognition was sought and welcomed (with London, historically, providing the metropolis of letters). Writers who published abroad, however, often suffered delayed recognition in their own country: the most prominent examples among the now older generation of novelists would be Christina Stead and Patrick White, who from the beginnings of their careers have published in London and New York. Although today the more artificial aspects of this

distinction between local and international writing have faded, there still remains a "metropolis," a perceived source of influence, of critical and financial success, but it is now much more likely to be located by Australian writers in New York than London.

For Australian readers, conspicuous recent examples of novelists who are winning "international" recognition through publication in the United States would include: Thomas Keneally with *Confederates* (Sydney and London: Collins, 1979; New York: Harper and Row, 1980), David Malouf with *An Imaginary Life* (London: Chatto and Windus, 1978; New York: Braziller, 1978), and Roger McDonald with his first novel, *1915* (St. Lucia: University of Queensland, 1979; New York: Braziller, 1980). As well, the new generation of short fiction writers has appeared in American magazines, including Murray Bail, Morris Lurie, and Michael Wilding in the *New Yorker*; and Peter Carey's collection *The Fat Man in History* has been published simultaneously by prestigious houses in New York and London (New York: Random House, 1980; London: Faber, 1980). Such examples could be multiplied, yet (and to come to the point), well-deserved as this recognition is, an element of adventitiousness enters into its achievement, in that the writers who attain it are not the only ones whose reputations are high among Australian readers. Conspicuously absent from the examples just given is Frank Moorhouse, who is generally seen as among the most original and substantial of the writers who emerged in the late 1960s and the early 1970s. There seems some perversity in his not having received international recognition through publication in America, because the impact of American culture on Australia is a recurring subject in his fiction—and the book with which he first established his reputation is entitled ***The Americans, Baby.***

I

Moorhouse's most recent collection of stories, ***The Everlasting Secret Family*** (1980), appears after a decade in which he published five others, including his first. It was also a period of distinct social, political, and cultural change, a period he has captured in his latest book, an anthology of "new journalism," chiefly his own, titled *Days of Wine and Rage* (1980). Like this—but for the imaginative registering of cultural change in his fiction—***The Everlasting Secret Family*** also has aspects of a retrospective collection. The early books—***Futility and Other Animals*** (1969), ***The Americans, Baby*** (1972), and ***The Electrical Experience*** (1974)—were each subtitled "a discontinuous narrative"; this is the form that Moorhouse has made his distinctive, though varied, means of structuring his fictions, and employed in ***Conference-ville*** (1976) and ***Tales of Mystery and Romance*** (1977). While individual stories can be read (and some have been published) separately, the interlinking of characters and themes relates them in each volume. As well, some characters reappear from volume to volume; and a story from the first recurs in the second, one from that in the third, underscoring the sense of a "family" relationship, or, one might say (not inappropriately, given its psychological associations), a "polymorphous" relationship within each collection and among them all. The effect is that while the stories move through discrete social levels, generations, and locales, they also imply an elusive pattern of interaction, one in which connections are *not* made as they would be in a traditional novel.

Although Moorhouse is committedly a writer of stories rather than novels, his composed collections are among the most original, extended fictions of the past decade, and his discontinuous forms are essential to his view of the ways things happen and of the discreteness and fragmentation of individual experience. What happens does not "develop" as in a continuous narrative, yet there is the sense that all is not random, disconnected, arbitrary. *The Everlasting Secret Family* develops, in the senses of further revealing and imaginatively extending, these relationships underlying his work to date. Although not subtitled "a discontinuous narrative" as the first collections were, *The Everlasting Secret Family* contains such sequences in the first and third of its four sections. Readers expecting again a "family" relationship among all the stories (and they would be right to do so) will find that in mode, mood, and subject these form more radically distinct groups than in any of the previous collections. The book appears a "retrospective" in that each section develops different aspects of Moorhouse's characteristic manners and concerns, whereas the book as a whole (as its predecessors did successively) moves into different areas and new stylistic modulations.

The first group of stories, "Pacific City," offers scenes from provincial life in an earlier generation—a classic subject of realist, and ironic, fiction. Although in comparison with other writers of "contemporary" fiction (and his near contemporaries) like Murray Bail, Peter Carey, and Michael Wilding, Moorhouse is not so manifestly experimental in style and has tended to locate his fictions in immediate experience, to be ostensibly more the realist than the artificer, the realism of this opening sequence is in a very literary, artistically self-conscious mode. The town which is to be the site of the projected Pacific City is already familiar from earlier collections, especially *The Electrical Experience,* and is perhaps not unlike the town a hundred miles south of Sydney that the author himself (born 1938) came from. But it is also, with traditional literary and cultural associations, the Town as against the City, and a microcosm of the Society (as well as of a society in a particular time and place) that in all times frustrates the Artist and the Seer. In this consciousness of— even parodic awareness of—archetypes, the "Pacific City" sequence is closer to Patrick White's first novel, *Happy Valley,* than it is to traditional fiction about Australian country town life. And Moorhouse's style, in the particulars of his relocating classic themes in an alien environment, is not essentially different from White's: the predominant sense of "slice of life" realism is, at the same time, working figuratively, to transcend (and render arbitrary) that notional categorical separation into metonymic and metaphoric modes of writing posited by some theorists.

Irving Bow, "the proprietor of darkness" in the story so titled, and proprietor of the Odeon Cinema, is the focus for the ironic comedy in these stories which contrast mundane existence in the small town with the Life of the Imagination, of dreams and visions, but also of deception and delusions. Left money by his mother, Bow has built his Odeon facing away from the town toward the projected Pacific City (the year is 1927). With its plaster statues of the Muses in the foyer, it is his temple of art and promise of the Golden Age to come, advanced by electricity, when Pacific City will be a pleasure resort like Baden or Nice and the Odeon the center of its public life. But unsuspected by the townspeople who accept as real the illusions the cinema offers them, it is also a most transporting theater (an archaic flourish; but justified by **"The Crying Organ"** story, in which a troupe of strolling players protests at competition from the cinema and topples the statue of Thalia). In the stories' own images, it is Bow's castle Romanesque balcony and all, his retreat from the desert of the town; and, as keeper of his temple's mysteries, Bow is the proprietor of darkness in another sense—he is the dark stranger in the lives of the town's more attractive pubescents whom, with their compliance, he temporarily enslaves while he poses as a jaded Emperor. Or he shows "Passion's Slave" again to Dr. Trenbow in a private screening. His associates in the town are others who feel apart from it: Trenbow, whose ambition is to pursue the study of human psychology in Vienna; Backhouse, the newspaper editor, who aspires to Fleet Street; Scribner, the town's Bohemian of mysterious means, who is reputed to be an old Balliol man. **"The Town Philosophers' Banquet"** gathers together these and other luminaries, including Branton, who is regarded as a classics scholar, although he teaches something else at the local school, and Selfridge the athlete returned from the Amsterdam Olympics, who brings a body balm back from Greece (or Bow wants to think it's from Greece). Bow entertains them in the cinema's banquet room; as the guests discuss physical pleasure over the wine, the children of a Sicilian immigrant dressed in Grecian costume, dance before them, their performance culminating in a mime of seduction. Afterward Bow is left with the athletic but sleeping Selfridge, trying to delude himself from his balcony that "Pacific City and its glittering noise, automobiles, and neon gas lights, had already arrived."[1]

The ironically Platonic associations of the title and the Hellenic allusions (including pederasty) within the story convey the timeless nature of Irving Bow's dissatisfactions and his idealization of the City. His "lonely unrespectability" is both specific to this town and time and also to the romantic idealist's universal and perennial sense of estrangement. The other "philosophers" also feel exiled from an ideal metropolis. **"The Science Club Meets"** brings them together again, around the body of a two-headed calf, to hear Bow lecture on the cinematograph. Afterward, the secretary reads a letter from the Institute of Patentees, London:

"Our correspondent says that little groups of patentees were still discussing points from the lecture among themselves on the stairs well after the close of the meeting."

The secretary looked up. "That's all."

They sat there in silence, wanting so badly to have been among the small groups of patentees who gathered on the musty but well-polished stairs of the Institute in Westminster, the portraits of Faraday, Edison, Stephenson and Isambard Kingdom Brunel on the walls, the gas lights being turned out by the caretakers who told them to hurry along as they talked excitedly about Rynder's talk and spilled out into the spring air, pulling on their caps, going then maybe to a comfortable English public house for a pint, each giving guarded information about his latest theory, invention or calculation.

McDowell broke the wistful silence by moving in a quiet voice that the report of the Institute of Patentees be received.

(*ESF,* p. 51)

This sense of not fully belonging, of being spiritually estranged, remote from the true cultural center (whether it be a fanciful classical Athens or Rome, in imagined contemporary London or Vienna, or the idealized but never to be built Pacific City) pervades these stories. At the realistic level it captures the colonialist and provincial consciousness of this generation. At the metaphoric, and consciously literary, level, it insinuates the irony that such delusions of a finer, fuller life in some other place and time are perennial. The "Pacific City" sequence closes with "To Be Continued," quietly underscoring this recognition of the timeless conflict between the real and the ideal.

The complex play against the conventions of local literature which implicitly present man at home in such an environment comes out especially in **"The Illegality of the Imagination,"** a reworking of the traditional subject of the child lost in the bush. Conventionally, this subject should oppose a sense of community to the inhospitality of the bush, but Bow's alienation from both the landscape and the people of the countryside expresses the author's rejection of conventions that would sentimentalize life in this place, at this time. After a premonition of death, Bow finds the child, which is then thrashed by its father, and later loses itself in the bush again, never to be found. The "illegality" of Bow's imagination in conjuring up an image of the boy's skull on his naked body, and then remembering how the boy clung to him, corresponds with Moorhouse's own in venturing outside the conventions which traditionally prescribe how such subjects should be presented.

If Irving Bow, the corrupt master of illusions, is perceived as a type of the artist, forced into silence and exile, finding no one amongst his kindred to take his confession, but speaking the truth cunningly to the townspeople "in a way that it would not be understood" (*ESF,* p. 8), then the next section, **"The Dutch Letters,"** can also be seen as having problematical implications for art. The author-narrator tells us that he has found some letters in the student's room he is occupying during a conference, and he divulges their contents in full. The discovery is not accidental: the writer, curious to the point of invading the privacy of others, has actually broken into the student's locker and searched for the secret trap that conceals the letters in a writing cabinet. For the reader, the "status" of this story is uncertain: is it a *conte trouvé* (to use the title of one of Moorhouse's uncollected stories), and are the letters genuine? Or are the letters, and the writer-narrator, the invention of another writer who likes to play on the boundary between fact and fiction? The writer in this fiction is unable imaginatively to penetrate the lives, empathetically enter the relationships, that the letters present. All he can do is to document these documents, producing a jumble of discordant footnotes. The writers of the letters refuse to be "written"; their experiences remain intractable to this writer. From him the reader has a confession, such as Bow, another furtive voyeur, wanted to make. From Moorhouse, the writer "behind" this narrator, we have—what? Either the dramatic presentation of the gap between the recorded experience of others and the missing imaginative version that a "real" writer would create from it, or a confession of a violation of others' secrets and of imaginative failure on the part of the real writer.

The third section, **"Imogene Continued,"** is the most extended example of "discontinuous narrative" within *The Everlasting Secret Family* (though the possibility of the whole collection being a variation on this form needs to be kept open). It is in the mode most frequently associated with earlier collections, in which the author plays the roles of acute, ironic observer of contemporary manners and comic realist who blurs the edges between fact and fiction. Although such a characterization ignores the variations that exist between the previous collections, it has its point in summarizing readers' expectations that Moorhouse will speak the truth about social and sexual relationships (even though, like Irving Bow, he may speak it in such a way that it is not understood). Set at the same conference as the preceding **"Dutch Letters,"** this section introduces a range of contemporary intellectual and political types, some at least being sketched from life; and the ritualistic procedures and group behavior at the conference are so drolly observed that the sequence reads rather more like "new journalism" than fiction. Yet the sequence raises problematical questions about the relationships between these ostensibly distinct categories of "reportage" and "fiction" and contains its own authorial confessions.

Cindy, one of the academics attending the conference, and a former lover of the narrator (the same writer-narrator who had searched the student's room in the previous section), is raped by some delegates from the Aboriginal ghetto in Sydney. Her reaction to this, complicated by her vicarious guilt over the injustices accorded the Aboriginals historically, and the fact that the conference is being held in Queensland, where the police have a reputation for brutality and racism; the narrator's own reaction, affected by his past conditioning and earlier affair with Cindy; and the further complication introduced by their discovering that one of the Aboriginals involved is a convicted child molester: these confuse their attempts to make rational, detached, mature responses. They find, in a variation of the wording in a lecture they attend, "only the interaction of confusing things." The subject of this lecture, John Anderson, Professor of Philosophy at the University of Sydney from 1927-1958, had provided, through his empiricist rejection of totalizing systems of thought, a rationale for generations of "Libertarian" Sydney Bohemians. Cindy and the narrator (like Moorhouse himself) had been Libertarians in their youth; the irony is that they find themselves experiencing, emotionally and confusedly, that "interaction of complex things" which intellectually they hold as their understanding of life. It is an irony at the expense of the narrator, who establishes himself first of all as jauntily detached and self-possessed. While in public he retains this confidence, continuing to clown and to participate in the regressive antics of the conference, inwardly he is under the pressure of these personal confusions. In the context of Moorhouse's work as a whole, these admissions of uncertainty by the writer-narrator must seem confessional for the author also. The Libertarian subculture, influenced by Anderson's thinking, is presented in Moorhouse's earliest collections, and their discontinuous narrative structures can be seen as fictional demonstrations of Anderson's "interaction of complex things." Cindy is a character in these collections, and a story from the first reappears in this latest among the documenting notes to **"Imogene Continued"**—in which she admits to lying about the experience on which that earlier story was based. Such a play with fact and fiction seems designed to counter conventional distinctions between the author "in the story" (who reveals Cindy's secret to others) and the "real" author (who reveals it to us) and to be an admission that Moorhouse shares his narrator's or persona's uncertainties which he draws so confidently into his fiction.

The final (title) sequence begins by asserting the conventional distinction between author and narrator. The author notes that this "erotic memoir in six parts" has been prepared from various sources; the narrator remarks: "This was originally to be published privately and circulated privately. I do not in any way wish to harm the conservative forces in this country. In so far as this memoir touches on political things (and caution delimited this severely) it does so simply as a fact of our lives." But having come to this after the preceding sections of the book, the reader is likely to be wary of such a disclaimer from one of Moorhouse's narrators and to suspect the opposite is being hinted at. Yet **"The Everlasting Secret Family"** departs from realistic modes to embrace the conventions of high pornography: the vaguely specified setting in time and place, Gothic suggestions of sacrilege and defilement associated with rites and vestments, and a classic concentration less on luridly described physical encounters than on the psychology of dominance and submission. But this classic, conventional theme of the abasement of self and the subjugation of others through the senses is played upon by

this being a homosexual confession. A decadent set of conventions is revitalized by regaining its power to shock and disturb the imagination.

The narrator had been seduced by his lover, a politician, when he was a schoolboy; now he is a willingly submissive slave, chained by the telephone to his master's fickle whims, abused and manipulated, but also furtively rebellious in his promiscuity. In time, he obeys the instruction to initiate his master's son into the "secret family":

> I was joined to a line through history which went back to the first primitive tribal person who went my way, who took a virgin boy lover, and every boy who became a man and took, in due turn, a boy lover, through to Socrates. I had played a part now in the continuation of that chain. I had played my first part as a child in becoming a man's lover. I had now played my second part. I now belonged fully in that historical line. It was a way of passing on and preserving the special reality, a way of giving new life, the birth for the boy of a new reality, a joining of him to a secret family, the other family. To belong to that chain is to belong to another life.

> (*ESF*, p. 204)

In the high artificiality of its mode, this sequence departs from the varieties of realism preceding it in the collection. It can be seen as purely imaginative, fictional play, a calculatingly provocative virtuoso flourish by an author who, like Irving Bow, is a "proprietor of darkness," indulging the "illegality" of his imagination and, uncertainly, as a fable to be read, decoded, in political and psychological terms. In its engagement with taboo subjects and its revelation of secrets, it teasingly suggests possible "secret" and "family" relationships with the earlier sections in different modes: the politics of personal, and especially sexual, relationships—the dissembling, manipulativeness, and treachery that enter into these—and the deceptiveness, even deviousness, of the art that presents them. Where, though, there is only "the interaction of complex things" in the earlier sections, in **"The Everlasting Secret Family"** there is the narrator's discovering in his transported imagination a significance, a continuity, and an order in life—but a travesty of these traditional moral and literary positives. Here, clearly, the collection is implicitly rejecting any simple disjunction between the realistic, true-to-life, and the consciously fictional, true-to-art. Playing with the complicating possibilities between these opposed extremes, it constitutes a retrospective of Moorhouse's development to date.

II

Moorhouse's first collection, in which the story Cindy alludes to in *The Everlasting Secret Family* appears, was first issued by a publisher of "girlie" magazines at the end of the 1960s. With the success of *The Americans, Baby*, it was later reissued by Angus and Robertson, traditionally the major publisher of Australian writing since the late colonial period. Angus and Robertson have continued to reis-sue *Futility and Other Animals* to meet rising demand and have published all of Moorhouse's subsequent collections of fiction. The early stories were, in the main and on the surface, about being young in Sydney during the Vietnam war and experiencing the tensions induced by the prevailing subcultural ideology of "liberation"—political and sexual. A number of these stories had been rejected by editors of literary magazines (hence publication in popular but hardly cultural "girlies"), not only because they were considered as riskily indecent but also because they were counter to what it was felt an "Australian" short story should be about: more "representative" characters and a more normative set of attitudes. Moorhouse was consciously opposing such stereotypes and in an interview has commented upon his own earlier attempts to write such stories:

> They were humanistic. They were kind to the working class. They were sympathetic to kangaroos. They were everything that Australian short stories should have been at that time. Social realism writing. It has to pretend to be realistic, and also at the same time to be the vehicle for sentiments, liberal sentiments.[2]

The narrative manner of *Futility and Other Animals* is realistic, but it is not the vehicle for liberal humanist sentiment. Rather, the stories present detachedly, without conventional judgment, the pressures of immediately contemporary experience and the conflicts between how the characters feel and the way they think they ought to feel.

In a prefatory note the author describes these characters as a "tribe—a modern, urban tribe" sharing an environment that is "both internal—anxieties, pleasures, and confusions—and external—houses streets, hotels. . . ." These experiences, the inner Sydney ambience, and the reappearance of various characters in different stories provide the common elements in this "discontinuous narrative." Although unconventional when it first appeared, because of its departure from the more "representative" characters and settings and the more "normal" situations of short stories then, it now seems more obviously a "first" collection, preoccupied with youthful rites of passage (and it is a book that has continued to appeal to new generations of readers). In the main, its stories are about growing up, leaving home, coming to the city from the country, or returning there; first love affairs, hetero- or homosexual; and finding a peer group, a life style, an ideology, especially the anti-ideology of Libertarianism. "Liberation" imposes its own stresses, conflicting with the desire for simple, secure relationships on the part of those who have rejected the "bourgeois" romantic concept of love, and, additionally, for the women, with their desire to have children. While the characters' emotional experiences are often "immature," Moorhouse's ironic distance from them is characteristic of his own mature manner, which is marked by direct, dramatic presentation of a voice or voices and by a preference for freshly colloquial, metaphoric language. Even the authorial "stage directions" for the dialogue (as later quotation will show) are conveyed by "low" or

homely concrete diction and comic metaphor rather than by abstract and polysyllabic description. The first story in *Futility and Other Animals* would seem implicitly to acknowledge an early debt to Hemingway for this astringency of style and dramatic shaping.

The Americans, Baby opens with a fine example of this mature and characteristically ironic manner, **"Dell Goes into Politics,"** which carries over some of the concerns of the first collection. It looks (or it did when it first appeared) very much a stereotypical "Australian" short story about the return of a girl to her family in a small country town after living in the city. Her "going into" politics is no more than her shouting out in the local pub, traditionally a male preserve, the anti-Vietnam slogans she has acquired from her Trotskyist lover in Sydney. Her family and friends, the rural working class, are embarrassed, even frightened. Dell's father tells her, "'There's only one way to get along in this world—shut up.'" "'What do you know about politics?' her mother said, suspicious, as though she's suspected she might also know about sex" (*AB,* p. 7), and then comforts herself with the ignorant thought that "They don't let women into Parliament anyhow" (*AB,* p. 8). Harry, the boy Dell had thought of marrying on her return, looks "as if he'd got a bee flying around him" when she asks if the politician in the pub is State or Federal—"Christ, Harry, that's about the least you can know" (*AB,* p. 4). The ironic registering of the impact of the war on public consciousness depends on the story being read against the conventions of a rural realism that sentimentalize the workers as a progressive class. As well, there is the impact of the war on individual consciousness with the revelation of Dell's bad faith. Her shouted "Why don't you bring the boys back from Vietnam?" is a displacement of her real concern, an evasion of the fact that she has come back home because she is pregnant. The nexus between politics and sex assumed by the revolutionaries in Sydney is here played with ironically.

The second story, **"The American Paul Johnson,"** introduces Carl, a radical student in Sydney, who thinks he should exploit an American he meets because he represents ideologically the "enemy," but instead discovers his own homosexuality through the encounter. Like the first story, this is a study in bad faith that reveals the private, emotional anxiety beneath a public involvement in politics. **"Becker and the Boys from the Band,"** which like many of Moorhouse's titles contains an ironic allusion (here to the play, then current, about New York homosexuals) introduces Becker, a Coca-Cola executive from Atlanta, Georgia. He seems another inauthentic figure, the creature of the corporation who would rather be back home, preferably playing piano in a jazz club; but his consciousness of his "inauthenticity," his shrugging acceptance of his own limitations, makes him the most positive character in the book. In a time-honored American tradition, Becker is the innocent abroad, in a country as remote to him as the moon (**"Becker on the Moon,"** written after the U.S. moon landing, is another story in the collection), but, with a twist to the conventions, he is, ambiguously, liberated or corrupted in this New World of speed freaks, drag queens, and aggressively emancipated women. Two other Americans appear in the first group of stories. Angela, in **"The Girl from The Family of Man"** (she claims her photograph as a child appears in that collection), is the epitome of a new variety of primness—countercultural self-righteousness—whereas the narrator, who beds her, is uninhibitedly vulgar, lecherous, and aggressive. Hugo, in **"The Story of Nature"** (who is carried over from *Futility and Other Animals*), is a "nuclear refugee" from the States, a scientist turned primitive who piously throws away Cindy's contraceptive pills in attempting to impose his values on their relationship. These stories present variations on a conflict between instinct and ideology over a range of characters who seem unrelated and socially peripheral—an impression important to the collection as a whole for the way changing sexual attitudes and radical political attitudes recur in the different worlds of city and country, business and the counter-culture, but in no simple, coherent pattern.

The sixth story, **"The American Poet's Visit,"** is one of two described as an "interlude," and these, strategically placed in the collection, move to the center of contemporary consciousness in the "metropolitan" Libertarian subculture influenced by Anderson's critical, or negative, ideology. The interludes also move closer to the author, who is elsewhere "invisible"; in the interludes he is the author as schlemiel, employing a self-deprecating irony as his defense against both life and the reader. **"The American Poet's Visit"** fictionally recounts Kenneth Rexroth's actual reception by Sydney Libertarians during the late 1960s, capturing their ingroup smugness and also their doubts and defensiveness when confronted by a figure from the truly metropolitan, indeed cosmopolitan, counter-culture:

> "We saw a reference to your magazine in the Provo stuff in Amsterdam," says Rexroth.
>
> "Yes, in a list of fraternal publications," his secretary amplifies, "published as a supplement to their own publication, *Provo,* in November."
>
> "She's well detailed," I comment to Gillian who tells me to belt up.
>
> But we all shuffle. We haven't published an issue for a year. We don't know why.
>
> "What are you guys doing in the way of protest these days?" he asks, moving away from the magazine, about which we are still formulating excuses.
>
> We try now to think about protest.
>
> "Actually we don't hold much interest in protest these days," says Wayne.
>
> These days of all days, I think, these days of rapid change and dehumanisation. And we choose to relax on protest. Our lives, I observe, are spent wading against trend.
>
> "Some of us might be what you call existential protestors," I say, "but not reformist protestors." Everyone in the room looks at me except Gillian who looks up at the ceiling.

> "We see the protest thing more as a permanent thing—you know . . . a way of life . . . in conflict with the authoritarian nature of society," Cooper puts in.
>
> The rest look at him gratefully.
>
> We walk up the historical escalator the wrong way. That's what we do.
>
> "That's our bag," I say, but no one admits to hearing me.
>
> "That's our bag," I say.
>
> Gillian makes a nauseated face.
>
> "Oh you people should see what the Provos are doing," his secretary says, with the enervating enthusiasm common to American business executives, folk singers, and tourists.
>
> I listen. Perhaps, I think, it will transmute our political ennui into go-man-go. I always feel that Americans are about to launch me into the space of endeavour. But it never happens.
>
> They don't drink much. But we do.
>
> We sit on the polychromatic poufs trying not to look at each other through the fluorescent clear silence. I move to sit on the edge of the table—edge of the world—nonchalantly ill at ease. Of course, I say to myself, it had to be like this. This was the way it had to be.

(*AB,* pp. 55-56)

And so the exquisitely embarrassing evening proceeds with the Libertarians aware of their remoteness but, with some satisfaction, also their critical distance from the real or imagined centers of change. The second interlude, **"The Girl Who Met Simone de Beauvoir in Paris,"** captures comically the threatening aspects of the women's movement for insecure males, and there is another painful reminder of their provincialism in the fact that de Beauvoir was met *in Paris.*

Between these comic interludes are stories about Dell's boyfriend Kim and his revolutionary friends, about Becker, another about Hugo; and there is **"Five Incidents Concerning the Flesh and the Blood,"** which, in tone and form, is quite distinct from these other stories about characters already introduced. Yet the thematic contrast it establishes between the rational, organized, and lifeless, *and* the spontaneous, instinctual, and vital, between "the fleeting pleasures" and "the groaning hours," opens up implications of a wider vision of life than the characters in the other stories, immersed in their subcultural preoccupations, can discern. In a self-consciously literary, perhaps too explicit way it points to a preference dramatically implied elsewhere in the collection for the vital and honest if also messy and vulgar, as against the controlled and rationalized. The structuring of the collection also seems to assert this preference. Although after the second interlude there are stories about Becker's "liberation" from life in the corporation (he ends up playing piano at the Silver Spade, Surfer's Paradise) and the story of Dell's rebelling against sexual indoctrination before returning home, to emphasize these narrative lines would be to give too "nov-elettish" an account. *The Americans, Baby* has the length and the substance—in terms of psychological density, significant themes, contrasting characters, and social settings—for a novel, yet it deliberately avoids developing situations and relationships as a novel would. It even wilfully resists conclusion, the drawing together of latent relationships between characters and events, by ending with **"The Letters to Twiggy,"** which shows an exceedingly "rational" but obsessive and sexually repressed mind quite out of control.

Through its structure, the collection presents a different view of the way things happen, the ways in which they do not form a simple, coherent, significant literary pattern, nor, in social terms, constitute a "community" of experiences. It implies a view of contemporary Australian society that departs from received literary and sociological stereotypes such as the city and the country, "Sydney or the Bush," an imposed Anglo-European tradition and a native, populist culture, "authentic" working class values and "inauthentic" middle class attitudes. Moorhouse's characters include Coca-Cola executives (as Americans, the transmitters of the dominant contemporary culture), a self-made, small town businessman, T. George McDowell, rural working class Dell, and varied representatives of the new class of predominantly young, predominantly middle class intellectuals, or lumpen-intellectuals; but all feel displaced, feel peripheral to their sense of a cultural center. The discontinuous form, which sets up subtle and elusive refractions between the stories, cannot be considered in purely formal terms: it raises questions beyond these, and some of the most analytical commentary has come from social historians and cultural critics. But the drawing out of the ideological implications of what is dramatized, although an essential part of a full reading, cannot alone account for the book's qualities: its usually wry but at times exuberantly comic observation of the ways of the contemporary world, and its underlying perception of life as conflict, which cannot be resolved or avoided by observing abstract precepts. More abruptly than any other book of its decade, *The Americans, Baby* moved Australian fiction into the contemporary.

With this second collection, Moorhouse won national recognition and the reputation of being an accurate and acute observer of contemporary manners and morals, a reputation reinforced by his journalism and writings on the media. In the period which saw the emergence of a self-consciously "new" fiction, Moorhouse clearly appeared more the realist than the fabulator. He continued to play a traditional role of the imaginative writer—a critical observer of social life—that many of his contemporaries were prepared to relinquish for formal and stylistic experimentation. Yet such broad distinctions, as were then forced, between "realistic" and more "imaginative" writing can have a dubious validity in particular cases. Not accorded equal recognition with his realism was Moorhouse's own, if less flamboyant, concern to "make it new" formally and stylistically, as well as mimetically. This commitment has

become more apparent as each book since *The Americans, Baby* has departed in its own way from its predecessors, and from readers' expectations formed by the first collections.

The Electrical Experience begins with the elderly businessman T. George McDowell in his small town talking to Becker about his daughter Terri and the problems of young people today. Terri is the disturbed young woman in *The Americans, Baby* who "liberates" Becker from the corporation and launches him on his uncertain career as a jazz pianist. The finest of the Becker stories in that preceding collection reappears here, but in the very different context of McDowell's life. George is a self-made and successful manufacturer of soft drinks, who had first visited the United States as a youth in 1923 and been influenced by the efficiency and technological progress he found there. The stories present, out of strict chronological order, revealing moments in George's life: Terri's birth during the bush fires of 1939; her conception, or at least George's conception of family planning; his changing his name to follow progressive business practice; George as a young man struggling to overcome shyness and meeting Zane Grey during the depression and the approach of the second World War; and finally as an old man suffering a stroke. Externally, he lives in the same South Coast town as in the later "Pacific City" stories—in which he also appears (as do Backhouse, Trenbow, and Scribner in these). Yet the town, or his perception of it, is different from Irving Bow's, that historical and spiritual outsider. George's town is located much more specifically, and more one dimensionally in time—especially through the photographs, recipes, technical tips, and folk sayings which are included among the collection's "fragments"—though it is still as much a mental as a physical environment. He identifies with the town in a way that Bow cannot, believing that "You had to find the right-size place for the size of man you were" (*EE,* p. 4), and the town is George externalized and extended.

With his Elbert Hubbard individualism and rural communalism, his Rotarian's respect for service and efficiency, and his sexual repression, he epitomizes a past ethos that conflicts with that of his daughter's generation, the contemporary urban intelligentsia whom he sees as "gypsies." The contradictions in his life—psychologically, between his instincts and his sense of propriety; philosophically, between his individualism and his communalism and between his rationalism and the larger questions that Rotary cannot answer—are "discontinuities" articulated through the stories. But the major discontinuity of the book is that between his generation and his daughter's, which is brilliantly emphasized in the final story, **"Filming the Hatted Australian."** In it, a group of young film makers in Sydney, which includes Terri, is making a documentary about "the prejudices, the beliefs, the life-style" (*EE,* p. 184) of the self-contained Australian of George's generation. They corner their specimen as though he were a primitive anthropological survivor and then proceed verbally to flay and dissect him. The sudden shift in temporal perspective and the disturbing shift in values capture the discontinuities within apparent social-historical continuity.

At this mimetic level, *The Electrical Experience* is immediately impressive as imaginative social history—both for its capturing of the individual's experience of social change through McDowell and through the motif of the transforming and dislocating effects of electricity. Like Moorhouse's other collections, this is *not* discontinuous with the world outside the book; yet neither are the language and the form transparent means of presenting a simple fictional version of historical processes, as the account above might suggest. In form and language, the book (a discontinuous *unity* in a way the thematically more complex *The Americans, Baby* is not) departs from conventions of literary and cultural realism, from received notions of "the typical," and from deterministic assumptions about personal and social development. The chronologically disordered structure works against naturalistic assumptions of causation; and George McDowell is not a representative "product" of his time and region—when the film crew in the last story selects a "subject" to fit its stereotype of George's generation, it chooses someone quite different from the same town. George expresses an ethos that in his own mind is more American than Australian; and it is through his expressing it, his language, that the reader is made conscious of Moorhouse's artistic concerns, which go together with his critical engagement with Australian society.

McDowell is a simple man with a simple language: "I do not care for words in top hats. I believe in shirt sleeve words" (*EE,* p. 9). The "invisible" Flaubertian narrator, using George's lexicon, creates gently, even affectionately, with superior irony, the gap between how George thinks and speaks and how we perceive him. This stylistic method is capable of the most delicate and subtle comedy when the author detaches himself by isolating George's favorite words and phrases within quotes. Like Irving Bow at the very beginning of the "Pacific City" sequence, and the narrators of the other collections which follow *The Electrical Experience,* George has a preoccupation with language. Language expresses and creates the contradiction between his outward confidence, his gregariousness and garrulity, and his inner shyness and uncertainty. This contradiction is apparent in the opening story, when he reflects that:

> Life's experience had taught him that never once had speaking to a stranger been anything but to his advantage. Although inherently shy as a young man, he had learned early to talk to someone as if they owed you money. In all his life, including his world travel, the only person with whom he had been unable to converse in good fellowship was his daughter Terri, and this was a source of some distress to both [him] and Thelma.
>
> (*EE,* p. 10)

Yet even with his wife, Thelma, intimacy is inhibited; and his inhibitions reveal themselves through the embarrassed and evasive syntax of his thought:

> He observed that the limitations and restrictions on the matter of sexual indulgence, placed by Thelma in their marriage, sometimes aroused him, her unwillingness, he had perhaps the sort of personality which was, which savoured, well, the restraint she imposed, the limitations on when, and her refusals. And now and then, though rarely, he imposed himself on her, and the silent, wordless impositions he enjoyed too. It had to do, he speculated, with the basic economic principle of scarcity. Though really, this aspect of their lives he did not truly understand and did not ponder over much and which was not to say, either, that they did not conduct their married life *correctly.*
>
> (*EE,* p. 16)

George is fond of such economic notions—"Man's know how was his personal capital. The bank inside his head" (*EE,* p. 52)—and mechanical metaphors—he sees children as society's "replacement parts." They encapsulate the rationalized view of life which his language systematizes. His language defines his character and ethos. It cannot comfortably accommodate intimacy, nor what he alludes to as the "Great Mysteries," his dim and resisted apprehensions of the more transcendent values of religion and art, which would demand different vocabularies.

Through his language, T. George McDowell creates his public and speechifying self; and his adoption of this form of his name (which Backhouse tells him looks "Americanized") suggests his consciousness of verbal role playing. Moorhouse's own consciousness of language, as an essential part of his "content" and not merely the vehicle for presenting it, is displayed with mastery in the final story. The abrupt shift, in diction and pace, into the speech of the young urban intellectuals contrasts them with their "subject" and his generation. They make aggressive, even sadistic verbal assaults on Frederick Victor Turner to provoke and then to destroy his defences. They are self-righteous both in their presumed artistic justification for their deceptions and provocations, and in their assumed moral superiority to the racism and sexism of a stereotype they despise (but have relentlessly "created" for the film). The easy ironies they achieve are not approved by the author-narrator in the story, nor are they consistent with the more comprehending, affectionate ironies of the book as a whole. Implicitly, the intention is the opposite of the film makers': toward an empathetic understanding of what it was like to be George McDowell, to see the world his way, and to feel that it is collapsing in the present. With *The Electrical Experience,* Moorhouse's ironic range, and the flexibility and precision of his control over dramatized language, made it obvious that as well as being a powerful "realist" he was also among the very finest of "stylists."

The first of the dozen "episodes" comprising *Conferenceville* is entitled **"In Flight Sadism"**; in it, the author-narrator flying to a conference meets "a conversational sadist," the academic who is going to introduce his paper, that is, he adds, if the conference eventuates. In this book (and "book" rather than "collection" seems even more appropriate here than with *The Electrical Experience*), language is more markedly an essential dimension of what is being realistically, and critically, presented. Moorhouse, playing the same uncertainly fictional role of author-narrator as in the middle sections of *The Everlasting Secret Family,* registers confusions that are not only expressed through language but arise from it, as he attempts to define his "position" in response to conflicting information and demands from others. At the conference there is incessant squabbling over and playing with words, the counter for counter interpretations of reality, while the author inwardly broods over his inability to find a coherent grammar of response for the comically varied situations he discovers himself in. Others have their confident positions, readily identifiable and entailing ready linguistic responses for interpersonal political skirmishes; the author has only his critically detached awareness of how their language reveals their positions, and the inadequacy of his own.

As a serially arranged collection of "episodes" (part of its original conception was that it could be issued as a magazine serial), *Conference-ville* differs from the earlier books in having a linear narrative development (though what "develops" remains problematic). It is closer to the novel, or at least novella form, but its more simple coherence can be seen as issuing from the author's preoccupation with what would prevent him from writing a novel. It is a non-novel about the difficulties, the impossibility of writing, in a form so traditional and confident of its conventions as the novel, about how we live now, in Australia in January 1976. The novel that is "unwritable," because about experiences which cannot be engaged truthfully and fictionally at the same time, would be about the effects of the *coup d'état* of November 1975 when the reformist Labor government, the first for a quarter of a century, was dismissed by the Governor-General, with suspicions that this unprecedented "destabilization" had been engineered by the C.I.A. The resulting "cold civil war" and the impossibility for the author of reaching a confident "position" in interpreting these events provide the subject of Moorhouse's non-novel. Lacking such a position, and being in actual circumstances which created confusion and induced "paranoia" (but then there was Chile), he cannot present a clear, coherent fictional interpretation, even a confidently paranoid, "new" fictional response to a plausibly paranoid political reality. The implicit discontinuity—or "interface," as some would say—becomes that between confident fiction and uncertain experience.

Ostensibly personalized "new journalism," with many public figures referred to as appearing at the actual conference on which it is based, *Conference-ville* also engages with some concerns of the "new" fiction. It is literature as process, writing about being a writer, confessing inadequacies and betrayals ("You could've changed the names at least," one character reproaches the author [*C,* p. 116] in the last episode). The author-narrator engages with the "unwritability" of contemporary life, registering his defeat in assuming honestly an authorial position that would allow him to organize, control, develop, and shape meaningfully

the "interaction of complex things" he has encountered. This uncommitted, sceptical position of the author-narrator, so precisely caught by the other author, or other self, behind him is this book's artistic strength: it turns the apparent negations of commitment into a positive open stance and shapes the uncertainties of writing about the contemporary into a taut set of images.

In the opening episode of *Conference-ville,* the academic "conversational sadist" mentions another (and actual) Australian writer who had been "the darling of the literary scene in the late fifties," who had broken "new ground" but whom no one reads today. The author-narrator winces:

> He meant me. It could happen to me. Not yet the darling, not yet unread.
>
> I chattered on, but damned Markham had set my mind on anxious literary introspection . . . will my other books be just obsessional pacing over the same initial life experiences . . . or attempts to reproduce what had succeeded earlier . . . worse, self-conscious attempts to "break" with the preoccupations of earlier work . . . rationally conceived fiction . . . no heat . . . no madness.
>
> (*C,* pp. 4-5)

Moorhouse's next book shares with its predecessors the characteristic of breaking "new ground," and although it is exceedingly self-conscious, in a problematical way, the "heat" and the "madness" are there from the very beginning:

> The Malaya restaurant, city of Sydney, my mouth burning with sambal, splashed with chilled beer, tasting only hot and cold. My psyche also running hot and cold. They are back. Milton and Hestia are back from the States.
>
> Milton's hand on my shoulder. Our first physical touching since his return. It rings through me. I can't hear the message. It's a confused line.
>
> 'Well, I'm glad you're both back,' I say suddenly, pleased with my spontaneity and correctness.
>
> (*TMR,* p. 2)

Contrary to the fears of the author in *Conference-ville,* *Tales of Mystery and Romance* impresses less as a "rationally-conceived fiction" than as a series of virtuoso stylistic performances by the author, who as a zany version of the same narrator, or set of clowning variations on the authorial self, dances with desperate playfulness on the indeterminate boundary between truth-telling and story-telling—or lying.

The title suggests a self-conscious literariness, with its nineteenth-century Gothic evocations of the fantastic and the erotic; and the preoccupations with perversion, incest, metamorphoses, drug-induced fantasies, and death of an earlier decadence are comically translated into a contemporary version here. The "tales" (the tale being to the story as the romance is to the novel, in claiming a greater imaginative "latitude"?) are set in a variety of typefaces to correspond with the discontinuities in mood between them; but despite this visual reinforcement of their tonal differences, the personality of their common narrator and the pattern of his emotional life emerge progressively. He is a thirty-seven year old poet-philosopher from Concord—the Sydney suburb, not the rural seat of Transcendentalism—who finds himself between two worlds. One, which is lost to him, is that of his family, childhood security, first love, marriage and fatherhood, the world of conventional domesticity: "A cold quandary blows permanently on the moors of abnormality. The cheery lighted house of normality is a distant stage set" (*TMR*, p. 94). The other is the world of Milton, his distant and never-to-be-attained love, his erstwhile intimate friend (but never, fully, his lover), his academic alter ego. Milton is now into a whole new "scene"—Transcendental Meditation, Yoga, the occult, living in a commune with Lance and Karrine, Hildergarde, Margit, Tina, Sheena . . . all, the narrator ruefully observes, under-thirties names. Although scornful, the lad from Concord with his Low Anglican, Boy Scout, small capitalist, individualist background is hurt by Milton's serenely frenetic pursuit of the now scene. He remembers that last year they were supposed to be nonhappy people, always freaking out; now it's satori, meditation, and deep relaxation. In a classic display of displaced, frustrated rage, he attacks a member of the Hare Krishna who accosts him on the street, embarrassing Milton and Milton's *new* friend: a most droll presentation of his insecurities which have been intensified by Milton's countercultural cant.

For Milton, the narrator is pathetically passé, vulgar in his pursuit of "volupté," inauthentic:

> 'Look around you,' he said, and I did, and he exasperatedly said, 'no, I mean around your scene—not the oval—hasn't it come home to you. Haven't you noticed we are all into a different trip now. It isn't champagne breakfasts. It's not watching the rosy fingers of dawn at the Taxi Club. It isn't throwing people into swimming pools, it isn't expensive dinners and mock speeches, and it isn't going to ethnic night clubs and joining in the handkerchief dance, having your photograph taken with the belly dancer, putting dollar notes down the crevice of her breast, it isn't getting your photograph in the newspapers wearing a cowboy hat, it isn't appearing in public places in drag, it isn't being seen arm-in-arm with two negresses in New Orleans. Oh you know that I mean, the scene has changed. And look at your age.'
>
> Listening carefully to what he said, I replied, 'You make it sound *first class*. The long years of penury have led me into wild excesses. Like Raphael de Valentin, I have dreamed of a life on a princely scale and now I can make the dream come true. My bills for champagne alone are enormous. Under the influence of Eugene Sue I see myself as a dandy, for I have a horror of the solemn imbecilities indulged in by the English with their much vaunted sang froid. I suppose you are troubled by my white house gowns with gold tasselled girdles?'

> 'Your dabbling in effeminacy doesn't interest me. But I'll tell you another thing it isn't—it isn't dodging being a real person by hiding in irony, self-concealing humour, hiding behind ambiguity, double-edged humour, switching of persona, self-deprecation—that's all so much shit.'

(*TMR*, pp. 97-98)

The dynamics of their conflict are verbal; the systems that clash, linguistic. Milton tells him that, "You must let go of words like 'decide,' 'intellectualize,' 'explain'" (*TMR*, p. 122). (The "must" is good.) The narrator suspects that Milton's copy of the "Desiderata," purportedly found in Old St. Paul's, Baltimore, and dated 1692, is a fraud on internal linguistic evidence. Yet beneath his verbal braggadocio and glib sententiousness is the underlying sadness of the clown. The central, revealing story here, **"The Loss of a Friend by Cablegram,"** is also the central story of the collection structurally.

In this, the narrator, visiting his ex-wife, receives Milton's telegram rejecting him for his new lifestyle. As he is attempting defensively to explain, she is reading from his notebook cryptic entries, some in the first person, others in the third, that reveal the confusion of his thoughts and values, and his theory of "the distortion of information by fictional suction": "The attention of the audience, the reporter's expectations, the audience's expectations even in conversation, drag you away from the complicated, ragged reality, from say, pointlessness, away from stray and unrelated material towards a distorting order, a distorting sensationalism" (*TMR*, p. 83). The discontinuities of mode and mood throughout the collection find their center here in the discontinuities of a personality that is overwhelmed by consciousness of the "complicated, ragged reality" and refuses to accept "a distorting reality" from among those offered in the language and value systems embraced by others. The narrator is vulnerable, exposed, accused by his wife of being on the very edge of reality; and in tone this is much more a "confessional" story than most of the others (excepting the one in the form of letters to the same ex-wife), bringing out the lonely and uncomfortable integrity underlying the comic surface elsewhere.

Tales of Mystery and Romance is both satisfying and enigmatic. A book of brilliant comic surfaces and rhetorical flourishes, yet one that conceals or complicates as much as it reveals. The presentation of the narrator's various selves is as much the real action as his encounters with Milton and his ex-wife; but the confusions and uncertainties of this narrator are dramatized with such confidence that we cannot completely identify him with the author. The implications for art are enigmatic. "Lying and fiction are brothers? But not twins," we are told (*TMR*, p. 79), but which is which here—which lies, which secrets? Is the author, again like Irving Bow in the next collection, speaking the truth in a way that it will not be understood? Or, in accordance with the jottings in the narrator's notebook, is the truth being presented without the distortion and sensationalization of fiction? With *Tales of Mystery and Romance,* Moorhouse may seem to have moved across the spectrum from his early critical, realistic engagement with social experience to that mode in which the only sure subject is the style, and the only true value the act of writing itself. Yet the pattern of his work is not so simple, as such a simplistic distinction would assume, and as, in its retrospective aspect, *The Everlasting Secret Family* makes clear.

III

In form, in theme, in social "subject matter," and personal preoccupations, the latest collection looks back but, appropriately from a writer who has emphasized discontinuities between all levels of experience, including the artistic, in no simple way. "Pacific City" returns to the lost world of T. George McDowell, but from a different perspective, and shows Moorhouse the subtle, delicately ironic stylist. **"The Dutch Letters"** and **"Imogene Continued"** return to the narrative stance of *Conference-ville,* to the immediacies of personal and public life, and to the tensions between them; they show Moorhouse in his most commonly recognized and easily identified role as the witty, acute, but sceptical intelligence critically engaged in defining and interpreting contemporary social reality. While the title sequence apparently disrupts this emerging retrospective pattern, it also exhibits another characteristic of his writing: his continuing to break "new ground" and old taboos, and to break also from his readers', his patrons' expectations, which could otherwise imprison him like the narrator in this sequence. In drawing together and further developing these different aspects of his work to date, *The Everlasting Secret Family* makes apparent the continuance throughout his varied books of his simultaneous concerns with experience and art: with finding the appropriate forms, styles, and authorial stances for engaging experience—past and present, personal and social, real and imaginative. Each may be discontinuous with the other, but discontinuity would seem to presuppose some continuity to depart from, and this latest collection suggests the "familial" though "secret" relationships between them all which provide his work with its unique, imaginative pattern.

Notes

1. Frank Moorhouse, *The Everlasting Secret Family and Other Stories* (Sydney: Angus & Robertson, 1980), p. 36; referred to hereafter parenthetically as *ESF.* All subsequent references to *Futility and Other Animals* (Sydney: Gareth Powell Associates, 1969), *The Americans, Baby* (Sydney: Angus & Robertson, 1972), *The Electrical Experience* (Sydney: Angus & Robertson, 1974). *Conference-ville* (Sydney: Angus & Robertson, 1976), and *Tales of Mystery and Romance* (Sydney: Angus & Robertson, 1977) will be noted parenthetically in the text with titles abbreviated, respectively, as follows: *FOA, AB, EE, C,* and *TMR.* Moorhouse has also published recently a nonfiction anthology, *Days of Wine and Rage* (Ringwood, Victoria: Penguin Books, 1980).

2. "There's no such thing as a gay novel," interview with Frank Moorhouse by Martin Smith, (Sydney) *Campaign,* 21 (1977), p. 19.

C. Kanaganayakam (essay date 1985)

SOURCE: "Form and Meaning in the Short Stories of Frank Moorhouse," in *World Literature Written in English,* Vol. 25, No. 1, Spring, 1985, pp. 67-76.

[*In the following essay, Kanaganayakam explores the complexity of Moorhouse's narrative style and thematic concerns.*]

The short stories of Frank Moorhouse have remained so consistently complex and open-ended during the last thirteen years that any attempt to identify them as realistic, experimental or internationalist can be misleading. Since each collection explores new dimensions of experience and fresh possibilities of expression, the reader is constantly called upon to shift his focus and seek different modes of interpretation. Not that one cannot speak of the evolution of Moorhouse in terms of a diachronic axis, but in doing so one is also leaving out significant aspects of his writing. On the other hand one cannot totally ignore the process of evolution which is germane to the author's mode of writing. The present [essay] is an attempt to explore certain aspects of form and meaning in order to suggest a reading of Moorhouse's short stories.

Moorhouse's own statements about his writing provide a useful starting point. In a prefatory note to *Futility and Other Animals,* Moorhouse draws attention to three aspects of his writing that define the scope of his stories and that implicitly suggest the genuine ambivalence of his work. He claims that

> In some ways, the people in the stories are a tribe; a modern, urban tribe which does not fully recognise itself as a tribe. Some of the people are central members of the tribe while others are hermits who live on the fringe.[1]

In calling the fictional characters of his "Comédie Humaine de Balmain" a tribe, he suggests, in anthropological terms, a pre-feudal group, linked by a common ideology and firmly rooted within a scale of values. He also implies unity, a sense of history and a definite identity. Commenting on the form, he asserts that "These are interlinked stories and, although the narrative is discontinuous and there is no single plot, the environment and characters are continuous."

The form of linked stories is by no means new, although Moorhouse's imaginative use of it might well be called innovative. The same characters appear in different stories and define themselves differently each time they appear. There are also similarities in social milieu, plot and central concern. Instead of repetition, there is a sense of superimposition with multiple facets of reality appearing simultaneously.

Finally, in a reference to thematic concerns, he says, "The central dilemma is that of giving birth, of creating new life." The anthropological connotations of "tribe" are caught up again in the reference to "creating new life." Evidently he is concerned with the process of history, with the sense of continuity. The comment also implies a concern with the child motif, which becomes a crucial issue in *Futility* and which appears in various guises in his subsequent collections. Metaphorically speaking, creating new life might well imply a struggle with the form itself, a desire to create a form which would express his dual purpose: to write history and to write fiction.

These assertions, characteristically, are paradoxical as well. There is, for instance, a paradox in juxtaposing "urban" with "tribe." We realize that what characterizes the *lumpen* groups of his stories is a lack of unity, a confusion of values and a loss of identity. Each character is isolated with his own problems, and we are told repeatedly that there is very little possibility of communication. There is no indication of people consciously deciding to form themselves into an anti-establishment group. As the narrator says in **"Writing Yourself a Proper Narrative,"**

> Originally most of us came to work in the city or go to university . . . and we found ourselves—it came about imperceptibly, one didn't *join,* it was all imperceptible, accidents of time, age and occupation.[2]

The characters in this story and elsewhere are a loosely knit group at best. Equally paradoxical is the statement about the "discontinuous narrative" form. Here again, "discontinuous" implies dislocation and fragmentation, while "narrative" implies movement and continuity.

These apparent discrepancies point towards some of the fundamental differences in coming to terms with Moorhouse's fiction. In many ways, Moorhouse is a traditional writer. Brian Kiernan, in his note on Moorhouse in *The Most Beautiful Lies,* concedes that "In a number of ways, his stories seem more 'realistic' than those of most of the other writers here."[3] In fact, in a *Meanjin* interview, asked to comment on his writing methods, Moorhouse states emphatically, "They're not very unorthodox, that's all."[4] If we associate modern writing with foregrounding of style, rejection of chronological time sequence, cancellation, contradiction and permutation, then we find little of it in Moorhouse. He usually has a clear sense of plot, and his stories do have a sense of movement from one point to another. In some stories, the plot begins *in medias res* and then moves backward and forward. The characters are fairly well defined, and the backdrop is convincingly evoked. Rarely do sudden shifts of focus leave the reader stranded between the worlds of reality and dream. The structure of his sentences follows a conventional pattern, and there is hardly any attempt at defamiliarization through

abrupt permutation and contradiction. John Docker sums up the conventionality of *The Americans, Baby* by saying

> There is nothing in *The Americans, Baby* which suggests significant innovation or experiment—that Moorhouse's work has been noticed for its treatment of sexuality does not distinguish him from, for example, Norman Lindsay or A. D. Hope who received similar attention in previous times. Basically, Moorhouse's book presents a set of moral and metaphysical positions which reveal him an unwitting heir to older literary attitudes.[5]

Docker's argument can be extended to include Moorhouse's thematic concerns as well. He is not obsessively concerned with the psyche or the unconscious, although they are not unimportant in a total evaluation of his work. He deals with the Vietnam war, American imperialism, women's liberation, racism, the conflict between generations and the impact of American cultural values. He is conscious of the inventiveness of fiction, of the impossibility of arriving at a well-defined reality, but these do not prevent him from immersing himself in political and social issues. As he admits, "Formal, aesthetic consideration *and* social, moral, political issues interest me and show up in my fiction." He adds, "I do not think that an awareness of political and social questions is necessary for good imaginative work of all kinds. Only for my kind."[6]

And yet Moorhouse is not a writer who could be classified as a social realist. For one thing, he is writing after the Vietnam war, which, like the fall of Singapore in World War II, shook Australia out of its cultural insularity. As Michael Wilding says in "The Tabloid Story Story," "The Vietnam war was one of the biggest; it drew Australia out of a comfortable, non-political ease into a society dramatically divided within itself once again."[7] He is also alive to the various liberation movements—women's, gay and black. For another, he is confronted with the problem of giving expression to a new consciousness while using the tools of a writing designed to express a different consciousness. Basically the problem is language and convention. The moment he adopts the language of the previous generation, he unconsciously accepts a scale of values within which the language operates. This is a problem with which all writers, but specifically Commonwealth writers, are confronted time and again. To adopt a language is to adopt an identity, and Moorhouse is attempting to have it both ways. On the surface at least he is adopting the linguistic patterns and conventions of an earlier generation. And yet he is describing a world which is no longer sure of its values, which can no longer distinguish between reality and fiction. All these factors combine to lift Moorhouse out of the realm of realist fiction.

In *The Electrical Experience,* Moorhouse jettisons the old reality by jettisoning its conventions. Bruce Clunies Ross explains this process:

> Once a writer begins to tamper with the conventions by which fiction renders a model of "reality" and is distin-

guished from it, the whole question of our perception of reality is thrown into doubt.[8]

The quotation captures the foregrounding of form achieved in **The Electrical Experience.** The book becomes a multi-media object with its own process of communication. The two photographs which "frame" the beginning and the end, the photographs of machines, advertisements, the black pages with white print, typographical communication and fancy lettering have a visual impact that heightens and shapes the verbal meaning. Anecdotes, recipes, little sermons, quotations and other bits of information are also interspersed with the narrative. The idea of fiction as a self-conscious medium which draws attention to itself and which creates its own imaginary world comes across partly through the format. Although the success of the book depends partly on these devices and partly on the language of the narrative, Moorhouse jettisons this mode and returns to a more traditional pattern in his subsequent works.

Even in his more conventional stories, however, the intuitive feeling of a careful craftsman at work is evident in the subjective response of the reader, which is sometimes diametrically opposed to what the stories communicate on the surface. Take, for instance, **"The Story of the Knife"** in **Futility.** The story begins with the imminent possibility of separation, but the crisis is averted and the couple decide to forget their differences. This constitutes the moral frame of the story. Paradoxically, the reader is left with a sense of fragmentation. The language, imagery and the subjective associations cut across the harmony of the couple. The final section of **The Everlasting Secret Family** is concerned obsessively with homosexual erotica. The story is shocking, even revolting in its exploration of homosexual practices. At the same time the language suggests a preoccupation with politics, with the master-slave relationship.

The complexity of the stories is inextricably linked with the cumulative effect of the "discontinuous narrative" pattern. Says Clunies Ross:

> His recent volumes are not clusters of stories on the way to becoming novels: they form a genre of their own, quite different from story cycles on the one hand, or novels on the other. It is a genre founded on the arts of short fiction, employing its narrative strategies and potential intensity, while exploring the possibilities of linkage between the pieces to chart an extended imaginary world and shift the reader's perspective on it.[9]

The linkage that Ross speaks of goes through all the collections with remarkable consistency. Cindy, for instance, appears in all the books, adopting different attitudes, changing her partners and defying all attempts at classification. The rather erratic Cindy in **Futility,** who cannot decide whether she wants a child or not, who cannot resolve her emotional pressures, is quite different from the woman in **The Everlasting Secret Family,** who is raped by three aboriginals but is prepared to defend them and even speak up for them. Terri, who wants a child in **Futility,** becomes

totally liberated and sexually aggressive in **The Americans, Baby,** only to become extremely subdued in **The Electrical Experience.** The point is that the reader is given a series of fragments, but any attempt to unify them is frustrated. The reader becomes familiar with the city, its pubs, motels, seminars and parties, with the South Coast and the suburbs. But the characters are always in a state of change. Similar relationships are regarded from different angles. Multiple realities begin to emerge. The author/narrator stance keeps altering, and the reader is constantly confused. The way characters and themes are played off against each other performs the dual function of distancing the reader and also challenging the reader's views. Why, for instance, does the Carl-Johnson relationship seem romantic and the relationship in **The Everlasting Secret Family** seem repulsive? By creating this continual state of flux Moorhouse achieves the effect of open-endedness and ambivalence. Asked in an interview why the Becker-Terri affair breaks down, Moorhouse replies: "No it doesn't break down. We don't know where it's gone, but they're still together."[10] The tentativeness that the author points out is a characteristic feature in the interesting stories dealing with Dell. In one story, she flaunts her politics, her freedom and her fantasies about sex. In another, she fails to cope with the politics of Kim and abandons herself to promiscuity. The reader is left guessing. Very much like a novel, the discontinuous narrative form creates its own world within which the characters operate. At the same time, unlike the novel, the reader is permitted to enter and leave this world at any point. This is why Moorhouse works equally well in an anthology like **The Most Beautiful Lies** and in a collection like **Futility.** The effect on the reader is of course different in each case, but that difference is crucial to Moorhouse's writing.

As in all good modern writing, the narrative voice is a powerful element in Moorhouse's strategy. Speaking primarily of **Tales of Mystery and Romance** and **Conference-Ville,** Ian Reid argues that the narrator adopts the "Third Position" as against the didactic "Missionary Position." Defining the Third Position, Reid says that

> The Third Position is on the border, the margin or limbo-line, which we have already recognised in his previous work: a personal and social dilemma which also shapes the narrative structure itself.[11]

This is not true of all his collections, but he certainly makes use of it in all except **The Electrical Experience,** which employs an omniscient narrator. The self-congratulatory first-person narrator justifies himself at every possible turn and employs magnificent rhetoric to stress his point of view, but the reader is always conscious of multiple ironies, of how the narrator is creating his own fiction to cope with reality. In **"Across the Plains. . ."**[12] the self-conscious narrator's fictionalized version of reality is punctured when his ex-girlfriend tells him that she cannot remember a thing of what he said. In **"I Am a Very Clean Person"**[13] Moorhouse introduces both the third-person and the first-person narrative, thus giving the reader two equally plausible versions. The use of the first person narrator is at its best in **"The American Poet's Visit."**[14] In this story, as in **"The Dance of the Chain"** in *The Everlasting Secret Family,* the link between the narrator and the author is clear, perhaps intentionally so. In **"The Dance of the Chain,"** the narrator says that he is from Balmain and takes delight in conferences—both of which are true of Moorhouse. In **"The American Poet's Visit,"** the narrator says at one point, "I write for a girlie magazine—a sort of imitation *Playboy*" (p. 59), evidently a playful reference to the initial publishing problems of the author. The narrator in this story is the odd man out, always guilty of one *faux pas* or another, distrusting his own language. He must follow up a joke by saying "J-O-K-E" so that he will not be misunderstood. The narrator contributes immensely to the sense of play, the sheer inventiveness of the whole fiction. His bumbling exposes the sham, the elaborate game played by both the visiting poet and his Australian counterparts to mask their hypocrisy. In this story the main thrust is satiric and the narrator achieves it by becoming the butt of ridicule. Quite a different effect is gained by the first-person narrator in the final section of *The Everlasting Secret Family.* In all Moorhouse's writing, **"An Erotic Memoir in Six Parts"** is the most explicitly sexual, and the most disgusting. The sado-masochistic narrator's obvious delight in repeating the sordid details of his sexual encounters is a conscious device to alienate the reader. The repetitive mention of confined spaces such as the car, the motel room, the townhouse and lavatories create the oppressive, claustrophobic atmosphere that permeates the narrative. The narrator's grim parody of prayer by obliging a man in a church is intentionally shocking. His self-pity, self-abasement, his malice in dressing up as a woman to alienate his partner's wife, his incest in humiliating his "child" and his perverse loitering around lavatories have the cumulative effect of undercutting the final assertion that he "was joined to a line through history which went back to the first primitive tribal person . . . who took a virgin boy lover" (p. 204). The narrative voice is instrumental in transforming a celebration of homosexuality into a castigation of it.

As important as the narrative voice is Moorhouse's use of recurring motifs, symbols, sexuality and language. These often shape, alter or determine the meaning. Take, for instance, the use of the child motif. Significantly, the author begins his first collection, *Futility,* by referring to the dilemma of giving birth, and goes back to it at the end of his recent work, *The Everlasting Secret Family.* Here, the narrator, having humiliated a boy, who is also his "child," says that

> It was a way of passing on and preserving the special reality, a way of giving new life, the birth for the boy of a new reality, a joining of him to a secret family, the other family.

> (p. 204)

This morbid assertion after the "initiation ritual" is that of the narrator, not the author. In any case, nothing is conclusive in Moorhouse, and hence the episode does not in any way invalidate the other dimensions generated by the child motif. Often in *Futility,* and occasionally in *The Americans, Baby,* the issue of child bearing becomes a central concern. At one level, characters do not want children simply because they are a nuisance and would become a hindrance to their lifestyle. Anderson, for instance, dreams of going abroad, and hence opposes the idea of having a child. But even as the characters argue about it, the reader is aware of other psychological factors. For the women, the child means a denial of freedom, an assertion of their vulnerability. For both sexes the child implies a future which they do not wish to face. It is also a reminder of another world of stable values which they have rejected yet secretly long for.

The complex working out of the child motif is perhaps best illustrated in the three stories involving Cindy. In the first story, she walks out on Hugo because he throws away the contraceptives and suggests that they have children. To deny her the pill is to deny her freedom, and she sees his act as an attempt to reassert male domination. As she tells him, "You're like all men—you think we can be used for your—fantasies."[15] In the second story, Cindy desperately wants a child. She becomes aware that the pill in giving her freedom from sexual responsibility has trapped her into yet another enslavement—enslavement to the pill. She says,

> Women are free now because they control contraception and it is premeditated contraception and she can be free of pregnancy and unhampered by devices and totally relaxed about it, but it means a sexual routine, a medical regimen . . . and I've broken the regimen and am exposed to pregnancy . . . and giving up control of my body and reliant on a man to care for me, to be my . . . hunter and my soldier.

> (p. 152)

The shifting narration, the continuous, hysterical movement of the lines and the fantasy implied in "hunter" and "soldier" undercut the assertion of freedom and create a fruitful ambivalence. Ironically, she discovers that she is not, after all, pregnant. In the third story, she actually conceives but rejects the assistance of her mother who comes to look after her. She can neither tolerate the order and discipline of her mother nor the freedom and slovenliness of her "husband." Her pregnancy, in the final analysis, instead of resolving the problems, only heightens them.

The notion of child bearing also implies the notion of sex, which figures prominently as a controlling device in Moorhouse. In fact, Moorhouse's reputation as an avant-garde writer is inextricably linked with his explicit treatment of sex, although critics strangely do not often draw attention to it. In a general way, Michael Wilding says that "New Writing often deals with sex. Not always, not compulsively, not inevitably—but often,"[16] although he does not specifically refer to Moorhouse. On the other hand, John Docker states that sexuality and politics are directly linked to Moorhouse. Commenting specifically on *The Americans, Baby,* he says that "Throughout the book there is an opposition between sexuality and politics."[17] In a literal sense, this is true of a number of stories where sex becomes a means of undercutting political commitment or expressing political domination. But to insist on it would be to claim that Moorhouse is essentially a political writer and that sexuality is a device to explore its dimensions.

Sexuality appears in various forms—promiscuity, masturbation, homosexuality, fantasy and perversion. By dramatizing the fantasies associated with sex, the writer brings to the surface the anxieties, guilt feelings and repressed desires of the reader. In a country which has denied quite deliberately the reality of the id, such explicit treatment of it is a challenge to the reader. It does not, however, usually evoke a negative response as the characters tend to pay a heavy price for the domination of the id. The process of displacement is so subtle and effective that the reader is able to view the expression of the id with a certain degree of detachment.

In terms of theme, however, sexuality is associated with fantasy, with a way of coming to terms with uncertain and shifting values. All Moorhouse characters are uprooted, alienated and in perpetual conflict with internal pressures. For them sex becomes a means of temporary escape. Nish and McDowell are two characters who cannot indulge in satisfying sex, and hence must fantasize about it. McDowell carefully conceals his sexual fantasies and does not let them affect his pattern of respectable social behaviour. His fantasies help him to cope with the reality of an unattractive wife. Nish cannot control his obsessive fantasies, and is fast becoming neurotic through unfulfilled desires.

Other characters, particularly in *Futility* and *The Americans, Baby,* indulge compulsively in sex, yet Moorhouse rarely depicts a truly satisfying sexual experience. Certainly nothing conveys the impression that sex is a biological need. For some, it is a desperate way of affirming identity. In **"Dell Goes into Politics."**[18] Dell's thoughts constantly revolve around sex. She cannot even look at her younger brother, who is a mere child, without vividly picturing his sexual potential. We recognize at the end that these thoughts become a means of allaying her feelings of anxiety regarding her pregnancy. The connection between sexuality and fantasy comes across vividly in **"The Etiquette of Deception."**[19] Irving, the proprietor of the Odeon cinema, reprimands the children for indulging in the pure fantasy of the illusory world of the film, and then he walks "along the passage under the floor of the cinema, thinking of the young white bottoms and groins squirming with nervous excitement" (p. 12). The significance of walking along an underground passage and the tonal irony confirm the relation between sex and fantasy.

The element of fantasy disappears from the treatment of homosexuality, which is always presented as a compulsive force which breaks up the conventional man-woman relationship. In many stories, there is a sense of dormant homosexuality which is captured through symbols. The author's attitude to homosexuality, however, remains uncertain. If there is a celebration of it in the Carl-Johnson stories, there is a definite rejection of it in *The Everlasting Secret Family.* In both cases, homosexuality is associated with the process of self-discovery. The self-discovery initiated by homosexuality does not lead to any alternation of social behaviour, but that is in keeping with the open-endedness of his stories.

Another aspect of form which determines the complexity of the stories is the constant recourse to symbols. In the very first story in *Futility,* the knife is a symbol. On the surface, it is a phallic symbol expressing male sexuality, and at least one character sees it as such. But the couple's unconscious response to it suggests other possible meanings. For the woman, it is possibly a symbol of destruction, a way of punishing herself, presumably to expiate a sense of guilt. For the man, it is a symbol of homosexuality, and he needs it in order to consummate his love for the woman. Significantly, his desire for the woman comes at moments when he is handling the knife. Another classic use of symbolism occurs in the Irving Bow stories, where the cinema operates at various levels. It becomes a symbol of Irving's lasciviousness, his repressed desires and his subconscious. All the underground passages, the rooms that are never opened, the images of the temple and the dragon coalesce to produce the symbolic undertones which provide the essential tension of the stories—the tension between public and private life.

All these aspects eventually lead to the question of language, which, after all, is the medium within which the author operates. Moorhouse is not a conscious stylist, and he doesn't often foreground style to achieve his effects. But he is confronted with the problem of finding a language to express a new sensibility. In other words, the language he has inherited is associated with certain basic assumptions regarding social behaviour and the universe. That world is no longer available and hence language too must undergo a process of adaptation. At its most obvious, the author makes use of "new" terms like "square," "camp," "kook" and so forth. He also insists on naming sexual organs and sexual acts. These words, in their own way, help to create a world which is distinct from that of the earlier generation. He also uses a tonal irony which becomes functional in controlling the response of the reader. There is, for instance, the title, **"The Town Philosopher's Banquet."**[20] The characters in this story are anything but philosophers, and the banquet is an orgy. When the two children come in and provide vicarious sexual indulgence, George says very correctly that it is "artistic too" (p. 32). Language here becomes a means of concealing thought, and the writer deliberately draws attention to the ambivalence of language. In quite a different way, the language of sexuality in *The Everlasting Secret Family* becomes indirectly the language of politics as well. The rape of Cindy by the three aboriginals and the homosexuality between the minister and the boy are described in a language which points to the political concern of the writer. The rape turns out to be a confrontation between the blacks and the whites.

Moorhouse's awareness and exploitation of the potential of language promises further development. But if the past is anything to go by, then he is likely to remain a writer who is continually looking forward while being aware of the reverberations of what has already been achieved. Keeping track of certain recurring aspects of form and language thus becomes one possible way of interpreting the significance of Moorhouse's short stories.

Notes

1. *Futility and Other Animals* (1969; Sydney: Angus and Robertson, 1973). Prefatory material is unpaginated.

2. *The Everlasting Secret Family and Other Secrets* (Sydney: Angus and Robertson, 1980), pp. 120-21.

3. Brian Kiernan, ed., *The Most Beautiful Lies* (Sydney: Angus and Robertson, 1977), p. 149.

4. Interview with Frank Moorhouse, *Meanjin,* 36 (1977), p. 170.

5. John Docker, *Australian Cultural Elites* (Sydney: Angus and Robertson, 1974), p. 160.

6. In his response to "Questionnaire to Authors," *Australian Literary Studies,* 10 (1981), p. 222.

7. Michael Wilding, ed., *The Tabloid Story Pocket Book* (Sydney: Wild and Woolley, 1978), p. 307.

8. Bruce A. Clunies Ross, "Laszlo's Testament or Structuring the Past and Sketching the Present in Contemporary Short Fiction, Mainly Australian," *Kunapipi,* 1, No. 2 (1979), p. 112.

9. Bruce Clunies Ross, "Some Developments in Short Fiction, 1960-1980," *Australian Literary Studies,* 10 (1981), p. 177.

10. Interview with Moorhouse, p. 160.

11. Ian Reid, "Writing from the Third Position: Frank Moorhouse's Recent Fiction," *Meanjin,* 37 (1978), p. 170.

12. *Futility,* pp. 39-42.

13. *Futility,* pp. 70-6.

14. *The Americans, Baby* (Sydney: Angus and Robertson, 1972), pp. 53-63.

15. *Futility,* p. 54.

16. Wilding, p. 310.

17. Docker, p. 61.

18. *The Americans, Baby*, pp. 1-8.

19. *The Everlasting Secret Family,* pp. 10-20.

20. *The Everlasting Secret Family,* pp. 28-37.

Simone Vauthier (essay date 1988)

SOURCE: "Ventriloquist's Act: Frank Moorhouse's 'Pledges, Vows and Pass This Note,'" in *Recherches Anglaises et Nord-Americaines*, Vol. XXI, 1988, pp. 97-112.

[*In the following essay, Vauthier offers a close reading of Moorhouse's short story "Pledges, Vows and Pass the Note," and analyzes thematic and stylistic aspects of the story.*]

By now, the relevance to "post-modernist" fiction of John Hawkes's "assumption that the true enemies of the novel were plot, character, setting and theme" hardly needs pointing out.[1] That in the process of doing away with the old elements of narrative, contemporary fictionists have also been playing games with the traditional "modes" has not received as much critical attention.[2] Yet in many short stories, *description* has often taken over from *report,* or *comment*—including narratorial comment, that bugaboo—recovered a place it had lost in modernist fiction. In **"Pledges, Vows and Pass this Note,"** Australian writer Frank Moorhouse offers a very good example of a radical manipulation of modes which, together with his selection of material, results in effects very close to those of American fictionists of the period.[3]

The Title

On the threshold of the story the title already signals a departure from narrative conventions with its rupture of syntactical and semantic expectations: after two nouns isotopically related, we expected another, perhaps contrastive, noun—a sequence like pledges, vows and betrayals. What we encounter is a verb or rather a clause, which recontextualizes the first two words. The nominal half of the title designates actions and constitutes a simple statement: it suggests that pledges and vows have been made in an unspecified time and place which we are going to be told about. But the verbal syntagm has illocutionary force. A socio-cultural formula, it implies that the locutor is passing on the note and it requires the allocutor to hand it on. Since we are the ultimate receivers of "this note" we too are committed. The title therefore operates a sort of reversal: by nominalizing "vows" and "pledges" it has evacuated the performative value of the corresponding verbs, but recovers illocutionary power with the verbal syntagm. It is as if the events to be narrated were devalorized in advance while the act of writing retains some efficacy. At the same time, "vows" and "pledges" connote the solemnity of contracts between two main parties while "pass this note", on the contrary, involves a third unconcerned party and connotes a school-room atmosphere. In short, we are jostled into an anticipation of ruptures and nudged into a serio-comic mode.

A Montage of Fragmented Discourses

"Pledges" does deviate from narrative conventions in that it relies exclusively on the mode of speech.[4] The text is a series of acts of interlocution, most of which take place between a man and a woman—not always the same one. It is a mosaic of utterances in free direct discourse, juxtaposed without even minimal connective tissue. As we embark on the story, only the content and illocutionary force of the sentences tell us that they are supposed to be oral utterances: "Pass this note. He wants an answer. Pass this note and do not read it. He wants an answer. Will you be my girl-friend? I like you: do you like me?"(85). And so on for 23 lines after which the lay-out changes: each statement is isolated in a discrete paragraph:

Please don't do that.

Not there, not yet.

I'm not that sort of girl.

(86)

Because only snatches of dialogue are offered, the story is not a scene or a sequence of scenes but a montage of fragmented discourses.

As we shall see, **"Pledges"** amply proves that one can "do things with words" and that "speech" can therefore supplant "report". Interestingly, the absence of "description" is perhaps more immediately felt: among other things, the characters have no physical features and events occur in a sort of limbo. (The very few places mentioned, *not described,* in the exchanges do not belong to the topic space, but to some paratopic space as in "But I saw you with her in the coffee shop", 87). The reader, at first, feels called upon to supply a backdrop and easily conjures up a school setting for the first part of the story. But as the story proceeds and the locus of the transactions keeps changing, this placelessness becomes more than absence—a positive feature intended to block visualization: we no longer feel compelled to construct, however vaguely, the missing background; rather we hear disembodied voices speaking not out of a stage setting but, as it were, against a white screen, the blankness of the page. Meanwhile, the story has provided us with an opportunity to test, *in absentia,* the role of description.

THE NARRATIVE AGENT

Because the words seem to come to us unmediated, **"Pledges"** also draws attention to the role of the narrator. According to Seymour Chatman, the term "narrator" should be used only to mean "the someone—person of presence—actually telling the story to an audience, no matter how minimally evoked his voice or the audience's listening ear. A narrative that does not give the sense of this presence, one that has gone to noticeable lengths to efface it, may reasonably be called "non-narrated" or "un-narrated" (33-34). To be sure, no such "voice" or "listening ear" is evoked in **"Pledges."** But if one defines the narrator more inclusively as a set of narrative procedures, some of these procedures become in our story all the more important precisely because the strictly narrating function has been eliminated.[5] To simplify the discussion I will personify the functions operating in the narrative.

Although the narrative agent does not use "report", the strictly narrative mode, he nevertheless exercises some of a narrator's (or should I say a scriptor's) major responsibilities: he selects and arranges his material. Purporting to transcribe a series of oral communications, he in fact pro-

duces a montage of fragments of conversation, even fragments of sentences, which presuppose an absent context. Thus a phrase like "The cold light of day" is evidently a segment of a longer utterance. Moreover the women characters are granted many more lines than the man. The disproportion, which comforts two gender stereotypes, points to the control of the narrator: since the woman's utterances are often replies [e.g. "Not on the first date", (87) "Of course it's yours . . . I resent that", (88)] the man's side of the exchange has been suppressed and the succession of statements does not reproduce dialogues as they might be recorded on a tape, thereby hinting at the true nature of fiction.

Out of such ruthlessly selected and discontinuous snatches, the narrating agent makes a *narrative, that is to say a sequence* which has a *thematic and temporal* unity. All these fragments are arranged in chronological order and tell the story of a male character's sexual relationships: it has a beginning in the schoolboy's interest in female schoolmates, a protracted middle—the young man's sexual experiences, his marriage when the girl, after several "false alarms", is pregnant—and an end—his extra-marital adventures and finally the break-up of the marriage, his joining "the race of men" who "roam the world at will". The ending is therefore marked inasmuch as the male actor, so far only glimpsed in his relationships with women, seems to be leaving the world of women behind, yet open inasmuch as the pattern of repetition is so insistent as to make us doubt the protagonist's ability to escape from the "compulsion to repeat". In fact, the macro-story is itself composed of similar micro-stories with beginning, middle and end. Although the full pattern is not always deployed, they go from "What is your name?" (85, 87) to "One-track mind" (87, 88) to "We've broken up". Thus although there are no time markers, the sequence is strongly temporal. "I'm interested in time-frame traps", Frank Moorhouse said in an interview (323). **"Pledges"** is such a time-frame trap.

Within the chronological order, however, the narrator still uses his privilege of *manipulating time*. His use of ellipsis may be forceful [as in "It's all over between us. / I missed you too", (87)] or more transparent. In any case, the selection subordinates the sequencing of the reported conversations to that of the overall story for we do not have discrete interactions complete with beginning, middle and end. A question like "What's your name?" inagurates both a specific act of communication and a narrative "function" (Barthes) but since the ensuing dialogue is not quoted, it is the opening of the "function" which is privileged. More innovatively, the narrator finds ways to circumvent the temporal limitations of utterances that only concern present feelings or attitudes. In the following example, the repetition of an identical formula in which only the love-object's initials change serves as a capsule of many identical boyish infatuations and hence a *summary*: "FM L NJ true. FM L JS true. FM L FL true. FM L JJ true" (85). (Needless to say, the succession and the fact that the one uncoded word is "true" make the declaration ironical and the reduction of "love" to L quasi prophetic of the movement from "love" to loss.) Generally the frequent regrouping of paradigmatic units serves to suggest the recurrence of similar scenes, hence the passing of time. Take for instance

> I don't want to feel guilty about it.
>
> I don't want it to be furtive.
>
> I don't want it to be something we just do.
>
> (86)

The alignment of the statements serves to convey some kind of duration. Such anaphoric regroupings, moreover, reveal the highly fabricated character of the syntagmatic chain which is chronological but not mimetically so, as is amusingly illustrated in these three lines:

> But how could you: She's my best friend!
>
> But how could you: She's old enough to be your mother!
>
> But how could you: She's been with everyone in town.
>
> (89)

The anaphora underlines the boring sameness of these jealous outbursts, while the change in reference of "She" indicates that time has passed between each of the scenes, a time which may well have been filled with the complaints that, paradigmatically gathered together, precede the passage just quoted: "Talk to me once in a while. / It may have escaped your notice but I live here too. / You'd feel better if you talked about it" (89). We might say, to paraphrase Jakobson, that the narrator projects the principle of equivalence from the axis of selection upon the axis of structural combination. In other words, he is showing his poetic hand. Conversely, some lines only add up synonymous phrases. "Going out together. Going around together. Going steady. / Sort of engaged. On together" (87). In such "syllepses" (Genette, 121) the flow of time is almost abrogated. Similarly, "We've broken up. We've busted up. He broke it off" (87) makes a temporal synthesis of several statements which presumably were not uttered at the same moment and do not carry the same aspectual status. The conclusion is inescapable: all these apparently discontinuous utterances that seem to reach us without mediation have been arranged into a skillful montage.

VOICES

While speech is made to serve the purposes of narrative, it cannot fulfill its own role unambiguously because of the lack of *narrative* relay. Normally, inquits and even quotation marks assign ownership. In **"Pledges"** it is not always possible to decide to which locutor a statement must be ascribed or whether two consecutive lines belong to two different locutors or not. We must rely on the content or the context of the utterance for this distribution. Clearly, the exchange "I've never kissed a girl like this before. I bet you say that to all the girls" (85) offers no problem. Nor does "No . . . I won't find out the name of a doctor"

(88). But if we say that "we were made for each other" (88) sounds more female than male, we are depending on socio-cultural gender images. And what about "We'll call it off then" (87)? There is no stichomythic pattern to guide us. In addition, the syllepses I have mentioned raise the question of their origin. To give another example, is the following list to be accepted as a single statement emanating from the character: "I'm pregnant. I'm with child. I'm expecting. I'm in the pudding club. I'm in the family way. Bun in the oven" (88)? It would seem not. Such recurring thesaurus-like entries appear to be *narratorial* micromontages within the overall macro-montage.

To complicate things, the speakers are only identified through initials (given only once in the women's case) and through the use of pronouns, I and You, the reference of which keeps shifting with each speech act, so that the pronoun I cannot serve as a name, as it does in traditional narratives (Barthes 1970, 74-75). Consider the line "We've broken up. We've busted up. I broke it off" (87). This is a repetition with one pronominal variation of an earlier line "We've broken up. We've busted up. He broke it off" (87), the last sentence of which is spoken by the woman. But the variation "*I* broke it off" makes it impossible to assign the utterance to either speaker with grammatical certainty. So the variation may either signal a change in the attitude of the woman, now desirous to be the one who took the initiative of the break-up—an idea which the recurrence of the two we's somewhat undermines. Or it may signal the man's pleasure at having escaped from a tiresome entanglement; his belief in mastery is similarly undercut by the two we's and the two intransitive verbs. And who utters that conjunctive "we" which in the immediate context (and the macrocontext) is rather ironical?[6]

Sometimes, then, we do not know who is speaking. If it hardly matters for our understanding of the events, it matters for our interpretation of the narration. The point is that the presentation of their exchanges disoriginates the characters' voices, which are unassigned, unlocatable.

Such dis-originating, certainly, does not simply result from the presentational process but also from the nature of the presented world, which is the world of the *cliché*.[7] Before we come to this, however, I must briefly examine the other voices in the text.

So far I have only referred to the characters' discourses. But **"Pledges"** is also a *collage* in which pre-existing texts—popular songs, ballads, religious ritual, poems—are embedded in the montage of fragments of conversation. Considered from the point of view of their insertion, their textual status differs. For instance the fragment of the marriage service (89) can be attributed to the minister: "Dearly beloved we are gathered together here in the sight of God, and in the face of this congregation, to join together this Man and this Woman in holy Matrimony" (89). The utterance therefore stands on the same level as the others, although of course two voices can be heard, the collective voice of ritual and the voice of the celebrant. Some of the other collage elements, on the other hand, are quotations within quotations. When we read "They tried to tell us we're too young, too young to be really in love" we recognize lines from a popular song inserted into the speech of either or both the youthful lovers. The typography indeed indicates as much in the following example:

> True love has a guardian angel on high with nothing to do but to care for you and to care for me, love forever true. But that's all you want to do now when we go out.

(88)

From the lay-out, the two statements seem part of the same fragment, ascribable to the woman. (Needless to say the idea of the angel in the second-degree quotation clashes comically with the young man's intentions implied in the first-degree quotation.) Such quotations are never acknowledged by the characters who appropriate them. Hence the possibility of confusion. Faced with the reluctance of his girl, the young man quotes four lines from Donne's "The Flea" and, since this does not persuade her, four more lines from Marvell's "To his coy Mistress". If for the reader, the voice of the poet supersedes that of the plagiarizing character, the woman addressed, not recognizing the poem and apparently oblivious to the poetic form of the utterance, focusses on the content of the message and responds to the poet's words as if they were her lover's: "But we have our whole life ahead of us" (86). The commonsense remark can only strike the reader as funny and ironical in its effects. Apparently Marvell's rhetoric does not work either so that further down Donne's "How little that which thou deny'st me is . . ." turns up again. The single line, however, has a different effect on the reader; thus isolated and with the three dots at the end, it sounds like a form of shorthand for a longer speech, which the narrating agent feels no need to reproduce in its entirety.[8] Furthermore, it is followed by another quotation from a well-known American folk song: "Love oh love oh careless love" (86).[9] Who quotes from this lament of a woman seduced and betrayed? Certainly not the young man. The woman? But in all her arguments against yielding to his advances, this would be the only one in which she indirectly expresses doubts about him. So it is tempting to hear through the refrain another *voice* which counterpoints with mild cynicism the declarations of lovers, whether the diegetic lovers, or those of Donne, who has just been cited, or of Marvell, etc. In this view, the collage and montage of out-referential speech serves the purpose of *comment,* and these lines constitute an exception to the absence of a *narrative voice.* But in any case, this voice is hidden behind that of the quoted utterances and only perceptible in the dialogism (Bakhtin) of the word.

THE TRIUMPH OF THE CLICHÉ

The illustrations intended to throw light on various aspects of the short story must also have demonstrated the importance of clichés. To start with larger units, **"Pledges"** accumulates what Laurent Jenny calls "clichés narratifs"

(501), set sequences of actions the model of which exists prior to the text.[10] Here, of course, it is the familiar pattern, boy meets girl—boy wins girl—boy loses girl, which prevails. When considered from a thematic angle, these sequences give rise, for instance, to the formula X loves Y, a theme whose stereotyped nature is such that it can be expressed through a code "FM L WH true" (88), or they generate the fixed phrases denoting the end of a relationship, "we've broken up", "it's all over", etc.[11] Another cliché of the seduction scene is the lover's quoting poetry.

Furthermore, such narrative clichés, which bring together the out-referential world and the fictional world, also return as in-referential clichés within the text. The narrative is riddled with repetitions. These repetitions can link different micro-stories, like the opening gambit "What's your name" (two occurrences on page 85 and one on page 87) or the mid-affair reproach, "one-track mind" (87, 88). Thus the two main love stories offer such striking parallels that the narrative clichés become clichés of the narration itself which jells, as it were, into recurring set situations. Even within one love affair, the exchange between the partners is a rehashing of the same situations and words. In the following quotation, the lines which are either repeats, or announcements of another, will give an idea of the intrication of the structure:

> You only like me because I let you do it.
>
> But I saw you with her in the coffee shop.
>
> How could you?
>
> I'm not jealous.
>
> I just don't like two-timers.
>
> You're free to do what you want and I'm free to do what I want.
>
> I think it will give us time to see if we really love each other.
>
> We'll call it off then.
>
> We've broken up. We've busted up. He broke it off.
>
> It's all over between us.
>
> I missed you too.
>
> The best part of breaking up is making up.
>
> This time it is for keeps.
>
> But don't ever to that to me again, promise?
>
> Don't you ever think of anything else?
>
> You only like me because I let you do it.
>
> But I saw you looking at her.
>
> Really, I'm different.
>
> We'll call it off then.
>
> We've broken up. We've busted up. I broke it off.
>
> I've given him up as a bad job.
>
> It's all over between us.

(87)

Every communication rings with the hollow echo of past communications. The language of love and lust is mechanical.

In such cases the distinction between the clichéd situation and the verbal cliché becomes very tenuous. The characters' language indeed is so hackneyed that the individual clichés do not really stand out against a neutral background (Riffaterre, 175). One may at best find a difference between contextual clichés as in: "There is something you should know. / I can't tell you over the telephone" and general clichés as in "I am overdue. / False alarm.: [. . .] I am in the pudding club. I'm in the family way. Bun in the oven." (88) Foregrounding of the clichés under the circumstances is provided by a non-linguistic device, the blanks in the lay-out.

The only evident binary opposition is between verse and prose. Yet some of the verse quoted is itself clichéd. After his wife's reproaches, the husband justifies his wandering eye with a quotation from a ballad—which earns him the reply "Poetry doesn't mend anything" (89). The lines given are themselves built on a series of stereotypes and fixed expressions:

> There's a race of men that don't fit in,
> It's a race that can't be still,
> So they break the hearts of kith and kin,
> And they roam the world at will.[12]

(89)

Line 3, indeed, is produced by the conjoining of two set phrases. If the Donne and Marvell poems defamiliarize, in different ways, lyrical *topoi,* investing them with a note of parody, **"Pledges,"** by having the protagonist use the lines in his various attempts at seduction, turns them into clichés in its own system. Yet, at the same time, their insertion into the diegetic conversation confers upon them a new value; and if the speaker intends them to serve the same purpose of persuading a coy mistress, they nevertheless assume a new illocutionary force because they are part of a supposedly 'real' exchange. The narrative therefore both confirms the superior authority of classic poetry over ordinary language and undercuts that authority by debasing it and showing that life and art are continuous, dialectically linked through an ongoing process of stereotyping/defamiliarizing/re-stereotyping. (As a consequence, the woman's somewhat improbable acceptance of Donne's verse as simply her lover's words can be read as a metafictional questioning of the boundary between literature and life.)

After this examination of some of the story's technical features, we are now in a position to recapitulate what has happened to the conventional narrative elements.

CHARACTERS?

Although the most important function of speech "and certainly the one most productive of interest and variety" is widely held to be "the presentation and development of character (Page, 51), Frank Moorhouse in **"Pledges"** uses speech to undermine character in its interest and variety.

What the characters mouth is so humdrum and repetitive that the number of features their speech enables us to attach to them is very limited. The two women heap the same reproaches on the man: the accusation, "one-track mind", on page 87 is echoed on page 88, the rhetorical question "Don't you ever think of anything else?" (87) picked up on page 88,—and the irony is that the two complaints, dissimilar on the discourse level, actually boil down to the same semantic message. Although the second woman has a few more features (a child, marriage, a greater awareness of the passing of time), she is only a copy of the first, who anyway believed herself married "even if the world doesn't know it", (87). Similarly the man resorts to the same plots and quotations with both—until the end when metaphysical poetry has become irrelevant and the ballad of the roaming men provides him with a justifying generalization. These people can only say what has been said, heard, read countless times, can only speak a sort of mechanical sociolect. For instance, the women's early coyness, expressed only through clichés,—"I'm not that sort of girl" (86) or "Not on the first date" (87)—is deflated to the socially coded language of Western middle-class culture before the "sexual revolution".[13] 'Listening' in to the characters' exchanges, we keep hearing other voices.

The word "character" which I have employed so far is therefore inappropriate, albeit convenient. These paper beings have neither the "psychological depth" associated with the traditional story nor even the elaborate linguistic surfaces attached to some contemporary characters. Cartoon-like, they could come out of a book by Claire Brétecher. The initials—sparingly used at that—which designate them slyly mock their individuality and even humanity. "Ce qui est caduc aujourd'hui dans le roman, ce n'est pas le romanesque, c'est le personnage; ce qui ne peut plus être écrit, c'est le Nom Propre" (Barthes, 1970, 102). Their redundant speech shows them up as reduced to roles—actorial gender roles (experimenting boy/sex-driven adolescent/wandering lover and husband, or coy mistress/jealous lover/nagging wife) determined by socio-cultural patterns.[14] Such "existents" (Chatman) deviate from a basic law of "novelistic character [which] is conceived as a challenge to repetition, a rupture in the duty imposed on all men to breed and multiply, to create and recreate oneself unremittingly and repeatedly" (Said, 117). In Barthes's terms, they are not *personnages* but *figures* inasmuch as they are restricted to a configuration of symbolic relations. As such, however, they become Everyman/Everywoman. Disturbing mirrors of ourselves. Disconcerting echoes of our voices.

PLOT?

While the narrator, as we have seen, structures a sequence out of montage of utterances, nevertheless the whole concept of plot as causal organization is questioned.

Linear succession prevails, imposing on the story its "pseudo-natural status" and proving Shlomith Rimmon-Kenan's argument that "temporal succession is sufficient as a *minimal* requirement for a group of events to form a story" (18). A second principle of combination in the macro-sequence is the linking of micro-sequences which develop through increasing expansion a similar pattern (meeting-winning-losing): this seems akin to the second "formative principle" of "dialogue" in the Bakhtin-Kristeva sense, which combines "transfinite sequences that are next-larger to the preceding causal series" and in which "symbolic relationships and analogy take precedence over substance-causality connexions" (Julia Kristeva, 72). If we may say that there is no plot at the macro-level, on the other hand, we may remark that there is almost too much of it at the micro-level where the Aristotelian basics of beginning, middle and end are very much in evidence. Thus the idea of plot is undermined from two opposing directions. What with the flagrant stereotyping of the events and the repetitiveness of the narrative sequences, which are ways of "laying bare" the conventions of plot, **"Pledges"** comes close to being an anti-story.

THEMES

Of all the fundamental elements of narrative, theme is the one which seems to survive unimpaired. To begin with the most obvious, **"Pledges"** is undoubtedly "about" man/woman relationships, the comedy of sexuality. And "about" the breaking of pledges and vows. But the structural features of the story modalize, as it were, the thematic pitch, making **"Pledges"** an anti-*love* story. For instance, since pledges and vows are only mentioned in the title, the absence of the words in the text invites us to consider the place of promises, which though not explicitly made are yet broken, in the narrated lives, and perhaps to regard them as part of a schoolchildren's code which has no relevance to sexual reality. (Should I pass this note?) The structure of repetition which informs the narrative cannot fail to have repercussions of the reader's construction of meaning. In the first place, it makes breaking-up seem inevitable, thereby forestalling moral judgment. In the second, it points to the "futility" of it all.[15] Any change will only bring a return of the same. Sexuality is reduced to a mechanical function and love deprived of its vital spontaneity. In the third place, the repetition structure raises the problem of story telling: why weave a thematic web that can only appear threadbare?

Similarly the other major theme to emerge constitutes a *topos* of literature: even if Moorhouse's actors believe that they express their feelings, the text denounces the characters' illusions that they are persons, making free choices, including linguistic choices. It ironically shows up that they can only repeat and unconsciously parody what other lovers have said through the ages whether in a pedestrian mode or in a more elevated one. The *topos,* however, is to some extent renewed by its treatment. **"Pledges"** *enlarges* the theme of how shopworn and debased the language of *love* is into a more radical investigation of language for

which the speech of lovers offers a synecdochic test case. The most intimate choice of a human being—his or her sexual relationships—is in fact moulded through a *public language,* a *socio-cultural code,* even if the code uses great love poetry. When the locutor believes he is most fully a "subject", he or she is being revealed as fully subjected to the law of language which speaks him or her, and therefore as *dispossessed* of his/her speech. Creating 'characters' which are only disembodied voices, the narration ultimately deprives them of their speech. But the failure of the actors is the failure of language itself, the codes of which always fall short of desire and of the real. This, rather than the (anti) love story, is the overarching theme of the text.

It would seem then that the 'new' form of the story is no obstacle to thematization. However, we must recall that thematization is a virtuality to be observed only through the mediation of the reader's interpretation. "[L]a limite entre l'autothématisation du texte et son hétérothématisation par le lecteur est vouée à être, non par insufissance d'analyse mais par principe, l'enjeu d'une indécidable querelle de frontière" (Claude Brémond, 61). On this indecidable frontier, who is to say that it is not my need to thematize, nurtured by the old forms of narrative, which prevails over the self-reflexivity of the text? As Laurent Jenny remarks (517), "la multiplicité des clichés tend de plus à discréditer la capacité de vraisemblable de toute rhétorique. La rhétorique est dénoncée par le cliché comme ne renvoyant à rien d'autre qu'à elle-même. Le cliché devient métalangage". Here, however, metalanguage maintains the elusive link which exists between language and social "reality". In answer to a questionnaire, Frank Moorhouse 1981, 323) stated that "formal, aesthetic considerations *and* social, moral, political issues interest me and show up in my fiction. I have in my work, dialogues which are endless—with gender, with the notion of 'commitment', with nationality, with self—and with form". To construct the themes of **"Pledges"** is the reader's way of entering this dialogue with contributions that must remain tentative, or at least open. Yet, to the extent that the problematics of language is a familiar concern of post-modern fiction, this participation is likely to embroil him/her in a discussion that is on the way to being a commonplace of contemporary criticism. Unlike the helpful schoolmate who is not to read the note, the critic is intended to read the story and to become the included third, as I know, to my own risk.

On the other hand, the dialogue with form in **"Pledges"** involves defamiliarizing the clichés which it trots out. Normally, renewing a cliché implies transformation of the set phrase through various substitutions (see Riffaterre, 169-70). But **"Pledges"** which strings together clichés in all their pristine purity, has to find other forms of defamiliarization.

THE CLICHÉS AGAIN

After the first page, the typographical presentation of the characters' utterances break away from narrative norms and from dramatic norms as well.[16] In fact these utterances look like verse (and the quotations from poems or songs cannot be differentiated at one glance).[17] To be sure, the blank spaces at the end of lines do not suffice to turn the text into versified prose. But they enable it to function partly like a poem: they emphasize the equivalence relation between units;[18] they impose a different attitude upon the reader, a certain rhythm to his/her reading, which is not that of prose, a certain delay. They make the text more readable—to go through pages of stereotypes aligned without pause, as in the first paragraph, might be very tiresome—yet to some extent less easy to decipher. The clichés stand out in their psitaccism, yet, being "made strange" (Shklovski), recover some pregnance, or the possibility of an added meaningfulness. Or take another instance of foregrounding: "My darling. Darling. Yours forever. Only yours. SWALK. With all the love in my heart" (86). In the accumulation of professions of love, the ostentatious acronym, visually drawing attention to itself and to the sequence, introduces a new semantic possibility (walk) absent from its other version (SWAK, sealed with a kiss), a possibility which enters into the isotopy of walking away and sets in relief the nature of the accumulated formulae, which are letter *ends*. Thus the characters' statements are doubled for the reader by a metaphoric meaning which goes counter to the first-level content.

The text further plays on the ambivalence of clichés by making them necessary to an understanding of what is going on. We make sense of the narrative in spite of all its lacunae and shifters ("it" crops up again and again) because we know the clichés, whether linguistic or narrative, in which the narration is grounded. We easily decode the line "I am not that sort of girl" because in such a context there are only two sorts, the sort who does and the sort who doesn't; we have no trouble constructing the event which occurs in the wings, in-between the utterances, "I'm very nervous. / Be gentle. / You must never tell anyone" (86) because the situation is hackneyed. It is our familiarity with stereotypes and their social and cultural background which enables us to leap over gaps, supply missing links and missing words. We are therefore just as implicated as the characters but our implication means that the narrator's act of communication is successful. In short, it is the *dialogism* of the cliché—understood as the two-dimensional intersection of speaking subject, addressee and cultural context—which enables communication to take place.[19]

Revivifying of clichés is also obtained through the collage effects, and the ensuing dialogic interplay of the high mode of the poetry quoted by the male actor and the low mode of his own sexual adventures. Moreover, Donne's poem itself embeds *en abyme* this very interplay, with the introduction of the trivial flea, which refreshes the age-old motif of erotic persuasion; while "To his Coy Mistress" illustrates the possibility of cliché renewal through the little twists that turn *topos* (*carpe diem*) and set phrases, (to have time enough, Time's chariot) into new linguistic forms. Again, of course, the reader is involved in the on-

going dialogue between low and high modes and between stereotype and revived form, that is to say, he is both compromised and—comforted. For as "post-modernist" Canadian writer, George Bowering, writes in an optimistic mood (126), "It beats talking back to the electrowave oven. Voice, speech, is a means of bonding or asking; it is what connects people with one another & with the world, or reaching from the post modern world, with the universe".

As for the narrator, we can appreciate that his artfulness lies in his refusal to speak in his own voice—since in any case it could not be his. Nevertheless he is compromised too by the hundred-times told tale he puts together. Nor is the author free of guilt: he is even implicated within the text since the initials of the male character FM may stand for Frank Moorhouse. But if **"Pledges"** is "autobiographical", it nevertheless only inscribes the already inscribed. The author is not passing judgment but himself standing on trial.

Derision then permeates the text. Derision of the illusion men and women entertain about themselves and about each other. Derision of desire. But also self-derision which mocks fictional mimesis, itself mimesis of mimesis endlessly repeated, with the added irony that speech, the most mimetic of modes, should be used to undercut the mimetic dimension. Self-derision directed at the speaking/writing/reading subject.

Nevertheless we cannot conclude on this note. For one thing, as Barthes (1964, 273) noted, "toute subversion du langage se confond contradictoirement avec une exaltation du langage, car se soulever contre le langage au moyen du langage même, ce n'est jamais que prétendre libérer un langage "second" qui serait l'énergie profonde, "anormale" (soustraite aux normes) de la parole. . . ." However dubious language may be, however denied personality, "Pledges" is a story that asks from us a sort of commitment to language and its energy and even to these puppets which are so unlife-like and so like us. Beyond or in between the stale statements, linguistic activity is going on, narrative structure has been rejuvenated, ordinary "dreck", to use Donald Barthelme's well known term, reshaped into a unique art form, which breaks away from the repetition it stages. In the dialogic performance thus enacted language brings joy to the writing/reading subject, and literature recovers its *bonding* function. Or as Moorhouse himself (1981, 324) has written of good short fiction: "We are presenting primarily, [sic] an *aesthetic experience*. This aesthetic experience shifts the boundaries of perceptions and gives the readers possibilities and room for reactions which they can take and use for their own growth, in their own time and in their own way." Please pass this note.

Notes

1. John Hawkes interviewed by J. J. Enck in *Wisconsin Studies in Contemporary Literature*, VI, 2, Summer 1964, quoted in Bradbury, p. 7.

2. I am adopting the term, because it is convenient if not entirely adequate, from Helmut Bonheim, who

classifies description, report, comment and speech as the four narrative modes. Similarly I am not happy about the word "postmodernist" which I use for lack of a better.

3. Frank Moorhouse (1938-) was a journalist and a union organizer before he became a full-time writer. He started publishing stories in 1957 but found it difficult at first to have his work accepted by the established literary quarterlies partly because of the explicitness of his fiction, partly because he "developed", as he said (Moorhouse 1977), "away from the humanist tradition of the Australian story—sympathetic to the working class and kind to kangaroos". He has now published several collections of stories, edited anthologies, written screenplays. In 1972 he co-founded with Michael Wilding the alternative story magazine *Tabloid*. *The Oxford Companion to Australian Literature* from which I draw the preceding information concludes that he is generally regarded as one of the finest contemporary prose stylists. Brian Kiernan, in his introduction to *The Most Beautiful Lies* defines Moorhouse as "the most consistently 'realistic' of all the [new writers in his anthology] being very much concerned with social stereotypes (including those of the counter-culture), not to fictionally flesh out these abstractions but to test them critically and humorously" (xiv).

I have been using the 1985 edition of "Pledges, Vows and Pass this Note" but I have no way now, in my corner of the world, of checking whether this was the first appearance of the story.

4. Predecessors of Moorhouse include Hemingway (e.g. "The Killers"), Dorothy Parker (e.g. "The Sexes"), Ivy Compton-Burnett. But they still rely on tags to identify the speakers ("Nick asked", and Parker's recurrent "he said", "she said") as well as on a minimum of 'stage directions' and description, all of which point straight to the narrator's activities. Some contemporary American writers have gone further and eliminated inquits (for instance, Donald Barthelme in "The Crisis"). In "Said", Stephen Dixon also plays with the mode of speech in just the opposite way from Moorhouse's, by eliminating it; he narrates a marital quarrel by giving us only narrative tags and stage directions. "He said, she said. / She left the room, he followed her" etc. (*Boundary 2,* Spring 1980, pp. 99-100).

5. See Gérard Genette: "Il peut sembler étrange, à première vue, d'attribuer à quelque narrateur que ce soit un autre rôle que la narration proprement dite, c'est-à-dire le fait de raconter l'histoire, mais nous savons bien en fait que le discours du narrateur, romanesque ou autre, peut assumer d'autres fonctions" (*Figures III,* p. 261).

6. The pronominal system of the story would deserve close investigation, which I cannot undertake within the scope of this article.

7. "Lorsque les thèmes-fonctions s'organisent en séquences figées (ou suites de séquences) identifiables globalement, on a alors affaire à des 'clichés narratifs' dont l'importance varie avec le nombre des séquences enchaînées les unes aux autres" (Jenny, 501).

8. Both the Donne and the Marvell excerpts are taken up again in the story of the second sexual affair and this time they are reduced to their central message: "How little that which thou deny'st me is. . . ." and "Had we but World enough and Time / This coyness Lady were no crime. . . ." (88).

9. It is listed as American in Margaret Bradford Boni, *Fireside Book of Folk Songs,* N.Y., Simon & Schuster, 1947. Note that when "Love oh love oh careless love" is quoted again, it is sandwiched between another quotation "I love you and I'll love you until the twelfth of never and that's a long time" and the statement "FM L WH true" (88), thus throwing an ironic light on both framing utterances.

10. I will use the word "cliché" to designate true clichés like "one-track mind", "bun in the oven", i.e. set phrases which cannot be modified without a stylistic effect and which could ideally be listed in a dictionary, and stereotyped phrases like "how could you?" "Men are all the same". The difference is not particularly pertinent to my analysis. See Anne Hershberg-Pierrot, ("Clichés, Stéréotypie et Stratégie Discursive dans le discours de Lieuvain", *Poétique,* 43, Septembre 80, p. 89: "S'il paraît assez artificiel de distinguer cliché verbal et stéréotype verbal, on peut avancer que le stéréotype possède une extension plus large que le cliché: verbal ou non le stéréotype désigne toute répétition impensée d'un habitus social, opérant la confusion du prescriptif et du descriptif, de la norme et de son usage (il est *ce qui se fait* [. . .] ou *ce qui se dit*)".

11. The use of abbreviations (cf. also the acronym SWALK) and of formulae, like "Yours forever. Only yours" shows that the narrator occasionally reports written, not oral, statements.

12. I haven't been able to locate this ballad. Is it one of Kipling's? Of Henry Lawson's? If the last, it would introduce an Australian reference, where the other quoted texts are either American or British. Since the other poems figure in school anthologies, it may be presumed that the last ballad must also be fairly well-known. On the other hand, the thought crossed my mind that Moorhouse may have invented it.

13. To some extent these clichés date the 'characters' assuming them. They have not heard of the new permissiveness. In many of his stories, in contrast, Moorhouse explores the changes in sexual mores.

14. This is not the place to discuss at length the actantial roles (Greimas) which are not modified by the elimination of description, comment or even report since speech takes over the narrative function.

To put it succinctly, there is a double *Actantial pattern:* the Subject (now male now female) seeks an Object of the opposite sex (now female now male). Reversible, the pattern is not, however, symmetrical. The two Subjects invest the Object of their respective quests with different values, the man with dominantly sexual, the woman with dominantly social, values: hence the conflicts in the relationship. The other actantial roles receive actorial manifestations which may differ in each pattern: for instance, if the role of Helper is filled for both boy and girl Subjects by the schoolmate passing the note, one may say that the child, an auxiliary in the woman's quest, is an Opponent (though not for long) in the man's. All this should be investigated closely.

15. "Futility and Other Animals" (1969) is the title of Frank Moorhouse's first collection of stories.

16. Cf. Barthelme's 'dialogue stories' in *Great Days* (1969): although their layout, with the dash introducing utterances, is not that of a traditional narrative, they do not create the same visual, verse-like impact.

17. Conversely, first quoted with the typography proper to verse, the ballad of the roaming men, when repeated, is not set out in lines.

18. "Poetic texts are characterized by their setting up of equivalence relations, whether codified or not, between different points of the discourse, relations which are defined on superficial levels—where by 'superficial' we mean phonetic, phonological, morphological and/or surface syntax" (Ruwet, p. 98).

19. See Kristeva, 65 and 66: the "three dimensions or coordinates of dialogue are writing subject, addressee and exterior texts. The word's status is thus defined *horizontally* (the word in the text belongs to both writing subject and addressee) as well as *vertically* (the word in the text is oriented toward an anterior or synchronic literary corpus)".

Works Cited

Moorhouse, Frank, "Pledges, Vows and Pass this Note," in *Room Service, Comic Writings of Frank Moorhouse,* Ringwood, Vict., Viking, 1985, 85-90.

———. "Questionnaire on Fiction: Statements," *Australian Literary Studies,* 8, 2, October 1977, 189-90.

———. "Authors' Statements: Questionnaire to the Authors," *Australian Literary Studies,* 10, October 1981, 323-324.

Barthes, Roland, *Essais Critiques,* Paris, Seuil, 1964.

———. *S/Z,* Paris, Seuil, 1970.

Bonheim, Helmut, *The Narrative Modes: Techniques of the Short Story,* Cambridge, D.S. Brewer, 1982.

Bowering, George, *The Mask in Place, Essays on Fiction in North America,* Winnipeg, Turnstone Press, 1982.

Bradbury, Malcolm, *The Novel Today, Contemporary Writers on Modern Fiction,* London, Fontana, 1982.

Bremond, Claude, "En lisant une fable," *Communications,* 47, 1988, 41-62.

Chatman, Seymour, *Story and Discourse, Narrative Structure in Fiction and Film,* Ithaca, Cornell University Press, 1978.

Genette, Gérard, *Figures III,* Paris, Seuil, 1972.

Jenny, Laurent, "Structures et fonctions du cliché, A propos des 'Impressions d'Afrique,'" *Poétique,* 12, 1972, 495-517.

Kiernan, Brian, ed., *The Most Beautiful Lies,* A collection of stories by five major contemporary fiction writers: Bail, Carey, Lurie, Moorhouse and Wilding, Sidney, Angus & Robertson, 1977.

Kristeva, Julia, *Desire in Language, a Semiotic Approach to Literature and Act,* edited by Leon S. Roudiez and translated by Thomas Gora, Alice Jardine and Leon S. Roudiez, N.Y., Columbia University Press, 1980.

Page, Norman, *Speech in the English Novel,* London, Longman, 1973.

Riffaterre, Michael, *Essais de stylistique structurale,* Paris, Flammarion, 1971.

Rimmon-Kenan, Shlomith, *Narrative Fiction: Contemporary Poetics,* London, Methuen, 1983.

Ruwet, Nicolas, "Parallelisms and deviation in poetry" in Tzvetan Torodov, *French Literary Theory Today, A Reader,* Cambridge, Cambridge University Press, 1982, 92-124.

Said, Edward, *The World, the Text and the Critic,* Cambridge, Harvard University Press, 1983.

Gay Raines (essay date 1990)

SOURCE: "The Short Story Cycles of Frank Moorhouse," in *Australian Literary Studies,* Vol. 14, No. 4, October, 1990, pp. 425-35.

[*In the following essay, Raines compares Moorhouse's use of the short story cycle to that of Sherwood Anderson, William Faulkner, and James Joyce.*]

In 1981, at the end of his article 'Frank Moorhouse: A Retrospective', Brian Kiernan wrote the following comment about the stories in *The Everlasting Secret Family*:

Each may be discontinuous with the other, but discontinuity would seem to presuppose some continuity to depart from, and this latest collection suggests the 'familial' though 'secret' relationships between them all which provide his work with its unique, imaginative pattern.

(94)

The first section of Kiernan's discussion noted the 'polymorphous' relationship within and between collections of stories and commented that these 'composed collections' are amongst 'the most original extended fictions of the past decade' (75). Between this opening and the conclusion quoted above Kiernan explored the themes Moorhouse pursues, his examination of manners and the cultural implications, his irony and his use of language, thus diversifying the focus of discussion and failing to push his observations on Moorhouse's structural patterns home in such a way as to displace the familiar description of them as 'discontinuous narratives'.

Doubtless it is in the nature of Moorhouse's work itself to beget diversifying commentary which does not press a (single) argument home. Its variety of tone and style, its multiplicity of observation, are found equally, if not more, fascinating than the structural experiment. The overall arrangement of form, once noted by the critic, is inclined to disappear within the various kinds of other discourse which have been triggered.[1] My present purpose is to argue that there is, in seven of the eight Moorhouse collections, a 'closed' aspect which suggests that it is more accurate to describe them as developments of the short story cycle rather than as 'discontinuous narratives'.

> . . . a book of short stories so linked to each other by their author that the reader's successive experience on various levels of the pattern of the whole significantly modifies his experience of each of the component parts.

In the twentieth century, he continued, 'the devices by which the "many" become component patterns of the "one" are more subtle, generally, than the devices used in past ages' (19). Frank Moorhouse has contributed markedly to this development. He has taken and retained the orderly basis of the story cycles of Sherwood Anderson and James Joyce, creating more sinuous connections within individual cycles, and developing ways in which a number of cycle can be interlaced with each other so that their sequence can constitute what Kanaganayakam has called a kind of 'Comédie Humaine de Balmain' (67).

In *Yacker 3* Moorhouse recalls that he 'had been particularly excited by Salinger's stories, all about the same family but appearing at different times and places' and that 'another book which influenced me . . . was Sherwood Anderson's *Winesburg, Ohio* . . . the story was told from different characters' points of view in the town, but with all the characters overlapping' (224). Anderson's cycle was published in 1919, modelled upon and complicating the structure of James Joyce's *Dubliners* (1914). Other cycles, Hemingway's *In Our Time* (1925), Steinbeck's *Pastures of Heaven* (1932) and Salinger's story cycles about the Glass family (from 1953 on) failed to achieve

the complexity of interrelation between stories which marks *Winesburg,* let alone develop or improve upon it.

The American author closest to Moorhouse in awareness of the possibilities of manipulating cycle structure was William Faulkner. *Go Down, Moses* (1942) is a cycle which touches on the theme of the retreat of the wilderness before the concrete urban onslaught, in stories about different generations of one Southern family nexus, from the end of the eighteenth century to the middle of the twentieth. One story in it, 'The Bear', has a section which Faulkner regarded as belonging to the story when it appeared in *Go Down, Moses* but not belonging to it when it appeared in separate anthologies. Faulkner also used 'The Bear' in *Big Woods,* a collection specifically on the theme of the deteriorating countryside, together with another story from *Go Down, Moses,* 'The Old People', and a rewritten version of a third story, 'Delta Autumn'. Material from one collection was thus 're-cycled' by Faulkner, carrying with it some of the force of its earlier context, varying the inferences to be drawn in the new context, and relating each volume to the other. Moorhouse's work develops such possibilities over a number of cycles.

The first three volumes of Moorhouse's conventionally published stories were described on their title pages as 'discontinuous narratives'. In *Yacker 3* Moorhouse recalls that this description came to him when the publisher of his first collection said: 'These stories all link up . . . but it's not a novel. What are we going to call it?' (224). The definition was useful in the early days, as an attempt to embrace both the use of varying styles and methods within individual stories, and the thematic unity which Moorhouse found himself continually creating within and between his collections. After the third book, ***The Electrical Experience,*** the term was not used again, an appropriate decision for, by that time, organisation within the collections was becoming too structured for discontinuity to remain the dominant impression.

Futility and Other Animals was published in 1969. The stories are about a group of people, mainly in their twenties. The action reaches back and forth through time—occasionally reflecting over the length of a relationship, occasionally flashing back to childhood. There is no chronological order. Themes are sometimes started in one story and pursued backward into the past in subsequent stories. All these explorations into earlier stages of story lines are interleaved with each other, and with other story lines as well. But there is an overall forward movement in which Roger of the first story and Cindy of the fifth and seventh stories move forward to some kind of relationship at the end of the cycle, starting a baby together, something which others among the characters had felt unable to face.

In *Winesburg, Ohio* and *Dubliners* place was the unifying environment of the stories, and disillusion and depression the typical spirit of those places. In ***Futility and Other Animals*** the place is sometimes the city, sometimes the bush, sometimes the old home town, and although there is a spirit of confusion about, there is an overall lift of optimism. Differing from his antecedents in these respects Moorhouse nevertheless uses Anderson's technique of recurring characters and the forward movement of the most important ones as a method of linking the stories. Also, like Joyce, who grouped stories of childhood, young manhood and maturity, Moorhouse groups his stories according to aspects named 'Confusion', 'Sickness' and 'Bravery'. In later collections he was to find further ways of defining a cycle's shape.

As well as refining such received techniques Moorhouse was also developing greater flexibility in style. Borges, in his experiments, had attempted to break the traditional structure of short stories and turn them into intellectual games. Moorhouse is more old-fashioned. His experiments—counterpointing plain print and italics, slipping into lists, use of the short line, unexpected headings mid-story, disappearing speech marks, the use of poetic monologue, and deliberately casual titles—all these are used to promote more varied awareness of the narrator or character-of-current-focus and his, or her, insight. In short, he is attempting, by the variety of his technique, to extend the illusion of reality rather than to fracture it. It is not until subsequent volumes that readers are occasionally invited to become aware that the author is, at times deliberately, balancing on a fine line between fiction and autobiography, tantalising us with the puzzle as to which is which, bringing the lovingly polished form under constant question and incipient threat.

The Americans, Baby, published in 1972, maintained for the most part the traditional distance between the author and his work. The characters emerge distinctly. The opening story (Del returning home to have Kim's baby) fixes the country environment. The rest of the stories are then set in the city. Again, Moorhouse interleaves the experiences of several of the characters through the sequence of stories. In this collection, however, the story lines move forward, rather than backward and forward. The one exception to this is the eighteenth, **"Anti-bureaucratisation and the Apparatchiki,"** which is a flashback, but it does have the effect of tying the near-end of the cycle back to its beginning, with the same care to establish an overall form for the collection as had been evident in *Futility and Other Animals.* After the last Becker story a coda is attached in the shape of **"Letters to Twiggy."** Seemingly unrelated to the rest of the book this coda provides a last comic image of a basically chauvinist man sent slightly mad by the seduction of media images and his inability to break through to any reality behind. It is an image which refers cogently to some of the main confusions explored elsewhere in the book and reveals Moorhouse drawing the cycle together at its end with no uncertain intention.

The reprinting in *The Americans, Baby* of **"The Story of Nature"** from *Futility and Other Animals* is the first of many subsequent re-placings of stories which occur throughout the eight collections. Together with the reappearance of the characters of Roger and Cindy it indi-

cates the continuum between the two volumes. The experiences explored in the second volume are, in many ways, different from those in the first. But the connections with the first cycle signal that this is still the same group of people whose typical experiences are being further explored.

By contrast, *The Electrical Experience* effectively reaches back to before Moorhouse's generation and focusses instead on T. George McDowell, an 'Australian of the first half of the century'. The diagnosis of McDowell's case has the effect of throwing new light on subsequent generations. He is the father of the wayward girl who had proved to be the distraction of Becker, the Coca Cola salesman, in *The Americans, Baby* and he is part of the explanation of why she is as she is. When Terri, representative of the next generation—which McDowell had believed it was his responsibility to 'hold'—breaks down and rejects her father, it is the moment of collapse for him too. The examination of T. George McDowell is a discovery of roots, an attempt to uncover the spiritual legacy, the psyche of the community.

In an attempt to extend visual tactics beyond those already in use (of varying the appearance and layout of words on the page) Moorhouse inserts, between each of the stories in this volume, a number of black pages with white printed fragments, photographs and charts. The blackness of these pages satirically suggests the darkness of a world without, or before, the achievement of George's passion, electric light. The inserts catch and carry undercurrents already implicit in the text, and start some new ones of their own, 'tricking fresh meaning from the form' or creating a 'new exchange between the reader and the form'.[2] When, for example, George's suggested "Creed for New South Wales Country Schools" is printed after **"The St. Louis Rotary Convention 1923, Recalled"** it is not only an example of Rotary thinking as George understands it but its pompous optimism and confidence lends greater pathos to his state of almost-breakdown in the previous story, **"An Interesting Point."** At the same time it recalls the quotation from 'The Man with the Hoe', a similarly pompous piece of proselytising from an earlier time and place, printed after **"Rules and Practices for Overcoming Shyness."** Ambrose Bierce is quoted as saying that "The Man with the Hoe" had "all the life of a dead fish" (76), which comment reverberates when two pictures of dead fish occur later in the book. They come on either side of "The Secret of Endurance" which features Zane Grey, the American writer and self-styled big-game fisherman. After the second fish picture comes a note entitled "A Literary Coincidence" which blandly observes that Zane Grey once went eighty-three days without a bite while Hemingway's Old Man in *The Old Man and the Sea* once went eighty-four! George's brave and empty "Creed" is thus carefully placed in a network of expanding, ironic, cultural and literary references. Not only is an underlying symbolism, referring to the national character and experience, evoked by some of the details, and strengthened by tight cross-referencing between moments in different stories, but the whole thing is enhanced by the interplay of, or the dialogue created by, the interspersed fragments.

As in **The Americans, Baby** a focussing and qualifying coda is attached at the end of the cycle, in the shape of a story satirically recording the antics of a film crew who are trying to 'trick' their own preconceived version of 'the Australian of the first half of the century' out of an unaware and inarticulate man in a hat, picked out at random at a football ground. A black page preceding the story carries a fragment from **"An Application for a Film Grant"**. It says:

> . . . as the material covers a lengthy time-span a styl-
> ised form of story telling is used . . . . Each sequence
> will either fade or iris in and out. There will be enough
> emotive, even perhaps heart-rending, material without
> building up melodrama by cutting. . . .
>
> (178)

An analogy is suggested between the method of the film-maker and the method of the storyteller in the previous stories. Some of the scepticism with which the film-makers are treated, as they 'trick' their own story out of a dull reality, doubtless reflects back on the storyteller who has tried to 'trick' out of the dull T. George McDowell the inner truths of a half-century's history.

In his first two books Moorhouse interleaves groups of differing characters to cumulative advantage. In the third, one character's life and place in history is examined in increasing depth, from discontinuous vantage points. In the next collection, **Conference-ville,** Moorhouse employs one narrator progressing through a short, conventional time sequence, both of which techniques contribute to shaping the cycle. The narrator here is older than the people in **The Americans, Baby.** While they had progressed from the private world of **Futility and Other Animals** into a more social context, this narrator now moves amongst intellectuals who apparently have some prestige in the world. He tries very hard to be open-minded when the younger fringe attempt to break the traditional conference format, but his instincts are now rather inclined to the conservative. His behaviour is revealing in spite of himself. When the rebellious youngsters video the older participants on the conference platform, his body language is revealed as that of a 'bourgeois elitist. Or something' (89). The narrator is even mortified to note that he conducts himself in a *fawning* manner to the man of greater prestige than himself. In relating this anecdote the author is calling up another kind of imaging technique, which should undermine the dominantly realist method of his text. Ironically, the effect is to deliver an extra level of realistic insight instead. The traditional distinction between image and reality is both reinforced and scrutinised in this episode.

At the same time, the distinction between fiction and autobiography begins to come into question. The writer in **"Pictures of Corruption"** seems to have exactly the picture of himself which we might expect Moorhouse to have,

given all that we can deduce about him from *Days of Wine and Rage,* his introductions to his own work and to collections of stories, and from the interviews he has given. The last story in the volume is reprinted in *Days of Wine and Rage* (Moorhouse's 1980 documentary collection from the seventies) as one which 'recreates an actual incident at Tony's in the old days' (269). The narrator is also described as a writer poking about for material, who discovers some letters in a student room he visits during the conference (94), an idea which provides the basis for another story collection, in **The Everlasting Secret Family and Other Secrets.**

Tales of Mystery and Romance continues the use of a first person narrator throughout, and hovers even more tantalisingly on the edge of sounding autobiographical. The restaurants of Sydney, the philosophical arguments, the well-publicised break-ups between friends, all bespeak the Push as recorded in *Days of Wine and Rage.* The narrator is a writer and philosopher who enjoys seminars and conferences. In the fifth story he refers to a Moorhouse story from **The Americans, Baby** but does not go so far as to lay direct claim to it. Instead, Moorhouse declares in his Preface that 'the events, characterisation, and locations are used fictionally and to seek identification would be unjustified and a disservice to the book'. Moreover, the clarity and edge of the writing, the bold and rueful encapsulation of events, achieve a comic stylisation which is clearly a fictionalising technique rather than an attempt at faithful recording of people and events.

The opening story of **Tales of Mystery and Romance** suggests that the narrator and his male friend Milton, who is a university lecturer, serve each other in an 'alter ego' capacity. '"I'm your down town self," I say, "and you're my academic self"' (13)—a clear indication that more self-conscious imaging techniques are being exercised in the pursuit of a fictional self-analysis. The second story, **"Letters to an Ex-wife Concerning a Reunion in Portugal,"** is a loosely grouped collection of extracts from letters, and private notes reflecting on the circumstances surrounding the letters. A somewhat old-fashioned technique, it is nevertheless used to reveal the interplay between the front which meets the world and the inner reactions of the mind, over an extended period of time. In other stories such interplay is recorded directly by a sharp and economical registering of minute shifts of feeling and insight between characters in interchange.

The last story, as in the three previous volumes, acts as a kind of coda, comically reflecting what has gone before, and rounding the cycle off. **"The Chain Letter Story"** shows the kind of communication which plays on fear and the desire to belong while having no basic rationale and being ultimately phoney. We may conclude that communes, mysticism, civilised attempts to communicate with either male or female partners, or even our own families (the topics explored in the preceding stories) are as pointless and anxiety-driven as the instinct which the chain letter aims to work upon.

The Everlasting Secret Family and Other Secrets is presented in a slightly different way from the other books. Here there are four separate mini-cycles which have the effect of bringing the areas of interest from earlier cycles together between one set of covers. In **"The Mystery of the Time Piece"** (*Tales of Mystery and Romance*), in answer to his sister's comment, 'There was a time when you were going overseas', the narrator had said, 'One should travel the same ground again and again until it speaks to you'; and, a little later, 'Travel gives irrelated, lineal experience. Staying put gives vertical, corporated experience' (51). Moorhouse stays with the same kind of settings and themes throughout his cycles, constantly reinforcing the same imaginative ground by repetition of stories and episodes from book to book, increasing the significance with each repetition.

"Pacific City" continues the study of the George McDowell period; **"Imogene Continued"** develops *Conference-ville*; and **"The Everlasting Secret Family"** explores even more specifically the theme of homosexual relationships which had been touched upon in *Futility and Other Animals,* and further developed in *The Americans, Baby* and *Tales of Mystery and Romance.* The title story of the mini-cycle **"Imogene Continued"** (it is about Cindy of *Futility* and *Americans,* now seen in an extension of *Conference-ville,* whom the narrator says he has always privately called Imogene) and the note "To Be Continued", at the end of "Pacific City," affirms the homogeneity and ongoing movement of the cycles taken together.

In this context **"The Dutch Letters"** cycle fits a little uneasily. Like *The Americans, Baby* it presents an outsider's view of Australians. The use of the letter format is like a return to the early novel structures of the eighteenth century. But it is also an example of Moorhouse's use of any kind of writing method, from diaries, letters, notebooks, advertisements, recipe books and so on, to vary and fill out the ways of recording life. In 'Writing Yourself a Proper Narrative' from **"Imogene Continued"** the narrator observes of one of the other characters: 'I really thought that she was novelising her fairly decent affluent life, giving herself a part in some feminist narrative . . . and not doing it well' (124). Rendering their lives into fiction is one of the ways human beings use to understand themselves and lay a hold on life.

Although each of the other three mini-cycles in *The Everlasting Secret Family* had roots in somewhat different earlier volumes, they share the common theme of ways of negotiating or living with sexual experiences which are conventionally felt to be unsavoury. The "Pacific City" stories feature Irving Bow, the proprietor of the darkness of the early cinema who, even though he molests children, is someone who dreams of the future. His urge to confess to his weakness, so reminiscent of *Winesburg, Ohio,* is never allowed to surface by those who silently connive, knowing what the confession might be and not wanting to receive it. The etiquette of deception is examined, and the illegal behaviour of the imagination is recorded; the stories

become an image of the pain and guilt of everyman, rather than the study of an isolated pervert. The mini-cycle **"Imogene Continued"** records the sense of guilt and muddle which besets thinking white Australians on the question of how to behave towards Aborigines. This is presented through the outraged but comic dilemma of Cindy, an emancipated lady at a conference who is raped by an Aborigine, a fellow delegate. **"The Everlasting Secret Family"** stories record various moments in the life of a 'kept' homosexual boy, and projects a history of homosexuality back into classical times and forward as a subculture into all time. Apart from **"The Dutch Letters,"** the cycles in this book reveal Moorhouse exploring the corners of living which many readers are fastidious about. They are another kind of technical adventure helping to develop ways of writing about what had hitherto been deemed unmentionable.

In author's notes to four of his earlier volumes Moorhouse had referred to his 'stories'. In his note to *Room Service* he refers to 'these pieces' which have been collected from his journalism and revised for this book. It does not constitute a cycle, but the interests encountered in the book seem, in general, to be those of the narrator of *Futility*, *The Americans*, *Conference-ville*, *Tales* and "Imogene," and to cast further light upon him. It belongs in its chronological place in the overall *oeuvre,* the 'comédie humaine' and, especially in the rhythmical experimentation in Part Two, in the structural exploration and adventure which constitute Moorhouse's work in the short story genre.

In *Forty-Seventeen* Moorhouse returns to the cycle proper, and to a deepening of the kind of personal exploration begun in **"The Mystery of the Time Piece"** story in *Tales of Mystery and Romance.* The now familiar but un-named protagonist who, in the course of the emerging volumes, has scrutinised life from first relationships and first political activities to being in the second rank of importance in *Conference-ville,* has now arrived at the age of some public status when he is invited to sit on an international commission. He is still an actively sexual being, fascinated by extremes of sexuality. He still likes to think of himself as a bushman and to ponder about relations with the past. He now has quite a strong drive to identify his own roots and see them materialise in his present. And the time has come at which he begins to encounter mortality and to try to recognise what difference, if any, it makes. He is forty and his thoughts are polarised by relationships with a girl of seventeen and a woman of seventy.

The opening story, **"Buenaventura Durruti's Funeral,"** begins with another American poet's visit, and reference back to an earlier such visit included in *The Americans, Baby.* The protagonist of *Forty-Seventeen* is inclined to identify with the hero of a film which he outlines; by the end of the collection we realise that a plotline, or structure for the cycle has thus been projected. This particular story is constructed by compiling a collection of short descriptions, notes, extracts from journalism and letters, and ends with the thought that his relationship with the young girl has become no more than footnotes to a poem. Life will fade into fiction, as it so often does in a Moorhouse cycle.

Between reflections on drink and life at forty is set an uncharacteristically Borgesian story. **"The White Knight"** is about a sequence of meaningless coincidences, connecting a story the protagonist had intended to write, some moments in his own activities, and reports of a mass suicide. His ex-wife had been enamoured of coincidences and he had always derided her for this. Now, perhaps as a result of illness, these coincidences put him under the kind of strain which causes him to give up writing, but the cycle nevertheless continues, creating the usual Moorhouse anomaly of almost apparent autobiography retreating back into fiction before the reader can pin it down. In 1981 Moorhouse had written in *Australian Literary Studies*: 'One of the things which I am doing more, is writing fiction which returns, within itself, to autobiography and reportage. I see it as a controlled oscillation within the story' (222). In this case, the distancing effect of reported narrative resumes its usual force, an underlying drive reasserts itself, and **"The White Knight"** falls into a parodic perspective. Although Moorhouse constantly experiments, to 'trick new meaning from the form', it is not his practice to undercut it completely, or to depart from a mainly realist base, nor has he yet explored the ways in which 'magic realists' subsume the extravagant and impossible into their realism.

A more traditional format comes next, in a collection of the letters the narrator's wife, Robyn, had written to him in the early days of their courtship; and this is followed by **"The Story Not Shown"** which he, as a young writer, had felt unable to let his virginal girlfriend read. The two contrasting pieces of writing accurately and sympathetically record, and gently mock, the way he and Robyn had been, in the days of their youth. The passing of time spoils many relationships. The man who breaks the news to him of Robyn's death, a man he can no longer stand, is Madden from **"Rambling Boy"** in Moorhouse's first volume, *Futility and Other Animals.* In that story, which is repeated here, the narrator had shared with Madden, for 'four sweet seasons', a romantic homosexual rapport. The repetition of that story here reopens past time and extends the perspectives within the present cycle.

In subsequent stories the narrator pursues the fates predicted both by the film in the opening story of the cycle, and by the genetic inheritance from his grandmother, whose career as a whore anticipated his own sensuality as well as the uncertainty of his own freelance (and parasitic?) career as a journalist. But the last entry in the book is a postcard from his young girlfriend in London proposing that they get together again: 'Isn't it time the footnotes became their own story?' she wrote. This is at once a return full circle to the opening story, and a moment of recognition for the reader that the foregoing stories were already footnotes on life. The cycle structure has allowed both the pursuit of differing lines of exploration, and the attempt to draw the lines into some kind of meaningful relation. It is

a form which recognises and reveals that any attempt to understand or structure a life can only ever be partial, but that literature can be a tool in such a process. The attempt to formulate a pattern is, at the least, a gesture against chaos. Moorhouse's work has extended the range of his chosen genre in this attempt.

Through the complete collection of his cycles Moorhouse has progressed from exploring the interpersonal and public relations of the young and the middle aged and aspects of the history of the Australian community in the early twentieth century to, in his most recent volume, the history of an individual psyche. His main characteristic as a writer is to fictionalise, and to render comic without demeaning them, records which might otherwise be too painful to read. His originality is in the almost pyrotechnical display of a multiplicity of kinds of writing within the prose story form, which delights by its virtuosity and yet is sinuously and flawlessly blended to achieve new dimensions for story and cycle form.

In *The State of the Art* Moorhouse wrote:

> . . . there is something I call the 'journey of the form': the results that come from working at a particular art form over a long period . . . finding where it leads . . . the pursuit of form produces a dialogue with the writer's own work as well as the inescapable dialogue with what has been written by other writers, past and contemporary.
>
> (4)

It is in extending the use of the short story cycle, to create a series of interlinked cycles, capable of following a life experience through, that Moorhouse seems to me to have continued the 'journey of the form', after his inescapable dialogue with what has been written by others. In *Yacker 3,* after referring to his interest in the way Salinger, Anderson and Lawson wrote stories which were connected, he went on to speak of the kind of writing he now liked to do:

> It works as a structure and allows me to do bigger things than just stories, and I think I now do different, more interesting things with the form than those writers I admired—while, admittedly, having to climb on their backs to begin with. I see it as circuitry, circuits within the larger assembly, with the books coming in, one on another.
>
> (225)

I would like to suggest that, while 'discontinuous narrative' is still a term which can be used to describe the basic prose method in Moorhouse's work, it is no longer an adequate description of the formal properties of each collection as a whole, or of the body of works taken together. Moorhouse's own description of his work as 'circuits within a larger assembly' is another way of saying that he is developing grouped short story cycles. It is in doing this that he is making a unique contribution to the development of the short story genre.

Notes

1. For example: Docker, John. *Australian Cultural Elites: Intellectual Traditions in Sydney and Melbourne.* Sydney: Angus and Robertson, 1974. Concentrates on Moorhouse the 'ideologue'. Reid, Ian. 'Writing From the Third Position: Frank Moorhouse's Recent Fiction.' *Meanjin* 37 (1978): 165-70. Argues that the focal position of the stories, 'an uneasy one on the margins', was the main determinant of form. Rowse, Tim. 'The Pluralism of Frank Moorhouse.' *Nellie Melba and Ginger Meggs and Friends.* Ed. Susan Dermody, John Docker, and Drusilla Modjeska. Victoria: Kibble Books, 1982. 250-267. Suggests that the early preference for discontinuous narrative was the rendering within fiction of a plurality of subcultures. Arens, Werner. 'The Ironical fate of "The Drover's Wife": Four Versions from Henry Lawson (1892) to Barbara Jefferis (1980).' *The Story Must Be Told.* Ed. Peter O. Stummer. Würzburg: Königshausen-Neumann, 1986. 119-133. Smith, Graeme Kinross. 'Liberating Acts—Frank Moorhouse, his Life, his Narratives.' *Southerly* 46 (1986): 391-423. Provides a biography of Moorhouse; and offers the conclusion that his work is essentially provincial. Kirby, Stephen. 'Homosexual Desire and Homosexual Panic in the Fiction of David Malouf and Frank Moorhouse.' *Meanjin* 46 (1987): 385-93.

2. When selecting stories for *The State of the Art* Moorhouse wrote: '. . . dialogue with form is one of the things I looked for . . . prising or tricking fresh meaning from the form releasing verbal energy . . . a new exchange between reader and the form' (3).

Works Cited

Baker, Candida. *Yacker 3.* Sydney: Pan, 1989.

Ingram, Forrest L. *Representative Short Story Cycles of the Twentieth Century.* The Hague: Mouton & Co., 1971.

Kanaganayakam, C. 'Form and Meaning in the Short Stories of Frank Moorhouse.' *World Literature Written in English* 25.1 (1985): 67-76.

Kiernan, Brian, 'Frank Moorhouse: A Retrospective.' *Modern Fiction Studies* 27 (1981): 73-94.

Moorhouse, Frank. *Futility and Other Animals.* Sydney: Angus & Robertson, 1969. Rev. Arkon ed. 1981.

———. *The Americans, Baby.* Sydney: Angus & Robertson, 1972. Arkon ed. 1978.

———. *The Electrical Experience.* Sydney: Angus & Robertson, 1974. Rev. Arkon ed. 1980.

———. *Conference-ville.* Sydney: Angus & Robertson, 1976.

———. *Tales of Mystery and Romance.* Sydney: Angus & Robertson, 1977. Rev. Arkon ed. 1980.

———. *The Everlasting Secret Family.* Sydney: Angus & Robertson, 1980.

———. ed. *Days of Wine and Rage.* Ringwood: Penguin, 1980.

———. 'Authors' Statements: Frank Moorhouse. *Australian Literary Studies* 10.2 (1981): 222-23.

———. ed. *The State of the Art.* Ringwood: Penguin, 1983.

———. *Room Service.* Ringwood: Viking, 1985. Penguin, 1987.

———. *Forty-Seventeen.* Ringwood: Viking, 1988.

FURTHER READING

Criticism

Bennett, Bruce. "Asian Encounters in the Contemporary Australian Short Story." *WLWE* 26, No. 1 (Spring 1986): 49-61.

    Examines the portrayal of Asian characters in Moorhouse's short fiction.

Lewis, Peter. "Reclaiming Realism." *Stand Magazine* 32, No. 3 (Summer 1991): 78-84.

    Compares the careers of Moorhouse and Michael Wilding.

Ross, Bruce Clunies. "Some Developments in Short Fiction, 1969-1980." *Australian Literary Studies* 10, No. 2 (October 1981): 165-80.

    Traces the development of the Australian short story through a survey of the work of Moorhouse, Peter Carey, and Michael Wilding.

Smith, Graeme Kinross. Liberating Acts: Frank Moorhouse, His Life, His Narratives." *Southerly* 46, No. 4 (1986): 391-423.

    Provides an overview of Moorhouse's life and career.

Arthur Morrison
1863–1945

English novelist, journalist, and short story writer.

INTRODUCTION

Morrison's literary reputation is mostly based on his realistic novels and short stories about slum life in London. In addition, he wrote detective fiction that is openly derivative of Arthur Conan Doyle's Sherlock Holmes stories. Possessed with a wide and free-ranging curiosity, Morrison wrote both fiction and nonfiction works on diverse subjects, from Japanese art to occultism, and participated in English literary life well into World War II.

BIOGRAPHICAL INFORMATION

Morrison was born in London's East End slums on November 1, 1863. While he apparently wanted to live down his working-class origins, and never gave any specific accounting of his early years, this never prevented him from displaying his penetrating understanding of slum life in his work. Commentators consider it likely that he was largely, if not entirely self-educated. In 1886 he began working as a clerk for the "People's Palace," a social-improvement charity organized by novelist and critic Walter Besant. By 1889, Morrison was working as an editor for Besant's *Palace Journal*, and made a brief appearance on the editorial staff of the *Globe* as well. His East End sketch, "A Street," published in *Macmillan's Magazine* in 1891, garnered some popular and critical attention. His work began appearing in newspapers and periodicals regularly, and a collection of his short stories about London slum life, *Tales of Mean Streets*, was published in 1894.

By 1910, Morrison had less interest in literature. He acquired a taste for Eastern art, especially Japanese painting and printmaking. He assembled an extensive collection of Japanese and other Eastern art, as well as works by a number of English masters, including William Hogarth, Thomas Gainsborough, John Constable, and J. M. W. Turner. His literary output continued to dwindle, even as he was elected to the Royal Society of Literature. Morrison eventually became a professional art dealer. He died in 1945 at the age of eighty-two.

MAJOR WORKS OF SHORT FICTION

Morrison's short fiction can be classified into two main categories; realistic East End chronicles and detective stories. His first collection, *Tales of Mean Streets*, chronicles

the plight of the urban poor in London's East End. This collection, along with his subsequent East End novel *A Child of the Jago*, fed into the ongoing controversy over literary realism, a debate involving such authors as Stephen Crane and Emile Zola. In 1894 Morrison began publishing detective stories in the *Strand* and *Windsor Magazine*. The protagonist of these stories, Martin Hewitt, was thought to be a response to the death of Sherlock Holmes, to whom Hewitt is often compared. The Hewitt stories were collected in four volumes: *Martin Hewitt, Investigator, Chronicles of Martin Hewitt, Adventures of Martin Hewitt,* and *The Red Triangle*. In addition to his Hewitt stories, Morrison made two other forays into the detective field: *The Dorrington Deed-Box,* which introduces the quasi-criminal antihero Dorrington; and *The Green Eye of Goona,* a pastiche of Willkie Collins's *The Moon-Stone*.

CRITICAL RECEPTION

Although he was accused of overemphasizing and exploiting the gloomier and more fatalistic side of East End life,

Morrison garnered considerable praise and attention for his collection *Tales of Mean Streets*. The stories in the collection figured in an ongoing debate about literary realism and were esteemed and criticized for its grimly vivid depictions of the bleakness and the squalor of lower-class existence in London's East End. Morrison's detective fiction suffered by inevitable comparison with Sherlock Holmes, but enjoyed moderate popularity all the same. As far as modern critics are concerned, many have observed that his work has fallen into undeserved obscurity and merits serious reconsideration.

PRINCIPAL WORKS

Short Fiction

Martin Hewitt, Investigator 1894
Tales of Mean Streets 1894
Chronicles of Martin Hewitt 1895
Zig-Zags at the Zoo 1895
Adventures of Martin Hewitt 1896
The Dorrington Deed-Box 1897
The Red Triangle: Being Some Further Chronicles of Martin Hewitt, Investigator 1903
Divers Vanities 1905
Green Ginger 1909
Short Stories of Today and Yesterday 1929
Fiddle O'Dreams 1933

Other Major Works

The Shadows around Us: Authentic Tales of the Supernatural (nonfiction) 1891
A Child of the Jago (novel) 1896
To London Town (novel) 1899
Cunning Murrell (novel) 1900
The Hole in the Wall (novel) 1902
The Green Eye of Goona (novel) 1904
Exhibition of Japanese Screens Painted by the Old Masters (criticism) 1910
The Painters of Japan 2 Vols. (criticism) 1911
Guide to an Exhibition of Japanese and Chinese Paintings (criticism) 1914

CRITICISM

The Bookman (review date 1895)

SOURCE: A review of *Tales of the Mean Streets*, in *The Bookman*, Vol. 1, No. 1, February, 1895, pp. 121-22.

[*The following review praises Morrison's* Tales of Mean Streets.]

[*Tales of Mean Streets*] is an unmistakably strong book. The East End and its dwellers have never before been painted from the same standpoint, nor in so vigorous and independent a fashion. That it gives the inevitable picture which sojourners in the neighbourhood must carry away, we certainly do not assert. It is distinctly limited, but limited because its point of view is individual, its purpose scrupulously truthful. Mr. Morrison's intention has been to tell just what he has seen, idealising nothing and keeping back little. He has carried it out with a frankness which no doubt some readers will term brutal, and which certainly wants some courage to face. They are pictures of misery, cruelty, sordidness, he gives us for the most part, pictures rather than descriptions; the moral showman never appears at all to pull a long face, or shake his head, or say "How pitiful!" or "How wrong!" The reader is left to make his own reflections, and they will not be comfortable ones, on **"Lizerunt," "Without Visible Means,"** and **"On the Stairs."** Mr. Morrison has plainly a bias; and who has not? With the right or wrong of that bias literary criticism has nothing to do, provided he give it logical and forcible expression. It is, however, perfectly legitimate to take objection to the long monotony of dreariness, which the slight facetiousness of **"The Red Cow Group,"** the comic mixture of rascality and hysteria in **"A Conversion,"** the patient pluck in **"Three Rounds,"** and the grim independence of **"Behind the Shade,"** are not enough, and hardly of a kind, to relieve. It is fair to say that there is something wanting in his picture—something pertaining to rational happiness and unselfish endeavour, which experience has led one to expect in streets however mean. We need not accept his as the whole picture, but who will dare to say it is not true in great part? The book is far from heartless; indeed, possibly it is just because the observer's feelings were not of that easy kind that can be relieved by mere words of pity that his stories are so grim and so ungenial. So much for the effect of the tales on our emotions. Regarded merely from the point of fiction, they are the work of an unusually vigorous writer, whose vision is clear and whose dramatic sense is vivid, and who, in putting his scenes and pictures into words, invariably takes the best and shortest way. An introduction has been written for the American edition; and a portrait of Mr. Morrison will be found among our News Notes.

The Bookman (review date 1909)

SOURCE: "Novels Notes," in *The Bookman*, Vol. XXXV, No. 210, March, 1909, p. 281.

[*In the following review, the anonymous critic lauds the humor in* Green Ginger.]

It is evidently time that we revised our judgment of Mr. Arthur Morrison. Whilst we have been persistently classing him as a grim and sombre realist, he has been developing into one of the most delightfully irresponsible of humorists. Of course we knew from **"That Brute Simmons,"** in his *Tales of Mean Streets,* and from certain of the tales in his *Divers Vanities,* that he had an abundant sense of humour, but we had not credited him with possessing the breezy, broadly farcical spirit of fun that fills the pages of *Green Ginger* with the best and heartiest food for laughter that you will find nowadays anywhere outside a book by Jacobs. Now and then, as in such stories as **"Cap'en Jollyfax's Gun"** or **"The Copper Charm,"** he gives you quaint and excellent character-sketches; everywhere the descriptions of persons and places are touched in vividly and with his accustomed skill; but when all's said you come back to the story—the tale's the thing, and though it might be easy to decide which of them has the most ingenious plot, which embodies the most gloriously odd or ludicrous incident, it is very difficult indeed to look back over them and say, where all are so wholly amusing, which is the liveliest and most laughable. Perhaps it is enough to say that the present reviewer, a hardened specimen of his tribe, has read every one of them, taking them in their order, and was only sorry they were not twice as many, and that if you would like to laugh, and to keep on laughing through three hundred and twenty-eight pages, you cannot do better than ask for *Green Ginger,* and see that you get it.

Jocelyn Bell (essay date 1952)

SOURCE: "A Study of Arthur Morrison," in *Essays and Studies,* Vol. 5, 1952, pp. 77-89.

[*In the following essay, Bell provides a biographical survey of Morrison's writing.*]

At a distance of half a century an age is no longer dismissed as old-fashioned; its historical importance and period singularity are recognized. The Victorians and Edwardians are reappearing, freshly presented in reprints and radio serials and revalued in biography and criticism. Arthur Morrison is among them. Born in 1863, he belongs in literature to the 1890's and the turning century, finishing his best work by 1902 but writing throughout the Edwardian reign until he retired in 1913. He was one of those contemporary best-sellers who could be found on every Edwardian bookshelf, but who vanished in the Great War and were unknown to the new and changed generation which followed; and now that, once again, the novels which made his name are in the bookshops, it is not out of place to attempt an assessment of his literary talent, to determine how much he achieved, and why he did not achieve more.

The 1890's were brilliant, chaotic years: gay, sombre; irresponsible, earnest; years which saw Lottie Collins at the Gaiety and Mrs. Pat Campbell as Paula Tanquerary; which saw Keir Hardie's first Labour Party and the Diamond Ju-

bilee; the Sidney Webbs, Beardsley, and the trial of Oscar Wilde. The literary world introduced its own novelties, from the "incomparable Max" to George Bernard Shaw, and the dramatic explosion of Ibsen had been preceded but a few years previously by that of Zola, when in the 1880's his novels were first translated into English, immediately suppressed, and their publisher imprisoned. If it was an age of aesthetic adventure, it was also an age of moral revolution.

The translations of the French "realistic" novelists, Zola and Flaubert, the Goncourts and Maupassant, had raised a sharp and violent controversy in the English periodical press as to the place of frankness in literature, an outcry which had been countered successfully by prominent critics like Edmund Gosse[1] and lesser known pioneers like Hubert Crackanthorpe,[2] and by 1894 the "new" realistic fiction, though still experimental, was recognized in literary circles and developed by major writers like George Moore and George Gissing, and by minor ones like Henry Harland, "George Egerton", Crackanthorpe, and Grant Allen. Taking its main inspiration from the French writers, it was concerned with the direct portrayal of the social conditions and moral problems of contemporary life, and novelists, claiming broader horizons for their art, asserted their right to deal with any subject, fine or ugly, beautiful or sordid, which was a genuine aspect of human existence. Arthur Morrison belongs to the forefront of this realistic movement, and his *Tales of Mean Streets* which appeared in 1894, were not only the first examples of "mean street" studies, but also a collection of best-sellers which provided a neat generic title for the subsequent studies of slum life which followed in rapid succession from other writers. Morrison's "mean street" realism, however, is in a different category from that of George Moore or Gissing, who used such surroundings as background to the main play of character and moral problem, for he is not a moralist, nor does he attempt studies of psychology and temperament; he presents the slum surroundings, not as the background, but as the main theme. It is a serious theme, too, plainly spoken. Slums and poverty were not, of course, new to literature; they were in Dickens, Mrs. Gaskell and Charles Kingsley, or, nearer to hand, in books like Walter Besant's *Children of Gideon*—a romance in the dismal East End setting of Hoxton which is at the same time a plea for social reform; and in Gissing's *The Nether World* there are descriptions of Pennyloaf Candy's wretched home in Clerkenwell which foreshadow Morrison's *Child of the Jago.* But Morrison was the first to set out deliberately to record slum life as it really was: "In my East End stories," he said, "I determined that they must be written in a different way from the ordinary slum story. They must be done with austerity and frankness, and there must be no sentimentalism, no glossing over. I felt that the writer must never interpose himself between his subject and his reader. I could best bring in real life by keeping myself and my . . . moralizings out of it. For this I have been abused as hard and unsympathetic, but I can assure you it is far more painful for me to write stories than for you to read them." How far in this attitude he saw himself as part of a literary trend it is difficult to say, for he was undoubtedly aware of the realistic movement and had seen its possibilities; he belonged to his time. Yet he was a journalist rather than a man of letters, and literary historians are sometimes prone to over-emphasize "influences"; however much he may have read of contemporary English and French realism, his primary inspiration came without question direct and at first hand from his own experience in the East End.

The People's Palace, founded by Walter Besant, had been opened at Mile End in 1887, and Morrison worked for many years as Secretary of the People's Palace Trust, being a close friend of its Chairman, Sir Edmund Currie, and living, as he said, "in the very heart of that part of London". When he turned to journalism it was from these days that he drew material for his tales. The publication of the first of them in *Macmillan's Magazine* attracted the attention of W. E. Henley, then editing the famous *National Observer.* Morrison wrote, at Henley's request, further short stories which appeared in the *National Observer* and were later collected into the one volume: *Tales of Mean Streets.* Henley was an exacting editor; he demanded brevity, incisiveness and finish from his contributors, and Morrison, though he wrote many more stories, does not again achieve the variety and skill of these sketches and descriptive incidents, drawn objectively, but with a strong undercurrent of feeling, and detailing facets of East End life—its brutality, its heartlessness, its shoddy gentility and grey monotone. The first tale: **"A Street"**—where he tries to paint the empty sameness of average slum life, is perhaps the least successful, though it struck an original note when it was written, but there is a touch of genuine drama ending the story **"In Business,"** as the patient, stupid husband, driven at last to protest against his wife's nagging victimization, walks out quietly one morning and leaves her; a touch of comedy in the lighter treatment of a similar relationship in **"That Brute Simmons"**—a tale which he afterwards dramatized. There is the stringent cynicism of **"Conversion,"** in which light-fingered Scuddy Lond slips neatly back to iniquity after an emotional spasm of grace in the local mission hall; or the unblinking horror of **"Lizerunt"** (once christened, but long forgotten as, Elizabeth Hunt), her courtship and marriage. They are plain tales in plain language, in which, from a present-day vantage-point, it is easier to see omissions than achievement, since there is neither subtlety nor sophistication, depth of character study nor creation of mood, no sensuous appeal nor lyric grace. They possess, on the other hand, a firm and even economy of line, etched with a dry restraint which can deepen into caustic terseness; the subject-matter is genuine, the treatment honest, and, while in accordance with his purpose he sternly avoids emotionalism and sensationalism, he is never detached—the pressure of his own keen feeling is perceptible, strengthening his style.

The short story was becoming a popular form, and realism was a new vogue; *Tales of Mean Streets,* in addition to their intrinsic merit, came appropriately. Critics were impressed, and the author's reputation was established. Other writers like W. Pett Ridge and Edwin Pugh pursued the "mean street" theme in sketches of suburban types—shop girls, clerks, domestic servants, but played for Cockney comedy rather than serious comment. Nearer to Morrison in spirit were Richard Whiteing, who wrote *No. 5. John Street* as a picture of life in a London tenement, and Somerset Maugham, whose first novel, *Liza of Lambeth,* was in 1897 considered shockingly daring and quite improper for young ladies, since it told of an illicit love affair followed by a miscarriage. The style in its immature simplicity is tepid beside Morrison's, although the gift of sharp and accurate observation, the acute interest in people and their behaviour, which were ultimately to make him a more accomplished writer, are already apparent. Morrison took his own East End studies further two years later in a full-length novel, *Child of the Jago.* The Jago was his name for that part of Shoreditch known as the Nichol, from the name of Old Nichol Street, and it comprised the Boundary Lane area skirted by the Shoreditch High Street and the Bethnal Green Road. Nothing of it remains today, except the faded name-plate of Old Nichol Street; there is merely a commonplace agglomeration of shops, houses, prefabs, and bomb damage, buttressed by the stolid barrack-like buildings of the L.C.C. housing estate. Contemporary nineteenth-century reports, however, described it as "a nest of vice and disease" comprising "congeries of filthy and insanitary courts and alleys," and it was a notorious slum. It is claimed by those who know Morrison's book and something of the background against which it was written, that its publication was finally responsible for urging the London County Council to act and clear this district; unfortunately the compliment is without foundation, for the facts disprove it. The L.C.C. had been formed in 1889, and had started slum clearance in this part of Shoreditch as a pressing priority in 1891. Morrison himself stated, in a long interview in the *Daily News* for December 12th, 1896, that when he first went to the Nichol it was "on the point of being pulled down," although encroachment was slow. He lived in the Nichol, working and talking with the inhabitants, for eighteen months, and his novel is a record of his experience, which he completed in 1896 "just as the last houses were coming down." Building of the new estate began immediately, and it was opened by the Prince of Wales in 1900. Yet, although Morrison could not be credited with instigating the reform, he did receive tribute for commemorating it, for the Prince when speaking at the opening ceremony said that "few, indeed will forget this site who have read Mr. Morrison's pathetic tale of *Child of the Jago.* Certainly the book made its mark, and its frank honesty may have influenced later housing schemes. It is as a sidelight on social history rather than as a novel that it is now valuable; the Jago, though vanished, is as symptomatic as Gin Lane. As a novel, the book is but average, but as a documentary it is illuminating. Critics complained, not without reason, of the technical faults in construction, and deplored the unpleasantness of the subject-matter, shifting a little uneasily, no doubt, before such an uncompromising statement of the facts, while Morrison in reply agreed that the Nichol was one of the isolated plague spots and not typical of the sheer dreariness of most East End life, which was "respectable to the gloomiest point of monotony"; on the other hand, he rewarded his critics with chapter and verse for the origin of some of the incidents they had picked out as improbable: "Critics have considered that Sally Green, my fighting heroine, was exaggerated. Indeed she is not. She is alive now, and her particular mode of fighting . . . is spoken of to this hour." Glass bottles, deliberately broken and jagged, were "quite a feature of East End life" as aggressive weapons. Those who argued that he had "nothing new to say" and that in any case the evil he exposed was already being remedied were answered in the preface to a later edition of the novel, as well as in newspaper articles: "I have remarked in more than one place the expression of a foolish fancy that because the houses of the old Jago have been pulled down the Jago difficulty has been cleared out of the way. That is far from being the case. The Jago, as mere bricks and mortar, is gone. But the Jago in flesh and blood still lives. . . ." Slum clearance was only the first step in social reform, which would not be really effective until organized and authoritative action was taken for dealing with the human problem which the slums produced.

Morrison's intention in writing the book can also be given in his own words. It was "to tell the story of the horrible Nichol . . . and of a boy who, but for his environment, would have become a good citizen." The tale is of Dicky Perrott, whose parents, though once boasting an honest if shabby livelihood, have sunk to Jago level. The mother is an inert weakling, the father a thief. Dicky, too, shows an early aptitude for theft which is promptly exploited by the cunning fence, Aaron Weech, while his childish gropings towards a better way of life are fostered by the local missionary, Father Sturt, who finds him a job as a shop boy in the Bethnal Green Road. The evil Mr. Weech, however, thereby losing a client, negotiates the boy's dismissal, and Dicky, bewildered and only half-comprehending the forces stronger than himself, returns to his old haunts, accepting the Jago dictum: "Spare nobody and stop at nothing, for the Jago's got you, and it's the only way out, except the gaol and the gallows." The father, Josh Perrott, does end on the gallows for murdering Aaron Weech, but Dicky is knifed in a street brawl and so is spared the worst excesses of Jago life.

Morrison had excellent narrative skill, and could reproduce all the pert pungency of the Cockney dialect. His style is swift and direct, his descriptions forceful. Yet one of his critics[3] put the paradoxical view that, in spite of the realistic immediacy, the final effect of the book was one of unreality, which led him to suggest that Morrison could succeed better within the compass of the short story than in the full-length novel. That the latter was not the case Morrison was to prove when he wrote *The Hole in the Wall,* but the paradox holds, and can be explained. As in *Tales of Mean Streets* the author was writing from deep conviction about what he knew, but what in the former work was a source of strength is here a source of weakness. His very feeling about his subject blunts his vision,

leading him to record rather than interpret his experience. He is too near to be able to shed irrelevancies and distil the essential features, or to illuminate the heart of his story by throwing it into relation with a broader background. His emotions are too violent to be a creative inspiration; they break through, upsetting poise and perspective, leading him into acid sarcasm, or over-description. He seeks to emphasize by repetition rather than selection. He portrays facts, but not the motives which underlie them, and material circumstance alone does not make a living novel any more than genuine cups and saucers on the stage made a living drama; it is the old confusion between realism and reality. We are led ingeniously on through a series of vivid incidents, but one street fight follows another very like it—Morrison was an expert boxer himself, and no doubt enjoyed describing what he understood so well—but in the end we have arrived nowhere; we have experienced movement without progression. In the same way, his characters live in sharp and convincing outline, but they do not grow; they are solid enough when in action, but revert to pasteboard stuff when they have to think or feel. Dicky Perrott is a real child when he steals the Bishop's watch or runs for his life from his pursuers, but when faced with an emotional experience tends to become mawkish or theatrical. Morrison's ability to create character was limited to what was outwardly visible; had he had George Eliot's penetrating insight into character he might have drawn a child as memorable as Maggie Tulliver, for he had a theme full of potentialities.

Morrison had been introduced to the Nichol by the Reverend Osborne Jay, Vicar of Holy Trinity, Shoreditch, a man for whom he had profound affection and respect, and he dedicated the book to him, incorporating him in the Jago story as Father Sturt. Jay must indeed have been a man of fine and powerful character, for since his appointment to the living in 1886 he had carried out reforms in the face of heartbreaking odds which eventually won the acknowledgement even of the Jagos: "He had an influence among them such as they had never known before. . . . The mean cunning of the Jago, subtle as it was, and baffling to most strangers, foundered miserably before his relentless intelligence, and crafty rogues . . . soon gave up all hope or effort to deceive him. . . . Thus he was respected. . . . Then there became apparent in him qualities of charity and loving-kindness, well-judged and governed, that awoke in places a regard that was in a way akin to affection." Offset against this are sarcastic criticisms of the church mission and popular philanthropy, whether justified or not it is not easy to say at this distance; certainly the Shoreditch Committee of the London Charity Organization Society was admitting defeat in 1888: "An examination of cases has shown a great mass of hopeless poverty, with which private charity is not strong enough to cope. . . . In many instances efforts were made to help, but the results have not been encouraging. . . ." In face of the dire need for drastic and official social reforms, Morrison had no use for fashionable "slumming" or for genteel charity operated from a safe distance, and he had seen the futility of the methods of the sentimental pietist in a district like the

Nichol where poverty bred crime and criminal bred criminal in rapid and progressive deterioration. "The false sentiment of the day is the curse of the country", he wrote in one newspaper article,[4] and he aimed to show that "Father Jay's method is the only one it is possible to employ in such a district". If the book is a social indictment, it is also a tribute to a man's work.

Those who did not care for hard facts in fiction could choose elsewhere, and the choice was wide and varied. There were the early stories of Kipling, glowing with unfamiliar colour; the gentler mood of Barrie, or Kenneth Grahame; *The Time Machine* had appeared in 1895 and was quickly followed by more of Wells's scientific romances, while those who preferred historical romance could turn to Anthony Hope, Gilbert Parker, or Stanley Weyman, and Marie Corelli's unique sensationalism was drawing its own readers—*The Sorrows of Satan,* produced in 1895, reached its fortieth reprint within a few years. Emerging as a new genre was the detective story, for Arthur Conan Doyle had won immediate popularity with the first Sherlock Holmes stories in the late 1880's and early 90's, and readers who had enjoyed these could turn back to Arthur Morrison for further adventures in the same vein. He came as a quick successor to Conan Doyle, and alongside *Tales of Mean Streets* in 1894 came a close imitation of *The Adventures of Sherlock Holmes* in *Martin Hewitt, Investigator.* This in turn was continued in further volumes as the *Adventures* and *Chronicles* of the same hero. The comparison with Conan Doyle, who is still good entertainment, is an amusing one. Hewitt and his staunch friend, Brett, replace Holmes and the blunt-witted Watson, and Brett, like Watson, acts as the chronicler of his brilliant friend's exploits. Hewitt, like Holmes, is encyclopaedic. As Holmes has only to see a Chinese tattoo mark to launch into a description of the art, so Hewitt is equally fluent on Chinese seals or the chemical decomposition of burnt boot buttons, and proves himself just as instantaneous in decoding a cypher or summing up a character's past history from his personal appearance. In short, "Hewitt's infallible intuition", as his *Times* critic phrased it, "is positively stupefying". Morrison copied Doyle's method of exposition by explanatory narrative dialogue which is long and sometimes unwieldy, though Morrison could write good dialogue when on his own ground, as his Cockney stories show. Conan Doyle's style in general is crisper than Morrison's, and the incidents he invents are more bizarre and exotic. Hewitt does not possess Holmes's exceptional flair for disguises, nor is he ever called in to help the crowned heads of Europe out of their intrigues. Sherlock Holmes's creator endowed him with an eccentric personality: a tall, spare figure with pipe and silk dressing-gown, aquiline features and long, nervous fingers, with moody and unpredictable habits and a fondness for solving his problems by sitting up all night smoking, cross-legged on a pile of silk cushions. Morrison, on the contrary, insists on the ordinariness of his detective; Hewitt is just a plain fellow, an ex-barrister enjoying a hobby, a "pleasant and companionable" chap, of ordinary height and even inclined to stoutness; in detective literature he marks a distinct break-away from the established eccentric type of crime-investigator. Working in a plainer style than Holmes, he deals with more homely crimes, which, in fact, recur a little monotonously, as do the attendant circumstances of burnt papers, forged cheques and locked doors. Morrison is not very inventive, and does not stray far from jewel robberies, forgery and simple murder, although in a later sequence, *The Red Triangle,* Hewitt does have to pit his wits against a dangerous hypnotist, and Morrison gives the genre a new twist in *The Dorrington Deed-Box,* where the unravelling of crime is done by Dorrington as a fake inquiry-agent who turned his talents to his own profit. Moreover, he avoids cheap sensationalism, and the incident in *The Dorrington Deed-Box* where the dupe wakes up to find himself drowning in an iron tank and is rescued miraculously at the last minute by a workman providently employed next door, is a rare lapse from his usual good sense. To modern readers these early detective stories seem unsubtle in their directness and one-sided in their purely intellectual exercise, forerunners in period dress of what is now an ingenious and intricate literature; yet they have their assured place in the history of detective fiction. Sherlock Holmes has become immortal, and though Martin Hewitt will not be known to many readers, the historian recognizes that Morrison's sound style and good craftsmanship was a solid contribution to a genre which was too readily debased by third-rate hack-writing.

Detective stories were a diversion. Morrison returned at the close of the century to an authentic background of an entirely different kind from the East End of London in his next two novels: *To London Town* and *Cunning Murrell.* The former is competent but undistinguished, employing his knowledge of Epping Forest and the stretch of country through Leytonstone into north-east London to Blackwall Cross and Harbour Lane, where the widowed Mrs. May comes to find a livelihood in shopkeeping while her son Johnny is apprenticed as a ship engineer. *Cunning Murrell* is well worth remembering as a real record of witchcraft in Essex in the 1850's, against a background of smuggling around the coast of Leigh and Hadleigh, which were then quiet rural backwaters. It is incredible but true that in such parts of Essex belief in witchcraft lingered throughout the nineteenth century and even into the twentieth. Contemporary newspapers provide evidence of actual cases brought before the local courts from time to time, as near our own day as 1908. The real James Murrell, the original of Morrison's novel, belongs to the mid-nineteenth century period, and he lived in Hadleigh as a shoemaker by trade, who made an additional income by telling fortunes, casting spells, and discovering witches, and, as a practising herbalist, by administering drugs and potions. He was widely known and feared for his occult powers, and when he died in 1860 a large number of letters and papers were disclosed which revealed the extent of his practices and influence. Morrison had seen these—he mentions them in his foreword—and it is from them that he weaves this tale of how Murrell casts out an innocent old woman as a witch, with the intricate train of events which follow. In spite of its unusual and potentially sinister theme, it is more genial in tone and better-made as a novel than *Child of the Jago* and with descriptions of Hadleigh, its castle and Essex landscape as a background the story flows with just sufficient movement, mystery and suspense to keep the reader turning the next page, the next chapter, to the end.

Morrison knew his Essex as intimately as he knew his East End. He had married in 1892 and probably settled at Loughton soon afterwards, for we find him giving an address there in 1896, though of course he continued for many years to work in London. His connection with the People's Palace Trust ended in 1902 when Sir Edmund Currie resigned the chairmanship, and he devoted all his time to journalism, working on the editorial staff of a London newspaper. Later his Essex address changes to High Beech, in the heart of Epping Forest, where W. W. Jacobs also lived. No doubt his best writing went into newspaper articles which were often unsigned or written under an assumed name, for although in the Edwardian period he published further collections of short stories: *Divers Vanities, Green Ginger* and *The Green Eye of Goona,* they do not disclose any development of talent, but repeat, albeit skillfully, the same patterns grouped round earlier East End characters, or those Essex characters which appeared in *Cunning Murrell.* His former trenchancy has gone, and here comedy is uppermost, resting on Cockney humour which exploits situation and dialogue, in which there is much genuine comedy in spite of a tendency to jauntiness. One misses the warmer, more human, quiet comedy of Jacobs.

He did, however, write one more full-length novel, which V. S. Pritchett has claimed to be "one of the minor masterpieces of this century". This is a just estimate of *The Hole in the Wall,* though out of focus, for the book belongs to its period and it would be a truer definition to call it a "minor Edwardian masterpiece." The Hole in the Wall is a public-house, in the notorious Radcliffe Highway of the mid-nineteenth century, which by 1902, when the book was written, had been purged and re-named St. George Street. The tale is of the small orphaned boy, Stephen, who is brought up there by his grandfather, and surrounded by murder, violence and swindling. Morrison can be trusted to deal with a sensational theme unsensationally, and the economy and quiet forcefulness with which the sinister plot unfolds produce a vivid, concise narrative; indeed, this narrative gift, always his first asset, is here seen at its best. Instead of the unrelieved sordidness which marred the after-effect of *Child of the Jago,* the dark episodes are lightened by comedy, derived from the flowing Cockney dialogue with which he is always at home, and in particular from the character of Mr. Cripps, the scoundrel artist who haunts the pub for what he can gain and who cannot resist interfering—to his own ultimate discomforture—in other people's affairs. Such moments are among Morrison's most enjoyable, and one remembers the incident in the otherwise tepid story of *To London Town* where the pretentious Mr. Butson is accosted on dockside by the half-drunk Emma Pacey and badgered to lend her twopence. It is broad, simple comedy, but effective.

Morrison's device of telling the *The Hole in the Wall* story partly as "Stephen's tale" and partly as direct narrative is an imaginative stroke which heightens the effect considerably. Intensity and perspective vary as the angle of vision shifts from the child's personal story to the author's, lighting the stage now this way, now that, as, for example, where the screams of the woman who has fallen over a certain dead body which she dreaded finding in the dark, are heard in Blue Gate by the last pub-stragglers and at the same time by Stephen, lying in bed listening with innocence but apprehension to the creaking house. The honest simplicity of the child's nature throws an even murkier shadow over the evil which surrounds him.

The central theme is the change wrought in Grandfather Nat—by no means a virtuous character—by his incurred responsibility towards the child, and by the child's unquestioning affection for him. It has already been suggested that Morrison's ability to draw character was limited, and that although his people live and move with enough conviction to propel the story, they do not develop, but then portrayal of temperament and personal relationship was not his first concern. He draws types rather than individuals, and having drawn them, tends to repeat the pattern, or he will draw a slightly eccentric personality by emphasizing one feature at the expense of the rest, so giving characters like Aaron Weech in *Child of the Jago* or Long Hicks in *To London Town* a superficial Dickensian resemblance—superficial, because the two authors have little really in common except their social anger and London background. In *The Hole in the Wall* however, he achieves a much closer interrelation of character and event than hitherto, and attempts to show, at least in the case of Grandfather Nat, a character modified by experience. Furthermore, action springs from character as well as from incident: it is Mag's devotion to Dan Ogle—her one virtue—which ironically focuses suspicion on him; it is Mr. Cripps's officious self-importance which precipitates the unmasking of Mrs. Grimes; it is the enraged vanity of Blind George, who, malicious as he is towards others, cannot bear taunts about his own blindness, which incenses him to blind Dan Ogle in revenge, and indirectly to change the end of the story. In the other novels characters were either good or bad; here at times they suggest a deeper complexity, with moods of doubt and fear.

The author's descriptive method is direct photography—a recording of things as they are. That this is not always successful is illustrated by his description of the notorious pub, for he devotes a page to drawing its twisted geometry, whereas a few significant strokes and a touch of imagery would have created for the reader a less exact but more impelling impression. But such instances are few, and are more than offset by the controlled incisiveness of such scenes as Mag's journey across Limehouse flats, the blinding of Dan Ogle, or the fire which destroys the public-house. These, and passages from his other East End books, leave memorable pictures of the London river with its docks and wharfs, its warehouses and murky dockside streets, its marshy flats and sullen skies, of slum squalour and the humdrum traffic of poverty.

After the excellence of *The Hole in the Wall* Morrison's failure to develop as an Edwardian novelist is disappointing, and possible reasons for this are by now apparent; he was, in the final count, a skilled craftsman rather than a creative artist, and lacked the imaginative power to sustain original work; moreover, he was a busy practising journalist and perhaps had neither the time nor the ambition to attempt literary eminence. One further reason may have lain in the fact that he was at this time compiling a work of very different dimensions. Morrison devoted his spare time to the collection of works of art, and he was a keen connoisseur not only of English painting, but also, and of more importance, of Oriental art. His last published work before he retired in 1913 was a two-volume survey of the painters of Japan, which became, and is still regarded as, a leading work on the subject, while his fine collection of Chinese and Japanese drawings was acquired by the British Museum on his retirement.

His career as a writer was therefore over, but his interest in literature by no means waned. After the 1914-18 war he returned from Epping Forest to live in London, and settled in Cavendish Square, off Regent Street. In December, 1924, through his close friendship with Sir Henry Newbolt, he was elected a member of the Royal Society of Literature by unanimous invitation of its Council. Eleven years later he was invited to join the Council itself, on which he served as a keen and active member until his death in his Buckinghamshire home in 1945.

It was perhaps the circumstance of his death, together with the returning taste for this period of literature, which brought about the re-issue of his best work, and present-day readers owe much to publishers like Eyre and Spottiswoode, whose Century Library series is designed to save such authors as Morrison from oblivion, for they deserve to be reinstated on our bookshelves. Yesterday's best-sellers can be more than today's curiosities; with an assured and honest craftsman they exhibit talents which both inform and entertain.

Notes

1. The National Review, 1892: The tyranny of the novel.
2. The Yellow Book, 1894.
3. H. D. Traill: The new fiction, and other essays on literary subjects. Hurst & Blackett, 1897.
4. *Daily News,* 12th December, 1896.

P. J. Keating (essay date 1971)

SOURCE: "Arthur Morrison and the Tone of Violence," in *The Working Classes in Victorian Fiction,* Routledge & Kegan Paul, 1971, pp. 167-98.

[*In the following essay, Keating provides a thematic and stylistic analysis of Morrison's fiction dealing with working-class life in the East End of London.*]

I

In the 1890s Arthur Morrison wrote three books which deal with working-class life in the East End: *Tales of Mean Streets* (1894), *A Child of the Jago* (1896) and *To London Town* (1899). . . . Morrison's work is an amalgam of Besant, who supplies a new image of the East End; Charles Booth, who clarifies the class structure of that image; and Kipling, from whom Morrison derives his objective, amoral, literary method. To these diverse influences he brings considerable personal experience of working-class life, carefully acquired skill as a reporter, and a simple but vivid prose style. More than any other author it is Arthur Morrison who establishes the tone of slum fiction in the nineties.

Very little of a personal nature is known about his early life, though it is now possible to construct a sound outline of his activities in the nineties. His birth certificate shows that he was born in Poplar, the son of an engine fitter, and from a few obviously autobiographical remarks in his published writings it seems reasonable to assume that at least some of his childhood was spent in the East End, but it is impossible to draw any definite conclusions about this period of his life. Nothing further is known of him until, at the age of twenty-three, his signature appears on a cash receipt in respect of one month's salary (September 1886) as Clerk to the Beaumont Trustees, the philanthropic foundation that administered the People's Palace. Once again he disappears from the scene until 6 March 1889 when he was appointed sub-editor of the *Palace Journal,* then under the control of Walter Besant, from whom it was later claimed he 'received some hints on the technical ABC of fiction'.[1] As sub-editor of the *Journal* he compiled a weekly column of general information about the Palace and, more interestingly, published three signed descriptive sketches of the East End. After about nine months Morrison relinquished his post as sub-editor and six months later resigned from the Beaumont Trustees.[2] From this time onwards he chiefly earned his living as a free-lance journalist. In October 1891, he published an article in *Macmillan's Magazine* called "A Street" which, in a revised form, later became the famous introduction to *Tales of Mean Streets.* This article attracted the attention of W. E. Henley who invited Morrison to write a series of working-class stories for *The National Observer.* Apart from the *Mean Streets* stories he probably also contributed unsigned articles to the *Observer* and was usually labelled as one of 'Henley's young men' with, among others, Rudyard Kipling, who remained a life-long friend.

The three descriptive sketches published in the *Palace Journal* show Morrison striving, with little success, to develop an individual approach to the difficult problem of writing about the East End. The first of them, **"Whitechapel"** (24 April 1889), challenges the 'graphically-written descriptions of Whitechapel, by people who have never seen the place.' Morrison distinguishes between two types of description. The one:

> A horrible black labyrinth . . . reeking from end to end
> with the vilest exhalations; its streets, mere kennels of

horrent putrefaction; its every wall, its every object, slimy with the indigenous ooze of the place; swarming with human vermin, whose trade is robbery, and whose recreation is murder; the catacombs of London—darker, more tortuous, and more dangerous than those of Rome, and supersaturated with foul life.

This approach, as we have already seen, belongs to the Newgate-novel-Dickens-Kingsley-early-Gissing tradition, and during the late-Victorian period was still commonly used in the working-class romance. The other type of description is that of 'outcast' London:

> Black and nasty still, a wilderness of crazy dens into which pallid wastrels crawl to die; where several families lie in each fetid room, and fathers, mothers, and children watch each other starve; where bony, bleareyed wretches, with everything beautiful, brave, and worthy crushed out of them, and nothing of the glory and nobleness and jollity of this world within the range of their crippled senses, rasp away their puny lives in the sty of the sweater.

Morrison admits there are places in Whitechapel that fit these descriptions, but because of the size of the district and the variety of life to be found in it, neither can be said to be representative. In order to paint a fair picture of Whitechapel, he argues, one should take into account the ancient industries, colourful street traders, booksellers, and its many literary and historical associations, as well as the suffering poor and the foul slums. This is very similar to the kind of East End image that, under Besant's influence, the *Palace Journal* usually advanced, save at the close of Morrison's sketch a note of despair creeps in. While mocking the 'slummers' Morrison agrees that 'something must be done' about the black spots. But what?

> Children must not be left in these unscoured corners. Their fathers and mothers are hopeless, and must not be allowed to rear a numerous and equally hopeless race. Light the streets better, certainly; but what use in building better houses for these poor creatures to render as foul as those that stand? The inmates may ruin the character of a house, but no house can alter the character of its inmates.

These words, written while Morrison was actually working in 'The Palace of Delight,' hardly represent a vote of confidence for Besant's particular brand of optimism, but at this stage of his development Morrison was obviously not sure in his own mind just what attitude he should adopt towards the East End and the working classes. The other two sketches he wrote for the *Palace Journal* show the same uncertainty. **"On Blackwall Pier"** (8 May 1889) attempts to describe the strange extremes of life to be found side by side in a working-class setting. The gay coarseness of lovers on a pier is contrasted with the half-drowned body of an attempted suicide that is dragged from the Thames. The third sketch is virtually a plagiarism of Dickens's *A Christmas Carol,* in which tradesmen and shoppers swop jokes amid a plethora of fruit, meat and spirits. In this East End jolly policemen fall over chil-

dren's slides, gentlemen's hats fly off, bells chime, and the foulness of the slums is made picturesque by a sparkling frost.

By the time Morrison wrote **"A Street"** in 1891 he had rid his mind of these conflicting attitudes and had firmly established the compound of realistic observation and quiet despair that he made peculiarly his own:

> There is about one hundred and fifty yards of our street, all of the same pattern. It is not a picturesque street; a dingy little brick house twenty feet high with three square holes to carry the windows and an oblong hole to carry the door is not picturesque; and two or three score of them in a row, with one front wall in common, represent either side of our street and suggests stables.

Morrison has here completely accepted Besant's view that monotony not poverty is the most serious problem of East End life, but he has rejected Besant's cultural antidote. For Morrison monotony is a quality endemic in working-class life; it is not merely a sickness to be cured by building libraries or Palaces of Delight: 'And this is the record of a day in our street,—of any day,—of every day . . . Of every day excepting Sunday . . . This is Sunday in our street, and every Sunday is the same as every other Sunday.'[3]

To the social influence of Besant can be added the literary influence of Kipling, for the tone of *Tales of Mean Streets* owes much to 'Badalia Herodsfoot.' Short, simple, yet rhythmic sentences, tellingly used to create an air of authorial disinterest, is one of the techniques, coming from Kipling, that most distinctly separates the slum novelists of the nineties from their predecessors:

> Nobody laughs in our street,—life is too serious a thing—nobody sings. There was a woman who sang once,—a young wife from the country. But she bore children, and her voice cracked; then her man died, and she sang no more. They took away her home, and with her children about her skirts the woman left our street for ever. The other women did not think much of her. She was 'helpless.'[4]

Morrison himself wrote that he intended **"A Street"** to convey 'the deadly monotony and respectability of the mean streets so characteristic of the East End, for hopeless monotony is more characteristic than absolute degradation such as you find in the Jago.'[5] And this is the theme of not merely the introduction but the majority of *Mean Streets* tales. This point is of some importance as Morrison's reputation for concentrating upon the violent aspects of slum life was established even before he wrote *A Child of the Jago* (1896).

When *Tales of Mean Streets* was first published, critical attention, which was on the whole very favourable, focused so exclusively on **"Lizerunt,"** the one really violent story in a collection of fourteen, that Morrison, who was generally shy of publicity, wrote to one periodical denying that he had 'generalized half London as a race of Yahoos'.[6] At this time he had already begun to write *To London*

Town which, because of its gentleness of tone, might have been intended as a rebuke to his critics, but for some unknown reason he abandoned this work and published instead his study of East End criminal life *A Child of the Jago*. Once again he found himself at the centre of a debate on the extent and nature of violence in working-class life and fiction. Just as he had earlier pointed out that **"Lizerunt"** represented only one part of life in the East End, now he was forced to explain that *A Child of the Jago* dealt with a specific East End criminal ghetto, and at no time had he intended to offer it as representative of working-class life as a whole.[7] The critics paid little attention to his disavowals, and the phrase 'Jagodom' (used as a synonym for hooliganism, itself a word of recent coinage) passed, with 'mean streets,' into common usage. In spite of the fact that the greater part of Morrison's work was not concerned with the working classes at all, and that most of his working-class fiction did not deal with violent themes, it was **"Lizerunt"** and *A Child of the Jago* that established his literary reputation in the nineties.

Even today Morrison's critics find it difficult to regard his work in a rational manner. Julian Franklyn, concentrating entirely on **"Lizerunt,"** claims that: 'There could be such a monster [as Billy Chope, the hero] but in *Tales of Mean Streets* one gathers the impression that all Cockneys are like this. To Morrison, poverty and criminality are synonymous.'[8] And Alan Sillitoe, himself an outstanding working-class novelist, ironically in the Morrison tradition, finds that Morrison's characters 'lived in a zoo, and were to be regarded with fear, hostility, and derision.'[9]

Judgements such as these are extremely unfair to Morrison. While it is true that his most successful work is on the violent side of working-class life (in artistic terms *To London Town* is a complete failure), violence is never used for sensational reasons, but is always part of a well-defined total pattern. Furthermore Morrison's novels and stories possess considerable historical importance. When he first decided to write some short stories about the working classes he determined that 'they must be done with austerity and frankness and there must be no sentimentalism, no glossing over.'[10] Almost every working-class novelist before him had vowed the same, but, as we have already seen, in these earlier novels scenes which deal with the more debased or violent aspects of working-class life, such as wife-beating, drunkenness or hooliganism, are so handled as to indicate the author's personal disappropriation of the behaviour described. This may be done in two ways. Either some kind of terrible retribution comes to the debased character, or the way of life of other characters in the novel (either a substitute-working-class or a middle-class hero) provides a constant moral standard against which the debased scenes can be measured. Morrison, following the example of Kipling, rejected these moral middle-men. In his role of 'realist' he demanded absolute freedom to write on whatever subject he wished:

> If the community have left horrible places and horrible lives before [the novelist's] eyes, then the fault is that of the community; and to picture these places and these lives becomes not merely his privilege, but his duty.[11]

As Morrison's reference to the 'duty' of the novelist suggests, he did not believe in the total abnegation of social responsibility, but he interpreted 'responsibility' to mean presenting the simple, objective truth as it appeared to him. He angrily attacked those critics who demanded that in his novels he should always clearly indicate his own moral position:

> It is not that these good people wish me to write 'even weeping': for how do they know whether I weep or not? No: their wish is not that I shall weep, but that I shall weep obscenely in the public gaze. In other words that I shall do their weeping for them, as a sort of emotional bedeman.[12]

Morrison owes his historical and literary importance to precisely this—that he refused to be an 'emotional bedeman' for the reading public. Like Kipling, he felt that the only justifiable way of presenting the working classes in fiction was in terms of their own attitudes and values. The East End world that he knew seemed to comprise three main qualities, monotony, respectability and violence. It is the interrelationship of these qualities that Morrison tries to express in his novels and stories.

"Lizerunt" traces the brief life of a factory girl, Elizabeth Hunt, from her courting days, through the early years of marriage and fertile motherhood, to the moment when her brutal husband throws her out of the house to earn money street-walking. Several aspects of his kind of story had already been handled by novelists. The Bank Holiday courtship which is used to contrast the rowdy horse-play of cockney love-making with the brutal violence that takes its place once the marriage ceremony is over, had been used by Gissing in *The Nether World*. And the theme of a feeble, terrorized wife devotedly defending her debased husband had also been superbly handled by Gissing in his portrait of Pennyloaf Candy, by Kipling in "Badalia Herodsfoot," and by many other writers stretching back to Dickens in *Sketches by Boz*. The tone of **"Lizerunt"** owes everything to Kipling. As in "Badalia Herodsfoot," the action centres upon several violent moments in Lizer's life, each of which is described dispassionately by the author. Moral comment is made obliquely by using incongruous metaphors and images. Thus, Lizer watching two men fighting over her is elated and 'for almost five minutes she was Helen of Troy.'[13] This use of the mock heroic—like pastoral, a technique favoured by many working-class novelists—serves not merely to describe but also to ridicule. The same is true of some of Morrison's observations on working-class behaviour. When Billy Chope meets Lizer in the street he 'caught and twisted her arm, bumping her against the wall':

> 'Garn', said Lizerunt, greatly pleased: 'Le' go!' For she knew that this was love.[14]

Morrison does not point out (as for instance Gissing does) that rough physical contact is an important part of slum courtship, but allows the incident to speak for itself. The effect, however, is immediately destroyed by the implied sneer in his next sentence.

Yet in spite of these faults **"Lizerunt"** is very effective. By concentrating a period of about three years into a series of graphically presented moments, Morrison captures one of the aspects of slum life that had always horrified the working-class novelist—the collapse of a slum girl's feeble prettiness into the shapeless sluttishness of the young slum mother. She is by no means an innocent victim (as are both Badalia Herodsfoot and Pennyloaf Candy), but lives by a moral code little different from that of her husband. Driven solely by mercenary motives, she plays each of her two boy friends off against the other, until the issue is resolved by Billy Chope having Sam Cardew beaten up. For a while she is smitten by something very like conscience, but soon tires of a quiet life and returns to the person responsible for Sam's beating. She is fully aware of what she is doing. The period of enjoyment she can expect from life is short, and to waste time taking oranges to a bandaged, bed-ridden hero, is to make it even shorter. Life with Sam Cardew might have been better than it offers to be with Billy Chope, but in a world where pleasure is immediate and mainly violent, a choice between the two men is, at bottom, meaningless. This, for instance, is one of the courtship scenes:

> 'Ullo, Lizer! Where *are* y' a-comin' to? If I 'adn't laid 'old 'o ye—!' But here Billy Chope arrived to demand what the 'ell Sam Cardew was doing with his gal. Now Sam was ever readier for a fight than Billy was; but the sum of Billy's half-pints was large: wherefore the fight began. On the skirt of an hilarious ring, Lizerunt, after some small outcry, triumphed aloud. Four days before she had no bloke; and here she stood with two, and those two fighting for her! Here in the public gaze, on the Flats! For almost five minutes she was Helen of Troy.[15]

If a person accepts this as pleasure, and all three participants obviously do, then there can be no complaint when the triumphant girl-friend becomes the victimized wife:

> 'Two bob? Wot for?' Lizer asked.

> "Cos I want it. None o' yer lip.'

> 'Ain't got it,' said Lizer sulkily.

> 'That's a bleed'n lie.'

> 'Lie yerself.'

> 'I'll break y'in'arves, ye blasted 'eifer!' He ran at her throat and forced her back over a chair.

> 'I'll pull yer face auf! If y' don't give me the money, gawblimey, I'll do for ye!'[16]

For Morrison it is a simple matter of logic that the first of these scenes could quite easily, although not inevitably, lead to the second. The emphasis that earlier writers had placed on the possibilities of escape from the slums disappear in Morrison. Billy Chope is by no means presented as the ordinary working man (Morrison later described him as 'in a minority, a blackguard')[17] but the forces which control his outlook and actions, press down upon, and thus limit, the aspirations of even the most respectable mem-

bers of the mean streets. When Morrison says, in the introduction, that no one sings in the street and then in the very first story shows Lizer and Billy Chope shouting and dancing with glee at the Whitsun Fair, he is not contradicting himself. He means that no one sings for long as the country girl sang; no one can bridge two separate worlds once they inhabit this street. The country girl sings of a world outside of her present environment; the simple desire she expresses is for gentle happiness, which has no relevance in the East End. Once she suffers some of the everyday tragedies she collapses—she is 'helpless'—she cannot establish a working compromise with her physical surrounding, and anyone who cannot do that must be crushed. It is for this reason that, unlike Besant, Morrison can suffer no aristocrats living in his world, and unlike Gissing, cannot allow his characters to spend their evenings reading Greek tragedy. The slums would not allow such things to happen. If anyone should move in this direction, then, like the country girl, their voices would crack and they would sing no more.

Yet the theme of escape occurs frequently in Morrison's stories—escape from monotony or from violence, from one section of working-class life into another. More than any other author he uses as a framework for his stories the deadening desire for respectability (as passionate as in any middle-class world) that is the only viable means of escape from association with the twin evils of violence and social pity. A majority of the stories in *Tales of Mean Streets* deal with this theme of respectability, and it is indicative of the depth of Morrison's pessimism that all such strivings are shown as pointless or self-defeating.

In **"That Brute Simmons"** a farce is enacted in which an intensely house-proud woman believing herself to be a widow marries again. When her first husband reappears and tries to blackmail her successor, the two men vie with each other in trying to run away from this respectable hell. In **"Behind the Shade"** a mother and daughter, fallen from a higher social position, starve themselves to death rather than let their neighbours know they can no longer keep up the façade of respectability. **"In Business"** and **"All that Messuage"** have similar plots. In the former, a family dominated by a respectable mother use a small inheritance to set up a genteel shop in Bromley. In the latter, some hard-saved money is used to buy a house so that a couple can live on the rent. In both cases these plans collapse because of the inability of the working-class aspirants to understand the most elementary commercial principles. **"Squire Napper"** is similar but far more successful. A labourer inherits a small sum of money and immediately gives up his work, and while he wonders what to do with his new-found wealth, indulges in the only form of entertainment he knows—drinking. His money slowly disappears and with it the opportunity, of which he is never really aware, to better himself. In one scene, very reminiscent of the Boffin-Wegg relationship in *Our Mutual Friend*, Squire Napper hires a street-corner orator so that he can listen to revolutionary speeches in his own home. In another story **"On the Stairs,"** a mother, influenced by her neighbours' snobbery, determines to give her dying son a decent funeral. When a sympathetic doctor gives her some money, she saves it rather than spend it on medicine. The son dies and the mother is proud that she can afford the ultimate funereal status symbol—plumes.

These stories with their stale, hackneyed plots, do not live up to the promise offered by the introduction and **"Lizerunt,"** but they are saved from being excessively sentimental or pathetic by Morrison's terse style and relentless insistence that the slum is an autonomous world which forbids the miraculous character transformation so common in working-class romance. The characters are not fools—in **"The Red Cow Group,"** for instance, they neatly turn the tables on an anarchist seeking converts—but the environment within which they live has eaten into their souls, so that their social ambitions, humble as they may be, are utterly beyond their capabilities. In one of the best sketches—there is no plot to make it a story—**"To Bow Bridge,"** the narrator is one of a handful of respectable working-class people taking a bus journey late at night. When the pubs turn out, a crowd of rowdy men and women clamber on to the bus in order to cross to the other side of Bow Bridge where the drinking hours are extended to midnight. Morrison carefully and impartially describes the coarse, drunken, noisy but non-violent behaviour of the crowd until their destination is reached and they get off, leaving the respectable workers to continue their journey. This sketch epitomizes Morrison's attitude in *Tales of Mean Streets.* The journey that all the passengers are making is dull and dreary; for some of them it is only made bearable by hooliganism. The novelist sits by, noting behaviour patterns but passing no comparative judgement. For Morrison the working classes are neither more nor less corrupt than other social groups—at least not in a moral sense. Their behaviour, habits and customs are part of a pattern which possesses its own impetus, scale of values, class system and taboos. Above all else what interested Morrison about working-class life was the way that this predominantly dreary world could suddenly explode into physical violence. In **"To Bow Bridge"** he merely stated the problem; in *A Child of Jago* he tried to explore it fully.

Shortly after the publication of *Tales of Mean Streets* Morrison received a letter of appreciation from the Reverend A. Osborne Jay, vicar of the Holy Trinity, Shoreditch. Jay praised the truthfulness of Morrison's East End portrait and invited the author to visit his parish. At this time Morrison was already planning to write a full-length novel which would explore the effects of heredity and environment on a young boy, but was uncertain where exactly in the East End to set his story. The meeting with Jay helped him to make up his mind, and for a period of eighteen months he frequented Jay's parish, exploring the alleys and courts, sitting with the parishioners in their homes, drinking with them in pubs, and even for a spell letting them teach him how to make matchboxes (at this date still one of the standard occupations for the London destitute).[18] The real name of this tiny area that later came to be called the Jago, was the Old Nichol. It stood on the boundaries of Shoreditch and Bethnal Green, a square block of some half-a-dozen streets containing one of the worst slums in East London.[19] On Charles Booth's maps it is shaded a deep black denoting inhabitants of the 'lowest class of occasional labourers, loafers and semi-criminals,' as far removed from the dreary, respectable workers of *Mean Streets* as it was possible to be. Here Billy Chope would have been completely at home. Jay had taken charge of the parish that contained the Old Nichol in 1886 and, realizing the futility of pursuing a purely religious policy in such an area, had gradually improvised an idiosyncratic technique for dealing with his unruly flock. He opened a social club, encouraged boxing matches in which he often took part, painstakingly acquired a working knowledge of criminal language and habits, and wrote three excellent books describing his work: *Life in Darkest London* (1891), *The Social Problem* (1893) and *A Story of Shoreditch* (1896). In the first of these he described a street scene in the Old Nichol:

> Women, sodden with drink, fighting and struggling like wild creatures; men, bruised and battered, with all the marks and none of the pleasures of vice upon them; outcasts, abject and despairing, without food or shelter; the very children, with coarse oaths and obscene jests, watching, like wild beasts, for anything, dishonest or otherwise, which might come their way.[20]

As so much of the criticism later aimed at *A Child of the Jago* questioned the veracity of Morrison's portrait, it is worth mentioning that Jay, although in some ways eccentric, was no sensationalist. He always maintained that the Old Nichol was a special case: that the East End had 'portions which are really delightful,'[21] and he later vigorously defended Morrison against his incredulous critics.[22] Neither Jay nor Morrison claimed to be writing about the 'working classes' as a whole. Their subject was Charles Booth's 1.2 per cent of the East End population and unlike many writers before and after they were fully aware that they were dealing with only a minority section of the working classes, albeit a minority that posed a permanent threat to the well-being of its decent neighbours.

Morrison knew that he was compiling a social document in the form of a novel, a work in which problems of character and personality would be subordinated to a sociologically exact, yet at the same time symbolic, image of the Jago. In *A Child of the Jago,* the Jago itself is the true hero. This seems to suggest that Morrison was writing under the direct influence of Zola's dramshop or coal mine, but the novel as it finally appeared is a curious mixture of the English social-moralizing tradition and French naturalistic objectivity. Morrison, for instance, outlining his reasons for writing the novel, sounds just like Mrs Gaskell Kingsley or Dickens:

> I resolved therefore to write the *Child of Jago* which should tell the story of a boy, who, but for his environment, would have become a good citizen; also, the story of the horrible Nichol; and, lastly, I wished to

show that Father Jay's method is the only one that is possible in such a district.[23]

And it is interesting to find repeatedly details in Morrison's novel which seem to be unashamedly borrowed from Jay's various slum memoirs.[24] Yet *A Child of the Jago* is not merely a *Tendenzroman*. Only at the close of the book is a moral clearly stated. Until that moment Morrison succeeds in absorbing the reader in this strange and violent world, not by pointing a social lesson but by bringing the slum vividly alive.

The long opening description of the Jago shows Morrison rejecting the 'austere' objectivity of **Mean Streets** in favour of the death, disease and hell imagery traditionally found in slum descriptions. But he now has a specific reason for doing this. Unlike Gissing's nether world or Kipling's Gunnison Street, which were representative districts of areas totally rotten, the Jago is a solitary diseased spot which threatens to contaminate the whole of the East End.

It was past the mid of a summer night in the Old Jago. The narrow street was all the blacker for the lurid sky; for there was a fire in a farther part of Shoreditch, and the welkin was an infernal coppery glare. Below, the hot, heavy air lay, a rank oppression, on the contorted forms of those who made for sleep on the pavement: and in it, and through it all, there rose from the foul earth and the grimmed walls a close, mingled stink—the odour of the Jago.[25]

The usual inhabitants of this hell are not the suffering poor but the very dregs of London: 'What was too vile for Kate Street, Seven Dials, and Ratcliff Highway in its worst day, what was too useless, incapable and corrupt—all that seemed in the Old Jago.' In this world 'cosh carrying was near to being the major industry'; 'front doors were used merely as firewood' (which provides as we later see not merely warmth but easy escape passages from the police); and 'the elementary Education Act ran in the Jago no more than any other Act of Parliament.'[26] Law in the jago is determined by the feuding gangs of Ranns and Learys who, while usually content to fight each other, are also capable of joining forces to face a common enemy; and by Father Sturt (modelled faithfully on Jay), whose philosophy of good-neighbourliness interests few of his parishioners. The Perrott family, as newcomers to the Jago, owe allegiance to neither the gangsters nor the priest. Josh Perrott, the father, is a tradesman who, having fallen on evil days, discovers that earning a living Jago-style is more attractive than plastering. It is his son Dicky who is the 'child' of the Jago.

In choosing to centre his novel on a slum child Morrison was following a very conventional line, and it is possible that he deliberately did this as an implied criticism of the golden-haired child or the aristocratic changeling of working-class romance. The novel that set the tone for this romantic mid-Victorian treatment was *Oliver Twist* which was often seen in the later 'realistic' period as the father of the slum novel.[27] Certainly there are sufficient similarities

between *Oliver Twist* and *A Child of the Jago* to suggest that Morrison had the earlier novel in mind. Aaron Weech, who battens on Dicky Perrott and cunningly trains him as a thief, recalls Fagin, while Josh Perrott's flight from the police, especially the moment when he is spotlighted in an upstairs window, is very reminiscent of Bill Sikes's death scene. Finally, Josh's trial is virtually a plagiarism of Fagin's. Where the novels differ most is in their treatment of the slum child. Dicky Perrott could never be mistaken for a lost aristocrat, nor will he escape by virtue of a superior education. At times Morrison appears to be mocking this convention, as when Beveridge offers Dicky some advice:

'Now, Dicky Perrott, you Jago whelp, look at them— look hard. Someday, if you're clever—cleverer than anyone in the Jago now—if you're only scoundrel enough, and brazen enough, and lucky enough—one of a thousand—maybe you'll be like them: bursting with high living, drunk when you like, red and pimply. There it is—that's your aim in life—there's your pattern. Learn to read and write, learn cunning, spare nobody and stop at nothing, and perhaps—' he waved his hand towards the Bag of Nails. 'It's the best the world has for you, for the Jago's got you, and that's the only way out, except the gaol and the gallows.[28]

The model life being held up for Dicky's approval is that of the High Mobsman: the alternatives, as pointed out by Beveridge, are the gallows and the gaol. Father Sturt's attempt to find Dicky a regular job is frustrated, not simply because Aaron Weech is lurking round the corner, but because the power of the slum is greater than that of the priest. In the Jago crime is attractive, respectability non-existent. There is only the East End Elevation Mission and Pansophical Institute to provide an alternative way of life and this is bitterly satirized by Morrison as a place where 'a number of decently-dressed and mannerly young men passed many evenings . . . in harmless pleasures, and often with an agreeable illusion of intellectual advancement'.[29] The only good it does for the Jago is to provide Dicky with the opportunity to steal a watch. It is his first 'click' and after the sheer joy of this moment he has no chance at all. From now on he accepts as a moral guide the single rule of the Jago—'Thou shalt not nark'— and he abides by this even when he lies dying, stabbed in a street brawl.

There is much about *A Child of the Jago* that is unsatisfactory. Some of the characters (Pigeony Poll the golden-hearted prostitute, and Aaron Weech the fence, in particular) are conventional and rather wooden figures, while the portrait of Dicky does have, as H. D. Traill pointed out, 'odd touches of old-fashioned melodrama' about it.[30] More seriously, the fatalistic tone is too heavy for the slight structure of the story. Even allowing for the Jago as a special case, the reader feels that the dice are too heavily loaded against the Perrott family, the options open to them unjustifiably narrow and soul-destroying.

What really impresses is Morrison's handling of violence. The gang fights evoke an atmosphere of crude reality that the English working-class novel had never seen before:

Norah Walsh, vanquished champion, now somewhat re-covered, looked from a window, saw her enemy vul-nerable, and ran out armed with a bottle. She stopped at the kerb to knock the bottom off the bottle, and then, with an exultant shout, seized Sally Green by the hair and stabbed her about the face with the jagged points. Blinded with blood, Sally released her hold on Mrs. Perrott, and rolled on her back, struggling fiercely; but to no end, for Norah Walsh, kneeling on her breast, stabbed and stabbed again, till pieces of the bottle broke away. Sally's yells and plunges ceased, and a man pulled Norah off. On him she turned, and he was fain to run, while certain Learys found a truck which might carry Sally to the hospital.[31]

It is not so much the actual description that is new as the assumption by the novelist that this kind of behaviour, at least in the Jago, is the norm. So infectious is the battle that everyone is caught up in it:

As for old Beveridge, the affair so grossly excited him that he neglected business (he cadged and wrote beg-ging screeves) and stayed in the Jago, where he strode wildly about the streets, lank and rusty, stabbing the air with a carving knife, and incoherently defying 'all the lot' to come near him.[32]

Violence of various kinds and degrees dominates the novel. Josh Perrott's boxing match with Billy Leary in Jago Court is a public festival, honoured with the attendance of the High Mobsmen who put up the stake money. Only Mrs Perrott is frightened: for everyone else the fight is a high spot of their week, the moment when Kingship (in a non-criminal sense) is firmly decided. Josh's victory in the fight brings him a larger sum of money than he had ever possessed before, and while he is fêted as a hero, news ar-rives that his baby has died: 'The rumour went in the Jago that Josh Perrott was in double luck. For here was insur-ance money without a doubt.'[33] In this world the formula that Gissing felt typified working-class attitudes in *The Nether World*—'Get by whatever means so long as with impunity'—reigns absolutely. When a later fight breaks out in a pub, the rotten floor gives way and the Jagos and Dove Laners are hurled into the cellar. They immediately forget their feud and plunder the pub. The children born and bred in the Jago naturally follow the example of their parents in forming gangs and settling private quarrels by premeditated violence.

In the Jago there is no tenderness or love—save that pro-fessionally administered by Father Sturt—for such emo-tions would undermine the basic Jago philosophy of social anarchism; they would encourage people to build whereas the only thing the Jagos understand is destruction. Nor, in spite of his careful attempts to recreate the speech of the Jago, does Morrison allow his characters the cockney's traditional fund of wit for fear that this would weaken the horror of his portrait. What he does neatly capture, and make good use of, is the sardonic side of cockney humour, as in the first conversational lines of the book: 'AH-h-h-h,' he said, 'I wish I was dead: an' kep' a cawfy shop;' and in the same character's immediate comment on his friends'

refusal to speak to him: 'This is a bleed'n' unsocial sort o evenin' party, this is.'[34] But where Morrison is once agai truly successful is in presenting working-class speech a moments of violence:

'Won't sing yer hymn? There ain't much time!

My boy was goin' straight, an' earnin' wages:

someone got 'im chucked. A man 'as time to

think things out, in stir! Sing, ye son of

a cow! Sing! Sing!'[35]

It is one of the main themes of the novel that those wh live violently, die violently. Josh Perrott is hanged for murder of revenge and his son is stabbed in a childis vendetta. These are the victims. But the Ranns and th Learys do not come to grief. When the County Counci begins to demolish the Jago, most of the inhabitants mov on, seeking a new district as much like the old as possible for even if they could afford to live in the new flats, the would be unable to change their way of life. Kiddo Cook now a respectable costermonger and married to Pigeon Poll, does take a council flat. He is the only 'Jago-rat' t escape. It is interesting to compare the end of this nove with that of *The Nether World*. Gissing openly stated tha life in the new flats was worse than in the old slums, bu this judgement did not fit easily with the working-clas life we were shown. It was Gissing talking about himse rather than about his characters. Morrison quite clearly be lieved that the flats represent a step forward for society but recognizes that they are not for the Ranns and Learys This fits in perfectly with the way they have been pre sented in the novel. The flats would impose restriction upon them, it would break up the clan basis of their life, would destroy the only thing they have to enjoy—the vig orous, brutal excitement of slum violence.

In a prefatory note to *To London Town* (1899), Morriso wrote:

I designed this story, and, indeed, began to write it, be-tween the publication of **Tales of Mean Streets** and that of *A Child of the Jago,* to be read together with those books: not that I pretend to figure in all three— much less in any one of them—a complete picture of life in the eastern parts of London, but because they are complementary, each to the others.

To London Town attempts to strike a balance between th monotony of **Mean Streets** and the criminal violence of *Child of the Jago.* The opening scenes show the May fam ily living on the borders of Epping Forest which the Eas End invades in the form of some London visitors gettin drunk in a country pub. When the grand father dies th mother and her son Johnny move to the East End wher he is apprenticed to an engineering firm, and she remar ries. Morrison traces the adventures of Johnny and hi mother to the moment when the son falls in love, and th mother's marriage breaks down.

To London Town is perhaps not so dull as this summar makes it sound, but it is certainly less successful than th other two books in the trilogy. Its comparative failure does, however, raise interesting issues regarding the narrow range of working-class experience normally presented in fiction. So long as Morrison is dealing with working-class characters in extreme situations then his fiction comes vividly alive, but the same is not true of his treatment of the more ordinary, less sensational, aspects of working-class life. We have already seen that this is true of most earlier fiction, where street characters, cartoon types, suffering poor, melodramatic villains, or a political mass, act as working-class representatives. The most important contribution made by Kipling and Morrison was to break down the old view that one code of manners could be used to cover the behaviour of different class groups. They showed that drunkenness, swearing, and even violence, could be regarded as genuine forms of expression for people who did not respond to situations in a rational, intellectual or 'educated' way. But this in itself was only a partial solution. If, for instance, a novelist tries to write about working-class life from a point of view other than, on the one hand, violence, and on the other, escape, then what does he place at the core of his novel? What frame of reference can he use to interrelate the various experiences he is describing? This line of thought must be returned to in the next chapter; here we can briefly see how it applies to Morrison, as in *To London Town* he was obviously trying to solve such a problem. Johnny May is the kind of boy Dicky Perrott might have hoped to be had he not been brought up in the Jago. Morrison takes great care when outlining Johnny's development—his apprenticeship, work at night school, membership of a social club and his falling in love—to present him as an 'ordinary' member of the working classes. Johnny's mother is presented in a similar manner. In *Tales of Mean Streets* those working-class women whose highest ambition was to run a small shop had been treated harshly by Morrison. Mrs May, however, has enough business sense to make a success of her shop by providing a much needed service to the working-class community. But when it comes to turning this observed behaviour into material for a novel Morrison's own good sense breaks down. The girl Johnny falls in love with turns out to be, after a series of mysterious disappearances, the daughter of 'Old-Mother-Born-Drunk', the most disreputable character in the neighbourhood; and the man Johnny's mother marries is not merely a drunkard but also a bigamist. The novel is thus a curious mixture of the new realism and the old melodrama.

By the time he came to write this novel Morrison's influence was already at work on other slum novelists of the nineties. In his two early books he had shown that, provided great care was observed, the objective use of violence was a new and fruitful way of presenting the working classes in fiction. He had also shown that working-class characters could be placed at the heart of a novel; that the substitute working-class hero common in earlier fiction was unnecessary so long as the novelist did not entertain ambitious views of presenting a cross-section of society in his work. In this he was following the example of Kipling who had concentrated on the working class as a

separate cultural entity by using as his media the short story, sketch and ballad, rather than the full-scale social novel. Morrison had both limited and expanded the scope of working-class fiction, and there were many novelists who were willing to learn from him.

II

Late in life, looking back upon his long career as a novelist, Somerset Maugham wrote of his first novel *Liza of Lambeth* (1897):

> Any merit it may have is due to the luck I had in being, by my work as a medical student, thrown into contact with a side of life that at that time had been little exploited by novelists. Arthur Morrison with his *Tales of Mean Streets* and *A Child of the Jago* had drawn the attention of the public to what were then known as the lower classes and I profited by the interest he had aroused.[36]

Maugham owed a greater debt to Morrison than this would suggest. Apart from the change of setting from East to South London, much of *Liza of Lambeth* suggests Morrison's influence. The three principal qualities that Morrison believed dominated working-class life (monotony, a yearning for respectability and violence) all feature in Maugham's novel. The opening description of Vere Street with its subdued evocation of environmental monotony is typical of the *Mean Streets* approach:

> It has forty houses on one side and forty houses on the other, and these eighty houses are very much more like one another than ever peas are like peas, or young ladies like young ladies. They are newish, three-storied buildings of dingy grey brick with slate roofs, and they are perfectly flat, without a bow-window or even a projecting cornice or window-sill to break the straightness of the line from one end of the street to the other.[37]

The houses themselves are dead, but the street is full of life, with children playing cricket in the road, and women gossiping in doorways. Liza burst upon this scene with great vivacity and humour. She is dressed in the standard coster costume of 'brilliant violet, with great lappets of velvet, and she had on her head an enormous black hat covered with feathers'.[38] Her appearance transforms the mood of the street. She sings Albert Chevalier's latest music-hall song, 'Knocked 'em in the Old Kent Road,' jokes with the gossips, flirts with the men, plays cricket with the children, and finally gets the whole street dancing round a barrel-organ. Like Badalia Herodsfoot and Lizerunt, these are Liza's 'days of fatness' and this carefree moment signifies the beginning of her tragic decline.

The most unusual feature of *Liza of Lambeth* is that it deals at some length with a working-class love affair. The Pennyloaf Candy/Bob Hewett and Lizerunt/Billy Chope marriages are not really 'love' matches at all. Gissing and Morrison both merely note what they regarded as rather curious courting habits and then moved the stories on to their violent conclusions. Maugham, however, makes the love affair central to his book, and furthermore treats it seriously and sympathetically. This is all the more unusual because Liza's love for Jim Blakeston is adulterous, and although adultery had long been a stock subject for the novelist, its fictional treatment had been limited to the middle and upper classes. There are two main reasons for this: Gissing's novels can supply one, Kipling's and Morrison's the other. As was pointed out earlier, Gissing usually allowed his working-class heroines to be sexually attractive only in proportion as they possessed upper-class qualities. This was in order that they might be worthy of their substitute working-class lovers. The three genuine working-class girls in his novels are handled in a different manner. Pennyloaf Candy is spineless and totally subservient to Bob Hewett, and is also shown to be physically anaemic. Clem Peckover is extremely sensual but she is more animal than human. Totty Nancarrow in *Thyrza* is much nearer in personality to Liza than Clem Peckover or Pennyloaf Candy, but, for Gissing, her ceaseless chatter and coarse manners made her sexually undesirable. In this respect it is significant that she finally marries Joe Bunce, one of the least important people in the novel. It is impossible to imagine Gissing regarding any of these women as fit subjects for a prolonged, adulterous, love affair. Kipling and Morrison did not share Gissing's snobbery in this respect, but their reason for avoiding the subject of adultery is just as strange. They blindly accepted the belief that working-class sexual amorality was a natural condition of slum life, and that therefore the term adultery possessed no meaning. Badalia Herodsfoot is shown to be sexually attractive, but when her husband leaves her, Kipling goes out of his way to stress how strange it was that she did not immediately pair off with someone else: 'With rare fidelity she listened to no proposals for a second marriage according to the customs of Gunnison Street, which do not differ from those of the Barralong.'[39] Morrison, for all his claims of dealing frankly and fearlessly with life in the East End, rarely shows sex to be a part of it, but that he would have agreed with Kipling on this subject can be seen from his reference to Dicky Perrott as 'not married, either in the simple Jago fashion or in church.'[40] In the final instance Kipling and Morrison are little different from Gissing, for like him they could not conceive of a working-class couple possessing the sensitivity or emotional depth which, as participants in an adulterous love affair, they would require.

Maugham was not so inhibited. All the normal trappings of a fictional middle- or upper-class love affair are there, simply translated into working-class terms. Liza and Jim meet in the street, on a Bank Holiday outing, in the gallery of a theatre, and in pubs. The initial seduction scene is a curious instance of Maugham interpreting the horseplay of courtship for animal violence:

> He looked at her for a moment, and she, ceasing to thump his hand, looked up at him with half-opened mouth.
>
> Suddenly he shook himself, and closing his first gave her a violent, swinging blow in the stomach.

'Come on,' he said.

And together they slid down into the darkness of the passage.[41]

Liza is not presented as a naturally immoral person. She treats Tom, her faithful working-class suitor, gently; becomes the outcast object of her neighbours' respectability, and when called a 'prostitute' fights the slanderer. She is also, for the sake of love, willing to shoulder her guilt, rather than act as, for instance, Kipling thought natural for one of her class. In this respect Jim Blakeston is the innocent:

> 'Well, I'll marry yer. Swop me bob, I wants ter badly enough.'
>
> 'Yer can't; yer married already.'
>
> 'Thet don't matter! If I give the missus so much a week aht of my screw, she'll sign a piper ter give up all clime ter me, an' then we can get spliced. One of the men as I works with done thet, an' it was arright.'[42]

Jim's innocence is a form of self-protection. In this world men determine the physical and women the moral code of behaviour. So long as Jim can respond to any situation with an immediate show of strength, he is safe. Liza cannot so easily escape retribution. Because of her adultery she has lost all chance of gaining the much-coveted badge of respectability. For the men she becomes merely an object of their semi-serious bawdry: 'Yer might give us a chanst, Liza; you come aht with me one evenin'. You oughter give us all a turn, jist ter show there's no ill-feelin'.'[43] But for the women Liza is a constant threat to their own marital stability: 'A woman's got no right ter tike someone's 'usbind from 'er. An' if she does she's bloomin' lucky if she gits off with a 'idin'—thet's wot I think.'[44] The public beating that Mrs Blakeston gives Liza is not merely personal revenge; it is a ritualistic cleansing approved by the whole female community of Lambeth. It is only at this moment that Liza, pregnant, physically beaten and rejected by the other women, ever appears to be promiscuous. Moved by Tom's faithfulness, she offers herself to him, but he refuses to understand anything except marriage. At the same time as this conversation is taking place the husbands are reasserting their supremacy. Jim Blakeston knocks his wife senseless, and when a neighbour attempts to get her own husband to intervene, he refuses:

> 'But 'e's killin' 'er,' repeated Polly, trembling with fright.
>
> 'Garn!' rejoined the man; 'she'll git over it; an' p'haps she deserves it, for all you know.'[45]

The relationship between Liza and Jim had been tender and happy, but in this world violence ultimately decides every issue of importance. As a young girl Liza had managed to impose her personality on the neighbourhood, by singing louder, dressing flashier, being cheekier than her friends. The older women can no longer act in this way.

They have already faced the brutality and violence that later must also come to Liza, and now they have replaced their early gaiety with a staid, and largely hypocritical, cover of respectability. This is their protection against the physical superiority of the men. So long as Liza strictly acts out the part allotted to her then the older women approve her actions, but once she steps into their domain, they temporarily adopt the masculine form of dealing with trouble and then retreat once again into respectability.

This behaviour pattern is presented directly in Mrs Blakeston's thrashing of Liza, and is also worked out in a more subdued tone through the presentation of Liza's mother. Mrs Kemp has only two aims in life—to be drunk whenever she can, and to be regarded as eminently respectable by her neighbours. She alone of the Lambeth women knows nothing of Liza's affair. When she learns that her daughter has had a miscarriage she can only say, 'Well, you surprise me . . . I didn't known as Liza was thet way. She never told me nothin' abaht it.'[46] She exhibits no emotion on hearing that Liza is dying, but just sits with the nurse discussing the 'respectable' funerals the district has known, and swopping tales about the 'respectability' of their late husbands. Only when Jim Blakeston, huge and bearded, comes to sit by the death bed does Mrs Kemp show any interest: 'Fancy it bein' 'im!. . . Strike me lucky, ain't 'e a sight!'[47]

Maugham's treatment of working-class life is thus very similar to Morrison's. The natural condition of the slums is bleak monotony, and life is only made bearable by adopting rowdiness, violence or respectability as a means of expression. Each of these is self-defeating. They produce a narrow, enclosed, vicious society that will tolerate no deviation from what it regards as normal or everyday. Jim Blakeston's proposed solution of running away to another district is not countenanced by Liza. To do this would be to surrender her individuality. Elsewhere, living with Jim as man and wife she would be obliged to conform to the very hypocrisy she condemns in Lambeth.

If Maugham relies heavily on Morrison for his literary method and philosophy of working-class life, he does instill into *Liza of Lambeth* that genuine sense of working-class humanity so lacking in Morrison's work. Liza's love affair is an obvious example of this, but there is also the greater emphasis that is placed on working-class speech. Maugham captures just as well as Morrison the grim jesting and the free-flowing abuse of the sardonic or the angry cockney, but he also manages to convey raucous humour:

> 'Na, I can't,' she said, trying to disengage herself. 'I've got the dinner ter cook.'

> 'Dinner ter cook?' shouted one small boy. 'Why, they always cook the cats' meat at the shop.'[48]

The humour in *Liza of Lambeth* is the true humour of a realist—it conveys a joke which is funny to the characters rather than to the reader. It also attempts to express briefly but forcefully the truth about their life without passing judgement upon it:

> 'Them's not yer ribs,' shouted a candid friend—'Them's yer whale-bones yer afraid of breakin'.'

> 'Garn!'

> ''Ave yer got whale-bones?' said Tom, with affected simplicity, putting his arm round her waist to feel.

> 'Na then,' she said, 'Keep off the grass!'

> 'Well, I only wanted ter know if you'd got any.'

> 'Garn; yer don't git round me like thet.' He still kept as he was.

> 'Na then,' she repeated, 'tike yer 'and away. If yer touch me there you'll 'ave t'er marry me.'[49]

It is by successfully relating moments such as this to the wider framework provided by the monotony-violence-respectability philosophy that Maugham manages to expand, if only slightly, the narrow cultural world of Morrison. One scene in Liza of Lambeth shows Maugham falling short of the austere standard set by Morrison in *Jago* and reverting to one of the weaknesses of **"Liz-erunt."** The Bank Holiday outing, from which the above extract comes, is at one point sub-titled 'The Idyll of Corydon and Phyllis.' For a few inexplicable pages Liza becomes a 'shepherdess' and Tom her 'swain.' With incongruous irony Corydon and Phyllis are shown swilling beer from a pint pot and when it is finished holding a spitting contest. For all their successful presentation of certain aspects of working-class life, neither Morrison nor Maugham could completely escape the lingering influence of pastoral.

III

The popular success of Kipling's and Morrison's work inspired many writers to try to produce novels and short stories in the same vein, but, apart from Somerset Maugham, they possessed little talent and added nothing new to working-class fiction. Lacking Kipling's profound personal involvement with working-class culture or Morrison's sociological common sense, they were unable to make any worthwhile use of the lessons offered them by 'Badalia Herodsfoot', **Mean Streets** and *A Child of the Jago*. Certain important aspects of these three books—the new system of phonetics to indicate working-class speech, a changing image of the East End, violence as a means of slum expression and the doctrine of authorial objectivity—are widely used by later novelists. But so ignorant do they seem of the real issues involved, so careless are they with the exact social and literary qualifications made by Kipling and Morrison, that instead of further expanding the scope of working-class fiction, they actually pervert their models' original intentions. This process can be understood most clearly by looking at the influence of Morrison on first the working-class romance, and secondly, the later 'realists.'

In the nineties the romance retained its faith in a plot based upon change of identity or individual philanthropy and thus an overall tone of cheerful optimism. It also continued to concentrate on the problems of middle- or upper-class characters acted out against a working-class back-cloth, but changed the model for its working-class scenes from the 'Newgate' novel or Dickens to a mixture of Besant and Morrison, with an occasional dash—for the more serious-minded reader—of Mrs Humphry Ward. Some examples of these 'realistic' romances are: Joseph Hocking's *All Men are Liars* (1895) and *The Madness of David Baring* (1900); Harry Lander's *Lucky Bargee* (1898); Richard Whiteing's *No. 5 John Street* (1899); John A. Stewart's *Wine on the Lees* (1899); Robert Blatchford's *Julie* (1900); and Morley Roberts's *Maurice Quain* (1897), which has a special interest in that the middle-class hero living in the slums is almost certainly a portrait of George Gissing. We can see the influence of Morrison by looking at just two of these novels. *Wine on the Lees* tells the story of an aristo-cratic brewer's conversion to the cause of temperance and in most respects is no different from many such novels written earlier, but there are certain scenes in it that belong only to the nineties. Jenny Goodman, a gentle working-class wife, explains to the woman who once employed her as a maid, why she doesn't want to return to London:

> 'Oh my Lady!' she cried, the tears coming afresh, 'you can never understand what it is to be poor and live in the East End of London. My Lady, you say it is hor-rible—it's worse, it's worse.'[50]

But she does go back to London and is soon resigned to her fate:

> It no longer paralysed her to come upon groups of muscular sluts whooping and clawing each other's faces, tearing rags from grimy shoulders and dancing jigs on them in the gutter. Marks of death on stairs and pavement ceased to make her sick. Even when in great orgies wives tucked and bled over their fallen men she did not swoon or feel faint.[51]

Here the slum dwellers are no longer the suffering poor, the drearily respectable people of **Mean Streets,** or the ghetto criminals of the Jago—they are the ordinary inhab-itants of the East End. Charles Booth's 1.2 per cent has become the whole population, and Morrison's careful at-tempt to show that slum violence was either a reaction against the bleak monotony of the East End or the normal behaviour of certain kinds of criminal, has been trans-formed into widespread working-class animalism. Further-more, in contradiction to the central social philosophy of the realistic romance, there frequently appears a sneering and condescending attitude towards organized philan-thropy: 'Missionaries, indeed, there were whose wry, re-proachful faces and tactless ways made redemption sour and excited resentment and ridicule.'[52] Here, without any attempt to relate it to a total pattern, is one of the standard ironic devices employed by Kipling and Morrison. Their social criticism is turned into a meaningless platitude.

No. 5 John Street is not so crude a novel as *Wine on the Lees* but it differs in degree rather than kind. An extremely popular novel in its day, it provides a perfect example of the old-fashioned romance that has had elements of the new 'realism' grafted uneasily on to it. Whiteing was an old man when he suddenly attained his first commercial success. Over thirty years earlier he had written *Mr. Sprouts: His Opinions* (1867), a lively if superficial satire on working-class manners, and in 1888 he had published *The Island,* a satirical examination of English society in the year of the Jubilee. Whiteing had thus been interested in the working classes for many years, but there is nothing in *No. 5 John Street* to suggest that his latest novel was a natural product of artistic development. Like *Wine on the Lees* it has a hackneyed plot. A wealthy young man deter-mines to find out for himself how the working classes live. His first thought is to join a settlement in the East End but 'it proved to be a mere peep-hole into the life I wanted to see, with the Peeping Tom still a little too much on the safe side'.[53] As this implies he is obviously on the look-out for violence and he goes to live in a West End slum, hop-ing to find the real workers there. On his first night in the slums he hears a scream and tries to draw it to the atten-tion of Low Covey, his working-class friend:

> 'Did you hear that fearful cry?'
>
> 'Ah!, I 'eerd somethink.'
>
> 'There's murder going on—a woman, I think.'
>
> 'Dessay; it's Sat'd'y night.'
>
> 'I'm going to see.'
>
> 'S'pose so; you're fresh to the place.'[54]

The meaning of this scene is perfectly clear. The working man accepts murder as a natural condition of his life, or at least of his Saturday nights, and the fact that the victim appears to be a woman does not disturb him in the least. In Kipling, Morrison or Maugham, there is always a rea-son specified as to why a working man might, in a given situation, remain indifferent to a scene of violence. Whiteing feels there is no need for an explanation of Low Cov-ey's curious behaviour. In all other respects he is shown to be gentle and friendly, but by clumsily following what had come to be a stale literary convention, Whiteing uncon-sciously shows Low Covey, in this instance at least, to be morally corrupt. When the two men do stir themselves they find an 'Amazon' towering over a sailor who has been knocked to the ground:

> Her gown torn open in the scuffle, exposes the heaving breast. Her black hair streams over her shoulders. Her sleeves are turned up to the elbows for battle. One stout fist is streaked with the blood of the man with the knife. The lips are parted with her quick breathing; the flashing eyes outshine the moonlight.[55]

No working-class romance of this time would have been complete without one scene describing a half-naked working-class woman fighting in the streets, and once again this example shows how hollow the convention had become. Clem Peckover, Pennyloaf Candy, Lizerunt, Bada-lia Herodsfoot, and Liza Kemp, in their different ways, had all been the victims of slum violence. They had suffered and had ultimately been destroyed by either accepting the code of violence or by being unable to avoid it. In *No. 5 John Street* the genuine pathos of these earlier working-class heroines becomes merely a lifeless, romantic posture.

Wine on the Lees and *No. 5 John Street* demonstrate how the working-class romance, in trying to inject itself with new life drawn from Morrison's studies of slum violence, only succeeded in establishing a new set of stale attitudes and conventions. The same is even more true of the writers who produced plagiarisms of *Tales of Mean Streets.* W. J. Dawson's *London Idylls* (1895), Arthur St John Adcock's *East End Idylls* (1897), Edith Ostlere's *From Seven Dials* (1898), J. Dodsworth Brayshaw's *Slum Silhouettes* (1898) and K. Douglas King's *The Child who will Never Grow Old* (1898), attempt to re-create not isolated scenes from Morrison's work but the overall tone of dispassionately described monotony and violence. The stories in these collections exhibit a bizarre mixture of pastoral (strikingly epitomized by the recurrent, ironic use of the word 'Idyll') and objective realism. As with working-class romance the result is a crude perversion of Morrison's original intentions. A closer look at two of these stories will be sufficient to demonstrate this.

Katherine Douglas King's 'Lil: an Idyll of the Borough' tells the story of a slum girl who has the chance to escape from her environment by going to live in 'pagan unconventionality' as the mistress of a wealthy aesthete. Lil's moral dilemma is made acute by the presence of her working-class boy friend, Jim, and her two sisters, Liz, and Louie, a four-year-old cripple. The basic plot is, of course, ages old. Lil's beauty is of 'a restless, passion-swayed, unangelic nature' even though she is only a 'starving seamstress,' and her beauty alone gives her the opportunity to escape from slum life. But the trappings of this feeble plot are so brutal, the attitudes that come through to the reader so tasteless, that it could have been written at no earlier period. While trying to decide what to do Lil wonders what her life will be like if she stays in the Borough:

> She knew . . . that a lamp flung by a drunken husband into her face; a kick of his nailed boots on her prostrate body; his fists in her eyes; and a chair-back on her breasts, do not improve a woman's looks, nor compensate for the bearing of many sickly babies.

This will happen to her not because Jim is exceptionally violent but because most of the women in her street have already suffered the same fate. In this story the only kind of response permitted to the working-class characters, in any situation, is violence, if not upon someone else then upon themselves. When Lil's scandalous behaviour is made public, her sister's boy friend takes this opportunity to run away:

> A little quiver passed over Liz's strained stunted features, when Dick's footsteps had died away. Her teeth met on her tongue until her mouth was full of blood . . . When she had washed out her mouth she set about getting tea for Louie.

In the Borough this kind of behaviour represents the norm. In one scene Jim comes to the house to try to discover Lil's new address. At first he attempts to bribe the cripple with sweets and 'custid tarts' but when the four-year-old child bites him in anger, he gives her a 'blow on the ear that half-killed her.' Finally Lil leaves to join her pagan lover and is pursued down the street by Jim swearing he will beat her up while 'his new girl' is waiting for him round the corner.[56]

With stories such as this (and if not always quite so crudely employed, the same elements constantly recur) the portrayal of working-class violence and amorality reaches its lowest point. What makes this story so horrifying is the author's belief that she should not pass any kind of moral or social judgement on the actions of her characters. In Kipling and Morrison objectivity was necessary if they were to show that in certain circumstances slum violence could be exciting for some if not all of the participants. In 'Lil' the treatment of slum violence is blatantly vicarious. Katherine King's characters behave as they do for no other reason than that they are working class.

In its approach to working-class life Edith Ostlere's 'Any Fla-ars or Po-t Ferns' is just as insensitive as 'Lil' but it shows Morrison's influence working in a slightly different manner. Nell, a local beauty (not idealized like Lil) and flower-seller, is courted by two costers—Bill Gubbins who is ugly but kind hearted, and Jack Standing, who is handsome and rakish. Much to Bill Gubbins's surprise Nell chooses him. The scene then switches to the marriage night:

> A thrill of passion swept over him. His heart felt bursting.
>
> 'Nell,' he whispered hoarsely, 'there ain't nobody lookin', give us a kiss.'
>
> 'Lor', Bill, giv' hover, yer fat-'eaded sawney, yer! I ain't a-goin' to do nothink of the sort!'
>
> All the same she did.

Then one evening he returns from work to find that Nell is missing. She has left a note reading, in part: 'i am goin ome to mother's for a week abart dont kum arter me wen I kum ome Praps i shall ave Sumthink 2 Sho yew.'[57] Neighbouring gossips persuade Bill that his wife has run off with Jack Standing and when ten days later she knocks on the door Jim curses her and drives her away. The next day he meets Jack and the two men fight. Bill is beaten and then learns that Jack has had nothing to do with Nell's disappearance. A year passes while Bill searches for his wife, until one day he sees a street accident involving a woman and a child. They are, of course, his wife and child. Nell dies in agony but not before she has told Bill that she left him to have the baby 'nice an' easy like, an' I'd be no trouble to yer, nor cost yer nothink neither, an' I meant ter bring it back to yer as a s'prise like.' Nell then dies and Bill is left with the baby.[58]

It is impossible to imagine a story like this, completely serious as it is, being written about people of any other class. Unlike the writer of a temperance novel who is able to justify his grotesque treatment of the working classes in moral terms, or the 'Condition-of-England' reformer who can defend his shock tactics on social grounds, Edith Ostlere has no excuse for writing as she does. From Morrison she has learnt the lesson that because of the corrupting effect of the slums upon the working classes they cannot be held responsible for their actions. Therefore, she reasons, one pattern of behaviour is just as plausible as any other. So long as the author does not interfere, the working classes cannot be presented as too degraded or ignorant.

These working-class romances and stories written during the closing years of the nineteenth century are bizarre travesties of Morrison's carefully observed, deeply felt and sociologically qualified work. Although limited, in both artistic and social terms, his novels and short stories were genuinely experimental. More than any other working-class novelist of the late-Victorian period he had broken with past conventions; attacking, though not destroying, the pastoral myth, and claiming the right of the urban working classes to a place in serious fiction. Unfortunately Morrison did not continue to write working-class fiction, and Somerset Maugham, the only important writer of the nineties with a talent similar to Morrison's and a far greater potential as a novelist, also turned to other subjects. With no one to provide a lead, popular novelists seized upon isolated aspects of Morrison's work and by employing them with a crude lack of imagination, crushed all meaning from them. The nineteenth century passed on to the twentieth two distinct images of the working man, both of which were popular corruptions taken from experimental fiction of the nineties. The first, a working man, violent, debased and lacking any decent or humane qualities, came from Morrison; the second, which must be examined in more detail now, came from the Cockney School.

Notes

1. 'Arthur Morrison,' *The Bookman* VII (January 1895), 107.

2. For Morrison's early years and his association with the People's Palace, see P. J. Keating, 'Arthur Morrison: A Biographical Study,' introduction to *A Child of the Jago* (1969).

3. 'A Street,' *Macmillan's Magazine* LXIV (October 1891), 460-3 *passim.* By the time this article was republished as the introduction to *Tales of Mean Streets,* Morrison's style had grown even more terse. The quotations given here are from the original. In the *Mean Streets* introduction Morrison also significantly omitted a paragraph containing the sentence: 'A Palace of Delight was once set in the midst of this street, but Commissioners brandished their pens over it and it became a Polytechnic Institution.'

4. *Ibid.,* 462.

5. Interview with Morrison, *Daily News,* 12 December 1896.

6. *Spectator* LXXIV (16 March 1895), 360.

7. 'What is a Realist?', *New Review* XVI (March 1897), 326-36.

8. *The Cockney* (1953), 39.

9. Introduction to Robert Tressell, *The Ragged Trousered Philanthropists* (Panther Books, 1965), 8.

10. *Daily News* interview.

11. 'What is a Realist?', 328.

12. *Ibid.,* 330.

13. *Tales of Mean Streets,* 37.

14. *Ibid.,* 32.

15. *Ibid.,* 36-7.

16. *Ibid.,* 45-6.

17. *Spectator* letter.

18. See the *Daily News* interview, and 'The Methods of Mr. Morrison,' *Academy* L (12 December 1896), 531.

19. See T. Harper Smith, 'A Child of the Jago,' *East London Papers* II, (April 1959), No. 1.

20. *Life in Darkest London* (1891), 14.

21. *A Story of Shoreditch* (1896), 98-9.

22. In a letter to the *Fortnightly Review* LXVII (February 1897), 324.

23. *Daily News* interview.

24. Cf. Jay's methods of dealing with his criminal parishioners with those of Father Sturt: *Life in Darkest London,* 35-43, *A Child of the Jago,* Ch. XIV. Also Jay's and Morrison's treatment of gang feuds: *A Story of Shoreditch,* Ch. VI, and *A Child of the Jago,* Ch. IV.

25. *A Child of the Jago* (1896), 1.

26. *Ibid.,* 2, 5, 9, 78.

27. See Jane Findlater, 'The Slum Movement in Fiction,' *Stones from a Glass House,* 67-73: Robert Blatchford, 'On Realism,' *My Favourite Books* (1901), 222-53 *passim.*

28. *A Child of the Jago,* 112.

29. *Ibid.,* 20.

30. *The New Fiction and Other Essays* (1897), 13. It was the title essay of this collection, challenging the 'realism' of Morrison's Jago portrait, that forced him to publish his defensive article 'What is a Realist?'.

31. *A Child of the Jago,* 51-2.

32. *Ibid.,* 47.

33. *Ibid.,* 141.

34. *Ibid.,* 4.

35. *Ibid.,* 313.

36. *The Summing Up* (1938), 166.

37. *Liza of Lambeth,* Collected Edition of Maugham's Works (1934), 1. All page references are to this edition.

38. *Ibid.,* 5.

39. "Badalia Herodsfoot," *Many Inventions,* 296.

40. *A Child of the Jago,* 281. A similar phrase had been used earlier by Jay: 'only married, not churched' (*Life in Darkest London,* 110).

41. *Liza of Lambeth,* 89.

42. *Ibid.,* 114.

43. *Ibid.,* 109.

44. *Ibid.,* 134.

45. *Ibid.,* 145-6.

46. *Ibid.,* 160.

47. *Ibid.,* 168.

48. *Ibid.,* 30.

49. *Ibid.,* 42-3.

50. *Wine on the Lees* (1899), 58.

51. *Ibid.,* 65.

52. *Ibid.,* 101.

53. *No. 5 John Street* (1899), 11.

54. *Ibid.,* 28-9.

55. *Ibid.,* 31.

56. K. Douglas King, 'Lil: an Idyll of the Borough,' *The Child who will Never Grow Old* (1898), 143-56 *passim.*

57. The extreme crudity of Nell's spelling is a further example of Edith Ostlere misunderstanding an important aspect of the slum novels. The use of phonetics to indicate illiteracy rather than the sound of a voice has a long ancestry in fiction, though the late-Victorian novelists in the main rarely used phonetics for this purpose. Gissing's explanation why he does not faithfully reproduce the letter that Carrie Mitchell sends to Arthur Golding, is particularly relevant: 'The handwriting was extremely bad, so bad in places as to be almost undecipherable, and the orthographical errors were abundant. I have chosen to correct the latter fault, lest the letter should excite amusement' (*Workers in the Dawn,* II, 285-6).

58. Edith Ostlere, 'Any Fla-ars or Po-t Ferns,' *From Seven Dials* (1898), 1-33 *passim.*

E. F. Bleiler (essay date 1976)

SOURCE: In an introduction to *Best Martin Hewitt Detective Stories,* Dover Publications, Inc., 1976, pp. vii-xiv.

[*In the following overview of Morrison's detective stories, Bleiler contrasts Martin Hewitt and Sherlock Holmes.*]

In detective stories the last decade of the nineteenth century was dominated by Sherlock Holmes. "A Scandal in Bohemia," the first story of *The Adventures of Sherlock Holmes,* appeared in the July 1891 issue of *The Strand Magazine,* and was followed by a succession of stories that continued for some three years. But unfortunately for the publishers of *The Strand Magazine,* Holmes and A. Conan Doyle had to rest occasionally, and substitutions had to be made.

During the interregnum between the first and second series of *The Adventures of Sherlock Holmes,* the editors of *Strand* ran as a stopgap a collection of cases by Dick Donovan, one of the hacks of the day. But recognizing that Donovan's work was not what the readership was clamoring for, the editors placed at the bottom of Donovan's last case the following frosty notice: "Next month will appear the first of the new series of 'The Adventures of Sherlock Holmes.'"

Over the next few years the editors of *The Strand Magazine* and its rival variety periodicals used other authors in an attempt to match popularity with Doyle: Guy Boothby, Fred White, L. T. Meade, B. Fletcher Robinson, Baroness Orczy and others. The most successful of these authors, it is generally agreed, was Arthur Morrison, the chronicler of London slum life, whose sleuth Martin Hewitt is probably the second-best detective from the period 1891-1905, or the Age of Sherlock Holmes.

To many of his contemporaries, Arthur Morrison must have seemed unlikely as the creator of Martin Hewitt, since he was much in the public eye for a different sort of writing: painstakingly accurate, unsentimental, naturalistic studies of the seamy side of London's slums. The stories, which were later gathered together as **Tales of Mean Streets,** had been appearing in *Macmillan's Magazine* and *The National Observer,* where they had attracted much favorable attention. Morrison's shift from original, perceptive naturalism to what amounted to a classical pastoral was unexpected and, it must be admitted, sometimes severely criticized by his contemporaries.

Morrison's contemporaries knew very little about Morrison the man, and we, today, know only a little more. He was a very shy, retiring man who avoided publicity as much as he could. He was more respected than known by his greater contemporaries. He was very sensitive about his family, which had been quite low on the British social scale, and he seemed to have found it painful to talk about his early life. He either evaded questions or deliberately offered misleading information, and his wife, who apparently shared his feelings, at his death burned all his private papers.

Morrison was born in 1863 in a slum district of London known as Poplar, a little to the north of the Isle of Dogs, and he grew up there and in other similar slums in East London. His father was a steam-fitter, and the inference is reasonable that there was a persistent milieu of temporary unemployment, poverty, moving and relocation, and domestic unhappiness. All of these themes—plus the dominant central concept of the boy who tries to escape the slums—occur throughout his serious fiction, and are probably based on his own life pattern.

Almost no details are known of this earlier life. We do not know the exact locations where he lived; we do not know where he received his education; nor do we know how he spent the years after he must have left the local schools. He is first found working as a clerk at the People's Palace in East London in 1887, when he was twenty-three or twenty-four years old. This People's Palace was an organization much like our modern community houses, where free lectures, exhibitions, concerts and vocational training were offered to slumdwellers, with the intention of fitting them better for life. It was here that Morrison probably received his true education, gaining the momentum that carried him on up to the fulfillment he wished. He worked on accounts and correspondence, and eventually became a subeditor of the *Palace Journal.*

By 1890 or so the People's Palace was undergoing internal difficulties, and Morrison, taking advice from Walter Besant, decided that he was now capable of making a living at journalism. He moved to West London—a symbolic gesture in those days—and took a position on a local newspaper, also working at freelance writing. Much of this early work is probably now lost, since anonymous publication in periodicals was still very common, but his first book publication came in 1891 with a collection of rather weak ghost stories entitled *Shadows Around Us.*

The same year, 1891, however, saw in *Macmillan's Magazine* the first appearance of **"The Street,"** one of the components of *Tales of Mean Streets.* **"The Street"** caught the eye of W. E. Henley, one of the leading editors of the day, who accepted further stories for *The National Observer.* When *Tales of Mean Streets* was published in 1894, it became a manifesto for the New Writing.

Naturalistic themes and treatment had occurred previously in English literature, but Morrison portrayed depths of brutality and squalor that had never before been described. Although his contemporaries did not know it, and saw his work as a tour de force, Morrison was writing about things that he knew from his own witness. Possibly because of his own implication, he did not sentimentalize, glorify or preach. Dispassionately, with complete detachment, Morrison described the lives of broken charwomen, pimping parasites and shattered workers who drifted down to destruction; he showed shabby attempts to retain respectability and the perpetual edging or slipping into crime.

The horror-filled slums of London again served as literary material in Morrison's second classic of degradation, *A Child of the Jago.* After *Tales of Mean Streets* had been published, Morrison received a letter from Rev. A. Osborne Jay, a missionary to the slums and author of books on the East End. Father Jay asked Morrison to investigate the Old Nichol, then one of the worst areas in London. Morrison responded by devoting eighteen months to the project. Aided by Father Jay he became acquainted with the denizens. He interviewed them with a persistence and precision worthy of a modern anthropologist, recorded their utterance and even took part in the events of their daily life. His knowledge of boxing, which he had picked up at the People's Palace, is said to have stood him in good stead on several occasions when he was mugged by natives of the Old Nichol. (All this, of course, is in great contrast with Jack London, who spent a couple of desultory weeks in London before writing *People of the Abyss,* his study of a slum.) Carefully selecting incidents that had taken place, Morrison, his eighteen months passed, wrote his best-known work, *A Child of the Jago.* It is the story of a good-hearted boy who grows up among pickpockets, muggers, prostitutes, sneak thieves, fences and burglars, and is destroyed by his environment. *A Child of the Jago* was immediately recognized as a work of stature, and by 1912 had been translated into several Continental languages. It went through seven British printings.

Six years after *A Child of the Jago,* Morrison wrote his third important book. This was *The Hole in the Wall* (1902), which I consider his finest work. As V. S. Pritchett put it, it is a minor classic of the twentieth century, still as vivid, as gripping, as inevitable in development as when it was first written. It is set in the mid-nineteenth century, not too far away in time from the years when Morrison himself was growing up in an East End slum. Told by varying narrators, it is the story of a small boy in the incredibly foul waterfront area near the Ratcliffe Highway. The boy's grandfather, whose hands are not unstained with murder and theft, operates a low dive, The Hole in the Wall. Both boy and grandfather are caught up in a complex intertwining of crimes, plotted and committed.

After *The Hole in the Wall* Arthur Morrison, writer of European stature, disappeared from the new book lists. For two or three years he continued to write light fiction, then even this ceased. Why he stopped writing fiction we can only speculate. Perhaps his newspaper work took up too much of his time. Perhaps with easy financial circumstances he no longer had to write. Or perhaps as P. J. Keating in his fine introduction to the MacGibbon and Kee edition of *A Child of the Jago* has suggested, there were psychological reasons. His serious fiction obviously recapitulates themes from his own life, and these psychological configurations may eventually have lost their power. With *The Hole in the Wall,* which is deeply felt, in contrast to the dispassionate earlier works, Morrison may finally have gotten something out of his system. If so, *pace* Morrison's own feelings, the world lost a good writer.

Around 1902 a new facet of Arthur Morrison, however, had become public. This was Arthur Morrison, art historian and critic. He had become a most enthusiastic collector of Japanese prints, and he haunted the waterfront shops and shipping in the harbor area, looking for Oriental art work brought home by sailors. He often completed his purchases in low taverns in the small hours of the night, and would hasten back to the West End, routing his friends out of bed, to show what he had acquired.

Morrison was not a dilettante, and his knowledge of Japanese art soon became exhaustive. It culminated in a two-volume work, *The Painters of Japan* (1911), which was published in both England and America, and is still highly regarded. In 1913 he sold his collection to the British Museum for the rumored price of £4,000 (perhaps $80,000 in present value) and retired.

Arthur Morrison lived until 1945, but little is known of his life during his last thirty years. He was elected to the Royal Literary Society and in the 1920's served on its council. When he died in 1945 the world was more astonished to learn that he had been still living than that he was dead.

In this brief biographical sketch only Morrison's more important work has been considered. Morrison wrote a fair amount of ephemeral journalism as well as several other books. His relatively unknown work ***Zig-Zags at the Zoo*** (1895) popularized natural history, sometimes a little fancifully, while ***The Dorrington Deed-Box*** (1897) is a series of connected short stories about a rogue who also does occasional detective work for his own benefit. *To London Town* (1899), the experiences of a young man in lower-class London, is much less vivid than the books about the slums, and is not regarded very highly. Journalistic expertise, but little else, is to be found in *Cunning Morrell* (1899), a sentimental historical romance set in early nineteenth-century Essex. The title character is a historical white witch, about whom Morrison wrote more satisfyingly in a periodical article. *The Green Eye of Goona* (known in America as *The Green Eye*) (1904) is a detective adventure in quest of a stolen gem secreted in a magnum of Imperial Tokay. Anticipatory of *The Twelve Chairs,* it has some ingenious touches and is amusing. ***Divers Vanities*** (1905) and ***Green Ginger*** (1909) are collections of earlier work. An occasional story in them has crime elements, but the general mode is that of W. W. Jacobs, and does not fit Morrison well. This is all quite far from Morrison's true detective stories.

．　．　．　．　．

Martin Hewitt first met the reader's eye in **"The Lenton Croft Robberies"** in the March 1894 issue of *The Strand Magazine.* This was the first of six stories which were thereupon issued in book form under the title ***Martin Hewitt, Investigator.*** The second and third series of Hewitt's adventures, however, appeared in *The Windsor Magazine* in 1895 and 1896; these were later published as *(The)* ***Chronicles of Martin Hewitt*** and *(The)* ***Adventures of Martin Hewitt.*** All in all there are eighteen of these short stories. An episode-serial, ***The Red Triangle,*** is also concerned with Hewitt; it appeared in *The London Magazine* in 1903, and described Hewitt's campaign against a master criminal from the West Indies who uses hypnotism to control his servitors. It is much inferior to the short stories.

The short stories about Martin Hewitt seem to have been quite popular in both England and America. They were novel and imaginative in subject matter; plotted with greater meticulousness than most of their contemporary counterparts; and they were intelligent and pleasantly written, without the crude sensationalism of L. T. Meade or Fred White, or the blatant, aggressive vulgarity of C. Cutcliffe Hyne's or Guy Boothby's lesser work.

Seen in retrospect Hewitt is obviously based on Sherlock Holmes via the identity of opposites. Whereas Holmes is tall and gaunt, Hewitt is of medium stature and plump; whereas Holmes is egotistical and arrogant, Hewitt is pleasant and unctuously affable; whereas Holmes scorns Scotland Yard, Hewitt is grateful for cooperation, reflecting that the Metropolitan Police can perform operations he cannot. Holmes's adventures are set at high key; Hewitt is deliberately low key. All in all, the Holmes-Hewitt relationship reminds one of the motion pictures in the 1910's and 1920's: a comedian anxious to appear distinct from Charles Chaplin would wear clothes that were too small rather than too large, would sport a large moustache rather than a small one, and might walk pigeon-toed rather than duck-footed. It all came to the same thing.

If part of Hewitt is Sherlock Holmes facing in the opposite direction, the remainder is probably an emergence of Arthur Morrison's financial situation. Morrison wrote the stories for the large fees paid by the rival variety magazines, and did not consider them as important as his naturalistic work. As far as can be determined—apart from the negative criterion of avoiding the lower-class crime that might have memory links—the Martin Hewitt stories had no personal meaning for Morrison. Nor did he desire to experiment, as he had done in his serious work. He consciously wrote in a tradition that had suddenly become frozen into a classical form: the bourgeois detective story of the Doyle sort, where the roles of detective and supplicant are fixed, the emergence of story is close and circular, and the resolution is clear. The subject matter is genteel, the crimes are passionate or commercial, and the mores of society are fulfilled.

This adherence to traditional pattern is something of a pity, since Morrison should have been the New Writer in the detective story. Along among his writing contemporaries he knew true crime: he had lived among it as a child and young man, and had studied it intensively as an adult. In his later work, like *The Hole in the Wall,* he had mastered a literary technique at least the equal of any of his contemporaries, and he showed the capability of breaking form. Morrison should have taken the detective story out of 221B Baker Street.

This development took place a generation later in America, when a group of writers, most notably Dashiell Hammett and Raymond Chandler, came to recognize that a broad spectrum of choices surrounded the detective, and that a detective story need not be limited to a single secant of experience. This is not to say that the classical British drawing-room story is aesthetically immoral, as some theorists of the hard-boiled school imply, but simply to say that there are many modes of detection, all equally valid, and that Morrison was in a unique position to enhance the form and did not.

But to consider Arthur Morrison simply as a lost horizon and Hewitt as a Pathfinder who went around a single tree is probably too negative, and ultimately unfair. One should not judge criminals by crimes they did not commit, writers by stories they did not write, nor detectives by cases or experiences that did not befall them. One cannot weigh negatives.

Morrison's Martin Hewitt remains the second-best detective of the period of Doyle, before the emergence of G. K. Chesterton and R. A. Freeman. Original crime motifs, ingenious plotting and good characterizations keep the best of Hewitt's adventures fresh and appealing.

A selection of Hewitt's most interesting cases follows. This selection has been difficult to make, for Morrison's stories are very even in quality. To bring the reader a little closer to Morrison's epoch, we have reproduced the original magazine pages in photographic facsimile.

Michel Krzak (essay date 1979)

SOURCE: "Arthur Morrison's East End of London," in *Victorian Writers and the City,* edited by Jean-Paul Hulin and Pierre Coustillas, De l'universite de lile III, 1979, pp. 147-82.

[*In the following essay, Krzak describes Morrison's personal and professional connections to London's East End.*]

Arthur Morrison, who died in December 1945 at the age of 82, is still described as a native of Kent in many reference books—for instance in the 1974 edition of the *Encyclopaedia Britannica*—despite new data found notably in P. J. Keating's introduction to the 1969 edition of *A Child of the Jago.* Such an indication is unfortunate since it may lead readers to think that his was an outsider's picture of London.

We may wonder what prompted Arthur Morrison to provide false information about his origins to *Who's Who's* first biographical enquiry in 1897, at a time when he was an established short-story writer and the novelist of *A Child of the Jago.* If we dismiss ignorance on his part—although we can understand why he chose Kent, his mother's native county, rather than Essex which he had adopted as his home—, we are faced with a riddle, only partially and unsatisfactorily solved by charges of deceit or social snobbery. Not that a deliberate wish to stand aloof was out

of character in a man who, judging by the testimonies of acquaintances, was reserved and secretive. But there remains a mystery when we realize that this information would have provided an overwhelming argument to counter the fierce reactions and bitter attacks after the publication of *Tales of Mean Streets* and *A Child of the Jago,* especially during the controversy on realism initiated by H. D. Traill. Perhaps he felt that Victorian society could not acknowledge his rise from a working-class background. Whatever his true motives, personal and social, there is no need to capitalize on his mystification at this juncture. Indeed, we can reinstate him as a man of the people, born in Poplar, and the son of an engine fitter. Though we have no documents about his education, we know, from the 1871 census, that he was still in the East End at the age of eight; and, as he became an office boy at fifteen, he must have spent all his childhood east of Aldgate. Thanks to the encouragements of W.E. Henley, he made his way to realistic literature in the 1890s, via his secretaryship at the People's Palace in Mile End Road and journalism in Fleet Street.

The biography, as well as the historical and social context, underlines the significance of Morrison's work. In the closing decades of the nineteenth century, a new outlook on the environment of industrial cities prevailed—London being regarded as an epitome and a development of the basic traits of urban life. Special emphasis was laid on hidden features, and fresh evidence was brought forward to question society's achievement, notably its policy towards the poor. *The Bitter Cry of Outcast London,* which forcefully sounded the alarm in 1883, was by no means an isolated appeal for changes and reforms. Several other publications and reports—Walter Besant's *All Sorts and Conditions of Men* in 1882 and George Gissing's *The Nether World* in 1889 are prominent literary examples—exposed shameful facts and were instrumental in arousing acute concern for city slum dwellers in the 1880s and 1890s.

Naturally, Mayhew's studies of London labour, Chadwick's and Greenhow's investigations of the 1840s and 1850s should be kept in mind when examining Morrison's descriptions of the 1890s, even though their perspective was different. The image of the unknown country was still used to describe the poverty-stricken areas, but Morrison's main interest focused on the urban growth of London as the cause of severe negligence despite successive reports and subsequent reforms. His presentation can be seen as resulting from a long investigation into living conditions which started with an enquiry into the paupers of mid-century London to end with Booth's study of the submerged population. From the "Cockney Corners", which appeared as early as 1888, through the trilogy *Tales of Mean Streets, A Child of the Jago* and *To London Town,* to *The Hole in the Wall,* published in 1902, Morrison followed a path leading from fact to fiction, from a factual account to a more elaborate description of city life, from journalism to naturalism and realism.

. . . . .

Morrison's earliest contribution to *The People* provides his first approach to a picture of London. As the announcement made it clear, this series of independent "sketches" was to "deal with localities and their peculiarities, rather than with individuals".[1] Its aim was to introduce the reader to several districts of London and to pinpoint their characteristic traits—Poplar and its Saturday market, Clerkenwell and its clockmakers and jewellers, the French restaurants of Soho, Bow Street Police Court, Whitechapel with its rows of houses, its homecrafts and ethnical groups, Jacob's Island, and the contrapuntal areas of Greenwich Park and Epping Forest.

Morrison successfully gives the impression of a dense population at certain key points of the capital, on London Bridge for instance every Saturday at noon, when "the pavement is filled by two solid streams of steadily hurrying human beings" and when pedestrians must dodge an incessant flow of traffic. Similarly on Saturday nights another gathering of people busy shopping in the East End is depicted in these words: "The broad Whitechapel road swarms with laughing, shouting, noisy human life. Buyers and sellers, rogues and dupes, drinkers and fighters. Each for himself and the thought of the moment!". The struggle for life is felt all the more acutely as economic competition is magnified by the thick crowd and as London Hospital looms up in the vicinity, looking after those who "have come to grief in some of the thousand ways so easy among the dense population, the large works, and the traffic". Urban concentration is an unquestionable factor of accidents in this "great cosmorama of life and death, joy and sorrow, health, sickness, and pain". Morrison excels in drawing accurate sketches of people in the streets, but on the whole he sticks to a general description and watches with a critical eye both setting and city dwellers. His "explorer's mind" notices in Soho "bell-handles, thick on the door-posts, like stops on an organ, front door never shut, children rolling down the steps, dirty babies nursed by premature little women and 'Apartments to Let' everywhere", as so many signs of overcrowding, of the conditions of tenant and sub-tenant families, and of the corollary questions of child care and hygiene.[2]

In contrast with city life and to balance or counter the effects of urban overcrowding and pollution, Epping Forest is a godsend, whose proximity and advantages should be realized by the busy population of London, for, as Morrison puts it in his sketch, "Epping Forest is a Cockney Corner, from Epping to Wanstead Flats, and from Walthan Abbey to Chigwell, but one without smoke, chimney pots, noise and dirt; with whispering thickets, noble trees, grassy hollows and cool waters; with singing birds, humming insects, all sweet sounds. . . ." How surprising to find this quasi-lyrical description of nature coming from Morrison's pen! The author so appreciated this wholesome "lung" of the city, the benefits of which should fall to the working East Ender, that he settled on the outskirts of the forest, at Chingford, and later at Loughton.[3] He publicly stated his marked preference for life in Essex,[4] never far from London it is true, and was well aware of the threat of industrial or urban growth, of the continual encroachment of the town upon nature, upon the Hainault Forest for instance.[5] The notion of an antithesis between town and country life, not original in itself, refers to a duality inscribed in Morrison's life and literary career. His emigration may be seen as corresponding to the typical aspiration of the East Ender he was. Rooted in the East End, he later developed a professional life in London and a private life in the country, chiefly in Essex. This parallel is present in the double current of his production—his East End studies and his Essex stories, united by the same insight into place and character, and an earnest commitment to faithful treatment. Besides, if his interest in oriental art lies beyond this duality, his commitments to the literature of detection, to journalism and to humorous short stories are essentially urban.

Whereas ***Tales of Mean Streets*** and *A Child of the Jago* are set in London only, *To London Town* depicts a migration to London from the country for economic reasons. Actually, several migratory movements, illustrating a general situation, are outlined in the plot. First, sons and daughters leave their rustic parents to come and work in the job-supplying East End of London; secondly, when an emergency arises, if the father dies for instance, the family returns to the parents or grandparents in the country; thirdly, when the latter source of supporting income becomes extinct, a new economic migration takes place—the industrious widow enters the labour market as head of the family while the elder son becomes an apprentice at the firm which used to employ his father. The facts and the events are exemplary in so far as the Mays are drawn by the centripetal force of London; the country is their native soil as well as a temporary refuge or source of comfort—it is motherly on both counts. Indeed, even though this orphaned family is uprooted and plunged into a highly competitive world, it is hardly touched by urban morality; only the younger generation represented by Johnny proves more adapted to a tougher milieu and more wary of city sharks or spongers. The Mays are still endowed with sturdy rustic qualities; they have retained a filial love for the country of their forbears, which they semi-consciously uphold as their ideal.

Contrasted with a world ruled by the economic struggle for bread, the country is idyllically associated with the notions of peace and quiet. But this position is far from being immune to change. As London keeps expanding, nature is slowly and relentlessly the victim of urbanization and industrialization. If the air in Essex is still "healthier and cleaner" than in London, the country has become a "poorer hunting ground" for butterflies, a prey to "the great smoky province that lay to the south-west".[6] London is a magnetic and tentacular force which draws the lifeblood from the provinces through migration and impairs the country's unadulterated state through pollution.

. . . . .

Apart from this image of the city threatening the countryside, Morrison's early descriptions of the outer environment of the poorer classes of London lay stress on the sameness of streets and houses. He notices in "Jacob's Is-land" a "very dull street" with "mean, black little dwelling houses", and draws attention to the depressing atmosphere pervading this dreary, matter-of-fact world:

> Back from the river, what a sorry blank is Jacob's Is-land! It is to-day, without exception, the saddest Cock-ney Corner we know. Not eminently crime-saddened, or poor or starved. Colourless, blank . . . Mean little houses, not old enough to be interesting and not new enough to be clean, cluster thick about Jacob Street, London Street, Hickman's Folly and their alleys (. . .) Jacob's Island is comparatively respectable, but, oh!, how fearsomely dull!

As in another sketch, **"On Blackwall Pier,"** which takes up the identical themes of sordid street monotony and hard living conditions, the crude facts are attended by pessimis-tic comment.[7] This particular emphasis paves the way for his highly praised study entitled **"A Street,"** which dwells obsessively upon the drabness of surroundings.

If the setting in "Cockney Corners" can be regarded as a décor in the sense of a somewhat neutral visual presenta-tion, in his subsequent work it loses its picturesqueness to assume social significance since it is directly, if negatively, related to its counterparts in more favoured districts. The architectural impression is strengthened by a parallel view of the inhabitants' way of life. Morrison establishes an in-evitable link between outer appearance and actual exist-ence, although this interpretation, which sets the tone for a realistic approach, is not borne out in all the "tales of mean streets", for life is not necessarily dreary where liv-ing conditions are grim.

Morrison was not the first nor the last of his generation to have observed the uniformity of the streets and houses in London. Hubert Crackanthorpe for instance depicts the monotony of "shabbily symmetrical" streets, with "a double row of insignificant, dingy-brick houses".[8] In *To London Town* Morrison offers a similar description when the Mays come to the East End. If "the road narrowed and grew fouler, and the mouths of unclean alleys dribbled slush and dirty children across the pavements", they even-tually reach "a place of many streets lying regularly at right angles, all of small houses, all clean, every one a counterpart of every other" (*TLT,* pp. 76-7). Unlike some other areas, Shipwrights Row is renowned for its cleanli-ness and the colour pattern of the outside paintwork. Yet, monotony is spreading—the children travelling to Essex notice "close, regular streets of little houses, all of one pattern, (that) stared in raw brick, or rose, with a forlorn air of crumbling sponginess, amid sparse sticks of scaf-folding" (*TLT,* p. 186)—as if London kept exporting a mass-produced housing pattern. The depressing monotony in certain quarters is intensified by overcrowding. Families gather near their places of work, in districts which soon become congested. These districts change character ac-cording to their inhabitants, whose number keeps increas-ing. People pile into quickly saturated lodgings—"eight, ten or a dozen human sleepers" in one room, in the ex-treme case of the Jago.[9]

Foul nooks and crannies inevitably developed in the tex-ture of Victorian London, as backhouses enjoyed the cheap rents a working-class family could afford. Different types of slum dwellings emerged as demands rose and rents al-tered, tenancy being more or less temporary. The poorer labourers had to resort to these lodging ghettos, motivated by proximity of work and their financial resources. The ironically named Pleasant Court in Crackanthorpe's *Vi-gnettes* (1896) is a good example—"To find it, you must penetrate a winding passage, wedged between high walls of dismal brick". And Jago Court, the focal point in Mor-rison's novel, is a typical, though extreme, example of re-claimed backyards where all kinds of needy people have come to settle. Dr. Barnardo's article entitled "A Tale of a Mean Street" provides a parallel depiction of a narrow, ill-paved, East-End street and a dark cellar-like kitchen.[10] An identical impression of an underground world pervades the crowded courts, typical of those built-in areas which have long passed saturation point, depicted by Octavia Hill in the 1870s. The spatial confinement becomes unbearable in the sultry atmosphere. In "a narrow paved court with houses on each side, the sun has heated them all day, till it has driven nearly every inmate out of doors". The children especially are "crawling or sitting on the hard hot stones till every corner of the place looks alive".[11] The opening pages of *A Child of the Jago* offer an exact parallel. The Jago is the "blackest pit in London" and Jago Court, "the blackest hole in all that pit". In the sultry and smelly at-mosphere of summer nights, it is filled with rat-like human shapes. Because the contemporary picture, with its rheto-ric, is so consistent, we may infer that Morrison's fiction is based on reliable facts, and insist on his first-hand knowledge of the places he describes—a knowledge he re-peatedly stressed in reply to criticisms. His four years as secretary to the People's Palace, his observations as a journalist, and his careful documentation prior to writing (notably his "intimate study" of the parish of Trinity Church at Shoreditch which lasted a year and a half), bear witness to the credibility of his account.

There is both a gradation and an evolution in presentment. **"A Street"** underlines the bleak monotony of city streets in Poplar, where spectacular aspects are deliberately dis-carded. Yet, his denunciation of false, biased views of the East End as "an evil plexus of slums that hide human creeping things",[12] is contradicted by the image of the Jago in his first novel. Again, if the docks in *To London Town,* where the Mays used to live, are described in a subdued manner, and if the busy riverside at Blackwall Pier is less colourful (*TLT,* p. 35-7, 244), the dockland and Wapping area in *The Hole in the Wall* is much more picturesque and dangerous with its maze of "crooked lanes" and "small, ill-lighted streets".[13] Off the notorious Ratcliff Highway, lies Blue Gate, hazardous and ill-famed, set in mid-nineteenth-century London.

Habitation and reputation varied according to the district and the economic situations of the inhabitants of the East End. While regular workers lived in rather characterless though clean lodgings, casual labourers and new immigrants had to be content with unsuitable dwelling places, for financial reasons. They had to join other urban categories—marginal groups such as criminal types—, running the risk, repeatedly stressed, of being contaminated. As for the densely crowded areas, or rookeries, inhabited by a fluctuating, unstable population, they were often considered dangerous quarters—a threat to civilized society. The traditional haunts of disreputable characters, thieves and criminals, such as Whitechapel, Limehouse, Ratcliff Highway, were often painted in this light.

In point of fact, as the slum dwellers had little inclination to stay confined in their small dingy rooms, they repaired to the street, which was the meting place of natives and visitors, and a vantage point for the observant novelist. The streets in the East End were busy places at any hour, but on a number of regular and special occasions, people gathered in large numbers. While fun fairs, bank holiday rejoicing, and street fights tended to draw people from far and near, street markets assembled a more local crowd. Apart from adults, loafers or busy tradesmen and housewives, observers noticed the presence of a great number of children, which seemed to corroborate the idea of a prolific East End. Although school attendance was compulsory, it was seldom or inadequately enforced, so that, when unemployed, children were left on their own. Because of the absence of their fathers, ill or dead or in jail, which obliged mothers to rule the home, the children had to fend for themselves, unsupervised. As bread, not to mention money, was lacking, many of them became self-sufficient at an early age. They regarded the streets as a spectacle—witness the boys watching the clockmakers in a sketch called **"Clerkenwell"** (*CC*)—, but they were also on the lookout for a favourable opportunity—picking up an odd job like parcel carrying, or snatching things. Maturity soon fell upon their young shoulders, especially when, like Mother Sister Julia in Edwin Pugh's *A Street in Suburbia* (1895), the elder children helped to bring up little brothers and sisters, or when new family or social responsibilities prevailed. Early moral and economic independence was not a new fact in the late Victorian period, but a characteristic feature of the working-class children of East London. Dicky Perrott is the archetype of boys who, rather than playing games, were in search of food, or objects to exchange for bread, and who, like adults, had to rely on themselves only.

The documentary realism used by Morrison and some of his contemporaries to present a vivid description of the environment in East London also provided a basis for reflection. Many aspects of this environment seemed unworthy of a modern Victorian city; they were at variance with the ideals and principles expounded by contemporary society. These writers implicitly demanded that efforts should be made to relieve those shameful areas, those dark recesses which bore witness to obvious neglect in town planning, and also to abolish the actual and latent dangers of a marginal, segregated life to the population at large, but especially to children left without proper material care and moral support. If the later Morrison seems to have been

more cautious about such possibilities, the young writer of the "Cockney Corners" did not hesitate to dwell on the positive merits of Epping Forest and public parks as essential lungs for oppressed East-Enders, just as he provided guidance in organizing the activities of young members when he was at the People's Palace.

. . . . .

Morrison reveals that there is a definite physical and moral pattern of life in the East End of London, people being identified with their streets and their districts. From his descriptions of the drab lives in mean streets and the violent life in the Jago, we can gather that urban structures had a direct bearing on the material and mental conditions of people.

A direct consequence of the sanitary conditions, already exposed by Edwin Chadwick in the 1840s, was the high death-rate in slum areas. Shoreditch is an exemplary case, even in 1898: "Nowhere else in London can you gaze on such a scene of wretchedness. Houses hardly fit to be dog-kennels, breeding disease which brings the children of Shoreditch to the grave with terrible rapidity and suddenness. Four graves are dug here for every one in any other part of London".[14] Statistics showing population density and mortality rates were used to show the consequences of deplorable circumstances. Morrison did not fail to stress the phenomenon dramatically:

> Albeit the Jago death-rate ruled full four times that of all London beyond, still the Jago rats bred and bred their kind unhindered, multiplying apace and infecting the world (p. 107).

Infant mortality was markedly more widespread in cities, and among poor urban working-class families. The death registers at Somerset House bear numerous mentions of still-born babies. Moreover, neglect and lack of food caused the untimely deaths of frail children, as we may observe in *A Child of the Jago,* in little Looey's case. Dicky Perrott's sister is soon replaced, however, by little Em and baby Josh, which demonstrates the high birth-rate prevailing in East London. For the same environmental reasons, children like Dicky "would never get really tall" (p. 109). In those substandard lodgings and insanitary conditions, the children were the first to suffer, as poverty was the cause of undernourishment and malnutrition, which accelerated disease and death.

Poverty was also related to, and aggravated by, drinking. In view of the social context, it is not surprising that drinking should have been so popular. The public houses were attractive, brightly lit places which stood out against the dreary surroundings, and afforded an outlet, a release from outer struggles and family troubles. Octavia Hill clearly points out the effect of the close, stifling courts on people's behaviour—during the hot evenings "the drinking is wildest, the fighting fiercest, and the language most violent",[15] while Robert Sherard indicates that "it is indeed rather on account of the physical exigencies of their work (and, we may add, of their lodgings) that these people, as a class, exceed and are intemperate".[16] Naturally, drinking was considered an aggravating factor in those unfavoured districts of the East End. Not only did it divert money from more immediate needs, but it also brought people into contact with disreputable characters. The pubs were indeed places where shady business transactions were often settled. Apart from "The Hole in the Wall" which chiefly enjoys an underground activity, there are several types of public houses in the Jago. "The Feathers" is described as "the grimiest and vilest of the four", and in all of them there were frequent "bar riots". At Mother Gapp's, fighting and rejoicing alternate. On great occasions, such as the homecoming of a released convict—Josh Perrott in the novel—the public house fulfils a social function, in that it proclaims reintegration and asserts its communal feelings. Hannah Perrott has to "prove herself not unduly proud" and indulge in gin-drinking, lest she should incur her neighbours' rebukes (p. 164).

Much of the money is spent on drinking—in poor districts shopping is done on Sunday morning after Saturday's drink, with what is left of the week's wages. The search for food and the basic necessities of life takes several forms, according to the ability of the housewife. Morrison points out in "A Workman's Budget", published in 1901,[17] that although generalization is difficult, the working-class woman is "commonly no fool and no idler". Yet, recalling his personal experience—"I have met with perfectly amazing cases of masterly household management on slender means; and brilliant instances aside, the average workman's missis is a very good housewife"—, he implicitly infers that there are less happy cases. In fact, he acknowledges the existence of wide differences—"between the drunkard, whose household starves while he soaks away his wages, and the weakling, whose wife takes every penny and scarce gives him one back, there lie many degrees"—, between a Jago family and the Ropers or the Mays.

Hunting for the money necessary for subsistence and lodging involves a daily struggle. When illness strikes a working-class family, hardships increase. **"Chrisp Street, Poplar"** (*CC*), after a picturesque description of the streets, introduces the reader to the pathetic story of a couple emerging from a pawnshop:

> Times have been hard with Joe and the missis. Joe has had rheumatic fever, and has spent his entire convalescence in hunting for a job. Day after day he has started out, good fellow, with a mendacious assurance to the missis that he didn't feel up to any breakfast, well knowing the little he left for her and the small Barkers even then. Evening after evening he has come home again—feetsore, hungry, disappointed, and well-nigh heartbroken—unsuccessful. And evening after evening his noble little missis has met him with a smile—poor soul, it gets harder to smile as the face grows thinner and the brain feels duller—with a smile and a kiss as warm and as true as even when she was a plump-faced nursemaid and he was a jolly 'prentice lad over on the island.

If the outlook is optimistic and the tone slightly sentimental, as the family is seen climbing uphill with courage and

perseverance, this vignette depicting representatives of the "industrious poor" is nonetheless truthful enough.

To overcome adversity, pawning is the usual solution. From the "Cockney Corners" onwards, Morrison mentioned it in his works. When Josh Perrott is injured and is unable to work, his wife Hannah pawns a coat at a "leaving shop in a first floor back in Jago Row" (*CJ*, p. 138). In *To London Town,* Norah's dress is pledged as a direct consequence of the drinking habits of her mother. The same means was used to pay the rent. Otherwise, as a long term solution, it was possible to sub-let, or take in lodgers, but Hannah Perrott would not hear of this simply because "she doubted her ability to bully the rent out of them, or to turn them out if they did not pay" (*CJ*, p. 158)—which indicates that the practice was frequent.

Circumstances drove people along various paths, even beyond the limits of morality, to obtain basic necessities. Several methods were used to get money and clothing from the "profitable sentimentalist" in the Jago, although these methods were held in contempt by the "sturdier ruffians", who preferred stealing. One of the devices consisted of "a profession of sudden religious awakening" (*CJ*, pp. 104-5), which reminds us of the study called **"A Conversion"** (*TMS*). Hesitant potential converts received "the boots, the coats, and the half-crowns used to coax weak brethren into the fold". Similar behaviour is seen in children who do not normally attend school except when free gifts—coal or food—are distributed. Dicky, for instance, goes to school "at irregular intervals", but "whenever anything was given away, he attended as a matter of course" (*CJ*, pp. 105, 109).

Hardships tend to favour a realistic approach to daily problems. Several examples of the suffering poor are given in "Cockney Corners", especially in **"London Hospital"** (*CC*), where disease or injury leads to crises. A bricklayer, who has fallen from his scaffolding, is happy to see his wife, courageous and smiling:

> His wife is sitting by him, with her little boy. See what a brave, bright face she keeps, and how gaily she reports her own well-doing, although the poor fellow himself well knows how few shillings there were in hand a month ago, when he first came in, and how she is charring hard for every mouthful she and the child eat.

The poignancy of the picture is enhanced if we are aware that Morrison's mother may have gone through a similar experience when his father was in hospital suffering from phthisis.

Diseases, death, brutal or violent events steel people to a stern, often stoic, attitude to life. Harsh realities and constant worries are not conducive to pleasure and laughter. Indeed, women with a tendency towards merriment or singing are regarded with suspicion and judged mercilessly, like the young countrywife in **"A Street."**[18] Lizerunt, in the opening "tale", hardly experiences any pleasure in her almost inevitable progression from work at a pickle factory to charring, mangling, and finally to forced prostitution. Robert Sherard, who also describes "the mean miseries of the very poor", insists on work as being their all-encompassing activity, which means that they have "no time for relaxation" and that "their entire energy is taken up in the hunting of the loaf".[19]

Yet "the utter remoteness from delight", which closes **"A Street"** and sets the tone for the *Tales of Mean Streets*, must be qualified. Even in **"Lizerunt"** courting represents a pleasant, if brief, spell of comparative happiness before marriage. Elsewhere life is brightened up, if not illuminated, on a few rare occasions, especially when a little time or money can be spared. Drinking can be a special occasion, even in the Jago, when Josh Perrott wins his fight for instance. In more favoured spots, a funfair (as in **"Lizerunt"**), or a ball at the Institute (as in *To London Town,* though it comes to naught for the young pair), are events that lit up the dull, workaday routine. Brief, fleeting pleasures, with no time wasted in refinement, characterize life in the East End.

Socially, if anonymity prevails in all great cities and particularly in the urban pattern of the East End, there is also a definite sense of community. Neighbours, because of proximity and promiscuity, exert a more or less overt pressure on each other, seemingly inspired by both a sense of bondage in poverty and a desire to be protected against social annihilation. On the positive side we see in *To London Town* the exchange of paint as a mark of good neighbourly relationship and solidarity; on the negative, the compulsory leave-taking of the May family once the shame of quarrelling and the accusation of adultery and bigamy have stained the shop's good name and the family's character. Respectability varies according to districts, but, as often as not, the fear of scandal and loss of people's esteem are compelling forces in matters of behaviour. Even in a district like the Jago, the Ropers find it hard to preserve their working-class decency. Their presence in the Jago results from unemployment; they are not integrated. Mrs. Roper is disliked because of her neatness and cleanliness, and her "aloofness from gossip", just as her husband is rejected, for not drinking, or brawling, or beating his wife. This reluctance to comply with the Jago norm is a cause of antagonism; the Ropers are a disruptive example, or, as Morrison puts it, "a matter of scandalous arrogance, impudently subversive of Jago custom and precedent". The tension is so acute that the Ropers, who have complained of robbery, are accused of "assailing the reputation of the neighbourhood" and, because they are but "pestilent outsiders", are beaten up and plundered by their neighbours, only to be saved by the parson's timely intervention (*CJ,* pp. 72-3, 77). The Ropers are in fact an alien graft and are physically and morally rejected by the community; they are fought as a threat to its identity. Brian Harrison gives corroborative evidence when he points out that "slum dwellers disliked working men" who "gave themselves airs", and that teetotallers were often insulted.[20]

Hannah Perrott experiences similar difficulties at first, because her background is different and she is "an alien who has never entirely fallen into Jago ways". She neither drinks, nor gossips; nor is she beaten by her husband—a side reference to the normal relationship between husbands and wives. Her attitude is regarded as scornful aloofness and resented by other women, "irritated by such superiorities", to the point of causing her harm—she is in fact beaten up as she belongs neither to the Ranns nor the Learys, the two families in feud (*CJ,* p. 65). Noncompliance thus exposes people to reprisal. In Hannah's case though, a slow process of acceptance and integration takes place, the physical preceding the moral change.

Respectability can be demonstrated in various ways. In **"Behind the Shade"** (*TMS*), two women, a widow and her daughter, live in a cottage at the end of "the common East End street", but the neighbours disapprove of the independence enjoyed by this one isolated family, and gossip over the "piano-forte lessons" advertised in the window. Gradually their situation deteriorates and rather than appeal to public charity, they let themselves die of hunger. Two features are revealed; on the one hand a sense of conformity to a general "code of morals" even if it is a warped one, and self-respect on the other. To starve rather than beg stems from an attitude of stoic defiance. Echoes of the same notion were common enough at the time: a commentator noted in 1898 that "the reticence and reserve of the respectable struggling poor, who would prefer to starve in a garret rather than apply for the charitable doles, was not understood".[21] The idea expressed here establishes categories among the poor and the destitute, and takes for granted that charitable money was there for the asking, though there undoubtedly were misuses. What Morrison and his contemporaries often insisted upon, was the extreme point to which self-respect could lead. Typical is the attitude towards funerals—everything becomes subservient to the profound, stubborn urge to stage a "handsome funeral". **"On the Stairs"** portrays an old mother who fails to help her dying son and keeps the money that could have brought him relief in order to procure the "mutes" and "plooms" required for a respectable departure, to be acknowledged by the whole neighbourhood. There are similar observations in *To London Town,*[22] also in George Gissing's *The Nether World.* Elsewhere the characters express their horror of a cheap, plain coffin, and long for a "lovely" one— vainly in the case of Jack Randall in **"All That Messuage."** Such an attitude may be the sign of imported middle-class notions, but it represents a characteristic outburst of self-respect or pride in the harsh life of the poor.

If we now return to the problem of the precarious existence of the working classes, we are led to note how often the chase for subsistence was frustrated, since work was insecure for the labourer whose hands were his sole property. In addition to the bad housing and sanitary conditions, the lack of security endangered the health and life of the working population. But unlike Sherard, who exposed the harsh and dangerous conditions in industry, Morrison did not dwell upon life in factories—except an engineering firm in *To London Town.* Instead, he depicted women at home, engaged in various occupations, such as rush-bag, sack or matchbox making. The latter especially enjoyed popularity among late Victorian observers. *A Child of the Jago* provides us with a well-documented picture—Morrison himself claimed to have assembled a few boxes. Hannah Perrot's case is typical in so far as "temporarily widowed" wives were numerous in the Old Nichol-Jago area since many men were "in the country", i.e. in jail (p. 151). Several such activities, like shirt-mending, were in great demand, and were reserved for these more or less permanent widows. In the course of one of their removals, the Perrotts come to a room "wherein a widow had died over her sack-making two days before", leaving hungry children (p. 118). She presumably tried to avoid going to the workhouse, to which her children were eventually sent. Hannah, like the other women, would rather be exploited by manufacturers, and work for a pittance, than depart to the "house". Dr. T. J. Barnardo, in an article on the East End working classes, described their dread of the workhouse:

> The workhouse? Ah! Well you hardly know, perhaps, the loathing and horror with which the industrious and decent poor contemplate the prospect of breaking up their little homes, of being separated from their children, and of committing themselves, without hope of deliverance, to the Union.[23]

The "Union" or the "house" meant the break up of families, since the sexes as well as children and parents were separated, and imposed restrictions on the independence of the poor. Outdoor relief was rarely given, but even when people were entitled to it and even though they were at the end of their tether, they radically refused the provisions of the Poor Law. Individualism and self-respect prevailed again.

Thinking of the slum population in this light, sociologists have divided families into clear-cut categories. Mayhew proposed several divisions according to the "honesty" of the poor, and distinguished between those "who *will* work", those "who *can't* work", and those "who won't work", in other words, the "striving", the "disabled" and the "dishonest".[24] The range of people presented by Morrison provides a parallel with this classification. Just as there were various types of slums, so there were different classes of East Enders, "working class" being an ambiguous or inadequate term when applied to the second and third categories. The third one also includes criminals of the Jago type, as well as spongers on charity organizations or even on women like Mr. Burton in *To London Town.* In the preface to this story, Morrison described his new novel on the East End as forming with ***Tales of Mean Streets*** and *A Child of the Jago* "a trilogy intended to point a picture of a certain portion of life in the East End". Although he insisted on the limits of his representation, he claimed that "in these three books there is a fairly wide range, from thieves and blackguards, through decent workmen and their wives, to the best classes of workmen, the last of whom make up the characters in *To London Town.*[25] P. J.

Keating's distinction between the poverty-stricken, the criminals and the respectable artisans in Morrison's work is another convenient way of describing the same three classes.[26]

Morrison tried to restore a truer perspective in an interview published in *Cassell's Saturday Journal,* stating that:

> The 'East-Ender' is, more often than not, a respectable, hard-working man, who does his duty to his wife and children, and goes cleanly and honestly through the world. The great majority of the men work regularly and live in decent houses.

Here, the pendulum undoubtedly swung too far the other way, but the author at least tried to justify his view by adding that:

> There is still in the East End an enormous multitude of people who seem almost of another race than ours, who bring up large families in poverty, live in dens rather than houses, and eat tomorrow what they earn to-day.[27]

It is refreshing to see him leave aside moral characteristics, and stress physical and genetic as well as social and environmental features. No doubt his exposure of the daily life of representative sections of East End Londoners led to a wholesome and salutary reaction. The realistic portrayal of the living conditions of the poor and the working classes resulting from the urban environment in the East End was to disturb consciences and to challenge the unruffled complacency of the time. Characteristic of the contemporary reception of Morrison's studies was the enlightened appraisal in the *Literary Year Book* for 1898 which commended their direct sociological significance: "In his two studies of the East End, ***Tales of Mean Streets*** and *A Child of the Jago,* Mr. Morrison has made his mark both as an artist and as a sociological observer. He gives as it were the subjective side of one of Mr. Charles Booth's pictures".[28]

. . . . .

Because of the complex interaction of several factors it is hard to assess exactly the negative influence of urban conditions upon people's lives. If overcrowding and poverty were sometimes perceived as leading to delinquency and crime, the mere association of urban and social evils was more often observed than their causality. The back streets and backyards in the slum areas of East London certainly created conditions which were conducive to crime. These blights in the urban fabric made it possible for people to evade both the Victorian sanitation and policing laws. In the crowded rookeries, criminals of all descriptions could find shelter, secure as they were from police interference, while the streets and main thoroughfares were regarded by them as hunting grounds. Jago Court is described by Morrison as "an unfailing sanctuary, a city of refuge ever ready, ever secure", to the extent that higher rents had to be paid for "the privilege of residence in the Jago" (*CJ,* pp. 116-18), however questionable this advantage was in respect of sanitation and housing. Arthur Mee recalls Orange Court, in the Old Nichol area of Shoreditch, which "was approached by a tunnel from the street, and was on this account the favourite haunt of thieves", adding that "the police dare not enter the court, as the men would watch them emerge from the tunnel and throw bricks at them".[29] It is not surprising in this context that people should have developed special norms of behaviour, verging on, if not altogether steeped in, criminality. Contagion did play a role. As J. J. Tobias points out in general terms, "groups of people, living in distinctive areas, had evolved a way of life of their own based on crime", which forced other people to adopt the "same techniques, habits and attitudes".[30] A minority was thus capable of influencing a whole group and of giving a peculiar reputation to a given area.

Because of their unreachable recesses, the dockland and riverside areas of London, which play such prominent parts in *A Child of the Jago* and *The Hole in the Wall*, used to harbour and even favour dishonest deals and shady transactions performed by unscrupulous characters. The environment also palpably told on people's physical and mental health. William Booth insisted upon the "disease-breeding, manhood-destroying character" of congested housing, statistically involving about three million "submerged" people.[31] Quite naturally, contemporary writers dwelt on the notion of degradation to bestiality, and resorted to animal imagery when depicting slum dwellers. Crowded courts would be compared to dens, unfit for human habitation. Morrison uses this image extensively in his description of the Jago, where people are debased into "slinking" rats living in foul dens.

The danger of contagion, previously mentioned, menaced young people especially. The children were often in the streets, and, for want of parental authority, were submitted to various harmful influences. R. L. Shoenwald, studying Chadwick's investigations in the 1830s, observes that exclusion of children from factories or reduced hours, has often turned them "out into the streets and swollen the ranks of juvenile delinquents".[32] Even after the creation of School Board inspectors there were many ways of playing truant. Moreover, the milieu had such a powerful impact on the children that they could not improve in it. They were "schooled, not educated", as William Booth deplored. Many were born in workhouses, or were orphaned, experiencing, instead of a protective—though often inadequate—parenthood, the "competitive city life". In that context of indiscipline and laissez-faire, young minds were an easy prey to social determinism.

A prison chaplain, the Reverend W. D. Morrison, observed in 1896 that "Juveniles in all ranks of life are exceedingly sensitive to public opinion, and, unless gifted with great inborn force of character, are apt to become what the world in general considers them to be"[33]—which pinpoints the pressure weighing on those young shoulders. The young were expected to behave the way their parents did; they had to bear the burden of their social origins as if they had

committed unredeemable faults. Everyone was induced to follow the code of morals prevailing in his neighbourhood. Self-appropriation, for instance, was the means of defeating necessity in the Jago, and even "the one way to riches" (p. 81). Typical of this unwritten law is Dicky's reflection over his first theft, that "by all Jago custom and ethic it was his if only he could get clear away with it" (pp. 165-66). For those quick-maturing, self-sufficient boys, who modelled their conduct on the general pattern, the atmosphere was conducive to delinquency.

Yet, the notion of determinism seems to be absent from the following statement by W. D. Morrison:

> There is a population of habitual criminals which form a class by itself. Habitual criminals are not to be confounded with the working or any other class; they are a set of persons who make crime the object and business of their lives; to commit crime is their trade; they deliberately scoff at honest ways of earning a living, and must accordingly be looked upon as a class of separate and distinct character from the rest of the community.[34]

This viewpoint, which in 1891 was by no means new, reminds us of the distinction made in 1851 by Mary Carpenter between the "perishing classes", in danger of falling into crime, and the "dangerous classes", living by theft. Logically, all reformatory endeavours were directed towards the former, the latter being judged unredeemable. The moral distinction between the deserving and the underserving poor became a sociological one, so that, despite this clear-cut categorization, it was still thought possible to alter conditions and circumstances so as to salvage endangered people, without examining the direct correlation between poverty and crime.

The existence of a criminal class was so much taken for granted that it found its way into fiction. In *A Child of the Jago* the criminal class is inseparable from the milieu that gives it nurture and support, and, behind the apparently individualistic and empirical character of its actions, it has developed an internal discipline and a structure capable of stimulating the young. Dicky Perrott entertains two hopes—owning a shop, and achieving the status of a mobsman, i.e. a first class thief. In his eyes both objectives are praiseworthy; they would earn him consideration on the economic and social levels. A high mobsman, like the Mogul, commands general respect in the underground world—he is a tyrannical ruler exerting his sway over a given urban territory. He generally enjoys "suburban respectability" (p. 143) and police immunity because of his established position based on wealth, so that he can operate safely as the brain behind important swindles or robberies. He is the ruthless captain at the top of the criminal hierarchy, and there is intense rivalry among cabin-boys, or street urchins—young Dicky is a good example—to resemble most closely the man they at once admire and dread.

The actions performed are measured with a special yardstick which distinguishes several categories of crime, from

pilfering to shoplifting, and from house-breaking to burglary, just as thieves fall into classes and are manipulated
by fences and mobsmen. The latter control people, super-
vise fights and organize betting in the Jago. Once a young
boy like Dicky has proved his worth, he may be contacted
and engaged by a receiver—Aaron Weech uses food and
flattery to coax the hungry boy into working for him. A
whole substructure is thus revealed. When the chase after
the thief becomes too hot, stolen goods are dropped into
the fence's yard, conveniently concealed from the public
eye. On the other hand, when Josh Perrott wants to sell
the watch he has stolen from the Mogul, or King of the
High Mobsmen, the news has already got abroad and he
vainly goes from Mother Gapp to pawnbrokers and to
Weech. The latter treacherously informs the Mogul in the
hope of a reward from this powerful protector. This incident points to an active underground organization, which
controls individuals to preserve its cohesion.

For a better understanding of environmental influences on
young people, we may examine Dick Perrott's exemplary
case, and try to grasp the meaning of the rise and eventual
downfall of a talented boy who could have made his way
to the top. Forced to fend for himself at an early age, he
soon realizes that "he must take his share, lest it fall to
others" (p. 71). Necessity accelerates maturity and self-
sufficiency. The lack of food in the cupboard and the fact
that "there seemed nothing at home worth staying for" (p.
73), reduce him to loitering and pilfering, then to petty lar-
ceny with groups of other boys where he is noticed for his
efficiency. He soon becomes an expert thief, and wins
grades, the birchrod being part of his experience. This progression follows the lines traced by Old Beveridge in his
advice to Dicky, when he urged him to become a high
mobsman, "one of a thousand"—which implies that luck
is necessary in the strife to find room at the top. All means
are justified to reach this end—"Learn to read and write,
learn all you can, learn cunning, spare nobody and stop at
nothing, and perhaps"—Dicky might become one of the
High Mob. "It's the best the world has for you, for the Jago's got you", Old Beveridge adds (p. 91). The moral
standard of behaviour directly originates from this East
End corner.

The second pole of his potentiality is presented by Father
Sturt, but it presupposes a transformation in outlook. No
doubt Dicky senses that it is "a chance of life", but the
dream of becoming "a tradesman, with a shop of his own
and the name 'R. Perrott', with a golden flourish, over the
door" (p. 122), is soon shattered by the jealous villainy of
Weech the fence, and the shopkeeper's prejudices. Old
Beveridge's lessons and Weech's philosophy cannot be ignored, especially when life proves too firmly rooted in
Jago reality. Dicky's defeat confirms his predestination—
"He was of the Jago, and he must prey on the outer world,
as all the Jago did" (p. 130)—and should not long after an
impossible ideal. The other—and better—way out, somewhat artificially reiterated by the dying Dicky, is impossible. He feels further branded and rejected when his father is executed: "Now he went doubly sealed of the

outcasts: a Jago with a hanged father . . . He was a Jago
and the world's enemy" (p. 185). He is inexorably
doomed: he is destined either for the Gallows or for the
High Mob.

One is led to think that such children become outcasts because they are cast out by society, and restricted to their
self-contained world of crime. Dicky's position is conditioned by two driving forces: hunger or necessity on the
one hand—theft or crime are alternatives to starvation—,
ambition on the other—the desire to reach a high criminal
status. These forces, especially the second, must be related
to pressures and influences stemming, not only from congested slums, but also from the jungle-like atmosphere
people have been steeped in from their childhood. These
are hereditary causes, not in the sense of genetic developments due to alcoholism for instance, though this factor is
not to be neglected, but because criminal fathers, parents
and neighbours are the models on which children frame
their image of the world. The street is their school. Old
Beveridge is Dicky's real teacher; Father Sturt only an occasional preceptor from the outside who has neither the
time nor the influence necessary to alter the situation.
Conditioning affects adults as well as children; because
they are unable to bear physical or moral rejection, individuals are sucked under. The phenomenon that Jocelyn
Bell calls "sinking to Jago level"[35] reaches the Ropers—
who are later offered a chance to escape—and also affects
Hannah Perrott.

Social commentators seem to have been especially aware
of the inversion or distortion of moral values, though
criminality was seen as an inherent product of the environment. Of the same district in Shoreditch a writer observed:
"There are men here whom it is impossible to convince
that stealing is a crime. They were born into evil, bred on
stealing, and it is their means of livelihood".[36] In the
fiercely competitive street life of late Victorian London, a
certain type of class war was being waged. In Morrison's
Jago, people not only take to plundering each other's property, but keep delivering attacks on the well-stocked shops
in Meakin Street, and on wealthy passers-by—walking in
some streets of East London was actually fraught with
dangers for everyone. But their predatory instinct carries
them further afield. Dicky ventures as far as St Paul's,
while Josh takes the train to Canonbury to commit burglary, disturbing the suburban tranquillity enjoyed by a
High Mobsman who directly exploits East End thieves
(pp. 139-40). Warehouses are also visited—the "great
goods depot of a railway company" at the end of Bethnal
Green Road and the neighbouring tobacco factories are
preyed upon by the Jagos. The "fat's a-running" industry,
i.e. snatching goods from vehicles and running away, is
part of the sport practised by the able-bodied and younger
members. "To venture a load of goods up Luck Row" was
perilous indeed, the narrator observes when describing the
experience of a newly-appointed carman who rashly chases
a thief into the Jago area (pp. 109-13). After plundering,
the compromising objects are quickly disposed of. Other
instances of stealing, burgling, peter-claiming, swindling

are also depicted in *Divers Vanities* (1905). In *The Hole in the Wall,* fighting, smuggling, violence and murder flourish unhindered by the river. Dicky himself sometimes resorts to the riverside area, as well as to the market-places in Mile End and Stepney, or to Liverpool Street Station to do some bag-carrying, though the struggle is all the more savage as he intrudes upon territories where the local boys claim their hunting right. He is more secure in his own district and shares this feeling with his father. In the Jago's movement from exposure to shelter, from enemy territory to family or community (and *vice versa*), can be seen a pattern characteristic of hunters in primitive societies: the man roams abroad, till he finds the food or the articles necessary for his sustenance and that of his family.

As in tribal groups there is an endless feud between families, the Ranns and the Learys inside the Jago, but also an eternal feud, racial in character, between the Jago area and Dove Lane, with peaceful spells between the battles underlined by bouts of general rejoicing at Mother Gapp's. Nevertheless, they are united by a common feeling against the police: hostility and distrust. Their code of morals forbids them to "nark", and retaliation threatens informers— Aaron Weech is thus murdered by Josh Perrott when the latter is released from prison. As for Dicky, he refuses to tell the name of his young assassin. "Thou shalt not nark" is one of the first commandments of the Jago creed. Any police intervention is resented as a violation; people observe the law of silence or attempt to baffle any investigation.[37] In Darkest England there can be no intrusion or trespassing.

This specifically urban type of criminality was partially due to the presence of uncleared, foul spots, notably in East London. Distressing slum-dwelling conditions, coupled with destitution and disease, could not but sharpen the moral and social problem of criminality, which became all the more acute as urban growth gathered pace and as the rift between East and West, the poor and the rich, widened. Moreover those facts were variously perceived by the public. The existence of a hard core of criminals amidst a working class community did cast a shadow over the East End as a whole. Morrison's descriptions were sometimes misread and their actual bearing misinterpreted. A book reviewer went so far as to warn his readers: "let us not delude ourselves into imagining that half London is inhabited by a race of Yahoos". This sweeping statement prompted the author to react in a letter to the editor of the *Spectator* in which he insists on his personal knowledge of life in East London and rejects the unfair generalization.[38] The concept of dangerous classes, mentioned above, was part of the prejudiced associations latent in the mind of the middle-class public. Though Morrison's work has no strictly statistical basis, it has sometimes been incorrectly judged, just as Mayhew's description of street folk has been made to encompass all the poor and working-class population of London. Despite his protests, Morrison may nonetheless have unwittingly contributed, through the very forcefulness of his East End studies, to lay an undue emphasis on the question of urban violence and criminality

among the poor, east of Aldgate. His stories have given the city poor a metaphorical dimension which appears to be responsible for simplified modern visions of the "brutal, murderous London of the late 19th century", to cite V.S. Pritchett's words.[39]

If determinism is sometimes blurred or hard to define, human behaviour proceeding both from a broadly genetic process and an environmental phenomenon, *A Child of the Jago* is clearly basically naturalistic in character. Théodore de Wyzewa, a contemporary French critic, perceived it to be so in his article entitled "Un naturaliste anglais", published in 1897.[40] Although the English equivalent of Zola did not develop as a naturalist, his picture is sociologically significant. The existence of criminal rookeries was known, but a detailed description was needed to throw the issues into sharp relief, to shake the sensibilities and rouse the conscience of the middle-class. The demonstration agrees with J. J. Tobias's insistence on the strict relation between environment and crime when he writes: "These youngsters were criminal in England because of lack of work and because of the pernicious effects of a morally unhealthy urban environment".[41] In Dicky Perrott's tragedy we find a striking exposure of society's sly ways of rejecting an individual's attempt to better his condition. Society maintains and safeguards its rigid hierarchy. In the same way as the Jago dictates its law to its immigrants, the world outside the ghetto keeps the *status quo.* The novel may in fact be seen as presenting a realistic and pessimistic view of urban and social mobility.

H. D. Traill, in his attack of the book in *The Fortnightly Review,* to which Morrison replied in *The New Review,*[42] asserted that it was not impossible to escape from the Jago, thus refuting Dicky's predicament. In an interview given in 1907,[43] Morrison himself indicated this possibility if only in the form of a radical break—transplantation through the adoption of children for example. In the same interview the author expressed his intentions and expounded his views of the "curse of environment":

> In *A Child of the Jago* it was my desire to show that, no matter how good a boy might be, or how great his abilities, there was no chance for him if he was put in the wrong environment, and that if his lot was thrown among the habitual criminals, he was inevitably bound to become a criminal.

More explicit of the naturalistic nature of his picture is his earlier analysis published in 1900 where he stresses the fundamentally deterministic value of his demonstrative case:

> The root of the whole problem is the child, and it was to show this that I wrote the story of the Jago, one of the worst of all the districts in the East End. I took a boy through the whole of his life in the environment of the Jago, and tried to show how he was crushed at every turn, and how helpless any effort to uplift him was.[44]

Upbringing and environment are powerful influences: "stealing became a moral habit" to the boy—which means that, as Dicky is morally determined, the moral debate is irrelevant and the social one is essential. "So criminals are made and paupers are brought into the world", Morrison concludes, implicitly accusing society.

If statistical data are rare in Morrison's novel—we know that there are seventy males on ticket of leave in Old Jago Street alone (p. 151)—, William Booth's work, *In Darkest England,* provides us with figures on criminality and suicide which substantiate his idea of the oppressing forces bearing on the population that is "partially, no doubt, bred to prison, the same as other people are bred to the army and to the bar". In his mind society is to blame for the existence of "the hereditary criminal", since in many cases such causes as poverty or "sheer starvation" are determining factors:

> Absolute despair drives many a man into the ranks of the criminal class, who would never have fallen into the category of criminal convicts if adequate provision had been made for the rescue of those drifting to doom. When once he has fallen, circumstances seem to combine to keep him there.[45]

Dicky Perrott's life is a study in depth of the impossible emergence of a talented boy. Family education and experience in the street are too powerful to be discarded, so that, despite a brave attempt at improvement—through decent, honest work—, the criminal context proves the victor. The Jago frustrates his higher ambitions, plunges him into its murderous ways, and eventually, causes his death.

. . . . .

Morrison's presentation of East London constitutes a social indictment, a statement of failure on several counts, which spells out the crying need for adequate organization. As far as town planning is concerned, *A Child of the Jago* is a realistic story based on a slum clearance scheme. While the crowded, insanitary district moulds characters and shapes events, the transformation of the structure by demolition serves as a background to the crisis. Only at the end does the changed area defeat Josh Perrott who can no longer find a refuge in his flight. It is unquestionable that the destruction of rookeries cleared dangerous quarters where policing was difficult, besides providing more wholesome lodgings. But Morrison did not fail to highlight the contradictions and inadequacies of such schemes.

If the demolition of "the foul old lanes" and the "subterraneous basements where men and women had swarmed, and bred, and died, like wolves in their lairs" (*CJ,* p. 121), can be regarded as a positive achievement, as it also served to deter criminality in that particular area, the planning scheme which intended to "wipe out the blackest spot in the Jago" (p. 105) was a partial failure. In the novel, Morrison mocks the eager philanthropic movement which intended to "abolish poverty and sin" in that part of the East End, and points out that people were very reluctant to leave the Jago. They devised all sorts of pretexts to postpone their eviction and, when they left, preferred to rent a room in another area. Morrison ironically notes this tendency to crowd neighbouring districts.

> They did not return to live in the new barrack-buildings; which was a strange thing, for the County Council was charging very little more than double the rents which the landlords of the Old Jago had charged.

(p. 165)

The only successful case presented is Kiddo Cook, whose prosperity enables him to take *two* rooms in the new County Council dwellings. Similarly, H. J. Dyos and D. A. Reeder point to the paradox of these urban improvements, which were

> hailed as a means of clearing the slums, though they had hardly ever failed to aggravate them, for their effect always was to reduce the supply of working class housing, either absolutely or in terms of the kind of houses which those turned out of doors by their operations could afford or wish to occupy.[46]

The complaint was not new in the 1890s though the range of it had altered: the lowest strata of slum-dwellers were the worst hit. Moreover, in the case of the Old Nichol Area, the number of people to be rehoused was gradually reduced, as indicated in *The Housing Question in London* (1900). On the one hand, townplanners were concerned, as they are to-day, with problems of expenditure and rent; on the other, people shrank from living in lodgings so rationally, or impersonally, laid out—they resented any interference. What was more subjective but nonetheless real was the ineradicable habits of the destitute deplored by Octavia Hill in *House of the London Poor* in 1875: "Transplant them tomorrow to healthy and commodious houses, and they would pollute and destroy them". She disbelieved in public intervention and favoured individual initiative, with good results in some cases only. Many medical officers were reluctant to act forcefully through the Sanitation Acts, because they rightly thought that expulsion meant further overcrowding. Also, though various bodies were conscious of the relation between rent-paying and wage-earning, it was not until the turn of the century that adequate solutions were realistically examined. The Public Health Act of 1875 was insufficiently enforced. Yet, on the credit side, some progress was made towards a better grasp of the social problems of overcrowding and slum-dwelling.

Even though the clearance scheme was already in progress when Morrison gathered his material in the district of the Old Nichol in Shoreditch, his novel had a definite, if tardy, influence, as testifies the reference made by the Prince of Wales in 1900 at the official opening of the new lodgings. It is no mean achievement on the author's part to have illustrated the problem so well.[47] But Morrison's outlook was pessimistic. To the objection that the slums were slowly disappearing, he replied in 1900:

> Are you quite sure of that? You drive the people away by pulling down their houses, but you drive them to another place—that is all. One slum goes, another comes. The lower East-End, as we know it to-day, will disappear, but it will appear farther out (. . .).The same evils we are seeking to destroy in Central London are growing up in the suburbs. In many of the larger subur-

ban towns the people are being crowded together, and some day Greater London will be face to face with the slum problem as we have it in the East-End to-day.[48]

Starting from the observation that the load was merely transferred from one area to another, and that the movement generated from the centre, he reached the conclusion that the centrifugal shift would affect the suburbs. Fortunately the prophecy of an outgrowing housing problem was not to be realized in such terms.

Correspondingly the problem of criminality could not be solved simply by wiping out criminals' haunting places—the root causes could not be obliterated overnight. Young Dicky Perrott, as we have seen, inevitably relapses into his former habits despite the advice and protective support of a priest, which proves that moral precepts and honest living are defeated. In fact, harsh contact with daily reality has abated the ideals and the enthusiasm of both the surgeon and the missioner in the Jago. In an enlightening dialogue, the surgeon acknowledges the failure of medicine to deal with the consequence of the high birth rate, but advocates the right to curb the proliferation of children in such a dangerous environment:

Is there a child in all this place that wouldn't be better dead—still better unborn? (. . .)

Here lies the Jago, a nest of rats, breeding, breeding, as only rats can; and we say it is well. On high moral grounds we uphold the right of rats to multiply their thousands.

As for Father Sturt, he confesses that the situation is hopeless, while stoically insisting on the duty he has to perform (*CJ*, pp. 156-8).

These ideas are taken up in the *Saturday Journal* article where Morrison voices his private views on the impossibility of influencing the race of criminals and paupers. Because the latter frustrate any hope of improvement he proposes a strict control: "Personally I should be in favour of almost any means which would restrict the growth of such a race" in order "to eliminate danger to the community". And he suggests segregation and transportation. If this solution, and indeed the notion of a race apart, is rather unpalatable in the 1970s, it nevertheless stems from a keen wish to protect vulnerable individuals, and, first and foremost, children—"the care of the children is really of grave importance", he adds—, which may mitigate the brutality of the proposal.

Poverty increased certain types of criminal offence, because the Poor Law was inadequate and the workhouses were considered to be worse than prisons. They dissuaded needy people from applying for relief and were even regarded as schools for gaolbirds. As for the failure of penal measures, Morrison is more precise when he examines the problem of hooliganism. Condemning the leniency of justice, he recommends a deterrent punishment—the cat-o'-nine-tails in cases of violence. This proposition recalls two features in *A Child of the Jago*. When Josh Perrott weighs

the pros and cons before committing his burglary, or robbery with violence, he shudders at the thought of the cat, like all the Jago toughs. Dicky Perrott, on the other hand, would rather take a whipping than go to a reformatory (*CJ*, p. 140, p. 154). Although Morrison's analysis is correct on the whole, the problem of urban hooliganism included elements and factors beyond his ken. His was a plea for an unsentimental, hence realistic, apprehension of the bankruptcy of religious, social and judicial measures.

Education was also inadequate in the East End. The Education Acts left loopholes in their regulations, and inspectors could not enforce the measures capable of schooling the young East Londoners. If the number of juvenile delinquents alarmed the authorities, compulsory education contributed in no negligible way to diminish the rate of criminality, if only because it kept young children from the streets where they were "learning their lessons of evil".[49] Besides, the opening of Institutes proceeded from an attempt to find an appropriate cultural and educational means of reaching working-class people, and of catering for the masses in dense urban districts. In *To London Town*, Johnny attends evening courses at the Institute founded by a shipbuilder, which includes a gymnasium, a cricket club and activities like boxing, also cookery and dressmaking for girls. This recalls the example of the People's Palace as a way of educating the culturally underdeveloped working-class area of Poplar in the East End. Morrison, who had quitted the post of secretary to the Beaumont Trust administering this scheme after four years of active work, later criticized the development of the institution into a polytechnic, seemingly because it had ceased to fulfil its vaster cultural and social role. Yet this venture was not lost, it paved the way for the one University in East London, Queen Mary College, an outpost of culture and advancement set in this essentially working-class district.

In his article in the *Saturday Journal*, he reveals his disappointment at the non-realization of cultural plans for the masses: "Such places as the People's Palace, and a hundred others—excellent institutions all of them—do not reach the people they are started for". He also pinpoints the delusion, which affected outside visitors, of "imagining that these well-dressed people were once the dirty, ragged, vulgar people these institutions were built for", and then condemns the misdirection of otherwise praiseworthy endeavours. His purpose is clearly to debunk his contemporaries' dangerous complacency. "Let us be honest", he concludes, "and not pretend that we are reaching people who are quite beyond our influence". This is a statement of failure and incompetence, stemming from a pessimistic view of the possibility of social improvements. Equally pessimistic is the description of miscarried ventures in the rookeries. Slumming led to philanthropic blunders, which are satirized in *A Child of the Jago*, notably in the form of the East End Elevation Mission and Pansophical Institute. Superior or paternalistic attitudes were ill-suited to the character of the East-Ender; ill-adapted too, was the sentimental approach, mocked in the novel (*CJ*, p. 104). Most charitable institutions fell short of their promises.

As positive evidence there remains Arthur Osborne Jay's (or Father Sturt's) example—a model of muscular approach to Christianity and to social problems. His down-to-earth principles, his iron discipline, his directness and singeing irony, seem to have had good results in his East End parish. Clubs could unite people, and boxing was a sport that suited their temperament and kept them away from street fights. But he refused to take advantage of their presence in the club to force religion into them. His was a new pedagogy, adapted to a tough milieu; it represented a breakaway from stale and sterile patronizing attitudes. Yet Jay was rather fatalistic as he noted only slight improvements in the Old Nichol area. Morrison probably inherited this pessimistic outlook on human nature. But both men wanted change. Jay wished to "wake up the authorities as to the state of the district", as he put it in the opening pages of *A Story of Shoreditch* (1896), and demanded reform for those who "enter life heavily handicapped". Morrison, too, still believed in social reform, if not in a social revolution:

> There is not likely to be any great upheaval. The East-End is no revolutionist. And in the main it is much better than its reputation. But there will always be room for the social reformer, as there will be in every great city, and the most hopeful aspect of his work, I think, will be that which aims at the child.[50]

This is an appeal to concentrate duly on the future generation in the city.

. . . . .

Arthur Morrison's record of East End life should be examined in relation to the sociological works of men like Booth and of social workers and reformers like Octavia Hill. Morrison is one of the few writers who wrote forcefully and convincingly of the "People of the Abyss" in the 1890s, to refer to the title of Jack London's social novel published in 1902. If Morrison's books had such an enduring impact, it is partly because his account of East London represented a shock treatment for the public, but also and essentially because his presentation supported as well as foreshadowed other descriptions and parallel images drawn by contemporary writers and social historians. His work both crystallized and perpetuated a portrayal of an East End calling for reform.

His exposure of the physical and moral degradation of the poor and working-class population in the East End implies that determinism of the environment should not prevail, and that alleviation, if not complete eradication, of hardships and handicaps, are possible by eliminating the causal errors, the blameful shortcomings of social structures. If the Jago already represented an old battle when Morrison published his fictional account, the problems raised reach beyond its contemporary, documentary value. It is exemplary of the housing question whenever society relinquishes its responsibilities and fails to cater for its needy members—especially the children whose expectancies are frustrated.

Although W. C. Frierson correctly sees the naturalistic current in *A Child of the Jago,* one must question his conclu-

sion that "Morrison draws no lesson and preaches a sermon" and that "he accepts the low creature's depravity".[51] The author's quotation from Ezekiel, which heads the novel, is indicative of his intention to rouse public opinion. The message borne out by Morrison's work is the necessity for a solution to the larger issue of urban poverty and criminality—still a relevant problem to-day when unfavourable environment favours unsocial or delinquent attitudes. In Lizerunt's fate and in Dicky Perrott's tragic life, the reader may feel a desire for a truly equalitarian city, where equal opportunities should be made available to all its inhabitants, a plea for improving the material conditions and for raising the educational and moral standards of the disinherited through supporting bodies, which should be organized yet flexible. This desired urban therapy depends on a reform of social legislation, which ultimately rests on the politico-economic plane.

His social exposures paved the way for the welfare state, but there remain issues on which the battle to be waged is sure to be a long one. One can cite for example two present-day problems: the question of battered wives and the dockland redevelopment program in East London. The former is more universal in its bearing—with some reservation one is tempted to say that Lizerunt is with us still. It involves family morals as well as social legislation, whereas the second more specifically concerns town planning policy. In a pamphlet issued by the London Docklands Study Team in April 1973,[52] one may read: "Some parts of the Area have interest and character, but the general impression of the physical environment is of drabness and deterioration", and one of the first alternatives proposed is "to provide housing for families living in overcrowding conditions or in dilapidated property". Mean streets and mean lodgings still. The East End has witnessed a radical alteration due to the closure of the docks; it is ironic that industry should now be asked to migrate to the East End to meet the labour supply of this essentially working-class community. In this period of economic crisis in Britain, redeployment has come to a head, though the long term programme will be carried to the nineties—the 1990s. As in Victorian times, there are housing problems and planning misjudgements, and social priorities are still matter for debate in East London.

Notes

Abbreviations: *CC* ("Cockney Corners"), *TMS* (*Tales of Mean Streets*), *CJ* (*A Child of the Jago*), *TLT* (*To London Town*).

1. *The Globe,* 20 October 1888, p. 7.

2. The quotations in this paragraph are taken from the sketches entitled "London Bridge," "London Hospital," and "Soho". They are part of a series called "Cockney Corners," which provides a new and most interesting source material, as it refers to an early period in Morrison's career, six years before the publication of *TMS*. Chronologically the *CC* were published as follows in *The People,* always on page 2:

"Chrisp Street, Poplar," 28 October 1888;

"A Patch of Clerkenwell," 4 November 1888;

"London Hospital," 11 November 1888;

"Greenwich," 18 November 1888;

"The Polytechnic Institution," 25 November 1888;

"Soho," 2 December 1888;

"Bridge and Borough," 9 December 1888;

"Epping Forest," 16 December 1888;

"Christmas Eve in the Street," 23 December 1888 (reprinted in *The Palace Journal,* 25 December 1889);

"Bow Street," 30 January 1889;

"Whitechapel," 6 January 1889 (reprinted in *The Palace Journal,* 24 April 1889);

"The People's Palace," 13 January 1889;

"Jacob's Island," 20 January 1889.

"On Blackwall Pier," which I have not traced in *The People,* was published in *The Palace Journal,* 8 May 1889.

3. After his death in Buckinghamshire, he was buried at Loughton.

4. See *The Bookman* (London), November 1908, p. 88.

5. "Epping Forest" (see note 2).

6. *TLT* (Methuen, 1889), p. 25.

7. Morrison seems to be more optimistic when he observes people choosing less gloomy places: "Be a town never so poor and dreary, be any district never so uniformly mean and sordidly uninteresting, there are always some among the humble inhabitants thereof, who, by an instinct they may be highly credited with, habitually resort to the least dull and ugly spot in its vicinity." The adjectives and adverbs are sufficiently eloquent, however, of urban drabness.

8. *Vignettes* (1896), p. 56.

9. *CJ,* p. 159. All subsequent references are taken from the Panther edition, 1971 (reprint of MacGibbon & Kee edition with introduction and notes by P. J. Keating, 1969).

10. *The Home Magazine,* 23 April 1898, p. 16.

11. *Homes of the London Poor* (1875), p. 197.

12. Quotation from "A Street."

13. *The Hole in the Wall* (1902) pp. 103-4.

14. *The Home Magazine,* 11 June 1898, p. 156.

15. See note 11.

16. *The White Slaves of England* (1897), p. 34.

17. *Cornhill Magazine,* March 1901, pp. 446-58.

18. "Nobody laughs here—life is too serious a thing; nobody sings. There was one a woman who sang—a young wife from the country. But she bore children, and her voice cracked. Then her man died, and she sang no more. They took away her home, and with her children about her skirts she left this street for ever. The other women did not think much of her. She was 'helpless.'" (*TMS,* pp. 17-8).

19. *Op. cit.,* p. 32.

20. In Dyos, H. J. and Wolff, M., *The Victorian City* (1973), Ch. 6, p. 183.

21. "Toynbee Hall," *The Home Magazine,* 9 Dec. 1899, p. 239.

22. See *TLT,* pp. 57-9. Because of the distance and the old man's disapproval, Johnny's grandfather does not get the "proper" funeral London would have required.

23. See note 10.

24. See Gertrude Himmelfarb, "The Culture of Poverty," in Dyos, *op. cit.,* ch. 30, p. 707.

25. *P.T.O.,* 7 December 1907, p. 545.

26. See P. J. Keating's introduction to the 1969 edition of *CJ.*

27. 19 September 1900, p. 24.

28. *Op. cit.,* p. 63.

29. "A Transformation in Slumland," *The Temple Magazine,* pp. 453-4.

30. *Crime and Industrial Society in the Nineteenth Century,* Penguin Books (1972), p. 42.

31. *In Darkest England* (1890), p. 24.

32. "Training Urban Man," in Dyos, *op. cit.,* ch. 28, p. 677.

33. Cited in J. J. Tobias, *op. cit.,* p. 63.

34. *Ibid.,* pp. 59-62.

35. "A Study of Arthur Morrison" in *Essays and Studies,* John Murray, 1952, p. 82.

36. *The Home Magazine,* 11 June 1898, pp. 256-8.

37. See *CJ,* end of Ch. 33 and *The Hole in the Wall,* Ch. 24.

38. *The Spectator,* 9 March 1895, pp. 329-30 and 16 March 1895, p. 360.

39. *New Statesman and Nation,* 22 January 1944, p. 61.

40. *Revue des Deux Mondes,* 1897, pp. 933-45. Although he calls the novel "un Assommoir national," and states that Morrison had "aimed at the most orthodox naturalism," he soon stresses the social and moral aspects of this "Public Prosecutor's charge."

41. J. J. Tobias, *op. cit.,* p. 286.

42. "The New Realism," *The Fortnightly Review,* 1 January 1897, pp. 65-70; "What is a Realist?", *The New Review,* March 1897, pp. 326-36.

43. See note 25.

44. See note 27.

45. *Op. cit.,* p. 58.

46. "Slums and Suburbs," in Dyos, *op. cit.,* ch. 15, p. 365.

47. See *CJ,* pp. 118-9, 158-60, 165-6.

48. See note 27.

49. Octavia Hill, *op. cit.,* p. 203.

50. See note 27.

51. See Frierson, W. C., *L'influence du naturalisme français sur les romanciers anglais de 1885 à 1900* (Paris, 1925); *The English Novel in Transition* (University of Oklahoma Press, 1942).

52. *Rebuilding Dockland. What Choice for the Future?,* T. Travers, p. 3.

Michel Krzak (essay date 1983)

SOURCE: In a preface to *Tales of Mean Streets,* The Boydell Press, 1983, pp. 7-17.

[*In the following essay, Krzak examines the circumstances surrounding the publication of Morrison's* Tales of Mean Streets.]

In 1907, thirteen years after the publication of *Tales of Mean Streets,* Arthur Morrison stated in an interview: 'the stories were built entirely on what I had heard and seen in the East End. I have reason for believing that they shocked a good many very respectable people.' Morrison repeatedly claimed that his presentation was true-to-life, and it must be realised at the outset that his portrayal of East London rests on a first-hand knowledge of the area. It is an insider's view of working-class life. Despite misleading statements regarding his birthplace, whether prompted by personal reserve or social consideration, Arthur Morrison was born in Poplar on 1st November 1863. His father was an engine fitter who worked in the docks, and his mother had recently migrated from Kent. There is no reason to believe that the Morrisons moved out of Poplar during his childhood, considering census data for 1871 and 1881. The family must have suffered hardships; in 1871 the father died of consumption after being ill for three years, leaving the mother with three children. There are autobiographical references to that situation in Morrison's works, particularly in *To London Town* (1899) and *The Hole in the Wall* (1902). But the circumstances improved in 1880 as Jane Morrison took over a haberdasher's shop in Grundy Street (probable reminiscences are to be found in the story **"In Business"**), when Arthur, her eldest son, had already been employed for a year. Since nothing is known of his school days—life in the East End was certainly essential in his formation—it can be assumed that he followed special courses before his appointment in February 1879, at fifteen and a half, as 'office boy' in the architect's department of the School Board of London, with a weekly salary of 7 shillings. He remained there until 1886, rising to junior and finally to 'third class' clerk. For comparable educational and career advancement from the working-class East End one can cite the cases of Edwin Pugh and H. M. Tomlinson. During that period Morrison no doubt read extensively, and he practised some sports, mainly boxing and cycling (there are recurring references to them in his stories), and wrote a few articles for cycling magazines under a pseudonym.

Probably backed by E. R. Robson, the official architect of the London School Board who designed the People's Palace, he was chosen in 1886 for the post of secretary to the Beaumont Trust, which administered the Palace, that bold venture to bring education and culture right into the heart of East London. The scheme, inspired by Walter Besant's idealistic concepts, was realised by the Beaumont Trust with the help of the Drapers' Company, under the active chairmanship of Sir Edmund Hay Currie. This return to the East End was a fruitful experience for the young man with wide-ranging interests. Morrison was in charge of the administration of the various facilities offered by the 'Palace of Delight'—clubs and societies, evening classes, cultural and sporting events, debates, lectures and exhibitions. From 1889 he also became sub-editor of the *Palace Journal,* and occasionally even replaced the editor, Walter Besant. In this capacity he gathered and publicised news on the past and future activities of the Palace, voicing his own comments; he tried to instil a sense of responsibility into the young members, stressing the need to improve the community spirit, especially since there were hostile reactions to the scheme from the start. His editorials also reflect his social concerns. He imparts information on the sufferings caused during the long dockers' strike of 1889 or on the conditions of the poor, drawn from medical reports. His interest in literature is equally apparent; he is persuasive when he urges the Palace members to join the Literary Society, to know and to read under proper guidance the works of the great English writers; he encourages those who have literary ambition, going so far as to advise the beginner to 'pour out every atom of knowledge, power, and ability which the subject needs—but no more'. The budding author, already writing for Fleet Street, knew from his journalistic experience the need for simplicity, clarity and suitability of style. Although the Literary Society was a failure, which Besant admitted in his *Autobiography* (1902), Morrison certainly benefited from the advice of the confirmed novelist, just as he did from his strategic position as secretary to the Beaumont Trust and sub-editor of the *Palace Journal,* where he was a spokesman for the controversial institution. His responsibilities fostered the development of his reflections on social issues and his evolution as a committed writer.

Three East End studies from his pen appeared in 1889 in the *Palace Journal.* They were reprints of earlier contributions—a series of thirteen independent sketches, under the heading 'Cockney Corners', in which he started to develop an original style. This series, published in the *People* in 1888, was designed to introduce several districts of London by underlining their specific features—Poplar and its Saturday market, Clerkenwell with its clockmakers and jewellers, Soho and its French restaurants, Bow Street Police Court, Whitechapel with its rows of houses, its home-crafts and ethnical groups, Jacob's Island, and the contrasting areas of Greenwich Park and Epping Forest. One can picture Morrison scouting about in these various places, noting down his impressions. He successfully conveys the image of the dense population, on London Bridge, where 'the pavement is filled by two solid streams of steadily hurrying human beings', and in the East End. Although he mainly observes the general setting critically, he excels in drawing accurate sketches of people in the street, which go beyond his initial plan to be picturesque. One vignette, for instance presents, with a sentimental touch, the sad story of Joe in Poplar, desperately hunting for a job and regularly visiting the pawnshop with his wife, while in **"London Hospital"** other types of stoical suffering are described, notably the case of an injured mason's wife who must go 'charring hard for every mouthful she and the child eat'. The hardships undergone by working-class people, when adverse circumstances, like an illness, drive them to a crisis, could not fail to stir Morrison's childhood memories. The writer is in search of his material, its full expression depending on accurate observation and personal insight into live situations. In the almost Dickensian-**"Christmas Eve in the Streets"** (December 1888), when all is rejoicing and feasting, a mere glance at the public house dispels the festive atmosphere: 'a wretched woman, with a baby at her breast, and a ragged child of uncertain sex crying at her skirts, grasps the coat of a drunken rascal in an attempt to draw him out of the door, and receives a blow which sends her staggering across the pavement'. This description foreshadows **"Lizerunt."** In his early sketches of the environment of the poorer classes, Morrison paints the dismal atmosphere pervading some dreary areas such as Blackwall Pier or Jacob's Island, defined as a 'sorry blank', respectable but 'fearsomely dull'—impressions coherently translated three years later in **"A Street."** He reveals in **"Whitechapel"** the heavy, depressing climate and the ghetto-like foul slums, with a pessimistic commentary and an urgent appeal for a change of living conditions, particularly for the children's sake. The material necessary for the treatment of both *Tales of Mean Streets* and *A Child of the Jago* is there, in an embryonic state. Morrison is thus gradually developing themes and reflections on already individual lines.

He became a professional journalist after his resignation from the People's Palace in July 1890, which took effect on 30th September. He joined the editorial staff of the *Globe,* an old-established evening paper, and took lodgings near the Strand. The general articles he wrote daily for about six months are a mixed bag of humorous and serious paragraphs on social matters. Some indication of his life in Fleet Street can be found in Brett, the journalist and narrator in the Martin Hewitt detective stories, which appeared later in the *Strand* and the *Windsor Magazine.* There was a large public demand for popular stories at that time; numerous periodicals were created, competing with each other to cater for new tastes. In newspapers and magazines it was a booming period for the short story, a modern genre reflecting contemporary socio-historical trends. In 1889 and 1890 Morrison had a story published in the *People* together with a whole series of narratives, under the general title *Shadows Around Us.* Their subject was the supernatural. Even if the *Globe* recommended these stories to its readers as very 'effectively written', Morrison later disavowed them as what he termed a 'pot-boiling compilation' of his youth. They should be considered in the wave of interest for the occult in some Victorian circles, exemplified by the Society for Psychical Research founded in 1882. This interest was sufficiently persistent to inspire **"The Legend of Lapwater Hall,"** a ghost story which created a sensation in *Macmillan's Magazine* in October 1892; it forms the basis for several detective stories; and it led Morrison to study the strange customs and superstitions in Essex, presented in *Cunning Murrell* (1900) and a number of Essex stories. On the humorous and anecdotal plane, he started to contribute to the *Million,* a new colour weekly, which was short-lived, and to the *Strand,* for which he wrote until the First World War.

The more ambitious vein, the painting of life in the East End, remained unexploited. In fact, this major literary line could not but be strengthened by his recent experience as a responsible secretary in East London and as a journalist, Morrison viewing his function critically. He soon resented his daily stint in journalism because it precluded any development of his talent, the expression 'in fiction' of what he 'had to say', if we refer to an interview he gave in 1896. **"A Street,"** a short description of the East End, was published in *Macmillan's Magazine* in October 1891, and drew the attention of several influential critics, notably W. E. Henley, editor of the *National Observer,* who was forming a team of young authors to write for his review. In August 1892, just before his marriage at Forest Gate and his move to Chingford in Essex, Morrison met Henley who, according to another interview published in the *Bookman* in 1895, 'confirmed him in his idea of writing a series of short stories and studies, presenting East End life with austerity, restraint and frankness'. These three qualities are remarkable as they reveal a new artistic perception in Morrison's development of a realistic style, under the advice and charisma of an exacting editor. Among the 'bright young men' thus handpicked by Henley there were Rudyard Kipling, J. M. Barrie, Thomas Hardy, Charles Whibley, H. G. Wells, W. B. Yeats and H. D. Lowry. This was no doubt a stimulating literary environment for Arthur Morrison who probably came into early contact with Kipling's 'Record of Badalia Herodsfoot', so influential in its description of slum conditions, and who developed a friendship with Henley, sharing his tastes for sports and the graphic arts for instance (a collector of oriental art, Morrison published *The Painters of Japan* in 1911).

The series of studies illustrating life in the East End appeared in the *National Observer* from December 1892 to the first quarter of 1894. **"Two of a Trade,"** published in

April 1893, was probably judged too pathetic to appear in *Tales of Mean Streets.* After Henley quitted the review, two stories were published in the *Pall Mall Budget*: **"A Conversion"** and **"That Brute Simmons"** in August and September 1894. By that time Morrison had already signed the publication agreement with Methuen for a volume collecting these stories, initially called 'Lizerunt', in which he included one new study, **"The Red Cow Group."** Apart from the title change, several alterations in the text and arrangements in the order of the stories were made. **"A Street"** provided the background of the tales, and **"Lizerunt"** had a first part added to **"Lizer's First"** and **"A Change of Circumstances,"** to lead the collection dedicated to W. E. Henley which was published on 15th November 1894.

Whereas writers of the mid-Victorian period were concerned with the situation of the poor in industrial cities, those of the last two decades turned their attention to the problem of urban slum conditions. The East End of London became by the mid-eighties 'as potent a symbol of late-Victorian urban poverty as Manchester had been of industrial conditions in the 1840s', to quote P. J. Keating in his well-researched study, *The Working Classes in Victorian Fiction* (1971). Arthur Morrison's achievement must be placed in the context of sociological inquiries into the lower classes, which began in the middle of the century with Henry Mayhew's *London Labour and the London Poor* and Edwin Chadwick's investigations, and ended with Charles Booth's *Life and Labour of the People in London* in the 1890s, if we are to understand why *Tales of Mean Streets* caused such a considerable stir in the social and literary world in 1894, comparable to the alarm sounded by *The Bitter Cry of Outcast London* in 1883. The upsurge of interest in the East End was produced by newspaper articles, such as George R. Sims's 'How the Poor Live', literary works such as Walter Besant's *All Sorts and Conditions of Men* (1882) and George Gissing's *The Nether World* (1889), and also by religious and charitable establishments in the area—the Oxford University settlement with Canon Barrett and Toynbee Hall, General William Booth and the Salvation Army, and the People's Palace where Morrison himself was employed. The closing years of the decade especially raised public concern for the East End: the strikes and demonstrations by matchgirls and dockers, the Jack the Ripper murders, and Charles Booth's first volume of his extensive and scientific study, *East London* in 1889. It was actually a discovery that upset the social structure and the Victorian conscience.

Arthur Morrison's forceful picture of the East End was instrumental in arousing further concern for the deprived working-classes in East London. But it also revived and developed the controversy on realism, at a time when the outcry generated by the translation of the French realists—Zola, Flaubert, Maupassant and the Goncourts—had not yet died down. The author was hailed as a new literary force and his *Tales of Mean Streets* became emblematic of the works of the new English school of fiction, which included notably Edwin Pugh, Somerset Maugham (in *Liza of Lambeth*), William Pett Ridge and Richard Whiting. He was a pioneer because he chose to record slum and working-class life without authorial comments—'there must be no sentimentalism, no glossing over', he stated. Yet, whenever he was disparagingly labelled a 'realist', or whenever the truthfulness of his descriptions was questioned, he not only vindicated the artist's right to treat his material in his own way, but never failed to stress the accuracy of his picture and his adherence to fact.

Even though there was now more tolerance towards French naturalism and realism in fiction, the content and viewpoint of *Tales of Mean Streets* generated reactions so extreme in some cases that the book was banned and boycotted. For instance in Clerkenwell, the volume was removed from the public library, following a decision of the local authorities—a few months later it was the turn of *Jude the Obscure*. What is more, the distributors W. H. Smith and Sons temporarily removed the title from their list and refused to supply the circulating libraries, six months after *Esther Waters* had suffered the same fate. The adverse criticisms were levelled at the violence and darkness of this picture of East London, and questioned the truth of such a 'naïve' presentation of reality. The *Spectator* wrote in its review: 'do not let us delude ourselves into imagining that half London is inhabited by a race of Yahoos'. Morrison was cut to the quick, even though his art and sincerity were praised. In a letter to the editor, he refuted some of the arguments, insisting on his personal experience and his direct contact with the milieu he described, so as to counter

> 'some misconception of my view of life in East London,—life which, if I may say so, I *do* happen to know at first hand, and without the help of a note-book. I do not present Billy Chope as a type of all dwellers in the East End; an effort to typify the people of a city in one character would be foolish indeed. Chope is a blackguard in a book of all sorts, among whom the blackguards are in what is, I hope, a just minority. There are fourteen members in the collection, of which the story of Lizerunt is only one. In whatever terms your reviewer might have thought fit to judge a book as a written performance, I should not, of course, have attempted to challenge them, but I am loth to be considered to have generalised half London as a race of Yahoos,—as loth as to be thought to suppose the world (which I did not attempt to cram into my book) a place without light and sunshine.'

Morrison tried to restore the balance inevitably upset by **"Lizerunt."** Later he also put his work into perspective, claiming that with *A Child of the Jago* and *To London Town* it forms 'a trilogy intended to paint a picture of a certain portion of life in the East End'. The suffering poor of *Tales of Mean Streets* are to be contrasted with the criminal types of the Jago, and with the more successful classes of working men.

But many reviewers were quick to praise unreservedly Morrison's skilful and truthful representation of the poorer classes, even comparing him to Hogarth, Phil May, or

Balzac. *Tales of Mean Streets* generated profound reflections on the social implications of such a bold picture. Typical of this was the *Realm*'s assertion that 'such a volume does more to make the West End realise the misery and degradation of the East than a score of mass meetings in Hyde Park, a wilderness of turgid oratory, a month of sermons'—a view echoed by Arthur Waugh, and the *Sun* for which it was 'a human document' and 'a plea for the poor'. The social import of the picture is far from being extinct when we consider the hard, sombre lives of some of the underprivileged people in our large industrial cities. Read in the light of unsolved problems of urban development, notably in the Dockland area, combined with economic and cultural issues, Morrison's description transcends its primitive Victorian setting to acquire a universal significance.

"A Street" sets the tone of the whole collection of short stories. It outlines the relentless sameness of the surroundings, through a terse style where repetitive, negative turns of phrases suggest that the point of reference is elsewhere, and the ideal unattainable—'for the air of this street is unfavourable to the ideal'. In a seemingly objective description, this study stresses the stultifying effect of the dreary surroundings, a case already stated by Besant and Gissing. The drab environment is an inescapable trap. Against this urban backdrop, individual lives are presented as illustrations of the little dramas and serious tragedies of everyday life in East London. And events do occur in this street a hundred miles long, despite the basic or outward monotony, perceived by the keen eye of the experienced journalist, selected and processed by the writer of fiction. Thus, if the starting point is a generalised presentation, the emphasis shifts from the typical to the individual in the stories.

A cross-section of East Enders is portrayed in their varied circumstances, faced with the daily struggle against poverty, unemployment and illness. The economic realities bear heavily on the working classes who depend for their living on the dockyards, the gas works or the factories. Lack of employment and industrial action has crippling effects on many; they are prominent features in a number of stories, some more historically marked than others. "The Red Cow Group" is rather grotesque in character, though it reveals the good sense and the scepticism of the workers in the context of anarchist movements in the 1890s, while "Without Visible Means" is a moving story set at the time of the great dock strikes of 1889, which caused the migration of workers towards the industrial northern cities. The three characters may symbolise human types on their way towards an unseen goal. The threat of the workhouse, or failure, looms large in their minds, and the weakest succumb, under the Darwinian law of survival of the fittest. The lonely struggle of the individual is seen differently in "Three Rounds," with a deft delineation of character. Boxing is especially congenial to the East Ender, but the starving young boxer is fighting against huge odds before the profit-making bookmakers and sponsors.

Set in this context of harsh socio-economic realities "Lizerunt" stands out more prominently because the tale is fraught with violence. It also rises above both its Limehouse and late Victorian setting—it is the three-tiered tragedy of a woman physically and morally crushed by circumstances. Although determinism is less marked on her personality, there prevails a naturalistic strain à la Zola which paves the way for the characterisation of the 'Child of the Jago'. The environment of poverty and violence shapes Lizerunt's life, while her stoical stance against adversity is both astounding and appalling. The 'love's light' of her brief courting days is extinguished in her memory long before she is brutally compelled to resort to prostitution. When the situation becomes desperate, it means the workhouse (the 'Union'), the pawn-shop being a half-way stage.

Apart from economic factors, there are other determining influences conditioning life in the East End community. Social values, such as the notions of respectability and conformity are also motivating forces in Morrison's stories. Several characters aspire to a betterment of their social status, but they fail more or less miserably to realise their ambitions. "Squire Napper" is the proud inheritor who spends away his fortune ostentatiously, on 'outward and visible signs of wealth', although he takes it lightheartedly. Social rise by taking over a shop, with the efforts not to be 'low' miscarries in the tale called "In Business." More tragic still, in "All That Messuage," is the downfall of Jack Randall who became a landlord, 'the ultimate dignity', as it is more 'genteel' than shopkeeping. He is the victim of estrangement in his neighbourhood, and later of the overt hostility of strikers, before being sent to the workhouse where he is bound to be buried in the plain coffin he had abhorred all his life. Changes in behaviour are thus thwarted when conformity is threatened. Oppressive social forces deny individual desires. Moreover, this wish of the poor to be buried decently is typical of their sense of respectability. "On the Stairs" reveals the pathetic behaviour of an old woman who refuses to prolong the life of her dying son, to be able to afford a decent funeral with 'mutes and plooms'. Morrison explained this special feeling of cheerless respectability of the poor: 'While I was in the East End I saw a good deal of poverty among people who did not make any fuss about it—they took no part in procession of the unemployed, and refused to go to charitable organisations in order to be helped, but, with the characteristic pride of the very poor, concealed their misery.' Illustrating this, "Behind the Shade" is the humble tragedy of two women whose slow agony is witnessed from the street, as their changing circumstances and their independent sense of self-respect bring them inexorably to starvation.

A subdued sense of hopelessness and even despair pervades many tales, although humour relieves some of their gloom. "That Brute Simmons" is the caricature of the case of a husband who deserts his unbearable wife and her thrifty working-class household—a farcical comedy which was dramatised as a one-act play in 1904. A similar domestic drama is described in **"A Poor Stick,"** with the husband equally a butt for ridicule. More cynical in its humour is the linear portrayal of a petty thief in **"A Conversion,"** with its ironic snub at the close. In all three the usual social references anchor the story firmly in its East End background.

Despite his detached standpoint, a seeming objectivity, Morrison evinces a genuine concern for contemporary social issues. An undercurrent of feeling runs through his narrative. His original realistic representation shifts the viewpoint from the outside to the inside, from newspaper reporting to imaginative studies, and confirms his talent as a writer of short fiction, before achieving breadth of vision in his novels. Whether in his East London or Essex stories he is at his best when he draws real-life characters, with their peculiarities, their specific manners and expressions. In the *Tales* he sometimes resorts to the traditional indirect speech but more often he reproduces the characteristic Cockney speech of the slums, to the very slang and swear words, transcribing them phonetically and using punctuation marks extensively to recreate the erratic delivery and uneven flow of language.

The originality of Morrison's short stories stems from the realistic treatment of social situations: they highlight the tension between individual desires, concrete or secret, and the over-powering urban and socio-economic conditions. An illustration of Morrison at work in East London is to be found in his description entitled **"To Bow Bridge."** Here the narrator is on board the tramcar, like a cameraman on a travelling platform. He shoots inside action and outside scenery, closes in on individuals, while he records cries and dialogues. In this street on the move, with a representative sample of the East End population, and amidst a threatening rowdy crowd, he manages to capture the longing look of a street-walker who gazes at children—'as a shoeless brat looks at the dolls in a toy-shop window'. In short, this sociological exploration of the East End bears the stamp of Morrison's keen insight and individualized approach.

Robert Calder (essay date 1985)

SOURCE: "Arthur Morrison: A Commentary with an Annotated Bibliography of Writings About Him," in *English Literature in Transition 1880-1920,* Vol. 28, No. 3, 1985, pp. 276-97.

[*In the following essay, Calder briefly surveys the critical response to Morrison's work.*]

In his introduction to the 1969 edition of *A Child of the Jago,* P. J. Keating points out that little is known of Arthur Morrison's life before the beginning of his career as an author in the early 1890s and that little is known of his years following his retirement from writing in 1911. The scant facts are that he was born in Poplar, in the East End

of London, on 1 November 1863, the son of an engine fitter. In his early twenties, he was employed in the administration of the People's Palace, the charitable institution established by Walter Besant. Following a year as sub-editor of *The Palace Journal,* he worked for a West End evening newspaper in 1890, and then quit to become a free-lance journalist.

In 1892, Morrison married Elizabeth Adelaide, and their only son, Guy, died in 1921. Morrison retired in 1913 to High Beech, Essex, and moved to Chalfont St. Peter, Buckinghamshire, in 1930. He died in December 1945. Biographically, he remains an obscure figure, and it is unlikely that a full account of his life will ever be written.

In a similar way, little is known or acknowledged today about Morrison's literary achievements. While he became a controversial figure in the debate about realism in England in the 1890s, and although he was fairly widely reviewed, often favourably, the number of substantial critical studies of his writing is small. Since the end of his career the only serious examinations of his work have been the few written by William C. Frierson, V. S. Pritchett, Jocelyn Bell, T. Harper Smith, Vincent Brome, and P. J. Keating. In literary surveys, if Morrison is recognised at all, as is, for example in Legouis' and Cazamian's *A History of English Literature,* more often than not merely in a footnote. Today, even in the academic world, he is little read or studied.

The lack of critical consideration of Morrison is regrettable, and certainly surprising when one examines his writing. In a sense, he was a writer with three distinct areas of accomplishment, each differing enough from the others to seem to be written by another person. After beginning his career by publishing stories in Macmillan's Magazine, Morrison established his reputation with books about slum life—*Tales of Mean Streets* (1894) and *A Child of the Jago* (1896)—certainly his best work. But at the same time he was producing the Martin Hewitt detective stories, and, while reviewers pointed out that they suffered by comparison with Doyle's Sherlock Holmes adventures, they praised their ingenious plots and well-wrought suspense. It has been suggested that Morrison is in fact better known today for these stories than for his slum writing. Finally, his two-volume study *The Painters of Japan* (1911) was widely praised as a pioneer work, and Morrison was for many years considered one of the most knowledgeable of European students of Oriental art.

Largely because of its social implications, Morrison's slum literature usually generated an ambivalent reaction in reviewers: while admitting that he demonstrated considerable technical skill, critics often found his subject matter unacceptable. *Tales of Mean Streets,* a collection of stories which reveal the monotony and dreariness of slum life, was on the whole well received. Athenaeum found "absolutely convincing," *Bookman* (London) called "scrupulously truthful," and *Spectator* wrote of its "great power." But while reviews praised Morrison's character sation and sensitive observation of ghetto life, several journals regretted that he failed to show any happiness or positive aspects in working-class life. *Spectator*, for example, argued that he presented the worst East End characters as representative figures and that he ultimately interpreted slum life through the eyes of a middle-class outsider.

It was *A Child of the Jago*, however, that earned Morrison the most notoriety. Once again his vigour, sympathy, economy of style, and vivid characterisation were praised. But, having admitted this, many reviewers went on to raise questions about the veracity of his slum pictures or the artistic justification for explicit scenes of violence and degradation—questions which reveal as much about the attitudes of the reviewers or periodicals as about Morrison. *Athenaeum* deplored the concentration on revolting details, descriptive passages which *Bookman* (London) called "orgies of physical violence" and "the useless riot of brutality." *Blackwood's* argued that fiction is the wrong form for such material, and protested that a reader looking for recreation and relaxation should not be confronted by such misery. Similarly, *Critic* (New York), while calling it a "tract for the times," felt that it might remain unread because of the "unrelieved wretchedness, pessimism and ugliness," and *Nation* argued that the despair was so overwhelming that no sympathetic action would be initiated in the reader.

A stronger attack, and the most important critical attention given to Morrison during his career, came from H. D. Traill, in *Fortnightly* in 1897. Traill charged that *A Child of the Jago* gives the impression of extraordinary unreality, a "fairyland of horrors" no more realistic than Book IV of *Gulliver's Travels*. This "idealisation of ugliness" was seen as part of a general corruption of realism in English literature. The same argument was taken up several years later by Robert Blatchford in *My Favorite Books* (1900) and in "The Novel of Misery," in *Quarterly Review* (1902). Traill's article also drew a response from the Rev. A. Osborne Jay, in which he attested to the truth of Morrison's picture of the East End, and in turn Traill countered with additional evidence when his essay was reprinted in *The New Fiction* (1897).

Nothing that Morrison wrote after *A Child of the Jago* was as good or as controversial, and later reviews expressed either relief that he moved away from harrowing slum stories or regret that he had not developed as a writer. In a summing up of Morrison's work in 1897, *Academy* argued, astutely it now seems, that he was at a critical stage of his career, a point where it would soon be seen whether his potential would be realised. It urged him to throw off the influence of Dickens, Kipling, Daudet, and Zola, and develop his original qualities. To some degree, *The Hole in the Wall* (1902) answered this challenged, and it was praised for its vivid and perceptive descriptions, careful workmanship, and sympathetically drawn characters.

The Hole in the Wall was applauded as well for its humour and lack of despair, a reaction that had also greeted *To London Town* (1899). *Spectator* argued that it refuted the idea that Morrison was filled with "conscious and incorrigible pessimism"; *Bookman* (London) and the *Times* (London) saw it as proof that he did not write only brutal stories. *Green Ginger* (1909) was similarly commended for its high spirits and farcical tone. *Bookman* (London) and the *New York Times* saw Morrison becoming a delightful humorist, and *Athenaeum* relished the mellow and kindly wit.

In his last major work, *The Painters of Japan* (1911), Morrison became an art historian, and with few exceptions he was given laudatory notices. Both Laurence Binyon in *Saturday Review* and the critic of the *Times Literary Supplement* called it "magnificent." Some reviewers felt that more illustrations from wider sources would have improved the book, but Morrison was praised for his observation, enthusiasm, shrewdness, and power of deduction.

Except for several collections of short stories, *The Painters of Japan* was Morrison's last book, and with his retirement came a return to obscurity. With the absence of notices in the popular press and literary journals, post-World War I readers did not discover Morrison's writing, and he soon became a figure of the past or simply not known at all.

The number of studies of Morrison published since the end of his career is small. William C. Frierson, in *The English Novel in Transition 1885-1940* (1940) did much to assess his place in the realistic movement of the Nineties. V. S. Pritchett, calling *The Hole in the Wall* "one of the minor masterpieces of the last forty years," drew attention to Morrison in the *New Statesmen and Nation* in 1944; and Jocelyn Bell, in *Essays and Studies for the English Association* (1952), provided a perceptive survey of his writing. In 1965 Morrison was one of four English realistic novelists analysed by Vincent Brome in the British Council series of "Writers and their Work."

The most recent criticism of Morrison, and the most important to date, is that undertaken by P. J. Keating of the University Leicester. Keating provides the most substantial biographical material yet available in his introduction to *A Child of the Jago*; he has written the most knowledgeable and intelligent critical commentary on Morrison in the introduction to *Working Class Stories of the 1890's* (1971) and especially in *The Working Classes in Victorian Fiction* (1971).

Roger Henkle (essay date 1992)

SOURCE: "Morrison, Gissing, and the Stark Reality," in *Novel*, Vol. 25, No. 3, Spring, 1992, pp. 302-20.

[*In the following essay, Henkle discusses Morrison's portrayal of the urban poor in the context of the late nineteenth-century debate concerning realism and naturalism.*]

I.

Finally, in the early 1890s, the urban poor acquire a voice. Not the ventriloquized voice of Henry Mayhew, but the voice of one who was born in the East End of lower working-class parents, grew up there, worked there, and chose it as his subject. Arthur Morrison was born in Poplar in 1863, the son of an engine fitter who worked on the docks. His father died of consumption when Arthur was a boy, and his mother raised the three children by running a haberdasher's shop in Grundy Street. Arthur himself took a job early as office boy in the architect's department of the School Board of London at a weekly salary of seven shillings, and moved up to junior and then "third class" clerk in 1886, when he left to become secretary of the Beaumont Trust, which administered Besant's People's Palace. There he started a Dickensian kind of journalistic ascent, publishing pieces on the East End in the *Palace Journal,* honing his journalistic skills at the evening *Globe,* and finally attracting attention, like Boz, with the publication in *Macmillan's Magazine* (October 1891) of his sketch of **"A Street"** in the East End.[1]

As his brief biography might suggest, Morrison underwent an *embourgeoisement* that took him beyond his East End roots. The dialogue that his writings create is with a middle-class reading audience. But he saw himself as an authentic voice of the urban slum experience, and his early works provided such a strikingly different version of the East End that they immediately created a small critical sensation. They were unlike the representations of the poor that had dominated the literature for half a century. Thus Morrison rejects the sentimental and the melodramatic for a laconic, unmodulated prose that rarely rises to a dramatic climax. He portrays of world of gratuitous violence or enervating degradation which offers up no *meaning* to the middle-class reader; it cannot be integrated into the systems of value, psychology, or material relations of the middle class. Morrison's world seems to be of a different order altogether.

The bourgeois feminine sensibility, . . . [once] the site of affective connection between the middle class and the urban underclass, . . . no longer provides a focal point around which to construct even the effect of subjectivity. In **"Lizerunt,"** the most famous story in Morrison's first book, *Tales of Mean Streets* (1894), the protagonist Elizabeth Hunt differs significantly from the pure and "unexpressive" young women who became the channels for middle-class ethical projection. As the corruption of her name to **"Lizerunt"** signifies, she has scarcely any chance to assert her own integrity and separate identity. Her time as a saucy young flirt, playing off the boys against each other, proves to be short; she attaches herself to Billy Chope in spite of his viciousness, and descends quickly into a life of steadily increasing degradation, in which she gradually becomes coarsened. Morrison graphically renders the *relationships* of East End existence that had been missing from the earlier journalistic and sociological accounts. They are not uplifting.

. . . Billy, rising at ten with a bad mouth, resolved to stand no nonsense, and demanded two shillings.

"Two bob? Wot for?" Lizer asked.

"Cos I want it. Non o' yer lip."

"Ain't got it," said Lizer sulkily.

"That's a bleed'n' lie."

"Lie yerself."

"I'll break y'in 'arves, ye blasted 'eifer!" He ran at her throat and forced her back over a chair. "I'll pull yer face auf! If y' don't give me the money, gawblimy, I'll do for you!"

Lizer strained and squalled. "Le' go! You'll kill me an' the kid too!" she grunted hoarsely. Billy's mother ran in and threw her arms about him, dragging him away. "Don't Billy," she said, in terror. "Don't Billy—not now! You'll get in trouble. Come away! She might go auf, an' you'd get in trouble!"

Billy Chope flung his wife over and turned to his mother. "Take yer 'ands auf me," he said: "go on, or I'll gi' ye somethin' for yerself." And he punched her in the breast by way of illustration.[2]

Billy later tries to abuse Lizer within hours after she has given birth to their unwanted baby and has to be thrown out of the house by the attending medical student, who is then roundly attacked by both Lizer and Billy's mother for interfering. He is an outsider who clearly does not understand the codes of East End life, which follows its own brutal logic. When Billy's mother dies from overwork, too poor for a decent burial because he has stolen all her savings, Lizer then feels the full brunt of his meanness. And the story ends with him forcing her into prostitution.

"Lizerunt" follows Rudyard Kipling's remarkable story, "The Record of Badalia Herodsfoot,"[3] in detailing the "creed and law" that governs slum life. Badalia is recruited into service by the local curate to help distribute alms because she is streetwise enough to spot a fraudulent claim and because she is not above smashing the face of any woman who tries to steal food or money meant for those in need. The story tells of her struggle between maintaining the trust that has been placed in her and her adherence to the slum code of womanhood that says she will be faithful to her drunken husband to the end. The struggle proves fatal; her husband beats her mercilessly in an attempt to get the almsmoney out of her. Yet even on her deathbed she refused to accuse him—thus keeping both "trusts."

Morrison and Kipling sketch out an East End that is more complexly—and fatalistically—coded than that of earlier accounts. It is no longer a land of shadows cast by the projections of middle-class subjectivity, no longer a terra incognita to be read in line with the dominant class anxieties and desires. It constitutes its own social order: a subsystem of gender relations that exert a power within their own domain that cannot be interpolated into bourgeois categories of self-agency. The slums of Morrison and Kipling acquire a density of customs and personal patterns that had rarely been observed in earlier accounts, as if, in Morrison's case especially, there were an effort to say that the East End is not simply an object of upper-class anxiety or domination, but an entity in and of itself. At the same time that he asserts this, Morrison also insists upon the enclosed, immobilizing fatality of that world: its immersion in violence, its deadened submission to poverty, its constricting social containment. The vicious circularity of the poor is symptomized by the frequent set pieces of Amazonian brawls between women, such as this one from a later Morrison work:

> Down the middle of Old Jago Street came Sally Green: red-faced, stripped to the waist, dancing, hoarse and triumphant. Nail-scores wide as the finger striped her back, her face, and her throat, and she had a black eye; but in one great hand she dangled a long bunch of clotted hair, as she whooped in defiance to the Jago. It was a trophy newly rent from the scalp of Norah Walsh, champion of the Rann womenkind, who had crawled away to hide her blighted head, and be restored with gin.[4]

For all the efforts of social services to confirm the woman as the ethical center of lower-class life, she turns out, in many of these stories, to be as uncontrollable as the men, at her worst, or too passive to resist her own victimization, at her best. . . .

The conditions of Morrison's East End not only diminish the capacity of women to act as an ethical force in family and neighborhood; the economic isolation of the slums also eliminates them as figures of commodity desire. Ironically, the objectifying in the upper classes of women into fetishes of style, beauty, even spiritual worth, transposes them into symbols of social and economic status and advancement. Clearly this is a form of dehumanization, but it has the effect of masking or finessing whatever subjection of the women is occurring. In a subsociety such as Morrison's urban slums, in which women cannot be conceived as icons of aesthetic or ethical value because there is no role for such values in the social order—no possibilities for women to be the means of financial or social improvement, no function for them to fulfill as the conservers of money and ideals—their status will be severely reduced. Their subjection will be all the more evident.

Correspondingly, the diminishment of women refigures the literary form, for the heroine as the register of morality, and as the focal point at which aesthetic and social ideals were brought together, had been essential to the English novel itself. The great experiment in the naturalist novel of the lower classes—Emile Zola's *L'Assommoir,* Edmond and Jules de Goncourt's *Germinie Lacerteux,* and George Moore's *Esther Waters*—had been to dramatize the moral and emotional issues of poverty and struggle through women whose victimization, and in some cases, personal weaknesses, stripped them of much of the auratic power of the conventional heroine. Moore, in particular, compensated by sentimentalizing his heroine, and it is telling that

the prominent English example relies on the bourgeois ethos of feeling to sustain a measure of attraction to his protagonist. Morrison will have none of that, and, as a consequence, his writing in **Mean Streets** has different rhetorical rhythms; it resembles in many respects the uninflected, neutral style of Margaret Harkness's *A City Girl.*[5]

The circumstances of life in the slums affect the possibilities for writing a traditional masculine text as well. The wave of optimism that prevailed at the beginning of the Victorian period, and which allowed the writers of Mayhew's generation to balance all their misgivings about the rapaciousness of the new competitive order and the loss of scope for mythicized action in men's lives against the excitement of change and social mobility . . . has disappeared from the scene of lower-class London. The dynamism that converts the somewhat puerile fantasy of masculine adventure and power into a vibrant, if often bizarre, scene of small entrepreneurialism and vivid sensory impression is gone. In its place is misogyny. The lower classes had always been depicted as misogynist, and we are quite aware how poverty leads to abuse and the self-hatred that goes with it, but the East End of Morrison's and Kipling's streets is the logical deterioration of the propensities of the illusory, gender-fixed compensations of the 1840s and '50s representations of an alternative underworld. . . . The misogynist social texts that we get of the slums thus . . . undermine any attempt to construct a generative male subjectivity. Morrison's male protagonists are to a man unfulfilled, fated to frustration. Economic and social conditions force this upon them, but the inchoate natures of all the characters indicate that a full, mutually interdependent code of subject construction is absent. A system such as that of the middle class, in which a female ethical subject balances and validates the agency that is granted to the male, is missing in the nether world.

This is, after all, the primary reason that the myth of a realm of primarily male adventure and "freedom" cannot be represented except in the hermetic form of the boys' adventure story, in which the protagonist never has to come of age. There is something of the same limitation in Morrison's novels about the slums, all of which focus on boyhood and young adolescence. It is only natural, in a way, that Morrison should turn to some form of the *Bildungsroman* for his accounts of life in the East End, since the likely course that the slum culture would take would be to imitate the middle class in its effort to establish for itself a masculine-based, if not patriarchal, order. The *Bildungsroman* is the form that epitomizes that effort, and we can surmise that Arthur Morrison had in mind, as a kind of model, the century's best known book about poverty, Dickens's *Oliver Twist.* Morrison's most famous and most compelling book on East End life, *The Child of the Jago* (1896), and his later novels touching on the urban slums, *To London Town* (1899) and *The Hole in the Wall* (1902), focus, therefore, on the issue of the formation of the male in the slums: the classic patriarchal story. Tellingly enough, the protagonist in each of these novels is a boy, as if to indicate that mature or "full" subjectivity is never attained in lower urban existence.

Morrison selected as his setting for *A Child of the Jago* one of the most anarchic and violent quarters of the East End, the Old Nichol area in Bethanl Green, a nest of streets just to the east of what is now Shoreditch High Street (about ten blocks north of Liverpool Station). The Old Nichol (which Morrison calls "The Jago"), was known as the warren of some of the most impoverished and depraved wretches in London, a pocket of narrow streets and courts that was on the verge of being demolished by the London County Council in the 1890s. Morrison spent eighteen months there, gathering impressions under the tutelage of the Reverend Arthur Osborne Jay, a well regarded and intrepid slum minister. In a later interview with *The Daily News,* Morrison contended that the "majority of the Jago people are semi-criminal, and an ordinary respectable working man would quickly be hounded out. . . ."[6] Morrison's Jago denizens eke out an existence in robbery, burglary, picking pockets, or "coshing" unwary strangers (a "cosh" is an iron bar); the women survive making match boxes or through other marginal activities. The men and women entertain themselves with massive and bloody brawls between rival gangs, and *A Child of the Jago* has several unforgettable accounts of the pitched battles between the Ranns and the Learys, which rage back and forth throughout the novel. There is no quarter given to delicate Victorian sensibilities in *Jago,* and the popularity of the novel was matched only by the critical outrage over its alleged grossness. Yet the violence is so spectacular, and so emblematic of the ferocity that comes out of lives of depravity and idleness, that the pathology becomes *symbolic.* The opening chapter establishes an atmosphere in which the specific details—of the restlessness in the Jago on a typical night, as a victim is coshed and robbed—are transposed into a symbolic setting: "Old Jago Street lay black and close under the quivering red sky: and slinking forms, as of great rats, followed one another quickly between the posts in the gut by the High Street, and scattered over the Jago" (45). Even the violated human body auratically conveys a social pathology:

> Out in the Jago the pale dawn brought a cooler air and the chance of sleep. From the paving of Old Jago Street sad grey faces, open-mouthed, looked upward as from the Valley of Dry Bones. Down by Jago Row the coshed subject, with the blood dry on his face, felt the colder air, and moved a leg.
>
> (52)

The ostensible protagonist of the story is the Child of the Jago, Dickie Perrott, who roams its streets, participating in its random violence, its crime, and its occasional play. He is a lad of strong familial instincts, attached to his younger brother and sister, but he shares some of the community's meanness, especially toward a crippled boy, Bobby Roper, who becomes Dickie's nemesis and stands for the perverse crippling of Dickie's own conscience. Under the influence of Father Sturt (modeled after Arthur Osborne Jay), Dickie makes one effort to go straight, and work his way out of the Jago, but it is condemned to failure. Indeed, any effort to get out of the Jago, by virtuous work or by crime, is doomed, and the "moral" of the story is intoned by old

Beveridge, regarded . . . as a trifle 'balmy', though anything but a fool," who points to a gathering of the super-criminals, the High Mobsmen, and tells Dickie,

> "Now, Dickie Perrott, you Jago whelp, look at them—look hard. Some day, if you're clever—cleverer than anyone in the Jago now—if you're only scoundrel enough, and brazen enough, and lucky enough—one of a thousand—maybe you'll be like them: bursting with high living, drunk when you like, red and pimply. There it is—that's you aim in life—there's your pattern. Learn to read and write, learn all you can, learn cunning, spare nobody and stop at nothing, and perhaps—It's the best the world has for you, for the Jago's got you, and that's the only way out, except gaol and the gallows. So do your devilmost, or God help you, Dickie Perrott—though He won't: for the Jago's got you!"
>
> (95-96)

If the only way out of the Jago is to emulate the High Mobsmen, it is a route through a parodic Jago-vision of the "better world" of money and power. "Those of the High Mob were the flourishing practitioners of burglar, the mag, the mace, and the broads, with an outer fringe of such dippers—such pickpockets—as could dress well, welshers, and snidesmen. These, the grandees of rascality, lived in places far from the Jago, and some drove in gig and pony traps" (95). The Mobsmen and their circle mimic and exaggerate upper-class clothing and upper-class airs—those with their gigs and pony traps—and parade before their inferiors a bizarre parody of privilege and grand manners. Their affectations transmit the felt presence of upper-class power—they play out a crude image of another realm of life—but they have the upper-class code all wrong. . . . Swept up in the centrifugal vortex of its ignorance and self-violence, the Jago denizen cannot conceive of the alternative world in a way that would allow him or her psychological access to it (at least in any terms that are "real"). It is as if the two spheres—the urban slums and the social world above it—are sealed off from each other. . . .

A social formation so detached from the prevalent order can, however, be conceived symbolically. This was, as it turned out, the very thing that Morrison's middle-class reviewers refused to allow him to do. The minute they read the disquieting book, they called it a "realistic" novel. And by "realism" they meant the English literary establishment's conception of "naturalism," a literature that deal with lower social orders, with distasteful and debasing material, and that was characterized by graphic detail, violence, and physicality.[7]

II.

The late nineteenth-century English debate over realism and naturalism, then, involves much more than literary taste and style: it embodies the effort by the cultural establishment to assure that all depiction and expression of lower-class life will be kept within the power of the middle class to assimilate it and represent it. One of the major pitched battles occurred between Morrison and the prominent literary critic H. D. Traill and it is worth pursuing briefly because it focuses the issues at stake. Remarkably enough, Traill perceives at some level that *Jago* is a symbolic text, and it makes him so uneasy that he rushes to dismiss the possibility. He acknowledges that what "has most astonished" him "is the impression of extraordinary unreality which, taken as a whole, [the novel] leaves behind it. To a critic opposed to the theories and methods of so-called realism, this is naturally rather disconcerting." Girded to show that the realism of *Jago* has sacrificed art for a false and exaggerated naturalism, Traill "comes out from the Jago with the feelings, not, as he had expected, of a man who has just paid a visit to the actual district under the protection of the police, but of one who has just awakened from the dream of a prolonged sojourn in some fairyland of horror. This, to be sure, may be the effect which Mr. Morrison desired to produce: it is certainly not difficult, I think, to show that his methods are distinctly calculated to produce it; but then those methods cannot be exactly the methods which the realist professes to employ, nor that effect at which he is commonly supposed to aim."[8] Traill insists that Morrison's work be treated as realism, that it be measured by a truth-factor and be shown to be untrue to actuality. "But I will make bold to say that as described by Mr. Morrison—described, that is to say, as a place of which, with [a] half-dozen exceptions . . . every single inhabitant out of 'swarming thousands' is either a thief, or a harlot, or a 'cosher' or a decoy, or a 'fence,' or a professional mendicant—it never did and never could exist.. . . If it is not what you would have actually found in exploring the Jago, it is no doubt what you might have found if all London had happened to pour its manifold streams of corruption into that particular *sentina*."[9]

Several things bother Traill here. First, he rejects Morrison's premise that the urban slums constitute a fully fleshed-out subsociety, with its own set of codes so antithetical to bourgeois norms for the lower classes. Second, he recoils from the notion that there might be a place where people live who cannot be reached and redeemed by either sentiment or economic "logic." Realism for Traill (and others of his time) means that characters will always stand in for human subjects, and by this he means figures whose sensibility are registered on terms readily associated with middle-class values: who desire what we desire. And finally, Traill's determination to categorize Morrison as a "realist" will assure that Morrison's vision will always be grounded in *material* terms. . . .

Morrison's Jago is not accessible to that scheme. The physical details in his novel attest, paradoxically, to the estrangement of the lower classes. Amy Kaplan has noted this in American realist works, saying that they "often assume a world which lacks solidity, and the weightiness of descriptive detail—one of the most common characteristics of the realistic text—often appears in inverse proportion to a sense of insubstantiality, as though description could pin down the objects of an unfamiliar world to make it real."[10] The spareness of Morrison's prose, its stark

ness—held in place only by a half-Dickensian ironic narrative commentary—constitutes not realism, at least as the English and French middle-class literary culture knew it, but a symbolic text. So disturbing is his version of slum existence, so alien, so intractable is it to middle-class representation and hegemonizing, that he has to be content with the charges that what he describes *isn't there*.

Consequently, an almost absurd exchange took place between Morrison and his supporters and Traill and his. The publication of Traill's essay on Morrison in his book *The New Fiction* was accompanied by a letter from a Mr. Woodland Erlebach, "who speaks from a thirty years' acquaintance with the district (Mr. Morrison's Jago)," and who writes, "I boldly say that the district, though bad enough, was not even thirty years ago so hopelessly bad and vile as this book paints it." Traill then appends the names and addresses of eight other people who had written letters protesting Morrison's picture of the East End.[11] Morrison, for his part, rallied Arthur Osborne Jay to his defense, and argued his bona fides in *Daily News* interview. In a separate article titled "What Is a Realist?" in the *New Review*, he summed up all the strategies used against him:

> There is a story current in the East End of London, of a distracted lady who, assailed with a request for the loan of a sauce pan, defended herself in these words:—"Tell yer mother I can't lend 'er the saucepan, consekince o' 'avin lent it to Mrs. Brown, besides which I'm a-usin' of it meself, an' moreover it's gone to be mended, and what's more I ain't got one." In a like spirit of lavish objection it has been proclaimed in a breath that I transgress:—because in the first place I should not have written about the Jago in its nakedness; next, that my description is not in the least like; moreover, that it is exaggerated; further, that though it may be true, it was quite unnecessary, because the Jago was already quite familiar, and everybody knew all about it; beyond this, that the Jago houses have been pulled down; and finally that there never was any such place as the Jago.[12]

When the journalist Clarence Rook tried to follow in the line of Arthur Morrison in his book *The Hooligan Nights* (1899), a reputedly first-hand account of the life of a young criminal named Alf from the slums of South London, he seemed prepared for some of the same objections to his "realism." Thus in the Preface, he stresses that [he has written] "neither a novel, nor in any sense a work of imagination. Whatever value or interest the following chapters possess must come from the fact that their hero has a real existence. . . ." Rook goes on, however, to paint a picture of a slum career with a romance to it that is a long way from Dickie Perrot's existence:

> When the Daily Chronicle published portions of the history of young Alf early in the year the editor received numerous complaints from well-meaning people who protested that I had painted the life of a criminal in alluring colours. They forgot, I presume, that young Alf was [a] study in reality, and that in real life the villain does not invariably come to grief before he has

come of age. Poetic justice demands that young Alf should be very unhappy; as a matter of fact, he is nothing of the sort. And when you come to think of it, he has had a livelier time than the average clerk on a limited number of shillings a week. He does not know what it is to be bored. Every day has its interests, and every day has its possibility of the unexpected, which is just what the steady honest worker misses.[13]

Young Alf is something of an original: he was trained as a boy by an acrobat to be able to creep about in absolutely complete silence; he modeled himself after South London's Patrick Hooligan, with whom, "as with the lives of Buddha and of Mahomet, legend has been at work" (14); and he apprenticed himself to the celebrated Billy the Snide, the most accomplished passer of false coin of his time. He lives a life along the undersides of society that often approaches, in Peter Keating's term, the "pastoral" in its freedom from moral self-doubt and in its removal from the harsh realities of the economic system. Alf glides in and out of Rook's view at times like a phantom, losing himself in back alleys, stairways, and the crowded stalls of the South London slums. He insinuates himself upon victims through his charm, and eludes capture by the same means; in one bold house burglary he saves a baby from choking to death on its night-dress and is toasted with wine by its grateful parents, the burglary victims. The Artful Dodger lives again.

A similar romanticism creeps into another Morrison-inspired novel, W. Somerset Maugham's early work *Lisa of Lambeth*.[14] Liza, though a product of the margins of the slums and the lower working classes, charms the reader in ways that no denizen of the urban depths had done before her:

> It was a young girl of about eighteen, with dark eyes, and an enormous fringe, puffed-out and curled and frizzed, covering her whole forehead from side to side, and coming down to meet her eyebrows. She was dressed in brilliant violet, with great lappets of velvet, and she had on her head an enormous black hat covered with feathers. . . .
>
> Liza had been so intent on her new dress and the comment it was exciting that she had not noticed the organ.
>
> "Oo, I say, let's 'ave some dancin'," she said as soon as she saw it. "Come on, Sally," she added, to one of the girls, "you an' me'll dance togither. Grind away, old cock!"[15]

Spirited, genial, fun-loving, engagingly flamboyant in dress and gesture, Liza is perhaps the most affecting figure in late nineteenth-century representations of the poor. Yet the dark futility of the slums quickly casts its shadow upon her. She proves vulnerable to the charms of a married man who will not leave his family to marry her, and she is turned into a pariah among the Lambeth lower working class. Caught up in an awful determinism, she slips into social ruin, finally beaten so severely by her lover's wife, in one of those celebrated fights among women which seemed to have become staples of the novel of the lower

classes after Zola and Morrison, that she miscarries the child she is carrying, and dies of its complications. The paradigm is similar to that of a *Mean Streets* story, but the difference is that a winsome, vital figure emerges briefly in the portrait of Liza. A personality is created and possibilities for self-definition are suggested, as if in an effort to open up a space for a gentler, happier experience among the lowest of the working classes and the urban poor. Liza has time to dream, to fall in love, to play cricket in the streets with the neighborhood children, to go off with her boyfriend on a lively, pleasurable bank holiday excursion. Maugham, who observed many of the conditions of Lambeth poverty during his years there as a medical student and clerk to physicians, shared some of Morrison's pessimism about the bridging of social spheres—and Liza's death symbolizes the futility of it—yet the tenor of *Liza of Lambeth* differs greatly from that of **"Lizerunt"**. A new element has been infused into the line of slum novels so dramatically begun by Morrison. Just as Alf's *joie de vivre* absolves us from the depressing fatality of poverty and petty criminality, so we can find solace in Liza's sharing of the same desires that any lower middle-class girl might. Her instinctive good-heartedness can pass for a lower-class version of ethics; she is potentially redeemable, transformable within the system. The fact that she cannot rise above her blighted circumstances may make her, in an odd way, more comforting to the reader, for she enacts the myth that says that the lower class share bourgeois English traits and are resigned to exercise them in even the most unpromising of circumstances.

Rook's and Maugham's novels belong to the line of late nineteenth-century literature that Peter Keating categorizes as the Cockney School of novel. These novels generally dealt with the urban lower working class, and only occasionally with the hard-core poor, but they proved to have a greater influence on the nature of the fiction of the lower class than Morrison's graphic accounts, largely because they provide a means of appropriating the lower classes into formulas recognizable to the upper strata. The writers of the "cockney school" such as Henry Nevinson and Edwin Pugh created an individual subject that could be brought within the hegemonizing of middle-class English culture. "Because of [the cockney's] determination to remain free," Keating writes, "he has developed the ability to take whatever life has to offer without complaint; take it wittily, cheerfully or philosophically. Such a man is of inestimable use to a democratic society. So long as his wit, drunkenness, violence, sentimentality and love of freedom are expressed in individual terms, he is socially harmless; so long as these qualities are viewed from a distance he is even attractive and picturesque."[16] He epitomizes, in Regenia Gagnier's words, the optimistic liberal view that the lower class individual is "an apparently autonomous and universal human spirit."[17] The cockney is typecast as the English "common man" individualistic, spirited, jingoistic, hard-playing, blunt, beef-eating, beer-drinking, and for all that, ultimately law-abiding. Certainly the portrait has its truth value—all the visitors to the working-class areas in the East End attest to its vital popular culture and to the remarkable resilience of the people—but one is reminded of the critique by the Frankfurt School that mass culture transforms originally realistic accounts into representations that one can read as repetitive diversions which present no danger to the dominant system.[18]

The separation of depictions of the lower orders of London that we noted before thus takes place. On the one hand, the Cockney Novel reiterates the redeemable nature of the working class; it can be hegemonized through its own yeoman image. While the culturalistic programs of Besant and the settlement house workers sought to absorb working-class popular culture into a more refined expression, the Cockney Novel makes use of the more raw versions of that culture to achieve the same ideological objectives. On the other hand, Morrison's *Jago* and **Mean Streets** . . . and George Gissing's *The Nether World* confront the reader with an essentially alienated domain.

III.

George Gissing's powerful novel of the London slums, *The Nether World* (1889), directly confronts the insidious integration of the London poor into the social discourses of popular culture, and like Morrison's work, it resists the easy representation of slum life that facilitates such an appropriation. Indeed, as we shall see, Gissing resists the absorption of the "experience" of the East End into any of the forms of culture—high or low—that we have seen to have been the social strategy of the 1880s. Gissing himself came to the slums from a lower middle-class background, driven into poverty by a dishonorable act and by his tortured fidelity to Nell Harrison, a prostitute and an alcoholic, whom he married in order to save, and who added to the misery of years of a dreary existence in wretched rented rooms in lower-class London neighborhoods. *The Nether World* is the greatest of a set of four novels Gissing wrote about the working classes and the slums, and it appears to confirm Morrison's abiding sense of the futility of the struggles of the underprivileged to rise out of their circumstances. The protagonist of the novel, Sidney Kirkwood, marries a woman who has been ruined in looks and spirit, and who burdens him with her near suicidal despair and her spiteful selfishness. The young woman he should have married, Jane Snowden, resigns herself to celibacy and poverty, and when they come together in a scene at the close of the book, the narrator can find hope only in their courage and determination: "Sorrow certainly awaited them, perchance defeat in even the humble aims that they had set themselves; but at least their lives would remain a protest against those brute forces of society which fill with wretchedness the abysses of the nether world."[19]

Long before then, however, the reader has learned that there is no passage from the nether world to the spheres above it. To move across it in a train is to travel "over the pest-stricken regions of East London, sweltering in sunshine which served only to reveal the intimacies of abomination; across miles of a city of the damned, such as thought never conceived before this age of ours; above

streets swarming with a nameless populace, cruelly exposed by the unwonted light of heaven. . . ." (164). A place called Shooter's Gardens epitomizes the heart of the nether world, and the narrator snarls that it is "needless to burden description with further detail; the slum was like any other slum; filth, rottenness, evil odours, possessed these dens of superfluous mankind and made them gruesome to the peering imagination. The inhabitants of course felt nothing . . . here was . . . the liberty to be as vile as they pleased. How they came to love vileness, well that is quite another matter, and shall not for the present concern us" (74). Charity cannot redeem such creatures: "of all forms of insolence there is none more flagrant than that of the degraded poor receiving charity which they have come to regard as a right" (253). Indeed, none of the apparatuses of the social order have any effectiveness in this dismal land. The novel seems for awhile to turn upon the device of charity, for Jane Snowdon's grandfather, having come into wealth, and haunted with guilt for his past omissions, concocts a scheme to turn Jane into an angel of mercy; since she grew up as a poor, abused servant girl in the slums she would be, he thinks, the ideal figure to administer a charitable project. This would be no visiting lady from the upper classes come to pass out alms, but a woman who knows the true contours of need. Unfortunately, the scheme is as impracticable as any of the others, and it is thwarted in the plot of the novel, as if Gissing were bent on exposing the fecklessness of the entire concept of such wish-fulfilling, guilt-dispelling interventions. . . .

Yet in *The Nether World,* the isolation of the lower classes seems to provide for an integrity of experience that Gissing values. In his rejection of all the efforts of philanthropy, social intervention, and acculturation of the poor and marginal workers, Gissing asserts—albeit ambivalently—the authenticity of the qualities of suffering, struggle, and anger that he has discovered among the disenfranchised. This integrity of experience is embodied in Jane Snowden and Clara Hewitt, the two women whom Sidney Kirkwood loves.

We first encounter Jane when she is an abused servant girl: pale, thin, constitutionally weak, intimidated by her cruel employers, slavishly attached to Sidney, the only man who is kind to her. Her grandfather liberates her, and gradually we see her develop into a quiet figure of determined compassion, with a muted but solid sense of social justice. As she comes upon the poor, "With wide, pitiful eyes, Jane looked at each group she passed. Three years ago she would have seen nothing but the ordinary and the inevitable in such spectacles, but since then her moral and intellectual being had grown on rare nourishment; there was indignation as well as heartache in the feeling with which she had learnt to regard the world of her familiarity" (130).

But for all the philosophy Jane imbibes, and all the strength of character she acquires, she is still indelibly marked by her earlier suffering:

> Two effects of the time of her bondage were, however, clearly to be distinguished. Though nature had endowed

her with a good intelligence, she could only with ex-treme labour acquire that elementary book-knowledge which vulgar children get easily enough; it seemed as if the bodily overstrain at a critical period of life had affected her memory, and her power of mental applica-tion generally. . . . The second point in which she had suffered harm was of more serious nature. She was subject to fits of hysteria, preceded and followed by the most painful collapse of that buoyant courage which was her supreme charm and the source of her influ-ence. Without warning, an inexplicable terror would fall upon her; like the weakest child, she craved protec-tion from a dread inspired solely by her imagination and solace from an anguish of wretchedness to which she could give no form in words.

(135-36)

As we shall see again, the body, as a site of material be-ing, asserts itself to complicate the ideological solutions of the text. In Jane, it recalls the fear of past wretchedness, the inexplicable terror of abuse, and it disfigures the ratio-nal consciousness indelibly. Jane signifies the real suffer-ing, the psychic injury of poverty, the humbling that pre-cludes rebellion. Hers has been an experience that provides its own probity, which depends in large part upon her be-ing a witness to the social injustices of the nether world. And it assures that, for all her improvement in learning and manners, she will never be assimilable into a higher culture of the middle and upper classes. She cannot be ap-propriated into her grandfather's charitable project—her mind and body rebel against it whenever he demands it of her. She cannot be philanthropized. Although in many re-spects she is the idealized, cheerful, industrious little worker among the poor that brighten many popular cul-tural accounts of life in the lower classes, she cannot be commodified. She is damaged goods. In almost perverse terms, she maintains the *integrity* of the nether world's message of social inequality and political failure.

Sidney Kirkwood recognizes this significance in her. When he is deeply attracted to her, the narrator recounts, "of a sudden he experienced a kind of shame, the result of com-parison between himself and the simple girl who stood be-fore him; she was so young, and the memory of passions from which he had suffered years ago affected him with a sense of unworthiness, almost of impurity" (168). While the specific, conscious impulses of his sense of shame are the comparisons of his own worldly desires with her inno-cence, he unconsciously associates Jane with the social suffering of the nether world, for the text has so deeply implicated her in the conditions of her class that she has come to represent the essentiality of that experience to her being—and to those whose lives she represents. For him to love Jane, and to be a party to elevating her out of the slums, would be in some way to break faith with his mis-sion (really Gissing's mission), which is to assert the in-tegrity of the message of that suffering. The logic of the book, as well as the logic of the social conditions it de-picts, dictate that Jane will remain as the troubled victim and consciousness of the nether world.

While Gissing respects the endurance of the lower classes, he is scarcely an unqualified admirer of the life that they

live. He can be as unsparing as Morrison in sketching the meanness, the wanton brutality, and the shiftlessness of slum dwellers and the lower working classes. His account of the leisure activities of such people seethes with con-tempt. Several of the characters take a bank holiday excur-sion to the Crystal Palace, the emblem of popular diver-sions:

How they gape, what listless eyes most of them have! The stoop in the shoulders so universal among them merely means over-toil in the workroom. Not one in a thousand shows the elements of taste in dress; vulgarity and worse glares in all but every costume. . . . Mark the men in their turn; four in every six have visages so deformed by ill-health that they excite disgust; their hair is cut down to within half an inch of the scalp; their legs are twisted out of shape by evil conditions of life from birth upwards.

(109)

Gissing is no more disposed toward the Cockney Novel hegemonizing of the lower orders than Morrison is. Al-though he perceives the growing separation of the classes in London that was taking place late in the century, he is conscious that they are mediated through the discourse of consumerism, leisure, and nationalism that is subsumed under popular culture, and he deplores the kind of identity that is being constructed among the lower working classes. Furthermore, long years of semi-obscurity scribbling for little recompense had hardened Gissing against the merce-nary nature of writing in a popular vein for a mass audi-ence.[20] Not only is the popular culture vision of the work-ing classes and poor untrue to their conditions, but it is actively implicated in the propagation of a mindless, ani-malistic hedonism symbolized in the Crystal Palace itself.

Gissing's antagonism to the consumerist aspects of both popular culture and the literary marketplace explains as well the particular nature of his own relationship to cul-ture, a relationship that in a sense governs Kirkwood's characterization in *The Nether World* and the animus that book contains toward the programs of acculturation of the lower classes taking place in England. Clearly the conflu-ence of the Arnoldian "high culture" movement and the rise of consumerism produced among Gissing's generation a certain amount of uneasiness. Since the very notion of higher culture was to establish a body of thought, art works, and activities that was uncontaminated by commer-cialism, a conscious effort was made to reconceive culture as a discourse that was outside the marketplace. Culture was made to reside in the realm of the sumptuary, outside use and exchange value (even if that ran the danger of fe-tishizing the work of art). Needless to say, this realm is one that has been traditionally occupied by the upper reaches of the middle class and by the aristocracy, for it requires a certain degree of immunity from the exigencies of a market economy in order to assign arbitrary worth to objects of art and to a cultured style of living. Gissing confirms this in his own writing and thinking, for the realm of art for him was explicitly associated with a higher class, all the more intensely because of his resignation to the fact that he would never inhabit that world (although he frequently visited it). This defines him in his concept of himself as an exile, as a man who is of the "unclassed.". . .

Fredric Jameson suggests that what we have here is a sign or trace of the ideologeme of Nietzschean *ressentiment,* where, among victimized groups (and those who think themselves victimized), the only way of reaction—that of deeds—is unavailable, so it is replaced by an imaginary vengeance. The primary effect is the revolutionary activity of the underclasses, but a secondary effect is seen in those dissatisfied intellectuals who foment imaginary violence as well, but now against the putative revolutionaries rather than against established power.[21] Gissing thus appreciates the antagonism of the lower classes toward their social conditions—even shares at some level their resentment of the arrogance and indifference of privilege—and yet believes that the poor and lower working classes must keep in their place. While an "exile" from the comforts and assurances of upper-class society, Gissing nonetheless disavows any sympathetic identification with the underclasses. We can now supplement Jameson's insight by factoring in the specific social configuration in which this all takes place: the culturalism of the late century, and Gissing's own particular relation to it.[22]

Indeed, just as Gissing could not comfortably be a part of the acculturation process of his time and class, he also presents (as does Morrison) an image of the nether world that seems to remove it from the discourse of the cultural altogether. To understand this image, we need to examine the "affect" of a novel such as *The Nether World* and also focus for a moment on the other major female character, Clara Hewitt. The affect of the novel is particularly vexing because it consists both of a deadening, despondent fatalism and of surges of intense melodrama. Sidney Kirkwood epitomizes the former, for at every stage he seems to repress both his desire and his anger. We are told that he originally aspired to be an artist, and showed some talent at it, but unfortunately his father suffered severe economic reverses and, troubled by Sidney's lack of direction, apprenticed him to a jeweler. The narrator ironically remarks that this saved Sidney from sowing his wild oats, and as the novel progresses, we watch him ossify into a kind of stoic, acting out of a severe personal morality, a man "reckless of the pain he gave to others so long as his own self-torture was made sufficiently acute" (235). Circumstances, but also something in his own nature, make Kirkwood into a figure of deflected desire, whose passion for Clara, then for Jane, is kept in check—the presence of the male body always obscured.

Clara Hewitt, on the other hand, unleashes desire with melodramatic force. Born into poverty, but born stunningly beautiful and quick of mind, "many a time had she sobbed out to herself, 'I wish I could neither read nor write! I wish I had never been told that there is anything better than to work with one's hands and earn daily bread!'" (82). She has no friends, except for Sidney, whose love she disdains, largely from her determination to spite herself and others in every way. She burns—and, as we shall see, the feverish language carries special connotations—with desire to rise above the nether world, and she risks everything to do so by becoming an actress: one of the last honorable of careers for a woman but the one that fits creatures who can be no better than impostors in the world above their own:

> Self-assertion; to be no longer an unregarded atom in the mass of those who are born only to labour for others; to find play for the strength and the passion which, by no choice of her own, distinguished her from the tame slave. Sometimes in the silence of night she suffered from a dreadful need of crying aloud, of uttering her anguish in a scream like that of insanity.
>
> (86)

For Gissing, then, Clara Hewitt constitutes a site of class desire, of *political* resistance to the injustices of society. As often as the narrator describes Clara's self-ruinous, haughty, spiteful nature—her essential selfishness—in melodramatic expositions, he attempts to lay the blame for it upon the "social forces" that have condemned her to poverty. "Suppose she'd been the daughter of a rich man, then everything we now call a fault in her would either have been of no account or actually a virtue" (102). Her rejection of Sidney's apparently disinterested love is described as a "fierce, unscrupulous rebellion" (86). "The access of self-pity" in her "was followed, as always, by persistent sense of intolerable wrong, and that again by a fierce desire to plunge herself into ruin, as though by such an act she could satiate her instincts of defiance. It is a phase of exasperated egotism common enough in original natures frustrated by circumstance—never so pronounced as in those who suffer from the social disease" (94).

The correlation between "social disease" and the passionate destructive urges of Clara has to be taken on faith. Withheld from the story of Clara Hewitt is the description of the *process* through which she became so alienated—the indignities and sufferings of growing up poor and of being intelligent and sensitive enough to perceive them—and absent, also, are accounts of the workings of the larger social order (the economic and political constructions) that create such circumstances. For Gissing the causes of Clara's misery almost have to be extrapolated:

> Natures such as hers are as little to be judged by that which is conventionally the highest standard as by that which is the lowest. The tendencies which we agree to call good and bad became in her merely directions of a native force which was at all times in revolt against circumstance. Character thus moulded may go far in achievement, but can never pass beyond the bounds of suffering. . . . As often as our conventions give us the opportunity, we crush them out of being; they are noxious, they threaten the frame of society. Oftenest the crushing is done in such a way that the hapless creatures seem to have brought about their own destruction.
>
> (295)

Such ruminations expose as much as they seem to dissemble, for such a passage reveals some of the uneasiness with which the observing consciousness confronts this site of rebellion—a site so melodramatically cast as female sexuality. Once again in the Victorian period the sexually vital woman has been crosscoded with class desire; not, as in Dickens, with the middle-class male's ambivalence toward competitiveness, but now with the bitterness and potential dangerousness of the underclasses. . . .

In Gissing's novel, Clara joins a traveling acting troupe as an understudy, and when the female star walks out on the show, she is invited to fill in as the lead in a melodrama. The episode is sexually charged, for it is clear that the manager of the company wants Clara as a mistress. On the night when Clara is to act in her first great part, however, a jealous fellow actress dashes vitriol into her face, scarring her horribly. What follows is one of the most melodramatic meetings in all of literature. When Sidney visits Clara after the incident, she wears a veil to prevent him from seeing her. Not only is she faceless—and thus unrepresentable—but she has almost lost the power of speech: "yet it was with difficulty that she commanded utterance . . . her voice failed again . . . her faltering voice sank lower and lower. . . ." (283-84). Almost at the point of erasure, Clara makes a final effort to assert herself, in an uncanny scene:

> There came a marvellous change—a change such as it needed either exquisite feeling or the genius of simulation to express by means so simple. Unable to show him by a smile, by a light in her eyes, what mood had come upon her . . . by her mere movement as she stepped lightly towards him, by the carriage of her head . . . she prepared him for what she was about to say. . . . He knew that she smiled, though nothing of her face was visible; he knew that her look was one of diffident, half-blushing pleasure.
>
> (287)

At one level, this passage attempts to reassert the primacy of the male observer: for Clara can only be read and articulated by Sidney. The dangers that Clara represents—of sexuality, resentment, and of social resistance—are subordinated to the interpretive male gaze. Yet the passage also tells of Clara's ability to communicate through the movements of her *body*. Later, in fact, the text will insist on the continued allure of her graceful, willowy frame and the felt presence of this faceless, almost inarticulate body. In addition, the narrative persistently refers to the feverish state in which she is often gripped: "the fever that then sustained her was much the same as she used to know before she had thoroughly accustomed herself to appearing in front of an audience. . . . With burning temples, with feverish lips, she moved about her little room like an animal in a cage" (291-92, 293). . . .

Fever, of course, is a symptom of real bodily illness. It is more than an impression; it is a pathological characteristic. Some quality beyond the representation of emotion thus intrudes itself into Gissing's text; the body makes its presence felt. On the symbolic level, Gissing negates the rebellion of the lower orders—signified in Clara's female

sexuality—by making its face unrecognizable, unrepresentable, and yet allows it to manifest itself, as the body is manifested by fever. Lower-class resentment acquires palpability and intensity.

The condition of the nether world in Gissing (and in Morrison) codes itself as pathology—not a cultural phenomenon but a condition represented through symptoms of the body. As *The Nether World* says, there is something called "a social disease." This is less a medicalization of the social vision than an effort to convey, in a physiological metaphor, a particular sensation of social experience. It is ironic that the effort is made in *The Nether World* to read those symptoms through the female body (as you recall, Jane, too, was at the mercy of the almost autonomous rebellions of her body), for the male body cannot be made the register. It is still able to suppress the fever; it is still inviolate in some way, as rigorous as Sidney Kirkwood is in self-repression. Yet the slums and the world of the underclasses had entered the Victorian discourse as a sphere for the registering of male energies and fantasies. And it is clear from a reading of Morrison's slum novel that it is male experience that has gone awry. The intensification of misogynistic brutality illustrates an inability to establish any coherence to masculine desires and rebellions. The frustration and anger manifests itself, in its clinically repressed form, all the way up from the Jago through Sidney Kirkwood to George Gissing and those who think like him—frustration and anger over social inequality, the futility of revolution, the diminution of passion, the sterility of cultural experience. And it is all the more tightly bound because the male body cannot be allowed to register the symptoms. Having become, through the pathology of the representation of the lower orders in the 1880s and '90s, the emblem of this malaise, the body, and especially the male body, must seek new forms in which it is able to express that ill.

Notes

1. I am indebted for the biographical material to Peter Keating's "Biographical Study," in *A Child of the Jago* (Suffolk: Boydell Press, 1969), 11-36, and to Michel Krzak's "Preface" to *Tales of Mean Streets* (Suffolk: Boydell Press, 1983), 7-10.

2. *Tales of Mean Streets,* 37-38. References hereafter will appear in parentheses in the text.

3. *Many Inventions,* 1893 (New York: Doubleday, Doran, 1941), 355-85.

4. *A Child of the Jago,* 64. References hereafter will appear in parentheses in the text.

5. While I recognize that *Mean Streets* is a collection of short stories, and shares with the late nineteenth-century short story in general its Chekhovian and Maupassantian restraint and relative absence of dramatic modulation, nonetheless, I would argue that the subject matter of many of the late nineteenth-century English short stories affects the form. For another instance in which the refusal

to treat the heroine as an auratic object of commodity desire dictates the style, I would point to Dorothy Richardson's *Pilgrimage.*

6. "The Children of the Jago," *Daily News* (Saturday, December 12, 1896): 6.

7. For a particularly lurid critique of naturalism, see Arthur Symons's essay, "A Note on Zola's Method," collected in his *The Symbolist Movement in Literature* (New York: E.P. Dutton, 1919), 154-64. See also Henry James, "Nana," 1880, in *The Future of the Novel: Essays on the Art of Fiction* (New York: Vintage, 1956), 84-96.

8. H. D. Traill, "The New Fiction," in *The New Fiction and Other Essays on Literary Subjects* (London: Hurst and Blackett, 1897), 9-10.

9. *Ibid,* 13-14.

10. *The Social Construction of American Realism* (Chicago: University of Chicago Press, 1988), 9.

11. Traill, 25-26.

12. *New Review* 16, 94 (March 1897): 329.

13. (Oxford: Oxford University Press, 1979), xxi-xxii.

14. For accounts of Morrison's influence, see Ted Morgan, *Maugham* (New York: Simon and Schuster, 1980), and Edward Garnett's reader's report on "A Lambeth Idyll" (its first title) for T. Fisher Unwin, reprinted in Anthony Curtis and John Whitehead, eds., W. *Somerset Maugham: The Critical Heritage* (London: Routledge & Kegan Paul, 1987), 22.

15. (Harmondsworth: Penguin, 1967), 8, 9.

16. Keating, *Working Classes,* 221.

17. Gagnier, 124. See Gagnier's wonderful description of Henry Nevinson's short stories, 124-31.

18. See "The Culture Industry: Enlightenment as Mass Deception," in Max Horkheimer and Theodor W. Adorno, *Dialectic of Enlightenment,* trans. John Cumming, 1944 (New York: Continuum, 1990).

19. *The Nether World* (London: The Harvester Press, 1974), 392. References hereafter will appear in parentheses in the text.

20. In Pierre Coustillas, ed., *George Gissing: Essays and Fiction* (Baltimore: Johns Hopkins, 1970), 96, 95.

21. Jameson, 201-02.

22. This helps account for the particular style, the dead classicism, that Jameson says characterizes Gissing's writing, for it is in itself a symptom of the particular culturalism of the alienated late nineteenth-century intellectual, Linda Dowling.

FURTHER READING

Bibliography

Calder, Robert. "Arthur Morrison: A Commentary with an Annotated Bibliography of Writings about Him." *English Literature in Transition: 1880-1920* 28, No. 3 (1985): 276-97.
     Provides a secondary bibliography on Morrison.

Criticism

Morrison, Arthur. A review of *Divers Vanities. The Bookman* XXIX, No. 170 (November 1905): 91.
     A mixed review of Morrison's *Divers Vanities.*

Priestman, Martin. "Detective Fiction and Ideas." *Detective Fiction and Literature: The Figure on the Carpet,* pp. 105-35. New York: St. Martin's Press, 1991.
     A brief survey of Morrison's detective stories.

Additional coverage of Morrison's life and career is contained in the following sources published by the Gale Group: *Contemporary Authors,* **Vols. 120, 157;** *Dictionary of Literary Biography,* **Vols. 70, 135, 197; and** *Twentieth-Century Literary Criticism,* **Vol. 72.**

How to Use This Index

The main references

> **Calvino, Italo**
> 1923-1985 .... **CLC 5, 8, 11, 22, 33, 39,**
> **73; SSC 3**

list all author entries in the following Gale Literary Criticism series:

BLC = *Black Literature Criticism*
CLC = *Contemporary Literary Criticism*
CLR = *Children's Literature Review*
CMLC = *Classical and Medieval Literature Criticism*
DA = *DISCovering Authors*
DAB = *DISCovering Authors: British*
DAC = *DISCovering Authors: Canadian*
DAM = *DISCovering Authors: Modules*
      DRAM: *Dramatists Module;* **MST:** *Most-Studied Authors Module;*
      MULT: *Multicultural Authors Module;* **NOV:** *Novelists Module;*
      POET: *Poets Module;* **POP:** *Popular Fiction and Genre Authors Module*
DC = *Drama Criticism*
HLC = *Hispanic Literature Criticism*
LC = *Literature Criticism from 1400 to 1800*
NCLC = *Nineteenth-Century Literature Criticism*
NNAL = *Native North American Literature*
PC = *Poetry Criticism*
SSC = *Short Story Criticism*
TCLC = *Twentieth-Century Literary Criticism*
WLC = *World Literature Criticism, 1500 to the Present*

The cross-references

> See also CANR 23; CA 85-88;
> obituary CA116

list all author entries in the following Gale biographical and literary sources:

AAYA = *Authors & Artists for Young Adults*
AITN = *Authors in the News*
BEST = *Bestsellers*
BW = *Black Writers*
CA = *Contemporary Authors*
CAAS = *Contemporary Authors Autobiography Series*
CABS = *Contemporary Authors Bibliographical Series*
CANR = *Contemporary Authors New Revision Series*
CAP = *Contemporary Authors Permanent Series*
CDALB = *Concise Dictionary of American Literary Biography*
CDBLB = *Concise Dictionary of British Literary Biography*
DLB = *Dictionary of Literary Biography*
DLBD = *Dictionary of Literary Biography Documentary Series*
DLBY = *Dictionary of Literary Biography Yearbook*
HW = *Hispanic Writers*
JRDA = *Junior DISCovering Authors*
MAICYA = *Major Authors and Illustrators for Children and Young Adults*
MTCW = *Major 20th-Century Writers*
SAAS = *Something about the Author Autobiography Series*
SATA = *Something about the Author*
YABC = *Yesterday's Authors of Books for Children*

Literary Criticism Series
Cumulative Author Index

20/1631
See Upward, Allen

A/C Cross
See Lawrence, T(homas) E(dward)

Abasiyanik, Sait Faik 1906-1954
See Sait Faik
See also CA 123

Abbey, Edward 1927-1989 .... **CLC 36, 59**
See also CA 45-48; 128; CANR 2, 41; DA3;
MTCW 2

Abbott, Lee K(ittredge) 1947- .... **CLC 48**
See also CA 124; CANR 51; DLB 130

Abe, Kobo 1924-1993 ...... **CLC 8, 22, 53, 81;
DAM NOV**
See also CA 65-68; 140; CANR 24, 60;
DLB 182; MTCW 1, 2

Abelard, Peter c. 1079-c. 1142 ...... **CMLC 11**
See also DLB 115, 208

Abell, Kjeld 1901-1961 .... **CLC 15**
See also CA 111

Abish, Walter 1931- .... **CLC 22**
See also CA 101; CANR 37; DLB 130

Abrahams, Peter (Henry) 1919- .... **CLC 4**
See also BW 1; CA 57-60; CANR 26; DLB
117; MTCW 1, 2

Abrams, M(eyer) H(oward) 1912- ... **CLC 24**
See also CA 57-60; CANR 13, 33; DLB 67

Abse, Dannie 1923- .... **CLC 7, 29; DAB;
DAM POET**
See also CA 53-56; CAAS 1; CANR 4, 46,
74; DLB 27; MTCW 1

Achebe, (Albert) Chinua(lumogu)
1930- ...... **CLC 1, 3, 5, 7, 11, 26, 51, 75,
127; BLC 1; DA; DAB; DAC; DAM
MST, MULT, NOV; WLC**
See also AAYA 15; BW 2, 3; CA 1-4R;
CANR 6, 26, 47; CLR 20; DA3; DLB
117; MAICYA; MTCW 1, 2; SATA 38,
40; SATA-Brief 38

Acker, Kathy 1948-1997 .... **CLC 45, 111**
See also CA 117; 122; 162; CANR 55

Ackroyd, Peter 1949- .... **CLC 34, 52**
See also CA 123; 127; CANR 51, 74; DLB
155; INT 127; MTCW 1

Acorn, Milton 1923- .... **CLC 15; DAC**
See also CA 103; DLB 53; INT 103

Adamov, Arthur 1908-1970 .... **CLC 4, 25;
DAM DRAM**
See also CA 17-18; 25-28R; CAP 2; MTCW
1

Adams, Alice (Boyd) 1926-1999 .. **CLC 6, 13,
46; SSC 24**
See also CA 81-84; 179; CANR 26, 53, 75,
88; DLBY 86; INT CANR-26; MTCW 1,
2

Adams, Andy 1859-1935 .... **TCLC 56**
See also YABC 1

Adams, Brooks 1848-1927 .... **TCLC 80**
See also CA 123; DLB 47

Adams, Douglas (Noel) 1952- .... **CLC 27, 60;
DAM POP**
See also AAYA 4, 33; BEST 89:3; CA 106;
CANR 34, 64; DA3; DLBY 83; JRDA;
MTCW 1; SATA 116

Adams, Francis 1862-1893 .... **NCLC 33**

Adams, Henry (Brooks)
1838-1918 .... **TCLC 4, 52; DA; DAB;
DAC; DAM MST**
See also CA 104; 133; CANR 77; DLB 12,
47, 189; MTCW 1

Adams, Richard (George) 1920- ... **CLC 4, 5,
18; DAM NOV**
See also AAYA 16; AITN 1, 2; CA 49-52;
CANR 3, 35; CLR 20; JRDA; MAICYA;
MTCW 1, 2; SATA 7, 69

Adamson, Joy(-Friederike Victoria)
1910-1980 .... **CLC 17**
See also CA 69-72; 93-96; CANR 22;
MTCW 1; SATA 11; SATA-Obit 22

Adcock, Fleur 1934- .... **CLC 41**
See also CA 25-28R, 182; CAAE 182;
CAAS 23; CANR 11, 34, 69; DLB 40

Addams, Charles (Samuel)
1912-1988 .... **CLC 30**
See also CA 61-64; 126; CANR 12, 79

Addams, Jane 1860-1945 .... **TCLC 76**

Addison, Joseph 1672-1719 .... **LC 18**
See also CDBLB 1660-1789; DLB 101

Adler, Alfred (F.) 1870-1937 .... **TCLC 61**
See also CA 119; 159

Adler, C(arole) S(chwerdtfeger)
1932- .... **CLC 35**
See also AAYA 4; CA 89-92; CANR 19,
40; JRDA; MAICYA; SAAS 15; SATA
26, 63, 102

Adler, Renata 1938- .... **CLC 8, 31**
See also CA 49-52; CANR 5, 22, 52;
MTCW 1

Ady, Endre 1877-1919 .... **TCLC 11**
See also CA 107

A.E. 1867-1935 .... **TCLC 3, 10**
See also Russell, George William

Aeschylus 525B.C.-456B.C. .. **CMLC 11; DA;
DAB; DAC; DAM DRAM, MST; DC
8; WLCS**
See also DLB 176

Aesop 620(?)B.C.-(?)B.C. .... **CMLC 24**
See also CLR 14; MAICYA; SATA 64

Affable Hawk
See MacCarthy, Sir(Charles Otto) Desmond

Africa, Ben
See Bosman, Herman Charles

Afton, Effie
See Harper, Frances Ellen Watkins

Agapida, Fray Antonio
See Irving, Washington

Agee, James (Rufus) 1909-1955 ...... **TCLC 1,
19; DAM NOV**
See also AITN 1; CA 108; 148; CDALB
1941-1968; DLB 2, 26, 152; MTCW 1

Aghill, Gordon
See Silverberg, Robert

Agnon, S(hmuel) Y(osef Halevi)
1888-1970 .... **CLC 4, 8, 14; SSC 30**
See also CA 17-18; 25-28R; CANR 60;
CAP 2; MTCW 1, 2

Agrippa von Nettesheim, Henry Cornelius
1486-1535 .... **LC 27**

Aguilera Malta, Demetrio 1909-1981
See also CA 111; 124; CANR 87; DAM
MULT, NOV; DLB 145; HLCS 1; HW 1

Agustini, Delmira 1886-1914
See also CA 166; HLCS 1; HW 1, 2

Aherne, Owen
See Cassill, R(onald) V(erlin)

Ai 1947- .... **CLC 4, 14, 69**
See also CA 85-88; CAAS 13; CANR 70;
DLB 120

Aickman, Robert (Fordyce)
1914-1981 .... **CLC 57**
See also CA 5-8R; CANR 3, 72

Aiken, Conrad (Potter) 1889-1973 .... **CLC 1,
3, 5, 10, 52; DAM NOV, POET; PC 26;
SSC 9**
See also CA 5-8R; 45-48; CANR 4, 60;
CDALB 1929-1941; DLB 9, 45, 102;
MTCW 1, 2; SATA 3, 30

Aiken, Joan (Delano) 1924- .... **CLC 35**
See also AAYA 1, 25; CA 9-12R, 182;
CAAE 182; CANR 4, 23, 34, 64; CLR 1,
19; DLB 161; JRDA; MAICYA; MTCW
1; SAAS 1; SATA 2, 30, 73; SATA-Essay
109

Ainsworth, William Harrison
1805-1882 .... **NCLC 13**
See also DLB 21; SATA 24

Aitmatov, Chingiz (Torekulovich)
1928- .... **CLC 71**
See also CA 103; CANR 38; MTCW 1;
SATA 56

Akers, Floyd
See Baum, L(yman) Frank

Akhmadulina, Bella Akhatovna
1937- .... **CLC 53; DAM POET**
See also CA 65-68

Akhmatova, Anna 1888-1966 ..... **CLC 11, 25,
64, 126; DAM POET; PC 2**
See also CA 19-20; 25-28R; CANR 35;
CAP 1; DA3; MTCW 1, 2

Aksakov, Sergei Timofeyvich
1791-1859 .... **NCLC 2**
See also DLB 198

Andersen, Hans Christian
1805-1875 .... **NCLC 7, 79; DA; DAB; DAC; DAM MST, POP; SSC 6; WLC**
See also CLR 6; DA3; MAICYA; SATA 100; YABC 1

Anderson, C. Farley
See Mencken, H(enry) L(ouis); Nathan, George Jean

Anderson, Jessica (Margaret) Queale
1916- .... **CLC 37**
See also CA 9-12R; CANR 4, 62

Anderson, Jon (Victor) 1940- . **CLC 9; DAM POET**
See also CA 25-28R; CANR 20

Anderson, Lindsay (Gordon)
1923-1994 .... **CLC 20**
See also CA 125; 128; 146; CANR 77

Anderson, Maxwell 1888-1959 .... **TCLC 2; DAM DRAM**
See also CA 105; 152; DLB 7; MTCW 2

Anderson, Poul (William) 1926- ...... **CLC 15**
See also AAYA 5, 34; CA 1-4R, 181; CAAE 181; CAAS 2; CANR 2, 15, 34, 64; CLR 58; DLB 8; INT CANR-15; MTCW 1, 2; SATA 90; SATA-Brief 39; SATA-Essay 106

Anderson, Robert (Woodruff)
1917- .... **CLC 23; DAM DRAM**
See also AITN 1; CA 21-24R; CANR 32; DLB 7

Anderson, Sherwood 1876-1941 ..... **TCLC 1, 10, 24; DA; DAB; DAC; DAM MST, NOV; SSC 1; WLC**
See also AAYA 30; CA 104; 121; CANR 61; CDALB 1917-1929; DA3; DLB 4, 9, 86; DLBD 1; MTCW 1, 2

Andier, Pierre
See Desnos, Robert

Andouard
See Giraudoux, (Hippolyte) Jean

Andrade, Carlos Drummond de CLC 18
See also Drummond de Andrade, Carlos

Andrade, Mario de 1893-1945 .... **TCLC 43**

Andreae, Johann V(alentin)
1586-1654 .... **LC 32**
See also DLB 164

Andreas-Salome, Lou 1861-1937 ... **TCLC 56**
See also CA 178; DLB 66

Andress, Lesley
See Sanders, Lawrence

Andrewes, Lancelot 1555-1626 .... **LC 5**
See also DLB 151, 172

Andrews, Cicily Fairfield
See West, Rebecca

Andrews, Elton V.
See Pohl, Frederik

Andreyev, Leonid (Nikolaevich)
1871-1919 .... **TCLC 3**
See also CA 104; 185

Andric, Ivo 1892-1975 .... **CLC 8; SSC 36**
See also CA 81-84; 57-60; CANR 43, 60; DLB 147; MTCW 1

Androvar
See Prado (Calvo), Pedro

Angelique, Pierre
See Bataille, Georges

Angell, Roger 1920- .... **CLC 26**
See also CA 57-60; CANR 13, 44, 70; DLB 171, 185

Angelou, Maya 1928- .... **CLC 12, 35, 64, 77; BLC 1; DA; DAB; DAC; DAM MST, MULT, POET, POP; WLCS**
See also AAYA 7, 20; BW 2, 3; CA 65-68; CANR 19, 42, 65; CDALBS; CLR 53; DA3; DLB 38; MTCW 1, 2; SATA 49

Anna Comnena 1083-1153 .... **CMLC 25**

Annensky, Innokenty (Fyodorovich)
1856-1909 .... **TCLC 14**
See also CA 110; 155

Annunzio, Gabriele d'
See D'Annunzio, Gabriele

Anodos
See Coleridge, Mary E(lizabeth)

Anon, Charles Robert
See Pessoa, Fernando (Antonio Nogueira)

Anouilh, Jean (Marie Lucien Pierre)
1910-1987 .... **CLC 1, 3, 8, 13, 40, 50; DAM DRAM; DC 8**
See also CA 17-20R; 123; CANR 32; MTCW 1, 2

Anthony, Florence
See Ai

Anthony, John
See Ciardi, John (Anthony)

Anthony, Peter
See Shaffer, Anthony (Joshua); Shaffer, Peter (Levin)

Anthony, Piers 1934- .... **CLC 35; DAM POP**
See also AAYA 11; CA 21-24R; CANR 28, 56, 73; DLB 8; MTCW 1, 2; SAAS 22; SATA 84

Anthony, Susan B(rownell)
1916-1991 .... **TCLC 84**
See also CA 89-92; 134

Antoine, Marc
See Proust, (Valentin-Louis-George-Eugene-) Marcel

Antoninus, Brother
See Everson, William (Oliver)

Antonioni, Michelangelo 1912- .... **CLC 20**
See also CA 73-76; CANR 45, 77

Antschel, Paul 1920-1970
See Celan, Paul
See also CA 85-88; CANR 33, 61; MTCW 1

Anwar, Chairil 1922-1949 .... **TCLC 22**
See also CA 121

Anzaldua, Gloria 1942-
See also CA 175; DLB 122; HLCS 1

Apess, William 1798-1839(?) .... **NCLC 73; DAM MULT**
See also DLB 175; NNAL

Apollinaire, Guillaume 1880-1918 .. **TCLC 3, 8, 51; DAM POET; PC 7**
See also Kostrowitzki, Wilhelm Apollinaris de
See also CA 152; MTCW 1

Appelfeld, Aharon 1932- .... **CLC 23, 47**
See also CA 112; 133; CANR 86

Apple, Max (Isaac) 1941- .... **CLC 9, 33**
See also CA 81-84; CANR 19, 54; DLB 130

Appleman, Philip (Dean) 1926- .... **CLC 51**
See also CA 13-16R; CAAS 18; CANR 6, 29, 56

Appleton, Lawrence
See Lovecraft, H(oward) P(hillips)

Apteryx
See Eliot, T(homas) S(tearns)

Apuleius, (Lucius Madaurensis)
125(?)-175(?) .... **CMLC 1**
See also DLB 211

Aquin, Hubert 1929-1977 .... **CLC 15**
See also CA 105; DLB 53

Aquinas, Thomas 1224(?)-1274 ..... **CMLC 33**
See also DLB 115

Aragon, Louis 1897-1982 .. **CLC 3, 22; DAM NOV, POET**
See also CA 69-72; 108; CANR 28, 71; DLB 72; MTCW 1, 2

Arany, Janos 1817-1882 .... **NCLC 34**

Aranyos, Kakay
See Mikszath, Kalman

Arbuthnot, John 1667-1735 .... **LC 1**
See also DLB 101

Archer, Herbert Winslow
See Mencken, H(enry) L(ouis)

Archer, Jeffrey (Howard) 1940- ...... **CLC 28; DAM POP**
See also AAYA 16; BEST 89:3; CA 77-80; CANR 22, 52; DA3; INT CANR-22

Archer, Jules 1915- .... **CLC 12**
See also CA 9-12R; CANR 6, 69; SAAS 5; SATA 4, 85

Archer, Lee
See Ellison, Harlan (Jay)

Arden, John 1930- .... **CLC 6, 13, 15; DAM DRAM**
See also CA 13-16R; CAAS 4; CANR 31, 65, 67; DLB 13; MTCW 1

Arenas, Reinaldo 1943-1990 . **CLC 41; DAM MULT; HLC 1**
See also CA 124; 128; 133; CANR 73; DLB 145; HW 1; MTCW 1

Arendt, Hannah 1906-1975 .... **CLC 66, 98**
See also CA 17-20R; 61-64; CANR 26, 60; MTCW 1, 2

Aretino, Pietro 1492-1556 .... **LC 12**

Arghezi, Tudor 1880-1967 .... **CLC 80**
See also Theodorescu, Ion N.
See also CA 167

Arguedas, Jose Maria 1911-1969 .... **CLC 10, 18; HLCS 1**
See also CA 89-92; CANR 73; DLB 113; HW 1

Argueta, Manlio 1936- .... **CLC 31**
See also CA 131; CANR 73; DLB 145; HW 1

Arias, Ron(ald Francis) 1941-
See also CA 131; CANR 81; DAM MULT; DLB 82; HLC 1; HW 1, 2; MTCW 2

Ariosto, Ludovico 1474-1533 .... **LC 6**

Aristides
See Epstein, Joseph

Aristophanes 450B.C.-385B.C. .... **CMLC 4; DA; DAB; DAC; DAM DRAM, MST; DC 2; WLCS**
See also DA3; DLB 176

Aristotle 384B.C.-322B.C. .... **CMLC 31; DA; DAB; DAC; DAM MST; WLCS**
See also DA3; DLB 176

Arlt, Roberto (Godofredo Christophersen)
1900-1942 .... **TCLC 29; DAM MULT; HLC 1**
See also CA 123; 131; CANR 67; HW 1, 2

Armah, Ayi Kwei 1939- . **CLC 5, 33; BLC 1; DAM MULT, POET**
See also BW 1; CA 61-64; CANR 21, 64; DLB 117; MTCW 1

Armatrading, Joan 1950- .... **CLC 17**
See also CA 114; 186

Arnette, Robert
See Silverberg, Robert

Arnim, Achim von (Ludwig Joachim von Arnim) 1781-1831 ..... **NCLC 5; SSC 29**
See also DLB 90

Arnim, Bettina von 1785-1859 .... **NCLC 38**
See also DLB 90

Arnold, Matthew 1822-1888 ..... **NCLC 6, 29; DA; DAB; DAC; DAM MST, POET; PC 5; WLC**
See also CDBLB 1832-1890; DLB 32, 57

Arnold, Thomas 1795-1842 .... **NCLC 18**
See also DLB 55

Arnow, Harriette (Louisa) Simpson
1908-1986 .... **CLC 2, 7, 18**
See also CA 9-12R; 118; CANR 14; DLB 6; MTCW 1, 2; SATA 42; SATA-Obit 47

Arouet, Francois-Marie
See Voltaire

Arp, Hans
See Arp, Jean

Arp, Jean 1887-1966 .... **CLC 5**
See also CA 81-84; 25-28R; CANR 42, 77

Arrabal
See Arrabal, Fernando

Benjamin, Walter 1892-1940 .... **TCLC 39**
See also CA 164
Benn, Gottfried 1886-1956 .... **TCLC 3**
See also CA 106; 153; DLB 56
Bennett, Alan 1934- .... **CLC 45, 77; DAB; DAM MST**
See also CA 103; CANR 35, 55; MTCW 1, 2
Bennett, (Enoch) Arnold
1867-1931 .... **TCLC 5, 20**
See also CA 106; 155; CDBLB 1890-1914; DLB 10, 34, 98, 135; MTCW 2
Bennett, Elizabeth
See Mitchell, Margaret (Munnerlyn)
Bennett, George Harold 1930-
See Bennett, Hal
See also BW 1; CA 97-100; CANR 87
Bennett, Hal CLC 5
See also Bennett, George Harold
See also DLB 33
Bennett, Jay 1912- .... **CLC 35**
See also AAYA 10; CA 69-72; CANR 11, 42, 79; JRDA; SAAS 4; SATA 41, 87; SATA-Brief 27
Bennett, Louise (Simone) 1919- ...... **CLC 28; BLC 1; DAM MULT**
See also BW 2, 3; CA 151; DLB 117
Benson, E(dward) F(rederic)
1867-1940 .... **TCLC 27**
See also CA 114; 157; DLB 135, 153
Benson, Jackson J. 1930- .... **CLC 34**
See also CA 25-28R; DLB 111
Benson, Sally 1900-1972 .... **CLC 17**
See also CA 19-20; 37-40R; CAP 1; SATA 1, 35; SATA-Obit 27
Benson, Stella 1892-1933 .... **TCLC 17**
See also CA 117; 155; DLB 36, 162
Bentham, Jeremy 1748-1832 .... **NCLC 38**
See also DLB 107, 158
Bentley, E(dmund) C(lerihew)
1875-1956 .... **TCLC 12**
See also CA 108; DLB 70
Bentley, Eric (Russell) 1916- .... **CLC 24**
See also CA 5-8R; CANR 6, 67; INT CANR-6
Beranger, Pierre Jean de
1780-1857 .... **NCLC 34**
Berdyaev, Nicolas
See Berdyaev, Nikolai (Aleksandrovich)
Berdyaev, Nikolai (Aleksandrovich)
1874-1948 .... **TCLC 67**
See also CA 120; 157
Berdyayev, Nikolai (Aleksandrovich)
See Berdyaev, Nikolai (Aleksandrovich)
Berendt, John (Lawrence) 1939- ...... **CLC 86**
See also CA 146; CANR 75; DA3; MTCW 1
Beresford, J(ohn) D(avys)
1873-1947 .... **TCLC 81**
See also CA 112; 155; DLB 162, 178, 197
Bergelson, David 1884-1952 .... **TCLC 81**
Berger, Colonel
See Malraux, (Georges-)Andre
Berger, John (Peter) 1926- .... **CLC 2, 19**
See also CA 81-84; CANR 51, 78; DLB 14, 207
Berger, Melvin H. 1927- .... **CLC 12**
See also CA 5-8R; CANR 4; CLR 32; SAAS 2; SATA 5, 88
Berger, Thomas (Louis) 1924- .. **CLC 3, 5, 8, 11, 18, 38; DAM NOV**
See also CA 1-4R; CANR 5, 28, 51; DLB 2; DLBY 80; INT CANR-28; MTCW 1, 2
Bergman, (Ernst) Ingmar 1918- ...... **CLC 16, 72**
See also CA 81-84; CANR 33, 70; MTCW 2
Bergson, Henri(-Louis) 1859-1941 . **TCLC 32**
See also CA 164

Bergstein, Eleanor 1938- .... **CLC 4**
See also CA 53-56; CANR 5
Berkoff, Steven 1937- .... **CLC 56**
See also CA 104; CANR 72
Bermant, Chaim (Icyk) 1929- .... **CLC 40**
See also CA 57-60; CANR 6, 31, 57
Bern, Victoria
See Fisher, M(ary) F(rances) K(ennedy)
Bernanos, (Paul Louis) Georges
1888-1948 .... **TCLC 3**
See also CA 104; 130; DLB 72
Bernard, April 1956- .... **CLC 59**
See also CA 131
Berne, Victoria
See Fisher, M(ary) F(rances) K(ennedy)
Bernhard, Thomas 1931-1989 ..... **CLC 3, 32, 61**
See also CA 85-88; 127; CANR 32, 57; DLB 85, 124; MTCW 1
Bernhardt, Sarah (Henriette Rosine)
1844-1923 .... **TCLC 75**
See also CA 157
Berriault, Gina 1926-1999 .... **CLC 54, 109; SSC 30**
See also CA 116; 129; 185; CANR 66; DLB 130
Berrigan, Daniel 1921- .... **CLC 4**
See also CA 33-36R; CAAS 1; CANR 11, 43, 78; DLB 5
Berrigan, Edmund Joseph Michael, Jr.
1934-1983
See Berrigan, Ted
See also CA 61-64; 110; CANR 14
Berrigan, Ted CLC 37
See also Berrigan, Edmund Joseph Michael, Jr.
See also DLB 5, 169
Berry, Charles Edward Anderson 1931-
See Berry, Chuck
See also CA 115
Berry, Chuck CLC 17
See also Berry, Charles Edward Anderson
Berry, Jonas
See Ashbery, John (Lawrence)
Berry, Wendell (Erdman) 1934- .. **CLC 4, 6, 8, 27, 46; DAM POET; PC 28**
See also AITN 1; CA 73-76; CANR 50, 73; DLB 5, 6; MTCW 1
Berryman, John 1914-1972 ... **CLC 1, 2, 3, 4, 6, 8, 10, 13, 25, 62; DAM POET**
See also CA 13-16; 33-36R; CABS 2; CANR 35; CAP 1; CDALB 1941-1968; DLB 48; MTCW 1, 2
Bertolucci, Bernardo 1940- .... **CLC 16**
See also CA 106
Berton, Pierre (Francis Demarigny)
1920- .... **CLC 104**
See also CA 1-4R; CANR 2, 56; DLB 68; SATA 99
Bertrand, Aloysius 1807-1841 .... **NCLC 31**
Bertran de Born c. 1140-1215 .... **CMLC 5**
Besant, Annie (Wood) 1847-1933 ..... **TCLC 9**
See also CA 105; 185
Bessie, Alvah 1904-1985 .... **CLC 23**
See also CA 5-8R; 116; CANR 2, 80; DLB 26
Bethlen, T. D.
See Silverberg, Robert
Beti, Mongo CLC 27; BLC 1; DAM MULT
See also Biyidi, Alexandre
See also CANR 79
Betjeman, John 1906-1984 ...... **CLC 2, 6, 10, 34, 43; DAB; DAM MST, POET**
See also CA 9-12R; 112; CANR 33, 56; CDBLB 1945-1960; DA3; DLB 20; DLBY 84; MTCW 1, 2
Bettelheim, Bruno 1903-1990 .... **CLC 79**
See also CA 81-84; 131; CANR 23, 61; DA3; MTCW 1, 2

Betti, Ugo 1892-1953 .... **TCLC 5**
See also CA 104; 155
Betts, Doris (Waugh) 1932- ...... **CLC 3, 6, 28**
See also CA 13-16R; CANR 9, 66, 77; DLBY 82; INT CANR-9
Bevan, Alistair
See Roberts, Keith (John Kingston)
Bey, Pilaff
See Douglas, (George) Norman
Bialik, Chaim Nachman
1873-1934 .... **TCLC 25**
See also CA 170
Bickerstaff, Isaac
See Swift, Jonathan
Bidart, Frank 1939- .... **CLC 33**
See also CA 140
Bienek, Horst 1930- .... **CLC 7, 11**
See also CA 73-76; DLB 75
Bierce, Ambrose (Gwinett)
1842-1914(?) .... **TCLC 1, 7, 44; DA; DAC; DAM MST; SSC 9; WLC**
See also CA 104; 139; CANR 78; CDALB 1865-1917; DA3; DLB 11, 12, 23, 71, 74, 186
Biggers, Earl Derr 1884-1933 .... **TCLC 65**
See also CA 108; 153
Billings, Josh
See Shaw, Henry Wheeler
Billington, (Lady) Rachel (Mary)
1942- .... **CLC 43**
See also AITN 2; CA 33-36R; CANR 44
Binyon, T(imothy) J(ohn) 1936- .... **CLC 34**
See also CA 111; CANR 28
Bion 335B.C.-245B.C. .... **CMLC 39**
Bioy Casares, Adolfo 1914-1999 ... **CLC 4, 8, 13, 88; DAM MULT; HLC 1; SSC 17**
See also CA 29-32R; 177; CANR 19, 43, 66; DLB 113; HW 1, 2; MTCW 1, 2
Bird, Cordwainer
See Ellison, Harlan (Jay)
Bird, Robert Montgomery
1806-1854 .... **NCLC 1**
See also DLB 202
Birkerts, Sven 1951- .... **CLC 116**
See also CA 128; 133; 176; CAAE 176; CAAS 29; INT 133
Birney, (Alfred) Earle 1904-1995 .. **CLC 1, 4, 6, 11; DAC; DAM MST, POET**
See also CA 1-4R; CANR 5, 20; DLB 88; MTCW 1
Biruni, al 973-1048(?) .... **CMLC 28**
Bishop, Elizabeth 1911-1979 ..... **CLC 1, 4, 9, 13, 15, 32; DA; DAC; DAM MST, POET; PC 3**
See also CA 5-8R; 89-92; CABS 2; CANR 26, 61; CDALB 1968-1988; DA3; DLB 5, 169; MTCW 1, 2; SATA-Obit 24
Bishop, John 1935- .... **CLC 10**
See also CA 105
Bissett, Bill 1939- .... **CLC 18; PC 14**
See also CA 69-72; CAAS 19; CANR 15; DLB 53; MTCW 1
Bissoondath, Neil (Devindra)
1955- .... **CLC 120; DAC**
See also CA 136
Bitov, Andrei (Georgievich) 1937- ... **CLC 57**
See also CA 142
Biyidi, Alexandre 1932-
See Beti, Mongo
See also BW 1, 3; CA 114; 124; CANR 81; DA3; MTCW 1, 2
Bjarme, Brynjolf
See Ibsen, Henrik (Johan)
Bjoernson, Bjoernstjerne (Martinius)
1832-1910 .... **TCLC 7, 37**
See also CA 104
Black, Robert
See Holdstock, Robert P.

Author Index

Bourjaily, Vance (Nye) 1922- .... **CLC 8, 62**
See also CA 1-4R; CAAS 1; CANR 2, 72;
DLB 2, 143

Bourne, Randolph S(illiman)
1886-1918 .... **TCLC 16**
See also CA 117; 155; DLB 63

Bova, Ben(jamin William) 1932- ...... **CLC 45**
See also AAYA 16; CA 5-8R; CAAS 18;
CANR 11, 56; CLR 3; DLBY 81; INT
CANR-11; MAICYA; MTCW 1; SATA 6,
68

Bowen, Elizabeth (Dorothea Cole)
1899-1973 . **CLC 1, 3, 6, 11, 15, 22, 118;
DAM NOV; SSC 3, 28**
See also CA 17-18; 41-44R; CANR 35;
CAP 2; CDBLB 1945-1960; DA3; DLB
15, 162; MTCW 1, 2

Bowering, George 1935- .... **CLC 15, 47**
See also CA 21-24R; CAAS 16; CANR 10;
DLB 53

Bowering, Marilyn R(uthe) 1949- .... **CLC 32**
See also CA 101; CANR 49

Bowers, Edgar 1924- .... **CLC 9**
See also CA 5-8R; CANR 24; DLB 5

Bowie, David CLC 17
See also Jones, David Robert

Bowles, Jane (Sydney) 1917-1973 ..... **CLC 3,
68**
See also CA 19-20; 41-44R; CAP 2

Bowles, Paul (Frederick) 1910-1999 . **CLC 1,
2, 19, 53; SSC 3**
See also CA 1-4R; 186; CAAS 1; CANR 1,
19, 50, 75; DA3; DLB 5, 6; MTCW 1, 2

Box, Edgar
See Vidal, Gore

Boyd, Nancy
See Millay, Edna St. Vincent

Boyd, William 1952- .... **CLC 28, 53, 70**
See also CA 114; 120; CANR 51, 71

Boyle, Kay 1902-1992 .... **CLC 1, 5, 19, 58,
121; SSC 5**
See also CA 13-16R; 140; CAAS 1; CANR
29, 61; DLB 4, 9, 48, 86; DLBY 93;
MTCW 1, 2

Boyle, Mark
See Kienzle, William X(avier)

Boyle, Patrick 1905-1982 .... **CLC 19**
See also CA 127

Boyle, T. C. 1948-
See Boyle, T(homas) Coraghessan

Boyle, T(homas) Coraghessan
1948- .... **CLC 36, 55, 90; DAM POP;
SSC 16**
See also BEST 90:4; CA 120; CANR 44,
76, 89; DA3; DLBY 86; MTCW 2

Boz
See Dickens, Charles (John Huffam)

Brackenridge, Hugh Henry
1748-1816 .... **NCLC 7**
See also DLB 11, 37

Bradbury, Edward P.
See Moorcock, Michael (John)
See also MTCW 2

Bradbury, Malcolm (Stanley)
1932- .... **CLC 32, 61; DAM NOV**
See also CA 1-4R; CANR 1, 33, 91; DA3;
DLB 14, 207; MTCW 1, 2

Bradbury, Ray (Douglas) 1920- .... **CLC 1, 3,
10, 15, 42, 98; DA; DAB; DAC; DAM
MST, NOV, POP; SSC 29; WLC**
See also AAYA 15; AITN 1, 2; CA 1-4R;
CANR 2, 30, 75; CDALB 1968-1988;
DA3; DLB 2, 8; MTCW 1, 2; SATA 11,
64

Bradford, Gamaliel 1863-1932 .... **TCLC 36**
See also CA 160; DLB 17

Bradley, David (Henry), Jr. 1950- ... **CLC 23,
118; BLC 1; DAM MULT**
See also BW 1, 3; CA 104; CANR 26, 81;
DLB 33

Bradley, John Ed(mund, Jr.) 1958- . **CLC 55**
See also CA 139

Bradley, Marion Zimmer
1930-1999 .... **CLC 30; DAM POP**
See also AAYA 9; CA 57-60; 185; CAAS
10; CANR 7, 31, 51, 75; DA3; DLB 8;
MTCW 1, 2; SATA 90; SATA-Obit 116

Bradstreet, Anne 1612(?)-1672 ...... **LC 4, 30;
DA; DAC; DAM MST, POET; PC 10**
See also CDALB 1640-1865; DA3; DLB
24

Brady, Joan 1939- .... **CLC 86**
See also CA 141

Bragg, Melvyn 1939- .... **CLC 10**
See also BEST 89:3; CA 57-60; CANR 10,
48, 89; DLB 14

Brahe, Tycho 1546-1601 .... **LC 45**

Braine, John (Gerard) 1922-1986 . **CLC 1, 3,
41**
See also CA 1-4R; 120; CANR 1, 33; CD-
BLB 1945-1960; DLB 15; DLBY 86;
MTCW 1

Bramah, Ernest 1868-1942 .... **TCLC 72**
See also CA 156; DLB 70

Brammer, William 1930(?)-1978 ...... **CLC 31**
See also CA 77-80

Brancati, Vitaliano 1907-1954 .... **TCLC 12**
See also CA 109

Brancato, Robin F(idler) 1936- .... **CLC 35**
See also AAYA 9; CA 69-72; CANR 11,
45; CLR 32; JRDA; SAAS 9; SATA 97

Brand, Max
See Faust, Frederick (Schiller)

Brand, Millen 1906-1980 .... **CLC 7**
See also CA 21-24R; 97-100; CANR 72

Branden, Barbara CLC 44
See also CA 148

Brandes, Georg (Morris Cohen)
1842-1927 .... **TCLC 10**
See also CA 105

Brandys, Kazimierz 1916- .... **CLC 62**

Branley, Franklyn M(ansfield)
1915- .... **CLC 21**
See also CA 33-36R; CANR 14, 39; CLR
13; MAICYA; SAAS 16; SATA 4, 68

Brathwaite, Edward (Kamau)
1930- ...... **CLC 11; BLCS; DAM POET**
See also BW 2, 3; CA 25-28R; CANR 11,
26, 47; DLB 125

Brautigan, Richard (Gary)
1935-1984 .... **CLC 1, 3, 5, 9, 12, 34, 42;
DAM NOV**
See also CA 53-56; 113; CANR 34; DA3;
DLB 2, 5, 206; DLBY 80, 84; MTCW 1;
SATA 56

Brave Bird, Mary 1953-
See Crow Dog, Mary (Ellen)
See also NNAL

Braverman, Kate 1950- .... **CLC 67**
See also CA 89-92

Brecht, (Eugen) Bertolt (Friedrich)
1898-1956 .... **TCLC 1, 6, 13, 35; DA;
DAB; DAC; DAM DRAM, MST; DC
3; WLC**
See also CA 104; 133; CANR 62; DA3;
DLB 56, 124; MTCW 1, 2

Brecht, Eugen Berthold Friedrich
See Brecht, (Eugen) Bertolt (Friedrich)

Bremer, Fredrika 1801-1865 .... **NCLC 11**

Brennan, Christopher John
1870-1932 .... **TCLC 17**
See also CA 117

Brennan, Maeve 1917-1993 .... **CLC 5**
See also CA 81-84; CANR 72

Brent, Linda
See Jacobs, Harriet A(nn)

Brentano, Clemens (Maria)
1778-1842 .... **NCLC 1**
See also DLB 90

Brent of Bin Bin
See Franklin, (Stella Maria Sarah) Miles
(Lampe)

Brenton, Howard 1942- .... **CLC 31**
See also CA 69-72; CANR 33, 67; DLB 13;
MTCW 1

Breslin, James 1930-1996
See Breslin, Jimmy
See also CA 73-76; CANR 31, 75; DAM
NOV; MTCW 1, 2

Breslin, Jimmy CLC 4, 43
See also Breslin, James
See also AITN 1; DLB 185; MTCW 2

Bresson, Robert 1901- .... **CLC 16**
See also CA 110; CANR 49

Breton, Andre 1896-1966 .. **CLC 2, 9, 15, 54;
PC 15**
See also CA 19-20; 25-28R; CANR 40, 60;
CAP 2; DLB 65; MTCW 1, 2

Breytenbach, Breyten 1939(?)- .. **CLC 23, 37,
126; DAM POET**
See also CA 113; 129; CANR 61

Bridgers, Sue Ellen 1942- .... **CLC 26**
See also AAYA 8; CA 65-68; CANR 11,
36; CLR 18; DLB 52; JRDA; MAICYA;
SAAS 1; SATA 22, 90; SATA-Essay 109

Bridges, Robert (Seymour)
1844-1930 ... **TCLC 1; DAM POET; PC
28**
See also CA 104; 152; CDBLB 1890-1914;
DLB 19, 98

Bridie, James TCLC 3
See also Mavor, Osborne Henry
See also DLB 10

Brin, David 1950- .... **CLC 34**
See also AAYA 21; CA 102; CANR 24, 70;
INT CANR-24; SATA 65

Brink, Andre (Philippus) 1935- . **CLC 18, 36,
106**
See also CA 104; CANR 39, 62; INT 103;
MTCW 1, 2

Brinsmead, H(esba) F(ay) 1922- ...... **CLC 21**
See also CA 21-24R; CANR 10; CLR 47;
MAICYA; SAAS 5; SATA 18, 78

Brittain, Vera (Mary) 1893(?)-1970 . **CLC 23**
See also CA 13-16; 25-28R; CANR 58;
CAP 1; DLB 191; MTCW 1, 2

Broch, Hermann 1886-1951 .... **TCLC 20**
See also CA 117; DLB 85, 124

Brock, Rose
See Hansen, Joseph

Brodkey, Harold (Roy) 1930-1996 ... **CLC 56**
See also CA 111; 151; CANR 71; DLB 130

Brodskii, Iosif
See Brodsky, Joseph

Brodsky, Iosif Alexandrovich 1940-1996
See Brodsky, Joseph
See also AITN 1; CA 41-44R; 151; CANR
37; DAM POET; DA3; MTCW 1, 2

Brodsky, Joseph 1940-1996 ..... **CLC 4, 6, 13,
36, 100; PC 9**
See also Brodskii, Iosif; Brodsky, Iosif Alexandrovich
See also MTCW 1

Brodsky, Michael (Mark) 1948- .... **CLC 19**
See also CA 102; CANR 18, 41, 58

Bromell, Henry 1947- .... **CLC 5**
See also CA 53-56; CANR 9

Bromfield, Louis (Brucker)
1896-1956 .... **TCLC 11**
See also CA 107; 155; DLB 4, 9, 86

Bullins, Ed 1935- .... **CLC 1, 5, 7; BLC 1; DAM DRAM, MULT; DC 6**
See also BW 2, 3; CA 49-52; CAAS 16; CANR 24, 46, 73; DLB 7, 38; MTCW 1, 2

Bulwer-Lytton, Edward (George Earle Lytton) 1803-1873 .... **NCLC 1, 45**
See also DLB 21

Bunin, Ivan Alexeyevich 1870-1953 .... **TCLC 6; SSC 5**
See also CA 104

Bunting, Basil 1900-1985 ..... **CLC 10, 39, 47; DAM POET**
See also CA 53-56; 115; CANR 7; DLB 20

Bunuel, Luis 1900-1983 .. **CLC 16, 80; DAM MULT; HLC 1**
See also CA 101; 110; CANR 32, 77; HW 1

Bunyan, John 1628-1688 ... **LC 4; DA; DAB; DAC; DAM MST; WLC**
See also CDBLB 1660-1789; DLB 39

Burckhardt, Jacob (Christoph) 1818-1897 .... **NCLC 49**

Burford, Eleanor
See Hibbert, Eleanor Alice Burford

Burgess, Anthony CLC 1, 2, 4, 5, 8, 10, 13, 15, 22, 40, 62, 81, 94; DAB
See also Wilson, John (Anthony) Burgess
See also AAYA 25; AITN 1; CDBLB 1960 to Present; DLB 14, 194; DLBY 98; MTCW 1

Burke, Edmund 1729(?)-1797 .... **LC 7, 36; DA; DAB; DAC; DAM MST; WLC**
See also DA3; DLB 104

Burke, Kenneth (Duva) 1897-1993 ... **CLC 2, 24**
See also CA 5-8R; 143; CANR 39, 74; DLB 45, 63; MTCW 1, 2

Burke, Leda
See Garnett, David

Burke, Ralph
See Silverberg, Robert

Burke, Thomas 1886-1945 .... **TCLC 63**
See also CA 113; 155; DLB 197

Burney, Fanny 1752-1840 .. **NCLC 12, 54, 81**
See also DLB 39

Burns, Robert 1759-1796 . **LC 3, 29, 40; DA; DAB; DAC; DAM MST, POET; PC 6; WLC**
See also CDBLB 1789-1832; DA3; DLB 109

Burns, Tex
See L'Amour, Louis (Dearborn)

Burnshaw, Stanley 1906- .... **CLC 3, 13, 44**
See also CA 9-12R; DLB 48; DLBY 97

Burr, Anne 1937- .... **CLC 6**
See also CA 25-28R

Burroughs, Edgar Rice 1875-1950 . **TCLC 2, 32; DAM NOV**
See also AAYA 11; CA 104; 132; DA3; DLB 8; MTCW 1, 2; SATA 41

Burroughs, William S(eward) 1914-1997 .. **CLC 1, 2, 5, 15, 22, 42, 75, 109; DA; DAB; DAC; DAM MST, NOV, POP; WLC**
See also AITN 2; CA 9-12R; 160; CANR 20, 52; DA3; DLB 2, 8, 16, 152; DLBY 81, 97; MTCW 1, 2

Burton, SirRichard F(rancis) 1821-1890 .... **NCLC 42**
See also DLB 55, 166, 184

Busch, Frederick 1941- .... **CLC 7, 10, 18, 47**
See also CA 33-36R; CAAS 1; CANR 45, 73; DLB 6

Bush, Ronald 1946- .... **CLC 34**
See also CA 136

Bustos, F(rancisco)
See Borges, Jorge Luis

Bustos Domecq, H(onorio)
See Bioy Casares, Adolfo; Borges, Jorge Luis

Butler, Octavia E(stelle) 1947- .... **CLC 38, 121; BLCS; DAM MULT, POP**
See also AAYA 18; BW 2, 3; CA 73-76; CANR 12, 24, 38, 73; CLR 65; DA3; DLB 33; MTCW 1, 2; SATA 84

Butler, Robert Olen (Jr.) 1945- .... **CLC 81; DAM POP**
See also CA 112; CANR 66; DLB 173; INT 112; MTCW 1

Butler, Samuel 1612-1680 .... **LC 16, 43**
See also DLB 101, 126

Butler, Samuel 1835-1902 . **TCLC 1, 33; DA; DAB; DAC; DAM MST, NOV; WLC**
See also CA 143; CDBLB 1890-1914; DA3; DLB 18, 57, 174

Butler, Walter C.
See Faust, Frederick (Schiller)

Butor, Michel (Marie Francois) 1926- .... **CLC 1, 3, 8, 11, 15**
See also CA 9-12R; CANR 33, 66; DLB 83; MTCW 1, 2

Butts, Mary 1892(?)-1937 .... **TCLC 77**
See also CA 148

Buzo, Alexander (John) 1944- .... **CLC 61**
See also CA 97-100; CANR 17, 39, 69

Buzzati, Dino 1906-1972 .... **CLC 36**
See also CA 160; 33-36R; DLB 177

Byars, Betsy (Cromer) 1928- .... **CLC 35**
See also AAYA 19; CA 33-36R, 183; CAAE 183; CANR 18, 36, 57; CLR 1, 16; DLB 52; INT CANR-18; JRDA; MAICYA; MTCW 1; SAAS 1; SATA 4, 46, 80; SATA-Essay 108

Byatt, A(ntonia) S(usan Drabble) 1936- ..... **CLC 19, 65; DAM NOV, POP**
See also CA 13-16R; CANR 13, 33, 50, 75; DA3; DLB 14, 194; MTCW 1, 2

Byrne, David 1952- .... **CLC 26**
See also CA 127

Byrne, John Keyes 1926-
See Leonard, Hugh
See also CA 102; CANR 78; INT 102

Byron, George Gordon (Noel) 1788-1824 .... **NCLC 2, 12; DA; DAB; DAC; DAM MST, POET; PC 16; WLC**
See also CDBLB 1789-1832; DA3; DLB 96, 110

Byron, Robert 1905-1941 .... **TCLC 67**
See also CA 160; DLB 195

C. 3. 3.
See Wilde, Oscar (Fingal O'Flahertie Wills)

Caballero, Fernan 1796-1877 .... **NCLC 10**

Cabell, Branch
See Cabell, James Branch

Cabell, James Branch 1879-1958 .... **TCLC 6**
See also CA 105; 152; DLB 9, 78; MTCW 1

Cable, George Washington 1844-1925 .... **TCLC 4; SSC 4**
See also CA 104; 155; DLB 12, 74; DLBD 13

Cabral de Melo Neto, Joao 1920- ... **CLC 76; DAM MULT**
See also CA 151

Cabrera Infante, G(uillermo) 1929- . **CLC 5, 25, 45, 120; DAM MULT; HLC 1; SSC 39**
See also CA 85-88; CANR 29, 65; DA3; DLB 113; HW 1, 2; MTCW 1, 2

Cade, Toni
See Bambara, Toni Cade

Cadmus and Harmonia
See Buchan, John

Caedmon fl. 658-680 .... **CMLC 7**
See also DLB 146

Caeiro, Alberto
See Pessoa, Fernando (Antonio Nogueira)

Cage, John (Milton, Jr.) 1912-1992 . **CLC 41**
See also CA 13-16R; 169; CANR 9, 78; DLB 193; INT CANR-9

Cahan, Abraham 1860-1951 .... **TCLC 71**
See also CA 108; 154; DLB 9, 25, 28

Cain, G.
See Cabrera Infante, G(uillermo)

Cain, Guillermo
See Cabrera Infante, G(uillermo)

Cain, James M(allahan) 1892-1977 .. **CLC 3, 11, 28**
See also AITN 1; CA 17-20R; 73-76; CANR 8, 34, 61; MTCW 1

Caine, Hall 1853-1931 .... **TCLC 97**

Caine, Mark
See Raphael, Frederic (Michael)

Calasso, Roberto 1941- .... **CLC 81**
See also CA 143; CANR 89

Calderon de la Barca, Pedro 1600-1681 .... **LC 23; DC 3; HLCS 1**

Caldwell, Erskine (Preston) 1903-1987 .. **CLC 1, 8, 14, 50, 60; DAM NOV; SSC 19**
See also AITN 1; CA 1-4R; 121; CAAS 1; CANR 2, 33; DA3; DLB 9, 86; MTCW 1, 2

Caldwell, (Janet Miriam) Taylor (Holland) 1900-1985 .. **CLC 2, 28, 39; DAM NOV, POP**
See also CA 5-8R; 116; CANR 5; DA3; DLBD 17

Calhoun, John Caldwell 1782-1850 .... **NCLC 15**
See also DLB 3

Calisher, Hortense 1911- ..... **CLC 2, 4, 8, 38; DAM NOV; SSC 15**
See also CA 1-4R; CANR 1, 22, 67; DA3; DLB 2; INT CANR-22; MTCW 1, 2

Callaghan, Morley Edward 1903-1990 ...... **CLC 3, 14, 41, 65; DAC; DAM MST**
See also CA 9-12R; 132; CANR 33, 73; DLB 68; MTCW 1, 2

Callimachus c. 305B.C.-c. 240B.C. .... **CMLC 18**
See also DLB 176

Calvin, John 1509-1564 .... **LC 37**

Calvino, Italo 1923-1985 .... **CLC 5, 8, 11, 22, 33, 39, 73; DAM NOV; SSC 3**
See also CA 85-88; 116; CANR 23, 61; DLB 196; MTCW 1, 2

Cameron, Carey 1952- .... **CLC 59**
See also CA 135

Cameron, Peter 1959- .... **CLC 44**
See also CA 125; CANR 50

Camoens, Luis Vaz de 1524(?)-1580
See also HLCS 1

Camoes, Luis de 1524(?)-1580
See also HLCS 1

Campana, Dino 1885-1932 .... **TCLC 20**
See also CA 117; DLB 114

Campanella, Tommaso 1568-1639 .... **LC 32**

Campbell, John W(ood, Jr.) 1910-1971 .... **CLC 32**
See also CA 21-22; 29-32R; CANR 34; CAP 2; DLB 8; MTCW 1

Campbell, Joseph 1904-1987 .... **CLC 69**
See also AAYA 3; BEST 89:2; CA 1-4R; 124; CANR 3, 28, 61; DA3; MTCW 1, 2

Campbell, Maria 1940- .... **CLC 85; DAC**
See also CA 102; CANR 54; NNAL

Campbell, (John) Ramsey 1946- ..... **CLC 42; SSC 19**
See also CA 57-60; CANR 7; INT CANR-7

Campbell, (Ignatius) Roy (Dunnachie) 1901-1957 .... **TCLC 5**
See also CA 104; 155; DLB 20; MTCW 2

Dickens, Charles (John Huffam)
1812-1870 .... **NCLC 3, 8, 18, 26, 37, 50, 86; DA; DAB; DAC; DAM MST, NOV; SSC 17; WLC**
See also AAYA 23; CDBLB 1832-1890; DA3; DLB 21, 55, 70, 159, 166; JRDA; MAICYA; SATA 15

Dickey, James (Lafayette)
1923-1997 .... **CLC 1, 2, 4, 7, 10, 15, 47, 109; DAM NOV, POET, POP**
See also AITN 1, 2; CA 9-12R; 156; CABS 2; CANR 10, 48, 61; CDALB 1968-1988; DA3; DLB 5, 193; DLBD 7; DLBY 82, 93, 96, 97, 98; INT CANR-10; MTCW 1, 2

Dickey, William 1928-1994 .... **CLC 3, 28**
See also CA 9-12R; 145; CANR 24, 79; DLB 5

Dickinson, Charles 1951- .... **CLC 49**
See also CA 128

Dickinson, Emily (Elizabeth)
1830-1886 ..... **NCLC 21, 77; DA; DAB; DAC; DAM MST, POET; PC 1; WLC**
See also AAYA 22; CDALB 1865-1917; DA3; DLB 1; SATA 29

Dickinson, Peter (Malcolm) 1927- .. **CLC 12, 35**
See also AAYA 9; CA 41-44R; CANR 31, 58, 88; CLR 29; DLB 87, 161; JRDA; MAICYA; SATA 5, 62, 95

Dickson, Carr
See Carr, John Dickson

Dickson, Carter
See Carr, John Dickson

Diderot, Denis 1713-1784 .... **LC 26**

Didion, Joan 1934- .... **CLC 1, 3, 8, 14, 32, 129; DAM NOV**
See also AITN 1; CA 5-8R; CANR 14, 52, 76; CDALB 1968-1988; DA3; DLB 2, 173, 185; DLBY 81, 86; MTCW 1, 2

Dietrich, Robert
See Hunt, E(verette) Howard, (Jr.)

Difusa, Pati
See Almodovar, Pedro

Dillard, Annie 1945- .. **CLC 9, 60, 115; DAM NOV**
See also AAYA 6; CA 49-52; CANR 3, 43, 62, 90; DA3; DLBY 80; MTCW 1, 2; SATA 10

Dillard, R(ichard) H(enry) W(ilde)
1937- .... **CLC 5**
See also CA 21-24R; CAAS 7; CANR 10; DLB 5

Dillon, Eilis 1920-1994 .... **CLC 17**
See also CA 9-12R, 182; 147; CAAE 182; CAAS 3; CANR 4, 38, 78; CLR 26; MAICYA; SATA 2, 74; SATA-Essay 105; SATA-Obit 83

Dimont, Penelope
See Mortimer, Penelope (Ruth)

Dinesen, Isak CLC 10, 29, 95; SSC 7
See also Blixen, Karen (Christentze Dinesen)
See also MTCW 1

Ding Ling CLC 68
See also Chiang, Pin-chin

Diphusa, Patty
See Almodovar, Pedro

Disch, Thomas M(ichael) 1940- ... **CLC 7, 36**
See also AAYA 17; CA 21-24R; CAAS 4; CANR 17, 36, 54, 89; CLR 18; DA3; DLB 8; MAICYA; MTCW 1, 2; SAAS 15; SATA 92

Disch, Tom
See Disch, Thomas M(ichael)

d'Isly, Georges
See Simenon, Georges (Jacques Christian)

Disraeli, Benjamin 1804-1881 ... **NCLC 2, 39, 79**
See also DLB 21, 55

Ditcum, Steve
See Crumb, R(obert)

Dixon, Paige
See Corcoran, Barbara

Dixon, Stephen 1936- .... **CLC 52; SSC 16**
See also CA 89-92; CANR 17, 40, 54, 91; DLB 130

Doak, Annie
See Dillard, Annie

Dobell, Sydney Thompson
1824-1874 .... **NCLC 43**
See also DLB 32

Doblin, Alfred TCLC 13
See also Doeblin, Alfred

Dobrolyubov, Nikolai Alexandrovich
1836-1861 .... **NCLC 5**

Dobson, Austin 1840-1921 .... **TCLC 79**
See also DLB 35; 144

Dobyns, Stephen 1941- .... **CLC 37**
See also CA 45-48; CANR 2, 18

Doctorow, E(dgar) L(aurence)
1931- .... **CLC 6, 11, 15, 18, 37, 44, 65, 113; DAM NOV, POP**
See also AAYA 22; AITN 2; BEST 89:3; CA 45-48; CANR 2, 33, 51, 76; CDALB 1968-1988; DA3; DLB 2, 28, 173; DLBY 80; MTCW 1, 2

Dodgson, Charles Lutwidge 1832-1898
See Carroll, Lewis
See also CLR 2; DA; DAB; DAC; DAM MST, NOV, POET; DA3; MAICYA; SATA 100; YABC 2

Dodson, Owen (Vincent)
1914-1983 .... **CLC 79; BLC 1; DAM MULT**
See also BW 1; CA 65-68; 110; CANR 24; DLB 76

Doeblin, Alfred 1878-1957 .... **TCLC 13**
See also Doblin, Alfred
See also CA 110; 141; DLB 66

Doerr, Harriet 1910- .... **CLC 34**
See also CA 117; 122; CANR 47; INT 122

Domecq, H(onorio) Bustos)
See Bioy Casares, Adolfo

Domecq, H(onorio) Bustos
See Bioy Casares, Adolfo; Borges, Jorge Luis

Domini, Rey
See Lorde, Audre (Geraldine)

Dominique
See Proust, (Valentin-Louis-George-Eugene-) Marcel

Don, A
See Stephen, SirLeslie

Donaldson, Stephen R. 1947- .... **CLC 46; DAM POP**
See also CA 89-92; CANR 13, 55; INT CANR-13

Donleavy, J(ames) P(atrick) 1926- .... **CLC 1, 4, 6, 10, 45**
See also AITN 2; CA 9-12R; CANR 24, 49, 62, 80; DLB 6, 173; INT CANR-24; MTCW 1, 2

Donne, John 1572-1631 .... **LC 10, 24; DA; DAB; DAC; DAM MST, POET; PC 1; WLC**
See also CDBLB Before 1660; DLB 121, 151

Donnell, David 1939(?)- .... **CLC 34**

Donoghue, P. S.
See Hunt, E(verette) Howard, (Jr.)

Donoso (Yanez), Jose 1924-1996 ... **CLC 4, 8, 11, 32, 99; DAM MULT; HLC 1; SSC 34**
See also CA 81-84; 155; CANR 32, 73; DLB 113; HW 1, 2; MTCW 1, 2

Donovan, John 1928-1992 .... **CLC 35**
See also AAYA 20; CA 97-100; 137; CLR 3; MAICYA; SATA 72; SATA-Brief 29

Don Roberto
See Cunninghame Graham, Robert (Gallnigad) Bontine

Doolittle, Hilda 1886-1961 . **CLC 3, 8, 14, 31, 34, 73; DA; DAC; DAM MST, POET; PC 5; WLC**
See also H. D.
See also CA 97-100; CANR 35; DLB 4, 45; MTCW 1, 2

Dorfman, Ariel 1942- ...... **CLC 48, 77; DAM MULT; HLC 1**
See also CA 124; 130; CANR 67, 70; HW 1, 2; INT 130

Dorn, Edward (Merton) 1929- ... **CLC 10, 18**
See also CA 93-96; CANR 42, 79; DLB 5; INT 93-96

Dorris, Michael (Anthony)
1945-1997 .... **CLC 109; DAM MULT, NOV**
See also AAYA 20; BEST 90:1; CA 102; 157; CANR 19, 46, 75; CLR 58; DA3; DLB 175; MTCW 2; NNAL; SATA 75; SATA-Obit 94

Dorris, Michael A.
See Dorris, Michael (Anthony)

Dorsan, Luc
See Simenon, Georges (Jacques Christian)

Dorsange, Jean
See Simenon, Georges (Jacques Christian)

Dos Passos, John (Roderigo)
1896-1970 ... **CLC 1, 4, 8, 11, 15, 25, 34, 82; DA; DAB; DAC; DAM MST, NOV; WLC**
See also CA 1-4R; 29-32R; CANR 3; CDALB 1929-1941; DA3; DLB 4, 9; DLBD 1, 15; DLBY 96; MTCW 1, 2

Dossage, Jean
See Simenon, Georges (Jacques Christian)

Dostoevsky, Fedor Mikhailovich
1821-1881 . **NCLC 2, 7, 21, 33, 43; DA; DAB; DAC; DAM MST, NOV; SSC 2, 33; WLC**
See also DA3

Doughty, Charles M(ontagu)
1843-1926 .... **TCLC 27**
See also CA 115; 178; DLB 19, 57, 174

Douglas, Ellen CLC 73
See also Haxton, Josephine Ayres; Williamson, Ellen Douglas

Douglas, Gavin 1475(?)-1522 .... **LC 20**
See also DLB 132

Douglas, George
See Brown, George Douglas

Douglas, Keith (Castellain)
1920-1944 .... **TCLC 40**
See also CA 160; DLB 27

Douglas, Leonard
See Bradbury, Ray (Douglas)

Douglas, Michael
See Crichton, (John) Michael

Douglas, (George) Norman
1868-1952 .... **TCLC 68**
See also CA 119; 157; DLB 34, 195

Douglas, William
See Brown, George Douglas

Douglass, Frederick 1817(?)-1895 .. **NCLC 7, 55; BLC 1; DA; DAC; DAM MST, MULT; WLC**
See also CDALB 1640-1865; DA3; DLB 1, 43, 50, 79; SATA 29

Dourado, (Waldomiro Freitas) Autran
1926- .... **CLC 23, 60**
See also CA 25-28R; 179; CANR 34, 81; DLB 145; HW 2

Dwyer, K. R.
  See Koontz, Dean R(ay)
Dwyer, Thomas A. 1923- .... **CLC 114**
  See also CA 115
Dye, Richard
  See De Voto, Bernard (Augustine)
Dylan, Bob 1941- .... **CLC 3, 4, 6, 12, 77**
  See also CA 41-44R; DLB 16
E. V. L.
  See Lucas, E(dward) V(errall)
Eagleton, Terence (Francis) 1943- . **CLC 132**
  See also Eagleton, Terry
  See also CA 57-60; CANR 7, 23, 68;
    MTCW 1, 2
Eagleton, Terry CLC 63
  See also Eagleton, Terence (Francis)
  See also MTCW 1
Early, Jack
  See Scoppettone, Sandra
East, Michael
  See West, Morris L(anglo)
Eastaway, Edward
  See Thomas, (Philip) Edward
Eastlake, William (Derry)
  1917-1997 .... **CLC 8**
  See also CA 5-8R; 158; CAAS 1; CANR 5,
    63; DLB 6, 206; INT CANR-5
Eastman, Charles A(lexander)
  1858-1939 .... **TCLC 55; DAM MULT**
  See also CA 179; CANR 91; DLB 175;
    NNAL; YABC 1
Eberhart, Richard (Ghormley)
  1904- .. **CLC 3, 11, 19, 56; DAM POET**
  See also CA 1-4R; CANR 2; CDALB 1941-
    1968; DLB 48; MTCW 1
Eberstadt, Fernanda 1960- .... **CLC 39**
  See also CA 136; CANR 69
**Echegaray (y Eizaguirre), Jose (Maria
    Waldo)** 1832-1916 .... **TCLC 4; HLCS 1**
  See also CA 104; CANR 32; HW 1; MTCW
    1
Echeverria, (Jose) Esteban (Antonino)
  1805-1851 .... **NCLC 18**
Echo
  See Proust, (Valentin-Louis-George-
    Eugene-) Marcel
Eckert, Allan W. 1931- .... **CLC 17**
  See also AAYA 18; CA 13-16R; CANR 14,
    45; INT CANR-14; SAAS 21; SATA 29,
    91; SATA-Brief 27
Eckhart, Meister 1260(?)-1328(?) ... **CMLC 9**
  See also DLB 115
Eckmar, F. R.
  See de Hartog, Jan
Eco, Umberto 1932- .... **CLC 28, 60; DAM
    NOV, POP**
  See also BEST 90:1; CA 77-80; CANR 12,
    33, 55; DA3; DLB 196; MTCW 1, 2
Eddison, E(ric) R(ucker)
  1882-1945 .... **TCLC 15**
  See also CA 109; 156
Eddy, Mary (Ann Morse) Baker
  1821-1910 .... **TCLC 71**
  See also CA 113; 174
Edel, (Joseph) Leon 1907-1997 .. **CLC 29, 34**
  See also CA 1-4R; 161; CANR 1, 22; DLB
    103; INT CANR-22
Eden, Emily 1797-1869 .... **NCLC 10**
Edgar, David 1948- .. **CLC 42; DAM DRAM**
  See also CA 57-60; CANR 12, 61; DLB 13;
    MTCW 1
Edgerton, Clyde (Carlyle) 1944- ...... **CLC 39**
  See also AAYA 17; CA 118; 134; CANR
    64; INT 134
Edgeworth, Maria 1768-1849 .... **NCLC 1, 51**
  See also DLB 116, 159, 163; SATA 21
Edmonds, Paul
  See Kuttner, Henry

Edmonds, Walter D(umaux)
  1903-1998 .... **CLC 35**
  See also CA 5-8R; CANR 2; DLB 9; MAI-
    CYA; SAAS 4; SATA 1, 27; SATA-Obit
    99
Edmondson, Wallace
  See Ellison, Harlan (Jay)
Edson, Russell CLC 13
  See also CA 33-36R
Edwards, Bronwen Elizabeth
  See Rose, Wendy
Edwards, G(erald) B(asil)
  1899-1976 .... **CLC 25**
  See also CA 110
Edwards, Gus 1939- .... **CLC 43**
  See also CA 108; INT 108
Edwards, Jonathan 1703-1758 .... **LC 7, 54;
    DA; DAC; DAM MST**
  See also DLB 24
Efron, Marina Ivanovna Tsvetaeva
  See Tsvetaeva (Efron), Marina (Ivanovna)
Ehle, John (Marsden, Jr.) 1925- ...... **CLC 27**
  See also CA 9-12R
Ehrenbourg, Ilya (Grigoryevich)
  See Ehrenburg, Ilya (Grigoryevich)
Ehrenburg, Ilya (Grigoryevich)
  1891-1967 .... **CLC 18, 34, 62**
  See also CA 102; 25-28R
Ehrenburg, Ilyo (Grigoryevich)
  See Ehrenburg, Ilya (Grigoryevich)
Ehrenreich, Barbara 1941- .... **CLC 110**
  See also BEST 90:4; CA 73-76; CANR 16,
    37, 62; MTCW 1, 2
Eich, Guenter 1907-1972 .... **CLC 15**
  See also CA 111; 93-96; DLB 69, 124
Eichendorff, Joseph Freiherr von
  1788-1857 .... **NCLC 8**
  See also DLB 90
Eigner, Larry CLC 9
  See also Eigner, Laurence (Joel)
  See also CAAS 23; DLB 5
Eigner, Laurence (Joel) 1927-1996
  See Eigner, Larry
  See also CA 9-12R; 151; CANR 6, 84; DLB
    193
Einstein, Albert 1879-1955 .... **TCLC 65**
  See also CA 121; 133; MTCW 1, 2
Eiseley, Loren Corey 1907-1977 .... **CLC 7**
  See also AAYA 5; CA 1-4R; 73-76; CANR
    6; DLBD 17
Eisenstadt, Jill 1963- .... **CLC 50**
  See also CA 140
Eisenstein, Sergei (Mikhailovich)
  1898-1948 .... **TCLC 57**
  See also CA 114; 149
Eisner, Simon
  See Kornbluth, C(yril) M.
Ekeloef, (Bengt) Gunnar
  1907-1968 ... **CLC 27; DAM POET; PC
    23**
  See also CA 123; 25-28R
Ekelof, (Bengt) Gunnar
  See Ekeloef, (Bengt) Gunnar
Ekelund, Vilhelm 1880-1949 .... **TCLC 75**
Ekwensi, C. O. D.
  See Ekwensi, Cyprian (Odiatu Duaka)
Ekwensi, Cyprian (Odiatu Duaka)
  1921- ...... **CLC 4; BLC 1; DAM MULT**
  See also BW 2, 3; CA 29-32R; CANR 18,
    42, 74; DLB 117; MTCW 1, 2; SATA 66
Elaine TCLC 18
  See also Leverson, Ada
El Crummo
  See Crumb, R(obert)
Elder, Lonne III 1931-1996 .... **DC 8**
  See also BLC 1; BW 1, 3; CA 81-84; 152;
    CANR 25; DAM MULT; DLB 7, 38, 44

Eleanor of Aquitaine 1122-1204 ... **CMLC 39**
Elia
  See Lamb, Charles
Eliade, Mircea 1907-1986 .... **CLC 19**
  See also CA 65-68; 119; CANR 30, 62;
    DLB 220; MTCW 1
Eliot, A. D.
  See Jewett, (Theodora) Sarah Orne
Eliot, Alice
  See Jewett, (Theodora) Sarah Orne
Eliot, Dan
  See Silverberg, Robert
Eliot, George 1819-1880 ...... **NCLC 4, 13, 23,
    41, 49; DA; DAB; DAC; DAM MST,
    NOV; PC 20; WLC**
  See also CDBLB 1832-1890; DA3; DLB
    21, 35, 55
Eliot, John 1604-1690 .... **LC 5**
  See also DLB 24
Eliot, T(homas) S(tearns)
  1888-1965 ...... **CLC 1, 2, 3, 6, 9, 10, 13,
    15, 24, 34, 41, 55, 57, 113; DA; DAB;
    DAC; DAM DRAM, MST, POET; PC
    5; WLC**
  See also AAYA 28; CA 5-8R; 25-28R;
    CANR 41; CDALB 1929-1941; DA3;
    DLB 7, 10, 45, 63; DLBY 88; MTCW 1,
    2
Elizabeth 1866-1941 .... **TCLC 41**
Elkin, Stanley L(awrence)
  1930-1995 .. **CLC 4, 6, 9, 14, 27, 51, 91;
    DAM NOV, POP; SSC 12**
  See also CA 9-12R; 148; CANR 8, 46; DLB
    2, 28; DLBY 80; INT CANR-8; MTCW
    1, 2
Elledge, Scott CLC 34
Elliot, Don
  See Silverberg, Robert
Elliott, Don
  See Silverberg, Robert
Elliott, George P(aul) 1918-1980 .... **CLC 2**
  See also CA 1-4R; 97-100; CANR 2
Elliott, Janice 1931- .... **CLC 47**
  See also CA 13-16R; CANR 8, 29, 84; DLB
    14
Elliott, Sumner Locke 1917-1991 ..... **CLC 38**
  See also CA 5-8R; 134; CANR 2, 21
Elliott, William
  See Bradbury, Ray (Douglas)
Ellis, A. E. CLC 7
Ellis, Alice Thomas CLC 40
  See also Haycraft, Anna (Margaret)
  See also DLB 194; MTCW 1
Ellis, Bret Easton 1964- ..... **CLC 39, 71, 117;
    DAM POP**
  See also AAYA 2; CA 118; 123; CANR 51,
    74; DA3; INT 123; MTCW 1
Ellis, (Henry) Havelock
  1859-1939 .... **TCLC 14**
  See also CA 109; 169; DLB 190
Ellis, Landon
  See Ellison, Harlan (Jay)
Ellis, Trey 1962- .... **CLC 55**
  See also CA 146
Ellison, Harlan (Jay) 1934- ... **CLC 1, 13, 42;
    DAM POP; SSC 14**
  See also AAYA 29; CA 5-8R; CANR 5, 46;
    DLB 8; INT CANR-5; MTCW 1, 2
Ellison, Ralph (Waldo) 1914-1994 .... **CLC 1,
    3, 11, 54, 86, 114; BLC 1; DA; DAB;
    DAC; DAM MST, MULT, NOV; SSC
    26; WLC**
  See also AAYA 19; BW 1, 3; CA 9-12R;
    145; CANR 24, 53; CDALB 1941-1968;
    DA3; DLB 2, 76; DLBY 94; MTCW 1, 2
Ellmann, Lucy (Elizabeth) 1956- ..... **CLC 61**
  See also CA 128

Farquhar, George 1677-1707 ... **LC 21; DAM DRAM**
See also DLB 84

Farrell, J(ames) G(ordon)
1935-1979 .... **CLC 6**
See also CA 73-76; 89-92; CANR 36; DLB 14; MTCW 1

Farrell, James T(homas) 1904-1979 . **CLC 1, 4, 8, 11, 66; SSC 28**
See also CA 5-8R; 89-92; CANR 9, 61; DLB 4, 9, 86; DLBD 2; MTCW 1, 2

Farren, Richard J.
See Betjeman, John

Farren, Richard M.
See Betjeman, John

Fassbinder, Rainer Werner
1946-1982 .... **CLC 20**
See also CA 93-96; 106; CANR 31

Fast, Howard (Melvin) 1914- .. **CLC 23, 131; DAM NOV**
See also AAYA 16; CA 1-4R, 181; CAAE 181; CAAS 18; CANR 1, 33, 54, 75; DLB 9; INT CANR-33; MTCW 1; SATA 7; SATA-Essay 107

Faulcon, Robert
See Holdstock, Robert P.

Faulkner, William (Cuthbert)
1897-1962 .... **CLC 1, 3, 6, 8, 9, 11, 14, 18, 28, 52, 68; DA; DAB; DAC; DAM MST, NOV; SSC 1, 35; WLC**
See also AAYA 7; CA 81-84; CANR 33; CDALB 1929-1941; DA3; DLB 9, 11, 44, 102; DLBD 2; DLBY 86, 97; MTCW 1, 2

Fauset, Jessie Redmon
1884(?)-1961 .... **CLC 19, 54; BLC 2; DAM MULT**
See also BW 1; CA 109; CANR 83; DLB 51

Faust, Frederick (Schiller)
1892-1944(?) .... **TCLC 49; DAM POP**
See also CA 108; 152

Faust, Irvin 1924- .... **CLC 8**
See also CA 33-36R; CANR 28, 67; DLB 2, 28; DLBY 80

Fawkes, Guy
See Benchley, Robert (Charles)

Fearing, Kenneth (Flexner)
1902-1961 .... **CLC 51**
See also CA 93-96; CANR 59; DLB 9

Fecamps, Elise
See Creasey, John

Federman, Raymond 1928- .... **CLC 6, 47**
See also CA 17-20R; CAAS 8; CANR 10, 43, 83; DLBY 80

Federspiel, J(uerg) F. 1931- .... **CLC 42**
See also CA 146

Feiffer, Jules (Ralph) 1929- ..... **CLC 2, 8, 64; DAM DRAM**
See also AAYA 3; CA 17-20R; CANR 30, 59; DLB 7, 44; INT CANR-30; MTCW 1; SATA 8, 61, 111

Feige, Hermann Albert Otto Maximilian
See Traven, B.

Feinberg, David B. 1956-1994 .... **CLC 59**
See also CA 135; 147

Feinstein, Elaine 1930- .... **CLC 36**
See also CA 69-72; CAAS 1; CANR 31, 68; DLB 14, 40; MTCW 1

Feldman, Irving (Mordecai) 1928- ..... **CLC 7**
See also CA 1-4R; CANR 1; DLB 169

Felix-Tchicaya, Gerald
See Tchicaya, Gerald Felix

Fellini, Federico 1920-1993 .... **CLC 16, 85**
See also CA 65-68; 143; CANR 33

Felsen, Henry Gregor 1916-1995 ..... **CLC 17**
See also CA 1-4R; 180; CANR 1; SAAS 2; SATA 1

Fenno, Jack
See Calisher, Hortense

Fenollosa, Ernest (Francisco)
1853-1908 .... **TCLC 91**

Fenton, James Martin 1949- .... **CLC 32**
See also CA 102; DLB 40

Ferber, Edna 1887-1968 .... **CLC 18, 93**
See also AITN 1; CA 5-8R; 25-28R; CANR 68; DLB 9, 28, 86; MTCW 1, 2; SATA 7

Ferguson, Helen
See Kavan, Anna

Ferguson, Samuel 1810-1886 .... **NCLC 33**
See also DLB 32

Fergusson, Robert 1750-1774 .... **LC 29**
See also DLB 109

Ferling, Lawrence
See Ferlinghetti, Lawrence (Monsanto)

Ferlinghetti, Lawrence (Monsanto)
1919(?)- .... **CLC 2, 6, 10, 27, 111; DAM POET; PC 1**
See also CA 5-8R; CANR 3, 41, 73; CDALB 1941-1968; DA3; DLB 5, 16; MTCW 1, 2

Fern, Fanny 1811-1872
See Parton, Sara Payson Willis

Fernandez, Vicente Garcia Huidobro
See Huidobro Fernandez, Vicente Garcia

Ferre, Rosario 1942- .... **SSC 36; HLCS 1**
See also CA 131; CANR 55, 81; DLB 145; HW 1, 2; MTCW 1

Ferrer, Gabriel (Francisco Victor) Miro
See Miro (Ferrer), Gabriel (Francisco Victor)

Ferrier, Susan (Edmonstone)
1782-1854 .... **NCLC 8**
See also DLB 116

Ferrigno, Robert 1948(?)- .... **CLC 65**
See also CA 140

Ferron, Jacques 1921-1985 .... **CLC 94; DAC**
See also CA 117; 129; DLB 60

Feuchtwanger, Lion 1884-1958 .... **TCLC 3**
See also CA 104; DLB 66

Feuillet, Octave 1821-1890 .... **NCLC 45**
See also DLB 192

Feydeau, Georges (Leon Jules Marie)
1862-1921 .... **TCLC 22; DAM DRAM**
See also CA 113; 152; CANR 84; DLB 192

Fichte, Johann Gottlieb
1762-1814 .... **NCLC 62**
See also DLB 90

Ficino, Marsilio 1433-1499 .... **LC 12**

Fiedeler, Hans
See Doeblin, Alfred

Fiedler, Leslie A(aron) 1917- .. **CLC 4, 13, 24**
See also CA 9-12R; CANR 7, 63; DLB 28, 67; MTCW 1, 2

Field, Andrew 1938- .... **CLC 44**
See also CA 97-100; CANR 25

Field, Eugene 1850-1895 .... **NCLC 3**
See also DLB 23, 42, 140; DLBD 13; MAICYA; SATA 16

Field, Gans T.
See Wellman, Manly Wade

Field, Michael 1915-1971 .... **TCLC 43**
See also CA 29-32R

Field, Peter
See Hobson, Laura Z(ametkin)

Fielding, Henry 1707-1754 ..... **LC 1, 46; DA; DAB; DAC; DAM DRAM, MST, NOV; WLC**
See also CDBLB 1660-1789; DA3; DLB 39, 84, 101

Fielding, Sarah 1710-1768 .... **LC 1, 44**
See also DLB 39

Fields, W. C. 1880-1946 .... **TCLC 80**
See also DLB 44

Fierstein, Harvey (Forbes) 1954- .... **CLC 33; DAM DRAM, POP**
See also CA 123; 129; DA3

Figes, Eva 1932- .... **CLC 31**
See also CA 53-56; CANR 4, 44, 83; DLB 14

Finch, Anne 1661-1720 .... **LC 3; PC 21**
See also DLB 95

Finch, Robert (Duer Claydon)
1900- .... **CLC 18**
See also CA 57-60; CANR 9, 24, 49; DLB 88

Findley, Timothy 1930- . **CLC 27, 102; DAC; DAM MST**
See also CA 25-28R; CANR 12, 42, 69; DLB 53

Fink, William
See Mencken, H(enry) L(ouis)

Firbank, Louis 1942-
See Reed, Lou
See also CA 117

Firbank, (Arthur Annesley) Ronald
1886-1926 .... **TCLC 1**
See also CA 104; 177; DLB 36

Fisher, Dorothy (Frances) Canfield
1879-1958 .... **TCLC 87**
See also CA 114; 136; CANR 80; DLB 9, 102; MAICYA; YABC 1

Fisher, M(ary) F(rances) K(ennedy)
1908-1992 .... **CLC 76, 87**
See also CA 77-80; 138; CANR 44; MTCW 1

Fisher, Roy 1930- .... **CLC 25**
See also CA 81-84; CAAS 10; CANR 16; DLB 40

Fisher, Rudolph 1897-1934 .. **TCLC 11; BLC 2; DAM MULT; SSC 25**
See also BW 1, 3; CA 107; 124; CANR 80; DLB 51, 102

Fisher, Vardis (Alvero) 1895-1968 ...... **CLC 7**
See also CA 5-8R; 25-28R; CANR 68; DLB 9, 206

Fiske, Tarleton
See Bloch, Robert (Albert)

Fitch, Clarke
See Sinclair, Upton (Beall)

Fitch, John IV
See Cormier, Robert (Edmund)

Fitzgerald, Captain Hugh
See Baum, L(yman) Frank

FitzGerald, Edward 1809-1883 .... **NCLC 9**
See also DLB 32

Fitzgerald, F(rancis) Scott (Key)
1896-1940 .. **TCLC 1, 6, 14, 28, 55; DA; DAB; DAC; DAM MST, NOV; SSC 6, 31; WLC**
See also AAYA 24; AITN 1; CA 110; 123; CDALB 1917-1929; DA3; DLB 4, 9, 86; DLBD 1, 15, 16; DLBY 81, 96; MTCW 1, 2

Fitzgerald, Penelope 1916-2000 . **CLC 19, 51, 61**
See also CA 85-88; CAAS 10; CANR 56, 86; DLB 14, 194; MTCW 2

Fitzgerald, Robert (Stuart)
1910-1985 .... **CLC 39**
See also CA 1-4R; 114; CANR 1; DLBY 80

FitzGerald, Robert D(avid)
1902-1987 .... **CLC 19**
See also CA 17-20R

Fitzgerald, Zelda (Sayre)
1900-1948 .... **TCLC 52**
See also CA 117; 126; DLBY 84

Flanagan, Thomas (James Bonner)
1923- .... **CLC 25, 52**
See also CA 108; CANR 55; DLBY 80; INT 108; MTCW 1

Flaubert, Gustave 1821-1880 .... **NCLC 2, 10, 19, 62, 66; DA; DAB; DAC; DAM MST, NOV; SSC 11; WLC**
See also DA3; DLB 119

Author Index

Freud, Sigmund 1856-1939 .... **TCLC 52**
See also CA 115; 133; CANR 69; MTCW
1, 2

Friedan, Betty (Naomi) 1921- .... **CLC 74**
See also CA 65-68; CANR 18, 45, 74;
MTCW 1, 2

Friedlander, Saul 1932- .... **CLC 90**
See also CA 117; 130; CANR 72

Friedman, B(ernard) H(arper)
1926- .... **CLC 7**
See also CA 1-4R; CANR 3, 48

Friedman, Bruce Jay 1930- ...... **CLC 3, 5, 56**
See also CA 9-12R; CANR 25, 52; DLB 2,
28; INT CANR-25

Friel, Brian 1929- .... **CLC 5, 42, 59, 115; DC
8**
See also CA 21-24R; CANR 33, 69; DLB
13; MTCW 1

Friis-Baastad, Babbis Ellinor
1921-1970 .... **CLC 12**
See also CA 17-20R; 134; SATA 7

Frisch, Max (Rudolf) 1911-1991 ... **CLC 3, 9,
14, 18, 32, 44; DAM DRAM, NOV**
See also CA 85-88; 134; CANR 32, 74;
DLB 69, 124; MTCW 1, 2

Fromentin, Eugene (Samuel Auguste)
1820-1876 .... **NCLC 10**
See also DLB 123

Frost, Frederick
See Faust, Frederick (Schiller)

Frost, Robert (Lee) 1874-1963 .. **CLC 1, 3, 4,
9, 10, 13, 15, 26, 34, 44; DA; DAB;
DAC; DAM MST, POET; PC 1; WLC**
See also AAYA 21; CA 89-92; CANR 33;
CDALB 1917-1929; DA3; DLB 54;
DLBD 7; MTCW 1, 2; SATA 14

Froude, James Anthony
1818-1894 .... **NCLC 43**
See also DLB 18, 57, 144

Froy, Herald
See Waterhouse, Keith (Spencer)

Fry, Christopher 1907- .... **CLC 2, 10, 14;
DAM DRAM**
See also CA 17-20R; CAAS 23; CANR 9,
30, 74; DLB 13; MTCW 1, 2; SATA 66

Frye, (Herman) Northrop
1912-1991 .... **CLC 24, 70**
See also CA 5-8R; 133; CANR 8, 37; DLB
67, 68; MTCW 1, 2

Fuchs, Daniel 1909-1993 .... **CLC 8, 22**
See also CA 81-84; 142; CAAS 5; CANR
40; DLB 9, 26, 28; DLBY 93

Fuchs, Daniel 1934- .... **CLC 34**
See also CA 37-40R; CANR 14, 48

Fuentes, Carlos 1928- .. **CLC 3, 8, 10, 13, 22,
41, 60, 113; DA; DAB; DAC; DAM
MST, MULT, NOV; HLC 1; SSC 24;
WLC**
See also AAYA 4; AITN 2; CA 69-72;
CANR 10, 32, 68; DA3; DLB 113; HW
1, 2; MTCW 1, 2

Fuentes, Gregorio Lopez y
See Lopez y Fuentes, Gregorio

Fuertes, Gloria 1918- .... **PC 27**
See also CA 178, 180; DLB 108; HW 2;
SATA 115

Fugard, (Harold) Athol 1932- . **CLC 5, 9, 14,
25, 40, 80; DAM DRAM; DC 3**
See also AAYA 17; CA 85-88; CANR 32,
54; MTCW 1

Fugard, Sheila 1932- .... **CLC 48**
See also CA 125

Fukuyama, Francis 1952- .... **CLC 131**
See also CA 140; CANR 72

Fuller, Charles (H., Jr.) 1939- .... **CLC 25;
BLC 2; DAM DRAM, MULT; DC 1**
See also BW 2; CA 108; 112; CANR 87;
DLB 38; INT 112; MTCW 1

Fuller, John (Leopold) 1937- .... **CLC 62**
See also CA 21-24R; CANR 9, 44; DLB 40

Fuller, Margaret **NCLC 5, 50**
See also Fuller, Sarah Margaret

Fuller, Roy (Broadbent) 1912-1991 ... **CLC 4,
28**
See also CA 5-8R; 135; CAAS 10; CANR
53, 83; DLB 15, 20; SATA 87

Fuller, Sarah Margaret 1810-1850
See Fuller, Margaret
See also CDALB 1640-1865; DLB 1, 59,
73, 83, 223

Fulton, Alice 1952- .... **CLC 52**
See also CA 116; CANR 57, 88; DLB 193

Furphy, Joseph 1843-1912 .... **TCLC 25**
See also CA 163

Fussell, Paul 1924- .... **CLC 74**
See also BEST 90:1; CA 17-20R; CANR 8,
21, 35, 69; INT CANR-21; MTCW 1, 2

Futabatei, Shimei 1864-1909 .... **TCLC 44**
See also CA 162; DLB 180

Futrelle, Jacques 1875-1912 .... **TCLC 19**
See also CA 113; 155

Gaboriau, Emile 1835-1873 .... **NCLC 14**

Gadda, Carlo Emilio 1893-1973 .... **CLC 11**
See also CA 89-92; DLB 177

Gaddis, William 1922-1998 ... **CLC 1, 3, 6, 8,
10, 19, 43, 86**
See also CA 17-20R; 172; CANR 21, 48;
DLB 2; MTCW 1, 2

Gage, Walter
See Inge, William (Motter)

Gaines, Ernest J(ames) 1933- ...... **CLC 3, 11,
18, 86; BLC 2; DAM MULT**
See also AAYA 18; AITN 1; BW 2, 3; CA
9-12R; CANR 6, 24, 42, 75; CDALB
1968-1988; CLR 62; DA3; DLB 2, 33,
152; DLBY 80; MTCW 1, 2; SATA 86

Gaitskill, Mary 1954- .... **CLC 69**
See also CA 128; CANR 61

Galdos, Benito Perez
See Perez Galdos, Benito

Gale, Zona 1874-1938 .... **TCLC 7; DAM
DRAM**
See also CA 105; 153; CANR 84; DLB 9,
78

Galeano, Eduardo (Hughes) 1940- . **CLC 72;
HLCS 1**
See also CA 29-32R; CANR 13, 32; HW 1

Galiano, Juan Valera y Alcala
See Valera y Alcala-Galiano, Juan

Galilei, Galileo 1546-1642 .... **LC 45**

Gallagher, Tess 1943- ...... **CLC 18, 63; DAM
POET; PC 9**
See also CA 106; DLB 212

Gallant, Mavis 1922- .. **CLC 7, 18, 38; DAC;
DAM MST; SSC 5**
See also CA 69-72; CANR 29, 69; DLB 53;
MTCW 1, 2

Gallant, Roy A(rthur) 1924- .... **CLC 17**
See also CA 5-8R; CANR 4, 29, 54; CLR
30; MAICYA; SATA 4, 68, 110

Gallico, Paul (William) 1897-1976 ..... **CLC 2**
See also AITN 1; CA 5-8R; 69-72; CANR
23; DLB 9, 171; MAICYA; SATA 13

Gallo, Max Louis 1932- .... **CLC 95**
See also CA 85-88

Gallois, Lucien
See Desnos, Robert

Gallup, Ralph
See Whitemore, Hugh (John)

Galsworthy, John 1867-1933 .... **TCLC 1, 45;
DA; DAB; DAC; DAM DRAM, MST,
NOV; SSC 22; WLC**
See also CA 104; 141; CANR 75; CDBLB
1890-1914; DA3; DLB 10, 34, 98, 162;
DLBD 16; MTCW 1

Galt, John 1779-1839 .... **NCLC 1**
See also DLB 99, 116, 159

Galvin, James 1951- .... **CLC 38**
See also CA 108; CANR 26

Gamboa, Federico 1864-1939 .... **TCLC 36**
See also CA 167; HW 2

Gandhi, M. K.
See Gandhi, Mohandas Karamchand

Gandhi, Mahatma
See Gandhi, Mohandas Karamchand

Gandhi, Mohandas Karamchand
1869-1948 .... **TCLC 59; DAM MULT**
See also CA 121; 132; DA3; MTCW 1, 2

Gann, Ernest Kellogg 1910-1991 ..... **CLC 23**
See also AITN 1; CA 1-4R; 136; CANR 1,
83

Garber, Eric 1943(?)-
See Holleran, Andrew
See also CANR 89

Garcia, Cristina 1958- .... **CLC 76**
See also CA 141; CANR 73; HW 2

Garcia Lorca, Federico 1898-1936 . **TCLC 1,
7, 49; DA; DAB; DAC; DAM DRAM,
MST, MULT, POET; DC 2; HLC 2;
PC 3; WLC**
See also Lorca, Federico Garcia
See also CA 104; 131; CANR 81; DA3;
DLB 108; HW 1, 2; MTCW 1, 2

Garcia Marquez, Gabriel (Jose)
1928- .... **CLC 2, 3, 8, 10, 15, 27, 47, 55,
68; DA; DAB; DAC; DAM MST,
MULT, NOV, POP; HLC 1; SSC 8;
WLC**
See also Marquez, Gabriel (Jose) Garcia
See also AAYA 3, 33; BEST 89:1, 90:4; CA
33-36R; CANR 10, 28, 50, 75, 82; DA3;
DLB 113; HW 1, 2; MTCW 1, 2

Garcilaso de la Vega, El Inca 1503-1536
See also HLCS 1

Gard, Janice
See Latham, Jean Lee

Gard, Roger Martin du
See Martin du Gard, Roger

Gardam, Jane 1928- .... **CLC 43**
See also CA 49-52; CANR 2, 18, 33, 54;
CLR 12; DLB 14, 161; MAICYA; MTCW
1; SAAS 9; SATA 39, 76; SATA-Brief 28

Gardner, Herb(ert) 1934- .... **CLC 44**
See also CA 149

Gardner, John (Champlin), Jr.
1933-1982 ...... **CLC 2, 3, 5, 7, 8, 10, 18,
28, 34; DAM NOV, POP; SSC 7**
See also AITN 1; CA 65-68; 107; CANR
33, 73; CDALBS; DA3; DLB 2; DLBY
82; MTCW 1; SATA 40; SATA-Obit 31

Gardner, John (Edmund) 1926- ...... **CLC 30;
DAM POP**
See also CA 103; CANR 15, 69; MTCW 1

Gardner, Miriam
See Bradley, Marion Zimmer

Gardner, Noel
See Kuttner, Henry

Gardons, S. S.
See Snodgrass, W(illiam) D(e Witt)

Garfield, Leon 1921-1996 .... **CLC 12**
See also AAYA 8; CA 17-20R; 152; CANR
38, 41, 78; CLR 21; DLB 161; JRDA;
MAICYA; SATA 1, 32, 76; SATA-Obit 90

Garland, (Hannibal) Hamlin
1860-1940 .... **TCLC 3; SSC 18**
See also CA 104; DLB 12, 71, 78, 186

Garneau, (Hector de) Saint-Denys
1912-1943 .... **TCLC 13**
See also CA 111; DLB 88

Garner, Alan 1934- ..... **CLC 17; DAB; DAM
POP**
See also AAYA 18; CA 73-76, 178; CAAE
178; CANR 15, 64; CLR 20; DLB 161;
MAICYA; MTCW 1, 2; SATA 18, 69;
SATA-Essay 108

Garner, Hugh 1913-1979 .... **CLC 13**
See also CA 69-72; CANR 31; DLB 68
Garnett, David 1892-1981 .... **CLC 3**
See also CA 5-8R; 103; CANR 17, 79; DLB
34; MTCW 2
Garos, Stephanie
See Katz, Steve
Garrett, George (Palmer) 1929- .. **CLC 3, 11,
51; SSC 30**
See also CA 1-4R; CAAS 5; CANR 1, 42,
67; DLB 2, 5, 130, 152; DLBY 83
Garrick, David 1717-1779 .... **LC 15; DAM
DRAM**
See also DLB 84
Garrigue, Jean 1914-1972 .... **CLC 2, 8**
See also CA 5-8R; 37-40R; CANR 20
Garrison, Frederick
See Sinclair, Upton (Beall)
Garro, Elena 1920(?)-1998
See also CA 131; 169; DLB 145; HLCS 1;
HW 1
Garth, Will
See Hamilton, Edmond; Kuttner, Henry
Garvey, Marcus (Moziah, Jr.)
1887-1940 ...... **TCLC 41; BLC 2; DAM
MULT**
See also BW 1; CA 120; 124; CANR 79
Gary, Romain **CLC 25**
See also Kacew, Romain
See also DLB 83
Gascar, Pierre **CLC 11**
See also Fournier, Pierre
Gascoyne, David (Emery) 1916- .... **CLC 45**
See also CA 65-68; CANR 10, 28, 54; DLB
20; MTCW 1
Gaskell, Elizabeth Cleghorn
1810-1865 .... **NCLC 70; DAB; DAM
MST; SSC 25**
See also CDBLB 1832-1890; DLB 21, 144,
159
Gass, William H(oward) 1924- . **CLC 1, 2, 8,
11, 15, 39, 132; SSC 12**
See also CA 17-20R; CANR 30, 71; DLB
2; MTCW 1, 2
Gassendi, Pierre 1592-1655 .... **LC 54**
Gasset, Jose Ortega y
See Ortega y Gasset, Jose
Gates, Henry Louis, Jr. 1950- .... **CLC 65;
BLCS; DAM MULT**
See also BW 2, 3; CA 109; CANR 25, 53,
75; DA3; DLB 67; MTCW 1
Gautier, Theophile 1811-1872 .. **NCLC 1, 59;
DAM POET; PC 18; SSC 20**
See also DLB 119
Gawsworth, John
See Bates, H(erbert) E(rnest)
Gay, John 1685-1732 .. **LC 49; DAM DRAM**
See also DLB 84, 95
Gay, Oliver
See Gogarty, Oliver St. John
Gaye, Marvin (Penze) 1939-1984 ..... **CLC 26**
See also CA 112
Gebler, Carlo (Ernest) 1954- .... **CLC 39**
See also CA 119; 133
Gee, Maggie (Mary) 1948- .... **CLC 57**
See also CA 130; DLB 207
Gee, Maurice (Gough) 1931- .... **CLC 29**
See also CA 97-100; CANR 67; CLR 56;
SATA 46, 101
Gelbart, Larry (Simon) 1923- .... **CLC 21, 61**
See also CA 73-76; CANR 45
Gelber, Jack 1932- .... **CLC 1, 6, 14, 79**
See also CA 1-4R; CANR 2; DLB 7
Gellhorn, Martha (Ellis)
1908-1998 .... **CLC 14, 60**
See also CA 77-80; 164; CANR 44; DLBY
82, 98

Genet, Jean 1910-1986 .. **CLC 1, 2, 5, 10, 14,
44, 46; DAM DRAM**
See also CA 13-16R; CANR 18; DA3; DLB
72; DLBY 86; MTCW 1, 2
Gent, Peter 1942- .... **CLC 29**
See also AITN 1; CA 89-92; DLBY 82
Gentile, Giovanni 1875-1944 .... **TCLC 96**
See also CA 119
Gentlewoman in New England, A
See Bradstreet, Anne
Gentlewoman in Those Parts, A
See Bradstreet, Anne
George, Jean Craighead 1919- .... **CLC 35**
See also AAYA 8; CA 5-8R; CANR 25;
CLR 1; DLB 52; JRDA; MAICYA; SATA
2, 68
George, Stefan (Anton) 1868-1933 . **TCLC 2,
14**
See also CA 104
Georges, Georges Martin
See Simenon, Georges (Jacques Christian)
Gerhardi, William Alexander
See Gerhardie, William Alexander
Gerhardie, William Alexander
1895-1977 .... **CLC 5**
See also CA 25-28R; 73-76; CANR 18;
DLB 36
Gerstler, Amy 1956- .... **CLC 70**
See also CA 146
Gertler, T. **CLC 34**
See also CA 116; 121; INT 121
Ghalib **NCLC 39, 78**
See also Ghalib, Hsadullah Khan
Ghalib, Hsadullah Khan 1797-1869
See Ghalib
See also DAM POET
Ghelderode, Michel de 1898-1962 ..... **CLC 6,
11; DAM DRAM**
See also CA 85-88; CANR 40, 77
Ghiselin, Brewster 1903- .... **CLC 23**
See also CA 13-16R; CAAS 10; CANR 13
Ghose, Aurabinda 1872-1950 .... **TCLC 63**
See also CA 163
Ghose, Zulfikar 1935- .... **CLC 42**
See also CA 65-68; CANR 67
Ghosh, Amitav 1956- .... **CLC 44**
See also CA 147; CANR 80
Giacosa, Giuseppe 1847-1906 .... **TCLC 7**
See also CA 104
Gibb, Lee
See Waterhouse, Keith (Spencer)
Gibbon, Lewis Grassic **TCLC 4**
See also Mitchell, James Leslie
Gibbons, Kaye 1960- .... **CLC 50, 88; DAM
POP**
See also AAYA 34; CA 151; CANR 75;
DA3; MTCW 1; SATA 117
Gibran, Kahlil 1883-1931 .... **TCLC 1, 9;
DAM POET, POP; PC 9**
See also CA 104; 150; DA3; MTCW 2
Gibran, Khalil
See Gibran, Kahlil
Gibson, William 1914- .. **CLC 23; DA; DAB;
DAC; DAM DRAM, MST**
See also CA 9-12R; CANR 9, 42, 75; DLB
7; MTCW 1; SATA 66
Gibson, William (Ford) 1948- ... **CLC 39, 63;
DAM POP**
See also AAYA 12; CA 126; 133; CANR
52, 90; DA3; MTCW 1
Gide, Andre (Paul Guillaume)
1869-1951 . **TCLC 5, 12, 36; DA; DAB;
DAC; DAM MST, NOV; SSC 13; WLC**
See also CA 104; 124; DA3; DLB 65;
MTCW 1, 2
Gifford, Barry (Colby) 1946- .... **CLC 34**
See also CA 65-68; CANR 9, 30, 40, 90

Gilbert, Frank
See De Voto, Bernard (Augustine)
Gilbert, W(illiam) S(chwenck)
1836-1911 .... **TCLC 3; DAM DRAM,
POET**
See also CA 104; 173; SATA 36
Gilbreth, Frank B., Jr. 1911- .... **CLC 17**
See also CA 9-12R; SATA 2
Gilchrist, Ellen 1935- ...... **CLC 34, 48; DAM
POP; SSC 14**
See also CA 113; 116; CANR 41, 61; DLB
130; MTCW 1, 2
Giles, Molly 1942- .... **CLC 39**
See also CA 126
Gill, Eric 1882-1940 .... **TCLC 85**
Gill, Patrick
See Creasey, John
Gilliam, Terry (Vance) 1940- .... **CLC 21**
See also Monty Python
See also AAYA 19; CA 108; 113; CANR
35; INT 113
Gillian, Jerry
See Gilliam, Terry (Vance)
Gilliatt, Penelope (Ann Douglass)
1932-1993 .... **CLC 2, 10, 13, 53**
See also AITN 2; CA 13-16R; 141; CANR
49; DLB 14
Gilman, Charlotte (Anna) Perkins (Stetson)
1860-1935 .... **TCLC 9, 37; SSC 13**
See also CA 106; 150; DLB 221; MTCW 1
Gilmour, David 1949- .... **CLC 35**
See also CA 138, 147
Gilpin, William 1724-1804 .... **NCLC 30**
Gilray, J. D.
See Mencken, H(enry) L(ouis)
Gilroy, Frank D(aniel) 1925- .... **CLC 2**
See also CA 81-84; CANR 32, 64, 86; DLB
7
Gilstrap, John 1957(?)- .... **CLC 99**
See also CA 160
Ginsberg, Allen 1926-1997 .... **CLC 1, 2, 3, 4,
6, 13, 36, 69, 109; DA; DAB; DAC;
DAM MST, POET; PC 4; WLC**
See also AAYA 33; AITN 1; CA 1-4R; 157;
CANR 2, 41, 63; CDALB 1941-1968;
DA3; DLB 5, 16, 169; MTCW 1, 2
Ginzburg, Natalia 1916-1991 .... **CLC 5, 11,
54, 70**
See also CA 85-88; 135; CANR 33; DLB
177; MTCW 1, 2
Giono, Jean 1895-1970 .... **CLC 4, 11**
See also CA 45-48; 29-32R; CANR 2, 35;
DLB 72; MTCW 1
Giovanni, Nikki 1943- .... **CLC 2, 4, 19, 64,
117; BLC 2; DA; DAB; DAC; DAM
MST, MULT, POET; PC 19; WLCS**
See also AAYA 22; AITN 1; BW 2, 3; CA
29-32R; CAAS 6; CANR 18, 41, 60, 91;
CDALBS; CLR 6; DA3; DLB 5, 41; INT
CANR-18; MAICYA; MTCW 1, 2; SATA
24, 107
Giovene, Andrea 1904- .... **CLC 7**
See also CA 85-88
Gippius, Zinaida (Nikolayevna) 1869-1945
See Hippius, Zinaida
See also CA 106
Giraudoux, (Hippolyte) Jean
1882-1944 .... **TCLC 2, 7; DAM DRAM**
See also CA 104; DLB 65
Gironella, Jose Maria 1917- .... **CLC 11**
See also CA 101
Gissing, George (Robert)
1857-1903 .... **TCLC 3, 24, 47; SSC 37**
See also CA 105; 167; DLB 18, 135, 184
Giurlani, Aldo
See Palazzeschi, Aldo
Gladkov, Fyodor (Vasilyevich)
1883-1958 .... **TCLC 27**
See also CA 170

Gudjonsson, Halldor Kiljan 1902-1998
  See Laxness, Halldor
  See also CA 103; 164
Guenter, Erich
  See Eich, Guenter
Guest, Barbara 1920- .... **CLC 34**
  See also CA 25-28R; CANR 11, 44, 84;
  DLB 5, 193
Guest, Edgar A(lbert) 1881-1959 ... **TCLC 95**
  See also CA 112; 168
Guest, Judith (Ann) 1936- .... **CLC 8, 30;**
  DAM NOV, POP
  See also AAYA 7; CA 77-80; CANR 15,
  75; DA3; INT CANR-15; MTCW 1, 2
Guevara, Che CLC 87; HLC 1
  See also Guevara (Serna), Ernesto
Guevara (Serna), Ernesto
  1928-1967 .... **CLC 87; DAM MULT;**
  HLC 1
  See also Guevara, Che
  See also CA 127; 111; CANR 56; HW 1
Guicciardini, Francesco 1483-1540 ..... **LC 49**
Guild, Nicholas M. 1944- .... **CLC 33**
  See also CA 93-96
Guillemin, Jacques
  See Sartre, Jean-Paul
Guillen, Jorge 1893-1984 .... **CLC 11; DAM**
  MULT, POET; HLCS 1
  See also CA 89-92; 112; DLB 108; HW 1
Guillen, Nicolas (Cristobal)
  1902-1989 ... **CLC 48, 79; BLC 2; DAM**
  MST, MULT, POET; HLC 1; PC 23
  See also BW 2; CA 116; 125; 129; CANR
  84; HW 1
Guillevic, (Eugene) 1907- .... **CLC 33**
  See also CA 93-96
Guillois
  See Desnos, Robert
Guillois, Valentin
  See Desnos, Robert
Guimaraes Rosa, Joao 1908-1967
  See also CA 175; HLCS 2
Guiney, Louise Imogen
  1861-1920 .... **TCLC 41**
  See also CA 160; DLB 54
Guiraldes, Ricardo (Guillermo)
  1886-1927 .... **TCLC 39**
  See also CA 131; HW 1; MTCW 1
Gumilev, Nikolai (Stepanovich)
  1886-1921 .... **TCLC 60**
  See also CA 165
Gunesekera, Romesh 1954- .... **CLC 91**
  See also CA 159
Gunn, Bill CLC 5
  See also Gunn, William Harrison
  See also DLB 38
Gunn, Thom(son William) 1929- .. **CLC 3, 6,**
  18, 32, 81; DAM POET; PC 26
  See also CA 17-20R; CANR 9, 33; CDBLB
  1960 to Present; DLB 27; INT CANR-33;
  MTCW 1
Gunn, William Harrison 1934(?)-1989
  See Gunn, Bill
  See also AITN 1; BW 1, 3; CA 13-16R;
  128; CANR 12, 25, 76
Gunnars, Kristjana 1948- .... **CLC 69**
  See also CA 113; DLB 60
Gurdjieff, G(eorgei) I(vanovich)
  1877(?)-1949 .... **TCLC 71**
  See also CA 157
Gurganus, Allan 1947- . **CLC 70; DAM POP**
  See also BEST 90:1; CA 135
Gurney, A(lbert) R(amsdell), Jr.
  1930- ..... **CLC 32, 50, 54; DAM DRAM**
  See also CA 77-80; CANR 32, 64
Gurney, Ivor (Bertie) 1890-1937 ... **TCLC 33**
  See also CA 167
Gurney, Peter
  See Gurney, A(lbert) R(amsdell), Jr.

Guro, Elena 1877-1913 .... **TCLC 56**
Gustafson, James M(oody) 1925- ... **CLC 100**
  See also CA 25-28R; CANR 37
Gustafson, Ralph (Barker) 1909- ..... **CLC 36**
  See also CA 21-24R; CANR 8, 45, 84; DLB
  88
Gut, Gom
  See Simenon, Georges (Jacques Christian)
Guterson, David 1956- .... **CLC 91**
  See also CA 132; CANR 73; MTCW 2
Guthrie, A(lfred) B(ertram), Jr.
  1901-1991 .... **CLC 23**
  See also CA 57-60; 134; CANR 24; DLB
  212; SATA 62; SATA-Obit 67
Guthrie, Isobel
  See Grieve, C(hristopher) M(urray)
Guthrie, Woodrow Wilson 1912-1967
  See Guthrie, Woody
  See also CA 113; 93-96
Guthrie, Woody CLC 35
  See also Guthrie, Woodrow Wilson
Gutierrez Najera, Manuel 1859-1895
  See also HLCS 2
Guy, Rosa (Cuthbert) 1928- .... **CLC 26**
  See also AAYA 4; BW 2; CA 17-20R;
  CANR 14, 34, 83; CLR 13; DLB 33;
  JRDA; MAICYA; SATA 14, 62
Gwendolyn
  See Bennett, (Enoch) Arnold
H. D. CLC 3, 8, 14, 31, 34, 73; PC 5
  See also Doolittle, Hilda
H. de V.
  See Buchan, John
Haavikko, Paavo Juhani 1931- .. **CLC 18, 34**
  See also CA 106
Habbema, Koos
  See Heijermans, Herman
Habermas, Juergen 1929- .... **CLC 104**
  See also CA 109; CANR 85
Habermas, Jurgen
  See Habermas, Juergen
Hacker, Marilyn 1942- ...... **CLC 5, 9, 23, 72,**
  91; DAM POET
  See also CA 77-80; CANR 68; DLB 120
Haeckel, Ernst Heinrich (Philipp August)
  1834-1919 .... **TCLC 83**
  See also CA 157
Hafiz c. 1326-1389(?) .... **CMLC 34**
Hafiz c. 1326-1389 .... **CMLC 34**
Haggard, H(enry) Rider
  1856-1925 .... **TCLC 11**
  See also CA 108; 148; DLB 70, 156, 174,
  178; MTCW 2; SATA 16
Hagiosy, L.
  See Larbaud, Valery (Nicolas)
Hagiwara Sakutaro 1886-1942 ..... **TCLC 60;**
  PC 18
Haig, Fenil
  See Ford, Ford Madox
Haig-Brown, Roderick (Langmere)
  1908-1976 .... **CLC 21**
  See also CA 5-8R; 69-72; CANR 4, 38, 83;
  CLR 31; DLB 88; MAICYA; SATA 12
Hailey, Arthur 1920- ..... **CLC 5; DAM NOV,**
  POP
  See also AITN 2; BEST 90:3; CA 1-4R;
  CANR 2, 36, 75; DLB 88; DLBY 82;
  MTCW 1, 2
Hailey, Elizabeth Forsythe 1938- ... **CLC 40**
  See also CA 93-96; CAAS 1; CANR 15,
  48; INT CANR-15
Haines, John (Meade) 1924- .... **CLC 58**
  See also CA 17-20R; CANR 13, 34; DLB
  212
Hakluyt, Richard 1552-1616 .... **LC 31**
Haldeman, Joe (William) 1943- .... **CLC 61**
  See also Graham, Robert

See also CA 53-56, 179; CAAE 179; CAAS
  25; CANR 6, 70, 72; DLB 8; INT
  CANR-6
Hale, Sarah Josepha (Buell)
  1788-1879 .... **NCLC 75**
  See also DLB 1, 42, 73
Haley, Alex(ander Murray Palmer)
  1921-1992 . **CLC 8, 12, 76; BLC 2; DA;**
  DAB; DAC; DAM MST, MULT, POP
  See also AAYA 26; BW 2, 3; CA 77-80;
  136; CANR 61; CDALBS; DA3; DLB 38;
  MTCW 1, 2
Haliburton, Thomas Chandler
  1796-1865 .... **NCLC 15**
  See also DLB 11, 99
Hall, Donald (Andrew, Jr.) 1928- ...... **CLC 1,**
  13, 37, 59; DAM POET
  See also CA 5-8R; CAAS 7; CANR 2, 44,
  64; DLB 5; MTCW 1; SATA 23, 97
Hall, Frederic Sauser
  See Sauser-Hall, Frederic
Hall, James
  See Kuttner, Henry
Hall, James Norman 1887-1951 ..... **TCLC 23**
  See also CA 123; 173; SATA 21
Hall, Radclyffe
  See Hall, (Marguerite) Radclyffe
  See also MTCW 2
Hall, (Marguerite) Radclyffe
  1886-1943 .... **TCLC 12**
  See also CA 110; 150; CANR 83; DLB 191
Hall, Rodney 1935- .... **CLC 51**
  See also CA 109; CANR 69
Halleck, Fitz-Greene 1790-1867 .... **NCLC 47**
  See also DLB 3
Halliday, Michael
  See Creasey, John
Halpern, Daniel 1945- .... **CLC 14**
  See also CA 33-36R
Hamburger, Michael (Peter Leopold)
  1924- .... **CLC 5, 14**
  See also CA 5-8R; CAAS 4; CANR 2, 47;
  DLB 27
Hamill, Pete 1935- .... **CLC 10**
  See also CA 25-28R; CANR 18, 71
Hamilton, Alexander
  1755(?)-1804 .... **NCLC 49**
  See also DLB 37
Hamilton, Clive
  See Lewis, C(live) S(taples)
Hamilton, Edmond 1904-1977 .... **CLC 1**
  See also CA 1-4R; CANR 3, 84; DLB 8
Hamilton, Eugene (Jacob) Lee
  See Lee-Hamilton, Eugene (Jacob)
Hamilton, Franklin
  See Silverberg, Robert
Hamilton, Gail
  See Corcoran, Barbara
Hamilton, Mollie
  See Kaye, M(ary) M(argaret)
Hamilton, (Anthony Walter) Patrick
  1904-1962 .... **CLC 51**
  See also CA 176; 113; DLB 191
Hamilton, Virginia 1936- ...... **CLC 26; DAM**
  MULT
  See also AAYA 2, 21; BW 2, 3; CA 25-28R;
  CANR 20, 37, 73; CLR 1, 11, 40; DLB
  33, 52; INT CANR-20; JRDA; MAICYA;
  MTCW 1, 2; SATA 4, 56, 79
Hammett, (Samuel) Dashiell
  1894-1961 .... **CLC 3, 5, 10, 19, 47; SSC**
  17
  See also AITN 1; CA 81-84; CANR 42;
  CDALB 1929-1941; DA3; DLBD 6;
  DLBY 96; MTCW 1, 2
Hammon, Jupiter 1711(?)-1800(?) . **NCLC 5;**
  BLC 2; DAM MULT, POET; PC 16
  See also DLB 31, 50

Heyward, (Edwin) DuBose
1885-1940 .... **TCLC 59**
See also CA 108; 157; DLB 7, 9, 45; SATA
21

Hibbert, Eleanor Alice Burford
1906-1993 .... **CLC 7; DAM POP**
See also BEST 90:4; CA 17-20R; 140;
CANR 9, 28, 59; MTCW 2; SATA 2;
SATA-Obit 74

Hichens, Robert (Smythe)
1864-1950 .... **TCLC 64**
See also CA 162; DLB 153

Higgins, George V(incent)
1939-1999 .... **CLC 4, 7, 10, 18**
See also CA 77-80; 186; CAAS 5; CANR
17, 51, 89; DLB 2; DLBY 81, 98; INT
CANR-17; MTCW 1

Higginson, Thomas Wentworth
1823-1911 .... **TCLC 36**
See also CA 162; DLB 1, 64

Highet, Helen
See MacInnes, Helen (Clark)

Highsmith, (Mary) Patricia
1921-1995 .... **CLC 2, 4, 14, 42, 102;
DAM NOV, POP**
See also CA 1-4R; 147; CANR 1, 20, 48,
62; DA3; MTCW 1, 2

Highwater, Jamake (Mamake)
1942(?)- .... **CLC 12**
See also AAYA 7; CA 65-68; CAAS 7;
CANR 10, 34, 84; CLR 17; DLB 52;
DLBY 85; JRDA; MAICYA; SATA 32,
69; SATA-Brief 30

Highway, Tomson 1951- .... **CLC 92; DAC;
DAM MULT**
See also CA 151; CANR 75; MTCW 2;
NNAL

Higuchi, Ichiyo 1872-1896 .... **NCLC 49**

Hijuelos, Oscar 1951- .... **CLC 65; DAM
MULT, POP; HLC 1**
See also AAYA 25; BEST 90:1; CA 123;
CANR 50, 75; DA3; DLB 145; HW 1, 2;
MTCW 2

Hikmet, Nazim 1902(?)-1963 .... **CLC 40**
See also CA 141; 93-96

Hildegard von Bingen 1098-1179 . **CMLC 20**
See also DLB 148

Hildesheimer, Wolfgang 1916-1991 .. **CLC 49**
See also CA 101; 135; DLB 69, 124

Hill, Geoffrey (William) 1932- ...... **CLC 5, 8,
18, 45; DAM POET**
See also CA 81-84; CANR 21, 89; CDBLB
1960 to Present; DLB 40; MTCW 1

Hill, George Roy 1921- .... **CLC 26**
See also CA 110; 122

Hill, John
See Koontz, Dean R(ay)

Hill, Susan (Elizabeth) 1942- .... **CLC 4, 113;
DAB; DAM MST, NOV**
See also CA 33-36R; CANR 29, 69; DLB
14, 139; MTCW 1

Hillerman, Tony 1925- . **CLC 62; DAM POP**
See also AAYA 6; BEST 89:1; CA 29-32R;
CANR 21, 42, 65; DA3; DLB 206; SATA
6

Hillesum, Etty 1914-1943 .... **TCLC 49**
See also CA 137

Hilliard, Noel (Harvey) 1929- .... **CLC 15**
See also CA 9-12R; CANR 7, 69

Hillis, Rick 1956- .... **CLC 66**
See also CA 134

Hilton, James 1900-1954 .... **TCLC 21**
See also CA 108; 169; DLB 34, 77; SATA
34

Himes, Chester (Bomar) 1909-1984 .. **CLC 2,
4, 7, 18, 58, 108; BLC 2; DAM MULT**
See also BW 2; CA 25-28R; 114; CANR
22, 89; DLB 2, 76, 143; MTCW 1, 2

Hinde, Thomas **CLC 6, 11**

See also Chitty, Thomas Willes

Hine, (William) Daryl 1936- .... **CLC 15**
See also CA 1-4R; CAAS 15; CANR 1, 20;
DLB 60

Hinkson, Katharine Tynan
See Tynan, Katharine

Hinojosa(-Smith), Rolando (R.) 1929-
See Hinojosa-Smith, Rolando
See also CA 131; CAAS 16; CANR 62;
DAM MULT; DLB 82; HLC 1; HW 1, 2;
MTCW 2

Hinojosa-Smith, Rolando 1929-
See Hinojosa(-Smith), Rolando (R.)
See also CAAS 16; HLC 1; MTCW 2

Hinton, S(usan) E(loise) 1950- .... **CLC 30,
111; DA; DAB; DAC; DAM MST,
NOV**
See also AAYA 2, 33; CA 81-84; CANR
32, 62; CDALBS; CLR 3, 23; DA3;
JRDA; MAICYA; MTCW 1, 2; SATA 19,
58, 115

Hippius, Zinaida **TCLC 9**
See also Gippius, Zinaida (Nikolayevna)

Hiraoka, Kimitake 1925-1970
See Mishima, Yukio
See also CA 97-100; 29-32R; DAM DRAM;
DA3; MTCW 1, 2

Hirsch, E(ric) D(onald), Jr. 1928- .... **CLC 79**
See also CA 25-28R; CANR 27, 51; DLB
67; INT CANR-27; MTCW 1

Hirsch, Edward 1950- .... **CLC 31, 50**
See also CA 104; CANR 20, 42; DLB 120

Hitchcock, Alfred (Joseph)
1899-1980 .... **CLC 16**
See also AAYA 22; CA 159; 97-100; SATA
27; SATA-Obit 24

Hitler, Adolf 1889-1945 .... **TCLC 53**
See also CA 117; 147

Hoagland, Edward 1932- .... **CLC 28**
See also CA 1-4R; CANR 2, 31, 57; DLB
6; SATA 51

Hoban, Russell (Conwell) 1925- . **CLC 7, 25;
DAM NOV**
See also CA 5-8R; CANR 23, 37, 66; CLR
3; DLB 52; MAICYA; MTCW 1, 2; SATA
1, 40, 78

Hobbes, Thomas 1588-1679 .... **LC 36**
See also DLB 151

Hobbs, Perry
See Blackmur, R(ichard) P(almer)

Hobson, Laura Z(ametkin)
1900-1986 .... **CLC 7, 25**
See also CA 17-20R; 118; CANR 55; DLB
28; SATA 52

Hochhuth, Rolf 1931- .. **CLC 4, 11, 18; DAM
DRAM**
See also CA 5-8R; CANR 33, 75; DLB 124;
MTCW 1, 2

Hochman, Sandra 1936- .... **CLC 3, 8**
See also CA 5-8R; DLB 5

Hochwaelder, Fritz 1911-1986 .... **CLC 36;
DAM DRAM**
See also CA 29-32R; 120; CANR 42;
MTCW 1

Hochwalder, Fritz
See Hochwaelder, Fritz

Hocking, Mary (Eunice) 1921- .... **CLC 13**
See also CA 101; CANR 18, 40

Hodgins, Jack 1938- .... **CLC 23**
See also CA 93-96; DLB 60

Hodgson, William Hope
1877(?)-1918 .... **TCLC 13**
See also CA 111; 164; DLB 70, 153, 156,
178; MTCW 2

Hoeg, Peter 1957- .... **CLC 95**
See also CA 151; CANR 75; DA3; MTCW
2

Hoffman, Alice 1952- ... **CLC 51; DAM NOV**
See also CA 77-80; CANR 34, 66; MTCW
1, 2

Hoffman, Daniel (Gerard) 1923- . **CLC 6, 13,
23**
See also CA 1-4R; CANR 4; DLB 5

Hoffman, Stanley 1944- .... **CLC 5**
See also CA 77-80

Hoffman, William M(oses) 1939- ..... **CLC 40**
See also CA 57-60; CANR 11, 71

Hoffmann, E(rnst) T(heodor) A(madeus)
1776-1822 .... **NCLC 2; SSC 13**
See also DLB 90; SATA 27

Hofmann, Gert 1931- .... **CLC 54**
See also CA 128

Hofmannsthal, Hugo von
1874-1929 ...... **TCLC 11; DAM DRAM;
DC 4**
See also CA 106; 153; DLB 81, 118

Hogan, Linda 1947- .. **CLC 73; DAM MULT**
See also CA 120; CANR 45, 73; DLB 175;
NNAL

Hogarth, Charles
See Creasey, John

Hogarth, Emmett
See Polonsky, Abraham (Lincoln)

Hogg, James 1770-1835 .... **NCLC 4**
See also DLB 93, 116, 159

Holbach, Paul Henri Thiry Baron
1723-1789 .... **LC 14**

Holberg, Ludvig 1684-1754 .... **LC 6**

Holcroft, Thomas 1745-1809 .... **NCLC 85**
See also DLB 39, 89, 158

Holden, Ursula 1921- .... **CLC 18**
See also CA 101; CAAS 8; CANR 22

Holderlin, (Johann Christian) Friedrich
1770-1843 .... **NCLC 16; PC 4**

Holdstock, Robert
See Holdstock, Robert P.

Holdstock, Robert P. 1948- .... **CLC 39**
See also CA 131; CANR 81

Holland, Isabelle 1920- .... **CLC 21**
See also AAYA 11; CA 21-24R, 181; CAAE
181; CANR 10, 25, 47; CLR 57; JRDA;
MAICYA; SATA 8, 70; SATA-Essay 103

Holland, Marcus
See Caldwell, (Janet Miriam) Taylor
(Holland)

Hollander, John 1929- .... **CLC 2, 5, 8, 14**
See also CA 1-4R; CANR 1, 52; DLB 5;
SATA 13

Hollander, Paul
See Silverberg, Robert

Holleran, Andrew 1943(?)- .... **CLC 38**
See also Garber, Eric
See also CA 144

Hollinghurst, Alan 1954- .... **CLC 55, 91**
See also CA 114; DLB 207

Hollis, Jim
See Summers, Hollis (Spurgeon, Jr.)

Holly, Buddy 1936-1959 .... **TCLC 65**

Holmes, Gordon
See Shiel, M(atthew) P(hipps)

Holmes, John
See Souster, (Holmes) Raymond

Holmes, John Clellon 1926-1988 ...... **CLC 56**
See also CA 9-12R; 125; CANR 4; DLB 16

Holmes, Oliver Wendell, Jr.
1841-1935 .... **TCLC 77**
See also CA 114; 186

Holmes, Oliver Wendell
1809-1894 .... **NCLC 14, 81**
See also CDALB 1640-1865; DLB 1, 189;
SATA 34

Holmes, Raymond
See Souster, (Holmes) Raymond

Holt, Victoria
See Hibbert, Eleanor Alice Burford

Jones, Edward P. 1950- .... **CLC 76**
See also BW 2, 3; CA 142; CANR 79

Jones, Gayl 1949- ..... **CLC 6, 9, 131; BLC 2; DAM MULT**
See also BW 2, 3; CA 77-80; CANR 27, 66; DA3; DLB 33; MTCW 1, 2

Jones, James 1921-1977 ...... **CLC 1, 3, 10, 39**
See also AITN 1, 2; CA 1-4R; 69-72; CANR 6; DLB 2, 143; DLBD 17; DLBY 98; MTCW 1

Jones, John J.
See Lovecraft, H(oward) P(hillips)

Jones, LeRoi **CLC 1, 2, 3, 5, 10, 14**
See also Baraka, Amiri
See also MTCW 2

Jones, Louis B. 1953- .... **CLC 65**
See also CA 141; CANR 73

Jones, Madison (Percy, Jr.) 1925- ...... **CLC 4**
See also CA 13-16R; CAAS 11; CANR 7, 54, 83; DLB 152

Jones, Mervyn 1922- .... **CLC 10, 52**
See also CA 45-48; CAAS 5; CANR 1, 91; MTCW 1

Jones, Mick 1956(?)- .... **CLC 30**

Jones, Nettie (Pearl) 1941- .... **CLC 34**
See also BW 2; CA 137; CAAS 20; CANR 88

Jones, Preston 1936-1979 .... **CLC 10**
See also CA 73-76; 89-92; DLB 7

Jones, Robert F(rancis) 1934- .... **CLC 7**
See also CA 49-52; CANR 2, 61

Jones, Rod 1953- .... **CLC 50**
See also CA 128

Jones, Terence Graham Parry
1942- .... **CLC 21**
See also Jones, Terry; Monty Python
See also CA 112; 116; CANR 35; INT 116

Jones, Terry
See Jones, Terence Graham Parry
See also SATA 67; SATA-Brief 51

Jones, Thom (Douglas) 1945(?)- .... **CLC 81**
See also CA 157; CANR 88

Jong, Erica 1942- .... **CLC 4, 6, 8, 18, 83; DAM NOV, POP**
See also AITN 1; BEST 90:2; CA 73-76; CANR 26, 52, 75; DA3; DLB 2, 5, 28, 152; INT CANR-26; MTCW 1, 2

Jonson, Ben(jamin) 1572(?)-1637 .. **LC 6, 33; DA; DAB; DAC; DAM DRAM, MST, POET; DC 4; PC 17; WLC**
See also CDBLB Before 1660; DLB 62, 121

Jordan, June 1936- .... **CLC 5, 11, 23, 114; BLCS; DAM MULT, POET**
See also AAYA 2; BW 2, 3; CA 33-36R; CANR 25, 70; CLR 10; DLB 38; MAI-CYA; MTCW 1; SATA 4

Jordan, Neil (Patrick) 1950- .... **CLC 110**
See also CA 124; 130; CANR 54; INT 130

Jordan, Pat(rick M.) 1941- .... **CLC 37**
See also CA 33-36R

Jorgensen, Ivar
See Ellison, Harlan (Jay)

Jorgenson, Ivar
See Silverberg, Robert

Josephus, Flavius c. 37-100 .... **CMLC 13**

Josiah Allen's Wife
See Holley, Marietta

Josipovici, Gabriel (David) 1940- ...... **CLC 6, 43**
See also CA 37-40R; CAAS 8; CANR 47, 84; DLB 14

Joubert, Joseph 1754-1824 .... **NCLC 9**

Jouve, Pierre Jean 1887-1976 .... **CLC 47**
See also CA 65-68

Jovine, Francesco 1902-1950 .... **TCLC 79**

Joyce, James (Augustine Aloysius)
1882-1941 .. **TCLC 3, 8, 16, 35, 52; DA; DAB; DAC; DAM MST, NOV, POET; PC 22; SSC 3, 26; WLC**
See also CA 104; 126; CDBLB 1914-1945; DA3; DLB 10, 19, 36, 162; MTCW 1, 2

Jozsef, Attila 1905-1937 .... **TCLC 22**
See also CA 116

Juana Ines de la Cruz 1651(?)-1695 .... **LC 5; HLCS 1; PC 24**

Judd, Cyril
See Kornbluth, C(yril) M.; Pohl, Frederik

Juenger, Ernst 1895-1998 .... **CLC 125**
See also CA 101; 167; CANR 21, 47; DLB 56

Julian of Norwich 1342(?)-1416(?) . **LC 6, 52**
See also DLB 146

Junger, Ernst
See Juenger, Ernst

Junger, Sebastian 1962- .... **CLC 109**
See also AAYA 28; CA 165

Juniper, Alex
See Hospital, Janette Turner

Junius
See Luxemburg, Rosa

Just, Ward (Swift) 1935- .... **CLC 4, 27**
See also CA 25-28R; CANR 32, 87; INT CANR-32

Justice, Donald (Rodney) 1925- .. **CLC 6, 19, 102; DAM POET**
See also CA 5-8R; CANR 26, 54, 74; DLBY 83; INT CANR-26; MTCW 2

Juvenal c. 60-c. 13 .... **CMLC 8**
See also Juvenalis, Decimus Junius
See also DLB 211

Juvenalis, Decimus Junius 55(?)-c. 127(?)
See Juvenal

Juvenis
See Bourne, Randolph S(illiman)

Kacew, Romain 1914-1980
See Gary, Romain
See also CA 108; 102

Kadare, Ismail 1936- .... **CLC 52**
See also CA 161

Kadohata, Cynthia **CLC 59, 122**
See also CA 140

Kafka, Franz 1883-1924 . **TCLC 2, 6, 13, 29, 47, 53; DA; DAB; DAC; DAM MST, NOV; SSC 5, 29, 35; WLC**
See also AAYA 31; CA 105; 126; DA3; DLB 81; MTCW 1, 2

Kahanovitsch, Pinkhes
See Der Nister

Kahn, Roger 1927- .... **CLC 30**
See also CA 25-28R; CANR 44, 69; DLB 171; SATA 37

Kain, Saul
See Sassoon, Siegfried (Lorraine)

Kaiser, Georg 1878-1945 .... **TCLC 9**
See also CA 106; DLB 124

Kaletski, Alexander 1946- .... **CLC 39**
See also CA 118; 143

Kalidasa fl. c. 400- .... **CMLC 9; PC 22**

Kallman, Chester (Simon)
1921-1975 .... **CLC 2**
See also CA 45-48; 53-56; CANR 3

Kaminsky, Melvin 1926-
See Brooks, Mel
See also CA 65-68; CANR 16

Kaminsky, Stuart M(elvin) 1934- ..... **CLC 59**
See also CA 73-76; CANR 29, 53, 89

Kandinsky, Wassily 1866-1944 .... **TCLC 92**
See also CA 118; 155

Kane, Francis
See Robbins, Harold

Kane, Paul
See Simon, Paul (Frederick)

Kanin, Garson 1912-1999 .... **CLC 22**
See also AITN 1; CA 5-8R; 177; CANR 7, 78; DLB 7

Kaniuk, Yoram 1930- .... **CLC 19**
See also CA 134

Kant, Immanuel 1724-1804 ..... **NCLC 27, 67**
See also DLB 94

Kantor, MacKinlay 1904-1977 .... **CLC 7**
See also CA 61-64; 73-76; CANR 60, 63; DLB 9, 102; MTCW 2

Kaplan, David Michael 1946- .... **CLC 50**

Kaplan, James 1951- .... **CLC 59**
See also CA 135

Karageorge, Michael
See Anderson, Poul (William)

Karamzin, Nikolai Mikhailovich
1766-1826 .... **NCLC 3**
See also DLB 150

Karapanou, Margarita 1946- .... **CLC 13**
See also CA 101

Karinthy, Frigyes 1887-1938 .... **TCLC 47**
See also CA 170

Karl, Frederick R(obert) 1927- .... **CLC 34**
See also CA 5-8R; CANR 3, 44

Kastel, Warren
See Silverberg, Robert

Kataev, Evgeny Petrovich 1903-1942
See Petrov, Evgeny
See also CA 120

Kataphusin
See Ruskin, John

Katz, Steve 1935- .... **CLC 47**
See also CA 25-28R; CAAS 14, 64; CANR 12; DLBY 83

Kauffman, Janet 1945- .... **CLC 42**
See also CA 117; CANR 43, 84; DLBY 86

Kaufman, Bob (Garnell) 1925-1986 . **CLC 49**
See also BW 1; CA 41-44R; 118; CANR 22; DLB 16, 41

Kaufman, George S. 1889-1961 ...... **CLC 38; DAM DRAM**
See also CA 108; 93-96; DLB 7; INT 108; MTCW 2

Kaufman, Sue **CLC 3, 8**
See also Barondess, Sue K(aufman)

Kavafis, Konstantinos Petrou 1863-1933
See Cavafy, C(onstantine) P(eter)
See also CA 104

Kavan, Anna 1901-1968 .... **CLC 5, 13, 82**
See also CA 5-8R; CANR 6, 57; MTCW 1

Kavanagh, Dan
See Barnes, Julian (Patrick)

Kavanagh, Julie 1952- .... **CLC 119**
See also CA 163

Kavanagh, Patrick (Joseph)
1904-1967 .... **CLC 22**
See also CA 123; 25-28R; DLB 15, 20; MTCW 1

Kawabata, Yasunari 1899-1972 ..... **CLC 2, 5, 9, 18, 107; DAM MULT; SSC 17**
See also CA 93-96; 33-36R; CANR 88; DLB 180; MTCW 2

Kaye, M(ary) M(argaret) 1909- .... **CLC 28**
See also CA 89-92; CANR 24, 60; MTCW 1, 2; SATA 62

Kaye, Mollie
See Kaye, M(ary) M(argaret)

Kaye-Smith, Sheila 1887-1956 .... **TCLC 20**
See also CA 118; DLB 36

Kaymor, Patrice Maguilene
See Senghor, Leopold Sedar

Kazan, Elia 1909- .... **CLC 6, 16, 63**
See also CA 21-24R; CANR 32, 78

Kazantzakis, Nikos 1883(?)-1957 .... **TCLC 2, 5, 33**
See also CA 105; 132; DA3; MTCW 1, 2

Kazin, Alfred 1915-1998 ..... **CLC 34, 38, 119**
See also CA 1-4R; CAAS 7; CANR 1, 45, 79; DLB 67

Keane, Mary Nesta (Skrine) 1904-1996
See Keane, Molly
See also CA 108; 114; 151

Keane, Molly CLC 31
See also Keane, Mary Nesta (Skrine)
See also INT 114

Keates, Jonathan 1946(?)- .... **CLC 34**
See also CA 163

Keaton, Buster 1895-1966 .... **CLC 20**

Keats, John 1795-1821 ...... **NCLC 8, 73; DA; DAB; DAC; DAM MST, POET; PC 1; WLC**
See also CDBLB 1789-1832; DA3; DLB 96, 110

Keble, John 1792-1866 .... **NCLC 87**
See also DLB 32, 55

Keene, Donald 1922- .... **CLC 34**
See also CA 1-4R; CANR 5

Keillor, Garrison CLC 40, 115
See also Keillor, Gary (Edward)
See also AAYA 2; BEST 89:3; DLBY 87; SATA 58

Keillor, Gary (Edward) 1942-
See Keillor, Garrison
See also CA 111; 117; CANR 36, 59; DAM POP; DA3; MTCW 1, 2

Keith, Michael
See Hubbard, L(afayette) Ron(ald)

Keller, Gottfried 1819-1890 .... **NCLC 2; SSC 26**
See also DLB 129

Keller, Nora Okja CLC 109

Kellerman, Jonathan 1949- .. **CLC 44; DAM POP**
See also BEST 90:1; CA 106; CANR 29, 51; DA3; INT CANR-29

Kelley, William Melvin 1937- .... **CLC 22**
See also BW 1; CA 77-80; CANR 27, 83; DLB 33

Kellogg, Marjorie 1922- .... **CLC 2**
See also CA 81-84

Kellow, Kathleen
See Hibbert, Eleanor Alice Burford

Kelly, M(ilton) T(errence) 1947- ...... **CLC 55**
See also CA 97-100; CAAS 22; CANR 19, 43, 84

Kelman, James 1946- .... **CLC 58, 86**
See also CA 148; CANR 85; DLB 194

Kemal, Yashar 1923- .... **CLC 14, 29**
See also CA 89-92; CANR 44

Kemble, Fanny 1809-1893 .... **NCLC 18**
See also DLB 32

Kemelman, Harry 1908-1996 .... **CLC 2**
See also AITN 1; CA 9-12R; 155; CANR 6, 71; DLB 28

Kempe, Margery 1373(?)-1440(?) ... **LC 6, 56**
See also DLB 146

Kempis, Thomas a 1380-1471 .... **LC 11**

Kendall, Henry 1839-1882 .... **NCLC 12**

Keneally, Thomas (Michael) 1935- ... **CLC 5, 8, 10, 14, 19, 27, 43, 117; DAM NOV**
See also CA 85-88; CANR 10, 50, 74; DA3; MTCW 1, 2

Kennedy, Adrienne (Lita) 1931- ..... **CLC 66; BLC 2; DAM MULT; DC 5**
See also BW 2, 3; CA 103; CAAS 20; CABS 3; CANR 26, 53, 82; DLB 38

Kennedy, John Pendleton
1795-1870 .... **NCLC 2**
See also DLB 3

Kennedy, Joseph Charles 1929-
See Kennedy, X. J.
See also CA 1-4R; CANR 4, 30, 40; SATA 14, 86

Kennedy, William 1928- .. **CLC 6, 28, 34, 53; DAM NOV**
See also AAYA 1; CA 85-88; CANR 14, 31, 76; DA3; DLB 143; DLBY 85; INT CANR-31; MTCW 1, 2; SATA 57

Kennedy, X. J. CLC 8, 42
See also Kennedy, Joseph Charles
See also CAAS 9; CLR 27; DLB 5; SAAS 22

Kenny, Maurice (Francis) 1929- ..... **CLC 87; DAM MULT**
See also CA 144; CAAS 22; DLB 175; NNAL

Kent, Kelvin
See Kuttner, Henry

Kenton, Maxwell
See Southern, Terry

Kenyon, Robert O.
See Kuttner, Henry

Kepler, Johannes 1571-1630 .... **LC 45**

Kerouac, Jack CLC 1, 2, 3, 5, 14, 29, 61
See also Kerouac, Jean-Louis Lebris de
See also AAYA 25; CDALB 1941-1968; DLB 2, 16; DLBD 3; DLBY 95; MTCW 2

Kerouac, Jean-Louis Lebris de 1922-1969
See Kerouac, Jack
See also AITN 1; CA 5-8R; 25-28R; CANR 26, 54; DA; DAB; DAC; DAM MST, NOV, POET, POP; DA3; MTCW 1, 2; WLC

Kerr, Jean 1923- .... **CLC 22**
See also CA 5-8R; CANR 7; INT CANR-7

Kerr, M. E. CLC 12, 35
See also Meaker, Marijane (Agnes)
See also AAYA 2, 23; CLR 29; SAAS 1

Kerr, Robert CLC 55

Kerrigan, (Thomas) Anthony 1918- .. **CLC 4, 6**
See also CA 49-52; CAAS 11; CANR 4

Kerry, Lois
See Duncan, Lois

Kesey, Ken (Elton) 1935- ..... **CLC 1, 3, 6, 11, 46, 64; DA; DAB; DAC; DAM MST, NOV, POP; WLC**
See also AAYA 25; CA 1-4R; CANR 22, 38, 66; CDALB 1968-1988; DA3; DLB 2, 16, 206; MTCW 1, 2; SATA 66

Kesselring, Joseph (Otto)
1902-1967 .... **CLC 45; DAM DRAM, MST**
See also CA 150

Kessler, Jascha (Frederick) 1929- ...... **CLC 4**
See also CA 17-20R; CANR 8, 48

Kettelkamp, Larry (Dale) 1933- .... **CLC 12**
See also CA 29-32R; CANR 16; SAAS 3; SATA 2

Key, Ellen 1849-1926 .... **TCLC 65**

Keyber, Conny
See Fielding, Henry

Keyes, Daniel 1927- ...... **CLC 80; DA; DAC; DAM MST, NOV**
See also AAYA 23; CA 17-20R, 181; CAAE 181; CANR 10, 26, 54, 74; DA3; MTCW 2; SATA 37

Keynes, John Maynard
1883-1946 .... **TCLC 64**
See also CA 114; 162, 163; DLBD 10; MTCW 2

Khanshendel, Chiron
See Rose, Wendy

Khayyam, Omar 1048-1131 .... **CMLC 11; DAM POET; PC 8**
See also DA3

Kherdian, David 1931- .... **CLC 6, 9**
See also CA 21-24R; CAAS 2; CANR 39, 78; CLR 24; JRDA; MAICYA; SATA 16, 74

Khlebnikov, Velimir TCLC 20

See also Khlebnikov, Viktor Vladimirovich

Khlebnikov, Viktor Vladimirovich 1885-1922
See Khlebnikov, Velimir
See also CA 117

Khodasevich, Vladislav (Felitsianovich)
1886-1939 .... **TCLC 15**
See also CA 115

Kielland, Alexander Lange
1849-1906 .... **TCLC 5**
See also CA 104

Kiely, Benedict 1919- .... **CLC 23, 43**
See also CA 1-4R; CANR 2, 84; DLB 15

Kienzle, William X(avier) 1928- ..... **CLC 25; DAM POP**
See also CA 93-96; CAAS 1; CANR 9, 31, 59; DA3; INT CANR-31; MTCW 1, 2

Kierkegaard, Soren 1813-1855 ..... **NCLC 34, 78**

Kieslowski, Krzysztof 1941-1996 .... **CLC 120**
See also CA 147; 151

Killens, John Oliver 1916-1987 .... **CLC 10**
See also BW 2; CA 77-80; 123; CAAS 2; CANR 26; DLB 33

Killigrew, Anne 1660-1685 .... **LC 4**
See also DLB 131

Killigrew, Thomas 1612-1683 .... **LC 57**
See also DLB 58

Kim
See Simenon, Georges (Jacques Christian)

Kincaid, Jamaica 1949- .... **CLC 43, 68; BLC 2; DAM MULT, NOV**
See also AAYA 13; BW 2, 3; CA 125; CANR 47, 59; CDALBS; CLR 63; DA3; DLB 157; MTCW 2

King, Francis (Henry) 1923- .... **CLC 8, 53; DAM NOV**
See also CA 1-4R; CANR 1, 33, 86; DLB 15, 139; MTCW 1

King, Kennedy
See Brown, George Douglas

King, Martin Luther, Jr.
1929-1968 .... **CLC 83; BLC 2; DA; DAB; DAC; DAM MST, MULT; WLCS**
See also BW 2, 3; CA 25-28; CANR 27, 44; CAP 2; DA3; MTCW 1, 2; SATA 14

King, Stephen (Edwin) 1947- .... **CLC 12, 26, 37, 61, 113; DAM NOV, POP; SSC 17**
See also AAYA 1, 17; BEST 90:1; CA 61-64; CANR 1, 30, 52, 76; DA3; DLB 143; DLBY 80; JRDA; MTCW 1, 2; SATA 9, 55

King, Steve
See King, Stephen (Edwin)

King, Thomas 1943- ... **CLC 89; DAC; DAM MULT**
See also CA 144; DLB 175; NNAL; SATA 96

Kingman, Lee CLC 17
See also Natti, (Mary) Lee
See also SAAS 3; SATA 1, 67

Kingsley, Charles 1819-1875 .... **NCLC 35**
See also DLB 21, 32, 163, 190; YABC 2

Kingsley, Sidney 1906-1995 .... **CLC 44**
See also CA 85-88; 147; DLB 7

Kingsolver, Barbara 1955- .... **CLC 55, 81, 130; DAM POP**
See also AAYA 15; CA 129; 134; CANR 60; CDALBS; DA3; DLB 206; INT 134; MTCW 2

Kingston, Maxine (Ting Ting) Hong
1940- .... **CLC 12, 19, 58, 121; DAM MULT, NOV; WLCS**
See also AAYA 8; CA 69-72; CANR 13, 38, 74, 87; CDALBS; DA3; DLB 173, 212; DLBY 80; INT CANR-13; MTCW 1, 2; SATA 53

Krutzch, Gus
　　See Eliot, T(homas) S(tearns)
Krylov, Ivan Andreevich
　　1768(?)-1844 .... **NCLC 1**
　　See also DLB 150
Kubin, Alfred (Leopold Isidor)
　　1877-1959 .... **TCLC 23**
　　See also CA 112; 149; DLB 81
Kubrick, Stanley 1928-1999 .... **CLC 16**
　　See also AAYA 30; CA 81-84; 177; CANR
　　33; DLB 26
Kueng, Hans 1928-
　　See Kung, Hans
　　See also CA 53-56; CANR 66; MTCW 1, 2
Kumin, Maxine (Winokur) 1925- ..... **CLC 5,**
　　13, 28; DAM POET; PC 15
　　See also AITN 2; CA 1-4R; CAAS 8;
　　CANR 1, 21, 69; DA3; DLB 5; MTCW
　　1, 2; SATA 12
Kundera, Milan 1929- . **CLC 4, 9, 19, 32, 68,**
　　115; DAM NOV; SSC 24
　　See also AAYA 2; CA 85-88; CANR 19,
　　52, 74; DA3; MTCW 1, 2
Kunene, Mazisi (Raymond) 1930- ... **CLC 85**
　　See also BW 1, 3; CA 125; CANR 81; DLB
　　117
Kung, Hans 1928- .... **CLC 130**
　　See also Kueng, Hans
Kunitz, Stanley (Jasspon) 1905- .. **CLC 6, 11,**
　　14; PC 19
　　See also CA 41-44R; CANR 26, 57; DA3;
　　DLB 48; INT CANR-26; MTCW 1, 2
Kunze, Reiner 1933- .... **CLC 10**
　　See also CA 93-96; DLB 75
Kuprin, Aleksander Ivanovich
　　1870-1938 .... **TCLC 5**
　　See also CA 104; 182
Kureishi, Hanif 1954(?)- .... **CLC 64**
　　See also CA 139; DLB 194
Kurosawa, Akira 1910-1998 .... **CLC 16, 119;**
　　DAM MULT
　　See also AAYA 11; CA 101; 170; CANR 46
Kushner, Tony 1957(?)- .... **CLC 81; DAM**
　　DRAM; DC 10
　　See also CA 144; CANR 74; DA3; MTCW
　　2
Kuttner, Henry 1915-1958 .... **TCLC 10**
　　See also CA 107; 157; DLB 8
Kuzma, Greg 1944- .... **CLC 7**
　　See also CA 33-36R; CANR 70
Kuzmin, Mikhail 1872(?)-1936 ...... **TCLC 40**
　　See also CA 170
Kyd, Thomas 1558-1594 .... **LC 22; DAM**
　　DRAM; DC 3
　　See also DLB 62
Kyprianos, Iossif
　　See Samarakis, Antonis
La Bruyere, Jean de 1645-1696 .... **LC 17**
Lacan, Jacques (Marie Emile)
　　1901-1981 .... **CLC 75**
　　See also CA 121; 104
Laclos, Pierre Ambroise Francois Choderlos
　　de 1741-1803 .... **NCLC 4, 87**
Lacolere, Francois
　　See Aragon, Louis
La Colere, Francois
　　See Aragon, Louis
La Deshabilleuse
　　See Simenon, Georges (Jacques Christian)
Lady Gregory
　　See Gregory, Isabella Augusta (Persse)
Lady of Quality, A
　　See Bagnold, Enid
La Fayette, Marie (Madelaine Pioche de la
　　Vergne Comtes 1634-1693 .... **LC 2**
Lafayette, Rene
　　See Hubbard, L(afayette) Ron(ald)

La Fontaine, Jean de 1621-1695 .... **LC 50**
　　See also MAICYA; SATA 18
Laforgue, Jules 1860-1887 . **NCLC 5, 53; PC**
　　14; SSC 20
Lagerkvist, Paer (Fabian)
　　1891-1974 ...... **CLC 7, 10, 13, 54; DAM**
　　DRAM, NOV
　　See also Lagerkvist, Par
　　See also CA 85-88; 49-52; DA3; MTCW 1,
　　2
Lagerkvist, Par SSC 12
　　See also Lagerkvist, Paer (Fabian)
　　See also MTCW 2
Lagerloef, Selma (Ottiliana Lovisa)
　　1858-1940 .... **TCLC 4, 36**
　　See also Lagerlof, Selma (Ottiliana Lovisa)
　　See also CA 108; MTCW 2; SATA 15
Lagerlof, Selma (Ottiliana Lovisa)
　　See Lagerloef, Selma (Ottiliana Lovisa)
　　See also CLR 7; SATA 15
La Guma, (Justin) Alex(ander)
　　1925-1985 .... **CLC 19; BLCS; DAM**
　　NOV
　　See also BW 1, 3; CA 49-52; 118; CANR
　　25, 81; DLB 117; MTCW 1, 2
Laidlaw, A. K.
　　See Grieve, C(hristopher) M(urray)
Lainez, Manuel Mujica
　　See Mujica Lainez, Manuel
　　See also HW 1
Laing, R(onald) D(avid) 1927-1989 . **CLC 95**
　　See also CA 107; 129; CANR 34; MTCW 1
Lamartine, Alphonse (Marie Louis Prat) de
　　1790-1869 . **NCLC 11; DAM POET; PC**
　　16
Lamb, Charles 1775-1834 ..... **NCLC 10; DA;**
　　DAB; DAC; DAM MST; WLC
　　See also CDBLB 1789-1832; DLB 93, 107,
　　163; SATA 17
Lamb, Lady Caroline 1785-1828 ... **NCLC 38**
　　See also DLB 116
Lamming, George (William) 1927- ... **CLC 2,**
　　4, 66; BLC 2; DAM MULT
　　See also BW 2, 3; CA 85-88; CANR 26,
　　76; DLB 125; MTCW 1, 2
L'Amour, Louis (Dearborn)
　　1908-1988 ...... **CLC 25, 55; DAM NOV,**
　　POP
　　See also AAYA 16; AITN 2; BEST 89:2;
　　CA 1-4R; 125; CANR 3, 25, 40; DA3;
　　DLB 206; DLBY 80; MTCW 1, 2
Lampedusa, Giuseppe (Tomasi) di
　　1896-1957 .... **TCLC 13**
　　See also Tomasi di Lampedusa, Giuseppe
　　See also CA 164; DLB 177; MTCW 2
Lampman, Archibald 1861-1899 ... **NCLC 25**
　　See also DLB 92
Lancaster, Bruce 1896-1963 .... **CLC 36**
　　See also CA 9-10; CANR 70; CAP 1; SATA
　　9
Lanchester, John CLC 99
Landau, Mark Alexandrovich
　　See Aldanov, Mark (Alexandrovich)
Landau-Aldanov, Mark Alexandrovich
　　See Aldanov, Mark (Alexandrovich)
Landis, Jerry
　　See Simon, Paul (Frederick)
Landis, John 1950- .... **CLC 26**
　　See also CA 112; 122
Landolfi, Tommaso 1908-1979 .... **CLC 11, 49**
　　See also CA 127; 117; DLB 177
Landon, Letitia Elizabeth
　　1802-1838 .... **NCLC 15**
　　See also DLB 96
Landor, Walter Savage
　　1775-1864 .... **NCLC 14**
　　See also DLB 93, 107

Landwirth, Heinz 1927-
　　See Lind, Jakov
　　See also CA 9-12R; CANR 7
Lane, Patrick 1939- ... **CLC 25; DAM POET**
　　See also CA 97-100; CANR 54; DLB 53;
　　INT 97-100
Lang, Andrew 1844-1912 .... **TCLC 16**
　　See also CA 114; 137; CANR 85; DLB 98,
　　141, 184; MAICYA; SATA 16
Lang, Fritz 1890-1976 .... **CLC 20, 103**
　　See also CA 77-80; 69-72; CANR 30
Lange, John
　　See Crichton, (John) Michael
Langer, Elinor 1939- .... **CLC 34**
　　See also CA 121
Langland, William 1330(?)-1400(?) ... **LC 19;**
　　DA; DAB; DAC; DAM MST, POET
　　See also DLB 146
Langstaff, Launcelot
　　See Irving, Washington
Lanier, Sidney 1842-1881 ..... **NCLC 6; DAM**
　　POET
　　See also DLB 64; DLBD 13; MAICYA;
　　SATA 18
Lanyer, Aemilia 1569-1645 .... **LC 10, 30**
　　See also DLB 121
Lao-Tzu
　　See Lao Tzu
Lao Tzu fl. 6th cent. B.C.- .... **CMLC 7**
Lapine, James (Elliot) 1949- .... **CLC 39**
　　See also CA 123; 130; CANR 54; INT 130
Larbaud, Valery (Nicolas)
　　1881-1957 .... **TCLC 9**
　　See also CA 106; 152
Lardner, Ring
　　See Lardner, Ring(gold) W(ilmer)
Lardner, Ring W., Jr.
　　See Lardner, Ring(gold) W(ilmer)
Lardner, Ring(gold) W(ilmer)
　　1885-1933 .... **TCLC 2, 14; SSC 32**
　　See also CA 104; 131; CDALB 1917-1929;
　　DLB 11, 25, 86; DLBD 16; MTCW 1, 2
Laredo, Betty
　　See Codrescu, Andrei
Larkin, Maia
　　See Wojciechowska, Maia (Teresa)
Larkin, Philip (Arthur) 1922-1985 ... **CLC 3,**
　　5, 8, 9, 13, 18, 33, 39, 64; DAB; DAM
　　MST, POET; PC 21
　　See also CA 5-8R; 117; CANR 24, 62; CD-
　　BLB 1960 to Present; DA3; DLB 27;
　　MTCW 1, 2
Larra (y Sanchez de Castro), Mariano Jose
　　de 1809-1837 .... **NCLC 17**
Larsen, Eric 1941- .... **CLC 55**
　　See also CA 132
Larsen, Nella 1891-1964 .... **CLC 37; BLC 2;**
　　DAM MULT
　　See also BW 1; CA 125; CANR 83; DLB
　　51
Larson, Charles R(aymond) 1938- ... **CLC 31**
　　See also CA 53-56; CANR 4
Larson, Jonathan 1961-1996 .... **CLC 99**
　　See also AAYA 28; CA 156
Las Casas, Bartolome de 1474-1566 ... **LC 31**
Lasch, Christopher 1932-1994 .... **CLC 102**
　　See also CA 73-76; 144; CANR 25; MTCW
　　1, 2
Lasker-Schueler, Else 1869-1945 ... **TCLC 57**
　　See also CA 183; DLB 66, 124
Laski, Harold 1893-1950 .... **TCLC 79**
Latham, Jean Lee 1902-1995 .... **CLC 12**
　　See also AITN 1; CA 5-8R; CANR 7, 84;
　　CLR 50; MAICYA; SATA 2, 68
Latham, Mavis
　　See Clark, Mavis Thorpe
Lathen, Emma CLC 2

Lustig, Arnost 1926- .... **CLC 56**
  See also AAYA 3; CA 69-72; CANR 47;
  SATA 56
Luther, Martin 1483-1546 .... **LC 9, 37**
  See also DLB 179
Luxemburg, Rosa 1870(?)-1919 ..... **TCLC 63**
  See also CA 118
Luzi, Mario 1914- .... **CLC 13**
  See also CA 61-64; CANR 9, 70; DLB 128
Lyly, John 1554(?)-1606 .... **LC 41; DAM
  DRAM; DC 7**
  See also DLB 62, 167
L'Ymagier
  See Gourmont, Remy (-Marie-Charles) de
Lynch, B. Suarez
  See Bioy Casares, Adolfo; Borges, Jorge
  Luis
Lynch, B. Suarez
  See Bioy Casares, Adolfo
Lynch, David (K.) 1946- .... **CLC 66**
  See also CA 124; 129
Lynch, James
  See Andreyev, Leonid (Nikolaevich)
Lynch Davis, B.
  See Bioy Casares, Adolfo; Borges, Jorge
  Luis
Lyndsay, Sir David 1490-1555 .... **LC 20**
Lynn, Kenneth S(chuyler) 1923- ...... **CLC 50**
  See also CA 1-4R; CANR 3, 27, 65
Lynx
  See West, Rebecca
Lyons, Marcus
  See Blish, James (Benjamin)
Lyre, Pinchbeck
  See Sassoon, Siegfried (Lorraine)
Lytle, Andrew (Nelson) 1902-1995 ... **CLC 22**
  See also CA 9-12R; 150; CANR 70; DLB
  6; DLBY 95
Lyttelton, George 1709-1773 .... **LC 10**
Maas, Peter 1929- .... **CLC 29**
  See also CA 93-96; INT 93-96; MTCW 2
Macaulay, Rose 1881-1958 .... **TCLC 7, 44**
  See also CA 104; DLB 36
Macaulay, Thomas Babington
  1800-1859 .... **NCLC 42**
  See also CDBLB 1832-1890; DLB 32, 55
MacBeth, George (Mann)
  1932-1992 .... **CLC 2, 5, 9**
  See also CA 25-28R; 136; CANR 61, 66;
  DLB 40; MTCW 1; SATA 4; SATA-Obit
  70
MacCaig, Norman (Alexander)
  1910- .... **CLC 36; DAB; DAM POET**
  See also CA 9-12R; CANR 3, 34; DLB 27
MacCarthy, Sir(Charles Otto) Desmond
  1877-1952 .... **TCLC 36**
  See also CA 167
**MacDiarmid, Hugh CLC 2, 4, 11, 19, 63; PC
  9**
  See also Grieve, C(hristopher) M(urray)
  See also CDBLB 1945-1960; DLB 20
MacDonald, Anson
  See Heinlein, Robert A(nson)
Macdonald, Cynthia 1928- .... **CLC 13, 19**
  See also CA 49-52; CANR 4, 44; DLB 105
MacDonald, George 1824-1905 .... **TCLC 9**
  See also CA 106; 137; CANR 80; DLB 18,
  163, 178; MAICYA; SATA 33, 100
Macdonald, John
  See Millar, Kenneth
MacDonald, John D(ann)
  1916-1986 .. **CLC 3, 27, 44; DAM NOV,
  POP**
  See also CA 1-4R; 121; CANR 1, 19, 60;
  DLB 8; DLBY 86; MTCW 1, 2
Macdonald, John Ross
  See Millar, Kenneth
Macdonald, Ross CLC 1, 2, 3, 14, 34, 41

  See also Millar, Kenneth
  See also DLBD 6
MacDougal, John
  See Blish, James (Benjamin)
MacDougal, John
  See Blish, James (Benjamin)
MacEwen, Gwendolyn (Margaret)
  1941-1987 .... **CLC 13, 55**
  See also CA 9-12R; 124; CANR 7, 22; DLB
  53; SATA 50; SATA-Obit 55
Macha, Karel Hynek 1810-1846 .... **NCLC 46**
Machado (y Ruiz), Antonio
  1875-1939 .... **TCLC 3**
  See also CA 104; 174; DLB 108; HW 2
Machado de Assis, Joaquim Maria
  1839-1908 ..... **TCLC 10; BLC 2; HLCS
  2; SSC 24**
  See also CA 107; 153; CANR 91
Machen, Arthur TCLC 4; SSC 20
  See also Jones, Arthur Llewellyn
  See also CA 179; DLB 36, 156, 178
Machiavelli, Niccolo 1469-1527 ..... **LC 8, 36;
  DA; DAB; DAC; DAM MST; WLCS**
MacInnes, Colin 1914-1976 .... **CLC 4, 23**
  See also CA 69-72; 65-68; CANR 21; DLB
  14; MTCW 1, 2
MacInnes, Helen (Clark)
  1907-1985 .... **CLC 27, 39; DAM POP**
  See also CA 1-4R; 117; CANR 1, 28, 58;
  DLB 87; MTCW 1, 2; SATA 22; SATA-
  Obit 44
Mackenzie, Compton (Edward Montague)
  1883-1972 .... **CLC 18**
  See also CA 21-22; 37-40R; CAP 2; DLB
  34, 100
Mackenzie, Henry 1745-1831 .... **NCLC 41**
  See also DLB 39
Mackintosh, Elizabeth 1896(?)-1952
  See Tey, Josephine
  See also CA 110
MacLaren, James
  See Grieve, C(hristopher) M(urray)
Mac Laverty, Bernard 1942- .... **CLC 31**
  See also CA 116; 118; CANR 43, 88; INT
  118
MacLean, Alistair (Stuart)
  1922(?)-1987 .. **CLC 3, 13, 50, 63; DAM
  POP**
  See also CA 57-60; 121; CANR 28, 61;
  MTCW 1; SATA 23; SATA-Obit 50
Maclean, Norman (Fitzroy)
  1902-1990 .... **CLC 78; DAM POP; SSC
  13**
  See also CA 102; 132; CANR 49; DLB 206
MacLeish, Archibald 1892-1982 ... **CLC 3, 8,
  14, 68; DAM POET**
  See also CA 9-12R; 106; CANR 33, 63;
  CDALBS; DLB 4, 7, 45; DLBY 82;
  MTCW 1, 2
MacLennan, (John) Hugh
  1907-1990 . **CLC 2, 14, 92; DAC; DAM
  MST**
  See also CA 5-8R; 142; CANR 33; DLB
  68; MTCW 1, 2
MacLeod, Alistair 1936- .... **CLC 56; DAC;
  DAM MST**
  See also CA 123; DLB 60; MTCW 2
Macleod, Fiona
  See Sharp, William
MacNeice, (Frederick) Louis
  1907-1963 .... **CLC 1, 4, 10, 53; DAB;
  DAM POET**
  See also CA 85-88; CANR 61; DLB 10, 20;
  MTCW 1, 2
MacNeill, Dand
  See Fraser, George MacDonald
Macpherson, James 1736-1796 .... **LC 29**
  See also Ossian
  See also DLB 109

Macpherson, (Jean) Jay 1931- .... **CLC 14**
  See also CA 5-8R; CANR 90; DLB 53
MacShane, Frank 1927-1999 .... **CLC 39**
  See also CA 9-12R; 186; CANR 3, 33; DLB
  111
Macumber, Mari
  See Sandoz, Mari(e Susette)
Madach, Imre 1823-1864 .... **NCLC 19**
Madden, (Jerry) David 1933- .... **CLC 5, 15**
  See also CA 1-4R; CAAS 3; CANR 4, 45;
  DLB 6; MTCW 1
Maddern, Al(an)
  See Ellison, Harlan (Jay)
Madhubuti, Haki R. 1942- . **CLC 6, 73; BLC
  2; DAM MULT, POET; PC 5**
  See also Lee, Don L.
  See also BW 2, 3; CA 73-76; CANR 24,
  51, 73; DLB 5, 41; DLBD 8; MTCW 2
Maepenn, Hugh
  See Kuttner, Henry
Maepenn, K. H.
  See Kuttner, Henry
Maeterlinck, Maurice 1862-1949 ... **TCLC 3;
  DAM DRAM**
  See also CA 104; 136; CANR 80; DLB 192;
  SATA 66
Maginn, William 1794-1842 .... **NCLC 8**
  See also DLB 110, 159
Mahapatra, Jayanta 1928- .... **CLC 33; DAM
  MULT**
  See also CA 73-76; CAAS 9; CANR 15,
  33, 66, 87
Mahfouz, Naguib (Abdel Aziz Al-Sabilgi)
  1911(?)-
  See Mahfuz, Najib
  See also BEST 89:2; CA 128; CANR 55;
  DAM NOV; DA3; MTCW 1, 2
Mahfuz, Najib CLC 52, 55
  See also Mahfouz, Naguib (Abdel Aziz Al-
  Sabilgi)
  See also DLBY 88
Mahon, Derek 1941- .... **CLC 27**
  See also CA 113; 128; CANR 88; DLB 40
Mailer, Norman 1923- ... **CLC 1, 2, 3, 4, 5, 8,
  11, 14, 28, 39, 74, 111; DA; DAB;
  DAC; DAM MST, NOV, POP**
  See also AAYA 31; AITN 2; CA 9-12R;
  CABS 1; CANR 28, 74, 77; CDALB
  1968-1988; DA3; DLB 2, 16, 28, 185;
  DLBD 3; DLBY 80, 83; MTCW 1, 2
Maillet, Antonine 1929- .. **CLC 54, 118; DAC**
  See also CA 115; 120; CANR 46, 74, 77;
  DLB 60; INT 120; MTCW 2
Mais, Roger 1905-1955 .... **TCLC 8**
  See also BW 1, 3; CA 105; 124; CANR 82;
  DLB 125; MTCW 1
Maistre, Joseph de 1753-1821 .... **NCLC 37**
Maitland, Frederic 1850-1906 .... **TCLC 65**
Maitland, Sara (Louise) 1950- .... **CLC 49**
  See also CA 69-72; CANR 13, 59
Major, Clarence 1936- . **CLC 3, 19, 48; BLC
  2; DAM MULT**
  See also BW 2, 3; CA 21-24R; CAAS 6;
  CANR 13, 25, 53, 82; DLB 33
Major, Kevin (Gerald) 1949- . **CLC 26; DAC**
  See also AAYA 16; CA 97-100; CANR 21,
  38; CLR 11; DLB 60; INT CANR-21;
  JRDA; MAICYA; SATA 32, 82
Maki, James
  See Ozu, Yasujiro
Malabaila, Damiano
  See Levi, Primo
Malamud, Bernard 1914-1986 .. **CLC 1, 2, 3,
  5, 8, 9, 11, 18, 27, 44, 78, 85; DA;
  DAB; DAC; DAM MST, NOV, POP;
  SSC 15; WLC**
  See also AAYA 16; CA 5-8R; 118; CABS
  1; CANR 28, 62; CDALB 1941-1968;
  DA3; DLB 2, 28, 152; DLBY 80, 86;
  MTCW 1, 2

Martinez, Jacinto Benavente y
  See Benavente (y Martinez), Jacinto
Martinez Ruiz, Jose 1873-1967
  See Azorin; Ruiz, Jose Martinez
  See also CA 93-96; HW 1
Martinez Sierra, Gregorio
  1881-1947 .... **TCLC 6**
  See also CA 115
Martinez Sierra, Maria (de la O'LeJarraga)
  1874-1974 .... **TCLC 6**
  See also CA 115
Martinsen, Martin
  See Follett, Ken(neth Martin)
Martinson, Harry (Edmund)
  1904-1978 .... **CLC 14**
  See also CA 77-80; CANR 34
Marut, Ret
  See Traven, B.
Marut, Robert
  See Traven, B.
Marvell, Andrew 1621-1678 .. **LC 4, 43; DA;**
  DAB; DAC; DAM MST, POET; PC
  10; WLC
  See also CDBLB 1660-1789; DLB 131
Marx, Karl (Heinrich) 1818-1883 . **NCLC 17**
  See also DLB 129
Masaoka Shiki TCLC 18
  See also Masaoka Tsunenori
Masaoka Tsunenori 1867-1902
  See Masaoka Shiki
  See also CA 117
Masefield, John (Edward)
  1878-1967 ..... **CLC 11, 47; DAM POET**
  See also CA 19-20; 25-28R; CANR 33;
  CAP 2; CDBLB 1890-1914; DLB 10, 19,
  153, 160; MTCW 1, 2; SATA 19
Maso, Carole 19(?)- .... **CLC 44**
  See also CA 170
Mason, Bobbie Ann 1940- ... **CLC 28, 43, 82;**
  SSC 4
  See also AAYA 5; CA 53-56; CANR 11, 31,
  58, 83; CDALBS; DA3; DLB 173; DLBY
  87; INT CANR-31; MTCW 1, 2
Mason, Ernst
  See Pohl, Frederik
Mason, Lee W.
  See Malzberg, Barry N(athaniel)
Mason, Nick 1945- .... **CLC 35**
Mason, Tally
  See Derleth, August (William)
Mass, William
  See Gibson, William
Master Lao
  See Lao Tzu
Masters, Edgar Lee 1868-1950 .... **TCLC 2,**
  25; DA; DAC; DAM MST, POET; PC
  1; WLCS
  See also CA 104; 133; CDALB 1865-1917;
  DLB 54; MTCW 1, 2
Masters, Hilary 1928- .... **CLC 48**
  See also CA 25-28R; CANR 13, 47
Mastrosimone, William 19(?)- .... **CLC 36**
  See also CA 186
Mathe, Albert
  See Camus, Albert
Mather, Cotton 1663-1728 .... **LC 38**
  See also CDALB 1640-1865; DLB 24, 30,
  140
Mather, Increase 1639-1723 .... **LC 38**
  See also DLB 24
Matheson, Richard Burton 1926- .... **CLC 37**
  See also AAYA 31; CA 97-100; CANR 88;
  DLB 8, 44; INT 97-100
Mathews, Harry 1930- .... **CLC 6, 52**
  See also CA 21-24R; CAAS 6; CANR 18,
  40

Mathews, John Joseph 1894-1979 .. **CLC 84;**
  DAM MULT
  See also CA 19-20; 142; CANR 45; CAP 2;
  DLB 175; NNAL
Mathias, Roland (Glyn) 1915- .... **CLC 45**
  See also CA 97-100; CANR 19, 41; DLB
  27
Matsuo Basho 1644-1694 .... **PC 3**
  See also DAM POET
Mattheson, Rodney
  See Creasey, John
Matthews, (James) Brander
  1852-1929 .... **TCLC 95**
  See also DLB 71, 78; DLBD 13
Matthews, Greg 1949- .... **CLC 45**
  See also CA 135
Matthews, William (Procter, III)
  1942-1997 .... **CLC 40**
  See also CA 29-32R; 162; CAAS 18; CANR
  12, 57; DLB 5
Matthias, John (Edward) 1941- .... **CLC 9**
  See also CA 33-36R; CANR 56
Matthiessen, Peter 1927- ... **CLC 5, 7, 11, 32,**
  64; DAM NOV
  See also AAYA 6; BEST 90:4; CA 9-12R;
  CANR 21, 50, 73; DA3; DLB 6, 173;
  MTCW 1, 2; SATA 27
Maturin, Charles Robert
  1780(?)-1824 .... **NCLC 6**
  See also DLB 178
Matute (Ausejo), Ana Maria 1925- .. **CLC 11**
  See also CA 89-92; MTCW 1
Maugham, W. S.
  See Maugham, W(illiam) Somerset
Maugham, W(illiam) Somerset
  1874-1965 ... **CLC 1, 11, 15, 67, 93; DA;**
  DAB; DAC; DAM DRAM, MST, NOV;
  SSC 8; WLC
  See also CA 5-8R; 25-28R; CANR 40; CD-
  BLB 1914-1945; DA3; DLB 10, 36, 77,
  100, 162, 195; MTCW 1, 2; SATA 54
Maugham, William Somerset
  See Maugham, W(illiam) Somerset
Maupassant, (Henri Rene Albert) Guy de
  1850-1893 . **NCLC 1, 42, 83; DA; DAB;**
  DAC; DAM MST; SSC 1; WLC
  See also DA3; DLB 123
Maupin, Armistead 1944- ..... **CLC 95; DAM**
  POP
  See also CA 125; 130; CANR 58; DA3;
  INT 130; MTCW 2
Maurhut, Richard
  See Traven, B.
Mauriac, Claude 1914-1996 .... **CLC 9**
  See also CA 89-92; 152; DLB 83
Mauriac, Francois (Charles)
  1885-1970 .... **CLC 4, 9, 56; SSC 24**
  See also CA 25-28; CAP 2; DLB 65;
  MTCW 1, 2
Mavor, Osborne Henry 1888-1951
  See Bridie, James
  See also CA 104
Maxwell, William (Keepers, Jr.)
  1908- .... **CLC 19**
  See also CA 93-96; CANR 54; DLBY 80;
  INT 93-96
May, Elaine 1932- .... **CLC 16**
  See also CA 124; 142; DLB 44
Mayakovski, Vladimir (Vladimirovich)
  1893-1930 .... **TCLC 4, 18**
  See also CA 104; 158; MTCW 2
Mayhew, Henry 1812-1887 .... **NCLC 31**
  See also DLB 18, 55, 190
Mayle, Peter 1939(?)- .... **CLC 89**
  See also CA 139; CANR 64
Maynard, Joyce 1953- .... **CLC 23**
  See also CA 111; 129; CANR 64

Mayne, William (James Carter)
  1928- .... **CLC 12**
  See also AAYA 20; CA 9-12R; CANR 37,
  80; CLR 25; JRDA; MAICYA; SAAS 11;
  SATA 6, 68
Mayo, Jim
  See L'Amour, Louis (Dearborn)
Maysles, Albert 1926- .... **CLC 16**
  See also CA 29-32R
Maysles, David 1932- .... **CLC 16**
Mazer, Norma Fox 1931- .... **CLC 26**
  See also AAYA 5; CA 69-72; CANR 12,
  32, 66; CLR 23; JRDA; MAICYA; SAAS
  1; SATA 24, 67, 105
Mazzini, Guiseppe 1805-1872 .... **NCLC 34**
McAlmon, Robert (Menzies)
  1895-1956 .... **TCLC 97**
  See also CA 107; 168; DLB 4, 45; DLBD
  15
McAuley, James Phillip 1917-1976 .. **CLC 45**
  See also CA 97-100
McBain, Ed
  See Hunter, Evan
McBrien, William (Augustine)
  1930- .... **CLC 44**
  See also CA 107; CANR 90
McCaffrey, Anne (Inez) 1926- .... **CLC 17;**
  DAM NOV, POP
  See also AAYA 6, 34; AITN 2; BEST 89:2;
  CA 25-28R; CANR 15, 35, 55; CLR 49;
  DA3; DLB 8; JRDA; MAICYA; MTCW
  1, 2; SAAS 11; SATA 8, 70, 116
McCall, Nathan 1955(?)- .... **CLC 86**
  See also BW 3; CA 146; CANR 88
McCann, Arthur
  See Campbell, John W(ood, Jr.)
McCann, Edson
  See Pohl, Frederik
McCarthy, Charles, Jr. 1933-
  See McCarthy, Cormac
  See also CANR 42, 69; DAM POP; DA3;
  MTCW 2
McCarthy, Cormac 1933- ...... **CLC 4, 57, 59,**
  101
  See also McCarthy, Charles, Jr.
  See also DLB 6, 143; MTCW 2
McCarthy, Mary (Therese)
  1912-1989 .. **CLC 1, 3, 5, 14, 24, 39, 59;**
  SSC 24
  See also CA 5-8R; 129; CANR 16, 50, 64;
  DA3; DLB 2; DLBY 81; INT CANR-16;
  MTCW 1, 2
McCartney, (James) Paul 1942- . **CLC 12, 35**
  See also CA 146
McCauley, Stephen (D.) 1955- .... **CLC 50**
  See also CA 141
McClure, Michael (Thomas) 1932- ... **CLC 6,**
  10
  See also CA 21-24R; CANR 17, 46, 77;
  DLB 16
McCorkle, Jill (Collins) 1958- .... **CLC 51**
  See also CA 121; DLBY 87
McCourt, Frank 1930- .... **CLC 109**
  See also CA 157
McCourt, James 1941- .... **CLC 5**
  See also CA 57-60
McCourt, Malachy 1932- .... **CLC 119**
McCoy, Horace (Stanley)
  1897-1955 .... **TCLC 28**
  See also CA 108; 155; DLB 9
McCrae, John 1872-1918 .... **TCLC 12**
  See also CA 109; DLB 92
McCreigh, James
  See Pohl, Frederik

Meyers, Jeffrey 1939- .... **CLC 39**
 See also CA 73-76; CAAE 186; CANR 54;
 DLB 111

Meynell, Alice (Christina Gertrude
 Thompson) 1847-1922 .... **TCLC 6**
 See also CA 104; 177; DLB 19, 98

Meyrink, Gustav TCLC 21
 See also Meyer-Meyrink, Gustav
 See also DLB 81

Michaels, Leonard 1933- .... **CLC 6, 25; SSC**
 16
 See also CA 61-64; CANR 21, 62; DLB
 130; MTCW 1

Michaux, Henri 1899-1984 .... **CLC 8, 19**
 See also CA 85-88; 114

Micheaux, Oscar (Devereaux)
 1884-1951 .... **TCLC 76**
 See also BW 3; CA 174; DLB 50

Michelangelo 1475-1564 .... **LC 12**

Michelet, Jules 1798-1874 .... **NCLC 31**

Michels, Robert 1876-1936 .... **TCLC 88**

Michener, James A(lbert)
 1907(?)-1997 .... **CLC 1, 5, 11, 29, 60,**
 109; DAM NOV, POP
 See also AAYA 27; AITN 1; BEST 90:1;
 CA 5-8R; 161; CANR 21, 45, 68; DA3;
 DLB 6; MTCW 1, 2

Mickiewicz, Adam 1798-1855 .... **NCLC 3**

Middleton, Christopher 1926- .... **CLC 13**
 See also CA 13-16R; CANR 29, 54; DLB
 40

Middleton, Richard (Barham)
 1882-1911 .... **TCLC 56**
 See also DLB 156

Middleton, Stanley 1919- .... **CLC 7, 38**
 See also CA 25-28R; CAAS 23; CANR 21,
 46, 81; DLB 14

Middleton, Thomas 1580-1627 .... **LC 33;**
 DAM DRAM, MST; DC 5
 See also DLB 58

Migueis, Jose Rodrigues 1901- .... **CLC 10**

Mikszath, Kalman 1847-1910 .... **TCLC 31**
 See also CA 170

Miles, Jack CLC 100

Miles, Josephine (Louise)
 1911-1985 .. **CLC 1, 2, 14, 34, 39; DAM**
 POET
 See also CA 1-4R; 116; CANR 2, 55; DLB
 48

Militant
 See Sandburg, Carl (August)

Mill, John Stuart 1806-1873 .... **NCLC 11, 58**
 See also CDBLB 1832-1890; DLB 55, 190

Millar, Kenneth 1915-1983 ... **CLC 14; DAM**
 POP
 See also Macdonald, Ross
 See also CA 9-12R; 110; CANR 16, 63;
 DA3; DLB 2; DLBD 6; DLBY 83;
 MTCW 1, 2

Millay, E. Vincent
 See Millay, Edna St. Vincent

Millay, Edna St. Vincent
 1892-1950 .... **TCLC 4, 49; DA; DAB;**
 DAC; DAM MST, POET; PC 6;
 WLCS
 See also CA 104; 130; CDALB 1917-1929;
 DA3; DLB 45; MTCW 1, 2

Miller, Arthur 1915- ...... **CLC 1, 2, 6, 10, 15,**
 26, 47, 78; DA; DAB; DAC; DAM
 DRAM, MST; DC 1; WLC
 See also AAYA 15; AITN 1; CA 1-4R;
 CABS 3; CANR 2, 30, 54, 76; CDALB
 1941-1968; DA3; DLB 7; MTCW 1, 2

Miller, Henry (Valentine)
 1891-1980 .... **CLC 1, 2, 4, 9, 14, 43, 84;**
 DA; DAB; DAC; DAM MST, NOV;
 WLC
 See also CA 9-12R; 97-100; CANR 33, 64;
 CDALB 1929-1941; DA3; DLB 4, 9;
 DLBY 80; MTCW 1, 2

Miller, Jason 1939(?)- .... **CLC 2**
 See also AITN 1; CA 73-76; DLB 7

Miller, Sue 1943- .... **CLC 44; DAM POP**
 See also BEST 90:3; CA 139; CANR 59,
 91; DA3; DLB 143

Miller, Walter M(ichael, Jr.) 1923- ... **CLC 4,**
 30
 See also CA 85-88; DLB 8

Millett, Kate 1934- .... **CLC 67**
 See also AITN 1; CA 73-76; CANR 32, 53,
 76; DA3; MTCW 1, 2

Millhauser, Steven (Lewis) 1943- .... **CLC 21,**
 54, 109
 See also CA 110; 111; CANR 63; DA3;
 DLB 2; INT 111; MTCW 2

Millin, Sarah Gertrude 1889-1968 ... **CLC 49**
 See also CA 102; 93-96

Milne, A(lan) A(lexander)
 1882-1956 ..... **TCLC 6, 88; DAB; DAC;**
 DAM MST
 See also CA 104; 133; CLR 1, 26; DA3;
 DLB 10, 77, 100, 160; MAICYA; MTCW
 1, 2; SATA 100; YABC 1

Milner, Ron(ald) 1938- .... **CLC 56; BLC 3;**
 DAM MULT
 See also AITN 1; BW 1; CA 73-76; CANR
 24, 81; DLB 38; MTCW 1

Milnes, Richard Monckton
 1809-1885 .... **NCLC 61**
 See also DLB 32, 184

Milosz, Czeslaw 1911- ...... **CLC 5, 11, 22, 31,**
 56, 82; DAM MST, POET; PC 8;
 WLCS
 See also CA 81-84; CANR 23, 51, 91; DA3;
 MTCW 1, 2

Milton, John 1608-1674 .... **LC 9, 43; DA;**
 DAB; DAC; DAM MST, POET; PC 19,
 29; WLC
 See also CDBLB 1660-1789; DA3; DLB
 131, 151

Min, Anchee 1957- .... **CLC 86**
 See also CA 146

Minehaha, Cornelius
 See Wedekind, (Benjamin) Frank(lin)

Miner, Valerie 1947- .... **CLC 40**
 See also CA 97-100; CANR 59

Minimo, Duca
 See D'Annunzio, Gabriele

Minot, Susan 1956- .... **CLC 44**
 See also CA 134

Minus, Ed 1938- .... **CLC 39**
 See also CA 185

Miranda, Javier
 See Bioy Casares, Adolfo

Miranda, Javier
 See Bioy Casares, Adolfo

Mirbeau, Octave 1848-1917 .... **TCLC 55**
 See also DLB 123, 192

Miro (Ferrer), Gabriel (Francisco Victor)
 1879-1930 .... **TCLC 5**
 See also CA 104; 185

Mishima, Yukio 1925-1970 .... **CLC 2, 4, 6, 9,**
 27; DC 1; SSC 4
 See also Hiraoka, Kimitake
 See also DLB 182; MTCW 2

Mistral, Frederic 1830-1914 .... **TCLC 51**
 See also CA 122

Mistral, Gabriela TCLC 2; HLC 2
 See also Godoy Alcayaga, Lucila
 See also MTCW 2

Mistry, Rohinton 1952- .... **CLC 71; DAC**
 See also CA 141; CANR 86

Mitchell, Clyde
 See Ellison, Harlan (Jay); Silverberg, Robert

Mitchell, James Leslie 1901-1935
 See Gibbon, Lewis Grassic
 See also CA 104; DLB 15

Mitchell, Joni 1943- .... **CLC 12**
 See also CA 112

Mitchell, Joseph (Quincy)
 1908-1996 .... **CLC 98**
 See also CA 77-80; 152; CANR 69; DLB
 185; DLBY 96

Mitchell, Margaret (Munnerlyn)
 1900-1949 . **TCLC 11; DAM NOV, POP**
 See also AAYA 23; CA 109; 125; CANR
 55; CDALB 3; DA3; DLB 9; MTCW 1, 2

Mitchell, Peggy
 See Mitchell, Margaret (Munnerlyn)

Mitchell, S(ilas) Weir 1829-1914 .... **TCLC 36**
 See also CA 165; DLB 202

Mitchell, W(illiam) O(rmond)
 1914-1998 .. **CLC 25; DAC; DAM MST**
 See also CA 77-80; 165; CANR 15, 43;
 DLB 88

Mitchell, William 1879-1936 .... **TCLC 81**

Mitford, Mary Russell 1787-1855 ... **NCLC 4**
 See also DLB 110, 116

Mitford, Nancy 1904-1973 .... **CLC 44**
 See also CA 9-12R; DLB 191

Miyamoto, (Chujo) Yuriko
 1899-1951 .... **TCLC 37**
 See also CA 170, 174; DLB 180

Miyazawa, Kenji 1896-1933 .... **TCLC 76**
 See also CA 157

Mizoguchi, Kenji 1898-1956 .... **TCLC 72**
 See also CA 167

Mo, Timothy (Peter) 1950(?)- .... **CLC 46**
 See also CA 117; DLB 194; MTCW 1

Modarressi, Taghi (M.) 1931- .... **CLC 44**
 See also CA 121; 134; INT 134

Modiano, Patrick (Jean) 1945- .... **CLC 18**
 See also CA 85-88; CANR 17, 40; DLB 83

Moerck, Paal
 See Roelvaag, O(le) E(dvart)

Mofolo, Thomas (Mokopu)
 1875(?)-1948 .. **TCLC 22; BLC 3; DAM**
 MULT
 See also CA 121; 153; CANR 83; MTCW 2

Mohr, Nicholasa 1938- .... **CLC 12; DAM**
 MULT; HLC 2
 See also AAYA 8; CA 49-52; CANR 1, 32,
 64; CLR 22; DLB 145; HW 1, 2; JRDA;
 SAAS 8; SATA 8, 97; SATA-Essay 113

Mojtabai, A(nn) G(race) 1938- ..... **CLC 5, 9,**
 15, 29
 See also CA 85-88; CANR 88

Moliere 1622-1673 ..... **LC 10, 28; DA; DAB;**
 DAC; DAM DRAM, MST; WLC
 See also DA3

Molin, Charles
 See Mayne, William (James Carter)

Molnar, Ferenc 1878-1952 .. **TCLC 20; DAM**
 DRAM
 See also CA 109; 153; CANR 83

Momaday, N(avarre) Scott 1934- ...... **CLC 2,**
 19, 85, 95; DA; DAB; DAC; DAM
 MST, MULT, NOV, POP; PC 25;
 WLCS
 See also AAYA 11; CA 25-28R; CANR 14,
 34, 68; CDALBS; DA3; DLB 143, 175;
 INT CANR-14; NNAL; MTCW 1, 2; NNAL;
 SATA 48; SATA-Brief 30

Monette, Paul 1945-1995 .... **CLC 82**
 See also CA 139; 147

Monroe, Harriet 1860-1936 .... **TCLC 12**
 See also CA 109; DLB 54, 91

Monroe, Lyle
 See Heinlein, Robert A(nson)

Montagu, Elizabeth 1720-1800 .... **NCLC 7**

Montagu, Elizabeth 1917- .... **NCLC 7**
 See also CA 9-12R

Montagu, Mary (Pierrepont) Wortley
 1689-1762 .... **LC 9, 57; PC 16**
 See also DLB 95, 101

Montagu, W. H.
See Coleridge, Samuel Taylor
Montague, John (Patrick) 1929- ..... **CLC 13, 46**
See also CA 9-12R; CANR 9, 69; DLB 40; MTCW 1
Montaigne, Michel (Eyquem) de 1533-1592 .... **LC 8; DA; DAB; DAC; DAM MST; WLC**
Montale, Eugenio 1896-1981 ... **CLC 7, 9, 18; PC 13**
See also CA 17-20R; 104; CANR 30; DLB 114; MTCW 1
Montesquieu, Charles-Louis de Secondat 1689-1755 .... **LC 7**
Montgomery, (Robert) Bruce 1921(?)-1978
See Crispin, Edmund
See also CA 179; 104
Montgomery, L(ucy) M(aud) 1874-1942 .... **TCLC 51; DAC; DAM MST**
See also AAYA 12; CA 108; 137; CLR 8; DA3; DLB 92; DLBD 14; JRDA; MAICYA; MTCW 2; SATA 100; YABC 1
Montgomery, Marion H., Jr. 1925- .... **CLC 7**
See also AITN 1; CA 1-4R; CANR 3, 48; DLB 6
Montgomery, Max
See Davenport, Guy (Mattison, Jr.)
Montherlant, Henry (Milon) de 1896-1972 ..... **CLC 8, 19; DAM DRAM**
See also CA 85-88; 37-40R; DLB 72; MTCW 1
Monty Python
See Chapman, Graham; Cleese, John (Marwood); Gilliam, Terry (Vance); Idle, Eric; Jones, Terence Graham Parry; Palin, Michael (Edward)
See also AAYA 7
Moodie, Susanna (Strickland) 1803-1885 .... **NCLC 14**
See also DLB 99
Mooney, Edward 1951-
See Mooney, Ted
See also CA 130
Mooney, Ted CLC 25
See also Mooney, Edward
Moorcock, Michael (John) 1939- ...... **CLC 5, 27, 58**
See also Bradbury, Edward P.
See also AAYA 26; CA 45-48; CAAS 5; CANR 2, 17, 38, 64; DLB 14; MTCW 1, 2; SATA 93
Moore, Brian 1921-1999 ... **CLC 1, 3, 5, 7, 8, 19, 32, 90; DAB; DAC; DAM MST**
See also CA 1-4R; 174; CANR 1, 25, 42, 63; MTCW 1, 2
Moore, Edward
See Muir, Edwin
Moore, G. E. 1873-1958 .... **TCLC 89**
Moore, George Augustus 1852-1933 .... **TCLC 7; SSC 19**
See also CA 104; 177; DLB 10, 18, 57, 135
Moore, Lorrie CLC 39, 45, 68
See also Moore, Marie Lorena
Moore, Marianne (Craig) 1887-1972 .... **CLC 1, 2, 4, 8, 10, 13, 19, 47; DA; DAB; DAC; DAM MST, POET; PC 4; WLCS**
See also CA 1-4R; 33-36R; CANR 3, 61; CDALB 1929-1941; DA3; DLB 45; DLBD 7; MTCW 1, 2; SATA 20
Moore, Marie Lorena 1957-
See Moore, Lorrie
See also CA 116; CANR 39, 83
Moore, Thomas 1779-1852 .... **NCLC 6**
See also DLB 96, 144
Moorhouse, Frank 1938- .... **SSC 40**
See also CA 118

Mora, Pat(ricia) 1942-
See also CA 129; CANR 57, 81; CLR 58; DAM MULT; DLB 209; HLC 2; HW 1, 2; SATA 92
Moraga, Cherrie 1952- .... **CLC 126; DAM MULT**
See also CA 131; CANR 66; DLB 82; HW 1, 2
Morand, Paul 1888-1976 .... **CLC 41; SSC 22**
See also CA 184; 69-72; DLB 65
Morante, Elsa 1918-1985 .... **CLC 8, 47**
See also CA 85-88; 117; CANR 35; DLB 177; MTCW 1, 2
Moravia, Alberto 1907-1990 .... **CLC 2, 7, 11, 27, 46; SSC 26**
See also Pincherle, Alberto
See also DLB 177; MTCW 2
More, Hannah 1745-1833 .... **NCLC 27**
See also DLB 107, 109, 116, 158
More, Henry 1614-1687 .... **LC 9**
See also DLB 126
More, Sir Thomas 1478-1535 .... **LC 10, 32**
Moreas, Jean TCLC 18
See also Papadiamantopoulos, Johannes
Morgan, Berry 1919- .... **CLC 6**
See also CA 49-52; DLB 6
Morgan, Claire
See Highsmith, (Mary) Patricia
Morgan, Edwin (George) 1920- .... **CLC 31**
See also CA 5-8R; CANR 3, 43, 90; DLB 27
Morgan, (George) Frederick 1922- .. **CLC 23**
See also CA 17-20R; CANR 21
Morgan, Harriet
See Mencken, H(enry) L(ouis)
Morgan, Jane
See Cooper, James Fenimore
Morgan, Janet 1945- .... **CLC 39**
See also CA 65-68
Morgan, Lady 1776(?)-1859 .... **NCLC 29**
See also DLB 116, 158
Morgan, Robin (Evonne) 1941- .... **CLC 2**
See also CA 69-72; CANR 29, 68; MTCW 1; SATA 80
Morgan, Scott
See Kuttner, Henry
Morgan, Seth 1949(?)-1990 .... **CLC 65**
See also CA 185; 132
Morgenstern, Christian 1871-1914 .. **TCLC 8**
See also CA 105
Morgenstern, S.
See Goldman, William (W.)
Moricz, Zsigmond 1879-1942 .... **TCLC 33**
See also CA 165
Morike, Eduard (Friedrich) 1804-1875 .... **NCLC 10**
See also DLB 133
Moritz, Karl Philipp 1756-1793 .... **LC 2**
See also DLB 94
Morland, Peter Henry
See Faust, Frederick (Schiller)
Morley, Christopher (Darlington) 1890-1957 .... **TCLC 87**
See also CA 112; DLB 9
Morren, Theophil
See Hofmannsthal, Hugo von
Morris, Bill 1952- .... **CLC 76**
Morris, Julian
See West, Morris L(anglo)
Morris, Steveland Judkins 1950(?)-
See Wonder, Stevie
See also CA 111
Morris, William 1834-1896 .... **NCLC 4**
See also CDBLB 1832-1890; DLB 18, 35, 57, 156, 178, 184

Morris, Wright 1910-1998 .. **CLC 1, 3, 7, 18, 37**
See also CA 9-12R; 167; CANR 21, 81; DLB 2, 206; DLBY 81; MTCW 1, 2
Morrison, Arthur 1863-1945 .... **TCLC 72; SSC 40**
See also CA 120; 157; DLB 70, 135, 197
Morrison, Chloe Anthony Wofford
See Morrison, Toni
Morrison, James Douglas 1943-1971
See Morrison, Jim
See also CA 73-76; CANR 40
Morrison, Jim CLC 17
See also Morrison, James Douglas
Morrison, Toni 1931- . **CLC 4, 10, 22, 55, 81, 87; BLC 3; DA; DAB; DAC; DAM MST, MULT, NOV, POP**
See also AAYA 1, 22; BW 2, 3; CA 29-32R; CANR 27, 42, 67; CDALB 1968-1988; DA3; DLB 6, 33, 143; DLBY 81; MTCW 1, 2; SATA 57
Morrison, Van 1945- .... **CLC 21**
See also CA 116; 168
Morrissy, Mary 1958- .... **CLC 99**
Mortimer, John (Clifford) 1923- ..... **CLC 28, 43; DAM DRAM, POP**
See also CA 13-16R; CANR 21, 69; CDBLB 1960 to Present; DA3; DLB 13; INT CANR-21; MTCW 1, 2
Mortimer, Penelope (Ruth) 1918- ...... **CLC 5**
See also CA 57-60; CANR 45, 88
Morton, Anthony
See Creasey, John
Mosca, Gaetano 1858-1941 .... **TCLC 75**
Mosher, Howard Frank 1943- .... **CLC 62**
See also CA 139; CANR 65
Mosley, Nicholas 1923- .... **CLC 43, 70**
See also CA 69-72; CANR 41, 60; DLB 14, 207
Mosley, Walter 1952- .... **CLC 97; BLCS; DAM MULT, POP**
See also AAYA 17; BW 2; CA 142; CANR 57; DA3; MTCW 2
Moss, Howard 1922-1987 ...... **CLC 7, 14, 45, 50; DAM POET**
See also CA 1-4R; 123; CANR 1, 44; DLB 5
Mossgiel, Rab
See Burns, Robert
Motion, Andrew (Peter) 1952- .... **CLC 47**
See also CA 146; CANR 90; DLB 40
Motley, Willard (Francis) 1909-1965 .... **CLC 18**
See also BW 1; CA 117; 106; CANR 88; DLB 76, 143
Motoori, Norinaga 1730-1801 .... **NCLC 45**
Mott, Michael (Charles Alston) 1930- .... **CLC 15, 34**
See also CA 5-8R; CAAS 7; CANR 7, 29
Mountain Wolf Woman 1884-1960 .. **CLC 92**
See also CA 144; CANR 90; NNAL
Moure, Erin 1955- .... **CLC 88**
See also CA 113; DLB 60.
Mowat, Farley (McGill) 1921- .... **CLC 26; DAC; DAM MST**
See also AAYA 1; CA 1-4R; CANR 4, 24, 42, 68; CLR 20; DLB 68; INT CANR-24; JRDA; MAICYA; MTCW 1, 2; SATA 3, 55
Mowatt, Anna Cora 1819-1870 ..... **NCLC 74**
Moyers, Bill 1934- .... **CLC 74**
See also AITN 2; CA 61-64; CANR 31, 52
Mphahlele, Es'kia
See Mphahlele, Ezekiel
See also DLB 125
Mphahlele, Ezekiel 1919- ... **CLC 25; BLC 3; DAM MULT**
See also Mphahlele, Es'kia

Percy, Walker 1916-1990 .... **CLC 2, 3, 6, 8, 14, 18, 47, 65; DAM NOV, POP**
See also CA 1-4R; 131; CANR 1, 23, 64; DA3; DLB 2; DLBY 80, 90; MTCW 1, 2

Percy, William Alexander
1885-1942 .... **TCLC 84**
See also CA 163; MTCW 2

Perec, Georges 1936-1982 .... **CLC 56, 116**
See also CA 141; DLB 83

Pereda (y Sanchez de Porrua), Jose Maria de 1833-1906 .... **TCLC 16**
See also CA 117

Pereda y Porrua, Jose Maria de
See Pereda (y Sanchez de Porrua), Jose Maria de

Peregoy, George Weems
See Mencken, H(enry) L(ouis)

Perelman, S(idney) J(oseph)
1904-1979 .. **CLC 3, 5, 9, 15, 23, 44, 49; DAM DRAM; SSC 32**
See also AITN 1, 2; CA 73-76; 89-92; CANR 18; DLB 11, 44; MTCW 1, 2

Peret, Benjamin 1899-1959 .... **TCLC 20**
See also CA 117; 186

Peretz, Isaac Loeb 1851(?)-1915 ... **TCLC 16; SSC 26**
See also CA 109

Peretz, Yitzhok Leibush
See Peretz, Isaac Loeb

Perez Galdos, Benito 1843-1920 ... **TCLC 27; HLCS 2**
See also CA 125; 153; HW 1

Peri Rossi, Cristina 1941-
See also CA 131; CANR 59, 81; DLB 145; HLCS 2; HW 1, 2

Perlata
See Peret, Benjamin

Perrault, Charles 1628-1703 ... **LC 3, 52; DC 12**
See also MAICYA; SATA 25

Perry, Anne 1938- .... **CLC 126**
See also CA 101; CANR 22, 50, 84

Perry, Brighton
See Sherwood, Robert E(mmet)

Perse, St.-John
See Leger, (Marie-Rene Auguste) Alexis Saint-Leger

Perutz, Leo(pold) 1882-1957 .... **TCLC 60**
See also CA 147; DLB 81

Peseenz, Tulio F.
See Lopez y Fuentes, Gregorio

Pesetsky, Bette 1932- .... **CLC 28**
See also CA 133; DLB 130

Peshkov, Alexei Maximovich 1868-1936
See Gorky, Maxim
See also CA 105; 141; CANR 83; DA; DAC; DAM DRAM, MST, NOV; MTCW 2

Pessoa, Fernando (Antonio Nogueira)
1888-1935 .... **TCLC 27; DAM MULT; HLC 2; PC 20**
See also CA 125; 183

Peterkin, Julia Mood 1880-1961 ...... **CLC 31**
See also CA 102; DLB 9

Peters, Joan K(aren) 1945- .... **CLC 39**
See also CA 158

Peters, Robert L(ouis) 1924- .... **CLC 7**
See also CA 13-16R; CAAS 8; DLB 105

Petofi, Sandor 1823-1849 .... **NCLC 21**

Petrakis, Harry Mark 1923- .... **CLC 3**
See also CA 9-12R; CANR 4, 30, 85

Petrarch 1304-1374 .... **CMLC 20; DAM POET; PC 8**
See also DA3

Petronius c. 20-66 .... **CMLC 34**
See also DLB 211

Petrov, Evgeny TCLC 21
See also Kataev, Evgeny Petrovich

Petry, Ann (Lane) 1908-1997 ... **CLC 1, 7, 18**
See also BW 1, 3; CA 5-8R; 157; CAAS 6; CANR 4, 46; CLR 12; DLB 76; JRDA; MAICYA; MTCW 1; SATA 5; SATA-Obit 94

Petursson, Halligrimur 1614-1674 .... **LC 8**

Peychinovich
See Vazov, Ivan (Minchov)

Phaedrus c. 18B.C.-c. 50 .... **CMLC 25**
See also DLB 211

Philips, Katherine 1632-1664 .... **LC 30**
See also DLB 131

Philipson, Morris H. 1926- .... **CLC 53**
See also CA 1-4R; CANR 4

Phillips, Caryl 1958- . **CLC 96; BLCS; DAM MULT**
See also BW 2; CA 141; CANR 63; DA3; DLB 157; MTCW 2

Phillips, David Graham
1867-1911 .... **TCLC 44**
See also CA 108; 176; DLB 9, 12

Phillips, Jack
See Sandburg, Carl (August)

Phillips, Jayne Anne 1952- .... **CLC 15, 33; SSC 16**
See also CA 101; CANR 24, 50; DLBY 80; INT CANR-24; MTCW 1, 2

Phillips, Richard
See Dick, Philip K(indred)

Phillips, Robert (Schaeffer) 1938- .... **CLC 28**
See also CA 17-20R; CAAS 13; CANR 8; DLB 105

Phillips, Ward
See Lovecraft, H(oward) P(hillips)

Piccolo, Lucio 1901-1969 .... **CLC 13**
See also CA 97-100; DLB 114

Pickthall, Marjorie L(owry) C(hristie)
1883-1922 .... **TCLC 21**
See also CA 107; DLB 92

Pico della Mirandola, Giovanni
1463-1494 .... **LC 15**

Piercy, Marge 1936- .... **CLC 3, 6, 14, 18, 27, 62, 128; PC 29**
See also CA 21-24R; CAAS 1; CANR 13, 43, 66; DLB 120; MTCW 1, 2

Piers, Robert
See Anthony, Piers

Pieyre de Mandiargues, Andre 1909-1991
See Mandiargues, Andre Pieyre de
See also CA 103; 136; CANR 22, 82

Pilnyak, Boris TCLC 23
See also Vogau, Boris Andreyevich

Pincherle, Alberto 1907-1990 .... **CLC 11, 18; DAM NOV**
See also Moravia, Alberto
See also CA 25-28R; 132; CANR 33, 63; MTCW 1

Pinckney, Darryl 1953- .... **CLC 76**
See also BW 2, 3; CA 143; CANR 79

Pindar 518B.C.-446B.C. .... **CMLC 12; PC 19**
See also DLB 176

Pineda, Cecile 1942- .... **CLC 39**
See also CA 118

Pinero, Arthur Wing 1855-1934 ... **TCLC 32; DAM DRAM**
See also CA 110; 153; DLB 10

Pinero, Miguel (Antonio Gomez)
1946-1988 .... **CLC 4, 55**
See also CA 61-64; 125; CANR 29, 90; HW 1

Pinget, Robert 1919-1997 .... **CLC 7, 13, 37**
See also CA 85-88; 160; DLB 83

Pink Floyd
See Barrett, (Roger) Syd; Gilmour, David; Mason, Nick; Waters, Roger; Wright, Rick

Pinkney, Edward 1802-1828 .... **NCLC 31**

Pinkwater, Daniel Manus 1941- .... **CLC 35**
See also Pinkwater, Manus

See also AAYA 1; CA 29-32R; CANR 12, 38, 89; CLR 4; JRDA; MAICYA; SAAS 3; SATA 46, 76, 114

Pinkwater, Manus
See Pinkwater, Daniel Manus
See also SATA 8

Pinsky, Robert 1940- .... **CLC 9, 19, 38, 94, 121; DAM POET; PC 27**
See also CA 29-32R; CAAS 4; CANR 58; DA3; DLBY 82, 98; MTCW 2

Pinta, Harold
See Pinter, Harold

Pinter, Harold 1930- .. **CLC 1, 3, 6, 9, 11, 15, 27, 58, 73; DA; DAB; DAC; DAM DRAM, MST; WLC**
See also CA 5-8R; CANR 33, 65; CDBLB 1960 to Present; DA3; DLB 13; MTCW 1, 2

Piozzi, Hester Lynch (Thrale)
1741-1821 .... **NCLC 57**
See also DLB 104, 142

Pirandello, Luigi 1867-1936 ...... **TCLC 4, 29; DA; DAB; DAC; DAM DRAM, MST; DC 5; SSC 22; WLC**
See also CA 104; 153; DA3; MTCW 2

Pirsig, Robert M(aynard) 1928- ... **CLC 4, 6, 73; DAM POP**
See also CA 53-56; CANR 42, 74; DA3; MTCW 1, 2; SATA 39

Pisarev, Dmitry Ivanovich
1840-1868 .... **NCLC 25**

Pix, Mary (Griffith) 1666-1709 .... **LC 8**
See also DLB 80

Pixerecourt, (Rene Charles) Guilbert de
1773-1844 .... **NCLC 39**
See also DLB 192

Plaatje, Sol(omon) T(shekisho)
1876-1932 .... **TCLC 73; BLCS**
See also BW 2, 3; CA 141; CANR 79

Plaidy, Jean
See Hibbert, Eleanor Alice Burford

Planche, James Robinson
1796-1880 .... **NCLC 42**

Plant, Robert 1948- .... **CLC 12**

Plante, David (Robert) 1940- ...... **CLC 7, 23, 38; DAM NOV**
See also CA 37-40R; CANR 12, 36, 58, 82; DLBY 83; INT CANR-12; MTCW 1

Plath, Sylvia 1932-1963 ..... **CLC 1, 2, 3, 5, 9, 11, 14, 17, 50, 51, 62, 111; DA; DAB; DAC; DAM MST, POET; PC 1; WLC**
See also AAYA 13; CA 19-20; CANR 34; CAP 2; CDALB 1941-1968; DA3; DLB 5, 6, 152; MTCW 1, 2; SATA 96

Plato 428(?)B.C.-348(?)B.C. ... **CMLC 8; DA; DAB; DAC; DAM MST; WLCS**
See also DA3; DLB 176

Platonov, Andrei TCLC 14; SSC 38
See also Klimentov, Andrei Platonovich

Platt, Kin 1911- .... **CLC 26**
See also AAYA 11; CA 17-20R; CANR 11; JRDA; SAAS 17; SATA 21, 86

Plautus c. 251B.C.-184B.C. ... **CMLC 24; DC 6**
See also DLB 211

Plick et Plock
See Simenon, Georges (Jacques Christian)

Plimpton, George (Ames) 1927- .... **CLC 36**
See also AITN 1; CA 21-24R; CANR 32, 70; DLB 185; MTCW 1, 2; SATA 10

Pliny the Elder c. 23-79 .... **CMLC 23**
See also DLB 211

Plomer, William Charles Franklin
1903-1973 .... **CLC 4, 8**
See also CA 21-22; CANR 34; CAP 2; DLB 20, 162, 191; MTCW 1; SATA 24

Plowman, Piers
See Kavanagh, Patrick (Joseph)

Plum, J.
See Wodehouse, P(elham) G(renville)

Plumly, Stanley (Ross) 1939- .... CLC 33
See also CA 108; 110; DLB 5, 193; INT 110

Plumpe, Friedrich Wilhelm 1888-1931 .... TCLC 53
See also CA 112

Po Chu-i 772-846 .... CMLC 24

Poe, Edgar Allan 1809-1849 ..... NCLC 1, 16, 55, 78; DA; DAB; DAC; DAM MST, POET; PC 1; SSC 34; WLC
See also AAYA 14; CDALB 1640-1865; DA3; DLB 3, 59, 73, 74; SATA 23

Poet of Titchfield Street, The
See Pound, Ezra (Weston Loomis)

Pohl, Frederik 1919- .... CLC 18; SSC 25
See also AAYA 24; CA 61-64; CAAS 1; CANR 11, 37, 81; DLB 8; INT CANR-11; MTCW 1, 2; SATA 24

Poirier, Louis 1910-
See Gracq, Julien
See also CA 122; 126

Poitier, Sidney 1927- .... CLC 26
See also BW 1; CA 117

Polanski, Roman 1933- .... CLC 16
See also CA 77-80

Poliakoff, Stephen 1952- .... CLC 38
See also CA 106; DLB 13

Police, The
See Copeland, Stewart (Armstrong); Summers, Andrew James; Sumner, Gordon Matthew

Polidori, John William 1795-1821 . NCLC 51
See also DLB 116

Pollitt, Katha 1949- .... CLC 28, 122
See also CA 120; 122; CANR 66; MTCW 1, 2

Pollock, (Mary) Sharon 1936- .... CLC 50; DAC; DAM DRAM, MST
See also CA 141; DLB 60

Polo, Marco 1254-1324 .... CMLC 15

Polonsky, Abraham (Lincoln) 1910- .... CLC 92
See also CA 104; DLB 26; INT 104

Polybius c. 200B.C.-c. 118B.C. ...... CMLC 17
See also DLB 176

Pomerance, Bernard 1940- ... CLC 13; DAM DRAM
See also CA 101; CANR 49

Ponge, Francis 1899-1988 . CLC 6, 18; DAM POET
See also CA 85-88; 126; CANR 40, 86

Poniatowska, Elena 1933-
See also CA 101; CANR 32, 66; DAM MULT; DLB 113; HLC 2; HW 1, 2

Pontoppidan, Henrik 1857-1943 .... TCLC 29
See also CA 170

Poole, Josephine CLC 17
See also Helyar, Jane Penelope Josephine
See also SAAS 2; SATA 5

Popa, Vasko 1922-1991 .... CLC 19
See also CA 112; 148; DLB 181

Pope, Alexander 1688-1744 .... LC 3, 58; DA; DAB; DAC; DAM MST, POET; PC 26; WLC
See also CDBLB 1660-1789; DA3; DLB 95, 101

Porter, Connie (Rose) 1959(?)- .... CLC 70
See also BW 2, 3; CA 142; CANR 90; SATA 81

Porter, Gene(va Grace) Stratton 1863(?)-1924 .... TCLC 21
See also CA 112

Porter, Katherine Anne 1890-1980 ... CLC 1, 3, 7, 10, 13, 15, 27, 101; DA; DAB; DAC; DAM MST, NOV; SSC 4, 31
See also AITN 2; CA 1-4R; 101; CANR 1, 65; CDALBS; DA3; DLB 4, 9, 102; DLBD 12; DLBY 80; MTCW 1, 2; SATA 39; SATA-Obit 23

Porter, Peter (Neville Frederick) 1929- .... CLC 5, 13, 33
See also CA 85-88; DLB 40

Porter, William Sydney 1862-1910
See Henry, O.
See also CA 104; 131; CDALB 1865-1917; DA; DAB; DAC; DAM MST; DA3; DLB 12, 78, 79; MTCW 1, 2; YABC 2

Portillo (y Pacheco), Jose Lopez
See Lopez Portillo (y Pacheco), Jose

Portillo Trambley, Estela 1927-1998
See also CANR 32; DAM MULT; DLB 209; HLC 2; HW 1

Post, Melville Davisson 1869-1930 .... TCLC 39
See also CA 110

Potok, Chaim 1929- ... CLC 2, 7, 14, 26, 112; DAM NOV
See also AAYA 15; AITN 1, 2; CA 17-20R; CANR 19, 35, 64; DA3; DLB 28, 152; INT CANR-19; MTCW 1, 2; SATA 33, 106

Potter, Dennis (Christopher George) 1935-1994 .... CLC 58, 86
See also CA 107; 145; CANR 33, 61; MTCW 1

Pound, Ezra (Weston Loomis) 1885-1972 .. CLC 1, 2, 3, 4, 5, 7, 10, 13, 18, 34, 48, 50, 112; DA; DAB; DAC; DAM MST, POET; PC 4; WLC
See also CA 5-8R; 37-40R; CANR 40; CDALB 1917-1929; DA3; DLB 4, 45, 63; DLBD 15; MTCW 1, 2

Povod, Reinaldo 1959-1994 .... CLC 44
See also CA 136; 146; CANR 83

Powell, Adam Clayton, Jr. 1908-1972 .... CLC 89; BLC 3; DAM MULT
See also BW 1, 3; CA 102; 33-36R; CANR 86

Powell, Anthony (Dymoke) 1905- . CLC 1, 3, 7, 9, 10, 31
See also CA 1-4R; CANR 1, 32, 62; CDBLB 1945-1960; DLB 15; MTCW 1, 2

Powell, Dawn 1897-1965 .... CLC 66
See also CA 5-8R; DLBY 97

Powell, Padgett 1952- .... CLC 34
See also CA 126; CANR 63

Power, Susan 1961- .... CLC 91
See also CA 145

Powers, J(ames) F(arl) 1917-1999 ..... CLC 1, 4, 8, 57; SSC 4
See also CA 1-4R; 181; CANR 2, 61; DLB 130; MTCW 1

Powers, John J(ames) 1945-
See Powers, John R.
See also CA 69-72

Powers, John R. CLC 66
See also Powers, John J(ames)

Powers, Richard (S.) 1957- .... CLC 93
See also CA 148; CANR 80

Pownall, David 1938- .... CLC 10
See also CA 89-92, 180; CAAS 18; CANR 49; DLB 14

Powys, John Cowper 1872-1963 ... CLC 7, 9, 15, 46, 125
See also CA 85-88; DLB 15; MTCW 1, 2

Powys, T(heodore) F(rancis) 1875-1953 .... TCLC 9
See also CA 106; DLB 36, 162

Prado (Calvo), Pedro 1886-1952 ... TCLC 75
See also CA 131; HW 1

Prager, Emily 1952- .... CLC 56

Pratt, E(dwin) J(ohn) 1883(?)-1964 .... CLC 19; DAC; DAM POET
See also CA 141; 93-96; CANR 77; DLB 92

Premchand TCLC 21
See Srivastava, Dhanpat Rai

Preussler, Otfried 1923- .... CLC 17
See also CA 77-80; SATA 24

Prevert, Jacques (Henri Marie) 1900-1977 .... CLC 15
See also CA 77-80; 69-72; CANR 29, 61; MTCW 1; SATA-Obit 30

Prevost, Abbe (Antoine Francois) 1697-1763 .... LC 1

Price, (Edward) Reynolds 1933- ... CLC 3, 6, 13, 43, 50, 63; DAM NOV; SSC 22
See also CA 1-4R; CANR 1, 37, 57, 87; DLB 2; INT CANR-37

Price, Richard 1949- .... CLC 6, 12
See also CA 49-52; CANR 3; DLBY 81

Prichard, Katharine Susannah 1883-1969 .... CLC 46
See also CA 11-12; CANR 33; CAP 1; MTCW 1; SATA 66

Priestley, J(ohn) B(oynton) 1894-1984 .... CLC 2, 5, 9, 34; DAM DRAM, NOV
See also CA 9-12R; 113; CANR 33; CDBLB 1914-1945; DA3; DLB 10, 34, 77, 100, 139; DLBY 84; MTCW 1, 2

Prince 1958(?)- .... CLC 35

Prince, F(rank) T(empleton) 1912- .. CLC 22
See also CA 101; CANR 43, 79; DLB 20

Prince Kropotkin
See Kropotkin, Peter (Alekseievich)

Prior, Matthew 1664-1721 .... LC 4
See also DLB 95

Prishvin, Mikhail 1873-1954 .... TCLC 75

Pritchard, William H(arrison) 1932- .... CLC 34
See also CA 65-68; CANR 23; DLB 111

Pritchett, V(ictor) S(awdon) 1900-1997 ...... CLC 5, 13, 15, 41; DAM NOV; SSC 14
See also CA 61-64; 157; CANR 31, 63; DA3; DLB 15, 139; MTCW 1, 2

Private 19022
See Manning, Frederic

Probst, Mark 1925- .... CLC 59
See also CA 130

Prokosch, Frederic 1908-1989 ...... CLC 4, 48
See also CA 73-76; 128; CANR 82; DLB 48; MTCW 1

Propertius, Sextus c. 50B.C.-c. 16B.C. .... CMLC 32
See also DLB 211

Prophet, The
See Dreiser, Theodore (Herman Albert)

Prose, Francine 1947- .... CLC 45
See also CA 109; 112; CANR 46; SATA 101

Proudhon
See Cunha, Euclides (Rodrigues Pimenta) da

Proulx, Annie
See Proulx, E(dna) Annie

Proulx, E(dna) Annie 1935- .. CLC 81; DAM POP
See also CA 145; CANR 65; DA3; MTCW 2

Proust, (Valentin-Louis-George-Eugene-) Marcel 1871-1922 .... TCLC 7, 13, 33; DA; DAB; DAC; DAM MST, NOV; WLC
See also CA 104; 120; DA3; DLB 65; MTCW 1, 2

Prowler, Harley
See Masters, Edgar Lee
Prus, Boleslaw 1845-1912 .... **TCLC 48**
Pryor, Richard (Franklin Lenox Thomas)
1940- .... **CLC 26**
See also CA 122; 152
Przybyszewski, Stanislaw
1868-1927 .... **TCLC 36**
See also CA 160; DLB 66
Pteleon
See Grieve, C(hristopher) M(urray)
See also DAM POET
Puckett, Lute
See Masters, Edgar Lee
Puig, Manuel 1932-1990 .... **CLC 3, 5, 10, 28,
65; DAM MULT; HLC 2**
See also CA 45-48; CANR 2, 32, 63; DA3;
DLB 113; HW 1, 2; MTCW 1, 2
Pulitzer, Joseph 1847-1911 .... **TCLC 76**
See also CA 114; DLB 23
Purdy, A(lfred) W(ellington) 1918- ... **CLC 3,
6, 14, 50; DAC; DAM MST, POET**
See also CA 81-84; CAAS 17; CANR 42,
66; DLB 88
Purdy, James (Amos) 1923- .... **CLC 2, 4, 10,
28, 52**
See also CA 33-36R; CAAS 1; CANR 19,
51; DLB 2; INT CANR-19; MTCW 1
Pure, Simon
See Swinnerton, Frank Arthur
Pushkin, Alexander (Sergeyevich)
1799-1837 . **NCLC 3, 27, 83; DA; DAB;
DAC; DAM DRAM, MST, POET; PC
10; SSC 27; WLC**
See also DA3; DLB 205; SATA 61
P'u Sung-ling 1640-1715 .... **LC 49; SSC 31**
Putnam, Arthur Lee
See Alger, Horatio Jr., Jr.
Puzo, Mario 1920-1999 .... **CLC 1, 2, 6, 36,
107; DAM NOV, POP**
See also CA 65-68; 185; CANR 4, 42, 65;
DA3; DLB 6; MTCW 1, 2
Pygge, Edward
See Barnes, Julian (Patrick)
Pyle, Ernest Taylor 1900-1945
See Pyle, Ernie
See also CA 115; 160
Pyle, Ernie 1900-1945 .... **TCLC 75**
See also Pyle, Ernest Taylor
See also DLB 29; MTCW 2
Pyle, Howard 1853-1911 .... **TCLC 81**
See also CA 109; 137; CLR 22; DLB 42,
188; DLBD 13; MAICYA; SATA 16, 100
Pym, Barbara (Mary Crampton)
1913-1980 .... **CLC 13, 19, 37, 111**
See also CA 13-14; 97-100; CANR 13, 34;
CAP 1; DLB 14, 207; DLBY 87; MTCW
1, 2
Pynchon, Thomas (Ruggles, Jr.)
1937- ...... **CLC 2, 3, 6, 9, 11, 18, 33, 62,
72; DA; DAB; DAC; DAM MST, NOV,
POP; SSC 14; WLC**
See also BEST 90:2; CA 17-20R; CANR
22, 46, 73; DA3; DLB 2, 173; MTCW 1,
2
Pythagoras c. 570B.C.-c. 500B.C. . **CMLC 22**
See also DLB 176
Q
See Quiller-Couch, SirArthur (Thomas)
Qian Zhongshu
See Ch'ien Chung-shu
Qroll
See Dagerman, Stig (Halvard)
Quarrington, Paul (Lewis) 1953- ..... **CLC 65**
See also CA 129; CANR 62
Quasimodo, Salvatore 1901-1968 ..... **CLC 10**
See also CA 13-16; 25-28R; CAP 1; DLB
114; MTCW 1

Quay, Stephen 1947- .... **CLC 95**
Quay, Timothy 1947- .... **CLC 95**
Queen, Ellery **CLC 3, 11**
See also Dannay, Frederic; Davidson,
Avram (James); Lee, Manfred
B(ennington); Marlowe, Stephen; Stur-
geon, Theodore (Hamilton); Vance, John
Holbrook
Queen, Ellery, Jr.
See Dannay, Frederic; Lee, Manfred
B(ennington)
Queneau, Raymond 1903-1976 ..... **CLC 2, 5,
10, 42**
See also CA 77-80; 69-72; CANR 32; DLB
72; MTCW 1, 2
Quevedo, Francisco de 1580-1645 .... **LC 23**
Quiller-Couch, SirArthur (Thomas)
1863-1944 .... **TCLC 53**
See also CA 118; 166; DLB 135, 153, 190
Quin, Ann (Marie) 1936-1973 .... **CLC 6**
See also CA 9-12R; 45-48; DLB 14
Quinn, Martin
See Smith, Martin Cruz
Quinn, Peter 1947- .... **CLC 91**
Quinn, Simon
See Smith, Martin Cruz
Quintana, Leroy V. 1944-
See also CA 131; CANR 65; DAM MULT;
DLB 82; HLC 2; HW 1, 2
Quiroga, Horacio (Sylvestre)
1878-1937 .... **TCLC 20; DAM MULT;
HLC 2**
See also CA 117; 131; HW 1; MTCW 1
Quoirez, Francoise 1935- .... **CLC 9**
See also Sagan, Francoise
See also CA 49-52; CANR 6, 39, 73;
MTCW 1, 2
Raabe, Wilhelm (Karl) 1831-1910 . **TCLC 45**
See also CA 167; DLB 129
Rabe, David (William) 1940- .. **CLC 4, 8, 33;
DAM DRAM**
See also CA 85-88; CABS 3; CANR 59;
DLB 7
Rabelais, Francois 1483-1553 ...... **LC 5; DA;
DAB; DAC; DAM MST; WLC**
Rabinovitch, Sholem 1859-1916
See Aleichem, Sholom
See also CA 104
Rabinyan, Dorit 1972- .... **CLC 119**
See also CA 170
Rachilde
See Vallette, Marguerite Eymery
Racine, Jean 1639-1699 . **LC 28; DAB; DAM
MST**
See also DA3
Radcliffe, Ann (Ward) 1764-1823 ... **NCLC 6,
55**
See also DLB 39, 178
Radiguet, Raymond 1903-1923 ...... **TCLC 29**
See also CA 162; DLB 65
Radnoti, Miklos 1909-1944 .... **TCLC 16**
See also CA 118
Rado, James 1939- .... **CLC 17**
See also CA 105
Radvanyi, Netty 1900-1983
See Seghers, Anna
See also CA 85-88; 110; CANR 82
Rae, Ben
See Griffiths, Trevor
Raeburn, John (Hay) 1941- .... **CLC 34**
See also CA 57-60
Ragni, Gerome 1942-1991 .... **CLC 17**
See also CA 105; 134
Rahv, Philip 1908-1973 .... **CLC 24**
See also Greenberg, Ivan
See also DLB 137

Raimund, Ferdinand Jakob
1790-1836 .... **NCLC 69**
See also DLB 90
Raine, Craig 1944- .... **CLC 32, 103**
See also CA 108; CANR 29, 51; DLB 40
Raine, Kathleen (Jessie) 1908- ..... **CLC 7, 45**
See also CA 85-88; CANR 46; DLB 20;
MTCW 1
Rainis, Janis 1865-1929 .... **TCLC 29**
See also CA 170; DLB 220
Rakosi, Carl 1903- .... **CLC 47**
See also Rawley, Callman
See also CAAS 5; DLB 193
Raleigh, Richard
See Lovecraft, H(oward) P(hillips)
Raleigh, Sir Walter 1554(?)-1618 .. **LC 31, 39**
See also CDBLB Before 1660; DLB 172
Rallentando, H. P.
See Sayers, Dorothy L(eigh)
Ramal, Walter
See de la Mare, Walter (John)
Ramana Maharshi 1879-1950 .... **TCLC 84**
Ramoacn y Cajal, Santiago
1852-1934 .... **TCLC 93**
Ramon, Juan
See Jimenez (Mantecon), Juan Ramon
Ramos, Graciliano 1892-1953 .... **TCLC 32**
See also CA 167; HW 2
Rampersad, Arnold 1941- .... **CLC 44**
See also BW 2, 3; CA 127; 133; CANR 81;
DLB 111; INT 133
Rampling, Anne
See Rice, Anne
Ramsay, Allan 1684(?)-1758 .... **LC 29**
See also DLB 95
Ramuz, Charles-Ferdinand
1878-1947 .... **TCLC 33**
See also CA 165
Rand, Ayn 1905-1982 ...... **CLC 3, 30, 44, 79;
DA; DAC; DAM MST, NOV, POP;
WLC**
See also AAYA 10; CA 13-16R; 105; CANR
27, 73; CDALBS; DA3; MTCW 1, 2
Randall, Dudley (Felker) 1914- .... **CLC 1;
BLC 3; DAM MULT**
See also BW 1, 3; CA 25-28R; CANR 23,
82; DLB 41
Randall, Robert
See Silverberg, Robert
Ranger, Ken
See Creasey, John
Ransom, John Crowe 1888-1974 .. **CLC 2, 4,
5, 11, 24; DAM POET**
See also CA 5-8R; 49-52; CANR 6, 34;
CDALBS; DA3; DLB 45, 63; MTCW 1,
2
Rao, Raja 1909- ..... **CLC 25, 56; DAM NOV**
See also CA 73-76; CANR 51; MTCW 1, 2
Raphael, Frederic (Michael) 1931- ... **CLC 2,
14**
See also CA 1-4R; CANR 1, 86; DLB 14
Ratcliffe, James P.
See Mencken, H(enry) L(ouis)
Rathbone, Julian 1935- .... **CLC 41**
See also CA 101; CANR 34, 73
Rattigan, Terence (Mervyn)
1911-1977 .... **CLC 7; DAM DRAM**
See also CA 85-88; 73-76; CDBLB 1945-
1960; DLB 13; MTCW 1, 2
Ratushinskaya, Irina 1954- .... **CLC 54**
See also CA 129; CANR 68
Raven, Simon (Arthur Noel) 1927- .. **CLC 14**
See also CA 81-84; CANR 86
Ravenna, Michael
See Welty, Eudora

Rawley, Callman 1903-
See Rakosi, Carl
See also CA 21-24R; CANR 12, 32, 91

Rawlings, Marjorie Kinnan
1896-1953 .... **TCLC 4**
See also AAYA 20; CA 104; 137; CANR
74; CLR 63; DLB 9, 22, 102; DLBD 17;
JRDA; MAICYA; MTCW 2; SATA 100;
YABC 1

Ray, Satyajit 1921-1992 .. **CLC 16, 76; DAM
MULT**
See also CA 114; 137

Read, Herbert Edward 1893-1968 ..... **CLC 4**
See also CA 85-88; 25-28R; DLB 20, 149

Read, Piers Paul 1941- .... **CLC 4, 10, 25**
See also CA 21-24R; CANR 38, 86; DLB
14; SATA 21

Reade, Charles 1814-1884 .... **NCLC 2, 74**
See also DLB 21

Reade, Hamish
See Gray, Simon (James Holliday)

Reading, Peter 1946- .... **CLC 47**
See also CA 103; CANR 46; DLB 40

Reaney, James 1926- .. **CLC 13; DAC; DAM
MST**
See also CA 41-44R; CAAS 15; CANR 42;
DLB 68; SATA 43

Rebreanu, Liviu 1885-1944 .... **TCLC 28**
See also CA 165; DLB 220

Rechy, John (Francisco) 1934- ...... **CLC 1, 7,
14, 18, 107; DAM MULT; HLC 2**
See also CA 5-8R; CAAS 4; CANR 6, 32,
64; DLB 122; DLBY 82; HW 1, 2; INT
CANR-6

Redcam, Tom 1870-1933 .... **TCLC 25**

Reddin, Keith **CLC 67**

Redgrove, Peter (William) 1932- . **CLC 6, 41**
See also CA 1-4R; CANR 3, 39, 77; DLB
40

Redmon, Anne **CLC 22**
See also Nightingale, Anne Redmon
See also DLBY 86

Reed, Eliot
See Ambler, Eric

Reed, Ishmael 1938- .. **CLC 2, 3, 5, 6, 13, 32,
60; BLC 3; DAM MULT**
See also BW 2, 3; CA 21-24R; CANR 25,
48, 74; DA3; DLB 2, 5, 33, 169; DLBD
8; MTCW 1, 2

Reed, John (Silas) 1887-1920 .... **TCLC 9**
See also CA 106

Reed, Lou **CLC 21**
See also Firbank, Louis

Reese, Lizette Woodworth 1856-1935 . **PC 29**
See also CA 180; DLB 54

Reeve, Clara 1729-1807 .... **NCLC 19**
See also DLB 39

Reich, Wilhelm 1897-1957 .... **TCLC 57**

Reid, Christopher (John) 1949- .... **CLC 33**
See also CA 140; CANR 89; DLB 40

Reid, Desmond
See Moorcock, Michael (John)

Reid Banks, Lynne 1929-
See Banks, Lynne Reid
See also CA 1-4R; CANR 6, 22, 38, 87;
CLR 24; JRDA; MAICYA; SATA 22, 75,
111

Reilly, William K.
See Creasey, John

Reiner, Max
See Caldwell, (Janet Miriam) Taylor
(Holland)

Reis, Ricardo
See Pessoa, Fernando (Antonio Nogueira)

Remarque, Erich Maria
1898-1970 ... **CLC 21; DA; DAB; DAC;
DAM MST, NOV**
See also AAYA 27; CA 77-80; 29-32R;
DA3; DLB 56; MTCW 1, 2

Remington, Frederic 1861-1909 ..... **TCLC 89**
See also CA 108; 169; DLB 12, 186, 188;
SATA 41

Remizov, A.
See Remizov, Aleksei (Mikhailovich)

Remizov, A. M.
See Remizov, Aleksei (Mikhailovich)

Remizov, Aleksei (Mikhailovich)
1877-1957 .... **TCLC 27**
See also CA 125; 133

Renan, Joseph Ernest 1823-1892 .. **NCLC 26**

Renard, Jules 1864-1910 .... **TCLC 17**
See also CA 117

Renault, Mary **CLC 3, 11, 17**
See also Challans, Mary
See also DLBY 83; MTCW 2

Rendell, Ruth (Barbara) 1930- . **CLC 28, 48;
DAM POP**
See also Vine, Barbara
See also CA 109; CANR 32, 52, 74; DLB
87; INT CANR-32; MTCW 1, 2

Renoir, Jean 1894-1979 .... **CLC 20**
See also CA 129; 85-88

Resnais, Alain 1922- .... **CLC 16**

Reverdy, Pierre 1889-1960 .... **CLC 53**
See also CA 97-100; 89-92

Rexroth, Kenneth 1905-1982 .... **CLC 1, 2, 6,
11, 22, 49, 112; DAM POET; PC 20**
See also CA 5-8R; 107; CANR 14, 34, 63;
CDALB 1941-1968; DLB 16, 48, 165,
212; DLBY 82; INT CANR-14; MTCW
1, 2

Reyes, Alfonso 1889-1959 .. **TCLC 33; HLCS
2**
See also CA 131; HW 1

Reyes y Basoalto, Ricardo Eliecer Neftali
See Neruda, Pablo

Reymont, Wladyslaw (Stanislaw)
1868(?)-1925 .... **TCLC 5**
See also CA 104

Reynolds, Jonathan 1942- .... **CLC 6, 38**
See also CA 65-68; CANR 28

Reynolds, Joshua 1723-1792 .... **LC 15**
See also DLB 104

Reynolds, Michael S(hane) 1937- ..... **CLC 44**
See also CA 65-68; CANR 9, 89

Reznikoff, Charles 1894-1976 .... **CLC 9**
See also CA 33-36; 61-64; CAP 2; DLB 28,
45

Rezzori (d'Arezzo), Gregor von
1914-1998 .... **CLC 25**
See also CA 122; 136; 167

Rhine, Richard
See Silverstein, Alvin

Rhodes, Eugene Manlove
1869-1934 .... **TCLC 53**

Rhodius, Apollonius c. 3rd cent.
B.C.- .... **CMLC 28**
See also DLB 176

R'hoone
See Balzac, Honore de

Rhys, Jean 1890(?)-1979 ...... **CLC 2, 4, 6, 14,
19, 51, 124; DAM NOV; SSC 21**
See also CA 25-28R; 85-88; CANR 35, 62;
CDBLB 1945-1960; DA3; DLB 36, 117,
162; MTCW 1, 2

Ribeiro, Darcy 1922-1997 .... **CLC 34**
See also CA 33-36R; 156

Ribeiro, Joao Ubaldo (Osorio Pimentel)
1941- .... **CLC 10, 67**
See also CA 81-84

Ribman, Ronald (Burt) 1932- .... **CLC 7**
See also CA 21-24R; CANR 46, 80

Ricci, Nino 1959- .... **CLC 70**
See also CA 137

Rice, Anne 1941- .. **CLC 41, 128; DAM POP**
See also AAYA 9; BEST 89:2; CA 65-68;
CANR 12, 36, 53, 74; DA3; MTCW 2

Rice, Elmer (Leopold) 1892-1967 ...... **CLC 7,
49; DAM DRAM**
See also CA 21-22; 25-28R; CAP 2; DLB
4, 7; MTCW 1, 2

Rice, Tim(othy Miles Bindon)
1944- .... **CLC 21**
See also CA 103; CANR 46

Rich, Adrienne (Cecile) 1929- ... **CLC 3, 6, 7,
11, 18, 36, 73, 76, 125; DAM POET;
PC 5**
See also CA 9-12R; CANR 20, 53, 74;
CDALBS; DA3; DLB 5, 67; MTCW 1, 2

Rich, Barbara
See Graves, Robert (von Ranke)

Rich, Robert
See Trumbo, Dalton

Richard, Keith **CLC 17**
See also Richards, Keith

Richards, David Adams 1950- .... **CLC 59;
DAC**
See also CA 93-96; CANR 60; DLB 53

Richards, I(vor) A(rmstrong)
1893-1979 .... **CLC 14, 24**
See also CA 41-44R; 89-92; CANR 34, 74;
DLB 27; MTCW 2

Richards, Keith 1943-
See Richard, Keith
See also CA 107; CANR 77

Richardson, Anne
See Roiphe, Anne (Richardson)

Richardson, Dorothy Miller
1873-1957 .... **TCLC 3**
See also CA 104; DLB 36

Richardson, Ethel Florence (Lindesay)
1870-1946
See Richardson, Henry Handel
See also CA 105

Richardson, Henry Handel **TCLC 4**
See also Richardson, Ethel Florence
(Lindesay)
See also DLB 197

Richardson, John 1796-1852 .... **NCLC 55;
DAC**
See also DLB 99

Richardson, Samuel 1689-1761 ...... **LC 1, 44;
DA; DAB; DAC; DAM MST, NOV;
WLC**
See also CDBLB 1660-1789; DLB 39

Richler, Mordecai 1931- ...... **CLC 3, 5, 9, 13,
18, 46, 70; DAC; DAM MST, NOV**
See also AITN 1; CA 65-68; CANR 31, 62;
CLR 17; DLB 53; MAICYA; MTCW 1,
2; SATA 44, 98; SATA-Brief 27

Richter, Conrad (Michael)
1890-1968 .... **CLC 30**
See also AAYA 21; CA 5-8R; 25-28R;
CANR 23; DLB 9, 212; MTCW 1, 2;
SATA 3

Ricostranza, Tom
See Ellis, Trey

Riddell, Charlotte 1832-1906 .... **TCLC 40**
See also CA 165; DLB 156

Ridge, John Rollin 1827-1867 ...... **NCLC 82;
DAM MULT**
See also CA 144; DLB 175; NNAL

Ridgway, Keith 1965- .... **CLC 119**
See also CA 172

Riding, Laura **CLC 3, 7**
See also Jackson, Laura (Riding)

Riefenstahl, Berta Helene Amalia 1902-
See Riefenstahl, Leni
See also CA 108

Riefenstahl, Leni **CLC 16**
See also Riefenstahl, Berta Helene Amalia

Riffe, Ernest
See Bergman, (Ernst) Ingmar

Riggs, (Rolla) Lynn 1899-1954 ..... **TCLC 56;
DAM MULT**
See also CA 144; DLB 175; NNAL

Saintsbury, George (Edward Bateman)
  1845-1933 .... **TCLC 31**
  See also CA 160; DLB 57, 149
Sait Faik TCLC 23
  See also Abasiyanik, Sait Faik
Saki TCLC 3; SSC 12
  See also Munro, H(ector) H(ugh)
  See also MTCW 2
Sala, George Augustus NCLC 46
Saladin 1138-1193 .... **CMLC 38**
Salama, Hannu 1936- .... **CLC 18**
Salamanca, J(ack) R(ichard) 1922- .. **CLC 4,
  15**
  See also CA 25-28R
Salas, Floyd Francis 1931-
  See also CA 119; CAAS 27; CANR 44, 75;
  DAM MULT; DLB 82; HLC 2; HW 1, 2;
  MTCW 2
Sale, J. Kirkpatrick
  See Sale, Kirkpatrick
Sale, Kirkpatrick 1937- .... **CLC 68**
  See also CA 13-16R; CANR 10
Salinas, Luis Omar 1937- ..... **CLC 90; DAM
  MULT; HLC 2**
  See also CA 131; CANR 81; DLB 82; HW
  1, 2
Salinas (y Serrano), Pedro
  1891(?)-1951 .... **TCLC 17**
  See also CA 117; DLB 134
Salinger, J(erome) D(avid) 1919- .. **CLC 1, 3,
  8, 12, 55, 56; DA; DAB; DAC; DAM
  MST, NOV, POP; SSC 2, 28; WLC**
  See also AAYA 2; CA 5-8R; CANR 39;
  CDALB 1941-1968; CLR 18; DA3; DLB
  2, 102, 173; MAICYA; MTCW 1, 2;
  SATA 67
Salisbury, John
  See Caute, (John) David
Salter, James 1925- .... **CLC 7, 52, 59**
  See also CA 73-76; DLB 130
Saltus, Edgar (Everton) 1855-1921 . **TCLC 8**
  See also CA 105; DLB 202
Saltykov, Mikhail Evgrafovich
  1826-1889 .... **NCLC 16**
Samarakis, Antonis 1919- .... **CLC 5**
  See also CA 25-28R; CAAS 16; CANR 36
Sanchez, Florencio 1875-1910 .... **TCLC 37**
  See also CA 153; HW 1
Sanchez, Luis Rafael 1936- .... **CLC 23**
  See also CA 128; DLB 145; HW 1
Sanchez, Sonia 1934- .... **CLC 5, 116; BLC 3;
  DAM MULT; PC 9**
  See also BW 2, 3; CA 33-36R; CANR 24,
  49, 74; CLR 18; DA3; DLB 41; DLBD 8;
  MAICYA; MTCW 1, 2; SATA 22
Sand, George 1804-1876 ..... **NCLC 2, 42, 57;
  DA; DAB; DAC; DAM MST, NOV;
  WLC**
  See also DA3; DLB 119, 192
Sandburg, Carl (August) 1878-1967 . **CLC 1,
  4, 10, 15, 35; DA; DAB; DAC; DAM
  MST, POET; PC 2; WLC**
  See also AAYA 24; CA 5-8R; 25-28R;
  CANR 35; CDALB 1865-1917; DA3;
  DLB 17, 54; MAICYA; MTCW 1, 2;
  SATA 8
Sandburg, Charles
  See Sandburg, Carl (August)
Sandburg, Charles A.
  See Sandburg, Carl (August)
Sanders, (James) Ed(ward) 1939- ... **CLC 53;
  DAM POET**
  See also CA 13-16R; CAAS 21; CANR 13,
  44, 78; DLB 16
Sanders, Lawrence 1920-1998 .... **CLC 41;
  DAM POP**
  See also BEST 89:4; CA 81-84; 165; CANR
  33, 62; DA3; MTCW 1

Sanders, Noah
  See Blount, Roy (Alton), Jr.
Sanders, Winston P.
  See Anderson, Poul (William)
Sandoz, Mari(e Susette) 1896-1966 .. **CLC 28**
  See also CA 1-4R; 25-28R; CANR 17, 64;
  DLB 9, 212; MTCW 1, 2; SATA 5
Saner, Reg(inald Anthony) 1931- .... **CLC 9**
  See also CA 65-68
Sankara 788-820 .... **CMLC 32**
Sannazaro, Jacopo 1456(?)-1530 .... **LC 8**
Sansom, William 1912-1976 .... **CLC 2, 6;
  DAM NOV; SSC 21**
  See also CA 5-8R; 65-68; CANR 42; DLB
  139; MTCW 1
Santayana, George 1863-1952 .... **TCLC 40**
  See also CA 115; DLB 54, 71; DLBD 13
Santiago, Danny CLC 33
  See also James, Daniel (Lewis)
  See also DLB 122
Santmyer, Helen Hoover 1895-1986 . **CLC 33**
  See also CA 1-4R; 118; CANR 15, 33;
  DLBY 84; MTCW 1
Santoka, Taneda 1882-1940 .... **TCLC 72**
Santos, Bienvenido N(uqui)
  1911-1996 .... **CLC 22; DAM MULT**
  See also CA 101; 151; CANR 19, 46
Sapper TCLC 44
  See also McNeile, Herman Cyril
Sapphire
  See Sapphire, Brenda
Sapphire, Brenda 1950- .... **CLC 99**
Sappho fl. 6th cent. B.C.- ..... **CMLC 3; DAM
  POET; PC 5**
  See also DA3; DLB 176
Saramago, Jose 1922- ..... **CLC 119; HLCS 1**
  See also CA 153
Sarduy, Severo 1937-1993 .... **CLC 6, 97;
  HLCS 1**
  See also CA 89-92; 142; CANR 58, 81;
  DLB 113; HW 1, 2
Sargeson, Frank 1903-1982 .... **CLC 31**
  See also CA 25-28R; 106; CANR 38, 79
Sarmiento, Domingo Faustino 1811-1888
  See also HLCS 2
Sarmiento, Felix Ruben Garcia
  See Dario, Ruben
Saro-Wiwa, Ken(ule Beeson)
  1941-1995 .... **CLC 114**
  See also BW 2; CA 142; 150; CANR 60;
  DLB 157
Saroyan, William 1908-1981 ... **CLC 1, 8, 10,
  29, 34, 56; DA; DAB; DAC; DAM
  DRAM, MST, NOV; SSC 21; WLC**
  See also CA 5-8R; 103; CANR 30;
  CDALBS; DA3; DLB 7, 9, 86; DLBY 81;
  MTCW 1, 2; SATA 23; SATA-Obit 24
Sarraute, Nathalie 1900- . **CLC 1, 2, 4, 8, 10,
  31, 80**
  See also CA 9-12R; CANR 23, 66; DLB
  83; MTCW 1, 2
Sarton, (Eleanor) May 1912-1995 ..... **CLC 4,
  14, 49, 91; DAM POET**
  See also CA 1-4R; 149; CANR 1, 34, 55;
  DLB 48; DLBY 81; INT CANR-34;
  MTCW 1, 2; SATA 36; SATA-Obit 86
Sartre, Jean-Paul 1905-1980 . **CLC 1, 4, 7, 9,
  13, 18, 24, 44, 50, 52; DA; DAB; DAC;
  DAM DRAM, MST, NOV; DC 3; SSC
  32; WLC**
  See also CA 9-12R; 97-100; CANR 21;
  DA3; DLB 72; MTCW 1, 2
Sassoon, Siegfried (Lorraine)
  1886-1967 .... **CLC 36, 130; DAB; DAM
  MST, NOV, POET; PC 12**
  See also CA 104; 25-28R; CANR 36; DLB
  20, 191; DLBD 18; MTCW 1, 2
Satterfield, Charles
  See Pohl, Frederik

Satyremont
  See Peret, Benjamin
Saul, John (W. III) 1942- ...... **CLC 46; DAM
  NOV, POP**
  See also AAYA 10; BEST 90:4; CA 81-84;
  CANR 16, 40, 81; SATA 98
Saunders, Caleb
  See Heinlein, Robert A(nson)
Saura (Atares), Carlos 1932- .... **CLC 20**
  See also CA 114; 131; CANR 79; HW 1
Sauser-Hall, Frederic 1887-1961 ...... **CLC 18**
  See also Cendrars, Blaise
  See also CA 102; 93-96; CANR 36, 62;
  MTCW 1
Saussure, Ferdinand de
  1857-1913 .... **TCLC 49**
Savage, Catharine
  See Brosman, Catharine Savage
Savage, Thomas 1915- .... **CLC 40**
  See also CA 126; 132; CAAS 15; INT 132
Savan, Glenn 19(?)- .... **CLC 50**
Sayers, Dorothy L(eigh)
  1893-1957 .... **TCLC 2, 15; DAM POP**
  See also CA 104; 119; CANR 60; CDBLB
  1914-1945; DLB 10, 36, 77, 100; MTCW
  1, 2
Sayers, Valerie 1952- .... **CLC 50, 122**
  See also CA 134; CANR 61
Sayles, John (Thomas) 1950- . **CLC 7, 10, 14**
  See also CA 57-60; CANR 41, 84; DLB 44
Scammell, Michael 1935- .... **CLC 34**
  See also CA 156
Scannell, Vernon 1922- .... **CLC 49**
  See also CA 5-8R; CANR 8, 24, 57; DLB
  27; SATA 59
Scarlett, Susan
  See Streatfeild, (Mary) Noel
Scarron
  See Mikszath, Kalman
Schaeffer, Susan Fromberg 1941- ..... **CLC 6,
  11, 22**
  See also CA 49-52; CANR 18, 65; DLB 28;
  MTCW 1, 2; SATA 22
Schary, Jill
  See Robinson, Jill
Schell, Jonathan 1943- .... **CLC 35**
  See also CA 73-76; CANR 12
Schelling, Friedrich Wilhelm Joseph von
  1775-1854 .... **NCLC 30**
  See also DLB 90
Schendel, Arthur van 1874-1946 ... **TCLC 56**
Scherer, Jean-Marie Maurice 1920-
  See Rohmer, Eric
  See also CA 110
Schevill, James (Erwin) 1920- .... **CLC 7**
  See also CA 5-8R; CAAS 12
Schiller, Friedrich 1759-1805 . **NCLC 39, 69;
  DAM DRAM; DC 12**
  See also DLB 94
Schisgal, Murray (Joseph) 1926- .... **CLC 6**
  See also CA 21-24R; CANR 48, 86
Schlee, Ann 1934- .... **CLC 35**
  See also CA 101; CANR 29, 88; SATA 44;
  SATA-Brief 36
Schlegel, August Wilhelm von
  1767-1845 .... **NCLC 15**
  See also DLB 94
Schlegel, Friedrich 1772-1829 .... **NCLC 45**
  See also DLB 90
Schlegel, Johann Elias (von)
  1719(?)-1749 .... **LC 5**
Schlesinger, Arthur M(eier), Jr.
  1917- .... **CLC 84**
  See also AITN 1; CA 1-4R; CANR 1, 28,
  58; DLB 17; INT CANR-28; MTCW 1,
  2; SATA 61
Schmidt, Arno (Otto) 1914-1979 ...... **CLC 56**
  See also CA 128; 109; DLB 69

Silverstein, Virginia B(arbara Opshelor)
1937- .... **CLC 17**
See also CA 49-52; CANR 2; CLR 25;
JRDA; MAICYA; SATA 8, 69

Sim, Georges
See Simenon, Georges (Jacques Christian)

Simak, Clifford D(onald) 1904-1988 . **CLC 1, 55**
See also CA 1-4R; 125; CANR 1, 35; DLB
8; MTCW 1; SATA-Obit 56

Simenon, Georges (Jacques Christian)
1903-1989 .... **CLC 1, 2, 3, 8, 18, 47; DAM POP**
See also CA 85-88; 129; CANR 35; DA3;
DLB 72; DLBY 89; MTCW 1, 2

Simic, Charles 1938- .... **CLC 6, 9, 22, 49, 68, 130; DAM POET**
See also CA 29-32R; CAAS 4; CANR 12,
33, 52, 61; DA3; DLB 105; MTCW 2

Simmel, Georg 1858-1918 .... **TCLC 64**
See also CA 157

Simmons, Charles (Paul) 1924- .... **CLC 57**
See also CA 89-92; INT 89-92

Simmons, Dan 1948- .... **CLC 44; DAM POP**
See also AAYA 16; CA 138; CANR 53, 81

Simmons, James (Stewart Alexander)
1933- .... **CLC 43**
See also CA 105; CAAS 21; DLB 40

Simms, William Gilmore
1806-1870 .... **NCLC 3**
See also DLB 3, 30, 59, 73

Simon, Carly 1945- .... **CLC 26**
See also CA 105

Simon, Claude 1913- .... **CLC 4, 9, 15, 39; DAM NOV**
See also CA 89-92; CANR 33; DLB 83;
MTCW 1

Simon, (Marvin) Neil 1927- ... **CLC 6, 11, 31, 39, 70; DAM DRAM**
See also AAYA 32; AITN 1; CA 21-24R;
CANR 26, 54, 87; DA3; DLB 7; MTCW
1, 2

Simon, Paul (Frederick) 1941(?)- ..... **CLC 17**
See also CA 116; 153

Simonon, Paul 1956(?)- .... **CLC 30**

Simpson, Harriette
See Arnow, Harriette (Louisa) Simpson

Simpson, Louis (Aston Marantz)
1923- ...... **CLC 4, 7, 9, 32; DAM POET**
See also CA 1-4R; CAAS 4; CANR 1, 61;
DLB 5; MTCW 1, 2

Simpson, Mona (Elizabeth) 1957- .... **CLC 44**
See also CA 122; 135; CANR 68

Simpson, N(orman) F(rederick)
1919- .... **CLC 29**
See also CA 13-16R; DLB 13

Sinclair, Andrew (Annandale) 1935- . **CLC 2, 14**
See also CA 9-12R; CAAS 5; CANR 14,
38, 91; DLB 14; MTCW 1

Sinclair, Emil
See Hesse, Hermann

Sinclair, Iain 1943- .... **CLC 76**
See also CA 132; CANR 81

Sinclair, Iain MacGregor
See Sinclair, Iain

Sinclair, Irene
See Griffith, D(avid Lewelyn) W(ark)

Sinclair, Mary Amelia St. Clair 1865(?)-1946
See Sinclair, May
See also CA 104

Sinclair, May 1863-1946 .... **TCLC 3, 11**
See also Sinclair, Mary Amelia St. Clair
See also CA 166; DLB 36, 135

Sinclair, Roy
See Griffith, D(avid Lewelyn) W(ark)

Sinclair, Upton (Beall) 1878-1968 ..... **CLC 1, 11, 15, 63; DA; DAB; DAC; DAM MST, NOV; WLC**
See also CA 5-8R; 25-28R; CANR 7;
CDALB 1929-1941; DA3; DLB 9; INT
CANR-7; MTCW 1, 2; SATA 9

Singer, Isaac
See Singer, Isaac Bashevis

Singer, Isaac Bashevis 1904-1991 .. **CLC 1, 3, 6, 9, 11, 15, 23, 38, 69, 111; DA; DAB; DAC; DAM MST, NOV; SSC 3; WLC**
See also AAYA 32; AITN 1, 2; CA 1-4R;
134; CANR 1, 39; CDALB 1941-1968;
CLR 1; DA3; DLB 6, 28, 52; DLBY 91;
JRDA; MAICYA; MTCW 1, 2; SATA 3,
27; SATA-Obit 68

Singer, Israel Joshua 1893-1944 .... **TCLC 33**
See also CA 169

Singh, Khushwant 1915- .... **CLC 11**
See also CA 9-12R; CAAS 9; CANR 6, 84

Singleton, Ann
See Benedict, Ruth (Fulton)

Sinjohn, John
See Galsworthy, John

Sinyavsky, Andrei (Donatevich)
1925-1997 .... **CLC 8**
See also CA 85-88; 159

Sirin, V.
See Nabokov, Vladimir (Vladimirovich)

Sissman, L(ouis) E(dward)
1928-1976 .... **CLC 9, 18**
See also CA 21-24R; 65-68; CANR 13;
DLB 5

Sisson, C(harles) H(ubert) 1914- .... **CLC 8**
See also CA 1-4R; CAAS 3; CANR 3, 48,
84; DLB 27

Sitwell, Dame Edith 1887-1964 ..... **CLC 2, 9, 67; DAM POET; PC 3**
See also CA 9-12R; CANR 35; CDBLB
1945-1960; DLB 20; MTCW 1, 2

Siwaarmill, H. P.
See Sharp, William

Sjoewall, Maj 1935- .... **CLC 7**
See also CA 65-68; CANR 73

Sjowall, Maj
See Sjoewall, Maj

Skelton, John 1463-1529 .... **PC 25**

Skelton, Robin 1925-1997 .... **CLC 13**
See also AITN 2; CA 5-8R; 160; CAAS 5;
CANR 28, 89; DLB 27, 53

Skolimowski, Jerzy 1938- .... **CLC 20**
See also CA 128

Skram, Amalie (Bertha)
1847-1905 .... **TCLC 25**
See also CA 165

Skvorecky, Josef (Vaclav) 1924- ...... **CLC 15, 39, 69; DAC; DAM NOV**
See also CA 61-64; CAAS 1; CANR 10,
34, 63; DA3; MTCW 1, 2

Slade, Bernard CLC 11, 46
See also Newbound, Bernard Slade
See also CAAS 9; DLB 53

Slaughter, Carolyn 1946- .... **CLC 56**
See also CA 85-88; CANR 85

Slaughter, Frank G(ill) 1908- .... **CLC 29**
See also AITN 2; CA 5-8R; CANR 5, 85;
INT CANR-5

Slavitt, David R(ytman) 1935- ..... **CLC 5, 14**
See also CA 21-24R; CAAS 3; CANR 41,
83; DLB 5, 6

Slesinger, Tess 1905-1945 .... **TCLC 10**
See also CA 107; DLB 102

Slessor, Kenneth 1901-1971 .... **CLC 14**
See also CA 102; 89-92

Slowacki, Juliusz 1809-1849 .... **NCLC 15**

Smart, Christopher 1722-1771 .. **LC 3; DAM POET; PC 13**
See also DLB 109

Smart, Elizabeth 1913-1986 .... **CLC 54**
See also CA 81-84; 118; DLB 88

Smiley, Jane (Graves) 1949- ...... **CLC 53, 76; DAM POP**
See also CA 104; CANR 30, 50, 74; DA3;
INT CANR-30

Smith, A(rthur) J(ames) M(arshall)
1902-1980 .... **CLC 15; DAC**
See also CA 1-4R; 102; CANR 4; DLB 88

Smith, Adam 1723-1790 .... **LC 36**
See also DLB 104

Smith, Alexander 1829-1867 .... **NCLC 59**
See also DLB 32, 55

Smith, Anna Deavere 1950- .... **CLC 86**
See also CA 133

Smith, Betty (Wehner) 1896-1972 .... **CLC 19**
See also CA 5-8R; 33-36R; DLBY 82;
SATA 6

Smith, Charlotte (Turner)
1749-1806 .... **NCLC 23**
See also DLB 39, 109

Smith, Clark Ashton 1893-1961 .... **CLC 43**
See also CA 143; CANR 81; MTCW 2

Smith, Dave CLC 22, 42
See also Smith, David (Jeddie)
See also CAAS 7; DLB 5

Smith, David (Jeddie) 1942-
See Smith, Dave
See also CA 49-52; CANR 1, 59; DAM
POET

Smith, Florence Margaret 1902-1971
See Smith, Stevie
See also CA 17-18; 29-32R; CANR 35;
CAP 2; DAM POET; MTCW 1, 2

Smith, Iain Crichton 1928-1998 .... **CLC 64**
See also CA 21-24R; 171; DLB 40, 139

Smith, John 1580(?)-1631 .... **LC 9**
See also DLB 24, 30

Smith, Johnston
See Crane, Stephen (Townley)

Smith, Joseph, Jr. 1805-1844 .... **NCLC 53**

Smith, Lee 1944- .... **CLC 25, 73**
See also CA 114; 119; CANR 46; DLB 143;
DLBY 83; INT 119

Smith, Martin
See Smith, Martin Cruz

Smith, Martin Cruz 1942- .... **CLC 25; DAM MULT, POP**
See also BEST 89:4; CA 85-88; CANR 6,
23, 43, 65; INT CANR-23; MTCW 2;
NNAL

Smith, Mary-Ann Tirone 1944- .... **CLC 39**
See also CA 118; 136

Smith, Patti 1946- .... **CLC 12**
See also CA 93-96; CANR 63

Smith, Pauline (Urmson)
1882-1959 .... **TCLC 25**

Smith, Rosamond
See Oates, Joyce Carol

Smith, Sheila Kaye
See Kaye-Smith, Sheila

Smith, Stevie CLC 3, 8, 25, 44; PC 12
See also Smith, Florence Margaret
See also DLB 20; MTCW 2

Smith, Wilbur (Addison) 1933- .... **CLC 33**
See also CA 13-16R; CANR 7, 46, 66;
MTCW 1, 2

Smith, William Jay 1918- .... **CLC 6**
See also CA 5-8R; CANR 44; DLB 5; MAI-
CYA; SAAS 22; SATA 2, 68

Smith, Woodrow Wilson
See Kuttner, Henry

Smolenskin, Peretz 1842-1885 .... **NCLC 30**

Smollett, Tobias (George) 1721-1771 ... **LC 2, 46**
See also CDBLB 1660-1789; DLB 39, 104

Staunton, Schuyler
See Baum, L(yman) Frank

Stead, Christina (Ellen) 1902-1983 ... CLC 2, 5, 8, 32, 80
See also CA 13-16R; 109; CANR 33, 40; MTCW 1, 2

Stead, William Thomas 1849-1912 .... TCLC 48
See also CA 167

Steele, Richard 1672-1729 .... LC 18
See also CDBLB 1660-1789; DLB 84, 101

Steele, Timothy (Reid) 1948- .... CLC 45
See also CA 93-96; CANR 16, 50; DLB 120

Steffens, (Joseph) Lincoln 1866-1936 .... TCLC 20
See also CA 117

Stegner, Wallace (Earle) 1909-1993 .. CLC 9, 49, 81; DAM NOV; SSC 27
See also AITN 1; BEST 90:3; CA 1-4R; 141; CAAS 9; CANR 1, 21, 46; DLB 9, 206; DLBY 93; MTCW 1, 2

Stein, Gertrude 1874-1946 .... TCLC 1, 6, 28, 48; DA; DAB; DAC; DAM MST, NOV, POET; PC 18; WLC
See also CA 104; 132; CDALB 1917-1929; DA3; DLB 4, 54, 86; DLBD 15; MTCW 1, 2

Steinbeck, John (Ernst) 1902-1968 ... CLC 1, 5, 9, 13, 21, 34, 45, 75, 124; DA; DAB; DAC; DAM DRAM, MST, NOV; SSC 11, 37; WLC
See also AAYA 12; CA 1-4R; 25-28R; CANR 1, 35; CDALB 1929-1941; DA3; DLB 7, 9, 212; DLBD 2; MTCW 1, 2; SATA 9

Steinem, Gloria 1934- .... CLC 63
See also CA 53-56; CANR 28, 51; MTCW 1, 2

Steiner, George 1929- .. CLC 24; DAM NOV
See also CA 73-76; CANR 31, 67; DLB 67; MTCW 1, 2; SATA 62

Steiner, K. Leslie
See Delany, Samuel R(ay, Jr.)

Steiner, Rudolf 1861-1925 .... TCLC 13
See also CA 107

Stendhal 1783-1842 .... NCLC 23, 46; DA; DAB; DAC; DAM MST, NOV; SSC 27; WLC
See also DA3; DLB 119

Stephen, Adeline Virginia
See Woolf, (Adeline) Virginia

Stephen, SirLeslie 1832-1904 .... TCLC 23
See also CA 123; DLB 57, 144, 190

Stephen, Sir Leslie
See Stephen, SirLeslie

Stephen, Virginia
See Woolf, (Adeline) Virginia

Stephens, James 1882(?)-1950 .... TCLC 4
See also CA 104; DLB 19, 153, 162

Stephens, Reed
See Donaldson, Stephen R.

Steptoe, Lydia
See Barnes, Djuna

Sterchi, Beat 1949- .... CLC 65

Sterling, Brett
See Bradbury, Ray (Douglas); Hamilton, Edmond

Sterling, Bruce 1954- .... CLC 72
See also CA 119; CANR 44

Sterling, George 1869-1926 .... TCLC 20
See also CA 117; 165; DLB 54

Stern, Gerald 1925- .... CLC 40, 100
See also CA 81-84; CANR 28; DLB 105

Stern, Richard (Gustave) 1928- ... CLC 4, 39
See also CA 1-4R; CANR 1, 25, 52; DLBY 87; INT CANR-25

Sternberg, Josef von 1894-1969 .... CLC 20
See also CA 81-84

Sterne, Laurence 1713-1768 .. LC 2, 48; DA; DAB; DAC; DAM MST, NOV; WLC
See also CDBLB 1660-1789; DLB 39

Sternheim, (William Adolf) Carl 1878-1942 .... TCLC 8
See also CA 105; DLB 56, 118

Stevens, Mark 1951- .... CLC 34
See also CA 122

Stevens, Wallace 1879-1955 ...... TCLC 3, 12, 45; DA; DAB; DAC; DAM MST, POET; PC 6; WLC
See also CA 104; 124; CDALB 1929-1941; DA3; DLB 54; MTCW 1, 2

Stevenson, Anne (Katharine) 1933- .. CLC 7, 33
See also CA 17-20R; CAAS 9; CANR 9, 33; DLB 40; MTCW 1

Stevenson, Robert Louis (Balfour) 1850-1894 . NCLC 5, 14, 63; DA; DAB; DAC; DAM MST, NOV; SSC 11; WLC
See also AAYA 24; CDBLB 1890-1914; CLR 10, 11; DA3; DLB 18, 57, 141, 156, 174; DLBD 13; JRDA; MAICYA; SATA 100; YABC 2

Stewart, J(ohn) I(nnes) M(ackintosh) 1906-1994 .... CLC 7, 14, 32
See also CA 85-88; 147; CAAS 3; CANR 47; MTCW 1, 2

Stewart, Mary (Florence Elinor) 1916- .... CLC 7, 35, 117; DAB
See also AAYA 29; CA 1-4R; CANR 1, 59; SATA 12

Stewart, Mary Rainbow
See Stewart, Mary (Florence Elinor)

Stifle, June
See Campbell, Maria

Stifter, Adalbert 1805-1868 .. NCLC 41; SSC 28
See also DLB 133

Still, James 1906- .... CLC 49
See also CA 65-68; CAAS 17; CANR 10, 26; DLB 9; SATA 29

Sting 1951-
See Sumner, Gordon Matthew
See also CA 167

Stirling, Arthur
See Sinclair, Upton (Beall)

Stitt, Milan 1941- .... CLC 29
See also CA 69-72

Stockton, Francis Richard 1834-1902
See Stockton, Frank R.
See also CA 108; 137; MAICYA; SATA 44

Stockton, Frank R. TCLC 47
See also Stockton, Francis Richard
See also DLB 42, 74; DLBD 13; SATA-Brief 32

Stoddard, Charles
See Kuttner, Henry

Stoker, Abraham 1847-1912
See Stoker, Bram
See also CA 105; 150; DA; DAC; DAM MST, NOV; DA3; SATA 29

Stoker, Bram 1847-1912 .... TCLC 8; DAB; WLC
See also Stoker, Abraham
See also AAYA 23; CDBLB 1890-1914; DLB 36, 70, 178

Stolz, Mary (Slattery) 1920- .... CLC 12
See also AAYA 8; AITN 1; CA 5-8R; CANR 13, 41; JRDA; MAICYA; SAAS 3; SATA 10, 71

Stone, Irving 1903-1989 . CLC 7; DAM POP
See also AITN 1; CA 1-4R; 129; CAAS 3; CANR 1, 23; DA3; INT CANR-23; MTCW 1, 2; SATA 3; SATA-Obit 64

Stone, Oliver (William) 1946- .... CLC 73
See also AAYA 15; CA 110; CANR 55

Stone, Robert (Anthony) 1937- ... CLC 5, 23, 42
See also CA 85-88; CANR 23, 66; DLB 152; INT CANR-23; MTCW 1

Stone, Zachary
See Follett, Ken(neth Martin)

Stoppard, Tom 1937- ... CLC 1, 3, 4, 5, 8, 15, 29, 34, 63, 91; DA; DAB; DAC; DAM DRAM, MST; DC 6; WLC
See also CA 81-84; CANR 39, 67; CDBLB 1960 to Present; DA3; DLB 13; DLBY 85; MTCW 1, 2

Storey, David (Malcolm) 1933- . CLC 2, 4, 5, 8; DAM DRAM
See also CA 81-84; CANR 36; DLB 13, 14, 207; MTCW 1

Storm, Hyemeyohsts 1935- ..... CLC 3; DAM MULT
See also CA 81-84; CANR 45; NNAL

Storm, Theodor 1817-1888 .... SSC 27

Storm, (Hans) Theodor (Woldsen) 1817-1888 .... NCLC 1; SSC 27
See also DLB 129

Storni, Alfonsina 1892-1938 . TCLC 5; DAM MULT; HLC 2
See also CA 104; 131; HW 1

Stoughton, William 1631-1701 .... LC 38
See also DLB 24

Stout, Rex (Todhunter) 1886-1975 ..... CLC 3
See also AITN 2; CA 61-64; CANR 71

Stow, (Julian) Randolph 1935- ... CLC 23, 48
See also CA 13-16R; CANR 33; MTCW 1

Stowe, Harriet (Elizabeth) Beecher 1811-1896 .... NCLC 3, 50; DA; DAB; DAC; DAM MST, NOV; WLC
See also CDALB 1865-1917; DA3; DLB 1, 12, 42, 74, 189; JRDA; MAICYA; YABC 1

Strabo c. 64B.C.-c. 25 .... CMLC 37
See also DLB 176

Strachey, (Giles) Lytton 1880-1932 .... TCLC 12
See also CA 110; 178; DLB 149; DLBD 10; MTCW 2

Strand, Mark 1934- .... CLC 6, 18, 41, 71; DAM POET
See also CA 21-24R; CANR 40, 65; DLB 5; SATA 41

Straub, Peter (Francis) 1943- . CLC 28, 107; DAM POP
See also BEST 89:1; CA 85-88; CANR 28, 65; DLBY 84; MTCW 1, 2

Strauss, Botho 1944- .... CLC 22
See also CA 157; DLB 124

Streatfeild, (Mary) Noel 1895(?)-1986 .... CLC 21
See also CA 81-84; 120; CANR 31; CLR 17; DLB 160; MAICYA; SATA 20; SATA-Obit 48

Stribling, T(homas) S(igismund) 1881-1965 .... CLC 23
See also CA 107; DLB 9

Strindberg, (Johan) August 1849-1912 .... TCLC 1, 8, 21, 47; DA; DAB; DAC; DAM DRAM, MST; WLC
See also CA 104; 135; DA3; MTCW 2

Stringer, Arthur 1874-1950 .... TCLC 37
See also CA 161; DLB 92

Stringer, David
See Roberts, Keith (John Kingston)

Stroheim, Erich von 1885-1957 ..... TCLC 71

Strugatskii, Arkadii (Natanovich) 1925-1991 .... CLC 27
See also CA 106; 135

Strugatskii, Boris (Natanovich) 1933- .... CLC 27
See also CA 106

Strummer, Joe 1953(?)- .... **CLC 30**

Strunk, William, Jr. 1869-1946 ...... **TCLC 92**
See also CA 118; 164

Stryk, Lucien 1924- .... **PC 27**
See also CA 13-16R; CANR 10, 28, 55

Stuart, Don A.
See Campbell, John W(ood, Jr.)

Stuart, Ian
See MacLean, Alistair (Stuart)

Stuart, Jesse (Hilton) 1906-1984 ... **CLC 1, 8, 11, 14, 34; SSC 31**
See also CA 5-8R; 112; CANR 31; DLB 9, 48, 102; DLBY 84; SATA 2; SATA-Obit 36

Sturgeon, Theodore (Hamilton)
1918-1985 .... **CLC 22, 39**
See also Queen, Ellery
See also CA 81-84; 116; CANR 32; DLB 8; DLBY 85; MTCW 1, 2

Sturges, Preston 1898-1959 .... **TCLC 48**
See also CA 114; 149; DLB 26

Styron, William 1925- .... **CLC 1, 3, 5, 11, 15, 60; DAM NOV, POP; SSC 25**
See also BEST 90:4; CA 5-8R; CANR 6, 33, 74; CDALB 1968-1988; DA3; DLB 2, 143; DLBY 80; INT CANR-6; MTCW 1, 2

Su, Chien 1884-1918
See Su Man-shu
See also CA 123

Suarez Lynch, B.
See Bioy Casares, Adolfo; Borges, Jorge Luis

Suassuna, Ariano Vilar 1927-
See also CA 178; HLCS 1; HW 2

Suckling, John 1609-1641 .... **PC 30**
See also DAM POET; DLB 58, 126

Suckow, Ruth 1892-1960 .... **SSC 18**
See also CA 113; DLB 9, 102

Sudermann, Hermann 1857-1928 .. **TCLC 15**
See also CA 107; DLB 118

Sue, Eugene 1804-1857 .... **NCLC 1**
See also DLB 119

Sueskind, Patrick 1949- .... **CLC 44**
See also Suskind, Patrick

Sukenick, Ronald 1932- .... **CLC 3, 4, 6, 48**
See also CA 25-28R; CAAS 8; CANR 32, 89; DLB 173; DLBY 81

Suknaski, Andrew 1942- .... **CLC 19**
See also CA 101; DLB 53

Sullivan, Vernon
See Vian, Boris

Sully Prudhomme 1839-1907 .... **TCLC 31**

Su Man-shu .... **TCLC 24**
See also Su, Chien

Summerforest, Ivy B.
See Kirkup, James

Summers, Andrew James 1942- .... **CLC 26**

Summers, Andy
See Summers, Andrew James

Summers, Hollis (Spurgeon, Jr.)
1916- .... **CLC 10**
See also CA 5-8R; CANR 3; DLB 6

Summers, (Alphonsus Joseph-Mary Augustus) Montague
1880-1948 .... **TCLC 16**
See also CA 118; 163

Sumner, Gordon Matthew .... **CLC 26**
See also Sting

Surtees, Robert Smith 1803-1864 .. **NCLC 14**
See also DLB 21

Susann, Jacqueline 1921-1974 .... **CLC 3**
See also AITN 1; CA 65-68; 53-56; MTCW 1, 2

Su Shih 1036-1101 .... **CMLC 15**

Suskind, Patrick
See Sueskind, Patrick
See also CA 145

Sutcliff, Rosemary 1920-1992 .... **CLC 26; DAB; DAC; DAM MST, POP**
See also AAYA 10; CA 5-8R; 139; CANR 37; CLR 1, 37; JRDA; MAICYA; SATA 6, 44, 78; SATA-Obit 73

Sutro, Alfred 1863-1933 .... **TCLC 6**
See also CA 105; 185; DLB 10

Sutton, Henry
See Slavitt, David R(ytman)

Svevo, Italo 1861-1928 ...... **TCLC 2, 35; SSC 25**
See also Schmitz, Aron Hector

Swados, Elizabeth (A.) 1951- .... **CLC 12**
See also CA 97-100; CANR 49; INT 97-100

Swados, Harvey 1920-1972 .... **CLC 5**
See also CA 5-8R; 37-40R; CANR 6; DLB 2

Swan, Gladys 1934- .... **CLC 69**
See also CA 101; CANR 17, 39

Swanson, Logan
See Matheson, Richard Burton

Swarthout, Glendon (Fred)
1918-1992 .... **CLC 35**
See also CA 1-4R; 139; CANR 1, 47; SATA 26

Sweet, Sarah C.
See Jewett, (Theodora) Sarah Orne

Swenson, May 1919-1989 ...... **CLC 4, 14, 61, 106; DA; DAB; DAC; DAM MST, POET; PC 14**
See also CA 5-8R; 130; CANR 36, 61; DLB 5; MTCW 1, 2; SATA 15

Swift, Augustus
See Lovecraft, H(oward) P(hillips)

Swift, Graham (Colin) 1949- ...... **CLC 41, 88**
See also CA 117; 122; CANR 46, 71; DLB 194; MTCW 2

Swift, Jonathan 1667-1745 ..... **LC 1, 42; DA; DAB; DAC; DAM MST, NOV, POET; PC 9; WLC**
See also CDBLB 1660-1789; CLR 53; DA3; DLB 39, 95, 101; SATA 19

Swinburne, Algernon Charles
1837-1909 .... **TCLC 8, 36; DA; DAB; DAC; DAM MST, POET; PC 24; WLC**
See also CA 105; 140; CDBLB 1832-1890; DA3; DLB 35, 57

Swinfen, Ann .... **CLC 34**

Swinnerton, Frank Arthur
1884-1982 .... **CLC 31**
See also CA 108; DLB 34

Swithen, John
See King, Stephen (Edwin)

Sylvia
See Ashton-Warner, Sylvia (Constance)

Symmes, Robert Edward
See Duncan, Robert (Edward)

Symonds, John Addington
1840-1893 .... **NCLC 34**
See also DLB 57, 144

Symons, Arthur 1865-1945 .... **TCLC 11**
See also CA 107; DLB 19, 57, 149

Symons, Julian (Gustave)
1912-1994 .... **CLC 2, 14, 32**
See also CA 49-52; 147; CAAS 3; CANR 3, 33, 59; DLB 87, 155; DLBY 92; MTCW 1

Synge, (Edmund) J(ohn) M(illington)
1871-1909 . **TCLC 6, 37; DAM DRAM; DC 2**
See also CA 104; 141; CDBLB 1890-1914; DLB 10, 19

Syruc, J.
See Milosz, Czeslaw

Szirtes, George 1948- .... **CLC 46**
See also CA 109; CANR 27, 61

Szymborska, Wislawa 1923- .... **CLC 99**
See also CA 154; CANR 91; DA3; DLBY 96; MTCW 2

T. O., Nik
See Annensky, Innokenty (Fyodorovich)

Tabori, George 1914- .... **CLC 19**
See also CA 49-52; CANR 4, 69

Tagore, Rabindranath 1861-1941 ... **TCLC 3, 53; DAM DRAM, POET; PC 8**
See also CA 104; 120; DA3; MTCW 1, 2

Taine, Hippolyte Adolphe
1828-1893 .... **NCLC 15**

Talese, Gay 1932- .... **CLC 37**
See also AITN 1; CA 1-4R; CANR 9, 58; DLB 185; INT CANR-9; MTCW 1, 2

Tallent, Elizabeth (Ann) 1954- .... **CLC 45**
See also CA 117; CANR 72; DLB 130

Tally, Ted 1952- .... **CLC 42**
See also CA 120; 124; INT 124

Talvik, Heiti 1904-1947 .... **TCLC 87**

Tamayo y Baus, Manuel
1829-1898 .... **NCLC 1**

Tammsaare, A(nton) H(ansen)
1878-1940 .... **TCLC 27**
See also CA 164; DLB 220

Tam'si, Tchicaya U
See Tchicaya, Gerald Felix

Tan, Amy (Ruth) 1952- . **CLC 59, 120; DAM MULT, NOV, POP**
See also AAYA 9; BEST 89:3; CA 136; CANR 54; CDALBS; DA3; DLB 173; MTCW 2; SATA 75

Tandem, Felix
See Spitteler, Carl (Friedrich Georg)

Tanizaki, Jun'ichiro 1886-1965 ... **CLC 8, 14, 28; SSC 21**
See also CA 93-96; 25-28R; DLB 180; MTCW 2

Tanner, William
See Amis, Kingsley (William)

Tao Lao
See Storni, Alfonsina

Tarantino, Quentin (Jerome)
1963- .... **CLC 125**
See also CA 171

Tarassoff, Lev
See Troyat, Henri

Tarbell, Ida M(inerva) 1857-1944 . **TCLC 40**
See also CA 122; 181; DLB 47

Tarkington, (Newton) Booth
1869-1946 .... **TCLC 9**
See also CA 110; 143; DLB 9, 102; MTCW 2; SATA 17

Tarkovsky, Andrei (Arsenyevich)
1932-1986 .... **CLC 75**
See also CA 127

Tartt, Donna 1964(?)- .... **CLC 76**
See also CA 142

Tasso, Torquato 1544-1595 .... **LC 5**

Tate, (John Orley) Allen 1899-1979 .. **CLC 2, 4, 6, 9, 11, 14, 24**
See also CA 5-8R; 85-88; CANR 32; DLB 4, 45, 63; DLBD 17; MTCW 1, 2

Tate, Ellalice
See Hibbert, Eleanor Alice Burford

Tate, James (Vincent) 1943- ..... **CLC 2, 6, 25**
See also CA 21-24R; CANR 29, 57; DLB 5, 169

Tauler, Johannes c. 1300-1361 ...... **CMLC 37**
See also DLB 179

Tavel, Ronald 1940- .... **CLC 6**
See also CA 21-24R; CANR 33

Taylor, C(ecil) P(hilip) 1929-1981 .... **CLC 27**
See also CA 25-28R; 105; CANR 47

Taylor, Edward 1642(?)-1729 ..... **LC 11; DA; DAB; DAC; DAM MST, POET**
See also DLB 24

Wolfe, Thomas (Clayton)
1900-1938 ...... **TCLC 4, 13, 29, 61; DA; DAB; DAC; DAM MST, NOV; SSC 33; WLC**
See also CA 104; 132; CDALB 1929-1941; DA3; DLB 9, 102; DLBD 2, 16; DLBY 85, 97; MTCW 1, 2

Wolfe, Thomas Kennerly, Jr. 1930-
See Wolfe, Tom
See also CA 13-16R; CANR 9, 33, 70; DAM POP; DA3; DLB 185; INT CANR-9; MTCW 1, 2

Wolfe, Tom **CLC 1, 2, 9, 15, 35, 51**
See also Wolfe, Thomas Kennerly, Jr.
See also AAYA 8; AITN 2; BEST 89:1; DLB 152

Wolff, Geoffrey (Ansell) 1937- .... **CLC 41**
See also CA 29-32R; CANR 29, 43, 78

Wolff, Sonia
See Levitin, Sonia (Wolff)

Wolff, Tobias (Jonathan Ansell)
1945- .... **CLC 39, 64**
See also AAYA 16; BEST 90:2; CA 114; 117; CAAS 22; CANR 54, 76; DA3; DLB 130; INT 117; MTCW 2

Wolfram von Eschenbach c. 1170-c.
1220 .... **CMLC 5**
See also DLB 138

Wolitzer, Hilma 1930- .... **CLC 17**
See also CA 65-68; CANR 18, 40; INT CANR-18; SATA 31

Wollstonecraft, Mary 1759-1797 ..... **LC 5, 50**
See also CDBLB 1789-1832; DLB 39, 104, 158

Wonder, Stevie **CLC 12**
See also Morris, Steveland Judkins

Wong, Jade Snow 1922- .... **CLC 17**
See also CA 109; CANR 91; SATA 112

Woodberry, George Edward
1855-1930 .... **TCLC 73**
See also CA 165; DLB 71, 103

Woodcott, Keith
See Brunner, John (Kilian Houston)

Woodruff, Robert W.
See Mencken, H(enry) L(ouis)

Woolf, (Adeline) Virginia
1882-1941 .. **TCLC 1, 5, 20, 43, 56; DA; DAB; DAC; DAM MST, NOV; SSC 7; WLC**
See also Woolf, Virginia Adeline
See also CA 104; 130; CANR 64; CDBLB 1914-1945; DA3; DLB 36, 100, 162; DLBD 10; MTCW 1

Woolf, Virginia Adeline
See Woolf, (Adeline) Virginia
See also MTCW 2

Woollcott, Alexander (Humphreys)
1887-1943 .... **TCLC 5**
See also CA 105; 161; DLB 29

Woolrich, Cornell 1903-1968 .... **CLC 77**
See also Hopley-Woolrich, Cornell George

Woolson, Constance Fenimore
1840-1894 .... **NCLC 82**
See also DLB 12, 74, 189, 221

Wordsworth, Dorothy 1771-1855 .. **NCLC 25**
See also DLB 107

Wordsworth, William 1770-1850 .. **NCLC 12, 38; DA; DAB; DAC; DAM MST, POET; PC 4; WLC**
See also CDBLB 1789-1832; DA3; DLB 93, 107

Wouk, Herman 1915- ... **CLC 1, 9, 38; DAM NOV, POP**
See also CA 5-8R; CANR 6, 33, 67; CDALBS; DA3; DLBY 82; INT CANR-6; MTCW 1, 2

Wright, Charles (Penzel, Jr.) 1935- .. **CLC 6, 13, 28, 119**
See also CA 29-32R; CAAS 7; CANR 23, 36, 62, 88; DLB 165; DLBY 82; MTCW 1, 2

Wright, Charles Stevenson 1932- ... **CLC 49; BLC 3; DAM MULT, POET**
See also BW 1; CA 9-12R; CANR 26; DLB 33

Wright, Frances 1795-1852 .... **NCLC 74**
See also DLB 73

Wright, Frank Lloyd 1867-1959 .... **TCLC 95**
See also AAYA 33; CA 174

Wright, Jack R.
See Harris, Mark

Wright, James (Arlington)
1927-1980 .... **CLC 3, 5, 10, 28; DAM POET**
See also AITN 2; CA 49-52; 97-100; CANR 4, 34, 64; CDALBS; DLB 5, 169; MTCW 1, 2

Wright, Judith (Arandell) 1915- ..... **CLC 11, 53; PC 14**
See also CA 13-16R; CANR 31, 76; MTCW 1, 2; SATA 14

Wright, L(aurali) R. 1939- .... **CLC 44**
See also CA 138

Wright, Richard (Nathaniel)
1908-1960 .... **CLC 1, 3, 4, 9, 14, 21, 48, 74; BLC 3; DA; DAB; DAC; DAM MST, MULT, NOV; SSC 2; WLC**
See also AAYA 5; BW 1; CA 108; CANR 64; CDALB 1929-1941; DA3; DLB 76, 102; DLBD 2; MTCW 1, 2

Wright, Richard B(ruce) 1937- .... **CLC 6**
See also CA 85-88; DLB 53

Wright, Rick 1945- .... **CLC 35**

Wright, Rowland
See Wells, Carolyn

Wright, Stephen 1946- .... **CLC 33**

Wright, Willard Huntington 1888-1939
See Van Dine, S. S.
See also CA 115; DLBD 16

Wright, William 1930- .... **CLC 44**
See also CA 53-56; CANR 7, 23

Wroth, LadyMary 1587-1653(?) .... **LC 30**
See also DLB 121

Wu Ch'eng-en 1500(?)-1582(?) .... **LC 7**

Wu Ching-tzu 1701-1754 .... **LC 2**

Wurlitzer, Rudolph 1938(?)- .... **CLC 2, 4, 15**
See also CA 85-88; DLB 173

Wyatt, Thomas c. 1503-1542 .... **PC 27**
See also DLB 132

Wycherley, William 1641-1715 ...... **LC 8, 21; DAM DRAM**
See also CDBLB 1660-1789; DLB 80

Wylie, Elinor (Morton Hoyt)
1885-1928 .... **TCLC 8; PC 23**
See also CA 105; 162; DLB 9, 45

Wylie, Philip (Gordon) 1902-1971 ... **CLC 43**
See also CA 21-22; 33-36R; CAP 2; DLB 9

Wyndham, John **CLC 19**
See also Harris, John (Wyndham Parkes Lucas) Beynon

Wyss, Johann David Von
1743-1818 .... **NCLC 10**
See also JRDA; MAICYA; SATA 29; SATA-Brief 27

Xenophon c. 430B.C.-c. 354B.C. ... **CMLC 17**
See also DLB 176

Yakumo Koizumi
See Hearn, (Patricio) Lafcadio (Tessima Carlos)

Yamamoto, Hisaye 1921- .... **SSC 34; DAM MULT**

Yanez, Jose Donoso
See Donoso (Yanez), Jose

Yanovsky, Basile S.
See Yanovsky, V(assily) S(emenovich)

Yanovsky, V(assily) S(emenovich)
1906-1989 .... **CLC 2, 18**
See also CA 97-100; 129

Yates, Richard 1926-1992 .... **CLC 7, 8, 23**
See also CA 5-8R; 139; CANR 10, 43; DLB 2; DLBY 81, 92; INT CANR-10

Yeats, W. B.
See Yeats, William Butler

Yeats, William Butler 1865-1939 .... **TCLC 1, 11, 18, 31, 93; DA; DAB; DAC; DAM DRAM, MST, POET; PC 20; WLC**
See also CA 104; 127; CANR 45; CDBLB 1890-1914; DA3; DLB 10, 19, 98, 156; MTCW 1, 2

Yehoshua, A(braham) B. 1936- .. **CLC 13, 31**
See also CA 33-36R; CANR 43, 90

Yellow Bird
See Ridge, John Rollin

Yep, Laurence Michael 1948- .... **CLC 35**
See also AAYA 5, 31; CA 49-52; CANR 1, 46; CLR 3, 17, 54; DLB 52; JRDA; MAICYA; SATA 7, 69

Yerby, Frank G(arvin) 1916-1991 . **CLC 1, 7, 22; BLC 3; DAM MULT**
See also BW 1, 3; CA 9-12R; 136; CANR 16, 52; DLB 76; INT CANR-16; MTCW 1

Yesenin, Sergei Alexandrovich
See Esenin, Sergei (Alexandrovich)

Yevtushenko, Yevgeny (Alexandrovich)
1933- .. **CLC 1, 3, 13, 26, 51, 126; DAM POET**
See also CA 81-84; CANR 33, 54; MTCW 1

Yezierska, Anzia 1885(?)-1970 .... **CLC 46**
See also CA 126; 89-92; DLB 28, 221; MTCW 1

Yglesias, Helen 1915- .... **CLC 7, 22**
See also CA 37-40R; CAAS 20; CANR 15, 65; INT CANR-15; MTCW 1

Yokomitsu, Riichi 1898-1947 .... **TCLC 47**
See also CA 170

Yonge, Charlotte (Mary)
1823-1901 .... **TCLC 48**
See also CA 109; 163; DLB 18, 163; SATA 17

York, Jeremy
See Creasey, John

York, Simon
See Heinlein, Robert A(nson)

Yorke, Henry Vincent 1905-1974 ..... **CLC 13**
See also Green, Henry
See also CA 85-88; 49-52

Yosano Akiko 1878-1942 .... **TCLC 59; PC 11**
See also CA 161

Yoshimoto, Banana **CLC 84**
See also Yoshimoto, Mahoko

Yoshimoto, Mahoko 1964-
See Yoshimoto, Banana
See also CA 144

Young, Al(bert James) 1939- . **CLC 19; BLC 3; DAM MULT**
See also BW 2, 3; CA 29-32R; CANR 26, 65; DLB 33

Young, Andrew (John) 1885-1971 ...... **CLC 5**
See also CA 5-8R; CANR 7, 29

Young, Collier
See Bloch, Robert (Albert)

Young, Edward 1683-1765 .... **LC 3, 40**
See also DLB 95

Young, Marguerite (Vivian)
1909-1995 .... **CLC 82**
See also CA 13-16; 150; CAP 1

Young, Neil 1945- .... **CLC 17**
See also CA 110

SSC Cumulative Nationality Index

SSC Cumulative Title Index

471

Title Index

Title Index

Title Index

Title Index

Title Index

Title Index

ISBN 0-7876-3276-7

90000